D. Brynwyn Davies
The Baptist College
Pontypool.

The Acts and Monuments of John Foxe

As some months must necessarily elapse before the publication of the first volume of the Acts and Monuments, containing the Prefaces, Indexes, &c., the Editor feels called upon to state, that the present work is a reprint of the fourth edition of the original work of JOHN FOXE, published in 1583, with the exception of passages introduced from the first three English editions, and from the fifth, which latter, though published after the Author's death, was partially or completely corrected and revised by himself. Every material variation from the text of 1583 is properly distinguished; while, occasionally, obscure passages have been explained by a reference to the Latin edition of 1559.

In removing the Latin documents from the text, and placing them in the notes at the bottom of the pages, a slight variation in the context must obviously be necessary, but this arrangement has been thought desirable for the convenience of general readers.

For the same reason, modern orthography is introduced; grammatical errors corrected; dates inserted at the head of each page; while a few coarse expressions of a less cultivated age are either omitted or remodelled; but *these are carefully distinguished* by the insertion of the mark † in the margin.

The Engravings given in this edition will be about forty in number, and of their style, the Title-page of this volume will give a correct idea. Several of them are now ready, and might have been given in the present volume, had it not been thought more advisable to insert them in their proper places in the work. The portion now published, consisting chiefly of preliminary history, afforded no appropriate subject for pictorial illustration.

The Editor, in conclusion, gives this pledge to the public, that every insertion (with the above exceptions) is from the pen of John Foxe, and in no single instance has he infringed upon the original intent and meaning of the Author.

FULHAM,
December 15, 1836.

DEDICATED, BY PERMISSION,

TO

HIS MOST GRACIOUS MAJESTY.

THE ACTS AND MONUMENTS OF JOHN FOXE.

VOL. II.

LONDON
PRINTED BY R CLAY, BREAD-STREET-HILL,
DOCTORS' COMMONS

ACTES

and Monuments

of these latter and perillous dayes, touching matters of the Church,

wherein are comprehended and described the great persecutions & horrible troubles, that haue bene wrought and practised by the Romishe Prelates, speciallye in this Realme of England and Scotlande, from the yeare of our Lorde a thousande, unto the tyme nowe present.

Gathered and collected according to the true copies and wrytinges certificatorie as wel of the parties themselues that suffered, as also out of the Bishops Registers, which wer the doers therof, by *John Foxe*.

¶ *Imprinted at London by Iohn Day,*

dwellyng ouer Aldersgate.

Cum priuilegio Regie Majestatis.

THE ACTS AND MONUMENTS OF JOHN FOXE:

A NEW AND COMPLETE EDITION:

WITH A PRELIMINARY DISSERTATION,

BY THE

REV. GEORGE TOWNSEND, M.A.

OF TRINITY COLLEGE, CAMBRIDGE,

PREBENDARY OF DURHAM,

AND VICAR OF NORTHALLERTON, YORKSHIRE

EDITED BY THE

REV. STEPHEN REED CATTLEY, M.A.

OF QUEEN'S COLLEGE, CAMBRIDGE,

RECTOR OF BAGTHORP, NORFOLK,

AND CHAPLAIN TO THE RIGHT HONOURABLE THE EARL OF SCARBROUGH

VOL. II.

PUBLISHED BY R. B SEELEY AND W BURNSIDE,
AND SOLD BY L & G. SEELEY,
FLEET STREET, LONDON
MDCCCXXXVII.

CONTENTS.

VOL. II.

BOOK III.

CONTAINING THE THREE HUNDRED YEARS, FROM THE REIGN OF EGBERT TO THE TIME OF WILLIAM THE CONQUEROR.

BOOK IV.

CONTAINING ANOTHER THREE HUNDRED YEARS, FROM WILLIAM THE CONQUEROR TO THE TIME OF JOHN WICKLIFF.

BOOK V.

CONTAINING THE LAST THREE HUNDRED YEARS FROM THE LOOSING OUT OF SATAN.

ACTS AND MONUMENTS.

VOL. II.

ACTS AND MONUMENTS.

BOOK III.[1]

CONTAINING

THE THREE HUNDRED YEARS,

FROM THE REIGN OF KING EGBERT TO THE TIME OF

WILLIAM THE CONQUEROR

Now remaineth for me to do as before I did in describing the descent and diversity of the seven kings, together reigning and ruling in this land, namely, to prosecute in like order the lineal succession of those, who, after Egbert, king of the West Saxons, governed and ruled alone, until the conquest of William the Norman; first expressing their names, and afterwards recording such acts, as in their time happened in the Church worthy to be noted. Albeit, as touching the acts and doings of these kings, because they are sufficiently and at large described, and taken out of Latin writers into the English tongue, by divers and sundry authors, as in the History or Chronicle of Fabian; I shall not spend much travail thereupon, but rather refer the reader to him or to some other, where the troublesome tumults between the Englishmen and the Danes at that time may be seen, whoso listeth to read them. I have furnished a table of their names and reigns, and the acts done under their reigns, I have compendiously abridged, using such brevity as the matter would allow.

Therein is to be noted, that before the reign of Edward the Confessor, the Danes obtained the crown under Canute, their captain, who reigned nineteen years. Harold Harefoot, son of Canute, reigned about four years; Hardicanute, son of Canute, two years; Edward the Confessor, an Englishman, son of Ethelred, twenty-four years; Harold, son of Earl Godwin, an usurper, one year; and William the Conqueror, a Norman, reigned twenty-one years and ten months.

(1) Edition 1563, p 10 Ed 1583, p. 135 Ed 1596, p 126 Ed 1684, vol I p 150 —N B The first eight pages of the Latin Edition of 1559, bring the reader down to an account of the proceedings of a Convocation of Bishops, holden at Lambeth, in the time of Wickliff, A. D 1377 —Ed.

A TABLE OF THE KINGS WHO GOVERNED AND RULED ALONE, FROM THE TIME OF KING EGBERT THE GREAT, TILL THE CONQUEST OF WILLIAM THE NORMAN.

N. B. The Numbers attached to the Titles of the Sovereigns denote the Order in which they severally reigned.

The Saxon Line.

1. Egbert the Great, King of England, A. D. 827, died 836.

2. Ethelwolf, his son, d. 857, and had issue four sons, viz.

3. Ethelbald, d. 860; and Ethelbert, (reigned together.)

4. Ethelbert, d. 866; alone.
 Ethelwald.

5. Ethelred I., killed by the Danes, 871.

6. Alfred the Great, d. 901, and was succeeded by his son,

7. Edward I., d. 924.

8. Athelstan, his nat. son, d. 941.

9. Edmund I., d. 946.

10. Edred, d. 955.

11. Edwy, divided the Kingdom with Edgar, d. 959.

1st, the dau. of Earl Ordmer, ⁜ 12. Edgar, d. 975; married twice. ⁜ 2dly, Elfrida, dau. of the Earl of Devon, and had Issue

13. Edward II., murdered at Corfe Castle, by order of Elfrida, 978.

1st, Elgiva, by whom he had ⁜ 14. Ethelred II., d. 1016. ⁜ 2dly, Emma, sister to Richard II., Duke of Normandy.

16. Edmund II., surnamed Iron-side, m. Algitha, and was murdered at Oxford, 1017, by two accomplices of the traitor Edric, D. of Mercia.

Edwy, murdered by Canute.

Alfred, taken by the treachery of Earl Godwin, and died in prison.

20. Edward the Confessor, m. Editha, dau. of Earl Godwin, d. 1066.

21. Harold II., son of Earl Godwin, killed at Hastings by William the Conqueror, 14 Oct. 1066.

Edwin and Edward, who were both sent by Canute to the King of Sweden, with directions to put them to death; but he sent them to Solomon, King of Hungary, to be brought up. Edwin married Solomon's sister, and died without issue; and Edward married Agatha, the daughter of Henry I., Emperor of Germany, by whom he had Edgar Etheling (who died very old without issue,)—and Margaret, who married Malcolm, King of Scotland, by whom she had

Edgar, Alexander, and David, successively Kings of Scotland, from the last of whom descended James VI. of Scotland, and I. of England; consequently in him the Saxon and Norman Lines were united.

Matilda, mar. Henry I., King of England.

The Danish Line.

15. Sweyn, King of Denmark and England. He obliged Ethelred to fly into Normandy. The nobles swore allegiance to him, soon after which, in 1014, he died, and Ethelred returned.

17. Canute the Great, the son of Sweyn, m. Emma, the widow of Ethelred II.; he died 1035, leaving two sons, viz.

18. Harold I. d. 1040.

19. Hardicanute, d. 1042.

The Norman Line.

Rogvald, a Norwegian chieftain.
Rollo I., his son, Duke of Normandy, 912; d. 917.
William Longsword, his son, d. 943.
Richard I., brother to William, d. 1002.

Richard II., d. 1026.

Emma, m. Ethelred II., after whose death she m. Canute the Great.

Robert, who died 1035, kept a concubine, whose name was Harlotta, a tanner's daughter, by whom he had

22. William the Conqueror, who m. Matilda, daughter of Baldwin, Earl of Flanders, d. 1087.

Ed.

Egbert.

A.D. 800.

EGBERT THE GREAT,

KING OF THE WEST SAXONS, AFTERWARDS MONARCH OF THE WHOLE REALM.

In the reign of Brightric, a little before mentioned, about the year of grace 795, there was in his dominion a noble personage, of some called Egbert, of some Ethelbert, of some Ethelbright; who, being feared of the same Brightric, because he was of kingly blood and near unto the crown, was, by the force and conspiracy of the aforenamed Brightric, chased and pursued out of the land of Britain into France, where he endured till the death of the said Brightric; after the hearing whereof Egbert sped him quickly out of France, unto his country of West-Sax, where he so behaved himself that he obtained the regiment and governance of the kingdom.[1] The Danes first came into the north and parts, were driven out again.

Bernulph, king of Mercia abovementioned, and other kings, had this Egbert in such derision that they made of him divers scoffing jests and scorning rhymes, all which he sustained for a time. But when he was more established in his kingdom, and had proved the minds of his subjects, and especially God working withal, he afterward assembled his knights, and gave battle to the said Bernulph, in a place called Elinden, in the province of Hampton; and, notwithstanding in that fight were great odds of number, as six or eight against one, yet Egbert, through the might of the Lord, who giveth victory as pleaseth him, had the better, and won the field; which done, he seized that lordship into his own hand; and that also done, he made war upon the Kentish Saxons, and at length of them, in like manner, obtained the victory.[2] And, as it is in Polychronicon testified, he also subdued Northumberland,[3] and caused the kings of these three kingdoms to live under him as tributaries, or joined them to his kingdom.[4] This Egbert also won from the Britons or Welshmen the town of Chester, which they had kept possession of till that day. After these and other victories, he peaceably enjoying the land, called a council of his lords at Winchester, where, by their advice, he was crowned king and chief lord over this land, which before that day was called Britain; but then he sent out into all the coasts of the land his commandments and commissions, charging strictly that, from that day forward, the Saxons should be called Angles, and the land Anglia. A.D. 807. A.D. 826. A.D. 827. This land first called Anglia.

About the thirtieth year of the reign of Egbert, that heathenish people the Danes, that a little before had made horrible destruction in Northumberland, and especially in the isle of Lindisfarn, where they spoiled the churches, and murdered the ministers, with men, women, and children, after a cruel manner, entered now the second A.D. 833. Danes now the second time entered this land.

(1) On the 25th of December, A.D. 800, Charlemagne became Roman emperor, and Leo III., the ninety-fifth bishop of Rome, was in possession of the papal chair. After a reign of forty, and a war of thirty-three, years' duration, Charlemagne died at Aix-la-Chapelle, A.D. 804, aged 72.—ED.

(2) Of this victory went a proverb,—"Rivus cruore rubuit, ruina restitit, fœtore tabuit."

(3) See Malmsb. de gest. Reg. Angl. lib. i. c. 3. [Also Harpsfield, Hist. Eccl. Secul. 8, c. 21.—ED.]

(4) Ex Flor. Hist.

Egbert. A.D. 833. time, with a great host, into this land, and spoiled the isle of Sheppy in Kent, or near to Kent; where, Egbert hearing thereof, assembled his people, and met with them at Charmouth: in that conflict he sped not so well as he was wont in times before, but with his knights was compelled to forsake the field. Notwithstanding, in the A.D. 834. next battle, the said Egbert, with a small power, overthrew a great multitude of them, and so drave them back[1]. The next year following, the Danes presuming upon their victory before, made their return again into the land westward, where, joining with the Britons, by their help and power, they assailed the lands of Egbert, and did much harm in many places of his dominion and elsewhere; so that after this day they were continually abiding in one place of the realm of England or another, till the time of Hardicanute, last king of the Danes' blood; so that many of them were married to English women, and many that now be, or in times past were, called Englishmen, are descended of them. And albeit that they were many and sundry times driven out of the land, and chased from one country to another, yet, that notwithstanding, they ever gathered new strength and power, so that they abode still within the land.

England five times plagued by other nations.

And thus, as by the histories appears, this troublesome land of Britain, now called England, hath been hitherto by five sundry outward nations plagued: first, by the Romans; then by the Scots and Picts; thirdly, by the Saxons; fourthly, by the Danes, of whose outrageous cruelty and hostility our English histories[2] do most exclaim and complain; and fifthly, by the Normans, who, I pray God, may be the last.

Then it followeth in the story, that the time of this persecution of the aforesaid pagans and Danes continuing, King Egbert, when he had ruled the West Saxons, and over the more part of England, by the term of seven and thirty years, died, and was buried at Winchester, leaving to his son Ethelwolf, his kingdom, who first was bishop of Winchester, as Hoveden recordeth, and after, upon necessity, was made king, leaving withal, and pronouncing this saying to his son, "Felicem fore si regnum, quod multa rexerat industria, ille consueta genti illi non interrumperet ignavia."

ETHELWOLF.

A.D. 837. Ethelwolf, the son of Egbert, in his former age had entered into the order of sub-deacon, and as some others say, was made bishop of Winchester; but, afterwards, being the only son of Egbert, was made king through the dispensation, as Fabian saith, of Pope Paschal:[3] but that cannot be, for Paschal was not then bishop: so that by the computation of time, it should rather seem to be Gregory IV. This Ethelwolf (as being himself once nursed in that order) was always good and devout to holy church and religious orders, insomuch that he gave to them the tithe of all his goods and lands

(1) Fabian, c. 158. Rog. Hoved. lib. v. c. 1.
(2) Ex Rog. Hoved. lib. v. (3) Guliel. lib. de gest. Anglor. saith, this Pope was Leo IV.

Ethelwolf. A.D. 837.

among the West Saxons, with liberty and freedom from all service and civil charges; whereof his chart instrument beareth testimony after the tenor below[1], much like to the donation of Ethelbald, king of Mercians, above mentioned.

A.D. 844. The blind ignorance of those days.

By the privileges and donations given by King Ethelwolf to the clergy, it may appear, how and when the churches of England began first to be endowed with temporalities and lands; also how their privileges and exemptions were enlarged: moreover (and that which specially is to be considered and lamented), what pernicious doctrine this was, wherewith they were led thus to set remission of their sins and remedy of their souls, in this donation and such other deeds of their devotion, contrary to the information of God's word, and with no small derogation from the Cross of Christ.

These things thus done within the realm, the said Ethelwolf, the king, taking his journey to Rome with Alfred, his youngest son, committed him to the bringing up of Pope Leo IV., where he also re-edified the English school at Rome; which, being founded by King Offa, or rather by Ive, king of Mercians, as in the 'Flowers of Histories' is affirmed, was lately, in the time of King Egbert his father, consumed with fire. Further and besides, this king gave and granted there unto Rome, of every fire-house a penny to be paid through his whole land, as King Ive in his dominion had done before. Also, he gave and granted, yearly to be paid to Rome, 300 marks; that is, to the maintaining of the light of St. Peter, 100 marks; to the light of St. Paul, 100 marks; to the use of the Pope also another hundred. This done, he returning home through France, married there Judith, the daughter of Charles the Bald, the French king; whom he restored afterward (contrary to the laws of West Saxons) to the title and throne of a queen. For before, it was decreed among the West Saxons, by the occasion of the wicked Ethelburga, who poisoned Brigthric, her own husband, that after that, no king's wife there should have the name or place of a queen.

Peter-pence through the realm granted to Rome. Money bestowed to burn daylight.

And forasmuch as I have here entered upon the mention of Judith, daughter of Charles the Bald, the occasion thereof putteth me in memory here to insert by the way, a matter done, although not in this realm, yet not impertinent to this ecclesiastical history. And first, to deduce the narration thereof from the first original; the father of this Charles the Bald, whose name was Ludovicus, the first of that name called Pius, king of France, had two wives; by the first of whom he had three sons, Lothaire, Pepin, and Louis: which three sons unnaturally and unkindly conspiring against their father and his second wife, with her son, their youngest brother, persecuted him so that through a certain council of lords spiritual and

The wholesome counsel.

(1) "Regnante Domino nostro in perpetuum. Dum in nostris temporibus per bellorum incendiâ, et direptiones opum nostrarum, necnon et vastantium crudelissimas deprædationes hostium barbarorum, paganarumque gentium, multiplices tribulationes ad affligendum usque ad internecionem, tempora cernimus incumbere periculosa. Quamobrem, ego Ethelwulfus Rex occidentalium Saxonum, cum consilio Episcoporum et principum meorum, consilium salubre, et uniforme remedium affirmavi: ut aliquam portionem terrarum heræditariam, Deo et sanctæ Mariæ, et omnibus sanctis jure perpetuo possidendam concedam, scilicet partem terræ meæ, ut sit tuta et immunis ab omnibus secularibus servitiis, necnon regalibus tributis majoribus et minoribus sive taxationibus, quod nos dicimus Witterden: sitque libera omnium rerum, pro remissione animarum et peccatorum nostrorum, ad Deo soli deserviendum, sine expeditione, et pontis constructione, et arcis munitione: ut eo diligentius pro nobis ad Deum preces sine cessatione fundant, quo eorum servitutem in aliqua parte levigamus," etc.—Ex Flor. Hist.

Ethelwolf. A.D. 844.

temporal, they deposed the same their natural and right godly father, dispossessing and discharging him of all rule and dominion. Moreover, they caused him to renounce his temporal habit, enclosing him in the monastery of St. Mark, for a monk, or rather a prisoner. All which done, they divided his empire and kingdom among themselves.

and doings of the spiritual lords.

Thus was Ludovicus Pius, king of France, of impious sons left desolate. But the power of God which worketh, when all earthly power ceaseth, of his divine mercy, so aided and recovered him out of all his tribulation to this imperial dignity again, that it was to all his enemies confusion, and to all good men, a miracle. But this by the way. By his second wife, whose name was Judith,[1] he had this Charles the Bald, here mentioned. This Judith was thought, and so accused to the Pope, to be within such degree of alliance, that by the Pope's law, she might not continue his wife without the Pope's dispensation. It so fell out in the mean time, that this Ludovicus, the emperor, had promoted a young man named Frederic, to be bishop of Utrecht; and to him had given sad and good exhortation, that he remembering and following the constancy of his predecessors, would maintain right and truth without exception of any person, and punish misdoers with excommunication, as well the rich as the poor; with such like words of godly counsel. Frederic, hearing the king thus say, sitting at dinner with him as the manner was, being newly invested, in these words answered the emperor again: "I thank your majesty," saith he, "who with your so wholesome exhortation put me in mind of my profession. But I beseech you, of your benign favour and patience, that I may freely disclose that which hath long encumbered and pierced my conscience." To whom leave being given, thus he began: "I pray you, lord emperor, to show me herein your mind" (pointing to the fish before him), "whether it is more according to attain this fish here present, beginning first at the head or at the tail?" "What a tale is this," quoth the emperor, "of the tail and of the head?" "At the head," quoth he. Then Frederic, taking thereof his occasion, proceedeth: "Even so let it be, lord emperor," saith he, "as you have said. Let christian faith and charity first begin with yourself, as with the head, admonishing you to cease from your erroneous practices, that your subjects by that example be not emboldened to follow your misdoing. Wherefore first forsake you your unlawful wedlock, which you have made with Judith your near kinswoman." These words of the new bishop, although they moved Ludovicus the emperor, not a little, yet he with a gentle modesty and modest silence, was contented, suffering the bishop to go home in peace. But the word being uttered in such an audience could not be so concealed, but spread and burst out in much talk in the whole court, and especially among the bishops, consulting earnestly with themselves about the matter. Through whose counsel and labour so at length it fell, that the emperor was constrained to leave the company of his wife, till he had purchased a license of the bishop of Rome to retain her again, who then forgave the said bishop all that was past. But the woman hired two knights that slew him in his

Frederic, bishop of Utrecht.

Openly admonisheth the emperor at the table.

(1) There were two Judiths, one the mother of Charles the Bald, the other his daughter, whom King Ethelwolf married.

vestments, when he had ended his mass. Ranulphus[1] gave forth this story in his great commendation, that he died a martyr; whereof I have not to judge, nor here to pronounce, but that rather I think him to be commended in his dying, than the woman for her killing. *Ethelwolf.* A.D. 844. Judged of some a martyr.

And forasmuch as mention hath been made of Ludovicus Pius, here is to be noted, that in France then was used by priests and churchmen, precious and shining vestures, and golden and rich staring girdles, with rings and other ornaments of gold. Wherefore the said Ludovicus purchased of the bishop of Rome a correction for all such as used such disordinate apparel, causing them to wear brown and sad colours, according to their sadness.[2]

Of this Ludovicus the Papists do feign, that because he converted certain of their church-goods and patrimony to the wages of his soldiers, "his body," say they, "was carried out of his tomb by devils, and was no more seen."

And thus having digressed a little out of our course, now let us return out of France into England again. King Ethelwolf, coming from Rome by way of France, was now returned again into his own dominion, where he continued not long after.

This Ethelwolf had especially about him two bishops, whose counsel he was most ruled by, Swithin, bishop of Winchester, and Adelstan, bishop of Sherborne. Of the which two, the one was more skilful in temporal and civil affairs touching the king's wars, and filling of his coffers, and other furniture for the king. The other, who was Swithin, was of a contrary sort, wholly disposed and inclined to spiritual meditation, and to minister spiritual counsel to the king; who had been schoolmaster to the king before. Wherein appeared one good condition of this king's nature, among his other virtues, not only in following the precepts and advertisements of his old schoolmaster, but also in that he, like a kind and thankful pupil, did so reverence his bringer-up, and old schoolmaster (as he called him), that he ceased not, till he made him bishop of Winchester, by the consecration of Celnoch, then archbishop of Canterbury. But as concerning the miracles which are read in the church of Winchester, of this Swithin, them I leave to be read together with the Iliads of Homer, or the tales of Robin Hood. Swithin, bishop of Winchester. Monkish miracles feigned of Swithin.

This Gregory IV. in this present chapter abovementioned, was the third pope who succeeded after Paschal I., being but four years betwixt them: Paschal succeeded after Stephen IV., who followed after Leo III., the next pope to Adrian above in our history mentioned, where we treated of Charlemagne. From the time of that Adrian I. unto Pope Adrian III. the emperors had some stroke in the election, at least in the confirmation, of the Roman pope. Notwithstanding divers of those aforesaid popes in the mean time began to work their practices to bring their purpose about; but yet all their devices could take no full effect, before the said Adrian III., as hereafter (Christ willing) shall be declared; so that the emperors all this while bare some rule in choosing the popes, and in assembling general councils. Wherefore, by the commandment of Ludovicus, the emperor, in the time of this Gregory IV., a general synod was commenced at Aquis- A General Synod at Aquisgrane.

(1) Gul. lib. de Pontif. (2) Fabian.

Ethelwolf. A.D. 844. grane, where it was decreed by the said Gregory and his assistants: first, that every church should have sufficient of its own proper lands and revenues to find the priests thereof, that none should need to lack or go about a begging. Item, that none of the clergy, of what order or degree soever they be, should use any vesture of any precious or scarlet colours, neither should wear rings on their fingers, unless it be when prelates be at mass, or give their consecrations. Item, that prelates should not keep too great ports or families, or keep great horse, or use dice, or harlots, and that the monks should not exceed measure in gluttony or riot. Item, that none of the clergy, being either anointed or shaven, should use either gold or silver in their shoes, slippers, or girdles, like Heliogabalus. By this it may be conjectured, what pomp and pride in those days had crept in among the clergy. Moreover, by the said Pope Gregory IV., at the commandment of Ludovicus, the emperor, the feast of All Saints was first brought into the church.

Every Church to have sufficient to find its own priests.

The Feast of All Saints.

After this pope came Sergius II., who first brought in the altering of the popes' names, because he was named before 'Os porci,' that is, 'Swine's-snout:' who also ordained the 'Agnus,' thrice to be sung at the mass, and the host to be divided into three parts.

The Popes' names first altered.

The Host divided into three parts.

After him was Pope Leo IV., to whom this King Ethelwolf, as in this present chapter is above specified, did commit the tuition of his son Alfred. By this Pope Leo IV. it came in, and was first enacted in a council of his, that no bishop should be condemned under threescore and twelve witnesses; according as ye see in the witnesses at the condemnation of Stephen Gardiner orderly practised.

Also, contrary to the law of Gregory IV., his predecessor, this pope ordained the cross, all set with gold and precious stones, to be carried before him, like a pope.

The golden cross first borne before the Pope.

And here next now followeth and cometh in the whore of Babylon [Rev. xix. 2,] (rightly, in her true colours, by the permission of God, and manifestly without all tergiversation) to appear to the whole world: and that not only after the spiritual sense, but after the very letter, and the right form. For after this Leo abovementioned, the cardinals, proceeding to their ordinary election (after a solemn mass of the Holy Ghost, to the perpetual shame of them and of that see), instead of a man pope, elected a woman to minister sacraments, to say masses, to give orders, to constitute deacons, priests, and bishops; to promote prelates, to make abbots, to consecrate churches and altars, to have the reign and rule of emperors and kings: and so she did indeed, called by name Joan VIII. This woman's proper name was Gilberta, a Dutch woman of Mayence, who went with an English monk out of the abbey of Fulda, in man's apparel, unto Athens, and after, through her dexterity of wit and learning, was promoted to the popedom, where she sat two years and six months. At last, openly in the face of a general procession, she fell in labour and travail of child, and so died, by reason whereof the cardinals, even to this day, do avoid to come near by that street where this shame was taken.[1] By Benedict III. who succeeded next in the Romish see, was first ordained (as most writers record) the dirge to be said for the dead. Albeit before him, Gregory III. had done in that matter worthily for his part already.

A.D. 855

A woman pope, called Joan VIII.

Dirge for the dead.

(1) In reference to this event, which has proved a source of lengthened controversy, a monkish poet observes—"Papa Pater Patrum peperit Papissa Papellum." See Bower's Lives of the Popes: Joan. Also, Mosheim's Ecc. Hist. vol. ii. p. 271.—Ed.

After him sat Pope Nicholas I. who enlarged the pope's decrees with many constitutions, equalling the authority of them with the writings of the apostles. This Pope Nicholas ordained that no secular prince, nor the emperor himself, should be present at their councils, unless in matters concerning the faith; to the end that such as they judged to be heretics, they should execute and murder. Also, that no laymen should sit in judgment upon the clergy, or reason upon the pope's power. Also, that no christian magistrate should have any power upon any prelate, alleging that a prelate is called God. Also, that all church service should be in Latin; yet, notwithstanding, dispensing with the Sclavonians and Polonians to retain still their vulgar language. Sequences in the mass were by him first allowed. By this pope priests began to be restrained and debarred from marrying: wherefore Hulderickc, bishop of Augsburgh, a learned and a holy man, sending a letter unto the pope, gravely and learnedly refuteth and reclaimeth against his indiscreet proceedings touching that matter. The copy of which letter, as I thought it unworthy to be suppressed, so I judged it here worthy and meet for the better instruction of the reader to be inserted, the words whereof here follow, out of Latin into English translated. *Marriages of priests forbidden.*

A learned epistle of Huldericke, bishop of Augsburgh, sent to Pope Nicholas I., proving that priests ought not to be restrained from marriage.[1]

Huldericke, bishop only by name, unto the reverend Father Nicholas, the vigilant provisor of the holy church of Rome, with due commendation sendeth love as a son, and fear as a servant. Understanding, reverend Father, your decrees which you sent to me concerning the single life of the clergy, to be far discrepant from all discretion, I was troubled partly with fear, and partly with heaviness. With fear for that, as it is said, the sentence of the pastor, whether it be just or unjust, is to be feared. For I was afraid lest the weak hearers of the Scripture (who scarcely obey the just sentence of their pastor, much more despising this unjust decreement) through the onerous and importable transgression of their pastor, should show themselves disobedient. With heaviness I was troubled, and with compassion, for that I doubted how the members of the body should do, their head being so greatly out of frame. For what can be more grievous or more to be lamented, touching the state of the church, than for you, being the bishop of the principal see, to whom appertaineth the regiment of the whole church, to swerve ever so little out of the right way! Certes, in this you have not a little erred, in that you have gone about to constrain your clergy to singleness of life, through your imperious tyranny; whom rather you ought to stir up to the continency of marriage. For is not this to be counted a violence and tyranny to the judgment of all wise men, when a man is compelled by your decrees to do that which is against the institution of the gospel and the proceeding of the Holy Ghost? Seeing then there be so many holy examples both of the Old and New Testament, teaching us (as you know) due information, I desire your patience not to think it grievous for me to bring a few here out of many.

First, in the old law, the Lord permitteth marriage unto the priests, which afterward in the new law we do not read to be restrained, but in the gospel thus he saith, "There be some which have made themselves eunuchs for the kingdom of heaven, but all men do not take this word; he that can take it, let him take it." [Matt. xix. 12.] Wherefore, the apostle saith, "Concerning virgins, I have no commandment of the Lord, but only I give counsel." *Priests' marriage in the old law permitted, in the new law not forbidden.*

(1) Nicholao Domino et Patri, pervigili sanctæ Romanæ ecclesiæ provisori, Huldericus solo nomine episcopus, amorem ut filius, timorem ut servus. Cum tua (O Pater et Domine) decreta super clericorum continentiam, &c.

Ethelwolf. A.D. 858.

[1 Cor. vii. 25.] Which counsel also all men do not take, as in the commandment of the Lord before, but many there be, false dissemblers and flatterers, going about to please men, and not God, whom we see under a false pretence of continency to fall into horrible wickedness. And therefore, lest, through the infection of this wicked pestilence, the state of the church should too much go to ruin; he said, "Because of fornication, let every man have his own wife." [1 Cor. vii. 2.] Touching which saying, our false hypocrites falsely do lie and feign, as though only it pertained to the laity, and not to them. And yet they themselves, seeming to be set in the most holy order, are not afraid to commit adultery, and as we see, with weeping eyes, all they do outrage in the aforesaid wickedness.

These men have not rightly understood the Scripture, from whose breasts, while they suck so hard, instead of milk, they suck out blood. For the saying of the apostle, "Let every man have his own wife," [1 Cor. vii. 2,] doth except none in very deed, but him only who hath the gift of continency, settling with himself to keep and continue his virgin in the Lord. Wherefore, O reverend Father, it shall be your part to cause and oversee, that whosoever, either with hand or mouth, hath made a vow of continency, and afterward would forsake it, either should be compelled to keep his vow, or else by lawful authority should be deposed from his order.

And to bring this to pass, you shall not only have me, but also all other of my order, to be helpers unto you. But that you may understand, that those who know not what a vow doth mean, are not to be violently compelled thereunto, hear what the apostle saith to Timothy, "A bishop must be irreprehensible, the husband of one wife." [1 Tim. iii. 2—12.] Which sentence lest you should turn and apply only to the church, mark what he inferreth after, "He that knoweth not to rule his own household and family, how should he rule the church of God?" And likewise of the deacons, he saith, "Let them be the husband of one wife, which have knowledge to govern their own house and children." And this wife, how she is wont to be blest of the priest, you understand sufficiently, I suppose, by the decrees of holy Sylvester, the pope.

This decree contrary to the bishops and prelates in Queen Mary's time.

To these and such other holy sentences of the Scripture, agreeth also he that is the writer of the rule of the clergy, writing after this manner, "A clerk must be chaste and continent, or else let him be coupled in the bands of matrimony, having one wife." Whereby it is to be gathered, that the bishop and deacon are noted infamous and reprehensible, if they be divided in more women than one: otherwise, if they do forsake one under the pretence of religion, both they together, as well the bishop as the deacon, be here condemned by the canonical sentence, which saith, "Let no bishop or priest forsake his own wife, under the colour and pretence of religion. If he do forsake her, let him be excommunicated. And if he so continue, let him be degraded." St. Augustine also, a man of discreet holiness, hath these words, "There is no offence so great or grievous, but it is to avoid a greater evil."

Furthermore, we read in the second Book of the Tripartite History, that when the Council of Nice, going about to establish the same decree, would enact that bishops, priests, and deacons, after their consecration, either should abstain utterly from their own wives, or else should be deposed; then Paphnutius (one of those holy martyrs of whom the Emperor Maximus had put out the right eye, and hocked their left legs,) rising up amongst them, withstood their purposed decree: confessing marriage to be honourable, and calling the bed of matrimony to be chastity; and so persuaded the council from making that law, declaring thereby what occasion might come to themselves and their wives of fornication. And thus much did Paphnutius (being unmarried himself) declare unto them. And the whole council, commending his sentence, gave place thereto, and left the matter freely without compulsion, to the will of every man, to do therein as he thought right.

Six thousand heads of infants found in the Pope's moat.

Notwithstanding there be some who take St. Gregory for their defence in this matter, whose temerity I laugh at, and ignorance I lament; for they know not, being ignorantly deceived, how dangerous the decree of this heresy was (being made by St. Gregory), who afterwards well revoked the same, with condign fruit of repentance. For upon a certain day, as he sent unto his fishpond to have fish, and did see more than six thousand infants' heads brought to him, which were taken out of the same pond or moat, he did greatly repent in himself the decree made before touching the single life of priests,

Ethelwolf. A.D. 858.

which he confessed to be the cause of that so lamentable a murder.[1] And so purging the same with condign fruit of repentance, he altered again the things which he had decreed before, commending that counsel of the apostle, which saith, "It is better to marry than to burn," [1 Cor. vii. 9;] adding moreover of himself thereunto, and saying, "It is better to marry than to give occasion of death."

Peradventure if these men had read with me this which so happened, I think they would not be so rash in their doing and judging, fearing at least the Lord's commandment, "Do not judge, that you be not judged." [Matt. vii. 4.] And St. Paul saith, "Who art thou that judgest another man's servant? Either he standeth or falleth to his own master; but he shall stand; for the Lord is mighty and able to make him stand." Therefore let your holiness cease to compel and enforce those whom only you ought to admonish, lest through your own private commandment (which God forbid) you be found contrary as well to the Old Testament as to the New; for, as St. Augustine saith to Donatus, "This is only what we do fear in your justice, lest, not for the consideration of christian lenity, but for the grievousness and greatness of transgressions committed, you be thought to use violence in executing punishment of that which only we do desire you, by Christ, not to do. For transgressions are so to be punished, that the life of the transgressors may repent." Also another saying of St. Augustine we would have you to remember, which is this:—"Nil nocendi fiat cupiditate, omnia consulendi charitate, et nihil fiat immaniter, nihil inhumaniter;" that is, "Let nothing be done through the greediness of hurting, but all things through the charity of profiting; neither let any thing be done cruelly, nothing ungently." Also of the same Augustine it is written, "In the fear and name of Christ I exhort you, which of you soever have not the goods of this world, be not greedy to have them. Such as have them presume not too much upon them. For I say, to have them is no damnation, but if you presume upon them, that is damnation, if for the having of them you shall seem great in your own sight, or if you do forget the common condition of man through the excellency of any thing you have. Use therefore therein due discretion, tempered with moderation, the which cup of discretion is drawn out of the fountain of the apostolic preaching, which said, Art thou loose from thy wife? do not seek for thy wife. Art thou bound to thy wife? seek not to be loosed from her." [1 Cor. vii. 27.] Where also it followeth, "Such as have wives, let them be as though they had them not, and they that use the world, let them be as not using it."

A saying of Augustine.

Also concerning the widow, he saith, "Let her marry to whom she will, only in the Lord." [1 Cor. vii. 39.] To marry in the Lord is nothing else but to attempt nothing in contraction of matrimony, which the Lord doth forbid. Jeremy also saith, "Trust not in the words of lies, saying, The temple of the Lord, the temple of the Lord, the temple of the Lord." [Jer. vii. 4.] The which saying of Jeremy, Hierome expoundeth thus, "This may agree also, and be applied to such virgins as brag and vaunt of their virginity with an impudent face, pretending chastity when they have another thing in their conscience, and know not how the apostle defineth the virgin, that she should be holy in body, and also in spirit. For what availeth the chastity of the body, if the mind itself be unchaste, or if it have not the other virtues, which the prophetical sermon doth describe? the which virtues, forasmuch as we see partly to be in you; and because we are not ignorant that this discretion, although neglected in this part, yet in the other actions of your life is kept honestly of you, we do not despair but you will also soon amend the little lack which is behind; and therefore with as much gravity as we can, we cease not to call upon you, to correct and amend this your negligence. For although, according to our common calling, a bishop is greater than a priest, and Augustine was less than Hierome, notwithstanding, the good correction proceeding from the lesser

To marry in the Lord.

What a virgin is defined by the apostle.

(1) How far our author is correct in this awful statement the Editor has no means of proving. If the standard of religious faith and practice in the Romish Church, "Dens' Theology," must be viewed only as an incentive to crimes, the blackest and the deepest, in the nineteenth century, it would be inconsistent to expect that the darker ages of the ninth century, under the fostering care of the same Church, would be wanting in the most aggravated instances of human depravity. While the Church of Rome retains on her escutcheon, "forbidding to marry," she raises a barrier to human happiness, and opens a door to all iniquity; in a word, she enjoins that which *they* taught, who, the great apostle St. Paul declared, had "departed from the faith," were "giving heed to seducing spirits and doctrines of devils," "speaking lies in hypocrisy," and had "their conscience seared with a hot iron." 1 Tim. iv. 1—3.—Ed.

Ethelwolf. A.D. 858.

to the greater, was not to be refused or disdained, especially when he who is corrected is found to strive against the truth, to please men. For, as St. Augustine saith, writing to Boniface, "The disputations of all men, be they never so catholic or approved persons, ought not to be had instead of the canonical Scriptures, so that we may disprove or refuse (saving the honour and reverence which is due unto them) any thing that is in their writings, if any thing there be found contrary to truth. And what can be found more contrary to the truth than this? When, as the Truth himself, speaking of continency, not of one only, but of all together (the number only excepted of them which have professed continency), saith, "He that can take, let him take;" the which saying these men, moved, I cannot tell by what cause, do turn and say, "He that cannot take, let him be accursed." And what can be more foolish amongst men, than when any bishop or archdeacon run themselves headlong into all kinds of lust? yet shame not to say, that the chaste marriage of priests is in ill savour with them; and, as void of all compassion and true righteousness, do not *desire* or *admonish* their clerks, as their fellow-servants, to abstain, but *command* them, and *enforce* them as servants violently to abstain. Unto the which imperious commandment of theirs, or counsel (whichever you will call it) they add also this foolish and scandalous suggestion, saying, "that it is more honest privately to lead the life of a libertine, than apertly in the sight and consciences of many men to be bound to one wife." The which truly they would not say, if they were either of him, or in him, who saith, "Woe to you Pharisees, which do all things before men." And so the Psalmist, "Because they please men they are confounded, for the Lord hath despised them." [Ps. liii. 5.] These be the men who ought to persuade us that we should rather shame to sin privily in the sight of Him, to whom all things be open, than seem in the sight of men to be clean. These men therefore, although through their sinful wickedness they deserve no counsel of godliness to be given them, yet we, not forgetting our humanity, cease not to give them counsel, by the authority of God's word, which seeketh all men's salvation, desiring them by the bowels of charity, and saying, with the words of Scripture, "Cast out, thou hypocrite, first the beam out of thine own eye, and then thou shalt see to cast the mote out of the eye of thy brother."

The absurd saying and contrary doing of Papists.

Moreover, this also we desire them to attend to, what the Lord saith of the adulterous woman, "Which of you that is without sin, let him cast the first stone against her." As though he would say, "If Moses bid you, I also bid you." But yet I require you that be the competent ministers and executors of the law, take heed what you add thereunto; take heed also, I pray you, what you are yourselves: for if, as the Scripture saith, thou shalt well consider thyself, thou wilt never defame or detract from another.

Moreover, it is signified unto us also, that some there be of them, who, when they ought like good shepherds to give their lives for the Lord's flock, yet are they puffed up with such pride, that without all reason they presume to rend and tear the Lord's flock with whippings and beatings; whose unreasonable doings St. Gregory bewailing, thus saith, "Quid fiat de ovibus quando pastores lupi fiunt?" that is, "What shall become of the sheep when the pastors themselves be wolves?" But who is overcome, but he who exerciseth cruelty? Or who shall judge the persecutor, but he who gave patiently his back to stripes? And this is the fruit which cometh to the church by such persecutors, also which cometh to the clergy by such despiteful handling of their bishops, or rather infidels. For why may you not call them infidels, of whom St. Paul thus speaketh, and writeth to Timothy? That, "in the latter days there shall certain depart from the faith, and give heed to spirits of error and doctrine of devils: that speak false through hypocrisy, having their consciences marked with a hot iron, forbidding to marry, and commanding to abstain from meats." [1 Tim. iv. 1—3.] And this is, if it be well marked, the whole handful of the darnel and cockle growing amongst the corn: this is the covent of all madness; that while they of the clergy be compelled to relinquish the company of their own lawful wives, they become afterward fornicators and adulterers, and wicked ministers of other sinful filthiness. These be they that bring into the church of God this heresy, as blind guides leading the blind; that it might be fulfilled which the Psalmist speaketh of, as foreseeing the errors of such men, and accursing them after this manner, "Let their eyes be blinded, that they see not, and bow down always their back." [Ps. lxix. 23.] For so much then, O apostolical sir! as no man who knoweth you, is ignorant, that if you through the light of your discretion had understood and seen what poisoned pestilence might have come into the church through the sentence of this your decree, you would never have consented to the suggestions of certain wicked persons. Wherefore, we counsel you, by the fidelity of our due subjection, that with all diligence you would put away so great slander from the church of God; and through your discreet discipline, you will remove this Pharisaical doctrine from the flock of God: so that this only Shunamite of the Lord's (using no more adulterous husbands) do not separate the holy people and the kingly priesthood from her spouse which is Christ, through an irrecoverable divorcement: seeing that no man without chastity (not only in the virgin's state, but also in the state of matrimony) shall see our Lord, who, with the Father and the Holy Ghost, liveth and reigneth for ever. Amen.[1]

By the above epistle of Bishop Huldericke the matter is plain, gentle reader, to conceive what was then the sentence of learned men concerning the marriage of ministers: but here, by the way, the reader is to be admonished, that this epistle, which by error of the writer is referred to Pope Nicholas I., in my mind is rather to be attributed to the name and time of Nicholas II. or III.

After this Pope Nicholas succeeded Adrian II., John IX., and Martinus II. After these came Adrian III., and Stephen V. By this Adrian it was first decreed, That no emperor after that time should intermeddle or have any thing to do in the election of the pope; and thus began the emperors first to decay, and the papacy to swell and rise aloft. Thus much concerning Romish matters for this time.

To return to where we left off, touching the story of King Ethelwolf. About the latter end of his reign, the Danes, who before had invaded the realm, in the time of King Egbert, as is above declared, now made their entry again, with three and thirty ships arriving about Hampshire; through the barbarous tyranny of whom much bloodshed and murder happened here among the English, in Dorsetshire, about Portsmouth, in Kent, in East Anglia, in Lindsey, at Rochester, about London, and in Wessex, where Ethelwolf, the king, was overcome, besides divers other kings and dukes, whom the Danes, daily approaching in great multitudes, in divers victories had put to flight. At length King Ethelwolf, with his son Ethelbald, warring against them in Southery, at Oclea, drave them to the sea; where they hovering a space, after a while burst in again with horrible rage and cruelty, as hereafter (Christ willing) shall be declared, as much as to our purpose shall serve, professing in this history to write not of matters extern and politic, but only pertaining to the church. The cause of this great affliction sent of God unto this realm, thus I found expressed and collected in a certain old written story, which hath no name: the words of which writer, for the same cause as he thought to recite them, (writing, as he saith, "ad cautelam futurorum,") I thought also for the same here not to be omitted, albeit in all parts of his commendation I do not fully with him accord. The words of the writer be these:[2]—

(1) Invenitur hæc epistola in vetustis membranaceis libris (testante Illyrico in catalogo). Meminit ejusdem epistolæ Æneas Sylvius, in sua peregrinatione, et Germaniæ descriptione.
(2) "In Anglorum quidem Ecclesia primitiva, religio clarissime resplenduit: ita ut Reges et Reginæ, et Principes ac Duces, Consules, et Barones," etc.—Ex vetusto exemplo historiæ Carianæ. W. C. 1.

Ethelwolf

A.D. 858.

The causes of God's wrath, whereby the realm of England was scourged by the Danes.

"In the primitive church of the Englishmen, religion did most clearly shine, insomuch that kings, queens, princes and dukes, consuls, barons, and rulers of churches, incensed with the desire of the kingdom of heaven, labouring and striving among themselves to enter into monkery, into voluntary exile and solitary life, forsook all, and followed the Lord. Where, in process of time, all virtue so much decayed among them, that in fraud and treachery none seemed like unto them: neither was to them any thing odious or hateful, but piety and justice; neither any thing in price or honour, but civil war and shedding of innocent blood. Wherefore, Almighty God sent upon them pagan and cruel nations, like swarms of bees, which neither spared women nor children, as Danes, Norwegians, Goths, Suevians, Vandals, and Frisians: who, from the beginning of the reign of King Ethelwolf till the coming of the Normans, by the space of nearly two hundred and thirty years, destroyed their sinful land from the one side of the sea to the other, from man also to beast. For why? they, invading England ofttimes of every side, went not about to subdue and possess it, but only to spoil and destroy it. And if it had chanced them at any time to be overcome of the English, it availed nothing, since other navies with still greater power in other places were ready upon a sudden and unawares to approach upon them."

Thus far have you the words of mine author, declaring the cause which provoked God's anger: whereunto may be adjoined the wickedness, not only of them but of their forefathers also before them, who, falsely breaking the faith and promise made with the Britons, did cruelly murder their nobles, wickedly oppress their commons, impiously persecute the innocent Christians, injuriously possess their land and habitation: chasing the inhabitants out of house and country, besides the violent murder of the monks of Bangor, and divers foul slaughters among the poor Britons, who sent for them to be their helpers. Wherefore God's just recompence falling upon them from that time, never suffered them to be quiet from foreign enemies, till the coming of William the Norman.

The first entering of the Danes.

Moreover, concerning the outward occasions given on the part of the English, by which the Danes were first moved to invade the realm, I find in certain stories two most specially assigned; the one unjustly given, and justly taken, the other not given justly, and unjustly taken.[1] Of these two, the first was given in Northumberland, by means of Osbright, reigning under-king of the West Saxons, in the north parts. This Osbright upon a time journeying by the † way, turned into the house of one of his nobles called Bruer, who, having at home a wife of great beauty (he being absent abroad), the king after his dinner, allured with the excellency of her beauty, did † sorely ill treat her: whereupon, she being greatly dismayed and vexed in her mind, made her moan to her husband on his return, of this violence and injury received. Bruer consulting with his friends, first went to the king, resigning into his hands all such service and possessions as he did hold of him: that done, he took shipping and sailed into Denmark, where he had great friends, and had his bringing up before. There, making his moan to Codrinus the king, he desired his aid in revenging the great villany of Osbright against him and his wife. Codrinus hearing this, and glad to have some just quarrel to enter the land, levied an army with all speed, and preparing all things necessary for the same, sendeth forth Inguar and Hubba, two brethren, his chief captains, with an innumerable multitude of

Codrinus the king, and Inguar and Hubba, captains of the Danes.

(1) Ex Historia Jornalensi.

Danes, into England; who first arriving at Holderness, there burnt up the country, and killed without mercy both men, women, and children, whom they could lay hands upon. Then marching towards York, they joined in battle with the aforesaid Osbright, where he with the most part of his army was slain; and so the Danes obtained possession of the city of York. Others say, and it is by the most part of story writers recorded, that the chief cause of the coming of Inguar and Hubba with the Danes, was, to be revenged of King Edmund, reigning under the West Saxons over the East Angles in Norfolk and Suffolk, for the murder of a certain Dane, father to Inguar and Hubba, which was falsely imputed to King Edmund. The story is thus told.

Ethelwolf. A.D. 858.

A.D. 867.

Another cause of the coming of the Danes.

"A certain nobleman of the Danes, of the king's stock, called Lothbroke, father to Inguar and Hubba, entering upon a time with his hawk into a certain skiff or cock-boat alone, by chance, through tempest, was driven with his hawk to the coast of Norfolk, named Rudham, where he, being found and detained, was presented to the king. The king understanding his parentage, and seeing his case, entertained him in his court accordingly; and every day more and more perceiving his activity and great dexterity in hunting and hawking, bare special favour unto him, insomuch that the king's falconer, or master of game, bearing privy envy against him, secretly, as they were hunting together in a wood, did murder him, and threw him into a bush. This Lothbroke, being murdered, within two or three days began to be missed in the king's house; of whom no tidings could be heard, but only by a spaniel dog of his, which continuing in the wood, with the corpse of his master, at sundry times came and fawned upon the king so long, that at length they, following the trace of the hound, were brought to the place where Lothbroke lay. Whereupon, inquisition being made, at length, by certain circumstances of words and other evidences, it was known how and by whom he was murdered; that was, by the king's huntsman, named Berike; who thereupon being convicted, was put into the same boat of Lothbroke, alone, and without any tackling, to drive by seas, and thus either to be saved by the weather, or to be drowned in the deep. As it chanced that Lothbroke was driven from Denmark to Norfolk, so it happened that from Norfolk Berike was carried into Denmark, where the boat of Lothbroke being well known, hands were laid upon him, and inquisition made of the party. In fine, in his torments, to save himself, he uttered an untruth of King Edmund, saying, 'That the king had put Lothbroke to death in the county of Norfolk.' Whereupon grudge first was conceived, then an army appointed, and great multitudes sent into England to revenge that fact, where they, arriving in Northumberland, destroyed, as is said, those parts first. From thence sailing into Norfolk, they exercised the like tyranny there upon the inhabitants thereof, especially upon the innocent prince and blessed martyr of God, King Edmund." Concerning the further declaration of this hereafter shall follow (Christ our Lord so permitting) more to be spoken, as place and observation of time and years shall require.

Murder will out.

In the mean season, King Ethelwolf, as already noticed in this chapter, when he had chased the aforesaid Danes from place to

Ethelbald. A.D. 858. place, causing them to take the sea, in the mean while departeth himself both from land and life, leaving behind him four sons, who reigned every one in his order, after the decease of their father; the names of whom were Ethelbald, Ethelbright, Ethelred, and Alfred or Alured.

King Ethelwolf deceaseth.

ETHELBALD, ETHELBERT, AND ETHELRED I.

A.D. 858. King Ethelbald, the eldest son of Ethelwolf, succeeding his father in the province of West Sax, and Ethelbert in the province of Kent, reigned both together the term of five years, one with the other. Ethelbald left this infamy behind him in stories, namely, that of marrying his stepmother, wife to his own father, named Judith.

A.D. 867. Ethelred. After these two succeeded Ethelred, the third son, who, in his time, was so incumbered with the Danes bursting in on every side, especially about York, which city they then spoiled and burnt up, that he in one year stood in nine battles against them, with the help of Alfred his brother. In the beginning of this king's reign, the Danes landed in East England, or Norfolk and Suffolk. But, as Fabian writeth, they were compelled to forsake that country, and so taking shipping again, sailed northward, and landed in Northumberland, where they were met by the kings then reigning there, called Osbright and Ella, who gave them a strong fight; but, notwithstanding, the Danes, with the help of such as inhabited the country, won the city of York, and held it a certain season, as is above premised.

York burned by the Danes.

In the reign of this Ethelred I., the Northumberlanders rebelling against the king, thought to recover the former state of their kingdom out of the West Saxons' hands; by reason of which discord, as happeneth in all lands where dissension is, the strength of the English nation was not a little weakened, and the Danes the more thereby prevailed.

A.D. 870. In the latter time of the reign of this King Ethelred I., which was about A.D. 870, certain of the aforesaid Danes being thus possessed of the north country, after their cruel persecution and murder done there, as partly is noticed before, took shipping from thence, intending to sail toward the East Angles, who, by the way upon the sea, met with a fleet of Danes, whereof the captains or leaders were named Inguar and Hubba; who, joining together in one council, made all one course, and lastly landed in East England, or Norfolk, and in process of time came to Thetford. Thereof hearing, Edmund, then under-king of that province, assembled a host and gave them battle; but Edmund and his company were forced to forsake the field, and the king, with a few persons, fled unto the castle of Framlingham, whom the Danes pursued; but he a short while after yielded himself to the persecution of the Danes, answering in this manner to the messenger, who addressed him in the name of Inguar, prince of the Danes, "who most victoriously," saith he, "was come with innumerable legions, subduing both by sea and land many nations unto him; and so now arrived in those parts requireth him likewise to submit himself, yielding to him his hid treasures, and all other goods

St. Edmund, king of East Angles.

of his ancestors, and so to reign under him: which thing if he would not do, he should," said he, "be judged unworthy both of life and reign." Edmund, hearing of this proud message of the pagan, consulted with certain of his friends, and among others, with one of his bishops, who was then his secretary; who, seeing the present danger of the king, gave him counsel to yield to the conditions. Upon this the king pausing a little with himself, at length rendered this answer, bidding the messenger go tell his lord in these words, "that Edmund, a christian king, for the love of temporal life, will not submit himself to a pagan duke, unless he first would be a Christian." Immediately upon the same, the wicked and crafty Dane, approaching in most hasty speed upon the king, encountered with him in battle, as some say, at Thetford; where the king being put to the worse, and pitying the terrible slaughter of his men, thinking with himself rather to submit his own person to danger, than that his people should be slain, did fly, as Fabian saith, to the castle of Framlingham, or, as mine author writeth, to Halesdon, now called St. Edmundsbury, where this blessed man, being on every side compassed by his cruel enemies, yielded himself to their persecution. And, for that he would not renounce or deny Christ and his laws, they therefore most cruelly bound him unto a tree, and caused him to be shot to death; and, lastly, caused his head to be smitten from his body and cast into the thick bushes; which head and body at the same time by his friends were taken up, and solemnly buried at the said Halesdon, otherwise now named St. Edmundsbury: whose brother, named Edwold, notwithstanding of right the kingdom fell next unto him, setting apart the liking and pleasure of the world, became a hermit, of the abbey of Cerum, in the county of Dorset.

The persecution and martyrdom of St. Edmund, king of the East Angles, by the Danes.

After the martyrdom of this blessed Edmund, when the cruel Danes had sufficiently robbed and spoiled that country, they took again their ships, and landed in Southery, and continued their journey till they came to the town of Reading, and there won the town with the castle, where, as Cambrensis saith, within three days of their coming thither, the aforesaid Inguar and Hubba, captains of the Danes, as they went in pursuit of their prey or booty, were slain at a place called Englefield. These princes of the Danes thus slain, the rest of them kept whole together, in such wise that the West Saxons might take of them no advantage, but yet, within a few days after, the Danes were holden so short, that they were forced to issue out of the castle and to defend themselves in open battle; in the which, by the industry of King Ethelred and of Alfred his brother, the Danes were discomfited, and many of them slain, which discomfort made them fly again into the castle, and there keep them for a certain time. The king then committing the charge of them to Ethelwold, duke of Baroke, or Berkshire, departed. But when the Danes knew of the king's departure, they brake suddenly out of their hold, took the duke unprovided, and slew him and much of his people; and so, joining themselves with others that were scattered in the country, embattled them in such wise, that of them was gathered a strong host.

Reading taken by the Danes, and Inguar and Hubba slain.

Duke Ethelwold slain.

As the tidings hereof were brought to King Ethelred, which put

Ethelred. A.D. 871.

him in great heaviness, word also was brought the same time of the landing of Osrick, king of Denmark, who, with the assistance of the other Danes, had gathered a great host, and were embattled upon Ashdon. To this battle King Ethelred, with his brother Alfred, forced by great need, hastened, to withstand the Danes, at which time the king a little staying behind, being yet at his service, Alfred, who was come in before, had entered already into the whole fight with the Danes, who struck together with huge violence.[1] The king being required to make speed, and being then at service and meditations, such was his devotion, that he would not stir out one foot before the service was fully complete. In the meanwhile, the Danes so fiercely invaded Alfred and his men, that they won the hill, and the christian men were in the valley, and in great danger to lose the field. Nevertheless, through the grace of God, and their godly manhood, the king coming from his service, with his fresh soldiers, recovered the hill of the infidels, and so discomfited the Danes that day, that in flying away not only they lost the victory, but most part of them their lives also, insomuch that their duke or king, Osrick or Osege, and five of their other dukes, with much of their people were slain, and the rest chased unto Reading town.

Osrick, king of Denmark, landeth in England.

Invocation and prayer profitable in time of battle.

The Danes overthrown at Ashdon.

After this the Danes yet re-assembled their people, and gathered a new host, so that within fifteen days they met at Basingstoke, and there gave battle to the king, and had the better. Then the king again gathered his men, which at that field were dispersed, and with fresh soldiers accompanying them, met the Danes, within two months after, at the town of Merton, where he gave them a sharp battle, so that much people were slain as well of the Christians as of the Danes; but, in the end, the Danes had the honour of the field, and King Ethelred was wounded, and therefore fain to save himself.

Another battle at Merton.

After these two fields thus won by the Danes, they obtained great circuit of ground, and destroyed man and child that would not yield to them; and churches and temples they turned to the use of stables, and other vile occupations.

Thus the king, being beset with enemies on every side, seeing the land so miserably oppressed of the Danes, his knights and soldiers consumed, his own land of West Saxons in such desolation, he being also wounded himself, but specially for that he, sending his commissions into Northumberland, Mercia, and East Anglia, could have of them but small or little comfort, because they, through wicked rebellion, were more willing to take the part of the Danes than of their king, was sore perplexed therewithal, as the other kings were both before him and after him at that time, so that as Malmesbury witnesseth, "magis optarent honestum exitium, quam tam acerbum imperium:" that is, "they rather wished honestly to die, than with such trouble and sorrow to reign." And thus this king not long after deceased, when he had reigned, as Fabian saith, eight years, or, as Malmesbury writeth, but five years, during which time, notwithstanding his so great troubles and vexations in martial affairs (as is in some stories mentioned), he founded the house or college of canons

Death of Ethelred.

(1) Ex Guliel. Malmesboriensi. Ex Historia Jornalensi. Ex Fabiano et aliis.

at Exeter, and was buried at the Abbey of Winborn, or Woburn, after whose decease, for lack of issue of his body, the rule of the land fell unto his brother Alfred. *Alfred.* A.D. 871.

ALFRED,[1] OTHERWISE CALLED ALURED.

Among the Saxon kings hitherto in this history mentioned, I find few or none to be preferred, or even to be compared, to this Alfred, or Alured, for the great and singular qualities in this king, worthy of high renown and commendation—whether we behold in him the valiant acts and manifold travails which he continually, from time to time, sustained against his enemies in war, during almost all the time of his reign, for the public preservation of his people; or whether we consider in him his godly and excellent virtues, joined with a public and tender care, and a zealous study for the common peace and tranquillity of the weal public, appearing as well in his prudent laws by him both carefully set forth, and with the like care executed, as also by his own private exercises touching the virtuous institution of his life; or, lastly, whether we respect that in him, which with equal praise matcheth with both the others before, that is, his notable knowledge of good letters, with a fervent love and princely desire to set forth the same through all his realm, before his time being both rude and barbarous. All these heroical properties, joined together in one prince, as it is a thing most rare, and seldom seen in princes now a-days, so I thought the same the more to be noted and exemplified in this good king, thereby either to move other rulers and princes in these our days to his imitation, or else, to show them what hath been in times past in their ancestors, which ought to be, and yet is not found in them. Wherefore, of these three parts to discourse either part in order, first we will begin to treat of his acts and painful travails sustained in defence of the realm public, against the raging tyranny of the Danes, as they are described in the Latin histories of Roger Hoveden and Huntington, whom Fabian also seemeth in this part somewhat to follow. King Alfred, therefore, the first of all the English kings, taking his crown and unction at Rome of Pope Leo[2] (as Malmesbury and Polychronicon do record), in the beginning of his reign, perceiving his lords and people much wasted and decayed by reason of the great wars which Ethelred had against the Danes, yet, as well as he could, gathered a strength of men unto him; and, in the second month that he was made king, he met with the Danes beside Wilton, where he gave them battle; but being far over-matched through the multitude of the contrary part, he was put there to the worse, though not without a great slaughter of the pagan army, which army of the Danes,

King Alfred's valour, piety, and learning.

(1) Edition 1563, p. 11. Ed. 1583, p. 141. Ed. 1596, p. 127. Ed. 1684, vol. i. p. 157.—Ed.

(2) Pope John VIII., the hundred and sixth bishop of Rome, was chosen A.D. 872, the year that Alfred obtained the government of his realm. The Leo to whom our author refers, was Leo IV. to whom Alfred was sent at the age of four years, to be educated. [A.D. 854.] Aperius, who wrote Alfred's life, informs us that Leo confirmed him, adopted him for his son, and anointed him king ("took his crown and unction at Rome," as Foxe observes), but of what kingdom neither that writer, nor any other has informed us. . The kingdom of West Saxons was then held by his father, who had three sons older than Alfred.—Ed.

Alfred. A.D. 873. after that victory, by compact made with King Alfred to depart out of his dominion of West Sax, removed from Reading to London, where it abode all that winter. Halden their king, making truce there with Burthred, king of Mercia, the following year left those parts, and drew his men to Lindsey, robbing and spoiling the towns and villages as they went, and holding the common people under servitude. From thence they proceeded to Repingdon, where, joining with the three other kings of the Danes, called Surdrim, Osketell, and Hamond, they grew thereby to mighty force and strength: then, dividing their army into two parts, the one half remained with Halden in the country of Northumberland; the residue were with the other three kings, wintering and sojourning all the next year at Grantbridge, which was the fourth year of King Alfred. In that year King Alfred's men had a conflict on the sea with six of the Danes' ships, of which they took one, the others fled away. In the same year went Rollo, the Dane, into Normandy, where he was duke thirty years, and afterward was baptized in the faith of Christ, and named Robert. The aforesaid army of the three Danish kings above-mentioned, from Grantbridge returned again to West Saxony, and entered the Castle of Wareham, where King Alfred, with a sufficient power of men, was ready to assault them; but the Danes seeing his strength durst not encounter with him, but sought delays till more aid might come. In the mean season they were constrained to entreat for a truce, leaving also sufficient pledges in the king's hand; promising, moreover, upon their oath, to leave the country of the West Saxons. The king, upon this surety, let them go; but they, falsely breaking their league, privily in the night brake out, taking their journey toward Exeter, during which journey they lost six score of their small ships by a tempest at Sandwich, as Henry Huntingdon in his story recordeth. Then King Alfred followed after the horsemen of the Danes, but could not overtake them before they came to Exeter, where he took of them pledges and fair promises of peace, and so returned. Notwithstanding, the number of the pagans did daily more and more increase, insomuch (as one of my authors saith) that if in one day thirty thousand of them were slain, shortly after they increased to double as many.

Burthred expelled his kingdom, dies at Rome.

A.D. 874.

Rollo, a Dane, first duke of Normandy.

A.D. 876. After this truce taken with King Alfred, the Danes withdrew to the land of Mercia, part of which kingdom they kept themselves, and part they committed to one Ceolulphus, upon condition that he should be vassal to them, and at their commandment, with his people at all times.

A.D. 877. The next year ensuing, which was the seventh year of the reign of Alfred, the Danes now having all the rule of the north part of England, from the river Thames, with Mercia, London, and Essex, disdained that Alfred should have any dominion on the other side of Thames southward. Whereupon the aforesaid three kings, with all the forces and strength they could gather, marched toward Chippenham, in West Sax, with such a multitude, that the king with his people was not able to resist them; insomuch that of the people which inhabited there, some fled over the sea, some remained with the king, and divers submitted themselves to the Danes. Thus King Alfred being overset with a multitude of enemies, and forsaken of his people, having neither land to hold, nor hope to recover that which he had lost, withdrew himself with a few of his nobles about him, into a certain wood country in Somersetshire, called Etheling, where he had right scant to live upon, but such as he and his people might procure by hunting and fishing. This Edeling, or Etheling, or Ethelingsey, which is to say, the Isle of Nobles, standeth in a great marsh or moor, so that there is no access to it without ship or boat, and hath in it a great wood called Selwood, and in the middle a little plain, about two acres of ground: in this isle is venison, and other wild beasts, with fowl and fish in great plenty. In this wood King Alfred, at his first coming, espied a certain desert cottage of a poor swineherd, keeping swine in the wood, named Dunwolf; by whom the king, then unknown, was entertained and cherished with such poor fare as he and his wife could make him, for which King Alfred afterwards set the poor swineherd to learning, and made him bishop of Winchester.

Alfred. A.D. 877.

Alfred flieth into a wood.

A swineherd made bishop of Winchester.

In the mean time, while King Alfred, accompanied with a few, was thus in the desert wood, waiting the event of these miseries, according to certain stories a poor beggar there came and asked alms of the king; and the night following he appeared to the king in his sleep, saying, his name was Cuthbert, promising (as sent from God unto him for his good charity) great victories against the Danes. But let these dreaming fables pass, although they be testified by divers authors.[1] Notwithstanding, the king, in process of time, was more strengthened and comforted, through the providence of God, respecting the miserable ruin of the English. First, the brother of King Halden the Dane, before-mentioned, coming in with three and thirty ships, landed about Devonshire, where by chance being resisted by an ambushment of King Alfred's men, who for their safeguard there lay in garrison, they were slain to the number of 1300 men, and their ensign, called the Raven, was taken. Hoveden, in his book called 'Continuationes,' writeth, that in the same conflict both Inguar and Hubba were slain among the other Danes.[2] After this, King Alfred being better cheered, showed himself more at large; so that daily resorted to him men of Wiltshire, Somersetshire, and Hampshire, till he was strongly accompanied.

Then the king put himself in a bold and dangerous venture, as write Malmesbury, Polychronicon, and Fabian, who followeth them both. For he, apparelling himself in the habit of a minstrel, being very skilful in all Saxon poems, with his instrument of music, entered into the tents of the Danes, lying then at Eddington. There, while showing his interludes and songs, he espied all their sloth and idleness, and heard much of their counsel; and after, returning to his company, declared to them the whole manner of the Danes. Shortly upon this, the king suddenly in the night fell upon the aforesaid Danes, distressed and slew of them a great multitude, and chased them from that coast, insomuch that through his strong and valiant assaults upon his enemies out of his tower of Edeling newly fortified, he so incumbered them, that he clearly voided the country

Alfred ventures into the Danish tents.

A.D. 878.

(1) Guliel. Malmesb. lib. de Reg.; Polychronicon, Rog. Hoveden; Jornalensis; Henr. Hunting. lib. v. de Hist. Ang.
(2) See page 19.—Ed.

Alfred. A.D. 879. of them, between that and Selwood. His subjects soon hearing of these his valiant victories and manful deeds, drew to him daily out of all coasts; so that through the help of God, and their assistance, he held the Danes so short, that he won from them Winchester and divers other good towns. Briefly, he at length forced them to seek for peace, which was concluded upon certain covenants, whereof one, and the principal was, that the beforenamed Gutrum, their king, should be christened; the other was, that such as would not be christened should depart, and leave the country.

Gutrum, prince of the Danes, christened, and named Athelstan. Norfolk and Suffolk given to him. Upon these covenants, first the said Gutrum, the Danish prince, coming to Winchester, was there christened with twenty of his greatest dukes or nobles, which Gutrum, King Alfred, being his godfather at his baptism, named Athelstan. Having, after a certain season, feasted the said Danes, Alfred, according to his promise before made, gave unto their king the country of East Anglia, containing Norfolk and Suffolk, and part of Cambridgeshire. Moreover, as saith Polychronicon, he granted to the Danes that were christened, the country of Northumberland; so the residue that would not be christened departed the land, and sailed into France, where what vexation and harm they wrought, the chronicles of France do partly comprehend.

King Athelstan thus having the possession of these countries, had all East Anglia under his obedience; and, albeit that he held the said province as in fee of the king, and promised to dwell there as his liege man, yet, notwithstanding that, he continued more like a tyrant by the term of eleven years, and died in the twelfth year; during which space, King Alfred, having some more rest and peace, repaired certain towns and strong holds before by the Danes impaired; also he builded divers houses of religion, as the House of Nuns at Shaftesbury; another religious house at Etheling he founded; another in Winchester, named the New Monastery; and also endowed richly the Church of St. Cuthbert in Durham. He, likewise, sent to India to pay and perform his vows to St. Thomas of Ind, which he made during the time of his distress against the Danes.

The nunneries of Shaftesbury and Etheling, and the minster at Winchester built.

A.D. 885. About the fifteenth year of the reign of Alfred, the Danes returning from France to England, landed in Kent, and so came to Rochester and besieged that city, and there lay so long that they builded a tower of timber against the gates of the city: but, by strength of the citizens, that tower was destroyed, and the city defended, till King Alfred came and rescued them; whereby the Danes were so distressed, and so near trapped, that for fear they left their horses behind them, and fled to their ships by night. But the king, when he was thereof aware, sent after them, and took sixteen of their ships, and slew many of the Danes. This done, the king returned to London, and repaired the same honourably (as saith Hoveden), and made it habitable, which before was sore decayed and enfeebled by the Danes.

A.D. 889. The third year after this, which was the nineteenth year of the reign of King Alfred, the aforesaid Athelstan, the Danish king of Norfolk, who was before christened by Alfred, deceased. Not long after this, about the one and twentieth year of this king's reign, the Danes again landed in four places of this land; namely, in

East England, and in the north, and in two places in the west. Before the landing of these Danes it chanced that King Alfred, having heard of the death of King Athelstan, and of other complaints of the Danes, was in East Anglia when these tidings came to him. *Alfred.* A.D. 981.

When King Alfred was hereof assured that some of the Danes were landed on that coast, thinking with themselves the further they went in those parts the less resistance to have and the more speed, as they were wont to have before; Alfred, sending messengers in all haste to Ethelred, duke of Mercia, to assemble him a host to withstand the Danes, who landed in the west, made forth toward his enemies there, where he was in East Anglia, whom he pursued so sharply, that he drove them out from those parts. They then landed in Kent, whither the king with his people sped him; and in like manner drave the Danes from thence, without any great fight, so far as in our authors we can see. After this, the Danes took shipping again and sailed into North Wales, and there robbed and spoiled the Britons, and from thence returned by the sea into East Anglia, with a hundred ships, and there rested themselves, inasmuch as the king was then gone westward. **The Danes driven from Norfolk.** **Return to North Wales.**

The fourth host of the Danes the same year came to Chester, which at length they won; but the country adjoining pressed so sorely upon them, and besieged them so long, keeping them within the city, that at last, wearied with the long siege, they were compelled to eat their own horses for hunger. But, by appointment, at last they gave up the town, and went about by North Wales to Northumberland, which was about the three and twentieth year of King Alfred. In the mean while Alfred with his host sped him thitherward. Then the Danes, leaving their strong holds and castles, and furnished with men and victuals, again took shipping, and set their course in such wise that they landed in Sussex, and so came to the port of Lewes, and from thence toward London, and builded a tower or castle near the river Ley, twenty miles from London. But the Londoners hearing thereof, manned out a certain number of men at arms, who, with the assistance of them of that country, put the Danes from that tower, and afterwards beat it to the ground. Soon after, the king came down thither, and, to prevent the dangers that might ensue, commanded the river Ley to be divided into three streams, so that where a ship might sail in times before, a little boat might then scarcely row. From thence the Danes, leaving their ships and wives, were forced to fly that country, and took their way again toward Wales, and came to Quadruge, near the river Severn; where, upon the borders thereof, they builded a castle, and rested themselves for a time, but the king with his army soon pursued them. In the mean time the Londoners at Ley, taking the Danish ships, brought some of them to London, and the rest they fired. During these three years, from the first coming of the Danes to Ley, England was afflicted with three kinds of sorrows; with the Danes, with pestilence of men, and with murrain of beasts; notwithstanding which troubles the king manfully resisted the malice of his enemies, and thanked God always, what trouble soever fell to him, or to his realm, sustaining it with great patience and humility. These three years overpast, the next following, which was the eight and twentieth **Driven out of Chester.** **Driven from Lewes.** **The river Ley divided into three streams.** **Three plagues in England.**

Alfred. A.D. 897. of the reign of Alfred, the Danes divided their host, of whom part went to Northumberland, part to Norfolk; others sailed over to France, and some came to West Sax, where they had divers conflicts with the Englishmen, both by land, and especially upon the sea; of whom some were slain, many perished by shipwreck, divers others were taken and hanged, and thirty of their ships were captured.

The Danes' ships taken. A.D. 897.

A.D. 901. Not long after this, King Alfred, when he had reigned twenty-nine years and six months, exchanged this mortal life. And thus much, and more, peradventure, than will seem to this our ecclesiastical history appertaining, touching the painful labours and travails of this good king; which he no less valiantly achieved than patiently sustained, for the necessary defence of his realm and subjects.

Character of King Alfred.

Now, if there be any prince who listeth to see and follow the virtuous and godly disposition of this king, both touching the institution of his own life, and also concerning his careful government of the common-weal, thus the histories of him do record: that at what time he, being young, perceiving himself somewhat disposed to carnal indulgences, and thereby hindered from many virtuous purposes, did not, as many young princes and kings' sons in the world be now wont to do, that is, resolve themselves into all kind of carnal license and dissolute sensuality, running and following without bridle, whithersoever their license given doth lead them; as therefore, not without cause, the common proverb reporteth of them, that "kings' sons learn nothing else well but only to ride:" meaning thereby, that while princes and kings' sons have about them flatterers, who bolster them in their faults, their horses yield to them no more than to any other, but if they sit not fast, they will cast them. But this young king, seeing in himself the inclination of his fleshly nature, and minding not to give himself so much as he might take, but rather by resistance to avoid the temptation thereof, besought God that he would send him some continual sickness to quench that vice, whereby he might be more profitable to the public business of the commonwealth, and more apt to serve God in his calling.[1]

His godly prayer.

Then, at God's ordinance, he had the evil called Ficus till he came to the age of twenty years, whereof at length he was cured (as is said in some histories) by a virgin called Modwen, an Irish woman. After this sickness being taken away, to him fell another, which continued with him from the twentieth to the forty-fifth year of his age (according to his own petition and request, made unto God), whereby he was the more reclaimed and attempered from the other greater inconveniences, and less disposed to that which he did most abhor.

Moreover, to behold the bountiful goodness, joined with like prudence, in this man, in the ordering and disposing his riches and rents, it is not unworthy to be recited, how he divided his goods into two equal parts,[2] the one appertaining to uses secular, the other to uses spiritual or ecclesiastical; of the which two principal parts, the first he divided into three portions, namely, one to the

(1) Cestren. lib. v. cap. 1. Fab. cap. 17.
(2) Polychron. lib. v. cap. 1. Guliel. Malmesb. lib. de Regibus.

behoof of his house and family; one to the workmen and builders of his new works, wherein he had great delight and cunning; and one to strangers. Likewise the other second half upon spiritual uses, he did thus divide in four portions; one to the relieving of the poor, another to monasteries, the third portion to the schools of Oxford for the maintaining of good letters, the fourth he sent to foreign churches without the realm. This also is left in stories written in his commendation for his great tolerance and sufferance, that when he had builded the new monastery at Winchester, and afterward his son Edward had purchased of the bishop and the chapter a sufficient piece of ground for certain offices to be adjoined unto the same, and had given for every foot of ground, "marcam auri pleni ponderis" (which was, as I think, a mark of gold or more), yet Alfred therewithal was not greatly discontented to see his coffers so wasted.

His liberal heart.

Over and besides, how sparing and frugal he was of time, as of a thing in this earth most precious, and how far from all vain pastimes and idleness he was, this doth well declare, which in the story of Malmesbury and other writers is told of him; namely, that he so divided the day and night in three parts, if he were not let by wars or other great business, that eight hours he spent in study and learning, other eight hours he spent in prayer and almsdeeds, and other eight hours he spent in his natural rest, sustenance of his body, and the needs of the realm; which order he kept duly by the burning of waxen tapers kept in his closet by persons appointed for that purpose.[1]

How well and godly he spent his time.

How studious he was and careful of the commonwealth, and maintenance of public tranquillity, his laws, most godly set forth and devised by him, may declare; wherein especially by him was provided for the extirpation and abolishing of all theft and thieves out of the realm, whereby the realm, through his vigilant care, was brought into such tranquillity, or rather perfection, that in every cross or turning-way, he made to be set up a golden brooch, at least of silver gilded, throughout his dominions, and none so hardy, neither by day nor night, to take it down; for the more credit whereof, the words of the Latin story be these, "armillas aureas juberet suspendi, quæ viantium aviditatem irritarent, dum non essent qui eas abriperent."[2] And no great marvel therein, if the realm in those days was brought into such an order, and justice so well ministered, when the king himself was so vigilant in overseeing the doings of his judges and officers; whereof thus also we read in the said author testified: "judiciorum a suis hominibus factorum inquisitor perperam actorum asperrimus corrector," *i. e.* "he was," saith mine author, speaking of the king, "a vigilant inquisitor of the doings of his judges, and a strict punisher of their misdoings." Jornalensis also writing upon the same, saith, "he did diligently search out the doings of his officers, and especially of his judges, so that if he knew any of them to err, either through covetousness or unskilfulness, them he removed from their office."[3]

His godly laws.

(1) Guliel. Malmesb. lib. de regibus Angl. (2) Ibid.
(3) "Facta ministrorum suorum et potissime judicum diligenter investigavit, adeo ut quos ex avaritia aut imperitia errare cognosceret, ab officio removebat."—Ex Hist. Jornalensi.

Alfred. A.D. 901.

And thus much concerning the valiant acts and noble virtues of this worthy prince; whereunto, although there were no other ornaments adjoining besides, yet sufficient were they alone to set forth a prince worthy of excellent commendation. Now, besides these other qualities and gifts of God's grace in him above-mentioned, remaineth another part of his no little praise and commendation, which is his learning and knowledge of good letters, wherein he not only was excellently expert himself, but also a worthy maintainer of the same through all his dominions. Where, before his time, no use of grammar or other sciences was practised in this realm, especially about the west parts of the land, there, through the industry of this king, schools began to be erected and studies to flourish. Although among the Britons, in the town of Chester, in South Wales, long before that, in King Arthur's time, as Galfridus writeth, both grammar and philosophy, with other tongues, were taught. After that, some writers record that in the time of Egbert, king of Kent, this island began to flourish with philosophy. About which time some also think that the university of Granchester, near to that which now is called Cambridge, began to be founded by Bede, following this conjecture therein, for that Alcuinus, before-mentioned, who after went to Rome, and from thence to France, in the time of Charlemagne, where he first began the university of Paris, was first trained up in the exercise of studies at the same school of Granchester. Bede[1] also, writing of Sigebert, king of East Anglia, declareth how that king, returning out of France into England, according to the examples which he did there see, ordered and disposed schools of learning, through the means of Felix, then bishop, and placed in them masters and teachers, after the use and manner of the Cantuarites. And yet before these times, moreover, it is thought that there were two schools or universities within the realm; the one for Greek, at the town of Greglade, which afterward was called Kirkelade; the other for Latin, at a place then called Latinlade, afterward Lethelade, near Oxford.

King Alfred commended for learning. Learning first encouraged in England. Chester a place of learning. University of Granchester by Cambridge. University of Paris. King Sigebert a founder of schools. Two ancient schools in England, one for Greek, the other for Latin.

But, however it chanced that the knowledge and study of good letters, once planted in this realm, afterward went to decay, yet King Alfred deserveth no little praise for restoring, or rather increasing the same; after whose time they have ever since continued, albeit not continually through every age in like perfection. But this we may see, what it is to have a prince learned himself, who, feeling and tasting the price and value of science and knowledge, is thereby not only the more apt to rule, but also to instruct and frame his subjects from a rude barbarity, to a more civil congruity of life, and to a better understanding of things, as we see in this famous prince to happen. Concerning his first education and bringing up, although it was somewhat late before he entered on his letters, yet, such was the apt towardness and docility of his nature, that being a child he had the Saxon Poems, as they were used then in his own tongue, by heart and memory. Afterwards with years and time he grew up in such perfection of learning and knowledge that, as mine author saith, "nullus Anglorum fuerit vel intelligendo acutior, vel interpretando elegantior;" which

(1) Beda, lib. iii. cap. 18.

thing in him the more was to be marvelled at, for that he was twelve years of age before he knew any letter. Then his mother, careful and tender over him, having by chance a book in her hand, which he would fain have, promised to give him the same, so that he would learn it.[1] Whereupon he, for greediness of the book, soon learned the letters, having for his schoolmaster Pleimundus, afterwards bishop of Canterbury. And so daily grew he more and more in knowledge, that, at length, as mine author saith, "a great part of the Latin library he translated into English, converting to the uses of his citizens a notable prey of foreign ware and merchandize."[2] Of the books by him and through him translated, were Orosius, the Pastoral of Gregory, the History of Bede, Boëtius 'de Consolatione Philosophiæ;' also a book of his own making and in his own tongue, which in the English speech he called a Hand-book, in Greek called Enchiridion, in Latin a Manual. Besides the History of Bede, translated into the Saxon tongue, he also himself compiled a story in the same speech, called, 'The Story of Alfred,' both which books, in the Saxon tongue, I have seen, though the language I do not understand. As he was learned himself excellently well, so likewise did he inflame all his countrymen to the love of liberal letters, as the words of the story reporteth: "he exhorted and stirred his people to the study of learning, some with gifts, some by threats, suffering no man to aspire to any dignity in the court except he were learned."[3] Moreover, another story thus saith, speaking of his nobles: "also his nobles so much he did allure to the embracing of good letters, that they sent all their sons to school; or if they had no sons, yet their servants they caused to be learned;"[4] whereby the common proverb may be found, not so common as true, "such as is the prince, such be the subjects." He began, moreover, to translate the Psalter into English, and had almost finished the same, had not death prevented him.[5] In the prologue of the book,[6] thus he writeth, declaring the cause why he was so earnest and diligent in translating good books from Latin into English; showing the cause thereof why he so did, as followeth:[7] "the cause was, for that innumerable ancient libraries, which were kept in churches, were consumed with fire by the Danes; and that men had rather suffer peril of their life than follow the exercises of studies; and therefore he thought thereby to provide for the people of the English nation."[7]

Pleimundus teacher to King Alfred, afterwards bishop of Canterbury.

Books translated out of Latin by Alfred.

None advanced to any dignity except he were learned.

The Psalter translated into English by King Alfred.

It is told of him, both by Polychronicon, Malmesbury, Jornalensis, and other historians, whereof I have no names, that he, seeing his country to the westward, to be so desolate of schools and learning, partly to profit himself, partly to furnish his country and subjects with better knowledge, first sent for Grinbald, a learned

(1) Ex Hist. Guliel. Malmesb. de Regib. Ang.

(2) "Plurimam partem Romanæ Bibliothecæ Anglorum auribus dedit, optimam prædam peregrinarum mercium civium usibus convertens."

(3) "Illos præmiis, hos minis hortando neminem illiteratum ad quamlibet curiæ dignitatem aspirare permittens."

(4) "Optimates quoque suos ad literaturam addiscendam in tantum provocavit, ut sibi filios suos, vel saltem si filios non haberent, servos suos, literis commendarent."—Polychron. lib. vi. cap. 1.

(5) Guliel. Malmesb. de Regib. Ang.

(6) Entitled, "Pastorale Grego."

(7) "Quod Ecclesiæ in quibus innumeræ priscæ Bibliothecæ continebantur, cum libris a Danis incensæ sint: quodque in tota insula studium literarum ita abolitum esset, ut quisque minus timeret capitis periculum, quam studiorum exercitia adire. Quapropter se in hoc Anglis suis consulere," &c.

Alfred. A.D. 901. monk, out of France, to come into England: he also sent for another learned man out of Wales, whose name was Asserion, whom he made bishop of Sherborne; and out of Mercia he sent for Werefrith, bishop of Worcester, to whom he gave the Dialogues of Gregory to be translated. But chiefly he used the counsel of Neotus, who then was counted for a holy man, an abbot of a certain monastery, in Cornwall, by whose advisement he sent for the learned men above recited, and also first ordained certain schools of divers arts at Oxford, and enfranchised the same with many great liberties;[1] whereof perhaps the school now called New College first then begun by this Neotus, might take its name; which afterwards, peradventure, the bishops of Winchester, after a larger manner, did re-edify and enlarge with greater possessions.

Learned men sent for and placed about the king. Neotus an abbot. The schools and university of Oxford begun by King Alfred.

Johannes Scotus.

Moreover, among other learned men who were about King Alfred, histories make mention of Johannes Scotus, a godly divine and a learned philosopher; but not that Scotus whom now we call Duns, for this Johannes Scotus came before him many years. This Johannes is described to have been of a sharp wit and of great eloquence, and well expert in the Greek tongue, pleasant and merry of nature and conditions, as appeareth by divers of his doings and answers. First, he coming to France out of his own country of Scotland, by reason of the great tumults of war, was there worthily entertained, and for his learning had in great estimation of Charles the Bald, the French king; who commonly and familiarly used ever to have him about him, both at table and in chamber. Upon a time the king sitting at meat, and seeing something (belike in this John Scot) which seemed not very courtly, cast forth a merry word, asking him what difference there was betwixt a Scot and a sot? Whereunto the Scot, sitting over against the king somewhat lower, replied again suddenly rather than advisedly, yet merrily, saying, "mensa tantum," that is, "the table only;" importing thereby himself to be the Scot, and so calling the king a sot by craft; which word how other princes would have stomached I know not, but this Charles, for the great reverence he bare to his learning, turned it but to laughter among his nobles, and so let it pass.

His answer to the French king.

Another time the same king being at dinner was served with a certain dish of fish, wherein were two great fishes and a little one. After the king had taken thereof his repast, he set down to John Scot the aforesaid fish, to distribute unto the other two clerks sitting there with him, who were two tall and mighty persons, he himself being but a little man. John taketh the fish, of the which the two great ones he taketh and carveth to himself, while the little fish he reacheth to the other two. The king, perceiving his division thus made, reprehended the same. Then John, whose manner was ever to find out some honest matter to delight the king, answered him again, proving his division to stand just and equal: "for here," saith he, "be two great ones and a little one," pointing to the two great fishes and himself, "and likewise here again is a little one and two great;" pointing to the little fish, and the two great persons: "I pray you," saith he, "what odds is there, or what

(1) Guliel. Malmesb.; Jornalensis; Fabian, c. 171.

distribution can be more equal?" Whereat the king with his nobles being much delighted, laughed merrily. *Alfred.* A.D. 901.

At the request of this Charles, sirnamed Bald, the French king, this Scotus translated the book of Dionysius, entitled, "De Hierarchia," from Greek into Latin, word for word, "quo fit," as my author saith, "ut vix intelligatur Latina litera? quum nobilitate magis Græca, quam positione construitur Latina." He wrote also a book, 'De Corpore et Sanguine Domini,' which was afterward condemned by the Pope, 'in concilio Vercellensi.' The same John Scot, moreover, compiled a book of his own, giving it a Greek title, 'Περὶ φυσικῶν διαρέσεων,' that is, 'De naturæ divisione;' in which book (as saith my aforesaid author) is contained the resolution of many profitable questions, but so that he is thought to follow the Greek church rather than the Latin, and for the same was counted of some to be a heretic; because in that book some things there be which in all points accord not with the Romish religion. Wherefore the pope, writing to the said King Charles of this Scotus, complaineth, as in his own words here followeth:—"relation hath been made unto our apostleship, that a certain man called Johannes, a Scottish man, hath translated the book of Dionysius the Areopagite, of the names of God and of the heavenly orders, from Greek into Latin; which book, according to the custom of the church, ought first to have been approved by our judgment; namely, seeing the said John, albeit he be said to be a man of great learning and science, in time past, hath been noted by common rumour, to have been a man not of upright or sound doctrine in certain points."[1] For this cause, the said Scotus being constrained to remove from France, came into England, allured, as some testify, by the letters of Alured, or Alfred, by whom he was with great favour entertained, and was conversant a great space about the king; till, at length (whether before or after the death of the king, it is uncertain), he went to Malmesbury, where he taught certain scholars a few years, by whom at last most impiously he was murdered and slain with their penknives, and so died, as stories say, a martyr, buried at the said monastery of Malmesbury with this epitaph.

Johannes Scotus translates Dionysius de Hierarchia into Latin.

Is accused by the Pope as a heretic.

Slain by his own scholars.

> "Claudìtur in tumulo sanctus sophista Johannes,
> Qui ditatus erat jam vivens dogmate miro.
> Martyrio tandem Christi conscendere regnum
> Qui meruit, regnans secli per secula cuncta."

King Alfred having these helps of learned men about him, and no less learned also himself, past his time not only to the great utility and profit of his subjects, but also to a rare and profitable example of other christian kings and princes for them to follow. This aforesaid Alfred had by his wife, called Ethelwitha, two sons, Edward and Ethelward; and three daughters, Elfleda, Ethelgora, and Ethelguida: "quas omnes liberalibus fecit artibus erudiri;" that is, "whom he set all to their books and study of liberal arts," as my story testifieth. First, Edward, his eldest son, succeeded him

The children of Alfred.

(1) "Relatum est apostolatui nostro, quod opus Dionysii Areopagitæ, quod de divinis nominibus, et de cœlestibus ordinibus, Græco descripsit eloquio, quidam vir Johannes (genere Scotus) nuper transtulit in Latinum. Quod, juxta morem Ecclesiæ, nobis mitti, et nostro judicio debuit approbari; præsertim quum idem Johannes (licet multæ scientiæ esse prædicetur) olim non sane sapere, in quibusdam frequenti rumore dicatur," &c.

Alfred. A.D. 901.

in the kingdom; the second son, Ethelward, died before his father; Ethelgora, his middle daughter, was made a nun; the other two were married, the one in Merceland, the other to the earl of Flanders. Thus King Alfred, that valiant, virtuous, and learned prince, after he had thus christianly governed the realm for the term of twenty-nine years and six months, departed this life, 5 Cal. Novemb. A.D. 901, and lieth buried at Winchester. Of Alfred this I find, moreover, greatly noted and commended in history, and not here to be forgotten, for the rare example thereof, that, wheresoever he was, or whithersoever he went, he bare always about him in his bosom or pocket a little book containing the Psalms of David, and certain other orisons of his own collecting, whereupon he was continually reading or praying whensoever he was otherwise vacant, having leisure thereunto. Finally, what were the virtues of this famous king, this little table hereunder written, which is left in ancient writing in remembrance of his worthy and memorable life, doth sufficiently, in few lines, contain.[1]

Death of King Alfred. A.D. 901.

Arch-bishops of Canter-bury.

In the story of this Alfred, a little above, mention was made of Pleimund, schoolmaster to the said Alfred, and also bishop of Canterbury, as succeeding Ethered there bishop before him; which Pleimund governed that see thirty-four years. After Pleimund succeeded Athelm, who sat twelve years, and after him, Ulfelm, who sat thirteen years. Then followed Odo, a Dane, born in the said see of Canterbury, who governed the same twenty years, being in great favour with King Athelstan, King Edmund, and Edwin, as in process hereafter (Christ willing), as place and order doth require, shall more at large be expressed.

Ecclesiastical affairs.

Nine popes in nine years.

As touching the course and proceedings of the Romish bishops there, where I last made mention of them, I ended with Pope Stephen V.[2] After his time was much broil in the election of the bishops of Rome, one contending against another, insomuch that within the space of nine years were nine bishops, of whom the first was Formosus, who succeeded next unto the forenamed Stephen V.,

(1) "In Regis Alfredi, et virtutis illius claram memoriam:—Famosus, bellicosus, victoriosus; viduarum, pupillorum, et orphanorum, pauperumque, provisor studiosus; poetarum Saxonicorum peritissimus; suæ genti charissimus, affabilis omnibus, liberalissimus; prudentia, fortitudine, temperantia, justitia præditus; in infirmitate, qua continue laborabat, patientissimus; in exequendis judiciis indagator discretissimus, in servicio Dei vigilantissimus et devotissimus, Anglo-Saxonum Rex Alfredus, piissimi Ethelulfi filius, 29 annis sexque mensibus regni sui peractis mortem obiit. Indict. 4. quinto cal. Novemb. feria quarta, et Wintoniæ in novo monasterio sepultus, immortalitatis stolam, et resurrectionis gloriam cum justis expectat," &c.

Moreover, in the history of Henry of Huntingdon, these verses I find written in commendation of the same Alfred, made, as I suppose, and by his words appeareth, by the said author, whereof I thought not to defraud the reader. The words thereof here follow:

Epitaphium Regis Alfredi.

Nobilitas innata tibi probitatis honorem,
Armipotens Alfrede, dedit, probitasque laborem,
Perpetuumque labor nomen, cui mixta dolori
Gaudia semper erant, spes semper mixta timori.
Si modo victor eras, ad crastina bella pavebas,
Si modo victus eras, ad crastina bella parabas.
Cui vestes sudore jugi, cui sicca cruore
Tincta jugi, quantum sit onus regnare, probarunt.
Non fuit immensi quisquam per climata mundi,
Cui tot in adversis nil respirare liceret.
Nec tamen aut ferro contritus ponere ferrum,
Aut gladio potuit, vitæ finisse dolores.
Jam post transactos vitæ regnique labores,
Christus ei sit vera quies, sceptrumque perenne.

(2) See page 15. Stephen V.—Ed.

being made pope against the mind of certain in Rome, that willed rather Sergius, then deacon of the church of Rome, to have been pope, notwithstanding which Mars and money prevailed on Formosus' part. This Formosus, of whom also some mention is made in other places of this ecclesiastical history,[1] being before bishop of Pontiniake, or Portuake, had in time past, I know not for what cause, offended Pope John VIII., by reason whereof, for fear of the pope, he voided away, and left his bishopric, and because, being sent for again by the pope, he would not return, he was excommunicated. At length, coming into France to make there his satisfaction to the pope, he was degraded from a bishop into a secular man's habit, swearing to the pope that he would no more re-enter the city of Rome, nor claim his bishopric again; subscribing, moreover, with his own hand, to continue from that time in the state of a secular person. But Pope Martin, the next pope after John, released the said Formosus from his oath, and restored him again unto his bishopric; whereby Formosus not only entered Rome again, but also obtained shortly after the papacy. Thus he being placed in the popedom, there arose a great doubt or controversy among the divines about his consecration, whether it was lawful or not; some holding against him, that forasmuch as he was solemnly deposed, degraded, unpriested, and also sworn not to reiterate the state ecclesiastical, therefore he ought to be taken no otherwise than for a secular man. Others alleged again, that whatsoever Formosus was, yet for the dignity of that order, and for the credit of them whom he ordered, all his consecration ought to stand in force, especially seeing the said Formosus was afterward received and absolved by Pope Martin from that his perjury and degradation. In the mean time, as witnesseth Sigebert, this Formosus sendeth to King Arnulph for aid against his adversaries; who then marching towards Rome, was there prevented by the Romans from entering. But in the siege, saith the author, the Romans within so played the lions, that a poor hare, or such like thing, coming toward the city, the host of Arnulph followed after with such a main cry, that the valiant Romans upon the walls for very fear, and where there was no hurt, cast themselves desperately over the walls, so that Arnulph with little labour scaled the walls, and got the city. Thus Arnulph, obtaining the city of Rome, rescueth Pope Formosus, and beheadeth his adversaries; whom the pope to gratify with like recompence again, blesseth and crowneth for emperor. This Formosus, sitting fast about the space of four or five years, followed his predecessors; after whose time, as I said, within the space of nine years, were nine bishops, as followeth. But in the mean time, concerning the story of this Formosus declared by Sigebert, and many other chronicles, this thing would I gladly ask, and more gladly learn of some indifferent good Catholic person, who not of obstinacy, but of simple error being a papist, would answer it to his conscience, whether doth he think the holy order of priesthood, which he taketh for one of the seven sacraments, to be *character indelebilis* or not? If it be not *indelebilis*, that is, if it be such a thing as may be put off, why then

Ecclesiastical affairs.

Schisms among the popes.

(1) Ex Chronico Sigeberti.

Ecclesiastical affairs.

Whether the pope with his cardinals may err.

doth the pope's doctrine so call and so hold the contrary, pretending it to be *indelebilis*, unremovable? If it be indeed so as they teach and affirm, *indelebilis character*, why then did Pope John, or could Pope John annihilate and evacuate one of his seven pope-holy sacraments, making of a priest a non-priest or layman, uncharactering his own order, which is (as he saith) a character, which in no wise may be blotted out or removed? Again, howsoever Pope John is to be judged in this matter to do either well or not well, this would I know, if he did well in so dispriesting and discharactering Formosus for such private offences? If yea, how then standeth his doing with his own doctrine which teacheth the contrary? If he did not well, how then standeth his doctrine with his doings to be true, which teacheth that the pope with his synod of cardinals cannot err? Moreover, if this Pope John did not err in his disordering Formosus, how then did Martin, his successor, not err in repealing the said doing of his predecessor? or how did not Pope Formosus himself err, who being unpriested by Pope John, afterward, without reiterating the character or order of priesthood, took upon him to be Pope, and made acts and laws in the church? Again, if Formosus now pope did not err, how then did Pope Stephen his successor afterward not err, who did annihilate the consecration, and all other acts of the said Formosus, as erroneous? Or again, if we say that this Stephen with his synod of cardinals did right, then how could it be that Pope Theodore, and Pope John X., who came after the aforesaid Stephen, did not plainly err, who, approving the consecration of Formosus, did condemn and burn the acts synodal of Stephen and his cardinals, which before had condemned Formosus, according as in story here consequently may appear?

After Formosus had governed the see of Rome five years, succeeded first Boniface VI., who continued but five and twenty days. Then came Stephen VI., who so envied the name of his predecessor Formosus, that he abrogated and dissolved his decrees, and, taking up his body after it was buried, cut two fingers off his right hand, and commanded them to be cast into the Tiber, and then buried the body in a private or layman's sepulchre.[1]

Thus, after Stephen had sat in the chair of pestilence one year, succeeded to the same chair Pope Romanus, and sat three months, repealing the acts decreed by Stephen his predecessor, against Formosus. Next to him came Theodore II., who likewise taking part with Formosus against the aforesaid Stephen, reigned but twenty days. Then sat Pope John X., who did fight and repugn against the Romans, and, to confirm the cause of Formosus more surely, did hold a synod at Ravenna of seventy-four bishops, the French king Endo and his archbishops being present at the same, at the which council were ratified all the decrees and doings of Formosus, and the contrary acts of the synod of Stephen VI. were burned. This pope lived not as pope fully two years, after whom succeeded Benedict IV., who kept the chair three years. After him, Leo V. was next pope, who within forty days of his papacy, was, with strong

One council burneth another's decrees. A.D. 906.

(1) Ex Chron. Martini pænitentiarii. Ex Sigeberto. Ex Polych. et aliis.

hand, taken and cast into prison by one Christopher, his own household chaplain, whom he had long nourished in his house; which thing, saith Platina, could not be done without great conspiracy, and much slaughter of men. This Christopher, being pope about the space of seven months, was likewise himself hoisted from his papal throne by Sergius, like as he had done to his master before; and thus within the space of nine years had been nine popes, one after another. Then Sergius, after he had thrust down Pope Christopher, and shorn him monk into a monastery, occupied his room seven years. This Sergius, a rude man and unlearned, very proud and cruel, had before been put back from the popedom by Formosus above-mentioned; by reason whereof, to revenge himself upon Formosus again, Sergius being now in his papacy, caused the body of Formosus, where it was buried, to be taken up, and afterward sitting in the papal see (as in his pontificalibus), first degraded him, and then commanded his head to be smitten off, with the other three fingers that were left, as Sigebert writes; which done, he made his body to be thrown into the Tiber, deposing likewise all such as by the said Formosus before had been consecrated and invested. This body of Formosus, thus thrown into the Tiber, was afterwards, as our writers say, found and taken up by certain fishers, and so brought into St. Peter's temple; at the presence whereof, as they also say, certain images there standing by, bowed down themselves, and reverenced the same—with lie and all. But such deceivable miracles of stocks and images, in monkish and friary temples, be to us no news, especially here in England, where we have been so inured to the like, and so many, that such wily practices cannot be to us invisible, though this crown-shorn generation think themselves to dance in a net. But the truth is, while they think to deceive the simple, these wily beguilers most of all deceive themselves, as they will find, except they repent. By this Pope Sergius I. came up the use to bear about candles on Candlemas day, for the purifying of the blessed Virgin; as though the sacred conception of Jesus the Son of God, were to be purified as a thing impure, and that with candle-light!

Ecclesiastical affairs.

Pope Leo V. imprisoned and unpoped by his own chaplain.

A.D. 907.

Pope Formosus, after death, beheaded.

Feigned miracle upon the body of Formosus.

Bearing candles on Candlemas day, how it came up.

After Sergius entered Pope Anastasius III., in whose time the body of Formosus, aforenamed, is thought to be found of fishermen in the river Tiber, and so brought (as is said) into the temple to be saluted of the images; which thing may be quickly tainted as a lie; for how is it to be thought that the body of Formosus, so long dead before, and now lying seven years in the river, could remain whole all that while, that fishers might take it up, and discern it to be the same? After Anastasius had sat two years followed Pope Lando I., the father, as some think, of Pope John, which John is said to have been the paramour of Theodora, an infamous woman of Rome, and set up by her, either against Lando, or after Lando his father, to succeed in his room. There is a story writer, called Luithprandus,[1] who maketh mention of this Theodora and Pope John X., and saith, moreover, that this Theodora had a daughter, named Marozia, which Marozia had, by Pope Sergius above-mentioned, a son, who was afterward Pope John XI. The same Marozia afterwards chanced

A.D. 911.

A.D. 913. Harlots at this time ruled all at Rome.

(1) Luithprandus, de Imperatoribus, lib. ii. cap. 13.

Ecclesiastical affairs. to marry with Guido, marquis of Tuscia, through the means of which Guido and his friends at Rome, she brought to pass that this Pope John X. was smothered with a pillow laid to his mouth, after he had reigned thirteen years, and so that the aforesaid John XI., her son, might succeed next after him; but because the clergy and people of Rome did not agree to his election, Pope Leo VI. was in his place set up; thus, Pope John, the son of Sergius and Marozia, being dejected, Pope Leo reigned seven months. After him, Pope Stephen A.D. 929. VII. or VIII. reigned two years, who, being poisoned, Pope John XI. above-rehearsed, the son of Sergius and Marozia, was set up again in the papacy, where he reigned nearly the space of five years. Of the wickedness of Marozia, how she married two brethren, one after the death of the other, and how she governed all Rome and the whole church at that time, I let it pass. Although the Latin verses wherewith Luithprandus doth inveigh against such women as marry two brethren, were not unworthy here to be recited, and perhaps might be further applied than to that Marozia of Rome, yet for shortness I let them also pass. After John XI. followed Pope Leo VII. three years and four months; Pope Stephen VIII. three years and four A.D. 939. months; Pope Martin III. three years and six months; and, after him, Pope Agapetus II. eight years and six months;[1] about whose time, or a little before, began first the order of monks, called Ordo Cluniacensis. But now to leave off these monstrous matters of Rome, A.D. 946. and to return again to our country of England, where we last left off.

Pope John XI. restored.

Ordo Cluniacensis beginneth.

EDWARD THE ELDER.[2]

A.D. 901. After the reign of the famous King Alfred, his son Edward succeeded, sirnamed the Elder; where first is to be noted, that before the conquest of the Normans, there were in England three Edwards: first, this Edward the Elder; secondly, Edward the Martyr; thirdly, Edward the Confessor; whereof hereafter (by the grace of Christ) shall follow in order, as place shall give to be declared. This Edward began his reign A.D. 901,[3] and governed the land right valiantly and nobly four and twenty years. In knowledge of good letters and learning he was not to be compared to his father; otherwise, in princely renown, in civil government, and in martial prowess, he was nothing inferior, but rather excelled him, through whose valiant acts the princedom of Wales and kingdom of Scotland, with Constantine king thereof, were first to him subdued. He adjoined, moreover, to his dominion, the country of East Anglia, that is, of Norfolk, Suffolk, and Essex. All Merceland also he recovered, and Northumberland, out of the hands of the Danes. In all his wars he never lightly went without victory. The subjects of his provinces and dominions were so inured and hardened in continual practice and feats of war, that when they heard of any enemies coming (never tarrying for any

Three Edwards before the Conquest.

Alfred and his son Edward compared.

(1) On the authority of Mosheim, some obvious errors in the history of the popes of Rome have been here corrected.—Ed.

(2) Edition 1563, p. 10. Ed. 1583, p. 146. Ed. 1596, p. 132. Ed. 1684, vol. i. p. 163. Ed.

(3) Baronius calls the tenth century, an "iron age, barren of all goodness; a leaden age, abounding with all wickedness; and a dark age, remarkable above all the rest for the scarcity of writers and men of learning."—Ed.

bidding from the king or from his dukes), straightway they encountered with them; both in number and in knowledge of the order of war, excelling always their adversaries. Malmesbury saith, "So was the coming and assaulting of their enemies, to the people and common soldiers but a trifle, to the king but a ridicule."[1] Among other adversaries who were busy rather than wise, in assailing this king, was one called Clito Ethelwold, a young man, King Edward's uncle's son; who, first occupying the town of Woburn, and taking thence a nun with him, whom he had already married, fled by night to Northumberland, to unite himself unto the Danes, and was made chief king and captain over them. Being chased from thence, Clito fled over into France, but shortly returning again into England, he landed in East England, where, with a company of Danes of that country gathering to him, he destroyed and pillaged much of the country about Crekinford and Crikeland; and so passing over the Thames, after he had spoiled the land there to Bradenstock, returned again to Norfolk and Suffolk; where, meeting with an ambushment of Kentish men, which dragged and tarried after the main host of Edward, contrary to his commandment, he inclosed them, and slew the most part of them. Soon after, the two hosts meeting together, between the two ditches of St. Edmund's land, after a long fight, Clito and many of the Danes were slain, and the remnant were constrained to seek for peace, which, upon certain conditions, and under a tribute, was to them granted.

Edward the Elder. A.D. 901.

Clito Ethelwold rebels against King Edward. A.D. 904.

In process, about the twelfth year of his reign, the Danes repenting them of their covenants, and minding to break the same, assembled a host, and met with the king in Staffordshire, at a place called Tottenhall, and soon after at Wodenfield, at which two places the king slew two kings, two earls, and many thousands of Danes that occupied the country of Northumberland. A.D. 913.

Thus the importunate rage of the Danes being assuaged, King Edward having now some leisure given from wars to other studies, gave his mind to the building or repairing of cities, towns, and castles, that by the Danes were rased, shattered, and broken; as first, of Chester, which city he enlarged to double that it was before, compassing the castle within the walls of the same, which before stood without. That done, the king builded a strong castle at Hereford, on the edge of Wales. Also, for the strengthening of the country, he made a castle at the mouth of the water of Avon, and another castle at Buckingham, and the third fast thereby upon the river Ouse. Moreover, he builded or re-edified the towns of Towcester and Wigmoor, and destroyed the castle that the Danes had made at Demesford. Likewise upon the river Trent, against the old town of Nottingham, he builded a new town on the south side, and made a bridge over the river between the said two towns. Also by the river Mersey he builded a city or town in the north end of Mercia, and named it Thilwall; and after repaired the city of Manchester, that was sore defaced with wars of the Danes.

The new town of Nottingham builded.

In this renewing and building of towns and castles, for the more fortifying of his realm, his sister Elfleda, daughter of King Alfred, and married to the duke of Mercia, as is before-mentioned, was no small

(1) "Ita hostes militibus contemptui, regi risui erant."—Guliel. Malmesb. de Regib.

Edward the Elder. A.D. 913.

helper. Of this Elfleda, it is firmly of writers affirmed, that she being, as is said, married to Ethelred, duke of Mercia, after she had once assayed the pains of travail, did so much abhor them, that it seemed to her, she said, not seemly for a noble woman to desire that whereof so great sorrow and travail should ensue. Yet notwithstanding, the same Elfleda, for all her delicate tenderness, was so hardy in warlike dangers, which nature giveth not to women, that, fighting against the Danes, four of her next knights, who were guardians of her body, were slain fast by her. This Elfleda, among her other noble acts, whereby she deserved praise, was a great helper and stirrer up of her brother Edward, who builded and newly repaired many castles and towns, as Tamworth beside Lichfield, Stafford, Warwick, Shrewsbury, Watrisbury, Eldsbury beside Chester in the forest, now destroyed; also, in the north end of Mercia, upon the river Mersey, a castle called Runcorn; as well as a bridge over the Severn, named Brimmisbury bridge.

Character of Elfleda.

The laws of King Alfred and King Edward.

As touching the laws and statutes of this Edward, as also of his father Alfred, made before him, I omit here to record them for length of matter and waste of time; yet, notwithstanding, this admonition by the way I think good to note, that in the days of those ancient kings reigning in England, the authority both of conferring bishoprics and spiritual promotions, and also of prescribing laws as well to the churchmen as to the laity, and of ordering and intermeddling in matters merely spiritual, was then in the hands of kings ruling in the land, and not only in the hand of the pope, as appeareth by the laws of Alfred.[1]

Kings of England in times past had authority in spiritual causes.

By these and other such like constitutions it may appear, how the governance and direction of the church in those days depended not upon Monsieur le Pope of Rome, but upon the kings, who here, in their time (under the Lord), did govern the land. To this also the example of King Edward's time gives testimony; which Edward, with Pleimundus above-mentioned, archbishop of Canterbury, and with other bishops, in a synod assembled, assigned and elected seven bishops, in seven metropolitan churches of the realm; the first of whom was Fridelstan, the second Adelstan, the third Werstan, the fourth Adeleme, the fifth Edelfus, the sixth Dernegus, the seventh Kenulphus; in which election the king's authority seemed then alone to be sufficient.

A.D. 924. Children of King Edward the Elder.

This Edward, as in the beginning was said, reigned twenty-four years, who had three wives, Egwin, Elfled, and Ethelwid. Of Egwin he had his eldest son Athelstan, who next succeeded in the kingdom, and a daughter, married after to the duke of Northumberland. Of Elfled he received two sons, to wit, Ethelwald and Edwin, and six daughters. Ethelwald was excellently well seen in all knowledge of learning, much resembling, both in countenance and conditions, his grandfather Alfred; he died soon after his father. Of his six daughters, two of them, Elfled and Ethelhilda, were made nuns, the other

(1) "Si quis fornicetur cum uxore aliena, &c.
Si quis in quadragesima sanctum velum in publico vel in lecto, &c.
Ut Christiani Deum diligant et paganismo renuncient, &c.
Si quis Christianitatem mutet, &c.
Si quis ordinatus sacris furetur, &c.
Si Presbyter ad rectum terminum sanctum chrisma, &c.
Si duo fratres vel cognati cum una aliqua fornicentur, &c."

four were married; Edgina to Charles, the French king, in his father's time; Ethilda, by king Athelstan, was married to Hugo, the son of Duke Robert; Edgitha and Algina were both sent to Henry, prince of Almains. The latter the said Henry married to his son Otho, who was the first emperor of the Almains; the other sister, who was Edgitha, the aforesaid Henry married to a certain duke, about the borders of the Alps, in Italy. Of his third wife, Ethelwid, Edward received two sons, Edmund and Edred, who both reigned after Athelstan; and two daughters, Edburga, whom he made a nun, and Eadguina, who was married to Louis, prince of Aquitania, in France. These sons and daughters King Edward the Elder thus brought up; his daughters he set to spinning and to the needle; his sons he set to the study of learning, "to the end that they, being at first made philosophers, should be the more expert thereby to govern the commonwealth."[1] The bringing up of King Edward's children.

ATHELSTAN, OR ADELSTAN.[2]

ATHELSTAN, or Adelstan, after the death of Edward his father, began his reign in England, and was crowned at Kingston. He was a prince of worthy memory, valiant and wise in all his acts, and nothing inferior unto his father Edward. In like worldly renown of civil government, he joined, with much prosperous success, in reducing this realm under the subjection of one monarchy; for he both expelled the Danes, subdued the Scots, and quieted the Welshmen, as well in North Wales as also in Cornwall. The first enemy against this Athelstan, was one Elfred, who, with a faction of seditious persons conspiring against the said Athelstan, at Winchester, incontinently, after the death of his father, went about to put out his eyes. Notwithstanding, the king escaping that danger, through the help of God, was at that time delivered. Elfred, upon this, being accused, fled to Rome, there before the pope to purge himself by his oath. Being brought to the church of St. Peter, and there swearing, or rather forswearing, himself to be clear, who indeed was guilty thereof, he suddenly, upon his oath, fell down; and so being brought to the English house in Rome, within three days after departed. The pope sending word unto King Athelstan, whether he would have the said Elfred buried among Christians or no, at length, through the persuasions of his friends and kinsfolks, it was concluded that he should be buried with christian burial. This story, although I find it in no other writers mentioned, but only in the Chronicles of Gulielmus, yet, forasmuch as it beareth the witness and words of the king himself, as testified in an old deed of gift, given to the monastery of Malmesbury, I thought the same to be of the more credit. The words of the king proceed as follow in the note.[3]

A.D. 924.

Duke Elfred suddenly stricken by the hand of God for perjury.

(1) "Ut quasi philosophi ad gubernandam rempublicam non jam rudes procederent."—Guliel. Malmesb. de Regib.

(2) Edition 1563, p. 10. Ed. 1583, p. 147. Ed. 1596, p. 133. Ed. 1684, vol. i. p. 164.—ED.

(3) The copy of an old writing of King Athelstan, testifying of the miraculous death of Duke Elfred, suddenly stricken by the hand of God for perjury:—"Sciant sapientes regionis nostræ, non has præfatas terras me injuste rapuisse, rapinamque Deo dedisse. Sed sic eas accepi, quemadmodum judicaverunt omnes optimates regni Anglorum. Insuper et apostolicus papa Romanæ

Athelstan. A.D. 925.

In the second year of the reign of King Athelstan, for an unity and a peace to be had between the king and the Danes of Northumberland, he married the sister of Sitheric their king, whereof mention is made before; but shortly after, within one year, this Sitheric died, after whose death, King Athelstan seized that province into his own hands, putting out the son of the aforesaid Sitheric, called Alanus, who, with his brother Godfrid, fled, the one into Ireland, the other to Constantine, king of Scots; and, when he had thus accorded with the Danes of Northumberland, he shortly made subject unto him Constantine, king of Scots. But the said Constantine behaved himself so lowly to the king, that he restored him to his former dignity, saying, that it was more honour to make a king than to be a king.

Northumberland and the Scots subdued to the king of England.

Not long after, the said Constantine, king of Scots, did break covenant with King Athelstan; wherefore he assembled his knights, and made towards Scotland, where subduing his enemies, and bringing them again unto due subjection, he returned into England with victory. Here, by the way, in some story-writers, who, forgetting the office of historians, seem to play the poets, is written and recorded for a marvel, that the said Athelstan, returning out of Scotland into England, came to York, and so into the church of St. John of Beverly, to redeem his knife, which before he had left there for a pledge at his going forth; in the which place, he praying to God and to St. John of Beverly, that he might leave there some remembrance whereby they that came after might know that the Scots by right should be subdued to the English men, smote with a sword, they say, upon a great hard stone standing near about the castle of Dunbar, so that with the stroke thereof the stone was cut a large ell deep, with a lie also no less deep than was the stroke in the stone. But of this poetical or fabulous story, albeit Polychronicon, Fabian, Jornalensis, and others, constantly accord in the same, yet in Malmesbury and Huntington no mention is made at all. But peradventure, he that was the first inventor of this tale of the stone, was disposed to lie for the whetstone; wherefore in my mind he is worthy to have it. Of like truth and credit seemeth also to be this that followeth, about the same year and time under the reign of King Athelstan, in the eighth year of his reign, of one Bristan, bishop of Winchester, who succeeded Frithstan, in the same see, and governed that bishopric four years. This Bristan, being a devout bishop in prayer and contemplation, used much, among his solitary walks, to frequent late the church-yard, praying

Fabulous miracles.

A.D. 931.

ecclesiæ Johannes, Elfredo defuncto, qui nostræ felicitati et vitæ æmulus extitit, nequitiæ inimicorum nostrorum consentiens; quando me voluerunt (patre defuncto) cæcare in urbe Wintonia, si non me Deus sua pietate eripuisset. Sed denudatis eorum machinamentis, remissus est ad Romanam ecclesiam, ut ibi se coram Apostolico Johanne jurejurando defenderet. Et hoc fecit coram altare sancti Petri. Sed facto juramento, cecidit coram altare, et manibus famulorum suorum portatus est ad scholam Anglorum, et ibi tertia nocte vitam finivit. Et tunc apostolicus ad nos remisit, et quid de co ageretur a nobis consuluit, an cum cæteris Christianis corpus illius poneretur. His peractis, et nobis renunciatis, optimates regionis nostræ cum propinquorum illius turma efflagitabant omni humilitate, ut corpus illius per nostram licentiam cum corporibus poneretur Christianorum. Nosque flagitationi illorum consentientes Romam remisimus; et papa consentiente, positus est ad cæteros Christianos, quamvis indignus. Et sic judicata est mihi tota possessio ejus in magnis et in modicis. Sed et hæc apicibus literarum prænotavimus, ne quando aboleatur, unde mihi præfata possessio, quam Deo et sancto Petro dedi, donatur. Nec justius novi, quam Deo et sancto Petro hanc possessionem dare, qui æmulum meum in conspectu omnium cadere fecerunt, et mihi prosperitatem regni largiti sunt," &c.—Gulíel. Malmesb. lib. de Reg in Vita Ethelstani.

for the souls there, and all christian souls departed. Upon a time the said Bristan, after his wonted manner proceeding in his devotions, when he had done, came to "Requiescant in pace," whereunto suddenly a great multitude of souls answering together with one voice, said, "Amen." Of this miracle albeit I have not much to say, hasting to other matters, yet this question would I ask of some indifferent papist, who were not wilful, but of ignorance deceived, whether this multitude which here answered, "Amen," were the souls of them buried in the church-yard or not? If yea, then how were they in purgatory, what time they were heard in that place answering "Amen," except we should think purgatory to be in the church-yard at Winchester, where the souls were heard then so many answering and praying, "Amen?" And yet this story is testified by the accord of writers of that time, Malmesbury, Polychronicon, Hoveden, Jornalensis, and others. Much like miracles and prophecies also we read of Elphege who succeeded him; but because we haste to other things, let these fables pass.

Ye heard a little before, how King Athelstan, after the death of Sitheric, king of Northumberland, seized that land or province into his own hand, and put out his son Alanus, who, after flying into Scotland, married the daughter of Constantine, king of Scots, by whose stirring and exhortation he gathered a company of Danes, Scots, and others, and entered the mouth of the Humber with a strong navy of six hundred and fifteen ships. King Athelstan, with his brother Edmund, having knowledge of this, prepared an army, and at length joined in fight with him and his people, at a place called Brunanburh, or Brimford, where he, fighting with them from morning to even, after a terrible slaughter on both sides, the like of which hath not been often seen in England, had the victory. In this battle were slain five small and under-kings, with Constantine, king of Scots, and twelve dukes, with the more part of all the strangers which at that time they gathered to them. Here, also, our writers put in another miracle, how, in this battle, King Athelstan's sword miraculously fell into its sheath, through the prayer of Odo, then archbishop of Canterbury.

Battle fought at Brunanburh, A.D. 934.

Another unlikely miracle of king Ethelstan's sword.

Concerning this battle, I find in a certain written Chronicle, the underwritten verses, which, that they should not be lost, I thought not unworthy here of rehearsal.[1]

Odo, archbishop of Canterbury.

(1) "Transierat quinos, et tres, et quatuor annos,
Jure regens cives, subigens virtute tyrannos:
Cum redit illa lues Europæ noxia labes.
Jam cubat in terris fera barbaries aquilonis,
Et jacet in campis pelago pirata relicto.
Illicitas torvasque minas Analaus anhelans,
Bacchanti furiæ, Scotorum rege volente,
Commodat assensum borealis terra serenum.
Et jam grande tument, jam terrent aera verbis.
Cedunt indigenæ, cedit plaga tota superbis.
Nam quia rex noster fidens alacrisque juventa,
Emeritus pridem detriverat ocia lenta,
Illi continuis fædabant omnia prædis
Urgentes miseros injectis ignibus agros.
Marcuerant totis viridantia gramina campis,
Ægra seges votum deluserat agricolarum.
Tanta fuit peditum, tam barbara vis equitantum,
Innumerabilium concursus quadrupedantum.
Excivit tandem famæ querimonia regem,
Ne se cauterio tali pateretur inuri.
Quod sua barbaricæ cessissent arma securi,
Nec mora, victrices ducentia signa cohortes,

Athelstan. A.D. 934.

After this victory thus obtained over the Danes and Scots, King Athelstan also subdued, or at least quieted, the North Britons, whom he convening at Hereford, or thereabouts, forced them to grant unto him, as a yearly tribute, twenty pounds of gold, three hundred pounds of silver, and of heads of neat, five and twenty hundred, with hawks and dogs, to a certain number. This done, he went to Exeter, and there likewise subduing the South Britons about Exeter and Cornwall, repaired the walls of Exeter with sufficient strength, and so returned.

The North and South Britons brought to tribute, and subdued.

Among the victorious and noble acts of this king, one blot there is of him written and noted, wherein he is as much worthy to be reprehended as in the other before to be commended; that is, the innocent death and murder of his brother Edwin, the occasion whereof was this:—King Edward beforenamed, their father, in the time of his youth, coming by a certain village or grange where he had been nursed and brought up when a child, thought of courtesy to go to see how his nurse did, where he, entering into the house, espied a certain young damsel, beautiful, and right seemly attired, Egwina by name. This Egwina, being a poor man's daughter, had before had a vision by night, that from her sprang such a bright light of the moon, that the brightness thereof gave light to the realm of England, by reason whereof she was taken into the aforesaid house, and daintily brought up instead of their own daughter for hope of some advantage to ensue thereby, as afterward it came to pass; for King Edward, as is declared, coming into the house, and being ravished with the beauty of the maiden, had of her this Athelstan. Wherefore the said Athelstan being thus born of Egwina, the first wife to Edward, as is said, before he was married to her, and fearing his next brother Edwin, who was rightly born, especially being stirred thereunto through the sinister suggestion of his butler, did bear such displeasure towards the aforesaid Edwin his brother, being yet but young, that, notwithstanding his innocent submission and purgation made against his accusers, he caused him to be set in an old rotten boat in the broad sea, with only one esquire, and without any tackling or other provision to the same, where the young and tender prince being dismayed with the rage of the winds and the floods, and now weary of his life, cast himself overboard into the sea, and so was drowned. The esquire, however, shifting for himself as he could, and recovering the body of his master, brought it to Sandwich, where it was buried: which done, the king, afterwards coming to the remembrance of himself, was stricken with great repentance the space of seven years together, and at length was revenged of him that was the accuser of his brother. This accuser, as is said, was the king's cup-bearer, who, as God the righteous Judge of all things would have it, upon a certain solemn feast, bearing the cup unto the king, chanced in the middle of the floor to stumble

King Athelstan seeks the death of his own brother.

Explicat inventum vexilla ferocia centum,
Juncta virum virtus, decies bis millia quina,
Ad stadium belli comitantur prævia signa.
Hicque ciet strepitus armatorum legiones,
Terruit insignis venientum fama latrones,
Ut posita proprias præda repetant regiones.
At vulgus reliquum miseranda strage peremptum,
Infecit bibulas terris nidoribus auras.
Fugit Analanus de tot modo millibus unus," &c.

with one foot, helping and recovering himself with the other, saying these words, "Thus one brother, as you see, helpeth another." These words being thus spoken in the hearing of the king, so moved his mind, that forthwith he commanded the false-accuser of his brother to be had out to execution; whose just recompence I would wish to be a warning to all men, what it is to sow discord between brother and brother.

Athelstan. A.D. 933 to 941.

King Athelstan, besides his seven years' lamentation for this act, builded the two monasteries of Middleton and of Michlenes for his brother's sake, or, as the stories say, for his soul: whereby it may appear what was the cause most special in those days of building monasteries, to wit, for releasing the sins both of them departed, and them alive; which cause, how it standeth with the grace and verity of Christ's gospel, and of his passion, let the christian reader try and examine within himself. This cruel fact of the king towards Edwin, caused him afterward to be more tender and careful towards his other brethren and sisters left in his hands unmarried; which sisters, as is partly in the chapter before declared, he richly bestowed in great marriages, as one to the king of Northumberland, Sitheric; another to Louis, king of Aquitaine; and a third to Henry, duke of Almain, for his son Otho I. emperor of the Germans; whereby it is to be understood, that the empire at this time began first to be translated from France, where it had remained about one hundred years and a half unto Germany, where it hath ever since continued.

The cause of building abbeys.

Otho I. emperor of the Germans.

The fourth of his sisters, being a virgin of singular beauty, Hugo, the French king, required to be given to him; sending to King Athelstan precious and sumptuous presents, such as were not before seen in England: among which gifts, besides the rare odours of sundry favours and fine spices; and besides the precious and costly gems, namely, of smaragdine of most redolent green; besides also many and great coursers and palfries with rich trappings: especially of one jewel do writers make mention, which was a certain vessel finely and subtilely made of the precious stone onyx, so radiantly wrought, that in it appeared the lively corn growing, and men's images walking. Over and besides was sent also the sword of Constantine the Great, with the name of the possessor written in golden letters, and in the haft of the same all beaten in gold was one of the iron nails wherewith our Saviour on the cross was nailed. Of the verity of this I am not disposed at this present much to say what I suspect, but from the ecclesiastical story of Eusebius, it is evident, that two of the aforesaid nails of Christ were spent on the bridle of Constantine, the third he cast into the sea in a raging tempest; wherefore, if Christ were nailed with four nails, perhaps this nail might be one. If he were nailed but with three, I see not how this story can stand with other stories, neither how this fourth nail can stand with the truth. Among the rest, moreover, was the spear, as is reported, wherewith the side of our Saviour was opened, which also the said Constantine was wont to carry in the field against his enemies, with a portion likewise of the holy cross enclosed in crystal; also a part of the crown of thorns in like manner enclosed. Of these relics, part was given to

Jewels sent to Athelstan from the French king.

One of the nails wherewith our Saviour was crucified.

Athelstan.

A.D. 941.

Winchester, and part to the church of Malmesbury, where King Athelstan was buried. As this king was endued and enlarged by the gift of God (the setter-up and disposer of all kings) with great victories of worldly renown, having under his subjection both Scots and Britons, and the whole monarchy of the land; so he devised divers good and wholesome laws for the government of the same, as well concerning the state of the orders ecclesiastical, as also of the secular or lay people. Whereby it is to be understood, that the usurped power of the Bishop of Rome did not then extend itself so largely, nor so proudly derogate from the authority of kings and princes, but that every one in his own dominion had, under God, and not under the pope, the doing of all matters within the same his dominion contained, whether they were causes temporal or spiritual, as by the decrees and constitutions of this king, and also of others as well before him as after him, may evidently be testified; as where he, amongst other laws, thus ordaineth touching the bishop, in the words that follow underwritten.[1]

Kings of England governors as well in causes ecclesiastical as temporal.

A law concerning tithes.

The said Athelstan prescribed other constitutions also, as touching tithes-giving, where he saith, and proclaimeth: "I Athelstan, king, charge and command all my officers through my whole realm, to give tithes unto God of my proper goods, as well in living cattle as in the corn and fruits of the ground; and that my bishops, likewise, of their proper goods, and mine aldermen, and my officers and headmen, shall do the same.[2] Item, this I will, that my bishops and other headmen do declare the same to such as be under their subjection, and that to be accomplished at the term of St. John the Baptist. Let us remember what Jacob said unto the Lord, 'Of all things that thou givest to me I will offer tithes unto the Lord;'

(1) "Episcopo jure pertinet, omnem rectitudinem promovere, Dei videlicet, ac seculi. In primis, debet omnem ordinatum instruere, quid ei sit agendum jure, et quid hominibus secularibus judicare debeant.

"Debet etiam sedulo pacem et concordiam operari cum seculi judicibus, qui rectum velle diligunt, et in compellationum allegationem edocere, ne quis alii perperam agat in jurejurando, vel ordalio.

"Nec pati debet aliquam circumventionem injustæ mensuræ, vel injusti ponderis. Sed convenit ut per consilium et testimonium ejus omne legis rectum et burgi mensura, et omne pondus sit secundum ditionem [alias dictionem] ejus, institutum valde rectum; ne quis proximum suum seducat, pro quo decidat in peccatum.

"Et semper debet Christianis providere contra omnia quæ prædicta sunt, et ideo debet se de pluribus intromittere: ut sciat quomodo grex agat, quem ad Dei manum custodire suscepit, ne diabolus cum dilaniet, nec malum aliquod superseminet. Nunquam enim erit populo bene consultum, nec digne Deo conversabitur, ubi lucrum impium et magis falsum diligitur. Ideo debent omnes amici Dei quod iniquum est enervare, et quod justum est elevare, nec pati ut propter falsum et pecuniæ quæstum homines se forisfaciant erga vere sapientem Deum, cui displicet omnis injustitia.

"Christianis autem omnibus necessarium est, ut rectum diligant, et iniqua condemnent, et saltem sacris ordinibus evecti justum semper erigant, et prava deponant.

"Hinc debent episcopi cum judicibus judicia dictitare, et interesse, ne permittant (si possint) ut illinc aliqua pravitatum gramina pullulent. Et sacerdotibus pertinet in sua diœcesi, ut ad rectum sedulo quemcumque juvent, nec patiantur (si possint) ut Christianus aliquis alii noceat, non potens impotenti, non summus infirmo, non prælatus subditis, [minoribus] non dominus hominibus suis, servis, aut liberis. Et secundum ditionem [scriftes dictionum] et per mensuram suam, convenit per rectum, ut necessaria servi operentur [servi testimentales] super omnem scyram cui præest [cui insunt.]

"Et rectum est ut non sit aliqua mensurabilis virga longior quam alia, sed per Episcopi mensuram [scriftes mensuram] omnes institutæ sint, et exequatæ per suam diœcesin [in sua scriftscyra.] Et omne pondus constet secundum dictionem ejus, et si aliquid controversiarum intersit, discernat Episcopus.

"Uniuscujusque Domini proprium est et necesse, ut servis condescendat; et compatiatur, sicut indulgentius poterit: quia Domino Deo viventi sunt æque chari servus, et liber. Et omnes uno et eodem pretio redemit, et omnes sumus Deo necessario servi, et sic judicabit nos, sicut ante judicavimus eos, in quos potestatem judicii in terris habebimus. Et ideo opus est ut eis parcamus qui nobis parere debent, et tunc manutenebimur, in Dei Omnipotentis proprio judicio. Amen."—Extractum ex legib. Regis Ethelstani.

(2) "Ego Ethelstanus Rex, consilio Ulfelmi archiepiscopi mei et aliorum episcoporum, mando præpositis omnibus in regno meo, in nomine Domini et sanctorum omnium, ut imprimis reddant de meo proprio decimas Deo, tam in vivente capitali, quam in mortuis frugibus terræ: et episcopi mei similiter faciant de suo proprio, et aldermanni mei et præpositi mei," &c.

A.D. 941.

also, what the Lord saith in the Gospel of St. Matthew, 'To him that hath it shall be given, and he shall abound.' We must also consider how terribly it is written in books, that 'if we will not offer our tenths, from us nine parts shall be taken away, and only the tenth part shall be left us.'" And, in the same place, after that he hath assigned the church rights to be paid in the place whereto they belong, it followeth, "that the king would usurp no man's goods wrongfully."[1]

Among his other laws and ordinances, to the number of thirty-five, divers things are comprehended, pertaining as well to the spiritual, as also to the temporal jurisdiction.

Out of the laws of this king first sprang up the attachment of thieves, that such as stole above twelve pence, and were above twelve years old, should not be spared. Thus much, briefly, concerning the history of King Athelstan, and things in his time done, who reigned about the space of sixteen years:[2] as he died without issue, after him succeeded his brother Edmund, A.D. 940, who reigned six years.

EDMUND.[3]

EDMUND, the son of Edward the Elder by his third wife (as is declared) and brother of Athelstan, being of the age of twenty years, entered upon his reign, who had by his queen Elgina two sons, Edwin, and Edgar, surnamed Pacificus, who both reigned after him as followeth. This Edmund continued his reign six years and a half. By him were expelled the Danes, Scots, Normans, and all foreign enemies out of the land. Such cities and towns as before were in the possession of strangers, as Lincoln, Nottingham, Derby, Stafford, and Leicester, he recovered out of their hands. Thus the realm being cleared of foreign power for a time, the king set his mind upon redressing and maintaining the state of the church; which all stood then in building of monasteries, and furnishing of churches, either with new possessions, or in restoring the old, which were taken away before. In the time of this Edmund, this I find in an old written story borrowed of William Carey, a citizen of London, a worthy treasurer of most worthy monuments of antiquity. The name of the author I cannot allege, because the book beareth no title, lacking both the beginning and the latter end, but the words thereof faithfully recited be these, "In the time of this king, there was a scattering or dispersion made of the monks out of the monastery of Evesham, and canons substituted in their place, through the doing of Athelmus and Ulricus, laymen, and of Osulfus, bishop," &c.[4] A.D. 941. (A.D. 941 to 946.)

Here, as concerning this matter between monks and others of the clergy, first it is to be understood, that in the realm of England heretofore, before the time of Dunstan, the bishops' sees and cathedral (The difference between monks and priests.)

(1) "Facite etiam ut mihi mea propria capiatis, quæ mihi poteritis recte acquirere. Nolo ut aliquid mihi injuste conquiratis. Sed omnia vestra concedo vobis eo tenore, quo mihi mea similiter exoptetis, Cavete simul et vobis, et eis quos admonere debetis, ab ira Dei, et transgressione mea."

(2) Epitaph. in Ethelst. "Sol illustravit bisseno scorpion ortu: cum regem cauda percutit ille sua."

(3) Edition 1563, p. 11. Ed. 1583, p. 150. Ed. 1597, p. 135. Ed. 1684, vol. i. p. 167.—ED.

(4) "Hujus regis tempore facta est dispersio monachorum Eushmensis cœnobii, cum substitutione canonicorum per Athelmum et Ulricum laicos, et Osulphum episcopum," &c.

Edmund. A.D. 941 to 946.

churches were replenished with no monks, but with priests and canons, called then clerks, or men of the clergy. After this, beginneth to rise a difference or a sect between these two parties in strictness of life, and in habit; so that they who lived after a stricter rule of holiness were called monks, and professed chastity; that was, to live without wives, for so was chastity then defined in those blind days; as though holy matrimony were not chastity, according as Paphnutius did well define it in the Council of Nice. The other sort, who were not monks, but priests, or men of the clergy so called, lived more free from those monkish rules and observances, and were then commonly, or at least lawfully, married, and in their life and habit came nearer to the secular state of other Christians, by reason whereof great disdain and emulation were among them, insomuch that in many cathedral churches, where priests were before, there monks were put in; and on the contrary, where monks had intruded, there priests and canons again were placed, and monks thrust out; whereof more shall appear hereafter (by the grace of Christ), when we come to the life of Dunstan. In the mean time something to satisfy the cogitation of the reader, who peradventure either is ignorant, or else would know of the first coming in of monks into this realm and church of England in the Saxons' time, this is to be noted, according as I find in old chronicles, namely, in the Latin history of Malmesbury, recorded touching the same.[1]

About this time of King Edmund, or shortly after, hardness and strictness of life, joined with superstition, was had in veneration, and counted for great holiness: men, therefore, either to win public fame with men, or merits with God, gave themselves to lead a strict life, thinking thereby, the stranger their conversation was, and the further from the common trade of vulgar people, the more perfect to be towards God and man. There was at that time, and before that, a monastery in France named Floriake, after the order and rule of Benedict; from which monastery did spring a great part of our English monks, who being there professed, and afterward returning into England, did congregate men daily to their profession; and so, partly for strangeness of their rule, partly for outward holiness of their strict life, partly for the opinion of holiness that many had of them, were in great admiration, not only with the rude sort, but with kings and princes, who founded their houses, maintained their rules, and enlarged them with possessions. Among this order of monks coming from Floriake especially was one Oswald, first a monk of Floriake, then bishop of Worcester and York, a great patron and setter-up of monkery. Touching this Oswald, writing of his history, hath these words: "It was a common custom at that time among Englishmen, that if any good men were well-affected or minded toward religion, they went to the monastery of the blessed St. Benedict in France, and there received the habit of a monk, whereupon the first origin of this religion began,"[2] &c. But of this Oswald, bishop of York, and Dunstan, bishop of Canterbury, and Ethelwald, bishop of Winchester, how they replenished divers

(The monastery of Floriake.) (Oswald, Bishop of York, a great patron of monkery.) (Its origin.)

(1) Guliel. Malmesb. de Gestis Pontificum Anglorum, lib. ii.

(2) "Familiaris per id temporis Anglis consuetudo fuit, ut si qui boni afflati essent desiderio, in beatissimi Benedicti Monasterio cœnobialem susciperent habitum, a quo religionis hujusce manavit exordium," &c. Guil. Malmesb. lib. iii. de Pontif.

monasteries and cathedral churches with monks, and how they discharged married priests and canons out of their houses, to plant in monks in their cells, more shall be spoken, by the grace of Christ, hereafter.

Edmund. A.D. 941 to 946.

Let us now return to the matter where we left off, of King Edmund, who, besides his noble victories against his enemies, and recovering the cities above expressed into his own hands, did also subdue the province of Cumberland; and, after he had put out the eyes of the two sons of Dunmail, king of Cumberland, he committed the governance thereof to Malcolm, king of Scots, upon promise of his trusty service and obedience, when the king should stand in any need of him. In the time of this king, Dunstan was not yet archbishop of Canterbury, but only abbot of Glastonbury, of whom many fabulous narrations pass among writers, importing more vanity than verity, whereof this is one of the first. What time Edgar, called Pacificus, was born, Dunstan, being at the same time abbot of Glastonbury, heard, as the monkish fables dream, a voice in the air of certain angels singing after this tenor, "Now peace cometh to the church of England in the time of this child, and of our Dunstan," &c. This I thought to recite, that the christian reader might the better ponder with himself the impudent and abominable fictions of this Romish generation. But of the same mint also they have forged, how the said Dunstan heard the angels sing the Kyrieleson, usually sung at even-song in the church.[1] Which is as true as that the harp, hanging in a woman's house played by itself the tune of the anthem, called, "Gaudent in cœlis," &c. What would not these deceivers feign in matters something likely, who, in things so absurd and so inconvenient, shame not to lie and to forge so impudently, and also so manifestly? Through the motion of this Dunstan, King Edmund builded and furnished the monastery of Glastonbury, and made the said Dunstan abbot thereof.

Dunstan, abbot of Glastonbury.

The sons of King Edmund.

The impudent vanity of the Popes' church in forging false miracles.

The abbey of Glastonbury re-builded by King Ive.

Concerning the end and death of this king, sundry opinions there be. Alfridus and Marianus say, that while this King Edmund endeavoured himself to save his sewer from the danger of his enemies, who would have slain him at Pulcher church, the king, in parting the fray, was wounded, and died shortly after. But Malmesbury saith,[2] "that the king being at a feast at Pulcher church upon the day of St. Augustine, spied a felon sitting in the hall named Leof, whom he for his felony had exiled; and leaping over the table did fly upon him, and plucked the thief by the hair of the head to the ground; in which doing, the felon with a knife wounded the king to the death, and also with the same knife wounded many other of the king's servants, and at length was hewn down and died forthwith.

By the laws of King Edmund (ordained and set forth, as well for the redress of church matters, as also of civil regiment) it would appear, that the state of causes both temporal and spiritual, appertained then to the king's right (the false pretended usurpation of the bishop of Rome notwithstanding), as by these laws is to be seen: where he, by the advice of his lords and bishops did enact and determine concerning the chastity and pure life of ecclesiastical

The laws of King Edmund touching as well the state spiritual as temporal.

(1) Guliel. Malmesb. de Pontif. lib. i. (2) Idem, de Regib lib. ii.

Edmund. ministers, and such as were in the orders of the church, with the penalties also for those who transgressed the same.

A.D. 941 to 946.

Item, For tithes to be paid for every christian man, and for the church fees, and alms fees, &c.

Item, For defiling of women professed, whom we call nuns, &c.

Item, For every bishop to see his churches repaired of his own proper charge; and boldly to admonish the king, whether the houses of God were well maintained, &c.

Item, For flying into the church for sanctuary, &c.

Item, Concerning cases and determinations spousal or matrimonial, &c.

All which constitutions declare what interest kings had in those days in matters as well ecclesiastical as others, within their dominion; and that, not only in disposing the ordinances and rites that appertained to the institution of the church, but also in placing and setting bishops in their sees, &c.

In the time of this Edmund, Ulstan was archbishop of York, and Odo, archbishop of Canterbury, which Odo, being a Dane born, as is before said, was promoted to that see by King Athelstan, for that, as they say, he being first bishop of Wilton, and present with King Athelstan in the field against Analanus before-mentioned, what time the said Athelstan had lost his sword, he, through his intercession up to heaven, did see a sword from heaven come down into the sheath of the king. Whereof relation being made unto the king by the aforesaid bishop,[1] Athelstan upon the same was so affected towards Odo, that not only he accounted him a patron of his life, but also made him primate of Canterbury after the decease of Ulfelm. This Odo was the first from the coming in of the Saxons, who was archbishop of Canterbury, being no monk; for all the others before him were of the profession of monks, of whom a great part had been Italians unto Berctualdus.[2] Notwithstanding this, Odo, being also a stranger born, after he was elected to the bishopric, to answer to the old custom of others before him, sailed over into France, and there, at Floriake, after the usual manner above-mentioned of Englishmen, received the profession and habit of monkish religion, as saith Malmesbury.[3] And, like as the said Odo first being no monk, was made archbishop of Canterbury, so also Ulstan, being at the same time bishop of York and of Worcester, differed from divers of his predecessors before him in profession and habit; of whom the beforenamed author thus writeth in his third book, speaking of Ulstan, "Qui sanctitate discrepabat et habitu;" that is, "He differed in sanctimony and in habit." Whereby it is to be collected, that in those days there was a difference in habit and garment, not only between monks and bishops, but also between one bishop and another; albeit what difference it was, I do not find. But to return again to Odo, who, by the description of his manners, might seem not to be the worst who occupied that place, were it not that our lying histories, feigning false miracles about him, as they do of others, make him indeed to seem worse

Odo made monk at Floriake, after he was archbishop of Canterbury.

The difference of habit and garment among men of the church.

(1) Guliel. Malmesb. de Pontif. lib. i. Polychron. lib. vi. cap. 6.
(2) Idem, de Pontif. lib. i.
(3) Idem, lib. iii. de Pontif. Ebor.

than he was, as where they imagine that he should see from heaven a sword fall into the scabbard of King Athelstan; also, where he should cover and defend the church of Canterbury with his prayers from rain; and where he should turn the bread of the altar (as the writer termeth it) into lively flesh, and from flesh into bread again, to confirm the people who before doubted about it. Where note again, good reader! that albeit this miracle were true, as no doubt it is untrue, yet is it to be noted, that in those days was a great doubt amongst Englishmen about the popish sacrament, and that transubstantiation was not received into the christian creed. The like judgment is to be given also of that, where our English writers, testifying of the same Odo, say that he prophesied long before that Dunstan would be his successor in the church of Canterbury. But to let these phantasies and idle stories pass, this which we find of his own writing is certain, that the said Odo, in the reign of King Edmund, had a synod commenced of the chief prelates and men of the clergy in his time, to whom he directed this letter here following: the copy whereof I thought to give, for the reader to see what zealous care then reigned in archbishops toward the church of the Lord. The words of his epistle proceed in this tenor:—

Lying miracles of Odo.

Transubstantiation not yet received.

The letter or epistle of Odo, archbishop of Canterbury, sent to the other bishops and men of the clergy.[1]

By the divine grace of God, I Odo of the church of our Lord and Saviour Jesus Christ, archbishop and metropolitan of the city of Dover, to my fellow-bishops and fellow-planters of the Catholic faith, and my fellow-brethren in the spiritual bond of charity, with greeting, wish prosperity in this world present, and in the world to come felicity. If it were so, or by any means could be, that all the riches of this world were laid before mine eyes, so that I being emperor had all things universally under my subjection, all those things gladly would I give, yea and myself also I would offer willingly for the health of your souls, as who also do desire, and trust likewise myself to be strengthened with the fervency of your holiness, as appertaining to those things wherein the Lord our God hath set us to be workmen, &c.

And after a few other words to the like effect, wherein he doth declare the heavy burden of his office, it followeth after this manner:—

Wherefore most humbly, and as one unworthy, but yet a devout fellow-brother of yours, I beseech and exhort your holiness, that you will not show yourselves cold and negligent in the cure and regiment of souls, so that in the time of the fearful judgment, the Lord do not complain of you, saying, "My shepherds did not feed my flock, but they fed themselves;" and again, "They were princes of my flock, and I knew not of it." But rather let us take heed and be diligent over the household of the Lord, over which he hath set us to be the leaders, to give them meat and true measure of corn in time convenient; that is to say, wholesome doctrine. And, although upon mine own merits or worthiness, I do not presume to comfort or exhort any man, but as one being unworthy and faulty in transgressions innumerable, I am glad, and stand in need rather, to be strengthened by your brotherly admonitions; yet, for the ancient authority of my predecessors, as of Augustine of happy memory, and also of all other saints, by whose industry the rule of Christianity did first flourish and spring from this metropolitan see unto all quarters of England, therefore I have thought good to direct unto

(1) "Mirabili cuncti-potentis polorum præsulis clementia opitulante, ego Odo ecclesiæ salvatoris Domini nostri Jesu Christi archiepiscopus Doverniensis civitatis metropolitanus, coepiscopis fidei Catholicæ compagatoribus, spirituali charitatis vigore meis confratribus, præsentium prosperitatem æthereique decoris beatitudinem," &c.

Edmund. A.D. 941 to 946. you these my letters to the profit of you all; especially, for that our renowned and princely king Edmund, with all his people, doth joy to follow that which he heareth in you and of you; and also forasmuch as all his subjects, who be under his imperial dominion, do love and delight to follow most joyfully the same, and report of your sincere conversation, &c.

This Odo continued bishop the space of twenty years. After him Elsinus was elected and ordained by the king to succeed through favour and money; but, in going to Rome for the pope's pall, in his journey through the Alps, he decayed and died for cold. Hereupon succeeded Dunstan, as in time and place (by the leave of Christ) followeth to be declared.

King Edmund gave to St. Edmund the Martyr before-mentioned, the town of Bredrichworth, which is now called St. Edmundsbury, with great revenues and lands appertaining to the same. But concerning the frivolous miracles which our monkish story-writers here feign of this good Edmund, by the way, or rather out of the way, I let them pass. And thus much concerning King Edmund, who, after he had reigned six years and a-half, was slain, as it is said, at Pulcherchurch, and buried at Glastonbury by Dunstan, leaving behind him two children, Edwin and Edgar, by his wife Elgina. But because the two aforesaid children were yet young, and under age, therefore Edred, brother to King Edmund, and uncle to the children, governed as protector about the space of nine years and a half, till Edwin the eldest son came of age. This Edred, with great moderation and fidelity to the young children behaved himself, during the time of his government. In his time Dunstan was promoted, through the means of Odo the archbishop, from abbot of Glastonbury to be bishop of Worcester. By the counsel of this Dunstan, Edred was much ruled, and too much thereto addicted; insomuch that he is reported in stories to have submitted himself to much fond penance and castigation, inflicted on him by the said Dunstan. Such zealous devotion was then in princes, and more blind superstition in bishops. And here again is another miracle as fantastical as the other before, forged by Dunstan, that when that Edred being sick sent for Dunstan to be his confessor, by the way Dunstan should hear a voice declaring to him beforehand, that Edred was already departed; at the declaring whereof, Dunstan's horse fell immediately dead under him—with lie and all!

Children of King Edmund.

Edred, governor of the realm. A.D. 946 to 955.

Dunstan made bishop of Worcester.

EDWIN, OR EDWY.

A.D. 955 to 959. Edwin, the eldest son of King Edmund before-mentioned, after his uncle Edred, began his reign about A.D. 955, being crowned at Kingston by Odo, the archbishop of Canterbury. Of this Edwin it is reported by divers writers, that the first day of his coronation, sitting with his lords, he brake suddenly from them, and entered a secret chamber, to the company of a certain woman whom he inordinately retained, being, as some say, another man's wife, whose husband he had before slain; as others say, being of his alliance, to the great misliking of his lords, and especially of the clergy. Dunstan was as yet but abbot of Glastonbury; who, following the king into the chamber, brought him out by the hand, and accused him to Odo, the archbishop, causing him to be separate from the company of the aforesaid party, by which Odo, the king was for his deed suspended out of the church: by reason whereof the king, being displeased with Dunstan, banished him, and forced him for a season to fly into Flanders, where he resided in the monastery of St. Amand. About the same season the monastical order of Benedict monks, or black monks, as they were called, began to multiply and increase here in England; insomuch that where, beforetime, other priests and canons had been placed, there monks were in their rooms set in, and the secular priests (as they then were called) or canons, put out. But King Edwin, for the displeasure he bare to Dunstan, did so vex all the order of the said monks, that in Malmesbury, Glastonbury, and other places, he thrust them out, and set secular priests in their stead. Notwithstanding, it was not long before these priests and canons were again removed, and the said monks in their stead restored, both in the aforesaid houses, and in divers other cathedral churches besides, as in the next story of King Edgar (Christ willing) shall more at large appear.

Edwin. A.D. 955 to 959.

The king suspended by the archbishop.

Edwin an enemy to monks.

In fine, King Edwin being hated, by reason of his demeanour, by all his subjects, especially the Northumbrians and Mercians, was by them removed from his kingly honour, and his brother Edgar in his stead received, so that the river Thames divided both their kingdoms. Edwin, after he had reigned about the term of four years, departed, leaving no heir of his body, wherefore the rule of the land fell to Edgar, his younger brother.

His death.

EDGAR, SIRNAMED PACIFICUS.[1]

EDGAR, the second son of Edmund, and brother to Edwin, being of the age of sixteen years, began his reign over the realm of England, A.D. 959, but was not crowned till fourteen years after; the causes whereof hereunder follow (Christ willing) to be declared. In the beginning of his reign he called home Dunstan, whom King Edwin had exiled. Then was Dunstan, who before was abbot of Glastonbury, made bishop of Worcester, and then of London. Not long after, this Odo, the archbishop of Canterbury, deceased, after he had governed that church twenty-four years. Next after him, Brithilinus, bishop of Winchester, was elected; but because he was thought not sufficient to furnish that room, Dunstan was ordained archbishop, and the other sent home again to his old church.[2] Note here by the way, how in those days the donation and assigning of ecclesiastical dignities remained in the king's hand; only they fetched their pall from Rome as a token of the pope's confirmation.[3] Dunstan, being thus by the king made archbishop, took his journey to Rome for his pall of Pope John XIII., about the beginning of the king's reign; and, obtaining it, shortly after his return from Rome, entreateth King Edgar, that Oswald (who, as is said, was made monk at Floriake, and was nephew to Odo, late archbishop of Canterbury) might be promoted to the bishopric of Worcester, which

A.D. 959.

Dunstan made bishop of London, and presently archbishop of Canterbury.

Livings given by the king, and not by the pope.

(1) Edition 1563, p. 10. Ed. 1583, p. 152. Ed. 1596, p. 137. Ed. 1684, vol. i. p. 169.—ED.
(2) Ex Hist. Ro. Hoveden.
(3) The "pall" was the richly embroidered robe which every bishop received at his consecration at the hands of the pope, after the payment of *certain dues*.—ED.

Edgar.
A.D. 959.

thing to him was granted; and, not long after, through the means of the said Dunstan, Ethelwold, whom stories do feign to be the great patron of monkery, first a monk at Glastonbury, then abbot of Abingdon, was made bishop of Winchester. Of this Ethelwold, Malmesbury[1] recordeth, that what time he was a monk in the house of Glastonbury, the abbot had a vision of him, to this effect: how that there appeared to him in his sleep a certain great tree, the branches whereof extended throughout all the four quarters of the realm, which branches were all covered with many little monks' cowls; and that, in the top of the tree, there was one great master-cowl, which, in spreading itself over the other cowls, enclosed all the rest; which master-cowl mine author, in the interpretation, applieth to the life of this Ethelwold. Of such prodigious fantasies our monkish histories be full; and not only our histories of England, but also the heathen stories of the Gentiles be stuffed with dreams of much like effect.

Ethelwold, bishop of Winchester, a great maintainer of monkery.
A.D. 963.
Monkish dreams.

Of such a kind is the dream we read of the mother of Athelstan; how the moon did spring out of her, and give light to all England! Also that of King Charles the emperor, how he was led by a thread to see the torments of hell. Likewise that of Furceus, the hermit, mentioned in the third Book of Bede, who saw the joys of heaven, and the four fires that should destroy the world: the one was of lying, for breaking our promise made at baptism; the second fire of covetousness; the third of dissension; the fourth was the fire of impiety and wrongful dealing. Of a like sort was the dream of Dunstan, and the dream of that same Ethelwold, to whom appeared the three bishops, Bristan, Birin, and Swithin, &c. Again, there is the dream of the mother of this Ethelwold, who being great with him, did see a golden eagle fly out of her mouth, &c.; the dream likewise, or the vision of King Edgar, concerning the falling of the two apples; and of the pots, one being full of water, the other empty, &c.; also of King Edward the Confessor, touching the ruin of the land by the conquest of the Normans. We read also in the History of Astiages, how he dreamed of Cyrus, and likewise of many other dreams in the books of the monks and of the ethnic writers; for what cannot either the idle vanity of man's head, or the deception of the lying spirit work by man, in foreshowing such earthly events as happen commonly in this present world? But there is a difference to be understood between these earthly dreams, speaking of earthly things and matters of human superstition; and between other spiritual revelations sent by God touching spiritual matters of the church, pertaining to man's salvation. But, to our purpose: by this dream, and by the event which followed after, it may appear how, and by what means, the multitude of monks began first to swarm in the churches of England, that is, in the days of this Edgar, by the means of these three bishops, Dunstan, Ethelwold, and Oswald. Albeit Dunstan was the chief ringleader of this race, yet Ethelwold, being now bishop of Winchester, and Oswald bishop of Worcester, were not much behind for their parts. By the instigation and counsel of these three aforesaid, King Edgar is recorded in histories to build either new out of the ground, or to re-edify of monasteries decayed by the Danes, more than forty: as the house of Ely, Glastonbury, Abingdon, Burga by Stamford, Thorney, Ramsey, Wilton, Wenton,

How and when monks began to swarm in England.
Three setters up of monkish religion.

(1) Ex Guliel. Malmesb. lib. de Gestis Pontificum Anglorum.

Winchcomb, Thamstoke in Devonshire, with divers more, in the setting up and building of which the aforesaid Ethelwold was a great doer, and a founder under the king. Moreover, through the motion of this Dunstan and his fellows, King Edgar, in divers great houses and cathedral churches where prebendaries and priests were before, displaced the priests, and set in monks. Of this we read in the Chronicles of Roger Hovenden, in words and form as followeth:—"Ethelwold, bishop of Winchester, who was then one of the king's council, did urge the king chiefly to expel clerks out of monasteries, and in their room to bestow monks and nuns."[1] Thus the secular priests being put to their choice, whether to change their habit, or to leave their rooms, departed out of their houses, giving place for other better men to come in, and thus the houses and monasteries of religious men through all the realm rose up apace. *Edgar* A.D. 964.

After the king's mind was thus persuaded and incited by these bishops to advance monkery, then Oswald, bishop of Worcester, and also made archbishop of York after the decease of Oskitel, "Sui voti compos effectus," as Hoveden writeth, having his see in the cathedral church there of St. Peter, began first with fair persuasions to assay the minds of the canons and priests, whether they could be content to change their profession, and to be made monks or no; and when he saw it would not take effect, he practised this policy with them:—near to the said church of St. Peter, within the church-yard, he erected another church of our Lady,[2] which when he had replenished with monks, he continually frequented; there he kept, there he sat, and was ever there conversant, by reason whereof the other church was left naked and desolate, and all the people gathered there, where the bishop was. The priests seeing themselves so to be left and neglected both by the bishop and by the people, to whom nothing remained but shame and contempt, were driven by shame either to relinquish the house (such as would not enter the monkish profession), or else to become monks (such as had nothing else to depend upon). After the like superstition, although not after the same subtilty, did Ethelwold also drive out the canons and priests from the new monastery in Winchester, afterward called Hida, and place therein his monks. So in Oxford and in Mildune, with divers other places, the secular priests, with their wives, were expelled, to give place to monks. The cause thereof is thus pretended in certain story-writers, whom I see also Fabian to follow; for that the priests and clerks were thought slack and negligent in their church service, and set in vicars in their stead, while they lived in pleasure and mispent the patrimony of the church after their own lust. Then King Edgar gave to the vicars the same land which before belonged to the prebendaries; who also not long after showed themselves as negligent as the others. Wherefore King Edgar, as mine authors write, by the consent of Pope John XIII., voided clearly the priests, The policy of Oswald in driving out priests to place in monks. A.D. 969.

(1) "Hic namque Ethelwoldus regem, cujus eximius erat consiliarius, ad hoc maxime provocavit, ut clericos a monasteriis expelleret, et monachos sanctimonialesque in eis collocaret," &c. Ro. Hoveden, lib. Continuationum post Bedam. Chro. Jornalens. Guliel. Malmesb. de Gestis Pontif. lib. i. Whereunto accordeth likewise Jornalensis: "Hoc anno Ethelwoldus Wint. et Oswaldus Wigorniensis, episcopi, jussu Regis Edgari (Clericis de quibusdam majoribus ecclesiis expulsis) monachos instituerunt, aut de eisdem clericis et aliis monachos in eisdem fecerunt." Malmesbury also, writing of the time of Dunstan, maketh the matter somewhat more plain, where he saith, "Itaque clerici multarum ecclesiarum data optione, ut aut amictum mutarent, aut locis valedicerent, melioribus habitacula vacuefacientes. Surgebant itaque in tota insula religiosorum monasteria, cumulabantur mole pretiosi metalli sanctorum altaria," &c.

(2) Guliel. Malmesb. lib. iii. de Gest. Pont.; Chron. Jornalen. in Vita Edgari.

Edgar A.D. 966

and ordained there monks; though certain of the nobles and some of the prelates were therewith not well contented, as in the chapter following may partly appear.

Ecclesiastical affairs

But forasmuch as we have entered upon the mention of monks and nuns, and of their profession, which I see so greatly in our monkish stories commended; lest perhaps the simple reader may be deceived thereby, in hearing the name of monks in all histories of times to be such an ancient thing in christian life, even from the primitive church after the apostles' time, both commonly recited and well received: therefore, to help the judgment of the ignorant, and to prevent all error herein, it shall not be unprofitable, in following the present occasion here given, by way of a little digression, to intermeddle somewhat concerning the original institution of monks, what they were in the old time who were called Monachi; wherein the monks of the primitive time did differ from the monks of the middle time, and from these our monks now of this latter age; moreover, wherein all these three do differ from priests, as we call them, and from men of the clergy. Wherefore, to answer to the superstitious scruple of those who allege the old antiquity of the name and title of monks, first, I grant the name and order of monks to be of old continuance, nearly from the time of three hundred years after Christ; of whom divers old authors do discourse, as Augustine, Hieronymus, Basilius Magnus (who was also himself one of the first institutors and commenders of that superstition), Chrysostom, Nazianzen, Evagrius, Sozomen, Dionysius, and divers others. In the number of these monks, who then were divided into hermits or anchorites, and into Cœnobites, were Antonius, Paulus, and Johannes, with divers other recluses, among whom were Hierome, Basil, Macharius, Isidore, Pambus, Nilammon, Simeon, with infinite others, both in Palestine, Syria, Thebes, Mesopotamia, Egypt, Africa, and Scythia; insomuch that Cassianus[1] maketh mention of a certain monastery at Thebes, wherein were above 5,000 monks, under the government of one abbot. And here also in England mention is made before of Bangor, wherein were 2,200 monks under one man's ruling [A.D. 596]; whereby it appeareth that there were monks then, and two hundred years before, in the primitive time of the church. But what monks these were, is to be considered: such as by tyranny of persecution were driven into solitary and desert places, or else such as not constrained by any, but of their own voluntary devotion, joined with some superstition, for the love they had unto spiritual contemplation, and for hatred of the wicked world, withdrew themselves from all company, either having nothing to themselves proper, or else all things common with others. Now all these were then nothing else but laymen: of which laymen there were two sundry sorts, one of the vulgar and common people, who only were partakers of the sacraments; the others, through following a monastical kind of life, were called monks, being nothing but laymen leading a more severe and stricter trade of life than others.

The difference, order, and institution of monks

Two sorts in the primitive church

Monks in the old time were only lay men, leading a strict life.

By the authors quoted in the note,[2] it is evident that monks

(1) Cassian lib ii cap 4 De Canon Noctur Orat

(2) August lib de moribus ecclesiæ, cap 13 Item, lib de operibus Monachorum Item, Epistola ad Aurelium Also by Hierome ad Heliodorum, writing these words: "Alia monachorum

Edgar. *Ecclesiastical affairs.*

in the former age of the church, albeit they lived a solitary life, yet were they no other but laymen, differing from priests and also from the other monks who succeeded them afterwards in the middle age of the church, and that in three points: First, they were tied and bound to no prescribed form, either of diet or apparel, or any thing else, as we may see testified by the words of St. Augustine.[1] And Sozomen, speaking of the monks of the same time, who in cities had several mansions separate from others, saith, "Some live in cities, so behaving themselves, as seeming nothing worth, and they differed nothing from the multitude,"[2] &c. The second point wherein they were discrepant from the later monks was, that they remained in no other order but that of laymen, only being of a stricter life than the rest, and had nothing to do in matters and charges ecclesiastical; which was afterward broken by Pope Boniface IV., as followeth (the Lord willing) to be seen and said. Thirdly, the aforesaid monks of that age, albeit the most part of them lived sole and single from wives, yet some of them were married: certes, none of them were forbidden or restrained from marriage. Of such as were married, speaketh Athanasius, who says, "he knew both monks and bishops, as married men, and fathers of children."[3]

Monks in the primitive time differing from monks in the second age of the church.

Some were married, and none restrained from marriage.

The said monks of the old time, though they were better than the others who followed them, yet, all that notwithstanding, superstition with them, and among them, began then to creep into the church through the crafty subtilty of Satan, and all for the ignorance of our free justification by faith in Jesus Christ. Examples do declare the vain and prodigious superstition of these monastical sorts of men; which examples do not lack, if leisure rather did not lack to bring them in. But two or three shall suffice for many, which I purpose (the Lord willing) here to insert, to the intent the mind of the godly reader may the better consider and understand, how shortly after the time of Christ and his apostles, the doctrine of christian justification began to be forgotten, true religion turned to superstition, and the price of Christ's passion to be obscured through the vain opinion of men's merits, &c. A certain abbot, named Moses, thus testifieth of himself in the Collations of Cassianus, that he so afflicted himself with much fasting and watching, that sometimes, for two or three days together, not only he felt no appetite to eat, but also had no remembrance of any meat at all, and by reason thereof was driven also from sleep; insomuch that he was caused to pray to God but for some portion of the night to be given him, for a little refreshing of sleep.[4] In the same author mention is made of

Superstition crept in with monkery.

Ignorance of free justification by Christ, the cause of all superstition.

est causa, alia clericorum; clerici pascunt oves, ego pascor," &c. that is, "One thing pertaineth to monks, another thing unto them of the clergy; they of the clergy feed their flock. I am fed," &c. Et ex Dionysio. The same appeareth likewise by the fourth canon of the Council of Chalcedon, where it is provided, "Ne monachi se ecclesiasticis negotiis immisceant;" that is, "That monks should not intermeddle with matters of the church," &c. Et Leo, Epistola 62. vetat Monachos et Laicos, "etsi scientiæ nomine glorientur, admitti ad officium docendi et concionandi."

(1) "Neque inter hæc nemo urgetur in aspera, quæ ferre non potest: nulli quod recusat imponitur. Nec ideo contemnitur a cæteris, in quod eis imitandis se fatetur invalidum. Meminerunt enim quantopere commendata sit in scripturis charitas. Meminerunt omnia munda mundis, &c. 'Non quod intrat in os coinquinat hominem, sed quod exit.' Itaque non rejiciendis generibus ciborum quasi pollutis, sed concupiscentiæ perdomandæ, et dilectioni fratrum retinendæ invigilat omnis industria."—August. de Institutis Monachorum.

(2) "Alii in turba civitatum conversabantur, sic seipsos gerentes, ut nullius momenti viderentur et a multis nihil differrent," &c.—Lib. iii. cap. 16.

(3) "Se novisse et monachos et episcopos conjuges et liberorum patres," &c.—In Epistola ad Dracontium.

(4) Cassi. cap. 17. Collat. 2.

Edgar. *Ecclesiastical affairs.* a certain old man, a hermit, who, because he had conceived in himself such a purpose as never to eat meat without he had some guest or stranger with him, sometimes was constrained to abstain five days together until Sunday, when he went to the church, and thence brought some stranger or other home with him.

Two other examples more will I add out of the said Cassianus, to declare how the subtilty of Satan, through superstition and false colour of holiness, blindeth the miserable eyes of those who rather attend men's traditions than the word of God. The said author relates that a certain abbot named Johannes, in the desert of Scythia, sent two of his novices with figs unto one that was sick in the wilderness, eighteen miles off from the church. It chanced that these two young novices, missing the way, wandered so long in the wild forest or wilderness, unable to find the cell, that for emptiness and weariness they waxed faint and tired; and yet rather would they die than taste the figs committed to them to carry, and so they did, for shortly after they were found dead, their figs lying whole by them.[1]

Blind monkish superstition.

Another story also Cassianus reciteth, of two monastical brethren, who making their progress in the desert of Thebes, purposed with themselves to take no sustenance but such as the Lord himself should minister unto them. It happened, as they were wandering desolate in the desert, and fainting almost for penury, that certain Mazises, a kind of people by nature fierce and cruel, notwithstanding being suddenly altered into a new nature of humanity, came forth, and of their own accord, offered bread unto them; which bread, the one thankfully received as sent of God; the other, accounting it sent of man, and not of God, refused it, and so for lack perished.[2]

Another instance.

Hereunto might I also annex the story of Mucius, who, to declare his obedience, did not stick, at the commandment of his abbot, to cast his son into the water, not knowing whether any were appointed there ready to rescue him from drowning; so far were the monks in those days drowned in superstition. What is this, but for man's traditions and commandments to transgress the commandments of God, who saith, "Thou shalt do no murder;" "Thou shalt not tempt the Lord thy God?" What man is so blind, that seeth not by these, and infinite examples more, what pernicious superstition had begun by reason of this monkery, almost from the beginning, to creep into the church? whereat I cannot marvel enough, seeing that age of the church had in it so many learned and famous doctors, who not only did approve and allow these monastical sects of life, but also certain were themselves the authors and institutors of the same, yea, and of men's traditions made the service of God; in the number of whom may be reckoned Basilius Magnus, and Nazianzen, who, with immoderate austerity, did so pluck down themselves, that when they were called to the office of bishops, they were not able to sustain the labour thereof.

Another.

Monkery the mother of superstition and hypocrisy.

Monks of the middle and latter ages of the church.

After these aforesaid monks of that time, above-recited, followed other monks of the middle age of the church, who, as in multitude, so also in superstition increasing, began, by little and little, from their desolate dens in the vast wilderness, to approach more near to

(1) Cassi. lib. de Spiritu Gastrimarg. cap. 40. (2) Idem. lib. vi. cap. 2.

great towns, where they had solemn monasteries founded by kings and queens, and king's daughters, and other rich consuls, as is partly before touched upon, and also the causes withal for which they were first founded.[1] All these impious and erroneous titles and causes we find alleged in histories, as in Malmesbury, Jornalensis, Henricus, and others. In those histories I also note, that most of the monasteries were erected first upon some great murder, either by war in the field, or privately committed at home, as shall well appear to them that read their books to whom I have referred.

Edgar.

Ecclesiastical affairs.

Causes of the founding of monasteries and nunneries, tending to the derogation of Christ's passion, and the christian faith.

But, to return to our monks again, who, as is said, first began to creep from the cold fields into warm towns and cloisters, from towns then into cities, and at length from their close cells and cities, into cathedral churches (as here appeareth by this story of King Edgar), where, not only did they abound in wealth and riches (especially these monks of our later time), but much more did they swim in superstition and pharisaical hypocrisy, being yoked and tied in all their doings to certain prescribed rules and formal observances; in watching, in sleeping, in eating, in rising, in praying, in walking, in talking, in looking, in tasting, in touching, in handling, in their gestures, in their vestures, every man apparelled not as the proper condition of others would require, nor as the season of the year did serve, but as the compulsory rules and order of every sect did enforce.

Various orders of monks.

The number of monkish sects was infinitely divers: some, after Basilius's rule, went in white; some, after Benet's rule, in black; some, Cluniacenses, first set up by Otho in the time of this King Edgar, wore after the rule of Benet's order; some, after Hierome's rule, were leather-girdled, and coped above their white coat; some Gregorians were copper-coloured; some, 'De valle umbrosa,' were grey monks; some, Grandimontenses, wore a coat of mail upon their bare bodies, with a black cloak thereupon: some, Cistercians, had white rochets on a black coat; some, Celestines, all in blue, both cloak, cowl and cap; some, charter monks, wearing haircloth next their bodies; some, Flagellants, going barefoot in long white linen shirts, with an open place in the back, where they beat themselves with scourges on the bare skin every day before the people's eyes, till the blood ran down, saying, that it was revealed to them by an angel, that in so scourging themselves, within thirty days and twelve hours they should be made as pure from sin as they were when they first received baptism; some, starred monks; some, Jesuits, with a white girdle and russet cowl. Briefly, who can reckon up the innumerable sects and disguised orders of their fraternities? some holding of St. Benet, some of St. Hierome, some of St. Basil, some of St. Bernard, some of St. Bridget, some of St. Bruno, some of St. Lewis; as though it were not enough for Christians to hold of Christ only. So subject were they to servile rules, that no part of christian liberty remained among them; so drowned and sunk in superstition, that not only they had lost Christ's religion, but also almost the sense and nature of men. For where men naturally are and ought to be ruled

(1) "Pro remedio animæ meæ," "pro remissione peccatorum meorum," "pro redemptione peccatorum meorum," et "pro salute regnorum," quique meo subjacent regimini populorum. In honorem gloriosæ Virginis.

Edgar. *Ecclesiastical affairs.* by the discreet government of reason in all outward doings wherein no one rule can serve for all men, the circumstance of time, place, person and business being so sundry and divers; on the contrary, among these, not reason, but only the knock of a bell ruled all their doings: their rising, their sleeping, their praying, their eating, their coming in, their going out, their talking, their silence; and altogether, like insensible people, either not having reason to rule themselves, or else as persons ungrateful to God, neither enjoying the benefit of reason created in them, nor yet using the grace of Christ's liberty, whereunto he redeemed them.

Monks ruled by the knock of a bell.

Thus thou seest, gentle reader! sufficiently declared, what the monks were in the primitive time of the church, and what were the monks of the middle age, and of these our latter days of the church; whereunto join this withal, that whereas the monks of elder time, as is said, were mere laymen, and not spiritual ministers, afterwards Boniface IV. made a decree, that monks might use the offices of preaching, christening, and hearing confessions; and also, that of absolving them from their sins: so that monks, who, in the beginning, were but laymen, and not spiritual ministers, forbidden by the general council of Chalcedon, as is above related, to intermeddle with matters ecclesiastical, afterwards, in process of time, did so much encroach upon the office of spiritual ministers, that at length the priests were discharged out of their cathedral churches, and monks put in their places; because that monks in those days, leading a stricter life, and professing chastity, had a greater countenance of holiness among the people than had the priests, who then, in the days of King Edgar, had wives (at least so many as would), no law forbidding them till the time of Hildebrand, now called Gregory VII., whereof more shall be said (Christ willing) in the book next following.

A.D. 606.

Made spiritual ministers contrary to the decrees and custom of the church.

Priests had wives

A.D. 967. And thus much, by the way, as touching the order and profession of monks. Now, to turn in again from whence we digressed, that is, to the matter of King Edgar, who, following the counsel and leading of Dunstan, and the aforesaid Ethelwold, bishop of Winchester, was somewhat thereby inclined to superstition; but, otherwise, of his own nature, well given to all virtues and princely acts worthy of much commendation and famous memory. So excellent was he in justice, and sharp in correction of vices, as well in his magistrates as other subjects, that never before his days was less felony by robbers, nor less extortion or bribery by false officers. Such provinces and lordships as were not yet come under the king's subjection, he united and adjoined to his dominion; and so made one perfect monarchy of the whole realm of England, with all the islands and borders about the same. Such as were wicked he kept under; he repressed those that were rebels; the godly he maintained; he loved the modest; he was devout to God, and beloved of his subjects, whom he governed in much peace and quietness. And as he was a great seeker of peace, so God did bless him with much abundance of peace and rest from all wars, so that, as the history recordeth of him, "he neither tasted of any privy treason among his subjects, nor of any invasion of foreign enemies," for which he was called Pacificus. So studious he was of the public profit of his realm, and fruitful in his government,

The worthy laws of King Edgar.

England reduced to one perfect monarchy.

Edgar. A.D. 970.

that, as the said story saith of him, "no year passed in all the time of his reign, wherein he did not some singular and necessary commodity for the commonwealth."[1] A great maintainer he was of religion and learning, not forgetting herein the foresteps of King Alfred his predecessor. Among his other princely virtues this chiefly is to be regarded, that whereas other princes in much peace and quietness are commonly wont to grow into a dissolute negligence of life, or oblivion of their charge committed unto them; this king, in continuance of peace (that notwithstanding), kept ever with him such a watch, and a vigilant severity joined with a seemly clemency, that I cannot but recite here what our historians witness, testifying of his diligent and great care over the commonwealth, "that he would suffer no man, of what degree of nobility soever he were, to evade his laws without condign punishment."[2] And the same author adds, "in all his time there was neither any privy picker, nor open thief, but he that in stealing other men's goods, would venture, and suffer, as he was sure to do, the loss of his own life."[3]

Edgar and Alfred compared.

Moreover, as the studious industry of this prince was forward in all other points, so his prudent provision did not lack in this also, in driving out the devouring and ravening wolves throughout all his land, wherein he used this policy, in causing Llewellyn, prince or king of Wales, to yield him yearly, by way of tribute, 300 wolves; by means whereof, within the space of four years after, in England and Wales, might scarcely be found one wolf alive.

Wolves first driven out of England.

This Edgar, among other of his politic deeds, had in readiness 3600 ships of war to scour the seas in the summer-time, whereof 1200 kept the east seas; as many defended the west side; and again, as many were in the south seas to repulse the invasion of foreign enemies. Moreover, in the winter season, the use and manner of this virtuous king was this: during all the time of his life, to ride over the land in progress, searching and inquiring diligently (to use the words of mine author), "how the laws and statutes by him ordained were kept, and that the poor should suffer no prejudice, or be oppressed in any manner of way by the mightier,"[4] &c. Briefly, as I see many things in this worthy prince to be commended, so this one thing in him I cannot but lament, to see him, like a phenix, to fly alone; that of all his posterity so few there be that seek to keep him company. And although I have showed more already of this king than I think will well be followed, yet this more is to be added to the worthiness of his other acts, that whereas, by the multitude of the Danes dwelling in divers places of England, much excessive drinking was used, whereupon ensued drunkenness and many other vices, to the evil example and hurt of his subjects; he, therefore, to prevent that evil, ordained certain cups, with pins or nails set in them, adding thereunto a law, that what person drank past the mark at one draught should forfeit a certain penny, whereof

The provision of King Edgar for keeping the seas.

A notable example for all good princes to follow.

The device of King Edgar to prevent drunkenness.

(1) "Nullus fere annus in chronicis præteriit, quo non magnum et necessarium patriæ aliquid fecerit."

(2) "Ut nullum cujuscunque dignitatis hominem leges eludere impune permitteret."

(3) "Nemo ejus tempore privatus latro, nemo popularis prædo, nisi qui mallet in fortunas alienas grassari propriæ vitæ dispendio," &c. Guliel. Malmesb. de Reg.

(4) "Quomodo legum jura, et suorum statuta decretorum observarentur; et ne pauperes a potentibus præjudicium passi opprimerentur."

Edgar. A.D. 971.

one half should fall to the accuser, and the other half to the ruler of the borough or town where the offence was done.

Eight kings do homage to King Edgar.

It is reported of this Edgar, by divers authors, that about the thirteenth year of his reign, he being at Chester, eight kings, called in histories Subreguli, to wit, petty-kings, or under-kings, came and did homage to him; of whom the first was the king of Scots, called Kenneth, Malcolm of Cumberland, Mackus, or Mascusinus, king of Monia, and of divers other islands; and all the kings of Wales, the names of whom were Dufnal or Dunewald, Sifresh, Huwall, Jacob, and Ulkell or Juchel. All these kings, after they had given their fidelity to Edgar, the day following, for a pomp or royalty, he entered with these aforesaid kings the river Dee; where he, sitting in a boat, took the rule of the helm, and caused these eight kings, every person taking an oar in his hand, to row him up and down the river, to and from the church of St. John, unto his palace again, in token that he was master and lord of so many provinces, whereupon he is reported to have said in this manner: "Tunc demum posse successores suos gloriari, se Reges Angliæ esse, cum tanta prærogativa honorum fruerentur." But in my mind this king had done much better, if he had rather said with St. Paul, "Absit mihi gloriari, nisi in cruce Domini nostri Jesu Christi."

Edgar a superstitious upholder of monkery.

And thus ye have heard hitherto, touching the commendation of King Edgar, such reports as the old monkish writers thought to bestow upon him, as upon the great patron of their monkish religion, who had builded as many monasteries for them as there were Sundays in the year, as some say, or, but forty-eight, as Edmer reporteth.

Vices noted in Edgar.

Now, on the other side, what vices in him were reigning, let us likewise consider, according as we find in the said authors described, who most wrote to his advancement. The first vice is noted to be cruelty as well towards others, as especially towards a certain earl, being of his secret council, called Ethelwold. The story is this: Ordgar, duke of Devonshire, had a certain daughter, named Elfrida, whose beauty being highly commended to the king, and he being inflamed therewith, he sent this aforesaid Ethelwold (whom he especially trusted) to the party, to see and to bring him word again, and if her beauty were such as was reported, willing him also to make the match between them. Ethelwold well viewing the party, and seeing her beauty nothing inferior to her fame, and thinking first to serve his own turn, told all things contrary unto the king. Whereupon the king, withdrawing his mind otherwise, in the end it came to pass that Ethelwold himself did marry her.

Not long after, the king, understanding further by the complaints and rumours of certain, how he was prevented and beguiled, set a fair face upon the matter before Ethelwold, and merrily jesting with him, told him how he would come and see his wife; and indeed appointed the day when he would be there. Ethelwold, the husband, perceiving this matter to go hardly with him, made haste to his wife, declaring to her the coming of the king, and also opening the whole order of the matter how he had done; desiring her of all love, as she would save his life, to disgrace and deform herself with garments and such attire as the king might take no delight in her.

Elfrida hearing this, what did she, but, contrary to the request of her husband and promise of a wife, against the king's coming trim herself at the glass, and deck her in her best array; whom, when the king beheld, he was not so much enamoured with her as in hatred with her husband, who had so deceived him. Whereupon the king shortly after, making as though he would go to hunt in the forest of Harewood, sent for Ethelwold to come to him under the pretence of hunting, and there ran him through and slew him. After this the bastard son of Ethelwold coming to him, the king asked him how he liked that hunting? who answered, "That which pleaseth the king ought not to displease me." For the death of this Ethelwold, Elfrida afterwards builded a monastery of nuns, for remission of sins.

His cruelty

Another fault which Malmesbury noteth in him, was the coming in of strangers into this land, as Saxons, Flemings, and Danes, whom he with great familiarity retained, to the great detriment of the land, as the aforesaid story of Malmesbury recordeth, whose words be these: "whereby it happened that divers strangers, out of foreign countries, allured by his fame, came into the land, as Saxons, Flemings, and Danes also, all whom he retained with great familiarity; the coming of which strangers wrought great damage to the realm, and therefore is Edgar justly blamed in stories,"[1] &c. With this reprehension all the Saxon stories also do agree.

Great detriment to this realm by King Edgar

The third vice to him objected was his incontinency and his lasciviousness of life. He degraded a duke's daughter, being a nun, and a virgin named Wilfrida, or Wilstrud, of which Wilfrida was born Editha, a bastard daughter of Edgar. Also a certain other virgin in the town of Andover, who was privily conveyed into his chamber by this means: the lascivious king, coming to Andover, not far from Winchester, and thinking to have his desire of a certain other duke's daughter, of whose beauty he heard much speaking, commanded the maid to be brought unto him. The mother of the virgin, grieving to have her daughter so wronged, secretly, by night, conveyed to the king's chamber, instead of her daughter, another maiden of beauty and favour not uncomely, who, in the morning rising to her work, and so being known by the king who she was, had granted unto her by the king such liberty and freedom, that of a servant she was made mistress both to her master, and also to her mistress.[2]

His incontinent life †

Among other concubines Edgar had Egelfleda, or Elfleda, called Candida, the fair daughter of Duke Ordmer,[3] she being also a professed nun, of whom he had Edward; for which he was enjoined by Dunstan seven years' penance, which being complete, he took to him as his lawful wife,[4] Elfrida, the mother of Edmund and Ethelred, otherwise called Egelred, whereof more shall be said (the Lord willing) hereafter.

Edward born in bastardy of Elfled, King Edward's concubine

Over and besides all these vices, noted and objected to King Edgar, in our monkish story-writers, I also observe another no less, or rather a greater vice than the other before-recited, which was blind

(1) "Unde factum est, ut fama ejus per ora omnium volitante, alienigenæ, Saxones, Flandritæ, ipsi etiam Dani huc frequenter annavigarent, Edgaro familiares effecti. Quorum adventus magnum provincialibus detrimentum peperit. Inde merito jureque reprehendunt eum literæ," &c.
(2) Ex Matth. Paris. lib. de Regib. (3) Gulielm. Malmesb. (4) Idem.

Edgar. A.D. 975.

superstition, which brought idolatrous monkery into the church of Christ, with the wrongful expelling of lawful married priests out of their houses. Whereupon, what inconveniences ensued in this realm, especially in the house of the Lord, I leave to the consideration of those who have heard of the detestable enormities of those religious votaries: the occasion whereof, first and chiefly, began in this Edgar, through the instigation of Dunstan and his fellows; who, after they had inveigled the king, and had brought him over to their purpose, caused him to call a council of the clergy, where it was enacted and decreed that the canons of divers cathedral churches, collegiates, parsons, vicars, priests and deacons, with their wives and children, either should give over that kind of life, or else give room to monks, &c. For execution of which decree, two principal visitors were appointed; Athelwold, or Ethelwold, bishop of Winchester, and Oswald, bishop of Worcester, as is before mentioned.[1]

King Edgar seduced by Dunstan, and Ethelwold, bishop of Winchester.

And thus much concerning the history of King Edgar, and of such things as in his time happened in the church, which Edgar, after he had entered into the parts of Britany, to subdue the rebellion of the Welshmen, and there had spoiled the country of Glamorgan, and wasted that of Odo, within ten days after, when he had reigned the space of sixteen years, died, and was buried at Glastonbury, leaving after him two bastards, to wit, Editha and Edward, and one son lawfully begotten, named Ethelred, or otherwise by corruption called Egelred: for Edmund, the elder son, died before his father.

His death.

Ye heard before how King Edgar is noted in all stories to be an incontinent liver. In consequence of his connexion with Elfled, mother of Edward, he was stayed and kept back from his coronation, by Dunstan, archbishop of Canterbury, the space of seven years: and so the said king, beginning his reign in the sixteenth year of his age, being A.D. 959, was crowned at the age of one and thirty, A.D. 974, as is, by the Saxon Chronicle of Worcester Church, to be proved.[2] For the more evident declaration of this matter, concerning the coronation of the king restrained, and the presumptuous behaviour of Dunstan towards the king, and his penance by the said Dunstan enjoined, ye shall hear both Osberne, Malmesbury, and other authors speak in their own words, as followeth: "Perpetrato itaque in virginem velatam peccato," &c.[3] After Dunstan had understanding of the king's offence, perpetrated with the professed nun, and that the same was blazed amongst the people, with great ire and passion of mind he came to the king, who, seeing the archbishop coming, immediately of gentleness arose from his regal seat towards him, to take him by the hand, and to give him place. But Dunstan refused to take him by the hand, and with stern countenance, bending his brows, spake to this effect, as stories import, unto the king: "You that have not feared to corrupt a virgin maid, handfast to Christ, presume you to touch the consecrated hands of a bishop? You have defiled the spouse of your Maker, and think you by flattering service to pacify the friend of the bridegroom? No, Sir, his friend will not I be, who hath Christ for his enemy." The king, terrified with these thundering words of Dunstan, and seized with compunction and re-

Dunstan refused to take the king by the hand.

(1) Ex Osberno in Vita Dunstani, fol. 27; Malmesbur. de Vit. Pontif.; Rog. Hoved. et aliis.
(2) Ex Chronico Saxonico Ecclesiæ Wigorniensis. (3) Ex Osberno in Vita Dunstani.

Edgar. A.D. 975.

pentance for his crime perpetrated, fell down weeping at the feet of Dunstan, who, after he had raised him up from the ground again, began to utter to him the horribleness of his deed; and finding the king ready to receive whatsoever satisfaction he would lay upon him, enjoined him this penance for seven years' space, as followeth:—

Penance enjoined to Edgar

"That he should wear no crown all that space, that he should fast twice in the week; that he should distribute his treasure, left to him by his ancestors, liberally unto the poor, that he should build a monastery of nuns, at Shaftesbury; and that as he had robbed God of one virgin, through his transgression, so should he restore to him many again in times to come. Moreover, he should expel clerks of evil life (meaning such priests as had wives and children) out of churches, and place covents of monks in their room."

Edgar reigned but three years crowned king

It followeth, then, in the story of Osberne, that when the seven years of the king's penance were expired, Dunstan, calling together all the peers of the realm, with bishops, abbots, and other ecclesiastical degrees of the clergy, in the public sight of all the multitude, set the crown upon the king's head, at Bath, which was the one and thirtieth year of his age, and thirteenth of his reign; so that he reigned only three years crowned king. All the other years besides, Dunstan, it is likely, ruled the land as he listed. Furthermore, as touching the son of the said Elfleda, Osberne writeth to this effect, "The child also which was born of Elfred, he baptized in the holy fountain of regeneration, and so giving him the name of Edward, he did adopt him to be his son."[1] By this narration, agreeing also with the story of the Saxon book abovementioned, there is evinced a double untruth or error, either negligently overseen, or of purpose dissembled, in our later monkish story-writers, as in Malmesbury, Matthew Paris, Matthew of Westminster, and others; who, to conceal the fault of King Edgar, or to square with Dunstan's fact in setting up Edward for the maintenance of their monkish order, first do falsely affirm that Editha, the daughter of Wilfrida, was born after Edward, and that for her this penance was enjoined on King Edgar. This neither is, nor can be so, as in process hereafter (the Lord willing) shall appear.

Errors in Malmesbury and others

Secondly, they are deceived in this, that they affirm King Edgar to have two wives; and that Elfleda, the mother of Edward, was not a professed nun indeed, but dissembled so to be, to avoid the violence of the king, whereas, indeed, the truth of the story both giveth her to be a nun, and her son to be base, and she herself never to be married unto the king.

Now, forasmuch as we have hitherto made mention of Elfleda and Editha, and also of Ulfred and Dunstan, the opportunity should not be let pass to speak something of their lying miracles, falsely forged, to the great seduction of christian people, by superstitious monks, who cared not what fables and lies they brought into the church, so that they might have the advantage of poor men's purses and oblations. And first, here come in the fabulous miracles wrought at the tomb of Elfleda, the king's concubine, which William of Malmesbury in certain verses expresseth;[2] the English of

(1) "Puerum quoque ex peccatrice quondam progenitum, sacro fonte regeneratum lavavit, et aptato illi nomine Edwardo in filium sibi adoptavit."

(2) "Nam nonnullis passa annis morborum molestiam,
Dæfecatam et excoctam Deo dedit animam
Functas ergo vitæ fato beatas exuvias
Infinitis clemens signis illustravit Deitas

Inopes

Edgar. A.D. 975.

which it is needless here to recite. Briefly, the effect is this:—That both the blind, deaf, halt, and such as be mad, receive their health again, if they worship the tomb of this Elfleda. The like feignings and monstrous miracles we read also in chronicles of the doting Dunstan, drowned in all superstition, if he were not also a wicked sorcerer. First, how he, being yet a boy, chased away the devil, set about with a great company of dogs, and how the angels did open the church door for him to enter; then, how the lute or harp, hanging upon the wall, did sing or play without any finger these words: "The souls of the saints, who have followed the footsteps of Christ, and who have shed their blood for his love's sake, are rejoicing in heaven; therefore they shall reign with Christ for ever."[1] Item, where a certain great beam or master-post was loosed out of its place, he, by making the sign of a cross, set it in right frame again. Moreover, how the said Dunstan, being tempted upon a time by the devil, with impure cogitations, caught the devil by the nose with a hot pair of tongs, and held him fast. Item, how heavenly spirits often appeared to him, and used to talk with him familiarly. Item, how he prophesied of the birth of King Edgar, of the death of King Egelred, of the death of Editha, and of Ethelwald, bishop of Winchester. Also, how our Lady, with her fellows, appeared visibly to him, singing this song:

The idle fantasies and forged miracles of Dunstan.

Dunstan a post-setter. Catches the devil by the nose with a hot pair of tongs.

> "Cantemus domino sociæ, cantemus honorem,
> Dulcis amor Christi personet ore pio."

Again, how the angels appeared to him, singing the hymn called "Kyrie Rex splendens," and yet these prodigious fantasies, with others, are written of him in chronicles, and have been believed in churches.

A foul monkish miracle in the story of Editha.

Among many other false and lying miracles, forged in this corrupt time of monkery, the fabulous, or rather filthy legend of Editha, were not to be overpassed, if for shame and honesty it might well be recited. But to cast the dirt of these pope-holy monks in their own face, who so impudently have abused the church of Christ, and the simplicity of the people, with their ungracious vanities, let us see what this miracle is, and how honestly it is told.

Another dream of Dunstan.

Certain years after the death of Editha, saith William of Malmesbury, which years Capgrave in his new legend reckoneth to be thirteen, the said Editha, and also St. Dennis, holding her by the hand, appeared to Dunstan in a vision, willing and requiring him that the body of Editha, in the church of Wilton, should be taken up and shrined, to the intent it might be honoured here on earth by her servants, according as it is worshipped by her spouse in heaven. Dunstan, upon this, coming from Salisbury to Wilton, where Editha was interred, commanded her body to be taken up with much honour and solemnity; who, there, on opening her tomb (as both Malmesbury and Capgrave with shame enough record), found the whole body of † this Editha consumed to earth, save only her thumb, and a few other

> Inopes visus et auditus si adorant tumulum,
> Sanitati restituti probant sanctæ meritum.
> Rectum gressum refert domum, qui accessit loripes,
> Mente captus redit sanus, boni sensus locuples."

(1) "Gaudent in cœlis animæ sanctorum, qui Christi vestigia sunt sequuti, et qui pro ejus amore sanguinem suum fuderunt: ideo cum Christo regnabunt in æternum."

(2) What marvel, if certain books and epistles be falsely ascribed to the doctors, when the papists shame not to ascribe other men's verses also to the Virgin Mary herself?

relics. Whereof the said Editha, expounding the meaning, declared that her thumb remained sound for the much crossing she used with the same, and that the other parts were uncorrupted for a testimony of her abstinence and integrity.[1]

Edward the Martyr.

A.D. 975.

What Satan hath so envied the true sincerity of christian faith and doctrine, as to contaminate the same with such impudent tales, such filthy vanities, and such idolatrous fantasies as these? Such monks, with their detestable houses, where Christ's people were so abominably abused, and seduced to worship dead carcases of men and women, whether they deserved not to be rased and plucked down to the ground, let all chaste readers judge. But of these matters enough and too much.

Here followeth the Epitaph written by Henry, archdeacon of Huntingdon, upon the praise and commendation of King Edgar:—

An epitaph commendatory of King Edgar.

"Autor opum, vindex scelerum, largitor honorum,
Sceptiger Edgarus regna superna petit.
Hic alter Salomon, legum pater, orbita pacis,
Quod caruit bellis, claruit inde magis.
Templa Deo, templis monachos, monachis dedit agros,
Nequitiæ lapsum, justitiæque locum.
Novit enim regno verum perquirere falso,
Immensum modico, perpetuumque brevi."

Among his other laws, this king ordained that the Sunday should be solemnized from Saturday at nine o'clock till Monday morning.

EDWARD II., CALLED THE MARTYR.[2]

A.D. 975.

Contention amongst the lords about the putting in of monks.

AFTER the death of King Edgar no small trouble arose among the lords and bishops about the succession of the crown; the principal cause whereof arose on this occasion, as by the story of Simon of Durham, and Roger Hoveden, is declared. Immediately after the decease of the king, Alferus duke of Mercia, and many other nobles who held with Egelred, or Ethelred, the only right heir and lawful son of Edgar, disliking the placing and intruding of monks into churches, and the thrusting of the secular priests, with their wives and children, out of their ancient possessions, expelled the abbots and monks, and brought in again the aforesaid priests, with their wives; against whom, certain others there were on the contrary part that made resistance, as Ethelwin, duke of East Angles, Elfwold his brother, and the Earl Brithnoth, saying, in a council together assembled, "That they would never suffer the religious monks to be expelled and driven out of the realm, who held up all religion in the land;" and, thereupon, immediately levied an army, wherewith to defend by force such monasteries as were within the precincts of East Anglia.

Also for choosing the king.

In this hurly-burly amongst the lords, about the placing of monks, and putting out of priests, rose also the contention about the crown, who should be their king; the bishops and such lords as favoured the monks, seeking to advance such a king as they knew would incline

(1) Ex Guliel. Malmesb., et Capgravo, in legenda nova.
(2) Edition 1563, p. 11. Ed. 1583, p. 157. Ed. 1596, p. 142 Ed 1684, vol. i. p. 175. ED.

Edward the Martyr. A.D. 975.

to their side; so that the lords thus divided, some of them would have Edward, and some agreed upon Egelred, the lawful son. Then Dunstan, archbishop of Canterbury, and Oswald, archbishop of York, with other their fellow-bishops, abbots, and divers other lords and dukes, assembled together in a council; into which council Dunstan coming with his cross in his hand, and bringing Edward before the lords, so persuaded them, that, in the end, Edward, by Dunstan's means, was elected, consecrated, and anointed for their king.

Edward the Bastard made king, and the right heir put back.

And thus hast thou, good reader, the very truth of this story, according to the writing of authors of most antiquity who lived nearest to that age, as Osberne and others;[1] which Osberne, living in the days of William the Conqueror, wrote this story of Dunstan on the motion of Lanfranc, and allegeth, or rather translateth the same out of such Saxon stories as were written before his time. Besides this Osberne, we have also for witness hereof, Nicholas Trivet, in his English History, written in French, and also Johannes Paris, in his French History, written in the Latin tongue, where he plainly calleth Edward, "non legitimum filium," that is, "no lawful son." Whereunto add, moreover, the testimony of Vincentius and Antoninus, who in plain terms likewise report the same.

Editha not the child for whom Edgar was enjoined penance.

Now, having laid the foundation for the truth and ground of this matter, let us come to examine how truly our later writers do say, who write that Editha, and not Edward, was the child for whom Dunstan enjoined the king seven years' penance; and, also, how truly they report Edward to be the lawful heir, and Elfleda to be the lawful wife, to King Edgar. For first touching Editha, this is confessed by the said writers themselves, that she was of good years at the time Edgar, her father, was enjoined his penance; after which seven years of his penance were expired, he lived, at the most, but three years and a half; which seven years, and three years and a half, do make in all but ten years and a half. But now the said authors themselves do grant, that she was made abbess by her father, he being then alive. And how then can this stand with her legend, which saith, that she was not less than fifteen years of age? By which account it must needs fall out, that she could not be so little as five years old before the birth of that child for whom the king did penance. And thus much touching Editha.

The years of Editha and Edward.

Now, in like manner, to consider of the time of Edward. First, this by all writers is granted, that he was slain in the fifteenth year of his age, which age doth well agree to that bastard child which King Edgar had, and for which he did penance; for the more evidence whereof, let us come to the computation of the years in this sort: first, the penance of the king after the birth of this child lasted seven years; then, the king, after the same, lived three years and a half; after whose death Edward reigned other three years and a half, which in all make the full sum of fourteen years, about the count of which age, by their own reckoning, the said Edward, going on in his fifteenth year, was slain.

Thus have ye, by manifest demonstration, proved by the right casting up of the years, after their own grant and reckoning, that Editha, daughter of Wifrida, in no case can be the child that was

(1) Ex Osbern., Nic. Trivet., Johan. Paris., Vincentio, Antonino.

born after Edward, and for whom the king was enjoined penance; but that Edward rather was born after Editha, and was the child for whom the penance was enjoined, contrary to the opinion commonly received in the church, which, for ignorance of the story, hath hitherto holden Edward to be a holy martyr, and right heir to the crown. How this error and opinion first sprang up, and by whom, albeit it pertain not to my story to discuss, yet were it no hard matter to conjecture.

Edward the Martyr. A.D. 975.

First, after that Dunstan and Oswald, with other bishops, abbots, and certain lords and dukes of that faction, for the maintenance of monkery, had advanced Edward to be king, against Queen Elfrida, mother of Ethelred, and Alferus, duke of Mercia, and certain other nobles who held with the contrary side of the priests against the monks; in process of time, the monks that came to write stories, perceiving Dunstan to be reputed in the church of Rome for a holy saint, and the said King Edward for a holy martyr, and partly also to bolster up their own religion of monkery as much as they could, to the intent that they might save the credit both of Dunstan and the king, and especially bearing favour to their own religion, and partly that the reputation of the church of Rome should not be stained by opening the truth of this matter, either they did not see, or would not confess herein what they knew, but rather thought best to blanch the story, and colourably to hide the simple truth thereof; making the people falsely believe that Elfleda, the mother of Edward, was wife to King Edgar, and that Edward was lawfully born, and also that Editha was born after Edward, and was the child for which the king was enjoined penance. All which is false, and contrary both to the order of time above declared, and also to the plain words of Malmesbury, who, speaking of King Edgar's last concubine, saith in plain words, "Dilexit unice integram lecto uni diferens fidem, quoad legitimam uxorem accepit Elfthridem, filiam Ordgari:"[1] that is, "He had a concubine whom he loved entirely, keeping true faith to her alone, until the time he married for his lawful wife Elfrida, the daughter of Duke Ordgar:" whereby we have to understand, that whatsoever woman this was of whom Malmesbury speaketh, certain it is, that Edgar lived incontinently till the time he married his lawful wife. Furthermore, and to conclude: beside these arguments and allegations above-recited, let this also be appended, how the said Dunstan, with his accomplices, after the killing of King Edward, leaving the right heir of the crown, namely, Ethelred, went about (as Capgrave[2] in their own legend confesseth) to set up Editha, the other bastard, to possess the crown; but that she, more wise than her brother Edward, refused the same. Whereby what is to be thought of the doings of Dunstan, and what could be the cause why he preferred both Edward and Editha to the crown, rather than the lawful heir, I leave to all indifferent readers thereof to judge.

The cause why this story of Edward is so falsely corrupted in monkish histories.

Dunstan suborneth Editha to take the crown from the right heir.

After Dunstan and his fellows had thus set up Edward for their king, they were now where they would be, supposing all to be sure on their side, and that they had established the kingdom of monkery for ever, through the help of the young king, and the duke of East

(1) Guliel. Malmesb. in lib. de Regib.
(2) Capgrav. in Vita Sanctæ Edithæ.

Edward the Martyr. A.D. 976.

Angles, and certain other nobles whom they had drawn to their part. Howbeit, this matter passed not so well with them as they hoped; for, shortly after the coronation of this young king, Alferus, duke of Mercia, who followed much the deeds of the queen, with other great men, stoutly standing on the contrary side, drove out the monks from the cathedral churches, whom King Edgar before had set in, and

Priests with their wives restored.

restored the priests, as Ranulphus saith, with their *concubines;* but, in the history of the library of Jornalensis, I find it plainly expressed, with their *wives.* The very words of the author be these:—"Alferus, duke of Mercia, with other great men, drove out the monks from the great monasteries, whom King Edgar had there set in before,

Bishops and priests in those days married.

and restored again the priests with their wives."[1] Whereby it doth evidently appear that priests in those days were married, and had their lawful wives. The like before that, in King Ina's time, is plain, that bishops then had wives and children, as appeareth by the words of the law then set forth, and extant in the history of Jornalensis.[2] And thus much, by the way, for priests' wives and their children.

Now to our purpose again, which is to declare how the duke and nobles of England expelled the monks out of the monasteries after the death of King Edgar; whereof let us hear what the monkish

Great stir in the land about placing in monks, and displacing priests.

story of the abbey of Crowland recordeth:—"The monks being expelled out of certain monasteries, the clerks again were brought in, who distributed the manors or farms of the said monasteries to the dukes and lords of the land, that they being obliged to them, should defend them against the monks. And so were the monks of Evesham thrust out, and the secular clerks placed therein, and the lands of the church given to the lords; with whom the queen, the king's stepmother, holding at the same time, took part also with the said clerks against the king. On the contrary side stood the king and the holy bishops, taking part with the monks. Howbeit the lords and peers of the realm, staying upon the favour and power of the queen, triumphed over the monks."[3]

Priests' marriage noted for an old custom in England.

Thus, as there was much ado through all quarters of the realm about the matter among the lords, so arose no less contention between the priests and monks of England. The priests complaining to the king and Dunstan, said for themselves that it was uncomely, uncharitable, yea, and unnatural, to put out an old known dweller, for a new unknown; and that God was not pleased, that that should be taken from the ancient possessor, which by God was given him; neither that it could be of any good man accepted, to suffer any such injury to be done, lest peradventure the same thing, wherein he was prejudicial to another, might afterwards revert and redound upon himself at last.[4] The monks on the other side said for their

(1) "Alferus princeps Merciorum, cæterique plures, ejectis monachis de magnis monasteriis, quos Rex Edgarus nuper instituerat, Clericos cum uxoribus reduxerunt."—Historia Jornalensis, in Vita Edgari.—Idem.

(2) "Si quis filiolum alterius occidat vel patrinum, sit simile cognationi, et crescat emendatio secundum Weram ejus regi, sicut cognationi. Si de parentela sit qui occidit eum, tuncexcedat emendatio patrini, sicut mandata Domini. Si episcopi filiolus sit, sit dimidium hoc," &c.—Idem.

(3) "Monachis de quibusdam monasteriis ejectis, clerici sunt introducti, qui statim monasteriorum maneria ducibus terræ distribuebant, ut sic in suas partes obligati, eos contra monachos defensarent. Tunc de Monasterio Eveshamensi, monachis expulsis, clerici fuerunt introducti. Terræque tyranni de terris ecclesiæ præmiati sunt; quibus regina novercali nequitia, stans cum clericis in regis opprobrium, favebat. Cum monachis autem rex et sancti episcopi persistebant. Sed tyranni, fulti reginæ favore et potentia, super monachos triumphabant. Multus inde tumultus in omni angulo Angliæ factus est."—Ex Chronico Ingulphi Abbatis de Crowland.

(4) Guliel. de Regib. lib. ii.

part, that Christ allowed neither the old dweller, nor the new comer, nor yet looked upon the person, but whoso would take the cross of penance upon him, and follow Christ in virtuous living, should be his disciple.

Edward the Martyr. A.D. 977.

These and such other were the allegations of the monks; but whether a monk's cowl, or a wifeless life, make a sufficient title to enter into other men's possessions or no, I refer it to the judgment of the godly. The troublous cares in marriage, the necessary provision for housekeeping, the virtuous bringing up of children, the daily helping of poverty, and bearing of public charges, with other manifest perturbations and incumbrances daily incident to the state of matrimony, might rather appear, to godly wise men, to come nearer to the right cross of penance, than the easy and loitering idleness of monkery. In the end, upon this controversy, was holden a council of bishops and others of the clergy. First, at Reading, or at Winchester, as Malmesbury saith, where the greater part, both of the nobles and commons, judged the priests to be greatly wronged, and sought by all means possible to bring them again to their old possessions and dignities. Jornalensis here maketh rehearsal of an image of the crucifix, or a rood standing upon the frater-wall, where the council was holden. To this rood Dunstan required them all to pray, being belike not ignorant of some spiritual provision beforehand. In the midst of their prayer the rood (or else some blind monk behind it in a trunk) through the wall, is reported to speak these words, "Absit hoc ut fiat; absit hoc ut fiat: judicastis bene, mutaretis non bene." In remembrance whereof these verses were written under the rood's feet:

Married men's lives compared with those of monks.

A.D. 977.

A vain miracle of Dunstan's rood that spake. Here lacked a Thomas Cromwell to try out false juggling.

"Humano more crux præsens ædidit ore,
Cœlitus affata, quæ perspicis hic subarata;
Absit ut hoc fiat, et cætera tunc memorata."

Of this Dunstanical, or rather Satanical oracle, Henry maketh no mention, nor Ranulph, nor yet Hoveden, nor Fabian, in their histories. Malmesbury, in his book De Regibus, reporteth it, but by hearsay, in these words, saying, "Aliæ literæ docent," &c.; wherefore of the less credit it seemeth to be. Albeit if it were of credible truth, yet it proveth in this matter nothing else but Dunstan to be a sorcerer, as Polydore Virgil also himself seemeth to smell something in this matter.

A council at Calve.

Notwithstanding all this the strife ceased not; insomuch that a new assembly of the clergy and others was appointed afterwards at a place called the Street of Calve, where the council was kept in an upper loft. In this council many grievous complaints were made, as Malmesbury saith, against Dunstan; but yet he kept his opinion, and would not remove from that which he had begun to maintain. And while they were in great contention and argument which way should be admitted and allowed (if that be true which in the stories is written), suddenly the joists of the loft failed, and the people with the nobles fell down, so that certain were slain, and many hurt.[1] But Dunstan, they say, only standing upon a post of the gallery which remained unbroken, escaped without danger. Which

A sudden fall of the people at the council.

(1) Henricus, lib. v.; Malmesb., Ranulph, Jornalensis, Fabian.

Edward the Martyr. A.D. 978.

thing, whether it so happened to portend the ruin of the realm and of the nobles, as Henry Huntingdon doth expound it, which after ensued by the Danes, or whether it was so wrought by Dunstan's sorcery, as was not impossible, or whether it were a thing but feigned of the monkish writers, and not true; all this I leave to the readers to think therein what they like. The stories say further, that upon this, the matter ceased, and Dunstan had all his will.

These things thus done at Calve, it happened not long after, that King Edward, whom writers describe to be a virtuous and a meek prince, very pitiful and beneficial to the poor, about the fourth year of his reign came upon a time from hunting in the forest alone, without a company of his servants, to the place in the west country, where Queen Elfrida his mother, with her son Egelred, did live. When she was warned of his coming by her men, anon she calleth a servant of hers, who was of her special trust, opening to him all her conceived counsel, and showing him all points, how, and what to do, for the accomplishing of her wicked purpose. Which thing done, she made towards the king, and received him with all courtesy, desiring him to tarry that night; but he, in like courtesy, excused himself, and for speed desired to see his brother, and to take some drink upon his horse sitting, which was shortly brought. While the cup was at his mouth, the servant of the queen, being instigated, struck him in the body with a long two-edged dagger; after which stroke, the king took the horse with the spurs, and ran toward the way where he expected to meet with his company; but he bled so sore, that with faintness he fell from his horse, one foot remaining in the stirrup, by reason whereof he was drawn by his horse over fields and lands, till he came to a place named Corfegate, where he was found dead; and because neither the manner of his death, nor yet he himself, to be the king, was known, he was buried unhonourably at the town of Wareham, where the body remained the space of three years; after which it was taken up by Duke Alferus beforementioned, and with pomp and honour accordingly, was removed to the minster of Shaftesbury, and there bestowed in the place called Edwardstow.

The horrible wickedness of a queen-mother.

King Edward traiterously murdered. A.D. 978.

Edward buried, not known to be king; reinterred at Shaftesbury.

Many tales run, more perchance than be true, concerning the finding and taking up of his body, which our most common histories ascribe to miracles and great wonders wrought about the place where the king was buried. As first, how a poor woman, born blind, received her sight by the means of St. Edward, there where he did lie. Also, how a pillar of fire from heaven descended over the place of his burial. Then, how the aforesaid Queen Elfrida, taking her horse to go to the place, was stopped by the way, so that neither her horse could be driven by any means, nor she herself on foot was able to approach near to the place where the corpse of St. Edward was. Furthermore, how the said queen, in repentance of her deed, afterward builded two nunneries, one at Amesbury by Salisbury, the other at Werewell, where she kept herself in continual repentance all the days of her life. And thus, as ye have heard, was this virtuous young King Edward murdered, when he had reigned almost four years, leaving no issue behind him, whereby the rule of the land fell to Egelred, his brother.

Two nunneries founded upon murder.

Here by the way is to be noted, upon the name of this Edward, that there were three Edwards before the conquest. The first was King Edward the Elder; the second, King Edward the Martyr, who was this king; the third was King Edward, called the Confessor, of whom hereafter shall follow, Christ willing, to be declared. *Ecclesiastical affairs.* Edwards before the conquest.

In the order and course of the Roman bishops, mention was made last of Agapetus II., after whom next succeeded Pope John XIII., of whom Dunstan, archbishop of Canterbury, received his pall, as in the story of King Edward is before-minded. This pope is noted to be very wicked and infamous, replete, from his first bringing up, with abominable vices; an adulterer, incestuous, libidinous, a gamester, an extortioner, perjured, a fighter, a murderer, cruel and tyrannous. Of his cardinals, he put out the eyes of some, from some he cut off the tongues, from some the fingers, from some the noses. In a general council, before the Emperor Otho, the first of that name (who was the first emperor of the Germans), after the empire was translated out of France to Germany by Pope Agapetus, as is before related, these objections were articulate against him:[1]—"That he never said his service; that in saying his mass he did not communicate; that he ordained deacons in a stable; that he twice committed incest; that playing at dice he called for the devil to help; that for money he made boys bishops; that he turned the palace of the Lateran to the vilest of uses; that he put out the eyes of Bishop Benedict; that he caused houses to be set on fire; that he brake open houses; that he drank to the devil; that he never crossed himself." For these causes, and worthily, he was deposed by the consent of the emperor with the prelates, and Pope Leo substituted in his place; but after his departure, through the harlots of Rome, and their great promises, the said Pope John was restored again, and Leo, who had been set up by the emperor, was deposed. At length, about the tenth year of the popedom of this John, he being found without the city in company with another man's wife, was so wounded by her husband, that within eight days he died.

Continuation of the Romish bishops, or popes. A.D. 955. † A.D. 964. Pope John XIII. deposed, and afterwards restored.

After him, the Romans elected Pope Benedict V., without the consent of the Emperor Otho; whereupon, the emperor being not a little displeased for the displacing of Leo, whom he had before promoted, and also for the choosing of Benedict, came with his army and laid siege to Rome, and so set up Pope Leo again, being the eighth of that name, who, to gratify his benefactor in return, crowned Otho as emperor, and entitled him to be called Augustus. Also the power which Charlemagne had given before to the clergy and people of Rome, this Leo, by a synodal decree, granted to the emperor and his successors; that is, touching the election of the bishop of Rome. The emperor again restored to the see of Rome all the donations and possessions which either Constantine (as they falsely pretend), or which Charlemagne took from the Lombards, and gave to them.

A.D. 966. The election of the bishop of Rome given to the emperor.

After Pope Leo had reigned a year and three months, succeeded Pope John XIV., against whom, for holding with the emperor, Petrus the head captain of the city, with two consuls, twelve aldermen,

Pope John XIV.

(1) Luithprandus, lib. vi.

Ecclesiastical affairs.

and divers other nobles, gathering their power together, laid hands upon him in the church of Lateran, and clapped the pope in prison eleven months. The emperor hearing this, with all speed returned with his army again to Rome; who, after execution done upon the authors and chief doers of that deed, among other things committed the aforesaid Petrus to the pope's arbitrement, whom he caused first to be stripped naked; then, his beard being shaven, to be hanged by the hair a whole day together; after that to be set upon an ass with his face turned backward, and his hands bound under the ass's tail, and so to be led through the city, that all men might see him; that done, to be scourged with rods, and so banished the city. Thus ye see how the holy father followeth the injunction of the gospel, "Diligite inimicos vestros," "Love your enemies." [Luke vi. 35.] From this pope proceeded first the christening of bells, A.D. 971.

The cruel revenge of the pope.

Christening of bells begun.

After Leo, followed Pope Benedict VI., who in like manner was apprehended by Cinthius, a captain of Rome, and cast into prison, where he was strangled, or, as some say, famished to death.

Pope Benedict VI. slain in prison. A.D. 975.

Then came Pope Donus II.; after whom Boniface VII. was pope, who likewise seeing the citizens of Rome to conspire against him, was constrained to hide himself, and seeing no place there for him to tarry, took the treasure of St. Peter's church, and so privily stole away to Constantinople, in whose stead the Romans set up Pope John XV. Not long after, Boniface returning from Constantinople, by means of his money and treasure, procured a garrison or company to take his part, by which force Pope John was taken, and his eyes being put out, he was thrown into prison, where he was, as some say, famished; others say he was slain by Ferrucius; neither did Boniface reign many days after, but suddenly died, A.D. 976, whose carcass, after his death, was drawn by the feet through the streets of Rome after a most despightful manner, the people shrieking and exclaiming against him.

Two popes together.

Pope John slain.

A.D. 976.

Pope Boniface drawn through the streets of Rome.

The next pope was Benedict VII., by the consent of the Emperor Otho II., and who reigned nine years. In the time of this pope, Hugh Capet, the French king, took Charles, the right heir to the crown, by the treason of the bishop of Laon; and when he had imprisoned him, he also committed to prison Arnold, archbishop of Rheims, and placed in his room Gilbert, a monk of Floriack, a necromancer, who was schoolmaster to Duke Robert, the king's son. But this Pope Benedict, calling a council at Rheims, restored the said Arnold, and displaced Gilbert, who after, by the help of Otho, was made archbishop of Ravenna, and at length was pope, as in process hereafter (Christ granting) shall be declared.

Gilbert, a necromancer, made archbishop.

After Benedict, succeeded in the see of Rome Pope John XVI., who died the eighth month of his papacy; next to whom came John XVII., and after him Gregory V., A.D. 995. This Gregory, called before Bruno, was a German born, and therefore the more maliced of the clergy and people of Rome. Whereupon Crescentius, with the people and clergy, conventing against him, set up John XVIII., on which Gregory sped himself with all convenient haste to the Emperor Otho III. in Germany, who, hearing the complaint of Gregory, and understanding his wrongs, set forward with his army

A.D. 995.

Two popes again in Rome.

well-appointed to Italy, and getting possession of the city, there took both Crescentius the consul, and John the pope; which John first having his eyes put out, was afterwards deprived of his life. Crescentius, the consul, was set upon a vile horse, having his nose and ears cut off, and so was led through the city with his face turned to the horse's tail, and, then, having his members cut off, he was hanged upon a gibbet.

Egelred. A.D. 978.

Pope John had his eyes put out, and was put to death.

Pope Gregory, thus being restored to his former state, reigned four years in his papacy (although Marianus Scotus, and Martinus, say, that he sat but two years), during which time he assembled a council in Rome, where he, to establish the empire in his own country, by the consent and counsel of Otho, ordained seven princes of Germany to be electors of the emperor, which order yet to this day remaineth.[1] What be the names of these seven electors, and what their office, thus I find in the verses expressed below.[2]

Seven electors of the empire ordained in Germany.

These were the seven: three bishops, three princes, to wit, the Palatine, the duke of Saxony, and the Marquis Brandenburgh; to whom was added also the king of Bohemia, to give the odd voice, if the even voices could not agree. This constitution being first begun A.D. 997, was afterward established in Germany by Otho the emperor, A.D. 1002; and thus much by the way, or rather digression, concerning the rages and tumults of the Romish church. Now to our matter again.

EGELRED, OR ETHELRED II.

SIRNAMED THE UNREADY.[3]

KING EDWARD thus being murdered, as is aforesaid, the crown fell next to Egelred, his younger brother, and son to King Edgar by the aforesaid queen Alfrith, as we have declared. This Egelred had a long reign given by God, which endured thirty and eight years, but was very unfortunate and full of great miseries; and he himself, by the histories, seemeth to have been a prince not of the greatest courage to govern a commonwealth. Our English historians writing of him, report of his reign, that it was ungracious in the beginning, wretched in the middle, and hateful in the latter end. Of this Egelred we read, that when Dunstan the archbishop should christen him, as he did hold him over the font, something there happened that pleased not Dunstan, whereupon he sware, "By the mother of Christ, he will be a prince untoward and cowardly."[4] I find in William of Malmesbury,[5] that this Egelred being of the age of ten years, when he heard that his brother Edward was slain, made such sorrow and weeping for him, that his mother falling therewith in a rage, took wax candles, having nothing else at hand, wherewith she scourged him so sorely (well nigh till he swooned),

A.D. 978.

(1) Ex Chronico Martini.

(2) Maguntinensis, Treverensis, Coloniensis;
Quilibet imperii fit cancellarius horum.
Et Palatinus dapifex, dux portitor ensis,
Marchio præpositus cameræ, pincerna Bohemus.—Ib.

(3) Edition 1563, p. 10. Ed. 1583, p. 163. Ed. 1596, p. 144. Ed. 1684, vol. i. p. 179.—ED.

(4) "Per sanctam Mariam, iste ignavus homo erit."—Chron. de Crowland.

(5) Lib. ii. de Regib.

Egelred. A.D. 981. that afterwards he could never abide any wax candles to burn before him. After this, about A.D. 981, the day of his coronation had been appointed by the queen-mother and the nobles, Dunstan archbishop of Canterbury (who first refused so to do), and Oswald archbishop of York, were enforced to crown the king, which they did at Kingston. In doing whereof, the report of stories goeth that Dunstan said thus, prophesying unto the king,—"That forasmuch as he came to the kingdom by the death of his brother, and through the conspiracy of the wicked conspirators, and other Englishmen, they should not be without blood-shedding and sword, till there came a people of an unknown tongue, which should bring them into thraldom; neither should that trespass be cleansed, without long vengeance."[1]

The coronation of Egelred.

The prophecy of Dunstan, as monkish stories give it.

Not long after the coronation of this king, a cloud was seen throughout the land, which appeared the one half like blood, and the other half like fire, and changed afterwards into sundry colours, and vanished at last in the morning. Shortly after the appearance of this cloud, in the third year of his reign, the Danes arriving in sundry places of the land, first spoiled Southampton, either slaying the inhabitants, or leading them away captive. From thence they went to the Isle of Thanet; then they invaded Chester, from whence they proceeded to Cornwall and Devonshire, and so to Sussex, where in those coasts they did much harm, and then withdrew to their ships. Roger Hoveden, writing hereof,[2] saith that London at the same time, or, as Fabian saith, a great part of London, was consumed with fire. About this time happened a variance between the aforesaid Egelred and the bishop of Rochester, insomuch that he made war against him, and besieged the city; and, notwithstanding Dunstan required the king, sending him admonishment, to give over for the sake of St. Andrew, yet continued he his siege, till the bishop offered him an hundred pounds of gold, which he received, and so departed. The Danes, seeing the discord that then was in the realm, and especially the hatred of the subjects against the king, rose again, and did great harm in divers places of England; insomuch that the king was glad to grant them great sums of money, for peace to be had. For the assurance of this peace, Analaffe, captain of the Danes, became a christian man, and so returned home to his country, and did no more harm. Besides these miseries before-recited, a sore sickness of the bloody-flux and hot fevers fell among the people, whereof many died, with a like murrain, also, among the beasts. Moreover, for lack of justice, many thieves, rioters, and bribers, were in the land, with much misery and mischief.

The Danes return to England.

London consumed with fire. The king wars against the bishop of Rochester.

A.D. 990.

About the eleventh year (some say the ninth) of this king's reign died Dunstan; after whom succeeded Ethelgar, or, as Jornalensis writeth, Stilgar. After him Elfric, as affirmeth Malmesbury;[3] but as Polydore saith, Siric. After him Elfric came, but Siric according to Malmesbury, while Polydore saith, Aluric; then Elphege.

Death of Dunstan.

About the same time, A.D. 995, Aldunus, a bishop, translated the

(1) In the Chronicles of Crowland I find these words:—"Quoniam ascendisti ad thronum tuum, per mortem fratris tui, quem occidit mater tua, propterea audi verbum Domini: hoc dicit Dominus, non deficiet gladius de domo tua, sæviens in te omnibus diebus vitæ tuæ, et interficiens de semine tuo, et de gente tua, usque dum regnum tuum transferatur in regnum alienum: cujus ritum et linguam gens tua non novit, nec expiabitur nisi longa vindicta, et multa sanguinis effusione peccatum matris tuæ, et peccatum virorum pessimorum, qui consenserunt consilio ejus nequam, ut mitterent manum in Christum Domini, ad effundendum sanguinem innocentem."

(2) Hoveden. lib. Continuationum.

(3) Lib. i. de Pontif

body of St. Cuthbert, which first had been in a northern island, and then at Rochester, from Chester to Durham, or Dunelme; whereupon the bishop's see of Durham first began.[1]

Egelred. A.D. 991.

The see of Durham begins.

Not long after the death of Dunstan, the Danes again entered England, in many and sundry places of the land, in such sort, that the king had to seek to which coast he should go first, to withstand his enemies; and, in conclusion, for the avoiding of more harm, he was compelled to appease them with great sums of money. But when that money was spent, they fell anew to robbing of the people, and to assailing the land in divers places, not only about the country of Northumberland, but they at last besieged the city of London. Being repulsed, however, by the manhood of the Londoners, they strayed to other countries adjoining, as to Essex, Kent, Sussex, and Hampshire, burning and killing wheresoever they went, so that for lack of a good head or governor, many things in the land perished; for the king gave himself up to gross vices, and also to the polling of his subjects, and disinheriting men of their possessions, caused them to redeem the same again with great sums of money; for he paid great tribute to the Danes yearly, which was called Danegilt, which tribute so increased, that from the first tribute of 10,000*l.*, it was brought at last, in five or six years, to 40,000*l.*, which yearly, till the coming of St. Edward, and after, was levied of the subjects of this land.

London besieged by the Danes.

Great tribute levied, Danegilt. A.D. 991.

To this sorrow, moreover, were joined hunger and penury among the commons, insomuch that every one of them was constrained to pluck and steal from others, so that, what through the pillage of the Danes, and what by inward thieves and bribers, this land was brought into great affliction. Albeit the greatest cause of this affliction, as to me appeareth, is not so much to be imputed to the king, as to the dissention among the lords themselves, who then did not agree one with another; but when they assembled in consultation together, either they drew divers ways, or if any thing was agreed, upon any matter of peace between the parties, it was soon broken; or else, if any good thing were devised for the prejudice of the enemy, anon the Danes were warned thereof by some of the same counsel. Of these the chief doers were Edrike, duke of Mercia, and Alfrike, the admiral or captain of the ships, who betrayed the king's navy to the Danes; wherefore the king apprehended Alfagar, son of the said Alfrike, and put out his eyes, as did he afterwards to the two sons of duke Edrike.

The sorrowful affliction of the nation.

What discord doth among the nobles.

The Danes thus prevailing more and more over the English, grew to such pride and presumption, that when they, by strength, caused the husbandmen to ear and sow the land, and to do all other vile labour belonging to the house, they would sit at home holding the wife at their pleasure, with daughter and servant: and when the husbandman came home, he could scarcely have of his own, as his servants had; so that the Dane had all at his will and fill, faring of the best, when the owner scarcely had his fill of the worst. Thus the common people being of them oppressed, were in such fear and dread, that not only they were constrained to suffer them in their doings, but also glad to please them, and called every one of them in the house where they had rule, Lord-Dane, which word, afterwards, in process of time, when

The pride of the Danes towards the English.

Lord-Dane.

(1) On the 27th May, 1827, the tomb of St. Cuthbert, in Durham Cathedral, was opened, and the coffin and skeleton found within. See Account of St. Cuthbert, p. 180. By James Raine, M.A. Durham. 1828.—Ed.

Egelred. A.D. 1000. the Danes were got rid of, was, for despight of the Danes, turned by the Englishmen to a name of opprobrium, so that when one Englishman would rebuke another, he would for the more part call him "Lurdane."

The first joining between the Normans and English. And thus hitherto, through the assistance of Christ, we have brought this history down to the year of our Lord 1000.[1] During the continuance of these great miseries upon this English nation, the land was brought into great ruin by the grievous tributes of the Danes, and also by sustaining manifold villanies and injuries, as well as other oppressions within the realm. In this year Egelred, through the counsel of certain his familiars about him, in the one and twentieth year of his reign, began a matter, which was the occasion, either given by the one, or taken by the other, of a new plague to ensue upon the Saxons, who had formerly driven out the Britons; which was, by joining with the Normans in marriage. For the king, this year, for the more strength, as he thought, both of him and the realm, married Emma, the daughter of Richard, duke of Normandy, which Richard was the third duke of the Normans, and the first of that name. By reason of this marriage, King Egelred was not a little elated; and, by presumption thereof, sent secret and strict commissions to the rulers of every town in England, that upon St. Brice's day, at an hour appointed, the Danes should be suddenly slain; and so it was performed, which turned after to more trouble.

King Egelred married Emma, daughter of the duke of Normandy.

The Danes slain in every town of England. Nov. 13. A.D. 1002.

As soon as tidings came into Denmark of the murder of those Danes, Swanus, king of Denmark, with a great host and navy, landed in Cornwall; where, by treason of a Norman, named Hugh, who, by favour of Queen Emma, was made earl of Devonshire, the said Swanus took Exeter, and beat down the walls. From thence proceeding further into the land, they came to Wilton and Sherborne, where they cruelly spoiled the country, and slew the people. But, anon, Swanus hearing that the king was coming to him with the power of his land, took his ships and fetched his course about to Norfolk; where, after much wasting of that country, and spoiling the city of Norwich, and burning the town of Thetford, and destroying the country thereabout, at length duke Uskatel met him and beat him, and slew many of the Danes. Wherefore Swanus for that year returned to Denmark, and there made great provision to re-enter the land again the next year following; and so he did, landing at Sandwich about the five and twentieth year of the reign of King Egelred, and spoiled that country. A.D. 1003. And as soon as he heard of any host of Englishmen coming toward him, he took shipping again, so that when the king's army sought to meet him on one coast, he would suddenly land on another, and when the king provided to meet with him upon the sea, either they would feign to flee, or else they would with gifts blind the admiral of the king's navy. And thus wearied they the Englishmen, and in conclusion brought them into extreme and unspeakable misery, insomuch that the king was fain to make peace with them, and to give to King Swanus 30,000*l.*, after which peace thus made Swanus returned again to Denmark.

Tribute paid to the Danes of 30,000*l.*

Edric, or Earic, duke of Mercia. This peace continued not long, for the year next following, King Egelred made Edric, above mentioned, duke of Mercia, who was subtle

(1) Henry of Huntingdon, lib. vi.

of wit, glosing and eloquent of speech, untrusty, and false to the king and the realm; and soon after this, one Turkil, a prince of the Danes, landing in Kent with much people, did such harm there that the Kentishmen were fain to make peace with great gifts, on which they departed. But this persecution from the Danes, in one country or other in England, never ceased, nor did the king ever give them any notable battle; for when he was disposed to give them battle, this Edric would always counsel him to the contrary, so that the Danes ever spoiled and robbed, and waxed rich, and the Englishmen ever poor and bare.

Egelred. A.D. 1004. The persecution of Turkil. Evil counsel about a king, what hurt it doth.

After this, Swanus being in Denmark, and hearing of the increase of his people in England, brake his covenants before made, and with a great army and navy, in most defensible manner appointed, landing in Northumberland, proclaimed himself to be king of this land; where, when after much vexation he had subdued the people, and caused the earl with the rulers of the country to swear to him fealty, he passed over the river Trent to Gainsborough and to Northwatling-street, and, subduing the people there, forced them to give him hostages; these he committed with his navy unto Canute, his son, to keep, while he went further inland, and so, with a great host, came to Mercia, killing and slaying. He then took by strength Winchester and Oxford, and did there what he liked. This done, he came toward London, and hearing the king was there, passed by the river Thames, and came into Kent, and there besieged Canterbury, where he was resisted, the space of twenty days. At length, by the treason of a deacon, called Almaric, whom the bishop had preserved from death before, he won it, took the goods of the people, fired the city, and tithed the monks of St. Augustine's abbey; that is to say, they slew nine by cruel torment, and the tenth they kept alive as for their slave. They slew there of religious men to the number of 900 persons; of other men, with women and children, they slew above 8,000. And, finally, when they had kept the bishop Elphege in strait prison the space of seven months, because he would not condescend to give them 3,000*l*., after many villanies done unto him, they brought him to Greenwich, and there stoned him to death.

The return of Swanus into England. Canterbury, being besieged, is taken and burnt. A cruel murder by the Danes.

King Egelred, in the mean time, fearing the end of this persecution, sent his wife Emma, with his two sons, Alfred and Edward, to the duke of Normandy, with whom also he sent the bishop of London. The Danes proceeded still in their fury and rage, and when they had won a great part of West Saxony, they returned again to London, whereof the Londoners hearing, sent unto them certain great gifts and pledges. At last the king, about the five and thirtieth year of his reign, was chased unto the Isle of Wight, and, with a secret company, spent there a great part of the winter; and finally, without cattle or comfort, sailed into Normandy, to his wife. Swanus being informed thereof, inflamed with pride, levied exceeding impositions upon the people, and, among others, required a great sum of money of St. Edmund's lands, which the people there, claiming to be free from king's tributes, refused to pay. For this, Swanus entered the territory of St. Edmund, and wasted and spoiled the country, despising the holy martyr, and menacing also the place of his sepulture. Wherefore the men of that country, fearing his tyranny, fell to prayer and fasting, so that shortly after Swanus died suddenly, crying and

A.D. 1013. Egelred driven to the Isle of Wight, from thence to Normandy. The virtue of christian men's prayers.

Egelred. A.D. 1014.

Death of Swanus.

yelling among his knights. Some say that he was stricken with the sword of St. Edmund, whereof he died the third day after; in fear whereof Canute, his son, who ruled as king after his father, granted them the freedom of all their liberties, and, moreover, ditched the land of the said martyr with a deep ditch, and granted to the inhabitants thereof great freedoms, quitting them from all tax or tribute.

The abbey of St. Edmundsbury builded.

He afterwards builded a church over the place of his sepulture, and ordained there a house of monks, and endowed them with rich possessions. And after that time it was the usage of the kings of England, when they were crowned, to send their crowns for an offering to St. Edmund's shrine, and to redeem the same again, afterwards, with a suitable price.

Egelred returneth to England. Canute cutteth off the noses and hands of his pledges.

When King Egelred heard of the death of Swanus, he made provision and returned to England, for whose sudden coming Canute, being unprovided, fled to Sandwich, and there, cutting off the noses and hands of the hostages whom his father had left with him, sailed into Denmark, who the next year returned again with a great navy, and landed in the south country; wherefore the eldest son of King Egelred, called Edmund Ironside, made provision with the aid of Edric, duke of Mercia, to meet him. But Edric, feigning himself sick, came not, but deceived him; for, as it was after proved, Edric had promised his allegiance to Canute. By reason of this, Canute entered the country of the West Saxons, and forced the people to be sworn unto him, and to give him pledges. During this season, King Egelred being in London, was taken with great sickness, and there died, and was buried in the north side of Paul's church, behind the choir, after he had reigned unprosperously thirty-six years; leaving behind him his eldest son, Edmund Ironside, and Alfred and Edward, who were in Normandy, sent thither before, as is above-rehearsed. This Egelred, although he was miserably assailed and vexed of his enemies, yet he with his council gave forth wholesome laws, containing good rules and lessons for all judges and justices to learn and follow.[1]

Taketh Wessex.

A.D. 1016.

A wicked judge deposed by the king.

Of this King Egelred I find noted in the book of Roger Hoveden, that he deposed and deprived of his possessions, a certain judge or justice named Walgeatus, the son of one Leonet, for false judgment and other proud doings, whom, notwithstanding, he loved above all others.

(1) *Laws of King Egelred.*—" Omnis judex justus misericordiam et judicium liberet in omnibus, ut inprimis per rectam scientiam dicat emandationem secundum culpam, et eam tamen admensuret propter indulgentiam. Quædam culpæ reputantur a bonis judicibus secundum rectum emendandæ, quædam per Dei misericordiam condonandæ. Judicia debent esse sine omni haderunga, quod non parcatur diviti alicui; vel egeno amico vel inimico, jus publicum recitari. Nihil autem injustius est, quam susceptio munerum pro judicio subvertendo: quia munera excæcant corda sapientum, et subvertunt verba justorum. Dominus Jesus dixit: 'in quo judicio judicaveritis, judicabimini.' Timeat omnis judex ac diligat Deum judicem suum, ne in die judicii mutus fiat, et humiliatus ante oculos judicis cuncta videntis. Qui innocentem opprimit, et dimittit noxium pro pecunia, vel amicitia, vel odio, vel quacunque factione, opprimetur ab omnipotente judice. Et nullus dominus, nulla potestas, stultos aut improbos judices constituant, quia stultus per ignaviam, improbus per cupiditatem vitat quam didicit, veritatem. Gravius enim lacerantur pauperes a pravis judicibus, quam a cruentis hostibus. Nullus hostis acerbior, nulla pestis efficacior quam familiaris inimicus. Potest aliquoties homo fuga, vel defensione vitare pravos inimicos. Non ita possunt judices, quoties adversus subditos malis desideriis inflammantur. Sæpe etiam boni judices habent malos vicarios et ministros nefandos, quorum reatibus ipsi domini constringuntur, si non eos coerceant, et a rapacitate cohibeant. Quia Dominus et minister sæculorum ait, non solum male agentes, sed omnes consentientes digni sunt æterna morte. Sæpe etiam pravi judices judicium pervertunt, vel respectant, et non finiunt causam, donec voluntas eorum impleatur. Et quando judicant, non opera, sed munera considerant. Impii judices, juxta verbum sapientum, sicut rapaces lupi vespere nil residuant usque mane, id est, de præsenti solum vita cogitant, de futura nihil considerant. Malorum præpositorum mos est, ut quicquid possunt, auferant, et vix necessarium parum quid relinquant sustentationi. Iracundus judex non potest attendere rectam

EDMUND IRONSIDE, A SAXON, AND CANUTE, A DANE, KINGS TOGETHER IN ENGLAND.[1]

After the death of Egelred, there was variance among the Englishmen about the election of their king; for the citizens of London, with certain other lords, named Edmund, the eldest son of Egelred, a young man of lusty and valiant courage, in martial adventures both hardy and wise, and who could very well endure all pains; wherefore he was sirnamed Ironside. But the more part of the lords favoured Canute, the son of Swanus, especially the abbots, bishops, and men of the spiritualty, who before had sworn to his father. By means of this, many great battles were fought between these two martial princes, first in Dorsetshire, where Canute was compelled to fly the field, and after that, they fought another battle in Worcestershire, so sore that none could tell who had the better; but either for weariness, or for lack of day, they departed one from the other, and on the morrow fought again, but Canute was then compelled to forsake the field. After this they met in Mercia, and there fought again; where Edmund, as stories say, by the treason of that false Edric, duke of Mercia, whom he before had received to favour, had the worse. Thus there were many great conflicts between these two princes, but upon one occasion, when the hosts were ready to join, and a certain time of truce had been taken before battle, a knight, of the party of Edmund, stood up upon a high place, and said these words:—

Battles between Edmund and Canute.

"Daily we die, and none hath the victory: and when the knights be dead on either part, then the dukes, compelled by need, shall accord, or else they must fight alone, and this kingdom is not sufficient for two men, which sometimes sufficed seven. But if the covetousness of lordship in these twain be so great, that neither can be content to take part and live by the other, nor the one under the other, then let them fight alone, that will be lords alone. If all men fight, still, at the last, all men shall be slain, and none left to be under their lordship, nor able to defend the king that shall be, against strange enemies and nations."

A witty oration to stay blood between two armies.

These words were so well approved of by both the hosts and the princes, that all were content to try the quarrel between those two only. Then the place and time were appointed, at which they should both meet in sight of the two hosts, and when either had attacked the other with sharp swords and strokes, on the motion of Canute, as some write, hastily they were both agreed, and kissed each other, to the comfort of both hosts; and, shortly after, they agreed upon a partition of the land, and, after that, during their lives they loved as brethren. Soon after, a son of wicked Edric, by the instigation of his father, as appeared afterwards, espied when King Edmund was at the draught, and with a spear, some say with a long knife, gave him a secret thrust,

Two kings fight hand to hand.

A.D. 1017. Wicked murder of king Edmund.

judicii satisfactionem. Nam per furoris excæcationem, non perspicit rectitudinis claritatem. Justum judicium, ubi non persona consideratur. Scriptum est: non attendas personam hominis in judicio, nec pro aliquo facies, ut a vero declines, et injuste judices. Susceptio muneris est dimissio veritatis."—Ex Historia Bibliothecæ Jornalensi.

(1) Edition 1563, p. 11. Ed. 1583, p. 162. Ed. 1596, p. 146. Ed. 1684, vol. i. p. 181.—Ed.

Canute
A. D. 1017.

whereof the said Edmund shortly after died, after that he had reigned two years. He left behind two sons, Edmund and Edward, whom Edric, the wicked duke, after the death of their father, took from their mother, not knowing yet of the death of Edmund her husband, and presented them to King Canute, saluting him in these words, "Ave rex solus." Thus Canute, after the death of Edmund Ironside, was king alone of the whole realm of England, and afterwards, by the advice of his council, he sent the aforesaid sons of Edmund Ironside to his brother Swanus, king of Sweden, to be slain; who abhorring that deed, sent them to Salomon, king of Hungary, where Edmund being married to the king's daughter, died; Edward was married to Agatha, daughter of his brother, the emperor, Henry IV.

When Canute was established in the kingdom, he called a parliament in London, where, among other things there debated, it was propounded to the bishops, barons, and lords of parliament, present, whether, in the composition made between Edmund and Canute, there was any special remembrance made of the children or brethren of Edmund, by any partition of any part of the land. Whereunto the English lords, falsely flattering the foreign king, and speaking against their own minds, as also against their native country, answered, and said, "Nay." Affirming, moreover, with an oath (for the king's pleasure) that they, to the uttermost of their powers, would put off the blood of Edmund in all that they might; by reason of which answer and promise, many of them thought to have purchased with the king great favour. But, by the just retribution of God, it chanced far otherwise; for many of them, or the most part (such especially as Canute did perceive to be sworn before-time to Edmund and his heirs, and also considering that they were native Englishmen) he mistrusted and disdained ever after, insomuch that some he exiled, a great number he beheaded, and some, by God's punishment, died suddenly, among whom wicked Edric also, the traitor, although with his sugared words he continued a while in the king's favour, at length escaped not condign reward for his deceivable dealing. For, as the history of Jornalensis recordeth, as the king was in his palace beyond the Thames, this Edric, being probably accused, or else suspected of the king before, and coming unto him, began to reckon up his benefits and labours bestowed for his sake, first, in forsaking and betraying Egelred, then in slaying King Edmund's son, with many such other deeds, which all, for his sake, he had done. "Well," saith the king, "thou hast here rightly judged thyself, and worthily thou shalt die for slaying thy natural prince, and my sworn brother," and so commanded him to be bound immediately hand and foot, and to be thrown into the Thames. Some stories say, that when he had saluted the king with "Ave rex solus," and showed him the slaying of Edmund, Canute, promising that he would make him, therefore, higher than all the lords of the realm, commanded his head to be stricken off, and to be set upon London bridge, and his body to be cast into the town-ditch: and thus with shame ended he his wretched life; as all they commonly do, who, with like dissimulation, seek the destruction of their prince, and of their country.

Flattery, infidelity, and untruth, in English lords

Duke Edric, the false traitor and murderer of his king rewarded

The brother of Edmund Ironside slain

This Canute, shortly after the death of King Edmund, by the counsel of Edric, exiled Edwy, being brother unto King Edmund, called rex rusticorum, 'the king of churls;' but afterwards, he was reconciled again to the king's favour, and, lastly, slain by certain of the king's secretaries, or servants. Also, through the council of the said Edric, and of Emma his wife, he sent the two sons of Edmund Ironside, Edmund and Edward, to his brother Swanus, king of Denmark, to be slain, as is before said.

Canute. A.D. 1017.

Two sons of Edmund Ironside sent out to be slain.

In the mean time Swanus, king of Denmark, brother to Canute, died; wherefore that land fell to Canute, who soon after sailed thither, and took possession of it, and after he had set it in order, he returned to England and married Emma, late wife of Egelred, and by her he had a son, called Hardeknight, or Hardicanute. Moreover this Canute assembled a parliament at Oxford, where it was agreed that Englishmen and Danes should hold the laws made by King Edgar, because they were thought so good and reasonable above any other laws. Thus the Danes being in England began, by little and little, to be Christian men. Canute went to Rome, and returning again to England, governed that land the space of twenty years, leaving after him two sons, Harold and Hardicanute; which latter was made king of Denmark in his father's time.

Canute, king of Denmark, marries Emma, widow of Egelred.

A.D. 1035.

Harold I., called Harefoot for his activity and swiftness, son to Canute by Elgina, his first wife, began his reign over England A.D. 1035. Of him little is left in memory, save that he banished his step-mother Emma, and took her goods and jewels from her.

Harold Harefoot, a Dane.

Hardicanute, being king of Denmark, and second son to Canute by his last wife Emma, was next king of England. In the time of these Danish kings, there was one Godwin, an earl in England, who had been before in great favour with Canute, for his acts done in Denmark against the Norwegians; who afterwards married the sister (some say the daughter) of Canute. This Godwin was of a cruel and subtle wit, as is instanced not a little by the sons of King Egelred; for when those two, whose names were Alfred and Edward, came from Normandy into England, to visit their mother Emma, and brought with them a great company of Normans, this Godwin (having a daughter called Godith, whom he thought to marry to Edward, and set him up to be king), to bring his purpose about, used this device, namely, to persuade King Hardicanute, and the lords, not to suffer those Normans to be within the realm for jeopardy, but rather to punish them for example: by which means he obtained authority to order the matter himself, wherefore he met them on Guild down, and there most wretchedly murdered, or rather martyred the greater number of the Normans, and that without provocation. For, as Swanus before had tithed the monks of Canterbury, so he, with a cruel company of English soldiers, slew nine of the said Normans, and saved the tenth. And yet, passing the fury of Swanus, as not contented with that tyranny, he tithed again the said tithe, and slew every tenth knight, and that by cruel torment, as winding their entrails out of their bodies, as writeth Ranulphus. Among his other deeds, he put out the eyes of the elder brother, Alfred, and sent him to the abbey of Ely, where he, being fed with bread and water, endured not long. By some writers it is recorded, that he was there slain with the aforenamed torment, and that Edward was conveyed by some one to his mother; who, fearing the treason of Godwin, sent him soon over the sea into Normandy again. This cruel

Hardicanute, last of the Anglo-Danish kings.

A.D. 1040.

Cruelty of Earl Godwin against the Normans.

Alfred, son of Egelred, right heir to the crown, tormented to death.

Canute A.D. 1040. act of Godwin and his men against the innocent Normans, whether it came of himself, or of the king's setting on, seemeth to me to be the cause why the justice of God did shortly after revenge the quarrel of these Normans, in conquering and subduing the English nation by William the Conqueror, and the Normans who came with him. For so it was just and right, that as the Normans, coming with a natural English prince, were murdered of Englishmen; so afterwards, the Englishmen should be slain and conquered by the Normans, coming with a foreign king, not being of their natural country.

Why God suffered this land to be conquered by the Normans

Death of Hardicanute A.D 1042 Then it followeth in the story, that this King Hardicanute, when he had reigned two years, being merry at Lambeth, suddenly was stricken dumb, and fell down to the ground, and within eight days died without issue, A. D. 1042. He was the last that reigned in England of the blood of the Danes

Sons of Godwin. The aforesaid Godwin had, by the daughter of Canute, his wife, but one son, who was drowned By his second wife he had six sons, to wit, Swanus, Harold, Tostius, Wilmot, Sixth or Surth, and Leofric, with one daughter, called Goditha, who was afterwards married to King Edward the Confessor.

Concerning the story of this Alfred, I find it somewhat otherwise reported in our English chronicles, that it should be after the death of Hardicanute; forasmuch as the earls and barons after his death assembled and made a council, that never after, any of the Danes' blood should be king of England, for the despite that they had done to Englishmen. For ever before, if the English and the Danes happened to meet upon a bridge, the Englishmen were not so hardy as to move a foot, but stood still till the Danes had passed over. And, moreover, if the Englishmen had not bowed down their heads to do reverence to the Danes, they would have been beaten and defiled. For these despites and villanies they were driven out of the land after the death of Hardicanute, for they had no lord that might maintain them, and after this manner the Danes so evacuated England, that they never came again[1]

Abject state of the English

The earls and barons, by their common assent and council, sent into Normandy for these two brethren, Alfred and Edward, intending to crown Alfred, the elder brother, and to make him king of England; and to this the earls and barons made their oath. But the Earl Godwin of West Sax, falsely and traitorously thought to slay these two brethren, as soon as they came into England, to the intent that he might make Harold his son king; which son he had by his wife, Hardicanute's daughter, who was a Dane. So this Godwin went privily to Southampton, to meet the two brethren at their landing; and thus it fell out, that the messengers who went (saith mine author) into Normandy, found only Alfred the elder brother, for Edward his younger brother was gone to Hungary, to speak with his cousin, the outlaw, who was Edmund Ironside's son.

Alfred or Alured, son of King Egelred When Alfred had heard these messengers, and perceived their tidings, he thanked God, and hastening with all speed to England, arrived at Southampton. There Godwin, the false traitor, having knowledge of his coming, welcomed and received him with much joy,

(1) Taken out of the English story or chronicle compiled by certain English clerks

pretending to lead him to London, where the barons waited to make him king; and so they together passed forth toward London. But when they came to Guild down, the traitor commanded all his men to slay all that were in Alfred's company, who came with him from Normandy, and after that to take Alfred, and to lead him into the isle of Ely, where they should put out both his eyes, and so they did; for they slew all the company that were there, to the number of twelve gentlemen, who came with Alfred from Normandy, and after that they took Alfred, and in the isle of Ely they executed their commission. That done, they opened his body, took out his bowels, and setting a stake into the ground, fastened an end of his bowels thereunto, and with needles of iron they pricked his tender body, thereby causing him to go about the stake, till all his bowels were drawn out. So died this innocent Alfred or Alured, being the right heir to the crown, through treason of wicked Godwin. When the lords of England heard thereof, and how Alfred, who should have been their king, was put to death through the false traitor Godwin, they were wondrous wroth; and sware between God and them that he should die a worse death than did Edrith, who betrayed his lord, Edmund Ironside; and would immediately have put him to death, but that the traitor fled thence into Denmark, and there remained four years and more, losing all his lands in England.

Another Latin story I have, bearing no name, which saith that this coming in of Alfred and the Normans was in the time of Harold, Canute's son.[1] Also how Godwin, after he pretended great amity to them, suddenly in the night came upon them at Guildford, and after he had tithed the Normans, sent Alfred to Harold in London; who sent him to the isle of Ely, and caused his eyes to be put out. And thus much of Canute, and of his sons, Harold and Hardicanute.

Besides these two sons, Canute had also a daughter named Gunilda, married to Henry the emperor. Of her some write, that she being accused to the emperor of spouse-breach, and having no champion or knight that would fight for her, after the manner of that country, for trial of her cause, a certain little dwarf or boy, whom she brought with her out of England, stirred up of God, fought in her cause against a mighty big German, of a monstrous greatness; which silly dwarf, cutting by chance the sinews of his leg, afterwards struck him to the ground, and cut off his head, and so saved the life of the queen; if that be true which Malmesbury and Fabian report. *Gunilda, wife of Henry the emperor.*

Of this Canute it is storied that he, following much the superstition of Egelnoth, archbishop of Canterbury, went on a pilgrimage to Rome, and there founded an hospital for English pilgrims. He gave the pope precious gifts, and burdened the land with a yearly tribute, called the Rome-shot. He shrined the body of Berinus, and gave great lands and ornaments to the cathedral church of Winchester; he also builded St. Benet's in Norfolk, which was before a hermitage; likewise St. Edmundsbury, which King Athelstan before ordained for a college of priests, he turned to an abbey of monks of St. Benet's order. *Canute went to Rome, and founded the hospital for English pilgrims. Rome-shot confirmed by him.*

Henry, archdeacon of Huntingdon,[2] maketh mention of this Canute, as doth also Polydore,[3] that he, after his coming from Rome, walking

(1) Ex historia ignoti authoris. (2) Lib. vi. (3) Lib. vii.

Canute. A.D. 1042.

upon a time by the port of Southampton (but, as Polydore saith, and Fabian affirmeth the same, it was by the Thames' side in London), when his flatterers coming about him, began to exalt him with high words, calling him a king of all kings, most mighty, who had under his subjection both the people, the land, and also the sea: Canute, revolving this matter in his mind (whether for pride of his heart exalted, or whether to try and refel their flattering words), commanded his chair of state to be brought to the sea side, at what time the tide should begin to flow. Polydore saith that no seat was brought; but sitting upon his garments, being folded together under him, there charged and commanded the floods arising and coming towards his feet, that they should touch neither him nor his clothes. But the water, keeping its ordinary course, came nearer and nearer, first to his feet, and so growing higher, began to wash him well-favouredly; wherewith the king abashed, and partly also afraid, started back, and looking at his lords, "Lo," saith he, "ye call me such a mighty king, and yet I cannot command back this little water to stay at my word, but it is ready to drown me. Wherefore all earthly kings may know that all their powers be but vain, and that none is worthy to have the name of a king, but he alone who hath all things subject to the power and authority of his word, who is the Lord of heaven and earth, the Creator above of all things, the Father of our Christ and Lord, who with him for ever is to be glorified: him let us worship and extol for our King for ever." After this, as histories witness, he never suffered the crown to come upon his head, but went to Winchester, or, as some say, to Canterbury; but both those accounts may be true, for his going to Canterbury was to acknowledge that there was a Lord much higher, and of more power than he himself was, and therewithal to render up his crown for ever. With that, Egelnoth, archbishop of Canterbury, informed him of the image of the crucifix beforementioned, which dissolved the matter between married priests and life of monks, and did many other miracles more, being then at Winchester; whereupon the king, provoked to go to Winchester to the rood, there resigned his regal crown, and made the rood king over all the land.

Flatterers and claw-backs about princes.

Canute chargeth the sea to stand back.

God only, the King of kings, and Lord of lords.

The king's crown put on a rood or cross.

Here is also to be noted in this Canute, that although, as is said, he submitted in the beginning of his reign to King Edgar's laws, yet afterwards, in process of time, he set forth peculiar laws of his own, among which, divers there be that concern as well causes ecclesiastical, as also temporal. Whereby it may appear, that the government of spiritual matters did not then depend upon the bishop of Rome, but appertained to the lawful authority of the temporal prince, no less than did matters and causes temporal, as by certain ordinances of the aforesaid Canute may be well perceived.[1]

Kings of England have as much right in causes spiritual as temporal.

And here is an end of the Danish kings. Now to the English kings again, whose right line cometh in, in Edward here following.

(1) *Laws of Canute, in matters ecclesiastical.*—"Pecunia sepulturæ justum est ut aperta terra reddatur. Si aliquod corpus a sua parochia deferatur in aliam, pecunia sepulturæ," &c.

In English:—"It is meet and right, that in funerals, money be given for opening the earth.

"If any body, or corse, be carried out of its own parish into another, the money of the burial shall pertain by the law to its own parish church.

"All ordinances and ceremonies of God, let them be observed as need in all things requireth.

"Upon the Sunday we forbid all public fairs or markets, all synods or conventicles, huntings, or any such secular actions to be exercised, unless urgent necessity compel thereunto.

"Let every christian man prepare himself thrice a year, to approach to the receiving of the Lord's body: so to eat the same, as not to his judgment, but to his wholesome remedy.

"If

Edward the Confessor.

A.D. 1042.

EDWARD THE CONFESSOR.[1]

FORASMUCH as God, who is the only maker of heirs, of his mercy and providence, thought it so good, after the woeful captivity of this English nation, to grant now some respite of deliverance, in taking away the Danish kings without any issue left behind them; who reigning here in England, kept the English people in miserable subjection about the space of eight and twenty years, and, from their first landing in the time of King Brightric, wasted and vexed this land the term of 255 years: now their tyranny here coming to an end, the next election and right to the crown fell, as appertained, to Edward, the younger son of King Egelred and Emma, a true-bred Englishman, who had been now long banished in Normandy, as is above declared; a man of gentle and soft spirit, more appliable to other men's council, than able to trust to his own; of nature and condition so given from all war and bloodshed, that, being in his banishment, he wished rather to continue all his life long in that private estate, than by war or bloodshed to aspire to any kingdom. This Edward, after the death of Canute II., or Hardicanute, being sent for by the lords into Normandy, to take possession of the realm, although he something mistrusted the inconstant and fickle heads of Englishmen, yet, having sufficient pledges laid for him in Normandy, came over, accompanied by a few Normans, and not long after was crowned at Winchester, A.D. 1043, by Edsius, then archbishop of Canterbury. Not long after that, he married Goditha, or Editha, daughter of Earl Godwin, whom he treated after such a sort, that he lived with her as though she had not been his wife. Whether it were for hate of her kin, as most likely it was, or for love of chastity, it remaineth uncertain, but most writers agree that he continued his life in this manner; for the which he is highly exalted among our story-writers, and called holy King Edward. After he had thus taken upon him the government of the realm, he guided the same with much wisdom and justice for the space of four and twenty years, lacking two months; from whom issued, as out of a fountain, much godliness, mercy, pity, and liberality toward the poor; gentleness and justice toward all men; and, in all honest life, he gave a virtuous example to his people. He discharged the Englishmen from the great tribute called Dane-gilt, which beforetime was yearly levied to the great impoverishing of the people. He subdued the Scots and the Welshmen, who in their borders began to rebel against him. In much peace he continued his reign, having no foreign enemy to assault him: albeit, as some chronicles do show, certain Danes and Norwegians there were, who intended to set upon England, but as they were taking shipping, there was brought to them first one bowl, then another, of mead[2] or methe, to drink for a *bon*

England afflicted by the Danes for 255 years.

King Edward crowned. A.D. 1043

"If a minister of the altar do kill any man, or have entangled himself in any notorious crime, let him be deprived both of his order and his dignity.

"If any married woman, her husband being alive, have committed adultery, and the same be proved; to her open shame in the world, let her have her nose and ears cut off.

"Let every widow, after the death of her husband, remain sole twelve months; or if she marry, let her lose her jointure."

(1) Edition 1563, p. 11. Ed. 1583, p. 164. Ed. 1596, p. 148. Ed. 1684, vol. i. p. 183.—Ed.

(2) Μέθη, [methe], in Greek, signifieth drunkenness.

Edward, the Confessor.

A.D. 1043.

viage. Thus one cup coming after another, after drink came drunkenness, after drunkenness followed jangling, of jangling came strife, and strife turned unto stripes, whereby many were slain, and the others returned to their homes again; and thus, the merciful providence of the Lord disposed of that journey.

Accusation against Emma, the king's mother.

In the time of this Edward, Emma his mother was accused of being familiar with Alwin, the bishop of Winchester; upon which accusation, by counsel of Earl Godwin, he took from her many of her jewels, and caused her to be kept a deal more strictly in the abbey of Warwel, and the bishop to be committed to the examination of the clergy. Polydore saith they were both in prison at Winchester, where she, sorrowing the defame both of herself and the bishop, and trusting to her conscience, desired justice of them, offering herself as ready to abide any lawful trial, yea, although it were the sharpest. Then divers of the bishops made entreaty to the king for them both, and had obtained the suit, had not Robert, then archbishop of Canterbury, stopped it; who, not well content with their labour, said unto them, "My brethren, how dare you defend her who is so unworthy the name of a woman? She hath defamed her own son the king, and hath lowered herself with the bishop. And if it be so, that the woman will purge the priest, who shall then purge the woman, who is accused of consenting to the death of her son Alfred, and who procured venom to the poisoning of her son Edward? But, whether she be guilty or guiltless, if she will go barefoot for herself four steps, and for the bishop five, continually upon nine ploughshares fire hot, and escape harmless, he shall be assoiled of this challenge, and she also." To this she agreed, and the day was appointed, on which the king and a great part of his nobles were present, save only Robert, the archbishop. This Robert had been a monk of a house in Normandy, and a helper of the king in his exile, and so by the sending for of the king, came over and was made first bishop of London, and afterwards archbishop of Canterbury. Then was she led blindfold unto the place between two men, where the irons lay burning hot, and passed the nine shares unhurt. At last, said she, "Good Lord, when shall I come to the place of my purgation?" When they then opened her eyes, and she saw that she was past the pain, she kneeled down, giving God thanks. Then the king repented, saith the story, and restored unto her what he had before taken from her, and asked her forgiveness; but the archbishop fled into Normandy.

False accusation purged by hot iron.

A.D. 1052.

Great snow and mortality.

Near about this time, about the tenth year of this reign, fell passing great snow from the beginning of January, to the seventeenth day of March. After which ensued a great mortality of men, murrain of cattle, and by lightning the corn was wonderfully blasted and wasted.

Not long after this, a certain earl of Boulogne, who had married King Edward's sister, came into England, through the occasion of whom, when execution should be done upon the citizens of Dover for a fray between them and the earl's men, variance happened between King Edward and Earl Godwin; who, perceiving that he could not withstand the king's malice, although he gathered a great company to work therein what he could, fled into Flanders, and was outlawed with his five sons. King Edward repudiated

Earl Godwin outlawed.

his wife, the daughter of the said Godwin; but the second year after, by mediators, he was reconciled to the king again, and recalled from banishment, and for his good behaviour he gave for pledges his two sons, Biornon and Tostius, who were sent to the duke of Normandy, there to be kept.

Edward the Confessor. A.D. 1052.

During the time of the outlawry of Godwin, William the Bastard, duke of Normandy, came with a goodly company into England to see King Edward, and was honourably received: for whom the king made great cheer, and on his return enriched him with great gifts and pleasures; and there, as some write, made promise to him that if he died without issue, the said William should succeed him in the kingdom of England.

William, duke of Normandy, comes to England.

In this king's reign lived Marianus Scotus, the story-writer. As concerning the end of Earl Godwin, the cruel murderer of Alfred, and of the Normans, although divers histories do vary, yet in this the most part do agree, that as he sat at table with King Edward at Windsor, it happened that one of the cup-bearers, one of Earl Godwin's sons, stumbled and recovered again, so that he shed none of the drink, whereat Godwin laughed, and said, how the one brother had sustained the other.[1] With which words the king calling to mind the death of his brother who was slain by Godwin, beheld the earl, saying, "So should my brother Alfred have holpen me, had not Godwin been." Godwin then, fearing the king's displeasure to be newly kindled, after many words in excusing himself, said, "So might I safely swallow this morsel of bread, as I am guiltless of the deed;" but as soon as he had received the bread, forthwith he was choked. Then the king commanded him to be drawn from the table; and so he was conveyed by Harold his son to Winchester, and there buried.

The death of ungodly Godwin. A.D. 1053.

About the thirteenth year of this king's reign, the said King Edward sent Aldred, bishop of Worcester, to the Emperor Henry IV., praying him that he would send to the King of Hungary, that his cousin Edward, son of Edmund Ironside, might come to England, as he intended to make him king after him, who was called Edward the Outlaw; which request was fulfilled, so that he came into England with his wife Agatha, and with his children, to wit, Edgar Etheling, Margaret, and Christina. But the year after his return into the realm, this Edward deceased in London, and was buried at Westminster, or, as Jornalensis saith, at St. Paul's church in London. After his decease, the king received Edgar Etheling his son as his own child, thinking to make him his heir; but fearing partly the inconstancy and mutability of the Englishmen, partly the pride and malice of Harold, the son of Godwin, and of others (perceiving thereby that he could not bring his purpose well to pass), he directed solemn ambassadors unto William, duke of Normandy, his kinsman, admitting and assigning him to be his lawful heir, to succeed next after him to the crown.

Edward the Outlaw, son of Edmund Ironside sent for.

A.D. 1056. Death of Edward son of Edmund Ironside.

William, duke of Normandy, admitted heir to the crown.

After the death of Godwin, Harold his son waxed so in the king's favour, that he ruled the most and greatest causes of the realm, and was lieutenant of the king's army, who, with his brother Toston or Tostius sent by the king against the Welshmen, subdued their

(1) Ex Jornal.; Malmesb.; Polydor.; Fab. et aliis.

Edward the Confessor. A.D. 1056. rebellion. But afterwards, such envy grew between these two brethren, because Tostius saw his brother Harold so greatly advanced in the king's favour, that at Hertford Tostius slew all his brother's men; and when he had cut them in pieces, he powdered their quarters and mangled parts in barrels of salt, vinegar, wine, and other liquors. This done, he made a power against his brother Harold, being king, with the aid of certain Danes and Norwegians, and fought a battle with him in the North, as after shall follow (God willing) to be seen. So ungracious were these wicked children of Earl Godwin, that if they saw any fair mansion or manor-place, they would slay the owner thereof with all his kindred, and enter upon the possession thereof themselves.

Graceless children of a wicked father.

At length it came into the mind of Harold to sail over the sea, as Polydore saith, unto Normandy, to see his brother Wilmot, as also his cousin Hacus, whom the king had sent thither to be kept for pledges, as ye heard before. Polydore saith, "These pledges were Tostius and Biornan;" but that cannot be, for Tostius was then in England. But as Henry, archdeacon of Huntingdon, saith, his journey was into Flanders, as seemeth more like; for it is not to be thought that Harold, who was a doer in the cruel murder of Alfred and of the Normans, would venture into Normandy, and therefore more like it is, that his sailing was into Flanders. But, as the story proceedeth, he, being in the course of sailing, was weather-driven by tempest into the province of Pountith, where he was taken prisoner, and sent to Duke William, of Normandy, to whom he was made to swear, that he, in time following, should marry his daughter, and that, after the death of King Edward, he should keep the land of England to his behoof, according to the will and mind of Edward, as some writers say, and so live in great honour and dignity, next unto him in the realm. This promise having been faithfully made to the duke, Harold returneth to England, having had his cousin Hacus, the son of his brother Swanus, delivered unto him; but Wilmot, the brother of Harold, the duke keepeth still for performance of the covenants. Thus Harold, I say, returning home, showeth the king all that he had done in the aforesaid matters, wherewith the king was well contented. Whereby it may be gathered that King Edward was right willing that Duke William should reign after him, and also it seemeth not unlike but that he had given him his promise thereunto before.

Harold taken by the Normans, promiseth Duke William to marry his daughter, and to keep the realm for his behoof.

Among all that were true and trusty to King Edward, among the English nobility, none had such commendation as had Leofric, earl of Mercia and Chester. This Leofric purchased many great liberties for the town of Coventry, and made it free of all manner of things, except only of horse. This freedom was obtained by means of his wife Godina, by riding, as the fame goeth, after a strange manner through the town. This Leofric, with his wife Godina, builded also the abbey of Coventry, and endowed the same with great lands and riches.

Earl Leofric true and faithful to his prince.

The abbey of Coventry builded by Leofric.

You heard a little before of the coming over of Edward, called the Outlaw, son of King Edmund Ironside, whom King Edward had purposed to have made king after him; but soon after his coming over, he deceased in London. This Edward had, by his

Edward the Confessor. A.D. 1065.

wife Agatha, a son called Edgar Etheling, and a daughter Margaret, who, being afterward married to the king of Scots, was the mother of Matilda, or Maud, queen of England, and of David, king of Scots.

The death of King Edward.

This virtuous and blessed King Edward, after he had reigned three and twenty years and seven months, died, and was buried in the monastery of Westminster, which he had greatly augmented and repaired; but afterwards it was more enlarged after the form which it hath now, by Henry III., the son of King John.

They that write the history of this king, here make mention of a dream or revelation that should be showed to him in time of his sickness;[1] how that because the peers and bishops of the realm were servants, not of God, but of the devil, God would give this realm to the hand of others. And when the king desired utterance to be given him, that he might declare the same to the people, whereby they might repent, it was answered again, that they would not repent; still, if they did, it should not be given to another people: but because it is a dream, I let it pass.

Divers laws were before in divers countries of this realm used, as the law first of Dunuallo Molinucius, with the laws of Mercia, called Mercenelega: then the laws of West Saxon kings, as of Ive, Offa, Alfred, &c., which were called West Saxenelega: the third were the laws of Canute, and of the Danes, called Danelega. Of all these laws, which before were diversely in certain particular countries used and received, this Edward compiled one universal and common law for all people through the whole realm, called King Edward's laws; which, being gathered out of the best and chiefest of the other laws, were so just, so equal, and so serving the public profit and weal of all estates, that mine authors say, "The people long after did rebel against their heads and rulers, to have the same laws again (being taken from them), and yet could not obtain them."

William the Conqueror sworn to King Edward's laws, yet went from them.

Furthermore, I read and find in Matthew Paris, that when William the Conqueror, at his coming in, did swear to use and practise the same good laws of Edward, for the common laws of this realm; afterwards being established in his kingdom, he forswore himself, and placed his own laws in their room, much worse and obscurer than the others were.

Notwithstanding, among the said laws of Edward, and in the first chapter and beginning thereof, this I find among the ancient records of the Guildhall in London:—"The office of a king, with such other appurtenances as belong to the realm of Britain," set forth and described in the Latin style; which I thought here not unmeet to be expressed in the English tongue, for those who understand no Latin. The tenor and meaning of it is as followeth.[2]

A king, the vicar of God on earth.

"The king, because he is the vicar of the highest King, is appointed

(1) Ex Malmesb.; Jornalen.; Historia Richardi II. jussis composita.

(2) *De jure et appendiis regni Britanniæ, et quod sit officium Regis.*—"Rex autem, quia vicarius summi regis est, ad hoc est constitutus, ut regnum terrenum et populum Domini, et super omnia sanctam ejus veneretur ecclesiam et regat, et ab injuriosis defendat, et maleficos ab eo avellat et destruat, et penitus disperdat. Quod nisi fecerit, nomen regis non in eo constabit. Verum Papa Johanne testante, nomen regis perdit: cui Pipinus et Carolus filius ejus (nec dum reges, sed principes sub rege Francorum stulto) scripserunt, quærentes, si ita permanere deberent Francorum reges, solo regio nomine contenti. A quo responsum est, illos decet vocare reges, qui vigilanter defendunt et regunt ecclesiam Dei et populum ejus," &c.—*Ex* Libro Reg. Antiquorumi in Prætorio Londinensi.

Edward the Confessor. A.D. 1065. for this purpose, to rule the earthly kingdom, and the Lord's people, and, above all things, to reverence his holy church, to govern it, and to defend it from injuries; to pluck away wicked doers, and utterly to destroy them: which, unless he do, the name of a king agreeth not unto him, but he loseth the name of a king, as witnesseth Pope John; to the which pope, Pepin and Charles his son being not yet kings, but princes under the French king (not being very wise), did write, demanding this question, 'Whether the kings of France ought so to continue, having but only the name of a king?' Unto whom Pope John answereth again, that it was convenient to call them kings, who vigilantly do defend and govern the church of God and his people, following the saying of King David, the Psalmograph, 'He shall not dwell in my house which worketh pride,' &c. Moreover, the king, by right and by his office, ought to defend and conserve fully and wholly, in all ampleness, without diminution, all the lands, honours, dignities, rights, and liberties, of the crown of his kingdom: and, further, to reduce into their pristine state, all such things as have been dispersed, wasted, and lost, which appertain to his kingdom. Also the whole and universal land, with all islands about the same in Norway and Denmark, be appertaining to the crown of his kingdom, and be of the appurtenances and dignity of the king, making one monarchy and one kingdom, which sometime was called the kingdom of the Britons, and now the kingdom of England; such bounds and limits as are beforementioned be appointed and limited to the name of this kingdom."

Limits of the kingdom of England.

Moreover, in the aforesaid laws of this King Edward, it followeth in the same book, where the said Edward, describing the office of a king, addeth in these words:—"A king," saith he, "ought above all things to fear God, to love and to observe his commandments, and cause them to be observed through his whole kingdom. He ought also to keep, cherish, maintain, and govern the holy church within his kingdom with all integrity and liberty, according to the constitutions of his ancestors and predecessors, and to defend the same against all enemies, so that God, above all things, be honoured, and ever be before his eyes. He ought also to set up good laws and customs, such as be wholesome and approved; such as be otherwise, to repeal them, and thrust them out of his kingdom. Item, He ought to do judgment and justice in his kingdom, by the counsel of the nobles of his realm. All these things ought a king in his own person to do, taking his oath upon the evangelists, and the blessed relics of saints, swearing in the presence of the whole state of his realm, as well of the temporality as of the spirituality, before he be crowned of the archbishops and bishops. Three servants the king ought to have under him as vassals: fleshly lust, avarice, and greedy desire; whom if he keep under as his servants and slaves, he shall reign well and honourably in his kingdom. All things are to be done with good advisement and premeditation; and that properly belongeth to a king. For hasty rashness bringeth all things to ruin, according to the saying of the gospel, 'Every kingdom divided in itself shall be desolate.'"

The office of a king described.

Three servants a king ought to have under his subjection.

After the duty and office of princes have been thus described, followeth the institution of subjects, declared in many good and necessary ordinances, very requisite and convenient for public government; of which laws, William the Conqueror was compelled, through the clamour of the people, to take some, but the most part he omitted, contrary to his own oath at his coronation, inserting and placing the most of his own laws in his language, to serve his purpose, and which as yet, to this present day, in the Norman language do remain. Now, the Lord willing, let us proceed in the story as in order followeth.

KING HAROLD II.[1]

A.D. 1066.

HAROLD, the second son of Earl Godwin, and last king of the Saxons, notwithstanding that divers of the nobles went with Edgar Adeling, the next heir after Edmund Ironside, yet he, through force and might contemning the young age of Edgar, and forgetting also his promise made to Duke William, took upon him to be king of England, A.D. 1066. When Harold Harefager, son of Canute, king of Norway and Denmark, heard of the death of King Edward, he came into England with 300 ships or more, who then joining with Tostius, brother to the said Harold, king of England, entered into the north parts, and claimed the land after the death of Edward. But the lords of the country arose, and gave them battle; notwithstanding the Danes had the victory. Therefore Harold, king of England, repaired towards them in all haste, and gave them another strong battle, and had the victory, where also Harold the Dane was slain by the hand of Harold king of England; and Tostius was also slain in the battle. After this victory, Harold waxed proud and covetous, and would not divide the prey with his knights who had deserved it, but kept it to himself, whereby he lost the favour of many of his knights and people.

Harold king of Denmark and Tostius slain.

In the mean time, William, duke of Normandy, sent an ambassage to Harold, king of England, admonishing him of the covenant that was agreed between them; which was, to have kept the land to his use after the death of Edward. But because the daughter of Duke William, who had been promised to Harold, was dead, Harold thought himself thereby discharged, and said, "That such a nice foolish promise ought not to be holden concerning another's land, without the consent of the lords of the same; and especially because he was thereunto, for need or for dread, compelled."

Upon these answers received, Duke William, in the mean time, while the messengers went and came, gathered his knights and prepared his navy, and had the assent of the lords of his land to aid and assist him in his journey. And besides that, sending unto Rome to Pope Alexander concerning his title and voyage into England, the pope confirmed him as to the same, and sent unto him a banner, willing him to bear it in the ship wherein himself should sail. Thus Duke William, being purveyed of all things concerning his journey,

The pope sendeth a banner to Duke William for a boon voyage into England.

(1) Edition 1563, p 12 Ed 1583, p 166. Ed 1596, p 150 Ed 1684, vol i p 186—Ed

Harold II. A.D. 1066.

sped him to the sea-side, and took shipping at the haven of St. Valery, where he tarried a long time ere he might have a convenient wind, on which account his soldiers murmured, saying, "It was a woodness,[1] and a thing displeasing God, to desire to have another man's kingdom by strength; and, namely, when God was against it by sending contrary wind." At last the wind shortly after came about, and they took shipping with a great company, and landed at Hastings, in Sussex.

William landeth at Hastings.

For three causes Duke William entered this land to subdue Harold. One was, for that it was to him given by King Edward, his nephew. The second was to take wreak for the cruel murder of his nephew Alfred, King Edward's brother, and of the Normans, which deed he ascribed chiefly to Harold. The third was, to revenge the wrong done to Robert, archbishop of Canterbury, who was exiled by the means and labour of Harold, in the time of King Edward.

Thus, while Harold was in the north, Duke William made so great speed, that he came to London before the king; out of which he was holden, till he made good surety that he and his people should pass through the city without tarrying; which promise he well observing, passed the bridge, and went over to Sussex, from whence he sent a monk unto Harold, and proffered him three manner of ways. First, either to render to him the possession of the land, and so to take it again of him under tribute, reigning under him; secondly, or else to abide and stand to the pope's arbitrement betwixt them both; or, thirdly, to defend this quarrel in his own person against the duke, and they two only to try the matter by dint of sword, without any other bloodshedding.

Three conditions offered to Harold by William.

But Harold refused all these offers, saying, "It should be tried by dint of swords, and not by one sword;" and so gathered his people and joined battle with the Normans, in the place where afterward was builded the Abbey of Battle in Sussex. In the beginning of this fight, the Englishmen kept them in good array likely to vanquish the Normans; wherefore Duke William caused his men to give back, as though they fled, whereupon the Englishmen followed fast, and broke their array. Then the Normans, fiercely giving a charge upon them, in conclusion obtained the victory through the just providence of God. On which occasion King Harold, who before had so cruelly murdered Alfred, the true heir of the crown, with his company of Normans, was now wounded of the Normans in the left eye with an arrow, and thereof incontinent died; although Gerardus saith he fled away to Chester, and lived after that, a monk in the monastery of St. James. This, however, is not likely, but rather that he was there slain, after he had reigned nine months, and was buried at Waltham, which proveth that he died not at Chester; and so was he the last that reigned in England of the blood of Saxons, which continued to reckon from Hengist's first reign in Kent, by the space of 591 years; and if it be reckoned from the years of the West Saxons, then it endured the space of 565 years.

The fight betwixt them.

King Harold slain.

This Duke William and King Edward were by the father's side

(1) "Wilfulness"—Ed.

cousin-germans removed: for Richard, the first of that name, who was the third duke of Normandy after Rollo, was father to Duke Richard, the second of that name, and brother to Emma, mother to King Edward, which Duke Richard II. was father to Duke Robert, this Duke William's father.

Ecclesiastical affairs.

Consanguinity between King Edward and William the Conqueror.

Albeit in this matter some others may gather otherwise and better perchance, yet, if I may say what I think, verily I suppose, that consanguinity is not so much the cause why God of his unknown judgments suffered the Normans here to prevail, as was rather the cruel murder of Alfred and of the innocent Normans, wrought by the cruel despight of Harold and the Englishmen, as is before declared, which merciless murder God here justly in this conquest recompensed.

Murder recompensed.

Now it remaineth to these foreign affairs of kings and princes, to add something concerning the continuation of the archbishops of Canterbury, beginning where we left off, that is, with Elphege, whom we declared a little before to have been stoned by the Danes at Greenwich.[1] After Elphege next succeeded Lining, and after him Egelnoth, also abovementioned. Then Robert, a Norman, a great doer, as is declared, about King Edward, and a faithful counsellor unto him, but he abode not long. After whom Stigand invaded the see, as they report, by simony, being both archbishop of Canterbury, bishop of Winchester, and also abbot in another place, wherein he continued a great space, gathering and heaping goods together; till at length Duke William put him in prison, and there kept him, placing in his room Lanfranc, a Lombard, of whom more shall follow, Christ willing, hereafter to be declared.

A.D. 1012. Archbishops of Canterbury.

A.D. 1052.

A.D. 1070.

*Whereupon[2] cometh the latter age of the church. Here now beginneth the fresh flowering blood of the church to faint, and strength to fail, oppressed with cold humours of worldly pomp, avarice, and tyranny; here now cometh in blind superstition, with cloaked hypocrisy, armed with rigorous laws, and cruel murdering of saints; here cometh in the order and name of cardinals, whose name was not heard of before the time 1030 years after Christ, growing up in such excess and riches, that some of them now have two, some three hundred benefices at once. Here cometh in four orders of friars; here the supremacy of Rome raged in his ruff, which being once established in the consciences of men, the power of all other christian princes did quake and decay, for dread of the pope's interdict, suspense, and excommunication, which they feared no less than Christ's own sentence from heaven. Thus the Roman bishop, under the title of St. Peter, doing what he lusted, and princes not daring that which was right; in the mean while the people of Christ were miserably governed and abused, especially here in England and Scotland, as in this history, Christ so permitting, shall appear. For here then came in tyranny without mercy, pomp and ambition without measure, error and blindness without knowledge, articles and canons without number, avarice without end, impropriations, abalienations, reservations, vowsons, or

Decay of the church.

(1) See page 77.—ED.

(2) This passage in single asterisks is an extract from the edition of Foxe of 1563, p. 10, and is entitled "The Third Age of the Church."—ED.

Ecclesiastical affairs. expectations of benefices, translations of cathedral churches, contributions, annuities, Petershots (as in our old chronicles they are termed), preventions of patronage, bulls, indulgences, and cases papal; with innumerable other grievances and proud proceedings of the Romish prelates, wherewith they brought all realms, with their princes, underneath their girdles; insomuch that the emperors, at length, could not take their crown but by the pope's grace and license: and if any did otherwise, the pope's ban[1] was ready either to depose him, or to stir up civil war against him. Then began corruption to enter and increase; then turned the gold and good metal into dross and filthiness; then quenched the clear light of the gospel; the book of God's word obscured in a dark tongue, which book King Athelstan before caused to be translated from Hebrew into English, A.D. 930; then shepherds and watchmen became wicked wolves, Christ's friends changed into enemies. To be short, then came in the time that the Revelation speaketh of, when Satan, the old serpent, being tied up for a thousand years, was loosed for a certain space, of the which space, here, in these books, by the help and supportation of Christ our Lord, we intend something to entreat and speak of, though not of all things in general done in all places, yet that such things as be most principal may come to light, the knowledge whereof shall be necessary for all our countrymen to understand.*

Proud proceedings of the Romish prelates.

Although the church of Christ and the state of religion, first founded and grounded by Christ and his apostles, did not altogether and continually remain in its primitive perfection wherein it was first instituted, but in process of time began from better to worse, to decrease and decline into much superstition and inconvenience, partly through the coming in of Mahomet, A.D. 612, partly through the increase of wealth and riches, and partly through the decrease of knowledge and diligence in such as should be the guides of Christ's flock; yet the infection and corruption of that time, though it were great, did not so abound in such excessive measure as afterwards in the other later times now following, about the thousand years expired after Christ, whereof we have to treat, Christ so permitting; about which time and year came Sylvester II. who next succeeded after Gregory V. already mentioned, and occupied the see of Rome about A.D. 1000, lacking one or two.

Coming in of Mahomet.

A.D. 1000.

Pope Sylvester II. a foul sorcerer.

This Sylvester was a sorcerer, who, after the manner of those who work by familiars, as they call them, and by conjuration, compacted with the devil to be made pope; and so he was, through the operation of Satan, according to his request, which thing, some histories say, he did greatly repent before his death; but for a more ample declaration hereof, I will bring in the words of Johannes Stella, a Venetian, translated from Latin into English, concerning the said Sylvester, to the intent that our enchanters and sorcerers now-a-days, of whom there be too many in England, may the better, through his example, be admonished. The words of Stella be these, agreeing also with the narration of Benno, Platina, and many others.[2] "Gibert, a Frenchman, called Sylvester II., being pope, sat in his papacy four

A. D. 999.

(1) The pope's ban—a public proclamation: thus, "banns of marriage." It is used more commonly in a bad sense, as in Shakspeare, and means to curse, proscribe, excommunicate.—ED.

(2) Johannes Stella, Platina, Petrus Præmonstratensis, Nauclerus, Antoninus, Robertus Barnus. Johannes Baleus.

years, one month, and eight days. He entered into his papacy through wicked and unlawful means, who from his youth being a monk, and leaving his monastery, gave himself wholly to the devil, to obtain what he required. And first coming to Hispalis, a city in Spain, he there applied to his book, and profited therein so much that he was made doctor, having amongst his auditors, Otho the emperor's son, Robert the French king, Lotharius archbishop of Senon, with divers others; by whose advancement he was promoted, first to be bishop of Rheims, then bishop of Ravenna, and at last, through the operation of Satan, he was exalted to the papacy of Rome, upon this condition, that after his death he should give himself to the devil, by whose procurement he came to that promotion. Upon a certain time he demanded an answer of the devil, how long he should enjoy his popedom. To whom he answered again, 'Until thou say mass in Jerusalem thou shalt live.' At length, in the fourth year of his popedom, saying mass at Lent-time in the temple of the Holy Cross, being called then Jerusalem, he there knew the time was come when he should die. Whereupon, being struck with repentance, he confessed his fault openly before the people, desiring them to cut his body all in pieces (being so seduced by deceits of the devil); and thus, being hewn in pieces, that they would lay it upon a cart, and bury it wheresoever the horses would carry it of their accord. And so the saying is, that by the providence of God (whereby the wicked may learn, that there is yet hope of remission with God, so that they will repent them in their life), the horses of their own accord stayed at the church of Lateran, and there he was buried:[1] where commonly, by the rattling of his bones within the tomb, is portended the death of popes, as the common report goeth." Thus much out of Johannes Stella concerning Sylvester, by whom our sorcerers and enchanters, or magicians, may learn to beware of the deceitful operation of Satan, who in the end deceiveth and frustrateth all them that have to do with him, as the end of all such doth declare commonly, who use the like art or trade. The Lord and God of all mercy, through the Spirit of Jesus, our Redeemer, dissolve the works of Satan, and preserve the hearts of our nobles, and all other Englishmen, from such infection! Amen.

Ecclesiastical affairs.

A.D. 1003.

An admonition for sorcerers.

After Sylvester succeeded John XIX. by whom was brought in, as Volateran saith, the feast of All Souls, A.D. 1004, through the means and instigation of one Odilo, abbot of Cluniack, to be celebrated next after the feast of All Saints. This monk Odilo, thinking that purgatory, as he heard, should be in the Mount Etna, dreamed upon a time, in the country of Sicily, that he, by his masses, had delivered divers souls from thence: saying moreover, "That he did hear the voices and lamentations of devils, crying out for that the souls were taken from them by the masses and funeral dirges."[2] Not long after him, came John XX. and Sergius IV., after whom succeeded Benedict VIII., and then John XXI., who being promoted by art magic of Theophylact his nephew, Gratian, Brazutus, and other sorcerers, brought in first the fast of the even of John Baptist and St. Lawrence. After him followed Pope Benedict IX., also

The feast of All Souls brought in by Pope John XIX. or XVII.

A.D. 1012.

A.D. 1033.

(1) Ex Johanne Stella. (2) Ex Bakenthorpo. in prologo. iv. lib. sententiarum.

Ecclesiastical affairs. aspiring to his papacy by like magic, practising enchantments and conjuration in woods, after a horrible manner; who resisted the Emperor Henry III. son to Conrad, and placed in his room Peter the king of Hungary, with this verse—

"Petra dedit Romam Petro, tibi Papa coronam."

A.D.1044. Afterwards, for fear of Henry prevailing in battle, he was fain to sell his seat to his successor, Gratian, called Gregory VI., for 1500*l.* At this time there were three popes together in Rome, reigning and raging one against another; Benedict IX., Sylvester III., and Gregory VI.; for which cause Henry, sirnamed Niger, the emperor, coming to Rome, displaced these three monsters at one time, placing instead of them Clement II., and thereupon enacting that no bishop of Rome should henceforth be chosen, but by the consent and confirmation of the emperor. This constitution, though it was both agreeable, and also necessary for the public tranquillity of that city, the cardinals would not suffer long to stand, but did impugn it afterward by subtle practice and open violence, as in process, the Lord permitting, shall appear in the time of Henry IV. and Henry V. In the time of this Clement, the Romans made an oath to the emperor concerning the election of the bishops, that they would themselves intermeddle no further therein, but as the assent of the emperor should go withal. Howbeit the emperor departing thence into Germany again, by and by they forgat their oath, and within nine months after poisoned the bishop, which deed some impute to Stephen, his successor, called Damasus II. Others impute it to Brazutus, who, as histories record, within thirteen years poisoned six popes; that is, Clement II., Damasus II., Leo IX., Victor II., Stephen IX., and Nicholas II.

No pope to be chosen but by the confirmation of the emperor.

A.D.1046.

A.D.1048.

Thus Clement being poisoned, after him succeeded Damasus II., elected neither by consent of the people, nor of the emperor, but by force and invasion; who also within twenty-three days being poisoned,

A.D.1049. A.D. 1049, much contention and striving began in Rome about the papal seat; whereupon the Romans, through the counsel of the cardinal, sent to the aforesaid emperor, desiring him to give them a bishop: and so he did, whose name was Bruno, an Almain, and bishop of Cologne, afterward called Leo IX. This Bruno, being a simple man, and easily to be led by evil counsel, coming from the emperor towards Rome in his pontifical apparel like a pope, there meeteth him by the way the abbot of Cluniack, and Hildebrand a monk, who seeing him so in his pontificalibus, began to rate him, laying to his charge, that he would so take his authority of the emperor, and not rather of the clergy of Rome and the people thereof, as other his predecessors were wont to do; and so counselled him to lay down that apparel, and to enter in with his own habit, till he had his election by them. Bruno, following their counsel, and confessing his fault before the clergy of Rome, obtained their favour; and so was nominated Leo. IX., whereby Hildebrand was made a cardinal, and put in high room. Under this Pope Leo were two councils, one kept at Vercelli, where the doctrine of Berengarius against the real substance in the sacrament was first condemned, although Berengarius yet recanted not, which nevertheless was done after in the Council of Lateran, under Nicholas II. A.D. 1060; the other was kept at Moguntia, where, amongst many other decrees, it was enacted, That priests should be utterly excluded and debarred from marriage. Item, that no layman might give benefice or bishopric, or any spiritual promotion,[1] &c.

Ecclesiastical affairs.

Council of Moguntium.

This Leo IX. being at Worms with the emperor on Christmas-day, did excommunicate the sub-deacon; because in reading the epistle, he did it not in the Roman tune, he being there present. The archbishop, moved therewith, departed from the altar (being then at mass) saying, He would not proceed any further in his service unless his sub-deacon was restored, whereupon the pope commanded him to be released, and so they went forward in their service.

After the death of Leo, whom Brazutus poisoned the first year of his popedom, Theophylactus did strive to be pope:[2] but Hildebrand, to defeat him, went to the emperor (partly also being sent by the Romans for fear of the emperor's displeasure), who assigned another bishop, a German, called Victor II. This Victor holding a council at Florence, deposed divers bishops and priests for simony and fornication: for simony, in that they took of secular men their dignities for money; for fornication, in that, contrary to their canon, they were married, &c. The second year of his papacy, and little more, this pope also followed his predecessors, being poisoned by the aforesaid Brazutus, through the procurement of Hildebrand and his master.

A.D.1054.

Council of Florence.

A.D.1057.

Here now began the church and clergy of Rome to wring out of the emperor's hand the election of the pope: electing Stephen IX. for pope, contrary to their oath, and to the emperor's assignment. Here was the church of Milan first brought to obedience of the Romish church by this Stephen IX. bishop of Rome; who also shamed not to accuse the emperor Henry (of whom mention is made before) of heresy, for minishing the authority of the Roman see. So this was their heresy at that time, not to maintain the ambitious proceedings of the Romish prelate; and simony they called this, to take and enjoy any spiritual living at a secular man's hand. Wherefore Stephen hearing this simony to reign in divers places, namely, in the churches of Burgundy and Italy, sent forth the cardinal Hildebrand to reform the matter, who was no less earnest in that kind of commission to help the matter forward.

The Church of Milan first brought under the Church of Rome.

In the mean time, Stephen the pope tasting of Brazutus's cup fell sick. Hildebrand, hearing that, applieth home, with all speed. So being returned to Rome, he assembleth all the companies and orders of the clergy together, making them to swear that they would admit none to be bishop, but who should be appointed by the public consent of them altogether. This being done, Hildebrand taketh his journey into Florence, to fetch the bishop of Florence, to install him bishop; the clergy swearing unto him that no bishop should be ordained before his return again. But the people of Rome, not suffering the election to stand so long after the death of Stephen, elected one of their own city, called Benedict X. Hildebrand,

Hildebrand beginneth to stir.

A.D.1059.

(1) Nauclerus Crantz. (2) Alb. Crantz. Saxo. lib. iv. cap. 45.

Ecclesiastical affairs. hearing of this, was not a little offended; wherefore, returning to Rome with one Gerhard, bishop of Florence, he caused the clergy to proceed to a new election, saying, "That Benedict was not lawfully called, but came in by force and bribing." But the clergy, not daring to attempt any new election at Rome, went to Sens, and there elected this Gerhard, bishop of Florence, whom Hildebrand brought with him. So were two popes in Rome together: but Gerhard, named Nicholas II., holding a council at Sutrium, through the help of Duke Godfrid and Guibert, and other bishops about Italy, caused the other pope to be deposed. Benedict, understanding them to be set against him through the means of Hildebrand, unpoped himself, and went to Velitras; living there more quietly than he would have done at Rome.

Two popes together at Rome.

Benedict unpopes himself.

The gloss of the pope's decrees refuted.

Here is to be noticed by the way the error of the gloss upon the three and twentieth distinction, which falsely allegeth out of the chronicles, that Benedict X. who succeeded Stephen, was deposed; after whom came Johannes, bishop of Sabine, for money, and he again was deposed. Benedict was then restored, and afterwards displaced again, and then Johannes, archdeacon, 'ad portam latinam,' was made pope, and he again deposed by the emperor; and all this within one year: which history neither is found in any chronicle, nor agreeth upon any Benedict, save only that Benedict IX. who was deposed, and then reigned three popes together: Benedict IX. Sylvester III. and Gregory VI., who before was called Johannes ad portam latinam, whom the emperor deposed. But that Benedict neither was the tenth, neither did he succeed Pope Stephen, as the gloss recordeth. Nicholas thus being set up without the mind either of the emperor or of the people of Rome, after his fellow-pope was driven away, brake up the synod of Sutrium, and came to Rome, where he assembled another council, called Concilium Lateranum; in which council first was promulgated the terrible sentence of excommunication mentioned in the decrees, and that beginneth, "In nomine Domini nostri," &c.[1] The effect whereof is this: first, that he, after a subtle practice, as far and as plainly as he durst speak, undermineth the emperor's jurisdiction, and transferreth to a few cardinals and certain Catholic persons, the full authority of choosing the pope. Secondly, against all such as do creep into the seat of Peter by money or favour, without the full consent of the cardinals, he thundereth with terrible blasts of excommunication, accursing them and their children with devils, as wicked persons, to the anger of Almighty God, giving also authority and power to cardinals, with the clergy and laity, to depose all such persons, and call a council-general, wheresoever they will, against them.

Council of Lateran. A.D.1059.

A terrible curse of Nicholas.

Berengarius driven to recantation.

Item, in the said Council of Lateran, under Pope Nicholas II., Berengarius Andegavensis, an archdeacon, was driven to the recantation of his doctrine, denying the real substance of Christ's holy body and blood to be in the sacrament, otherwise than sacramentally and in mystery.

Transubstantiation brought in.

In the same council also was hatched and invented the new-found device and term of 'transubstantiation.'

(1) Dist. 23 cap. "In nomine," &c.

It were too long here to declare the confederation betwixt this Nicholas and Robert Guiscard, whom this pope (contrary to all right and good law, displacing the right heir) made duke of Apulia, Calabria, Sicily, and captain-general of St. Peter's lands; that through his force of arms and violence he might the better subdue all such as should rebel, to his obedience; and so did.[1] Now let all men, who be godly wise, judge and understand how this standeth with the doctrine of Christ, the example of Peter, or the spirit of a christian bishop, by outward arms and violence to conquer christian men and countries, under the obedience of a bishop's see.[2] Thus Pope Nicholas II., well answering to his Greek name, by might and force continued three years and a half; but, at length, he met with Brazutus's cup, and so turned up his heels.[3]

Ecclesiastical affairs.

A.D. 1062.

At the beginning of this Nicholas, or somewhat before, about A.D. 1057, Henry IV., after the decease of Henry III., was made emperor, being but a child, and reigned fifty years; but not without great molestation and much disquietness, and all through the ungracious wickedness of Hildebrand, as hereafter (the Lord so permitting) shall be declared.

The emperor Henry IV.

Here, by the way, cometh to be noted an example, whereby all princes may learn and understand how the pope is to be handled, whosoever looketh to have any goodness at his hand. If a man stand in fear of his curse, he shall be made his slave; but if he be despised of you, you shall have him as you list. For the pope's curse may well be compared to Domitian's thunder: if a man give ear to the noise and crack, it seemeth a terrible thing; but if you consider the causes and effect thereof, it is a most vain ridicule.

The pope's curse compared to Domitian's thunder.

In the reign of this Nicholas, A.D. 1060, Aldred, bishop of Worcester, after the decease of Kinsius, his predecessor, was made archbishop of York; who, coming to Rome with Tostius, earl of Northumberland, for his pall, as the manner was, could not obtain it, but was deprived of all his dignity, for some default (I cannot tell what) in his answer; and furthermore, after his return home, was spoiled of all that he brought with him. Whereupon, he returning again to Rome with Tostius, the aforesaid earl, there made his complaint, but could not be heard, till Tostius, a man of stout courage, taking the matter in hand, told the pope to his face, "That that curse of his was not to be feared in far countries, which his own neighbours, yea, and most vile vagabonds, derided and despised at home." Wherefore he required the pope either to restore Aldred again to his goods lost, or else that it should be known that they were lost through his means and subtilty. And, furthermore, it would come to pass that the king of England hearing this would debar him of St. Peter's tribute, taking it for a great shame to him and his realm, if Aldred should come from Rome both deprived of dignity, and spoiled also of his goods, &c. In fine, the pope thus persuaded by the argument of his purse, was content to send home Aldred with his pall, according to his request.

Tostius persuadeth the pope.

(1) Nauclerus, Platina, Eneas Silvius.
(2) "Potentia Papæ coactiva" standeth not with the gospel.
(3) The doctrine of the Nicolaitans is supposed first to have been taught by Nicholas, one of the seven deacons. Ancient writers agree in ascribing to them what our author seems disposed to ascribe to Pope Nicholas II. namely, the grossest kinds of immorality. See Eusebius, Eccl. Hist. lib. iii. c. 26.—Ed.

Ecclesiastical affairs.

After the death of Nicholas, the Lombards being oppressed before by Pope Nicholas, and brought under fear, were the more desirous, and thought it good to have a bishop of their company, and so elected the bishop of Parma, called Cadolus, to be pope: sending to the emperor, and desiring his favour and support therein; for the election of the pope (said they) most properly appertained unto him.

Cadolus, a Lombard, made pope by the emperor.

The emperor, well pleased and content, giveth his good leave and voice withal. Hildebrand, no less a wicked necromancer than a stout maintainer of popish liberties against good emperors, hearing this, setteth up, by a contrary faction, another bishop, Anselm, after called Alexander II. Cadolus, thus elected by the emperor and the cardinals, setteth forward to Rome with a sufficient army and strength of men. Alexander also, no less prepared, there received him with another army, where they had a great conflict, and many were slain on both sides; but Cadolus, as he had the better cause, so he had the worst fortune, who, being repelled, yet repaired himself, and came again with a greater power; albeit he prevailed not. The emperor, seeing this hurly-burly, to take up the matter, sent thither his ambassador, Otho, archbishop of Cologne; who, coming to Rome, beginneth sharply to chide the pope for taking so upon him without the leave or knowledge of the emperor, declaring how the election of that see ought chiefly to appertain to the right of the emperor, as it hath done for the most part in the time of his predecessors. But Hildebrand, all set on wickedness and ambition, and also puffed up not a little with his late victories, not suffering the ambassador to tell his tale to the end, interrupted him in the middle of it; affirming, that if they should stand to law and custom, the liberty of that election should rather belong to the clergy than to the emperor. To make short, Otho the ambassador, bearing more with the clergy than with the emperor, was content to be persuaded, only requiring, in the emperor's name, a council to be had, to decide the matter, whereat the emperor should be present himself; and so he was. In that council, held at Mantua, Alexander was declared pope; the other had his pardon granted. In this council, amongst many other considerations, it was concluded, concerning priests, that they should have no wives; that such as have concubines should say no mass; that priests' children should not be secluded from holy orders; that no benefices should be bought for money; and that Allelujah should be suspended in time of Lent out of the church. This also was decreed (which made most for Hildebrand's purpose) that no spiritual man whatsoever should enter into any church, by a secular person, and that the pope should be elected only by the cardinals. Benno the Cardinal writeth thus of Alexander, that after he perceived the frauds of Hildebrand, and of others the emperor's enemies, and understanding that he was set up and enthronized only for a purpose; being at his mass, as he was preaching to the people, told them he would not sit in that place, unless he had the license of the emperor; which when Hildebrand heard, he was stricken with such a fury, that scarcely he could keep his hands off him till mass was done. After the mass being finished, by force of soldiers and strength of men, he had Pope Alexander into a chamber, and there pommelled him all over with his fists, rating and rebuking him because he would seek for favour of

Two battles betwixt two popes for St. Peter's seat.

Council of Mantua.

No secular man to give spiritual promotion.

Pope Alexander knocked about the pate by Hildebrand.

the emperor. Thus, Alexander being kept in custody, and being stinted to a certain allowance, as about five groats a day, Hildebrand encroacheth all the whole revenues of the church to himself, procuring thereby much treasure. At length Alexander, under the miserable endurance of Hildebrand, died at eventide, after eleven years and a half of his popedom. And thus much of Romish matters. *Ecclesiastical affairs.*

These things thus discoursed concerning the matters of Rome, now to return to our own country story, and having the order thereof, would require to enter again into the reign of William the Conqueror, the next king following in England; but as a certain oration of king Edgar's, which should have been inserted before, chanced in the mean time to come to my hands, not unworthy to be read; I thought by the way, at the end of this Book to insert the same, although out of order; yet better I judge it out of order, than out of the book. A.D.1073.

THE ORATION OF KING EDGAR TO THE CLERGY.

"Because God hath shewed his great mercy to work with us, it is meet, most reverend Fathers! that with worthy works we should answer his innumerable benefits. "For we possess not the land by our own sword, and our own arm hath not saved us; but his right hand and his holy arm, because he hath been delighted in us." (Psal. xliv. 3.) Therefore it is meet that we should submit both ourselves and our souls to him, that hath subjected all these things under our government; and we ought stoutly to labour, that they whom he hath made subject to us, might be subject to his laws. It belongs to me to rule the lay people with the law of equity, to do just judgment between man and his neighbour, to punish church-robbers, to hold under rebels, to deliver the helpless from the hand of the stronger, the needy also and the poor from them that rob them. It belongs also to my care to provide necessary things to the ministers of the churches, to the flocks of the monks, to the company of virgins, and to provide for their peace and quiet. The examining of all whose manners belongeth unto us; whether they live chastely, if they behave themselves honestly toward them that be without, whether they be diligent at God's service, if they be earnest to teach the people, if they be sober in eating and drinking, if they keep measure in apparel, and if they be discreet in judgment. If ye had regarded these things with a trial of them, (O reverend Fathers! by your leaves I speak,) such horrible and abominable things of the clerks should not have come unto our ears. I omit to speak how their crown is not broad, nor their rounding convenient: the wantonness in your life, your pride in gesture, the filthiness in your words, do declare the evil of the inward man.

Furthermore, what negligence is in God's service, when scarce they will be present at the holy vigils! And when they come to mass, they seem rather to be gathered to play and laugh than to sing. I will tell that which good men be sorry for, and the evil laugh at. I will speak with sorrow (if so be I may express it) how they be riotous in banquetings, in chambering, in drunkenness, and in unshamefacedness; that now clerks' houses may be thought to be resorts of harlots and covents of players. There be dice, there is dancing and singing, there is watching to midnight, with crying and shouting. Thus the goods of kings, the alms of princes, yea, and what is more, the price of that precious blood, is not esteemed. Have our fathers then spent their treasure for this purpose? Have the king's coffers decayed by taking away many revenues, for this cause? Hath the king's liberality given lands and possessions to Christ's churches for this intent, that clerks' paramours should be decked with the same? that riotous feasts might be dressed? that hounds, and hawks, and such other toys might be gotten? The soldiers cry out at these things, the people grudge, minstrels sing and dance; and yet ye regard it not, ye spare it, ye dissemble it. Where is the sword of Levi, and the zeal of Simeon, (Gen. xxxiv. 25,) which killed the Shechemites and the circumcised, who bare the figure of them that defile Christ's church with filthy deeds, because they abused

Ecclesiastical affairs.

Jacob's daughter? Where is Moses's spirit, who spared not his own kinsfolk that worshipped the head of the calf? (Exod. xxxii. 27.)

Where is Phinehas, the priest's dagger, who pacified God's anger by holy zeal, when he killed him that played the harlot with the Midianite? (Num. xxv. 8.) Where is Peter's spirit, by whose power covetousness is destroyed, and simoniacal heresy is condemned? (Acts iv. 4.) Be earnest, ye priests! be earnest to follow the ways of the Lord, and the righteousness of our God. (Deut. v. 33.) It is time to do against them that have broken the law of God. I have Constantine's sword, and ye have Peter's sword in your hands; let us join right hands, let us couple sword to sword, that the lepers may be cast out of the temples, that the holy place of the Lord may be purged, and the sons of Levi may minister in his temple, who said to his father and mother, "I know you not," and to his brothers, "I know not you." Go to diligently, I pray you, lest we repent to have done that we have done, and to have given that we give, if we shall see that to be spent not in God's service, but on the riotousness of wicked men, through vile and corrupt liberty of life, for lack of chastisement. Let the relics of holy saints, which they despise, and the holy altars before which they play the madmen, move you. Let the great devotion of our ancestors move you, whose alms the madness of the clerks doth abuse. My great grandfather, as ye know, gave the tenth part of all his lands to churches and abbies. My great great grandfather, Alfred, of holy memory, thought it not meet to spare his treasures, his goods, or costs, or rents, that he might enrich the church. My grandfather, the elder Edward, your fatherhood is not ignorant how great things he gave to the churches. It becometh you to remember with what gifts my father and his brothers did enrich Christ's altars. O father of fathers, Dunstan! behold, I pray thee, the eyes of my father looking on thee, from that bright place of heaven; hearken to his complaining words sounding in thine ears, thus pitifully lamenting: "O father Dunstan, thou, thou I say, gavest me counsel to build abbies and churches, thou wast my helper and fellow-worker in all things; I chose thee as a shepherd and bishop of my soul, and a keeper of my manners. When did I not obey thee? What treasures did I prefer in respect of thy counsels? What possessions did I not despise, if thou badest me? If thou thoughtest meet to give any thing to the poor, I was ready. If thou thoughtest meet to give any thing to churches, I deferred not. If thou complainedst that monks or clerks wanted any thing, I supplied. Thou saidst that alms lasted for ever, and that there was none more fruitful than that which was given to abbies or churches; for with that both God's servants are sustained, and that which remaineth is given to the poor. O worthy alms! O worthy price of the soul! O wholesome remedy for our sins, which now doth stink in the sweet furs of priests' lemans,[1] wherewith they adorn their ears and deck their fingers, apparelling their delicate bodies with silk and purple! O father, is this the fruit of my alms, is this the effect of my desire, and of thy promise? What wilt thou answer to this complaint of my fathers? I know, I know: when thou didst see a thief, thou runnest not with him, neither hast thou put thy portion with adulterers. Thou hast rebuked, thou hast exhorted, thou hast blamed them; but words have been despised, now we must come to stripes of correction. Thou hast here with thee, the worshipful father Edward, bishop of Winchester. Thou hast the reverend prelate, Oswald, bishop of Worcester. I commit this business to you, that both by bishoply correction, and the king's authority, the filthy livers may be cast out of the churches, and they that live orderly may be brought in, &c.

Ignorance and superstition of the time of King Edgar.

In this oration of King Edgar, above prefixed, three things are chiefly to be noted and considered of them that have judgment to mark and understand; to wit, the religious zeal and devotion of kings, both in giving to the church, and also in correcting the manners of churchmen. Secondly, the dissolute behaviour and wantonness of the clergy, in then abusing the great donations and patrimonies of princes bestowed upon them. Thirdly, the blind ignorance and superstition

(1) "Lemans," paramours.—ED.

of that time in both states, as well ecclesiastical as temporal, in esteeming Christ's religion chiefly to consist in giving to churches, and in maintaining of monkery; falsely being persuaded that remission of their sins, and remedy of their souls therein, did lie in building monasteries, erecting churches and cloisters, and in placing monks in the same, and such other alms-deeds and works of devotion. Wherein appeareth how ignorant that time was of the true doctrine of Christ's faith, and of the free grace of the gospel, which promiseth life, remedy, and justification, not by any devout merits of ours, nor by any works either of the law of God, or of the inventions of man, but only and freely by our faith in Christ Jesus, the Son of God, in whom only consist all the promises of God.[1] *Amen.*

Ecclesiastical affairs.

The doctrine of justification by faith in Christ unknown.

Now remaineth, as in the former Book before, so in this likewise, to prosecute the order and race of archbishops of Canterbury, as we have done the race of kings, beginning with Ethelred, who succeeded next after Celnocke, the seventeenth archbishop of that see, mentioned where we left before.[2]

The Names and Order of the Archbishops of Canterbury, from the time of King Egbert to William the Conqueror.

18. Ethelred was archbishop of Canterbury for nineteen years.

19. Pleimund, who was schoolmaster to King Alfred, possessed the see of Canterbury for twenty-nine years.

20. Athelm was archbishop for twelve years.

21. Ulfelm for thirteen years.

22. Odo for twenty years. By the prayers of Odo, the monkish stories say that the sword of King Athelstan was brought again into his scabbard, as is noted before in that king's time.

23. Elfius, or Elfin, first bishop of Winchester, came to the see of Canterbury, which he occupied one year, by the commandment of King Edgar, some say by bribes, contrary to the mind of Odo. Whereupon, on the first day of his consecration, he insulting the tomb of Odo with despite, shortly after went to Rome for his pall, where in his journey upon the Alps he died for cold, insomuch that though his horses were killed, and he put in their warm bellies, yet could he get no heat.[3]

24. Dunstan,[4] who was archbishop for twenty years. Of Dunstan many monkish miracles be feigned, as of the harp[5] upon the wall playing by itself, "Gaudent in cœlis," &c.[6] Of our Lady with her company appearing to him singing, "Cantemus Domino sociæ, cantemus honorem; dulcis amor Christi personet ore pio." Also of the angels singing "Kyrie leisone." Item, of holding the devil by the nose with a pair of tongs, for tempting him with women.[7] Item,

(1) The reader can hardly fail to observe the sound and scriptural principles of our author here expressed, and how admirably they harmonize with the received doctrines of the protestant church of Christ. Vid. Art. XVIII.—Ed.

(2) See the names and order of the archbishops of Canterbury at the close of Vol. I.—Ed.

(3) Malmesbury.

(4) Polydore maketh Dunstan to be the twenty-third archbishop.

(5) "St. Dunstan's harp upon the wall,
Fast by a pin did hang a;
Without man's help, with lie and all,
And by itself did twang a."

(6) See page 64. Vol. II.—Ed.

(7) Malmesbury.

Ecclesiastical affairs. of seeing the Holy Ghost at his mass in likeness of a dove. Item, in delivering the soul of Edwin from the devil. Item, in foreseeing the death of King Edred, by the death and falling of his horse. Item, of his mother being great with Dunstan, when all the candles of others went out, her candle only remained alight: and many other like fables.

25. Ethelgar sat for one year.

26. Elfric for eleven years.

27. Siric was archbishop for five years, and was the counsellor to King Egelred, to redeem peace of the Danes with a great tribute.

28. Elphege for six years. Elphege, because he refused to pay the Danes a tribute, was stoned to death at Greenwich, and of some is called a martyr.

29. Livingus for seven years.

30. Egenold for seventeen years.

31. Edsius for eleven years.

32. Robert, who sat for two years, caused Godwin and his sons to be banished, accusing them of treason; but afterwards, they being restored, he went to Rome, and at his return died.

33. Stigand, being an Englishman, in the time of William the Conqueror, the Norman, after being archbishop for seventeen years, was, by the craft of the said William, conveyed into Normandy, where a while with great honour he was entertained. At length, the said William procured secretly the pope's letters to depose him, that he might place Lanfranc in his room. This Stigand died at last in prison.

34. Lanfranc, who held the see for nineteen years.[1]

(1) In the days of Egbert, A.D. 795, Leo III., the ninety-fifth pope, filled the chair. Alexander II., who died A.D. 1073, was the hundred and fifty-fourth pope, including Pope Joan; consequently, since Leo III., sixty individuals occupied the papacy. Of these, a few, either voluntarily or by constraint, had vacated it; but the short average of four years and three months, allotted to sixty popes in succession, leads us reluctantly to conclude, that as our author records, it was not always the progress of disease, or the hand of old age, which caused the vacancy in that high and envied office.—See p. 96 of this volume.—Ed.

END OF BOOK THE THIRD.

ACTS AND MONUMENTS.

BOOK IV.

CONTAINING

ANOTHER THREE HUNDRED YEARS, FROM WILLIAM THE CONQUEROR TO THE TIME OF JOHN WICKLIFF,

WHEREIN IS DESCRIBED THE PROUD AND MISORDERED REIGN OF ANTICHRIST, BEGINNING TO STIR IN THE CHURCH OF CHRIST.[1]

William the Conqueror. A.D. 1066.

WILLIAM, duke of Normandy, sirnamed Conqueror, base son of Duke Robert, the sixth duke of Normandy, and nephew to King Edward, after the aforesaid victory obtained against Harold and the Englishmen, was received king over the realm of England, not so much by assent, as for fear and the necessity of the time; for else the Londoners had promised their assistance to Edgar Etheling to the uttermost of their power. But being weakened and wasted so greatly in former battles, and the duke coming so fast upon them, and fearing that they could not make their party good, they submitted themselves. Whereupon the said William (of a duke made a king) was crowned upon Christmas-day, A.D. 1067, by the hands of Aldred, archbishop of York; forasmuch as at that time Stigand, archbishop of Canterbury, was absent, or else durst not, or would not come into the presence of the king. A little before the coming in of this duke, a terrible blazing star was seen for the space of seven days, which was the year before; in record whereof, as well of the conquest of the duke, as of the blazing star, these verses yet remain:— A.D. 1067. A blazing star.

> "Sexagenus erat sextus millesimus annus,
> Cum pereunt Angli stella monstrante cometa."[2]

William thus being crowned, did reign over the realm of England the space of one and twenty years and one month, with great severity and cruelty toward the Englishmen, burdening them with great tributes and exactions; which was, to pay for every hide of ground containing twenty acres, six shillings; by means whereof certain parts of the land rebelled, and especially the city of Exeter, but at last William overcame them, and won the city, and punished them grievously. But for that and other stern deeds of this prince, divers of the lords departed into Scotland: wherefore he kept the other

Rebellion. Earl Marcarus, and Earl Edwin, Edgar Atheling, with

(1) Edition 1563, p. 14. Ed. 1583, p. 171. Ed. 1596, p. 154. Ed. 1684, vol. i. p. 192.—ED.

(2) In the copy of these verses, p. 14, Ed. 1563, follows a third line:—
"Dux Normanorum transit mare, vicit Heraldum."—ED.

William the Conqueror. A.D. 1067.

lords that tarried the straiter, and exalted the Normans, giving to them the chief possessions of the land; and forasmuch as he obtained the kingdom by force and dint of sword, he changed the whole state of the governance of this commonweal, and ordained new laws at his own pleasure, profitable to himself, but grievous and hurtful to the people, abolishing the laws of King Edward, whereunto notwithstanding, he was sworn before, to observe and maintain them. On this account great commotions and rebellions remained long after among the people, as histories record, to have the said laws of King Edward revived again.

his mother and two sisters, Margaret and Christian, fled into Scotland. New king, new laws. King William forsworn in abolishing King Edward's laws.

* Here,[1] by the way, speaking of laws, this is memorable, that even in this king's time the authority of the temporal magistrate was distinct from that of the church; but yet in such sort, that if need required, he should deal in causes ecclesiastical, and be assistant to the bishop, whose jurisdiction, what it was, and how qualified by King William now holding the stern of government in his hand, the words following do declare.[2]

William, by the grace of God, king of England, to all sheriffs and under-sheriffs, and to all French-born and English, who, in the bishopric of Remigius, the bishop, have lands, greeting. Know you all, and the rest my faithful subjects, who abide in England, that the bishop's laws which have been not well, nor according to the precepts of holy canons, even to my time in the kingdom of England; by the common council and the council of mine archbishops, and the rest of the bishops and abbots, with all the princes of my kingdom, I have judged to be amended. Wherefore I command, and by my royal authority give in charge, that no bishop or archdeacon do hold any more pleas of law in the hundred by the bishop's laws, nor bring any cause which pertaineth to the cure of souls unto the judgment of secular men: but whosoever, according to the bishop's laws, about any suit or default be troubled, shall come to the place, which to this end the bishop shall choose and name, and there answer his cause, and not according as in the hundred, but according to the canons and laws of the bishop, they shall do right unto God and to their bishop. And if any, puffed up with pride, being called once, twice, and thrice to the court of pleas, refuseth to come, and will not so be drawn to amendment, let him be excommunicated. And if need be, to correct and revenge this, let the power and justice of the king's under-sheriff be used. And he who, being called or summoned to the bishop's court, will not come, for every calling shall be put to his answer before the bishop, and make amends. And this I defend, and by mine authority forbid, that no under-sheriff or provost, or officer of the king, or any layman, meddle or make with the laws belonging to the bishop; nor that any layman bring or sue another out of the bishop's court of justice unto judgment. And as for judgment, let it be given in no place but in the bishop's see, or in that place which in this behalf the bishop shall appoint.

The jurisdiction ecclesiastical qualified and circumscribed in King William's time.

By this evidence of record it is manifest, as you see, that Duke William (now king) having assumed unto himself the absolute authority royal, endeavoured to establish a form of government both in the church and commonwealth answerable to his own mind: howbeit, this is to be noted, that he allowed unto the clergy a kind of jurisdiction of conventing persons before them, and likewise of exercising such ecclesiastical discipline as the quality of that age and time did use, whereon we will not stand to debate any thing at large, but proceed in the course of our story, as the Spirit of God shall vouchsafe to direct us.*

(1) This passage in single asterisks is not in the Edition of 1583, but it appears in that of 1596.—Ed.

(2) "Willielmus Gratia Dei Rex Anglorum, comitibus, vicecomitibus, et omnibus Francigenis et Anglis, qui in Episcopatu Remigii Episcopi terras habent, salutem. Sciatis," &c.—Turris Londin.

Over and besides this, *the aforesaid William, as he was a warrior, so he delighting in forts and bulwarks,*[1] builded four strong castles, two at York, one at Nottingham, and another at Lincoln, which garrisons he furnished with Normans. *William the Conqueror.* A.D. 1069.

About the third year of his reign, Harold and Canute, sons of Swanus, king of Denmark, entered into the north country. The Normans within York, fearing that the Englishmen would aid the Danes, fired the suburbs of the town; whereof the flame was so big, and the wind so strong, that it reached the city, and burnt a great part thereof, with the minster of St. Peter, where no doubt many worthy works and monuments of books were consumed, in the time whereof the Danes, by favour of some of the citizens, entered the city, and slew more than three thousand of the Normans. But not long after King William chased them out, and drove them to their ships, and took such displeasure with the inhabitants of that country, that he destroyed the land from York to Durham, so that nine years after the province lay waste and unmanured, except only St. John's land of Beverly; and the people thereof were so strictly kept in penury by the war of the king, that, as our English story saith, they eat rats, cats, and dogs, and other vermin. **York, with the minster, burnt.** **The north country wasted with war and famine.**

Also, in the fourth year of this king, Malcolm, king of Scots, entered into Northumberland, and destroyed the country, and slew there much of the people, both men, women, and children, after a lamentable sort, and took some prisoners. But within two years after, King William made such war upon the Scots, that he forced Malcolm their king to do him homage. **A.D. 1070. Malcolm III., king of Scots, subdued.**

And thus much concerning the outward calamities of this realm under this foreign conqueror, which is now the fifth time that the said land with the inhabitants thereof hath been scourged by the hand of God. First, by the Romans in the time of Julius Cæsar; then by the Scots and Picts, as hath been showed; afterward by the Saxons. Again, the Saxons or Englishmen did not enjoy the possession of Britain with long quiet, but were brought into as much subjection themselves under the Danes as they had brought the Britons before, and even much more, insomuch that through all England, if an Englishman had met a Dane upon a bridge, he might not stir one foot before the Lord Dane (otherwise Lurdane) were past. And then if the Englishman had not given low reverence to the Dane at his coming by, he was sure to be sharply punished, as above hath been declared. This subjection continued almost from the reign of King Ethelwolf till the reign of King Edward, for the space of two hundred and thirty years; and yet the indignation of God then ceased not, but stirred up the Normans against them, who conquered and altered the whole realm after their own purpose; insomuch that besides the innovation of the laws, coins, and possessions, there was almost in no church in England any English bishop, but only Normans and foreigners placed through all their dioceses.[2] To such misery was this land then brought, that not only of all the English nobility not one house was standing, but also it was thought reproachful to be called an Englishman. This punishment of God **Five conquests which have been in this realm.**

(1) This passage in italic is not in the Edition of 1583, but is found in that of 1596.—Ed.
(2) Ex Henr. Huntingdon. lib. vi.

William the Conqueror. A.D. 1070.

against the English nation, writers do assign diversely to divers causes, as partly before is touched; of whom some assign this to be the cause as followeth in the words of the story:—"That whereas kings and queens, dukes and prelates, in the primitive time of the English church, were ready, for religion, to forsake either liberty or country, and give themselves to a solitary life, in process of time they grew to such dissoluteness, that they left no other realm like unto them in iniquity,"[1] &c. Again some, writing of the vision of King Edward, a little before the invasion of the Normans, testify how the king, reporting of his own vision, should hear that for the great enormity and misbehaviour of the head dukes, bishops, and abbots of the realm, the kingdom should be given to the hand of their enemies after the decease of him, for the space of one hundred years and one day; which space was also seen by William the Conqueror, to be one hundred and fifty years, and that his progeny so long should continue. Again, some writers, treating of this so great wrath of God upon the English people, declare the cause thereof as followeth:—"Like as the Englishmen did subdue the Britons, whom God proposed for their deservings to exterminate, and them unjustly did dispossess of their land, so they should likewise be subdued and scourged with a double persecution, first by the Danes, and after by the Normans,"[2] &c. Moreover to these injuries and iniquities done and wrought by the Englishmen, hitherto recited, let us add also the cruel villany of this nation, in murdering and tithing the innocent Normans before, who coming as strangers with Alfred, the lawful heir of the crown, were despitefully put to death; which seemeth to me no little cause why the Lord, whose doings be always just and right, did suffer the Normans so to prevail. By the coming in of these Normans, and by their quarrel unto the realm, three things we may note and learn. First, to consider and learn the righteous retribution and wrath of God from heaven upon all iniquity and unrighteous dealing of men. Secondly, we may thereby note, what it is for princes to leave no issue or sure succession behind them. Thirdly, what dangers often do chance to realms public by foreign marriage with other princes.

Vision of King Edward.

Englishmen scourged for their unjust oppression of the Britons.

Cruelties against the Normans.

Three things in this conquest to be noted.

A.D. 1070. Council at Winchester. Divers bishops, abbots, and priors deposed.

In the same fourth year of this king, between Easter and Whitsuntide, was holden a solemn council of the clergy of England at Winchester, at which were present two cardinals sent from Pope Alexander II., Peter and John. In this council, the king being present, were deposed divers bishops, abbots, and priors, by the means of the king, without any evident cause; to the intent his Normans might be preferred to the rule of the church, as he had preferred his knights before to the rule of the temporality, thereby to stand in more surety of the land: amongst whom also Stigand, archbishop of Canterbury, was put down for three causes against him pretended.

(1) "In primitiva Angliæ ecclesia religio clarissime splenduit, ita ut reges et reginæ, duces et episcopi, vel monachatum, vel exilium pro Dei amore appeterent: processu vero temporis adeo omnis virtus in eis emarcuit, ut gentem nullam proditione et nequitia sibi parem esse permitterent," &c.—Ex Histor. Jornalens.

(2) "Nam sicut Angli, Britones quos Deus disterminare proposuerat (peccatis suis exigentibus) humiliaverant, et a terra Angliæ minus juste fugaverant: sic ipsi duplici persecutione," &c.

William the Conqueror.

A.D. 1070.

The first was for that he had holden wrongfully that bishopric, while Robert, the archbishop, above mentioned, was living.

The second was for that he had received the pall of Benedict V., bishop of Rome, who, for buying his popedom, had been deposed, as is showed before.

The third cause was, for that he occupied the said pall without license and lawful authority of the court of Rome.

A.D. 1070.

Then Stigand well proved the benevolence of King William, for whereas before, the king seemed in friendly countenance to make much of him, and did unto him great reverence, he then changed all his mildness into sternness, and excused himself by the bishop of Rome's authority, so that in the end Stigand was deprived of his dignity, and kept in Winchester as a prisoner during his life. This Stigand is noted for a man so covetous and sparing, that when he would take nothing of his own, and would swear that he had not a penny, yet by a key fastened about his neck, was found great treasure of his under ground.

Lanfranc, an Italian, archbishop of Canterbury.

At this time was preferred to the archbishopric of York, Thomas, a Norman, and canon of Bayonne. At the same time also Lanfranc, abbot of Cadomonency, a Lombard and Italian born, was sent for, and made archbishop of Canterbury, between which two archbishops, about their consecration, first began a contention for giving and taking the oath of obedience; but that contention was, at that time, appeased by the king, and Thomas was contented to subscribe to the archbishop of Canterbury's obedience.

The minster of York rebuilt.

The giving of the pall.

After this, it followed within short space, that the said Lanfranc, and Thomas, archbishop of York, who first builded the minster of York, and gave possessions thereunto, came to Rome with Remigius, bishop of Dorchester, for their palls, as the manner was; without which no archbishop nor bishop could be confirmed, although their election were never so lawful. This pall must be asked nowhere but of the pope or his assigns, and that within three months; also it must be asked not faintly, but mightily (Dist. 100, cap. "prisca"), which, as it was a chargeable thing to other nations, especially such as were far from Rome, so it was no small gain to the Romish see, as they did order it. For although, at the beginning, the pall was given without money according to the decree, Dist. 100,[1] or for little, as was the case in this time of Lanfranc;[2] yet, in process of years, it grew to such excess, that whereas the bishopric of Mentz was wont to give to Rome but ten thousand florins, afterwards, it arose so, that he who asked his confirmation, could not obtain it without twenty thousand; and from thence it exceeded to five and twenty thousand, and at length to seven and twenty thousand florins, which sum Jacob, archbishop of Mentz, was pressed to pay a little before the Council of Basil; insomuch that the said Jacob at his departing, which was within four years after, said, that his death did not so much grieve him as to remember his poor subjects, who should be constrained to pay so terrible a fine for the pope's pall. Now by this, what did arise to the pope in the whole of Germany, containing in it above fifty bishoprics, may be easily conjectured. Lanfranc thus coming to Rome, with the other two bishops, he, for

Eneas Silvius writeth that there be fifty

(1) Dist. 100, cap. "novit." (2) Ex lib. Gravaminum Nationis Germanicæ.

William the Conqueror.

A.D. 1070.

the estimation of his learning, obtained of Alexander two palls, one of honour, the other of love. Item, he obtained for the other two bishops also their confirmation. At this time, they being there present before Alexander, the controversy began first to be moved, or rather renewed, for the primacy betwixt the two metropolitans, that is, betwixt the archbishop of Canterbury and the archbishop of York, whether of them should have pre-eminence above the other; for Canterbury challenged to himself prerogative and primacy over the whole of Britain and Ireland. This contention continued a long season betwixt these two churches, and was often renewed in the days of divers kings after this; as in the reign of Henry I., betwixt Thurstin of York and Radulph of Canterbury; and again, in the seven and twentieth year of the said king, at his second coronation, for Radulph would not suffer the first coronation to stand, because it was done by the bishop of York, without his assent. Also, in the reign of Henry II., where Pope Alexander made a letter decretal betwixt these two metropolitans, for bearing the cross, A.D. 1159. Also, at another time, in the reign of the said king, betwixt Richard of Canterbury and Roger of York. Again, about A.D. 1170, when Thomas Becket, hearing the king to be crowned of Roger, bishop of York, complained thereof grievously to Pope Alexander III. Item, at another time, A.D. 1176, betwixt Richard and the said Roger, whether of them should sit on the right hand of Cardinal Hugo in his council in London. Moreover, in the beginning of the reign of King Richard, A.D. 1190, betwixt Baldwin of Canterbury and Godfrid of York.

Bishoprics in Germany.

Now to proceed in the story: after this question was brought, as is said, to the pope's presence, he being not disposed to decide the matter, sent them home to England, there to have their cause determined. Whereupon they, speeding themselves from Rome to England A.D. 1072, and in the sixth year, as it is said, of this William, brought the matter before the king and the clergy at Windsor. On this occasion, Lanfranc, first alleging for himself, brought in how that from the time of Austin to that of Bede (about one hundred and forty years), the bishop of Canterbury had ever the primacy over the whole land of Britain and Ireland; how he kept his councils divers times within the precints of York; how he did call and cite the bishops of York thereto, whereof some he did constitute, some he did excommunicate, and some he did remove: besides which he alleged divers privileges granted by princes and prelates to the primacy of that see.

To this Thomas, archbishop of York, replieth again, and first beginning with the first original of the Britons' church, declareth, in order of time, how the Britons, first possessors of this kingdom of Britain, which endured from Brutus and Cadwalladar two thousand and seventy-six years, under a hundred and two kings, at length receiving the christian faith A.D. 162, in the time of Lucius, their king, when Eleutherius, bishop of Rome, sent Faganus and Damanus as preachers unto them; at which time, after their conversion, they assigned and ordained in the realm eight and twenty bishops, with two archbishops, Theonus, the archbishop of London, and Theodosius, archbishop of York. Under those bishops and

Lucius, the first king of Britain, christened.

Theonus, first archbishop of London.

archbishops the church of Britain was governed after their conversion, almost three hundred years, till at length the Saxons, being then infidels, with Hengist their king, subduing the Britons by fraudulent murder, invaded their land, which was about A.D. 440.[1] After this, the Britons being driven into Cambria, which we now call Wales, the Saxons overrunning the land, divided themselves into seven kingdoms; and so, being infidels and pagans, continued till the time that Gregory, bishop of Rome, sent Augustine to preach unto them; who, coming first to Dover, being then the chief city of Kent (called in Latin Dorobernia), and there planting himself, converted first the king of Kent, called Ethelbert, who had then subdued certain other kings as far as the Humber. By reason of this Augustine was made archbishop of Dover, by the appointment of Gregory I., about A.D. 600, who sent him certain palls with his letter from Rome, as before is expressed,[2] which letter being recited, Thomas expounding upon the same, beginneth to declare for himself, how the meaning of Gregory in this letter was, to reduce the new church of Saxons or Englishmen to the order that was in the old time among the Britons; that is, to be under two metropolitans, one of London, the other of York; for so the church was ordered in the time of the Britons, as is before declared. Notwithstanding he giveth to Augustine this prerogative during his lifetime, to have authority and jurisdiction, not only over his twelve bishops, but upon all other bishops and priests in England; and after his decease then these two metropolitans, London and York, to oversee the whole clergy, as in times past amongst the Britons, whom he joineth together after the death of Augustine, to constitute bishops, and to oversee the church. That he meaneth London to be equal in authority with York, it appeareth by four arguments. First, in that he willeth London to be consecrated by no bishop, but of his own synod. Secondly, in that he willeth no distinction of honour to be betwixt London and York, but only according to that as each one of them is elder in time. Thirdly, in that he matcheth these two together in common council, and with one agreement to consent together in doing and disposing such things as they shall consult upon, in the zeal of Christ Jesus; and that, in such sort, that one should not dissent nor discord from the other. What meaneth this, but that they should govern together, whom he would not to dissent together? Fourthly, in that he writeth, that the bishop of York should not be subject to the bishop of London; what meaneth this, but that the bishop of London should be equivalent with the metropolitan of York, or rather superior unto him?

This was about 150 years after the coming of the Saxons.

And thus he expounded the meaning of Gregory to be in the aforesaid letter. To whom Lanfranc again answereth, that he was not the bishop of London, and that the question pertained not to London. Thomas replieth, having on his part many favourers, that this privilege was granted by Gregory to Augustine alone, to have all other bishops subject to him; but after his decease there should be equality of honour betwixt London and York, without any distinction of priority, save only that priority of time should make superiority between them. And although Augustine translated the see from London to Kent, yet Gregory, if his mind had been to give the same

(1) Ex Chronic. Sigeberti. (2) See vol. i.

William the Conqueror. A.D. 1072.

prerogative to the successors of Augustine, which he gave to him, would expressly have uttered it in the words of his epistle, writing thus to Augustine: "That which I give to thee, Augustine, I give also and grant to all thy successors after thee." But in that he maketh here no mention of his successors, it appeareth thereby, that it was not his mind so to do.

To this Lanfranc argueth again, "If this authority had been given to Augustine alone, and not to his successors, it had been but a small gift, proceeding from the apostolic see, to his special and familiar friend; especially seeing also that Augustine in all his life did constitute no bishop of York, neither was there any such bishop to be subject to him. Again, we have privileges from the apostolic see, which confirm this dignity in the successors of Augustine, in the same see of Dover. Moreover, all Englishmen think it both right and reason to fetch the direction of well living from that place, where first they took the sparkle of right believing. Further, whereas you say that Gregory might have confirmed with plain words the same thing to the successors of Augustine, which he gave unto him; all that I grant: yet notwithstanding, this is nothing prejudicial to the see of Canterbury. For, if you know your logic, that which is true in the whole is also true in the part; and what is true in the more, is also true in the less. Now the church of Rome is as the whole, to whom all other churches be as parts thereof; and as 'homo,' *i. e.* mankind, is 'genus,' *i. e.* the general in a certain respect to all his 'individua,' *i. e.* to all particular persons, yet in every particular person lieth the property of the general; so in like manner the see of Rome in a certain respect is the general, and the whole to other churches, and yet in every particular church is contained the whole fulness of the whole christian faith. As the church of Rome is greater than all churches, that which is wrought in it ought to work in the less churches also, so that the authority of every chief head of the church ought to stand also in them that do succeed, unless there be any precise exception made by name. Wherefore like as the Lord said to all bishops of Rome the same thing which he said to Peter, so Gregory in like manner said to all the successors of Augustine, that which he said to Augustine; so thus I conclude, likewise as the bishop of Canterbury is subject to Rome, because he had his faith from thence, so York ought to be in subjection to Canterbury, which sent the first preachers thither. Now, whereas you allege, that Gregory would Augustine to be resident in London, that is utterly uncertain, for how is it to be thought that such a disciple would do contrary to the mind of such a master? But grant, as you say, that Augustine removed to London, what is that to me, who am not bishop of London? Notwithstanding all this controversy ceasing betwixt us, if it shall please you to come to some peaceable composition with me, all contention set apart, you shall find me not out of the way, so far as reason and equity shall extend."

Dignity of Canterbury confirmed.

Well replied of an Italian.

If this similitude were formed into a syllogism, neither were the major true; and especially the minor were utterly false.

With these reasons of Lanfranc, Thomas gave over, condescending that his province should begin at the Humber. Whereupon it was then decreed that York from that time should be subject to Canterbury in all matters appertaining to the rites and regiment of the catholic church; so that wheresoever within England Canter-

William the Conqueror. A.D. 1072

bury should or would hold his council, the bishop of York should resort thither with his bishops, and be obedient to his decrees canonical. Provided moreover that when the bishop of Canterbury should decease, York should repair unto Dover, there to consecrate with others the bishops that should be elect. And if York should decease, his successor should resort to Canterbury, or else where the bishop of Canterbury should appoint, there to receive his consecration, making his profession there, with an oath of canonical obedience. Thomas being content withal, Lanfranc, the Italian, triumpheth with no small joy, and putteth the matter forthwith in writing, that the memory thereof might remain to the posterity of his successors. But yet that decree did not long stand; for, shortly after, the same scar, so superficially cured, burst out again, insomuch that in the reign of King Henry I., A.D. 1121, Thurstin, archbishop of York, could not be compelled to swear to the archbishop of Canterbury; and yet, notwithstanding, by the letters of Calixtus II., was consecrated without any profession made to the said bishop, with much more matter of contention, all which to recite it were too long. But this I thought to commit to history, to the intent men might see the lamentable decay of true Christianity amongst the christian bishops, who, inflamed with glorious ambition, so contended for honour, that without mere forcement of law, no modesty could take place.

Of divers such contentions among prelates of the clergy for superiority, we read in old chronicles, as in the history entitled Chronicon Hirfeldense, where is declared a bloody conflict, which twice happened in the church of Goslaria, between Hecelon, bishop of Hildesheime, and Wederatus, bishop of Fulda, and all for the superior place, who should sit next to the emperor; the emperor himself being there present, and looking on, and yet not able to stay them.

Thus I have described the troublous contention between Lanfranc and Thomas, metropolitan of York, in the days of Alexander, of which controversy, and of the whole discourse thereof, Lanfranc writeth to Pope Alexander.[1]

Bishops' sees translated in England.

In the story before of King Egelred, was declared, about A.D. 1016, how the bishopric of Lindisfarne, otherwise named Holy-island, in the flood of Tweed, was translated to Durham; so likewise in the days of this Lanfranc, archbishop of Canterbury, A.D. 1076, divers bishops' sees were altered and removed from townships to greater cities; as the bishopric of Selese to Chichester; of Cornwall to Exeter; of Wells to Bath; of Sherborne to Salisbury; of Dorchester to Lincoln; of Lichfield to Chester; the bishopric of Chester, Robert being then bishop, being reduced from Chester to Coventry. Likewise after that, in the reign of William Rufus, A.D. 1095, Herbert, bishop of Thetford, from thence reduced the see to Norwich, &c.

(1) The letter of Lanfranc sent to Pope Alexander begins thus —"Domino totius Christianæ religionis summo speculatori Alex papæ, Lancfrancus sanctæ Dorobernensis ecclesiæ antistes, debitam cum omni servitute obedientiam In concilio quod Angliæ per vestram authoritatem coactum est, ubi querelæ Thomæ Archiepiscopi prolatæ et ventilatæ sunt, allata est Ecclesiastica gentis Anglorum Historia, quam Eboracensis ecclesiæ Presbyter, et Anglorum doctor Beda composuit." and so forth, in a long process of words which follow, among which, in the middle of the epistle, speaking of Dover and Canterbury, he hath these words "Urbs namque, quæ nunc Cantuarberia nominatur, antiquis temporibus, ab ipsius terræ incolis Doroberina vocabatur," &c With many other words in the said epistle, which for brevity I here over-pass.

William the Conqueror. A.D. 1072.

As concerning Dover and Canterbury, whether the see was likewise translated from the town of Dover to the city of Canterbury in the time of Theodore, or whether Canterbury in old time had the name of Dorobernia, as the letter of Lanfranc to Pope Alexander abovementioned doth pretend, I find it not in histories expressly defined; save that I read in the words of William, being yet duke of Normandy, charging Harold to make a well of water for the king's use in the castle of Dorobernia, that the said Dorobernia then was taken for that which we now call Dover; but whether Dorobernia and the city of Canterbury be both one or divers, the matter is not great. Notwithstanding this I read in the epistle of Pope Boniface to King Ethelbert, as also in one to Justin, the archbishop; in one of Pope Honorius to Bishop Honorius; in one of Pope Vitalianus to Theodore; in one of Pope Sergius to King Ethelred, Alfred and Adulphus, and to the bishops of England; likewise in one of Pope Gregory III. to the bishops of England; of Pope Leo to Athelard, archbishop of Canterbury; of Formosus to the bishops of England; and of Pope John to Dunstan; that the names of Dorobernia and Canterbury indifferently are taken for one matter.

Council holden at London. A.D. 1075.

In this time, and by the procuring of this Lanfranc, the ninth year of this king, a council was holden at London, where among the acts thereof these were the principal things concluded:—

I. For the order of sitting, that the archbishop of York should sit on the right hand, and the bishop of London on the left hand; or in the absence of York, London should have the right, and Winchester the left hand of the archbishop of Canterbury sitting in council.

II. That bishops should translate their sees from villages into cities: (whereupon those sees abovenamed were translated.)

III. That monks should have nothing in proper; and if any so had, he dying unconfessed should not be buried in the churchyard.

IV. That no clerk or monk of any other diocese should be admitted to orders, or retained without letters commendatory or testimonial.

V. That none should speak in the council except bishops and abbots, without leave of the arch-metropolitans.

VI. That none should marry within the seventh degree, with any either of his own kindred, or of his wives departed.

VII. That none should either buy or sell any office within the church.

VIII. That no sorcery or any divination should be used or permitted in holy church.

IX. That no bishop or abbot, or any of the clergy, should be at the judgment of any man's death or dismembering, neither should be any fautor of the said judicants.

Bishops of England drive out monks, and place priests in their stead.

Moreover in the days of this Lanfranc divers good bishops of the realm began to take part with priests against the monks, in displacing these out of their churches, and in restoring the married priests again, insomuch that Walkelm, bishop of Winchester, had placed above forty canons instead of monks for his part; but this godly enterprize was stopped by stout Lanfranc, the Italian Lombard. This lusty prelate sat nineteen years, but, at his latter end, he was not so favoured of William Rufus, and died for sorrow. Although this Italian Frank being archbishop had little leisure to write, yet something he thought to do to set out his famous learning, and wrote a book against Berengarius, entitling it "Opus Scintillarum." The old church of Canterbury he plucked down, and builded up the new.

William the Conqueror.

A.D. 1073.

After the death of Pope Alexander II., abovementioned, next unto him followed Hildebrand, surnamed Gregory VII. This Hildebrand, as he was a sorcerer, so was he the first and principal cause of all this perturbation that is now, and hath been since his time, in the church; by reason that through his example all this ambition, stoutness, and pride, entered first into the church of Rome, and hath ever since continued. For before Hildebrand came to Rome, working there his feats, setting up and displacing what bishops he listed, corrupting them with pernicious counsel, and setting them against emperors, under pretence of chastity destroying matrimony, and under the title of liberty breaking peace, and resisting authority; before this, I say, the church of Rome was in some order, and bishops were quietly governed under christian emperors, and also were defended by the same; as Marcellus, Miltiades, and Sylvester were subdued, and under obedience to Constantine, A.D. 340; Siricius to Theodosius, A.D. 388; Hilary to Justinian, A.D. 528; Gregory to Mauritius, A.D. 600; Adrian and Leo to Charlemagne, A.D. 801; Paschal and Valentius to Ludovicus Pius, A.D. 830; Sergius II. to Lothaire, A.D. 840; Benedict III. and John IX., to Louis, son of Lothaire, A.D. 856.

Hildebrand, the cause of all the stoutness and pride in prelates.

The obedience of bishops in ancient time to emperors.

Against this obedience and subjection Hildebrand was the first who began to spurn, and by his example taught all other bishops to do the like; insomuch that at length they wrought and brought to pass that it should be lawful for a few courtesans and cardinals (contrary to ancient ordinance and statutes decretal) to choose what pope they list, without any consent of the emperor at all. And whereas before it stood in the emperors' gift to give and to grant bishoprics, archbishoprics, benefices, and other ecclesiastical preferments within their own limits, to whom they list; now the popes, through much wrestling, wars, and contention, have extorted all that into their own hands, and to their assigns, yea, have plucked in all the riches and power of the whole world; and not content with that, have usurped and prevailed so much above emperors, that, as before, no pope might be chosen without the confirmation of the emperor, so now no emperor may be elected without the confirmation of the pope, taking upon them more than princes to place or displace emperors at their pleasure for every light cause, and to put down or set up when and whom they listed; as Frederic I., for holding the left stirrup of the pope's saddle, was persecuted almost to excommunication; which cause moveth me to strain more diligence here, in setting out the history, acts, and doings of this Hildebrand, from whom, as the first patron and founder, sprang all this ambition and contention about the liberties and dominion of the Roman church; to the intent that such as cannot read the Latin histories may understand in English the original of evils: how and by what occasion they first began, and how long they have continued.

Popes have usurped more than princes.

Frederic I. for holding the pope's left stirrup, is persecuted.

And first, how this Hildebrand hitherto had behaved himself before he was pope, I have partly declared. For though he was not yet pope in name, yet he was then pope indeed, and ruled the popes and all their doings as him listed. Item, what ways and fetches he

William the Conqueror. A.D. 1073. had attempted ever since his first coming to the court of Rome, to magnify and maintain false liberty against true authority; what practice he wrought by councils, what factions and conspiracies he made, in stirring up popes against emperors, striving for superiority; and what wars followed thereof, I have also expressed. Now let us see further (by the help of Christ) the worthy virtues of this princely prelate, after he came to be pope, as they remain in histories of divers and sundry writers described.

The tragical history of Gregory VII., otherwise named Hildebrand.

A.D.1073. "Hitherto the bishops of Rome have been elected by voices and suffrages of all sorts and degrees, as well of the priests and the clergy, as of the nobility, people, and senate, all conventing and assembling together."[1] And this election I find to stand in force, if so be it were ratified and confirmed by the consent of Roman emperors who had authority to call and to assemble all these, as well as bishops, together unto councils as case required. Under the authority and jurisdiction of these emperors were contained both in Germany, France, and Italy, and throughout the whole dominion of Rome, all patriarchs, bishops, masters of churches and monasteries, by the decree of councils, according to the old custom of our ancestors, as is declared in a certain story in the life of Charlemagne. The holy and ancient fathers (like as Christ our Lord with his disciples and apostles both taught and did) honoured and esteemed their emperors as the supreme potestate next under God on earth, set up, ordained, elected and crowned of God, above all other mortal men, and so counted them, and called them their lords. To them they yielded tribute, and paid their subsidies, and also prayed every day for their life. Such as rebelled against them they took as rebels and resisters against God's ordinance and christian piety. The name of the emperor then was of great majesty, and received as given from God. Then these fathers of the church never intermeddled nor entangled themselves with politic affairs of the commonweal; much less occupied they martial arms and matters of chivalry. Only in poverty and modesty was all their contention with other christians, who should be poorest and most modest among them, and the more humbleness appeared in any, the higher opinion they conceived of him. The sharp and two-edged sword they took, given to the church of Christ, to save, and not to kill; to quicken, and not to destroy; and called it the sword of the Spirit, which is the word of God, the life and light of men, and revoketh from death to life, making of men, gods; of mortal, immortal. Far were they from that, to thrust out any prince or king (though he were ever so far out of the way, yea an Arian) from his kingdom, or to curse him, to release his subjects from their oath and their allegiance, to change and translate kingdoms, to subvert empires, to pollute themselves with christian blood, or to war with their christian brethren for rule and principality. This was not their spirit and manner then, but rather they loved and obeyed their princes. Again, princes loved them also like fathers

The state of the old church in times past.

Reverence and obedience given to princes.

The manner and virtue of the forefathers of the church.

(1) The words of the Latin History be these:—"Hactenus Pontifices Rom. comitiis curiatis, calatis, a sacerdotibus, equitatu, plebe, senatu," &c.—Ex Aventino.

William the Conqueror.

A.D. 1074.

and fellow-princes with them over the souls of men. Now this Gregory VII., otherwise named Hildebrand, trusting to the Normans, who then ruffled about Apulia, Calabria, and Campania, trusting also to the power of Matilda, a stout woman there about Rome; and partly again bearing himself bold for the discord among the Germans; first of all others, and contrary to the manner of elders, contemning the authority of the emperor, invaded the cathedral see of Rome, vaunting himself, as having both the ecclesiastical and temporal sword committed to him by Christ, and that fulness of power was in his hand, to bind and loose whatsoever he listed. Whereupon thus he presumed to occupy both the regiments, to challenge all the whole dominion, both of the east and west church, yea, and all power to himself alone, abiding none to be equal, much less superior unto him; derogating from others, and arrogating to himself their due right and honour, setting at light Cesars, kings and emperors, and who thus reigned but by his own god-a-mercy. Bishops and prelates as his underlings he kept in awe, suspending and cursing, and chopping off their heads, stirring up strife and wars, sowing of discord, making factions, releasing oaths, defeating fidelity and due allegiance of subjects to their princes. Yea, and if he had offended, or injured the emperor himself, yet notwithstanding he ought to be feared, as he himself glorieth in a certain epistle, as one that could not err, and had received of Christ our Saviour, and of Peter, authority to bind and unbind at his will and pleasure.[1] Priests then in those days had wives openly and lawfully, no law forbidding to the contrary, as appeareth by the deed and writings of their chapter-seals and donations, which were given to temples and monasteries, wherein their wives also be cited with them for witness, and were called Presbyterissæ. Also bishops, prelates, parsons of churches, governors of the clergy, masters of monasteries, and religious houses—all these were, in those times, by the emperor's ordination, to assign by voice or consent to whom he would. Now these two things this Pope Gregory could not abide; for which two causes only was all his striving and driving from his first beginning to abolish the marriage of priests, and to translate the authority imperial to the clergy; for to this scope only tended all his labour, practices, and devices, as appeared before in the council of Lateran under Pope Nicholas, and also in the council of Mantua under Alexander, making their marriage heresy, and the other to be simony. And that which before he went about by others, now he practiseth by himself, to condemn ministers that were married for Nicolaitans, and to treat any spiritual regiment of secular persons as simony, directing forth his letters upon the same to Henry the emperor; also to dukes, princes, potestates, tetrarchs; namely to Berchtold, to Rodolph of Suabia, to Welph, Adalberon, and to their wives; also to bishops, archbishops, priests, and to all the people. In these letters he denounceth them to be no priests, so many as were married, forbidding men to salute them, to talk, to eat, to keep company with them, to pay them tithes, or to obey them if they would not be obedient to him. Amongst others he directed special letters to Otho, bishop of Constance, concerning this matter; but Otho, perceiving the ungodly and unreasonable pretence

The ambitious presumption of Hildebrand.

Priests' wives called presbiterissæ.

Hildebrand a mortal enemy to priests' marriages.

A.D. 1074.

Priests' marriage made heresy, and spiritual regiment of secular persons held to be simony.

(1) Ex Aventino, qui invenit in instrumentis donationum.

William the Conqueror. of Hildebrand, would never separate those who were married from their wives, nor yet forbid those to marry who were unmarried."

A.D. 1074.

The copy of the letter of Hildebrand sent to the bishop of Constance, against priests' marriages.

Gregory, bishop, servant of the servants of God, to the clergy and laity, both more and less, within the diocese of Constance, salutation and benediction. We have directed to our brother Otho, your bishop, our letters exhortatory; wherein we enjoined him, according to the necessity of our duty, by the authority apostolical, that he should utterly abolish out of his church the heresy of simony, and also should cause with all diligence to be preached the chastity of priests. But he, neither moved with reverence for St. Peter's precept, nor yet with the regard of his duty, neglected to do these things, whereunto we so fatherly have exhorted him; incurring thereby a double offence, not only of disobedience, but also of rebellion, in that he hath gone and done clean contrary to our commandment, yea, rather the commandment of blessed St. Peter, so that he hath permitted his clergy, not only such as had wives, not to put them away, but also such as had none, to take unto them. Whereupon we being truly informed thereof, and grieved therewith, have directed to him another letter, declaring the motion of our displeasure and indignation. In which letters also we have cited him up to our council at Rome, there to appear and give account of his disobedience in the audience of the whole synod. And now therefore we thought it best to signify this to you (our dear children), whereby in this behalf we might the better provide for your health and salvation; for if your bishop shall continue so obstinately to repugn and resist against our commandment, he is not meet to sit over you, &c. Wherefore these shall be to command you, and all those that be obedient to God, and to blessed St. Peter, by our apostolical authority, that if this your bishop shall persist in his obstinacy, you that be his subjects hereafter give to him no service nor obedience; for the which thing doing, we here discharge you before God and your souls. For if your bishop shall seem contrary to the decreements and injunctions apostolical, we, through the apostolical authority of St. Peter, discharge and absolve you from the band of your allegiance to him. So that if you be sworn to him, so long as he is a rebel against God and the apostolic seat, we loose you from the peril of your oath, that you shall not need to fear therein any danger, &c.

Otho, bishop of Constance, cited to appear, for allowing priests their lawful wives.

The pope dispenseth for disobedience.

Otho, bishop of Constance, thus being cited, whether he did appear personally himself, I do not read. This I read and find, that in the said council holden at Rome, Hildebrand, with other bishops of Rome, did then enact, among many others, these three things most special:—First, that no priest, hereafter, should marry. Secondly, that all such as were married should be divorced. Thirdly, that none hereafter should be admitted to the order of priesthood, but should swear perpetual chastity, &c. This council of Rome being ended, forthwith the act of Hildebrand concerning the single life of priests was proclaimed and published in all places, and strict commandment given to bishops to execute the same.

Here cometh in the vow of chastity.

The copy of his Bull sent into Italy and Germany.

Gregory, the pope, otherwise Hildebrand, the servant of the servants of God, sendeth the apostle's blessing to all those within the kingdoms of Italy and Germany, who show their true obedience to St. Peter. If there be any priests, deacons, and subdeacons, that still will remain in the sin of fornication, we forbid them the church's entrance, by the omnipotent power of God, and by the authority of St. Peter, till in time they amend and repent. But, if they persevere in their sin, we charge that none of you presume to hear their service; for their blessing is turned into cursing, and their prayer into sin, as the Lord doth testify to us by his prophets, "I will turn your blessing," &c.

The bishops of France being called upon daily with the pope's letters, were compelled to obey the decree of the council; but the residue of the clergy, manfully and stoutly withstanding the pope's decree and enforcement of their bishops, would not agree, but repined thereat, and said that the council did manifestly repugn against the word of God, and that the pope did take from priests that which both God and nature had given them; and therefore that that person was a heretic, and author of a wicked doctrine, who ruled and governed not by the Spirit of God, but by Satan. That the decree and act set forth tended directly against the word of God and the saying of Christ,—"Non omnes capiunt verbum hoc:" "All men have not the gift and capacity of this word." Also that it was against the sound doctrine of St. Paul, writing these words,—"As concerning virginity, I have no commandment of the Lord," &c.; again; "He that cannot otherwise live continent, let him marry." Also, that it was against the canons both of the apostles and of the Nicene Council. Moreover, that it was against the course of nature, which he required, namely, that men being sequestered from their natural wives and women, should be coacted to live as angels; that is, to perform that which nature doth not give; and, therefore, that the bishop therein did open a pernicious window to uncleanness and to fornication. In sum, giving up their answer, thus they concluded: that they had rather give up their benefices than forsake their natural and lawful wives, against the word of Christ; and, finally, if married priests could not please them, they should call down angels from heaven to serve the churches. But Hildebrand, nothing moved, neither with honest reason nor with the authority of holy Scripture, nor with the determination of the Nicene Council, nor any thing else, followeth up this matter, and calling upon the bishops still, with his letters and legates, doth solicit their minds, accusing them of negligence and dastardliness, and threatening them with excommunication, unless they cause their priests to obey his decree enjoined them. Whereupon a great number of bishops, for fear of the pope's tyranny, laboured the matter with their priests, by all means possible, to bereave them of their accustomed matrimony.

William the Conqueror. A.D. 1074.

The clergy of France resist the bull.

Amongst others, the archbishop of Mentz, perceiving this act of taking away priests' marriage might breed him no little trouble, talketh with his clergy gently, admonisheth them of the pope's mind and decree, and giveth them half a year's respite to deliberate upon the case;[1] exhorting them diligently to show themselves obedient to the pope and to him, and to grant with good will that which at length, will they, nill they, they must needs be forced unto; and therefore of their own accord to stand content therewith, lest the pope should be compelled to attempt ways of sharper severity. The time of deliberation expired, the archbishop assembleth his clergy at Erspford, in the month of October, and there willeth them, according to the pontifical decree, either to abjure for ever all matrimony, or else to renounce their benefices and ecclesiastical livings. The clergy again defend themselves against the pope's decree with the Scriptures, with reason, with the acts of general councils, with the examples of their

Bishop of Mentz.

The priests of Germany stout against the pope's unlawful proceedings.

(1) Ex Lamberto Scafnaburgensi, in Hist. Germanorum.

William the Conqueror.

A.D. 1075.

ancestors, and with divers strong arguments, declaring the pope's decree not to be consonant nor one that ought to take effect; but the archbishop said he was compelled so of the pope, and could not otherwise do, but execute that which was enjoined him.

The clergy seeing that no reason nor prayer, nor disputation would serve, laid their heads together, consulting among themselves what was best to be done. Some gave counsel not to return again to the synod, some thought it good to return and thrust out the archbishop from his see, and to give him due punishment of death for his deserving, that by his example, others may be warned hereafter never to attempt that thing any more, to the prejudice of the church, and the rightful liberty of ministers. After that, there was signified to the archbishop, by certain spies that were amongst them, what the clergy intended to do; on which the archbishop, to prevent and salve the matter, sendeth to the priests as they were coming out, certain messengers, bidding them to be of good hope, and to return again to the metropolitan, and that they should have that which should content their minds. So, being persuaded, they come again to the council. The bishop promiseth he would do his endeavour what he could to revoke and turn the mind of the bishop of Rome from that sentence, willing them in the mean time to continue as they had done in their cure and
A.D. 1076. ministry. The next year following, Hildebrand, the soldier of Satan, sendeth his legate, who was a certain bishop called Curiensis, to the archbishop of Mentz, and assembled there a council, in which the archbishop again proposed the matter, commanding all the clergy, under pain of the pope's curse, there perpetually to renounce either their wives or their livings. The clergy defended their cause again with great constancy, but when no defension could take place, but all went by tyranny and mere extortion, it burst out in the end in an uproar and tumult, from which the legate and the archbishop being in great danger, hardly escaped with their lives; and so the council broke up. By this schism and tumult it followed, that the churches after that, in choosing their priests, would not send them to the bishops (the enemies and suppressors of matrimony) to be confirmed and inducted, but did elect them within themselves, and so put them in their office without all leave or knowledge of the bishops, who then agreed and were determined to admit no priests, but such as should take an oath of perpetual singleness, never to marry after; and thus first came up the oath and profession of single priesthood. Notwithstanding, if other nations had followed the constancy and concord of those German ministers, the devilish drift and decree of this Hildebrand, or rather 'Hellbrand,' had been frustrated and avoided; but this greediness of livings in weak priests made them yield up their godly liberty to wicked tyranny. Yet this remaineth in these Germans to be noted, what concord can do in repressing the inordinate requests of evil bishops if they constantly stand to the truth, and hold together. And thus much for banishing of matrimony.

Single priesthood, how it began.

Concord between priests and ministers.

Now let us proceed to the contests between wicked Hildebrand and the godly emperor. But before, by the way of digression, it shall not be much from the purpose to touch a little on the properties of this pope, as we find them described in certain epistles of Benno, a cardinal, writing to other cardinals of Rome; which

Benno lived in the same time of Hildebrand, and detecteth the prodigious acts and doings of this monstrous pope. First he declares that he was a sorcerer most notable, and a necromancer, an old companion of Sylvester, of Laurentius and Theophylact, called otherwise Benedict IX. Amongst others, Benno the cardinal writeth this history of him:

"Upon a certain time this Gregory, coming from Albanus to Rome, had forgot behind him his familiar book of necromancy, which he was wont commonly to carry always with him. Whereupon remembering himself, on entering the port of Lateran, he calleth two of his most trusty familiars to fetch the book, charging them on no account to look within it. But they being so restrained, were the more desirous to open it, and to peruse it, and so did. After they had read a little the secrets of the satanical book, suddenly there came about them the messengers of Satan, the multitude and terror of whom made them almost out of their wits. At length, they coming to themselves, the spirits were instant upon them to know wherefore they were called up, wherefore they were vexed; 'quickly,' said they, 'tell us what ye would us to do, or else we will fall upon you, if ye retain us longer.' Then spake one of the young men to them, bidding them go and pluck down yonder walls, pointing unto certain high walls there nigh to Rome, which they did in a moment. The young men crossing them for fear of the spirits, and scarcely recovering themselves, at length came to their master."

And it followeth, moreover, in the epistle of the said Benno to the cardinals,—

"We have made mention to you before of divers colleges of the church of Rome which refused to communicate with him; as Leo, then arch-priest of the cardinals, Benno, Ugobald, Johannes the cardinal, and Peter, chancellor and cardinal, being all instituted before this Hildebrand. These three also being consecrated by him, that is to say, Natro, Innocent, and Leo, forsook him, cursing the detestable errors which he held. In like case Theodinus, whom he constituted archdeacon, and other cardinals more, Johannes sirnamed Primicerius, Petrus Oblationarius, with all that appertained to them, saving one only man. And now, when this Hildebrand saw that the bishops also would forsake him, he called unto him the laymen and made them privy of his council, thinking thereby to separate the bishops, that they should have no conference with the cardinals. After that he called together those bishops, and being guarded with bands of laymen he enforced the bishops, partly for fear, and partly by his menacing words, to swear unto him, that they should never disagree unto that which he would have done, that they should never defend the king's quarrel, and that they should never favour or obey the pope that should in his stead be instituted. Which thing being done, he sent them, by means of the prince of Salernites, into Campania; and thus did he separate them from the company of the cardinals, and from the city of Rome. And not only the bishops, but also the priests of the city, and clerks of inferior orders, as also the laymen, he bound by their oaths, that at no time nor for any cause they should condescend unto the king.

Pope Hildebrand forsaken by divers of his cardinals.

He compelleth the bishops and priests of Rome to swear unto him.

"As soon as Pope Alexander was dead, who died somewhat before night, the same day, contrary to the canons, he was chosen pope of the laymen, but the cardinals subscribed not to his election, for the canons prescribed, under pain of cursing, that none should be chosen pope before the third day after the burial of his predecessor. But he, by sinister means thus climbing to the see, removed the cardinals of the said see from being of the council. With what persons, however, he consulted night and day, Rome well heard and saw. And he now putting the cardinals from his council, his life, faith, and doctrine, no man could accuse or bear witness of; whereas in the canons is commanded, that in every place wheresoever the pope is, should be with him three cardinals, being priests, and two deacons, because of his ecclesiastical testimony, and style of verity; at which canonical decree look, gentle reader, before. He violently wrested the sacred Scriptures to cover his falsehood, which kind of idolatry how great it is, manifestly, throughout all the Scripture, appeareth. Contrary

Pope Hildebrand unorderly made pope.

William the Conqueror.

A.D. 1076.

to the minds and counsel of the cardinals, and beside the determinate order of pronouncing judgment by the canons, he rashly did excommunicate the emperor, being in no synod solemnly accused before. The sentence of which excommunication, after rehearsal of these presents, shall also be manifested (Christ willing), to the which excommunication (saith Benno) none of the cardinals would subscribe. As soon as he arose out of his seat papal, to excommunicate the emperor, the same seat, being made but a little before with big timber, suddenly, by the appointment of God, was rent and shivered in pieces; so that all men might plainly understand, what and how great and terrible schisms that lubber had sown against the church of Christ, against the seat of St. Peter, and how cruelly he had aspersed the chair of Christ, in defiling the laws of the church, ruling by might and austerity in that his so perilous and presumptuous excommunication.

The emperor wrongfully excommunicated. The pope's chair breaks under him as he rises to excommunicate the emperor.

"In the description of the same excommunication he inserteth those things wherein he himself erred, when he absolved the emperor, being unjustly excommunicated, and the bishops also communicating with him; and to the uttermost thus cutting and mangling the unity of the church, and those that communicated with them, he did as much as in him lay to make two churches.

The pope divideth the unity of the church.

"Also the same bold merchant commanded that the cardinals should fast, to the intent that God would reveal whose opinion was better, whether that of the church of Rome, or of Berengarius, touching the controversy of the Lord's body in the sacrament. And hereby he proved himself to be a manifest infidel, for that in the Nicene Council it is written, 'He that doubteth is an infidel.'

"Further, he sought for a sign to establish his faith concerning the article of the Lord's body; as did Gregory to confirm the woman's faith, when the consecrated bread was transubstantiated into the form of a fleshly finger. He also sent two cardinals, Attones and Cunones, unto Anastasie, that with the arch-priest of the same church they should begin a fast of three days' space, and that every of them, every day during those three days, should say over the Psalter, and sing masses, that Christ would show unto them some such like sign of his body, as he did to the aforesaid Gregory; which thing they could not see.

Of this miracle we read in no approved history.

"The emperor was wont oftentimes to go to St. Mary's church, in the mount Aventine, to pray. Hildebrand, when he had by his espials searched out and knew all the doings of the emperor, caused the place where the emperor was accustomed, either standing or prostrate on his face, to pray, to be marked, and for money he hired a naughty pack like himself, to gather and lay together a heap of great stones directly over the place in the vault of the church where the emperor would stand, that in throwing the same down upon his head, he should slay the emperor. About which purpose as the hireling hasted, and was busy removing to the place a stone of great hugeness and weight, it broke the plank whereon it lay, and the hireling standing thereupon, both together fell down from the roof to the pavement of the church, and with the same was dashed all in pieces. After the Romans had understanding of the handling of this matter, they fastened a rope to one of the feet of this hireling, and caused him to be drawn through the streets of the city three days together in example to others. The emperor, notwithstanding, according to his wonted clemency, caused him to be buried.

The pope hireth one to slay the emperor.

"Johannes, bishop of Portua, being one of the secret council of Hildebrand, came up into the pulpit of St. Peter, and amongst other things, in the hearing both of the clergy and people, said, "Hildebrand and we have committed such a deed, and so horrible, for the which we are all worthy to be burned alive;" meaning of the sacrament of the body of Christ, which sacrament Hildebrand, when he thereof required a divine answer against the emperor, and it would not speak, threw into the fire and burned it, contrary to the persuasion of the cardinals who were there present, and would have resisted the same.

Hildebrand casteth the sacrament of the Lord's body into the fire, because it would give him no answer.

"In the second holy day, in the Easter-week, when the clergy and the people were assembled at St. Peter's church to hear mass, after the gospel he went up into the pulpit, as he was in his pontifical attire, and, in the presence of divers bishops and cardinals (a great company both of the senate and the people of Rome being gathered together) openly preached, among many other words of divination, that the king, whose name was Henry, should die, without all peradventure, before the feast of St. Peter next ensuing; or else, at leastwise, that he should be so dejected from his kingdom, that he should not be able any more to gather together above the number of six knights. This he preached to the bishops and cardinals, and to all that were present, crying out of the pulpit in these words, "Never accept me for pope any more, but pluck me from the altar, if this prophecy be not fulfilled by the day appointed." About the same time he went about, by help of privy murderers, to kill the emperor, but God preserved him. And many there were, even at that time, who thought Pope Hildebrand to be guilty, and to be the deviser of the treason, because that then he, before the deed was put in execution, presumed of the death of the king, being by him falsely prophesied of before, which words of his wounded many men's hearts. And it came to pass that Hildebrand, by his words, was openly condemned in the congregation, which, as it is said, gave judgment of himself to be no pope, neither that he would be counted for pope any longer, but thought to be both a belier and a traitor, unless that before the feast of St. Peter, next coming, the emperor should die, or else should be deprived of all kingly honour, insomuch that he should not be able to make above six knights on his part. And thus, by the appointment of God, it came to pass, that by his own mouth he was condemned for a heretic.

William the Conqueror. A.D. 1076.

The pope seeketh again to murder the emperor.

The pope by his own mouth condemned for a heretic.

"Thus saith the Lord, The prophet who of arrogancy will prophesy in my name those things I have not commanded him, or else will prophesy in the name of other gods, let him be slain. And if thou shalt say with thyself, How shall I know what thing it is that the Lord hath not commanded to be spoken? this token shalt thou have to know it by: whatsoever thing the prophet, in the name of God, shall prophesy, and the same come not to pass, that mayest thou be sure the Lord hath not spoken, but the prophet hath imagined, through the haughtiness of his own mind, and therefore thou shalt not be afraid of him.'

"When the time was expired that Hildebrand in his divination had set, and that neither the king was dead, neither the power of the empire impaired; and fearing, lest by the words of his own mouth he should be reprehended and condemned, subtilely he turned his tale, saying, and persuading the ignorant people, that he meant not of the body of the king, but of his soul; as though the soul of the king had lost all, saving six of his knights or soldiers, or else had been dead during that space; and thus, by these sleights he beguiled the ignorant people. Against such prophets, St. Gregory on Ezekiel saith, 'Between true prophets and false this difference there is, that true prophets, if they speak any thing of their own mind, they be soon rebuked, but the false prophets both tell lies, and, not having the spirit of truth, persevere in their falsity.'

The emperor preserved by the power of God, and the pope a false prophet.

"Over and besides, the said Hildebrand judged to death three men, before they were convicted, or else confessed their crime, without the sentence of any secular judge, and caused them to be hanged upon a pair of gallows, over against the church of St. Peter, in a place called Palatiolum, without any delay or advisement, contrary to the laws which command, that every public offender should have thirty days' space before he be put to execution; which thing even amongst the pagans is in use and observed, as teacheth the authority of St. Ambrose, and the martyrdom of holy Marcelianus and Marcus.

Three persons put to death by Hildebrand against all law.

"He cast Centius the son of Stephen, the alderman, into prison, being before his trusty friend; and, in a vessel thick set with sharp nails, he tormented him to the point of death, who, after he was escaped, apprehended the said Hildebrand. Of this apprehension, before he was set at liberty, he openly forgave all the conspirators; which thing afterwards, contrary to his fidelity, he brake and revenged, and caused Centius, to whom he had forgiven all offences, to be taken, and hanged him, and nine of his men, upon the gallows before St. Peter's porch.

Centius tortured by the pope.

"There was, at the apprehension of Pope Hildebrand, a certain widow's son, to whom and to others more, for their penance, he had enjoined a year's banishment; which time being expleat, or run out, the widow, in token of more ample satisfaction, thinking thereby to have appeased the mind of Hildebrand, put a halter about her son's neck, and, drawing him by the rope to the foot of Hildebrand, said, 'My lord pope, at your hands will I receive again my son, who one whole year hath endured banishment, and other penance, by your holiness enjoined.' Then the said Hildebrand for that instant, because of those who were with him in company, dissembling his wrath, delivered her her son, very churlishly, saying, 'Get thee hence, woman, I bid

William the Conqueror. A.D. 1076.

thee, and let me be at rest.' After this he sent his officers, and apprehended the widow's son, and gave commandment to the justices to put him to death, who all together making answer, said, 'That they could no more condemn or meddle with him, for that he had for his crime committed appealed once to the pope, and abidden the banishment, and done the penance by him enjoined.' Hereupon this glorious Hildebrand, displeased with the judges, caused the foot of the widow's son to be cut off, making neither repentance, nor the laws and ordinances, to be of any estimation with him: and thus, his foot being cut off, he died within three days after with the pain thereof. Many other wicked deeds did this Hildebrand, upon whom the blood of the church crieth vengeance, shed by the sword, that is, the miserable treachery of his tongue; for which things, and that justly, the church refused to communicate with him."[1]

The villany of the pope in killing a widow's son.

Another Epistle of Benno to the Cardinals.

To the reverend fathers of the church of Rome, and to his beloved in Christ, and to his brethren who shall for ever be beloved, Benno, the cardinal of the church of Rome, wisheth faithful service, health, and communion with the servants of the catholic church: of the which communion, discipline, and power, *he* vainly braggeth, who, by the presumption of his authority, shall unjustly bind or loose any manner of person. And he doth unjustly bind, whatsoever he be, who curseth any man, being willing to make satisfaction, and bewailing his boldness, being also unconvicted, and not confessing the crime; but rather by cursing that party in vain, he curseth and condemneth himself, turning his weapon upon his own person to his destruction. O strange and new found treachery, proceeding from the sanctuary, nay, rather from him who, as high-priest, seemeth to rule the church, and to be a judge over the judges!

Hildebrand setting the bishops against the emperor.

Hildebrand was earnestly in hand with the emperor, that he should deprive those bishops who came in by simony. The emperor, thinking, as a zealous prince, that this commission had proceeded from the throne of God, without delay obeyed the same, and, forthwith, without any consideration, or judicial order, deprived certain bishops, and thought that by this his obedience to Hildebrand he offered an acceptable sacrifice to God; not knowing the crafty handling of him. But Hildebrand then again replaced those whom the emperor for simony at his commandment had before deposed, and those whom by that means he made to bear a hateful heart to the emperor, he reconciled again to himself in great familiarity; and by many and great oaths taken of them, for their fidelity towards him, he promoted them above all the rest. And thus, by these pranks, the imperial seat of the king being shortly after impaired, and destitute almost of friends, he, craftily purchasing the friendship and favour of the greatest princes, the better to bring his matters to pass, suddenly again, without any lawful accusation, without any canonical vocation, without all judicial order, excommunicated the emperor (so obedient always unto him), and set the princes of the empire all against him. And notwithstanding, as the apostle saith, that no man ought to circumvent his brother in his business, as much as in him lay, he rather mortified and killed him, than brotherly corrected him. Thus the emperor being many ways circumvented, as excommunicated besides of the canonical order, and by the consent and counsel of Hildebrand, spoiled of the greatest part of his imperial honour, and overcharged with great wars and slaughters of his own subjects, in vain desired and sued to have the canon read and heard, causing him, by force and violence, at Canusium, in the presence of Hildebrand, to accuse himself by his own confession.

The emperor caused by Hildebrand to accuse himself.

Say you now, I pray you, all such as love justice, and love not to lean either to the left hand, or to the right, in favour of any person; say your minds, whether that such a confession being forced upon never so poor a man (much less upon an emperor) ought at such a time to be prejudicial or not? or whether he who extorted the same confession is guilty of the canon, or he who, being so perversely judged, suffered the injury of a most perverse judge? who also most patiently and publicly suffered this violence with lamentable affliction upon his bare feet, clothed in thin garments, in the sharp winter, to which he never was used, and

The great patience of the godly emperor.

(1) Hæc Benno. Rom. Cardinal.

was three days together at Canusium made a spectacle both of angels and men, and a ludibrious mocking-stock to that proud Hildebrand. Never trust me, if fourteen cardinals, the archdeacon himself, and he that is called Primicerius, being all wise and religious men, besides many others of the clerks of Lateran, (to the judgment and privilege of whose holy seat the whole world is obedient,) weighing and considering his intolerable apostasy, departed not from participating, and refused to communicate with him.

William the Conqueror. A.D. 1076.

This glorious Hildebrand, and his affinity, by their new authority, breaking the decrees of the Chalcedon Council, not only in words, but also in public writings, have agreed, that it is tolerable both to baptise and communicate, being out of the church of God: and how blind these men were, and also what heretics they be, their own writings do declare. What a mischief is this (saith Benno) that they presume to judge of the church, who swarm themselves in all errors, who also esteem the verity but as a lie; and lest their poisoned falsehood both in words and writings should appear, they have, like subtle poisoners, the sooner to deceive, mixed honey therewithal. A lie, saith St. Augustine, is every thing pronounced with the intent of deceiving others.

What a lie is.

It were too long and tedious here to recite all the detestable doings, and diabolical practices of conjurings, charms, and filthy sorceries, exercised between him, and Laurentius, and Theophylact, otherwise named Pope Benedict IX., whereof a long narration followeth, in the aforesaid epistle of Benno to the cardinals, to be seen, to which the reader may repair, whoso hath either leisure to read or mind to understand more of the abominable parts and devilish acts of this Hildebrand.

Pope Hildebrand a worker of sorcery and conjuring.

Thus having sufficiently alleged the words and testimonies of Benno and Aventinus, concerning the acts and facts of this pope; now let us proceed, in the order as followeth in his story, to set forth the miserable vexation which the virtuous and godly emperor sustained by that ungodly person.

About what time Hildebrand was made pope, Henry IV., the emperor, was encumbered and much vexed with civil dissention in Germany, by reason of certain grievances of the Saxons against him and his father, Henry III.; whereupon the matter growing to sedition, sides were taken, and great wars ensued betwixt Otho, duke of Saxony, and Henry, the emperor. This busy time seemed to Hildebrand very opportune to work his feats, whose study and drift was ever from the beginning to advance the dominion of the Romish seat above all other bishops, and also to press down the authority of the temporal rulers, under the spiritual men of the church. And although he went about the same long before, by subtle trains and acts set forth concerning simony, yet now he thought more effectuously to accomplish his purposed intent, after that he was exalted thither where he would be. And therefore now bearing himself the bolder, by the authority of St. Peter's throne,[1] first he began to pursue the act set out by his predecessor, as touching simony, cursing and excommunicating, whosoever they were, that received any spiritual living or promotion at laymen's hands, as also all such as were the givers thereof. For this he then called simony, that under that colour he might defeat the temporal potestates of their right, and so bring the whole clergy at length to the lure of Rome. And forasmuch as the emperor was the head, thinking first to begin

Henry IV. emperor.

(1) "Much boast is made of Peter's throne,
But his life they let alone."

William the Conqueror.

A.D. 1076.

with him, he sendeth for him, by letters and legates, to appear in the council of Lateran at Rome. But the emperor, busied in his wars against the Saxons, had no leisure to attend to councils. Notwithstanding Gregory, the pope, proceedeth in his council, rendering there the cause and reason before the bishops, why he had excommunicated divers of the clergy, as Herman, bishop of Bamberg, counsellor to the emperor, and other priests besides, for simony. And there, moreover, in the said council he threateneth to excommunicate likewise the emperor himself, and to depose him from his regal kingdom, unless he would renounce the heresy of simony, and do penance. The council being ended, Guibert, archbishop of Ravenna, persuaded one Centius, a Roman, the captain's son, whom the pope had excommunicated, to take the emperor's part against the pope, who, watching his time in the temple of St. Mary, upon Christmas-day in the morning, taketh the pope and putteth him fast in a strong tower. The next day the people of Rome hearing this, harness themselves with all expedition to help the bishop, and when they loosed him out of prison, they besieged the house of Centius, and plucked it down to the ground; his family having their noses cut off were cast out of the city. Centius himself escaping, fled to the emperor. Guibert, the archbishop, pretending good will to the pope, departed from Rome; who, likewise, had wrought with Hugo Candidus, a cardinal, and with Theobald, archbishop of Milan, also with divers other bishops about Italy, to forsake the pope and take the emperor's part. Gregory the pope, called Hildebrand, hearing of the conspiracy, layeth the sentence of excommunication upon them all, and depriveth them of their dignity. The emperor, being moved not unworthily, with the arrogant presumption of the proud prelate, called together a council at Worms, in which all the bishops not only of Saxony, but of all the whole empire of the Germans, agree and conclude upon the deposition of Hildebrand, and that no obedience hereafter should be given to him. This being determined in the council, Rowland, a priest of Parma, was sent to Rome with the sentence, who, in the name of the council, should command Gregory to yield up his seat, and also charge the cardinals to resort to the emperor, for a new election of another pope. The tenor of the sentence sent up by Rowland was this:—

Herman excommunicated by Hildebrand.

Hildebrand cast in a tower.

Council of Worms.

A.D. 1076.

The sentence of the Council of Worms against Hildebrand.

Forasmuch as thy first ingress and coming in, hath been so spotted with so many perjuries, and also the church of God brought into no little danger through thine abuse and new-fangleness: moreover, because thou hast defamed thine own life and conversation with so much and great dishonesty, that we see no little peril or slander to arise thereof; therefore the obedience, which yet we never promised thee, hereafter we utterly renounce, and never intend to give thee. And as thou hast never taken us yet for bishops (as thou hast openly reported of us), so neither will we hereafter take thee to be apostolic. Vale.

The council of Rome against the council of Worms.

Gregory the pope, tickled with this sentence, first condemneth it in his council of Lateran with excommunication. Secondly, he depriveth Sigifrid, archbishop of Mentz, of his dignities and ecclesiastical livings, with all other bishops, abbots, and priests, as many as took the emperor's part. Thirdly, he accuseth the emperor Henry himself, depriving him of his kingdom and regal possession, and releasing all his subjects of their oath of allegiance given unto him, after this form and manner.

William the Conqueror. A.D. 1076.

The tenor of the sentence excommunicatory against Henry the emperor, by Pope Hildebrand.

O blessed St. Peter, prince of the apostles! bow down thine ears I beseech thee, and hear me thy servant, whom thou hast brought up even from mine infancy, and hast delivered me unto this day from the hands of the wicked, who hate and persecute me, because of my faith in thee. Thou art my witness, and also the blessed mother of Jesus Christ, and thy brother St. Paul, fellow-partner of thy martyrdom, how that I entered this function not willingly, but enforced against my will; not that I take it so as a robbery, lawfully to ascend into this seat, but because that I had rather pass over my life like a pilgrim or private person, than for any fame or glory to climb up to it. I do acknowledge, and that worthily, all this to come of thy grace, and not of my merits, that this charge over christian people, and this power of binding and loosing, are committed to me. Wherefore, trusting upon this assurance for the dignity and tuition of holy church in the name of God Omnipotent, the Father, the Son, and the Holy Ghost, I do here depose Henry, the son of Henry, once the emperor, from his imperial seat and princely government, who hath so boldly and presumptuously laid hands upon thy church. And, furthermore, all such as heretofore have sworn to be his subjects, I release them of their oath, whereby all subjects are bound to the allegiance of their princes; for it is meet and convenient, that he should be void of dignity, who seeketh to diminish the majesty of thy church. Moreover, for that he hath contemned my monitions, tending to his health and to the wealth of his people, and hath separated himself from the fellowship of the church, which he, through his seditions,[1] studieth to destroy, therefore I bind him by virtue of excommunication, trusting and knowing most certainly, that thou art Peter, on the rock of whom, as on the true foundation, Christ, our king, hath built his church.[2]

Mark this, ye papists, that say, the pope cannot err.

The emperor, thus assaulted with the pope's censure, sendeth abroad his letters through all nations to purge himself, declaring how wrongfully, and against all right, he was condemned. The princes of Almany, partly fearing the crack of the pope's thunder-clap, partly again rejoicing that occasion was renewed to rebel against the emperor, assembled a commencement, where they did consult and so conclude; to elect another emperor, and so fall from Henry, unless the pope would come to Germany, and he would there be content to submit himself and obtain his pardon. Wherein is to be considered the lamentable affections of the Germans in those days, so to forsake such a valiant emperor, and so much to repute a vile bishop: but this was the rudeness of the world then, for lack of better knowledge. The emperor, seeing the chief princes ready to forsake him, promiseth them with an oath, that if the pope would repair to Germany, he would ask forgiveness.

The Saxons take the pope's part against the emperor.

Upon this the bishop of Treves was sent up in commission to Rome, to entreat the pope to come into Germany. The pope, at the instance of the legate and the princes, was content. He entered into Germany, thinking to come to Augsburgh. After he was come to Vercelli (the bishop of that city being the chancellor of Italy, and desirous to disturb peace for the old grudge he had to the emperor),

(1) Quis tulerct Gracchos de seditione querentes?—Juven. (2) Ex Platina.

William the Conqueror. A.D. 1076. falsely persuaded the pope, that he was certain the emperor was coming with a mighty great army against him, counselling him therefore to provide betimes for his own safeguard in some stronger place; whereby the pope's mind being altered, he retired back to Canusium, or Canossa, a city being subject to Matilda, a countess of Italy, where he should not need to fear the emperor.

Henry, understanding the false fear of the pope, and of his retiring to Canusium, incontinent (coming out of Spires with his wife and his young son, in the deep and sharp winter) resorteth to Canusium. All his peers and nobles had left him for fear of the pope's curse, neither did any accompany him. Wherefore the emperor, being not a little troubled, and laying apart his regal ornaments, came barefooted with his wife and child to the gate of Canusium, where he from morning to night (all the day fasting) most humbly desireth absolution, craving to be let in, to the speech of the bishop: but no ingress might be given him once within the gates. Thus, he continuing three days together in his petition and suit, at length answer came, that the pope's majesty had yet no leisure to talk with him. The emperor, nothing moved therewith, that he was not let into the city, patient and with an humble mind, abideth without the walls, with no little grievance and painful labour; for it was a sharp winter, and all frozen with cold. Notwithstanding, yet through his importunate suit, at length it was granted, through the entreating of Matilda, the pope's paramour, and of Arelaus, earl of Sebaudia, and of the abbot of Cluniack, that he should be admitted to the pope's speech. On the fourth day being let in, for a token of his true repentance, he yieldeth to the pope's hands his crown, with all other ornaments imperial, and confessed himself unworthy of the empire, if ever he do against the pope hereafter, as he hath done before, desiring for that time to be absolved and forgiven. The pope answereth, he will neither forgive him, nor release the bond of his excommunication, but upon conditions. First, to promise that he shall be content to stand to his arbitrement in the council, and to take such penance as he shall enjoin him; also that he shall be prest and ready to appear, in what place or time the pope shall appoint him. Moreover, that he, being content to take the pope as judge of his cause, shall answer in the said council to all objections and accusations laid against him, and that he shall never seek any revengement herein. Item, that he, though he be quit and cleared therein, shall stand to the pope's mind and pleasure, whether to have his kingdom restored, or to lose it. Finally, that before the trial of his cause, he shall use neither his kingly ornaments, sceptres, nor crown, nor usurp the authority to govern, nor exact any oath of allegiance upon his subjects, &c. These things being promised to the bishop by an oath, and put in writing, the emperor is only released of excommunication.

A wondrous submission of a valiant emperor to a vile pope.

Proud conditions of the pope.

Here the beast of the Apocalypse appeareth in his colours.

The form and tenor of the oath, which Henry made to the pope.

I Henry, king, after peace and agreement made to the mind and sentence of our lord Gregory the Seventh, promise to keep all covenants and bonds betwixt us, and to provide that the pope go safely wheresoever he will, without any danger either to him, or to his retinue; especially in all such places as he subject to our empire.... And that I shall not at any time stay or hinder him, but that he may do what belongeth to his function, where and whensoever his pleasure shall be. And these things I bind myself with an oath to keep."[1] *William the Conqueror.*

A.D. 1079.

Thus, the matter being decided between them after the pope's own prescribement, the emperor taketh his journey to Papia. The pope, with his cardinals, did vaunt and triumph with no little pride, that they had so quailed the emperor, and brought him on his knees to ask them forgiveness. Yet, notwithstanding, mistrusting themselves, and misdoubting time, what might befall them hereafter if fortune should turn, and God give the emperor to enjoy a more quiet kingdom; therefore, to prevent such dangers betimes, they study and consult privily with themselves how to displace Henry clean from his kingdom, and how that device might safely be conveyed. They conclude and determine to divert the empire unto Rodolph, a man of great nobility amongst the chiefest states of Germany; and also to incite and stir up all other princes and subjects, being yet free and discharged from their oaths, against Henry, and so, by force of arms, to expel the emperor out of his kingdom. To bring this purpose the better to pass, legates were sent down from the pope, Sighard patriarch of Aquilia, and Altiman bishop of Padua, who should persuade through all France, that Henry the emperor was rightfully excommunicated, and that they should give to the bishop of Rome their consents in choosing Rodolph to be emperor. This being done, there was sent to the said Rodulph, duke of Suabia, a crown from the pope with this verse:—

The crafty conspiracy of the cardinals against the emperor.

A.D. 1080.

"Petra dedit Petro, Petrus diadema Rodulpho."
"The Rock gave the crown to Peter,
Peter giveth it to Rodolph."

Here, by the way of digression, to make a little gloss upon this barbarous verse, two notable lies are to be noted. One, where he lieth about Christ, the other, where he lieth about St. Peter. First, that Christ gave any temporal diadem to Peter, it is a most manifest lie, and against the Scriptures, whereas he would not take it, being given to himself, saying, "My kingdom is not of this world." Again, where he saith that Peter giveth it to Rodolph, here he playeth the poet; for neither had Peter any such thing to give; and if he had, yet he would not have given it to Rodolph from the right heir; neither is it true that Peter did give it, because Hildebrand gave it. For it is no good argument Hildebrand did give it—ergo, Peter did give it, except ye will say, Hildebrand stirred up great wars and bloodshed in Germany—ergo, Peter stirred up great wars in Germany. So Peter neither could, nor would, nor did, give it to Rodolph, but only Hildebrand, the pope; who, after he had so done, gave commandment to the archbishop of Mentz and of Cologne to elect this Rodolph for emperor, and to anoint him king, and also to defend him with all the force and strength they might.

The pope proved a double liar.

While this conspiracy was in hand, Henry the emperor was

(1) Actum Canos. v. Calend. Februarii, Indic. xv.

William the Conqueror.

A.D. 1080.

absent, and the pope's ambassadors with him also. In the mean space Rodolph was elected emperor, unknown to Henry. Upon this cometh the bishop of Strasburg to the emperor, certifying him what was done. He, suspecting and seeing the stomach and doings of the Saxons so bent against him, mustereth his men with expedition, and marcheth forward to defend his right; but first sendeth to Rome, trusting to the league betwixt him and his pope, and requireth the bishop to proceed with his sentence against Rodolph for the rebellious invasion of his empire. But the bishop, minding nothing less, sendeth word again, that it was not right to condemn any person, his cause being not heard; thus, under pretence of the law, colouring his unlawful treachery. Henry, thus disappointed, and forsaken on every side, with his men about him, attempteth battle against Rodolph; in which battle there was a marvellous great slaughter on both sides, but the victory on neither part was certain, so that both the captains still challenged the empire. After the battle, and great murder on both sides, they both sent to Rome to know of the pope's determination, to whether of them two he judged the right title of the empire to appertain. The bishop commanded them both to break up their armies, and depart the field, promising that he shortly would call a council, where this matter should be disputed: in the mean time they should cease from war. But before the messengers returned, their armies being refreshed, they had another conflict together, but no victory got on either part. Thus both the captains being wearied in wars, the Romish beast, the bishop, who was the cause thereof, perceiving whither these cruel wars would tend, to the great calamity not only of the Germans, but also of other nations, and trusting to find another way to help Rodolph and his adherents, sendeth down a commission by Otho, archbishop of Treves, Bernard a deacon, and Bernard, abbot of Massilia, to whom he gave in charge that they should call together a council or sitting in Almany, and that there it should be defined to which party the empire should pertain, by most right and public consideration; promising that what they should therein determine, he (looking upon the matter through the authority of God omnipotent, and of St. Peter and St. Paul) would ratify the same. Moreover, for that no let nor impeachment should happen to the legates by the way, he giveth them letters to the princes and nations of Germany, whereof the contents be declared briefly in Platina, if any list to read them.

The pope traitor to the emperor.

Great wars stirred up by the pope.

But the emperor would not permit the legates to have any council within Germany, except they would first deprive Rodolph of his kingdom. The legates, considering that to be against the drift and intention of the pope, returned again from whence they came. The pope hearing this, and seeing his purpose was thus disappointed by the emperor, draweth out another excommunication against him, and again bereaveth him of his kingdom; sending about his letters excommunicatory throughout all places, thinking thereby to further the part of Rodolph the better. Platina hath in his book the whole effect of the writing, which tendeth after this sort.

William the Conqueror.

The copy of the second excommunication of Hildebrand against the Emperor.

A.D. 1080.

Blessed St. Peter, prince of the apostles, and thou St. Paul also, the teacher of the Gentiles, give ear unto me, I beseech you, a little, and gently hear me, for you are the disciples and lovers of truth! The things that I shall say are true. This matter I take in hand for truth's sake, that my brethren, whose salvation I seek, may the more obsequiously obey me, and better understand, how that I, trusting upon your defence, next to Christ, and his mother, the immaculate Virgin, resist the wicked, and am ready to help the faithful. I did not enter this seat of mine own accord, but much against my will and with tears, for that I accounted myself unworthy to occupy so high a throne. And this I say, not that I have chosen you, but you have chosen me, and have laid this great burden upon our shoulders. And now, whereas by this your assignment I have ascended up this hill, crying to the people, and showing them their faults, and to the children of the church their iniquities, the members of Satan have risen up against me, and have laid hands together to seek my blood. For the kings of the earth have risen up against me,[1] and the princes of this world, with whom also have conspired certain of the clergy, subjects against the Lord, and against us his anointed, saying, "Let us break asunder their bands, and cast off from us their yoke." This have they done against me, to bring me either to death or to banishment; in the number of whom is Henry, whom they call king, the son of Henry the emperor, who hath lift up so proudly his horns and heel against the church of God, making conspiracy with divers other bishops, both Italians, French, and Germans; against the pride of whom, hitherto, your authority hath resisted; who, rather being broken than amended, coming to me in Cisalpina, made humble suit to me for pardon and absolution. I, thinking nothing else but true repentance in him, received him again to favour, and did restore him to the communion only, from which he was excommunicate; but to his kingdom, from which in the synod of Rome he was worthily expelled, I did not restore him, nor to the rents and fruits thereof, that he might return to the faith again; that I granted not to him. And that I did, for this purpose, that if he should defer to fall to agreement with certain of his neighbours whom he hath always vexed, and to restore again the goods both of the church and otherwise, then he might be compelled by the censures of the church and force of arms thereunto: whereby divers and sundry bishops and princes of Germany (such as he had long troubled) being helped by this opportunity, elected Rodolph, their duke, to be king in the place of Henry, whom they for his transgressions had removed and despatched from his empire. But Rodolph, first in this matter using a princely modesty and integrity, sent up his messengers to me, declaring how he is constrained (wild he, nild he) to take that regal government upon him, albeit he was not so desirous thereof, but that he would rather show himself obedient to us, than to the other that offered him the kingdom; and, whatsoever our arbitrement should be therein, he would be under obedience both of God and of us. And, for more assurance of his obedience, he hath sent his own children hither for pledges. Upon this Henry began to snuff, and first entreated us to restrain and inhibit Rodolph, through the pain of our curse, from the usurpation of his kingdom. I answered again, I would see whether of them had more right and title thereunto, and so send our legates thither upon the same, to know the whole state of the matter; and thereupon I would decide betwixt them, whether of them had the truer part. But Henry would not suffer our legates to come to take up the matter, and slew divers, both secular men, and of the clergy, spoiling and profaning churches; and so by this means hath endangered himself in the bonds of excommunication. I, therefore, trusting in the judgment and mercy of God, and in the supportation of the blessed Virgin, also bold upon your authority do lay the sentence of curse upon the said Henry and all his adherents; and here again I take his regal government from him, charging and forbidding all christian men that have been sworn unto him, whom I discharge here of their oath, that hereafter they obey him in

O pestiferous hypocrite!

The pope prayeth St. Peter to dishonour his king. And St. Peter bindeth the pope to honour his king.

Crocodili lachrymæ.

Scripture well applied.

Let all papists mark here well the holiness of their holy father.

As if he were not set up by you, rather than by them.

(1) A figure called ἀντιμεταβολή, cujus contrarium verum est. Vim faciunt scripturis, ut plenitudinem accipiant potestatis.

William the Conqueror

A.D. 1083

nothing, but that they take Rodolph to their king, who is elected by many princes of the province. For so right it is and convenient, that as Henry, for his pride and stubborness, is deprived of his dignity and possession, so Rodolph, being grateful to all men, for his virtue and devotion be exalted to the imperial throne and dominion

The more to blame emperors to suffer you to be so saucy with them. Nego argumentum. Confer this clause with the history of the story hereafter. O double hypocrite!

Therefore, O you blessed princes of the apostles! grant to this, and confirm with your authority what I have said, so that all men may understand, if you have power to bind and loose in heaven, you have also power in earth to give and take away empires, kingdoms, principalities, and whatsoever here in earth belongeth to mortal men. For if you have power to judge in such matters as appertain to God, what then should we think you have, of these inferior and profane things? And if it be in your power to judge the angels, ruling over proud princes, what then shall it beseem you to do upon their servants? Therefore let the kings understand by this example, and all other princes of the world, what you be able to do in heaven, and what you are with God, that thereby they may fear to contemn the commandment of holy church. And now do you exercise this judgment quickly upon Henry, whereby all men may see this son of iniquity to fall from his kingdom, not by any chance, but by your provision and only work. Notwithstanding this, I would crave of you, that he, being brought to repentance through your intercession, still in the day of judgment may find favour and grace with the Lord.—Actum Romæ, nonis Martii, Indictione iii.

Furthermore, Hildebrand, not yet content with this, interdicteth and deposeth also Guibert, archbishop of Ravenna, for taking the emperor's part, commanding all priests to give no manner of obedience to him, and sendeth thither to Ravenna another archbishop with full authority.

Fourth battle betwixt Henry and Rodolph

After and upon this, Henry and Rodolph, to try the matter by the sword, coped together in battle, not without bloodshed, where Henry, by the favour of God, against the judgment of Hildebrand, had the victory. Rodolph, there greatly wounded in the conflict, was had out of the army, and carried to Hyperbolis, where he commanded the bishops and chief doers of his conspiracy to be brought before him. When they came, he lifted up his right hand, in which he had taken his deadly wound, and said, "This is the hand which gave the oath and sacrament unto Henry my prince, and which, through your instigation, so oft hath fought against him in vain; now go and perform your first oath and allegiance to your king, for I must to my fathers;" and so died. Thus the pope gave battle, but God gave the victory.

Rodolph at his death repenteth. The pope giveth war. God giveth victory

Henry, after his enemy had been thus subdued, and wars had ceased in Germany, forgat not the old injuries received of Hildebrand, by whom he was twice excommunicated, and expelled from his kingdom, and to whom he was three days making humble suit, yea, and that in sharp winter, but could find no favour with him. Besides that, he incited moreover, and aided his enemy against him. Wherefore he calleth together a council, or assembly of divers bishops of Italy, Lombardy, and Germany, at Brixia, A.D. 1083, where he purged himself, and accused the bishop Hildebrand of divers crimes, as being an usurper, a perjured, a necromancer, and a sorcerer, a sower of discord, complaining, moreover, of wrongs and injuries done by the bishop and church of Rome, in that the church of Rome preferred the bishop before him, when that his father, being emperor before him, had enthronized and set in divers and sundry bishops there by his assignment, without any other election. And now this

Council at Brixia A.D. 1083

bishop, contrary to his oath and promise made, thrust in himself without the will and knowledge of him, being their king and magistrate. For, in the time of his father Henry III., this Hildebrand, with others, bound themselves with a corporal oath, that so long as the emperor and his son, now being king, should live, they should neither themselves presume, nor suffer any other to aspire to the papal seat, without the assent and approbation of the aforesaid emperors; which now this Hildebrand, contrary to his corporal oath, had done. Wherefore the aforesaid council, with one agreement, condemned this Gregory, that he should be deposed; the tenor of which condemnation is thus expressed in the abbot Urspergensis.

William the Conqueror.

A.D. 1084.

No bishop of Rome can be chosen without consent of the emperor.

The sentence of the council of Brixia against Hildebrand.[1]

Because it is not unknown that this bishop was not elected of God, but intruded himself by fraud and money, who hath subverted all ecclesiastical order, who hath disturbed the government of the christian empire, menacing death of body and soul against our catholic and peaceable king, who hath set up and maintained a perjured king, sowing discord where concord was, causing debate amongst friends, slanders and offences amongst brethren, divorcements and separation amongst the married, for he took away the marriage of priests, as Henry Mutius witnesseth, and finally disquieting the peaceable state of all quiet life: Therefore we, here in the name and authority of God congregated together, with the legates and hands of nineteen bishops, the day of Pentecost at Mentz, do proceed in canonical judgment against Hildebrand, a man most wicked, preaching sacrilege and burning, maintaining perjury and murders, calling in question the catholic faith of the body and blood of the Lord, a follower of divination and dreams, a manifest necromancer, a sorcerer, and infected with a Pythonical spirit, and therefore departed from the true faith; we judge him to be deposed and expelled, and unless he hearing this, shall yield and depart the seat, to be perpetually condemned.—Enacted vii. Calend. Julii, feria. v. Indictione iii.

The pope judged and deposed by the council.

This being enacted and sent to Rome, they elected Guibert, archbishop of Ravenna, in the place of Hildebrand, to govern the church of Rome, named Clement III. But when Hildebrand neither would give over his hold, nor give place to Clement, the emperor, gathering an army to send to Italy, came to Rome to depose Gregory, and to place Clement in his room. But Hildebrand, sending to Matilda, the countess beforementioned, required her, in remission of all her sins, to withstand Henry the emperor; and so she did. Notwithstanding, Henry prevailing, came to Rome, where he besieged the city all Lent, and after Easter got it, the Romans being compelled to open the gates unto him; so he coming to the temple of St. Peter, there placeth Clement in his papacy. Hildebrand straight flieth into Adrian's tower with his adherents, where he, being beset round about, at length sendeth for Robert Guiscard, his friend, a Norman. In the mean time, while Robert collecteth his power, the abbot of Cluniack, conferring with Gregory, exhorteth him to crown Henry emperor in Lateran; which if he would do, the other promiseth to bring about, that Henry should depart with his army into Germany; whereunto the people of Rome also did likewise move him. To whom Gregory answered, "That he was content so to do, but upon condition that the emperor would submit himself to ask pardon, to amend his fault, and to promise obedience." The emperor not

The pope seeketh succour of his paramour.

The first example to fight for remission of sins began in Hildebrand.

A.D. 1084.

(1) Edition 1563, p. 29.

William the Conqueror

agreeing to those conditions, went to Senas, taking Clement, the newly stalled pope, with him.

A.D. 1085.

After the return of the emperor, the aforesaid Robert Guiscard, approaching with his soldiers, burst in at one of the gates, and spoileth the city, and, not long after, delivereth Hildebrand out of his enemies' hands, and carried him away to Campania, where he not long continuing, afterwards died in exile.[1]

Antoninus writeth, that Hildebrand, as he did lie a dying, called to him one of his chief cardinals, bewailing to him his fault and misorder of his spiritual ministry, in stirring up discord, war, and dissension; whereupon he desired the cardinal to go to the emperor, and desire of him forgiveness, absolving from the danger of excommunication both him and all his partakers, both quick and dead.

Hildebrand, the author and patron of all misrule.

Thus hast thou, gentle reader, the full history of Pope Gregory VII., called Hildebrand, which I have laid out more at large, and desire thee to mark, because that from this pope, if thou mark well, springeth all the occasions of mischief, of pomp, pride, stoutness, presumption, and tyranny, which since that time have reigned in his successors hitherto, in the cathedral church of the Romish clergy. For here came first the subjection of the temporal regiment under the spiritual jurisdiction; and emperors, which before were their masters, now are made their underlings. Also here came in the suppression of priests' marriage, as is sufficiently declared. Here came in, moreover, the authority of both the swords spiritual and secular into spiritual men's hands, so that christian magistrates could do nothing in election, in giving bishoprics or benefices, in calling councils, in hearing and correcting the excesses of the clergy, but only the pope must do all. Yea, moreover, no bishop or pastor in his own parish could excommunicate or exercise any discipline among his flock, but only the pope challenged that prerogative to himself. Finally, here came in the first example to persecute emperors and kings with rebellion and excommunication, as the clergy themselves hereafter do testify and witness in proceeding against Paschal. Thus, these notes being well observed, let us, by the grace of Christ, now repair again to our country history of England.

A.D. 1087. The death of William the Conqueror.

About the death of Pope Hildebrand, or not long after, followed the death of King William the Conqueror, A.D. 1087, after he had reigned in England the space of one and twenty years and ten months. The cause of his sickness and death is said to be this: for that Philip, the French king, upon a time jestingly said, that "King William lay in childbed, and nourished his fat belly." To this the aforesaid William, hearing thereof, answered again and said, "When he should be churched, he would offer a thousand candles to him in France, wherewithal the king should have little joy." Whereupon King William, in the month of July, when the corn, fruit, and grapes, were most flourishing, entered into France, and set on fire many cities and towns in the west side of France. And lastly, coming to the city of Meaux, where he, burning a woman being as a recluse, in a wall enclosed (or as some say, two men anchorites

(1) Platina, Nauclerus, Sabellicus, Crantzius, Benno, &c.

enclosed) was so fervent and furious about the fire, that with the heat partly of the fire, partly of the time of year, he fell sick and died.

By the life and acts of this king it may appear true, as stories of him report, that he was wise, but guileful; rich, but covetous; a fair speaker, but a great dissembler; glorious in victory, and strong in arms, but rigorous in oppressing those whom he overcame, and in levying of tasks passing all others; insomuch that he caused to be enrolled and numbered in his treasury every hide of land and owner thereof, what fruit and revenues surmounted of every lordship, of every township, castle, village, field, river, and wood, within the realm of England. Moreover, how many parish churches, how many living cattle there were, what and how much every baron in the realm could dispend, what fees were belonging, what wages were taken, &c.: the tenor and contents of which taskment yet remaineth in rolls. After this tasking or numbering, which was in the year before his death, followed an exceeding murrain of cattle and barrenness of the ground, with much pestilence and hot fevers among the people, so that such as escaped the fever were consumed with famine. Moreover, at the same season, among certain other cities, a great part of the city of London, with the church of St. Paul's, was wasted with fire, A.D. 1085.

Doomsday Book.

Pestilence in England and murrain of beasts

London with the church of St Paul's burnt

In hunting and in parks the aforesaid king had such pleasure, that in the county of Southampton, for the space of thirty miles, he cast down churches and townships, and there made the New Forest; loving his deer so dearly, as though he had been to them a father, making sharp laws for the increasing thereof, under pain of losing both the eyes. So hard he was to Englishmen, and so favourable to his own country, that as there was no English bishop remaining, but only Wolstan of Worcester, he, being commanded of the king and Lanfranc to resign his staff, partly for inability, partly for lack of the French tongue, refused to resign it, except to him that gave it, and so went to the tomb of King Edward, where he thought to resign it, but was permitted to enjoy it still; so likewise in his days there was almost no Englishman that bare office of honour or rule in the land, insomuch that it was half a shame at that time to be called an Englishman. Notwithstanding he a good deal favoured the city of London, and granted unto the citizens the first charter that ever they had, written in the Saxon, sealed with green wax, and contained in few lines.

Wolstan, bishop of Worcester

Among his other conditions, this in him is noted, that so given he was to peace and quiet, that any maiden being laden with gold or silver, might pass through the whole realm without harm or resistance. This William in his time builded two monasteries, one in England, at Battle in Sussex, where he won the field against Harold, called the abbey of Battle; besides another, named Barmondsey, in his country of Normandy.

England peaceable from thieves

The abbies of Battle and Barmondsey.

After the life and story of King William, thus briefly described, with the acts and order of battle between him and King Harold (although much more might have been written of that matter, if the book had come sooner to my hands, which afterwards I saw), now remaineth in the end of this story to describe the names of such barons and nobles of Normandy, as entered with him into

William the Conqueror. A.D. 1087.

this land, as well of them who were embarked with him; and also the slain, as appeareth, in the battle; as also of those who were planted and advanced, by the said conqueror, in the lands and possessions of English lords, whom he either expelled, or else beheaded: the names of which Normans here follow underwritten.

Out of the Annals of Normandy, in French, whereof one very ancient book in parchment remaineth in the custody of the writer.

The day after the battle, very early in the morning, Odo, bishop of Bayeux, sung mass for those that were departed. The duke, after that, desirous to know the state of his battle, and what people he had therein lost and were slain, he caused to come unto him a clerk who had written their names when they were embarked at St. Valeries, and commanded him to call them all by their names, who called them that had been at the battle, and had passed the seas with Duke William. And hereafter follow their names.

THE NAMES OF THOSE THAT WERE AT THE CONQUEST OF ENGLAND.

Odo, bishop of Bayeux.
Robert, conte de Mortaign. These two were brethren unto Duke William by their mother.
Baudwin de Buillon,
Roger, conte de Beaumont, surnamed 'With the Beard,' of whom descended the line of Meullent.
Guillaume Malet,
Le sire de Monfort sur Rille,
Guillaume de Viexpont,
Neel de S. Sauveur le viconte,
Le sire de Fougiers,
Henry seigneur de Ferieres,
Le sire Daubemare,
Guillaume, sire de Rommare,
Le sire de Lithehare,
Le sire de Touque,
Le sire de la Mare,
Le sire de Neauhou,
Le sire de Pirou,
Robert, sire de Beaufou,
Le sire Danou,
Le sire de Soteuille,
Le sire de Margneville,
Le sire de Tancarville,
Eustace Dambleville,
Le sire de Marngneville,
Le sire de Grantmesnil,
Guillaume Crespin,
Le sire de S. Martin,
Guillaume de Moulins,
Le sire de Puis,
Geoffray, sire de Mayenne,
Auffroy de Bohon,
Auffroy et Maugier de Cartrait,
Guillaume de Garrennes,
Hue de Gournay, sire de Bray,
Le conte Hue de Gournay,
Euguemont de l'aigle,
Le viconte de Touars,
Richard Dauverénchin,
Le sire de Biars,
Le sire de Solligny,
Le bouteiller Daubigny,
Le sire de Maire,
Le sire de Vitry,
Le sire de Lacy,
Le sire du val Dary,
Le sire de Tracy,
Hue, sire de Montfort,
Le sire de Piquegny,
Hamon de Kayeu,
Le sire de Despinay,
Le sire de Port,
Le sire de Torcy,
Le sire de Jort,
Le sire de Riviers,
Guillaume Moyonne,
Raoul Tesson de Tingueleiz,
Roger Marmion,
Raoul de Guel,
Avenel des Byars,
Paennel du Monstier Hubert,
Robert, Bertran le Tort,
Le sire de Seulle,
Le sire de Dorival,
Le sire de Breval,
Le sire de S. Jehan,
Le sire de Bris,
Le sire du Homme,
Le sire de Sauchoy,
Le sire de Cailly,
Le sire de Semilly,
Le sire de Tilly,
Le sire de Romelli,
Marq. de Basqueville,
Le sire de Preaulx,
Le sire de Gonis,
Le sire de Sanceaulx,
Le sire de Moulloy,
Le sire de Monceaulx.

The Archers du val du Ruel, and of Bretheul, and of many other places.

Le sire de S. Saen, i. de S. Sydonio,
Le sire de la Kiviere,
Le sire de Salnarville,
Le sire de Rony,
Eude de Beaugieu,
Le sire de Oblie,
Le sire de Sacie,
Le sire de Nassie,
Le Visquaius de Chaymes,
Le sire du Sap,
Le sire de Glos,
Le sire de Mine,
Le sire de Glanville,
Le sire de Breençon,
Le Vidam de Partay,
Raoul de Morimont,
Pierre de Bailleul, sire de Fiscamp,
Le sire de Beausault,
Le sire de Tillieres,
Le sire de Pacy,
Le seneschal de Torcy,
Le sire de Gacy,
Le sire de Doully,
Le sire de Sacy,
Le sire de Vacy,
Le sire de Tourneeur,
Le sire de Praeres,
Guil. de Coulombieres,
Hue, sire de Bollebec,
Richard sire Dorbeck,
Le sire de Bonneboz,
Le sire de Tresgoz,
Le sire de Montfiquet,
Hue le Bigot de Maletot,
Le sire de la Haye,
Le sire de Mombray,

William the Conqueror A.D. 1037

Le sire de Saye,
Le sire de la Ferte,
Boutevillain,
Troussebout,
Guillaume Patric de la Laund,
Hue de Mortemer,
Le sire Danvillers,
Le sire Donnebaut,
Le sire de S. Cler
Rob le filz Herneys, duc d'Orleans,
Le sire de Harecourt,
Le sire de Crevecœur,
Le sire de Deyncourt,
Le sire de Brimetot,
Le sire Combray,
Le sire Daunay,
Le sire de Fontenay,
Le conte Deureux,
Le sire de Rebelchil,
Alain Fergant, conte de Bretaigne,
Le sire de S Vallery,
Le conte Deu,
Gualtier Gifford, conte de Longeville,
Le sire Destouteville,
Le conte Thomas Daubmalle,
Guill, conte de Hoymes et Darques,
Le sire de Bereville,
Le sire de Breante,
Le sire de Freanville,
Le sire de Pavilly,
Le sire de Clere,
Toustan du Bec,
Le sire Maugny,
Roger de Montgomery,
Amaury de Touars :—

Over and besides the great number of knights and esquires that were under them; in the same battle between the said William the Bastard, duke of Normandy, on the one part, and King Harold, on the other part, there were slain on King Harold's side, of Englishmen, 66,654; and on Duke William's side, there were slain 6,013 men, as is to be found in the Chronicle of St. Peter of Westminster, besides those that were drowned in the river Thames.

When the abovenamed and many other great lords were so called, some of them appeared, and others did not, for some of them were slain there in the field, and others so wounded, that they could not come forth to show themselves. Then gave the duke commandment that the dead should be buried, and those that were sick comforted, and eased the best that might.

Out of the ancient Chronicles of England, touching the names of other Normans who seemed to remain alive after the battle, and who were advanced to the seigniories of this land.

John de Maundevile,
Adam Undevile,
Bernard de Frevile,
Richard de Rochvile,
Gilbard de Frankvile,
Hugo de Dovile,
Symond de Rotevile,
R de Evyle,
B. de Knevuile,
Hugo de Morvile,
R de Colevile,
A. de Warvile,
C. de Karvile,
R. de Rotevile,
S. de Stotevile,
H. Bonum,
J. Monum,
W. de Vignoum,
K. de Vispount,
W. Bailbeof,
S de Baleyne,
H de Marreys,
J. Aguleyne,
G. Agilon,
R. Chamburlayne,
N. de Vendres,
H. de Verdon,
H. de Verto,
C de Vernon,
H. Hardul,
C. Cappan,
W. de Camvile,
T. de Cameyes,
R de Rotes,
R de Boys,
W. de Waren,
T. de Wardboys,
R. de Boys,
W. de Audeley,
K Dynham,
R. de Vaures,
G. Vargenteyn,
I de Hastings,
G. de Hastank,
L. de Burgee,
R. de Butuileyn,
H. de Malebranche,
S. de Malemain,
G de Hautevile,
H. Hauteyn,
R. de Morteyn,
R de Mortimere,
G de Kanovile,
E. de Columb,
W Paynel,
C. Panner,
H. Pontrel,
I. de Rivers,
T. Revile,
W. de Beauchamp,
R. de Beaupale,
E de Ou,
F. Lovel,
S. de Troys,
I. de Artel,
John de Montebrugg,
H. de Mounteserel,
W. Trussebut,
W Trussel,
H Byset,
R. Basset,
R. Molet,
H. Malovile,
G Bonet,
P. de Bonvile,
S de Rovile,
N. de Norbec,
I. de Corneux,
P de Corbet,
W. de Mountague,
S. de Mountfychet,
I de Genevyle,
H. Gyffard,
I. de Say,
T Gilbard,
R. de Chalons,
S de Chauward,
H. Feret,
Hugo Pepard,
J. de Harecourt,
H. de Haunsard,
J. de Lamare,
P. de Mautrevers,
G. de Ferron,
R. de Ferrers,
I. de Desty,
W. de Werders,
H de Bornevyle,
J. de Santenys,

William the Conqueror. A.D. 1087.

S. de Seucler,
R. de Gorges,
E. de Gemere,
W. de Feus,
S. de Filberd,
H. de Turbervyle,
R. Troblenuer,
R. de Angon,
T. de Moier,
T. de Rotelet,
H. de Spencer,
E. de Saintquinten,
I. de Saint Martin,
G. de Custan,
Saint Constantin,
Saint Leger et Saint Med.
M. de Cronu et de St Viger,
S. de Crayel,
R. de Crenker,
N. Meyuell,
I. de Berners,
S. de Chumli,
E. de Charers,
J. de Grey,
W. de Grangers,
S. de Grangers,
S. Baubenyn,
H. Vamgers,
E. Bertram,
R. Bygot,
S. Tieoly,
I. Trigos,
G. de Feues,
H. Filiot,
R. Taperyn,
S. Talbot,
H. Santsaver,
T. de Samford,
G. de Vandien,
C. de Vautort,
G. de Mountague,
Thomas de Chambernon,
S. de Montfort,
R. de Feinevaux,
W. de Valence,
T. Clarel,
S. de Clervaus,
P. de Aubemarle,
H. de Saint Arvant,
E. de Auganuteys,
S. de Gant,
G. de Malearbe,
H. Mandut,
W. Chesun,
L. de Chandut,
B. Filzurs,
B. vicount de Low,
G. de Cantemere,
T. de Cantlow,
R. Breaunce,
T. de Broxeboof,
S. de Bolebec,
B. Mol de Boef,
J. de Muelis,
R. de Brus,
S. de Brewes,
J. de Lylle,
T. de Bellyle,
I. de Watervile,
G. de Nevyle,
R. de Neuburgh,
H. de Burgoyne,
G. de Bourgh,
S. de Lymoges,
L. de Lyben,
W. de Helyoun,
H. de Hildrebron,
R. de Loges,
S. de Seintlow,
I. de Maubank,
P. de Saint Malow,
R. de Leoferne,
J. de Lovotot,
G. de Dabbevyle,
H. de Appetot,
W. de Percy,
H. de Lacy,
C. de Quincy,
E. Tracy,
R. de la Souche,
V. de Somery,
I. de Saint John,
T. de Saint Gory,
P. de Boyly,
Richard de Saint Valery,
P. de Pinkeni,
S. de Pavely,
G. de Monthaut,
T. de Mountchesy,
R. de Lymozy,
G. de Lucy,
J. de Artoys,
N. de Arty,
P. de Grenvyle,
I. de Greys,
V. de Ciesty,
F. de Courcy,
T. de Lamar,
H. de Lymastz,
J. de Monbray,
C. de Morley,
S. de Gorney,
R. de Courtenay,
P. de Gourney,
R. de Cony,
I. de la Huse,
R. de la Huse,
V. de Longevyle,
P. Longespye,
J. Pouchardon,
R. de la Pomercy,
J. de Pountz,
R. de Pontlarge,
R. Estraunge,
Thomas Savage.

Hirman the first bishop of Salisbury. A little above, mention was made of the bishop's see of Sherborne, translated from thence to Salisbury. The first bishop of Salisbury was Hirman, a Norman, who first began the new church and minster of Salisbury. After him succeeded Osmund, who finished the work, and replenished the house with great living, and much good singing. This Osmund first began the ordinary, *The use and order of Sarum, how and when disused.* which was called 'Secundum usum Sarum.' an. 1076, the occasion whereof was this, as I find in an old story-book, entitled 'Eulogium.'[1] A great contention chanced at Glastonbury between Thurstan the abbot, and his convent, in the days of William the Conqueror. This Thurstan the said William had brought out of Normandy from the abbey of Cadonum, and placed him as abbot of Glastonbury. The cause of this contentious battle was, for that Thurstan, contemning their choir-service, then called 'The use of St. Gregory,' compelled his monks to 'The use of William,' a monk of Fiscam, in Normandy. Whereupon came strife and contentions amongst them, first in

(1) "Ordinale ecclesiastici officii secundum asum Sarum." Ex Eulogio Histor lib iii

William Rufus — A.D. 1087.

words, then from words to blows, after blows then to armour. The abbot, with his guard of harnessed men, fell upon the monks, and drave them to the steps of the high altar, where two were slain, and eight were wounded with shafts, swords, and pikes. The monks, then driven to such a strait and narrow shift, were compelled to defend themselves with forms and candlesticks, wherewith they did wound certain of the soldiers. One monk there was, an aged man, who instead of his shield took an image of the crucifix in his arms for his defence, which image was wounded in the breast by one of the bowmen, whereby the monk was saved. My story addeth more, that the striker, incontinent upon the same, fell mad, which savoureth of some monkish addition besides the text. This matter being brought before the king, the abbot was sent again to Cadonum, and the monks, by the commandment of the king, were scattered in far countries. Thus, by the occasion hereof, Osmund, bishop of Salisbury, devised that ordinary, which is called, 'The use of Sarum,' and was afterward received in a manner through all England, Ireland, and Wales. And thus much for this matter, done in the time of this King William.

This William, after his death, by his wife Matilda, or Maud, left three sons, Robert Courtsey, to whom he gave the duchy of Normandy; William Rufus, his second son, to whom he gave the kingdom of England; and Henry, the third son, to whom he left and gave treasure, and warned William to be to his people loving and liberal, Robert to be to his people stern and sturdy.

Example of God's judgment upon a bishop, who being unmerciful to the poor was eaten by rats and mice.

In the history called 'Jornalensis,' it is reported of a certain great man, who about this time of King William was compassed about with mice and rats, and flying to the midst of a river, yet when that would not serve, came to the land again, and was of them devoured. The Germans say that this was a bishop, who dwelling between Cologne and Mentz, in time of famine and dearth, having store of corn and grain, would not help the poverty crying to him for relief, but rather wished his corn to be eaten up of mice and rats. Wherefore, being compassed with mice and rats, by the just judgment of God, to avoid the annoyance of them, he built a tower in the midst of the river Rhine, which yet to this day the Dutchmen call 'Rat's Tower;' but all that would not help, for the rats and mice swam over to him in as great abundance as they did before, of whom at length he was devoured.

WILLIAM RUFUS.[1]

A.D. 1087.

William Rufus, the second son of William the Conqueror, began his reign A.D. 1087, and reigned thirteen years, being crowned at Westminster by Lanfranc; who, after his coronation, released out of prison, by the request of his father, divers English lords, who before had been in custody. It chanced that, at the death of William the Conqueror, Robert Courtsey, his eldest son, was absent in Almany, who, hearing of the death of his father, and how William, his younger brother, had taken upon him the kingdom, was therewith

(1) Edition 1583, p 184 Ed 1596, p 166. Ed 1684, vol i p 207 —Ed

William Rufus. greatly moved; insomuch that he laid his dukedom to pledge unto his brother Henry, and with that good gathered unto him an army,
A.D. 1087. and so landed at Hampton, to the intent to have expelled his brother from the kingdom. But William Rufus, hearing thereof, sent to him fair and gentle words, promising him dedition and subjection, as to the more worthy and elder brother; this thing only requiring, that seeing he was now in place and possession, he might enjoy it during his life, paying to him yearly three thousand marks, on condition that which of them overlived the other should enjoy the kingdom. The occasion of this variance between these brethren wrought a great dissension between the Norman lords and bishops, both in England and in Normandy, insomuch that all the Norman bishops within the realm almost rebelled against the king, taking part with Duke Robert, except only Lanfranc, and Wolstan, bishop of Worcester, above-mentioned, an Englishman; who, for his virtue and constancy, was so well liked and favoured of his citizens, that emboldened with his presence and prayer, they stoutly maintained the city of Worcester against the siege of their enemies, and at last vanquished them with utter ruin. But Duke Robert, at length, by the advice of his council (hearing the words sent unto him, and wagging his head thereat, as one conceiving some matter of doubt or doubleness), was yet content to assent to all that was desired, and so returned shortly after into Normandy, leaving the bishops, and such others, in the briars, who were in England, taking his part against the king.

Worcester stoutly defended.

This Rufus was so ill liked of the Normans, that between him and his lords was oft dissension; wherefore well near all the Normans took part against him, so that he was forced of necessity to draw to him the Englishmen. Again, so covetous he was, and so immeasurable in his tasks and takings, in selling benefices, abbies, and bishoprics, that he was hated of all Englishmen.

A.D. 1090. Death of Lanfranc, archbishop of Canterbury.

In the third year of this king died Lanfranc, archbishop of Canterbury, from whose commendation and worthiness, as I list not to detract any thing (being so greatly magnified of Polydore, his countryman) so neither do I see any great cause why to add any thing thereunto. This I think, unless that man had brought with him less superstition, and more sincere science into Christ's church, he might have kept him in his own country still, and have confuted Berengarius at home. After the decease of Lanfranc, the see of Canterbury stood empty four years.

Lincoln minster builded.

After the council of Lanfranc above mentioned, wherein was concluded for translating of bishops' sees from villages into head cities, Remigius, bishop of Dorchester, who, as ye heard, accompanied Lanfranc to Rome, removed his bishop's see from Dorchester to Lincoln, where he builded the minster, situated upon a hill within the said city of Lincoln. The dedication of that church Robert, archbishop of York, did resist, saying, that it was builded within the ground of his precinct; but afterwards it had his Romish dedication by Robert Bleuet, next bishop that followed. By the same Remigius, also, was founded the cloister or monastery of Stow, &c.

Stow abbey builded.

A.D. 1091. In the fourth year of this king great tempests fell in sundry

William Rufus. A.D. 1091.

places in England, specially at Winchcombe, where the steeple was burned with lightning, the church wall burst through, the head and right leg of the crucifix, with the image of our Lady on the right side of the crucifix, thrown down, and such a stench left in the church, that none might abide it. In London the force of the weather and tempest overturned six hundred houses. In the same tempest the roof of Bow church was hurled up in the wind, and by the vehemency thereof was pitched down a great deepness into the ground.

Six hundred houses blown down with wind. The roof of Bow church overthrown.

King William, as ye have heard, an exceeding pillager, or ravener rather, of church goods, after he had given the bishopric of Lincoln to his chancellor, Robert Bleuet, above mentioned, began to cavil; avouching the see of Lincoln to belong to the see of York, till the bishop of Lincoln had pleased him with a great sum of money, of five thousand marks, &c.

Robert Blevet paid five thousand marks for his bishopric.

As nothing could come in those days without money from the king, so Herbert Losinga, paying to the king a piece of money, was made bishop of Thetford, as he had paid a little before to be abbot of Ramsey; who, likewise, at the same time, removing his see from Thetford to the city of Norwich, there erected the cathedral church, with the cloister, in the said city of Norwich, where he furnished the monks with sufficient living and rents of his own charges, besides the bishop's lands. Afterward, repenting of his open and manifest simony, he went to Rome, where he resigned into the pope's hands his bishopric, but so that immediately he received it again. This Herbert was the son of an abbot called Robert, for whom he purchased of the king to be bishop of Winchester, whereof run these verses:

Norwich minster builded by Herbert Losinga.

> "Filius est præsul, pater abba, Simon uterque:
> Quid non speremus si nummos possideamus?
> Omnia nummus habet, quod vult facit, addit et aufert.
> Res nimis injusta, nummus fit præsul et abba."

Ye heard a little before of the death of Pope Hildebrand, after the time of which Hildebrand the German emperors began to lose their authority and right in the pope's election, and in giving of benefices. For next after this Hildebrand came Pope Victor, by the setting up of Matilda, and the duke of Normandy, with the faction and retinue of Hildebrand, who likewise showed himself stout against the emperor. But God gave the shrewd cow short horns, for Victor being poisoned, as some say, in his chalice, sat but one year and a half. Notwithstanding the same imitation and example of Hildebrand continued still in them that followed after. And, like as the kings of Israel followed for the most part the steps of Jeroboam, till the time of their desolation; so, for the greatest part, all popes followed the steps and proceedings of this Hildebrand, their spiritual Jeroboam, in maintaining false worship, and chiefly in upholding the dignity of the see, against all rightful authority, and the lawful kingdom of Sion. In the time of this Victor began the order of the monks of Charterhouse, through the means of one Hugo, bishop of Gracianople, and of Bruno, bishop of Cologne.

Pope Victor poisoned in his chalice. A comparison between Hildebrand, pope of Rome, and Jeroboam, king of Israel. The order of Charter monks began.

Next to Victor sat Urban II., by whom the acts of Hildebrand were confirmed, and also new decrees enacted against Henry the

William Rufus

A.D. 1095

Two popes in Rome

The order of Cistercian or white monks began

emperor. In this time were two popes at Rome, Urban and Clement III., whom the emperor set up. Under Pope Urban came in the white monks of the Cistercian order, by one Stephen Harding, a monk of Sherborne, an Englishman, by whom this order had its beginning in the wilderness of Cistery, within the province of Burgoin, as witnesseth Cestrensis. Others write that this Harding was the second abbot of that place, and that it was first founded by the means of one Robert, abbot of Molesme, in Cistercium, a forest in Burgundy, A.D. 1098, persuaded perchance by Harding; and afterwards, A.D. 1135, it was brought into England by a certain man called Espek, who builded an abbey of the same order, called Merinale. In this order the monks did live by the labour of their hands; they paid no tithes nor offerings; they wore no fur nor lining; they wore red shoes, their cowls white, and coats black, they were all shorn save a little circle; they eat no flesh but only on their journey. Of this order was Bernard.

Council of Rome.

This Urban held divers councils; one at Rome, where he excommunicated all such lay persons as gave investure of any ecclesiastical benefice, also all such of the clergy as subjected themselves to be underlings or servants to lay persons for ecclesiastical benefices, &c.

A.D. 1095 Council of Clermont

The voyage unto the Holy Land

Another council he held at Clermont[1] in France, A.D. 1095, where among other things, the bishop made an oration to the lords there present, concerning the voyage and recovery of the Holy Land from the Turks and Saracens. The cause of this voyage first arose through one Peter, a monk or hermit, who, being in Jerusalem, and seeing the great misery of the Christians under the pagans, made thereof declaration to Pope Urban, and was therein a great solicitor to all christian princes. By reason of this, after the aforesaid oration of Pope Urban, thirty thousand men, taking on them the sign of the cross for their cognizance, made preparation for that voyage, whose captains were Godfrey duke of Lorrain, with his two brethren, Eustace and Baldwin, the bishop of Pody, Bohemund duke of Puell, and his nephew Tancred, Raymund earl of St. Egidius, Robert earl of Flanders, and Hugh le Grand, brother of Philip the French king:

(1) The first crusade arose out of the deliberations of a council held at Placentia, in March, A.D. 1095, and from the one here mentioned held in November following, at Clermont, at which Pope Urban presided. The origin of these destructive and chimerical undertakings appears to be this. The infidels in a few years had obtained possession of above one half of the empire of the East; churches and monasteries had been plundered, and priests, monks, and christian laity, cruelly massacred, while unoffending pilgrims, who from feelings of real piety, or superstition, were accustomed to visit the holy city suffered the most cruel oppression, slavery, and death.—[See William, Archb. of Tyre's Hist. of the Holy Wars, book i. c. 9. A.D. 1095.] Three hundred thousand men from France, Italy, and Germany, commenced their march to the East, but as the object of their undertaking was to extirpate the enemies of the christian faith, Jews as well as infidels fell a sacrifice to their fury. At Verdun, Spires, Worms, Cologne, and Mentz, the most horrible atrocities were committed against those unhappy outcasts, whose only chance of safety consisted in professing themselves Christians, and renouncing their religion.—[Bertold in Chron. ad ann. 1096.] Such unholy conduct, however, on the part of the crusaders, induced the inhabitants of the countries through which they passed, who were continually the victims of their plunder, to resent the injuries which they suffered. So effectual was the opposition which they offered, that by the 1st of August in the same year, on the arrival of the last division of the army under Peter the Hermit at Constantinople, he was scarcely able to add twenty thousand men to the two divisions which had already arrived in an equally enfeebled condition. This army, after committing the most unjustifiable excesses upon their friends the Greeks, crossed the Hellespont, and in two divisions were defeated and cut to pieces by the Turks. In A.D. 1099, another better disciplined army assembled at Constantinople, which, after crossing the Hellespont, amounted to about five hundred thousand foot, and one hundred thousand horse. After a most severe, although victorious campaign, with a very reduced force, Jerusalem was taken by scalade, on Friday, the 15th July, 1099. Twenty thousand Turks were massacred, and after eight days devoted to processions and religious ceremonies, Godfrey of Bouillon, who was the second to scale the wall, was unanimously elected king of Jerusalem. Pope Urban II., however, did not live to hear of these successes; he died on the 29th day of July in the same year, and the news of the victory had consequently not reached Rome; this was communicated to Paschal II. who succeeded him in the papal chair.—ED.

William Rufus. A.D. 1096.

to whom also was joined Robert Curthoyse, duke of Normandy, with divers other noblemen, along with the aforesaid Peter the Hermit, who was the chief cause of that voyage.

At that time many of the said noblemen put their lands and lordships out to mortgage, to provide for the aforenamed voyage; as Godfrey, duke of Lorrain, who sold the dukedom of Bologna to the bishop of Eburone, for a great sum of money. Also Robert Curthoyse, duke of Normandy, laid his dukedom to pledge to his brother William, king of England, for ten thousand pounds. &c.

A.D.1096.

Thus, the Christians, who passed first over the Bosphorus, having for their captain Peter the Hermit, a man perchance more devout than expert to guide an army, being trapped of their enemies, were slain and murdered in great numbers among the Bulgarians, and near to the town called Civita.

The acts of the Christians in their voyage to win Jerusalem.

When the nobles and the whole army met together at Constantinople, where Alexius was emperor, passing over by the Hellespont, going to Jerusalem, they took the cities of Nice, Heraclea, Tarsis, and subdued the country of Cicilia, appointing the possession thereof to certain of their captains.

Antioch taken by the Christians.

Antioch was besieged, and in the ninth month of the siege it was yielded to the Christians, by one Pyrrhus, about which season were fought many strong battles, to the great slaughter and desolation of the Saracens, and not without loss of many christian men. The governance of this city was committed to Bohemund, duke of Puell, whose martial knighthood was often proved in time of the siege thereof. And not long after Carbona, master of the Persian chivalry, was vanquished and slain, with a hundred thousand infidels. In that discomfiture were taken fifteen thousand camels.

A.D.1098. The slaughter of the Persian infidels.

Jerusalem conquered by the Christians.

Jerusalem, on the nine and thirtieth day of the siege, was conquered by the Christians, and Robert, duke of Normandy, was elect to be king thereof.[1] Howbeit, he refused it, hearing of the death of King William Rufus of England; wherefore he never sped well in all his affairs after the same. Then Godfrey, captain of the christian army, was proclaimed the first king of Jerusalem. At the taking of the city there was such a murder of men that blood was congealed in the streets the thickness of a foot. Then after Godfrey reigned Baldwin, his brother; after him Baldwin the second, his nephew. Then Gaufrid, duke of Gaunt; and after him Gaufrid, his son, by whom many great battles were fought there against the Saracens, and all the country thereabout subdued, save Ascalon, &c. And thus much hitherto touching the voyage to the Holy Land: now to our own land again.

The king of England's judgment against the pope.

About this time, as Matthew Paris writeth, the king of England favoured not much the see of Rome, because of the impudent and insatiable exactions which they required; neither would he suffer any of his subjects to go to Rome, alleging these words, "Because they follow not the steps of Peter, hunting for rewards; neither have they the power and authority of him, whose holiness they declare themselves not to follow."[2]

(1) Ex Hen. lib. vii.
(2) "Quod Petri non inhærent vestigiis, præmiis inhiantes, non ejus potestatem retinent, cujus sanctitatem probantur non imitari."—Ex Matt. Paris.

William Rufus

A.D. 1093.

By the same Urban, the seven hours, which we call 'septem horas canonicas,' were first instituted in the church.

Decrees of Pope Urban

Item, By this pope it was decreed, that no bishop should be made but under the name and title of some certain place.

Item, That matins and hours of the day should every day be said.[1]

Item, That every Saturday should be said the mass of our Lady, and that all the Jews' Sabbath should be turned to the service of our Lady, as in the council of Turin, to the which service was appointed the anthem, "Ora pro populo, interveni pro clero, intercede pro devoto fœmineo sexu."[2]

Item, That all such of the clergy as had wives should be deprived of their order.[3]

Item, That it should be lawful for subjects to break their oath of allegiance, with all such as were by the pope excommunicated.

Item, That it should not be lawful for husband and wife to christen one child both together; with many more matters.[4]

Example of God's righteous judgment in punishing murder

In the sixth year of the reign of William Rufus, Malcolm king of Scots, who four times before had made great slaughter of old and young in the north parts, as is before showed, burst into Northumberland, with all the power he could make, and there, by the right judgment of God, was slain with his son Edward, and also Margaret his wife, sister to Edgar Etheling, above-minded, a virtuous and devout lady, within three days after.

The same year he gave the archbishopric of Canterbury, after that he had detained the same in his own hands four years, to Anselm, abbot of Beck, in Normandy.

This Anselm was an Italian, in the city of Augsburgh, born and brought up in the abbey of Beck, in Normandy; where he was so strict a follower of virtue, that, as the story recordeth, he wished rather to be without sin in hell, than in heaven with sin. This saying and wish of his, if it were his, may seem to proceed out of a mind, neither speaking orderly according to the phrase and understanding of the Scripture, nor yet sufficiently acquainted with the justification of a christian man. Further, they report him to be so far from singularity, that he should say, it was the vice which first thrust the angels out of heaven, and afterwards man out of paradise.

Of this Anselm it is, moreover, reported, that he was so unwilling to take the archbishopric, that the king had much ado to thrust it upon him; and he was so desirous to have him take it, that the city of Canterbury, which before Lanfranc did hold but at the king's good will and pleasure, he gave now to Anselm wholly, which was about A.D. 1093. But as desirous as the king was then to place the said Anselm there, so much did he repent it afterward, seeking all manner of means to defeat him if he might such strife and contention arose between them two for certain matters, the first ground and occasion whereof was this.

Strife and contention between the king and Anselm, archbishop of Canterbury

After Anselm had been thus elected to the see of Canterbury, before he was fully consecrated, the king communed with him,

(1) Vid John Stella (2) Vid Nauclerus (3) Dist 31 Eos qui 15 q 6 Juratos.

(4) By the same pope thus many chapters stand written in the canon law, dist 7 Sanctorum, dist 31 Eos qui 1 q 1 Si qui dist 56 Presbyterorum, 11 q 3 quibus 15 q 6 Juratos 16 p 7 Congregatio 19. q 2 Statuimus, 23 q 8 Tributum, 30 q 4 quod autem 30 q 8 quod autem, &c.

assaying by all gentle manner of words to entreat him, that such lands and possessions of the church of Canterbury as the king had given and granted to his friends since the death of Lanfranc, they might still enjoy as their own lawful possessions through his grant and permission. But to this Anselm in no case would agree. Whereupon the king, conceiving great displeasure against him, did stop his consecration a great season, till at length in long process of time the king, enforced by the daily complaints and desires of his people and subjects, for lack of an archbishop to moderate the church, was constrained to admit and authorize him unto them. Thus Anselm, with much ado, taking his consecration, and doing his homage to the king, went to his see of Canterbury; and not long after the king sailed over to Normandy.

William Rufus. A.D. 1098.

About this time there were two striving in Rome for the popedom, as is afore-noticed, Urban and Guibert,—divers realms diversely consenting, some to the one, some to the other. England, taking with their king, was rather inclined to Guibert, called Clemens III.; but Anselm did fully go with Urban, making so his exception with the king on entering his bishopric. After the king was returned again from Normandy, the archbishop cometh to him, and asketh leave to go to Rome to fetch his pall of Pope Urban; which when he could not at first obtain, he maketh his appeal from the king to the pope. Whereat the king, being justly displeased, chargeth the archbishop with breach of his fealty, contrary to his promise made; that is, if he, without his license, should appeal either to Urban or to any other pope. Anselm answereth again, that it was to be referred unto some greater council, where it is to be disputed whether this be to break a man's allegiance to a terrene prince, if he appeal to the vicar of St. Peter. And here much arguing and contending was on both sides. The king's reason proceedeth thus: "The custom," saith he, "from my father's time hath been in England, that no person should appeal to the pope without the king's license. He that breaketh the customs of the realm, violateth the power and crown of the kingdom. He that violateth and taketh away my crown, is a traitor and enemy against me," &c. To this Anselm replieth again, "The Lord," saith he, "easily discusseth this question, briefly teaching what fidelity and allegiance we ought to give unto the vicar of St. Peter, where he saith, 'Thou art Peter, and upon this rock will I build my church,' &c.: and, 'To thee I will give the keys of the kingdom of heaven, and whatsoever thou shalt bind in earth, it shall be bound in heaven; and, whatsoever thou loosest in earth, shall be loosed in heaven,' &c. Again, to them all in general he saith, 'He that heareth you, heareth me; and whoso despiseth you, despiseth me.' And in another place, 'He that toucheth you, toucheth the apple of mine eye.' On the other side, what duty we owe to the king, he showeth also: 'Give,' saith he, 'to the emperor, what belongeth to the emperor, and to God, that which to God belongeth.' Wherefore, in such things as belong to God I will yield, and must yield by good right and duty, my obedience to the vicar of St. Peter, and in such things as belong again to terrene dignity of my prince, in those I will not deny to him my faithful help and counsel, so far as they can extend."

Urban and Clement striving for the papacy.

Anselm charged for a traitor.

Custom of England from William the Conqueror's time, not to appeal to the pope.

Anselm here ignorantly calleth the pope the vicar of St. Peter, whereas the canon law calleth him but the successor of Peter, and vicar of Christ.

William Rufus. A.D. 1098.

Thus have ye the grounded arguments of this prelate to stand so stiffly against his prince, whereunto peradventure was joined also some piece of a stubborn heart. But in this conclusion none of his fellow-bishops durst take his part, but were all against him; namely, William, bishop of Durham, to whom Anselm thus protesteth, saying, "Whosoever he were that would presume to prove it any breach of allegiance or fealty to his sovereign, if he appealed to the vicar of St. Peter, he was ready to answer at all times to the contrary." The bishop of Durham answereth again, "That he who would not be ruled by reason, must with force be constrained," &c. The king, having on his part the agreement of the bishops, thought both to deprive the archbishop of his pastoral see, and to expel him out of the realm. But he could not perform his purpose; for Anselm, as he was ready to depart the realm, said, wheresoever he went, he would take his office and authority with him, though he took nothing else; whereupon that matter was deferred till a longer time. In the mean season the king had sent privily two messengers to Pope Urban, to entreat him to send his pall to the king, for him to give it where he would, which messengers, by this time, were returned again, bringing with them from Rome Gualter, bishop of Alban, the pope's legate, with the pall to be given unto Anselm. This legate, first landing at Dover, from thence came privily (unknown to Anselm) to the king, declaring and promising, that if Urban was received pope in England, whatsoever the king required to be obtained, he, by his privilege from the apostolical see, would ratify and confirm the same, save only, that when the king required of the legate that Anselm might be removed, the legate thereunto would not agree, saying, "that it was impossible to be obtained, that such a man as he, being lawfully called, should be expelled without manifest cause." In conclusion, so it followed, that although he could not obtain his request of the legate, yet the legate so wrought with the king, that Urban was proclaimed lawful pope throughout all the realm."

All the bishops of the realm on the king's side against Anselm.

Gualter the pope's legate cometh to England.

The pope taketh this as no fault, for a subject to resist his king.

Then were sent to Anselm certain bishops to move and prove his mind, declaring what charges and pains the king had been at in his behalf, to procure the pall for him from Rome, which otherwise would have stood him in a great expense, and that all this the king had done for his sake, wherefore it were good reason and convenient, that he, to gratify the king, should somewhat condescend to his request again. But with all this Anselm, the stout archbishop, would not be moved. Wherefore the king, seeing no other remedy, was compelled to grant unto him the full right of his archbishopric. And so on the day appointed, when the pall should be brought to Canterbury, it being carried with all solemnity in a thing of silver, the archbishop, with a great concourse of people, came forth barefoot with his priestly vestments, after a most goodly manner, to meet the same; and so being brought in, it was laid upon the altar, while Anselm, spreading over his shoulders his popish vestments, proceeded unto his popish mass.

The manner of bringing Anselm's pall into Canterbury.

Thus agreement being made between the king and the bishop, so long as it would hold, it happened, in the year following, that the king with his army entered into Wales, to subdue such as there rebelled against him. After the victory gotten, the king returned home again with triumph; to whom Anselm thought to have come to congratulate him on his prosperous success. But the king prevented him by messengers, laying to the bishop's charge both the small number and the evil service of his soldiers sent to him at his need. At the hearing hereof, all the hope of Anselm was dashed, who at the same present had thought to have obtained and done many great matters with the king touching the state of the church; but here all turned contrary to his expectation, insomuch that he was charged, against the next court of parliament, to make his answer, which he avoided by appealing to Rome; wherefore he made his suit and friends to the king for license to go to the pope. To that suit the king answered, that he should not go, neither was there any cause for him so to do; for that both he knew him to be of so sound a life, that he had done no such offence, whereof he needed to crave absolution at Rome, neither was there any such lack of science and knowledge, that he needed to borrow any counsel there: "insomuch," saith the king, "that I dare say Pope Urban hath rather to give place to the wisdom of Anselm, than Anselm to have need of Urban. Wherefore, as he hath no cause to go, so I charge him to tarry. And if he continue in his stubbornness still, I will assuredly seize upon his possessions, and convert his archbishopric into my coffers, for that he transgresseth and breaketh his fidelity and obeisance, promising before to observe all the customs of my kingdom; neither is it the fashion in this realm, that any of my nobles should go to Rome without my sending. And therefore let him swear unto me that he shall not for any grievance appeal hereafter to the see of Rome, or else let him void my realm."

William Rufus

A.D 1098.

Another quarrel of the king against Anselm, who appealeth to Rome

No prelate or nobleman to go to Rome without the king's sending

Against these words of the king, Anselm thinking not best to reply again by any message, but by word of mouth, coming himself personally to the king, placeth himself, after his order, on the right hand of the prince, where he made his reply unto the message sent to him by the king.

"Whereas you say, I ought not to go to Rome, either in regard of any trespass, or for abundance of counsel and knowledge in me, (albeit I grant neither of them to be true,) yet what the truth is therein, I refer it to the judgment of God. And whereas ye say that I promised to keep and observe your customs; that I grant, but with a condition, so far to keep them, and such of them to observe, as were consonant to the laws of God, and ruled with right and equity. Moreover, whereas ye charge me with breach of my fidelity and allegiance, for that contrary to your customs I appeal to the see apostolic, (my reverence and duty to your sovereignty reserved) if another would say it, that is untrue For the fidelity and obeisance that I owe to thee, O king, I have it of the faith and fidelity of God, whose vicar St Peter is, to whose seat I do appeal. Further, whereas, as ye require me to swear that I shall for no cause hereafter at any time appeal to Rome, I pronounce openly that a christian prince requireth such an oath of his archbishop unjustly, for if I should forswear St. Peter, I should deny Christ. And when I shall at any time deny Christ, then shall I be content and ready to stand to the satisfaction of my transgression to you, for asking license to go to Rome. And peradventure, when I am gone, the goods of the church shall not so serve your temporal desires and commodities as ye ween for."

Anselm's answer to the king

Note the high reasons of Anselm.

At these words of the bishop, the king and his nobles were not a little incensed, they defending again, that in his promise of observing the king's customs, there was neither condition nor any clause put

William Rufus.

A.D. 1098.

in, either of God or right. "There was not," said Anselm. "If so be that in your customs was neither mention made of God nor of right, of what was there mention then? For God forbid that any Christian should be bound to any customs which go contrary to God and to right." Thus on both sides passed much altercation between them.

The bishops leave Anselm alone.

At length the king, after many threatening words, told him he should carry nothing out of the realm with him. "Well," said the bishop, "if I may neither have my horse nor garments with me, then will I walk on foot;" and so addressed him toward his journey, all the other bishops forsaking him, whereof none would take his part; but if he came to them for counsel, they said he was wise enough, and needed not their counsel, as who for his prudence knew best what was to be done, as also for his holiness was willing and able to prosecute the same that he did know. As for them, they neither durst nor would stand against the king, their lord, whose favour they could not lack, for the peril that might happen both to themselves and their kindred; but for him, because he was both a stranger, and void of such worldly corruption in him, they willed him to go forward as he had begun; their secret consent he should have, but their open voice they would not give him. Thus Anselm, remaining at Dover fifteen days, tarrying for wind, at last sped him toward his passage; but his packing being secretly known in the court, the king's officer, William Warlwast, prevented his purpose, searching, by the king's commandment, all his trusses, coffers, satchels, sleeves, purse, napkin, and bosom, for letters and for money; and so let him pass. Anselm, sailing into France, first rested a while at Lyons, and from thence came to Rome to complain to Pope Urban, according to the tenor and form of a certain epistle of his, wherein, among many other things in the same epistle contained, these words he writeth to Pope Paschal, the third year after his banishment, after the death of Urban, and a little before the death of the king.

Anselm flying out of England.

Anselm searched by the king's officer for letters and money.

To the Lord and Reverend Father Paschal, high bishop, Anselm, servant of the church of Canterbury, offereth due subjection from his heart, and prayers, if they can stand in any stead, &c. &c.[1]

A fragment or portion of a letter.

I see in England many evils, whose correction belongeth to me, and which I could neither amend, nor suffer without mine own fault. The king desireth of me, that under the name of right, I should consent to his pleasures, which were against the law and will of God. For he would not have the pope received nor appealed unto in England without his commandment; neither that I should send a letter unto him, or receive any from him, or that I should obey his decrees. He suffered not a council to be kept in his realm now these thirteen years since he was king. In all these things, and such like, if I asked any counsel, all my suffragan bishops of his realm denied to give me any counsel, but according to the king's pleasure. After that I saw these and such other things that are done against the will and law of God, I asked license of him to go to Rome, unto the see apostolical, that I might there take counsel for my soul, and the office committed unto me. The king said, that I offended against him for the only asking of license; and propounded to me, that either I should make him amends for the same as a trespass, (assuring him never to ask his license any more to appeal to the pope at any time hereafter,) or else that I should quickly depart out of his land. Wherefore, choosing rather to go out of the

The king would not have the pope received nor appealed unto in England.

(1) Ex Legend. Anselm. aut Eadmero. Et ex Epist. Anselm. 36, paulo post initium.

land than agree to so wicked a thing, I came to Rome, as you know, and declared the whole matter to the lord pope. The king, by and by, as soon as I went out of England, invaded the whole archbishopric, and turned it to his own use, taxing the monks only with bare meat, drink, and cloth. The king being warned and desired of the lord pope to amend this, contemned the same, and yet continueth in his purpose still. And now is the third year since I came thus out of England, and more. Some men, not understanding, demand why I did not excommunicate the king. But the wiser sort, and such as have understanding, counsel me that I do not this thing; because it belongeth not unto me both to complain and to punish. To conclude, I was forewarned by my friends that are under the king, that my excommunication (if it should be done) would be laughed to scorn and despised," &c.

William Rufus.

A.D. 1098.

Anselm complaineth of the king and of his suffragan bishops. The king contemneth the pope's warning.

By these here above prefixed, appeareth how Anselm the archbishop, coming unto Rome, made his complaint to Pope Urban of the king; and how the pope writing unto the king in behalf of Anselm, his letters and commandments were despised. And now to our story. In the mean time, while the pope's letters were sent to the king, Anselm was bid to wait about the pope to look for answer back, who perceiving, at length, how little the king reputed the pope's letters, began to be weary of his office, desiring the pope that he might be discharged thereof; but the pope in no case would thereto consent, charging him upon his obedience, that wheresoever he went, he should bear with him the name and honour of the archbishop of Canterbury. Whereunto Anselm again said, his obedience he neither durst nor would refuse, as who for God's cause was ready to suffer whatsoever should happen, yea, though it were death itself, as he thought no less would follow thereof. "But what should we think," saith he, "is there to be done, where justice not only taketh no place, but is utterly oppressed? And whereas my suffragans do not only not help, for dread, the righteous cause, but also for favour do impugn the same?" "Well," saith the pope, "as touching these matters, we shall sufficiently provide at the next council to be holden at Bayonne, whereas I will you the same time and place to be present."

Council of Bayonne.

When the time of the council was come, Anselm, amongst others, was called for, who, first sitting on an outer side of the bishops, afterwards was placed at the right foot of the pope, with these words, "Includamus hunc in orbe nostro, tanquam alterius orbis papam." Whereupon the same place after him was appointed to the successors of the see of Canterbury, in every general council, by the decree of Pope Urban, to sit at the right foot of the pope. In this said council great stir and much reasoning there was against the Grecians, concerning the matter and order of proceeding of the Holy Ghost. Here is to be noted, that the Greek[1] church hath of long time dissented from the Latin church in many and sundry points, to the number of twenty, or almost twenty-nine articles, as I have them collected out of the register of the church of Hereford; whereof, as occasion hereafter may serve (God willing) for a further and more ample tractation to be made; so here, by the way, partly I mean to touch some. The first is—

Anselm and his successors of Canterbury, placed at the right foot of the pope in his general councils.

De processione spiritus sancti.

(1) This dissention commenced in the seventh century; suspended for a time it was revived in 1053. Gregory IX., in 1232, endeavoured to effect a reconciliation; nor were these laudable attempts abandoned till the death of Urban IV., in 1264. Again, in the eighteenth century, the church of Rome attempted to make proselytes from the Greek church, but without success, and they remain, to this day, separate communions.—Ed.

William Rufus. A.D. 1098.

Articles and Opinions wherein the Greek Church differeth from the Latin.

The articles wherein the Greek church altereth from the Latin or Romish church, are these:[1]—

The difference between the Greek and the Latin churches.

I. They are not under the obedience of the church of Rome, because the church of Constantinople is not subject, but equal, to the same.

II. They hold that the bishop of the apostolic see of Rome hath not greater power than the four patriarchs; and whatsoever the pope doth beside their knowledge, or without their approbation, it is of no value.

III. Also, they say whatsoever hath been done or concluded, since the second general council, it is of no full authority; because from that time they recount the Latins to be in error, and to be excluded out of the holy church.

IV. Item, "Dicunt eucharistiam consecratam per Romanam ecclesiam non esse verum corpus Christi." That is, they hold the eucharist consecrated by the church of Rome not to be the very body of Christ. Also, where the Romish church doth consecrate in unleavened bread, they consecrate in bread leavened.

V. Further, they say that the Romish church doth err in the words of baptism, for saying, "I baptize thee;" when they should say, "Let this creature of God be baptized," &c.

VI. They hold moreover that there is no purgatory, and that the suffrages of the church do not avail the dead, either to lessen the pain of them that be destined to hell, or to increase the glory of them that be ordained to salvation.

VII. Also, they hold that the souls out of the bodies departed (whether they have done good or evil) have not their perfect pain or glory, but are reserved in a certain place till the day of judgment.

VIII. Also, they condemn the church of Rome for mixing cold water in their sacrifice.

IX. Also, they condemn the church of Rome, for that as well women as priests anoint children (when they baptize them) on both shoulders.

X. Item, "Dicunt panem nostrum panagiam." That is, they call our bread *panagia*.

XI. Further, they blame the church of Rome for celebrating their mass on other days besides Sundays, and certain other feasts appointed.

XII. Also, in this the Greek church varieth from the Latin; for they have neither cream nor oil, nor sacrament of confirmation.

XIII. Neither do they use extreme unction, or annoiling after the manner of the Roman church, expounding the place of St. James of the spiritual infirmity, and not corporal.

XIV. Also, they enjoin no satisfaction for penance, but only that they show themselves to the priests, anointing them with simple oil in token of remission of sins.

XV. Also, only on Maunday Thursday they consecrate for the sick, keeping it for the whole year after, thinking it to be more holy upon that day consecrated than upon any other: neither do they fast any Saturday through the whole year, but only on Easter-even.

XVI. Also, they give but only five orders, as of clerks, subdeacons, deacons, priests, and bishops; whereas the Roman church giveth nine orders, after the nine orders of angels.

XVII. Moreover, the Grecians in their orders make no vow of chastity, alleging for them the fifth canon, "Ego, presbyter vel diaconus, uxorum causa honestatis non rejiciam," &c.; that is, "I, N. priest or deacon, will not forsake my wife for honesty' sake."[2]

XVIII. Also, every year the Grecians use, on certain days, to excommunicate the church of Rome, and all the Latins as heretics.

XIX. Also further, among the said Grecians they are excommunicated that beat or strike a priest; neither do their religious men live in such priestly chastity as the Roman priests do.

(1) "Quod sunt extra obedientiam Romanæ ecclesiæ, pro eo quod ecclesia Constantinopolitana non est subjecta, sed ei æqualis. Dicunt dominum apostolicum non habere majorem potestatem, quam quatuor patriarchæ. Et quicquid fit præter scientiam eorum per papam, vel sine eorum approbatione, nullius est valoris," &c.—Ex Registro Eccles. Herefordiensis.

(2) My copy here seemeth to want somewhat.

XX. Also, their emperor amongst them doth ordain patriarchs, bishops, and others of the clergy, and deposeth the same at his pleasure; also, he giveth benefices to whom he listeth, and retaineth the fruits of the same benefices, as pleaseth him. *William Rufus.* A. D. 1098.

XXI. Item, they blame the Latin church because they eat no flesh, eggs, and cheese on Fridays, and do eat flesh on Saturdays.[1]

XXII. Item, they hold against the Latin men for celebrating without the consecrated church, either in the house or in the field, and for fasting on the Sabbath-day; also for permitting menstruous women to enter into the church before their purifying; and for suffering dogs and other beasts to enter into the church.

XXIII. The Grecians use not to kneel in all their devotions, not even to the body of Christ, (as the register termeth it,) but one day in the whole year; saying and affirming that the Latins be goats and beasts, for they are always prostrating themselves upon the ground in their prayers.

XXIV. The Grecians, moreover, permit not the Latins to celebrate upon their altars. And if it chance that any Latin priest do celebrate upon their altar, by and by they wash their altar, in token of abomination and false sacrifice; and diligently they observe, that, whensoever they do celebrate, they do but one liturgy or mass upon one altar or table that day.

XXV. Further, they dissent from the church of Rome touching the order and manner of the proceeding of the Holy Ghost.

These articles, wherein is declared the difference between the east and west church, of the Grecians and Romans, as I found them articulated and collected in an ancient and authentic register of the church of Hereford, so I thought here to insert them, and leave them to the consideration of the reader. Other four articles more in the same register be there expressed concerning simony and usury, not with them forbidden; and touching also their emperor; and how they teach their children to hurt or damnify, by any manner of way, the Latin priests, &c.; which articles, for that either they seem not truly collected out of their teachings, or else not greatly pertinent to the doctrine of religion, I overpass them. To the purpose now of our story again.

When certain of these above prefixed were moved in the aforesaid council to be discussed, namely concerning the assertion of the proceeding of the Holy Ghost, and concerning leavened bread in the ministration of the Lord's supper, Anselm, as is above said, was called for, who, in the tractation of the same articles, so bestirred him in that council, that he well liked the pope and them about him, as mine author recordeth. Whereupon, touching the matter of unleavened bread, how indifferently he seemed there to reason, and what he writeth to Waltram, or Valerame, bishop of Nurenburgh, thereof ye shall hear by a piece of his letter sent to the said bishop, the copy whereof here ensueth. Anselm a stout champion against the Grecians.

Anselm, servant to the church of Canterbury, to Waltram, bishop of Nurenburgh.[2]

As concerning the sacrifice in which the Grecians think not as we do, it seemeth to many reasonable Catholic men, that which they do not to be against the christian faith; for both he that sacrificeth unleavened and leavened, sacrificeth bread. And where it is read of our Lord (when he made his body of bread) that he took bread and blessed, it is not added unleavened or leavened. Yet it is certain that he blessed unleavened bread, peradventure not because the

(1) This article seemeth not to be rightly collected out of the Grecians.
(2) Ex Epist. Anselm. 325, post initium.

William Rufus. A.D. 1098.

thing that was done required that, but because the supper in which this was done did give that. And where in another place he calleth himself and his flesh bread, because that as man liveth temporally with this bread, so with that bread he liveth for ever. He saith not unleavened nor leavened, because both alike are bread; for unleavened and leavened differ not in substance, as some think, like as a new man before sin, and an old man rooted in the leaven of sin, differ not in substance. For this cause only, therefore, he might be thought to call himself and his flesh bread, and to have made his body of bread, because that this bread, unleavened or leavened, giveth a transitory life; and his body giveth everlasting life, not for that it is either leavened or unleavened. Although it be a commandment in the law to eat unleavened bread in the Passover, where all things are done in a figure, that it might be declared that Christ, whom they looked for, was pure and clean; and we that should eat his body were admonished to be likewise pure from all leaven of malice and wickedness: but now after we are come from the old figure to the new truth, and eat the unleavened flesh of Christ, that old figure in bread, of which we make that flesh, is not necessary for us. But manifest it is, to be better sacrificed of unleavened than of leavened, &c.

Bread in the communion to be unleavened is not necessary.

To this letter I have also adjoined another epistle of his to the said Waltram, appertaining to matters not much unlike; wherein the variety and divers usages of the sacraments in the church are treated of; whereby such as call and cry so much for uniformity in the church, may note, peradventure, in the same something for their better understanding.

Part of another Letter of Anselm to the said Waltram, Bishop of Nurenburgh.[1]

To the reverend father and his friend Waltram, by the grace of God, the worshipful bishop of Nurenburgh, Anselm, the servant of the church of Canterbury, greeting, &c.

Your worship complaineth of the sacraments of the church, that they are not made every where after one sort, but are handled in divers places after divers sorts. And truly if they were ministered after one sort, and agreeing through the whole church, it were good and laudable. Yet, notwithstanding, because there be many diversities which differ not in the sum of the sacrament, in the strength of it, or in the faith, or else can be gathered into one custom, I think that they are rather to be borne with in agreement of peace, than to be condemned with offence: for we have this from the holy fathers, that if the unity of charity be kept in the catholic faith, the diversity of customs hurteth nothing. But if it be demanded whereof this diversity of customs doth spring, I perceive no other cause thereof but the diversity of men's wits, which, although they differ not in strength and truth of the thing, yet they agree not in the fitness and comeliness of the ministering: for that which one judgeth to be meeter, oftentimes another thinketh less meet; wherefore, not to agree in such diversities, I think it not to swerve from the truth of the thing, &c.

Diversity of usages in the church to be borne with peace, rather than condemned with offence.

Then in the story it followeth, after long debating and discussing of these matters in the council, when they had given forth their determination upon the same, and the pope had blasted out his thundering excommunications against the Grecians, and all that took their part, at length were brought in the complaints and accusations against the king of England, upon the hearing whereof, Pope Urban, with his adherents, was ready to proceed in excommunication against the king; but Anselm, kneeling before the pope, after he

Excommunication denounced against the Grecians; also threatened against King William.

(1) Ex Epist. Anselm. 327.

had first accused his king, then afterwards obtained for him longer time to be given upon further trial.

William Rufus.

A.D. 1099.

Thus the council breaking up, the pope returned again to Rome, directing down his letters to the king, and commanding him that Anselm, with all his partakers, in speedy wise should be revested again in his archbishopric, and all other possessions thereunto appertaining. To this the king sendeth answer again by messengers, who, coming to the pope, declared in the king's behalf on this wise, That the king, their master, did not a little marvel what came into his mind to command Anselm to be revested and reseized again into his former archbishopric; seeing he told him before plainly, that if he went out of England without his leave, he would so do unto him. "Well," saith the pope, "have ye no other matter against Anselm but only this?" "No," quoth they.* "And have ye taken all this travail," saith the pope, "to come hither so far to tell me this, that the primate of your country is therefore disseized and dispossessed, because he hath appealed to the see and judgment apostolical? Therefore, if thou lovest thy lord, speed thee home and tell him, if he will not be excommunicated, that he quickly revest Anselm again in all that he had before. And lest I make thee to be hanged for thy labour, look to thy term, and see that thou bring me answer again from him into this city against the next council, the third week after Easter." The messenger, or speaker, being somewhat astonied at the hearing of this so tragical answer, thinking yet to work something for his king and master, came secretly to the pope, saying, that he would confer a certain mystery from his king privately with his holiness, between them two. What mystery that was, or what there passed from the king to the pope and the court of Rome, mine author does not show; but so cunningly that mystery was handled, that, with a full consent, both of the pope and all the court of Rome, a longer day was given, from Easter to Michaelmas; and the pope's choleric heat so assuaged, that when the council came, which then was holden at St. Peter's church in Rome, albeit great complaints were then denounced against the king, yet such favour was found, that he took no harm; only the sentence of excommunication was there pronounced against such lay persons as gave investiture of churches, and them that were so invested; also, against them that do consecrate such, or which gave themselves in subjection to laymen for ecclesiastical livings, as is before touched upon.

First break his head, and then give him a plaster.

A loud crack of thunder, but without a thunderbolt.

A bribing mystery handled at Rome.

Optimus Causidicus nummus. Acts of the Council of Rome.

This council being finished, the archbishop, seeing the unstedfastness of the pope, which pleased him but little, took his journey to Lyons, where he continued his abode a long time, till the death, first of Pope Urban, and then of the king.

Of this King William many things be diversely recorded, some to his commendation, and some to his discommendation; whereof this is one which some will ascribe to hardiness, but I rather to rashness in him. As this king upon a time was in his disport of hunting, suddenly word came to him that Cenourona, a city in Normandy, was besieged. The king, without longer tarrying or advisement, took the straight way toward the sea-side, sending to his lords that they should follow after. They, being come to his presence, advised him to stay till the time his people were assembled; but he would

The hardiness, or rather rashness, of King William.

William Rufus A D 1100

not be stayed, saying, that such as him loved, he knew, would follow him shortly; and so went to take ship. The shipmaster, seeing the weather so dark and cloudy, was afraid, and counselled the king to tarry till the wind did turn about, and the weather was more favourable. But the king, persisting in his journey, commanded him to make all the speed he might for his life; saying, that he never heard that any king yet was ever drowned; and so passed the sea in safety, and came to Normandy.

A saying of King William

The thirteenth year of his reign, the said King William, having the same time in his hand three bishoprics—Canterbury, Winchester, and Sarum, also twelve abbies in farm, as he was in his disport of hunting in the New Forest, by glancing of an arrow shot by a knight named Walter Tyrrell, was wounded to death, and so, speechless, was carried to Westminster, and there was buried. Here also is to be noted, that Richard, the cousin-german of King William, and son to Duke Robert his brother, was likewise slain in the aforesaid forest. See the just hand of God upon kings usurping wrongfully upon other men's grounds, as did William the Conqueror, their father, in making this new forest, plucking down divers churches and townships for the compass of thirty miles about. Here therefore appeareth, that although men cannot revenge, yet God revengeth, either in them or in their posterity. This king, as he always used concubines, so left he no issue legitimate behind him. His life was such, that it is hard for a story that should tell the truth to say whether he was more to be commended or reproved. Among other vices in him, especially is to be rebuked in him unmeasurable and unreasonable covetousness; insomuch that he coveted, if he might, to be every man's heir. This one example of a liberal and princely nature I find in him, that upon a time when a certain abbot of a place was dead, there came to his court two monks of the same house, who before had gathered much money, and made their friends to the king, and offered large offers, both of them to be promoted to that dignity. There was also a third monk of the same place, who of meekness and humility followed the other two, to the intent that upon him whom the king had admitted for abbot, he should give attendance, and as his chaplain with him return. The king called before him the two monks severally, of whom the one outproffered the other. As the king cast his eye aside, he espied the third monk standing by, supposing that his coming had been also for the like cause. Then the king, calling him, asked what he would do, whether he would give more than his brethren had offered to be abbot. He answered the king, and said, that he neither had, nor would (if he might) offer any penny for it by any such unlawful means. When the king had well pondered this third monk's answer, he said that he was best worthy to be abbot, and to have the rule of so holy a charge: and so gave unto him that benefice without taking any penny.

The death of William Rufus

Example of God revenging the faults of kings in their posterity.

Covetousness of King William

Urban, bishop of Rome, who, as is said, succeeded after Victor, ruled the church of Rome about the space of twelve years; and amongst his other acts he excommunicated the emperor, Henry IV., as a man not much devout to that see of Rome. But yet a worthy and victorious prince he was, in whom, albeit some vice perchance might be noted, yet none such wherefore any prelate or minister of

Christ ought to excite his subjects to rebel against public authority of God appointed. This emperor Henry IV. was by four popes severally excommunicated,—by Hildebrand, Victor, Urban, and Paschal; which excommunication wrought so in the ignorant and blind hearts of the people, that many, as well of the nobles as of the multitude, contrary to their sworn allegiance, rebelliously conspired against their king and emperor; in the number of whom was one certain earl, named Ludovic, to whom Waltram, bishop of the church of Mergburgh, (a godly and faithful man, as appeareth,) doth write letters of fatherly admonition, exhorting and instructing him in the office of obedience; unto the which letters he likewise doth answer again by cavilling sophistication, and by mere affection rather disposed to discord, than seeking sincerity of truth. And forasmuch as in these two letters the argument of christian obedience on both sides is so debated by proofs and reasons as may be profitable for the reader to peruse and understand, I thought therefore not to defraud the English reader of the same, whereof peradventure some utility might be taken. The tenor of the bishop's letter to the earl here followeth.

Henry IV. excommunicated by four popes. Earl Ludovic rebels against the emperor.

The Epistle of Waltram, bishop of Mergburgh, to the Earl Ludovic, exhorting to concord and obedience.[1]

Waltram, by the grace of God being that he is, to Ludovic, the noble prince, with instance of prayer, offereth himself serviceable for all things. To every realm concord is a thing profitable, and justice is much to be desired. For this virtue is the mother of godliness and the consecration of all honesty. Whosoever seeketh after civil dissension, and incenseth others to effusion of blood, he is a murderer, and a partaker with him who, ever gaping and thirsting for another's blood, goeth about seeking whom he may devour. You therefore considering with yourself, most noble prince, how God is the God of peace, and not of dissension, as much as in you doth lie, have peace with all men. God is charity; the devil is hatred. The whole law and prophets consist in love and charity. He that hateth and maligneth his brother is a murderer, and hath no part with Christ in the kingdom of God. This we read testified and protested both by him who is the Truth himself, and by him who was the scholar of the Truth, who, upon the breast of the Lord, drinking a more full draught of the gospel, rejoiceth the city of God with abundance of plentiful floods. In like manner, that worthy vessel of election, who, being rapt up to the third heaven, (not by man, but by revelation of Jesus Christ,) protesteth also, saying, "Let every soul submit himself to the higher powers: there is no power," saith he, "but of God. He that resisteth the power resisteth the ordinance of God." [Rom. xiii. 1, 2.] If that be true, therefore, which certain of our friends do jangle among women and the vulgar sort, that we ought not to be subdued to kingly power, then is it false which the apostle teacheth, that every soul must submit himself unto power and superiority. But can the Verity lie? or do we seek for experiment of him who spake in the apostle, Christ the Lord? Or do we provoke the Lord? Be we stronger than he? For what doth he but think himself stronger than the Lord that resisteth the ordinance of God? for "there is no power but of God." But what saith the prophet? "Confounded be all they that strive against thee, O Lord; and the men which repugn against thee shall perish." Rodolph, Hildebrand, Egbert, with many other princes, resisted the ordinance of God in Henry the emperor; and lo, even as they had never been, so are they now perished; and as their end was evil, so their beginning could not be good.

Concord and just obedience necessary in a commonwealth.

Disobedience punished by God.

(1) "Waltramus Dei gratia id quod est, Ludovico, serenissimo principi, cum instantia orationum semetipsum ad omnia devotissimum, omni regno utilis est concordia, desiderabilis est justitia," &c —Ex Appendice Mariani Scoti.

William Rufus.

A.D. 1100.

"Now therefore, forasmuch as they who be contrary to us do earnestly strive against us with their own arguments, whereas of right (I dare refer me to your judgment) we ought to use the authority of Christ and ancient fathers before that which our adversaries take out of their own treasury. And, because I will not refuse the order of law in this behalf, let it be the end of the strife, that either I may be openly ashamed before the people, or else that the victory falling on my side, we may win you to the obedience of our sovereign lord the emperor. Also take you heed to this saying, "If any man do preach otherwise than that which is preached, let him be of you accursed." [Gal. i. 8.] This curse, I say, doth not proceed from any new profane authority, but is thundered down from the third heaven. And of them who "know not the righteousness of God, but go about to establish their own righteousness," and therefore "be not subject to the righteousness of God." [Rom. x. 3.], I may boldly say, "Let such be accursed." So may you well say, "Confounded be all they that proudly rise up against the Lord; but thy servant, O Lord, shall rejoice." For, as thou hast well said, "Without me you can do nothing," [John xv. 5;] so, in judging of the wicked, thou dost not condemn the just. "Who art thou that judgest another man's servant? to his own Lord he doth either stand or fall." [Rom. xiv. 4.]

The railing answer of Earl Ludovic to the former letter of Bishop Waltram.

The Earl Ludovic to the Lord Waltram, howsoever unworthy or unmeet he be for the name. Like as a good man from the good treasure of the heart bringeth forth good fruit, so doth the evil man from the evil treasure of the heart bring forth evil fruit. What arrogancy hath so possessed you to provoke my displeasure with such injurious contumelies? for, indeed, those my good lords and spiritual fathers, who strengthen me in the way of righteousness, you railingly call bloody men like unto Satan; and the wholesome lessons which they teach, you say, are but dreams of the common people amongst foolish women. Hath God any need of your judgment, that you should speak leasings of him? Iniquity hath taught your mouth to follow blasphemous tongues; so that well may the prophet say of you, "He would not understand to do well; he hath devised wickedness upon his bed." Although, therefore, you, being altogether froward, have only spoken froward things, yet we have determined to set a watch before our mouth, as if a shameless person should stand up before us; and the word of God doth provoke us, saying, "Answer a fool according to his own foolishness, lest he should seem wise in his own opinion." Shall folly speak, and wisdom hold her peace? Shall lies be freely uttered, and truth compelled to keep silence? Shall darkness cover the earth, and shall not the Lord arise and shine? yea, rather the light hath lightened the darkness, and darkness hath not comprehended it: in consideration hereof our hearts have melted, and our zealous meditations have set us on fire. We therefore speak and cry, and the little foxes which undermine the Lord's vineyards (as much as in us is) we drive away, fearing the threatening prophecy—"You have not withstood our adversaries, neither have you made a bulwark for the defence of the house of Israel, that you might be able to stand in battle in the day of the Lord." Let them hear—I speak not to you who have ears and hear not, eyes and see not; who have made dark the light that is in you—but let them hear, I say, that be well disposed, and have ears to hear withal. As for you, you have no understanding; and if you have, you cloak it. Neither have you any thing to say or to prove by what reason we should be subject to the Lord Henry, whom you call emperor. And yet, as it is given us to understand, you go about to persuade that of necessity we ought to be subject to him, and that by the argument of St. Paul, "Let every soul be subdued to the higher powers, for there is no power but of God; he therefore that doth withstand power, doth resist God's ordinance:" which sentence of the apostle we say that you do evil conceive, and therefore evil interpret; for if every power be of God, as you understand, what is meant by that, that the Lord doth speak of some by the prophet, "They did reign, and were not made princes by me, and I knew them not." If every power be of God, as you take it, what is to be thought of that that the Lord doth say, "If thine eye offend thee, pluck it out, and cast it from thee?"

Well said, when you are not able to withstand his wisdom, call him a fool.

Note how the earl here calleth light darkness, and darkness light.

He hath uttered more reason than you are able ever to answer to.

Whether every power is to be obeyed or no.

for what is power but the eye? Certainly Augustine, in the exposition of this sentence of the apostle, "Let every soul," &c. doth say, that "if the powers do command any thing against God, then have them in contempt: but yet nevertheless fear them." Is there any iniquity with God? Is Christ the minister of sin? God forbid. What shall we therefore say? Doth the apostle preach contrary to truth? Augustine saith, "No. One wind filleth many pipes of divers tunes." Therefore let us hear the apostle agreeing and expounding himself, and destroying his enemy and avenger: "There is," saith he, "no power but of God." What followeth? "He therefore," saith he, "that doth resist the power," &c. God forbid:—doth nothing follow? But what doth follow? "Those powers which be ordained of God:" truly, that is it we look for. O crafty tongue! O heart imagining mischief! O consuming breath, that shall not return! Why hast thou lied to the Holy Ghost? Thine own conscience shall accuse thee. Behold the wicked fleeth, and no man doth pursue him.

If every power that offendeth his subjects is to be cast out, then hath this earl made a fair argument.

Why would you suppress the truth to the intent to deceive? Why have you stolen away the pith and effect of the sentence? for if these words should be taken away from the midst of the sentence, it should lie (contrary to itself) inconvenient and half dead. The word of the Lord is herein fulfilled, "He that diggeth a pit for his neighbour shall fall therein himself." Verily you can neither excuse yourself of theft, neither avoid the punishment due for the same. What, O unhappy man! what shall you answer to the Judge when he shall require an account of his servants of whom he putteth you in trust, seeing you shall be set before him in the midst, and proved a picker of your master's treasure? Wherefore did you not fear the judgment and execution, when the guiltiness of offence doth require condign punishment? The apostle, through the Holy Ghost, did foresee that you, and such heretics as you are, should spring up in the church, who should call good evil and evil good, and that should put darkness in the place of light, and light in place of darkness; who also should take occasion, by the sentences of truth, to bring in error: whereas he did set this before, "There is no power but of God," to the intent he might take away the conjecture of false understanding. "For," saith he, "those powers that be are ordained of God." Give therefore an ordinary power, and we do not resist; yea, we will forthwith do our homage. But I do marvel (if at the least there remain in you any one drop of blood) that you are not ashamed to call the Lord Henry king, or to allow him any ordinary place.

How lively these papists describe themselves in their own colours! But Paul judged the emperor to be an ordinary power when he appealed to him.

Is this a seemly order, think you, to give place to wickedness, and to make a general confusion in mixing good and evil, God's and man's devices together? Either do you think this good order for man to sin against his own body, as (O shameful wickedness!) to make his own wife a harlot, a mischief not heard of at any time since the beginning of the world before now? Or do you allow this for good order, when the Lord saith, "defend the widows, especially such as require equity of justice," and then to send them away most filthily defiled? Mad Orestes[1] doth protest him to be out of his wits that will say these things to be orderly or well done. Until this most miserable time, nature hath ever loved secrecy; but your king, given up to a reprobate sense, hath not scrupled to lay abroad all shamefacedness.

This is likely, that the emperor would make his own wife a harlot!

†

We will not speak of other things which cannot be numbered, that is to say, burning of churches, robberies, firing of houses, manslaughters, murders, and such like, the number whereof he knoweth, and not we; for let us speak chiefly of those things which most grieve the church of God. Hearken, therefore, to true and not feigned things: hearken, I say, to matters of earnest, and to no trifles. Every one that doth sell spiritual dignities is a heretic. But the Lord Harry, whom they call a king, doth sell both bishoprics and abbacies; for truly he sold for money the bishoprics of Constance, Babembarge, Mentz, and many others. The bishoprics of Ratisbon, Augsburgh, and Strasburg, he sold for a sword, and the abbey of Fulda and the bishopric of Mons, for the gratification of his lusts. Wickedness it is to speak or hear of such a fact. The which things, if without shame ye will deny, he is to be condemned by the witness of heaven and earth; yea, and of the silly poor idiots that come from the smith's forge. Wherefore the Lord Harry is a heretic; for the which most wicked evils he is excommunicated from the see apostolic, so that he may not exercise either kingdom

Evil will never said well.

(1) The writer seems to refer to Orestes, who, having committed the most fearful murders, is said to have been tormented to madness, by the Furies. Æschyl. in Eumen. Agam.—Ed.

William Rufus.

A.D. 1100.

or power over us who be catholic. And whereas you burden us with hatred of our brethren, know you that we purpose not to hate any of affection, but of a godly zeal. God forbid that we should think Harry worthy to be accounted amongst our christian brethren, who indeed is reputed for an ethnic and publican, in that he refused to hear the church which so oft hath reproved him; the hatred of whom we offer unto God for a great sacrifice, saying with the Psalmist, "Lord, shall not I hate them that hate thee? and shall not I triumph over thine enemies? I hate them with an inward hatred that be enemies to me for thy sake." The Truth itself, commending the worthiness of this hatred, doth say, "If any do not hate father and mother, brethren and sisters, for my sake, he cannot be my disciple." We are not therefore justly to be reproved of hatred, who do give over our own soul, to be in the way of God; who indeed are commanded to hate father and mother, and every affection which doth withstand us for walking in the path of God. Hereof it cometh, that we labour with all our study and endeavour to beware of the enemies of the church, and them to hate; not for that they be our enemies, but God's. Further, where you persuade peace to be had with all men, you must remember what the apostle doth put before, "If it may be." But if it cannot be that we can have peace with them, who can be contrary to God? Who doth not know the Lord our Saviour not only to commend peace, when, as he saith, "My peace I give unto you, my peace I leave unto you;" but that he is the peace; as saith the apostle, "He is the peace which made of both one;" for he calleth him our peace, speaking in commendation of the peace: "Think not," saith he, "that I came to send peace, for I came not to send peace, but the sword." What is meant by this? why is peace called a sword? or doth peace bid battle? Yea, truly, to destroy the peace of the devil; for the devil hath his peace, whereof the Lord speaketh, "When as the strong man keepeth his house, he doth possess all his substance in peace." Oh how mightily doth the devil keep his soldiers and his house in this time! who, with the shield of falsehood and the helmet of untruth, so doth defend him, that he will not suffer either arrow or dart of truth to pierce him. Nevertheless our Lord being more strongly armed, and fiercely coming upon your giant, is able to overcome him, and to take away his weapons, wherein he putteth his trust. We are not therefore to be blamed, if we do detest that peace, more cruel than any war, the which the Truth itself did reprove, weeping over Jerusalem, and saying, Truly, it grieveth me this day to see sinners in peace, being like unto that peace whereat the Psalmist was offended. Whereas you condemn Pope Gregory, King Rodolph, and Marquis Eggerbert, as men that have died an unhappy death, and do magnify your Lord, because he doth outlive them, it doth plainly, forsooth, appear that you remain void of all spiritual consideration. Is it not better to die well than to live ill? They be truly happy who suffer persecution for righteousness' sake. By the same reason may you esteem Nero, Herod, and Pilate happy, in that they outlived Peter, Paul, James, the apostles, and Jesus Christ. What can be said more foolish and wicked than this opinion? Wherefore refrain your babbling tongue from this blasphemy, lest you place yourself in the number of those who, seeing the end of the just to be glorious, themselves doing late and unfruitful penance, bewailing in the anguish of the Spirit, shall say, "These be they whom sometimes we had in derision, and laughed to scorn; we, being out of our wits, thought their lives madness, and their end to be without honour. Behold how they be allowed to be amongst the children of God, and their portion is amongst the saints. Wherefore we have erred from the way of truth, and the brightness of righteousness did not shine upon us. What did our pride avail us? and what profit did the boasting of our riches bring us? They are all vanished away like a shadow." The which words we have registered up into perpetual memory, and we do despise every attempt that shall lift up itself against the truth of God; and rejoicing in troubles, we may be reproved, put to shame and rebuked, yea, and finally be slain and killed, but we will neither yield nor be overcome. And with great triumph will we rejoice in our fathers' doings, of whom you, as a beardless boy, and of small knowledge, have nothing rightly conceived; who indeed, despising princes' commandments, have deserved everlasting reward.

A zeal, but far from knowledge. And when they shall slay you, they shall think they do God great service.—Yea true, if he had compelled you to forsake the name of Christ, which he never did.

Oh, how craftily doth Satan here shape himself to an angel of light!

There is a certain chronicle in old English metre, which, among other matters, speaking of William Rufus, declareth him to be so sumptuous and excessive in pompous apparel, that he not being contented with a pair of hose[1] at a low price, which was three shillings, caused a pair to be bought at a mark, whereupon his chamberlain, procuring a pair much worse than the other before, said, *Henry I* — A.D. 1100

> "That they costen'd a mark, and unneth he them so bought:
> Yea, Belamy (quoth the king) these are well bought!"

Whereby is to be noted what difference is to be seen between the hose of princes then, and the hose of serving-men now.

Appendix Historiæ.

After the time of this King William, the name of King ceased in the country of Wales among the Britons, since King Ris, in the reign of this king, A. D. 1093, was slain in Wales.[2] Kings ceased in Wales

HENRY THE FIRST.[3]

HENRY I, the third son of William the Conqueror, succeeding his brother Rufus, began his reign in England A. D. 1100, who, for his knowledge and science in the Seven Liberal Arts, was surnamed Clerk, or Beauclerk. In this prince may well appear how knowledge and learning do greatly conduce to the government and administration of any realm or country. At the beginning he reformed the state and condition of the clergy, released the grievous payments, and reduced again King Edward's laws, with emendation thereof; he reformed the old and untrue measures, and made a measure after the length of his arm; he greatly abhorred excess of meats and drinks; many things misused before his time he reformed, and used to vanquish more by counsel than by sword. Such persons as were nice and wanton he secluded from his court. This man, as appeareth, little favoured the usurped power of the bishop of Rome. Soon after he was king, he married Matilda, or Maud, daughter of Malcolm, king of Scots, and of Margaret his wife, daughter of Edward the Outlaw, as is before specified, being a professed nun at Winchester, whom, notwithstanding, and without the pope's dispensation, he married by the consent of Anselm, by the which Maud he received two sons, William and Richard, and two daughters, Matilda and Mary, which Matilda afterwards was married to the emperor, Henry V.[4]

A.D. 1100

Henry Beau-clerk, king of England

The measure of England made after the length of King Henry's arm

In the second year of his reign, Robert, his elder brother, duke of Normandy, being occupied in the christian wars against the Turks, and being elected, as you heard, king of Jerusalem, hearing of the death of Rufus, refused the kingdom thereof; for the which, as is thought, he never sped well after. Thus the said Robert, leaving off the Lord's business, and returning into Normandy, made there his preparations, and came over into England with a great host to challenge the crown; but, by mediation of the lords, it was agreed A.D. 1101

Example, what it is to leave off the Lord's business.

(1) This anecdote is told with great life and spirit by Malmesbury. "One morning," says he, "as he was putting on a pair of new boots, he asked his gentleman of the bedchamber, in waiting, what they cost? he was answered 'three shillings' 'Away, base fellow,' said the king, 'did you ever hear of a king wearing such pitiful boots as those? go, bring a pair of a mark of silver' The bedchamber-man went and brought a pair much worse, but told his master they cost what he had ordered 'Ay,' replied William, 'these are boots fit for a king to wear,' and so put them on"—ED

(2) Ex continuatione Roger Hoved

(3) Edition 1563, p 30 Ed 1583, p 191 Ed 1596, p 173 Ed 1684, vol i. p 216.—ED

(4) Ex Mat. Paris Flor Hist.

Henry I. A. D. 1102.

that Robert should have yearly, during his life, three thousand marks, as were likewise promised him before by King Rufus, his brother; and that whether of them outlived the other, should be the other's heir. On this Robert departed again into Normandy, to the great discontent of his lords there; but, in a few years after, the aforenamed tribute of three thousand marks, through the means of Queen Matilda, was released to the king his brother. In process of time, variance happening between King Henry and the said Robert his brother, at length Robert in his wars was taken prisoner, and brought over into England, and was put into the castle of Cardiff in Wales, where he continued as a prisoner while he lived.

Duke Robert taken prisoner.

The hospital of Bartholomew founded.

In this time, as about the third year of this king, the hospital of St. Bartholomew in Smithfield was founded, by means of a minstrel belonging unto the king, named Rayer, and it was afterwards finished by Richard Whittington, alderman and mayor of London. This place of Smithfield was at that day a laystall of all ordure or filth, and the place where the felons and other transgressors of the king's laws were put to execution.

Divers strict laws were by this king provided, especially against thieves and felons:

First, That whoso should be taken in that fault, no money should save him from hanging.

Item, That whoso should counterfeit false money, should have both his eyes put out, and the nether parts of his body cut off.

Item, In the same council was decreed an order for priests to be sequestered from their wives, which before was not forbidden.[1]

Item, It was then decreed that monks and priests should bear no rule over lay persons.

Item, It was decreed concerning broidering of hair, and wearing of garments.

† Item, That the secret contract between a young lad and a young maid should not stand, with other things concerning the excommunication of more gross offenders.

In the story of William Rufus before was declared how Anselm, the archbishop of Canterbury, departing out of the realm, went to the pope, who, after the death of King William, was sent for again by the aforesaid King Henry, and so returned again, and was at the council of the king at Westminster; where the king, in the presence of the lords, as well temporal as spiritual, ordained and invested two bishops, Roger bishop of Salisbury, and Roger bishop of Hereford. During that parliament or council of the king, Anselm in his convocation deposed and displaced divers abbots and other prelates from their rooms and dignities, either for that they lawfully came not by them, or uprightly did not administer the same.

The king ordains and invests bishops without the pope.

After this council and the other before set forth by Anselm, Herbert, bishop of Norwich, had much ado with the priests of his diocese, for they would neither leave their wives, nor yet give over their benefices. On this he wrote to Anselm, the archbishop, for counsel what was to be done therein, who required him, as he did others at the same time by writing, to persuade the people of Norfolk and Suffolk, that as they professed Christianity, they should subdue them as rebels against the church, and utterly drive both them and

Anselm cruel and fierce against married priests.

(1) The words of mine author are these: "Anselmus prohibuit uxores sacerdotibus Anglorum ante non prohibitas. Quod quibusdam mundissimum visum est, quibusdam periculosum, ne dum mundicias viribus majores appeterent, in immundicias horribiles ad Christiani nominis summum dedecus inciderent," &c.—Ex Hen. Hunt. lib. vii. Anselm.

their wives out of the country, placing monks in their room, as by the epistles of the said Anselm doth appear;[1] whereof certain parcels shall hereafter, by the grace of Christ, ensue, for the better evidence of this and his other acts above recited.

The like business also had Gerard, the archbishop of York, in depriving the priests of his province of their wives; which thing, with all his excommunications and thunderings, he could hardly bring about. Upon this ruffling of Anselm with married priests, were rhyming verses made to help the matter withal, when reason could not serve, which verses, for the folly thereof, I thought here to annex.[2]

A.D. 1104. A strife between King Henry and Anselm, archbishop of Canterbury.

About the end of the third year of this king, which was by computation A.D. 1104, a variance happened between King Henry and Anselm, the occasion whereof was this:—Ye heard a little before how Henry, the aforesaid king, had, of his own authority, invested two bishops, one Roger, who was chancellor, bishop of Salisbury, and another, bishop of Hereford. Besides them divers also he invested, and divers other like things took he upon him in the ecclesiastical state, which he might lawfully do, God's word allowing well the same; but because he was restrained by the bishop of Rome, and forbidden so to do, this Anselm swelled, fretted, and waxed so mad, that he would neither consent to it, nor yet confirm them, nor communicate nor talk friendly with those whom the king had instituted and invested; but opprobriously called them abortives, or children of destruction, disdainfully rebuking the gentle king as a defiler of religion, and polluter of their holy ceremonies; as witnesseth Polydore. With this uncomely outrage the king was much displeased, as he might full well, and required Gerard, the archbishop of York, as he owed him allegiance, to consecrate them; who, without delay, did so, well performing the same, saving that one William Gifford, to whom the king had given the bishopric of Winchester, refused to take his consecration by the hands of the archbishop of York, for which cause the king, worthily with him offended, deprived him both of bishopric and goods, and banished him the realm.

Gifford, bishop of Winchester, refused to be consecrated by the archbishop of York.

Moreover, the king required of Anselm, the archbishop of Canterbury, to do unto him homage, after the manner of his ancestors, as witnesseth Malmesbury.[3] Also it was asked of the said Anselm, whether he would be with the king in giving investitures, as Lanfranc, his predecessor, was with his father. To whom Anselm said, that he promised not at any time that he would enter into this order to keep the law or custom of his father, as Lanfranc did. Moreover, as concerning homage to be done to the king, that he refused; alleging the censures of the pope's excommunication, who, in his council of Rome a little before, had given forth open sentence of excommunication upon all such lay persons, whatsoever they were, that should from henceforth confer or give any spiritual promotions, and also

Acts of the Roman council against laymen giving any spiritual promotions.

(1) Ex Epist. Ansel. 176.

(2) "O male viventes, versus audite sequentes;
Uxores vestras, quas odit summa potestas,
Linquite propter eum, tenuit qui morte trophæum,
Quod si non facitis, inferna claustra petetis.
Christi sponsa jubet, ne Presbyter ille ministret,
Qui tenet uxorem, Domini quia perdit amorem:
Contradicentem fore dicimus insipientem:
Non ex rancore loquor hæc, potius sed amore."
Versus male feriati, ex Bibliis Ramsay.

(3) Ex Guliel. Malmesb. lib. i. de Gestis Pontif. Anglo.

Henry I. A.D. 1104.

upon them that received them at their hands, either yet should consecrate any such receivers. Moreover, he accursed all them that for benefices or other ecclesiastical promotions should subject themselves under the homage or service of any great man, king, prince, duke, or earl of the laity. For it was unseemly, said the pope, and a thing very execrable, that the hands which were converted into so high a working as was granted to no angel (that is, to create him with their crosses, who created all, and to offer up the same before the sight of the Father for the salvation of the whole world), should be brought to such a slavery as to be subject to those filthy hands, which both day and night are polluted with shameful touchings, robberies, and bloodshed, &c.[1] This decree of Pope Urban, Anselm alleging for himself, denied to subject himself to the king's homage, fearing, as he said, the pope's excommunication. Upon this, messengers were sent to Rome on both parts unto the pope, then Pope Paschal, who, stoutly standing to the steps and determinations of Urban, his predecessor, would in no case yield to the king's investing.[2]

No spiritual person to be under subjection to a lay personage.

Anselm refuseth to do homage to his king.

In the mean time, while there was long disputation on both sides for investing, the nobles of the realm contended, that investings did belong to the king's dignity: wherefore the king, calling for Anselm again, required him either to do homage to him, or else to void his kingdom. To whom Anselm replying again, required the pope's letters to be brought forth, and, according to the tenor thereof, so the matter to be decided; for now the messengers were returned from Rome, with the pope's answer, altogether siding with Anselm. Then said the king, "What have I to do with the pope's letters? I will not forego the liberties of my kingdom for any pope." Thus the contention continued between them. Anselm saith, he would not out of the realm, but depart home to his church, and there see who would offer him any violence: and so he did. Not long after, message came from the king to Anselm, requesting him, after a gentle sort, to repair to the king's presence again, to put an end to the controversy, whereunto Anselm yielded and came. Then were new ambassadors sent again to the pope, that he would something qualify and moderate, or rather abolish, the strictness of the Roman decree beforementioned. On the part of Anselm went two monks, Baldwin and Alexander. On the king's behalf were sent two bishops, Robert, bishop of Lichfield, and Herbert, bishop of Norwich, with the king's letters written to the pope, containing in form as followeth.[3]

The king hath nothing to do with the pope's letters.

Messengers sent again to Rome.

Letter of King Henry I

To the reverend father Paschal, the chief bishop. Henry, by the grace of God, king of England, greeting. For this your promotion unto the see of the holy

(1) Ex Jornalensi. Bibliothecæ Historia.

(2) Ex Matthæo Paris. Ex Guliel. Malmesb. lib. i. de Gestis Pont. Ang.

(3) "Patri venerabili Paschali summo pontifici, Henricus Dei gratia rex Anglorum, salutem. Promotioni vestræ in sedem sanctæ Romanæ ecclesiæ plurimum congaudeo, petens ut amicitia quæ patri meo cum antecessoribus vestris fuit, inter nos quoque illibata permaneat. Unde, ut dilectio et benignitas a me videatur sumere initium, beneficium quod ab antecessoribus meis beatus Petrus habuit, vobis mitto: eosque honores et eam obedientiam quam tempore patris mei antecessores vestri in regno Angliæ habuerunt, tempore meo ut habeatis volo, eo videlicet tenore, ut dignitatis usus et consuetudines, quas pater meus tempore antecessorum vestrorum in regno Angliæ habuit, ego tempore vestro in eodem regno meo integre obtineam. Notumque habeat sanctitas vestra, quod me vivente (Deo auxiliante) dignitates et usus regni Angliæ non minuentur Et si ego (quod absit) in tanta me dejectione ponerem; optimates mei (imo totius Angliæ populus) id nullo modo pateretur. Habita igitur (charissime pater) utiliori deliberatione, ita se erga nos moderetur benignitas vestra, ne quid invitus faciam, et a vestra me cogatis recedere obedientia."

church of Rome, as I am heartily glad, so my request is to you, that the friendship and amity, which hath been heretofore between my father and your predecessors in times past, may now also between us in like manner continue undiminished; and, that love and gentleness may first begin on my part, here I send to you that gift that St. Peter had in former time of my predecessors. And likewise the same honours and obedience which your predecessors have had in the realm of England before in the time of my father, I will you to have the same in my time also: after this form I mean and tenor, that the usage and manner of dignity, and such customs, as my father hath had in this realm of England, in the time of your ancestors, I in like ample manner also now, in your time, may fully enjoy the same in this the said realm of England. Thus, therefore, be it known to your holiness, that during this life of mine (God Almighty enabling me to the same) these abovenamed dignities, usages, and customs of this realm of England, shall in no part be lessened. Yea, and if that I (as God forbid I should) would so much deject myself unto such cowardness, yet my nobles, yea, the whole people of England, in no case would suffer it. Wherefore, dear father, using with yourself a better deliberation in this matter, let your gentleness so moderate itself toward us, lest ye compel me, which I shall do against my will, to recede and depart utterly from your obedience.

Henry I. A.D. 1104.

Spoken like a king.

The king is at a point to leave the pope's obedience.

At the same time, also, he sent another letter or epistle to the said pope, craving of him the pall for Gerard, archbishop of York, the form whereof here also followeth:[1]—

To the reverend and well-beloved father universal, Pope Paschal, Henry, by the grace of God, king of England, greeting. The great love which I bear to you, and the no less gentleness in you, which not a little beautifieth your doings, ministereth to me boldness to write. And whereas I thought to have retained still this Gerard with me, and to have craved your pall for him by letters; yet, notwithstanding, when his desire could not otherwise be satisfied, but he would needs present himself before your presence, by his own heart to crave of you the same, I have sent him up unto you, desiring your benign fatherhood in this behalf, that he, obtaining the pall at your hands, may be sent home again to me. And thus, requiring the assistance of your prayers, I pray the Lord long to preserve your apostleship.

Another letter of King Henry I. to the pope.

This second letter of the king in sending for the pall was well taken of all the court of Rome, which (as mine author saith) procured such favour to Gerard, archbishop of York, and bringer thereof, that no complaint of his adversaries afterwards could hurt him with the pope. Notwithstanding, he was accused grievously for divers things, and specially for not standing to the consecration of Anselm, archbishop of Canterbury.

Polydore, in his eleventh book of his English history, affirmeth, that Anselm also went up to Rome with Gerard about the same cause. But both the premises and sequel of the story argue that to be untrue, for what need the two monks to be sent up on Anselm's side, if he had gone up himself?[2] Again, how could the pope write down by the said messengers to Anselm, if he had been present there himself? for so proceedeth the story by the narration of Malmesbury and others.

A place of Polydore Virg. found faulty.

After the ambassadors, thus on both sides sent up to Rome, had laboured their cause with instant suit one against the other, the pope, glad to gratify the king, yet loath to grant his request, being against his own profit, and therefore more inclining to Anselm's side,

The pope loath to go against his own profit.

(1) "Reverendo et diligendo patri universali papæ Paschali, Henricus Dei gratia rex Anglorum, salutem. Amor quem plurimum erga vos habeo, et benignitas quæ multum vestros actus exornat," &c.
(2) Ex Guliel. Malmesb. lib. viii. de Pont. Ang.

Henry I. A.D. 1104.

sendeth down his letters to the said Anselm, signifying that he would not repeal the statutes of his holy fathers for one man's pleasure; charging him, moreover, not only not to yield in the cause of investing, but constantly to adhere to the aforesaid decreement of Pope Urban, his predecessor, &c. Besides this letter to Anselm, he directed also another to the king himself, which, mine author saith, the king suppressed and did not show, only declaring, by word of mouth, what the ambassadors had said unto him from the pope, which was, that he permitted unto him the license of investing, upon condition that in other things he would execute the office of a good prince, &c. To this, also, the testimony of the two bishops above mentioned did accord, which made the matter more probable. But the two monks on the other side replied, bringing forth the letter of Anselm to the contrary, &c. To them it was answered, that more credit was to be given to the degree and testimony of the bishops, than to theirs; and that as for monks, they had no suffrage nor testimony in secular matters, and therefore they might hold their peace. "But this is no secular matter," said Baldwin, abbot of Ramsey. Whereunto, again, the nobles of the king's part answered, saying, that he was a good man, and of such demeanour, that they had nothing to say against him, neither so would, if they might; but that both human and divine reason taught them to yield more credit and confidence to the testimony of three bishops, than to that of two monks: whereby may well appear, that Anselm at that time went not with them. Then Anselm, seeing how the king and his peers were bent, and hearing also the testimony of the three bishops, against whom he saw he could not prevail, and also having the pope's seal, which he saw to be so evident on the contrary side, made his answer again, that he would send to Rome for more certainty of truth: adding, moreover, that he neither would, nor durst give over his cause, though it should cost him his life, to do or proceed against the determination of the church of Rome, unless he had a perfect warrant of absolution from thence for his discharge. Then was it agreed by the king and his nobles, that he should not send, but go himself to Rome, and much entreaty was made that he would take that journey himself, in his own person, to present himself to the pope for the peace of the church and of his country. And so, at length, by persuasion, he was content to go to Rome and speak with the pope. In a short time after followeth also the king's ambassador, William Warlwast, the newly elected bishop of Exeter, who there pleading on the king's side for the ancient customs of the realm, and for the king's right of investing, &c., first declared, how England, of a long continuance, had ever been a province peculiar to the church of Rome, and how it payed duly its yearly tribute unto the same; inferring, moreover, how the king, as he was of nature very liberal, so also of courage he was a prince stout and valiant. Then what a shame would he think it to be to him, as it would indeed be, if he, who in might and dignity far exceeded all his progenitors, should not defend and maintain the liberties and customs by them procured. Wherefore he desired the pope to see to the matter, so that it might stand both with the king's honour, and also with his own profit and advantage, who, otherwise, no doubt should lose a great piece of

He meaneth beside the two bishops, Gerard, who made the third.

The oration of William Warlwast at the pope's court.

money out of the realm, unless he did remit something of the severity of his canons and laws decretal. *Henry I. A.D. 1106.*

With these and such other like persuasions to the same effect, the court of Rome was well contented, agreeing that the king's request ought with all favour to be granted. But the pope and Anselm sat still marking their doings. The ambassador, supposing their silence to be half a yielding unto him, added moreover and said; that the king, no not for the crown of his realm, would lose the authority of investing or admitting his prelates within his dominion.[1] Whereunto the proud pope answering again, burst out in these words: "Nor I," said he, "for the price of his head, as thou sayest, will lose the giving of spiritual promotions in England;" and, confirming it with an oath, "before God," saith he, "I speak it; know it for a certainty,* for the whole price of his head, I will not permit it unto him, neither shall he have it.*[2] Then it followeth in the story of Malmesbury, that with this word of the pope the minds of the rest were changed, saying, "Benedicta sit cordis tui constantia, benedicta oris tui loquela." The king's attorney also was therewith dashed, who, notwithstanding, brought it to pass, that certain of the king's customs, used before of his father, were released unto him. At that time, in the same court, it was decreed,—the king only, who had invested them, being excepted,—that the others who were invested by the king should be excommunicated; the absolution and satisfaction of whom were left to Anselm, the archbishop.

A proud answer of the pope.

Excommunication abused.

Thus Anselm, being dismissed from Rome, took his journey towards England: but the ambassador, pretending to go to St. Nicholas, remained behind, to see whether he could win the pope's mind to the king's purpose; but when he saw it would not be, he overtaketh Anselm by the way, at Placentia, and openeth to him the king's pleasure. "The king," saith he, "giveth to you in charge and commandment, that if you will come to England, and there behave yourself to him, as your predecessors did to his father, you should be received and retained in the realm accordingly; if not, you are wise enough to know what I mean, and what will follow."[3] And so, with these words parting from him, he returned again to the king. Anselm remained at Lyons a year and a half, writing divers letters to the king, after this effect, and in words as followeth:—

To his reverend Lord, Henry, king of England, Anselm, archbishop of Canterbury, faithful service with prayers.[4]

Although ye understand by William Warlwast what we have done at Rome, yet I shall shortly show you that which belongeth to me. When I came to Rome, I declared the cause wherefore I came to the lord pope. He answered that he would not swerve from the statutes of his predecessors. Furthermore, he commanded me that I should have no fellowship with those who received investings of churches at your hands, after the knowledge of this prohibition, unless they would do penance, and forsake that which they had received, without hope of recovery; and that I should not communicate with the other bishops who had consecrated such men, except they would present themselves to the judgment of the apostolic see. The aforesaid William can be a witness of all these

(1) Ex Guliel. Malmesb. de Gestis Pont. lib. i. Ex. Matth. Paris. lib. iii.
(2) These words are inserted from Edition 1563, p. 31.—Ed.
(3) Ex Radulph. Londinensi. (4) Epist. 224.

Henry I. A.D. 1106.

things if he will. This William, when we departed asunder, reckoning up in your behalf the love and liberality which you have had always towards me, warned me as your archbishop, that I should show myself such an one, that if I would come into England, I might be with you as my predecessor was with your father, and ye might treat me with the same honour and liberty that your father treated my predecessor. By which words I understand, that except I should show myself such an one, you would not have me come into England. For your love and liberality I thank you; but that I should be with you as my predecessor was with your father, I cannot do it, for I dare not do homage to you, nor do I dare communicate with those who take investings of churches at your hands, because of the aforesaid inhibition made, I myself hearing it. Wherefore, I desire you to send me your pleasure herein, if it please you, whether I may return into England, as I said, with your peace and the power of mine office.

The proud stoutness of a prelate in a wrong cause.

In the mean while, great business there was, and much posting went to and fro between the king, the archbishop, and the pope, but nothing was done; for neither would the pope agree to the king, nor would the king condescend to the archbishop. At last the archbishop, seeing that by no means he could prevail against the king, thought to revenge himself by excommunication, and so went about the same. The king, having word thereof by the Countess Adela, his sister, desireth her to come to him into Normandy, and bring Anselm with her: whereupon, by the means of the countess, reconcilement was made, and the archbishop was restored to his former possessions; only his return into England was deferred, because he would not communicate with those whom the king had invested. So the king took his passage over into England, and Anselm made his abode at the abbey of Becke.

Reconcilement made between the king and Anselm.

Then were ambassadors again directed unto Rome, namely, William Warlwast, and Baldwin, above named, abbot of Ramsey; who, at length, concluded the long controversy between the king and the pope upon this agreement: that the king should take homage of the bishops elect, but should not deal with investing them by staff and ring. While the ambassadors were thus in their suit at Rome, divers complaints were daily brought from England to Anselm against the priests and canons, who, in his absence, contrary to the late council holden at London, received their wives into their houses again, and so were permitted by the king, paying him certain money for the same.[1] Anselm, the sore enemy against lawful marriage, grieved therewith, addresseth his letters unto the king, requiring him to refrain from any more taking of such exactions, declaring, moreover, and affirming, that the offences of all such ecclesiastical ministers must be corrected by the instance of bishops, and not of laymen. To this the king answereth gently again by letters, tempering himself; how he purposed shortly to come over into Normandy, and if he had done any thing amiss, either in these or other things, he would reform it by his obedience.

Priests received their wives again in the absence of Anselm.

The faults of ecclesiastical ministers belong to none but to bishops to correct, quoth Anselm.

Not long after, the messengers being now returned from Rome, the king, as he had promised, sped him into Normandy, where he, warring against his brother Robert, brought both him and the country of Normandy at last under his subjection. But first meeting with Anselm at the abbey of Becke, he covenanted and agreed with

The king brought under the archbishop.

(1) Guliel. Malmesb. lib. i. de Gestis Pontif.

him in all such points as the archbishop required. As first, that all his churches, which before were made tributary unto King William, his brother, now should remain free from all tribute. Item, that he should require nothing of the said churches or provinces, in the time of the seat being vacant. Moreover, concerning such priests and ministers as had given money to the king for their company with their wives, it was agreed that they should surcease from all ecclesiastical function for the space of three years, and that the king should take no more after such manner. Item, that all such goods, fruits and possessions, as had been taken away before from the archbishopric, should be restored at his coming again into England, &c. *Henry I.* A.D. 1106. Lawful matrimony punished.

This Anselm, the stout champion of popery and superstition, after this victory gotten over the king, for the which he so long fought, with joy and triumph saileth into England, having all his popish requests obtained. On his arrival he first flieth like a lion upon the married priests, contrary to the word of God, divorcing and punishing by man's authority, those whom the eternal and almighty God had coupled. Next, he looketh to them, who did hold any church by farm under the king. Against simony likewise, and against them that married within the seventh degree, he proceedeth with his full pontifical authority. Priests driven again from their wives.

Shortly after, as King Henry had finished his war in Normandy, and with victory had returned again into England, about the sixth year of his reign, Anselm, archbishop of Canterbury, by the permission of the king, assembled a great council at Westminster, in London, of the clergy and prelates of England, in which, by the bishop of Rome's authority, he so wrought with the king, that at length, albeit, as the story saith, not without great difficulty, it was newly confirmed and enacted, that no temporal man after that day should make investiture with cross or with ring, or with pastoral hook. In this council, sundry and divers injunctions were given forth to priests and deacons, as divers other synodal acts also by the same Anselm had been concluded in other councils before. And because mention is made here of the acts synodal concluded in the time of this Anselm, I thought good to pack them all in one general heap together, as I find them in Malmesbury, and in other sundry authors scatteringly recited. A.D. 1106.

The first thing decreed by this Anselm in his synodal councils, was touching the fault of simony, whereby divers, both bishops and abbots (as is aforesaid) were at the same time deposed. Laymen, also, were forbidden to confer any ecclesiastical promotion.[1]

Also, it was decreed, that no bishop should bear any office in secular men's business or meetings, and that such should not go apparelled as the laymen did, but should have their vestures decent, and meet for religious persons, and that in all places they should never go without some to bear witness of their conversation. Priests' apparel.

Item, That no archdeaconries should be let out to farm.

Item, That no archdeacon should be under the degree of a deacon.

Item, That no archdeacon, priest, deacon, subdeacon, colligener, or canon, should from thenceforth marry a wife, nor yet keep her, if he had been married to one before.

(1) Ex lib. Guliel. Malmesb. de Gestis Pontif. lib. i. Ex Jornalensi et aliis.

Henry. I.

A.D. 1106.

Item, That every subdeacon, being under the degree of a canon, after the profession of chastity marrying a wife, should be subject to the same rule.

They ordained also, that for a priest to keep company with his wife, should be reputed unlawful, and that he should say no mass, and if he said mass, he should not be heard.

They charged that none should be admitted to orders from that time forward, from the degree of a subdeacon, unless he did profess chastity.

That priest's sons should not claim by heritage the benefices of their fathers, as the custom had always been before.

How then was Stephen Gardiner lord chancellor in Queen Mary's time?

Item, That no spiritual person should sit in any secular office; as to be procurators or judges of blood.

Item, That priests should not resort to taverns or banquets, nor sit drinking by the fire-side.

That the garments of priests should be of one colour, and that their shoes should be decent.

Item, That monks, or any others of the clergy, if they forsook their order, either should come again, or be excommunicated.

Item, That the men of the clergy should wear broad crowns.

Item, That no tithes should be given but to the church.

Item, That no churches or prebends should be bought.

That no new chapels should be made without consent of the bishop.

That no church should be hallowed, before the necessary provision was made for the priest, and for the church to be maintained.

That abbots should send forth no men to war, and that they must both sleep and eat in the same house with their monks, unless some great necessity do let.

Item, That monks do enjoin no penance to any man without the knowledge of his abbot; and also that their abbots give no license therein, but only for such persons whose charge they have of soul.

That no monks should be godfathers, or nuns godmothers.

That monks should have no lordships to farm.

Item, That monks should take no churches but by the bishop, neither should so spoil and oppress the churches given unto them with their rents, that sufficient were not left for the ministers of the same.

That privy contracts between man and woman without witness should not stand, but be frustrated, if each party do go from the contract.

Item, That such of the clergy, as wear long hair, be so rounded, that part of their ear appear, and that their eyes be not covered.

Item, That there be no matrimonial connexion within the seventh degree of kindred, and that it do not continue if they be married, but that the marriage be broken. And that if any one privy to that incest, do not detect the same, he to be held guilty of the same crime.

Item, That no funerals or buryings be without their own parish church, so that the priest thereof do lose that which to him is due.

Item, That no man, upon any new-fangled rashness, do attribute any reverence or opinion of holiness to dead men's bodies, to fountains, or to any other thing, as the use hath been in time past, without authority of the bishop.

Item, That no buying and selling be used hereafter in England of men, as of other cattle.

† Also, after the restraint of priests' marriage, when grievous crimes began to come in the place thereof, they were forced to make another act, which was this.

† "With a grievous curse we condemn both those that occupy any nameless vice, and those also that willingly assist them, or be wicked doers with them in the same; till such time as they may deserve absolution by penance and confession.

"So that whatsoever he be that is noised or proved to be of this wickedness, if he be a religious person, he shall from thenceforth be promoted to no degree of honour, and that which he hath shall be taken from him.

"If he be a lay person, he shall be deprived of all his freedom within the land, and be no better than a foreigner.

"And because it shall be known, that the absolution of such as be secular belongs only to bishops; it was therefore enacted, that on every Sunday, in every parish church of England, the said excommunication should be published," &c. †

But mark in this great matter what followed; for, as Ranulphus Cestrensis witnesseth, this grievous general curse was soon called back again by the suit of certain who persuaded Anselm, that the publication, or opening of that vice, gave kindlings to the same in the hearts of lewd persons, ministering occasion of more boldness to them to do the like:[1] and so, to stop the occasion of this vice, the publication thereof was taken away; but the forbidding and restrainment of priests' lawful marriage, which chiefly was the cause thereof, remained still. And thus, ever since, this horrible crime remained among the clergy, both for lack of marriage being more used, and for lack of publication less punished. †

Besides all these synodal acts above comprehended, and given out by Anselm in his councils before, here also, in this present council at Westminster, in the year of this king aforesaid, he also directed other new injunctions to the priests.

First, That they and their wives should never more meet in one house, neither yet have dwelling in their territories. *Penalties and forfeits against priests that keep their wives*

Item, That the priests, deacons, and subdeacons, should retain no woman in their house, unless they were of their next kin.

Item, That such as had dissevered themselves from the society of their wives, and yet, for some honest cause, had to communicate with them, might do so if it were without door, and with two or three lawful witnesses

Item, If any one of them should be accused by two or three witnesses, and could not purge himself again by six able men of his own order, if he be a priest, or if he be a deacon by four, or if he be a subdeacon by two, then he should be judged a transgressor of the statutes, deprived of his benefice, and made infamous, or be put to open reproach of all men. *In the latter days shall come false teachers, forbidding marriage and eating of meats, &c*

Item, He that rebelled, and in contempt of this new statute held still his wife, and presumed to say mass, upon the eighth day after, if he made not due satisfaction, should be solemnly excommunicated.

Item, All archdeacons and deacons to be strictly sworn not to wink or dissemble at their meetings, or to bear with them for money And if they would not be sworn to this, then to lose their offices without recovery.

Item, Such priests, as forsaking their wives were willing to serve still, and remain in their holy order, first must cease forty days from their ministration, setting vicars for them in the mean time to serve, and taking such penance upon them, as by their bishop should be enjoined them. *Purification of priests that had been married.*

Thus have ye heard the tedious treatise of the life and doings of Anselm, how superstitious in his religion, how stubborn against his prince he was, what occasion of war and discord he would have ministered by his complaints, if they had been taken, what zeal without right knowledge, what fervency without cause he pretended, what pains without profit he took; who, if he had bestowed that time and travel in preaching Christ at home to his flock, which he took in gadding to Rome, to complain of his country, in my mind, he had been better occupied. Moreover, what violent and tyrannical injunctions he set forth of investing and other things, ye have heard; but especially against the lawful and godly marriage of priests. What a vehement adversary he was, in that respect, may appear by these minutes or extracts of letters, which we have here annexed; in form and effect as followeth:—

(1) Ranulph. Cestrensis, lib vii

Henry I.

A.D. 1106.

A Letter of Anselm.

Anselm, archbishop, to his brethren and dearest sons, the lord prior and others at Canterbury.[1]

King Henry permitted priests to have both churches and wives.

As concerning priests, of whom the king commanded that they should have both their churches and their women as they had in the time of his father, and of Lanfranc, archbishop: both because the king hath revested and reseized the whole archbishopric, and because so cursed a marriage was forbidden in a council in the time of his father and of the said archbishop: boldly I command, by the authority which I have by my archbishopric, not only within my archbishopric, but also throughout England, that all priests, who keep wives, shall be deprived of their churches and ecclesiastical benefices.

A Letter of Pope Paschal to Anselm.

Pascal, bishop, servant of God's servants, to his reverend brother Anselm, archbishop of Canterbury, greeting and apostolical blessing.[2]

Pope Paschal hath so decreed it at Rome. Ergo, priests must have no wives. If profit of the church may come by priests' children, what hurt then were it to the church for priests to have wives?

We believe your brotherhood is not ignorant what is decreed in the Romish church concerning priests' children. But because there is so great a multitude of such within the realm of England, that almost the greater and better part of the clerks are reckoned to be on this side, therefore we commit this dispensation to your care; for we grant these to be promoted to holy offices by reason of the need at this time, and for the profit of the church (such as learning and life shall commend among you), so that, yet notwithstanding, the prejudice of the ecclesiastical decree be taken heed to hereafter, &c.

Another Letter of Anselm for Investing.

To the Reverend Lord and loving Father Paschal, high bishop, Anselm, servant of Canterbury church, due subjection and continual prayers.

King Henry and his nobles ready to forsake the Romish church.

After I returned to my bishopric in England I showed the apostolical decree, which I being present heard in the Romish council. 1. That no man should receive investing of churches at the king's hand, or any lay person's, or should become his man for it, and that no man should presume to consecrate him that did offend herein. When the king and his nobles, and the bishops themselves, and others of the lower degree, heard these things, they took them so grievously, that they said, they would in no case agree to the thing, and that they would drive me out of the kingdom, and forsake the Romish church, rather than keep this thing. Wherefore, reverend father, I desire your counsel by your letter, &c.

Another Letter of Anselm.

Anselm, archbishop, to the Reverend Gudulph, bishop, and to Arnulph, prior, and to William, archdeacon of Canterbury, and to all in his diocese, greeting.[3]

Against priests receiving again their wives. Priests excommunicated for receiving again their wives.

William, our archdeacon, hath written to me, that some priests that be under his custody (taking again their women that were forbidden) have fallen unto the uncleanness from the which they were drawn by wholesome counsel and commandment. When the archdeacon would amend this thing, they utterly despised, with wicked pride, his warning and worthy commandment to be received. Then he, calling together many religious men and obedient priests, excommunicated worthily the proud and disobedient, who beastly despised the curse, and were not afraid to defile the holy ministry, as much as lay in them, &c.

Unto these letters above prefixed, I have also adjoined another of the said Anselm, touching a great case of conscience, of a monk's whipping himself. Wherein may appear both the blind and lamentable superstition of those religious men, and the judgment of this Anselm in the same matter.

(1) Ex epist. Ansel. 7; et 377. (2) Ex epist. 33. (3) Ex epist. 37.

Another Letter of Anselm.

Anselm, archbishop, to Bernard, monk of the abbey of St. Warburg, greeting and prayer.[1]

I heard it said of your lord abbot, that thou judgest it to be of greater merit, when a monk either beats himself, or desireth himself to be beaten of another than when he is beaten (not of his own will) in the chapter, by the commandment of the prelacy. But it is not as you think, for that judgment which any man commandeth to himself, is kingly; but that which he suffereth by obedience in the chapter, is monkish. The one is of his own will; the other is of obedience, and not of his own will. That which I call kingly, kings and rich proud men commanded to be done to themselves; but that which I call monkish, they take not commanding, but obeying. The kingly is so much easier, by how much it agreeth to the will of the sufferer; but the monkish is so much the more grievous, by how much it differeth from the will of the sufferer. In the kingly judgment, the sufferer is judged to be his own; in monkish he is proved not to be his own: for although the king, or rich man, when he is beaten, willingly showeth himself humbly to be a sinner; yet he would not submit himself to this humbleness at any other's commandment, but would withstand the commander with all his strength. But when a monk submitteth himself to the whip humbly in the chapter at the will of the prelate, the truth judgeth him to be of so much greater merit, by how much he humbleth himself more and more, and more truly than the other. For he humbleth himself to God only, because he knoweth his sins, but this man humbleth himself to man for obedience. But he is more lowly that humbleth himself both to God and man for God's cause, than he which humbleth himself to God only, and not to God's commandment. Therefore, if he that humbleth himself shall be extolled, ergo, he that more humbleth himself, shall be more exalted. And where I said, that when a monk is whipped, it differeth from his will, you must not so understand it, as though he would not patiently bear it with an obedient will, but because by a natural appetite he would not suffer the sorrow. But if ye say, I do not so much fly the open beating for the pains (which I feel also secretly), as for the shame; know then that he is stronger that rejoiceth to bear this for obedience' sake. Therefore be thou sure, that one whipping of a monk by obedience is of more merit than innumerable whippings taken by his own mind. But whereas he is such that he always ought to have his heart ready without murmuring obediently to be whipped, we ought to judge him then to be of a great merit, whether he be whipped privily or openly, &c.

Whether is more merit for a monk to cause himself in the chapter to be whipped, or to suffer obediently the whipping of his abbot.

The judgment of Anselm on the case.

And thus much concerning Anselm, archbishop of Canterbury, whose stout example gave no little courage to Thurstin and Becket, his successors, and others that followed after, to do the like against their kings and princes, as in process hereafter by the grace of Christ shall appear.

About this time, two famous archbishops of Mentz, being right virtuous and well-disposed prelates, were cruelly and tyrannously dealt withal, and treated by the bishop of Rome. Their names were Henry and Christian. This Henry, having intelligence that he was complained of to the pope, sent a learned man, a special friend of his, to excuse him, named Arnold; one for whom he had done much, and whom he had promoted to great livings and promotions. But this honest man Arnold, instead of an excuser, became an accuser, bribing the two chiefest cardinals with good gold; by which means he obtained of the pope, those two cardinals, to be sent as inquisitors and only doers in that present case. They, coming to Germany, summoned the said Henry, and deposed him from his archbishopric in spite of all he could do either by law or justice, substituting in his place the aforesaid Arnold, in hope, truly, of the

Judges corrupted.

(1) Ex epist. 255.

Henry I. A.D. 1100 to 1106

ecclesiastical gold. Whereupon that virtuous and honourable Henry, as the story telleth, spake unto those his perverse judges on this wise: "If I should appeal unto the apostolic see for this your unjust process had against me, perhaps the pope would attempt nothing more therein than ye have, neither should I win any thing by it, but only toil of body, loss of goods, affliction of mind, care of heart, and missing of his favour. Wherefore I do appeal unto the Lord Jesus Christ, as the most high and just judge, and cite you before his judgment, there to answer me before the high Judge; for neither justly nor godly, but by corruption as it pleaseth you, you have judged." Whereunto they scoffingly answered: "Go you first, and we will follow." Not long after, as the story goes, the said Henry died, whereof the said two cardinals having intelligence, said one to the other jestingly: "Behold, he is gone before, and we must follow according to our promise." And verily, they said truer than they were aware of; for within a while they died in one day. For the one, sitting upon a jakes to ease himself, voided out all his entrails into the draught, and miserably ended his life; the other, gnawing off the fingers of his hands, and spitting them out of his mouth, all deformed in devouring himself, died. And in like manner, not long after the end of these men, the aforesaid Arnold, most horrible, in a sedition was slain; and certain days, lying stinking above the ground unburied, lay open to the spoil of every rascal and harlot. The historiographer in declaring hereof crieth out upon the cardinals in this manner: "O ye cardinals, ye are the beginning and authors hereof. Come ye hither, and heap and carry unto your countries the devil, and offer yourselves to him with that money, whereof ye have been most gluttonous and insatiable."

A terrible example for corrupt judges to beware.

A.D. 1100.

About the same time and year in which King Henry began his reign, Pope Paschal entered his papacy, succeeding Urban, about A.D. 1100, nothing swerving from the steps of Hildebrand, his superior. This Paschal, being elected by the cardinals, after the people had cried thrice, "St. Peter hath chosen good Rainerus;" he then putting on a purple vesture, and a tiara upon his head, was brought upon a white palfrey into Lateran, where a sceptre was given him, and a girdle put about him having seven keys, with seven seals hanging thereupon for a recognisance or token of his sevenfold power, according to the sevenfold grace of the Holy Ghost, of binding, loosing, shutting, opening, sealing, resigning, and judging. After this Paschal was elected pope, Henry IV., the aforesaid emperor (of courage most valiant, if the time had served thereto,) thought to come up to Italy to salute the new pope; but, understanding the pope's mind bent against him, he changed his purpose. In the mean time, Paschal, to show himself inferior to Hildebrand in no point, began first to depose all such abbots and bishops as the emperor had set up. Also he banished Albert, Theodoric, and Maginulph, striving at the same time for the papacy. I spake before of Guibert, whom Henry, the emperor, had made pope against Hildebrand. Paschal made out an army against this Guibert, who, being put to flight, not long after departed.

The pope's attire.

The sevenfold power of the pope.

Antichrist born and manifest.

About the same time, A.D. 1101, the bishop of Florence began to teach and to preach of antichrist then to be born and to be manifest, as Sabellicus testifieth; whereupon Paschal assembling a council, put to silence the said bishop, and condemned his books. In this council at Trecas, priests who were married were condemned for Nicolaitans. Item, according to the decree of Hildebrand, all, of what degree or estate soever they were (being laymen) who gave any ecclesiastical dignities, were condemned of simony. Furthermore, the statute of priests' tithes he renewed there, counting the selling away thereof as a sin against the Holy Ghost. Concerning the excommunication and other troubles, that Hildebrand wrought against Henry IV. the emperor, it is declared sufficiently before. This excommunication Paschal, the pope, renewed afresh against the said Henry; and not only that, but also conventing the princes of Germany unto a general assembly, he set up his own son against him, causing the bishops of Mentz, Cologne, and Worms, to deprive him of his imperial crown, and to place his son Henry V. in his father's kingdom; and so they did.[1] Coming to the place at Hilgeshem, first they required from him his diadem, his purple, his ring, and other ornaments pertaining to the crown. The emperor demanded the cause, being then excommunicated and void of friends. They pretended again, I cannot tell what, —the selling of bishoprics, abbacies, and other ecclesiastical dignities for money; also alleging the pope's pleasure and that of other princes. Then required he first of the bishop of Mentz, and likewise of the other two, whom he had preferred to their bishoprics before, asking them in order, if he had received of them any penny for his promoting them to their dignities. This when they could not deny to be so, "Well," saith he, "and do you requite me again with this?" with divers other words of exhortation, admonishing them to remember their oath and allegiance to their prince. But the perjured prelates, neither reverencing his majesty, nor moved with his benefits, nor regarding their fidelity, ceased not for all this, but first plucked from him, sitting on his throne, his crown imperial, and then disvestured him, taking from him his purple and his sceptre. The good emperor, being left desolate and in confusion, saith to them: "Videat Deus et judicet:" that is, "Let God see and judge." Thus leaving him, they went to his son to confirm him in his kingdom, and caused him to drive his father out; who then being chased of his son, and having but nine persons about him, did flee by way of the dukedom of Limbrugh, where the duke being then hunting, and perceiving and hearing of him, made after to follow him. The emperor fearing no other than present death, for he had displaced the same duke before out of his dukedom, submitted himself, craving of him pardon, and not revenge. The duke, full of compassion, and pitying his estate, not only remitted all his displeasure, but also received him to his castle. Moreover, collecting his soldiers and men of war, he brought him to Cologne, and there he was well received. His son hearing this, besieged that city. But the father, by night escaping, came to Leodium, where resorted to him all such as were men of compassion and constant heart, insomuch that his power, being strong enough, he was now able to pitch a field against his enemies, and so he did, desiring his friends, that if he had the victory, they would spare his son. In fine, the battle joined, the father had the victory,

A council at Trecas.

A tragical history of Pope Paschal, setting the son against the father.

The prelates set the son against the father.

A grateful example of a good and thankful duke.

(1) Ex Historia Helmoldi.

Henry I. A.D. 1107.

the son being put to flight, and many slain on both sides. But shortly after, the battle being renewed again, the son prevailed, and the father was overcome and taken; who then, being utterly dispossessed of his kingdom, was brought to that exigency, that coming to Spires, he was feign to crave of the bishop there, whom he had done much for before, to have a prebend in the church: and for that he had some skill in his book, he desired to serve in our Lady's quire; yet could he not obtain so much at his hand, who swore by our Lady, he should have nothing there.[1] Thus the woeful emperor, most unkindly handled, and repulsed on every side, came to Leodium, and there for sorrow died, after he had reigned fifty years; whose body Paschal, after his funeral, caused to be taken up again, and to be brought to Spires, where it remained five years unburied.[2]

The unkindness of a proud prelate.

The emperor five years without burial.

After the decease of this emperor Henry IV., his son Henry V. reigned the space of twenty years. This prince coming to Rome to be crowned of the pope, could not obtain it, before he would fully assent to have this ratified, that no emperor should have any thing to do with the election of the Roman bishop, or with other bishoprics.[3] Besides that, about the same time, such a stir was made in Rome by the said bishop, that if the emperor had not defended himself with his own hands, he had been slain. But as it happened, the emperor having victory, amongst many other Romans slain or taken in the same skirmish, taketh also the pope and leadeth him out of the city; where he intendeth with him upon divers conditions, both of his coronation, and of recovering again his right and title in the election of the pope, and of other bishops: whereunto the pope assenting agreed to all. So the emperor, being crowned by Paschal, returned again with the pope of Rome.

A.D. 1107. Henry emperor.

The pope taken prisoner.

All the conditions between the emperor and the pope, so long as the emperor remained at Rome, stood firm and ratified; but as soon as the emperor was returned again to Germany, forthwith the pope, calling a synod, not only revoked all that he had agreed to before, but also excommunicated Henry, the emperor, as he had done his father before, reproving the former 'privilegium' for 'pravilegium.' The emperor, returning from Rome to France, there married Matilda, daughter to King Henry; who then hearing what the pope had done, (grieved not a little,) with all expedition marched to Rome, and putteth the pope to flight, and finally placeth another in his stead. In the mean time the bishops of Germany, the pope's good friends, slacked not their business, incensing the Saxons all that they might against their Cæsar; insomuch that a great commotion was stirred up, and it grew at length to a pitched field, which was fought in the month of February, by the wood called Sylva Catularia.

War raised by the pope and his papists.

The emperor seeing no end of these conflicts, unless he would yield to the pope, was fain to give over, and forego his privilege, falling to a composition, not to meddle with matters pertaining to the pope's election, nor with investing, nor such other things belonging to the church and churchmen; and thus was the peace between them concluded, and proclaimed to the no small rejoicing of both the armies, then lying by Worms, near the river Rhine.

Peace concluded between the emperor and the pope.

(1) Ex Helmoldo, et Gotfrido Viterbiensi. (2) Ex Helmodo.
(3) Ex Chronico Carionis, lib. iii.

In the time of this Paschal lived Bernard, called Abbot Claravallensis, A.D. 1108, of whom sprang the Bernardine monks.

About this time the city of Worcester was almost consumed with fire.

All this while Henry the emperor had no issue, having to wife Matilda, the daughter of Henry I., king of England, and that by the just judgment of God, as it may appear; for as he, having a father, persecuted him by the pope's setting on, contrary to the part of a natural son; so God's providence did not suffer him to be the father of any child, naturally to love him, or to succeed him.

Bernardine monks come in. The city of Worcester almost all consumed with fire. The Lord's just retribution and judgment.

After the death of Paschal, A.D. 1118, succeeded Pope Gelasius, chosen by the cardinals, but without the consent of the emperor, whereupon rose no little variance in Rome; and at length another pope was set up by the emperor, called Gregory VIII., and Gelasius was driven away into France, and there died. After him came Calixtus II., chosen likewise by a few cardinals, without the voice of the emperor, who, coming up to Rome to enjoy his seat, first sent his legate into Germany to excommunicate the emperor Henry; who then, having divers conflicts with his fellow pope Gregory, at length, drave him out of Rome. At this time, by this occasion, great disputation and controversy arose between the emperor and the pope's court, whether of them in dignity should excel the other; whereof reasons and arguments on both sides were alleged, which in the verses below are comprehended.

Two popes striving together. The pope excommunicateth the emperor.

Allegatio imperatoris contra papam.

Cæsar lex viva stat regibus imperativa,
Legeque; sub viva sunt omnia jura dativa,
Lex ea castigat, solvit et ipsa ligat.
Conditor est legis, neque debet lege teneri,
Sed sibi complacuit sub lege libenter haberi:
Quicquid ei placuit, juris adinstar erat.
Qui ligat ac solvit Deus ipsum protulit orbi,
Divisit regnum divina potentia secum,
Astra dedit superis, cætera cuncta sibi.

Responsio Romanæ curiæ contra imperatorem.

Pars quoque papalis sic obviat imperiali,
Sic dans regnare, quod Petro subjiciaris:
Jus etenim nobis Christus utrumque parit.
Spiritus et corpus mihi sunt subjecta potenter,
Corpora terrena teneo, cœlestia mente,
Unde, tenendo polum, solvo ligoque solum.
Æthera pandere, cœlica tangere, papa videtur.
Nam dare, tollere, nectere, solvere cuncta meretur,
Cui debit omne decus lex nova, lexque vetus:
Annulus et baculus quamvis terrena putentur,
Sunt de jure poli, quæ significare videntur:
Respice jura Dei, mens tua cedat ei, &c.

In conclusion, the emperor being overcome so much with the vain reasons of the pope's side, and fearing the dangerous thunderbolt of his curse, (talking with princes, and persuaded with his friends,) was

Henry I

A.D. 1109.

fain to condescend to the unreasonable conditions of the pope: first, to ratify his election, notwithstanding the other pope (whom the said emperor had set up) was yet alive, secondly, that he should resign his right and title in matters pertaining to the election of the pope, and investure of bishops.

This being done and granted, and the writings thereof set up in the church of Lateran, for a triumph over the emperor thus subdued, the pope maketh out after Gregory, his fellow-pope, being then in a town called Sutrium, which being besieged and taken, Gregory also was taken;[1] whom, Calixtus the pope, setting him upon a camel, with his face to the camel's tail, brought him thus through the streets of Rome, holding the tail in his hand instead of a bridle; and afterward, being shorn, he was thrust into a monastery.

Gregory brought unto Rome by the pope, his face to the camel's tail

Amongst many acts done by this glorious pope, first he established the decrees of the papal see against this emperor. He brought in the four quarter fasts, called Ember days.[2]

The Ember days, by whom they were brought in, and when

By the same Calixtus the order of monks, called Præmonstratenses, was brought in

The order of monks, Præmonstratenses

Further, by him it was decreed to be judged for adultery, if any person, during his lifetime, had put from him either bishopric or benefice; grounding upon this scripture of St. Paul to the Romans, "The wife is bound to the law of her husband, so long as the husband liveth; after he is dead she is loosed from the law of her husband," &c.

Scripture clerkly applied by the pope.

Item, the same Calixtus, holding a general council at Rheims, decreed that priests, deacons, and subdeacons, should put away their concubines and wives; and that whosoever was found to keep his wife, should be deprived of benefice, and all other ecclesiastical livings: whereupon a certain English writer made these verses following:—

Priests and ministers compelled to leave their wives

"O bone Calixte, nunc omnis clerus odit te
Quondam presbyteri poterant uxoribus uti,
Hoc destruxisti, postquam tu papa fuisti," &c.

That is, word for word,—

"The hatred of the clergy hast thou, good Calixtus,
For sometimes priests might use their wives right,
But that thou hast rejected, since pope thou wast elected."

A.D. 1109.

And thus much of the Roman matters. Now to our country story again After the death of Anselm beforementioned, who deceased 1109, after he had been in the see sixteen years, the church of Canterbury stood void five years; and the goods of the church were spent to the king's use. When he was prayed to help the church that was so long without a pastor, he in his answer pretended that as his father and brother had been accustomed there to set the best tried and approved men that might be found, so to the intent that he might do the same, in choosing those who either should equal the former examples of them before, or at least follow their footsteps as near as they could, he took therein the more time and leisure. And so with shift of answer he dallied out the time, while

(1) Ex Platina, Vincentio, Stella, &c. (2) Dist 70, cap Jejunium

Henry I. A.D. 1109.

he had filled his coffers with the commodities of that benefice. The same year, after the death of Anselm, the king converted the abbey of Ely to a bishopric, which before was under the bishopric of Lincoln; placing there Henry, bishop of Bangor, as the first bishop of that see. And, as of late years before this, divers wonders were seen, as stars falling from heaven so thick that they could not be numbered, at the setting forth of the Christians to the Holy Land;[1] a blazing star over Constantinople; a spring boiling out blood, seen at Finchamstead, in Berkshire, three weeks together, A. D. 1090.[2] After that, the firmament appeared so red, as if it had been all on fire; also two full moons appeared together, one in the east, the other in the west, on Maunday Thursday; with a blazing star, in the same year, appearing about the taking of Duke Robert, having a white circle enclosing it; A. D. 1106.[3] Also with an eclipse of the sun darkened after that. So likewise about this present year, A. D. 1110, was seen the flood of Trent, about Nottingham, so dried up from morning to three of the clock at afternoon, that men might go over it dry shod.[4] Also in Shrewsbury a great earthquake happened; and after that followed a sharp winter, great murrain of beasts and pestilence of men, as Gualter Gisburn recordeth.[5] Moreover the same author mentioneth, that about the same year the like vading of water also happened in the flood of Medway; and in the Thames, between the bridge and the Tower, and under the bridge, from midnight to the next evening, was so great an ebb, that an innumerable sort of people and children waded over, scarcely knee deep in the water, the sea withdrawing his tide ten miles from his accustomed course.[6] In this year also, as the said authors and Jornalensis do testify, the city of Worcester by casualty was consumed with fire; also the city of Chester, A. D. 1114.[7]

The bishopric of Ely first planted.

A.D. 1110. Trent dried up.

An earthquake, murrain, and pestilence.

A.D. 1113. Worcester consumed with fire.

A.D. 1114. Dissension between Thurstin, of York, and Rodulph, archbishop of Canterbury, for subjection.

The next year following, Rodulph, bishop of Rochester, an Englishman, was promoted to be archbishop of Canterbury; and Thurstin, the king's chaplain, was elected archbishop of York; who, being content to receive his benediction or consecration of the see of Canterbury, yet, because he refused to make his profession of obedience to the same see, was by the king deprived of his dignity.

Then Thurstin, by the instigation of certain of his clerks at York, took his journey to Rome; who, there making his complaint to Pope Paschal, brought with him a letter from the pope to the king, where, among other words was contained as followeth:[8] "We hear and understand, that the archbishop elect of the church of York, a discreet and industrious man, is sequestered from the church of York; which standeth against both divine justice and the institution of the holy fathers. Our purpose is, that neither the church of Canterbury should be impaired, nor again that the church of York should suffer any prejudice, but that the same constitution, which

A.D. 1115. The letter of Paschal to King Henry.

(1) Jornalensis. (2) Gisburn. (3) Jornalensis. (4) Gisburn.
(5) Gisburn. (6) Rog. Hoved, Gisburn, &c. (7) Rog. Hoved.
(8) "Audivimus electum Eboracencis ecclesiæ, virum sapientem et strenuum, sine judicio ab Eboracensi sequestratum ecclesia, quod nimirum divinæ justitiæ et sanct. patrum institutionibus adversatur. Nos quidem neque Cant. ecclesiam minui, neque Eboracensem volumus præjudicium pati, sed eam constitutionem quæ a beato Gregorio, Anglicæ gentis Apostolo, inter easdem ecclesias, constituta est, firmam censemus illibatamque servari. Idem ergo electus, ut justitia exigit, ad suam ecclesiam omnibus modis revocetur. Si quid autem quæstionis inter easdem ecclesias nascitur, presentibus utrisque partibus in vestra præsentia pertractetur," &c.—Ex Gualter. Gisburnens, ex Guliel. Malmesb. de Pontif. lib. iv. Ex Roger. Hoved, Fabian. &c.

Henry I. A.D. 1116. was by blessed Gregory, the apostle of the English nation, set and decreed between those two churches, should remain still in force and effect inviolate. Wherefore, as touching the aforesaid elect, let him be received again by any means, as right and meet it is, into his church. And if there be any question between the aforesaid churches, let it be handled and decided in your presence, both the two parties being there present."

A.D. 1116. Assembly of the nobles at Salisbury. Upon occasion of this letter there was a solemn assembly appointed at Salisbury, about the hearing of this controversy. The variance between these two prelates still increased more and more. Rodulph, archbishop of Canterbury, in no case would yield or condescend to give imposition of hands unto him, unless he would make his profession of obedience. Thurstin again said, he would willingly receive and embrace his benediction; but as touching the profession of his subjection, that he would not agree to. Then the king, declaring his mind therein, signified unto Thurstin, that, without his subjection and obedience professed to the archbishop of Canterbury, he should not enjoy his consecration to be archbishop of York. Whereunto Thurstin, nothing replying again, renounced his archbishopric, promising, moreover, to make no more claim unto it, nor to molest those who should enjoy it.

Thurstin refuseth to profess subjection to the archbishop of Canterbury, and to renounce his see.

A.D. 1118. Shortly after this, it happened that Pope Paschal died; after whom, as is above-rehearsed, succeeded Pope Gelasius, who lived not a year, and died in France. Whereupon the cardinals, who then followed the said Pope Gelasius unto Cluniack, created another pope of their own choosing, whom they called Calixtus II. The other cardinals who were at Rome did choose another pope, called Gregory, of whom mention before is made: about which two popes much stir there was in Christian realms. As this Calixtus was remaining in France, and there calling a general council at Rheims, as ye heard before, Thurstin, the archbishop of York, desired license of the king to go to the council, purposing there to open the cause of his church; which eftsoons he obtained: first promising the king that he would there attempt nothing that should be prejudicial to the church of Canterbury. In the mean time the king had sent secret word unto the pope by Rodulph and other procurators, that in no case he would consecrate Thurstin. Yet, notwithstanding the faithful promise of the pope made to the king, so it fell out, that the said pope, through the suit of his cardinals, whom Thurstin had won to him, was inclined to consecrate him, and gave him the pall. For this deed the king was sorely discontented with Thurstin, and warned him the entry of this land.

Thurstin consecrated archbishop of York by the pope against the king's mind.

Council at Rheims. In this council at Rheims, abovementioned, where were gathered 434 prelates, these five principal acts were concluded:

1. That no man should either buy or sell any bishopric, abbotship, deanery, archdeaconship, priesthood, prebendship, altar, or any ecclesiastical promotion or benefice, orders, consecration, church-hallowing, seat or stall within the quire, or any office ecclesiastical, under danger of excommunication if he did persist.

2. That no lay person should give investiture of any ecclesiastical possession; and that no spiritual man should receive any such at any layman's hand, under pain of deprivation.

3. That no man should invade, take away, or detain the goods or possessions

of the church; but that they should remain firm and perpetual, under pain of perpetual curse.

4. That no bishop or priest should leave any ecclesiastical dignity or benefice to any by way of inheritance. Adding, moreover, that for baptism, chrism, annoiling, or burial, no money should be exacted.

5. That all priests, deacons, and subdeacons, should be utterly debarred and sequestered from company of their wives and concubines, under pain of exclusion from all christian communion.

The acts thus determined were sent at once to Henry, the emperor, to see and try, before the breaking up of the council, whether he would agree to the canonical elections, free consecration, and investing of spiritual persons, and to other acts of the council. The emperor maketh answer again, that he would lose nothing of that ancient custom which his progenitors had given him. Notwithstanding, because of the authority of the general council, he was content to consent to the residue, save only the investing of ecclesiastical function to be taken from him, to which he would never agree.[1] Upon this, at the next return of the pope to the council, the emperor was appointed to be excommunicated; which thing, when divers of the council did not well like, and therefore did separate themselves from the rest, the pope applying against them the similitude of the seventy disciples who were offended at the Lord, when he taught them of eating of his flesh and blood, and therefore divided themselves from him, declaring, moreover, to them, how they who gathered not with him scattered, and they that were not with him were against him: by these, and such like persuasions, reduced them again to his side; and so, by that council, Henry the emperor was excommunicated.

The acts sent to the emperor.

The emperor agreeth not to the pope's investing.

Henry the emperor excommunicated.

It was not long after that the pope came to Gisortium, where Henry, king of England, resorted to him, desiring, and also obtaining of him, that he would send henceforth no legate, nor permit any to be sent from Rome to England, unless the king himself should so require, by reason of some occasion of strife, which else could not be otherwise decided by his own bishops at home. The cause why the king required this of the pope was, for that certain Roman legates had been in England a little before; to wit, one Guido, and another Roman, named Anselm, and another also called Peter, who had spoiled the realm of great treasure, as the accustomed manner of the proud pope's legates is wont to be.[2] Also he required of the pope that he might use and retain all the customs used before by his forefathers in England and in Normandy.

England to have no legate from Rome but the archbishop of Canterbury.

England spoiled by the pope's legates.

To these petitions the pope did easily consent, requiring again of the king that he would license Thurstin, the archbishop above-named, to return with favour into his realm. But that the king utterly denied, unless he would profess subjection to the church of Canterbury, as his predecessors had done before; and excused himself by his oath which he before had made. To this the pope answered again, that he, by his authority apostolical, both might, and would also, easily dispense with him for his promise or oath. Then the king said that he would talk with his council thereof, and so send him an answer of his mind; which answer was this, That for the love and request of the pope, he was content that Thurstin should re-enter his realm, and quietly enjoy his prelateship, upon this condition, that he would (as

All the customs of the realm granted of the pope.

(1) Ex Roger. Hoved. (2) Guliel. Malmesb. de Pont. lib. i.

Henry I. A.D. 1120. his predecessors did) profess his subjection to the church of Canterbury. Otherwise, said he, so long as he was king, he should never sit archbishop of the church of York. And thus ended that meeting between the king of England and the pope for that time.

A.D. 1120. The year following, which was A.D. 1120, the aforesaid pope, Calixtus, directeth his letters for Thurstin to the king, and to Rodulph, archbishop of Canterbury; in which epistles, by his full power apostolical, he doth interdict both the church of Canterbury and the church of York, with all the parish churches within the same cities, from all divine service, from the burial also of the dead, except only the baptizing of children, and the absolution of those who lie dying; unless, within a month after the receipt of the same, Thurstin, without any exaction of subjection made, were received and admitted to the see of York, and that the king likewise should doubtless be excommunicated, except he would consent unto the same. Whereupon Thurstin, for fear of the pope's curse, was immediately sent for and reconciled to the king, and was placed quietly in his archiepiscopal see of York.

The king compelled to receive Thurstin for fear of the pope's curse.

A.D. 1122. It followed not long after, within two years, that Rodulph, archbishop of Canterbury, departed; in whose see succeeded after him Gulielmus de Turbine. About this time, in the seven and twentieth year of the king's reign, the Grey Friars, by the procuring of the king, came first into England, and had their house first at Canterbury. About the same season, or a little before, the king called a council at London, where the spiritualty of England, not knowing to what purpose it was required, condescended to the king to have the punishment of married priests: by reason of which grant, whereof the spiritualty afterwards much repented, the priests, paying a certain fine to the king, were suffered to retain their wives still, whereby the king gathered no small sum of money.[1] At this time began the first foundation of the monastery called Gisburn, in Cleveland.

The Grey Friars first came into England. A.D. 1125.

Priests paid for their wives.

The abbey of Gisburn builded.

It was above touched, how Matilda, or Maud, daughter to King Henry, was married to Henry V. the emperor; who, after the decease of the said emperor, her husband, returned about this time with the imperial crown to her father in Normandy, bringing with her the hand of St. James; for joy whereof the king builded the abbey of Reading, where the said hand was reposed. This Matilda was received by the said council to be next heir to the king, her father, in possession of the English crown, for lack of issue male; and soon after she was sent over to Normandy, to marry Geoffrey Plantagenet, earl of Anjou, of whom came Henry II., who, after Stephen, was king of England. About this time also was founded the priory of Norton, in the province of Chester, by one William, the son of Nichelle.

Saint James's hand. Reading abbey founded. Henry II. born of Matilda, the empress A.D. 1130. The priory of Norton founded.

In the stories of Polychronicon, Jornalensis, and Polydore, is declared, how King Henry was troubled greatly with three sundry visions appearing unto him by night. The first was of a great multitude of husbandmen of the country, who appeared to fly upon him with their mattocks and instruments, requiring of him his debt which he did owe unto them. In the second, he saw a great number of soldiers and harnessed men coming fiercely upon him. In the third,

Three terrible visions of the king.

(1) Ex Roger. Hoved. 7; et Malmesb, Gisburnens, Hunting. lib. vii.

he saw a company of prelates and churchmen, threatening him with their bishops' staves, and fiercely approaching him; whereupon being dismayed, in all haste he ran and took his sword to defend himself, finding there none to strike. On asking counsel afterwards concerning these visions, he was admonished by one of his physicians named Grimbald, by repentance, alms, and amendment of life, to make some amends to God, and to his country, whom he had offended. Which three vows thus being made, the next year after he went to England; where, being upon the seas in a great tempest with his daughter Matilda, he remembered there his three vows; and so coming to the land, for performance of the same, first released unto the commons the Dane-gilt which his father and brother before had renewed. Secondly, he went to St. Edmundsbury, where he showed great benefits to the churchmen. Thirdly, he procured justice to be better administered throughout his realm, &c. Also he ordained and erected a new bishopric at Carlisle.

Henry I. A.D. 1130.

Three vows of Henry. A.D. 1131.

Dane-gilt released.

In the three and thirtieth year of the king's reign (as witnesseth a certain author) a great part of the city of London, with the church of St. Paul, was burned with fire in Whitsun week.

The city and Paul's church in London burned.

After Calixtus (whose story and time is before discoursed) succeeded Pope Honorius II.; notwithstanding that the cardinals had elected another, yet he, by the means of certain citizens, obtained the papacy, A.D. 1125. About the second year of his induction, as is to be read in Mat. Paris, there was a certain legate of his, called Johannes Cremensis, sent down to England from the pope for the redress I cannot well tell of what; but, indeed, the chief purpose of his coming, as of all others after him in those days, was to fill his pouch with English money, as may further appear by his proceedings. This legate coming then with the pope's letters directed both into England and into Scotland, after he had well refreshed himself in bishops' houses, and amongst the abbots, at length resorted to London, where he assembled the whole clergy together, inquired after priests' concubines, otherwise called their wives, and made thereupon a statute in the said synod of London, after this tenor:[1] "To priests, deacons, subdeacons, and canons, we do utterly inhibit, by authority apostolical, all manner of society and conversation with all kinds of women, except only their mother, sister, or aunt, or such whereof can rise no suspicion. And whosoever shall be found to violate this decree, being convict thereof, shall thereby sustain the loss of all that he hath by his order. Moreover, amongst kindred or such as be joined in affinity, we forbid matrimony unto the seventh generation." But see how God worketh against such ungodly proceedings. The next night after, it happened that the same cardinal, ruffling and revelling with his concubines, was apprehended in the same vice whereof he had so strictly given out precepts the day before, to the no little slander and shame, as Matthew Paris doth write, of the whole clergy.

Honorius II.

A Romish statute concerning priests' wives and concubines.

Marriage forbidden to the seventh degree.

Unto A.D. 1125, lived Henry V. the emperor, after he had reigned twenty years, dying without issue, as is before mentioned. Next

(1) "Presbyteris, diaconibus, subdiaconibus, et canonicis, uxorum, concubinarum, et omnium omnino fœminarum cantubernia, authoritate apostolica inhibemus, præter matrem, aut sororem, vel amitam, aut ejusmodi quæ omnino careant suspicione. Et qui decreti hujus violator extiterit (confessus vel convictus) ruinam ordinis patiatur. Inter consanguineos seu affinitate propinquos, usque ad septimam generationem, matrimonia contrahi prohibemus."

Henry I. after Henry, the imperial crown came unto Lothaire, duke of Saxony.

A.D. 1133.

Certain histories make mention of one Arnulph, in the time of this Pope Honorius II. Some say he was archbishop of Lugdune, as Hugo, Platina, Sabellicus. Trithimius saith he was a priest, whose history, as it is set forth in Trithimius, I will briefly in English express. About this time, saith he, in the days of Honorius II., one Arnulph, a priest, zealous, and of great devotion, and a worthy preacher, came to Rome, who, in his preaching, rebuked the dissolute and lascivious looseness, incontinency, avarice, and immoderate pride of the clergy, provoking all to follow Christ and his apostles in their poverty rather, and in pureness of life. By reason whereof this man was well accepted, and highly liked of the nobility of Rome for a true disciple of Christ; but of the cardinals and the clergy he was no less hated than favoured of the other, insomuch that privily, in the night season, they took him and destroyed him. This his martyrdom, saith he, was revealed to him before from God by an angel, he being in the desert, when he was sent forth to preach; whereupon he said unto them publicly these words: "I know," saith he, "ye seek my life, and know you will make away with me privily: but why? Because I preach to you the truth, and blame your pride, stoutness, avarice, incontinency, with your unmeasurable greediness in getting and heaping up of riches, therefore you be displeased with me. I take here heaven and earth to witness, that I have preached unto you that which I was commanded of the Lord. But you contemn me and your Creator, who by his only Son hath redeemed you. And no marvel if you seek my death, being a sinful person, preaching unto you the truth, when if St. Peter were here this day and rebuked your vices, which do so multiply above all measure, you would not spare him neither." And as he was expressing this, with a loud voice he said moreover: "For my part I am not afraid to suffer death for the truth's sake; but this I say unto you, that God will look upon your iniquities, and will be revenged. You, being full of all impurity, play the blind guides to the people committed unto you, leading them the way to hell; a God he is of vengeance." Thus the hatred of the clergy being incensed against him for preaching truth, they conspired against him, and so laying privy wait for him, took him and drowned him. Sabellicus and Platina say they hanged him.

The history of Arnulph, a worthy preacher.

Arnulph, a martyr.

In the second volume of the General Councils, printed at Cologne, is mentioned a certain book called "Opus Tripartitum," written, as the author supposeth, above four hundred years ago, either by this Arnulph, or just about the time.[1] In this book, the writer complaineth of many enormities and abuses in the church. First, of the number of holidays, declaring what occasions of vice grew thereby, according unto the common saying of naughty women, who, say they, vantage more in one holiday than in fifty other days besides.

A book called Tripartitum, written 400 years ago.

Item, he complaineth of the curious singing in cathedral churches, whereby many be occasioned to bestow much good time, yea, many years, about the same, which otherwise they might give to the learning of better sciences.

(1) Ex Trithimio.

Likewise he complaineth of the rabble and the multitude of begging friars, and religious men and professed women, showing what great occasion of idle and uncomely life cometh thereof.

Also of the inconsiderate promotion of evil prelates, and of their great negligence in correcting and reforming the evil demeanour of the people.

Item, of the great wantonness and lasciviousness in their servants and families, concerning their excessive wearing of apparel.

Item, he complaineth also of the outrageous and excessive gains that prelates and others under them take for their seal, especially of officials, scribes, and such like; who give out the seal they care not how, nor wherefore, so they may gain money.

He complaineth in like manner, that prelates be so slack and negligent in looking to the residents in their benefices.

Further, he lamenteth the rash giving of benefices to parsons, vicars, and curates, not for any godliness or learning in them, but for favour or friendship, or intercession, or else for hope of some gain, whereof springeth this great ignorance in the church.

After this, he noteth in prelates, how they waste and expend the goods of the church in superfluities; or upon their kinsfolks, or other worse ways, which should rather be spent on the poor.

Next, in the tenth chapter he complaineth, that through the negligence of men of the church, especially of the church of Rome, the books and monuments of the old councils, and also of the new, are not to be found, which should be reserved and kept in all cathedral churches.

Item, that many prelates be so cold in doing their duties. Also he reproacheth the unchaste and voluptuous demeanour of ecclesiastical persons, by the examples of storks, whose nature is, saith he, that if any of their company, leaving his own mate, joineth with any other, all the rest fly upon him, whether it be he or she, beat him, and pluck his feathers off: "What then," saith he, "ought good prelates to do to such a person of their company, whose filthiness and corrupt life both defile so many, and stinketh in the whole church?"

Amendment of life first to begin with the priests.

Again, forasmuch as we read in the second book of Esdras, (chap. ix.) that he, purging Israel of strange women, began first with the priests; so now likewise in the purging and correcting of all sorts of men, first the purgation ought to begin with these, according as it is written by the Prophet Ezekiel, "Begin first with my sanctuary," &c.

The realm of France interdicted. King of Portugal deposed.

Moreover, how that in the time of Philip, king of France, the whole realm was interdicted, for that the king had but one woman instead of his wife, who was not his wife by law. And again, seeing in these our days the king of Portugal hath been sequestered from his dominion, by the authority of the church, being thought not sufficient to govern: what then ought to be said to that prelate who abuseth other men's wives, and virgins and nuns, who also is found unable and insufficient to take upon him the charge of souls?

Knights of the Rhodes and Templars.

About A.D. 1128, the orders of the knights of the Rhodes, called Johannites, also the order of Templars, rose up.

After Honorius, next in the same usurpation succeeded Pope Innocent II., A.D. 1130. But as it was with his predecessors before

Henry I. A.D. 1135.

him, that at every mutation of new popes, came new perturbations, and commonly never a pope was elected but some other was set up against him, sometimes two, sometimes three popes together, so likewise it happened with this Innocent; for after he was chosen, the Romans elected another pope, named Anacletus. Betwixt these two popes there was much ado, and great conflicts, through the partaking of Roger, duke of Sicily, taking Anacletus's part against Innocent until Lothaire the emperor came; who, rescuing Innocent, drove Roger out of Italy. Our stories record, that King Henry was one of the great helps in setting up and maintaining this Pope Innocent against Anacletus.[1]

Hurly-burly between popes.

Amongst many other things, this pope decreed that whosoever did strike a priest or clerk, being shaven, he should be excommunicated, and not be absolved but only by the pope himself.

Death of King Henry II. A.D. 1135.

About the time of doing these things, A.D. 1135, King Henry, being in Normandy, as some say, by taking there a fall from his horse, or, as others say, by taking a surfeit in eating lampreys, fell sick and died, after he had reigned over the realm of England five and thirty years and odd months, leaving for his heirs Matilda, the empress, his daughter, with her young son Henry to succeed him, to whom all the prelates and nobility of the realm were sworn. But, contrary to their oath made to Matilda, in the presence of her father before, William, the archbishop of Canterbury, and the nobles of the realm, crowned Stephen, earl of Boulogne, and sister's son to King Henry, upon St. Stephen's day, in Christmas week; which archbishop the next year after died, being, as it was thought, justly punished for his perjury. And many other lords, who did accordingly, went not quit without punishment. In the like justice of punishment is numbered also Roger, bishop of Salisbury; who, contrary unto his oath, being a great doer in the coronation of Stephen, was apprehended of the same king, and miserably, but justly, extermined.

A certain written English story[2] I have, which addeth more, and saith, that King Stephen, having many foes in divers quarters keeping their holds and castles against him, went to Oxford, and took the bishop of Salisbury, and put a rope about his neck, and so led him to the castle of Vies, that was his, and commanded them to render up the castle, or he would slay and hang their bishop. Which castle being given up, the king took the spoil thereof. The like also he did unto the bishop of Lincoln, named Alexander; whom in like manner he led in a rope to a castle of that bishop's, that was upon Trent, and bade them deliver up the castle, or else he would hang their lord before their gate. Long it was before the castle was given up; yet at length the king obtaining it, there entered and took all the treasure of the bishop, &c. Roger Hoveden[3] and Fabian alleging a certain old author, whom I cannot find, refer a great cause of this perjury unto one Hugh Bigot, sometime steward with King Henry; who, immediately after the death of the said Henry, came into England, and before the said archbishop, and other lords of the land, took wilfully an oath, and swore, that he was present a little before the king's death, when King Henry admitted for his heir, to

The bishop of Sarum and Lincoln taken prisoners.

(1) Gisburn. (2) Ex Chron. Angli. incerti autoris.
(3) Roger Hoved. in Vit. Steph. Ex Fab. in Vit. Steph.

be king after him, Stephen his nephew, forasmuch as Matilda his daughter had discontented him. Whereunto the archbishop, with the other lords, gave too hasty credence. But this Hugh, saith he, scaped not unpunished, for he died miserably in a short time after.[1] Albeit all this may be supposed rather to be wrought not without the practice of Henry, bishop of Winchester, and other prelates by his setting on, which Henry was brother to King Stephen.

Stephen. A.D. 1135.

STEPHEN.[2]

Thus, when King Stephen, contrary unto his oath made before to Matilda, the empress, had taken upon him the crown, as is above said, he swore before the lords at Oxford, that he would not hold the benefices that were voided, and that he would remit the Danegilt, with many other things, which afterwards he little performed. Moreover, because he dreaded the coming of the empress, he gave license to his lords, every one to build upon his own ground strong castles or fortresses, as they liked. All the time of his reign he was vexed with wars, but especially with David, king of the Scots, with whom he was at length accorded: but yet the Scottish king did him no homage, because he was sworn to Matilda, the empress. Notwithstanding this, Henry, the eldest son to King David, did homage to King Stephen. But he, after repenting thereof, entered into Northumberland with a great host, and burnt and slew the people in most cruel wise, neither sparing man, woman, nor child. Such as were with child they ripped up; the children they tossed upon their spears' points; and laying the priests upon the altars, they mangled and cut them all to pieces, after a most terrible manner. But by the manhood of the English lords and soldiers, and through the means of Thurstin, archbishop of York, they were met withal, and a great number of them slain, David their king being constrained to give to Henry, his son, as hostage for surety of peace. In the mean time, King Stephen was occupied in the south countries, besieging divers castles of divers bishops and other lords, and took them by force, and fortified them with his knights and servants, with intent to withstand the empress, whose coming he ever feared.

A.D. 1135. Building of castles in England. The cruelty of the Scots towards the Englishmen.

About the sixth year of his reign, Matilda, the empress, came into England out of Normandy, and by the aid of Robert, earl of Gloucester, and Ranulph, of Chester, made strong war upon King Stephen. In the end the king's party was chased, and himself taken prisoner, and sent to Bristol, there to be kept in sure hold. The same day when King Stephen should join his battle, it is said in a certain old chronicle before mentioned, that he being at the mass (which then the bishop of Lincoln said before the king), as he went to offer up his taper, it brake in two; and when the mass was done, (at what time the king should have been houseled) the rope whereby the pix[3] did hang did break, and the pix fell down upon the altar.

A.D. 1140. Maud, the empress, came into England against Stephen. Stephen taken prisoner.

(1) Ex Fabian.
(2) Edition 1563, p. 34. Ed. 1583, p. 200. Ed. 1596, p. 182. Ed. 1684, vol. i. p. 226.—Ed.
(3) The pix is a small box containing the consecrated wafer, which the papists call the host, to which they may be seen paying their adorations.—Ed.

Stephen.

A.D. 1141.

After this battle, the queen, King Stephen's wife, lying then in Kent, made great labour to the empress and her council, to have the king delivered and put into some house of religion, but could not obtain it. Also the Londoners made great suit to the said empress, to have and to use again St. Edward's laws, and not the laws of her father, which were more strict and strange unto them than the others. When they could not obtain this of her and her council, the citizens of London, being therewith discontented, would have taken the empress; but she having knowledge thereof, fled privily from London to Oxford. But the Kentish-men and Londoners, taking the king's part, joined battle against the empress; when the aforesaid Robert, earl of Gloucester, and base brother to the empress, was taken, and so, by exchange, both the king and earl Robert were delivered out of prison. Then Stephen, without delay gathering to him a strong army, straitly pursued the aforesaid Matilda, or Maud, with her friends, besieging them in the castle of Oxford, in the siege whereof fell a great snow and frost, so hard, that a man well laden might pass over the water; upon which occasion, the empress bethinking herself, appointed with her friends and retinue, clothed in white sheets, and issuing out by a postern gate, went upon the ice over Thames, and so escaped to Wallingford.[1] After this, the king (the castle being gotten), when he found not the empress, was much displeased, and molested the country round about divers ways. In conclusion, he pursued the empress and her company so hard, that he caused them to fly the realm, which was in the sixth year of his reign.

Stephen, and Robert, earl of Gloucester, delivered by exchange

A.D. 1143. The second year after this, which was the eighth year of his reign, there was a parliament held in London, to which all the bishops of the realm resorted, and there denounced the king accursed, and all those with him, who did any hurt to the church, or to any minister thereof. Whereupon the king began somewhat to amend his conditions for a certain space, but afterward, as my story saith, was as ill as he was before; but what the causes were, my author maketh no mention.

The decease of Geoffery Plantagenet.

To return again to the story: the empress, compelled, as is said, to fly the realm, returned again into Normandy, to Geoffery Plantagenet her husband, who, after he had valiantly won and defended the duchy of Normandy, against the puissance of King Stephen a long time, ended his life, leaving Henry, his son, to succeed him in that dukedom. In the mean while, Robert, earl of Gloucester, and the earl of Chester, who were strong of people, had divers conflicts with the king, insomuch that at a battle at Wilton, between them, the king was well nigh taken, but yet escaped with much difficulty.

Henry, duke of Normandy, enters England.

It was not long before Eustace, son to King Stephen, who had married the French king's sister, made war on Duke Henry of Normandy, but prevailed not. Soon after, the said Henry, duke of Normandy, in the quarrel of his mother Matilda, with a great puissance entered England, and at the first won the castle of Malmesbury, then the Tower of London, and afterward the town of Nottingham, with other holds and castles, as of Wallingford, and other places. Thus, between him and the king were fought many battles, to the great annoyance of the realm. During that time, Eustace, the king's son, departed; upon which occasion the king caused Theobald, arch-

(1) Ex incerti authoris Chronico.

Stephen. A.D. 1154.

bishop of Canterbury, who succeeded next after William, above mentioned, to make overtures to the duke for peace, which was concluded between them upon this condition,—that Stephen, during his lifetime, should hold the kingdom, and Henry, in the mean time, be proclaimed heir apparent, in the chief cities throughout the realm. These things done, Duke Henry taketh his journey into Normandy, King Stephen and his son William bringing him on his way, where William, the king's son, taking up his horse before his father, had a fall, and brake his leg, and so was had to Canterbury. The same year, about October, King Stephen, as some say for sorrow, ended his life, after he had reigned nineteen years perjuredly.

Peace between King Stephen and Duke Henry.

Death of King Stephen.

As Theobald succeeded William, archbishop of Canterbury, so in York, after Thurstin, succeeded William, who was called St. William of York, and was poisoned in his chalice by his chaplains.

In the time of this king, in the sixteenth year of his reign, Theobald, archbishop of Canterbury, and legate to the pope, did hold a council in London. In this council first began new-found appellations from councils to the pope, found out by Henry, bishop of Winchester; for, as the words of mine author do record, "In Anglia namque appellationes in usu non erant, donec eas Henricus Wintoniensis episcopus, dum legatus esset, malo suo crudeliter intrusit. In eodem namque concilio ad Romani pontificis audientiam ter appellatum est," &c. That is, "for appellations before were not in use in England, till Henry, bishop of Winchester, being then the pope's legate, brought them cruelly in, to his own hurt. For in that council appeal was thrice made to the bishop of Rome." A. D. 1151.

In the time of King Stephen died Gratian, a monk of Bonony, who compiled a book called 'The Pope's Decrees;' also his brother, Peter Lombard, bishop of Paris, who is called 'the Master of Sentences,' compiled his four books of the 'Sentences.' These two brethren were the greatest doers in finding out and establishing this blind opinion of the sacrament, that only the similitude of bread and wine remained, but not the substance of them; and this they call the spiritual understanding of the mystery, and therefore no marvel if the sun in those days were seen black and dim.

Gratian, compiler of the pope's decrees. Peter Lombard, master of the sentences.

Some also affirm, that Petrus Comestor, writer of the Scholastical History, was the third brother to these above-named.

At the same time, and in the reign of the said King Stephen, was also Hugo, surnamed "De sancto victore;" about which time, as Polychronicon reciteth, lived and died Bernardus Clarevaliensis.

The author of the history called 'Jornalensis,' maketh also mention of Hildegard, the nun and prophetess, in Almain, as having lived in the same age; concerning whose prophecy against the friars, hereafter (by the grace of Christ) more shall be said, when we come to recite the order and number of friars and religious men crept into the church of Christ.

We read, moreover, of one named Johannes de Temporibus, who, by the affirmance of most of our old histories, lived three hundred and sixty-one years, servant once to Charlemagne, and in the reign of Stephen king of England died.[1]

In the days also of this king, and by him, was builded the abbey

(1) Polychron. lib. vii. Continuator Henr. Hunt. Jornalensis in Vita Steph. Nichol. Trivet, &c.

Stephen. A.D. 1154.

of Feversham, where his son and he were buried. He builded the monastery of Finerneis, and that of Fomitance; also the castle of Wallingford, with a number of other castles.

The Jews crucified a child at Norwich.

During the time of the said King Stephen, A.D. 1144, the miserable Jews crucified a child in the city of Norwich.[1]

The order of the Gilbertines.

Much about the same time came up the order of the Gilbertines, by one Gilbert, son to Jacoline, a knight of Lincolnshire.

Mention hath been made before of certain English councils holden in the time of this king, where, in one of them, under Theobald the archbishop of Canterbury, it was decreed that bishops should live more discreetly; should teach their flock more diligently; that reading of Scriptures should be more usual in abbeys; that priests should not be rulers of worldly matters; and that they should learn and teach the Lord's Prayer and Creed in English.[2]

The Lord's Prayer and the Creed in English.

Matthew Paris[3] writeth, how Stephen, king of England, in these days reserved to himself the right and authority of bestowing spiritual livings, and investing prelates. At that time, also, Lothaire, the emperor, began to do the like, in recovering again the right and privilege taken away from Henry, his predecessor, had not Bernard given him contrary counsel, A.D. 1133.

Cursing with book, bell, and candle.

Here came into the church the manner of cursing with book, bell, and candle, devised in the council of London, holden by William, bishop of Winchester, under Pope Celestine, who succeeded after Innocent, A.D. 1144.

Also to Lothaire, succeeded in the imperial crown, Conrad III.,[4] the nephew of Henry V. beforementioned, who alone, of many emperors, is not found to receive the crown at the pope's hand, A.D. 1138.

In the days of this emperor, who reigned fifteen years, were divers popes, as Celestine II., Lucius II., Eugene III., at which time the Romans went about to recover their former old manner of choosing their consuls and senators. But the popes, then being in their ruff, in no case would abide it; whereupon arose many commotions, with much civil war amongst them, insomuch that Pope Lucius, sending for aid to the emperor, who otherwise hindered at that time could not come, armed his soldiers, thinking to invade them, or else to destroy them in their senate-house. But this coming to their knowledge beforehand, the people were all in array, and much ado was among them; Pope Lucius being also among them in the fight, and well pelted with stones and blows, lived not long after. Likewise Pope Eugene after him, pursuing the Romans for the same matter, first did curse them with excommunication; and afterwards, when he saw that would not serve, he came with his host, and so compelled them at length to seek peace, and to take his conditions, which were

Pope Lucius II. warring against the senators.

Spiritual excommunication abused in temporal causes.

(1) Nichol. Trivet. et alii. (2) Malmesb. (3) Matth. Paris, lib. Chron. iv.

(4) In the reign of Conrad, in consequence of some advantages obtained by the Saracens in the East, Bernard of Clairvaux, a learned and eloquent man, whose lecture to the pope may be seen in Dupin's Eccles. Hist. cent. xii., began to rouse the minds of the western nations, and directed their thoughts to the second crusade, A.D. 1146. Conrad III., the emperor of Germany, set forward with a numerous army to the East; but in November, in the same year, he was unexpectedly attacked by the sultan of Iconium, and his army destroyed. We are told that his force consisted of 70,000 coats of mail, besides infantry and light-horse. The emperor escaped, and joined the French king, Louis VII., at Ephesus. Nor was the latter, who appeared at the head of a second armament, more fortunate; in January, the following year, he too, through an error in the movements of his troops, was surprised and defeated, in an impetuous attack of the Saracens; the army was destroyed, and the king and the emperor retired to Jerusalem. Eugene III. was pope at that time.—Ed.

these: — That they should abolish their consuls, and take such senators as he, by his papal authority, should assign them. *Henry II.* A.D. 1154.

Then followed Anastasius IV., and after him Adrian IV., an Englishman, by name called Breakspear, belonging once to St. Albans. This Adrian kept great stir, in like manner, with the citizens of Rome, for abolishing their consuls and senate, cursing, excommunicating, and warring against them with all the power he could make, till in time he removed the consuls out of their office, and brought them all under his subjection. The like business and rage he also stirred up against Apulia, and especially against the empire, blustering and thundering against Frederic, the emperor, as (the Lord granting) you shall hear anon, after we have prosecuted such matter as necessarily appertaineth first to the continuation of our English story. Pope Adrian an Englishman.

HENRY THE SECOND.[1]

Henry II., the son of Geoffery Plantagenet, and of Matilda, the empress, and daughter of King Henry I., began his reign after King Stephen, and continued five and thirty years. The first year of his reign he subdued Ireland; and not long after, Thomas Becket was made by him lord chancellor of England. This king cast down divers castles erected in the time of King Stephen. He went into the north parts, where he subdued William, king of Scotland, who at that time held a great part of Northumberland, as far as Newcastle-upon-Tyne, and joined Scotland to his own kingdom, from the south ocean to the north isles of Orcades. Also he put under his dominion the kingdom of Wales, and there felled many great woods, and made the ways plain, so that by his great manhood and policy the seigniory of England was much augmented, with the addition of Scotland, Ireland, the Orcades isles, Britanny, Poitou, and Guienne. Also he had in his rule Normandy, Gascony, Anjou, and Chinon; also Auvergne and the city of Tholouse he won, and were to him subject. Over and besides, by the title of his wife Eleanor, daughter to the earl of Poictou, he obtained the mount Pyrame in Spain; so that we read of none of his progenitors who had so many countries under his dominion. A.D. 1154. Thomas Becket, chancellor of England.

In England were seen in the firmament two suns, or (as it is in Chronica Chronicorum) in Italy appeared three suns by the space of three hours, in the west; the year following, A.D. 1158, appeared three moons, whereof the middle moon had a red cross athwart the face, whereby was betokened, in the judgment of some, the great schism which afterwards happened among the cardinals, for the election of the bishop of Rome; or else rather the business between Frederic, the emperor, and the popes, whereof partly now incidently occasion giveth us to discourse after that I have first written of Gerhardus and Dulcinus Navarensis; who, in their time, according to their gift, did earnestly labour and preach against the church of Rome, defending and maintaining, that prayer was not more holy in one place than in another; that the pope was antichrist; that the clergy and prelates of Rome were rejected, and the very whore of Babylon prefigured in the Apocalypse, &c. Peradventure these had received some light of knowledge of the Waldenses, who, at length, with a great number of Gerhardus and Dulcinus, preachers against Antichrist.

(1) Edition 1563, p. 35. Ed. 1583, p. 202. Ed. 1596, p. 183. Ed. 1684, vol. i. p. 223.—Ed.

Henry II. A.D. 1155.

their followers, were oppressed and slain by the pope.[1] And although some inconvenient points of doctrine and dishonesty in their assemblies be against them alleged by some, yet these times of ours do teach us sufficiently what credit is to be given to such popish slanders, forged rather through hatred of true religion, than upon any judgment of truth. Illiricus, in his book "De testibus," referreth the time of these two to A.D. 1280; but, as I find in the story of Robert Gisburne, these two, about A. D. 1158, brought thirty with them into England, who, by the king and the prelates, were all burnt in the forehead, and so driven out of the realm, and afterwards, as Illiricus writeth, were slain by the pope.

Frederic Barbarossa, emperor.

And now, according to my promise premised, the time requireth to proceed to the history of Frederic I., called Barbarossa, successor to Conrad in the empire, who marched up to Italy, to subdue there certain rebels. The pope, hearing that, came with his clergy to meet him by the way, in a town called Sutrium, thinking by him to find aid against his enemies. The emperor, seeing the bishop, lighteth from his horse to receive him, holding the stirrup to the prelate on the left side, when he should have held it on the right, whereat the pope showed himself somewhat aggrieved. The emperor, smiling, excused himself, by saying, that he was never accustomed to hold stirrups; and seeing it was done only of good will, and of no design, it was the less matter what side of the horse he held. The next day, to make amends to the bishop, the emperor sending for him, received him, holding the right stirrup to the prelate, and so all the matter was made whole, and he the pope's own white son again.

The pope displeased that the emperor did not hold his right stirrup.

After this, as they were come in and sat together, Adrian, the pope, beginneth to declare to him how his ancestors before him, such as sought to the see of Rome for the crown, were wont always to leave behind them some special token or monument of their benevolence for the obtaining thereof, as Charlemagne, in subduing the Lombards; Otho, the Berengarians; Lothaire, the Normans, &c.; wherefore he required some benefit to proceed likewise from him to the church of Rome, in restoring again the country of Apulia to the church of Rome. Which thing if he would do, he, for his part, again would do that which appertained unto him to do; meaning in giving him the crown, for at that time the popes had brought the emperors to fetch their crown at their hands, A. D. 1155.

The pope's old practice in setting princes together by the ears.

Frederic, with his princes, perceiving that unless he would of his own proper costs and charges get back Apulia out of Duke William's hands, he could not speed of the crown, was fain to promise all that the pope required, and so the next day after he was crowned. This done, the emperor returneth into Germany, to refresh his army and his other furnitures, for the subduing of Apulia. In the mean while Adrian, not thinking to be idle, first giveth forth censures of excommunication against William, duke of Apulia; and, not content with this, he sendeth also to Emmanuel, emperor of Constantinople, incensing him to war against the aforesaid William. The duke perceiving this, sendeth to the pope for peace, promising to restore to him whatsoever he would. But the pope, through the malignant counsel of his cardinals, would grant no peace, thinking to get more

War stirred up by the pope, being more gainful than peace.

(1) Ex Hist. Gisburnensis.

by war. The duke seeing nothing but war, prepareth himself with all expedition for the same. To be brief, making all his power out of Sicily, he arrived at Apulia, and there putteth the emperor Emmanuel to flight. This done, he proceedeth to the city of Bonaventum, where the pope and his cardinal were looking for victory. He planting there his siege, so straitly pressed the city, that the pope and his cardinals were glad to entreat for peace, which they refused before. The duke granted them peace upon certain conditions, that is, that he should not invade such possessions as belonged to Rome, and that the pope should make him king of both Sicilies. So the matter was concluded, and they departed. The bishop, coming to Rome, was no less troubled there about their consuls and senators, insomuch that when his curses and excommunications could not prevail nor serve, he was fain to leave Rome, and removed to Ariminum.

The pope driven to treat for peace.

The emperor all this while sitting quietly at home, began to consider within himself, how the pope had extorted from the emperors, his predecessors, the investing and endowing of prelates; how he had pilled and polled all nations by his legates, and also had been the sower of seditions through all his empery; he began therefore to require of all the bishops of Germany homage, and an oath of their allegiance; commanding also that the pope's legates, if they came into Germany without his sending for them, should not be received; charging, moreover, all his subjects that none of them should appeal to Rome. Besides this, in his letters he set and prefixed his name before the pope's name; whereupon the pope, being not a little offended, directed his letters to the aforesaid Frederic the emperor, after this tenor and form as following.

The godly proceedings of Frederic the emperor against the pope.

Copies of the Letters between Adrian, the pope, and Frederic, the emperor.[1]

Adrian, bishop, servant of the servants of God, to Frederic the emperor, health and apostolical benediction. The law of God, as it promiseth to them that honour father and mother long life, so it threateneth the sentence of death to them that curse father and mother. We are taught, by the word of truth, that every one that exalteth himself, shall be brought low. Wherefore, my well-beloved son in the Lord, we marvel not a little at your wisdom, in that you seem not to show that reverence to blessed St. Peter, and to the holy church of Rome, which you ought to show. For why? In your letters sent to us, you prefer your own name before ours, wherein you incur the note of insolency, yea rather, to speak it, of arrogancy. What! should I here recite unto you the oath of your fidelity, which you sware to blessed St. Peter, and to us, and how you observe and keep the same? Seeing you so require homage and allegiance of them that be gods, and all the sons of the High God, and presume to join their holy lands with yours, working contrary to us; seeing also you exclude, not only out of your churches, but also out of your cities, our cardinals, whom we direct as legates from our side; what shall I say then unto you? Amend therefore, I advise you, amend; for while you go about to obtain of us your consecration and crown, and to get those things you have not, I fear much your honour will lose the things you have. Thus fare ye well.

The emperor's name before the pope's.

The Answer of Frederic the emperor to the pope.[2]

Frederic, by the grace of God, Roman emperor, ever Augustus, unto Adrian, bishop of the Roman church, and unto all such as be willing to cleave

(1) Adrianus Episcopus, servus servorum Dei, Frederico imperatori salutem, et apostolicam benedictionem, &c. The Latin copy of this letter in the edition of 1563, p. 36.—Ed.
(2) This letter in Latin, appears in the edition of 1563, p. 36.—Ed.

Henry II. A.D. 1155.

unto those things which Jesus began to work and teach, greeting. The law of justice giveth to every person accordingly that which is his; neither do we derogate from our parents, of whom, according as we have received this our dignity of the imperial crown and governance, so in the same kingdom of ours we do render their due and true honour to them again. And forasmuch as duty in all sorts of men is to be sought out, let us see first in the time of Constantine, (Silvester then being bishop of Rome,) what patrimony or regality he had of his own, due to him, that he might claim. Did not Constantine, of his liberal benignity, give liberty, and restore peace unto the church? and whatsoever regality or patrimony the see of your papacy hath, was it not by the donation of princes given unto them? Revolve and turn over the ancient Chronicles (if either you have not read, or neglected that we do affirm); there it is to be found. Of those who be gods by adoption, and hold our lordships of us; why may we not justly require their homage, and their sworn allegiance, when, as he which is both your Master and ours, taking nothing of any king or any man, but giving all goodness to all men, paid toll and tribute for him and Peter, unto Cæsar? giving you example to do the like. And therefore he saith to you and all men, "Learn of me, for I am meek and humble of heart." &c. Wherefore either render again your lordships and patrimonies which ye hold of us, or else if ye find them so sweet unto you, then give that which is due to God, unto God; and that which is due to Cæsar, unto Cæsar. As for your cardinals, we shut them out both of churches and cities, for that we see them not preachers, but prowlers; not repairers of peace, but rakers for money; not pillars and upholders of the church, but pollers insatiable of the world, and moylers of money and gold. What time we shall see them to be other men, such as the church requireth them to be, members and makers of peace, shining forth like lights to the people, assisting poor and weak men's causes in the way of equity, then shall they find us prest and ready to relieve them with stipends, and all things necessary. And whereas you infer such questions as these unto secular men, little conducing to religion, you incur thereby no little note and blemish of your humility, which is keeper of all virtues, and of your mansuetude. Therefore let your fatherhood beware and take heed, lest in moving such matters as seem to us unseemly for you, ye give thereby offence to such as depend on your word, giving ear to your mouth, as it were to an evening shower; for we cannot but tell you of that we hear, seeing now the detestable beast of pride doth creep into the seat of Peter; providing always as much as we may, by God's grace, for the peace of the church. Fare ye well.

Upon this Adrian the pope directeth a bull against Frederic, excommunicating him with public and solemn ceremonies. Moreover conspiring with William, duke of Apulia, he sought all manner of ways to infest the emperor, and to set all men against him, especially the clergy. Amongst many others writing to Hillinus, bishop of Treves, to Arnulph, bishop of Mentz, and to Frederic, bishop of Cologne, he seeketh first to make them of his side. His epistle to them soundeth to this effect.

A seditious and proud letter of the pope to the bishops of Germany.

The empire of Rome was transferred from the Greeks to the Almains, so that the king of Almains could not be called emperor, before he were crowned of the bishop apostolical. Before his consecration he is a king, afterwards emperor. Whence hath he his empire then, but of us? By the election of his princes he hath the name of a king, by our consecration he hath the name of the emperor, of august, or of Cæsar; ergo, by us he reigneth as emperor. Search ancient antiquities. Pope Zacharias promoted Carolus and made him a great name, that he was made and called emperor; and after that, the king of Almains was ever named emperor and advocate to the see apostolical, so that Apulia, conquered by him, was subdued to the bishop of Rome; which Apulia, with the city of Rome, is ours, and not the emperor's. Our seat is at Rome; the seat of the emperor is at Aquis, in Arduenna, which is a wood in France. The emperor, whatsoever he hath, he hath it of us: as Zacharias did translate the empire from the Greeks to the Almains, so we may translate it again from the Almains to the Greeks. Behold, it lieth in our power to give it to whom we

Well bragged, and like a pope.

will, being therefore set up of God above Gentiles and nations, to destroy and pluck up, to build and to plant," &c.[1] *Henry II.*

A.D. 1157.

And yet further to understand the ambitious presumption of this proud see of Rome, it so chanced, that this emperor Frederic, at his first coming up to Rome, did behold there, in the palace of Lateran, a certain picture brought forth unto him, how Lothaire II., the emperor, was crowned of the pope, with the inscription of certain verses in Latin, declaring how the aforesaid emperor, coming to Rome, first did swear to the city, after was made the pope's man, and so of him received the crown. Frederic, offended with this picture, desired the pope it might be abolished, that it should be no cause of any dissension hereafter. The pope understanding the intent of the emperor, how loth he was to come under subjection to his see, devised by all crafty ways to bring it to pass; and first taking his occasion by the bishop of Laodicea, (being then detained in custody, I cannot tell by whom,) he sent divers and sharp letters unto him, and yet not so sharp, as proud and disdainful; wherein the first salutation by his legates was this: "Our most blessed father, the pope, greeteth you, and the universal company of the cardinals; he, as your father; they, as your brethren."[2] Meaning thereby that he should understand himself to be subject and underling to the pope, no less than the cardinals were. Moreover, in his letters, objecting divers things against him, he reciteth how many and great benefits he had received of the church of Rome, by the which church he had obtained the fulness of his honour and dignity, &c. The emperor, with his princes, perceiving whereunto the pope by his legates did shoot, being a prince of courage, could not abide such intolerable presumption of a proud message, whereupon much contention fell between the legates and the princes. "And of whom then," say the legates, "receiveth Cæsar the empire, if he take it not of the pope?" With that word the German princes were so much offended, that, had not the emperor stayed them with much ado, they would have used violence against the legates. But the emperor, not permitting that, commanded the legates away, straightly charging them to make no turn by the way, to any person or persons, but straight to depart home. And he, to certify the whole state of the empire, of the truth of the matter, directeth forth these letters that follow.

Scripture well wrested.

See the ambitious presumption of a proud priest.

The tenor of the Emperor's letter sent through all his empire.[3]

Forasmuch as the Providence of God, whereon dependeth all power both in heaven and earth, hath committed to us, his anointed, this our regiment and empire to be governed, and the peace of his churches by our imperial arms to be protected; we cannot but lament and complain to you, with great sorrow of heart, seeing such causes of dissension, the root and fountain of evils, and the infection of pestiferous corruption thus to arise from the holy church, imprinted with the seal of peace and love of Christ.

By reason whereof (except God turn it away), we fear the whole body of the church is like to be polluted, the unity thereof to be broken, and schism and division to be betwixt the spiritual and temporal regiment. For we being of late at Bisunze, and there treating busily of matters pertaining as well to the

(1) The Latin copy of this letter appears in the edition of 1563, p. 37.—Ed.
(2) "Salutat vos beatissimus pater noster papa, et universitas cardinalium, ille ut pater, hii ut fratres." Ex Radenico, in appendice Prisingen.
(3) The Latin copy of this letter is also in the edition of 1563, p. 38.—Ed.

Henry II. A.D. 1158.

honour of our empire, as to the wealth of the churches, there came ambassadors of the see apostolical, declaring that they brought a legacy to our majesty of great importance, redounding to the no small commodity of our honour and empire.

Who then, the first day of their coming, being brought to our presence, and received of us (as the manner is) with honour accordingly, audience was given them to hear what they had to say. They forthwith bursting out of the mammon of iniquity, haughty pride, stoutness, and arrogancy, out of the execrable presumption of their swelling heart, did their message with letters apostolical, whereof the tenor was this: That we should always have before our eyes, how that our sovereign lord, the pope, gave us the imperial crown, and that it doth not repent him, if so be we have received greater benefits at his hand. And this was the effect of that so sweet and fatherly legation, which should nourish peace both of the church and of the empire, to unite them fast together in the band of love.

At the hearing of this so false, untrue, and most vain-glorious presumption of so proud a message, not only the emperor's majesty conceived indignation, but also all the princes there present were moved with such anger and rage thereat, that if our presence and request had not stayed them, they would not have held their hands from these wicked priests, or else would have proceeded with sentence of death against them.

Furthermore, because a great number of other letters (partly written already, partly with seals ready signed, for letters to be written according, as they should think good, to the churches of Germany) were found about them, whereby to work their conceived intent of iniquity here in our churches, to spoil the altars, to carry away the jewels of the church, and to flay off the limbs and plates of golden crosses, &c.: to the intent their avaricious meaning should have no further power to reign, we gave them commandment to depart the same way they came. And now, seeing our reign and empire standeth upon the election of princes, from God alone, who in the passion of his Son, subdued the world to be governed with two swords necessary; and, again, seeing Peter, the apostle, hath so informed the world with this doctrine, "Deum timete, regem honorificate" that is, "Fear God, honour your king" therefore, who so saith that we have and possess our imperial kingdom by the benefit of the lord pope, is contrary both to the ordinance of God, and to the doctrine of Peter, and also shall be reproved for a liar.

Note here a courageous heart in a valiant emperor an example for all princes to follow.

Therefore as our endeavour hath been heretofore to help and to deliver the servile captivity of churches out of the hand, and from the yoke, of the Egyptians, and to maintain the right of their liberties and dignities, we desire you all with your compassion to lament with us this slanderous ignominy inferred to us and our kingdom, trusting that your faithful good-will, which hath been ever trusty to the honour of this empire (never yet blemished from the first beginning of this city, and of religion,) will provide, that it shall have no hurt through the strange novelty and presumptuous pride of such. Which thing rather than it should come to pass, know you this for certain, I had rather incur the danger of death, than suffer such confusion to happen in our days.

This letter of Cæsar fretted the pope not a little, who wrote again to the bishops of Germany, accusing the emperor, and willing them to work against him what they could. They answer again with all obedience to the pope, submitting themselves, and yet excusing the emperor, and blaming him rather, and exhorted him henceforth to temper his letters and legacies with more gentleness and modesty; which counsel he also followed, perceiving otherwise that he could not prevail.

Much trouble had good Frederic with this pope, but much more with the other that followed. For this pope continued not very long, the space only of four years and odd months. About his time rose up the order of the hermits, by one William, once duke of Aquitania, and afterwards a friar. This Adrian, walking with his

The order of hermits.

cardinals abroad, to a place called Anagnia, or Arignanum, as Volaterran calleth it, chanced to be choked with a fly getting into his throat, and so was strangled; who, in the latter time of his papacy, was wont to say, that there is no more miserable kind of life in the earth, than to be pope, and to come to the papacy by blood; that is, said he, not to succeed Peter, but rather Romulus, who, to reign alone, did slay his brother.

Henry II. A.D. 1159.

The judgment of Pope Adrian.

The popes rather successors to Romulus than to Peter.

Although this Adrian was bad enough, yet came the next much worse, one Alexander III., who yet was not elected alone; for beside him the emperor, with nine cardinals, (albeit Sabellicus saith but with three,) did set up another pope, named Victor IV. Between these two popes arose a foul schism and great discord, and long continued, insomuch that the emperor being required to take up the matter, sent for them both to appear before him, that in hearing them both he might judge their cause the better. Victor came, but Alexander, disdaining that his matter should come in controversy, refused to appear. Hereupon the emperor, with a full consent of his bishops and clergy about him, assigned and ratified the election of Victor to stand, and so brought him into the city, there to be received and placed. Alexander flying into France, accused them both, sending his letters to all Christendom against them, as men to be avoided and cast out of all christian company. Also, to get him friends at Rome, by flattery and money he got on his side the greatest part of the city, both to the favouring of him, and to the setting up of such consuls as were for his purpose. After this, Alexander, coming from France to Sicily, and from thence to Rome, was there received with much favour, through the help of Philip the French king.

Alexander curseth the emperor.

The emperor, hearing this rebellion and conspiracy in Rome, removed with great power into Italy, where he had destroyed divers great cities. Coming at length to Rome, he required the citizens that the cause betwixt the two popes might be decided, and that he who had the best right might be taken. If they would so do, he would restore again that which he took from them before. Alexander, mistrusting his part, and doubting the wills of the citizens, and having ships ready prepared for him, from William, duke of Apulia, fetched a course about to Venice. A.D. 1164.

To declare here the difference in histories, between Blondus, Sabellicus, and the Venetian chroniclers, with other writers, concerning the order of this matter, I will overpass. In this most do agree, that the pope being at Venice, and required to be sent by the Venetians to the emperor, they would not send him. Whereupon Frederic the emperor sent thither his son Otho, with men and ships well appointed, charging him not to attempt any thing before his coming. The young man, more hardy than circumspect, joining with the Venetians, was overcome, and so taken, was brought into the city. Hereby the pope took no small occasion to work his feats.

The father, to help the captivity and misery of his son, was compelled to submit himself to the pope, and to entreat for peace: so the emperor coming to Venice, (at St. Mark's church, where the bishop was, there to take his absolution,) was bid to kneel down at the pope's feet.

The proud pope, setting his foot upon the emperor's neck, said

Henry II. A.D. 1164.

the verse of the psalm, "Super aspidem et basiliscum ambulabis, et conculcabis leonem et draconem:" that is, "Thou shalt walk upon the adder and on the basilisk, and shalt tread down the lion and the dragon." To whom the emperor answering again, said, "Non tibi sed Petro:" that is, "Not to thee, but to Peter." The pope again, "Et mihi et Petro;" "Both to me and to Peter." The emperor, fearing to give any occasion of further quarrelling, held his peace, and so was absolved, and peace made between them. The conditions whereof were these. First, that he should receive Alexander for the true pope. Secondly, that he should restore again to the church of Rome all that he had taken away before. And thus the emperor, obtaining again his son, departed.

Holy scripture abused. The pope treading on the emperor's neck.

Here as I note in divers writers a great diversity and variety touching the order of this matter, of whom some say that the emperor encamped in Palestine, before he came to Venice, some say, after; so I marvel to see in Volatcran, so great a favourer of the pope, such a contradiction, who in his two and twentieth book saith, that Otho, the emperor's son, was taken in this conflict, which was the cause of the peace between his father and the pope. And in his three and twentieth book again saith, that the emperor himself was taken prisoner in the same battle: and so afterwards, peace concluded, took his journey to Asia and Palestine. This pope, in the time of his papacy, which continued one and twenty years, kept sundry councils both at Turin and at Lateran, where he confirmed the wicked proceedings of Hildebrand and others his predecessors, as to bind all orders of the clergy to the vow of chastity; which were not greatly to be reprehended, if they would define chastity aright. "For whoso liveth not a chaste life," saith he, "is not fit to be a minister." But herein lieth an error full of much blindness, and also peril, to think that matrimony immaculate, as St. Paul calleth it, is not chastity, but only a single life, that they esteem to be a chaste life.

Council of Lateran. The clergy bound to the vow of chastity.

Now forasmuch as our English pope-holy martyr, called Thomas Becket, happened also in the same time of this Pope Alexander, let us somewhat also story of him, so far as the matter shall seem worthy of knowledge, and to stand with truth: to the end that the truth thereof being sifted from all flattery and lies of such popish writers as paint out his story, men may the better judge of him, both what he was, and also of his cause.

The History of Thomas Becket.

If the cause make a martyr, as is said, I see not why we should esteem Thomas Becket to die a martyr, more than any others whom the prince's sword doth here temporally punish for their temporal deserts. To die for the church I grant is a glorious matter. But the church, as it is a spiritual and not a temporal church, so it standeth upon causes spiritual, and upon a heavenly foundation, as upon faith, religion, true doctrine, sincere discipline, obedience to God's commandments; and not upon things pertaining to this world, as possessions, liberties, exemptions, privileges, dignities, patrimonies, and superiorities. If these be given to the church, I pray God

Becket no martyr. A.D. 1117.

churchmen may use them well; but if they be not given, the church cannot claim them; or if they be taken away, that standeth in the prince's power. To contend with princes for the same, it is no matter, in my mind, material to make a martyr, but rather is it a rebellion against those to whom we owe subjection. Therefore, as I suppose Thomas Becket to be far from the cause and title of a martyr, neither can he be excused from the charge of being a plain rebel against his prince; yet would I have wished again the law rather publicly to have found out his fault, than the swords of men, not bidden nor sent, to have smitten him, having no special commandment either of the prince, or of the law so to do. For though the indignation of the prince, as the wise prince saith, is death, yet it is not for every private person straightways to revenge the secret indignation of his prince, except he be publicly authorized thereunto; and this had been, as I suppose, the better way, namely, for the laws first to have executed their justice upon him. Certes, it had been the safest way for the king, as it proved after, who had just matter enough, if he had prosecuted his cause against him; and also thereby his death had been without all suspicion of martyrdom, neither had there followed that shrining and sainting of him as there did. Albeit the secret providence of God, which governeth all things, did see this way, percase, to be best and most necessary for those days. And doubtless, to say here what I think, and yet to speak nothing against charity, if the emperors had done the like to the popes contending against them, what time they had taken them prisoners; that is, if they had used the law of the sword against them, and chopped off the heads of one or two, according to their traitorous rebellion, they had broken the neck of much disturbance, which long time after did trouble the church. But for lack of that, because emperors having the sword, and the truth on their side, would not use their sword; but standing in awe of the pope's vain curse, and reverencing his seat for St. Peter's sake, durst not lay hand upon him, though he were never so abominable and traitorous a malefactor: the popes, perceiving that, took upon them, not as much as the Scripture would give, but as much as the superstitious fear of emperors and kings would suffer them to take; which was so much, that it past all order, rule, and measure: and all, because the superior powers either would not, or durst not, practise the authority given unto them of the Lord, upon those inferiors, but suffered them to be their masters.

Henry II. A.D. 1117 to 1164.

But, as touching Thomas Becket, whatsoever is to be thought of them that did the act, the example thereof yet bringeth this profit with it, to teach all Romish prelates not to be so stubborn, in such matters not pertaining unto them, against their prince, unto whom God hath subjected them.

Now to the story, which if it be true that is set forth in Quadrilogo, by those four,[1] who took upon them to express the life and process of Thomas Becket, it appeareth by all conjectures, that he was a man of a stout nature, severe, and inflexible. What persuasion or opinion he had once conceived, from that he would in nowise be removed, or very hardly. Threatening and flattery were to him both

Thomas Becket described.

(1) Herbertus de Boscham, Johan Charnot, Alanus, abbot of Tewkesbury, William of Canterbury.

Henry II. A.D. 1117 to 1164.

one; in this point singular, following no man's counsel so much as his own. Great helps of nature there were in him, if he could have used them well, rather than of learning; albeit somewhat skilful he was of the civil law, which he studied at Bonony; in memory excellent good, and also well broken in courtly and worldly matters. Besides this, he was of a chaste and strait life, if the histories be true; although in the first part of his life, being yet archdeacon of Canterbury, and afterwards lord chancellor, he was very civil, courtly, and pleasant, given much both to hunting and hawking, according to the guise of the court; and highly favoured he was of his prince, who not only had thus promoted him, but also had committed his son and heir to his institution and governance. But in this his first beginning he was not so well-beloved, but afterwards he was again as much hated, and deservedly, both of the king, and also of the most part of his subjects, save only of certain monks and priests, and such others as were persuaded by them, who magnified him not a little for upholding the liberties of the church; that is, the licentious life and excess of churchmen. Amongst all others, these vices he had most notable, and to be rebuked; he was full of devotion, but without any true religion: zealous, but clean without knowledge. And, therefore, as he was stiff and stubborn of nature, so (a blind conscience being joined withal) it turned to plain rebellion. So superstitious he was to the obedience of the pope, that he forgot his obedience to his natural and most beneficent king: and in maintaining, so contentiously, the vain constitutions and decrees of men, he neglected the commandments of God. But herein was he most of all to be reprehended, that not only, contrary to the king's knowledge, he sought to convey himself out of the realm, being in that place and calling, but also, being out of the realm, he set matter of discord between the pope and his king, and also between the French king and him, contrary to all honesty, good order, natural subjection, and true Christianity. Whereupon followed no little disquietness after to the king, and damage to the realm, as here, in process and order following, by the grace of Christ, we will declare; first beginning with the first rising up of him, and so consequently prosecuting in order his story, as followeth:—

What cometh of blind zeal destitute of right knowledge.

And first, to omit here the progeny of him and of his mother, named Rose, whom Polydore Virgil falsely nameth to be a Saracen, when indeed she came out of the parts bordering near to Normandy; to omit also the fabulous vision of his mother, mentioned in Robert of Cricklade, of a burning torch issuing out of her body, and reaching up to heaven; his first preferment was to the church of Branfield, which he had by the gift of St. Alban.[1] After that, he entered into the service of the archbishop of Canterbury, by whom he was then preferred to be his archdeacon; and afterwards, by the said Theobald, he was put, as a man meet for his purpose, to King Henry, to bridle the young king, that he should not be fierce against the clergy; whom in process of time the king made lord chancellor, and then he left playing the archdeacon, and began to play the chancellor. He fashioned his conditions like to the king's both in weighty matters and trifles; he would hunt with him, and watch the time when the

Polydore mistaketh the mother of Becket.

(1) Ex Florilego.

king dined and slept. Furthermore, he began to love the merry jestings of the court, to delight himself with the great laud of men, and praise of the people. And, that I may pass over his household stuff, he had his bridle of silver, and the bosses of his bridle were worth a great treasure. At his table, and in other expenses, he passed any earl: so that, on the one side, men judged him little to consider the office of an archdeacon; and, on the other side, they judged him to use wicked doings. He played also the good soldier under the king in Gascony, and both won and kept towns. When the king sent Thomas, then being chancellor, home into England as ambassador with other nobles, after the death of the archbishop, he willed Richard Lucy, one of the chiefs, to commend in his name this Thomas to the covent of Canterbury, that they might choose him archbishop; which thing he did diligently. The monks said, it was not meet to choose a courtier and a soldier to be head of so holy a company, for he would spend, said they, all that they had; others had this surmise also, because he was in such great favour with the prince, the king's son, and was so suddenly discharged of the chancellorship which he had borne five years. In the four and fortieth year of his age, on Saturday in Whitsun-week, he was made priest, and the next day consecrated bishop, A.D. 1161.

Difference in chronicles.

As touching the priesthood of this man, I find the histories vary: for, if he were beneficed, and chaplain to Theobald, and afterwards archdeacon, as some say, it is not unlikely but that he was priest before; and not, as most of our English stories say, made priest one day, and archbishop the next.

But however this matter passeth, here is, in the mean time, to be seen, what great benefits the king had done for him, and what great love had been between them both. Now, after Becket was thus promoted, what variance and discord happened between them, remaineth to be shown: the causes of which variance were divers and sundry.

The causes of variance recited between the king and the archbishop.

As first, when, according to the custom, the king's officers gathered of every one hide-money through the realm, for the defence of their own country, the king would have taken it to his coffers. But the bishop said, that which every man gave willingly, he should not count as his proper rent.

Another cause was, that where a priest was accused of murder, and the king's officers and the friends of the dead accused the priest earnestly before the bishop of Salisbury, his diocesan, to whom he was sent, desiring justice to be done on him, the priest was put to his purgation. But when he was not able to defend himself, the bishop sent to the archbishop to ask what he should do. The archbishop commanded he should be deprived of all ecclesiastical benefices, and shut up in an abbey to do perpetual penance. After the same sort were divers others handled for like causes, but none put to death, nor lost joint, nor were they burned in the hand, or put to the like pain.

The third cause was, that, where a canon of Bruis did revile the king's justices, the king was offended with the whole clergy. For these and such like things, the archbishop, to pacify the king's answer, commanded the canon to be whipped and deprived of his

Henry II. A.D. 1164. benefices for certain years. But the king was not content with this gentle punishment, because it rather increased their boldness, and therefore he called the archbishop, bishops, and all the clergy, to assemble at Westminster. When they were assembled together, the king earnestly commanded that such wicked clerks should have no privilege of their clergy, but be delivered to the gaolers, because they suffered so little of the spiritual correction; and this he said also their own canons and laws had decreed. The archbishop, counselling with his bishops and learned men, answered plausibly: and in the end he desired heartily the king's gentleness, for the quietness of himself and his realm, that under Christ, our new king, and under the new law of Christ, he would bring no new kind of punishment into his realm, upon the newly chosen people of the Lord, contrary to the old decrees of the holy fathers; and oft he said, that he neither ought nor could suffer it. The king, moved therewith, and not without cause, allegeth again and exacteth the old laws and customs of his grandfather, observed and agreed upon by archbishops, bishops, prelates, and other privileged persons; inquiring likewise of him, whether he would agree to the same, or else now, in his reign, would condemn that which in the reign of his grandfather was well allowed? To which laws and customs the said Thomas did partly consent, and partly not consent. The copy of the aforesaid laws contains the number of eight or nine and twenty, whereof I thought here to recite certain not unworthy to be known.[1]

The copy of the old laws and customs whereunto Thomas Becket did consent.[2]

I. That no order should be given to husbandmen's children and bondmen's children, without the assent or testimonial of them, which be the lords of the country where they were born and brought up: and if their sons become clerks, they shall not receive the order of priesthood without license of their lords.

II. And if a man of holy church hold any lay fee in his hand, he shall do therefore the king the service that belongeth thereto, as upon juries, assize of lands and judgments; saving only at execution doing of death.

III. If any man were the king's traitor, and had taken to the church, that it should be lawful for the king and his officers to take him out.

IV. And if any felon's goods were brought to holy church, that there should none such keep there; for every felon's goods be the king's.

(1) In the edition of 1563, page 48, the following passage is given in place of the two containing the "old laws," and the "articles" above inserted.

"The copy and effect of certain laws and constitutions set forth and proclaimed in the days of King Henry II.

"Concerning the nomination and presentation unto benefices, if any controversy shall arise between the laity and clergy, or between one spiritual man with another, the matter to be brought into the king's temporal court, and there to be decided.

"Churches, such as be defendo regis, to be given at no time without the assent and permission of the king.

"All spiritual and ecclesiastical persons, being accused of any crime, whatsoever it be, cited by the king's justice to come and appear in the king's court, there to have answer, whether the matter pertain to the spiritual court or temporal; so that if the said person or persons be found guilty and convicted of any crime, the church not to defend him or succour him.

"No archbishop or bishop, or person being of any ecclesiastical dignity, to attempt to go over out of the realm, without the king's knowledge or permission; and in so doing, yet notwithstanding tarrying in any place, to be bound to procure no damage either to the king or to the realm.

"Such goods or chattels as be forfeited to the king, neither any sentry of church or church-yard to detain them, contrary to the king's justice, for that they belong to the king, whether they be found in the church or church-yard." Then follows the first clause of No. 1 in the copy of the old laws, with this observation, "Besides these constitutions were divers others also at the same time set forth, to the number of xxix. in all; but these were the chief namely and expressly condemned by the bishop of Rome, amongst all the rest."—Ed.

(2) Out of an English chronicle, as it appeareth, drawn out of French by Earl Rivers Lord Scales.

V. That no land should be given to the church or to any house of religion, without the king's license. *Henry II.* A.D. 1164.

These articles following, Thomas agreed not unto.

I. If that between a clerk and a layman were any striving for church goods, they would the plea should be done in the king's court.

II. That neither bishop nor clerk should go out of the land without the king's license, and then he should swear upon a book that he would procure no hurt against the king, or any of his.

III. If any man were denounced accursed, and were come again to amendment, the king would not that he should be sworn, but only find sureties to stand to that which holy church should award.

IV. That no man, who held of the king in chief, or in service, should be accursed without the king's license.

V. That all the bishoprics and abbeys, that were vacant, should be in the king's hands, until such time that he should choose a prelate thereto, and he should be chosen out of the king's chapels; and first, before he were confirmed, he should do his homage to the king.

VI. If any plea were brought to the consistory, they should appeal from thence to the archdeacon, and from thence to the bishop's court, and from the bishop's court to the archbishop's, and from thence to the king, and no further. So that in conclusion, the complaints of holy church must come before the king, and not the pope.

VII. That debts, that were owing through troth plight, should not be pleaded in spiritual, but in temporal courts.

VIII. That the Peter-pence, which to the pope were gathered, should be taken to the king.

IX. If any clerk for felony were taken and so proved, he should be first degraded, and then through judgment be hanged; or if he were a traitor, be drawn.

Other laws and constitutions made at Clarendon, in Normandy, A. D. 1164, and sent to England, whereunto Becket and the pope would not agree, the former being then fled out of the realm.

I. If any person shall be found to bring from the pope, or from the archbishop of Canterbury, any writing containing any interdict or curse against the realm of England, the same man to be apprehended without delay for a traitor, and execution to be done upon the same.

II. That no monk nor any clerk shall be permitted to pass over into England without a passport from the king or his justices: whoso doth the contrary, that man to be attached and imprisoned.

III. No man to be so bold as to appeal to the pope, or to the archbishop of Canterbury out of England.

IV. That no decree or commandment, proceeding from the authority of the pope, or the bishop of Canterbury, be received into England, under pain of taking and imprisoning.

V. In general, to forbid any man to carry over any commandment or precept, either of clerk or layman, to the pope, or to the archbishop of Canterbury, under pain of imprisonment.

VI. If any bishop, clerk, abbot, or layman, shall do contrary to this inhibition, or will keep the sentence of interdicting, the same incontinent to be thrust out of the land, with all his kindred, and to leave all his goods behind him.

VII. All the possessions, goods, and chattels, of such as favour the pope or the archbishop of Canterbury, to be seized and confiscated to the king.

VIII. All such of the clergy as be out of the realm, having their rents and profits out of the land, to be summoned and warned through every shire within three months to repair home, or else their rents and goods to return to the king.

IX. That St. Peter's-pence should be no more paid to the apostolical see, but be

Henry II. reserved diligently in the king's coffers, and there to be at his commandment.[1]

A.D. 1164.

X. That the bishops of Salisbury and Norwich be at the king's mercy, and be summoned by the sheriff and beadles, that they, before the king's justices, do right to the king and his justices; because, contrary to the statutes of Clarendon, by commandment they interdicted the land of Earl Hugh, and published the same in their diocese without license of the king's justices.[2]

By these and such other laws and decrees it may appear, that the abolishing of the pope is no new thing in the realm of England. This only difference there is, that the pope being driven out then, could not be kept out so long as now he is. The cause is, that the time was not yet come that antichrist should so fully be revealed; neither was his wickedness then so fully ripe in those days, as it hath been now in our time. Now, these things premised, let us return to where we left off, namely, to the matter between the king and Thomas Becket.

The communication and controversy between the king and Thomas Becket, with his clergy.

The king, as is aforesaid, conventing his nobles and clerks together, required to have the punishment of certain misdoers of the clergy; but Thomas Becket not assenting thereunto, the king came to this point: to know whether he would consent, with his clergy, that the customs then set forth in the realm (meaning the first part of those decrees above specified) should be observed. To which the archbishop, consulting together with his brethren, giveth answer again: that he was contented the king's ordinances should be observed, adding this withal, *Salvo ordine suo;* that is, *saving his order*. And so in like manner all the other bishops afterwards, being demanded in order, answered with the same addition, *Salvo ordine suo.* Only Hilary, bishop of Chichester, perceiving the king to be exasperated with that addition, instead of *salvo ordine*, agreed to observe them *bona fide.* The king hearing them not simply to agree unto him, but with an exception, was mightily offended; who then turning to the archbishop and the prelates, said, that he was not well contented with that clause of theirs, *salvo suo ordine*, which he said was captious and deceitful, having some manner of venom lurking under it; and therefore required an absolute grant of them, without any exception, to agree to the king's ordinances. To this the archbishop answered again, that they had sworn unto him their fidelity, both life, body, and earthly honour, *salvo ordine suo;* and that in the same earthly honour also these ordinances were comprehended, and to the observing of them they would bind themselves after no other form, but as they had sworn before. The king with that was moved, and all his nobility, not a little. As for the other bishops, there was no doubt but they would easily have relented, had not the stoutness of the archbishop made them more constant than otherwise they would have been. The day being well spent, the king, when he could get no other answer of them, departed in great anger, giving no word of salutation to the bishops; and likewise the bishops, every one to his own house, departed. The bishop of Chichester, amongst the rest, was greatly rebuked of his fellows for changing the exception, contrary

Becket's addition, *Salvo ordine suo.*

(1) Ex Quadrilogo. (2) This latter article is not found in the edition of 1563.—ED.

to the voice of all the others. The next day following, the king took from the archbishop all such honours and lordships as he had given him before, during the time that he was chancellor; whereby appeared the great displeasure of the king against him and the clergy. Not long after this, the king removing from London, unknown to the bishops, sailed over to Normandy, whither the bishop of London, called Gilbert, not long after resorted, to crave the king's favour, and gave him counsel withal to join some of the bishops on his side; lest, if all were against him, peradventure he might sooner be overthrown. And thus the greatest number of the bishops were by this means reconciled again to the king; only the archbishop, with a few others, remained in their stoutness still. The king, thinking to try all manner of ways, when he saw that neither fear nor threats could turn him, did assay him with gentleness; it would not serve. Many of the nobles laboured betwixt them both, exhorting him to relent to the king; it would not be. Likewise the archbishop of York, with divers other bishops and abbots, especially the bishop of Chester, did the same. Besides this, his own household daily called upon him, but no man could persuade him. At length, understanding partly by them that came to him what danger might happen, not only to himself, but to all the other clergy, upon the king's displeasure, and partly considering the old love and kindness of the king towards him in time past, he was content to give over to the king's request, and came to Oxford to him, reconciling himself about the addition, which displeased the king so much. Whereupon the king being somewhat mitigated, receiveth him with a more cheerful countenance, but yet not so familiarly as before, saying, "that he would have his ordinances and proceedings after the form confirmed in the public audience and open sight of all his bishops and all his nobles." After this, the king being at Clarendon, there called all his peers and prelates before him, requiring to have all that performed which they had promised, in consenting to the observing of his grandfather's ordinances and proceedings. The archbishop, suspecting I cannot tell what in the king's promise, drew backward, and now would not what he would before; at last, with much ado, he was enforced to give assent. First came to him the bishops of Salisbury and Norwich, who, for old matters endangered to the king long before, came weeping and lamenting to the archbishop, desiring him to have some compassion of them, and to remit this pertinacy to the king, lest if he so continued, through his stoutness, to exasperate the king's displeasure, happily it might redound to no small danger, not only of them who were in jeopardy already, but also of himself to be imprisoned, and the whole clergy to be endangered. Besides these two bishops, there went to him other two noble peers of the realm, labouring with him to relent and condescend to the king's desire: if not, they should be enforced to use such violence as would not stand with the king's fame, and much less with his quietness; but yet the stout stomach of the man would not give over. After this came to him two rulers of the temple, called Templars; one, Richard de Hast; the other, Costans de Hoverio, with their company, lamenting and bewailing the great peril, which they declared unto him to hang over his head: yet neither with their

The stubborn wilfulness of Becket.

He relenteth to the king.

Henry II. A.D. 1164.

tears, nor with their kneelings, would he be moved. At length came the last message from the king, signifying unto him with express words, and also with tears, what he should trust to, if he would not give over to the king's request.

Becket yieldeth to the king.

By reason of this message, he, either terrified, or else persuaded, was content to submit himself; whereupon the king incontinent assembling the states together, the archbishop first, before all others, beginneth to promise the king obedience and submission unto his custom, and that *cum bona fide*, leaving out his former addition, *salvo ordine*, mentioned before: instead whereof he promised, *in verbo veritatis*, to observe and keep the king's customs, and swear to the same. After him the other bishops likewise gave the like oath; whereupon the king commanded incontinent certain instruments obligatory to be drawn, of which the king should have one, the archbishop of Canterbury another, and the archbishop of York the third, requiring also the said archbishop to set to his hand and seal. To this the archbishop, though not denying but that he was ready so to do, yet desired respite in the matter, while that he, being but newly come to his bishopric, might better peruse with himself the aforesaid customs and ordinances of the king. This request, as it seemed but reasonable, so it was readily granted; so the day being well spent, they departed for that season and brake up.

Salvo ordine left out in composition.

Becket repenteth of his good deed.

Alanus, one of the four writers of the life of this Thomas Becket, recordeth, that the archbishop, in his journey towards Winchester, began greatly to repent what he had done before, partly through the instigation of certain about him, but chiefly of his cross-bearer, who, going before the archbishop, sharply and earnestly expostulated with him for giving over to the king's request, against the privilege and liberties of the church, polluting not only his fame and conscience, but also giving a pernicious example to those who should come after, with many like words. To make the matter short, the archbishop was touched upon the same with such repentance, that keeping himself from all company, lamenting with tears and fasting, and with much penance macerating and afflicting himself, he did suspend himself from all divine service, and would not receive comfort, before that (word being sent to his holy grandfather the pope) he should be assoiled by him; who, tendering the tears of his dear chicken, directed to him letters again, by the same messenger that Thomas had sent up to him before, in which not only he assoiled him from his trespass, but also with words of great consolation did encourage him to be stout in the quarrel he took in hand. The copy of which letters consolatory, sent from the pope to Bishop Becket, here followeth underwritten.

A letter of Pope Alexander to Thomas Becket.

Alexander, bishop, &c.—Your brotherhood is not ignorant that it hath been advertised us, how that upon the occasion of a certain transgression or excess of yours, you have determined to cease henceforth from saying of mass, and to abstain from the consecration of the body and blood of the Lord; which thing to do, how dangerous it is, especially in such a personage, and also what inconvenience may rise thereof, I will you advisedly to consider, and discreetly also to ponder. Your wisdom ought not to forget, what difference there is between those who advisedly and willingly do offend, and those who through ignorance and for necessity' sake do offend. For, as you read, so much the greater is wilful sin, as the same not being voluntary is a lesser sin. Therefore, if you remember yourself to have done any thing that your own conscience doth accuse you of, whatsoever it be, we counsel you, as a prudent and wise prelate, to acknowledge the same. Which thing done, the merciful and pitiful God, who hath more respect to the heart of the doer than to the thing done, will remit and forgive you the same according to his accustomed great mercy. And we, trusting in the merits of the blessed apostles, St. Peter and St. Paul, do absolve you from the offence committed, and by the authority apostolical we release you unto your fraternity, counselling you and commanding you, that henceforth you abstain not, for this cause, from the celebration of the mass.

This letter, with others of the like sort, the pope then wrote to him, animating and comforting him in this quarrel so nearly pertaining to the pope's profit: by the occasion whereof, Becket took no small heart and consolation; insomuch that therefrom seemeth to me to proceed all the occasion that made him so stout and malapert against his prince, as hereafter followeth to be seen by his doings. What the other letters were that the pope wrote unto him, shortly, when we come to the appellations made to the pope, shall appear, God willing. In the mean season, as he sat thus mourning at home, the king hearing of him, and how he denied to set his seal to those sanctions, which he condescended to before, took no small displeasure against him; insomuch that he, threatening him and his with banishment and death, began to call him to reckonings, and to burden him with payments, that all men might understand that the king's mind was sore set against him. The archbishop hereupon (whether more for the love of the pope, or dread of his prince) thought to make his escape out of the realm, and so went about in the night, with two or three with him, stealing out of his house to take the sea privily. Now amongst the king's ordinances and sanctions, this was one; that none of the prelacy or nobility, without the king's license, or that of his justices, should depart out of the realm. So Becket twice attempted the sea, to flee to the see of Rome, but the weather not serving, he was driven home again, and his device for that time frustrated. After his departure began to be known and noised abroad, the king's officers came to Canterbury to seize upon his goods in the king's behalf; but as it chanced, the night before their coming, Becket being returned and found at home, they did not proceed in their purpose.

Becket enterpriseth against the king's laws to fly out of the realm.

Upon this the archbishop, understanding the king sore bent against him, and the seas not to serve him, made haste to the court, lying then at Woodstock, where the king received him, after a certain manner, but nothing so familiarly as he was wont; taunting him jestingly and merrily, as though one realm was not able to hold them both. Becket, although he was permitted to go and come at his pleasure to the court, yet could not obtain the favour that he would, perceiving both in himself, and confessing no less to others, how the matter would fall out, so that either he should be constrained to give over with shame, or stoutly stand to that which he had so boldly taken in hand. The archbishop of York, in the mean time, going betwixt the king and the archbishop, laboured to make peace and love betwixt them; but the king in no case would be reconciled, unless the other would subscribe to his laws. So in the mean while, as neither the king would otherwise agree, nor yet the archbishop in any wise would subscribe, there was a foul discord; where the fault was, let the reader

Taunted by the king.

Henry II. A.D. 1164.

here judge between them both. The king, for his regal authority, thought it much that any subject of his should stand against him. The archbishop again, bearing himself bold upon the authority, and especially upon the letters, of the pope, lately written to him, thought himself strong enough against the king and all his realm. Again, such was his quarrel for the maintenance of the liberties and glory of the church, that he could lack no setters on and favourers in that behalf, in so sweet a cause amongst the clergy. Wherefore the archbishop, trusting to these things, would give no place; but, by virtue of his apostolical authority, gave censure upon these laws and constitutions of the king, condemning some, and approving others for good and catholic, as is before declared. Besides this, there came also to the king, Rotrodus, archbishop of Rothomage, sent by the pope, to make peace between the king and Canterbury; whereunto the king was well content, so that the pope would agree to ratify his ordinances;[1] but when that could in nowise be obtained at the pope's hands, then the king, being stopped and frustrate of his purpose by reason of Becket's apostolic legacy (being legatus a latere), thought good to send up to the pope, and so did, to obtain of him, that the same authority of the apostolic legacy might be conferred on another after his appointment, who was the archbishop of York; but the pope denied. Notwithstanding, at the request of the king's clergy, the pope was content that the king should be legate himself; whereat the king took great indignation, as Hoveden writeth, so that he sent the pope his letters again. Here the pope was perplexed on both sides.

The king to be the pope's legate.

If he should have denied the king, that was too hot for him; for the pope useth always to hold in with kings, howsoever the world speedeth. Again, if he should have forsaken such a churchly chaplain, the cause being so sweet and so gainful, that would have been against himself. What did he then? Here now cometh in the old practice of popish prelacy, to play with both hands; privily he conspireth with the one, and openly dissembleth with the other. First, he granted to the king's ambassadors their request, to have the legate removed, and to place in that office the archbishop of York, after his own contentation; and yet, notwithstanding, to tender the cause of Thomas Becket, he addeth this promise withal, that the said Becket should receive no harm or damage thereby. Thus the pope craftily conveying the matter between them both, gladly to further the archbishop for his own advantage, and yet loath to deny the king for displeasure, writeth to the king openly, and also secretly directeth another letter to Becket; the contents whereof here follow.

Crafty dissimulation of the pope.

Alexander the pope, to Thomas, archbishop of Canterbury.[2]

The pope's secret letter to Becket.

Although we, condescending to the king's request, have granted the gift of our legacy after his mind from you, yet let not your mind thereby be discomforted, nor brought into sighs of despair. For before that we had granted that, or given our consent thereunto, the king's ambassadors firmly promised by the word of truth, ready also to be sworn upon the same, if I would so have required, that their letters also which he had obtained, should not be delivered to the archbishop of York without our knowledge and consent. This is certain,

(1) Ex Rogero Hoved. pr. parte Historiæ continuatæ post Bedam.
(2) For the Latin of this letter, see Edition 1563, p. 50.—Ed.

and so persuade yourself boldly without any scruple, doubt, or mistrust, that it was never my mind or purpose, nor ever shall be, God willing, to subdue you or your church under the obedience of any person, to be subject to any, save only to the bishop of Rome. And, therefore, we warn you and charge you, that if you shall perceive the king to deliver these aforesaid letters, which we trust he will not attempt without our knowledge to do, forthwith by some trusty messengers, or by your letters, you will give us knowledge thereof; whereby we may provide upon the same both for your person, your church, and also your city committed to you, to be clearly exempt, by our authority apostolical, from all power and jurisdiction of any legacy.

Henry II.

A.D. 1164.

Upon these letters and such others, as is said before, Becket seemed to take all his boldness to be so stout and sturdy against his prince, as he was. The pope, beside these, sent secretly a chaplain of his, and directed another letter also unto the king, granting and permitting at his request, to make the archbishop of York legate apostolical.

The king, after he had received his letters sent from the pope, began to put more strength to his purposed proceedings against the archbishop, first beginning with the inferiors of the clergy, such as were offenders against his laws: as felons, robbers, quarrellers, breakers of the peace, and especially such as had committed homicide and murders, whereof more than an hundred at that time were proved upon the clergy;[1] urging and constraining them to be arraigned after the order of the law temporal, and justice to be ministered to them according to their deserts; as first, to be deprived, and so to be committed to the secular hands. This seemed to Becket to derogate from the liberties of holy church, that the secular power should pass in causes criminal, or sit in judgment against any ecclesiastical person. This law the roisters[2] (then of the clergy) had picked and forged out of Anacletus and Euaristus, by whose falsely alleged and pretended authority they have deduced this their constitution from the apostles, which giveth immunity to all ecclesiastical persons to be free from secular jurisdiction. Becket therefore, like a valiant champion, fighting for his liberties, and having the pope on his side, would not permit his clerks defamed, otherwise to be convented, than before ecclesiastical judges, there to be examined and deprived for their excess, and no secular judge to proceed against them: so that, after their deprivation, if they should incur the like offence again, then the temporal judge to take hold upon them; otherwise not. This obstinate and stubborn rebellion of the archbishop stirred up much anger and vexation in the king, and not only in him, but also in the nobles and all the bishops, for the greater part, so that he was almost alone, a wonderment to all the realm.

More than a hundred murders by the clergy.

The king's wrath daily increased more and more against him, as no marvel it was, and caused him to be cited up to appear by a certain day at the town of Northampton, there to make answer to such things as should be laid to his charge. So, when the day was come, all the peers and nobles, with the prelates of the realm, upon the king's proclamation, being assembled in the castle of Northampton, great fault was found with the archbishop, for that he, being personally cited to appear, came not himself, but sent another for him. The cause why he came not, Hoveden assigneth to be this: for that the

Becket cited to Northampton.

(1) Guliel. Neuburg. lib. ii. cap. 16. (2) "Roisters," the turbulent men of the age.—Ed.

Henry II. A.D. 1164.

king had placed his horse and horsemen in the archbishop's lodging (which was a house there of canons), wherewith he being offended, sent word again that he would not appear, unless his lodging were voided of the king's horsemen, &c. Whereupon, by the public sentence, as well of all the nobles as of the bishops, all his moveables were adjudged to be confiscated to the king, unless the king's clemency would remit the penalty. The stubborn archbishop again, for his part, quarrelling against the order and form of the judgment, complaineth, alleging for himself (seeing he is the primate and spiritual father, not only of all others in the realm, but also of the king himself,) that it was not convenient that the father should be so judged of his children, or the pastor of his flock so condemned; saying moreover, that the ages to come should know what judgment was done, &c. But especially he complaineth of his fellow-bishops, who, when they should rather have taken his part, did sit in judgment against their metropolitan; and this was the first day's action.

Condemned in the loss of all moveables.

The next day the king laid an action against him in behalf of one that was his marshal, called John, for certain injuries done to him, and required of the said archbishop the repaying again of certain money, which he, as is said, had lent unto him being chancellor, the sum whereof came to five hundred marks. This money the archbishop denied not but he had received of the king, howbeit, by the way and title of gift as he took it, though he could bring no probation thereof. Whereupon the king required him to put in assurance for the payment thereof; whereat the archbishop making delays (not well contented at the matter), was so called upon, that either he should be accountable to the king for the money, or else he should incur present danger, the king being so bent against him. The archbishop, being brought to such a strait, and destitute of his own suffragans, could here by no means have escaped, had not five persons, of their own accord, stepped in, being bound for him, every man for one hundred marks a piece; and this was upon the second day concluded.

Becket required to give an account.

On the morrow, which was the third day of the council, as the archbishop was sitting below in a certain conclave with his fellow-bishops about him, consulting together, the doors being fast locked on them, as the king had willed and commanded, it was propounded unto him on behalf of the king, that he had had divers bishoprics and abbacies in his hand which were vacant, with the fruits and revenues thereof due to the king for certain years, whereof he had rendered as yet no account to the king; wherefore it was demanded of him to bring in a full and clear reckoning of the same. This, with other such like things, declared to all the council, caused great displeasure in the king, and no less danger to the archbishop.

The advice of the Bishops to Thomas Becket.

* Thus, while the bishops and prelates were in council, advising and deliberating what was to be done, at length it came to voices, every man to say his mind, and to give sentence what were the best way for their archbishop to take. First began Henry, bishop of Winchester, who then took part with Becket as much as he durst for fear of the king, who said, he remembered that the said archbishop, first being

Henry, bishop of Winchester.

archdeacon, and then lord chancellor, at what time he was promoted to the church of Canterbury, was discharged from all bonds and reckonings of the temporal court, as all the other bishops could not but bear record to the same. *Henry II.* A.D. 1164.

Next spake Gilbert, bishop of London, exhorting and motioning the archbishop, that he should call to mind with himself, from whence the king took him, and set him up; what, and how great things he had done for him; also that he should consider with himself the dangers and perils of the time, and what ruin he might bring upon the whole church, and upon them all there present, if he resisted the king's mind in the things he required. And if it were to render up his archbishopric, although it were ten times better than it is, yet he should not stick with the king in the matter. In so doing it might happen, that the king, seeing that submission and humility in him, would release him peradventure from all the rest. To this the archbishop answering, "Well, well," saith he, "I perceive well enough, my lord, whither you tend, and whereabout you go." Then spake Winchester, inferring upon the same, "This form of counsel," saith he, "seemeth to me very pernicious to the catholic church, tending to our subversion, and to the confusion of us all. For, if our archbishop and primate of all England do lean to this example, that every bishop should give over his authority and the charge of the flock committed to him, at commandment and threatening of the prince, to what state shall the church then be brought, but that all should be confounded at his pleasure and arbitrement, and nothing stand certain by any order of law; and so as the priest is, so shall the people be?" Gilbert, bishop of London. Henry, of Winchester.

Hilary, the bishop of Chichester, replieth again to this, saying, "If it were not that the instance and the great perturbation of the time did otherwise require and force us, I would think this counsel here given were good to be followed. But now, seeing the authority of our canon faileth and cannot serve us, I judge it not best to go so strictly to work, but so to moderate our proceedings, that dispensation with sufferance may win that which severe correction may destroy. Wherefore my counsel and reason is, to give place to the king's purpose for a time, lest by over hasty proceeding, we exceed so far, that both it may redound to our shame, and also we cannot rid ourselves out again when we would." Hilary, of Chichester.

Much to the same end spake Robert, the bishop of Lincoln, after this manner: "Seeing," saith he, "it is manifest that the life and blood of this man is sought, one of these two must needs be chosen; that either he must part with his archbishopric, or else with his life. Now what profit he shall take in this matter of his bishopric, his life being lost, I do not greatly see." Robert, of Lincoln.

Next followed Bartholomew, bishop of Exeter, with his advice, who, inclining his counsel to the state of the time, confirmed their sayings before, affirming how the days were evil and perilous; and that, if they might so escape the violence of that raging tempest under the cover of bearing and relenting, it were not to be refused; but that, he said, could not be, except strict severity should give place to tractability; and that the instance and condition of the time then present required no less, especially seeing that persecution was not Bartholomew, of Exeter.

Henry II. A.D. 1164. general, but personal and particular; and he thought it more holy and convenient for one head to run into some part of danger, than that the whole church of England should be subject and exposed to inconvenience inevitable.

Roger, bishop of Worcester. The answer of Roger, bishop of Worcester, was devised in a double suspense, neither affirming the one, nor denying the other; whose saying was this,—that he would give no answer on either part; "for if I," saith he, "should say that the pastoral function and cure of souls ought to be relinquished at the king's will or threatening, then my mouth would speak against my conscience, to the condemnation of mine own head. And if I should give, again, contrary counsel, to resist the king's sentence, here be they that would hear it, and report it to his Grace, and so I should be in danger to be thrust out of the synagogue, and for my part to be accounted amongst the public rebels, with them to be condemned; wherefore neither do I say this, nor counsel that."

Becket, the archbishop, replieth against the bishops. And this was the consultation of the bishops in that place, assembled together by the king's commandment. Against these voices and censures of the bishops, Becket, the archbishop, replieth again, expostulating and checking them with rebukeful words:—"I perceive," saith he, "and understand ye go about to maintain and cherish but your own cowardliness, under the colourable shadow of sufferance; and, under pretence of dissembling softness, to choke the liberty of Christ's church. Who hath thus bewitched you, O insatiable bishops? What mean ye? Why do ye so, under the impudent title of forbearing, bear a double heart, and cloak your manifest iniquity? What! call ye this bearing with time, when it is to the detriment of the church of Christ? Let terms serve the matter. Why pervert you the matter that is good with vocables and terms untrue? For that ye say we must bear with the malice of time, I grant with you; but yet we must not heap sin to sin. Is not God able to help the state and condition of his church, but with the sinful dissimulation of the teachers of the church? Certes God is disposed to tempt you. And tell me, I pray you, whether should the governors of the church put themselves to dangers for the church, in time of tranquillity, or in time of distress? Ye will be ashamed to deny the contrary, but in distress. And now then, the church lying in so great distress and vexation, why should not the good pastor put himself into peril there-for? For neither do I think it a greater act or merit for the ancient bishops of the old time to lay the foundation of the then church, with their blood, than now for us to shed our blood for the liberties of the same. And to tell you plain, I think it not safe for you to swerve from an example which you have received from your holy elders." After these things were spoken, they sat all in silence for a certain space, being locked in together. At length, to find a shift to cause the door to be opened, "I will," saith the archbishop, "speak with two earls who are about the king," and named them who they were. They, being called, opened the door and came in with haste, thinking to hear something which should appease the king's mind. To whom the archbishop spake in this manner:—"As touching and concerning the matters between the king and us, we have here conferred together. And forasmuch as we

A great distress grown in the church, because bishops may not be above kings and princes.

have them not present with us now, who know more in the matter than we do, (whose advice we would be glad to follow,) therefore we crave so much respite as to the next day following, and then to give our answer to the king." With this message two bishops were sent to the king, who were the bishop of London and the bishop of Rochester. London, to help the matter, and to set quietness, as I take it, adding something more to the message, said to the king, that the archbishop craved a little time to prepare such writings and instruments, wherein he should set forth and declare his mind in accomplishing the king's desire, &c. Wherefore two barons were sent to him from the king, to grant him that respite or stay; so that he would ratify that which the messengers had signified to the king. To whom the archbishop answereth, that he sent no such message as was intimated in his name; but only that the next day he would come and give answer to the king, in that which he had to say. And so the convocation of the bishops was dissolved, and they were dismissed home; so that the most part of them that came with the archbishop, and accompanied him before, now, for fear of the king's displeasure, severed themselves from him. The archbishop, thus forsaken and destitute, as his story saith, sent about for the poor, the lame, and the halt, to come in and furnish his house, saying, that by them he might sooner obtain his victory, than by the others who had so slipped from him.

Becket destitute and forsaken

The next day following, because it was Sunday, nothing was done. So the day after, which was the second fery,[1] the archbishop was cited to appear. But the night before, being taken with a disease called *passio iliaca*, the cholic, all that day he kept his bed, and was not able, as he said, to rise. Every man supposing this to be but a feigned sickness, as it seemed no less, certain of the chief nobles were sent to try the matter, and to cite him to the court; namely, Robert, earl of Leicester, and Reginald, earl of Devonshire, to whom the archbishop answered, that that day he was so diseased that he could not come, yea, though he were brought in an horse-litter. So that day passed over. On the morrow, certain that were about him, fearing no less but that some danger would happen to him, gave him counsel in the morning to have a mass in honour of the holy martyr St. Stephen, to keep him from the hands of his enemies that day. When the morrow was come, being Tuesday, there came to him the bishops and prelates, counselling and persuading him covertly by insinuation, for apertly they durst not, that he would submit himself, with all his goods, as also his archbishopric, to the will of the king, if peradventure his indignation by that means might assuage. Adding, moreover, that unless he would so do, perjury would be laid against him; for that he being under the oath of fidelity to keep the king's laws and ordinances, now would not observe them. To this Becket, the archbishop, answereth again,—"Brethren, ye see and perceive well how the world is set against me, and how the enemy riseth and seeketh my confusion. And although these things be dolorous and lamentable, yet the thing that grieveth me most of all is this,—the sons of mine own mother be pricks and thorns against me. And albeit I do hold my peace, yet the posterity to come will know and

Taken with sickness when he should appear

A mass of St Stephen to save him from his enemies.

Becket's answer to the bishops.

(1) "Fery," or feria, a day, sometimes a holiday —Ed

Henry II. A.D. 1164.

report how cowardly you have turned your backs, and have left your archbishop and metropolitan alone in his conflict, and how you have sitten in judgment against me, although unguilty of crime, now two days together; and not only in the civil and spiritual court, but also in the temporal court, are ready to do the same. But in general, this I charge and command, by the virtue of pure obedience, and in peril of your order, that ye be present personally in judgment against me. And that ye shall not fail so to do, I here appeal to our mother, the refuge of all such as be oppressed, the church of Rome; and if any secular men shall lay hands upon me, as it is rumoured they will, I straitly enjoin and charge you, in the same virtue of obedience, that you exercise your censure ecclesiastical upon them, as it becometh you to do for a father and an archbishop. And this I do you to understand, that though the world rage, and the enemy be fierce, and the body trembleth, for the flesh is weak, yet, God so favouring me, I will neither cowardly shrink, nor yet vilely forsake my flock committed to my charge," &c.

Becket appealeth to Rome.

The bishop of London appealeth from the archbishop.

But the bishop of London, contrary to this commandment of the archbishop, did incontinent appeal from him; and thus the bishops departed from him to the court, save only two, Henry of Winchester, and Joceline of Salisbury, who returned with him secretly to his chamber, and comforted him. This done, the archbishop, who yesterday was so sore sick that he could not stir out of his bed, now addresseth himself to his mass of St. Stephen with all solemnity, as though it had been a high festival-day, with his metropolitan pall, which was not used, but upon holidays, to be worn. The office of the mass began,—"Sederunt principes et adversum me loquebantur;" that is, "Princes sat and spake against me," &c.—the king's servants being also there, and beholding the matter. For this mass, Gilbert, bishop of London, accused Becket afterwards, both for that it was done, "Per artem magicam, et in contemptum regis," as the words of Hoveden purport; that is, "both by art of magic, and in contempt of the king," &c.

A mass to charm away persecutors.

Becket carrieth with him the sacrament going to the king.

The mass being ended, the archbishop putting off his pall, his mitre, and his other robes, proceedeth to the king's court; but yet not trusting, peradventure, so greatly to the strength of his mass, to make the matter more sure, he taketh also the sacrament privily about him, thinking himself thereby sufficiently defended against all bugs. In going to the king's chamber, there to attend the king's coming, as he entered the door, he taketh from Alexander his crosier, the cross with the cross staff, in the sight of all that stood by, and carrieth it in himself, the other bishops following him, and saying, "He did otherwise than became him." Amongst others, Robert, bishop of Hereford, offered himself to bear his cross, rather than he should so do, for that it was not comely; but the archbishop would not suffer him. Then said the bishop of London unto him,—"If the king shall see you come armed into his chamber, perchance he will draw out his sword against you, which is stronger than yours, and then what shall this your armour profit you?"[1] The archbishop answereth again: "If the king's sword do cut carnally, yet my sword cutteth spiritually, and striketh down to hell. But you, my lord, as you have played

(1) Hoveden referreth not this saying to the bishop of London, but to the archbishop of York.

the fool in this matter, so you will not yet leave off your folly for any thing I can see;" and so he came into the chamber. The king hearing of his coming, and of the manner thereof, tarried not long, but came where Becket was set in a place by himself, with his other bishops about him. First, the crier called the prelates and all the lords of the temporalty together. That being done, and every one placed in his seat according to his degree, the king beginneth with a great complaint against the archbishop for his manner of entering into court, not as, saith he, a subject into a king's court, but as a traitor, showing himself in such sort as hath not been seen before in any christian king's court, professing christian faith. To this all there present gave witness with the king, affirming Becket always to have been a vain and proud man, and that the shame of his deed did not only redound against the prince himself, but also against his whole realm. Moreover, they said, that this had so happened to the king, for that he had done so much for such a beast, advancing him so highly to such a place and room next under himself. And so altogether with one cry, they called him traitor, on every side, as one that refused to give terrene honour to the king, in keeping, as he had sworn, his laws and ordinances, at whose hands also he had received such honour and great preferments; and therefore he was well worthy, said they, to be handled like a perjured traitor and rebel. Upon this, great doubt and fear was, what should befal him. The archbishop of York, coming down to his men, said, he could not abide to see what the archbishop of Canterbury was likely to suffer. Likewise, the tipstaves, and other ministers of the assembly, coming down with an outcry against him, crossed themselves to see his haughty stubbornness, and the business there was about him. Certain there were of his disciples sitting at his feet, comforting him softly, and bidding him to lay his curse upon them; others, on the contrary, bidding him not to curse, but to pray, and forgive them; and that if he lost his life in the quarrel of the church and the liberty thereof, he should be happy. Afterwards, one of them, named John Stephen, desired to speak something in his ear; but could not be suffered by the king's marshal, who forbad that any man should have any talk with him. Then he, because he could not otherwise speak to him, wrought by signs, making a cross, and looking up with his eyes, and wagging his lips, meaning that he should pray, and manfully stand to the cross. In the mean time cometh to him Bartholomew, bishop of Exeter, desiring him to have regard and compassion of himself, and also of them, or else they were all like to perish for the hatred of him; "for there cometh out," saith he, "a precept from the king that he shall be taken, and suffer for an open rebel, who hereafter taketh your part. It is said, moreover, that Joceline, bishop of Salisbury, and William, bishop of Norwich, are to be had to the place of execution, for their resisting and making intercession for the archbishop of Canterbury." When he had thus said, the archbishop, looking upon the said bishop of Exeter, "Avoid hence from me," saith he, "thou understandest not, neither dost savour those things that be of God."

Henry II. A.D. 1164.

Called traitor by the king and all his nobles.

Blind zeal for the proud liberties of the church.

Whoso taketh Becket's part is counted a rebel.

The bishops and prelates then going aside by themselves from the other nobles, the king so permitting them to do, took counsel together what was to be done. Here the matter stood in a doubtful perplexity,

Henry II. A.D. 1164. for either must they incur the dangerous indignation of the king, or else, with the nobles, they must proceed in condemnation against the archbishop, for resisting the king's sanctions; which thing they themselves neither did favour. In this strict necessity, they, devising what way to take, at length agreed upon this: that they with a common assent should cite the archbishop to the see of Rome on perjury; and that they should oblige and bind themselves to the king with a sure promise to work their diligence in deposing the archbishop; upon this condition, that the king should promise their safety, and discharge them from the peril of that judgment which was directed towards them. So all the bishops, obliging themselves thus to the king, went forth to the archbishop; of whom one speaking for the rest, who was Hilary, bishop of Chichester, had these words:—"Once you have been our archbishop, and so long we were bound to your obedience; but now, forasmuch as you, once swearing your fidelity to the king, do resist him, neglecting his injunctions and ordinances, concerning and appertaining to his terrene honour and dignity, we here pronounce you perjured; neither be we bound to give obedience to an archbishop thus being perjured; but, putting ourselves and all ours under the pope's protection, we do cite you up to his presence." And upon the same, they assigned him his day and time to appear. The archbishop answering again, said he heard him well enough; and upon this sendeth up to Rome in all haste, to the pope, signifying to him by letters, the whole matter, how, and wherefore, and by whom, he was cited; to whom the pope directed again his letters of comfort, as he had done divers before, the copy whereof here ensueth.

Becket cited to Rome upon perjury.

Becket condemned.

Pope Alexander to Thomas, Archbishop of Canterbury.[1]

Your brotherly letters, which you directed to us, and such other matters which your messenger by word of mouth hath signified unto us, we have diligently heard the reading thereof, and thereby fully understand the grievous vexations and dolorous griefs wherewith your mind is daily encumbered: by reason whereof, we, hearing and understanding, are not a little disquieted in our spirit for your sake, in whose prosperities we do both gladly rejoice, and no less do sorrow in your adversities, as for our most dear brother. You, therefore, as a constant and wise man, remember with yourself that which is written: "The apostles departed away, rejoicing, from the face of the council," &c. With like patience do you also sustain that man's molestations, and let not your spirit be troubled therein more than needeth, but receive in yourself consolation; that we also, together with you, may be comforted in the Lord, who hath preserved you to the corroboration of his catholic and christian verity, in this distress of necessity; and from whom also it hath pleased him to wipe away the blot of those things which have been unorderly of you committed, and here to punish the same through sundry afflictions: whereby, in the strict judgment of God, they might not be called to account hereafter. But, henceforth, let not this much grieve you; neither let your heart be so deject or timorous in the matter, (for that you are cited up to the apostolic see,) which to us is both grateful and accepted. And this we will you, that if they who have cited you shall chance to come, draw not you back, but follow the appeal, if you please, and spare not; all doubt and delay set apart: for the authority of the church, tendering this your constancy, may not do that which may put you in fear or doubt. But our diligence shall be, with all labour and study, to conserve the right and pre-eminence (God willing) of that church committed to you, so much as in us lieth, (saving our justice and equity), as to one whom, in working for the church, we find to be both a constant and a valiant champion. Further, this I brotherly

(1) The Latin copy of this is in the Edition of 1563, p. 52.—ED.

require you, to repair unto the church of Canterbury; and, retaining but a few clerks about you, such only as serve your necessity, make excursions out as little as you can, in that country. But in this especially I thought to premonish you, that in no case, neither for fear nor any adversity, whatsoever may happen, you be brought to renounce and give up the right and dignity of your church.

Henry II. A.D. 1164.

Written at Sens, the seventh before the Kalends of November.

As the archbishop was thus cited up to Rome, sitting with his cross waiting in the court, neither giving place to the king's request, nor abashed with the clamour of the whole court against him, calling him traitor on every side, neither following the advertisement of his fellow-bishops, at length the king, by certain earls and barons, sent commandment to him (Robert, earl of Leicester, doing the message), that he should without delay come and render a full account of all things that he had received, as the profits and revenues of the realm, in the time he was chancellor, and especially for the thirty thousand marks, for the which he was accountable to the king.[1] To whom the archbishop answereth again, the king knew how oft he had made his reckoning of those things which now were required of him. Further and besides, Henry, his son and heir of his realm, with all his barons, and also Richard Lucy, chief justice of England, told him, that he was free and quit to God and to holy church, from all receipts and computations, and from all secular exactions on the king's behalf. And so he, taking thus his discharge at their hands, entered into his office; and therefore other account besides this he would make none. When this word was brought to the king, he required his barons to do the law upon him; who, so doing, judged him to be apprehended and laid in prison. This done, the king sendeth to him Reginald, earl of Cornwall and Devonshire, and Robert, earl of Leicester, to declare to him what was his judgment. To whom the archbishop answereth,—"Hear, my son, and good earl, what I say unto you: how much more precious the soul is than the body, so much more ought you to obey me in the Lord, rather than your terrene king; neither doth any law or reason permit the children to judge or condemn their father. Wherefore, to avoid both the judgment of the king, of you, and of all others, I put myself only to the arbitrement of the pope, under God alone to be judged of him, and of no other; to whose presence, here before you all, I do appeal, committing the ordering of the church of Canterbury, my dignity, with all other things appertaining to the same, under the protection of God and him. And as for you, my brethren and fellow-bishops, who rather obey man than God, you also I call and cite to the audience and judgment of the pope, and depart henceforth from you, as from the enemies of the catholic church, and of the authority of the apostolic see."[2]

Called to a full account.

Judged to be laid in prison.

Appealeth to the pope.

Thinketh not the protection of God sufficient without the pope.

While the barons returned with this answer to the king, the archbishop, passing through the throng, taketh unto him his palfrey, holding his cross in one hand, and his bridle in the other, the courtiers following after, and crying, "Traitor! traitor! tarry and hear thy judgment." But he passed on till he came to the uttermost gate of the court, which being fast locked, there he had been staid, had not one of his servants, called Peter, surnamed Demunc-

Flieth out of the court.

(1) Ex Rogero Hovedeno. (2) Ex Quadripartita Hist. lib. i. c. 33.

Henry II. A.D. 1165. torio, finding there a bunch of keys hanging by, first proved one key, then another, till at last, finding the true key, he had opened the gate, and let him out. The archbishop went straight to the house of canons, where he did lie, calling unto him the poor where they could be found. When supper was done, making as though he would go to bed, which he caused to be made between two altars, privily, while the king was at supper, he prepareth his journey secretly to escape; and changing his garment and his name, being called Derman, first went to Lincoln, and from thence to Sandwich, where he took ship, and sailed into Flanders, and from thence journeyed into France, as Hoveden saith. Albeit Alanus, differing something in the order of his flight, saith, "That he departed not that night; but at supper-time came to him the bishops of London and Chichester, declaring to him, that if he would surrender up to the king his two manors of Otford and Wingcham, there were hope to recover the king's favour, and to have all remitted." But when the archbishop would not agree thereunto, forasmuch as those manors were belonging to the church of Canterbury, the king hearing thereof, great displeasure was taken, insomuch that the next day Becket was fain to send to the king two bishops and his chaplain for leave to depart the realm. To this message the king answered, that he would take pause thereof till the next day, and then he should have an answer. But Becket, not tarrying his answer, the same day conveyed himself away secretly, as is aforesaid, to Louis, the French king; but before he came to the king, Gilbert, the bishop of London, and William, the earl of Arundel, sent from the king of England to France, prevented him; requiring the said French king, in the behalf of the king of England, that he would not receive, nor retain in his dominion, the archbishop of Canterbury: moreover, that at his instance he would be a means to the pope, not to show any familiarity unto him. But the king of England, in this point, seemed to have more confidence in the French king, than knowledge of his disposition; for thinking that the French king would have been a good neighbour to him, in trusting him too much, he was deceived. Neither considered he with himself enough the manner and nature of the Frenchmen at that time against the realm of England; who then were glad to seek and take all manner of occasion to do some act against England.

Changeth his name, and is called Derman.

And therefore Louis, the French king, understanding the matter, and thinking, perchance, thereby to have some vantage against the king and realm of England, by the occasion hereof, contrary to the king's letters and request, not only harboureth and cherisheth this Derman, but also, writing to the pope by his almoner and brother, entreateth him, upon all loves, as ever he would have his favour, to tender the cause of the Archbishop Becket. Thus the king's ambassadors, repulsed of the French king, returned; at which time he sent another ambassage, upon the like cause, to Alexander, the pope, then being at Sens, in France. The ambassadors sent on this message were Roger, archbishop of York; Gilbert, bishop of London; Henry, bishop of Winchester; Hilary, bishop of Chichester; Bartholomew, bishop of Exeter; with other doctors and clerks: also William, earl of Arundel, with certain more lords and

The French king supporteth Becket against the king of England.

Ambassadors to the pope.

barons, who, coming to the pope's court, were friendly accepted of certain of the cardinals; amongst the which cardinals rose also dissension about the same cause, some judging that the bishop of Canterbury, in the defence of the liberties of the church, (as in a good cause,) was to be maintained; some thinking again, that he, being a perturber of peace and unity, was rather to be bridled for his presumption, than to be fostered and encouraged therein. But the pope, partly bearing with his cause, which only tended to his exaltation and magnificence, partly again incensed with the letters of the French king, did wholly incline to Becket, as no marvel was. Wherefore the day following, the pope sitting in consistory with his cardinals, the ambassadors were called for, to the hearing of Becket's matter; and first beginneth the bishop of London; next, the archbishop of York; then Exeter; and then the other bishops, every one in his order, began to speak: whose orations being not well accepted of the pope, and some of them also disdained, the earl of Arundel, perceiving that, and somewhat to qualify and temper the matter to the pope's ears, began after this manner:— *Henry II.* A.D. 1165.

The Oration of the Earl of Arundel to the Pope.

Although to me it is unknown, (saith he,) who am both unlettered and ignorant, what it is that these bishops here have said, neither am I, in that tongue, so able to express my mind as they have done: yet being sent and charged thereunto of my prince, neither can nor ought I but to declare, as well as I may, what the cause is of our sending hither: not, truly, to contend or strive with any person, nor to offer any injury or harm unto any man, especially in this place, and in the presence here of such an one, unto whose beck and authority, all the world doth stoop and yield. But for this time is our legacy hither directed: to present here before you, and in the presence of the whole church of Rome, the devotion and love of our king and master, which ever he hath had, and yet hath still, toward you. And, that the same might the better appear to your excellency, he hath assigned and appointed to the furniture of this legacy, not the least, but the greatest; not the worst, but the best and chiefest of all his subjects; both archbishops, bishops, earls, barons, with other potentates more, of such worthiness and parentage, that if he could have found greater in all his realm, he would have sent them, both for the reverence of your person, and of the holy church of Rome. Over and besides this, I might add more, which your sanctitude hath sufficiently tried and proved already, namely, the true and hearty fidelity of this our king and sovereign toward you, who, in his first entrance to his kingdom, wholly submitted himself, with all that is his besides, to your will and pleasure. And truly, to testify of his majesty how he is disposed to the unity of the catholic faith, we believe there is none more faithful in Christ than he, nor more devout to God, nor yet more moderate in keeping the unity of peace whereunto he is called. And as I may be bold this to protest for our king and master, so neither do I affirm the archbishop of Canterbury to be a man destitute or unfurnished with gifts and ornaments in his kind of calling, but to be a man both sage and discreet in such things as to him appertain, save only that he seemeth to some, more quick and sharp than needeth. This blot alone if it were not, and if the breach between our king and him had not so happened, both the regiments together (of the temporalty and spiritualty) might quietly have flourished one with the other in much peace and concord, both under a prince so worthy, and a pastor so virtuous. Wherefore, the case so standing as it doth, our message hither, and our supplication to your vigilant prudence is, that through your favour and wisdom, the neck of this dissension may be broken, and that reformation of unity and love, by some good means, may be sought.

This oration of his, although it was liked of them for the softness and moderation thereof, yet it could not persuade the Romish bishop

Henry II. A.D. 1165.

to condescend to their suit and request; which suit was, to have two legates or arbiters to be sent from his popish side into England, to examine and take up the controversy between the king and the archbishop. But the pope, incensed, as is said before, would not grant their petition: forasmuch as it should be (saith he) prejudicial, and tending to the oppression of the archbishop, to grant it, he being not present; and therefore he willed them to tarry his coming up; otherwise he being absent, he would not, he said, in any case proceed against him. But they alleging the time to be expired appointed to them of the king, having besides other lets and causes as they alleged, said that they could not there wait for the coming of Becket, but must return back, their cause frustrated, without the pope's blessing to the king. Within four days after, Becket cometh to the pope's court, where he, prostrating himself at his feet, brought out of his bosom a scroll containing the customs and ordinances of the king, before mentioned. The pope, receiving the aforesaid scroll, and reading it in the open hearing of his cardinals, condemned and accursed the most part of the said decrees of the king, which he called 'consuetudines avitas;' that is, 'his grandfather's ordinances.' Besides this, the pope moreover blameth Becket, for that he so much yielded to them at the beginning, as he did: yet notwithstanding, because he was repentant for his unadvised fact, he was content to absolve him for the same, and the rather, because of his great troubles, which he for the liberties of holy church did sustain; and so with great favour for that day dismissed him,

The pope tendereth Becket's cause against the king.

Becket complaineth of the king to the pope.

Repentance for his well-doing.

The next day (Alexander the pope assembling his cardinals together in his secret chamber) appeareth before them Archbishop Becket, having this oration to the pope and his popelings, which here I thought to set out in our vulgar English tongue (translated out of Latin), to the intent that the posterity hereafter may understand either the vain superstition or vile slavery of the churchmen in those days, who, being not content with their own natural prince and king given them of God, must seek further to the pope; thinking no ecclesiastical living to be given, which is not taken at his hands. The words of his oration be storied rightly thus.

The Oration of Becket on resigning his bishopric to the Pope.[1]

Fathers and Lords, I ought not to lie in any place, much less before God, and in your presence here. Wherefore, with much sighing and sorrow of heart, I grant and confess, that these perturbations of the church of England be raised through my miserable fault. For I entered into the fold of Christ, but not by the door of Christ; for that not the canonical election did call me lawfully thereunto, but terror of public power drove me in. And albeit I, against my will, took this burden upon me, yet not the will of God, but man's pleasure placed me in the room; and therefore no marvel though all things have gone contrary and backward with me. And, as for the resigning up again thereof; if I had so done, and given up to their hands the privilege of my bishoply authority, which I had granted to me at the commandment of the king (so as my fellow-bishops did instantly call upon me to do), then had I left a pernicious and dangerous example to the whole catholic church; by reason whereof I thought to defer that unto your presence. And now, therefore (recognising with myself my ingress not to be canonical, and therefore fearing it to have the worse end; and again pondering my strength and ability not to be sufficient for such a charge), lest I should be found to sustain

Becket's argument.

And why might ye not, Mr. Becket, resign it as well to his hands of whom ye took it?

(1) For this oration in Latin, see the Edition of 1563, p. 53.—Ed.

that room to the ruin of the flock, to whom I was appointed a pastor unworthy: I here render up to your fatherly hands the archbishopric of Canterbury. *Henry II.* A.D. 1165.

And so putting off his ring from his finger, and offering it to the pope, he desired a bishop for the church of Canterbury to be provided: seeing he thought not himself meet to fulfil the same, and so (with tears, as the story saith) he ended his oration.

This done, the archbishop was bid to stand apart. The pope conferring upon this with his cardinals, about the resignation of Becket, what was best to be done; some thought it best to take the occasion offered, thinking thereby the king's wrath might easily be assuaged, if the church of Canterbury were assigned to some other person; and yet the said Becket otherwise to be provided for notwithstanding. On the contrary, others thought otherwise, whose reason was, that if he, who, for the liberties of the church, had ventured not only his goods, dignity, and authority, but also his life, should now, at the king's pleasure, be deprived, as it might be a precedent hereafter to others in resisting their king in like sort, if his cause were maintained, so contrariwise, if it quailed, it should be an example to all others hereafter not to resist his prince in the like case; and so might it redound, not only to the weakening of the state of the catholic church, but also to the derogation of the pope's authority. Briefly, this sentence at length prevailed: and so Becket receiveth his pastoral office of the pope's hand again, with commendation and much favour. But forasmuch as he could not be well placed in England; in the mean while the pope sendeth him with a monk's habit into the abbey of Pontigny in France, where he remained two years; from thence he removed to Senon, where he abode five years. So the time of his exile continued seven years in all.

A consultation between the pope and the cardinals about Becket's matter.

Becket in banishment seven years.

Upon this, the king, being certified by his ambassadors of the pope's answer, how his favour inclined more to Becket than to him, was moved (and worthily) with wrathful displeasure; and upon the same sailing from England into Normandy, he sent over certain injunctions directed against the pope and the archbishop of Canterbury, as were recited before, the contents of which commence thus:—"If any person should be found to bring from the pope, or from the archbishop of Canterbury," &c.

Of these, and such other injunctions, Becket specifieth partly in a certain letter, writing to a friend of his in this manner:[1]

Thomas, archbishop of Canterbury, to his well-beloved friend, &c. Be it known to your brotherly goodness, that we, with all ours here, by God's grace, are safe and in good health. Having a good hope and trust in your faithful amity, I charge you and require you, that either by the bringer hereof, or by some other, whom ye know faithful and trusty to our church of Canterbury, and to us, you write with all speed what is done. As touching the king's decrees here set out, these they be: That all havens and ports should be diligently kept; that no letters of the pope's interdict or curse be brought in; and, if religious men bring them in, they shall have their feet cut off; if he be a priest or clerk, he shall lose his eyes;[2] if he be a layman, let him be hanged; if he be a leper let him be burned. And if any bishop, for fear of the pope's interdict, will depart, besides his staff only in his hand, let him have nothing

(1) For the Latin, see the Edition of 1563, p. 54.—Ed.
(2) "Si clericus, oculos et genitalia amittat."—Latin.—Ed.

Henry II. A.D. 1166. else. Also the king's will is, that all scholars and students beyond the seas shall repair home, or else lose their benefices. And if they yet shall remain, they shall lose the liberty of ever returning. Further, if any such priests shall be found, that for the pope's suspense or interdict will refuse to sing, they shall be shamefully mutilated.[1] In fine, all such priests as show themselves rebels to the king, let them be deprived of their benefices," &c.

A.D. 1166. Besides these and such like injunctions, it was also set forth by the king's proclamation, A.D. 1166, that all manner of persons, both men and women, whosoever were found of the kindred of Thomas Becket, should be exiled, without taking any part of their goods with them, and sent to him where he was; which was no little vexation to Becket to behold them. Moreover, forasmuch as he then was lying with Gwarine, abbot of Pontigny, to whom the pope, as is aforesaid, had commended him; therefore the king, writing to the same abbot, required him not to retain the archbishop of Canterbury in his house, for if he did, he would drive out of his realm all the monks of his order.[2] Whereupon Becket was enforced to remove from thence, and went to Louis, the French king, by whom he was placed at Sens, and there was found of him the space of five years, as is above mentioned.

Becket's kindred banished.

In the mean time, messengers went daily with letters between the king and the pope, between the pope again and him, and also between the archbishop and others, whereof, if the reader, peradventure, shall be desirous to see the copies, I have thought here to express certain of them, to satisfy his desire; first beginning with the epistle of Becket, complaining of his prince to the pope, in manner and form as followeth.

Becket complaineth of his prince to the pope.

The copy of an Epistle sent by Thomas Becket to Pope Alexander.[3]

To your presence and audience I flee, most holy father, that you, who have bought the liberty of the church with your so great danger, might the rather attend to the same, either being the only or chief cause of my persecution, using and following therein your example. It grieveth me that the state of the church should fall to any decay, and that the liberties thereof should be infringed through the avarice of princes. For the which cause I thought to resist betimes that inconvenience beginning so to grow; and the more I thought myself obliged to the same, my prince, unto whom next under God I am most chiefly bound, the more boldness I took to me, to withstand his unrightful attempts, till such as were on the contrary part, my adversaries, prevailed, working my disquietness, and incensing him against me. Whereupon, as the manner is amongst princes, they raised up against me citations and slanders, to the occasion of my persecution; but I had rather be proscribed than subscribe. Besides this, I was also called to judgment, and cited before the king to make answer there as a lay person, to secular accounts, and while they whom I most trusted did most forsake me; for I saw my fellow-brethren, the bishops, through the instigation of some, ready to my condemnation. Whereupon, all being set against me, and I thus oppressed on every side, I took my refuge to appeal to your goodness, which casteth off none in their extremities, being ready to make my declaration before you, that I ought neither to be judged there in that place, nor yet of them. For what were that, father, but to usurp to themselves your right, and to bring the spiritualty under the temporalty? which thing, once begun, may breed an example to many. And therefore so much the more stout I thought to be in withstanding this matter, how much more prone and inclined I saw the way to hurt, if they might once see us to be

(1) See Note 2, p. 219.—Ed.
(2) These monks were of the Cistercian order.
(3) For the Latin, see the Edition of 1563, p. 54.—Ed.

faint and weak in the same. But they will say to me here again: "Give to Cæsar that which belongs to Cæsar," &c. But, to answer again thereunto: albeit we are bound to obey our king in most things, yet not in such manner of things, whereby he is made to be no king; neither were they then things belonging to Cæsar, but to a tyrant; concerning the which points these bishops should not for me only, but for themselves, have resisted the king. For if the extreme judgment be reserved to him who is able to judge both body and soul, is it not then extreme pride for men there to judge, who judge but by themselves? If the cause of the bishops and of the clergy, which I maintain, be right, why be they set against me? why do they reprehend me? For if I appealed to him, before whom either it was not lawful, or else not expedient for me so to do, what seem they by this, but either to blame me causeless, or else to distrust your equity? For me to be convicted before your holiness, it had been a double confusion. Or wherein have I deserved to be persecuted of them, for whose cause I have set myself to stand in their behalf? And if they had willed, I had prevailed; but it is ill with the head, when it is left of its members and forsaken; as if the eyes should take the tongue to speak against the head. If they had had eyes to have foreseen the matter, they might understand themselves to speak their own destruction, and that the princes did use their help but to their own servitude. And what so great cause of hatred had they against me, to procure their own undoing in undoing of me? So while they neglected spiritual things for temporal, they have lost them both. What should I speak more of this, that I repugning them, and appealing to your audience, they yet durst presume to stand in judgment and condemnation against me, as children against their father. Yea, and not against me only, but against the universal church of God, conspiring together with the prince being with me offended. And this suspicion might also as well pertain to you, holy father. But to this they will say, that they owe their duty and service unto the king, as their lord, to whom they are bound upon their allegiance. To whom I answer, that to him they stand bound bodily, to me spiritually. But to whom ought they rather to stand bound, than to themselves? And were it not better to sustain the loss of corporal than of spiritual things? But here they will say again; at this time the prince was not to be provoked. How subtilly do these men dispute for their own bondage? Yea, they themselves provoke him by their own excess, ministering wings unto him to fight against them; for he would have rested if they had resisted. And when is constancy more to be required, than in persecution? Be not a man's chief friends most tried in persecution? If they give over still, how shall they obtain the victory? Sometimes they must needs resist. Condescend, therefore, holy father, to my exile and persecution, and remember that I also once was a great man, in the time when it was; and now for your sake thus injuriously I am treated. Use your rigour, and restrain them by whose instigation the name of this persecution began, and let none of these things be imputed to the king, who rather is to be accounted the repairer than the author of this business.

To keep under the pride of prelates is no cause sufficient to un-king a prince.

If ye mean by spiritual things, such as pertain to the spiritual part of man, I grant; but your liberties be not as pertain to the inward or spiritual man, but rather are things more corporal.

Persecution trieth a true friend, but every cause maketh not a true persecution.

Besides this epistle sent to the pope, he writeth also another, sent to the king, in Latin, the tenor whereof he that is disposed to read may peruse in our former edition,[1] with notes adjoined withal.

(1) An Epistle of Becket, archbishop of Canterbury, to King Henry, found only in the edition of 1563, at page 55, with the notes, probably of John Foxe, adjoined.—Ed.

Desiderio desideravi videre faciem vestram et loqui vobiscum.[1] Non multum quidem propter me, sed maxime propter vos: ut visa facie mea reduceretis ad memoriam servitia, quæ, dum agerem in obsequio vestro, exhibui vobis devote et fideliter juxta animi conscientiam. Sic me Deus adjuvet in examine ultimo, quando omnes astabunt ante tribunal ipsius, recepturi prout gesserunt in corpore, sive bonum, sive malum, et ut moveremini super me pietate, quem oportet mendicando vivere inter alienos. Licet tamen Dei gratia, cum abundantia victualia ad sufficientiam habeamus. Estque nobis consolatio multa, quod dicit apostolus: omnes qui pie volunt vivere in Christo, persecutionem patientur. Et propheta: non vidi justum derelictum, nec semen ejus quærens panem. Propter vos: tribus ex causis. Tum quia dominus meus estis: tum quia rex meus estis: tum quia filius meus spiritualis.[2] Eò quòd dominus debeo vobis et offero concilium meum et obse-

Certain Notes upon this Latin Epistle.

1. Imo maxime suum agit negocium etiamsi dissimulat sedulo.

2. Si dominus est, cur te non prebes illi servum? Si rex, cur non subditum ostendis? porro quum servus non sui sit juris, sed in possessione sui domini, quo jure ergo servum agis fugitium, ab eo aufugiens, qui jure tui vendicat possessionem? atque in te potestatem occupat? preterea si dominum tuum esse agnoscas falso igitur illi te consilium debere dicis. In servo enim non consilium spectatur, sed obsequium nisi is consilium exigat.

Henry II. A.D. 1066.

Besides which epistle to the king in Latin, he sent also one or two more to the said King Henry II., much after the like rate and sort: one thus beginning, "Loqui de Deo, liberæ mentis est et valde quietæ. Inde est quod loquar ad Dominum meum, et utinam ad omnes pacifi-

quium quodcunque debet episcopus secundum honorem Dei et sanctæ ecclesiæ, domino. Eo quod rex, teneor vobis ad reverentiam et commonitionem. Eò quod filius, officii ratione, ad castigationem teneor et cohercionem. Corripit enim pater filium nunc blandis nunc asperis, ut vel sic provocet eum ad benefaciendum. Nosse debetis vos gratia regem esse, primo quia vos ipsum regere debetis vitamque vestram optimis informare moribus, ut vestri exemplo cæteri provocentur ad melius.[3] Juxta illud sapientis: Componitur orbis regis ad exemplum. Secundo, alios hos demulcendo, alios puniendo potestatis auctoritate quam ab ecclesia recepistis tum sacramento unctionis, tum gladii officio, quem gestastis ad malefactores ecclesiæ conterendos. Inunguntur enim reges tribus in locis, in capite, in pectore, in brachiis. Quod significat gloriam, scientiam, et fortitudinem. Qui antiquis temporibus justificationes Dei non observabant, et prævaricati sunt mandata ejus; his sublata est gloria, scientia, et fortitudo,[4] et eorum generationi. Exemplo Pharaonis, Nebugodonosor, Saulis, Salomonis, aliorumque plurium. Qui vero post delictum suum, cordis contritione humiliaverunt se domino: his Dei gratia accessit cum omnibus supradictis abundantiis, et perfectius. Sicut David, Ezechiæ, aliisque quam plurimis Christus fundavit matrem ecclesiam, ejusque comparavit[5] libertatem sanguine proprio, sustinendo flagella sputa, clavos, mortis angustias, nobis relinquens exemplum at sequamur vestigia ejus. Unde dicit apostolus: si compatiamur ei, et conregnabimus: si commoriamur, et resurgemus. Ecclesia enim Dei in duobus constat ordinibus, clero, et populo. In clero sunt apostoli, apostolicique viri, episcopi, et cæteri doctores ecclesiæ, quibus commissa est cura et regnum ipsius ecclesiæ, qui tractare habent negocia ecclesiastica, ut totum reducant ad salutem animarum. Unde et[6] Petro dictum est, et in Petro aliis rectoribus ecclesiarum, non regibus, non principibus: Tu es Petrus, et super hanc petram ædificabo ecclesiam meam, et portæ inferi non prævalebunt adversus eam. In populo sunt reges, et principes, duces, comites, et aliæ potestates, qui secularia habent tractare negotia, et totum reducant ad pacem et unitatem ecclesiæ. Et quia certum est reges potestatem suam accipere ab ecclesia, non ipsam ab illis, sed a Christo, ut salva pace vestra loquar, non habetis episcopis[7] præcipere, absolvere aliquem, vel excommunicare, trahere clericos ad secularia examina judicare de decimis, vel ecclesiis, interdicere episcopis ne tractent causas, de transgressione fidei vel juramenti, et multa in hunc modum quæ scripta sunt inter consuetudines vestras, quas dicitis avitas. Dominus enim dicit: leges meas custodite. Et per prophetam: Væ qui condunt leges iniquas et scribentes scripserunt injustitias, ut opprimerent pauperes in judicio, et vim facerent causæ humilium populi Dei. Audiat namque, si placet, dominus meus concilium fidelis sui, commonitionem episcopi sui, castigationem,[8] patris sui. Ne cum schismaticis de cætero habeat aliquam familiaritatem, vel communionem, nec cum eis aliquo modo contrahat fœdus vel amicitiam. Notum est enim toti fere mundo, quam devote, quam honorifice dom. papam receperatis, quantum ecclesiam Romanam foveritis, et honoraveritis, quantumque dom. papa, et etiam ecclesia Romana personam vestram dilexerint, honoraverint, et in quibuscumque secundum Deum potuerint vos exaudierunt. Nolite, Domine mi, ergo si salutem animæ vestræ desideratis, eidem ecclesiæ, quod suum est, aliqua ratione subtrahere, seu in aliquo ei citra justitiam contraire. Imo eamdam ei permittatis in regno vestro habere[9] libertatem, quam in aliis regnis habere dinoscitur. Memores quoque sitis confessionis quam fecistis, et posuistis scriptam super altare apud Westminster, de servanda ecclesiæ libertate, quando consecrati fuistis, et uncti in regem a prædecessore nostro Theobaldo. Ecclesiam etiam Cantuariensem a qua promotionem et consecrationem accepistis, in eum statum restituatis et dignitatem, in quibus fuit temporibus prædecessorum nostrorum,[10] possessiones etiam ad ipsam ecclesiam et ad nos pertinentes villas, prædia, castella, et omnia quæ pro voluntate vestra distribuistis res et omnes ablatas tam nostras quam clericorum nostrorum et laicorum in integrum nobis restituatis. Permittatis etiam, si placet, nos libere, et in pace, et cum omni securitate redire in sedem nostram, officioque nostro libere uti, sicut debemus, et ratio exigit. Et nos vobis tanquam domino charissimo et regi parati sumus fideliter et devote pro viribus servire in quibuscunque potuerimus, salvo honore Dei et ecclesiæ Romanæ et salvo ordine nostro.[11] Alioque pro certo sciatis, quia divinam severitatem et ulcionem sentietis.

---

3. Subditorum est subjici suis principibus, non eos subdere episcopi sunt subditi, suis principibus. Ergo male conantur episc. suos sibi principes subjicere. Ad principis spectat officium legibus animadvertere in sontes: Becketus id non permittit, prohibens clericos suos ad supplicia vocari. Ergo Becketus non se prestat subditum suo regi.

4. Nego argument. Deus punivit malos principes contra mandata sua delinquentes. Ergo pontifices et episcopi punire reges debent, sua decreta transgredientes.

5. Fallacia est a falsa definitione libertatis ecclesiasticæ. Ea enim libertas quam Christus suo sanguine comparavit, ad conscientiam duntaxat attinet, non ad terrena privilegia, aut corporeas facultates. Christus igitur aliam nobis redemit libertatem, Becketus de alia argutatur.

6. Quod Petro dictum est, dictum est tantum rectoribus ecclesiæ. Principes non sunt rectores ecclesiæ. Ergo non dictum est principibus. Resp. Neganda est minor, deinde majorem sic intelligo ex Aug. Quod dictum est Petro, ductum est ecclesiæ universe fidelium, quatenus fidem habet in Christum. Super quam fidem edificatur ecclesia unde liquet dictum hoc non magis spectare ad clerum quam ad principes fideles, &c.

7. Fallacia est a divisis ad conjuncta. Sunt enim variæ in ecclesia Christi functionesque variæ sunt ad alios atque alios referendæ. Quæ vero foris sunt et juris ordinesque externi, et ad castigationē attinent, propria sunt principum. Tantum ad clerum spectat dispensatio sermonis Dei, et sacramentorum administratio. Jam hæc omniaque disjungenda erant, perperam confundit hic theologus in una persona.

8. Episcopi si probi fuerint dici fortasse patres possunt suorum principum, sed in Christo tamen, hoc est, non nisi in eisque ad salutis tantum curam, doctrinæ videlicet et sacramentorum spectant. In ceteris vero principes patres sunt, et curam gerunt episcoporum non ille principum.

9. Iterum hic peccatur in falsa libertatis definitione.

10. Ut facile hic intelligas lector suam dignitatem et possessiones quæri ab episcopis, potius quam gloriam Jesu Christi.

11. Proximus honor secundum Deum debetur regibus in sua cujusque ditione, juxta scripturæ theologiam, quæ dicit: Deum timete, regem honorificate: at contra hic theologus inverso scripturæ ordine arguit, honorem Deo proximum deberi, primum Romanæ sedi, deinde episcoporum ordini et post hæc regibus.

cum," &c. Which epistle, for that I would not overcharge the volume of these histories with too much matter superfluous, I thought here to omit. The other he sent afterwards, whereof the words be these:—

Another Letter of Becket, sent to King Henry II.[1]

To his lord and friend Henry, by the grace of God, king of England, duke of Normandy and Aquitain, earl of Anjou: Thomas, by the same grace, humble minister of the church of Canterbury, (sometime his temporally, but now more his in the Lord), health and true repentance with amendment. I have long looked for that the Lord would look upon you, and that you would convert and repent, departing from your perverse way; and cut off from you your wicked and perverse counsellors, by whose instigation, as it is thought, you are fallen into that deep, whereof the Psalm speaketh, "A sinner, when he cometh to the depth of mischiefs, is without all care or fear." And albeit we have hitherto quietly suffered and borne, considering and earnestly looking if there would any messenger come that would say: "Your sovereign lord, the king, who now a long time hath erred and been deceived, and led even to the destruction of the church, through God's mercy, with abundant humility, doth now again make speed for the deliverance of the church, and to make satisfaction and amendment;" yet notwithstanding we cease not, day by day, continually to call upon Almighty God with most humble devotion, that that which we have long desired for you, and by you, we may speedily obtain with abundant effect. And this is one point, that the care of the church of Canterbury, whereunto God hath presently appointed us albeit unworthy, you being king, doth specially constrain me, in that as yet we are detained in exile, to write unto your majesty letters commonitory, exhortatory, and of correction. But I would to God they were fully able to correct, lest that I be too great a cloaker of your outrages, if there be any, as indeed there are; for the which we are not a little sorry. I mean especially of them which are done by you in every place, about the church of God and the ecclesiastical persons, without any reverence either of dignity or person; and lest also that I appear negligent to the great danger of my soul; for without doubt he beareth the offence of him which doth commit any offence, who neglecteth to correct that which another ought to amend; for it is written, "Not only they which do commit evil, but also they that consent thereunto, are counted partakers of the same." For they verily do consent, who, when they both might and ought, do not resist, or at the least reprove; for the error which is not resisted is allowed, and the truth, when it is not defended, is oppressed; neither doth it lack a privy note of society in him, who ceaseth to withstand a manifest mischief.[2] For like as, most noble prince, a small city doth not diminish the prerogative of so mighty a kingdom as yours, so your royal power ought not to oppress or change the measure of the religious dispensation; for it is provided always by the laws, that all judgments against priests should proceed by the determination of priests; for whatsoever bishops they are, albeit that they do err as other men do, not exceeding in any point contrary to the religion of faith, they ought not, nor can in any case be judged of the secular power.[3] Truly it is the part of a good and religious prince to repair the ruinous churches, to build new, to honour the priests, and with great reverence to defend them, after the example of the godly prince of most happy memory, Constantine,[4] who said, when a complaint

Certain Notes or Elenches upon this Epistle.

1. The scope of this epistle is this, to prove that bishops and priests ought not to come under the covert and controlment of temporal power.

2. This similitude holdeth not. For, though the smallness of a city blemisheth not the prerogative of a kingdom, yet the evilness and rebellion of a city do worthily blemish its own prerogative.

3. So saith the pope's decree, (Dist. 10), but the scripture of God importeth otherwise. Abiathar the priest was deposed by King Solomon, not for any heresy, but for other causes; (3 Reg. 12). Jonathas took his priesthood of King Alexander; and Simon, of Demetrius, (1 Maccab. vii.) Christ offered tribute to Cæsar for himself and for Peter. Also Peter saith, "Be ye subject to every human creature;" and it followeth, "whether it be to the king as to the chief," &c. Also Pope Leo submitted himself to Ludovicus, the emperor, with these words: "And if we do any thing incompetently, and do swerve from the path of righteousness, we will stand to your reformation, or of them whom you shall send." (Quæst. ii. Hos. vii.)

4. Notwithstanding, the said Constantine, writing to the bishops congregated at Tyre, first chideth them, then commandeth them to resort unto his presence, to have their cause judged and decided. (Trip. Hist. lib. iii. cap. 7.)

Henry II. of the clergy was brought to him, "You," said he, "can be judged by no secular judge, who are reserved to the only judgment of God." And forsomuch as we

A.D. 1166. do read that the holy apostles and their successors, appointed by the testimony of God, commanded that no persecution nor troubles ought to be made, nor to envy those which labour in the field of the Lord, and that the stewards of the Eternal King should not be expelled and put out of their seats; who then doubteth, but that the priests of Christ ought to be called the fathers and masters of all other faithful princes? Is it not a miserable madness, then, if the son should go about to bring the father under obedience,[5] or the scholar his master? and by wicked bonds[6] to bring him in subjection, by whom he ought to believe that he may be bound and loosed, not only in earth, but also in heaven? If you be a good and a catholic king, and one as we hope, or rather desire you should be (be it spoken under your license), you are the child of the church, and not the ruler of the church. You ought to learn of the priests, and not to teach them; you ought to follow the priests in ecclesiastical matters,[7] and not to go before them, having the privilege of your power given you of God to make public laws, that, by his benefits, you should not be unthankful against the dispensation of the heavenly order, and that you should usurp nothing, but use them with a wholesome disposition.

Wherefore, in those things which, contrary unto that, you have, through your malicious counsel, rather than by your own mind wickedly usurped; with all humility and satisfaction speedily give place, that the hand of the Most Highest be not stretched out against you, as an arrow against the mark. For the Most Highest hath bended his bow openly to shoot against him that will not confess his offences. Be not ashamed, whatsoever wicked men say to you, or that traitors do whisper in your ear, to humble yourself under the mighty hand of God; for it is he who exalteth the humble, and throweth down the proud; who also revengeth himself upon princes; he is terrible, and who shall resist him? You ought not to have let slip out of your memory, in what state God did find you; how he hath preferred, honoured, and exalted you; blessed you with children, enlarged your kingdom, and established the same in despite of your enemies; insomuch that hitherto, in a manner, all men have said with great admiration, that this is he whom God hath chosen. And how will you reward, or can you reward him for all these things which he hath done unto you? Will you,—at the provocation and instance of those who are about you, that persecute the church, and the ecclesiastical ministers,[8] and always have according to their power persecuted them, rendering evil for good, bringing oppressions, tribulations, injuries, and afflictions upon the church and churchmen,—do the like? Are not these they of whom the Lord speaketh: "He that heareth you, heareth me; he that despiseth you, despiseth me; and he that toucheth you, toucheth the apple of mine eye." Verily, forsaking all that thou hast, take up thy cross, that thou mayest follow thy God, our Lord Jesus Christ. Yet will it scarcely be, or not at all, that thou shalt appear a thankful recompenser of the benefits received at his hand. Search the Scriptures with such as are learned, and you shall understand that Saul, albeit he was the elect of the Lord, perished with his whole house, because he departed from the ways of the Lord.[9]

Uzziah also, king of Judah, whose name is spoken of and spread over all, through the manifold victories given him of God, his heart was so puffed up to his destruction, because the Lord did help and strengthen him in every place,

5. "The father under obedience," &c. If fatherhood go by age, I suppose that King Henry was older than Becket. If fatherhood consist in authority, I judge the authority of a king to be above the authority of an archbishop. If the see of Canterbury make the fatherhood, yet had Becket no cause to claim fatherhood over the king, seeing the son ordained the father; that is, seeing the king made him his archbishop, and he made not him his king.

6. "By wicked bonds." All is wicked with the papists, that bringeth them in subjection to their princes.

7 Ecclesiastical matters be such, as properly belong to doctrine and divine knowledge, for the institution of the soul, and information of conscience. In which both princes and subjects ought to follow the pastors, so long as they go truly before them without error, or else not. But what maketh this for the lands and liberties of churchmen?

8. Punishment due to malefactors and rebels is not to be called persecution, but due correction.

9. Saul brake the commandment of God and was rejected. Ozias, contrary to the commandment of God, took the office of a priest, and was stricken. Oza, against the express word of the law, put his hand to the ark, and was punished. But what express word had King Henry, why he should not correct and punish rebellious bishops, and wicked priests, within his own realm? wherefore these similitudes accord not. As for Achas, he was not so much punished for taking the priest's office, as for spoiling the temple of the Lord, and offering to idols.

that he, contemning the fear and reverence of the Lord, would usurp unto himself that which was not his office, that is to say, the priesthood, and offer incense upon the altar of the Lord, for the which he was stricken with a leprosy, and cast out of the house of the Lord. Many other kings and holy men of great substance, because they have walked above their estate in the marvels of the world, presuming to rebel against God in his ministries, have perished, and, at the last, have found nothing of their substance in their power. Also King Ahaz, because he did usurp the office of priesthood, was likewise stricken with a leprosy by God.

Oza also, albeit he was not king, yet forasmuch as he touched the ark and held it, when it would have fallen by the unruliness of the oxen, which thing pertained not unto him, but unto the ministers of the church, was stricken by the wrath of God, and fell down dead by the ark. O king! it is a famous proverb, "That a man, forewarned by another man's misfortune, will take the better heed unto himself." For every man hath his own business in hand when his neighbour's house is on fire.

Dearly beloved king, God would have the disposing of those things which pertain unto the church, to belong only unto priests, and not unto the secular power. Do not challenge unto thyself therefore another man's right, neither strive against him by whom all things are ordained, lest thou seem to strive against his benefits from whom thou hast received thy power. For not by the common laws,[10] and by the secular power, but by the bishops and priests, Almighty God would have the clergy of the christian religion to be ordered and ruled. And christian kings ought to submit all their doings unto ecclesiastical rulers, and not to prefer themselves; for it is written, that none ought to judge the bishops but only the church, neither doth it pertain unto man's law to give sentence upon any such. Christian princes are accustomed to be obedient unto the statutes and ordinances of the church, and not to prefer their own power. A prince ought to submit himself unto the bishops, and not to judge the bishops; for there are two things wherewith the world is chiefly governed, that is to say, the sacred authority of bishops, and royal power,[11] in the which the bishops' charge is so much the more weighty, in that they shall at the latter judgment render account even of the kings themselves. Truly you ought to understand, that you depend upon their judgment, and cannot reduce them unto your own will; for many bishops have excommunicated both kings and emperors. And if you require an especial example thereof, Innocent, the pope, did excommunicate Arcadius, the emperor, because he did consent that John Chrysostome should be expulsed from his seat; and St. Ambrose also did excommunicate Theodosius, the great emperor,[12] for a fault which seemed not so weighty unto other priests, and shut him out of the church, who, afterwards, by condign satisfaction was absolved.

There are many other like examples. For David, when he had committed adultery and murder, the prophet Nathan was sent unto him by God to reprove him, and he was soon corrected: and the king (laying aside his sceptre and diadem, and setting apart all princely majesty) was not ashamed to humble himself before the face of the prophet, to confess his fault, and to require forgiveness for his offence. What will you more? He, being stricken with repentance, asked mercy, and obtained forgiveness. So likewise you, most beloved king and reverend lord! after the example of this good king David, of whom it is said, "I have found a man after mine own heart," with a contrite and humble heart turn to the Lord your God, and take hold of repentance for your transgressions. For you have fallen and erred in many things, which yet I keep in store still, if (peradventure) God shall inspire you to say with the

10. "Common laws." St. Austin, writing to Boniface, saith thus: "Whosoever obeyeth not the laws of the emperor, being made for the verity of God, procureth to himself great punishment. For in the time of the prophets, all the kings which did not forbid and subvert all such things as were used of the people against the law of God, are rebuked. And such as did withstand them, are commended above the rest."

11. Isidorus hath these words: "Let temporal princes know that they must render account to God for the church, which they have at the hands of God to govern," &c.

12. The cases of Arcadius, Theodosi[illegible]avid, and of this king, as touching this matter, have no similitude. In them was murder: this king doth nothing but claim that which is his due. And though by the spiritual sword those kings were resisted, yet it agreeth not therefore that the persons of those who have the use of the spiritual sword are above the persons of those who have the temporal sword.

Henry II. A.D. 1166.

prophet, "Have mercy on me, O God, according to thy great mercy, for I have sinned much against thee, and done evil in thy sight." Thus much I have thought good to write to you, my dear lord, at this present, passing other things in silence, till I may see whether my words take place in you, and bring forth fruits worthy of repentance; and that I may hear and rejoice with them that shall bring me word and say, "O king! thy son was dead, and is alive again; was lost, and is found again.'" But if you will not hear me, look where I was wont before the majesty of the body of Christ to pray for you in abundance of tears and sighs; there in the same place I will cry against you, and say, Rise up, Lord, and judge my cause; forget not the rebukes and injuries which the king of England doth to thee and thine; forget not the ignominy of thy church, which thou hast builded in thy blood. Revenge the blood of thy saints which is spilt; revenge, O Lord, the afflictions of thy servants, of which there is an infinite number. For the pride of them which hate and persecute thee is gone up so high, that we are not able to bear them any longer. Whatsoever your servants shall do, all those things shall be required at your hands: for he seemeth to have done the harm, who hath given the cause thereof. Doubtless, the Son of the Most Highest, except you amend and cease from the oppressing of the church and clergy, and keep your hand from troubling of them, will come in the rod of his fury, at the voices of such as cry to him, and at the sighs of them that be in bands; when the time shall come for him to judge the unrighteousness of men in equity and severity of the Holy Ghost. For he knoweth how to take away the breath of princes, and is terrible among kings of the earth. Your dear and loving grace, I wish well to fare. Thus fare ye well again and ever.

Note the judgment of God against this Becket, who was slain at his mass, making the body of Christ.

Besides these letters of the archbishop sent to the king,[1] the pope also, in the same cause, writeth to the king:[2] the whole tenor of whose letter I would here express, but for protracting of the time and for straitness of room, having so many things else in this story (by the grace of Christ) to be comprehended. But the letter tendeth to this effect: to exhort and charge the king to show favour to Thomas Becket; where, in the process of the epistle, it followeth to this effect: "Therefore we do desire, admonish, and exhort your honour, by these our apostolical writings, and also enjoin you upon the remission of your sins, in the behalf of Almighty God, and of St. Peter, prince of the apostles, by our authority, that you receive again the aforesaid archbishop into your favour and grace, for the honour of God, his church, and of your own realm," &c. Thus have you heard the pope's entreating letter. Now here is another letter sent unto the aforesaid king, wherein he doth menace him, as in the tenor thereof here followeth.

Bishop Alexander, servant of the servants of God, to Henry, king of England, health and blessing apostolical.[3]

How fatherly and gently we have ofttimes entreated and exhorted, both by legates and letters, your princely honour to be reconciled again with our reverend brother, Thomas, archbishop of Canterbury, so that he and his may be restored again to their churches and other possessions to them appertaining, your wisdom is not ignorant, seeing it is notified and spread almost throughout all Christendom. Forasmuch therefore as hitherto we could not prevail with you, neither move nor stir your mind with fair and gentle words, it lamenteth us not a

(1) The pope's letter beginneth after this sort: "Alexander papa ad Henricum regem. Et naturali ratione, et forma juris dictante, providentiam tuam credimus edoctam fuisse, quod quanto quis ab aliquo majora suscepisse dignoscitur, tanto ei obnoxior, et magis obligatus tenetur," &c.

(2) "Ea propter severitatem tuam per apostolica scripta rogamus, monemus, et exhortamur in Domino; necnon in remissionem peccatorum ex parte Dei omnipotentis, et beati Petri principis apostolorum, auctoritate nostra injungimus, ut memoratum archiepiscopum pro Deo et ecclesia sua, et honore tuo, necnon et totius regni tui, in gratiam et favorum tuum recipias," &c.

(3) The Latin copy is in the Edition of 1563, p. 57.—Ed.

little, so to be frustrated and deceived of the hope and expectation which we had conceived of you: especially seeing we love you so dearly, as our own dearly beloved son in the Lord, and understand such great jeopardy to hang over you.

But forasmuch as it is written; "Cry out, and cease not; lift up thy voice like a trumpet, and declare to my people their wickedness, and their sins to the house of Jacob:" also forasmuch as it is in Solomon commanded, that the sluggish person should be stoned with the dung of oxen: we have thought good therefore, not to forbear or support your stubbornness any longer against justice and salvation, neither that the mouth of the aforesaid archbishop should be stopped from henceforth any more; but that he may freely prosecute the charge of his office and duty, and revenge with the sword of ecclesiastical discipline, the injuries both of himself, and of his church committed to his charge.

And here I have sent unto you two legates, Petrus de ponte Dei, and Bernardus de Corilio, to admonish you of the same. But if ye will neither by us be advised, nor give ear unto them in obeying, it is to be feared, doubtless, lest such things as they shall declare to you from us in our behalf may happen and fall upon you. —Dated at Beneventum, the ninth day before the kalends of June.

To answer these letters again, there was a certain other writing drawn out and directed to the pope, made by some of the clergy, as it seemeth, but not without consent of the king, as by the title may appear, inveighing and disproving the misbehaviour of the archbishop. The tenor thereof here followeth, and beginneth thus:—

An Answer to the Pope.[1]

Time now requireth more to seek help than to make complaints. For so it is now, that the holy mother church (our sins deserving the same), lieth in a dangerous case of great decay, which is like to ensue, except the present mercy of the Lord support her.

Such is the wickedness now of schismatics, that the father of fathers, Pope Alexander, for the defence of his faith and for the love of righteousness, is banished out of his country, unable to keep free residence in his own proper see, by reason of the obdurate heart of Frederic, the Pharaoh.

Nay, rather for false treason, against the emperor his prince. Frederic falsely compared to Pharaoh; but this was to claw the pope withal.

Further and besides, the church also of Canterbury is miserably impaired and blemished, as well in the spiritual as in the temporal estate: much like a ship in the sea, destitute of her guide, tossed in the floods, and wrestling with the winds. The pastor, being absent from his province, dare not there return through the power of the king, who, being over wise (to the jeopardy of himself, his church, and us also), hath brought and entangled us likewise with himself in the same partaking of his punishments and labours, not considering how we ought to forbear, and not to resist superior powers. And also he showeth himself to us unkind, who with all our affections bear the burden with him of his afflictions, not ceasing yet to persecute us who stand in the same condemnation with him. For, betwixt him and our sovereign prince, the king of England, arose a certain matter of contention, whereupon they were both agreed, that a day should be appointed to have the controversy discussed by equity and justice.

The day being come, the king commanded all the archbishops, bishops, and other prelates of the church, to be called to a great and solemn frequency: so that the greater and more general this council was, the more manifest the detection of this stubborn malice should appear and be espied.

At the day therefore above mentioned, this troubler of the realm and of the church presenteth himself in the sight of our catholic king; who, not trusting the quality and condition of his cause, armeth him with the armour of the cross, as one who should be brought to the presence of a tyrant. By reason whereof, the king's majesty being somewhat aggrieved, yet, because he would be delivered from all suspicion, committeth the matter to the hearing of the bishops. This done, it rested in the bishops to decide and cease this contention, and to set agreement between them, removing all occasion of dissension. Which thing they going about, this aforesaid archbishop cometh in, forbidding and commanding, that no man proceed in any sentence of him before the king.

(1) The Latin copy is in the Edition of 1563, p. 57.—Ed.

Henry II.

A.D. 1166.

This being signified in the king's hearing, his mind was grievously provoked thereby to anger: whose anger yet notwithstanding had been easily assuaged, if the other would have submitted himself, and acknowledged his default. But he, adding stubbornness to his trespass, through the quantity and greatness of his excess, was the author of his own punishment; which now by the law civil he sustaineth, and yet shameth to crave pardon for his desert at the king's hand; whose anger he feared not to stir up, in such a troublesome time of the persecution of the church, greatly against the profit of the same; augmenting and increasing thereby the persecution which now the church lieth under. Much better it had been for him to have tempered himself with the bridle of moderation, in the high estate of his dignity; lest in exceeding too far in straining the strict points of things by overmuch presumption, peradventure through his presumption, being not in mean and tolerable things, he might fall from higher. And if the detriments of the church would not move him, yet the great benefits and preferments of riches and honours ought to persuade him not to be so stubborn against the king. But here peradventure his friend and our adversary will object, that his bearing and submitting to the king in this behalf, were prejudicial against the authority and see apostolical. As though he did not or might not understand, that although the dignity of the church should suffer a little detriment in that judgment, yet he might and ought to have dissembled (for the time) to obtain peace to the church. He will object again, alleging the name of father, that it soundeth like a point of arrogancy for children to proceed in judgment of condemnation against the father; which thing is not convenient. But he must understand again, that it was necessary that the obedience and humility of the children should temper the pride of the father; lest, afterward, the hatred of the father might redound upon the children. Wherefore, by these premises your fatherhood may understand, that the action of this our adversary ought to fall down as void, and of none effect, who only upon the affection of malice hath proceeded thus against us, having no just cause or reason to ground upon.

Becket a stubborn trespasser; ergo, no martyr.

And, forasmuch as the care and charge of all churches (as ye know) lieth upon us, it standeth upon us to provide concerning the state of the church of Canterbury, by our diligence and circumspection: so that the said church of Canterbury, through the excess of its pastor, be not driven to ruin or decay.

By this epistle it may appear to the reader thereof, that Becket, being absent from England, went about to work some trouble against certain of the clergy and the laity, belike in excommunicating such as he took to be his evil willers.

Now, to understand further what his working was, or who they were whom he did excommunicate, this letter, sent to William, bishop of Norwich, shall better declare the matter.

A Letter of Becket, to William, bishop of Norwich, wherein are contained the names of those whom he did excommunicate.[1]

He bindeth himself to the penalty of the crime, whosoever receiving power and authority of God, useth and exerciseth not the same with due severity, in punishing vice; but, winking and dissembling, doth minister boldness to wicked doers, maintaining them in their sin. For the blood of the wicked is required at the hand of the priest, who is negligent or dissembleth. And, as the Scripture saith, "Thorns and brambles grow in the hands of the idle drunkard." Wherefore, lest, through our too much sufferance and dissembling, the transgressions of manifest evildoers should also be laid to our charge, and redound to the destruction of the church through our guilty silence; we, therefore, following the authority of the pope's commandment, have laid our sentence of curse and excommunication upon the Earl Hugo: commanding you throughout all your diocese publicly to denounce the said earl as accursed; so that, according to the discipline of the church, he be sequestered from the fellowship of all faithful people. Also, it is not unknown to your brotherhood, how long we have borne with the transgressions of the bishop of London; who, amongst his other

(1) For the Latin, see Edition 1563, p. 58.—Ed.

Henry II. A.D. 1166.

acts, I would to God were not a great doer, and fautour of this schism, and subverter of the rites and liberties of holy church. Wherefore we, being supported with the authority of the apostolic see, have also excommunicated him; besides also the bishop of Salisbury, because of his disobedience and contempt, and others likewise, upon divers and sundry causes, whose names here follow subscribed: Hugo Bernard's son; Rodulph of Brock; Robert of Brock, a clerk; Hugo de St. Cleare, and Letard, a clerk of Norfolk; Nigel, of Scachanal, and Richard Chaplin; William of Hastings, and the friar who possesseth my church of Monchote. We therefore charge and command you, by the authority apostolical and ours, and by the virtue of obedience, and by the peril of salvation, and of your order, that ye cause these openly to be proclaimed excommunicate, throughout all your diocese, and command all the faithful to avoid their company. Fare ye well in the Lord. Let not your heart be troubled, nor fear; for we stand sure through the assistance of the apostolic see, God being our defence against the pretensed shifts of the malignant sort, and against all their appellations. Furthermore, all such as have been solemnly cited of us shall sustain the like sentence of excommunication, if God will, on the Ascension-day: unless they shall otherwise agree with me. That is, to wit, Geoffrey, archdeacon of Canterbury, and Robert his vicar; Rice of Wilcester, Richard of Lucy, William Giffard, Adam of Cherings, with such others more, who either at the commandment of the king, or upon their own proper temerity, have invaded the goods and possessions either appertaining to us, or to our clerks about us. With these also we do excommunicate all such as be known, either with aid or council, to have incensed or set forward the proceeding of our king against the liberties of the church, and exiling of the innocents, and such also as be known to impeach or hinder, by any manner of way, the messengers sent, either from the pope, or from us, for the necessities of the church. Fare you well again, and ever.

The bishop of London excommunicated; and Salisbury, because he set in the dean, without the license of him, being then beyond the seas.

Hitherto hast thou seen, gentle reader, divers and sundry letters of Thomas Becket, whereby thou mayest collect a sufficient history of his doings and demeanour, though nothing else were said further of him, concerning his lusty and haughty stomach, about that which beseemed either his degree or cause which he took in hand. And here peradventure I may seem, in the story of this one man, to tarry too long, having to write of so many others better than him: yet for the weaker sort, who have accounted him, and yet do account him a saint, having in themselves little understanding to judge or discern in the causes of men, I thought to add this letter more, wherein he complaineth of his king to a foreign power; doing what in him did lie to stir for his own cause mortal war to the destruction of many. For suppose wrong had been offered him of his prince, was it not enough for him to fly? What cause had he, for his own private revenge, to set potentates in public discord? Now, having no just cause, but rather offering injury in a false quarrel, so to complain of his prince; what is to be said of this, let every man judge who seeth this letter.

An Epistle of Thomas, archbishop of Canterbury, to Pope Alexander.[1]

To our most loving father and lord, Alexander, by the grace of God bishop, Thomas, the humble minister and servant of the church of Canterbury, due and reverend obedience. Long enough and too long, most loving father, have I forborn, still looking after amendment of the king of England, but no fruit have I reaped of this my long patience: nay rather, whilst that unwisely I do thus forbear, I augment and procure the detriment and diminishing of mine authority, as also of the church of God: for oftentimes have I, by devout and religious

A seditious complaint of Becket to the pope against his king.

(1) "Amantissimo patri et Dom. Alexandro, Dei gratia summo pont. Thomas Cant. ecclesiæ humilis minister, debitam et devotam obedientiam," &c. [The whole of this letter in Latin is given in the Edition of 1563, p. 59.—ED.]

Henry II. A.D. 1166.

messengers, invited him to make condign satisfaction; as also by my letters, the copies whereof I have sent you, intimated and pronounced God's severity and vengeance against him, unless he repent and amend. But he, that notwithstanding, groweth from evil to worse, oppressing and ravaging the church and sanctuary of God; persecuting both me and those who take part with me; insomuch that with fearful threatening words his purpose is to terrify such as, for God's cause and mine own, seek any way to relieve and help me. He wrote also letters unto the abbot of the Cistercian order, that, as he favoured the abbacy of that his order ("which was in his power," said he), he would not accept me into the fellowship thereof, nor do any thing else for me. Why should I use many words? So much hath the rigour and severity, as well of the king as of his officers, under our patience and sufferance, showed itself, that if a great number of men, yea, and that of the most religious sort, should show unto you the matter as it is indeed, and that upon their oath taken, I partly doubt whether your holiness would give credit unto them or not. With heaviness of mind, therefore, I considering these things, and beholding as well the peril of the king as of ourself, have publicly condemned not only those pernicious customs, but all those perversities and wicked doings whereby the church of England is disturbed and brought to confusion, as also the writing whereby they were confirmed; excommunicating generally, as well the observers and exactors thereof, as also the inventors and patrons of the same, with their favourers, counsellors, and coadjutors whatsoever, either of the clergy or laity; absolving also our bishops from their oath, whereby they were so strictly enjoined to the observation of the same. These are the articles which in that writing I have principally condemned:—That it is inhibited to appeal unto the see apostolical for any cause, but by the king's license. That a bishop may not punish any man for perjury, or for breaking of his troth. That a bishop may not excommunicate any man that holdeth of the king *in capite*, or else interdict either their lands or offices without the king's license. That clerks and religious men may be taken from us to secular judgment. That the king or any other judge may hear and decide the causes of the church and tithes. That it shall not be lawful for any archbishop or bishop to go out of the realm, and to come at the pope's call without the king's license: and divers others such as these. Namely, I have also excommunicated John of Oxenford, who hath communicated with the schismatic and excommunicate person, Reginald Coloniensis, who also, contrary to the commandment of the lord pope and ours, hath usurped the deanery of the church of Salisbury, and hath, to renew his schism, taken an oath in the emperor's court. Also I have denounced and excommunicated Richard of Worcester, because he is fallen into the same damnable heresy, and has communicated with that famous schismatic of Cologne; devising and forging all mischief possible, with the schismatics and Flemings, to the destruction of the church of God, and especially to the church of Rome, by composition made by the king of England and them. Also Richard de Lucy and Jocelin de Baliol, who have furthered the favours of the king's tyranny and workers of their heresies. Also Ranulph de Broc, and Hugo de Sancto Claro, and Thomas the son of Bernard, who have usurped the possessions and goods of the church of Canterbury without our license and consent. We have also excommunicated all those who, without our license, do stretch out their hands to the possessions and goods of the church of Canterbury. The king himself we have not yet excommunicated personally, still waiting for his amendment: whom, notwithstanding, we will not defer to excommunicate, unless he quickly amend, and be warned by that he hath done. And therefore, that the authority of the see apostolic, and the liberty of the church of God, which in these parts are almost utterly lost, may by some means be restored, it is meet and very necessary that what we have herein done, the same be of your holiness ratified, and by your letters confirmed. Thus I wish your holiness long to prosper and flourish.

Godly articles condemned by Becket.

By this epistle, he that listeth to understand of the doings and quarrels of Becket, may partly judge what is to be thought thereof; which doings of his, although in some part they may be imputed either to ignorance of mind or blindness of zeal, or human frailty,

Becket reprehended for complaining of his king.

yet, in this point, so vilely to complain of his natural prince, for the zeal of the pope, he can in no wise be defended. But such was the blindness of the prelates in those days, who measured and esteemed the dignity and liberty of Christ's church by no other thing, than only by goods and possessions flowing unto and abounding among the clergy; and who thought no greater point of religion to be in the church, than to maintain the same. For this cause they did most abominably abuse Christian discipline and excommunication of the church at that time; as by this aforesaid epistle may appear. And what marvel if the acts and doings of this archbishop seem now to us in these days both fond and strange, seeing the suffragans of his own church and clergy, writing to him, could not but reprehend him, as in this their epistle, translated out of Latin into English, may be seen.

Excommunication abused.

An effectual and pithy Letter, full of reason and persuasion, sent from all the suffragans of the church of Canterbury to Thomas Becket, their archbishop.[1]

Such troubles and perturbations as happened through the strangeness of your departure out of the realm, we hoped by your humility and prudence should have been reduced again (God's grace working withal) into a peaceable tranquillity. And it was no little joy to us, to hear so of you in those parts where you are conversant, how humbly you there behaved yourself, nothing vaunting yourself against your prince and king, and that you attempt no risings or wrestlings against his kingdom, but that you bore with much patience the burden of poverty, and gave yourself to reading and prayer, and to redeem the loss of your time spent, with fasting, watchings, and tears; and so, being occupied with spiritual studies, to tend and rise up to the perfection of virtue, &c. But now, through the secret relation of certain, we hear (that we are sorry of) that you have sent unto him a threatening letter, wherein there is no salvation premised; in the which also ye pretend no entreating nor prayers for the obtaining of favour, neither do use any friendly manner in declaring what you write, but, menacing with much austerity, threaten to interdict him, and to cut him from the society of the church. Which thing if you shall accomplish with like severity as in words ye threaten to do, you shall not only put us out of all hope of any peace, but also put us in fear of hatred and discord without measure, and without all redress amongst us. But wisdom will consider before the end of things, labouring and endeavouring to finish that which she wisely beginneth. Therefore your discretion shall do well diligently to forecast and consider whereto ye tend; what end may ensue thereof, and whereabout ye go. Certes, we, for our parts, hearing what we do hear, are discouraged from that we hoped for, who, having before some good comfort of tranquillity to come, are cast from hope to despair, so that while one is drawn thus against another, almost there is no hope or place left to make entreaty or supplication. Wherefore, writing to your fatherhood, we exhort and counsel you by way of charity, that you add not trouble to trouble, and heap injury upon injury; but that you so behave yourself, that, all menaces set aside, ye rather give yourself to patience and humility, and yield your cause to the clemency of God, and to the mercy of your prince; and in so doing you shall heap coals of charity upon the heads of many. Thus charity shall be kindled, and that which menacings cannot do, by God's help and good men's counsel, pity, peradventure, and godliness shall obtain. Better it were to sustain poverty with praise, than in great promotions to be a common note to all men. It is right well known unto all men, how beneficial the king hath been unto you; from what baseness to what dignity he hath advanced you; and also into his own familiarity hath so much preferred you, that from the North Ocean to the Mount Perineus he hath subdued all

(1) "Quæ vestro (pater) in longinquo discessu inopinata rei ipsius novitate turbata sunt; vestris sperabamus humilitate," &c.

Henry II. things to your authority: insomuch that they were amongst all others accounted for men right fortunate, whosoever could find any favour with you.

A. D. 1166. And furthermore, lest that your estimation should be over matched by any nobility, he (against the mind of his mother, and of his realm) hath placed and ratified you substantially in ecclesiastical dignity, and advanced you to this honour wherein ye stand; trusting, through your help and counsel, to reign more safely and prosperously. Now, if he shall find disquietness, wherein he trusted to have quietness, what shall all men say or think of you? What recompense or retribution shall this be thought to be for so many and great benefits taken? Therefore, if it shall please you, ye shall do well to favour and spare your fame and estimation, and to overcome your lord and sovereign with humility and charity; whereunto if our advertisement cannot move you, yet the love and fidelity you bear to the bishop and holy church of Rome ought to incline you thereunto, and not to attempt any such thing, whereby the troubles of the church, our mother, may increase, or whereby her dolour may be augmented in the loss of those, whose disobedience now she doth bewail: for what if it so happen through provocation, that the king, whom all his subjects and kingdoms obey, should relinquish the pope, which God forbid, and should deny all obedience to him, as he denieth to the king help or aid against you, what inconvenience would grow thereof? And think you he hath not great instigations, supplications, gifts, and many fair promises so to do? Yet he, notwithstanding, abideth firm hitherto in the rock, despising, with a valiant mind, all that the world can offer. This one thing feareth us, lest his mind whom no worldly offers can assail, no glory, riches, nor treasure can overturn, only through indignation of unkindness, be subverted; which thing if it chance to happen through you, then may you sit down and sing the song of the Lamentation of Jeremy, and weep your bellyful.

Consider therefore, if it please you, and foresee well with yourself, this purpose of yours, if it proceed, how hurtful and perilous it will be, not only to the pope, and to the holy church of Rome, but also to yourself most especially. But some, peradventure, about you, of haughty and high-minded stoutness, more stout perchance than wise, will not suffer you to take this way, but will give you contrary counsel, to prove rather and declare what ye are able to do against your lord and prince, and to practise against him and all his the uttermost of your power and authority; which power and authority of yours, to him that offendeth, is fearful, and to him that will not amend, terrible. Such counsel as this, some, peradventure, will whisper in your ear. But to these again this we say and answer for our king, whom notwithstanding to be without fault we do not affirm, but yet, that he is always ready to amend and make satisfaction, that we speak confidently and protest in his behalf.

The commendation of King Henry II., for his meekness and moderation.

The king, appointed for the Lord's anointed, provideth for the peace of his subjects all that he is able: and therefore, to the intent he may conserve this peace in his churches and amongst his subjects committed to him, he willeth and requireth such ordinances as are due to kings, and have been exhibited to them beforetime, also to be exhibited to him; wherein if there hath any contradiction sprung up betwixt him and us, he being thereupon convented, and admonished from the pope by the reverend bishops of London and Hereford, burst not out into any defiance, but meekly and humbly answered, That whereinsoever the church or any ecclesiastical person can show himself grieved, he would therein stand to the judgment of the church of his kingdom. This also he is ready no less to perform indeed, thinking nothing more sweet unto him than to be admonished of his fault, if he have offended the Lord, and to reform the same; and not only to reform and amend his fault, but also to satisfy it to the uttermost, if the law shall so require him. Wherefore, seeing he is so willing to recompense and satisfy the judgment of the church in all things appertaining to the church; refusing no order that shall be taken, but in all things submitting his neck to the yoke of Christ; with what right, by what canon, or reason, can you interdict him, or use excommunication against him? It is a thing laudable, and a virtue of great commendation in wise men, wisely to go with judgment and reason, and not to be carried with puffs of hasty violence. Whereupon, this is the only and common petition of us all, that your fatherly care will diligently provide for your flock and sheep committed to you, so that they miscarry not, or run to any ruin through any inconsiderate or too much heady counsel in you; but rather, through your softness and sufferance, they may obtain life, peace, and security. It doth move us all, what we hear of late to be done by you against the bishop of Salisbury, and the dean of the same church, prosperously, as some men suppose; against whom you have given out the sentence of excommunication and condemnation, before any question of their crime was; following therein, as seemeth, more the heat of hastiness than the path of righteousness. This is a new order of judgment, unheard of yet to this day in our laws and canons, first to condemn a man, and after to inquire of the fact committed. Which order lest you should hereafter attempt to exercise in like manner against our sovereign and king, or against us, and our churches and parishes committed to us, to the detriment of the pope, and the holy church of Rome, and to the no little confusion of us all; therefore, we lay here against you, for ourselves, the remedy of appellation. And as before, openly in the public face of the church, with lively voice, we appealed to the pope for fear of certain perils that might have happened, so now again, in writing, we appeal to the same, assigning as the term of our appellation the day of the Lord's ascension: most humbly and reverently beseeching your goodness, that you, taking a better way with you in this matter, will let your cause fall, sparing herein both the labours and charges, as well of yourself as ours also. And thus we wish you right well to fare, reverend in the Lord.

Henry II. A.D. 1167.

The rescript or answer of Thomas Becket to all his suffragans, not obeying, but confuting, the counsel sent.[1]

Your brotherly letters sent, albeit not by the whole assent of your wisdoms written, as I suppose, I received of late upon a sudden, the contents whereof seem to contain more sharpness than solace; and would to God they proceeded more of sincere zeal of godliness, or affection of charity, than of disobedience or froward wilfulness! for charity seeketh not the things that be her own, but which appertain to Jesus Christ. It had been your duty, if there be truth in the gospel, as most undoubtedly there is, and if you would faithfully have accomplished his business whose person you represent, rather to have feared Him, who can cast both body and soul to hell, than him whose power extendeth no further than to the body; rather to have obeyed God than man; rather your Father than your master or lord, after the example of him who was to his Father obedient unto the death; who died for us, leaving us an example to follow his steps. Let us die therefore with him, and lay down our lives for the deliverance of his church out of the yoke of bondage, and tribulation of the oppressor, which church he hath founded, and whose liberty he hath procured with his own proper blood; lest, if we shall do otherwise, it may haply fall upon us which is written in the gospel, "Whoso loveth his own life more than me, is not worthy of me." This ye ought to know, that if it be right which your Captain commandeth, your duty requireth to obey his will; if not, ye ought then rather to obey God than men.

Scriptures in words rightly alleged, but falsely applied. I deny your minor, Mr. Becket.

One thing I will say, if I may be so bold to tell it unto you; I have now suffered and abstained a long space, waiting if the Lord had given you to take a better heart unto you, who have turned cowardly your backs in the day of battle; or if any of you would have returned again to stand like a wall for the house of Israel, or at least if he had but showed himself in the field, making but the countenance of a warrior against those who cease not daily to infest the Lamb of God. I waited, and none came; I suffered, and none rose up; I held my peace, and none would speak; I dissembled, and none would stand with me in like semblance; wherefore, seeing I see no better towardness in you, this remaineth only, to enter action of complaint against you, and to cry against mine enemies; "Rise up, O Lord! and judge my cause; revenge the blood of the church, which is wasted and oppressed. The pride of them which hate his liberty riseth up ever, neither is there any that doth good, no, not one." Would to God, brethren beloved! there were in you any mind or affection to defend the liberty of the church; for she is builded upon a sure rock, so that although she be shaken, yet she cannot be overthrown. And why then seek ye to confound me? nay, rather yourselves in me, than me in you?

The church of Christ cannot be overthrown: ergo, Becket ought not to be resisted.

(1) "Fraternitatis vestræ scriptum (quod tamen prudentiæ vestræ communi concilio non facile credimus emanasse) nuper ex insperato suscipimus," &c.

Henry II. A.D. 1167.

a man who hath taken upon me all the peril, have sustained all the rebukes, have sustained all the injuries, have suffered also for you all, to very banishment.

And so it was expedient, that one should suffer for that church, that thereby it might be released out of servitude. These things discuss you simply with yourselves, and weigh the matter. Attend, I say, diligently in your minds, for your parts, that God, for his part, removing from your eyes all majesty of rule and empery, as he is no accepter of persons, may take from your hearts the veil, that ye may understand and see what ye have done, what ye intend to do, and what ye ought to do. Tell me which of you all can say, I have taken from him, since the time of my promotion, either ox or ass. If I have defrauded him of any penny, if I have misjudged the cause of any man wrongfully, or if, by the detriment of any person, I have sought mine own gain, let him complain, and I will restore him fourfold. And, if I have not offended you, what then is the cause that ye thus leave and forsake me in the cause of God? Why bend ye so yourselves against me in such a cause, that there is none more special belonging to the church?

Servitude and liberty of the church wrongly defined. The words of holy Scripture clerkly applied.

Brethren, seek not to confound yourselves and the church of God (so much as in you is), but turn to me, and you shall be safe; for the Lord saith, "I will not the death of a sinner, but rather he should convert and live." Stand with me manfully in the war; take your armour and your shield to defend me. Take the sword of the word of the mighty God, that we altogether may withstand more valiantly the malignant enemies, such as go about to take away the soul of the church, which is her liberty; without which liberty she hath no power against them that seek to encroach to their inheritance, the possession of God's sanctuary. If ye will hear and follow me, know ye that the Lord will be with you, and with us all in the defence of the liberty of his church. Otherwise, if ye will not, the Lord judge betwixt me and you, and require the confusion of his church at your hands; which church, whether the world will or no, standeth firmly in the word of the Lord, whereupon she is builded, and ever shall, till the hour come that she shall pass from this world to the Father; for the Lord ever doth support her with his hand.

Turn to thee? Nay turn thou to the Lord and thou shalt be saved.

The soul of the church is the liberty of the church, saith Becket.

Wherefore, to return to the matter: Brethren, remember well with yourselves (which thing ye ought not to forget) what danger I was brought unto, and the church of God also, while I was in England, at my departing out of England, and after my departure from thence; also in what danger it standeth at this present day; but especially at that time, when, at Northampton, Christ was judged again in my person, before the judgment seat of the high president. Who ever heard the archbishop of Canterbury, being troubled for injuries done to him and to his church, and appealing to the pope of Rome, to be judged, condemned, appealed, and put to his sureties, and that of his own suffragans? Where is this law seen, or the authority, nay rather perversity, of this canon heard of? And why yet shame ye not at this your enormity? Why are ye not confounded? Or why doth not this confusion work in you repentance, and repentance drive you to due satisfaction before God and men? For these and such other injuries done to God and to his church, and to me for God's cause (which with a good conscience I ought to suffer, because that without danger of soul I ought not to dissemble them), I choose rather to absent myself for a season, and to dwell quietly in the house of my Lord, than in the tabernacle of sinners, until the time that (their iniquity being complete) the hearts of the wicked, and the cogitations of the same, shall be opened; and these injuries were the cause both of my appeal from the king, and of my departure from thence, which ye term to be sudden. But if ye will speak the truth which ye know, it ought to be no less than sudden, lest, being foreknown, it might have been prevented and stopped; and, as God turned the matter, it happened for the best, both for the honour of the king, and better safety of those who, seeking my harm, should have brought slander on the king. If such troubles followed upon my departing as ye say, let them be imputed to him who gave cause; the fault is in the worker, not in the departer; in him that pursueth, not in him that avoideth injuries. What would ye more? I presented myself to the court, declaring both the causes of my coming and of my appeal, declaring also the wrongs and injuries done to me and to my church, and yet could have no answer, neither was there any that laid any thing against me, before we came to the king. Thus, while we stood

Unbeseeming words of high presumption. Christ is not judged in the person of any traitor.

Conscience made where there is none.

But he leaveth out here the manner of his coming to the court and the sturdiness of his behaviour.

waiting in the court, whether any would come against me or no, they sent to my officials; charging them not to obey me in my temporalities, nor to owe any service to me or to any of mine. After my appellation made in the court, my church was spoiled; we and they about us deprived of our goods, outlawed both of the clergy and of the laity, men, women, and infants; the goods of the church, that is, the patrimony of the crucifix, confiscated, and part of the money turned to the king's use, part to your own coffers. Brother bishop of London, if this be true that we hear of you, and that to the use of your own church ye convert this money, we charge you and require you forthwith, by virtue of obedience, that within forty days after the sight of these letters, all delay and excuse set aside, ye restore again within the time aforesaid, all such goods and parcels as you have taken away: for it is unmeet and contrary to all law for one church to be enriched with the spoil of another church. If ye stand upon the authority that set you to work, you must understand, that in matters concerning the church goods, he can give no lawful authority, who committeth violent injury, &c.

What authority and what Scripture giveth this prerogative to princes upon church goods, which you would attribute to them? What? will they lay for them the remedy of appeal? God forbid! It were evil with the church of God, if, when the sacrilegious extortioner hath violently invaded other men's goods, especially the goods of the church, he should after defend him with the title of appeal, &c.

Becket seemeth here more skilful of his mass-book than of the book of holy Scripture, otherwise he might see it no new thing in the old law for kings to deprive priests, and to place whom they would.

Do not, brethren, so confound altogether the right of the church and of the temporal regiment, for these two are very different, one borrowing its authority from the other. Read the Scriptures, and you shall find what and how many kings have perished for taking upon them the priestly office. Therefore let your discretion provide, lest for this your doing, God's punishment light upon you; which if it come, it will be hard for you very easily to escape. Provide also and see to your king, whose favour ye prefer before the wealth and profit of the church; lest it happen, which God forbid, that he doth perish with all his house, after the example of those who for the like crime were plagued. And if ye cease not off from that ye begin, with what conscience can I dissemble or forbear, but must needs punish you? Let him dissemble with you who lists, having authority so to do; truly I will not; there shall be no dissimulation found in me. And where you write in your letters concerning my promotion, that it was against the voice of the whole realm, and that the church did exclaim against it, what should I say to you, but that, which ye know right well, "The lie, which the mouth doth willingly speak, killeth the soul?" but especially the words of a priest's mouth ought ever to go with verity. As touching this matter, I appeal to your own conscience whether the form of my election stood not fully with the consent of them all to whom the election belonged, having also the assent of the prince by his son, and of those who were sent thereto. And if there were some that repugned the same, he that was troubled and is guilty, let him speak.

Kings in the old law did not intermeddle with the priests' office in some things that were forbidden: but yet kings were officers over priests to correct them when they did amiss.

Ye say, moreover, that I was exalted and promoted from a base and low degree to this dignity by him. I grant that I came of no royal or kingly blood; yet, notwithstanding, I would rather be in the number of those whom virtue of the mind, rather than birth, maketh noble. Peradventure I was born in a poor cottage, of poor parentage; and yet, through God's clemency, who knoweth how to work mercy with his servants, and who cherisheth the humble and low things, to confound the high and mighty, in this my poor and low estate, before I came to the king's service, I had abundantly and wealthily to live withal, as ye know, amongst my neighbours and friends. And David, even from the sheepfold, was taken up and made a king; Peter, of a fisher, was made a prince of the church, who, for his blood being shed for the name of Christ, deserved to have in heaven a crown, and in earth name and renown; would to God we could do the like! We be the successors of Peter, and not of kings and emperors.

If ye mean of Achas and Oza in the Old Testament, then we deny your minor.

And where ye seem to charge me, by insinuation, with the blot of ingratitude, thus I answer: There is no offence capital or infamous, unless it proceed from the heart and intention. As, if a man commit a murder unwillingly, although he be called a murderer, yet he is not thereby punishable: and so, although I owe my duty and service with reverence to my king, yet, if I have

They be the successors and sons of saints, not that

Henry II. A.D. 1167.

forborne him as my lord, if I have warned him, and talked with him fatherly and gently as with a son, and in talking with him could not be heard: if therefore, I say, being enforced thereunto, and against my will, I do exercise upon him the censure of due severity, in so doing I suppose I make rather with him than against him, and rather deserve at his hand thanks for my correction, than note or suspicion of unkindness or punishment for the fact. Sometimes a man, against his will, receiveth a benefit, as, when necessity causeth a man to be restrained from doing that which he ought not to do: he that doth so restrain him, though he stop him, doth not hurt him, but rather profiteth him for his soul's health. Another thing that defendeth us from ingratitude, is, our Father and Patron Christ, who, in that he is our Father, to whom we as children owe obedience, then are we bound, as children, by necessity, to obey his commandment, in warning the evildoer, in correcting the disobedient, and in bridling the obstinate: which, if we do not, we run into danger to have his blood required at our hands. Ye set forth likewise and show, what loss we thereby may sustain of our temporalities, but ye speak no word of the loss of our souls.

hold the places of saints, but that do the works of saints.—Hierome.

Moreover, as concerning the departure of the king from the homage of the church of Rome, which in your letters ye seem to pretend, or rather threaten: God forbid, I say, that the devotion or faith of our king should ever swerve away from the obedience and reverence of the church of Rome, for any temporal commodity or incommodity, which thing to do is very damnable in any private subject, much more in the prince who draweth many others with him; therefore, God forbid that ever any faithful man should once think so heinous a deed. And you, according to your discretion, take heed lest the words of your mouth infect any person or persons therein, occasioning to them by your words such dangers and damnable matter, like to the golden cup which is called the cup of Babylon, which for the outward gold no man will refuse to drink of, but after they have drunk thereof, they are poisoned.

If the king had been an adulterer, or tyrant against the new doctrine or preaching of Christ, then might this reason serve, and God more to be obeyed than man. Now where did Becket learn that the king in his temporal right was not to be obeyed? Take heed, ye marvel, if ye open that door.

And where ye lay to my charge for the suspending of the reverend father, the bishop of Salisbury, and for excommunicating of John,[1] dean of the same church, for a schismatic, by knowledge and process had of the matter, to this I answer, that both these are justly and condignly excommunicate; and if ye understand perfectly the condition of the matter, and the right order of judgments, ye will say no less. For this standeth with good authority, as ye know, that in manifest and notorious crimes, this knowledge and order of proceeding is not requisite. Perpend with yourselves diligently, what the bishop of Salisbury did concerning the deanery, after that he was prohibited of the pope and of us, under pain of excommunication; and then shall ye better understand, that upon such manifest disobedience, suspension did rightly follow, as ye read in the decree of St. Clement, saying, "If they do not obey their prelates, all manner of persons, of what order soever they be, whether they shall be princes of high or low degree, and all other people, shall not only be infamed, but also banished from the kingdom of God and the fellowship of the faithful." As concerning John of Oxford, this we say, that excommunication cometh divers ways; some are excommunicate by the law denouncing them excommunicate; some by the sentence of the prelate; some by communicating with those who are excommunicate. Now he that hath fallen into this damnable heresy, of participating with schismatics whom the pope hath excommunicated, he draweth to himself the spot and leprosy of like excommunication. Wherefore, seeing he, contrary to the pope's express commandment and ours, being charged under pain of excommunication to the contrary, took upon him the deanery of Salisbury, we have denounced him, and hold him excommunicate, and all his doings we disannul by the authority of the eighth synod, saying, "If any man, either privily or apertly, shall speak, or communicate with him that is excommunicate, he draweth unto himself the punishment of like excommunication." And now, forasmuch as you, brother, bishop of London, who ought to know that saying of Gregory VII.[2], "If any bishop shall consent to the fornication of priests, deacons, &c. within his precinct, for reward, favour, or petition, or doth not by authority of his office correct the vice, let him be suspended from his office." And again, that saying of Pope Leo which is this: "If any bishop shall insti-

Divers ways of excommunication.

The council speaketh of such as he worthily excommunicated.

(1) This John was called a schismatic, because he took part with Reginald, archbishop of Cologne, and the emperor, against Alexander, the pope.

(2) This Gregory, otherwise called Hildebrand, was he that first took away priests marriage, condemning all priests who had wives, of fornication.

tute or consecrate such a priest as shall be unmeet and unconvenient, if he escape with the loss of his own proper dignity, yet he shall lose the power of instituting any more," &c. Therefore forasmuch, I say, as you, knowing this, have double-wise offended against the sentence of these canons, we command you, and in the virtue of obedience enjoin you, that if it be so, within three months after the receipt hereof, you will submit and offer yourself to due correction and satisfaction to the council of our fellow-bishops, for these your so great excesses, lest others, through your example, run into the like offence, and we be constrained to proceed against you with severer sentence.

Finally, in the close of your letter, where ye bring in for your appellation against me, a safeguard for you, which rather indeed is an hindrance to you, that we should not proceed against the invaders of the church goods, nor against the king, in like censure as we have done against the bishop of Salisbury, as ye say, and his dean; to this I answer, God forbid that we have, or else should hereafter proceed or do any thing against the king or his land, or against you or your churches, inordinately or otherwise than is convenient. But what if you shall exceed in the same or like transgression, as the bishop of Salisbury hath done? Think ye then your appellation shall help you from the discipline of our severity, that ye shall not be suspended? Mark ye diligently whether this be a lawful appeal, and what is the form thereof. We know that every one that appealeth, either doth it in his own name, or in the name of another; if in his own, either it is for some grievance inferred already, or else for that he feareth after to be inferred against him. Now, concerning the first, I am sure there is no grievance that you can complain of as yet, God be thanked, that you have received at my hand, for the which you should appeal from me; neither have you, I trust, any cause special against me so to do. If ye do it for fear of what is to come, lest I should trouble you and your churches, consider whether this be the fear that ought to happen in constant men, or whether this be the appeal which ought to suspend or stay our power and authority that we have upon you and your churches. It is thought, therefore, by wise men, and we also judge no less, that your appeal is of no force. First, for that it hath not the right form of a perfect appellation, and also because it is not consonant to reason, and lacketh order and help of the law.

Furthermore, if your appellation be in another man's name, either it is for the king (as most like it is) or for some other. If it be for the king, then you ought first to understand that appellations are wont to be made to repel, and not to infer injury; or, to release such as be oppressed, that they should not be oppressed any more. Wherefore if any man shall enter any appellation, not trusting to the surety of his cause, but to delay the time, that sentence be not given upon him, that appellation is not to be received. For what state will there be of the church, if the liberty thereof being taken away, the goods of the church spoiled, and the bishops driven from their places, or at least not received with full restitution of their goods, the invaders and spoilers thereof may defend themselves by appealing, thereby to save themselves from the penalty of their desert?

The form of a true appellation.

What a ruin of the church will this be? See what ye have done, and what ye say. Are you not the vicars of Christ, representing him on earth? Is it not your office to correct and bridle ill-doers, whereby they may cease to persecute the church? and is it not enough for them to be fierce and to rage against the church, but that you should take their part, setting yourselves against us, to the destruction of the church? Who ever heard of such monstrous doings? Thus, it shall be heard and said of all nations and countries, that the suffragans of the church of Canterbury, who ought to stand with their metropolitan unto death in defence of the church, now go about by the king's command, so much as in them doth lie, to suspend his authority, lest he should exercise his discipline of correction upon them that rebel against the church. This one thing I know, that you cannot sustain two sorts of persons at once, both to be the appeal makers, and to be appealed to yourselves. You be they who have made the appellation; you be they against whom the appellation is made. Are there any more churches than one, and the body of the same? And how meet were it then, that you, being the members of the church, should hold together with the head thereof? I am afraid, brethren, lest it may be said of us, these be the priests who have said, "Where is the Lord?" and having the law, do not know

One person cannot both be the appeal maker and the party appealed.

Henry II. A.D. 1167.

the law. Furthermore, this I suppose, you, being discreet men, are not ignorant of, that such as enter any appellation there, are not wont to be heard, unless the matter of their appellation either belongeth to themselves, or except special commandment force them thereunto, or else unless they take another man's cause upon them. First, that it belongeth nothing unto you, it is plain, forasmuch as the contrary rather pertaineth to your duty; that is, to punish and to correct all such as rebel against the church. And, secondly, if he who subverteth the liberty of the church, and invadeth the goods thereof, converting them to his own use, be not heard appealing for his own defence, much less is another to be heard appealing for him. Wherefore, as in this case neither he can appeal for himself, nor yet command you so to do; so neither may you receive the commandment to appeal for him. Thirdly, as touching the taking of another man's cause or business upon you: to this I say and affirm, that ye ought in no manner of wise so to do, especially seeing the matter pertaineth to the oppression of the church, and whereupon ensueth great damage to the same.

Wherefore, seeing it neither appertaineth to you, neither ought ye to receive any such commandment, nor yet to take upon you any such cause as that is, your appeal is neither to be heard, nor standeth with any law. Is this the devotion and consolation of brotherly love which you exhibit to your metropolitan, being for you in exile? God forgive you this clemency! And how now? will ye look for your letters and messengers to be gently received here of us? Neither do I speak this, as though there were any thing in hand betwixt your part and ours, or that we have done any thing inordinately against the person of the king, or against his land, or against the persons of the church, or intend, by God's mercy, so to do. And therefore, we say briefly, and affirm constantly, that our lord the king cannot complain of any wrong or injury to be done unto him, if he (being often called upon by letters and messengers to acknowledge his fault, neither will confess his trespass, nor yet come to any satisfaction for the same) have the censure of severity by the pope and us laid upon him: for no man can say that he is unjustly treated, whom the law doth justly punish. And, briefly to conclude: know you this for certain, that extortioners, invaders, detainers of the church goods, and subverters of the liberties thereof, neither have any authority of the law to maintain them, nor doth their appealing defend them.

Though the pope's law will not defend them, yet the law of the Scripture will and doth.

A brief censure upon the former rescript of Becket to his suffragans, with a general resolution of the reasons therein contained.[1]

If the king of England had been an idolater, covetous, and adulterer, an incestuous person, a murderer, with such like; then the zeal of this archbishop, threatening the king and such as took his part, had deserved praise in this epistle, and the Scripture would have borne him out therein. For these and such causes should bishops prosecute the authority of the gospel against all persons. But, the matter standing only upon church goods, liberty (or rather licentiousness) of priests, making of deans, titles of churches, superiority of crowning the king, with such other matters: to stand so stiff in these, is not to defend the church, but to rebel against the king. Again, if the principles, which he here groundeth upon, were true—to wit, that the pope were to be obeyed before princes, that the liberty of the church standeth upon the immunity of priests exempted from princes' laws, or upon ample possessions of the church; or that the pope's law ought to prevail in all foreign countries, and to bind all princes in their own dominions; or that the sentence of the pope and his popelings (how or by what affection soever it is pronounced) may stand by the undoubted sentence of God: then all the arguments of this epistle do proceed and conclude well. But, if they stand not ratified by God's word, but tottering upon man's traditions, then, whatsoever he inferreth or concludeth thereupon, his assumption being false, cannot be true, according to the school saying: "One inconveniency being granted in the beginning, innumerable follow thereupon." So in this epistle it happeneth, as is above noted, that the major of this man is true, but the minor is clean false, and to be denied.

(1) From the style of this censure, it is clearly from the pen of our author, Foxe.—Ed.

The letter of Matilda, the empress, and mother of the king, to Thomas Becket.

Henry II. A.D. 1168.

My lord the pope commanded me, and upon the forgiveness of my sins enjoined me, that I should be a mediator and means of peace and concord between my son and you, by reconciling of yourself to him, whereunto, as you know, you requested me. Wherefore the earnester and with more affection, as well for the divine honour as for holy church, I took the enterprise upon me. But this by the way, I assure you, that the king, with his barons and council, taketh it grievously that you, whom he entirely loved, honoured, and made chiefest in all this realm, to the intent to have more comfort and better trust in you, should thus, as the report is, rebel, and stir his people against him. Yea and further, that as much as in you lieth, you went about to disinherit him, and deprive him of his crown. Upon the occasion whereof, I sent unto you our trusty and familiar servant Lawrence, archdeacon, by whom I pray you that I may understand your mind herein, and good will toward my son, and how you mean to behave yourself, if my prayer and petition may be heard of him in your behalf, toward his grace. But this one thing I assure you of, that unless it be, through your great humility and moderation, evident in you appearing, you cannot obtain the favour of the king. Herein what you mean to do, I pray you send me word, by your proper letters and messengers.

But to proceed further in the order of the history. After these letters sent to and fro, A.D. 1169, which was the fifteenth year of the reign of King Henry II., the king misdoubting and fearing with himself, that the archbishop would proceed, or exceed rather, in his excommunication against his own person, to prevent the mischief, made his appeal to the presence of the pope, requiring to have certain legates sent down from Rome from the pope's side, to take up the matter between the archbishop and him; requiring, moreover, that they might also be absolved who were interdicted. Whereupon two cardinals, being sent from Alexander, the pope, with letters to the king, came to Normandy, where they appointed the archbishop to meet them before the king upon St. Martin's day. But the archbishop, neither agreeing with the day nor the place, delayed his coming till the eighth day after, neither would go any further than to Grisortium, where the two cardinals and the archbishop, with other bishops conventing together, had a certain entreaty of peace and reconciliation: but it came to no conclusion. The contents of this entreaty or action, being sufficiently contained in the cardinals' letter, who were called Gulielmus and Otho, written to the pope, it shall require no further labour, but to show out the words thereof, where the sum of the whole may appear: the words of the letter be these. A.D. 1169.

The copy of the epistle written and sent by two cardinals to the pope, concerning the matter of the Archbishop Becket.

William and Otho, cardinals of the church of Rome, to Alexander, the pope, &c. Coming to the land of the king of England, we found the controversy betwixt him and the archbishop of Canterbury more sharp and vehement than we would; for the king, and the greater part of those about him, said, that the archbishop had stirred up the French king grievously against him; and also that he made the earl of Flanders, his kinsman, who bare no displeasure to him before, his open adversary, ready to war against him, as is by divers evidences most certain. Thus, when we came to Cadomus, first to the king's speech,[1] we gave the letters of your fatherhood to his hands: which after he had received and considered (bringing forth withal other letters received from you before, something diverse and altering from those which he received of us), he was

Becket stirring up the French king against the king of England.

(1) "First to the king's speech," a confidant.—Ed.

Henry II.

A.D. 1169.

moved and stirred with no little indignation; saying, that the archbishop, after our departure from you, had received of you other contrary letters, by the virtue whereof he was exempted from our judgment, so that he should not be compelled to answer us. Moreover, the said king to us added and affirmed, and so did the bishops there present, testifying the same, that concerning the old and ancient customs of his progenitors, whereof complaint was made to you, all that, for the most part, was false and untrue which was intimated to you; offering further to us, that if there were any such customs or laws in his time, as seemed prejudicial or disagreeable to the statutes of the church, he would willingly be content to revoke and disannul the same. Whereupon we, with other archbishops, bishops, and abbots of the land, hearing the king so reasonable, laboured by all the means we might, that the king should not utterly break from us, but rather should incline to us to have the matter brought before us betwixt him and the forenamed archbishop. By reason whereof, we directed our own chaplains with letters unto him, appointing him both time and place where safely he might meet us on the feast of St. Martin. Nevertheless he, pretending certain excuses, made his dilatories, driving off the time from the day of St. Martin to the octaves following, which thing stirred the king's heart more than is to be thought.

A communication between Becket and the cardinals.

Thus, although we offered to the archbishop safe coming, yet when he refused to meet us in the borders of the king, we, to satisfy his mind, condescended to meet him within the land of the French king, in the place where he himself appointed, because there should be no let in us, whereby to stop his profit. After we had entered upon communication, we began to exhort him, all that we could, to submit and humble himself to his sovereign and king, who had heaped upon him such benefits and dignities; whereby matter might be given us for further occasion of reconciling them together. He, being thus moved and exhorted by us, departed aside to consult with his council upon the matter. At length, after counsel taken, he cometh again, answering in this manner: that he would submit and humble himself to the king, "saving the honour of God, and liberty of the church; saving also the honesty of his person, and possessions of churches; and moreover, saving the justice of him and of all his in all things."[1] After which communication had amongst us, we moved and required him more instantly, that he would come to the specialities, when as yet he had brought nothing in, either which was certain or particular. Likewise we demanded of him, if he would, in all such things contained and comprehended in our letters, stand and submit himself to our letters, so as the king and the bishops before were contented to do. To the which he answering again, said, that he had received from you a commandment, not to answer before he and all his were restored full to all their possessions; and then he would so proceed in the matter, according as he should receive commandment from the see apostolical.

Becket's addition.

Thus we, breaking off communication, seeing that he neither would stand to judgment, nor come to conformity, thought to make relation thereof to the king, and so did; declaring that which he had expressed to us, yet not uttering all, but keeping back a great part of that which we had heard and seen. Which when the king with his nobles had understanding of, he affirmed to us again; that he therein was cleared so much the more, for that the archbishop would not stand to their judgment, nor abide their trial. After much heaviness and lamentation of the king, the archbishop, bishops, and abbots of the realm, requiring of us, whether we had any such power, by virtue of our commission to withstand him and proceed against him; and perceiving that our authority would not serve thereunto, and fearing lest the aforesaid archbishop, refusing all order of judgment, would work again disquietness to some noble personages of the realm; and seeing our authority could not extend so far to help them against him, taking a consultation among themselves; we agreed together, with one assent, to make their appellation to your audience, prefixing accordingly the term of their appeal.

Becket would neither stand to judgment nor trial.

And this is the epistle of these two cardinals sent to the pope, wherein may sufficiently appear all the discourse and manner of that

(1) "Salvo honore Dei, et ecclesiæ libertate; salva etiam honestate personæ suæ et possessionibus ecclesiarum: et amplius, sua et suorum in omnibus salva justitia."

assembly, although particularly every thing be not expressed, concerning the talk betwixt the cardinals and the archbishop. When William, who of the two cardinals was the more eloquent, amongst other communication, had reasoned long with him as concerning the peace of the church, which Becket said he preferred above all things, "Well then," saith the cardinal, "seeing all this contention between the king and you riseth upon certain laws and customs to be abrogated, and that you regard the peace of the church so much, what say you? Will you renounce your bishopric, and the king shall renounce his customs? The peace of the church now lieth in your hands, either to retain or to let go; then what say you?" To whom he answereth again, that the proportion was not like. "For I," saith he, "saving the honour of my church and my person, cannot renounce my bishopric. On the contrary, it standeth upon the king, for his soul's health and honour, to renounce these his ordinances and customs." Which thing he thus proved; because the pope had condemned those customs, and he, likewise, with the church of Rome had done the same.

Becket loveth better his bishopric than the peace of the church, for all his gay talk

THE TALK BETWEEN THE FRENCH KING, THE KING OF ENGLAND, AND BECKET.

After the cardinals were returned, the French king, seeing the king of England disquieted, and solicitous to have peace, or at least pretending to set an agreement between them, brought the matter to a communication among them, in which communication the French king made himself as umpire between them. The king of England, hearing that the archbishop would commit himself to his arbitrement, was the more willing to admit his presence. Whereupon, many being there present, the archbishop, prostrating himself at the king's feet, declared unto him, kneeling upon his knees, that he would commit the whole cause, whereof the dissension arose between them, unto his own arbitrement, adding thereunto, as he did before, "salvo honore Dei;" that is, "saving the honour of God." The king, as is said before, being greatly offended at this word, hearing and seeing the stiffness of the man sticking so much to this word, "salvo honore Dei," was highly therewith displeased, rebuking him with many grievous words, as a man proud and stubborn, and also charging him with sundry and great benefits bestowed upon him, as a person unkind, and forgetting what he had so gently done and bestowed upon him.

Becket cometh in with his old addition, Salvo honore Dei. Becket charged with unkindness.

And speaking to the French king there present, "See, sir, if it please you," saith the king of England, "whatsoever displeaseth this man, that he saith to be contrary to the honour of God; and so by this means he will vindicate and challenge to himself both what is his and mine also. And yet, notwithstanding, because I will not seem to do any thing contrary or prejudicial to God's honour, this I offer him: There have been kings in England before, both of greater and less puissance than I am; likewise there have been bishops of Canterbury many, both great and holy men. What the greatest and most holy of all his predecessors, before him, hath done to the least of my progenitors and predecessors, before me, let him do the same to me, and I am content." They that stood by, hearing these words of

The king's offer to Becket both charitable and reasonable

Henry II. A.D. 1169.

the king, cried all with one voice, "The king hath debased himself enough to the bishop." The archbishop staying a little at this in silence; "What!" saith the French king to him, "my lord archbishop, will you be better than those holy men? Will ye be greater than Peter? What stand you doubting? Here now have you peace and quietness put in your own hands, if ye will take it." To this the archbishop anwered again: "Truth it is," saith he, "that my predecessors before me were both much better and greater than I, and of them every one for his time, although he did not extirpate and cut off all, yet something he did pluck up and correct, which seemed adverse and repugnant against God's honour. For if they had taken all together away, no such occasion then had been left for any man to raise up this fire of temptation now against us, as is here raised to prove us withal, that we, being so proved with them, might also be crowned with them, being likewise partakers of praise and reward, as we are of their labour and travail. And though some of them have been slack, or exceeded their duty, in that we are not bound to follow their example. Peter, when he denied Christ, we rebuke; but when he resisted the rage of Nero, therein we commend him. And therefore, because he could not find in his conscience to consent unto that he ought in no wise to dissemble, neither did he; by reason whereof he lost his life. By such like oppressions the church hath always grown. Our forefathers and predecessors, because they would not dissemble the name and honour of Christ, therefore they suffered. And shall I, to have the favour of one man, suffer the honour of Christ to be suppressed?" The nobles standing by, and hearing him thus speak, were greatly grieved with him, noting in him both arrogancy and wilfulness, in perturbing and refusing such an honest offer of agreement. But especially one among the rest was most grieved, who there openly protested, that seeing the archbishop so refused the counsel and request of both the kingdoms, he was not worthy to have the help of either of them, but as the kingdom of England had rejected him, so the realm of France should not receive him.[1]

The words of the French king.

This major, if it had been joined with a good minor, had made a good argument.

Alanus Herbert and certain other of his chaplains, who committed to story the doings of Becket, do record, whether truly or not I cannot say, that the French king, sending for him, as one much sorrowing and lamenting the words that he had spoken, at the coming of Becket did prostrate himself at his feet, confessing his fault in giving counsel to him in such a cause, (pertaining to the honour of God,) to relent therein, and to yield to the pleasure of man; wherefore, declaring his repentance, he desired to be absolved thereof. Thus, after this, the French king and Becket were great friends together, insomuch that King Henry, sending to the king to entreat and desire him that he would not support or maintain his enemy within his realm, the French king utterly denied the king's request, taking part rather with the archbishop than with him.

Besides these quarrels and grudges betwixt the king and the archbishop above mentioned, there followed yet another, which was this. Shortly after this communication recited between the king and Becket, the king of England returning again from Normandy into

(1) Ex Quadrilogo.

England, A.D. 1170, in the sixteenth year of his reign, about Midsummer, kept his court of parliament at Westminster, in the which parliament he, with the consent both of the clergy and the lords temporal, caused his son Henry to be crowned king. This coronation was done by the hands of Roger, archbishop of York, with the assistance of other bishops ministering to the same, as Gilbert of London, Joselin of Salisbury, Hugo of Durham, and Walter of Rochester. By reason of this, Becket of Canterbury, being there neither mentioned nor called for, took no little displeasure; and so did Louis, the French king, hearing that Margaret, his daughter, was not also crowned with her husband; whereupon he, gathering a great army, forthwith marched into Normandy. But the matter was soon composed by the king of England, who, sending his son unto him in Normandy, entreated there and concluded peace with him, promising that his son should be crowned again, and then his daughter should be crowned also. But the archbishop not ceasing his displeasure and emulation, sent unto the pope, complaining of these four bishops, especially of the archbishop of York, who durst be so bold in his absence, and without his knowledge or his license, to intermeddle to crown the king, being a matter proper and peculiar to his jurisdiction; at the instance of whom, the pope sent down the sentence of excommunication against the bishop of London. The other three bishops, with the archbishop of York, he suspended, whose sentence and letters thereof, for avoiding prolixity, I here omit.

Henry II

A.D. 1170.

The bishop of London excommunicated, with four other bishops suspended.

Besides these aforesaid bishops excommunicated, divers other clerks also of the court he cited to appear before him, by virtue of his large commission which he got from the pope, whom they were bound to obey, by reason of their benefices; and some he commanded in virtue of obedience to appear, on pain of forfeiting their order and benefices; of whom when neither sort would appear, he cursed them openly. And also some laymen of the court and the king's familiars, as intruders and violent withholders of church goods, he accursed; as Richard Lucy, and Joselin Balliot, and Ralph Brock, who took the bells and goods that belonged to the church of Canterbury; and Hugh Sentclear, and Thomas, the son of Bernard, and all that should hereafter take any church goods without his consent; so that almost all the court were accursed either by name, or as partakers.

This being done, the archbishop of York, with the aforesaid bishops, resorted to the king with a grievous complaint, declaring how miserably their case stood, and what they had sustained for fulfilling his commandment. The king, hearing this, was highly moved, as no marvel was. But what remedy? the time of the ruin of the pope was not yet come, and what prince then might withstand the injurious violence of that Romish potestate?

The cause of the king's wrath against Becket

In the mean season the French king, for his part, his clergy and courtiers likewise, slacked no occasion to incite and solicit Alexander the pope, against the king of England, to excommunicate him also, seeking thereby and thinking to have some vantage against the realm. Neither was the king ignorant of this, which made him more ready to apply for some agreement of reconciliation. At length came down from the pope two legates, the archbishop of Rothomage and the

Henry II. A.D. 1170. bishop of Navern, with direction and full commission either to drive the king to be reconciled, or to be interdicted by the pope's censures out of the church. The king, understanding himself to be in greater straits than he could avoid, at length, through the mediation of the French king, and of other prelates and great princes, was content to yield to peace and reconciliation with the archbishop, whom he both received to his favour, and also permitted and granted him free return to his church again. Concerning his possessions and lands of the church of Canterbury, although Becket made great labour therefor, yet the king, being then in Normandy, would not grant him them, before he should repair to England, to see how he would there agree with his subjects.

Thus peace after a sort concluded between the king and him, the archbishop, after six years of his banishment, returned to England, where he was right joyfully received of the church of Canterbury; albeit of Henry, the young king, he was not so greatly welcomed, insomuch that coming up to London to the king, he was returned back to Canterbury, and there bid to keep his house. Roger Hoveden maketh mention in his Chronicle, that the archbishop, upon Christmas-day, did excommunicate Robert de Brooke for cutting off the tail of a certain horse of his the day before. In the mean time the four bishops before mentioned, whom the archbishop had excommunicated, sent to him, humbly desiring to be released of their censure; to whom when the archbishop would not grant clearly and simply, without reservations and exceptions, they went over to the king, declaring unto him and complaining of their miserable state and uncourteous handling of the archbishop. Whereupon the king conceived great sorrow in his mind, and displeasure toward the party, insomuch that he lamented oft and sundry times to those about him, that, amongst so many that he had done for, there was none that would revenge him of his enemy. By occasion of which words certain that were about the king, to the number of four, who hearing him thus complain and lament, addressed themselves in great heat of haste to satisfy the grieved mind and quarrel of their prince, who within four days after the said Christmas-day, sailing over into England, and having a forward and prosperous wind in their journey, being in the deep of winter, came to Canterbury, where Becket was commanded to keep. After certain advisements and consultations had among themselves, they pressed at length into the palace where the archbishop was sitting with his company about him; first, to assay him with words, to see whether he would relent to the king's mind, and come to some conformity. They brought to him, said they, commandment from the king, which, whether he had rather openly there in presence, or secretly, to be declared to him, they bade him choose. Then the company being bid to retire, as he sat alone, they said, "You are commanded from the king beyond the sea, to repair to the king's son here, and to do your duty to him, swearing to him your fidelity for your baronage and other things, and to amend those things wherein you have trespassed against him." Whereupon the archbishop refusing to swear, and perceiving their intent, called in his company again, and in multiplying of words to and fro, at length they came to the bishops who were excommuni-

Becket returneth out of banishment.

The words of the king which were the cause of Becket's death.

If the papists will needs measure the success of things by seasons and weather, then must they by that reason condemn the cause of Becket, his adversaries having such forwardness of weather in doing their feat.

The talk between the four soldiers

cated for the coronation of the king, whom they commanded in the king's name he should absolve and set free again. The archbishop answered, that he neither suspended nor excommunicated them, but the pope; wherefore, if that were the matter that grieved them, they should resort to the pope; he had nothing to do with the matter.

Henry II.
A. D. 1170.
and Thomas Becket

Then said Reginald, one of the four, "Although you in your own person did not excommunicate them, yet through your instigation it was done." To whom the archbishop said again, "And if the pope," said he, "tendering the injuries done unto me and my church, wrought this revenge for me, I confess it offendeth me nothing." "Thus then," said they, "it appeareth well by your own words, that it pleaseth you right well, in contempt and contumely of the king's majesty, to sequester his bishops from their ministry, who, at the commandment of the king, did service in the coronation of his son. And seeing you have so presumed thus to stand against the exaltation of this our sovereign, our new king, it seemeth likely that you aspired to take his crown from him, and to be exalted king yourself." "I aspire not," said he, "to the crown and name of the king, but rather if I had four crowns, to give him more, I would set them all upon him; such good-will I do bear him, that, only his father, the king, excepted, there is none whose honour I more tender and love. And as concerning the sequestering of those bishops, this I give you to understand, that nothing was done in that behalf without the knowledge and assent of the king himself; to whom when I had made my complaint at the feast of Mary Magdalene, of the wrong and injury done to me and my church therein, he gave me his good leave to obtain at the pope's hand such remedy as I could, promising, moreover, his help to me in the same." "What is this," quoth they, "that thou sayest? Makest thou the king a traitor, and a betrayer of the king's own son, that when he had commanded the bishops to crown his son, he would give thee leave afterward to suspend them for so doing? Certes, it had been better for you not to have accused so the king of this prodition." The archbishop said to Reginald, that he was there present at that time, and heard it himself. But that Reginald denied, and swore it was not so. "And think you," said they, "that we, the king's subjects, will or ought to suffer this?" And so approaching nearer him, they said he had spoken enough against his own head, whereupon followed great exclamation and many threatening words. Then said the archbishop, "I have, since my coming over, sustained many injuries and rebukes, concerning both myself, my men, my cattle, my wines, and all other goods; notwithstanding the king, writing over to his son, required him that I should live in safety and peace; and now, beside all others, you come hither to threaten me." To this Reginald answering again, said, "If there be any that worketh you any injury otherwise than right is, the law is open, why do you not complain?" "To whom," said Becket, "should I complain?" "To the young king," said they. "Then," said Becket, "I have complained enough, if that would help, and have sought for remedy at the king's hands, so long as I could be suffered to come to his speech; but now, seeing that I am stopped from that, neither can find redress of so great vexations and injuries as I have and do daily sustain, nor can have the benefits of the law

Henry II. A.D. 1170.

or reason; such right and law as an archbishop may have, that will I exercise, and let for no man." At these words one of them, bursting out in exclamation, cried, "He threateneth, he threateneth! What? will he interdict the whole realm and us altogether?" "Nay, that he shall not," saith another, "he hath interdicted too many already." And drawing more near to him, they protested and denounced him to have spoken words to the jeopardy of his own head. And so departing in great fury, and with many high words, they rushed out of the doors; who, by the way returning to the monks, charged them in the king's name to keep him forthcoming, that he should not escape away. "What," quoth the archbishop, "think ye I will flee away? Nay, neither for the king, nor any man alive, will I stir one foot from you." "No," say they, "thou shalt not escape though thou wouldst." And so they departing with many words, the archbishop followeth them out of the chamber door, crying after them, "Here, here, here shall you find me," laying his hand upon his crown.

The stout heart of Becket.

The names of the four soldiers above mentioned were these: the first, Reginald Bereson;[1] the second, Hugh Mortevil; the third, William Thracy; and the fourth, Richard Brito; who, going to harness themselves, returned the same day again, but finding the hall-door of the palace of Canterbury shut against them, they went to an inward back-door leading into the orchard; there brake they up a window, and opened the door, and so issued into the place. The monks, it being about even-song time, had got the archbishop into the church; who, being persuaded by them, caused his cross to be borne before him, and so through the cloister, by a door which was broken up for him, he proceeded into the choir. The harnessed men following after, at length came to the church-door, which door the monks would have shut against them; but, as the story saith, the archbishop would not suffer them. So they approaching into the church, and the archbishop meeting them upon the stairs, there he was slain; every one of the four soldiers striking him with his sword into the head; who afterward flying into the north, and at length, with much ado, obtaining their pardon of the pope by the king's procurement, as some stories record, went to Jerusalem.[2]

The death of Thomas Becket.

What is to be thought or judged of Thos. Becket.

Thus you have heard the life and death of this Thomas Becket, of whom what is to be judged, let his own acts and facts declare. And, albeit the Scripture ought to be the only rule for us to judge all things by, yet, if any shall require further testimony, partly to satisfy their minds therein, ye shall hear the judgments of certain men, in years and times almost as ancient as himself, what they write and affirm of him.

Whether he died a saint or not?

And first, to begin with the testimony of one of his own religion, and also not far, as it appeareth, from his own time, who, writing of his martyrdom and miracles, thus testifieth of the judgment and sentence of divers concerning his promotion and behaviour. The chronicle being written in Latin, and having the name of the author

(1) Hume says, Reginald Fitz-urse, and Sharon Turner, Fitzwiso.—Ed.

(2) On the eastern wall of the nave of Preston church, in Sussex, some very ancient paintings, relics of English art, have lately been discovered; among them is a very spirited one of the murder of Thomas à Becket, displaying, with great minuteness and much talent, the particulars of his tragical end. See the 'Archæologia,' vol. xxiii. No. 17.—Ed.

cut out, thus beginneth: "Quoniam vero multi," &c. And in the first book and eighth chapter it followeth in this manner:[1]—

The promotion of Becket judged not canonical.

"Divers notwithstanding there be, who, as touching his promotion, suppose the same not to be canonical, for that it was wrought rather by the instance of the king (thinking him to be a man ready and inclinable to his utility) than by the assent either of the clergy, or of the people. Further, it is noted in him for a point of presumption and lack of discretion, for that he, being scarce worthy to take the oar in hand and play the boatswain, would take upon him to sit at helm, and guide the ship; namely, in that church, where the covent, being in gesture and vesture religious, be wont to have their prelate taken out of the same profession. Whereas he, scant bearing the habit of a clerk, and going in his changes and soft apparel, is more conversant among the delicate rufflers in the court, savouring rather of worldly things; not refusing, moreover, without any dread, to climb up to the high preferment of such a holy dignity, but rather willingly, of his own accord, to aspire to it. Moses we read did otherwise, who, being the friend of God, and sent of him to conduct his people Israel out of Egypt, trembled at the message, and said, 'Who am I, Lord, that I should go to Pharaoh, and bring thy people Israel out of Egypt?' And again, 'I pray thee,' saith he, 'O Lord,' I am nothing eloquent, send him whom thou wilt send.' Likewise Jeremias also, being sent of the Lord to prophesy against Jerusalem, was abashed to take the office upon him, answering again with much dread of heart, 'A, a, a, Lord, I cannot utter my mind, for I am a child.'"

Becket charged with presumption and lack of discretion.

Ambition noted in Becket, in not refusing but taking his promotion.

Bishops against their wills thrust into their bishoprics.

In like manner we read of the saints of the New Testament, whereof many were preferred oftentimes to their bishoprics and functions of the church, by mere forcement and compulsion of others rather than by their own wills. So was blessed Gregory, after his flight and going away, brought back again, and placed in the see and chair of Rome. Likewise St. Ambrose, sore against his mind; who also, of purpose accusing and confessing his own defects, because he would be repealed, yet by the commandment of Valentinian, the emperor, was enforced to take the burden upon him, which he could by no wise shake off. St. Martin, in like sort, not knowing of any such matter, was circumvented by a certain godly train and wile of the citizens, before he could be brought to his consecration; which he did not so much take, as he was thrust into it with much pensiveness and sorrow of heart. By these and such other examples this chancellor likewise should have rather excused himself as unworthy and unmeet for that room, showing himself more willing to refuse than to take it: to the which this archbishop is judged to do clean contrary.[2]

And, although scarcely any testimony is to be taken of that age, being all blinded and corrupted with superstition, yet let us hear what Neuburgensis, an ancient historiographer, saith in his Chronicle, who, in the days of the son of this King Henry II., prosecuting his history unto King Richard I., hath to this effect, writing of Thomas Becket.[3]

(1) "Nonnullis tamen idcirco promotionem ejus visum est fuisse minus canonicam, quod ad eam magis operata est regis instantia, quam cleri vel populi voto. Præsumptionis quoque vel indiscretionis fuisse notatum est, quod qui remum tenere vix idoneus videbatur primum gubernaculi locum suscepit," &c. "Et mox, magis etiam secularia tum sapiens, tam sanctum tantæ dignitatis fastigium non horrens tenuisse, sed ultroneus ascendisse creditus," &c. "Aliter Dei amicus Moses," &c.

(2) Hæc ex chronico, cui titulus, 'De Passione et Miraculis beati Thomæ.'

(3) "Sane cum plerique soleant in his quos amant et laudant affectu quodam propensiori, sed prudentia parciori, quicquid ab eis geritur approbare; plane ego in viro illo venerabili, ea quæ ita ab ipso acta sunt, quum nulla exinde proveniret utilitas, sed fervor tantum accenderetur regius, ex quo tot mala postmodum pullulasse noscuntur, laudanda nequaquam censuerim, licet ex laudabili zelo processerint: sicut in beatissimo apostolorum principe, quod gentes suo exemplo judaizare coegit; in quo eum doctor gentium reprehensibilem declarat fuisse, licet eum constet laudabili hoc pietate fecisse," &c.

Henry II.

A.D. 1170.

Acts of Becket disproved.

"Whereas many be wont, in them whom they love and praise, judging them more by affection than prudence, to allow and approve whatsoever they do; yet for me to judge upon this reverend man, verily I think not his doings and acts to be praiseworthy, or to be allowed, for so much as thereof came no utility, but only the anger and stirring up of the king: whereupon, afterward, sprung so great mischiefs, although the thing that he did might proceed of a certain laudable zeal; like as in the blessed prince of the apostles, in that he taught the Gentiles by his example to play the Jews, Paul, the doctor of the Gentiles, did declare him therein to be rebukable, albeit it cannot be denied, but that he did it of a good affection," &c.

And in the same author, in another place, it followeth to the like effect.[1]

"The letters which were sent before for the suspending of the bishops, he pursued with burning zeal of justice; but whether according to knowledge, God knoweth it. It is not for my rude and slender wit to judge of the doings of such a person. But yet this I suppose, that he did not behave himself so circumspectly as he ought, considering the time; and that the concord between him and the king as yet was but soft and tender, who, for the consideration of the time, and for the recompense of peace might have forborne or dissembled such things, which without any peril of christian religion might be tolerated well enough, according to the prophetical saying, 'A wise man in that time will keep silence, because the time will not serve him.' Wherefore, as the doings of that reverend prelate I judge in that behalf not to be commended, so neither do I presume to discommend them. But this I say, that if that holy man, through immoderate violence of zeal, did exceed in a part therein, the same was excocted again, and purged by the fire of his suffering, which afterward ensued. And so far holy men are to be loved or praised of us, who know ourselves much inferior to their virtues; that in such things wherein they have been men, and also known to be men, therein we neither hold with them, nor commend them; but only in such things wherein without all danger or scruple we ought to imitate them. For who is able to say, that they are to be imitated in all that they do? And therefore are they not to be esteemed and praised in all things generally, whatsoever they do, but considerately and with advisement, wherein they deserve praise, so that the only prerogative in this behalf be reserved to God, in whose praise no man can exceed, how fervent soever he be in his praising," &c.

And hear yet more, what the said author writeth in the same cause of the king's wrath and Becket's faults.[2]

"More than a hundred murders are said to have been committed by the clergy under King Henry II., in punishing of whom the king was somewhat

(1) "Literas has in Angliam ad suspensionem episcoporum præmissas ipse sequebatur, zelo justitiæ fervidus; verum an plene secundum scientiam novit Deus. Nostræ enim parvitati nequaquam conceditur, de tanti viri actibus temere judicare. Puto enim quod in molli adhuc teneraque regis concordia minus provide egisset, et ea quæ sine fidei Christianæ periculo tolerari potuissent, ratione temporis et compensatione pacis dissimulanda dixisset; juxta illud propheticum: Prudens in tempore illo tacebit, quia tempus malum est. Itaque quod a venerabili pontifice tunc actum est, nec laudandum esse judico, nec vituperare præsumo: sed dico, si vel modice in hujusmodi a sancto viro per zeli, immoderatiorem impetum esse excessum, hoc ipsum est sacræ, quæ consecuta noscitur, igne passionis excoctum. Ita quippe sancti viri vel amandi vel laudandi sunt a nobis, qui nos illis longe impares esse cognoscimus, ut ea, in quibus homines fuerunt, vel fuisse noscuntur, nequaquam vel amemus vel laudemus: sed ea tantum, in quibus eos sine scrupulo imitari debemus. Quis enim eos dicat in omnibus, quæ ab ipsis fiant, esse imitabiles? Non igitur in omnibus, quæ faciunt, sed sapienter et caute debent laudari, ut sua Deo prærogativa servetur, in cujus utique laudibus nemo potest esse nimius, quantumcunque laudare conetur," &c.

(2) "Plusquam centum homicidia a clericis commissa sub Henrico secundo dicuntur. In quibus plectendis rex aliquanto vehementior. Sed hujus immoderationis regiæ nostri temporis episcopos tantum respicit culpa, quantum ab eis processit et causa. Cum enim sacri præcipiunt canones, clericos non solum facinorosos, et gravioribus irretitos criminibus, verum etiam leviorum criminum reos degradari, et tot millia talium, tanquam innumeras inter pauca grana paleas ecclesia Anglicana contineat, tamen quam paucos a multis retro annis clericos in Anglia contigit officio privari. Nempe episcopi dum defendendis magis clericorum libertatibus vel dignitatibus, quam eorum vitiis corrigendis resecandisque invigilant, arbitrantur obsequium se præstare Deo et ecclesiæ, si facinorosos clericos, quos pro officii debito canonicæ vigore censuræ coercere debeant, contra publicam tueantur disciplinam. Unde clerici, qui in sortem Domini vocati, tanquam stellæ in firmamento cœli positæ, vita et verbo lucere deberent super terram, habentes pro impunitate agendi quodcunque libuerit, licentiam et libertatem, neque Deum, cujus judicium tardare videtur, neque homines potestatem habentes reverentur, cum et episcopalis circa eos solicitudo sit languida, et seculari eos jurisdictione sacri eximat ordinis prærogativa."

too vehement. But the fault," saith he, "of this immoderate dealing of the king resteth most in the bishops of our time, forasmuch as the cause thereof proceedeth of them. For where it is decreed and commanded by the canon law, concerning the spiritual men of the clergy, that not only such as be notorious, but such as be spotted with lighter crimes, should be degraded, whereof we have so many thousands, and whole swarms of such now in England, as innumerable chaff among the little good grain; yet how few do we see, these many years in England, deprived of their office? For why? The bishops, while they labour more to maintain the liberties and dignities of churchmen, than to correct their vices, think they do God and the church great service if they rescue and defend the enormities of the churchmen against public discipline, whom they ought rather to punish by the virtue of the censure ecclesiastical. Whereupon the churchmen, such as be sorted peculiarly to the Lord, and who ought like stars to shine in the earth by word and example, taking license and liberty to do what they lust, neither reverence God, whose judgment seemeth to tarry, nor men set in authority; when both the bishops are slack in their charge doing, and also the prerogative of their order exempteth them from the secular jurisdiction," &c.

And thus much out of Neuburgensis.

To this matter also pertain the words of Cæsarius, the monk, in his eighth book of Dialogues, and sixty-ninth chapter, about the eight and fortieth year after the death of Thomas Becket, A. D. 1220. His words, in sum, come to this effect:[1]— Whether Thomas Becket be saved or damned.

"There was a question moved among the masters of Paris, whether Thomas Becket were saved or damned? To this question answereth Roger, a Norman, that he was worthy death and damnation, for that he was so obstinate against God's minister, his king.—Contrary, Peter Cantor, a Parisian, disputed, saying and affirming, that his miracles were great signs and tokens of salvation, and also of great holiness in that man; affirming, moreover, that the cause of the church did allow and confirm his martyrdom, for the which church he died."

And thus have ye the judgment and censure of the school of Paris touching this question, for the sainting of Thomas Becket; in which judgment, forasmuch as the greatest argument resteth in the miracles wrought by him after his death, let us therefore pause a little upon the same, to try and examine these miracles. In the trial of them we shall find one of these two things to be true; either that if they were true, they were not wrought by God, but by a contrary spirit, of whom Christ our Lord giveth us warning in his gospel, saying, "Whose coming shall be with lying signs and wonders, to deceive, if it were possible, the elect," (Matt. xxiv.) or else we shall find that no such were ever wrought at all, but were feigned and forged of idle monks and religious bellies, for the exaltation of their churches, and the profit of their pouches; which thing indeed seemeth rather to be true, and no less may appear by the miracles themselves, set forth by one of his own monks, and of his own time;[2] who, in five solemn books, hath comprehended all the revelations, virtues, and miracles of this archbishop; the which books (as yet remaining in the hands of William Stephenson, citizen of London) I have seen and perused; wherein is contained the whole sum of all his

(1) "Quæstio Parisiis inter magistros ventilata fuit, utrum damnatus an salvatus esset ille Thomas. Dixerat Rogerius tunc Normanus, fuisse illum morte ac damnatione dignum, quod contumax esset in Dei ministrum regem. Protulit contra Petrus Cantor Parisiensis, quod signa salvationis et magnæ sanctitatis essent ejus miracula: et quod martyrium probasset ecclesiæ causa, pro qua mortem subierat." If God in these latter days giveth no miracles to glorify his own Son; much less will he give miracles to glorify Thomas Becket.

(2) Liber de Miraculis Beati Thomæ, authore monacho quodam Cantuar.

Henry II. A.D. 1170.

miracles, to the number of two hundred and seventy, being so far off from all truth and reason, some ridiculous, some monstrous, vain, absurd, some also blasphemous, and some so impudent, that not only they deserve no credit, as altogether savouring of mere forgery, but also, for very shame, will abash an honest pen to write of them. First, if miracles serve for necessity and for infidels, what cause, or necessity was there, in a christian realm having the word of God, for God to work such miracles after his death, who never wrought any in all his life? Then, to consider the end of these miracles: whither do they tend, but only to bring men to Canterbury, with their vows and offerings to enrich the covent?

Miracles of Becket considered.

Besides the number of these miracles—which are said to be so many, that they lose their own credit—what disease is there belonging to man or woman in the curing whereof some miracle hath not been wrought by this θαυματοῦργος, as fevers, fistula, the gout, toothache, palsy, consumption, falling-sickness, leprosy, head-ache, broken arms, maimed legs, swelled throats, the raising up of the dead who have been two days departed; with infinite others. And, as all these have been healed, for the most part, by one kind of salve, as a certain panacea, namely, with only the water of Canterbury, like as a cunning smith, who would open with one key all manner of locks; so again, in reading of the story of these miracles, ye shall find the matter so conveyed that the power of this dead saint was never twice showed on any one disease, but that every diverse disease had a diverse miracle.

Aqua Cantuariensis.

To recite in order all these prodigious revelations and fantastical miracles, falsely imagined and ascribed to this archbishop, were nothing else but to write a legend of lies, and to occupy the people with trifles: which because it pertaineth rather to the idle possession of such dreaming monks and cloisterers, as have nothing else to maintain that religion withal, I will not take their profession out of their hands. Wherefore, to omit all such vain and lying apparitions and miracles, as how this angry saint, three days after his death, appeared by vision at the altar in his pontificalibus, commanding the choir not to sing, but to say this office of his mass, "Exurge, quare obdormis Domine," &c., which vision the author himself of the book doth say he did see. To omit also the blasphemous lie, how in another vision the said archbishop should say, that his blood did cry out of the earth to God, more than the blood of just Abel. Item, in another vision it was showed to a monk of Lewes, how St. Thomas had his place in heaven appointed with the apostles, above Stephen, Laurence, Vincent, and all other martyrs; whereof this cause is rendered, for that St. Stephen, Laurence, and such others, suffered only for their own cause; but this Thomas suffered for the universal church. Item, how it was showed to a certain young man, Ormus by name, twelve years before the death of this Becket, that among the apostles and martyrs in heaven there was a vacant place left for a certain priest, as he said, of England, who was credibly supposed to be this Thomas Becket. Item, how a certain knight's son, being two days dead, was revived again as soon as he had the water of Canterbury put into his mouth, and had by his parents four pieces of silver bended, to be offered in Canterbury in the child's behalf. All

Singing at the mass forbidden by Thomas Becket after his death.

A blasphemous lie.

Becket above the martyrs in heaven.

A place prepared in heaven for Becket twelve years before his death.

these, I say, with such others omitted, the number whereof cometh to an infinite variety, only this one story, or another that followeth, shall suffice to express the vanity and impudent forgery of all the rest.

In the fourth book of this fabulous author, and in the third chapter, a miracle is there contained of a certain countryman of Bedfordshire, in King's Weston, whose name was Eilward, which Eilward, in his drunkenness, bursting into another man's house who was his debtor, took out of his house a great whetstone and a pair of hedging-gloves. The other party, seeing this value not sufficient for his condemnation, by the counsel of the town clerk, entered an action of felony against him for other things besides, as for stealing his wimble, his axe, his net, and his clothes.[1] Whereupon Eilward, being had to the gaol of Bedford, and afterward condemned for the same, was judged to have both his eyes put out, and otherwise to be disgracefully mutilated. This punishment, by the malice of his adversary, being executed upon him, he, lying in great danger of death by bleeding, was counselled to make his prayer to this Thomas of Canterbury. Which done, (saith the miracle,) there appeared one to him by night, in white apparel, bidding him to watch and pray, and put his trust in God and our Lady, and holy St. Thomas. In conclusion, the miracle thus fell out: the next day at evening, the man rubbing his eye-lids, began to feel his eyes to be restored again; first, in a little; after, in a greater measure; so that one was of a grey colour, the other was black: and here was one miracle rung. After this followed another miracle also upon the same person; for, going but the space of four miles, when his eyes were restored, he chanced in like manner to rub the parts where he had been mutilated, which immediately on the same (to use the words of my story) were to him by degrees restored, and this he permitted every one to ascertain, and shamed not to deny; insomuch that he, first coming up to St. Thomas, at London, was received with joy of the bishop of Durham; who, then sending to the burghers of Bedford for the truth of the matter, received from them again letters testimonial, wherein the citizens there (saith this fabulous festival) confirmed, first to the bishop, then to the covent of Canterbury, the relation of this to be as hath been told. This one miracle, gentle reader! so shameless and impudent, I thought here to express, that by this one thou mightest judge of all the residue of his miracles; and by the residue thereof mightest judge, moreover, of the filthy wickedness of all these lying monks and cloisterers, who count it a light sport so impudently to deceive the simple souls of Christ's church with trifling lies and dreaming fables. Wherefore, as I said, if the holy sainting of Thomas Becket standeth upon no other thing but upon his miracles, what credit is to be given thereto? and upon what a weak ground his shrine so long hath stood, by this may easily be seen. Furthermore, another fable as notable as this, and no less worthy of the whetstone, we read in the story of Gervasius; namely, that Thomas Becket appearing to a certain priest, named Thomas, declared to him, that he had so brought to pass, that all the names of the monks of the church of Canterbury, with the names of

An impudent and a lying miracle.

A blasphemous vision.

A false and impudent miracle. +

(1) Ex Historia Monachi Cant. de Miraculis Becketi Thomæ.

Henry II. A.D. 1170.

the priests and clerks, and with the families belonging to that city and church of Canterbury, were written in the Book of Life.[1]

But whatsoever is to be thought of his miracles, or howsoever the testimony of the school of Paris, or of these ancient times, went with him or against him; certain it is, that this anthem or collect, lately collected and primered in his praise, is blasphemous, and derogateth from the praise of Him, to whom only all praise and honour are due, where it is said:[2]

The blasphemous anthem of Thomas Becket.

> "For the blood of Thomas,
> Which he for thee did spend,
> Grant us, Christ, to climb
> Where Thomas did ascend."

wherein is a double lie contained; first, that he died for Christ; secondly, that if he had so done, yet that his blood could purchase heaven; which thing neither Paul nor any of the apostles durst ever challenge to themselves, for if any man's blood could bring us to heaven, then the blood of Christ was shed in vain.

And thus much touching the testimony or censure of certain ancient times concerning the cause of Thomas Becket, in the explication of whose history I have now stood the longer (exceeding peradventure in over-much prolixity), to the intent that his cause being fully opened to the world, and duly weighed on every part, men's minds thereby, long deceived by ignorance, might come unto the more perfect certainty of the truth thereof, and thereby judge more surely what is to be received, and what to be refused. Where, by the way, is to be noted out of the testimony of Rob. Crickeladensis, that which in him I find; namely, that the peers and nobles of this land, near about the king, gave out in straight charge, upon pain of death, and confiscating of all their goods, that no man should be so hardy as to name Thomas Becket to be a martyr, or to preach of his miracles.

After the death of Thomas Becket, the king fearing the pope's wrath and curse to be laid upon him (whereunto Louis, the French king, also helped what he could to set the matter forward), sent to Rome the archbishop of Rothomage, with certain other bishops and archdeacons, unto the pope with his excuse, which the pope would in no wise hear. And afterwards, other messengers being sent, whom some of the cardinals received, it was showed to them that on Good Friday, (being then near at hand,) the pope of custom was used to assoil, or to curse, and that it was noised, how the king of England with his bishops should be cursed, and his land interdicted, and that they should be put in prison.[3] After this, certain of the cardinals showed the pope, that the messengers had power to swear to the pope, that the king should obey his punishment and penance, which was taken both of the king and the archbishop of York; so that in the same day the pope cursed the deed-doers, with such as were of their consent, who either aided or harboured them. Concerning these deed-doers, it is touched briefly before, how they, lying in

The king sendeth to Rome.

(1) Ex Gervas. fol. 6.
(2) "Tu per Thomæ sanguinem, quem pro te impendit,
Fac nos Christe scandere, quo Thomas ascendit."
(3) Ex Libro Annotationum Historicarum manuscripto, J. Stenii.

Gainsborough, fled into Yorkshire; who, after having in penance to go in their linen clothes barefoot (in fasting and prayer) to Jerusalem, by reason of this hard penance are said to have died a few years after. *Henry II.* A.D. 1172.

The king's ambassadors lying, as is said, in Rome, could find no grace nor favour for a long time at the pope's hands. At length, with much ado, it was agreed that two cardinals should be sent down to inquire out the matter concerning those who were consenting to Becket's death. The king, perceiving what was preparing at Rome, neither being yet certain whereto the intent of the pope and coming down of the cardinals would tend, in the mean time addressed himself with a great power to enter into Ireland, giving in charge and commandment, as Hoveden writeth, that no bringer of any brief or letter should come over into England, or pass out of the realm (of what degree or condition soever he were), without special license and assurance that he would bring nothing that should be prejudicial to the realm. The penance of the four knights.

This order being set and ordained, the king, with four hundred great ships, taketh his journey to Ireland, where he subdued in short time the whole land unto him, which at that time was governed under divers kings to the number of five, of whom four submitted themselves unto the said King Henry; the fifth, who was the king of Tonacta, denied to be subdued, keeping himself in woods and marshes. Ireland first subdued to England.

In the mean season, while the king was thus occupied in Ireland, the two cardinals who were sent from the pope, namely, Theodine and Albert, were come to Normandy. Unto them the king the next year following resorted about the month of October, A.D. 1172. A.D. 1172. But before this (during the time of the king's being in Ireland), the bishop of London, and Joseline, bishop of Salisbury, had sent to Rome, and procured their absolution from the pope. The king returning out of Ireland, by Wales, into England, and from thence to Normandy, there made his purgation before the pope's legates, as touching the death of the aforesaid Becket; to the which he sware he was neither aiding nor consenting, but only that he spake rigorous words against him, for that his knights would not avenge him against the said Thomas; for the which cause this penance was enjoined him under his oath:

First, That he should send so much into the Holy Land as would find two hundred knights or soldiers for the defence of that land. The king's penance for the death of Becket.

Item, That from Christmas-day next following, he should set forth in his own person to fight for the Holy Land, the space of three years together, unless he should be otherwise dispensed withal by the pope.

Item, That if he would make his journey into Spain (as his present necessity did require), there he should fight against the Saracens, and as long as he should there abide, so long space might he take in prolonging his journey toward Jerusalem.

Item, That he should not hinder, nor cause to be hindered, any appellations made to the pope of Rome.

Item, That neither he nor his son should depart or dissever from Pope Alexander, or from his catholic successors, so long as they should account him or his son for kings catholic.

Henry II. A.D. 1174.

Item, That the goods and possessions taken from the church of Canterbury should be restored again, fully and amply, as they stood the year before Thomas Becket departed the realm; and that free liberty should be granted, to all such as were outlawed for Becket's cause, to return again.

Item, That the aforesaid customs and decrees, by him established against the church, should be extinct and repealed, (such only excepted as concerned his own person, &c.) besides other secret fastings and alms enjoined him.

All these former conditions the king with his son did both agree unto, debasing himself in such sort of submission before the two cardinals, by the occasion whereof the cardinals took no little glory, using this verse of the Psalm:—"Which looketh upon the earth, and maketh it to tremble; which toucheth the hills, and they smoke."[1] Moreover, it is mentioned in histories of the said king, that a little after William, king of Scots, with his army, had made a road into the realm, he, returning out of Normandy into England, came first to Canterbury; who, by the way, as soon as he came to the sight of Becket's church, lighting off his horse, and putting off his shoes, went barefoot to his tomb, whose steps were found bloody through the roughness of the stones. And not only that, but also he received further penance; by every monk of the cloister, certain discipline of a rod. By which so great dejection of the king (if it were true), thou mayest see the blind and lamentable superstition and ignorance of those days.[2] If it were pretensed (as might so be in time of war, to get the hearts of the people), yet mayest thou, learned reader, see what slavery kings and princes were brought into at that time under the pope's clergy. The same year (as Hoveden writeth), which was A.D. 1174, the whole city of Canterbury was almost all consumed with fire, and the said minster-church clean burnt.

King Henry II. goeth on pilgrimage with bloody steps to Thomas Becket's tomb.

A.D. 1174.

The city of Canterbury almost consumed with fire.

The next year ensuing, which was A.D. 1175, a convocation of bishops was holden at Westminster, by Richard, archbishop of Canterbury. In that conventicle all the bishops and abbots of the province of Canterbury and of York being present, determined, as had been done a little before in the days of King Henry I. A.D. 1113, about the obedience that York should do to Canterbury; that is, whether the archbishop of York might bear his cross in the diocese of Canterbury or not? whereof something was touched before in the former process of this history. Also about the bishopric of Lincoln, of Chichester, of Worcester, and of Hereford, whether these churches were under the jurisdiction of the see of York or not? &c. Upon these and other like matters rose such controversy between these two sees, that the one appealed the other to the presence of the bishop of Rome.

A.D. 1175.

Controversy between the see of Canterbury and the see of York. The latter appealeth the former to the bishop of Rome.

In these and such like causes, how much better had it been if the supremacy had remained more near in the king's hands at home, whereby not only much labour and travail had been saved, but also the great and wasteful expenses bestowed at Rome might, with much more fruit and thank, have been converted to their cures and flocks committed unto them, and also, perchance, their cause, not less indifferently heard, at least more speedily might have been decided. But

(1) Ex Quadrilogo. (2) Ex Rogero Hovedeno, Quadrilogo, et aliis.

to the purpose again. In this controversy divers of the archbishop of York's clergy, such as were of Gloucester, belonging to the church of St. Oswald, were excommunicated by the archbishop of Canterbury, because they, being summoned, refused to appear before him, &c. At length the same year, which was A.D. 1175, there was a cardinal sent down from Rome by the king's procurement, who studied to settle a peace between the two archbishops. Whereupon, this way of agreement was taken, by means of the king, at Winchester, that, as touching the church of St. Oswald, at Gloucester, the archbishop of Canterbury should cease his claim thereon, molesting the see of York no more therein; also, that he should absolve again the clerks thereof, whom he had excommunicated before. And, as concerning the bearing of the cross and all other matters, it was referred to the archbishop of Rothomage, and to other bishops in France, so that for five years a league or truce was taken betwixt them, till they should have a full determination of their cause.

Henry II. A.D. 1175. The clerks of St Oswald in Gloucester excommunicated. Agreement between the archbishop of Canterbury and York

The next year following, the aforesaid King Henry II., dividing the realm of England into six parts, ordained upon every part three justices of assize. The circuit or limitation of these justices was thus disposed. The first upon Norfolk, Suffolk, Cambridgeshire, Huntingdonshire, Bedfordshire, Buckinghamshire, Essex, Hertfordshire. Two upon Lincolnshire, Nottinghamshire, Derbyshire, Stamfordshire, Warwickshire, Northamptonshire, Leicestershire. Three upon Kent, Surrey, Southamptonshire, Sussex, Berkshire, Oxfordshire. Four upon Herefordshire, Gloucestershire, Worcestershire, Salopshire. Five upon Wiltshire, Dorsetshire, Somersetshire, Devonshire, Cornwall. Six upon Everikeshire, Richmondshire, Lancaster, Copland, Westmoreland, Northumberland, Cumberland.

A.D. 1176. Justices of assize divided into six circuits

In the same year Richard, archbishop of Canterbury, made three archdeacons in his diocese, whereas before there was but one.[1] About this time also it was granted by the king to the pope's legate, that a clerk should not be called before a temporal judge, except for offence in the forest, or for his lay fee that he holdeth.

Item, that no archbishopric, bishopric, or abbey, should remain in the king's hands over one year without great cause. It chanced the same year that this was done, that there was at Canterbury one elected to be abbot in the house of St. Austin, named Albert, who made great labour and suit unto the archbishop that he would come to his church, and there consecrate him abbot of St. Austin;[2] to whom the archbishop sent word again, that he was not bound to come to him, but rather that the other should repair to the metropolitan church of Canterbury, there to receive his consecration. Whereupon, controversy arising between them, the aforesaid newly elect appealed to the audience of the pope, and so laboured up himself to Rome; where he so handled the matter, (by what means I cannot tell, unless with his golden bottle, wherewith he quenched the pope's thirsty soul, for abbots never travel lightly without fat purses to Rome,) that with short dispatch he procured letters from Alexander the pope, to Roger, bishop of Worcester; signifying to him, that he had given

A frivolous contention between the archbishop and the abbot of Canterbury.

(1) Ex epitome Matth. Paris. et aliarum historiarum

(2) Where was here the precept of the gospel, "He that will be greatest among you, let him be an underling to others?"

Henry II. A.D. 1176. in charge and commandment to the archbishop of Canterbury, in the behalf of his dear son Albert, that he should consecrate him within his own monastery, which monastery properly and solely, without mediation, belonged to the jurisdiction of Rome; and so likewise should do to his successors after him, without any exaction of obedience of them. Which thing, further he said, if the archbishop would refuse to do within the term appointed, that then he the aforesaid bishop of Worcester should, by the authority committed unto him, execute the same, all manner of appellation or other decree, whatsoever should come, notwithstanding. This letter being obtained, the abbot that would be, returneth home, supposing with himself all things to be sure. The archbishop understanding the case, and seeing himself to be so straitly charged, and yet loth to yield and stoop to the abbot, took to him policy where authority would not serve; and both to save himself, and yet to disappoint the abbot, he watched a time when the abbot was about the business of his house, and coming the same time to the monastery, as he was commanded to do, with all things appointed that to such a business appertained, he called for the abbot, pretending no less than to give him his consecration. The abbot, being called for, was not at home; the archbishop, feigning himself not a little grieved at his labour and good will so lost, departed, as one in whom no ready diligence was lacking, if in case that the abbot had been at home. Whereupon the abbot, being thus disappointed, was fain to fill his silver flagons afresh, and make a new course to Rome to his father, the pope, from whom he received his consecration, and so came home again, with as much wit as he went forth, but not with so much money, peradventure, as he went withal.

The tenor of the pope's letter to the bishop of Worcester.

We have declared a little before, touching the acts and doings of this Pope Alexander III., how he had brought the emperor's head under his foot in St. Mark's church at Venice, at which time and place peace was concluded, and a composition made between the pope and the said Frederic the emperor; which pacification Roger Hoveden and Walter Gisburn refer to this time, A.D. 1177, bringing in two several letters sent from the said Pope, to Richard, archbishop of Canterbury, to Roger, archbishop of York, and Hugh, bishop of Durham. Out of the said letters, so much as serveth our purpose, I have taken and here inserted.

A.D. 1177.

The Letter of Pope Alexander, sent to Roger, archbishop of York, and to the bishop of Durham.[1]

"Alexander, servant of the servants of God, to his reverend brethren, Roger, archbishop of York, and Hugh, bishop of Durham, greeting and apostolical blessing. The obsequy and service of your kind devotion, which hitherto you are known to have given both devoutly and laudably to us and to the church, requireth that we should describe to you, as to our special friends, the prosperous success of the church, and let you know, as spiritual children of the church, what hath happened to the same. For meet it is, convenient, and also honest, that you, whom we have had so firm and sure in our devotion, should now be cherished and made joyous in the prosperity of us, and of the church."

(1) The Latin of the two extracts here translated by our author may be found in the Edition of 1563, p. 68.—Ed.

And about the end of the epistle it followeth thus:—

"The next day following, which was the feast of St. James, (the said emperor so requesting), we came to the aforesaid church of St. Mark, there to celebrate our solemn mass; where, as we were coming in the way, the said emperor met us without the church, and placing us again on his right hand, brought us so into the church. After the mass was done, placing us again on his right hand, he brought us to the church door. And moreover, when we should take our palfrey, he held our stirrup, exhibiting to us such honour and reverence, as his progenitors were wont to exhibit to our predecessors. Wherefore these shall be to incite your diligence and study towards us, that you rejoice with us and the church in these our prosperous successes, and also that you shall open the same effect of peace to other devout children of the church; that such as be touched with the zeal of the house of the Lord, may congratulate and rejoice also in the Lord for the great working of peace which he hath given.—Given at Venice, in the deep river, the 26th of July."

A meek emperor, and a proud pope. The emperor holdeth the pope's stirrup.

This year the contention revived again, spoken of a little before, between the two archbishops of York and Canterbury, the occasion whereof was this; the manner and practice of the pope is, when he beginneth to lack money, he sendeth some limiting[1] cardinal abroad to fetch his harvest in. So there came this year into England, as lightly few years were without them, a certain cardinal from Rome, called Hugo, or, as Hoveden nameth him, Hugezim, who would needs keep a council at Westminster. To this council resorted a great confluence, about the middle of Lent, of bishops, abbots, priors, doctors, and such others of the clergy. As every one was there placed in his order, and after his degree, first cometh the archbishop of York, named Roger, who, thinking to prevent the other archbishop, came something sooner, and straightway placed himself on the right hand of the cardinal. Richard, the archbishop of Canterbury, following shortly after, and seeing the first place taken up, refuseth to take the second, complaining of the archbishop of York, as one prejudicial to his see. So, while the one would not rise, and the other not sit down, there rose no small contention between the two. The archbishop of Canterbury claimed the upper seat by the pre-eminence of his church; contrary, the archbishop of York alleged for him, the old decree of Gregory, whereof mention is made before, by which this order was taken between the two metropolitans of Canterbury and York, that whichever of them two should be first in election, he should have the pre-eminence in dignity to go before the other. Thus they, contending to and fro, waxed so warm in words, that at last they turned to hot blows. How strong the archbishop of York was in reason and argument, I cannot tell, but the archbishop of Canterbury was stronger at the arm's end; whose servants being more in number, like valiant men, not suffering their master to take such a foil, so prevailed against York (sitting on the right hand of the cardinal), that they plucked him down from the hand to the foot of the cardinal upon the ground, treading and trampling upon him with their feet, that marvel it was he escaped with life. His casule, chimer, and rochet,[2] were all rent and torn from his back. Here no reason would take place, no debating would serve, no praying could

Contention between two archbishops, who should sit on the right hand of the cardinal.

(1) Chaucer uses the word 'limitour' to express a friar, who had a license to beg within certain limits.—Ed.

(2) The "casule" is probably the under garment, the "chimer" is a short light under dress worn by the bishops; and the "rochet" is the lawn sleeves.—Ed.

Henry II. A.D. 1177.

be heard, such clamour and tumult were there in the house among them, much like to the tumult which Virgil describeth:—

> "Ac veluti in magno populo, cum sæpe coorta est
> Seditio, sævitque animis ignobile vulgus,
> Jamque faces et saxa volant, furor arma ministrat."[1]

Now, as the first part of this description doth well agree, so some peradventure will look again, that, according to the latter part also of the same, my lord cardinal, with sageness and gravity (after the manner of the old Romans standing up), should have ceased and allayed the disturbance, according to that which followeth in the poet:—

> "Tum pietate gravem meritis si forte virum quem
> Conspexere, silent, arrectisque auribus astant:
> Ille regit mentes dictis, et pectora mulcet."[2]

But what did the noble Roman cardinal? Like a pretty man of his hands, but a prettier man of his feet, standing up in the midst, and seeing the house in such a broil, committed himself to flight, and, as Hoveden writeth, "abscondit se a facie illorum." The next day the archbishop of York bringeth to the cardinal his rochet, to bear witness what injury and violence he had sustained; appealing and citing up the archbishop of Canterbury, with certain of his men, to the bishop of Rome. And thus the holy council, the same day it was begun, brake up and was dissolved.

The large dominion of Henry II. Under the reign of this King Henry II., the dominion and crown of England extended so far as hath not been seen in this realm before him. Histories record that he possessed under his rule and jurisdiction, *Homage of Scotland.* first, Scotland, to whom William, king of Scots, with all the lords temporal and spiritual, did homage both for them and for their successors (the seal whereof remaineth in the king's treasury); as also Ireland, England, Normandy, Aquitaine, Gaunt, &c., to the mountains of Pyrenees, which be in the uttermost part of the great ocean in the British Sea; being also protector of France, to whom Philip the French king yielded both himself and his realm wholly to his *Henry II. protector of France.* governance, A.D. 1181. Moreover, he was offered also to be the king of Jerusalem, by the patriarch and master of the hospital there; *Chosen king of Jerusalem and refuseth it.* who, being then distressed by the soldan, brought him the keys of their city, desiring his aid against the infidels; which offer he then refused, alleging the great charge which he had at home, and the rebellion of his sons, which might happen in his absence.

Aid not to be denied to our neighbours, the cause being godly. And here the old histories find a great fault with the king for his refusal; declaring that to be the cause of God's plagues, which after ensued upon him by his children, as the patriarch, in his oration, being offended with the king, prophesied should so happen to him for the same cause; which story, if it be true, it may be a lesson to good princes, not to deny their necessary help to their distressed neighbours, especially the cause appertaining unto God.[3]

(1) Virg. Æn. I. 148.
"As when in tumults rise the ignoble crowd,
Mad are their motions and their tongues are loud;
And stones and brands in rattling vollies fly,
And all the rustic arms that fury can supply."

(2) "If then some grave and pious man appear,
They hush their noise and lend a listening ear:
He soothes with sober words their angry mood,
And quenches their innate desire of blood."—Dryden.

(3) Ex Polychro. Ex Giraldo Cambriensi.

The wisdom, discretion, manhood, and riches of this prince were so spread and renowned through all quarters, that messages came from Emmanuel, emperor of Constantinople, Frederic, emperor of Rome, and William, archbishop of Treves in Almain, from the duke of Saxony, and from the earl of Flanders, and also from the French king (upon determination of great questions and strifes), to ask counsel and determination thereof of this King Henry, as of one most wise, and schoolmaster of all wisdom and justice, to have solution of their questions and doubts. Moreover Alphonsus, king of Castile, and Sancius, king of Navarre, being in strife for certain castles and other possessions, submitted them, of their free accord, and by their oath, to abide the award of this King Henry, who made award and pleased them both; whereby it is to be presupposed, that this king, to whom other princes did so resort, as to their arbiter and deciser, did not attend either to any sloth or vicious living. Wherefore it may seem that the acts of this prince were not so vicious as some monkish writers do describe.

Henry II

A.D. 1181.

Henry II chosen arbiter by two kings

Among many other things in this king memorable, this one is to be noted (follow it who can), that he reigned five and thirty years, and having such wars with his enemies, yet never upon his subjects put any tribute or tax, nor yet upon the spiritualty, first-fruits, and appropriations of benefices It is likely they were not known, or else not used. And yet his treasure after his death, weighed by King Richard, his son, amounted to above nine hundred thousand pounds, besides jewels, precious stones, and household furniture. Of this substance eleven thousand pounds came to him by the death of Roger, archbishop of York, who had procured a bull of the pope, that if any priest died within his province without testament, then he should have all his goods. And shortly after the archbishop died, and the king had all his goods, which extended, as is said, to eleven thousand pounds, besides plate, A.D. 1181.

The treasure of King Henry II

A covetous archbishop

But as there is no felicity or wealth in this mortal world so perfect, which is not darkened with some cloud of encumbrance and adversity; so it happened to this king, that among his other princely successors, this incommodity followed him withal, that his sons rebelled and stood in armour against him, taking the part of the French king against their father. First, at the coronation of Henry, his son, whom the father joined with him as king, he being both father and king, notwithstanding, took upon himself, as a steward, to set down the first dish as servant to his son, renouncing the name of a king. At what time the aforesaid archbishop of York, sitting on the right hand of the young king, said, "Sir, ye have great cause this day to joy, for there is no prince in the world that hath such an officer this day," &c. And the young king disdaining his words, said, "My father is not dishonoured in this doing, for I am a king and a queen's son, and so is not he." And not only this, but afterwards he also persecuted his father; and so, in his youth, when he had reigned but a few years, died, teaching us what is the price and reward of breaking the just commandment of God.

Pride destroyeth all

After him likewise Richard (who was called Richard Cœur de Lion) rebelled against his father, and also John, his youngest son, did not much degenerate from the steps of his brethren, insomuch that this

Henry II A.D. 1189.

aforesaid Richard, like an unkind child, persecuting and taking part against his father, brought him to such distress of body and mind, that for thought of heart he fell into an ague, and within four days departed, A.D. 1189, after he had reigned five and thirty years;[1] whose corpse, as it was carried to be buried (Richard his son coming by the way and meeting it, and beginning for compassion to weep), the blood brast incontinent out of the nose of the king at the coming of his son, giving thereby a certain demonstration how he was the only author of his death.

King Henry II persecuted by his sons His death, A.D. 1189 How the king, being dead, bled at the coming of his son

After the reign and death of this king, his children after him, worthily rewarded for their unnaturalness against their father, lacking the success which their father had, lost all beyond the sea that he had got before.

And thus much concerning the reign of Henry II., and the death of Thomas Becket, which (as is aforesaid) happened in the days of Pope Alexander III., who, usurping the keys of ecclesiastical regiment one and twenty years, or, as Gisburn writeth, three and twenty years, governed the church with much tumult; striving and contending with Frederic the emperor; not shaming, like a most proud Lucifer, to tread with his foot upon the neck of the said emperor, as is above described.

This pope, among many other acts, had certain councils, as is partly before touched, some in France, some at Rome, in Lateran; by whom it was decreed, that no archbishop should receive the pall, unless he should first swear obedience, A.D. 1179; concerning the solemnity of which pall, for the order and manner of giving and taking the same with obedience to the pope, as it is contained in their own words, I thought it good to set it forth unto thee, that thou mayest well consider and understand their doings therein.

The form and manner how, and by what words, the pope is wont to give the pall unto the archbishop.[1]

To the honour[1] of Almighty God, and of blessed Mary, the Virgin, and of blessed St Peter and St. Paul, and of our lord Pope N. and of the holy church of Rome, and also of the church of N. committed to your charge, we give to you the pall taken from the body[2] of St Peter, as a fulness of the office pontifical, which you may wear within your own church, upon certain days,[4] which be expressed in the privileges of the said church, granted by the see apostolic.

NOTES UPON THE SAME.

1 "To the honour," &c. With what confidence durst the pope couple the honour of Almighty God, and the honour of Mary, of St Peter, and of the pope, and of the Romish church all together, if he had not been a presumptuous Lucifer, equalling himself not only with such saints, but also even with him who is God alone, to be blessed for ever?

2. "Taken from the body," &c. If St. Peter's body be not all consumed, let him show it if he can If he cannot show it, how then is this pall taken from the body of St. Peter? or if he mean it to be of St. Peter's own wearing, then belike St. Peter had a goodly wardrobe of palls, when every archbishop in all Christendom receiveth from the pope a divers pall.

3. "As a fulness of the office," &c. Rather he might say, the fulness of his own purse, when archbishops paid so sweetly for it, insomuch that Jacobus, the archbishop of Mentz, as is above touched a little before, in the council of

(1) "Ad honorem omnipotentis Dei, et beatæ Mariæ Virginis, et beatorum Petri et Pauli, et domini nostri *N* Papæ, et sanctæ Romanæ ecclesiæ, necnon *N* ecclesiæ tibi commissæ, tradimus tibi pallium de corpore beati Petri sumptum, plenitudinem pontificalis officii, ut utaris eo infra ecclesiam tuam certis diebus, qui exprimuntur in privilegiis tibi ab apostolica sede concessis"

Basil, where the price was wont to be but a thousand florins, could not obtain it without six and twenty thousand florins.

4. "Upon certain days," &c. This difference there was between the pope and other archbishops: the pope might wear the pall at all times, and in all places, at his pleasure; archbishops might not wear it but upon certain days, and in their church only, within their province. Moreover this pall should not be asked but with great instance, and within three months; without which pall he is not to be named archbishop, but may be deposed, having it not after three months; and the same pall must also be buried with him when he dieth; and when it is given, some privilege must be given withal, or the old renewed.[1]

In like manner proceedeth the oath of every bishop swearing obedience to the pope in words as followeth:[2]—

"I, *N.*, bishop of *N.*, from this hour henceforth, will be faithful and obedient to blessed St. Peter, and to the holy apostolic church of Rome, and to my Lord *N.*, the pope. I shall be in no council, nor help either with my consent or deed, whereby either of them, or any member of them, may be impaired, or whereby they may be taken with any evil taking. The council which they shall commit to me, either by themselves, or by messenger, or by their letters, wittingly or willingly I shall utter to none to their hindrance and damage. To the retaining and maintaining the papacy of Rome, and the regalities of St. Peter, I shall be an aider (so mine order be saved) against all persons. The legate of the apostolic see, both in going and coming, I shall honourably treat and help in all necessities. Being called to a synod, I shall be ready to come, unless I be let by some lawful and canonical impeachment. The palace of the apostles every third year I shall visit either by myself or my messenger, except otherwise being licensed by the see apostolic. All such possessions as belong to the table and diet of my bishopric, I shall neither sell, nor give, nor lay to mortgage, nor lease out, nor remove away by any manner of means, without the consent and knowledge of the bishop of Rome:[3] so God help me and the holy gospels of God.

This was the clause that made Becket to be banished and slain.

A NOTE UPON THE SAME.

Hereby thou hast by the way, gentle reader, to note and consider, among other things which here may be understood, that since the time the oath began to be laid and thrust upon bishops, all general councils began to lose their liberty. For, how could any freedom remain for men to speak their knowledge in redress of things, being by their oath so bound to the pope to speak nothing but on his side, to maintain the papacy and the church of Rome in all times and places? Conjecture by thyself, christian reader, what more is hereby to be considered.

Besides this, it was also decreed in the said council at Rome of three hundred and ten bishops, by Pope Alexander, "That no man should have any spiritual promotion, except he were of lawful age, and born in wedlock. That no parish church should be void above six months. That none in orders should meddle with temporal business. That priests should have but one benefice, and that the bishops should be charged to find the priest a living till he be promoted. That open usurers should not communicate at Easter, nor be buried within the churchyard. That nothing should be taken

(1) Ex libro gravaminum nationis Germanicæ.

(2) "Ego, *N.*, Episcopus *N.*, ab hac hora in antea fidelis et obediens ero beato Petro, sanctæque apostolicæ Romanæ ecclesiæ, et domino meo, dom. *N.*, papæ, suisque successoribus canonice intrantibus. Non ero in consilio, seu auxilio, consensu, vel facto, ut vitam perdant aut membrum, seu capiantur mala captione Consilium vero quod mihi credituri sunt, per se aut per nuncium, seu literas ad eorum damnum, me sciente nemini pandam. Papatum Romanum et regalia S. Petri adjutor eis ero ad retinendum et defendendum salvo meo ordine, contra omnem hominem. Legatum apostolicæ sedis in eundo et redeundo honorifice tractabo, et in suis necessitatibus adjuvabo. Vocatus ad synodum veniam, nisi præpeditus fuero canonica præpeditione. Apostolorum limina singulis trienniis visitabo, aut per me, aut per meum nuncium, nisi apostolica absolvar licentia Possessiones vero ad mensam mei episcopatus pertinentes non vendam, neque donabo, neque oppignorabo, neque de novo infeudabo, nec aliquo modo alienabo inconsulto Rom. pontifice: sic me Deus adjuvet, et sancta Dei evangelia."

(3) And how be not those bishops then perjured, who, at the death of Queen Mary, set and let out a great part of their possessions from their successors?

Henry II. A.D. 1189. for ministering sacraments or burying. Also, that every cathedral church should have a master to teach children freely, without taking any thing for the same."

In this council the vow of chastity was obtruded and laid upon priests. Thomas Becket, also, and Bernard, were canonized for saints.

During the reign and time of this King Henry II., the city of Norwich was destroyed and burnt by the men of Flanders. Also the towns of Leicester and Nottingham were wasted, and the burgesses slain by the earl of Ferrers. The town of Berwick was destroyed by the Scots. The king of Scots was taken in war by the Englishmen, A.D. 1174. The town of Huntingdon was taken and burned. The town of Canterbury, by casualty of fire, was burnt with all the churches, especially the Trinity church, where Becket was worshipped, in the same year. In A.D 1170, William, king of Scots, with David, his brother, and all the barons of the realm, did homage to the king of England. Ireland was made subject to England. Decreed in a council in Normandy, that no boys or children should possess any benefice. A council of Lateran was holden at Rome, where were three and thirty articles concluded, A.D. 1179. The French king came in pilgrimage to Thomas Becket, the king of England meeting him by the way, A.D. 1184. After the death of Richard, archbishop of Canterbury, who followed after Thomas Becket, succeeded Baldwin, who, of a Cistercian monk being made a bishop, is said never to eat flesh in his life. A certain poor woman, bare and lean, meeting him in the street, desired to know of him whether it were true that was said of him, that he never did eat flesh: which thing when he had affirmed to be true, "Nay," saith she, "that is false, for you have eaten my flesh unto the bone, for I had but one cow wherewith I was sustained, and that have your deans taken from me." "True, true," said the bishop, "and thou shalt have another cow as good as that."[1]

Baldwin archbishop of Canterbury.

Moreover, in the reign of King Henry, about A.D. 1178, I find in the story of Roger Hoveden and others, that in the city of Toulouse there was a great multitude of men and women whom the pope's commissioners, to wit, Peter, cardinal of St. Chrysogoim, and the pope's legate, with the archbishops of Narbonne and Bituriensis, Reginald, bishop of Bath, John, bishop of Pictavia, Henry, abbot Clarevallensis, &c., did persecute and condemn for heretics; of whom some were scourged naked, some chased away, some compelled to abjure: concerning whose articles and opinions I have no firm ground to make any certain relation, forasmuch as I see the papists, many times so false in their quarrelling accusations, untruly collected men's sayings, not as they meant, and meaning not as they said, but wresting and depraving simple men's assertions after such a subtle sort as they list themselves to take them. But this I find, how one of the said commissioners or inquisitors, Henry the abbot, in a certain letter of his, wrote thus of them:[2]—"After a new opinion he affirmed

(1) Jornalensis.

(2) "Nam et panem sanctum vitæ æternæ, sacerdotis ministerio in verbo domini consecratum non esse corpus Domini, novo dogmate contendebat asserere."

Henry II

A.D. 1189.

Waldenses se pauperes de Lugduno Leonistæ, Sabbatati

Four archpillars of proud papistry

that the holy bread of eternal life, consecrated by the ministry of the priest, was not the body of the Lord," &c.

In the time of this Alexander sprang up the doctrine and name of those, who were then called 'pauperes de Lugduno,'[1] who, from one Waldus, a chief senator in Lyons, were named 'Waldenses;' also 'Leonistæ' and 'Insabbatati:' about A.D. 1109, or, as Laziardus writeth, 1170.

Not long before this time, as is expressed above, rose up Gratian, master of the decrees, and Peter the Lombard, master of the sentences, both archpillars of all papistry; after whom followed also two as evil, or worse than they, Francis and Dominic, maintaining blind hypocrisy, no less than the other maintained proud prelacy. As these laboured one way, by superstition and worldly advancement, to corrupt the sincerity of religion, so it pleased Christ, the contrary way, labouring against these, to raise up therefore the said Waldenses against the pride and hypocrisy of the others.

Thus we never see any great corruption in the church, but that some sparkle of the true and clear light of the gospel yet by God's providence doth remain; whatsoever the Doctors Augustinus, Reinerius, Sylvius, and Cranzius, with others in their popish histories, do write of them, defaming them through misreport, and accusing them to magistrates as disobedient to orders, rebels to the catholic church, and contemners of the Virgin Mary, yet they who carry judgment indifferent, rather trusting truth than wavering with the times, in weighing their articles, shall find it otherwise, and that they maintained nothing else but the same doctrine which is now defended in the church. And yet I suppose not contrary, but as the papists did

(1) *Waldenses.*—Our author has fallen into the very common error of confounding the Waldenses with the 'Pauperes de Lugduno,' or 'Poor men of Lyons,' and of deriving their origin from Waldus, or Peter Waldo, of Lyons. The earliest period assigned to Peter Waldo is the year 1160, but there is a document of the year 1100, 'La Nobla Leyczon,' which speaks of the Waldenses, or Vaudois, under the term Vaudés. It is therefore much more probable that Peter Waldo was named after the community called Vaudés, than that the Waldenses should take their name from his. Authors who assert the greater antiquity of the Waldenses, Vallenses, or Vaudois, maintain,

1. That the Waldenses are so called from certain secluded Alpine valleys, principally in Piedmont, where they have been settled from time immemorial.

2. That the simplest etymology is that which is deduced from a local, and not from a personal name—'Vallis,' Latin, 'Valle,' Italian, 'Val,' Provençal, 'Val,' pl. 'Vaux,' and 'Vallee,' French, 'Val,' Spanish, 'Val,' Celtic, 'Wald,' Teutonic, 'Valley,' English.

3. That traces are to be found in early ecclesiastical history (beginning with the works of Ambrose and Jerome), of Alpine churches, which held opinions similar to those of the Waldenses of later times.

4. That the most ancient of the state records of Piedmont, in which the Waldenses are noticed as a religious community at variance with the church of Rome, call them 'Huomini delle Valli,' or 'Men of the Valleys.'

5. That the antiquity of 'La Nobla Leyczon,' which presents internal evidence of having been written in the year 1100, and contains the term Vaudés, and applies it to a religious body, not in communion with the church of Rome, is proved by Raynouard, in his 'Choix de Poesies des Troubadours,' and by others, whose authority is of importance as to the period and language of that valuable document.

6. That surnames were not in use in the twelfth century, and that Peter of Lyons had his second appellation Waldus, or Waldo, given to him to distinguish him, as one who had adopted the opinions of the Vaudés, or Waldenses.

7. That the earliest public edicts, which make mention of the Waldenses (such as, 'Statuta Synodalia Odonis Episcopi Tullensis,' in 1192.—"De hæreticis autem qui vocantur Wadoys—præcipimus," and the edict of Ildefonsus, king of Arragon, in 1194), do not give any derivation of the term Waldenses, but simply call certain heretics by that name.

8. That the earliest treatises which profess to give the etymology of the name Waldenses, derive it from a word signifying 'Valley.'—Thus Bernard of Fonteaud, A.D. 1185—"Dicti sunt Valdenses nimirum a valle densa, eo quod profundis et densis errorum tenebris involvantur;" and Ebrard de Bethuno, in the year 1200—"Vallenses se appellant eo quod in valle lachrymarum maneant."

9. That the first treatise which pretends to derive the Waldenses from Peter Waldus, of Lyons, was written after these, namely, 'Petri Vallium Sarnaii monachi Historia Albigensium,' in 1218. See Leger's 'Histoire generale des Eglises Evangeliques de Vallees de Piémont,' Allix's 'Churches of Piedmont,' Gilly's 'Waldensian Researches,' Blair's 'History of the Waldenses.'—ED.

Henry II. A.D. 1189. with the articles of Wickliff and Huss, so they did in like manner with their articles also, in gathering and wrestling them otherwise than they were meant.

The History of the Waldenses,

CONCERNING THEIR ORIGINAL AND DOCTRINE, WITH THEIR PERSECUTIONS.[1]

The first original of these Waldenses, came of one Waldus, a man both of great substance, and no less calling in the city of Lyons, the occasion whereof is declared of divers writers thus to come. About A.D. 1160, it chanced that divers of the best and chiefest heads of the city of Lyons, talking and walking in a certain place after their old accustomed manner, especially in the summer-time, conferred and consulted together upon matters, either to pass over time, or to debate things to be done; amongst whom it chanced for one (the rest looking on) to fall down by sudden death. In the number of these this aforesaid Waldus, there being amongst them, was one; who, beholding the matter more earnestly than the others, and terrified with so heavy an example, being, as it is said, a rich man, and God's Holy Spirit working withal, was stricken with a deep and inward repentance, whereupon followed a new alteration, with a careful study to reform his former life; insomuch that he began first to minister large alms of his goods to such as needed: secondly, to instruct himself and his family in the true knowledge of God's word: thirdly, to admonish all that resorted to him on any occasion, to repentance and virtuous amendment of life. Thus, partly through his large giving to the poor, and partly through his diligent teaching and wholesome admonitions, more resort of people daily frequented about him; whom when he did see ready and diligent to learn, he began to give out to them certain rudiments of the Scripture, which he had translated himself into the French tongue, for as he was a man wealthy in riches, so he was also not unlearned.

Although Laziardus Volateranus, with others, note him utterly unlearned, and charge him with ignorance, as who should procure others to write and translate for him; by others, who have seen his doings yet remaining in old parchment monuments, it appeareth he was both able to declare and to translate the books of Scripture, and also did collect the doctors' mind upon the same.

The true nature of Antichrist: neither himself to further the word, nor suffer other men to do it.

But whatsoever he was, lettered or unlettered, the bishops and prelates seeing him so to intermeddle with the Scriptures, and to have such resort about him, albeit it was but in his own house, under private conference, could neither abide that the Scriptures should be declared by any other, nor would they take the pains to declare them themselves. So, being moved with great malice against the man, they threatened to excommunicate him if he did not leave off so to do. Waldus, seeing his doing to be but godly, and their malice stirred up upon no just nor godly cause, neglecting the threatenings and frettings of the wicked, said, that "God must be obeyed more than man." To be brief, the more diligent he was in setting forth the true doctrine of Christ against the errors of Antichrist, the more

(1) Edition 1563, p. 42.—Ed.

maliciously their fierceness increased; insomuch that when they did see their excommunication to be despised, and would not serve, they ceased not with prison, with sword, and with banishment, to persecute, till at length they had driven both Waldus, and all the favourers of his true preaching, out of the city.

Henry II. A.D. 1189.

Hereupon came first their name, that they were called 'Waldenses,' or 'Pauperes de Lugduno,' not because they would have all things common amongst them, or that they, professing any wilful poverty, would imitate to live as the apostles did, as Sylvius did falsely belie them, but because they, being thrust out both of country and goods, were compelled to live poorly, whether they would or no. And thus much touching the first occasion and beginning of these men, and of the restoring and maintaining of the true doctrine of Christ's gospel, against the proud proceedings of popish errors. Now concerning their articles, which I find in order and in number to be these:[1]—

The Articles of the Waldenses.

I. Only the holy Scripture is to be believed in matters pertaining to salvation, and no man's writing, or man besides.

II. All things which are necessary to salvation are contained in holy Scripture; and nothing is to be admitted in religion but only what is commanded in the word of God.

III. There is one only Mediator; other saints are in no wise to be made mediators, or to be invocated.

IV. There is no purgatory; but all men are either, by Christ, justified to life, or, without Christ, to be condemned: and, besides these two, there is neither any third nor fourth place.

V. All masses, namely, such as be sung for the dead, are wicked, and to be abrogate.

VI. All men's traditions ought to be rejected, at least not to be reputed as necessary to salvation; and therefore this singing and superfluous chanting in the chancel is to be left off: constrained and prefixed fasts bound to days and times, difference of meats, such variety of degrees and orders of priests, friars, monks, and nuns, superfluous holidays, so many sundry benedictions and hallowing of creatures, vows, peregrinations, with all the rabblement of rites and ceremonies brought in by man, ought to be abolished.

VII. The supremacy of the pope usurping above all churches, and especially above all politic realms and governments, or for him to occupy or usurp the jurisdiction of both the swords, is to be denied; neither is any degree to be received in the church, but only the degrees of priests, deacons, and bishops.

VIII. The communion under both kinds is necessary to all people, according to the institution of Christ.

IX. The church of Rome is the very Babylon spoken of in the Apocalypse; and the pope is the fountain of all error, and the very antichrist.

X. The pope's pardons and indulgences they reject.[2]

XI. The marriage of priests, and of ecclesiastical persons, they hold to be godly, and also necessary in the church.

XII. Such as hear the word of God, and have a right faith, they hold to be the right church of Christ; and to this church the keys of the church are to be given, to drive away wolves, and to institute true pastors, and to preach the word, and to minister the sacraments.

These be the principal articles of the Waldenses, albeit some there be that add more to them; some, again, divide the same into more parts: but these be the principal, to which the rest be reduced.

The same Waldenses, at length exiled, were dispersed in divers

(1) "Solis sacris literis credendum esse in iis, quæ ad salutem," &c.
(2) This article seemeth to be given of them in Bohemia, long after, for indulgences came not in before Boniface VIII.

Henry II. A.D. 1189.

and sundry places, of whom many remained long in Bohemia;[1] who, writing to their king, Uladislaus, to purge themselves against the slanderous accusations of one Dr. Austin, gave up their confession with an apology of their christian profession; defending, with strong and learned arguments, the same which now is received in most reformed churches, both concerning grace, faith, charity, hope, repentance, and works of mercy.

Thomas Aquinas first finder of purgatory.

As for purgatory, they say that Thomas Aquinas is the author thereof.

Concerning the supper of the Lord, their faith was, that it was ordained to be eaten, not to be showed and worshipped; that it was for a memorial, not for a sacrifice; to serve for the present ministration, and not for reservation; to be received at the table (not to be carried out of the doors), according to the ancient use of the primitive church, when they used to communicate sitting.[2] And this they prove, both by an old chronicle, called 'Chronica Gestorum,' as also by ancient Origen, upon the third book of Moses, bringing in his words, which be these, proving that this sacramental bread ought not to be reserved:—"Whosoever receiveth this bread of the supper of Christ upon the second or third day after, his soul shall not be blessed, but polluted. Therefore the Gibeonites, because they brought old bread to the children of Israel, it was enjoined them to carry wood and water," &c.[3]

The sacramental bread ought not to be kept or reserved.

Part of the disputation between Dr. Austin and the Waldenses.

Dr. Austin, of whom mention is made before, disputing against them about this matter of the holy eucharist, urgeth them with this interrogation: "Whether it be the same Christ present in the sacrament who is present at the right hand of the Father? If it be not the same Christ, how is it true in the Scripture, 'Una fides, unus Dominus noster, Jesus Christus'—'One faith, one Lord Jesus Christ?' If it be the same Christ, then how is he not to be honoured and worshipped here as well as there?"

A dilemma; that is, a captious question, conferring on both sides an inconvenience.

The answer of the Waldenses. What it is to receive after a sacramental manner.

To this the Waldenses answer again, and grant that Christ is one and the same with his natural body, in the sacrament, which he is at the right hand of his Father, but not after the same existence of his body: for the existence of his body in heaven is personal and local, to be apprehended by the faith and spirit of men. In the sacrament the existence of the body is not personal or local, to be apprehended or received of our bodies, after a personal or corporal manner, but after a sacramental manner; that is, where our bodies receive the sign, and our spirit the thing signified. Moreover, in heaven the existence of his body is dimensive and complete, with the full proportion and quantity of the same body wherewith he ascended. Here, the existence of his complete body, with the full proportion, measure, and stature thereof, doth not, neither can, stand in the sacrament. Briefly, the existence of his body in heaven is natural,

Natural.

(1) "Bohemia." Our author is here anticipating the chronological order of history, and rambling into an account of the Bohemian brethren. Properly speaking, the religious community of the Alpine valleys of Piedmont are the only people who should be called Waldenses. From the beginning of the eleventh century many Anti-Romanists came into notice in different parts of Europe; especially in France, Germany, Italy, and Spain; but it confuses ecclesiastical history to call them Waldenses, or Albigenses. The two latter might hold some opinions in common, but they were essentially distinct communities.—Ed.

(2) Ex Orthuino Gratio.

(3) "Quicunque hunc panem cœna Christi secunda vel tertia die sumpserit, non benedicitur anima ejus, sed inquinabitur. Propterea Gabaonitæ, quia antiquos panes," &c.—Chronica Gestorum. Origen, super tertium librum Mosis.

not sacramental; that is, to be seen, and not remembered: here it is sacramental, not natural; that is, to be remembered, not to be seen.

This answer being made to the captious proposition of Dr. Austin, the Waldenses, retorting the like interrogation to him again, demand of him to answer them in the like objection: Whether it be all one Christ substantially and naturally, who sitteth in heaven, and who is under the forms of bread and wine, and in the receivers of the sacrament? If he grant it to be, then they bid him say, seeing Christ is as well in the sacrament as in heaven, and as well in the receiver as in the sacrament, and all one Christ in substance and nature; why then is not the same Christ as well in the breast of the receiver to be worshipped, as under the forms of bread and wine in the sacrament, seeing he is there after a more perfect manner in man, than in the sacrament? for in the sacrament he is but for a time, and not for the sacrament's sake, but for the man's cause: in man he is not for the sacrament's cause, but for his own; and that not for a season, but for ever, as it is written, "Qui manducat hunc panem vivet in æternum;" that is, "He that eateth this bread shall live for ever," &c.

Sacramental. Another dilemma against transubstantiation.

Moreover, seeing transubstantiation is the going of one substance into another, they question again with him, whether the forms of bread and wine remaining, the substance thereof be changed into the whole person of our Lord Christ Jesus, that is, both into his body, soul, and divinity; or not into the whole Christ? If he grant the whole; then, say they, that is impossible, concerning the divinity, both to nature and to our faith, that any creature can be changed into the Creator. If he say, the bread is changed into the body and soul of Christ, not to his divinity, then he separateth the natures in Christ. If he say, into the body alone, and not the soul, then he separateth the natures of the true manhood, &c., and so it cannot be the same Christ that was betrayed for us; for that he had both body and soul. To conclude, to what part soever he would answer, this doctrine of transubstantiation cannot be defended without great inconvenience on all sides. Over and besides, Eneas Sylvius,[1] writing of their doctrine and assertions (perchance as he found them, perchance making worse of them than they taught or meant), reporteth them after this manner, which I thought here to set out as it is in the Latin.[2]

The English of the Same.

That the bishop of Rome is equal with other bishops. That amongst priests there is no difference of degree. That no priest is to be reputed for any dignity of his order, but for the worthiness of his life.

That the souls of men departed are either to enter into pain everlasting, or everlasting joy. That there is no fire of purgatory to be found. That to pray for the dead is vain, and a thing only found out for the lucre of priests.

That the images of God (as of the Trinity), and of saints, are to be abolished. That the hallowing of water and palms is a mere ridicule. That the religion of begging friars was found out by the devil. That priests should not encroach riches in this world, but rather follow poverty, being content with their tithes, and men's devotion. That the preaching of the word is free to all men called thereunto.

That no deadly sin is to be tolerated, for whatsoever respect of a greater

(1) Eneas Sylvius, Bohemica historia de Waldensium dogmatibus.

(2) "Romanum præsulem reliquis episcopis parem esse. Inter sacerdotes nullum discrimen. Presbyterum non dignitatem sed vitæ meritum efficere potiorem."—For the original in Latin, see Edition 1563, p. 44.—Ed.

Henry II. A. D. 1189.

commodity to ensue thereupon. That the confirmation, which bishops exercise with oil, and extreme unction, are not to be counted among the sacraments of the church. That auricular confession is but a toy; and that it suffices for every man to confess himself in his chamber to God. That baptism ought to be administered only with pure water, without any mixture of hallowed oil. That the temple of the Lord is the wide world. That the majesty of God is not to be restrained within the walls of temples, monasteries, and chapels, so that his grace is rather to be found in one place than in another.

The temple of the Lord, that is, the habitation wherein God most properly dwelleth and worketh. That is, the mere place maketh not the ministration of holy things either more or less holy.

That priest's apparel, ornaments of the high altar, vestments, corporaces, chalices, patines, and other church plate, serve in no stead. For the difference and respect of the very place makes no matter, where the priest doth consecrate, or doth minister to those who do require. That it is sufficient to use only the sacramental words, without any other superfluous ceremonies.

That the suffrages of saints, reigning with Christ in heaven, are craved in vain, they being not able to help us. That in saying or singing the hours and matins of the day, the time is but lost. That a man ought to cease from his labour no day, but only upon the Sunday.

That the feasts and festivals of saints ought to be rejected. Item, that such fasts as be coacted and enjoined by the church have no merit in them.

These assertions of the Waldenses being thus articled by Eneas Sylvius, I thought to give them abroad in English as they are in Latin, to the intent that as they are the less to be doubted, being set out by a pope's pen, so we may both the better know them hereby, what they were, and also understand how this doctrine, now preached and taught in the church, is no new doctrine, which here we see both taught and persecuted almost four hundred years ago. And as I have spoken hitherto sufficiently concerning their doctrine, so now we will briefly somewhat touch of the order of their life and conversation, as we find it registered in a certain old written book of inquisition.[1]

MANNERS AND CUSTOMS OF THE WALDENSES.

The whole process cometh to this effect. The manner of the Waldenses is this. Kneeling upon their knees, leaning against some bank or stay, they do continue in their prayers in silence, as long as a man may say thirty or forty times, Pater noster. And this they do every day with great reverence, being amongst themselves and such as be of their own religion, and no strangers with them, both before dinner and after; likewise before supper and after; also at what time they go to bed, and in the morning when they rise, and at certain other times also, as well in the day as in the night. Item, they use no other prayer but the prayer of the Lord, and that without any Ave Maria, and the creed, which they affirm not to be put in as any prayer by Christ, but only by the church of Rome. Albeit they have and use the seven articles of faith concerning the divinity, and seven articles concerning the humanity, and the ten commandments, and seven works of mercy, which they have compiled together in a compendious book, glorying much in the same, and thereby offer themselves ready to answer any man as to their faith.

Their manner of grace before meat

Before they go to meat they have this grace, "Benedicite, Kyrie eleyson, Christe eleyson, Kyrie eleyson, Pater noster." Which being said, then the elder amongst them beginneth thus, in their own tongue:

(1) Ex inquisitorio quodam libello, de moribus et consuetudine Waldensium.

"God who blessed the five barley loaves and two fishes in the desert before his disciples, bless this table, and what is set upon it, or shall be set upon it: in the name of the Father, of the Son, and of the Holy Ghost. Amen." And likewise again, when they rise from meat, the senior giveth thanks, saying, in the words of the Apocalypse, "Blessing, and worship, and wisdom, and thanksgiving; honour, virtue, and strength, to God alone, for ever and ever. Amen." And addeth, moreover, "God reward them in their bosoms, and be beneficial to all them that be beneficial to us, and bless us. And the God who hath given us corporal feeding, grant us his spiritual life, and God be with us, and we always with him." To which they answer again, "Amen." And thus saying grace, they hold their hands upward, looking up to heaven. After their meat and grace said, they teach and exhort amongst themselves, conferring together upon their doctrine, &c.

Their grace after meat.

In their doctrine and teaching they were so diligent and painful, that Reinerius, a writer about that time (an extreme enemy against them), in a long process, wherein he describeth their doctrine and teaching, testifieth that he heard of one who did know the party, "that a certain heretic," saith he, "only to turn a certain person away from our faith, and to bring him to his, in the night, and in the winter time, swam over the river called Ibis, to come to him, and to teach him." Moreover, so perfect they were then in the Scriptures, that the said Reinerius saith, he did hear and see a man of the country unlettered, who could recite over the whole book of Job word by word, without book, with divers others, who had the whole New Testament perfectly by heart.

Reinerius, an old inquisitor against Waldenses.

And although some of them rather merrily than skilfully expounded the words of St. John, "Sui non receperunt eum"—"Swine did not receive him;" yet were they not so ignorant and void of learning, nor yet so few in number, but that they did mightily prevail; insomuch that Reinerius hath these words: "There was none durst stop them for the power and multitude of their favourers. I have often been at their inquisition and examination, and there were numbered forty churches infected with their heresy, insomuch that in one parish of Cammach were ten open schools of them," &c.[1]

Pius videtur locus in lascivos sacerdotes.

The power and multitude of Waldenses.

And the said Reinerius, when he hath said all he can in depraving and impugning them, yet is driven to confess this of them, where he doth distinguish their sect from other sects, and hath these words: "This sect of Leonists hath a great show of holiness, in that they both live justly before men, and believe all things well of God, and hold all the articles contained in the creed; only they do blaspheme the Romish church, and hate it," &c.[2]

Waldenses in all points sound, but only for holding against the church of Rome.

Now to touch somewhat their persecutions:—After they were driven out of Lyons, they were scattered into divers and sundry places, the providence of God so disposing, that the sound of their doctrine might be heard abroad in the world. Some, as I said, went to Bohemia; many did flee into their provinces of France;

(1) "Non erat qui eos impedire auderet propter potentiam et multitudinem fautorum suorum. Inquisitioni et examinationi sæpe interfui, et computatæ sunt quadragenæ ecclesiæ, quæ heresi infectæ fuerunt, ac in una parochia Cammach fuerunt decem eorum scholæ," &c.

(2) "Hæc vero Leonistarum secta magnam habet speciem pietatis, eo quod coram hominibus juste vivant, et bene omnia de Deo credant, et omnes articulos, qui in symbolo continentur; solam Romanam ecclesiam blasphemant, et oderunt."—Ex Orthuino gratio.

Henry II. A.D. 1189

some into Lombardy; others into other places. &c. But as the cross commonly followeth the verity and sincere preaching of God's word, so neither could these be suffered to live in rest. There are yet to be seen the consultations of lawyers, archbishops, and bishops of France, as Narbonensis, Arelatensis, Aquensis, and Albanensis, devised amongst themselves, which yet remain in writing, for the abolishing and extirpating of these Waldenses, written above three hundred years ago, whereby it appeareth that there was a great number of them in France.

The cross commonly followeth the word. Waldenses persecuted more than three hundred years ago by Antichrist.

Besides, there was a whole council kept in Toulouse about three hundred and fifty-five years before, and all against these Waldenses, who also were condemned in another council at Rome before that.

What great persecutions were raised up against them in France by these four archbishops before mentioned, it appeareth by their writings; whereof I will recite some of their words, which towards the end be these: "Who is such a stranger that knoweth not the condemnation of the Waldenses, the heretics, done and past so many years ago, so famous, so public, followed upon with so great labours, expenses, and travail of the faithful, and sealed with so many deaths of these infidels, so solemnly being condemned and openly punished?"[1] Whereby we may see persecution to be no new thing in the church of Christ, when Antichrist so long before, even three hundred years, began to rage against these Waldenses. In Bohemia, likewise, after that, the same, called by the name of Thaborites, as Sylvius recordeth, suffered no little trouble. But never persecution was stirred up against them, or any other people more terrible than was in these latter years in France by the French king, A.D. 1545, which lamentable story is described in Sleidan, and hereafter, in the process of this book, as we come to the order of years, shall be set forth, by the grace of Christ, more at large; in the which persecution is declared, in one town, Cabriera, to be slain by the captain of Satan, Reinerius, eight hundred persons at once, without respect of women or children of any age; of whom forty women, and most of them great with child, thrust into a barn, and the windows kept with pikes, and so fire set to them, were all consumed. Besides, in a cave not far from the town Mussium, to the number of five and twenty persons with smoke and fire were at the same time destroyed. At Merindolum the same tyrant, seeing all the rest were fled away, and finding one young man, caused him to be tied to an olive-tree, and to be destroyed with torments most cruelly; with much other persecution, as shall appear hereafter in the history translated out of Sleidan into English.

Antichrist, with whom he first began his persecution.

A horrible murder of Christ's holy martyrs.

Reinerius a horrible persecutor.

But to return again to higher times, from whence we digressed. Besides that, Reinerius (above mentioned), speaketh of one in the town of Cheron, a glover, who was brought at this time to examination, and suffered. There is also an old monument of process, wherein appear four hundred and forty-three to be brought to examination in Pomerania, Marchia, and places thereabouts, about A.D. 1391.

A glover suffered martyrdom in Cheron. Four hundred and forty-three brought to examination.

(1) "Quis enim est solus ille peregrinus, qui condemnationem hæreticorum Valdensium ignoret a longe retro annis factam, tam famosam, tam publicam, tot et tantis laboribus, expensis et sudoribus fidelium insecutam, et tot mortibus ipsorum infidelium solenniter damnatorum, publiceque punitorum tam fortiter sigillatam?" &c.

And thus much touching the origin, doctrine, and lamentable persecutions of the Waldenses; who, as is declared, first began about the time of this King Henry II.

OTHER INCIDENTS HAPPENING IN THE REIGN OF THIS HENRY II.

Concerning the first origin of the Waldenses, springing up in the days of this king, sufficient is already declared. Now remaineth in the like order of time to story also such other incidents as chanced under the reign of the said king, not unworthy to be observed, keeping the order of the time as near as we may, and as authors do give unto us.

Mary, the daughter of King Stephen, being the abbess of Ramsey, was married in this king's days to Matthew, earl of Boulogne; which marriage Thomas Becket did work against, and did dissolve, by reason whereof he procured himself great displeasure with the said earl, &c. A.D. 1161.[1]

Becket a dissolver of marriages.

The same year a certain child was crucified of the Jews in the town of Gloucester.[2] After the same manner the wicked Jews had crucified another child before in the city of Norwich, in the days of King Stephen, A.D. 1145.

Two children crucified by the Jews.

A collection was gathered through all England and France, of two pence in every pound, for the succour of the East Christians against the Turks, A.D. 1167.[3]

Babylon was taken and destroyed, and never since repaired, by Almaric, king of Jerusalem, A.D. 1170.[4]

Babylon utterly destroyed.

In the year 1173, almost all England was diseased with the cough.[5] About this year also William, king of Scots, was taken in battle and imprisoned in England.

Great war happened in Palestine, wherein the city of Jerusalem, with the cross and king of the city, and others of the temple, was taken by the Saracens, and the most part of the Christians there were either slain or taken. Cruel murder and slaughter were used by the Turk, who caused all the chief of the Christians to be brought forth and beheaded before his face; insomuch that Pope Urban III. for sorrow died, and Gregory VIII., the next pope after him, lived not two months. Then, in the days of Pope Clement III., news and sorrow growing daily for the loss of Palestine, and the destruction of the Christians; King Henry of England, and Philip, the French king, the duke of Burgundy, the earl of Flanders, the earl of Campania, with divers other christian princes, with a general consent, upon St. George's day, took the mark of the cross upon them, promising together to take their voyage into the Holy Land. At this time the stories say, the king of England first received the red cross, the French king took the white cross, the earl of Flanders took the green cross; and so likewise other princes diversly divers colours, thereby to be discerned every one by his proper cross. But King Henry, after the three years were expired, in which he promised to perform his voyage, sent to the pope for further delay of his promise, offering for the same to erect three monasteries; which thing

The holy cross taken with the city of Jerusalem, by the Saracens.

A voyage against the Turks.

How the difference of the crosses first came in.

(1) Ex chronico bibliothecæ Cariensis. (2) Jornalensis. (3) Ibid.
(4) Ex vetusto manuscripto exemplari historiæ Cariensis. (5) Ex vetusto chron. Acephalo.

Henry II. A.D. 1189

he thus performed. in the church of Waltham he thrust out the secular priests, and set in monks instead of them. Secondly, he repaired Amesbury, and brought in the nuns again, who before were excluded for their incontinent life. And thus performed he his promise made before to the pope, A. D. 1173.

King of Scotland doing homage to the king of England

The king of Scots[1] did his homage and allegiance to the king of England and to his son, and to his chief lords; promising that all the earls and barons of Scotland should do the like with their posterity. Item, all the bishops and abbots of the church of Scotland promised subjection and submission to the archbishop of York, A. D 1175[2]

The custom was in this realm, that if any had killed any clerk or priest, he was not to be punished with the temporal sword, but only excommunicated and sent to Rome for the pope's grace and absolution; which custom, in the days of this king, began first to be altered by the procurement of Richard, archbishop of Canterbury, A. D. 1176.[3]

London bridge

London-bridge first began to be made of stone by one Peter, priest of Colechurch, A. D. 1176.[4]

St William of Paris was slain by the Jews on Maundy-Thursday, for which the Jews were burned, and he counted a saint, A. D. 1177.

Ireland subdued to England

Ireland subdued to the crown of England by this king, A.D. 1177.[5]

Pilgrimage to Canterbury sprang up from a lying vision

About the five and twentieth year of the reign of the said King Henry, Louis the French king, by the vision of Thomas Becket appearing unto him in his dream, and promising to him the recovery of his son, if he would resort to him at Canterbury, made his journey into England to visit St. Thomas at Canterbury, with Philip, earl of Flanders, where he offered a rich cup of gold, with other precious jewels, and one hundred vessels of wine yearly to be given to the covent of the church of Canterbury: notwithstanding, the said Philip in his return from England, taking his journey to Paris to visit St Dennis, in the same his pilgrimage was stricken with such cold, that he fell into a palsy, and was benumbed in the right side of his body, A. D. 1178[6]

Stephen, bishop of Retinio, was wont to make many rhymes and gaudish prose to delight the ears of the multitude; to whom a little before his death this verse was sounded in his ear, "Desine ludere temere, nitere propere surgere de pulvere:", A. D. 1178.[7]

Transubstantiation gainsaid

The Albigenses of the city of Toulouse, denied transubstantiation in the sacrament of Christ's body and blood; also that matrimony was a sacrament, &c. A D. 1178[8]

Queen Elenor imprisoned

King Henry separated himself from his wife Elenor, and held her many years in prison, as some think, for the love of Rosamond; which seemeth to me to be the cause why God afterward stirred up all his sons to war against him, and to work him much sorrow;

(1) William, brother of Malcolm IV, is the monarch here referred to He was taken prisoner before Alnwick, by a stratagem, by Stutterville and Ralph de Glanville, two of King Henry's nobility, and was transported to Falaise, in Normandy, where he was compelled to sign a disgraceful treaty He returned to Scotland, and in the year 1175 Henry summoned him to meet him at York All the nobility and landholders of Scotland accompanied him thither, the disgraceful treaty of Falaise was confirmed, and Scotland found herself under the protection of Henry, deprived of liberty and honour —Ed

(2) Nicol Trivet (3) Ibid

(4) Ex Chron cujus initium "In diebus sanctissimi regis Edvardi," &c Ex Biblioth Canens.

(5) Ex variis Chron (6) Jornalensis, et alii (7) Nic Trivet. (8) Ibid

A. D. 1179;[1] notwithstanding, the said Elenor was shortly after reconciled to him. *Henry II.*

St. Frideswide was translated unto Oxford in the same year. A.D. 1180.

In the year 1180, there came to the council of Pope Alexander, one Pisanus Burgundio, a man very cunning both in Greek and Latin, who brought and presented to the council the homilies of Chrysostome upon the gospel of St. John, translated out of Greek into Latin, and said that he had translated likewise a great part of his Exposition upon Genesis; saying moreover, that the said Chrysostome had made expositions in Greek of the whole of the Old Testament, and also of the New. **Expositions made by Chrysostom, of the Old and New Testament.**

The monks of Charterhouse first entered into this land, A. D. 1180.

In the year 1181, Richard Pech, bishop of Coventry, before his death renounced his bishopric, and became a canon in the church of St. Thomas by Stafford.[2] **The bishop of Coventry renounceth his bishopric.**

About the latter time of this King Henry, one Hugo, whom men were wont to call St. Hugh of Lincoln, born in Burgundy, and prior of the monks of Charterhouse, was preferred by the king to the bishopric of Lincoln, who after his death is said to have done great miracles, and therefore was counted a saint. A. D. 1186.[3] **St. Hugh of Lincoln**

Baldwin, archbishop of Canterbury, began the building of his new house and church of Lambeth; but by the letters of Pope Clement III., he was forbidden to proceed in the building thereof. A. D. 1187.[4]

I find likewise in the aforesaid old written chronicle remaining in the hands of one William Cary, citizen of London, that King Henry II. gave to the court and church of Rome for the death of Thomas Becket, forty thousand marks of silver, and five thousand marks of gold. A. D. 1187. **King Henry's gift to the church of Rome for the death of Becket.**

Mention was made a little above of Almaric, king of Jerusalem, who destroyed Babylon, so that it was never after to this day restored, but lieth waste and desolate; wherein was fulfilled that which by the prophets, in so many places, was threatened to Babylon before. This Almaric had a son named Baldwin, and a daughter called Sibylla. Baldwin, from the beginning of his reign, was a leper, and had the falling-sickness, being not able, for feebleness of body, although valiant in heart and stomach, to satisfy that function.

Sibylla, his sister, was first married to one Willerm, marquis of Mount Ferrat, by whom she had a son, called also Baldwin. After him she was married to another husband, named Guido de Liziniaco, earl of Joppa and of Ascalon. Upon this it befel that the aforesaid Baldwin the leper, son of Almaric, being thus feeble and infirm, as is said, called his nobles together, with his mother and the patriarch, declaring to them his inability, and by their consents committed the under-government of the city unto Guido, the husband of Sibylla, his sister. But he being found insufficient, or else not lucky in the government thereof, the office was translated to another, named Raimund, earl of Tripolis. In the mean while, the soldan with his Saracens mightily prevailed against the Christians, and overran the country of Palestine, during which time Baldwin the king departed; **A worthy story of Sibylla and Guido.**

(1) Nic. Trivet. (2) Ex Chronico pervetusto, cui initium, "In diebus sanctis. regis," &c. (3) Flores. Hist. (4) Nic. Trivet.

Henry II. A.D. 1189. whereby the kingdom fell next to Baldwin (the son of Sibylla, by her first husband, Willerm), who, being but five years old, was put to the custody of the above Raimund. This Baldwin also died in his minority, before he came to his crown, whereby the next succession by descent fell to Sibylla, the wife of Guido above mentioned. The peers and nobles, joining together in council, offered unto the said Sibylla, as to the lawful heir to the crown, that she should be their queen, with this condition, that she should sequester from her, by solemn divorcement, the aforesaid Guido, her husband; but she refused the kingdom offered to her on that condition, till at last the magistrates, with the nobles in general, granted unto her, and by their oaths confirmed the same, that whomsoever she would choose to be her husband, all they would take and obey as their king. Also Guido, her husband, with like petition among the rest, humbly requested her that the kingdom, for his sake, or for his private loss, might not be destitute of government. At length, she, with tears consenting to their entreaty, was contented, and solemnly was crowned their queen, who, after the custom, again received their fidelity by their oath; whereupon Guido, without any hope either of wife or kingdom, departed home quietly to his own. This done, the queen, assembling her states and prelates together, entered talk with them about the choosing of the king, according to that which they had promised, and sworn unto her, namely, to obey him as their king, whom she would name to be her husband. Thus, while they were all in great expectation, waiting every man whom she would nominate, the queen, with a loud voice, said to Guido, that stood amongst them: "Guido, my lord, I choose thee for my husband, and yielding myself and my kingdom unto you, openly I protest you to be the king." At these words all the assembly being amazed, wondered that one simple woman so wisely had beguiled so many wise men; and worthy was she, no doubt, to be commended and extolled for her singular virtue, both of faithful chastity and high prudence; so tempering the matter, that she both obtained to her husband the kingdom, and retained to herself again her husband, whom she so faithfully loved. A. D. 1186.[1]

A worthy example of a true wife to her husband.

As I have hitherto described the public acts of King Henry, so now I mean to touch something of his private conditions. He was of mean stature, eloquent and learned, manly and bold in chivalry, fearful of the mutability and chance of war, more lamenting the death of his soldiers dead, than loving them alive; none more courteous and liberal for the obtaining of his purpose; in peace and tranquillity none more rough; stubborn against the stubborn; sometimes merciful to those whom he had vanquished; straight to his household servants, but liberal to strangers; publicly, of public things, liberal, sparing of his own; whom once he took a displeasure against, hardly, or never, would he receive again to favour; somewhat lavish of his tongue; a willing breaker of his promise; a lover of his own ease, but an oppressor of his nobility; a severe avenger and furtherer of justice; variable of word, and crafty in his talk; an open adulterer; a nourisher of discord amongst his children; moreover, the papists, bearing him for Thomas Becket's quarrel and such

(1) Ex Historia manuscripta cui initium, "Rex Pictorum." Ex Bibliotheca Cariensi mutuata.

like, as may be gathered, no good will, term him an adversary of the faith, the mall and beetle of the church. *Henry II.* A.D. 1189.

Also in the chronicle entitled 'Scala Mundi,' I find of him, that he followed the steps, manners, and conditions of Henry I. his grandfather, in every point. He preserved firm peace, and executed strict justice, through all his dominions. He loved marvellous well his forests; and again, those who were transgressors either to his crown or person, he most severely punished.

Moreover, in a certain history entitled 'De Regibus Angliæ,' I find that this king was sundry times admonished to reform and amend his life, and first by one who was an old man, in the castle of Cardif, in Wales, at that time of the year called 'Dominica in albis,' the eighth day after Easter; where also, after that he heard mass, and was going to take his horse, there stood a certain man by him, somewhat yellowish, his hair being rounded, lean, and ill-favoured, having on a white coat, and being barefoot, who looked upon the king, and spake on this wise:—"Good old king;" that done, thus he proceedeth,—"the King saluteth you, and his blessed mother; John Baptist and Peter straitly charge you, that upon the Sundays, throughout all your dominions, there be no buying and selling, or other servile business (those only excepted which appertain to the preparation of meat and drink); which thing if thou shalt observe, whatsoever thou takest in hand, thou shalt happily finish and bring to pass." Then spake the king, in French, unto the knight that held his horse by the bridle: "Ask of this churl whether he dreamed this or not?" And in the mean while that the knight should have interpreted the king's words and message, he spake before, and said, "Whether this be a dream or not, mark well what day this is; for unless thou do these things and amend thy life, such news shalt thou hear within these twelve months, as will make thee lament and mourn till thy dying day." And when these words were spoken, the man vanished out of his sight; and within one year after, Henry, Gaufrid, and Richard, his sons, forsook him, their father, and took part with the French king. The king of Scots, and the earls of Chester and Leicester, made an insurrection against the king. Many other premonitions were given also to the king, but all these did he little esteem. The second who did admonish him, was a certain Irishman, giving him certain secret signs. And thirdly, a certain knight of Findesey, named Philip de Easterby, sailing with him over into France, declared unto the king, in Normandy, seven articles which he should amend; which thing if he would do, he should reign seven years most honourably, and should take the holy cross from his enemies; or else he, in the fourth year, should die in great ignominy. The three first things were these, which he at his coronation sware to observe, that is, to defend the church, to maintain good laws, and to condemn no man to death without judgment. The fourth was, for the restoring of inheritance wrongfully taken; the fifth was, in doing justice without reward; the sixth was, of ministers and officers' wages and stipends; the seventh was, of expelling the Jews, leaving them some money to depart withal. But the king not amending his life, there rose up against him three strong enemies; that is to say, his three sons, along with the French king. But, after the king, forsooth, had gone a pilgrimage to the

The king admonished to amend his life. Sunday to be free from buying and selling.

The second and third admonition to the king to reform his life.

The king's victory falsely imputed to his pilgrimage.

Richard I martyr's tomb, barefoot, William, king of Scots, and the earls of Chester and Leicester, were taken at Alnwick.

A.D. 1189 In the five and thirtieth year of his reign, being in the castle of Chinon, in Normandy, he died; at whose death those who were present were so greedy of the spoil, that they left the body of the king naked, and not so much could be found as a cloth to cover it, till a page, coming in, and seeing the king lying so ignominiously, threw his cloak upon him; wherein, saith the author, was verified the surname which from his youth he bare, being called Henry Court Mantil.

The death of Henry II

RICHARD THE FIRST.[1]

A.D. 1189 In the year above recited, which was A.D. 1189, King Richard. the eldest son of Henry II., succeeding his father, entered upon his crown; at which time Pope Clement sat at Rome, succeeding Gregory, who died a little before with sorrow for the loss of the holy cross.

No Jew to enter the palace or church during Richard's coronation.

During the time of his coronation, it befel, that notwithstanding the king, the day before his coronation, by public edict commanded both the Jews,[2] and their wives, not to presume to enter either the church or his palace, during the solemnization of his coronation, amongst his nobles and barons; yet, while the king was at dinner, the chieftain of the Jews, with divers others of his Jewish affinity and superstitious sect, against the king's prohibition, together with other press, entered the court gates. Whereat a christian man being offended, struck one of them with his hand or fist, and bid him stand further from the court gate, as the king had given commandment; whose example others also following, being displeased with the Jews, offered them the like contumely. Others also, supposing that the king had so commanded indeed, as using the authority of the king, fell upon all the Jews that stood by without the court gate. And first they beat them with their fists, but afterwards they took up stones and such other things as they could get, and threw at them. And thus driving them from the court gates, some of them they wounded, some they slew, and some they left for dead.

A Jew through fear baptized

There was amongst this number of the Jews one called 'the blessed Jew of York,' who was so sorely wounded and beaten with the rest, that, for fear of his life, he said he would become a Christian, and was indeed baptized of William, the prior of the church of St. Mary of York; whereby he escaped the great peril of death he was in, and the persecutors' hands. In the mean while there was a great rumour spread throughout the whole city of London, that the king had commanded to destroy all the Jews. Whereupon, as well the citizens, as innumerable people more, being assembled to see the king's coronation, armed themselves and came together. The Jews thus being for the most part slain, the rest fled into their houses, where for a time, through the strong and sure building of them, they

The Jews in London slain

(1) Edition 1563, p 70 Ed 1583, p 234 Ed. 1597, p 213 Ed 1684, vol i p 265 — Ed

(2) The atrocities against the unfortunate Jews here recorded, are fully related in Walter Hemingford, Gale Script vol ii pp 514—518 — Ed.

were defended. But at length their houses were set on fire, and they destroyed therein.

These things being declared to the king, whilst he with his nobles and barons were at dinner, he sendeth immediately Ranulfe de Glanvile, the lord high steward of England, with divers other noblemen to accompany him, that they might stay and restrain these so bold enterprises of the Londoners: but all was in vain, for in this so great a tumult, none there was that either regarded what the nobility said, or else any whit reverenced their personages, but rather with stern looks and threatening words, advised them, and that quickly, to depart. Whereupon they, with good deliberation, thinking it the best so to do, departed; the tumult and insurrection continuing till the next day. At that time also the king, sending certain of his officers into the city, gave them in commandment to apprehend and present some, such as were the chief of the malefactors: of whom three were condemned to be hanged, and so were; the one, for that he had robbed a Christian's house in this tumult; and the other two, for that they fired the houses, to the great danger of the city. After this, the king sent for him who from a Jew was converted to Christianity, and in the presence of those who saw where he was baptized, the king asked him whether he was become a Christian or not? He answering the king, said, No, but to the intent that he might escape death, he promised to do whatsoever the Christians would have him. Then the king asked the archbishop of Canterbury, other archbishops and bishops being present, what were best to be done with him? Who unadvisedly answering, said, "If he will not be a man of God, let him be a man of the devil:" and so revolted he again to Judaism.

The small regard to the nobility in tumults and insurrections.

An unadvised answer of an archbishop

Then the king sent his writs to the sheriffs of every county, to inquire for the authors and stirrers of this outrage; of whom three were hanged, divers were imprisoned. So great was then the hatred of Englishmen against the Jews, that as soon as they began to be repulsed in the court, the Londoners taking example thereof, fell upon them, set their houses on fire, and spoiled their goods. The country again, following the example of the Londoners, semblably did the like. And thus the year, which the Jews took to be their jubilee, was to them a year of confusion; insomuch, that in the city of York, the Jews obtaining the occupying of a certain castle for their preservation, and afterwards not being willing to restore it to the Christians again, when they saw no other remedy, but by force to be vanquished, first they offered much money for their lives, when that would not be taken, by the counsel of an old Jew amongst them, every one, with a sharp razor, cut another's throat, whereby a thousand and five hundred of them were at that time destroyed. Neither was this plague of theirs undeserved; for every year commonly their custom was, to get some christian man's child from the parents, and on Good Friday to crucify him, in despite of our religion.[1]

A miserable and deserved destruction of the Jews

King Richard, after the death of his father, coming unto remembrance of himself, and of his rebellion against his father, sought for absolution of his trespass; and, in part of satisfaction for the same, agreed with Philip, the French king, about Easter next ensuing, to take his voyage with him for the recovery of Christ's patrimony,

(1) Ex Chron. Westm cui initium, "Æneas cum Ascanio," &c.

Richard I. A.D. 1189. which they called the Holy Land. Whereupon the said King Richard, immediately after his coronation, to prepare himself the better for his journey, set to sale divers of his manors, whereof Godfrey Lucy, then bishop of Winchester, bought a couple for two thousand marks; to wit, Wergrave and Melenge. The abbot of Bury bought another, for a thousand marks, called Middlesay. Hugh Puzas, bishop of Durham, bought the lordship of Seggesfield, or Sedberga, with the wapentake, and all the appurtenances thereto belonging; he bought also the earldom of Northumberland, whom, when the king should solemnize after the manner of secular earls, merrily with a mocking jest, "Lo," said he, "of an old bishop I have made a young earl." And because the said bishop had professed before, by a solemn vow, to visit the Holy Land, to be released of his vow, he compounded with the pope for a great sum of money there-for; and moreover gave to the king a thousand marks to remain at home, as the chief justice of England. *At that time it appeareth that these taxes, tolls, exactions, and subsidies, either were not known, or not so much had in use; by reason whereof this king was driven to make other shifts, by selling offices, liberties, and privileges.*[1]

The covetous greediness of bishops, in buying great lordships.

Sleights to get money.

Over and besides, the king set out all that he had to sale, such as woods, castles, townships, lordships, earldoms, baronages, *and, as he said himself, he would have sold London also, if he could have found any able to buy it;* ordaining also divers new bishops, and not without some advantages, as appeared, to his purse; feigning moreover his old seal to be lost, that they which had lands to hold might be driven to renew their writings again by the new seal, whereby great substance of money was gained.

A tenth gathered through all England.

Above all this, by the commandment of Pope Clement III., a tenth also was exacted of the whole realm, in such sort as that the Christians should make up for the king seventy thousand pounds, the Jews six thousand pounds.[2] King Richard, after his coronation, sent certain earls and barons unto Philip the French king, in the time of his parliament at St. Denis, desiring him to remember his promise made for the recovery of Christ's holy patrimony out of the Saracens' hands. Unto whom he sent word again, in the month of December, certifying him how he had bound himself by solemn oath, deposing upon the evangelists, that he, the next year following, about the time of Easter, had certainly prefixed to address himself towards that journey; requiring him likewise not to fail, but to be ready at the term above limited, appointing also the place where both the kings should meet together.

Philip and Richard concluding to travel to the Holy Land.

A.D. 1190. In the year next ensuing, A.D. 1190, at the beginning of it, being Twelfth-even, fell out a foul northern brawl, which turned well near to a fray, between the archbishop newly elected of the church of York and his company, on the one side, and Henry, dean of the said church, with his catholic partakers, on the other side, upon occasion, as followeth: Gaufrid, or Geffrey, son of King Henry II. and brother to King Richard, whom the king had elected a little before to the archbishopric of York, upon the even of the Epiphany, which we call Twelfth-day, was disposed to hear evensong with all solemnity in

A northern brawl in the cathedral church of York.

(1) This and the succeeding passage, between single asterisks, are from the Edition of 1563, p. 89.—ED. (2) Ex Gerv. fol. 134.

the cathedral church, having with him Hammon the chanter, with divers other canons of the church. The archbishop tarrying something long, belike in adorning and attiring himself, in the mean while Henry the dean, and Bucard the treasurer, disdaining to tarry his coming, with a bold courage lustily began their holy evensong, with singing their psalms, ruffling of descant, and merry piping of organs. Thus, this catholic evensong, with as much devotion begun, as God's high service proceeding, was now almost half complete, when, at length (they being in the midst of their mirth) in cometh the newly elect with his train and guardians,[1] all full of wrath and indignation, for that they durst be so bold, not waiting for him, to begin God's service, and so eftsoons commanded the choir to stay and hold their peace. The chanter likewise, whose name was Hammon, by virtue of his office, commandeth the same. But the dean and treasurer, on the other side, willed them to proceed; and so they sung on, and would not stint. Thus, the one half crying against the other, the whole choir was in a roar, their singing was turned to scolding, their chanting to chiding; and if, instead of the organs, they had had a drum, I doubt they would have 'sol-fa-ed' by the ears together.

Henry, dean of York, and Bucard, begin service, not tarrying for their archbishop.

The dean and treasurer would not cease evensong at the archbishop's commandment.

At last, through the authority of the archbishop, and of the chanter, the choir began to surcease and give silence. Then the newly elect, not contented with what had been sung before, with certain of the choir, began the evensong over again. *The treasurer not thinking to take such a foil, caused all the tapers and candles to be put out, and so their unhappy evensong was ceased again.[2]* For, like as without the light and beams of the sun, there is nothing but darkness in all the world, even so you must understand the pope's church can see to do nothing, *and that the popish evensong is blind, without candlelight, yea, though the sun should shine in the choir never so clear and bright; by reason whereof they went away evensongless, and so left their God in the church, that night, unserved.* This being so, the archbishop, thus disappointed on every side of his purpose, made a grievous plaint, declaring to the clergy and to the people what the dean and treasurer had done; and so upon the same, suspended both them and the church from all divine service, till they should make to him due satisfaction for their trespass.

The archbishop beginneth evensong again.

The treasurer putteth out the candles.

The pope's church can do nothing without candle light.

The church of York suspended from service.

Where note, by the way, good reader, that either the singing of the popish service doth little serve to God's honour, or else how could this archbishop be so injurious to God, to stop him of his honour because they had dishonoured him? But to the purpose again.

The next day, which was the day of Epiphany, when all the people of the city were assembled in the cathedral church, as their manner was (namely, in such feasts), devoutly to hear divine service, as they call it, of the church, there were also present the archbishop and the chanter, with the residue of the clergy, looking when the dean and treasurer would come and submit themselves, making satisfaction for their crime. But they, still continuing in their stoutness, refused so to do, exclaiming and uttering contemptuous words against the archbishop and his partakers. When the people heard this, they in a great rage would have fallen upon them; but the archbishop would

The dean and treasurer do not submit to the archbishop.

The people incensed against them.

(1) "Gardevian," one who collects the spiritualities of a bishopric during a vacancy in the See.
(2) For this passage, with the two succeeding ones, see Ed. 1563, p. 70.—Ed.

Richard I. A.D. 1190.

not suffer that. The dean then and his fellows, perceiving the stir of the people, for fear, like pretty men, were fain to flee, some to the tomb of St. William of York; some ran unto the dean's house, and there shrouded themselves, whom the archbishop then accursed. And so, for that day, the people returned home without any service.[1]

King Richard prepareth for his journey.

After this time King Richard, preparing to set all things in order before his going, committed the whole government of the realm principally to William, bishop of Ely, his chancellor, and to Hugh, bishop of Durham, whom he ordained to be the chief justice of all England in his absence; the one to have the custody of the Tower, with the oversight of all other parts of the land on this side of Humber; the other, who was the bishop of Durham, to have charge over all other his dominions beyond Humber, sending, moreover, unto Pope Clement, in the behalf of the aforesaid William, bishop of Ely, that he might be made the pope's legate through all England and Scotland, which also was obtained. Thus the bishop being advanced in high authority, to furnish the king towards his setting forth, provideth out of every city in England two palfreys, and two sumpters, and also out of every abbey one palfrey and one sumpter.

The chief overseers of the realm in the king's absence.

These things and others thus set in a stay, the king, according to his former appointment, about the time of Easter, sailed to France, where the French king and he conferring together, because they could not make ready at that time of Easter, concluded to take a longer day, proroguing their voyage till after Midsummer. In the mean time, the king occupying himself in redressing and establishing such things as further were to be ordered, there determined that Gaufrid and John his brethren, should not enter into England for three years after his departure; nevertheless he released that bond afterward to his brother John. Then he appointed the captains and constables over his navy, and set laws to be observed in his journey upon the seas; but especially his care was to make unity and concord between parties that were at variance, and to set them together at one.

Contention betwixt Baldwin, archbishop of Canterbury, and the monks of Christchurch.

[2]At this time the long contention began to be appeased, which so many years had continued between Baldwin, archbishop of Canterbury, and his monks of Christchurch; the discourse whereof, although it be somewhat tedious to be set forth at large, being enough to make a whole tragedy, yet to the intent the age now present may see what great conflicts and disquietness, upon what little trifles, have been stirred up, what little peace and unity hath been not only in this church, but commonly in all other churches under the pope's catholic regiment; I thought it not labour ill bestowed somewhat to intermeddle in opening to the eyes of the reader the consideration of this matter; wherein first is to be understood, that the archbishops of Canterbury, commonly being set up by the pope, especially since the time of the Conquest, have put the kings of this land to much sorrow and trouble, as appeareth by William Rufus and Lanfranc, and also Anselm; by Henry I. and Anselm;[3] King Stephen and Theobald; Henry II. and Becket, &c. For this the kings of this land have used the more care and circum-

Archbishops of Canterbury commonly were wont to work the king of England much sorrow.

(1) Ex veteri Chronico manuscripto, cui initium, 'Anno gratiæ millesimo,' &c.
(2) Foxe enters here solely upon Ecclesiastical History, from the days of Lanfranc, to A.D. 1190.
(3) "Anselm, who brought in the conception of our Lady to be hallowed, stirred coals in England against his king, Henry." Ed. 1563, p. 31.—ED.

spection, to have such archbishops placed in the see as either should stand with them, or at the least should not be against them.[1] *Richard I* A.D. 1137 to 1190.

Now to the purpose of our matter intended. First, after Lanfranc, who was archbishop twenty years, the see standing vacant five years, succeeded Anselm, and sat seventeen years; after whom, the see standing vacant four years, succeeded Rodulph, and continued nine years; then followed William, who sat twelve years, and died A.D. 1137; after whom came Theobald, in the time of King Stephen. Or fifteen, as some reckon. This Theobald, being no great favourer of the monkish generation, fell out with Jeremias, prior of the house of Canterbury, for certain causes between them; for which the archbishop, taking stomach against the prior, would lay the sentence of interdiction against him. The prior, seeing that, to save himself, made his appeal to Pope Innocent. The archbishop, provoked the more by that, deposed him from his priorship, and placed one Walter in his room. Jeremias, notwithstanding, making his complaint and appeal to Rome, obtained letters from the pope to Henry bishop of Winchester, being the pope's legate, by virtue whereof, he, against the heart of the archbishop, was restored, and Walter displaced. Nevertheless, the said Jeremy, not willing there to continue with displeasure of the archbishop, shortly after, of his own accord, renounced his priory, and Walter again was received in his stead. Not long after this followed the general council at Rheims, A.D. 1140. To that council, Theobald, contrary to the commandment of the king, would needs resort, to show his obedience to the pope; wherefore, at his returning home again, the king took such displeasure with him, that, within a while after, the archbishop was driven to void the realm, and fly into France, where he, by censure of interdiction, suspended divers churches and religious houses which refused to come to the council; and also, hearing how the king had seized upon all his goods, he interdicted likewise all the king's land whatsoever, belonging to the crown: so that the king, in conclusion, was fain to compound with him, and fall to agreement, which was about A.D. 1148.[2] Jeremy, prior of Canterbury, appealeth to Pope Innocent.

After this, A.D. 1151, after the death of Hugh, abbot of St. Austin's in Canterbury, Silvester was elected by the covent to be their abbot in the reign of King Stephen. When this Silvester came unto Theobald the archbishop, to make his profession of subjection unto him, and to receive of him consecration, the archbishop was contented, if that the abbot would come to Christchurch in Canterbury, and there make his profession. But to this, Silvester in no case would yield to take his consecration there; but, in any other church, wheresoever the archbishop would, he was contented. To this, when the archbishop in nowise would agree, Silvester, making a great bag of money, went to Rome, where he obtained of the pope for money (for what cannot money do at Rome?) letters that the archbishop should consecrate the abbot in his own church of St. Austin, and also not exact of him any profession of canonical subjection. Hereupon the archbishop was compelled, against his will, to come to the abbot's church, and there, at the pope's commandment, to consecrate him simply, and without any further profession to be required. A frivolous strife between Theobald, archbishop, and Silvester, abbot of St Austin's. Silvester goeth up to Rome.

(1) Ex Chron Gervas. (2) Ibid.

Richard I. A.D. 1137 to 1190.

Then Walter, prior of Christchurch in Canterbury, seeing that, and perceiving how prejudicial and derogatory the example thereof would be to the honour and majesty of their church, through counsel of his brethren, went thither; and, notwithstanding the doors were straitly watched and kept, yet, by means, he at last got in; and as he saw the archbishop attired in his pontificalibus, ready to minister consecration to the abbot, he stepped straight to the archbishop, and at once appealeth him up to Rome, for the great injury wrought against the church of Canterbury, forbidding him in the name of him to whom he appealed, to proceed any further. And so this holy consecration was for the present time staid, for which Silvester, with a new purse of money, was fain to travel and trot again to Rome, where he, complaining of the archbishop, and accusing him of contempt of the pope, in not executing the commandment sent down, obtaineth again new letters with more effectual charge to the aforesaid archbishop, that he, without any profession, simply should give to Silvester his consecration in his own church, "omni occasione et appellatione remota," "all manner of stay, or let, or appellation to the contrary notwithstanding." And so, in conclusion, the abbot, contrary to whatsoever the archbishop and all the monks of Canterbury could do, was, in his own church, made abbot, and had the victory for that time. Notwithstanding, the archbishop left not the matter so, but within five years after obtained of Pope Adrian, that Silvester should make profession of his obedience to the archbishop, and so he did.[1]

The monks of Christchurch, against the monks of St. Austin.

Silvester trudgeth again to Rome.

Silvester consecrated abbot in his own church.

In a few years after this died King Stephen, A.D. 1154; and after him Theobald, the archbishop, A.D. 1159, after he had sat three and twenty years; after whom, through the instant procurement of King Henry II., was placed Thomas Becket, the king's chancellor, A.D. 1162, of whose sturdy rebellion against the king, because sufficient hath been said before, it shall not need to make a double labour now about the same.

After the death of Becket, much ado there was between King Henry II. and Odo, prior of Canterbury, about the election of a new archbishop. For the king seeing the realm so oftentimes encumbered by those popish archbishops, and fearing lest the monks of Canterbury should elect such another as would follow the steps of Thomas Becket, most humbly, with cap in hand, and courtesy of knee, desired Odo the prior, that at his request, and for contentation of his mind, such a one might be elected as he would appoint (appointing and naming a certain bishop, who was a good simple man after the king's liking); but the prior dissemblingly answering the king again, that he neither could nor would, without the consent of his covent, give promise to any man; in fine, contrary to the king's so humble request, he agreed to the election of another, who was the prior of Dover, called Richard, A.D. 1173, and who continued in that see eleven years.

Odo, prior of Canterbury.

Richard, prior of Dover, elected archbishop of Canterbury.

And here was renewed again the like variance between this archbishop, and Roger, abbot of the Austin monks in Canterbury, as was before mentioned between Theobald and Silvester; for, when

Another frivolous contention

(1) Ex Gervas.

the said Roger, after his election to be abbot, must needs take his consecration at the archbishop's hand, the archbishop would not grant it unto him, unless he made profession of obedience, according to the ancient custom of his predecessors. Then Roger, consulting with his monks, at first refused so to do; but at length was contented, so it might not be done in the archbishop's church, but in any other church where he would, underwriting this clause withal, "salvis utriusque ecclesiæ privilegiis;" that is, "saving the privileges of both churches." To this the archbishop said again, first, that he should make his due and canonical profession, and that he should not come to him with writing or underwriting, but should say in his heart, "salve sancta parens," or "salve festa dies," not "salvis privilegiis," or any such like thing. Whereunto when the Austin monks in no case would consent, nor the archbishop otherwise would grant his benediction, Roger the abbot was fain to post to Rome, and there to bring the archbishop in hatred in the court of Rome, and made his abbey tributary to Pope Alexander. A.D. 1177.

Richard I. A.D. 1137 to 1190.

The pope, well contented with this, not only granteth the abbot his desire, but also, in contumely of the archbishop, dubbeth the abbot with all such ornaments as to a prelate appertain; and so, A.D. 1178, sent home the abbot triumphantly with his ring and mitre, and other ensigns of victory, with letters also to the archbishop, enjoining him, immediately upon the sight thereof, to consecrate the abbot in his own church, and without making any profession. Although with these letters the archbishop was shrewdly pressed, yet, notwithstanding, his stout heart would not stoop for this; but he laid his appeal against the same, and so the consecration for that time was suspended.

Roger the abbot returneth home with triumph.

Then Roger, for his more defence, getting the king's letters, travelled up the second time to Rome, where grievously he complained to Pope Alexander of the archbishop. At the same time a general council was summoned to be kept at Lateran, where Richard the aforesaid archbishop was also looked for amongst other bishops to be present, who came as far as Paris, but, being there, durst approach no further, and so retired home again; whereupon the pope being offended with his contempt, without any more delay, exalted the abbot with his own consecration, and invested him with all pomp and glory; howbeit, providing before that the said consecration should redound to no prejudice against the liberties of the mother church of Canterbury, and so, upon the same, wrote to the archbishop his letters of certificate, with this addition annexed, "salvo jure et dignitate Cant. ecclesiæ:" that is to say, "saving the liberties and dignities of the church of Canterbury."

Concilium Lateranum sub Alexandro Papa.

Roger travelleth again to Rome.

Is consecrated.

The council ended, Roger the abbot returneth home, although with an empty purse, yet full of victory and triumph. The archbishop, again thinking to work some grievance to the Austin monks, had procured, in the mean time, letters from Pope Alexander to the bishop of Durham and the abbot of St. Alban's, that they should cause the said Roger, abbot of the Austin monks, to show unto the archbishop all the old privileges of his house; which indeed, being showed, seemed to be rased and new written, with bulls of lead, not after the manner or style of that age, nor pretending any such

Richard I. A.D. 1137 to 1190.

antiquity as should seem to reach from the time of Austin, but rather newly counterfeit.

All this notwithstanding, the abbot, bearing him bold upon the pope's favour, ceased not still to disquiet and overcrow the archbishop by all ways he could, in exempting all his priests and laymen belonging to his jurisdiction from the archbishop's obedience; forbidding also that any of his should come to his chapters or synods, or fear any sentence of his curse or excommunication. Whereupon the archbishop, about the month of November the same year, sailing over to Normandy, where the king was, thought to take his journey to the pope to complain of the abbot; but being stayed by the king, he was not suffered to pass any further, the king labouring what he could to bring them to agreement. Nevertheless the pope and his "Romans," saith my story, "caring more for gold and silver, than for justice, still stirred coals of sedition and debate between them."[1]

Richard, the archbishop, staid by the king.

The Romish court set men at variance to get their money.

In the year ensuing, which was A.D. 1184, died Richard, the archbishop aforesaid, in the eight and thirtieth year of King Henry II., after whose decease much trouble happened about the election of a new archbishop, between the king and the monks of Canterbury. And now, to enter here into the story of Baldwin, above mentioned: first, the king sent to the monks, that they should consider with themselves about the election of their archbishop, and be ready against the time that he would send for them to the court. Upon this the covent, gladly assembling together, agreed in themselves upon one, whom they thought chiefly to prefer; yet naming four more, that if the king should refuse one, the other yet might stand. Now the practice of the monks was, first, to keep the election in their own hands only, as much as they could. And secondly, ever to give the election either to some prior or monk of their own house, or to some abbot or bishop who sometimes had been of their company; whereby, as much inconvenience and blind superstition was bred in the church of England, so the same disliked both the king and the bishops not a little.

Monks of Canterbury sent for by Henry II. about choosing their archbishop.

As this past on, King Henry II., when he saw his time, willed the monks of Canterbury to be cited or sent for, to understand what they had concluded in their election. Whereupon the monks sent up their prior, called Alanus, with certain other monks, to Reading, where the king then lay, about the month of August; who at first were courteously entertained, but, after the king had intelligence whom they had nominated and elected, they were sent home again with cold cheer; the king willing them to pray better, and to advise more earnestly upon the matter amongst themselves. Alanus, the prior, with his fellows, thus departed; who coming home, in conclusion, so concluded amongst themselves, that they would remit no jot of their liberties to the king, without the pope's consent and knowledge. The king understanding hereof, sent his ambassadors likewise to the pope, for the fortifying of his cause, being in the mean time grievously offended with the prior, saying, that he was proud, and would make archbishop whom he listed, and would be the second pope in England, &c.

Sent for to the king a second time.

The king offended with Alan, the prior, and with the stubborn monks of Canterbury.

(1) "Aurum et argentum magis quam justitiam sitientes, seditiones inter eos et litigia commovebant."—Ex Historia Gervasii.

Not long after this, as these letters were sent up to Rome, the king sent for Alanus, the prior, and more of the monks, to come to him; whom he entreateth, desiring them in gentle speech that they would show as much gentleness and favour to him being their lord and king (as becometh his friends and subjects to do), as to confer with the bishops of the realm about this matter, and to take some better counsel, such as might redound to God's glory, his honour, and the wealth of the public state, with other like words to the same effect; to whom when the prior had answered again, with thanks and due reverence, according to the king's request, the bishops and monks went to confer together about the matter. And first, the bishops marvelled why the monks should exclude them out of the election, seeing they were professed and suffragans to the said church of Canterbury; "Neither is there any prince," quoth the bishop of Bath, "that will refuse our counsel." "There be some counsels," said the monks, "whereat you may be called; but as touching the doing of this election, it pertaineth not unto you further than to publish only, and denounce the party whom we have chosen." The bishop of London then asked if they had already made an election? "No election," said the prior, "as yet, but only we have denominated the persons." "Then have ye proceeded further," quoth he, "than ye ought, having commandment from the pope not to proceed without us." And with that was brought forth the pope's letter, commanding that within forty days the bishops of England, and the prior and covent of Canterbury, should elect an able and fit person for their archbishop. About the scanning of these letters was much ado. The bishops said, they were first named, and therefore ought to have most interest in this election. The monks said again, that they also were not excluded, and required to have a transcript of the letter, whereof much doubt was made.

Richard I. A.D. 1137 to 1190.

Bishops of England claim to have interest in the election of the archbishop of Canterbury.

The pope's letter.

After long concertation, when they could not agree, the king, coming between them both, called away the bishops from the monks; supposing, by separating the one from the other, to draw both parties to his sentence. But that would not be; for the monks, stiffly standing to their liberties, would lose no pre-eminence of their church, still alleging how, by the ancient privileges of the church of Canterbury, the covent should choose their pastor and bishop, and the prior was but to publish and denounce the person. The bishops again replied, "That it was their right to appoint their archbishop and metropolitan, who were bishops and suffragans; and namely, the bishop of London, also being dean of the said church of Canterbury." The king then, as umpire between them, yet favouring rather the side of the bishops, desired them to agree together in peace. When that would not prevail, he set the lord steward, and other noblemen, to entreat the prior to draw to some agreement; at least to be contented with this form of election, which was, that the bishop of London, or some other bishop, should declare the election in these words:—

King Henry II separateth the bishops from the monks.

The monks will lose no pre-eminence of their church.

"We bishops, and the prior and covent of Christ's church, in Canterbury, with the assent of our lord the king, do choose such a person to be archbishop," &c. Or else thus, that the prior should pronounce the election in these words, saying: "The bishops of

The form of election of the archbishop.

Richard I. A.D. 1137 to 1190.

England, and I prior, and the covent of Canterbury, with the assent of our lord and king, do choose such a person," &c.

Upon this, the prior said he would convent with his covent. The latter, with much ado, were content to yield to the king's desire; but afterward, being required to put down the same in writing, that they refused to do; yet notwithstanding, relented at last to the king. But when the bishops made excuses for the absence of their fellow bishops, the matter for that time staid; and the king, sending home the monks again to their house in peace, deferred that business to a further day, which was till the first day of December; commanding the prior with his fellows the same day not to fail, but to be at London about the choosing of the archbishop. A.D. 1184.

The bishops and monks could not agree about the form of election.

The election of the archbishop deferred.

As the day prefixed came, the prior with his company were also present; who, giving attendance all that day, and also the day following, were thus driven off till the third day after. At length the lord steward, with other nobles of the realm, were sent to them from the king, to declare, that whereas the king before had divided the bishops from the monks, that they both might have their election by themselves, after the form of a bill which was put down in writing: now, the mind of the king was, that the monks, taking another way, should join with the bishops, and so, having the matter in talk together, should proceed jointly in the election.

Against this, many things were alleged by the prior and his mates, complaining much of the bishops, who said, that the bishops had ever holden with the kings, against the liberties of their church and archbishops. As first, they stood against Anselm for King William; then against Theobald for King Stephen; after that against Becket for King Henry; and after him, did supplant the election of Richard, their archbishop; and now again, went about to practise and work against this their election present. At last, the prior with his fellows concluding, desired they might speak with the king himself; who, presently coming unto them, willed them as good men to be contented, and go talk with the bishops about the election, promising, that whom they agreed upon, he also would grant his assent unto the same. To whom, when the prior again had objected the writings that before were made; "True it is," said the king, "such writings were made, but I neither may nor will go against the council of my realm; and therefore agree," said he, "with my bishops and abbots, and remember that the voice of the people is the voice of God."

The monks of Canterbury compelled against their wills to join with the bishops, touching the election of the archbishop.

Upon this the prior with his monks, seeing no other remedy, went to the bishops to confer, according to the king's request, about the election; who then were willed by the bishops to nominate whom they would, and the bishops would likewise name theirs. So, when the prior with his accomplices had named three, after their choosing, the bishops said they would nominate but one; and so did, who was the bishop of Worcester; willing the prior to go home, and to confer with his covent about the same, to whom, shortly after, the bishops sent certain priests, to signify to the covent, that they, according to the pope's letters, should repair to the bishops concerning the election of the archbishop; and to declare, moreover, to them, that the persons whom they had named were good men, but that he whom they had nominated was a more worthy man, whom they both had nominated, and also would elect. The monks, marvelling hereat, sent two monks with the archdeacon of Canterbury to the king.

The bishops make their election without the monks of Canterbury.

This done, immediately after the return of the priests, the bishops caused all the bells of the city to be rung, and 'Te Deum' to be sung for the archbishop newly elect; and when the two monks brought tidings to the covent at Canterbury of what was done at London, they were all in a marvellous dump. The king hearing this, and perceiving the stiffness of the monks, in all haste sent messengers to Canterbury, with gentle words, to will the prior to come to the king, and certify him of the purpose of his monks. Unto whom the prior, soon coming, declareth in the name of the whole covent, that in no case he nor the monks would ever, while the world stood, agree to that election of the bishops, unless the king, in his own person, would come to Canterbury, and there openly, before the whole covent, would protest, by his own mouth, the aforesaid election to be nought and void; and so returning to London again, would likewise openly, before the clergy and people, repudiate and reject the same; and, furthermore, that the party also elected should openly, in the same place, protest and say, that he neither would nor ought to take that function upon him, unless he entered with the consent of the prior and covent of Canterbury; and that all this should be done in the same place where the bishops had made their election before; and so, peradventure, said they, at the king's so earnest suit and request, they would gratify his will, and ratify the said election with the voices of their consent. To make the story short, after great hold between the secular clergy on the one side, and the regular order on the other side, and after the king's indignation against the prior, and the swooning of the prior before the king, at length the king to take up the matter, and to save the prior's life, was fain to perform in his own person all those conditions above prescribed by the monks.[1] A.D. 1184.

Conditions prescribed to the king by the monks of Canterbury, for the ratification of the archbishop made by the bishops.

Baldwin bishop of Worcester elected archbishop of Canterbury.

And thus have ye heard the tragical election of the bishop of Worcester, named Baldwin, made archbishop of Canterbury. Now what a troublesome time the said Baldwin had with the monks in governing the church of Canterbury, here followeth likewise not unworthy to be considered.

THE TROUBLES BETWEEN BALDWIN, ARCHBISHOP OF CANTERBURY, AND THE MONKS OF THE SAME CHURCH.

A.D. 1184 to 1190.

In the first year the archbishop showed himself friendly and loving to the monks; the year following he began to appear somewhat rough unto them. The manner then was of the house of Christ-church, toward the time of the Nativity and of Easter, to receive certain presents or gifts of their farmers or tenants, which the cellarer should take and lay up. Those presents the archbishop began first to intercept from the monks, and to bestow them upon his secular clerks. After this he took three churches or benefices, which the

(1) Ex Gervas. fol. 100.

Richard I. A.D. 1084 to 1190.

monks claimed as proper to themselves, and placed in them three of his chaplains. After this he encroacheth to his hands certain tenements, revenues and victuals, belonging before to the monks, as they said, and committed the custody thereof to certain of his own clerks and household servants.

The monks of Canterbury appeal to the pope against their archbishop. Reconciliation between the archbishop and the monks, which did not hold long.

The monks, who had borne so much with the archbishop before, seeing this, could forbear with him no longer, but needs would make their appeal against him. The archbishop, not much regarding that, waxed thereby the more fierce against them, insomuch that such farms and tenements as he before had let alone, he now received to his own occupying, with many other grievances wherewith he greatly vexed the monks, so that three abbots were fain to come and reconcile the archbishop and the monks; which reconciliation was this, that the monks should let fall their appeal, and the archbishop should restore again to them their farms and tenements. But as touching the benefices and the presents, the archbishop still kept them in his hands for a further trial of their obedience and patience. Nevertheless, some there were of the ancient monks who in no case would give over the aforesaid appeal, before the archbishop made a full restitution of all together.

The archbishop sendeth to the pope.

After this agreement, such as it was, between the monks and him, the archbishop soon after sent up to Rome one of his chaplains, unto whom he had given one of the benefices aforementioned, partly for confirmation of his benefice, partly also to obtain license for the archbishop to build a church, which he intended to erect, of secular priests near unto the town of Canterbury. Which being obtained of the pope, the archbishop, not a little glad thereof, began now more and more to wax fierce against the monks, not only in taking from them their churches and oblations, but also in aggravating the whole state of their house, which he intended either to subvert or greatly to diminish, to pluck down the pride and stubbornness of the monks. Wherefore, taking with him certain other bishops, who, he knew, bare no good will to that monkish generation, he went to the king, declaring how he had a good purpose in his mind to erect a new and a solemn church, in honour of St. Thomas of Canterbury, of secular priests or canons, and therefore desired of the king to have his favourable license to the same. The king, right well perceiving the purpose of the archbishop whither it tended, as to the bridling of the stiff-necked monks, was the more willing to give assent, if he were not also the chief worker of that matter himself.

The archbishop goeth about to pluck down the pride of the monks.

The purpose of the archbishop in building his new church at Canterbury.

The intent of the archbishop in planting of that new church, was to found there divers prebends, and to make both the king and every bishop, being his suffragans, prebendaries thereof, so that every one of them should confer one prebendship on the same foundation; minding there to consecrate bishops, to make his chrismatory, to celebrate his synods, and to administer all other things belonging unto the function of his see, and the same to be called Hakington church.

Three causes alleged against the archbishop by the monks.

The monks, not ignorant how the archbishop privily intended the desolation and subversion of their house and liberties, consulting upon the matter, determined at length among themselves to appeal to the see of Rome, for these three causes against the archbishop; namely, first, for spoiling them of their gifts and oblations: secondly, for depriving them of their churches and benefices: and thirdly, for erecting a new foundation of secular canons, to the derogation and overthrow of their religious order; giving admonition to the archbishop beforehand by their monks sent to him, of this their appellation. To whom the archbishop answered, that the foundation, which he went about, was to no derogation, but rather to the fortification and honour of their house. Who answered again, that it was, and could not otherwise be, but to their subversion. "And what should let me then," said the archbishop, "but I may build on my own ground what I will?" "No," said they, "no ground of yours, but your ground is our ground, as all other things that you have by right are ours, forasmuch as you have them not of yourself, but of the church, and for the church's cause. All which things have been given neither to you nor to the archbishops, but unto the church of Christ; and therefore," said they, "all such as appertain unto us inwardly and outwardly, with the persons also, and the whole state of our church, we submit under the pope's protection, and now here make our appeal to the see apostolic, assigning also the term when to prosecute the same."

The monks claim all the goods of the archbishop. The monks put themselves and their house in the pope's protection.

The archbishop receiving this appellation, and saying that he would answer to the same either by himself or by his responsal, within three days after, which was the sixteenth of December, came to Canterbury, where the monks, understanding how he was in mind to place new secular priests in the church of St. Stephen, where the monks had served before, came to the church, to stop the proceeding of the archbishop by way of appeal. Whereof the archbishop having warning beforehand, deferred the matter till the next day, on which day the monks, again being sent by Honorius, the prior, into the church, charged the archbishop in the name of Almighty God, and by virtue of their appeal made to the apostolic see, to surcease those his doings; forbidding also the parson of the church in any wise to suffer those secular clerks to be admitted into the church: all which, yet notwithstanding, the archbishop proceedeth in his business. And first, placing in his clerks, he suspendeth the prior from his administration. Then he abjureth the porters of the gate, upon their oath, to let none of the monks pass out of the house without his license. The monks likewise he commanded, by virtue of obedience, not to stray any where abroad without his leave. And furthermore, one of the aforesaid monks, who served the appeal against him, he utterly banished from that covent. Upon this, on the day following, Honorius, the prior, trusting, saith the story, on God and St. Thomas, took his way to Rome, sent in commission by the covent, to prosecute the appeal against the archbishop.

The prior of Canterbury suspended.

In the mean season, a new jar began between the said archbishop and the monks, about their rents and revenues, which the archbishop would have committed to the receiving and keeping of three monks, but the sub-prior Geffery, with the covent, in no case would suffer that: whereabout there was a foul stir. The archbishop craving the aid of the king, first had three bishops sent down to him, namely, those of Coventry, Norwich, and Worcester, who, being instant with the monks to submit their cause into the king's hands, like as the archbishop had done, they utterly refused it; especially seeing they

Another jar between the monks and their archbishop.

Richard I. A.D. 1184 to 1190.

had already referred the whole state of their cause to the determination of the apostolical see. The king, seeing no other remedy, came himself with the archbishop into the chapter-house; where he commanded first the doors to be kept fast, that none should enter but those who by name were called for. Among whom were two bishops, to wit, those of Norwich and Durham, and one Peter Blesensis, a learned man, whose epistles be yet extant in libraries, a chief worker in this matter against the monks. Then was called in Geffery, the sub-prior, with a few other monks whom he brought with him. The king then first talking with the archbishop and his company, and afterwards with the monks, laboured to entreat them that they would let fall their appeal, and so stand to the arbitrement of him and of the bishops, concerning the cause which was between the archbishop and them in traverse.

The king cometh into the chapter of Canterbury.

The monks refuse to put their matter from the pope to the king's hearing.

To this the monks answered, that these were good words, but served not for that time, forasmuch as their cause was already translated to the court of Rome, and now was presently in hearing before the pope's holiness; and therefore they neither could nor would do that injury to their lord pope, to refuse him, and to put the matter unto the judgment of any other. Then was it required of the monks, that they would put the matter in compromise, in case the prior would consent thereto; upon this intent, that if the prior consented, and the monks not, then should they run in contempt and disobedience; or if the monks would consent, and the prior not, then should the prior be excluded the realm. The wily monks, being not unprovided of this subtilty, made their answer, that seeing they had sent their prior forth in their commission, it stood not with their honesty to give any determinate consent without the knowledge and before the return of the said prior, unless the archbishop first would promise to make full restitution of all that he had wrongfully wrested from them. When the king could get no other answer of the monks, neither could move the archbishop to release the sentence of their suspension, unless they would confess and acknowledge their fault, he, so parting from them, passed over into France.

The monks' excuse to the king.

The first letter of Pope Urban to Baldwin archbishop of Canterbury.

Not long after this came a messenger from Rome, bringing letters from Pope Urban to the archbishop, wherein the pope, considering and tendering, as he said, the enormous grievances done against the monks, straitly enjoined and commanded him, within ten days after the receiving thereof, to release the sentence of his suspension against the prior and others of the said covent, and also to retract and restore again to the monks whatsoever he had plucked from them since the time of their appeal first made. Who, in case he should deny, or foreslack the doing hereof, commission was given to three abbots, those of Battle, Feversham, and St. Austin's, with ample authority to perform the same, &c. The archbishop, receiving these letters brought to him by a monk of the aforesaid house, first made his excuse that the pope was misinformed. But the monks not contented with that excuse, when they would needs know what answer he would make to the pope's nuncio, his answer was, that "he had yet ten days given him of the pope." In the mean time the archbishop went to London, and there, in the church of St. Paul, consecrated his holy oil and cream (making one of the pope's seven sacraments), which was

The answer. The archbishop maketh his oil and cream at London.

grievously taken in the church of Canterbury. At last, the ten days being ended, when the archbishop refused to accomplish that which was in the pope's letter enjoined him, the three abbots aforesaid, to execute the pope's commandment, came at their day assigned to Canterbury, and there assoiled all such as the archbishop before had suspended, and, in the end, certified Pope Urban by letters what they had done.

The archbishop, hearing this, within four days after, sent two of his clerks, who appealed the three abbots aforesaid up to Rome; and he himself, in the mean time, prepared busily for the building of his church, sending to all churches in England upon releasement from their sins, to confer unto the same; and to make the more haste, for lack of freestone he made up his building with timber, and such other stuff as he could get.

The archbishop's new church made of wood.

The prior Honorius all this while remained still at the court of Rome, giving attendance upon the pope, who, having intelligence of the archbishop's doings, procured another letter of Pope Urban to the whole clergy of England, straitly enjoining them that none should confer with the new fraternity of Baldwin, archbishop of Canterbury. To these letters the archbishop showed such reverence, that whereas before he had planted his chapel of wood and boards, now he provided the same to be builded of lime and stone.

A letter of Pope Urban against the archbishop.

By this time Peter Blesensis, with other messengers of the archbishop, seeing that Honorius the prior was gone from the court of France, resorted to the court of Rome, bringing with them letters of credit from the king, from the archbishop, and also from other bishops of the realm; but the pope, reading only the king's letters, and the archbishop's, the residue he cast into a window by, saying, he would read them at further leisure. Then the pope giving audience in his consistory to hear their cause, first came in Peter Blesensis, with the agents of the archbishop, exhibiting their letters, and propounding their requests to the pope, which were, that restitution should be made by the monks to the archbishop, wherein they had injured him. Secondly, That the things which had been granted before to the prior in the court, might be called in again. Thirdly, That the archbishop might have license to proceed in building his college of canons, &c. After this was called in Master Pilleus, the attorney for the monks of Canterbury, who, alleging many great things against the archbishop, for his contempt and disobedience to the pope's precepts, required that he should rather make restitution to the monks for the injuries he had done to them; and also that his new foundation of secular canons, tending to the overthrow of the conventual church of Canterbury, should be utterly rased and thrown down to the ground. Thus between these parties pleaing and repleaing one against the other, much hard hold there was; but, in conclusion, for all the king's letters, and for all that the archbishop's and bishops could do, the matter went on the monks' side; so that there was no remedy, but the pope would needs have the archbishops new building to come down, and the monks to be restored again to their full possessions: the execution whereof was committed to the three abbots aforesaid, to wit, those of Battle, Feversham, and St. Austin's, Canterbury, and to Geffrey, sub-prior of Canterbury.

The archbishop's messengers come to the pope's court. Letters of the king, the archbishop, and of other bishops to the pope.

Mr. Pilleus, attorney in the pope's court for the monks of Canterbury.

Richard I. A.D. 1184 to 1190.

These things being thus determined at Rome, Radulph Granville, lord steward of England, writing to the said abbot of Battle, and to the sub-prior and covent of Canterbury, commandeth them, in the king's name, and upon their oath and fealty given unto him, that neither they nor any of them do proceed in this controversy between the monks and the archbishop of Canterbury, before they come and talk with him, there to know further of the king's pleasure: and, furthermore, charging the covent of Canterbury not to enter further into any examinations concerning the archbishop's matters; and also citing the sub-prior of the said house to appear before him in London, at the feast of St. James, the same year, which was A.D. 1187. Notwithstanding, he excusing himself by sickness, sent two monks in his stead, and so kept himself at home; to whom commandment was given, that the monks of Canterbury, within fifteen days, should sail over to Normandy to the king, and there show the tenor and evidences of their privileges; and also that such stewards and bailiffs as they had placed in their farms and lordships, contrary to the will of the archbishop, should be removed. And likewise the three abbots, in the king's name, were commanded in no wise to execute the pope's commandment against the archbishop. Not long after this, the archbishop took shipping at Dover, and went over to the king, where he ordained three principal officers over the monks of Christ-church—the sacrist, the cellarer, and the chamberlain, contrary to the will of the covent, with other grievances more, whereby the monks were not a little offended, so that upon the same they made a new appellation to the pope; whereupon Pope Urban, by the setting on of Honorius the prior, who was now come again to the court, wrote to him another letter after a sharper and more vehement sort, to the effect as followeth.

The pope holdeth to the monks, against the king and bishops of the realm. The pope's executors commanded not to proceed against the archbishop.

Another appellation of the monks against the archbishop.

The tenor of Pope Urban's Letters to Baldwin, Archbishop of Canterbury.[1]

In that we have borne with your brotherhood hitherto, and have not proceeded in such grievous a manner against you as we might, although being thereto greatly provoked; the chiefest cause was this, that we supposed your heart would have relented from the oppression of the conventual church of Canterbury, committed unto you; if not for our reverence, which you seem to have contemned more than became you, yet at least for fear of God's judgment. For well we hoped, our conscience persuading us to the same, that after you had obtained that high state and dignity in the church of England, you would have been an example to others of obedience and reverence to be given to the see apostolic of all ecclesiastical persons. Wherefore, at the first beginning both of our and also of your promotion, we did not spare to advance and honour you as we have done few others besides, thinking no less than that we had found a faithful friend of the church for our honour; wherein we perceive now, which maketh us not a little to marvel, our expectation greatly deceived, and him whom we well trusted to be a sure stay for the maintenance of our estate, we now find a persecutor against us in our members.

Note how the popes stand all upon their honour.

For whereas we sundry times have written to you in the behalf of our brethren, and the church committed to your charge, that you should desist from disquieting them, and not vex or disturb their liberties, at least for reverence of us; you, not only in this, but in other things more, as commonly is reported of you in all places, setting at light our letters and appellations made unto the apostolical see; what you have wrought against them after their so manifold

The pope expostulateth with Baldwin for contempt of his see.

(1) "Urbanus episcopus, servus servorum Dei, Baldwino Cantuar. archiepiscopo et apostolicæ sedis legato, salutem et apostolicam benedictionem," &c.

appellations laid unto us, and our inhibitions again unto you, we are ashamed to utter. But revolve and consider in your mind, if ye have well done, and advise in your own conscience what you have done. We, for our part, because we neither may nor ought with deaf ears to pass over the clamours of the brethren, and such contempt of the apostolic see, although our biddings and warnings given to you seem to be all in vain; yet, notwithstanding, we send our mandates again unto your brotherhood, in these apostolical writings, directly and in virtue of obedience, commanding you, that whether you be present in your church, or absent, all that notwithstanding, whatsoever you have done in building of your chapel, which you to the destruction of the monastery of Canterbury have erected, after the time of their appeal made to us, or our inhibition sent to you, you fail not of your proper costs and charges to demolish; undoing again and making void whatsoever ye have begun and innovated, concerning the institution of the canons, and other things belonging to the erection of the said chapel; accounting moreover and reputing the place where the chapel was, to be accursed and profane; and also that all such, whosoever have celebrated in the same place, shall stand suspended till the time they appear before our presence. Commanding, furthermore, that all those monks whom you have presumed to remove from their office, or to excommunicate, since the time of their appeal made, you shall restore and assoil again, rendering also and restoring all such farms, manors, tenements, and oblations, as you, after their appeal made, have inveigled from them; and, finally, that you innovate nothing touching the state of that monastery, during the time of this controversy depending before us: giving you to understand that in case you shall continue in your stubbornness and rebellion upon this present warning, or defer the execution of this precept thirty days after the receiving thereof, we shall appoint others to execute the same; enjoining also your suffragans, that as you shall show yourself disobedient and rebelling to us, so they all shall refuse likewise to give any obedience or reverence unto you, &c.—Given at Ferraria, 5th Non. Oct. 1187.

The archbishop to throw down the building of his new church, of his own costs.

To restore the monks whom he did deprive and excommunicate.

The archbishop threatened by the pope.

Another letter besides this the pope also sent to the three abbots aforesaid, for the correction of these enormities. Likewise another letter was sent to King Henry II., wherein the pope enjoineth and requireth him, upon remission of his sins, not to dissemble and bear with the archbishop in his oppression of his monks, but to help those things to be amended, wherein he hath trespassed against them.

The pope writeth to the abbots, and to the king.

These pontifical letters were written A.D. 1187, the third day of October; and in the nineteenth day after, the same month, the said Pope Urban died. In the same year, and about the same month, Baldwin, king of Jerusalem, was taken, with many noblemen, by Saladin the Saracen, and Jerusalem lost, after it had been in the possession of the Christians, and had so continued, the space of eighty-eight years and eighty days, from the time that Godfridus Bolonius did first win it from the infidels.

Pope Urban dieth. Baldwin, king of Jerusalem, with many nobles, taken of the Saracens, and the city won.

After the receiving of those letters of Pope Urban above specified, both the king and archbishop, with all the bishops of the realm, were marvellously quailed, glad now to please, and speak fair to the monks, promising all things to be done and restored to them after the best sort; neither were now the king and the archbishop so submissive, but the monks on the other side were as brag and jocund, being fully assured that all now was their own: in the narration of which history, as it is set forth in Gervasius at large, this we have to note by the way, in what fear and thraldom kings in those days were under the pope, who could not be masters over their own subjects, but that every pilled monk, or pelting prior, upon virtue of their appeal to the court of Rome, and making their house tributary to the

The monks get the upper hand over the archbishop and the king.

The miserable subjection of kings to the pope.

pope, was able not only to match, but to give checkmate unto the best king christened, as not in this story only may appear.

It followeth then in the story of these monks, that as they were thus in the midst of their joy and jollity, suddenly cometh news of the death of Pope Urban, their great caliph,[1] and also how that Gregory VIII. was placed in his room, who was a special friend and favourer of the archbishop; which as it did greatly encourage the king and the archbishop, so the monks, on the other side, were as much discomforted, so that now all was turned upside down. For whereas, before, the king and the archbishop thought they had lost all, and were glad to compound with the monks, and to seek their favour, now were the monks on the contrary side fain to crouch to the king, and glad to have a good countenance; who then resorting to him, and finding him altered both in word and gesture, desired he would confirm and grant that which of late before he had promised. To whom it was answered again by the king, that seeing the archbishop had granted to them their sacrist, their chamberlain, and their cellarer, they should have no more restored by him; neither would he suffer the liberties and privileges of the archbishop to be impaired, or take any wrong. "As touching the new chapel of St. Thomas," said he, "whereabout ye strive so long, with the canonships and other buildings belonging thereto, the same I receive into my hands, so that none shall have any thing to do therein but myself," &c. In like manner from the archbishop such another like answer they received, and from bishops little better. So the monks, sent away with a flea in their ear, went home again out of Normandy unto their cell.

The king's answer to the monks of Canterbury

Now the archbishop having the monks where he would, wrought them much grievance; but that continued not very long. For within two months after and less died Pope Gregory VIII., about the sixteenth day of the December following. After him succeeded Pope Clement III., who, following the steps of Urban, bent all his power with the monks against the archbishop, sending divers precepts and mandates in the year following, which was A.D. 1188, with an imperious letter, willing and commanding him to desist from his oppression of the monks, and to throw down his new chapel. Hereupon the archbishop made his appeal, and minded to go to Rome, but was called back by the king, being ready to sail over. In the same year Honorius, the prior, died at Rome of the plague, which was some help and comfort to the archbishop, for whom the archbishop made Roger Noris, prior, against the wills of the covent. After this, about the latter end of the same year, Pope Clement sent down his legate, called Radulph, a cardinal, to Canterbury, with another letter more sharply written to the same effect unto the archbishop.[2]

Pope Gregory VIII dieth. Pope Clement III. Letters to the archbishop. Honorius, the prior of Canterbury, died at Rome. The second letter of Pope Clement to the archbishop.

Furthermore, in the year next after, he wrote also the third letter to him. In the same year also died King Henry II., after whom succeeded King Richard, his son, who joining likewise with the archbishop, took his part strongly against the said monks. At last, after

Henry II died. Richard I joined with the archbishop.

(1) Caliph is the high priest of the Saracens sitting in Damascus, to whom all the sultans were subject, as our princes now are to the pope [Caliph is the title assumed by the successors of Mahomet.—ED.]

(2) Ex Hist. Gervas.

much ado on both parts, and after great disturbance, and imprisoning divers of the monks, King Richard, preparing his voyage towards Jerusalem, and studying first to set peace between them, consulted and agreed with the bishops and abbots about a final concord in this matter, between the archbishop and monks of Canterbury; which at length on both parts was made, upon these conventions which follow:—

Richard I. A.D. 1184 to 1190.

First, That Roger Noris should be deposed, whom the archbishop had made prior against their wills: whom the king then at the request of the archbishop promoted to be abbot of Eusham.

Item, That the archbishop should pluck down his chapel, which he builded in the suburbs of Canterbury, against the minds of the monks.

Item, That the aforesaid monks should make profession of their obedience and subjection to the archbishop, as they had done to his predecessors.

Item, As touching all other complaints and injuries (except only the chapel, and the deposition of Roger Noris, the prior), the monks should stand to the arbitrement of the king, the archbishop, and the prelates.

Item, That the monks kneeling down before the king in the chapter-house, should ask the archbishop forgiveness.[1]

This being done, they went altogether to the church, and sang Te Deum for this reformation of peace; the next day, the archbishop coming into the chapter, restored to the covent their manors and farms again; also he discharged the prior whom he had made before; desiring them likewise, that if he had offended them either in word or deed, they would, from their heart, remit him. This reconciliation having been made between the archbishop and the covent, the archbishop then going about to dissolve the building of his new church, though he changed the place, yet thought not to change his intent, and therefore, making exchange of lands with the bishop and monks of Rochester, purchased of them their ground in Lambeth, A.D. 1191. Which done, he came to his clerks whom he had placed to be canons in his new college of Hakington, and also willed them to remove all their goods and furniture to Lambeth, over against Westminster, where he erected for them another church, and there placed the said canons. About which college of Lambeth afterwards much trouble likewise ensued, by the stirring of the said monks of Canterbury, in the time of Hubert, the archbishop, in the reign of the said King Richard, A.D. 1196. Furthermore, after the deposing of Roger Noris, prior of Canterbury aforesaid, Baldwin, the archbishop, being enforced to grant them another prior by the assent of the king and of the covent, assigned Osbern to be their prior, who had taken part before with the archbishop; but the monks not pleased with him, after the death of Baldwin, the archbishop, removed him again.

Archbishop of Canterbury purchaseth land in Lambeth to build his house upon.

And thus have you the tedious discourse of this catholic tragedy between the monks of Canterbury and their archbishop, scarce worth the rehearsal; notwithstanding, this I thought to give the reader to see, in order, first, to show forth unto the world the stout sturdiness of this monkish generation, who, professing profound humility in their coat, what little humility they had in their heart, what pride and arrogancy in their conversation, and what hypocrisy in their religion, that one example, among a thousand others, may give some experience

Three things to be observed in this story of the monks.

Hypocrisy in monkery

(1) Ex lib. anonymo, et ex Hist. Gervasii Monachi Cantuariensis.

Richard I. A.D. 1184 to 1190.

Secondly, that posterity now may see how little kings could then do in their own realms, for the pope. And thirdly, to the intent it may more notoriously appear to all readers, what strife and debate, what dissension and division, what little unity and concord hath always followed the pope's catholic church, wheresoever the corrupt religion and usurped ambition of the pope prevailed. For, not to speak only of this monkish house of Canterbury, what church, cathedral, collegiate, or conventual; what see, church, monastery, or chapel, was entirely under the pope's government, but ever there happened some variance, either between the king and the archbishop, as between King William and Lanfranc, King Henry I. and Anselm, King Stephen and Richard, King Henry II. and Becket, King John and Stephen Langton, King Henry III. and Boniface, &c.; or else between archbishop and archbishop, for making profession, for carrying the cross, for sitting on the right hand of the pope's legate, &c.; or else between archbishops and their suffragans, or between archbishops and their covents, or between bishops and monks, between dean and chapter, between monks and secular priests, monks of one sort against another, friars of one order against another, students against friars, townsmen against scholars, &c. As for example:—What discord was between the archbishop of Canterbury and Richard, archbishop of York, between Lanfranc and Archbishop Thomas, between Theobald, archbishop of Canterbury, and Sylvester, abbot of St. Austin's; between Walter, of Christchurch, and Sylvester, abbot aforesaid; between William, archbishop of Canterbury, and Jeremias, prior of Canterbury, A.D. 1144; between the monks of Canterbury, and Odo, their prior, for translating the relics of Dunstan; between King Stephen, and Roger, bishop of Salisbury; between the bishop of Lincoln, and Roger, bishop of Ely, his son, A.D. 1138; between Pope Innocent and Anacletus, for the space of seven years; the cardinals for money (saith Gervasius) sometimes holding with the one, sometimes with the other; at last the election was determined by a sore battle between Lothaire, the emperor, and Roger, duke of Apulia, A.D. 1137; also between Pope Innocent IV. and the Emperor Frederic II.; between King Henry III. and William Rale, bishop of Winchester, when the king bade the gates of Winchester town to be shut against him, A.D. 1250; between Boniface, archbishop of Canterbury, and the canons of St. Paul.[1] Item, between the said Boniface and the monks of St. Bartholomew, who sat there in harness in his visitation, A.D. 1250; between the abbot of Westminster and monks of the same house, A.D. 1251. Item, between the aforesaid William Rale, bishop of Winchester, and Boniface, archbishop of Canterbury, for a priest of the hospital in Southwark, A.D. 1252; between the said Boniface and canons of Lincoln, after the death of Robert Grosthead, for giving of prebends, A.D. 1253; between the monks of Coventry and canons of Lichfield, for choosing their bishop in the time of King Henry III.

Kings made slaves under the pope.

No concord nor unity in popish churches.

What discord, and how little unity, is in the pope's church.

And what should I speak of the discord which cost so much money between Edmund, archbishop of Canterbury, and the monks of Rochester, for choosing Richard Wandor to be their bishop, A.D. 1328; between Robert Grosthead, bishop of Lincoln, and the

(1) Matth. Paris.

canons of the same house, for which both he and they were driven to travel to Rome, A.D. 1244; between Gilbert, bishop of Rochester, delegate to Archbishop Baldwin, and Robert, the pope's legate, for sitting on the right hand of the legate in his council at Westminster, A.D. 1190; between the abbot of Bardeny and the said Grosthead, about the visitation of their abbey, A.D. 1242. Item, between the covent of Canterbury and the said Robert, bishop of Lincoln, A.D. 1243; between Hugo, bishop of Durham, and Hubert, bishop of Sarum, and Geffery, archbishop of York, A.D. 1189; between William, bishop of Ely, the king's chancellor, and the canons of York, for not receiving him with procession, A.D. 1190; between the abbot of Westminster and his covent of Black Monks, whom King Henry III. had much ado to still and make to agree, A.D. 1249. Item, between the aforesaid bishop of Lincoln and the abbot of Westminster; likewise between Nicholas, bishop of Durham, and John, abbot of St. Albans, A.D. 1246; also between Hubert, archbishop of Canterbury, and the monks there, for the house of Lambeth, A.D. 1146; and what a stir was between the preaching friars and the grey friars, mentioned in Matthew Paris, for superiority, A.D. 1243; also between the said grey friars and the prelates and doctors of Paris, about nine conclusions, condemned of the prelates to be erroneous.

Conclusions of the friars condemned for erroneous, by the prelates of Paris

I. Concerning the Divine Essence, that it cannot be seen by the angels or by men glorified.

II. Concerning the Essence of the Holy Ghost.

III. Touching the proceeding of the Holy Ghost, as he is love.

IV. Whether men glorified shall be "in cœlo empyreo," or "in cœlo crystallino."

V. That the evil angel at his first creation was evil, and never good.

VI. That there have been many verities from the beginning which were not God.

VII That an angel in one instant may be in divers places.

VIII. That the evil angel never had whereby he might stand, any more than had Adam in his state of innocency.

IX. That he which hath "meliora naturalia," that is to say, more perfect strength of nature working in him, shall have more full measure of necessity to obtain grace and glory.

To these articles the prelates answering, did excommunicate the same as erroneous, affirming, that grace and glory shall be given according to that God, who hath elected and predestinated, &c.[1]

Contention between friars about the conception of our Lady

In like manner between the said Dominic friars, and the grey friars,[2] what a brawl and tumult there was about the conception of our Lady, whether she was conceived without original sin or not, in the reign of King Henry VII. and King Henry VIII, A.D. 1559. Add moreover to these, the four and twenty heinous schisms, and not so few, which happened between pope and pope, in the church and see of Rome. But why do I stand to recite the divisions and dissensions of the pope's church, which is as much almost as to reckon the sands of the sea? for what church, chapter, or covent, was there in all that religion, which either had not some variance with itself or with others? Upon which continual strife and variance among them, the readers hereof may judge of them and their religion

Continual variance in the pope's church

(1) Matth. Paris, fol 167. (2) See Harl MSS Brit Mus. No 419, art 49.—Ed.

Richard I. A.D. 1190.

as pleaseth them: in the mean time, my judgment is this; that where such dissension dwelleth, there dwelleth not the spirit of Christ.

These things thus discoursed, touching the tragical dissension between Baldwin, the archbishop, and the monks of Canterbury; now let us proceed, by the Lord's assistance, in continuation of our story. After King Richard had thus, as is declared, set the monks and the archbishop in some agreement, and had composed such things as were to be redressed within the realm, he advanced forward his journey, and came unto Touraine, to meet with Philip, the French king, and after that went to Vezelay, where the French king and he joining together, for the more continuance of their journey, assured themselves by solemn oath, swearing fidelity one unto the other; the form of whose oath was this:—That either of them should defend and maintain the honour of the other, and bear true fidelity unto him of life, members, and worldly honour; and that neither of them should fail one the other in their affairs; but that the French king should aid the king of England in defending his land and dominions, as he would himself defend his own city of Paris, if it were besieged; and that Richard, king of England, likewise should aid the French king in defending his land and dominions, no otherwise than he would defend his own city of Rouen, if it were besieged, &c.

King Richard taketh his journey toward Jerusalem. The oath and fidelity between Philip II. the French king, and Richard I.

But how slenderly this oath did hold between these two kings, and by whose chief occasion first it fell asunder, the sequel of the story (the Lord willing) shall declare hereafter.

Furthermore, touching the laws and ordinances appointed by this King Richard for his navy, the form thereof was this:—

I. That whosoever killed any person on shipboard, should be tied with him who was slain, and thrown into the sea.

II. And if he killed him on the land, he should in like manner be tied with the party slain, and be buried with him in the earth.

III. He that shall be convicted by lawful witness of drawing out his knife or weapon, to the intent to strike any man, or that hath stricken any to the drawing of blood, shall lose his hand.

IV. He that striketh any person with his hand, without effusion of blood, shall be plunged three times in the sea.

V. Whoso speaketh any opprobrious or contumelious words, in reviling or cursing another, for as often as he hath so reviled, shall pay so many ounces of silver.

VI. A thief or felon that hath stolen, being lawfully convicted, shall have his head shorn, and boiling pitch poured upon his head, and feathers or down strewed upon the same, whereby he may be known; and so at the first landing place they shall come to, there to be cast up, &c.

These things thus set in readiness, King Richard sending his navy by the Spanish seas, and by the straits of Gibraltar, between Spain and Africa, to meet him at Marseilles, he himself went (as is said) to Vezelay, to the French king. The two kings went from thence to Lyons, where the bridge over the Rhone, for press of people, brake, and many, both men and women, were drowned. By reason of this, the two kings, for the cumbrance of their trains, were constrained to dissever themselves during their journey, appointing both to meet together in Sicily; and so Philip, the

They come to Lyons.

French king, took his way to Genoa, and King Richard to Marseilles, where he remained eight days, appointing his navy to meet him there. From thence crossing over to Genoa, where the French king was, he passed forward by the coast of Italy, and entered the Tiber, not far from Rome, where meeting with Ottoman, the cardinal and bishop of Hostia, he did complain greatly of the filthy simony of the pope and the pope's court, for receiving seven hundred marks for consecrating the bishop Cenomanensis; also a thousand and five hundred marks of William, the bishop of Ely, for his office legantine; and likewise an infinite sum of money of the bishop of Bordeaux, for acquitting him when he should be deposed for a certain crime laid to his charge by his clergy, &c.

Richard complaineth of the pope's court.

The seventh day of August, in the year aforesaid, King Richard departed out of Marseilles, after he had there waited seven days for his navy, which came not, and so hiring twenty galleys, and ten great barks, to ship over his men, he sailed by the sea-coast of Italy, and came to Naples, and, partly by horse and waggon, partly by the sea, passing to Falernum, he came to Calabria; where, after that he had heard his ships were arrived at Messina, in Sicily, he made the more speed; and so, on the twenty-third of September, he sent to Messina, with such a noise of trumpets and shawms, with such a rout and show, that it was the great wonderment and terror both of the Frenchmen, and of all others that did hear and behold the sight.

The king's ships arrive at Messina.

To the said town of Messina the French king had come before the sixteenth day of the same month of September, and had taken up the palace of Tancred, king of Sicily, for his lodging. To him King Richard, after his arrival, eftsoons resorted; and when the two kings had communed together, immediately the same day the French king took shipping, and entered the seas, thinking to sail toward the land of Jerusalem; but after he was out of the haven, the wind arising contrary against him, returned him back again to Messina. Then King Richard, whose lodging was prepared in the suburbs without the city, after he had resorted again, and talked with the French king, and also had sent to Tancred, king of Sicily, for the deliverance of Joan, his sister (some time queen of Sicily), and had obtained her to be sent unto him, the last day of September passed over the flood of Delfar, and there getting possession of a stronghold called De la Bagmare, or Le Bamre, and placing therein his sister, with a sufficient garrison, he returned again to Messina. On the second of October King Richard won another certain stronghold, called 'Monasterium Griffonum,' situated in the midst of the river Delfar, between Messina and Calabria; from whence the monks being expelled, he reposed there all his store and provision of victuals, which came from England or other places.

Richard and Philip at Messina.

Richard obtaineth his sister Joan, queen sometime of Sicily, to be sent to him.

The citizens of Messina, seeing that the king of England had won the castle and island in De la Bagmare, and also the monastery of the Griffons, and doubting lest the king would extend his power further to invade their city, and get if he could, the whole isle of Sicily, began to stir against the king's army, and to shut the Englishmen out of the gates, and keep their walls against them. The Englishmen, seeing that, made to the gates, and by force would have broken them open; insomuch that the king, riding among them with his

Discord between the citizens of Messina and the English army.

Richard I. A.D. 1190. staff, and breaking divers of their heads, could not assuage their fierceness; such was the rage of the Englishmen against the citizens of Messina. The king, seeing the fury of the people to be such that he could not stay them, took boat, and went to the palace of King Tancred, to talk over the matter with the French king. In the mean time the matter was so taken up by the wise handling of the ancient of the city, that both parties laying down their armour went home in peace.

The king could not stay the rage of the people.

Communication about peace.

On the fourth day of October came to King Richard the archbishop of Messina, with two other archbishops, also the French king, and sundry other earls, barons, and bishops, for entreatance of peace. As they were together consulting, and had almost concluded upon the peace, the citizens of Messina issued out of the town, some going up upon the mountains, some with open force invading the mansion or lodging of Hugh Brun, an English captain. The noise of this coming to the ears of the king, he, suddenly breaking off talk with the French king and the rest, departed from them, and coming to his men, commanded them forthwith to arm themselves; who then with certain of his soldiers, making up to the top of a mountain, which seemed to pass their power to climb, there put the citizens to flight, chasing them down the mountain, unto the very gates of the city; whom also certain of the king's servants pursued within the city; of whom five valiant soldiers and twenty of the king's servants were slain, the French king looking on, and not once willing to rescue them, contrary to his oath and league before made with the king of England; for the French king, with his men, being there present, rode in the midst of them safely and without harm to and fro, and might well have eased the king's party more than he did, if he had so liked.

A skirmish between the citizens of Messina and the Englishmen.

The French king against the Englishmen.

This being known to the English host, how their fellows were slain, and the Frenchmen admitted into the city, and that they were excluded, and the gates barred against them, being also stopped from buying of victuals and other things; they in great indignation gathered themselves in arms, burst open the gates, and scaled the walls, and so, winning the city, set up their flags, with the English arms upon the walls. When the French king did see this, he was mightily offended; requiring the king of England, that the arms of France might also be set up and joined with his; but King Richard to that in no case would agree. Notwithstanding, to satisfy his mind, he was well contented to take down his arms, and commit the custody of the city to the Hospitallers and Templars of Jerusalem, till the time that Tancred, king of Sicily, and he should agree together upon conditions.

Englishmen win the city of Messina.

These things being done on the fifth and sixth days of October, it followed upon the eighth day that peace between the kings was concluded. In that peace King Richard, and Philip, the French king, first renewed their oath and league before made, concerning their mutual aid and society, during the time of that peregrination. Secondly, peace also was concluded between King Richard and Tancred, king of Sicily aforesaid, with this condition, that the daughter of Tancred, in case King Richard should die without issue, should marry Arthur, duke of Brittany, the king's nephew and next heir to this crown, whereof a formal chart was drawn, and

The league renewed between Richard and the French king.

Peace concluded between King Richard and Tancred.

letters were sent thereof to Pope Clement, dated the ninth day of November.

In the mean time, as these two kings of France and England were thus wintering at Messina, the emperor, Frederic I. (the same on whose neck Pope Alexander did tread in the church of Venice, saying the verse of the psalm, "Super aspidem et basiliscum ambulabis," &c. whereof read before), and his son Conrad, with a mighty army of Almains and others, were coming up likewise toward the land of Jerusalem to the siege of Acre; where, by the way, the good emperor, through a great mischance, falling off his horse into a river called Salef, was therein drowned. After his decease, Conrad, his son, taking the government of his army, came to the siege of Acre (in which siege also he died); upon whose coming, such a dearth followed in the camp, which lasted two months, that a loaf of bread, which, before their coming was sold for one penny, was afterwards sold for three pounds, by reason whereof many christian soldiers did there perish through famine. The chief food which the princes there had to feed upon, was horse-flesh. This famine being so miserable, some good bishops there were in the camp, namely, Hubert, bishop of Salisbury, with certain other good bishops, who, making a general collection through the whole camp for the poor, made such a provision, that in this penury of all things, no man was so destitute and needy, but somewhat he had for his relief; till, within a few days after, by the merciful providence of God, who is the feeder of all creatures, ships came unto them with abundance of corn, wine, and oil.

Frederic the emperor drowned in going to the siege of Acre.

God's providence in time of need.

The siege of this town of Acre endured a long season, which, as it was mightily oppugned by the Christians, so it was strongly defended by the Saracens, especially by the help of wild-fire, which the Latins call "Græcus ignis," so that there was great slaughter on both sides. During the time of this siege many noble personages, and also bishops, died, among whom was Conrad, the emperor's son; Radulph, earl of Fougiers; the earl of Pericio; Robert, earl of Leicester; Baldwin, archbishop of Canterbury; with four archbishops, and divers other bishops, abbots, earls, and also barons, to the number of four and thirty, and not so few. All this while King Richard, and King Philip of France, still kept at Messina, in Sicily, from the month of September till April, for lack, I suppose, of wind or weather, or else of necessity for repairing their ships. In the mean time King Richard, hearing of Joachim, abbot of Curacio, a learned man in Calabria (who was then thought to have the spirit of prophecy, and told many things of a people that should come), sent for him, with whom he and his bishops had much conference about the coming and time of antichrist; *to[1] whom the said Joachim expounding the place of St. John's Revelation—"There be seven kings, of whom five are fallen, one is now, and another is yet to come," &c.—declareth seven persecutors of the church to be thereby signified: Herod, Nero, Domitian, Marentius, Mahomet, Turca, and the last,

Siege of Acre. Greek fire much used by the Saracens.

(1) This passage, in single asterisks, is republished from the edition of Foxe of 1563, pp. 70, 71. It slightly differs from the Latin edition of 1559, p. 57; an extract from which is subjoined: "Reges 7, inquit, septem sunt persecutores: Herodes, Nero, Constantius, Mahumet, Melsemutus, Saladinus, Antichristus, &c. Hæc Hovedenus. Annus vero hujus abbatis erat 1290." Joachim flourished in the thirteenth century, and the first edition of his prophecies appeared at Venice in 1517.—Ed.

which he said was then to come, to be Antichrist. And this antichrist, he said, was already born in the city of Rome, and should be there exalted in the apostolical see; bringing to that purpose the saying of the apostle, "he is an adversary, and advanceth himself against all that is called God: and then shall the wicked man be revealed whom the Lord shall consume with the spirit of his mouth, and destroy with the brightness of his coming." "Why," said the king, "I had thought all this while that antichrist should have been born in Antioch, or Babylon, out of the tribe of Dan, and should have ruled in the Lord's temple at Jerusalem, and should have travailed in the land where Christ had travailed, and borne rule three years and a half in the same, and dispute against Enoch and Elias, and then put them to death, and then have died himself; after whose death the Lord should have given sixty days of repentance, wherein those that erred from the truth, and were seduced by the preaching of antichrist, and his counterfeit apostles, might repent."

This, and such like talk, had they together; and though the abbot declared at that time that antichrist was born at Rome, yet were there certain prelates, the very members of that wicked head, who in no wise could abide to hear the tale of truth, but devised somewhat to reply against it. Among these were Walter, the archbishop of Rouen, and the archbishop of Appenna; and Gerard, archbishop of Auxonne; and John, bishop of Ebron, and divers others of that stamp, whose replications and opinions, if they were here put down, they would appear in that behalf good and substantial gear, I do warrant you.*

Abbot Joachim condemned in the council of Lateran.

This Joachim, belike, in his book and revelations had uttered some things against the see and pride of Rome, for the which he was less favoured of the popes, and judged an enemy to their see; and so he was condemned with his books for a heretic by Pope Innocent III. in his idolatrous general council of Lateran, A.D. 1215, as ye may read in Antoninus.

Henry, son of Frederic, emperor.

After this, Henry king of Almains, son of Frederic the emperor, hearing of the decease of his father, standing now to be emperor, first restored to Henry duke of Saxony, and to others, whatsoever his father before had taken from them. That done, he sent to Clement and his cardinals, promising in all things to confirm the laws and dignities of the church of Rome, if they would grant him their assent to be emperor. Whereupon Pope Clement, by advice of the Romans, assigned him the term of Easter in the next year ensuing, for his coronation. But before the Easter came, Pope Clement died, after he had sat three years and about four months; after whom succeeded Celestine III., of whom more hereafter, God willing.

The time thus passing over, in the month of February, the next
A.D. 1191. year following, which was A.D. 1191, King Richard sent over his galleys to Naples, there to meet his mother Elenor, and Berengaria, the daughter of Sancius, king of Navarre, whom he was purposed to marry, who by that time were come to Brundusium, under the conduct of Philip, earl of Flanders, and so proceeding unto Naples, there found the king's ships, wherein they sailed to Messina. In the mean time, King Richard showed himself exceedingly bounteous

and liberal unto all men. To the French king first he gave divers ships; upon others likewise he bestowed rich rewards; and of his goods and treasure he distributed largely unto his soldiers and servants about him. Of him it was reported that he distributed more in one month, than ever any of his predecessors did in a whole year; by reason whereof he purchased great love and favour, which not only redounded to the advancement of his fame, but also to his singular use and profit, as the sequel afterwards proved.

Bountiful liberality of King Richard.

To proceed then in the progress of King Richard, it followeth: on the first day of March, he, leaving the city of Messina, where the French king was, went on unto Catana, a city where Tancred, king of Sicily, then lay, where he was honourably received, and there remained with King Tancred three days and three nights. On the fourth day, when he should depart, Tancred offered him many rich presents in gold and silver, and precious silks; whereof King Richard would receive nothing but one little ring for a token of his good will. For this King Richard again gave him a rich sword. At length, when King Richard should take his leave, King Tancred would not so let him part, but needs would give him four great ships and fifteen galleys; and furthermore, he himself would needs accompany him, the space of two days' journey, to a place called Tavernium.

Honourable entertainment of Richard by Tancred.

Then the next morning, when they should take their leave, Tancred declared unto him the message which the French king, a little before, had sent unto him by the duke of Burgundy, the purport whereof was this: "That the king of England was a false traitor, and would never keep the peace that was between them. And if the said Tancred would war against him, or secretly by night invade him, he, with all his power, would assist him, and join with him to the destruction of him and all his army." To whom Richard the king protested again, that he was no traitor, and never was; and, as touching the peace begun between them, the same should never be broken through him, neither could he believe that the French king, being his good lord, and his sworn copartner in that voyage, would utter any such words of him. Which, when Tancred heard, he bringeth forth the letters of the French king, sent to him by the duke of Burgundy; affirming, moreover, that if the duke of Burgundy would deny the bringing of the said letters, he was ready to try with him by any of his dukes. King Richard, receiving the letters, and musing not a little upon the same, returneth again to Messina The same day that King Richard departed, the French king cometh to Tavernium to speak with Tancred, and there abode with him that night, and on the morrow returned to Messina again.

Philip, the French king, traitorously seeketh the destruction of Richard.

Faithful part of Tancred towards Richard.

From that time King Richard, moved in stomach against King Philip, never showed any gentle countenance of peace and amity, as he before was wont; whereat the French king greatly marvelling, and inquiring earnestly what should be the cause thereof, word was sent him again by Philip, earl of Flanders, what words he had sent to the king of Sicily; and for the testimony thereof, the letters were showed, which he wrote by the duke of Burgundy to the king of Sicily. When the French king understood this, he first held his peace, as guilty in his conscience, not knowing well what to answer.

First occasion of discord between the French king and King Richard. King Richard chargeth the French

Richard I. A.D. 1191.

At length, turning his tale to another matter, he began to quarrel with King Richard, pretending as though he sought causes to break with him, and to malign him, and therefore he forged these lies (said he) upon him, and all because he by that means would void to marry with Alice, his sister, according as he had promised: adding, moreover, that if he would so do, and would not marry the said Alice his sister, according to his oath, but would marry another, he would be an enemy to him and his, while he lived.

King with falsehood. Quarrel about a marriage.

To this King Richard said again, that he could by no means marry that woman, forasmuch as his father had had by her a son: † for proof whereof he had there presently to bring forth divers and sundry witnesses to the king's face, to testify with him. In conclusion, through counsel and persuasion of divers about the French king, agreement at last was made, so that King Philip did acquit King Richard from his bond of marrying his sister; and King Richard again should be bound to pay to him every year, for the space of five years, two thousand marks; with certain other conditions besides, not greatly material in this place to be deciphered. Thus, peace between them being concluded, the eight and twentieth day of the said month of March, the French king, launching out of the haven of Messina, on the two and twentieth day after, in Easter week, came with his army to the siege of Acre.

Agreement between the two kings, with the conditions.

The French king cometh to Acre.

After the departure of the French king from Messina (King Richard, with his army, yet remaining behind), Queen Elenor, the king's mother, arrived, bringing with her Berengaria, the king of Navarre's daughter, to be espoused to King Richard. This done, Elenor, leaving Berengaria behind her, departed, taking her journey toward Rome, to entreat the pope for Gaufrid, her other son above mentioned, to be consecrated in the archbishopric of York, he having been before elected by the procurement of King Richard, his brother, as ye heard. At this time, as Queen Elenor was travelling toward Rome, Pope Clement, above mentioned, died about the sixth day of April, in whose room succeeded Pope Celestine III., who, the next day after his consecration, came from Lateran to St. Peter's church, where in the way met him Henry, the emperor, and Constantia, his wife, with a great rout of armed soldiers; but the Romans, making fast their gates, would not suffer them to enter their city. Then Pope Celestine, standing upon the stairs before the church door of St. Peter, received an oath of the said Henry, king of the Almains (his army waiting without), that he should defend the church of God, and all the liberties thereof, and maintain justice; also that he should restore again the patrimony of St. Peter, full and whole, whatsoever hath been diminished thereof; and finally, that he should re-surrender to the church of Rome the city of Tusculanum. Upon these conditions and grants, the pope then took him to the church, and there anointed him for emperor, and his wife for empress; who, there sitting in his chair pontifical, held the crown of gold between his feet, and so the emperor, bowing down his head to the pope's feet, received the crown; and in like manner the empress also. The crown thus being set upon the emperor's head, the pope, immediately, with his foot struck it off again from his head unto the ground, declaring thereby, that he had power to depose him in case he

Berengaria, or as some do call her, Berengara, daughter to the king of Navarre, brought to be married to King Richard.

The pope of Rome in the full top of his pride.

Pope Celestine crowneth Henry the emperor with his feet. The pope striketh so deserved. Then the cardinals, taking up the crown, set it upon his head again.[1]

Richard I. A.D. 1191. off the emperor's crown with his foot.

Not long after the departure of King Philip from Messina, which was in the month of March, King Richard, in April following, about the twentieth day of the said month, sailing from the haven of Messina with a hundred and fifty great ships, and three and fifty great galleys, well manned and appointed, took journey towards Acre; who being upon the seas on Good Friday, about the ninth hour there arose a mighty south wind, with a tempest, which dissevered and scattered all his navy, some to one place, and some to another. The king, with a few ships, was driven to the isle of Crete, and there, before the haven of Rhodes, cast anchor. The ship that carried the king's sister, the queen of Sicily, and Berengaria, the king of Navarre's daughter, with two other ships, were driven to the isle of Cyprus. The king, making great moan for the ship his sister was in, and Berengaria, his wife that should be, not knowing what had become of them, after the tempest was overblown, sent forth his galleys diligently to search for the rest of his navy dispersed, but especially for the ship wherein his sister was, and the maiden whom he should marry; who at length were found safe and merry at Port Limisso, in the isle of Cyprus. Notwithstanding the two other ships, which were in their company before in the same haven, were drowned, with divers of the king's servants, and men of worship; amongst whom was Master Roger, called 'Malus Catulus,' the king's vice-chancellor, who was found having the king's seal hanging about his neck. The king of Cyprus was then Isakius (called also the emperor of the Griffons), who took and imprisoned all Englishmen who by shipwreck were cast upon his land, also inveigling into his hands the goods and prizes of those who were found drowned about his coasts; neither would he suffer the ship wherein the two ladies were, to enter within the port.

Richard overtaken with a tempest going to Acre.

Isakius, king of Cyprus, a cruel enemy to Englishmen.

The tidings of this being brought to King Richard, he, in great wrath, gathering his galleys and ships together, boardeth the land of Cyprus, where he first in gentlewise signifieth to King Isakius, how he with his Englishmen, coming as strangers to the supportation of the Holy Land, were, by distress of weather, driven upon his bounds; and, therefore, with all humble petition besought him, in God's behalf, and for reverence of the Holy Cross, to let go such prisoners of his as he had in captivity, and to restore again the goods of those who were drowned, which he detained in his hands, to be employed for the behoof of their souls. And this the king, once, twice, and thrice, desired of the emperor. But he, proudly answering again, sent the king word, that he would neither let the captives go, nor render the goods of them that were drowned.

Richard maketh suit to the king of Cyprus for his soldiers in captivity.

The disdainful answer of Isakius.

When King Richard heard how little the Emperor Isakius made of his so humble and honest petition, and how nothing there could be gotten without violent force; immediately he giveth commandment through all his host, to put themselves in armour, and to follow him, to revenge such injuries received of that proud and cruel king

(1) Ex veteri chronico manuscripto anonymo, de gestis Richardi Regis, cui initium, "Anno gratiæ," &c. Item ex alio ejusdem vetustatis chronico manuscripto, cui initium, "Eneas cum Ascanio," &c.

Richard I. A.D. 1191.

of Cyprus; willing them to put their trust in God, and not to doubt but that the Lord would stand with them, and give them the victory. The emperor, in the mean time, with his people, stood warding the sea coasts, where the Englishmen should arrive, with swords, bills, and lances, and such other weapons as they had, setting boards, stools, and chests before them instead of a wall. Howbeit but few of them were harnessed, and for the most part all inexpert and unskilful in the feats of war. Then King Richard with his soldiers, issuing out of their ships, first set his bowmen before, who with their shot made a way for others to follow. The Englishmen, thus winning the land upon them, so fiercely pressed upon the Griffons, that after long fighting and many blows, at last, the emperor was put to flight; whom King Richard valiantly pursued, and slew many, and divers he took alive, and had gone near also to have had the emperor, had not the night come on and parted the battle. And thus King Richard, with much spoil and great victory returning to the port town of Limisso, which the townsmen had left for fear, found there great abundance of corn, wine, oil, and victuals.

Richard setteth upon Isakius, emperor of the Griffons, who is put to flight.

The same day after the victory, Joan, the king's sister, and Berengaria, the maiden, entered the port and town of Limisso, with fifty great ships, and fourteen galliots; so that all the whole navy there meeting together, were two hundred and fifty-four tall ships, and above threescore galliots. Then Isakius the emperor, seeing no way for himself to escape by the sea, the same night pitched his tents five miles off from the English army, swearing that the third day after he would surely give battle to King Richard. But he preventing him before, suddenly, the same morning before the day of battle should be, setteth upon the tents of the Griffons early (they being unawares and asleep,) and made of them a great slaughter; insomuch that the emperor was fain naked to run away, leaving his tents and pavilions to the Englishmen, full of horses and rich treasure, also with the imperial standard, the lower part whereof, with a costly streamer, was covered and wrought all with gold. King Richard then returning with victory and triumph to his sister and Berengaria, shortly after, in the month of May following, and the twelfth day of the same month, married the said Berengaria, daughter of Rancon, king of Navarre, at Limisso in the isle of Cyprus.

The king of Cyprus again put to flight.

King Richard marrieth Berengaria in the isle of Cyprus.

The king of Cyprus, seeing himself overmatched, was driven at length to yield himself with conditions; to give King Richard twenty thousand marks in gold, for amends of such spoils as he had gotten of them that were drowned; also to restore all his captives again to the king; and, furthermore, in his own person, to attend upon the king to the land of Jerusalem, in God's service and his, with four hundred horsemen, and five hundred footmen; in pledge whereof he would give into his hands his castles, and his only daughter, and would hold his kingdom of him. This done, and the emperor swearing fidelity to King Richard, before Guido king of Jerusalem, and the prince of Antioch (who were come thither to King Richard a little before), peace was taken, and Isakius was committed to the ward of certain keepers. Notwithstanding, shortly after, he, breaking from his keepers, was again at defiance with the king. Whereupon King Richard, besetting the island of Cyprus round about with ships and

Isakius yieldeth himself to King Richard.

He subsequently breaketh conditions.

Again submitteth himself, and

galleys, did in such sort prevail, that the subjects of the land were constrained to yield themselves to the king, and at length the daughter also of the emperor, and at last the emperor himself, whom King Richard caused to be kept in fetters of silver and gold, and to be sent to the city of Tripolis.

is kept in golden fetters.

Richard's journey to Acre.

These things thus done, and all set in order touching the possession of the isle of Cyprus, the keeping whereof he committed unto Radulph, son of Godfrey, lord chamberlain, being then the first day of June; upon the fifth of the said month, King Richard departed from the isle of Cyprus, with his ships and galleys towards the siege of Acre, and on the morrow came unto Tyre, where, by procurement of the French king, he was constrained by the citizens to enter. The next day after, which was the sixth day of June, crossing the seas, he met with a great bark, fraught with soldiers and men of war, to the number of one thousand five hundred; who, pretending to be Frenchmen, and setting forth their flag with the French arms, were indeed Saracens, secretly sent with wild-fire and certain barrels of unknown serpents, to the defence of the town of Acre. This King Richard at length perceiving, eftsoons set upon them, and so vanquished them; of whom the most were drowned, and some taken alive; which being once known in the city of Acre, as it was a great discomfort there, so it was a great help unto the Christians for winning the city. The next day after, which was the seventh of June, King Richard came to Acre, which at that time had been long besieged of the Christians; after whose coming it was not long before the pagans within the city seeing their walls to be undermined and towers overthrown, were driven by composition to escape with life and limb, to surrender the city to the two kings. Another great help to the Christians in winning the city was this: in the said city of Acre there was a secret Christian among the Saracens, who, in time of the siege there, used at sundry times to cast over the walls, into the camp of the Christians, certain bills written in Hebrew, Greek, and Latin, wherein he disclosed unto the Christians, from time to time, the doings and counsels of the enemies, advertising them how and in what way they should work, and of what to beware; and always his letters began thus: "In nomine Patris, et Filii, et Spiritus Sancti; Amen;" by reason whereof, the Christians were much advantaged in their proceedings. But this was a great heaviness unto them, that neither would he utter his name, nor, when the city was got, could they ever understand who he was.[1]

Saracens sent to the rescue of Acre, vanquished on the sea by King Richard.

The city of Acre yielded to the Christians.

Honest part of a secret Christian in the city of Acre.

To make of a long siege a short narration, upon the twelfth day of July in the year aforesaid, A.D. 1191, the princes and captains of the pagans, upon agreement, resorted to the tent of the Templars, to commune with the two kings touching peace and giving up of their city, the form of which peace was this: That the kings should have the city of Acre freely and fully delivered unto them, with all that was within; and that five hundred captives of the Christians should be restored unto them, which were in Acre: also that the holy cross should be to them rendered, and a thousand christian captives, with two hundred horsemen, whosoever they themselves would choose out

The form of peace concluded between the kings, and the princes of Acre.

(1) Ex chronico manuscripto, de gestis Richardi.

Richard I. A.D. 1191.

of all those which were in the power of Saladin: over and besides, they should give to the kings, two hundred thousand bisants, so that they themselves would remain as pledges in the kings' hands for the performance hereof; that if, in forty days, these aforesaid covenants were not accomplished, they would abide the kings' mercy touching life and limb. These covenants being agreed upon, the kings sent their soldiers and servants into the city, to take one hundred of the richest and best of the city, to close them up in towers under strong keeping, and the residue they committed to be kept in houses and streets, ministering unto them according to their necessities: to whom notwithstanding, this they permitted, that as many of them as would be baptized, and receive the faith of Christ, should be free to go whither they would. Whereupon, many there were of the pagans, who for fear of death pretended to be baptized, but who, afterwards, as soon as they could, revolted again to the Saladin; on which account it was afterwards commanded by the kings, that none of them should be baptized against their wills.

Religion should be taught and not coacted.

The thirteenth day of July, King Philip of France, and King Richard, after they had obtained the possession of Acre, divided between them all things therein contained, as well the people, as the gold and silver, with all other furniture whatsoever remaining in the city; who, in dividing the spoil, were such good carvers unto themselves, that many knights and barons, with other soldiers, who had there sustained the whole travail two years together about the siege, seeing the kings to take all unto themselves, and their part to be but little, retracted themselves without the uttermost trench; and there, after consultation had together, sent word to the kings, that they would leave and forsake them, unless they were made partakers also of the gains for which they had so long travailed. To whom answer was sent again by the kings, that their wills should be satisfied: howbeit, because of long deferring of their promise, many, constrained by poverty, departed from them.

The two kings divide the city of Acre, with all the spoil thereof, between themselves.

Commonly seen, whoso taketh most pains, their part to be the least.

The twentieth day of July, King Richard, speaking with the French king, desired him that they two with their armies would bind themselves by oath to remain there still in the land of Jerusalem the space of three years, for the winning and recovering again of those countries. But he would swear, he said, no such oath: and so the next day, King Richard, with his wife and sister, entereth into the city of Acre, and placed there himself in the king's palace; the French king remaining in the houses of the Templars, where he continued till the end of the month. About the beginning of the month of August, Philip, the French king, after he and King Richard had made agreement between Guido and Conrad, the marquis, about the kingdom of Jerusalem, went from Acre to Tyre; notwithstanding, King Richard and all the princes of the christian army, with great entreaty, desired him to tarry; showing what a shame it were for him to come so far, and now to leave undone that for which he came; and on the third of August he departed from Tyre, leaving his half part of the city of Acre in the hands of the aforesaid Conrad, the marquis. After Philip's departure, the pagans refused to keep their covenants; who neither would restore the holy cross, nor the money, nor their captives, sending word to King Richard, that if he beheaded the

King Richard requireth of the French king to remain three years with his army, but he would not.

pledges left with him at Acre, they would chop off the heads of such captives of the Christians as were in their hands. Shortly after this, the Saladin, sending great gifts to King Richard, requested the time limited for beheading of the captives to be prorogued, but the king refused to take his gifts, and to grant his request; whereupon the Saladin caused all the christian captives within his possession forthwith to be beheaded, which was the eighteenth day of August. Albeit King Richard understood this, yet would not he prevent the time before limited for the execution of his prisoners, being the twentieth of August. Upon that day he caused the prisoners of the Saracens, openly in the sight of the Saladin's army, to lose their heads; the number of whom came to two thousand five hundred, save only that certain of the principal of them he reserved for purposes and considerations, especially to make exchange for the holy cross, and certain others of the christian captives.

Richard I. A.D. 1191.

Christian captives slain by the Saladin.

Saracen captives slain by King Richard.

After this, King Richard purposed to besiege the city of Joppa; where, by the way, between Acre and Joppa, near to a town called Ashur, Saladin, with a great multitude of his Saracens, came fiercely against the king's rearward; but, through God's merciful grace, in the same battle the king's warriors acquitted them so well, that the Saladin was put to flight (whom the Christians pursued the space of three miles), and lost the same day many of his nobles and captives, in such sort that it was thought the Saladin had not been put to such confusion for forty years before; and but one christian captain, called James Avernus, in that conflict was overthrown. From thence King Richard, proceeding further, went to Joppa, and then to Ascalon, where he first found the city of Joppa forsaken of the Saracens, who durst not abide the king's coming. Ascalon, the Saladin threw down to the ground, and likewise forsook the whole land of Syria; through all which land the king had free passage without resistance, neither durst the Saracen prince encounter, after that, with King Richard. Of all his achievements the said King Richard sent his letters of certificate as well into England, as also to the abbot of Clara Valle, in France; well hoping that he, God willing, should be able to make his repair again to them by Easter next.

The Saladin put to flight.

A noble victory by God's power gotten by King Richard.

King Richard in possession of Syria.

A BRIEF STORY OF WILLIAM, THE PROUD BISHOP OF ELY, THE KING'S CHANCELLOR.

And now, to leave King Richard awhile in the field, let us make a step into England, and look a little at what is doing at home while the king is abroad, and so return to the king again. Ye heard before how King Richard, at his setting forth, committed the government of the realm to Hugo, bishop of Durham, and to William, bishop of Ely, so that to the bishop of Durham was committed the keeping of the castle of Windsor. The other, who was the bishop of Ely, had the keeping of the Tower of London, about which he caused a great ditch with a rampart to be made, which is yet remaining. Furthermore, to these two bishops the king also assigned four other chief justices, who, jointly with them, should have the hearing and oversight of all causes, as well to the clergy as to the laity apper-

A.D. 1190 to 1191.

Four chief justices with two bishops appointed overseers of the realm in the king's absence.

taining: to wit, Hugh Bardolf, William Marshal, Geoffrey Peterson, and William Brewer; but the bishop of Ely was the principal, or at least he that took most upon him, who both was the king's chancellor, and bought with his money to be the pope's legate through England, Ireland, and Scotland, as is before specified. *For[1] the said Ely being more ambitious, so practised with the king, that with the king's ambassadors sending his letters to the pope, he obtained there the authority legative upon the whole realm of England, as the pope's letters[2] to him again directed may appear.* Touching the excessive pride and pomp of this bishop, his rufflings outrageous, and fall most shameful, it would make a long tragedy to relate the whole circumstances at full; to demonstrate only certain specialities thereof, for our present purpose may suffice.

The church and bells of York suspended, because the lord legate was not ushered in with procession.

First, this William, called Longchamp, being thus advanced by the king to be his high chancellor, and chief justice of the realm, and also the pope's legate, to show abroad the authority of his legateship, began to suspend the canons, clerks, and vicars of the church of St. Peter in York, because they received him not with procession: under which interdiction he held them, till they were fain at last, both canons, clerks, and vicars, to fall down at his feet, causing all their bells to be let down out of the steeple. After this cometh Hugo, bishop of Durham, whom the king sent home out of Normandy with his letters; who, meeting with the aforesaid William, bishop of Ely, in the town of Ely, showed him the king's letters, wherein was granted to him the keeping of Windsor castle, and to be the king's justice from the river Humber to the borders of Scotland. To these letters the chancellor answered, that the king's commandment should be done, and so brought him with him to Suwel, where he took him and kept him fast, till he was forced at last to surrender to him the castle of Windsor, and other things which the king had committed to his custody; and moreover, he was constrained to leave with the said chancellor, Henry de Puteaco, his own son, and Gilbert Leigh, for pledges and hostages of his fidelity, to be true to the king and realm. And thus the bishop of Durham, being set at liberty, went to his town of Hoveden; where, after he had made his abode a few days, cometh thither Osbert Longchamp, the chancellor's brother, and William Stutiville, with a great company of armed men sent by the chancellor to apprehend him. But the said bishop of Durham, putting in sureties not to depart that town without license of the king and of the chancellor, there still remained till he got letters to be sent to the king, signifying how he was used. Whereupon the king, writing his letters from Marseilles to the bishop of Ely, set the said bishop of Durham free, and confirmed to him all the possessions and grants that he before had given him.

Bishop of Ely getteth the castle of Windsor from the bishop of Durham.

The excessive pride and enormities of

It is almost incredible to think how intemperately this bishop and chancellor misconducted himself, after the king's departure into Syria, in excess of pride, and in cruel exactions and oppressions of the

(1) For this passage, with Pope Clement's letter, see Edition 1563, p. 70.—Ed.

(2) *The Letter of Pope Clement III. to the Bishop of Ely.*—"Clemens Episcopus, &c. Juxta commendabile desiderium charissimi in domino filii nostri illustrissimi Anglorum regis, fraternitati tuæ, legationis officium in tota Anglia et Wallia tam per Cantuariensem quam per Eboracensem archiepiscopatum, et in illis Hyberniæ partibus, in quibus nobilis vir Joannes Comes Moretonii, frater ipsius regis potestatem habet et dominium, autoritate apostolica duximus committendum. Datum nono Junii pontif. Nostri anno. 3."

king's subjects. First, his fellow-justices, whom the king joined with him for government of the realm, he utterly rejected and refused to hear their counsel, reputing none to be equal with him in all the realm. Neither was he contented with the authority of a prelate, but played both king and priest in the realm. All castles, lordships, abbeys, churches, and all other appropriations belonging to the right of the king, he claimed to himself; and, by virtue of his legateship, when he came to any bishop's house, abbey, priory, or any other religious house, he brought with him such a superfluity of men, horses, dogs, and hawks, that the house was the worse for it three years after; for commonly he rode never under fifteen hundred horse, of chaplains, priests, and other serving-men waiting upon him. From the clergy and laity he took away their churches, their advowsons, their livings, and their lands, to bestow upon his nephews and other waiting chaplains, to serve his vain glory; or else converted them to his own use, to maintain his pomp and vanity. In getting and gathering of treasures he had no measure; in mis-spending the same he kept no order; and that no vice should be wanting where such avarice taketh root, the money, which he wrongfully got, he committed to the bank to be increased by usury. What wantonness and lasciviousness were used in that so riotous life, the stories do shame to declare. All ruffianly runagates, idle bellies, and light persons, wheresoever he went, hung upon his court. To increase the vain jollity of this royal prelate, there was lacking no kind of musical instruments and melodious noise, to refresh belike his wearied senses, too much beaten and macerated with continual labour and study of hunting, hawking, and gaming: of preaching and reading, I should have said.

Richard I. A.D. 1191.

William, bishop of Ely.

Bishop of Ely never rode under 1500 horse.

Briefly, this aforesaid prelate, bearing the authority both of the king and of the pope, kept such a stir in England, that the whole realm was at his beck, with cap and knee, crouching to him; neither durst any man, rich or poor, displease him; yea, there was none in all the realm so noble or worshipful, but was glad to please him, accounting himself happy if he might stand in his favour. At his table, all noblemen's children did serve and wait upon him, with whom he coupled in marriage his nieces and kinswomen; and, when any one that stood waiting before him, durst once cast up his eyes, or did not demurely look downward upon the ground, he had a staff in his hand with a prick, wherewith he used to prick him; learning, belike, by the carter his father, who used at the plough or cart to drive his oxen. Furthermore, as kings used to have their guard about them, so he, because he would not also be unguarded, refusing men of the English nation, had his waiters and warders mostly of Frenchmen and Flemings.

Playeth both king and priest.

It happened after this, A.D. 1191, that a great discord arose between John, earl of Morton, the king's brother, with other states of the realm, and the said William, bishop of Ely; so that, universally, they all wrote over to the king concerning the misgovernment and enormities of the said bishop. Richard, understanding the case, sent from Messina into England, Walter, archbishop of Rouen, and William Marshal, earl, unto the bishop of Ely, with letters, commanding him that in all his doings he should associate unto him the archbishop of Rouen, William Marshal, Geoffrey Peterson, William

General complaint to the king, of the bishop of Ely.

Richard I. A.D. 1191.

Bruer, and Hugo Bardolf above mentioned; who, when they came into England, durst not deliver their letters, dreading the displeasure of the chancellor, for he despised all the commandments of the king, nor would suffer any fellow to join with him in his kingdom.

Another dissension between John, the king's brother, and William, bishop of Ely.

Hitherto have you heard of the glorious vanity of this lordly legate and chancellor of the realm; now ye shall hear of his shameful fall, after his shameless exaltation. For shortly after this followeth another breach between the said Earl John the king's brother, and him, about the besieging of the castle of Lincoln. Concerning that castle the said John sent him word, that unless he raised his siege the sooner from thence, he would send him away by force of sword. The bishop, either not able to make his party good, or not daring to resist, thought best to fall to some composition with the earl, and so did. In that composition, he was contented, against his will, by mediation of divers bishops and others, to make surrender, not only of the castle of Lincoln, but also of Nottingham, Tickhill, Wallingford, and many more places, which were then committed to the custody of sundry men of worship and honour. And thus was that controversy settled, wherein the bishop of Ely began to be cut a little shorter.

Another broil between the chancellor and Geffrey, archbishop of York.

It followed then not long after, in the same year, that another like business began to kindle between Geffrey, the archbishop of York, the king's brother, and the aforesaid glorious bishop of Ely upon this occasion. Ye heard before how the king, at his setting out, left order that Earl John and Geffrey, his brethren, should not enter into the realm for the space of three years after his departure (howbeit his brother John was shortly after released of that bond), and also after that, how King Richard, being at Messina, sent his mother Elenor to the pope for his brother Geffrey (elected before to the see of York) to be consecrated archbishop. Whereupon the said Geffrey being consecrated through license of Pope Celestine by the archbishop of Turin; the said Geffrey, immediately upon his consecration, lost no time, but would needs come into England. Of this the bishop of Ely having intelligence, sent him word, being at Wissland in Flanders, not to presume to adventure into the realm, contrary to his oath before made to King Richard; commanding, moreover, that if he came, he should be apprehended. All which, notwithstanding, the archbishop letted not for all that, but needs would repair to his see, and so arrived at Dover in the month of September, where the chancellor's men stood on the sea-side to apprehend him; but he, by changing his apparel, and by the swiftness of his horse, escaped their hands, and came to the monks' house of Dover; but the chancellor's men, whom he sent to take him, beset the church of the monks round about, so that in nowise he could avoid their hands.

The cruel handling of Geffrey, archbishop of York, by the bishop of Ely, the pope's legate, and chancellor of England.

To make the story short: as the archbishop, on a day when he had said mass, was standing at the altar, with his garments yet about him, the rude soldiers having little good manners, and less devotion, spared not boldly to rush into the church, and there laid hands upon the archbishop as he stood; took him, bound him, and dragged him through dirt and mire (and, as we use to say, through thick and thin), and so committed him to Matthew Clark, their constable, to be kept; whereat the people greatly disdained, seeing that he was a king's son, and the brother of a king, who was so treated. The news whereof, when it came to the ears of Earl John, his brother, he being not a little offended therewith, sent to know of the chancellor, whether this was his doing or not. To whom when the chancellor sent answer again, and stoutly confessed the fact to be his, the earl sent commandment that his brother should be delivered up, and so he was; who, then coming to London, made his complaint to the earl, his brother, and to other nobles of the realm, of the injuries done to him by the chancellor. On this the earl sent for the aforesaid chancellor, and appointed a day peremptory for him to appear before the whole body of the council, to make answer to such injuries as he had done, both to the archbishop of York, and also to the bishop of Durham above mentioned; but the chancellor, driving off the time with delays, would neither come nor send. Then the earl, with the bishops about him, made their journey towards London, to have the matter there handled in a great audience.

Geffrey delivered out of prison.

The chancellor, seeing that, withdrew himself from Windsor to the city of London, where by the way it happened, that the servants of the earl and of the chancellor meeting, did skirmish together; in which fray one of the earl's family was slain, but yet his men had the better; and the chancellor with his men were put to flight, and so fled to the Tower, where they did hide themselves. The next day, which was about the twelfth day of October, Earl John, the king's brother, and the archbishop of Rouen, with all the bishops, earls, and barons, and citizens of London, assembled together in Paul's church, where many and great accusations were laid against the said chancellor; so that in fine it was agreed in that assembly, that the said chancellor should be deposed, and in his place was substituted the archbishop of Rouen, according to the tenor of the king's letters sent from Messina; which was, that certain other persons should be associated with the chancellor for the government of the realm, by whose counsel, if he would not be directed, the archbishop of Rouen should be set in his place, and he should be deposed. The third day after this, the chancellor firmly promised not to depart out of the realm, before he had delivered out of his hands all such castles, the keeping whereof he committed to certain foreigners and strangers; and, for assurance thereof, he gave his two brethren and his chamberlain for pledges, and so went to Canterbury, where, he said, he would take the cross of a pilgrim, and leave the cross of his legateship.

A skirmish between the servants of the bishop of Ely, and those of Earl John.

Nobles assembled in council against the bishop of Ely.

Bishop of Ely deposed, resigneth his castles.

Now when he was come to the castle of Dover, and there had remained a few days, contrary to his promise made, his purpose was to take ship, and to pass over the seas. And because he durst not do it openly, he devised a new kind of disguising, decking himself in the apparel of a woman; and so, gouty as he was, he went to the sea-side in his woman's weeds, having in his hand a measuring yard, and on his arm a piece of linen cloth. And, thus, as he was sitting upon a rock, waiting for his ship to come and convey him over, a certain fisherman espying him, and supposing him to be a harlot, came to him, and found him to be, as he was indeed, a man, in likeness of a woman; whereat he wondered and began to make an outcry upon him. But the bishop's servants, being not far off, came running, and stilled him as well as they could.

Clotheth himself in woman's apparel.

A fisherman taketh the bishop to be a woman.

†

Richard I. A.D. 1191.

The fisherman then going to the next village, and there belike, declaring what he had seen, to try out the matter further, came out certain women; who, seeing the linen cloth hanging on his arm, began to question with him of the price of his cloth, and what he would take for it; but to this he would answer never a word, but smiled upon them. Whereat they musing with themselves, and whispering one with another, at last with their hands were so bold as to pluck down his muffler, and there his Balaam's mark, or shaven crown, appeared on his head; and so, with a loud exclamation, raised the village upon him, and would have fallen upon him with stones. Then came running a great multitude both of men and women; who, wondering at him, as birds are wont at an owl, laid hands upon him, and plucked him down to the ground, hauling and drawing him by the sleeves and collar of his gown through stones and rocks, whereby he was shrewdly hurt. His servants once or twice made out to rescue their old master, or new mistress, but could not for the press of the people; who, beating him with their fists, and spitting at him, drew him through the whole town, and so, with shame enough at length laid him in a dark cellar instead of a prison, of whom all the country about wondered and cried out. In conclusion, Earl John, hearing thereof, within eight days after sent word, that they should deliver him and let him go.

Balaam's mark.

The bishop baited by women at the sea-side.

Cast into a dark cellar.

Set at liberty by John earl of Morton.

The bishop then, set at liberty, sailed over as he could to Flanders, where he had but cold welcoming; from thence he went to Paris, where he gave Maurice, their bishop, threescore marks of silver to be received into the city with procession, and so he was. Then returned he into Normandy, but the archbishop of Rouen there gave commandment that the church doors should be locked, and no service said so long as he there remained. The bishop, seeing that, directed his letters and messengers to Pope Celestine, and also to King Richard into Syria, signifying to them how John, earl of Morton, and his accomplices, had handled him, and expelled him out of the realm; requiring that he might be restored again to what was taken from him, and also offering himself to be tried by the law for what he had done; so that if the king should dislike in any thing what he had done, he was ready to satisfy the king's contentation in all things wherein justly he could be charged.

Complaineth to the king and the pope.

Upon this, Pope Celestine, inflamed with an apostolical zeal in behalf of the said bishop of Ely, his legate, wrote a sharp and thundering letter to the archbishops, bishops, and prelates of England; commanding them, by his authority apostolical, that, forasmuch as the injuries, done to his legate, did redound to the contumely of the whole mother church of Rome, they should not fail therefore, but with severe censures of the church, that is, with book, bell, and candle, proceed as well against the said John, earl of Morton, as also against all others, whosoever had, or should attempt any violence or injury against the said his legate, the bishop of Ely, with no less severity than if the said injury should be offered to the person of the pope himself, or any other of his brethren, the cardinals.

Letter of Pope Celestine in behalf of the bishop of Ely.

The bishop of Ely, the pope's legate, bearing himself bold upon the favour and letters of the pope, who took his part, writeth to Henry, bishop of Lincoln, charging and requiring, that he, in virtue of

The bishop bold upon the pope's favour.

obedience, should execute the pope's sentence and mandate in excommunicating all such as were offenders in that behalf, and there reciteth the names of divers, against whom he should proceed, as the archbishop of Rouen, the bishop of Winchester, William Marshal, Geoffrey Peterson, Brewer, and Bardolf, the earl of Salisbury, the earl of Mellent, Gilbert Basset, the archdeacon of Oxford, and especially Hugh, bishop of Coventry; also Master Benet, and Stephen Ridle, chancellor to Earl John, the king's brother; to the which earl he reserved a further day of respite before he should be excommunicated, with a number of others besides; howbeit the said bishop of Ely could find none to execute this commandment of the pope. Then they, with a general consent, wrote again to King Richard, complaining of the intolerable abuses of the said bishop, his chancellor. In like manner the said chancellor also, complaining of them, wrote his letters to the king, signifying how Earl John, his brother, went about to usurp his kingdom, and would also shortly set the crown upon his own head, unless he made the more speed homeward. The king then was busy in repelling the Saladin, and prepared to lay siege against Jerusalem, and got Sclavonia, with divers other towns, from the Saracens, A.D. 1192, having divers conflicts in the mean time with the Saladin, and ever putting him to the worse. As the king was thus preparing to lay siege to Jerusalem, the Saladin, glad to fall to some composition with the king, sent unto him, that if he would restore to him again Sclavonia, in as good state as it was when he took it, he would grant to him, and to all Christians in the land of Jerusalem, truce for three years, and offered himself thereunto to be sworn. The king, seeing the duke of Burgundy and the Frenchmen to shrink from him, and his own men to decay, and also his money and health to diminish; but especially for that he understood by the bishop of Ely, his chancellor, that the French king intended to set up John, his brother, to possess his kingdom, being counselled thereto by the Templars, took the truce offered by the Saracens, and so began to draw homeward.

Richard I. A.D. 1192.

Many who stood against the bishop of Ely, appointed to be excommunicated.

The bishop of Ely complaineth of the earl of Morton, his brother.

In the mean while much grudge and strife increased more and more between the bishop of Ely and the archbishop of Rouen, insomuch that the archbishop, being excommunicate, sent up his clerks to Pope Celestine to complain of the bishop; but the pope ever stood in his purgation. At last he sent two of his cardinals, to wit, Ottoman, bishop of Hostia, and Jordanus de fossa nova, to break off the strife between the bishop of Ely and the archbishop of Rouen.

Strife between the bishop of Ely and the archbishop of Rouen.

After this King Richard being taken, and in the custody of Henry the emperor, the bishop of Ely, resorting to him, was sent by him into England to Elenor, his mother, and other nobles; who, then returning into England again, not as chancellor, nor as legate, as he said, but as a simple plain bishop, was by that means received.[1]

But of this vain-glorious prelate enough and too much. Now to return again to Richard, concerning whose worthy acts done abroad in getting of Cyprus, Acre, and Ptolemaida, and in pacifying Joppa, is partly spoken of before. Many other valiant and famous acts were by him and the French king achieved, and more would have been, had not those two kings, falling into discord, dissevered themselves,

What discord doth.

(1) Ex Matth. Paris.; et ex aliis incerti nominis manuscriptis codicibus.

Richard I. A.D. 1193. by reason whereof Philip, the French king, returned home again within a short space; who, being returned, eftsoons invaded Normandy, exciting also John, the brother of King Richard, to take on him the kingdom of England, in his brother's absence. This John then made league upon the same with the French king, and did homage unto him, which was about the fourth year of King Richard; who, being then in Syria, and hearing thereof, made peace with the Turks for three years. Not long after, King Richard, the next spring following, returned also, who, on his voyage home, being driven by stress of weather about the parts of Istria, in a town called Synaca, was taken by Leopold, duke of the same country, and sold to the emperor of Germany for sixty thousand marks; who, for no small joy thereof, writeth to Philip, the French king, the letter inserted below.[1]

Philip returneth from Palestine A D 1193.

King Richard returneth from Palestine

King Richard, thus being traitorously taken and sold, was there kept in custody a year and three months.[2] In some stories it is affirmed, that King Richard, returning out of Asia, came to Italy with a prosperous wind, where he desired of the pope to be absolved from an oath made against his will, and could not obtain it, and so setting out from thence towards England, and passing by the country of Conrad the marquis, whose death (he being slain a little before) was falsely imputed by the French king to the king of England, he was there traitorously taken, as is before said, by Leopold, duke of Austria Albeit, in another story, I find the matter more credibly set forth, which saith thus: that King Richard slew the brother of this Leopold, playing with him at chess in the French king's court;

(1) *The Letter of the Emperor, to Philip the French King, concerning the taking of King Richard* — "Henricus, Dei gratia Romanorum imperator, et semper Augustus, dilecto et speciali amico suo Philippo, illustri Francorum Regi, salutem, et sinceræ dilectionis affectum Quoniam Imperatoria celsitudo non dubitat regalem magnificentiam tuam lætiorem effici, de universis, quibus omnipotentia creatoris nostri nos ipsos et Romanum imperium honoraverit et exaltaverit, nobilitati tuæ tenore præsentium declarare duximus, quod inimicus imperii nostri, et turbator regni tui, rex Angliæ, quum esset in transeundo mare ad partes suas reversurus, accidit ut ventus, rupta navi sua in qua ipse erat, induceret eum in partes Histriæ, ad locum qui est inter Aquileiam et Venetias, ubi rex, Dei permissione, passus naufragium, cum paucis evasit Quidam itaque fidelis noster comes Mainardus de Gooxce, et populus regionis illius, audito quod in terra erat, et considerato diligentius qualem nominatus rex in terra promissionis proditionem et traditionem, et proditionis suæ cumulum exercuerat, insecuti sunt, intendentes eum captivare, ipso autem rege in fugam converso, ceperunt de suis octo milites Postmodum processit rex ad Burgum in archiepiscopatu Salseburgensi, qui vocatur Frisorum, ubi Fredericus de Betesow, rege cum tribus tantum versus Austriam properante, noctu sex milites de suis cepit Dilectus autem consanguineus noster Leopoldus, dux Austriæ, observata strata, sæpe dictum regem juxta Denam in villa viciniori in domo despecta captivavit Cum itaque in nostra nunc habeatur potestate, et ipse semper tua molestavit et turbationis operam præstiterit, ea quæ præmisimus nobilitati tuæ insinuare curavimus, scientes ea dilectioni tuæ beneplacita existere, et animo tuo uberrimam importare lætitiam Datum apud Ritheounten, 5 Calendas Januar"

(2) Thus ended the third Oriental Crusade, A D 1192 But as, after a fruitlessly victorious career, the adverse events which accompanied one of the bravest men whom the world has produced, cannot fail to interest the reader, a few words which our history seems to require are added, respecting the dangers which subsequently befel King Richard Having arrived at a town, which was probably Goretz, he narrowly escaped detection, in consequence of a generous offer of a splendid ruby which he made to the chieftain of the province, aware of the suspicions which he excited, and the solicitous inquiries which were made respecting him, Richard thought it prudent to retire in the night Still new dangers awaited him, he travelled forward in company with a knight, and a lad, who understood German, and after three days arrived at Audberg, on the Danube, near Vienna Here, sojourning in a retired cottage, his lad inadvertently went to market with his prince's gloves in his girdle, the sight of these, and the unsatisfactory answers of the lad, induced the local authorities to examine him by torture, in the extremity of his agony, and under the threat of repeated sufferings, he disclosed the name of his royal master The result may be anticipated the duke of Austria, who unfortunately was in that neighbourhood, immediately surrounded the cottage, and Richard surrendered himself to the duke in person. He was sold to the Emperor of Germany, as some say, for sixty thousand pounds of silver, and England paid the price of the ransom of her brave monarch The reader doubtless remembers the romantic tale of the minstrel commencing a favourite ballad, and the king completing the stanza, which eventually betrayed the place of his confinement Mr Sharon Turner, to whom the Editor is indebted for the substance of the above remarks, refers to an interesting and detailed account of the captivity of Richard, in the "MS Chronicle of Johannes de Oxenedes, monachus St Benedicti de Hulmo, in the Cotton Library"—Ed.

and that Leopold, taking his advantage, was the more cruel against him, and delivered him, as is said, to the emperor, in whose custody he was detained during the time above mentioned, namely, a year and three months. During that time of the king's endurance, the French king stirred up war in Normandy, and Earl John, the king's brother, made stir and invaded England; but the barons and bishops of the land mightily withstood him, and besieged him in the castle of Windsor, where they took from him all the castles and munitions which before he had got. Thus the earl, seeing no hope of prevailing in England, and suspecting the deliverance of the king, his brother, made off into France, and kept with the French king. At length it was agreed and concluded with the emperor, that King Richard should be released for a hundred thousand pounds, part of which should remain to the duke of Austria, the rest should be the emperor's. The sum of this money was here gathered and made in England of chalices, crosses, shrines, candlesticks, and other church plate; also with public contribution of friaries, abbeys, and various subjects of the realm. Part of the money was presently paid, and, for the residue, hostages and pledges were taken; which was about the fifth year of the king's reign. At that time it was obtained of the pope, that priests might celebrate with chalices of latin and tin;[1] and so it was granted and continued long after, which mine author, in his chronicle, entitled 'Eulogium,' doth testify himself to have seen. At that time, this aforesaid money was paid, and the hostages were given for the ransom of the king. I have an old story that saith how the aforesaid duke of Austria, shortly after, was plagued by God with five sundry plagues: first, with burning of his chief towns; secondly, with the drowning of ten thousand of his men in a great flood, happening no man could tell how; thirdly, by turning all the ears of his corn fields into worms; fourthly, by taking away almost all the nobles of his land by death; fifthly, by breaking his own leg by falling from his horse, which leg he was compelled to cut off with his own hands, and afterwards died of the same; who is said at his death to have forgiven King Richard fifty thousand marks, and to have sent home the hostages that were with him.[2] The book entitled 'Eulogium,' before mentioned, declareth thus; that the said Leopold, duke of Austria, fell into displeasure with the bishop of Rome, and died excommunicate the year after, A.D. 1196.

Richard I.

A.D. 1194.

Confederacy of the French king and Earl John against King Richard.

A.D. 1194.

The just punishment of God upon the duke of Austria.

A.D. 1196.

Thus King Richard being ransomed, as hath been declared, from the covetous captivity of the emperor, was restored again, and repaired to England; at whose return Earl John, his brother, resorting unto him with humble submission, desired to be pardoned his transgressions. To whom King Richard answered again, "Would God," saith he, "this your trespass, as it dieth with me in oblivion, so it may remain with you in remembrance!" and so gently forgave him. The king, after he had recovered his holds and castles, caused himself to be crowned again; which done, he made head against the French king, and drove him out of Normandy. After that he turned his course against the Welshmen, and subdued them.

The answer of King Richard to his brother.

(1) As a substitute for this sacrifice of the precious metals, the priests were permitted to use chalices of 'latin,' that is, 'l'étain,' 'pewter,' and 'tin.'—Ed.

(2) Ex variis chron.

Richard I.

A.D. 1197

In the year following, A.D. 1197, Philip, the French king, brake the truce made between him and King Richard; whereupon the king was compelled to sail over again to Normandy, to withstand the malice of his enemy. About this time my story recordeth of one, called of some Fulco; some say he was the archbishop of Rouen, called Walter. This Fulco being then in England, and coming to the king's presence, said to him, with great courage and boldness, "Thou hast, O mighty king! three daughters, very vicious and of evil disposition; take good heed of them, and betimes provide for them good husbands; lest, by untimely bestowing of the same, thou shalt not only incur great hurt and damage, but also utter ruin and destruction to thyself." To whom the king, in a rage, said, "Thou lying and mocking hypocrite, thou knowest not where thou art, or what thou sayest: I think thou art mad, or not well in thy wits; for I have never a daughter, as all the world knoweth; and, therefore, thou open liar, get thee out of our presence." To whom Fulco answered, "No, and like your grace, I lie not, but say truth; for you have three daughters, who continually frequent your court, and wholly possess your person, and such three naughty packs, as never the like hath been heard of; I mean, mischievous Pride, greedy Covetousness, and filthy Luxury; and, therefore, again I say, O king! beware of them, and out of hand provide marriages for them, lest in not so doing, thou utterly undo both thyself and the whole realm."

Three daughters of the king noted

†

These words of Fulco the king took in good part, with correction of himself, and confession of the same; whereupon he incontinently called his lords and barons before him, unto whom he declared the communing and motion of Fulco, who had willed him to beware of his three daughters—Pride, Avarice, and Luxury, with counsel out of hand to marry them, lest further discommodity should ensue, both to him and to the whole realm: "whose good counsel, my lords, I intend to follow, not doubting of all your consents thereunto. Wherefore, here before you all, I give my daughter, swelling Pride, to wife unto the proud Templars; my greedy daughter, Avarice, to the covetous order of the Cistercian monks; and, last of all, my filthy daughter, Luxury, to the riotous prelates of the church, whom I think to be very meet men for her; and so severally well agreeing to all their natures, that the like matches in this our realm are not to be found for them." And thus much concerning Fulco.

Not long after this, it befel that a certain noble personage (lord of Lemonice, in Little Britain, Widomarus by name), found a great substance of treasure, both of gold and silver, hid in the ground, whereof a great part he sent to King Richard, as chief lord and prince over the whole country, which the king refused; saying, He would have all or none, for that he was the principal chieftain over the land. But the finder would not condescend to that; wherefore the king laid siege to a castle of his, called Galuz, thinking the treasure to lie there. But the keepers and warders of the castle, seeing themselves not sufficient to withstand the king, offered him the castle, desiring to depart with life and armour. This the king would in no wise grant, but bade them re-enter the castle again, and defend it in all the forcible wise they could. It so befel, that as the king, with the duke of Brabant, went about the castle, viewing the places

He that all would have, shall all forego

John. A.D. 1199.

thereof, a soldier within, named Bertrand Cordoun, struck the king with an arrow in the arm; whereupon, the iron remaining and festering in the wound, the king, within nine days after, died; who, because he was not content with the half of the treasure that another man found, lost all his own treasure that he had. The king, being thus wounded, caused the man that struck him to be brought unto him, and asked him the cause why he so wounded him? The man answered, as the story saith, 'that he thought to kill rather than to be killed; and what punishment soever he should sustain, he was content, so that he might kill him who had, before, killed his father and brethren.' The king, on hearing his words, freely forgave him, and caused a hundred shillings to be given him; albeit, as the story addeth, after the death of the king, the duke of Brabant, after great torments, caused him to be hanged.[1] The story of Gisburn saith, that the killer of King Richard, coming to the French king, thinking to have a great reward, was commanded to be drawn asunder by horses, and his quarters to be hanged up.[2]

Covetous greediness plagued.

Death of King Richard I.

Richard forgiveth him that had mortally wounded him.

Another story affirmeth, and Gisburn partly doth testify the same, that a little before the death of King Richard, three abbots, of the Cistercian order, came to him, to whom he was confessed: and when he saw them somewhat stay at his absolution, he spake these words:—'That he did willingly commit his body to the earth, to be eaten of worms, and his soul to the fire of purgatory, there to be tormented till the judgment, in the hope of God's mercy.'[3]

Vain fear of purgatory.

About the reign of this king, Jornalensis maketh mention of Roger, archbishop of York, who put out of his church the monks, and placed for them secular priests; saying, 'That he would rather wish ecclesiastical benefices to be given to wanton priests, than to abominable monks; and that Thurstin did sin never worse in all his life, than in building that house for monks.' Another story I have, which saith, that this was not the bishop of York, but of Coventry.

Monks put out, and secular priests put in.

The king, not long after, departing without issue, John, his brother, reigned after him; in whom, although some vices may worthily be reprehended, especially his incontinent and too licentious life, yet was he far from deserving that, for the which he hath been so ill reported of divers writers, who, being led more with affection to popery, than with true judgment and due consideration, depraved his doings more than the sincere truth of the history will bear. Concerning his history, after so many writers, we thought also to bestow a little labour; although in this matter we cannot be so long as we would, and as the matter requireth.

JOHN.[4]

After the death of King Richard, called Cœur de Lion, reigned his brother, John, Earl of Morton. Afterwards, the archbishop put the crown on his head, and sware him to defend the church and to

A.D. 1199.

(1) Ex Historia Regis Richardi Secundi, cui initium, "De patre istius Bruti," &c. Ex Bibliotheca Cariensi.
(2) Ex Gualtero Hemingford, monacho Gisburn.
(3) Ex Jornalens. Gisburn. et aliis.
(4) Edition 1563, p. 71. Ed. 1583, p. 219. Ed. 1596, p. 226. Ed. 1684, vol. i. p. 281.—Ed.

John. A.D. 1199. maintain the same in her good laws, and to destroy the evil; and except he thought in his mind to do this, the archbishop charged him not to presume to take on him this dignity. On St. John Baptist's day next following, King John sailed into Normandy and came to Rouen, where he was royally received, and truce concluded between him and the French king for a time. And thither came to him the earl of Flanders, and all the other lords of France that were of King Richard's band and friendship, and were sworn unto him.

Arthur of Brittany. Not long after this, Philip, the French king, made Arthur, knight, and took his homage for Normandy, Brittany, and all other his possessions beyond the sea, and promised him help against King John. After this, King John and the French king talked together with their lords about one hour's space; and the French king asked so much land for himself and Knight Arthur, that King John would grant him none; and so he departed in wrath.

The same year a legate came into France, and commanded the king, on pain of interdiction, to deliver one Peter out of prison, who was elected to a bishopric; and thereupon he was delivered.

After that the legate came into England, and commanded King John, under pain of interdiction, to deliver the archbishop whom he had kept as prisoner two years; which the king refused to do, till he had paid him six thousand marks, because he took him in harness in a field against him, and swore him, upon his deliverance, that he should never wear harness against any christian man.

At this time divorce was made between King John and his wife, daughter of the earl of Gloucester, because they were in the third degree of kindred; and afterwards, by the counsel of the French king, King John wedded Isabella, daughter of the earl of Angouleme; and then Arthur of Brittany did homage to King John, for Brittany and others.

Marriage in the third degree forbidden by the pope.

A.D. 1200. At this time arose strife between King John, and Geffrey the archbishop of York, for divers causes: first, because he would not suffer and permit the sheriff of York, in such affairs as he had to do for the king within his diocese. Secondly, because he did also excommunicate the said sheriff. Thirdly, because he would not sail with him into Normandy, to make the marriage between Louis, the French king's son, and his niece, &c.

A.D. 1202. After this, A.D. 1202,[1] Philip, the French king, in a communication between King John and him, required that the said King John should part with all his lands in Normandy and Pictavia which he had beyond the sea, unto Arthur, his nephew, and that incontinent, or else he would war against him; and so he did. For when King John denied that request, the next day following, the French king, with the said Arthur, set upon certain of his towns and castles in Normandy, and put him to much disquietness.[2] But he (the Lord so providing, who is the giver of all victory) had such repulse at the Englishmen's hands, that they pursuing the Frenchmen in their flight, did so follow them in their hold, and so pressed upon them, that not only they took the said Arthur prisoner, with many others of the Frenchmen, but also gave such an overthrow to the

The French king driven out of Normandy.

Prince Arthur taken.

(1) In A.D. 1202, the fourth Oriental Crusade set out from Venice, and Constantinople was taken by the French and Venetians.—Ed.
(2) Nat. Paretti in Vita Johannis Regis.

-est, that none was left to bear tidings home. This Arthur was nephew to King John, and son to Geffrey, who was the elder brother to John; for King Henry II. (to make the matter more evident) had eight children: one was William, who died in his childhood; the second, Henry, who died also, his father being yet alive; the third, Geffrey, earl of Brittany, who likewise deceased in his father's days, leaving behind him two children, Arthur and Brecca; the fourth, Richard Cœur de Lion, king; the fifth, John, now reigning; and three other daughters besides. The same Arthur, being thus taken in war, was brought before the king, at the castle of Falaise, in Normandy; who, being exhorted with many gentle words to leave the French king, and to incline to his uncle, answered again stoutly, and with great indignation; requiring the kingdom of England, with all the other dominions thereto belonging, to be restored to him, as to the lawful heir of the crown. By reason whereof, he, provoking the king's displeasure against him, was sent to the tower of Rouen, where at length (whether by leaping into the ditch, thinking to make his escape, or whether by some privy hand, or by what chance else, it is not yet agreed upon in stories) he finished his life; by occasion whereof, the aforesaid King John was had, after, in great suspicion, whether justly or unjustly, the Lord knoweth.

John. A.D. 1202.

Mysterious end of Prince Arthur.

The year following, historiographers write, that King John, for lack of rescue, lost all his holds and possessions in Normandy, through the force of the French king. After these losses came other troubles upon him, with other as great or greater enemies (that is, with the pope and his popelings), by occasion of choosing of the archbishop of Canterbury; as in this history following, by Christ's grace, is to be declared.

A D 1203.

Normandy lost, and gotten by the French

In the year of our Lord 1205, about the month of July, Hubert, the archbishop of Canterbury, deceased; whose decease, after it was known in Canterbury to the monks, and before his body was yet committed to the earth, the younger sort of the monks there gathered themselves together at midnight, and elected their superior, Reginald, and, without the king's license, or yet knowledge, privily placed him in the metropolitan seat, singing 'Te Deum' at midnight. And because the king should not make their election void, they charged him, by virtue of his oath, to keep all secret by the way, and to show nothing that was done before he came to the pope; but he, contrary to his oath, as soon as he came into Flanders, opened all abroad the matter, and uttered their counsel: whereupon the monks, being not a little grieved with him, sent him privily unto the court of Rome, out of hand. The next day, the elder monks sent to the king, desiring him, of his gracious license, canonically to choose their archbishop. The king most gently and favourably granted their petition, requiring them instantly, and desiring them for his sake, to show favour to John Gray, then bishop of Norwich; as they did indeed, erecting him into that seat of their high primacy. Moreover, because the authority of kings and princes was then but small in their own dominion, without the pope's consent and confirmation to the same, he sent also to Rome, of his own charges, to have the aforesaid election ratified by the pope. The suffragans of Canterbury then, being not a little offended at these two elections, sent

A D 1205

Striving for the election of the archbishop of Canterbury

John. A.D. 1205. speedily to Rome to have them both stopped, because they had not been of counsel with them; and hereupon at last grew a most prodigious tumult.

*[1] In this year the clergy grew so unruly, that they neglected their charge, and thereby incensed the king's displeasure so sorely against them, that he took order about the goods of such as in that case were faulty; as shall appear more manifestly by that which followeth.

A Letter of King John, touching the Lands and Goods of such Clerks as refuse to celebrate Divine Service.[2]

The king to all clerks and lay people within the bishopric of Lincoln, greeting: Know ye that from Monday next before the feast of Easter,[3] we have committed to William of Cornhill, archdeacon of Huntingdon, and to Joselin of Canvil, all the lands and goods of the abbots and priors, and of all the religious persons; and also of all clerks within the bishopric of Lincoln, which will not from that time celebrate divine service. And we command you, that from thence you assist them as our bailiffs; and believe them in those things which they shall tell you privately on our behalf. Witness ourself at A.D. 1206. Clarendon, the eighteenth day of March, in the ninth year of our reign.

Prelates of the church had then money enough, it seems, that they could keep play at Rome against their prince; which thing caused the princes afterwards to seek such means to cut them short.

The like was written to all within the bishopric of Ely. So that hereby we see the dissoluteness and wilfulness of those popish churchmen, whom conscience of discharging their duty did so little move, as that they thought upon nothing less, till the king was driven to use such austerity and sharpness against them. But to proceed in this troublesome election: you shall understand,* that the next year after, the suffragans of the province of Canterbury on the one side, and the monks of Canterbury on the other side, came before the pope with their brawling matter. First the monks, presenting Reginald, their superior, desired that their election might be confirmed. The suffragans likewise complained that the monks would presume to choose the archbishop without their consent, and therefore desired, by divers reasons, the first election to be of none effect. The pope, deciding the matter between both, pronounced with the monks; charging the suffragans and bishops to meddle no more with A.D. 1207. that election, but to let the monks alone. The monks of Canterbury, now having the whole election in their own hands, fell also at square among themselves, the younger sort with the elder. The younger sort, who had chosen Reginald their superior, would have that election to stand. The elder sort of the monks replied again, saying, that the first election was done by stealth, and by night, and by the younger part; also without the counsel of other monks. Over and besides, it was done without the king's license or appointment, and without the due solemnity thereunto belonging.

Dissension among the monks of Canterbury about the election of the archbishop.

And as concerning our election, said they, it was done in the clear light of the day, by which it had authority in presence of our liege lord the king, and his council being willing to the same.

This allegation thus proponed, the suffragans' proctor or man of law stood forth, and proved the former election to be good, and this latter to be void and of no value, after this sort. "Whether the

(1) This passage is not found in the Edition of 1583, but appears in that of 1596.—Ed.
(2) "Rex omnibus de episcopatu Lincolniæ clericis et laicis, salutem. Sciatis quod a die lunæ proxime ante Floridum paschatis commisimus," &c.—Turris Lond.
(3) Some think that 'Floridum paschatis' is Palm Sunday; but Easter is rather thought to be meant thereby, sith the Spaniards, at this day, call the same Florida.

first election," saith he, "were just or unjust, ye ought first by the law to have condemned it before ye should have presumed to the second; but thus ye did not: therefore is this your latter doing no election at all, and the first therefore is rather to be ratified than yours." When they had thus multiplied talk on both sides, with many frivolous allegations a long time, and could not agree upon one person, Pope Innocent condemned both their elections, commanding them to choose Stephen Langton, then cardinal of St. Chrysogon, for their archbishop. The monks then answered, that they durst not so do without consent of their king, and for that it was prejudicial to their ancient liberties. The pope by and by (saith the text), as one in a fury, taking the words out of their mouths, said thus unto them: "We will ye to know, that we have full power and authority over the church of Canterbury; neither are we wont to tarry the consent of princes, therefore we command you, on pain of our great curse, that ye choose him only whom we have appointed."

The pride and tyranny of the pope.

The monks, at these words abashed and terrified, though they much murmured in their hearts, yet consented they all in one, and thereupon sang Te Deum; only Dr. Elias Brantfield withdrew himself from that election, whom the king had sent for the admission of the bishop of Norwich.

Thus was Stephen Langton, in the high church of Witerby, by the pope's hand, made archbishop of Canterbury.

Stephen Langton made archbishop of Canterbury.

*[1]This election, thus passed with the pope's grace and favour, the said Stephen had in England, among others that solicited his cause to the king, a brother named Master Simon Langton, who also in course of time became archbishop of York, as appeareth in the course of this story, in the reign of Henry III. A.D. 1228. In this behalf the king seemed tractable, so he might have his sovereignty entire; against which, because the said Stephen had vowed to oppose himself, and the king misliked such demeanour, he sent abroad his letters certificatory about the realm; therein giving intimation to all people of proud Stephen Langton's countenance. The form of the said letters followeth.

Letters certificatory of King John, touching the contumacy of Stephen Langton, Archbishop of Canterbury, by the Pope's Election.[2]

The king to all men, &c. Know ye that Master Simon Langton came to us at Winchester, on the Wednesday next before Mid-lent, and, in presence of our bishops, besought us that we would receive his brother, Master Stephen Langton, to be archbishop of Canterbury. And when we spake unto him touching the reservation and saving of our dignity unto us, he told us that he would do no such thing for us, unless we would wholly rely ourselves upon his courtesy and gentleness. This therefore we command, that you know evil and wrong to be done unto us in this behalf: and we charge you, that you believe those things which Reginald of Cornhill shall tell you on our part, touching the aforesaid deed between us and the bishops above-named, &c.—Witness the king at Winchester, the fourteenth day of March, in the ninth year of his reign.*

(1) This passage is not in any edition previous to that of 1596.—Ed.
(2) "Rex omnibus hominibus, &c. Sciatis quod magister Simon de Langton venit ad nos apud Winton die Mercurii proxime ante mediam quadragesimæ," &c.—Turris Lond.

John. A.D. 1208.

Now, albeit the king took indignation at this proceeding in the election of Stephen, "yet, from thenceforth," saith Matthew Paris, "the pope could do no less than mightily defend him from all vexation and danger; considering that he was his own dear darling, and a child of his own creation."

Furthermore, upon this occasion King John conceived an extreme displeasure against the clergy and monks of Canterbury, as he had good cause, they doing so many evils against his princely prerogative. Without his license they elected their archbishop, and put by the bishop of Norwich, whom he had appointed. They wasted a great part of his treasure for the wars; and, to bring all to the devil, they made Stephen Langton their high metropolitan, whom he took for a grievous enemy to the whole realm, being always so familiar with the French king: wherefore, in his anger, he banished them out of the land, to the number of threescore and four, for this their contumacy, and contempt of his regal power.

Monks of Canterbury banished.

The monks of Canterbury thus being expulsed, the king forthwith sendeth messengers to the pope with his letters, wherein he doth sharply and expressly expostulate with the pope. First, for that so uncourteously he resisted the election of the bishop of Norwich, and set up one Stephen Langton, a man unknown to him, and brought up amongst his enemies a long time in the kingdom of France, consecrating him archbishop of Canterbury, and letting the other go. Also, which is more, for that it redoundeth to the subversion and derogation of the liberties appertaining to his crown; for, notwithstanding his consent passed (being before of the monks, not made privy, who should have so done), yet he rashly presumed to promote and prefer another. Wherefore he cannot marvel, he saith, enough, that neither the said pope, nor the court of Rome, doth consider and revolve with themselves, how necessary his love and favour hath been always hitherto to the see of Rome; and that they consider not what great profit and revenues have proceeded hitherto to them out of the realm of England; the like whereof hath not been received out of any other country besides on this side the Alps. He addeth moreover, and saith, that for his liberties he will stand, if need be, unto death, neither can he be so removed and shaken off from the election of the bishop of Norwich, which he seeth to be so commodious to him and profitable. Finally, he thus concludeth, saying, that in case in this his request he be not heard, he will so provide by the seas that there shall be no such gadding and coursing any more over to Rome, suffering the riches of the land no more to be transported over, whereby he should be himself the less able to resist his enemies. And, seeing he hath of his own at home, archbishops, bishops, and other prelates of the church, both of Englishmen and of others, sufficiently provided and instructed in all kind of knowledge, therefore, he shall not need greatly to seek for judgment and justice further abroad.

The king expostulates with the pope for consecrating Stephen Langton, archbishop of Canterbury.

His bold threatening.

When these things came to the pope's knowledge, he directeth this letter again to the king in these words:—

The Pope's Letter to King John.

Innocent, pope, servant of the servants of God, to our well-beloved son in Christ, the king of England, health, and apostolical blessing. Whereas we have written to you heretofore, exhorting and entreating you after an humble, diligent, and gentle sort (concerning the church of Canterbury), you have written to us again after a threatening sort and upbraiding manner, both spitefully and also frowardly. And whereas we have borne and given to you more and above what our right and duty required; you again, for your part, have given to us not so much as by right and duty you are bound to do. And though your devotion, as you say, hath been to us very necessary, yet consider again that ours also is not a little opportune and expedient for you. And whereas we, in such like cases, have not showed at any time the like honour to any prince as we have unto you, you again have so much derogated our honour, as no prince else hath presumed to do besides; pretending certain frivolous causes and occasions, I cannot tell what, why you would not condescend to the election of Stephen Langton, cardinal of St. Chrysogon, chosen by the monks of Canterbury; for that the said Stephen (as you say) hath been conversant and brought up amongst your enemies, and his person is to you unknown. But you know what is the proverb of Solomon.—"The net is cast, but in vain, in the sight of the flying birds," &c.

John

A.D. 1208.

It is pity but this pope should be honoured of kings and princes

With much other matter in the same epistle, wherein he falleth into the commendation of Stephen Langton his cardinal, declaring how learned he was in the liberal arts and in divinity, insomuch that he was prebendated at Paris; also that he was come of an honest stock, and was an Englishman born, and not unknown to the king, seeing the king had written his letters thrice to him before. Declaring, moreover, in the said letter, how the messengers of the king had specified to him another cause; which was, that the monks of Canterbury, who had to do in the election, came not to him before for his consent. Declaring, moreover, in the said letter, how the said messengers of the king entreated in the king's behalf, that forasmuch as the pope's letters (wherein the king was commanded to send his proctors to Rome, for the same matter) came not to the king's hand, neither did the monks direct any such letters or message to the king to have his consent; therefore the pope, considering the same, would grant so much for the regard of the king's honour, that the monks of Canterbury should not proceed without the king's assent therein. And forasmuch as that hath not been done as yet, therefore they desired some delay therein to be given, sufficient for the doing thereof. Whereunto he said, that he had granted and fulfilled their request, in sending his letters and messengers once or twice to the king for the same purpose, although he said it was not the manner of the see apostolic (which had the fulness of power over the church of Canterbury) to wait for princes' consents in such elections, who then could not be suffered to do that which they came for. Wherefore, in knitting up his letter, he thus concludeth in these words.—

A pitiful case that a king cannot constitute an archbishop within his own realm.

"And therefore, seeing the matter so standeth, we see no cause why we should require or tarry for the king's favour or consent any more therein, but intend so to proceed in this matter, neither inclining to the right hand nor to the left, according as the canonical ordinances of the holy fathers shall direct us; that is, (all impediments and delays set aside) so to provide, that the church of Canterbury be not any longer destitute of her pastor. Wherefore, be it known to your discretion or kingly prudence, that forasmuch as this election of Stephen Langton hath orderly and in concord thus proceeded without fraud or deceit, upon a person meet for the same; therefore we will not, for man's pleasure, neither may we, without danger of fame and of conscience, defer or protract any longer the consummation of the said election. Wherefore, my well-beloved son, seeing we have had respect to your honour, above what our right and duty requireth, study to honour us so much as your duty requireth

A glorious letter of a proud pope.

John.

A.D. 1208.

again, so that you may the more plentifully deserve favour, both at God's hand and ours; lest that by doing the contrary, you bring yourself into such a peck of troubles, as afterwards you shall scarce rid yourself of again. For this know for a certainty, in the end it must needs fall out, that he shall have the better, unto whom every knee (of heavenly, earthly, and infernal creatures) doth bow, whose turn I serve in earth, though I be unworthy. Therefore settle not yourself to obey their persuasions, who always desire your unquietness, whereby they may fish the better in the water when it is troubled; but commit yourself to our pleasure, which undoubtedly shall turn to your praise, glory, and honour. For it should not be much for your safety in this cause to resist God and the church; in whose quarrel that blessed martyr, and glorious bishop, Thomas [Becket] hath of late shed his blood; especially seeing your father and your brother of famous memory, then kings of England, did give over those three wicked customs into the hands of the legates of the see apostolic. But, if you yield yourself humbly into our hands, we will look that you and yours shall be sufficiently provided for, that no prejudice may arise hereupon to you-ward.—Given at Lateran the tenth year of our popedom."

Note the proceedings of this ambitious pope.

Princes must be subject to the pope

Thus hast thou, gentle reader! the glorious letter of the proud pope; I beseech thee mark it well. Now to the story.

After this letter was sent out, not long after proceedeth a charge and commandment sent into England, unto certain bishops there, requiring them, by authority apostolical, that if the said king would not receive the prior of Canterbury and his monks, then they should interdict him throughout all his realm. For the executing of this, four bishops were appointed by the usurped power of the pope's bulls: namely, William, bishop of London; Eustace, bishop of Ely; Walter, bishop of Winchester; and Giles, bishop of Hereford. These four bishops went unto the king, and showed their commission from the pope, as is aforesaid, willing him to consent thereto; but the said king refused the same, and would by no means grant their request. Whereupon they, departing from his grace, went on the morrow after the Annunciation of our Lady, and pronounced the said general interdiction throughout all England, so that the church-doors were shut up with keys, and other fastenings, and with walls.

Four bishops appointed to interdict the realm.

Now when the king heard of this, he began to be moved against them, and took all the possessions of the four bishops into his hands, appointing certain men to keep the livings of the clergy throughout the realm, and that they should enjoy no part thereof. This being done, the bishops, seeing the same, cursed all them that kept, or should meddle with church goods, against the will of them that owned them: and understanding, for all that, that the king nothing regarded their doings, they went over sea to the bishop of Canterbury, and informed him what had happened: who hearing the same, willed them again to return to Canterbury, and he would come thither to them, or else send certain persons thither in his stead, that should do as much as if he were there himself. Then when the bishops heard this, they returned again to England, to Canterbury; on which tidings came shortly to the king, that they were come again thither. And because he might not himself travel to them, he sent thither bishops, earls, and abbots, to entreat them that the Archbishop Stephen, whom he had chosen, might be admitted; promising the prior and all the monks of Canterbury in his behalf, that he should never take any thing of the church goods against the will of them that owned them, but would make amends to them from whom he had

Discipline of the church abused for private revenge.

taken any such goods, and that the church should have all her franchises in as ample manner as she had in St. Edward the Confessor's time. *John.* A.D. 1209.

When the form of agreement was thus concluded, it was engrossed in a pair of indentures, and the aforesaid four bishops, to the one part thereof, set their seals; and the other part the said bishops, earls, and abbots, carried to show the king. When the king saw the order thereof, he liked it well, saving he would not agree to make restitution of the church goods. So he sent to the four bishops again that they should put out that point of restitution. But they answered stoutly, that they would not put out one word. Then the king sent word to the archbishop, by the four bishops, that he should come to Canterbury to speak with him, and for his safe conduct to come and go again at his will, he sent his justices as pledges: Gilbert Peitewin, William de la Beurer, and John Letfitz. This done, the Archbishop Stephen came to Canterbury, and the king, hearing thereof, came to Chilham; from whence he sent his treasurer, the bishop of Winchester, to him, to have the king's name put out of the indentures in the clause of restitution aforesaid: who refusing to alter any word of the same, moved the king in such sort, that immediately it was proclaimed throughout England, at the king's commandment, that all those that had any church-livings, and went over the sea, should come again into England by a certain day, or else lose their livings for evermore. And further in that proclamation, he charged all sheriffs within the realm, to inquire if any bishops, abbots, priors, or any other churchman (from that day forward) received any commandment that came from the pope, and that they should take his or their body and bring it before him; and also that they should take into their hands, for the king's use, all the church lands that were given to any man through the Archbishop Stephen, or by the priors of Canterbury, from the time of the election of the archbishop: and further charged that all the woods that were the archbishop's should be cut down and sold.

The inconsiderate stoutness of the prelates against the king.

Stephen Langton stout against his king

The king moved against him.

When tidings came to the pope that the king had thus done, being moved thereby with fiery wrath, he sent to the king two legates, the one called Pandulph, and the other Durant, to warn him, in the pope's name, that he should cease his doings to holy church, and amend the wrong he had done to the archbishop of Canterbury, to the priors and monks of Canterbury, and to all the clergy of England. And further, that he should restore the goods again that he had taken of them against their will, or else they should curse the king by name; and to do this, the pope gave them his letters in bulls patent. These two legates, coming into England, resorted to the king to Northampton, where he held his parliament, and, saluting him, said, they came from the pope of Rome, to reform the peace of holy church. And first, said they, "we admonish you in the pope's behalf, that ye make full restitution of the goods, and of the lands, that ye have ravished from holy church; and that ye receive Stephen, the archbishop of Canterbury, into his dignity; and the prior of Canterbury and his monks; and that ye yield again unto the archbishop all his lands and rents without any withholding; and, sir, yet moreover, that ye shall make such restitution to them as the church shall think sufficient."

Two legates sent from the pope.

Restitution required of the king.

John. A.D. 1210.

Fierce altercation between the king and Pandulph.

Then answered the king, as touching the prior and his monks of Canterbury, "All that ye have said I would gladly do, and all things else that you would ordain; but as touching the archbishop, I shall tell you as it lieth in my heart. Let the archbishop leave his bishopric; and if the pope then shall entreat for him, peradventure I may like to give him some other bishopric in England; and upon this condition I will receive and admit him."

Then said Pandulph to the king, "Holy church was wont never to degrade archbishop without cause reasonable; but she was ever wont to correct princes that were disobedient to her."

"What? How now," quoth the king; "threaten ye me?" "Nay," said Pandulph, "but ye have now openly told us as it standeth in your heart; and now we will tell you what is the pope's will; and thus it standeth: he hath wholly interdicted and cursed you, for the wrongs you have done unto holy church, and unto the clergy. And, forasmuch as ye will dwell still in your malice, and will come to no amendment, you shall understand, that from this time forward the sentences upon you given have force and strength. And all those that with you have communed before this time, whether that they be earls, barons, or knights, or any other, whatsoever they be, we assoil them safely from their sins unto this day: and from this time forward, of what condition soever they be, we accurse them openly, and specially by this our sentence, that do commune with you. And we assoil, moreover, earls, barons, knights, and all other manner of men, of their homages, services, and fealties, that they should do unto you. And this thing to confirm, we give plain power unto the bishop of Winchester, and to the bishop of Norwich; and the same power we give against Scotland unto the bishop of Rochester, and of Salisbury; and in Wales we give the same power to the bishop of St. David, and of Landaff, and of St. Asaph."

The legate curseth all who commune with the king.

"Also, sir king," quoth Pandulph, "all the kings, princes, and the great dukes christened, have laboured to the pope to have license to cross themselves, and to war against thee, as upon God's great enemy, and to win thy land, and to make king whom it pleaseth the pope. And we here now assoil all those of their sins that will rise against thee here in thine own land."

The pope author of rebellion and disobedience of subjects towards their prince.

Then the king, hearing this, answered: "What shame may ye do more to me than this?"

Pandulph again: "We say to you in the name of God, that neither you, nor any heir that you have, after this day shall be crowned." So the king said, "By him that is Almighty God, if I had known of this thing before ye came into this land, and that ye had brought me such news, I should have made you tarry out these twelve months."

Then answered Pandulph, "Full well we thought, at our first coming, that ye would have been obedient to God and to holy church, and have fulfilled the pope's commandment, which we have showed and pronounced to you, as we were charged therewith. And now ye say, that if ye had wist the cause of our coming, ye would have made us tarry out a whole year; who might as well say, that ye would have taken a whole year's respite without the pope's leave; but for to suffer what death ye can ordain, we shall not spare to tell all the pope's message and will, that he gave us in charge."

Like master like man.

In another chronicle I find the words between the king and Pandulph something otherwise described, as though the king should first threaten him with hanging, if he had foreknown of his coming. To whom Pandulph again should answer, that he looked for nothing else at his hand, but to suffer for the church's right. Whereupon the king, being mightily incensed, departed. The king, the same time, being at Northampton, willed the sheriffs and bailiffs to bring forth all the prisoners there, that such as had deserved, should be put to death; to the intent, as some think, to make Pandulph afraid. Among them was a certain clerk, who, for counterfeiting the king's coin, was also condemned to be hanged, drawn, and quartered; and, moreover, the king commanded (thereby to anger Pandulph the more, as may be thought) that this clerk should be hanged up highest, above the rest. Pandulph, hearing thereof, notwithstanding he somewhat began to fear lest he should be hanged himself; yet, with such courage as he had, he went to the church to set out book, bell, and candle, charging that no man, under pain of accursing, should lay hands upon the clerk. Upon this the king and the cardinal departed in no little anger, and Pandulph went to Rome, and reported to the pope and the cardinals what had been done.

Pandulph more afraid than hurt.

Then the pope summoned all the bishops, abbots, and clerks of England, to come and repair to Rome, to consult what was to be done therein. This council began the first day of October. It was therein decreed, by the pope and his assembly, that John, king of England, should be accursed, with all such as held with him, every day so long as that council endured; albeit this was not yet granted, that the people should be crossed to fight against him, because as yet he had shed no blood. But afterwards the said Pope Innocent, seeing that King John would by no means stoop under his subjection, nor under the rule of his popish see, sent unto the French king, upon remission of all his sins, and those of all that went with him, that with all the power they might, they should take with them the livery and badge of the cross, to invade the realm of England, and revenge him of the manifold injuries done to the universal church, by that cursed Turk or Pagan, King John.

The pope stirreth up the French king to invade England.

This occasion given, Pope Innocent yet once again commanded, on pain of his great curse, that no man should obey King John, neither yet keep company with him: he forbade all persons to eat and drink with him, or talk with him, to commune or counsel with him; yea, his own familiar household to do him any kind of service either at bed or at board, in church, hall, or stable. And what followed thereof? The greater part of them, who after such sort fled from him, by the ordinance of God, of divers and sundry diseases the same year died; and between both nations, English and French, fell, for that year, great amity; but secret, subtile, and false, to the bitter betraying of England. Neither was the pope content only with this, but, moreover, the said Pope Innocent gave sentence definitive, by council of his cardinals, that King John should be put from his seat regal and deposed, and another put in his room. To the speedy execution of this he appointed the French king, Philip; promising to give him full remission of all his sins, and the clear

The pope's great curse.

The just punishment of God upon disobedient subjects.

John. A.D. 1212.

possession of all the realm of England, to him and his heirs, if he did either kill him or expel him.

The pope found a murderer.

The next year the French king began his attempt, in hope of the crown of England; being well manned with bishops, monks, prelates, priests, and their servants, to maintain the same; bragging of the letters which they had received from the great men there. But behold the work of God: the English navy took three hundred of the French king's ships, well loaden with wheat, wine, meal, flesh, armour, and such other stores, meet for the war; and one hundred ships they burnt within the haven, taking the spoils with them. In the mean time the priests in England had provided them a certain false counterfeit prophet, called Peter Wakefield, of Poiz, who was an idle gadder about, and a prattling merchant. This Peter they made to prophesy lies, rumouring his prophecies abroad, to bring the king out of all credit with his people. They noised it daily among the commons of the realm, that Christ had twice appeared to this prophet of theirs in shape of a child between the priest's hands, once at York, another time at Pomfret; and that he had breathed on him thrice, saying, "Peace! peace! peace!" and teaching many things which he anon after declared to the bishops; and bade the people amend their naughty living. Being rapt also in spirit, they said he beheld the joys of heaven, and the sorrows of hell. For scant were there three, saith the chronicle, among a thousand that lived christianly. This counterfeit soothsayer prophesied of King John that he should reign no longer than the Ascension Day, A.D. 1213, which was the fourteenth year from his coronation; and this, he said, he had by revelation. Then was it of him demanded, whether the king should be slain, or expelled, or should of himself give over the crown? He answered, That he could not tell; but of this he was sure, he said, that neither he, nor any of his stock or lineage, should reign, that day once finished. The king, hearing of this, laughed much at it, and made but a scoff thereof. "Tush," saith he, "it is but an idiot knave, and such a one as lacketh his right wits." But when this foolish prophet had so escaped the danger of the king's displeasure, and that he made no more of it, he gat him abroad, and prated thereof at large, as he was a very idle vagabond, and used to tattle and talk more than enough; so that they who loved the king caused him anon after to be apprehended as a malefactor, and to be thrown into prison, the king not yet knowing thereof.

French ships taken by the English.

Peter the false prophet.

His seditious practices.

Peter is thrown into prison.

The fame of this fantastical prophet soon went all the realm over, and his name was known every where, as foolishness is much regarded of people, where wisdom is not in place; especially because he was then imprisoned for the matter, the rumour was the larger, their wonderings were the wantoner, their practising the foolisher, their busy talks, and other idle occupyings, the greater. Continually from thence, as the rude manner of people is, old gossips' tales went abroad, new tales were invented, fables were added to fables, and lies grew upon lies; so that every day new slanders were raised on the king, and not one of them true: rumours arose, blasphemies were spread, the enemies rejoiced, and treasons by the priests were maintained, and what in like manner was surmised, or whatever subtlety was practised, all was then fathered upon this foolish prophet: as, "Thus saith Peter Wakefield," "Thus hath he prophesied," and, "This shall come to pass;" yea, many times when he thought nothing less. When the Ascension Day was come, which was prophesied of before, King John commanded his regal tent to be spread abroad in the open field, passing that day with his noble council, and men of honour, in greater solemnity than ever he did before, solacing himself with musical instruments and songs, most in sight, amongst his trusty friends. When that day was passed in all prosperity and mirth, his enemies being confused, turned all to an allegorical understanding, to make the prophecy good, and said, "He is no longer king, for the pope reigneth, and not he;" yet reigned he still, and his son after him, to prove that prophet a liar. Then was the king by his council persuaded that this false prophet had troubled all the realm, perverted the hearts of the people, and raised the commons against him; for his words went over the sea by the help of his prelates, and came to the French king's ear, and gave him great encouragement to invade the land: he had not else done it so suddenly; but he was most foully deceived, as all they are, and shall be, that put their trust in such dark, drowsy dreams of hypocrites. The king therefore commanded that he should be drawn and hanged like a traitor, and his son with him, lest any more false prophets should arise of that race.

John. A.D. 1212.

The false prophet proved a liar by King John.

The false prophet hanged.

After the popish prelates, monks, canons, priests, &c. saw this their crafty juggling by their feigned prophet would not speed, notwithstanding they had done no little harm thereby, to help the matter more forward, they began to travail and practise with Pope Innocent on the one side, and also with the French king on the other; besides subtle treasons which they wrought within the realm, and by their confessions in the ear, whereby they both blinded the nobility and commons. The king thus compassed about on every side with enemies, and fearing the sequel thereof, knowing the conspiracies that were in working against him, as well by the pope, in all that ever he might, as also by Philip, the French king, by his procurement; and moreover his own people, especially his lords and barons, being rebelliously incited against him; as by the pope's curses and interdictions against such as took his part; and also by his absolutions and dispensations with all those that would rebel against him, commanding them to detain from him such homage, service, duties, debts, and all other allegiance, as godly subjects owe and are bound to yield and give to their liege lord and prince: all which things considered, the king, in the thirteenth year of his reign, because the French king began to make sharp invasion upon him within his own realm, sent speedy ambassadors to the pope, as to the fountain of all this his mischief, pretended to work and entreat his peace and reconciliation with him, promising to do whatsoever the pope should will and command him in the reformation of himself, and restitution of all wrongs done to holy church, and to make due satisfaction there-for unto all men that could complain.

King John submitteth himself to the pope.

Entreateth for peace with the pope.

Then sent the pope again into England his legate Pandulph, with other ambassadors: the king also at Canterbury (by letters, as it should seem, certified from his own ambassadors) waited their coming; where, the thirteenth day of May, the king received

John. A.D. 1212.

them, making unto them an oath, That of and for all things wherein he stood accursed, he would make ample restitution and satisfaction. Unto whom also all the lords and barons of England, as many as there were with the king attending the legates' coming, sware in like manner, That if the king would not accomplish in every thing the oath which he had taken, then they would cause him to hold and confirm the same, whether he would or not, or "by strength," to use the author's words.

[1]The king, seeing the great danger that was like to follow, and himself to be brought to such a strait, that no other way could be found to avoid the present destruction both of his person and the realm also, but utterly to be subverted; and especially fearing the French king; was enforced to submit himself to that execrable monster and antichrist of Rome, converting his land into patrimony of St. Peter, as many others had done before him, and so became a sorry subject of the sinful seat of Rome, thinking thereby to avoid all imminent dangers; for of this he was sure, not without shame, that being under his protection, no foreign potentate throughout the whole empire was able to subdue him.

Submitteth himself, and resigneth his crown.

Then submitted the king himself unto the court of Rome, and to the pope; and, resigning, gave up his dominions and realms in England and Ireland for him and for his heirs for evermore that should come of him: with this condition, that the king and his heirs should take again these two dominions of the pope to farm, paying yearly for them to the court of Rome one thousand marks of silver. Then took the king the crown from his head, in the presence of all his lords and barons of England, kneeling upon his knees to Pandulph, the pope's chief legate, saying in this wise, "Here I resign the crown of the realm of England into the pope's hands, Innocent III., and put me wholly in his mercy and ordinance." Then took Pandulph the crown of King John, and kept it five days as a possession and seizin-taking of these two realms of England and Ireland, confirming also all things promised by his charter obligatory as followeth:—

The Copy of the Letter Obligatory that King John made to the Pope, concerning the yielding up of the crown and realm of England into the Pope's hands, and a certain sum of money yearly to be paid.

Christ was offered a kingdom and would none of it.

To all christian people throughout the world dwelling, John, by the grace of God, king of England, greeting: to your university known be it, that, for as much as we have grieved and offended God, and our mother, the church of Rome, and forasmuch as we have need of the mercy of our Lord Jesus Christ, and we may nothing so worthy offer, and competent satisfaction make to God and to holy church, even if it were our own body, as with our realms of England and of Ireland; then, by the grace of the Holy Ghost, we desire to meek us for the love of him, that meeked him to the death upon the cross. And through counsel of the nobles, earls, and barons, we offer, and freely grant to God, and to the apostles St. Peter and Paul, and to our mother church of Rome, and to our holy father Pope Innocent III., and to all the popes that come after him, all the realm, patronages of churches of England and of Ireland, with all the appurtenances, for remission of sins, and help and health of our kings' soul, and of

(1) From the Edition 1563, p. 65.—Ed.

all christian souls. So that from this time afterwards, we will receive and hold of our mother, the church of Rome, as in farm, doing fealty to our holy father the pope, Innocent III., and to all the popes that come after him, in the manner above said. And in the presence of the wise man, Pandulph, the pope's south-deacon, we make liege homage, as if it were in the pope's presence, and we before him were, and as if he himself should have done all manner of things above said, and thereto we bind us, and all that come after us, and our heirs for evermore, without any gainsaying, to the pope, and eke the ward of the church vacant. And, in token of this thing ever for to last, we will, confirm, and ordain, that he be our special renter of the aforesaid realms (saving St. Peter pence) in all things, to the mother church of Rome, paying by the year one thousand marks of silver at two times of the year, for all manner of customs that we should do for the said realms; that is to say, at Michaelmas and at Easter: that is, for England seven hundred marks, and three hundred marks for Ireland; saving to us and to our heirs, our justices, and our other franchises. And all these things, that have before been said, we will that they be firm and stable, without end: and to that obligation we, and all our successors, and our heirs, in this manner are bound, That if we, or any of our heirs, through any presumption, fail in any point again of these things above said, and he having been warned, will not right amend him, he shall then release the aforesaid realms for evermore. and this charter of obligation, and our warrant for evermore, shall be firm and stable without gainsaying. We shall from this day afterward be true to God, and to the mother church of Rome, and to thee, Innocent III., and to all that come after thee, and in the realms of England and of Ireland we shall maintain true faith, in all manner of points, against all manner of men, by our power through God's help.

King John yieldeth to farm his realm of the pope

The rent charges

Upon this obligation the king was discharged, on the second day of July, from that tyrannical interdiction under which he had continued six years and three months. But, before the releasement thereof, first, he was miserably compelled, as hath been declared, to give over both his crown and sceptre to that antichrist of Rome for the space of five days; and, as his client, vassal, feudary, and tenant, to receive it again of him at the hands of another cardinal; being bound obligatory, both for himself and for his successors, to pay yearly for acknowledgment thereof, one thousand marks for England and Ireland. Then came they thither from all parts of the realm, so many as had their consciences wounded for obeying their liege king, as blind idiots, and there they were absolved, every one by his own bishop, except the spiritual fathers and ecclesiastical soldiers, for they were compelled to seek to Rome, as captives reserved to the pope's own fatherhood. In this new ruffling the king easily granted that abbots, deans, and curates, should be elected freely every where, so that the laws of the realm were truly observed; but against that were the bishops, alleging their canonical decrees and rules synodal, determining the king therein to have nothing to do, but only to give his consent after they had once elected. But among this shaven rabble, some there were who consented not to this wicked error; a sort also there were of the prelates at that time, who were not pleased that the land's interdiction should cease, till the king had paid all that which their clergy in all quarters of the realm had demanded, without reason; yea, what every saucy Sir John for his part demanded, even to the very breaking of their hedges, the stealing of their apples, and their other occasional damages, which grew to an incredible sum, and impossible to be answered. Such was the outrageous cruel noise of that mischievous progeny of antichrist, against their natural king.

The unreasonableness of the clergy against their natural prince.

John. A.D. 1215.

Notwithstanding that which is uttered before concerning the bitter malice of the clergy against their prince, yet did the pope's legate and cardinal, Nicholaus Tusculanus, much favour his doings, and allow of his proceedings; wherefore they reported of him that he was exceedingly partial, and regarded not their matters ecclesiastical, as he should have done. For, leaving the account of their restitutions, he went with the king's officers, as the king's pleasure was, to the cathedral minsters, abbeys, priories, deaneries, and great churches vacant; and there, for the next incumbent, he always appointed two, one for the king, another for the parties. But upon him only whom the king nominated he compelled most commonly the election to pass, which vexed them wonderfully. Upon this, therefore, they raised a new conspiracy against the king's person, by help of their bishops, seditious prelates, and such noblemen as they had drawn to their parties. "We beheld," saith Hoveden, "about the same time many noble houses and assemblies divided in many places. The fathers and the aged men stood upon the king's part, but the younger sort contrary; and some there were that for the love of their kindred, and in other sundry respects, forsook the king again." "Yea, the fame went that time," saith he, "that they were confederated with Alexander, the Scottish king, and Llewellyn, the prince of Wales, to work him an utter mischief." A council at Oxford the archbishop called, whereat some would not tarry, considering the confusion thereof; the other sort, having very obstinate hearts, reviled the king most spitefully behind his back, and said, that from thenceforth he ought to be taken for no governor of theirs. Their outrageous and frantic clamour so much prevailed in those days, that it grew to a grievous tumult, and a most perilous commotion.

Great division of opinion respecting the king.

In the year of our Lord 1215, as witnesseth Paulus Æmilius, and other historians, Pope Innocent III. held a general synod at Rome, called the Council of Lateran. The chief causes of that council were these:—In the days of this Innocent, heresy (as he calleth the truth of God, or the doctrine that rebuketh sin) began to rise up very high, and to spread forth its branches abroad, by reason whereof many princes were excommunicated; as Otho, the emperor; John, the king of England; Peter, king of Arragon; Raimund, the earl of Toulouse, Aquitaine, Sataloni, and such others, as is aforesaid: so that it could be no otherwise, saith Hoveden, but with the sharp axe of the gospel (so called the pope his excommunications) they ought of necessity to have been cut off from the church. Therefore was this council provided and proclaimed, and prelates from all nations thereunto called. And, to colour those mischiefs which he then went about, he caused it by his legates and cardinals (very crafty merchants) to be noised abroad, that his intent therein was only to have the church universally reformed, and the Holy Land from the Turks' hands recovered. But all this was craft and falsehood, as the sequel thereof hath manifestly declared; for his purpose thereby was, to subdue all princes, and to make himself rich and wealthy. For there he made this antichristian act, and established it by public decree, that the pope should have, from thenceforth, the correction of all christian princes; and that no emperor should be admitted, except he were sworn before, and were also crowned of him. He ordained moreover, that whosoever he

Council of Lateran holden by Pope Innocent.

Craft and subtleties of the pope.

The pope to have jurisdiction of all churches.

were that should speak evil of the pope, he should be punished in hell with eternal damnation.[1] He provided confession to help these matters; he allowed their bread a pix to cover it, and a bell when it goeth abroad, and made the mass equal with Christ's gospel. *John.* A.D. 1215.

In this council was first invented, and brought in, transubstantiation; of which Johannes Scotus, whom we call Duns, maketh mention in his fourth book, writing in these words:—"The words of the Scripture might be expounded more easily and more plainly without transubstantiation; but the church did choose this sense, which is more hard; being moved thereunto, as it seemeth, chiefly, because that of the sacraments men ought to hold, as the holy church of Rome holdeth," &c. And in the same place he maketh mention of Innocent III. Transubstantiation first brought in.

Moreover, in the said council was established and ratified the wretched and impious act, compelling priests to abjure lawful matrimony. Whereupon these metres or verses were made the same time against him, which here follow underwritten, in English thus:[2]— Marriages of priests forbidden.

"Nocent, not innocent, he is that seeketh to deface
By word the thing, that he by deed, hath taught men to embrace;
Who being now a bishop old, doth study to destroy
The thing, which he, a young man once, did covet to enjoy.
Priest Zachary both had a wife, and had a child also,
By means of whom, there did to him great praise and honour grow.
For he did baptize him, who was the Saviour of mankind:
Ill him befal, that holdeth this new error in his mind.
Into the higher heavens, good Paul was lifted from below,
And many secret hidden things, he learned there to know:
Returned at length from thence to us, and teaching rules of life,
He said, Let each man have his own, and only wedded wife.
For this and other documents, of them that learned be,
Much better and more comely eke, it seemeth unto me,
That each should have his own alone, and not his neighbour's wife,
Lest with his neighbour, he do fall in hate and wrathful strife.
Thy neighbour's daughters or their wives, or nieces to defile,
Unlawful is; therefore beware, do not thy self beguile.
Have thou thine own true wedded wife, delight in her alway,
With safer mind that thou mayst look, to see the latter day."

Now let us return to King John again, and mark how the priests and their adherents were plagued for their humble handlings of his majesty's will. In the aforesaid council of Lateran, and the same

(1) Conradus, Urspergensis, Hieronymus, Marius.
(2) "Non est innocentius, imo nocens vere,
Qui, quod facto docuit, verbo vult delere:
Et quod olim juvenis voluit habere,
Modo vetus pontifex studet prohibere.
Zacharias habuit prolem et uxorem,
Per virum quem genuit adeptus honorem;
Baptizavit etenim mundi Salvatorem:
Pereat qui teneat novum hunc errorem.
Paulus cœlos rapitur ad superiores,
Ubi multas didicit res secretiores;
Ad nos tandem rediens instruensque mores,
Suas, inquit, habeant, quilibet uxores.
Propter hæc et alia dogmata doctorum,
Reor esse melius et magis decorum,
Quisque suam habeat et non proximorum,
Ne incurrat odium vel iram eorum.
Proximorum fœminas, filias, et neptes
Violare nefas est, quare nil deceptes,
Vere tuam habeas, et in hac delectes,
Diem ut sic ultimum tutius expectes."

John. A.D. 1215.

year, was Stephen Langton, archbishop of Canterbury, excommunicated by Pope Innocent, with all those bishops, prelates, priests, barons, and commons, who had been of counsel with him in the former rebellion. And when the said archbishop had made instant suit to him to be absolved, anon he made him this answer with great indignation: "Brother mine, I swear by St. Peter, thou shalt not so soon at my hand obtain the benefit of absolution: for why? thou hast not only done harm to the king of England, but also thou hast in a great many things injured the church of Rome here; and therefore thou shalt tarry my leisure." The archbishop was also at that time suspended out of the church, and commanded to say no mass at all, neither yet to exercise any other ecclesiastical office; because he would not, at time convenient, execute the pope's curse upon the rebellious barons. With them the said pope had been so deeply offended and angered a little before, that the great charter of the liberties of England, with great indignation and countenance most terrible, he rent and destroyed, by sentence definitive, condemning it for ever; and, by and by thereupon, cursed all the other rebels, with book, bell, and candle. The greater captains of them, with the citizens of London, for that assay were pronounced excommunicate by name, and remained still interdicted. They appealed then to the council general.

Stephen Langton suspended.

Appeal to the general council.

In the same year, A.D. 1215, were those great men also summoned to appear at Rome in that general synod, who would not consent to their king's expulsion, nor yet tyrannical deposing. Though they were called, they said, thereunto by the archbishop of Canterbury and others, and required by oath to subscribe unto the same, yet could they not of their conscience do it, because he had humbled himself, and also granted to keep peace with all men. Thus was the whole realm miserably then divided into two factions, through the malice of the clergy, so that strifes increased in the land every where; yet were there of the lords and gentlemen a great number at that time, who followed the king and allowed his doings.[1] But they who were on the other side, not a little suspecting the state that they were in, fled speedily to the French king, Philip, desiring him that he would grant them his eldest son Louis, and they would elect him, to be their king, and that without much tarriance. They besought him, moreover, that he would send with him a strong and mighty power, such as were able to subdue him utterly, that they might, they said, be delivered from such a wicked tyrant. Such was the report that those most wicked papists gave their christian governor, appointed over them by God, whom they ought to have obeyed, though he had been evil, even for very conscience' sake. [Rom. xiii. 7.] And as certain of the lords and barons were busy to choose the said Louis for their king, the pope sent thither one Gualo, the cardinal of St. Martin, to stay those rash and cruel attempts; charging the French king, upon his allegiance, that he, with all power possible, should favour, maintain,

The discord between the nobles and the king.

Gualo, cardinal, sent into England.

(1) Stowe, speaking of these times, confirms the account which our author gives of these internal commotions which unhappily prevailed in England, but especially of the revolting assaults to which the Jews were subjected, so frequently referred to by our author. "I read, that in the year 1215, the sixteenth of King John, the barons entering the city by Ealdgate (Aldgate), first took assurance of the citizens; then brake into the Jews' houses, searched their coffers to fill their own purses; and after, with great diligence, repaired the walls and gates of the city, with stones taken from the Jews' broken houses."—See Stowe's Hist. of Lond. p. 7.—Ed.

and defend King John of England, his feudary or tenant. The French king thereto made answer, as one not content with that arrogant precept: "The realm of England," said he, "was never yet any part of St. Peter's patrimony, neither is it now, nor yet, at any time, shall be hereafter." Thus spake he, for that he was in hope to obtain it for his son, by treason of the barons.

John

A. D. 1215.

"No prince or potentate," said Philip, the French king, "may pledge or give away his kingdom, which is (beside the realm) the government of his whole commonwealth, without the lawful consent of his barons, who are bound to defend the same. If the pope shall introduce or set up such a precedent in Christianity, he shall, at his pleasure, bring all christian kings and their kingdoms to nought. I like not this example in these days begun. I cannot therefore allow this act of King John of England: though he be my utter adversary, yet I much lament that he hath so endamaged his realm, and hath brought that noble ground, and queen of provinces, under miserable tribute." The chief lords and men of his nobility standing by, when he uttered these words, being, as it were, in a fury, cried with one voice, "By the blood of God, by which we trust to be saved, we will stick to this article to the losing of our heads. Let the king of England do therein what him liketh: no king may put his land under tribute, and so make his nobility captive servants." With that came in Louis, the king's eldest son, and said unto them all there present, "I beseech you, hinder not my purposed journey: the barons of England have elected me for their lord and king, and I will not surely lose my right, but I will fight for it even to the very death, yea, so long as heart shall stir within my breast; and I doubt not but I shall well obtain it, for I have friends among them." His father, the king, stood still as if he had been in a dump, and answered never a word, but fared as though he had dissembled the matter. Belike he mistrusted something therein, as he might well enough; for all was procured by the priests, that they might live licentiously, in all wealth, and in freedom from the king's yoke.

The French king and his son reasoning about England

About the same time, were such treasons and conspiracies wrought by the bishops, priests, and monks, throughout all the realm, that the king knew not where to go, or find trusty friends; he was then compelled, by the uncertainty of his subjects, to travel from place to place, but not without a great army of men, looking, every day, when his barons and their confederates would cruelly set upon him. At last he came to Dover, and there looked for aid from other quarters, which loved him better than did his own people. And thither resorted to him from Flanders, Brabant, and Holland, on one side, and from Guienne, Gascony, and Poictiers, on the other side, and from other countries besides, a wonderful number of men. The report then went, that the pope had written unto those countries mightily to assist him, for divers considerations: one was, for that King John had both submitted himself and his dominions, to his protection; another was, because he had taken upon him, a little before, the livery of the Cross, to win again Jerusalem; the third was, because the pope had gotten by him the dominion of England and Ireland, and feared to lose both, if he should chance to decay. For the space of three months the king remained in the Isle of Wight, abroad

Prelates and priests conspiring against the king.

John. A.D. 1216.

in the air, to quiet himself, for a time, from all manner of tumults, and led there a solitary life among rivers and watermen, rather coveting to die than to live, being so traitorously handled of his bishops and barons, and not knowing how to be justly avenged of them. Upon the Purification day of our Lady, therefore, he took upon him the Cross, or voyage against the Turks, for recovery of Jerusalem; moved thereto rather for the doubts which he had of his people, than for any other devotion else. And thus he said to his familiar servants: "Since I submitted myself and my lands, England and Ireland, to the church of Rome (sorrow come to it!) never a thing hath prospered with me, but all hath gone against me."

In the next year, A.D. 1216, was Simon Langton chosen archbishop of York; but that election soon after was dissolved; for information was given to the pope, that the said Simon was brother to Stephen Langton, the archbishop of Canterbury, who had been the occasion of all the tumults which were at that time in England. The pope had the more hate unto him, for that he had brought him up from nought, and did find him, at that time, so stubborn; wherefore he placed in his brother's place Walter Gray, the bishop of Winchester.

Gualo, the pope's legate, renews the great curse on the French king's son.

In the same year Gualo, the pope's legate, renewed his great curse upon Louis, the French king's son, for usurping upon King John; likewise upon Simon Langton, and Gervais Hobruge, for provoking him to the same, and that with a wonderful solemnity; for in doing that, he made all the bells to be rung, the candles to be lighted, the doors to be opened, and the book of excommunications or interdictions publicly to be read, committing them wholly to the devil, for their contumacy and contempt. He also commanded the bishops and curates to publish it abroad over all the whole realm, to the terror of all his subjects. The said Simon and Gervais laughed him to scorn, and derided much his doings in that behalf, saying, that for the just title of Louis, they had appealed to the general council at Rome.[1]

The pope's curse laughed to scorn.

The magistrates and citizens of London did, likewise, vilipend and disdainfully mock all that the pope had there commanded and done; and, in spite both of him and his legate, they kept company with them that were excommunicated, both at table and at church; showing themselves, thereby, as open contemners both of him and his laws. Louis, at London, taking himself for king, constituted Simon Langton for his high chancellor, and Gervais Hobruge for his chief preacher; by whose daily preachings (as well the barons as the citizens themselves being excommunicated) he caused all the church doors to be opened, and the service to be sung, and the said Louis was in all points fit for their hands. About this time Pandulph, the cardinal, was collecting the Peter-pence, that old pillage of the pope, taking great pains therein; and for his great labours in those affairs of holy church, and for other great miracles besides, he was then made bishop of Norwich, to the augmenting of his dignity and expenses.

Pandulph, the pope's collector, made bishop of Norwich.

It chanced, about this time, that the viscount of Melun, a very noble man of the realm of France, who came thither with Prince Louis, fell deadly sick in London, and being moved, in conscience, to

(1) Radulphus Niger, cap. 43, 44.

call certain of the English barons unto him, such as were there appointed to the custody of that city, said unto them: "I lament your sorrowful case, and pity, with my heart, the destruction that is coming towards you and your country.[1] The dangerous snares, which are prepared for your utter confusion, are hidden from you; you do not behold them; but take you heed of them in time. Prince Louis hath sworn a great oath, and sixteen of his earls and noblemen are of counsel with him, that, if he obtain the crown of England, he will banish all them from service, and deprive them of lands and goods, as many as he findeth now to go against their liege king, and are traitors to his noble person. And, because you shall not take this tale for a fable, I assure you on my faith, lying now at the mercy of God, that I was one of those who were sworn to the same. I have great conscience thereof, and, therefore, I give you this warning. I pity poor England, which hath been so noble a region, that now it is come to such extreme misery." And when he, with tears, had lamented it a space, he turned again unto them and said: "My friends, I counsel you earnestly to look to yourselves, and to provide the remedy in time, lest it come upon you unawares: your king for a season hath kept you under, but if Louis prevail, he will deprive you of all; of two extreme evils, choose the more easy, and keep that secret which I have told you of good will." With that he gave over, and departed this life.

John

A. D. 1216.

The great providence of God for the help of England

When this was once noised among the barons, they were in great heaviness, for they saw themselves entrapped every way, and to be in exceeding great danger. And this daily augmented that fear which then came upon them; they were extremely hated of the pope and his legates, and every week, came upon them new excommunications. Daily detriments they had besides in their possessions and goods, in their lands and houses, corn and cattle, wives and children, so that some of them were driven to such need, that they were enforced to seek preys and booties for sustaining their miserable lives. For look, whatsoever Prince Louis obtained by his wars, either territories or castles, he gave them all to his Frenchmen, in spite of their heads, and said that they were but traitors, like as they had warning before; and this grieved them worst of all. At last, perceiving that in seeking to avoid one mischief, they were ready to fall into another much worse, they began to lay their heads together, consenting to submit themselves wholly, with all humility, unto the mercy of their late sovereign and natural liege lord, King John; and, as they were somewhat in doubt of their lives for the treason before committed, many of the friends of those who were of most credit with him, made suit for them; so that a great number of them were pardoned, after instant and great suit made for them. I here omit his recovery of Rochester castle and city, with many other dangerous adventures against the aforesaid Louis, both at London, York, Lincoln, Winchester, Norwich, and other places, as things not pertaining to my purpose. And now I return to my matter again.

Perplexity and distress of the barons

Into Suffolk and Norfolk he consequently journeyed, with a very strong army of men, and there, with great mischief, he afflicted them, because they had given place and were sworn to his enemies. After

(1) Matth Paris, Radul Niger, cap 47.

John. A.D. 1216. that, he destroyed the abbeys of Peterborough and Crowland, for the great treasons which they also had wrought against him; and so he departed from thence into Lincolnshire.

Pope Innocent III dieth. In this year, A.D. 1216, about the seventeenth day of July, died Pope Innocent III., and was buried in a city called Perugia, in Italy; whither he had travelled to make a peace between the Genoese and Pisans, for his own commodity and advantage. After him, anon, succeeded one Centius, otherwise called Honorius III., a man of very great age; yet lived he, in the papacy, ten years and a half, and more. When this was once known in England, all those greatly rejoiced who were King John's enemies, especially the priests; yet had they small cause, as will appear hereafter. They noised it all the realm over, that this new pope would set up a new order, and not rule all things as the other pope did; thinking, thereby, that he would have done all things to their commodity, but they found it otherwise. For he made all those who were excommunicated, pay double and treble, ere they could be restored again to their former livings.

King John poisoned by a monk. And, in the self-same year, as King John was come to Swinstead abbey, not far from Lincoln, he rested there two days; where, as most writers testify, he was most traitorously poisoned by a monk of that abbey, of the sect of the Cistercians, or St. Bernard's brethren, called Simon of Swinstead. As concerning the noble personage of this prince, this witness giveth Roger Hoveden thereon: "Doubtless," saith he, "King John was a mighty prince, but not so fortunate as many were; not altogether unlike to Marius, the noble Roman, he tasted of fortune both ways; bountiful in mercy; in wars sometime he won, sometime again he lost." "He was also very bounteous and liberal unto strangers, but of his own people, for their daily treason's sake, he was a great oppressor, so that he trusted more to foreigners than to them."[1]

Among other divers and sundry conditions belonging to this king, one there was, which is not in him to be reprehended, but commended rather; for that, being far from the superstition which kings at that time were commonly subject to, he regarded not the popish mass, as in certain chronicles writing of him may be collected; for this I find testified of him by Matthew Paris: that the king, once upon a time, in his hunting, coming where a very fat stag was cut up and opened (or how the hunters term it, I cannot tell), the king beholding the fatness and the liking of the stag: "See," saith he, "how easily and happily he hath lived, and yet for all that, he never heard any mass." King John derideth the mass.

It is recorded and found in the chronicle of William Caxton, called "Fructus temporum," and in the seventh book, that the aforesaid monk Simon, being much offended with certain talk that the king had at his table, concerning Louis, the French king's son, who then had entered and usurped upon him, did cast, in his wicked heart, how he most speedily might bring him to his end. And, first of all, he counselled with his abbot, showing him the whole matter, and what he was minded to do. He alleged for himself the prophecy of Caiaphas (John xi.), saying, "It is better that one man die, than all the people should perish." "I am well contented," saith he, "to lose my life, and so become a martyr, that I may utterly destroy

Wo be to you that call good evil, and evil good.

(1) Ex chronico cui titulus "Eulogium."

this tyrant." With that the abbot did weep for gladness, and much commended his fervent zeal, as he took it. The monk, then, being absolved beforehand of his abbot for doing this act, went secretly into the backside of the garden, and finding there a most venomous toad, he so pricked him and pressed him, with his penknife, that he made him vomit all the poison that was within him. This done, he conveyed it into a cup of wine, and with a smiling and flattering countenance, he said thus to the king: "If it shall like your princely majesty, here is such a cup of wine as ye never drank better before, in all your lifetime; I trust this wassail shall make all England glad;" and, with that, he drank a great draught thereof, the king pledging him. The monk anon after went to the farmary, and there died, his entrails gushing out of his body, and had continually from thenceforth three monks to sing mass for his soul, confirmed by their general chapter. What became, after that, of King John, ye shall know right well in the process following. I would ye did mark well the wholesome proceedings of these holy votaries, how virtuously they obey their king, whom God hath appointed, and how religiously they bestow their confessions, absolutions, and masses.

John.

A.D. 1216.

Simon the monk absolved by his abbot for poisoning his king.

Dieth of his own poison.

The king, within a short space after, feeling great grief in his body, asked for Simon, the monk; and answer was made that he was departed this life. "Then God have mercy upon me," said he, "I suspected as much, after he had said that all England should thereof be glad; he meant, now I perceive, those of his own generation." With that he commanded his chariot to be prepared, for he was not able to ride. So went he from thence to Sleaford castle, and from thence to Newark-on-Trent, and there, within less than three days, he died. Upon his death-bed he much repented his former life, and forgave all them, with a pitiful heart, that had done him injury; desiring that his elder son, Henry, might be admonished by his example, and learn by his misfortunes to be natural, favourable, gentle, and loving to his native people. When his body was embalmed and spiced, as the manner is of kings, his bowels or entrails were buried at Croxton abbey, which was held by the sect of Premonstratenses, or canons of St. Norbert. His hired soldiers, both Englishmen and strangers, were still about him, and followed his corpse triumphantly in their armour, till they came to the cathedral church of Worcester, and there honourably was he buried by Silvester, the bishop, betwixt St. Oswald and St. Wolstan, two bishops of that church. He died A.D. 1216, the nineteenth day of October, after he had reigned in such calamity, by the subtile contrivance of his clergy, eighteen years and six months and odd days. Now, as soon as King John was dead and buried (as is said before), the princes, lords, and barons, as many as were of his part, as well of strangers as of them that were born here, by counsel of the legate Gualo, gathered themselves together, and all with one consent proclaimed Henry, his son, for their king. Of him more shall follow (the Lord willing) hereafter.

Death of King John.

A prince to be loving to his subjects.

King John buried at Worcester.

Many opinions are among the chroniclers of the death of King John. Some of them do write that he died of sorrow and heaviness of heart, as Polydore; some of surfeiting in the night, as Radulphus Niger; some of a bloody flux, as Roger Hoveden; some of a

Contradictory opinions respecting his end.

John. A.D. 1216. burning ague, some of a cold sweat, some of eating apples, some of eating pears, some of plums, &c.

Thus you see what variety is among the writers concerning the death of this King John. Of which writers, although the most agree in this, that he was poisoned by the monk above named, yet Matthew Paris,[1] something differing from the others, writeth thus concerning his death: that he, going from Lynn to Lincolnshire, and there hearing of the loss of his carriage and of his treasures upon the washes, gave way to great heaviness of mind, insomuch that he fell thereby into a fervent fever, being at the abbey of Swinstead. This ague he also increased, through evil surfeiting and naughty diet, by eating peaches and drinking new ciser, or, as we call it, cider. Thus, being sick, he was carried from thence to the castle of Sleaford, and from thence to the castle of Newark; where, calling for Henry, his son, he gave to him the succession of his crown and kingdom, writing to all his lords and nobles to receive him for their king. Shortly after, upon St. Lucy's even, he departed this life, and was buried at Worcester.

Another account of King John's death.

In Gisburn I find otherwise, who, dissenting from others, saith, that he was poisoned with a dish of pears, which the monk had prepared for the king, therewith to poison him; who, asking the king whether he would taste of his fruit, and being bid to bring them in, according to the king's bidding, so he did. At the bringing in whereof (saith the story) the precious stones about the king began to sweat; insomuch that the king misdoubting some poison, demanded, of the monk, what he had brought. He said, of his fruit, and that very good; the best that ever he did taste. "Eat," said the king. And he took one of the pears, which he did know, and did eat. Also, being bid to take another, he did eat that likewise, savourily, and so likewise the third. Then the king, refraining no longer, took one of the poisoned pears, and was therewith poisoned, as is before narrated.[2]

The first mayor of London.

In the reign of this King John, the citizens of London first obtained of the king to choose yearly a mayor. In this reign also the bridge of London was first builded of stone, which before was of wood.[3]

HENRY THE THIRD.[4]

A.D. 1216. After King John had reigned, as some say, seventeen years, or as others say, though falsely, nineteen years, he was, as is above stated, poisoned, and died. This king left behind him four sons and three daughters; the first, Henry; the second, Richard, who was earl of Cornwall; the third, William of Valentia; the fourth, Guido Disenaie: he had also another son, who afterwards was made bishop. Of his daughters, the first was Isabella, married afterward to Frederic, the emperor; the second, named Elenor, was married to William, earl marshal; the third, to Mountfort, the earl of Leicester, &c. Another story saith, that he had but two daughters, Isabella and

(1) Matth. Paris. in Vita Johannis Regis. (2) Ex Hist. Gualt. Gisburn. (3) Rastal.
(4) Edition 1563, p. 72. Ed. 1583, p. 257. Ed. 1596, p. 234. Ed. 1684, vol. i. p. 290.—Ed.

Elenor, or, as another calleth her, Joan, who was afterwards queen of Scotland.[1] *Henry III* A.D 1216.

This King John being deceased, who had many enemies both of earls and barons, and especially of the popish clergy, Henry, the eldest son, was then of the age of nine years, at which time, most of the lords of England, did adhere to Ludovic, or Louis, the French king's son, whom they had sent for before, in displeasure of King John, to be their king, and had sworn to him their allegiance. Then William, earl Marshal, a nobleman, and of great authority, and a grave and sound counsellor, friendly and quietly called unto him divers earls and barons, and taking this Henry, the young prince, son of King John, setteth him before them, using these words: "Behold," saith he, "right honourable and well-beloved, although we have persecuted the father of this young prince[2] for his evil demeanour, and worthily; yet this young child, whom here ye see before you, as he is in years tender, so is he pure and innocent from these his father's doings: wherefore, inasmuch as every man is charged only with the burden of his own works and transgressions, neither shall the child, as the scripture teacheth us, bear the iniquity of his father; we ought, therefore, of duty and conscience, to pardon this young and tender prince, and take compassion of his age, as ye see. And now, forasmuch as he is the king's natural and eldest son, and must be our sovereign and king, and successor of this kingdom, come, and let us appoint him our king and governor, and let us remove from us this Louis, the French king's son, and suppress his people, which is a confusion and a shame to our nation; and the yoke of our servitude let us cast off from our shoulders." To these words spake and answered the earl of Gloucester: "And by what reason or right," said he, "can we so do, seeing we have called him hither, and have sworn to him our fealty?" Saying of earl Marshal.

Whereunto the earl Marshal inferred again, and said: "Good right and reason we have, and ought of duty to do no less, for that he, contrary to our mind and calling, hath abused our affiance and fealties. Truth it is we called him, and meant to prefer him to be our chieftain and governor; but he, oftsoons, surprised in pride, hath contemned and despised us: and, if we shall so suffer him, he will subvert and overthrow both us and our nation, and so shall we remain a spectacle of shame to all men, and be as outcasts to all the world."

At these words all they, as inspired from above, cried all together with one voice, "Be it so, he shall be our king." And so the day was appointed for his coronation, which was the day of Simon and Jude. This coronation, A.D. 1216, was kept, not at Westminster, forasmuch as Westminster at that time was holden of the Frenchmen, but at Gloucester, the safest place, as was thought, at that time in the realm,[3] by Gualo, the pope's legate, through counsel of all the lords and barons that held with his father, King John; to wit, the bishop of Winchester, the bishop of Bath, the bishop of Chester, and the bishop of Worcester; the Earl Radulph, of Chester; William, earl Marshal; William, earl of Pembroke; William Tren, earl of King Henry III crowned

(1) Ex Chronico vetusto Angliæ.
(2) Truly said, that you persecuted him, for persecutors ye were of a true man, and your own natural king. But well might England cry out upon your blind guides and setters on
(3) Ex Chron. Gisburn.

Henry III. A.D. 1216. Ferers; William de Brewer; Serle, or Samarike de Mal, baron. These were at the crowning of the king at Gloucester. Many other lords and barons there were, who, as yet, held with Louis, the French king's son, to whom they had done their homage before. *[1]For this cause only, and not by testament, was King John buried at Worcester; because that place of the realm, in those days, appeared most sure and safe, where they, who were friends to the crown, might best deliberate with themselves what was best to be done in that matter. So went they from thence to the town of Gloucester, with William Marshal, earl of the same, and there was he anointed and crowned king, by the legate Gualo, assisted by Peter, bishop of Winchester, and Jocelin, the bishop of Bath, with others who were then in the realm, and called Henry III.; and this was done on the feastful day of St. Simon and St. Jude. The court of Rome, at that time, not being too slack in these affairs, sent hither with all speed, commanding them that they should mightily stand by the young king, then being not fully ten years of age, and to defend England with armour, and his thundering curses, as holy church's patrimony, against Louis and his accomplices; and then the new pope, Honorius III., not only confirmed his legate Gualo, but also committed to his discretion all that appertained to that office of his, no appellations to the contrary admitted. The legate, being emboldened by this authority, compelled the prelates of England to be sworn true to the young king; and those that refused to take the oath, to be punished very sore. And Peter, the bishop of Winchester, was not at all behind in that commission for his part, but brought a grievous tallage upon the beneficed men and priests of his diocese, to help the king in his wars against Louis; which was not at all amiss. Such as were great beneficed priests, and might well pay, the said Gualo reserved to his own authority, and, for great sums of money, at the latter, dispensed with them. Some there were obstinate and froward, whom he degraded; some he excommunicated, and sent to Rome for their absolutions; not leaving one priest unpunished, who had taken part with Louis, having, every where, his searchers and spies to find them out.*

Immediately after the crowning of this king, he held a council at Bristol, at St. Martin's feast; where were assembled eleven bishops of England and Wales, with divers earls, barons, and knights of England, all of whom did swear fealty to the king. After homage thus done to the king, the legate Gualo interdicted Wales, because they held with the aforesaid Louis; and also the barons and all others, as many as gave help or counsel to Louis; or any others that moved or stirred any war against King Henry, the new king, he accursed them. All which notwithstanding, the said Louis did not cease, but first laid siege to the castle of Dover fifteen days. When he could not prevail there, he took the castle of Berkhamstead, and also the castle of Hertford, doing much harm in the counties, by spoiling and robbing the people, where he went: by reason whereof, the lords and commons, who held with the king, assembled themselves together to drive Louis and his men out of the land. But some of the barons, with the Frenchmen, in the mean

Berkhamstead and Hertford taken by Louis.

(1) This paragraph is from the Edition of 1563 p. 69, * I. v.—Ed.

season went to Lincoln and took the city, and held it for the use of Louis. This being known, eftsoons a great power on the king's part made thither, as earl Randulph, of Chester; William, earl Marshal; and William de Brewer, earl of Ferers, with many other lords, and gave battle to Louis and his party; so that, in conclusion, Louis lost the field; and on his side were slain the earl of Perche; Saer de Quincy, earl of Winchester; Henry de la Bohun, earl of Hertford; and Sir Robert le Fitzwater; with divers others more. Whereupon Louis, for succour, fled to London, causing the gates there to be shut and kept, waiting there for more succour out of France. As soon as the king had knowledge of this, immediately he sent to the mayor and burgesses of the city, willing them to surrender them and their city to him, as their chief lord and king; promising to grant to them again all their franchises and liberties, as in times past, and to confirm the same by his great charter and seal. In the mean time, on Bartholomew eve, Eustace, a French lord, accompanied with many other lords and nobles of France, came with a grand power, to the number of one hundred ships, to aid and assist the said Louis; who, before they arrived, were encountered upon the seas by Richard, King John's bastard son; who, having no more but eighteen ships to keep the cinque ports, set eagerly upon them, and, through God's grace, overcame them, where presently he smote off the head of Eustace: the rest of the French lords, to the number of ten, he brought with him to the land, where he imprisoned them in the castle of Dover, and slew almost all the men that came with them, and sunk their ships in the sea; only fifteen ships, say some of my stories, escaped away. Ludovic, or Louis, hearing of this loss of his ships and men, and misdoubting his own life for the great mischief he had done to the realm, sought means by Gualo, and the archbishop of Canterbury, and by other lords, to be at accord with the king. With whom, at length, it was so concluded and agreed, that, for his costs and expenses, he should have a thousand pounds of silver given. Matthew Paris speaketh of fifteen thousand marks, which he borrowed of the Londoners, that he should depart the realm, never to return into England again, neither he nor any of his.[1]

Henry III. A.D. 1216.

Lincoln also taken.

A noble victory by God's grace given to King John's son.

This being done, he, with all the other barons that took his part, was assoiled of Gualo, the legate; and thus peace being confirmed at Merton, Louis took his leave, and being brought honourably to the sea with the bishop of Canterbury, and other bishops, earls and barons, he returned home into France.

Louis, the French king's son, driven out of England.

And here, saith Gisburn, that was truly verified which was before spoken of the French king, the father of Louis. At the time the said Louis was in England, his father, the French king, demanded of his messengers coming into France, where his son was? They replied, "at Stamford." And, on his asking again, whether his son had got the castle of Dover? they said, "No." Then the father swearing by the arm of St. James: "My son," quoth he, "hath not one foot in England;" as, afterwards, well proved true.[2]

But the chief help that repelled Louis and the Frenchmen out of the realm, and that most preferred King John's son to the crown,

(1) Ex Matth. Paris. (2) Ex Gualter. Gisburn.

Henry III.

A.D. 1217.

was the singular working of God's hand, whereof mention was made before: which was through the confession of a certain gentleman of the French host (as Florilegus doth testify), who, lying sore sick at the point of death, and seeing no hope to escape, was touched in conscience for danger of his soul's health, openly to confess and utter, to the barons of England, what was the purpose of the Frenchmen to do; who had conspired and sworn together among themselves, with a privy compaction, that so soon as they subdued the land, they should thrust all the chiefs and nobles thereof into perpetual exile out of the realm, whereout they should never return again. This, coming to the ears of the barons, as is said, gave them to consider more with themselves, whereby many of them were the more willing to leave Louis, and apply to their natural king and prince; which, no less, may also be an admonition to all times and ages for Englishmen to take heed, and not to admit or to place foreign rulers in the realm, lest, perhaps, it follow that they be displaced themselves.

An admonition to Englishmen not to admit foreign rulers into the realm.

A bad wind that bloweth no man profit

After the happy departure of Louis and his Frenchmen out of the land, A.D. 1217, whereby the state of this realm, long vexed before, was now somewhat more quieted; immediately Gualo, the legate, looking to his harvest, directeth forth inquisitors through every shire to search out all such bishops, abbots, priors, canons, and secular priests, of what order or degree soever they were, who, with any succour or counsel, did either help, or else consented to Louis; for all these were exempted out of the charter of pardon and absolution made before, between the king and Louis. By reason of this, no small gain grew to the pope and the cardinal, for all such were either put out of their livings and sent up to the pope, or else were fain to fine sweetly for them. Among whom (besides a great number of other clerks, both religious and secular) was Hugo, bishop of Lincoln, who, for the recovery of his bishopric, disbursed one thousand marks to the pope, and one hundred marks to the aforesaid Gualo, the legate, who now (as Paris recordeth) by this time had gathered in a fair crop of that which he did never sow.[1]

Hugo, bishop of Lincoln, redeemeth his bishopric for one thousand marks.

Death of Pope Innocent III.

About this season, or not much before, died Pope Innocent III., in the nineteenth year of his popedom, to whose custody Frederic, the nephew of Frederic Barbarossa, being yet young, was committed by the empress his mother, of whom more shall follow (the Lord willing) hereafter. After this Innocent succeeded Pope Honorius III., who, writing to young King Henry in a special letter, exhorteth him to the love of virtue, and to the fear of God; namely, to be circumspect with what familiars and resort he acquainted himself; but principally, above all other things, he admonisheth him to reverence the church, which is the spouse of Christ, and to honour the ministers thereof, in whom Christ himself, saith he, is both honoured or despised.—And this seemeth the chiefest article of that his writing to him.[2]

A strange tale of Pope Honorius, if it be true.

Of this Pope Honorius, abbot Urspergensis (who lived in the same time) reporteth a strange wonder, more strange peradventure than credible; which is this: Honorius being priest in Rome (whose name was then Centius) and procurator to Jacinth, a cardinal; so it befel, that his master sent him abroad about Rome, to borrow and

(1) Ex Matth. Paris. in Vita Reg. Henr. III. (2) Ex Matth. Paris.

procure money for him against his journey into Spain; for Pope Clement then intended to send this Jacinth, as his legate, into Spain. As this Centius was walking by himself, all sad and solicitous to speed his master's message, there cometh to him a certain aged and reverend father, and asketh him, what cause he had to walk so heavily and carefully? To whom he answered again, and signified the occasion of the business that he then had to do. Then the old father said to him, "Go and return home again, for thy master," saith he, "shall not, at this time, go to Spain." "How so," quoth the other; "how, is that true?" "As true," saith he, "as it is certain that the pope shall die, and thy master shall be pope after him." Centius, thinking that to be unlikely, said, "He could not believe that to be true." To whom the other inferreth again, "So know this," said he, "to be as certain, as it is true that the city of Jerusalem, this day, is taken of the Saracens, and shall not be recovered again from them before the time of thy papacy." And thus speaking, he vaded suddenly away.[1] All this, saith the same author, came afterwards to pass, and was testified of the same Honorius, being pope afterwards, in his public sermons at Rome. All which I grant may be; and yet, notwithstanding, this fabulous narration may be a piece of the pope's old practices, subtilely invented, to drive men forth to Jerusalem to fight. Again, after Honorius (when he had governed ten years) followed Gregory IX., which two popes were in the time of this King Henry III. and Frederic the emperor; of whom we mind (Christ willing) further to touch, after that we shall have prosecuted more concerning the history of King Henry, and matters of England.

After that, it so pleased the merciful providence of Almighty God to work this great mercy upon the stock of King John (notwithstanding the unkind prelates, with their false prophets, had declared before, that never any of them should succeed in the throne after that king), and also unto the whole commonwealth of the realm, in delivering them from the dangerous service of Louis, and the aforesaid Frenchmen. After their departure, the following year, A.D. 1218, which was the third of this king's reign, the Archbishop Stephen Langton, and the bishops, earls, and barons, resorted to London unto the king at the Michaelmas next following, and there held a great parliament, wherein were confirmed and granted by the king, all the franchises which were made and given by King John, his father, at Runnemede, and them he confirmed and ratified by his charter; which, long time after (saith mine author) unto his days did continue, and were holden in England. For this cause, by the nobles and commons, were given and granted again unto the king two shillings for every plough-land throughout England. At this time Hubert de Burgh was made chief justice of England, of whose troubles more is to be said hereafter. This was the third year of King Henry, and the fiftieth year after the death of Thomas Becket: wherefore, the said Becket, in the year following, was taken up and shrined for a new saint made of an old rebel. Thither came such resort of people of England and of France, that the country of Kent was not sufficient to sustain them.[2] About the same time, Isabella, the king's mother, was married to the earl of March; and William

King Henry confirms the liberties granted by King John.

Thomas Becket shrined.

(1) Ex Abbate Ursperg. in Chronico. (2) Ex Historia D. Scales

Henry III. A.D. 1218. Marshal, the good earl, who was the governor of the king and the realm, died, not without great lamentation of the people of England. Then was the king committed to the government of Peter, bishop of Winchester. This noble earl left behind him five sons and five daughters. *[1] This year, which was 1218 from Christ's incarnation, Gualo made a general inquisition, nearly all the realm over, for them who did not observe the interdiction published for rebels, in the first year of this young king; for whose transgression, both to priests and monks, he appointed divers and many penalties grievous; some he suspended from their offices, and some he deprived of their benefices; so that, as well the guiltless as the guilty were compelled largely to pay.*

A.D. 1219. Aliens commanded out of England. In the next year, A.D. 1219, it was ordained and proclaimed through all the land, that all aliens and foreigners should depart the realm, and not return to the same again; such only excepted as used traffic or trade of merchandise under the king's safe conduct. This proclamation was thought chiefly to be set forth for this cause, to rid the land of Foukes de Brent, Philip de Marks, Egelardus de Ciconia, William earl Albemarle, Robert de Veteri Ponte, Brihenne de Insula, Hugo de Bailluel, Roger de Gaugi, with divers other strangers, who kept castles and holds of the king's, against his will. Of these, the beforenamed Foukes, was the principal, who fortified and held the castle of Bedford, which he had by the gift of King John, with might and strength against the king and his power, nearly the space of three months. Moreover, he went about to apprehend the king's justices, at Dunstable; but they, being warned thereof, escaped, all except Henry Braybroke, whom he imprisoned in the said castle. The king, hearing hereof, and consulting with his clergy and nobles, made his power against the same; which, after long siege and some slaughter, at length he obtained, and hanged almost all that were within, to the number of ninety-seven; which was, as Paris writeth, about the seventh or eighth year of his reign. Foukes, at that time, was in Wales; who, hearing of the taking of the castle, conveyed himself to the church of Coventry. At length, submitting himself to the king's mercy, upon consideration of his service done before to the king's father, he was committed to the custody of Eustace, bishop of London; and afterwards, being deprived of all his goods, possessions, and tenements, within the realm, was forced to perpetual banishment, never to return to England again.

Rebels against King Henry.

Here, by the way, I find it noted in Matthew Paris, that after this aforesaid Foukes had spoiled and rased the church of St. Paul in Bedford, for the building up of his castle, the abbess of Helvestue,[2] hearing thereof, caused the sword to be taken from the image of St. Paul standing in the church, so long as Foukes remained unpunished. Afterwards, hearing that he was committed to the custody of St. Paul in London, she caused the sword to be put into the hands of the image again.[3]

A.D. 1220. Henry crowned the second time at Westminster. About this year the young king was crowned the second time at Westminster, about which period began the new building of our Lady church at Westminster. Shortly after Gualo, the legate, was

(1) For this passage see Edition 1563, p. 70 * I. v.—Ed.
(2) Now called Elstow.—Ed.
(3) Matth. Paris. in Vita Hen. III.

Henry III — A.D. 1220.

called home again to Rome; for the holy father (as Matthew Paris reporteth) being sick of a spiritual dropsy, thought this Gualo (having such large occupying in England, and for so long a time) would be able somewhat to cure his disease. *[1] For that legate, by that time, had well favouredly unladen the purses of the beneficed fathers and cloisterers.* And so this Gualo returned with all his bags well stuffed, leaving Pandulph behind him to supply that bailiwick of his great grandfather, the pope. *Hugh Wells, then bishop of Lincoln, not long before, paid a thousand marks for the recovery of his office, and a hundred marks to the legate for his favour also in that case: other holy bishops and prelates, likewise, were taught, by his good example, to qualify that great heat, or dry thirst of the pope; Robert Curson at that time being a priest cardinal in Rome.*

Heat, or dry thirst of the pope

The life and acts of Pope Innocent III. are partly described before, how he intruded Stephen Langton, against the king's will, into the archbishopric of Canterbury, stirring up also sixty-four monks of the same church of Canterbury privily to work against the king. Moreover, how he did excommunicate the said king as a public enemy of the church, so long as the said king withstood his tyrannical doings, putting him and his whole kingdom under interdiction for the space of five years and three months, and at length deposing and depriving him of his sceptre, and keeping it in his own hands for five days. How he absolved his subjects from their due obedience and subjection unto him. How he gave away his kingdoms and possessions to Louis, the French king's son, commanding the said Louis to spoil him both of lands and life. Whereupon the king, being forsaken of his nobles, prelates, and commons, was forced, against his will, to submit himself, and swear obedience to the pope, paying him a yearly tribute of one thousand marks, for receiving of his kingdom again; whereby both he, and his successors after him, were vassals afterwards unto the pope. These were the apostolical acts of this holy vicar in the realm of England. Moreover, he condemned Almeric, a worthy learned man and a bishop, for a heretic, for teaching and holding against images. Also he condemned the doctrine of Joachim the abbot, of whom we spake before, for heretical. This pope brought first into the church the paying of private tithes; he ordained the receiving once a year at Easter; unto the papal decretals he added the decree, "Omnes utriusque sexus," &c.; also the reservation of the sacrament, and the going with the bell and light before the sacrament was by him appointed. In the said council of Lateran he also ordained that the canon of the mass should be received with equal authority as though it had proceeded from the apostles themselves. He brought in transubstantiation.[2]

Deeds and decrees of Pope Innocent III

Almeric and Joachim condemned

Private tithes brought in

Bell and candle

The canon of the mass authorised.

Transubstantiation.

Item, the said Innocent III. ordained that none should marry in the third degree, but only in the fourth degree, and so under.

Marriage in the third degree forbidden

The said pope stirred up Otho against Philip, the emperor, because the said Philip was elected emperor against his will; upon the occasion whereof followed much war and slaughter in Germany.

(1) For this, and the sentence next but one, see Edition 1563, p. 70, * I v.—Ed.
(2) See the decretals, titulo, I. "De Summa Trinit. et fide Catholica," cap. "firmiter credimus."

Henry III. A.D. 1220.

The pope setteth kings and emperors together by the ears.

And afterwards, against the said Otho, whom he had made emperor, he set up Frederic, king of Sicily, and caused the archbishop of Mayence to pronounce him excommunicate in all his titles, and to be deposed of his empire; for the which cause the princes of Germany did invade his bishopric, spoiling and burning his possessions. The cause why the pope so did accurse and depose him, was that the said Otho did take and occupy cities, towns, and castles, which the pope said appertained to him.

Council of Lateran.

Item, the said pope ordained, that if any princes offended one another, the correction should appertain unto the pope. In the fourth council of Lateran, A.D. 1215, were archbishops and primates sixty-one, bishops four hundred, abbots twelve, priors and conventuals eight hundred, besides other ambassadors, legates, and doctors; and of lawyers an innumerable sort, &c.

Martyrs of Alsace, to the number of one hundred burned in one day.

In the history of Hermanus Mutius, we read how, A.D. 1212, in this pope's time divers noblemen, and others in the country of Alsace, contrary to the tradition of the Romish popes, did hold that every day was free for eating of flesh, so it be done soberly. Also that they did wickedly, who restrained priests and ministers from their lawful wives; for which cause (as is in the aforesaid author) by this Pope Innocent III. and his bishops, a hundred of them in one day were burned and martyred.

Collections sent from the brethren of Milan to them of Alsace.

Nauclerus, another historian, recordeth, that at the same time there were many in the city of Milan of the said doctrine, who used to send collections unto the aforesaid saints of Alsatia.

Observant friars began.

In the chronicle of Walter Hemingford, otherwise called Gisburnensis, it is recorded, that in the days of this King John and Pope Innocent, began the two sects, or orders of friars, one called 'the preacher's order, and black friars of St. Dominic;' the other called 'the minorites of St. Francis.' The preachers of the black friars' order began from one Dominic, a Spaniard, about the parts of Toulouse, who, after he had laboured ten years in preaching against the Albigenses,[1] and such others as did hold against the church of Rome, afterward coming up to the council of Lateran with Fulco, bishop of Toulouse, desired of the aforesaid Innocent III. to have his order of preaching friars confirmed, which the pope a great while refused to grant. At length he had a dream, that the church of Lateran was ready to fall; which, when he beheld, fearing and much sorrowing thereat, cometh in this Dominic, who, with his shoulders, under-propped the church, and so preserved the building thereof from falling. And right well this dream may seem verified, for the friars have always been the chief pillars and upholders of the pope's church. Upon this, the pope, waking out of his dream, called Dominic to him, and granted his

Friars, upholders of the pope's church.

(1) It may be proved from the writings of Romish ecclesiastics, and from the canons of councils, for two hundred years before the preaching of Dominic, that religious doctrines, in opposition to the corruptions of the Latin church, prevailed very generally in the south of France, particularly in Languedoc, and in that part of it which was called Albigensium, or Pays d'Albigeois. But the name Albigenses, as applied to designate the religious body opposed to the authority of the pope, does not occur in any document before the end of the twelfth or the beginning of the thirteenth century. A letter of Innocent III., to Simon de Montfort, in 1215, is one of the earliest authentic records, which gives the appellation *Albigenses* to the unhappy people, against whom papal vengeance was directed until they were exterminated. Peter of Vaux Sernay, who had put forth his work against the Albigenses in 1218, states, that the heretics of Languedoc were usually called the heretics of Toulouse and Provence, until the strangers who assumed the Cross and took up arms against them in the year 1068, styled them generally Albigenses, the diocese of Albi being the centre of the heretical population. See "Vaissette, Histoire Générale de Languedoc," vol. iii. p. 553. "Note sur l'origine du nom d'Albigeois."—ED.

petition: and so came up this wolfish order of the Dominics. I call it 'wolfish,' for his mother, when she was great with this Dominic, dreamed that she had within her a wolf, that had a burning torch in its mouth. This dream the preachers of that order do greatly advance, and expound to their order's glory, as well as they can; nevertheless, howsoever they expound it, they can make a wolf but a wolf, and this, a wolfish order. The rule which they follow seemeth to be taken out of St. Augustine, as who should say, that Christ's rule were not enough to make a christian man. Their profession standeth upon three principal points, as thus described: "Having charity, holding humility, and possessing wilful poverty."[1] Their habit and clothing is black.

Henry III. A.D. 1220.

Minorite friars descended from St. Francis.

The order of the minors or minorite friars descended from one Francis, an Italian of the city of Assisium. This Assisian ass, who I suppose was some simple and rude idiot, hearing, upon a time, how Christ sent forth his disciples to preach, thought to imitate the same in himself and his disciples, and so left off his shoes: he had but one coat, and that of coarse cloth. Instead of a latchet to his shoe, and of a girdle, he took about him a hempen cord, and so he apparelled his disciples; teaching them to fulfil (for so he speaketh) the perfection of the gospel, to apprehend poverty, and to walk in the way of holy simplicity. He left in writing, to his disciples and followers, his rule, which he called "Regulam Evangelicam," the rule of the gospel. As though the gospel of Christ were not a sufficient rule to all christian men, but it must take its perfection of frantic Francis. And yet, for all that great presumption of this Francis, and notwithstanding this his rule, sounding to the derogation of Christ's gospel, he was confirmed by this Pope Innocent. Yea, and such fools this Francis found abroad, that, not only he had followers of his doltish religion, both of the nobles and unnobles of Rome, but also some there were, who builded mansions for him and his friars. This Francis, as he was superstitious in casting all things from him, as his girdle, girding a cord about him; so, in outward chastising of himself, so strait he was to his flesh, leaving the ordinary remedy appointed by God, that in the winter season he covered his body with ice and snow. He called poverty his Lady; he kept nothing overnight. So desirous he was of martyrdom, that he went to Syria to the Saladin, who received him honourably; whereby it may be thought, that surely he told not the truth, as St. John Baptist did in Herod's house, for truth is seldom welcome in courts, and in the world. But it is hard to make a martyr of him who is no true confessor. I will here pass over the fable, how Christ and his saints did mark him with five wounds. These Franciscan or begging friars, although they were all under one rule and clothing of St. Francis, yet they be divided into many sects and orders; some go on treen shoes or pattens, some barefooted; some are regular Franciscans or observants, some minors or minorites, others be called 'minimi,' others of the gospel, others 'de caputio.' They all differ in many things, but accord in superstition and hypocrisy. And forasmuch as we have here entered into the matter of these two orders of friars, by the occasion hereof, I thought a little, by the way, to digress from our story, in reciting the

Divers sects of Franciscans.

(1) "Charitatem habentes, humilitatem servantes, et paupertatem voluntariam possidentes."

Henry III. — A.D. 1220

whole catalogue or rabblement of monks, friars, and nuns, of all sects, rules and orders, set up and confirmed by the pope. The names of whom here in order of the alphabet follow.

The Rabblement of Religious Orders.

	A.D.
Augustinians, the first order.	
Ambrosians, two sorts	490
Antony's Heremites	324
Austin's Heremites	498
Austin's Observants	490
Armenians' sect.	
Ammonites and Moabites.	
Basilius' order	384
Benet's order	524
Bernardus' order	1120
Barefooted Friars	1222
Bridget's order	1370
Beghearts, or White Spirits	1399
Brethren of Jerusalem	1103
Brethren of St John de civitate, Black Friars	1220
Brethren of wilful Poverty.	
Cluniacensis order	913
Canons of St Augustine	1080
Charterhouse order	1086
Cisterciensis order	1098
Crossbearers, or Crossed Friars	1216
Carmelites or White Friars	1212
Clare's order	1225
Celestine's order	1297
Camaldulensis order	950
Cross-starred Brethren.	
Constantinopolitanish order	
Crossbearers	
Chapter Monks.	
Dutch order	1216
Dominic Black Friars	1220
Franciscans	1224
Grandmontensis order	1076
Gregorian order	594
George's order	1407
Gulielmites	1246
Gerundinensis order.	
Galilei, or Galileans.	
Heremites.	
Helen's brethren. Humiliati	1166
Hospital Brethren.	
Holy Ghost order.	
Jerom's orders, two sorts	1412
John's Heremites.	
Justin's order	1432
John's order, Joannites, or Knights of the Rhodes	380, 1308
Injesuati	1365
Jerome's Heremites	490

	A.D.
Joseph's order	
Jacobites' sect.	
James's Brethren order	
James's Brethren with the Sword.	
Indians' order.	
Katharine of Sens's order	1455
Keyedmonks, Knights of Rhodes.	
Lazarites, or Mary Magdalenes, our Lady Brethren	1034
Lords of Hungary.	
Minorites, which be divided into Conventuales, Observantes, Reformate, Collectane, De Caputio, De Evangelio, Amedes, Clarini, and others	
Minors, or Minorites	1224
Mary's Servants	1304
Monks of Mount Olivet	1046
Marovinies sect	
Minorites' sect.	
Monachi and Monachæ.	
Morbonei and Meresti	
Menelaish and Jasonish sect.	
New Canons of St. Austin	1430
Nestorini.	
Nalheart Brethren.	
New Order of our Lady.	
Nazaræi.	
Paul's Heremites	345
Præmonstratensis order	1119
Preacher order, or Black Friars	
Peter the Apostle's order	1409
Purgatory Brethren.	
Rechabites.	
Sarrabites.	
Sambonites	1199
Scourgers, the first sect	1266
Soldiers of Jesus Christ	1323
Scopenites, or St. Salvator's order,	1367
Specularii, or the Glass order.	
Sepulchre's order.	
Sheer order.	
Swerd's order.	
Starred Monks.	
Starred Friars.	
Sclavony order.	

	A. D.
Scourgers, the second sect, called Ninevites.	
Stool Brethren.	
Scotland Brethren order.	
Sicarii.	
St. Sophy's order.	
Templar Lords	1110
Templar Knights	1120

	A. D.
The Vale of Josaphat's order.	
Vallis Umbrosæ	1400
Waldensis' sect.[1]	
Wentzelaus' order.	
Wilhelmer order.	
White Monks of Mount Olivet	1406
Zelotes' order.	

Henry III. A. D. 1220.

Thus hast thou, if thou please, gentle reader, the means of knowing what orders and what sects of religion have been set up by the pope; the catalogue and number of them all, so far as we could search them out, not only in books printed of late in Germany, namely, by the reverend father Martin Luther; but also conferred with another English book which came to our hands, containing the same like notes of ancient antiquity, the number of which rabblement of religious persons came to a hundred and one. Now as I have reckoned up the names and varieties of these prodigious sects, it cometh to mind consequently to refer to the prophecy of Hildegard, as well against the whole rout of Romish prelates, and the fall of that church, as especially against the begging friars and such other unprofitable bellies of the church. This Hildegard is holden, of the papists themselves, to be a great prophetess, whose prophecy proceedeth in this manner; first, against the priests and prelates of the Romish church, as followeth.

THE PROPHECY OF HILDEGARD OF THE RUIN OF ROME, AND AGAINST THE BEGGING FRIARS.[2]

Hildegard, a nun, and, as many judged, a prophetess, lived A. D. 1146. In her prophecies she doth most grievously reprehend, not only the wicked and abominable life of the spiritual papists, but also the contempt of the ecclesiastical office, and the horrible destruction of the church of Rome. In a certain place she hath these words: "And now is the law neglected among the spiritual people, who neglect to teach and to do good things; the masters likewise, and the prelates do sleep, despising justice and laying it aside." In a certain vision the church appeared to her in the shape of a woman, complaining that the priests had bewrayed her face with dust, and rent her coat, &c., and that they did not shine over the people, either in doctrine or in example of life; but rather the contrary, and that they have driven the innocent lamb from them. She said moreover, "That all

(1) For want of an accurate distinction between different sects, and different religious orders, Foxe has fallen into the error of placing "Waldensis' sect" amongst what he calls a "rabble of popish religious orders." In the year 1207, an enthusiast named Durand of Osca, or Huesca, obtained a license from Pope Innocent III., for the establishment of a fraternity to be called "The Order, or Society, of Poor Catholics." Durand, afterwards becoming an object of suspicion to the bishop of Languedoc, was accused of heresy, and he and his companions were then stigmatised with the name, then commonly given to all heretics, "Waldenses." Now the Waldenses having been previously confounded with the "Poor Men of Lyons," the new order of "Poor Catholics" fell under the same designation. Hence the mistake of our martyrologist, who, copying inadvertently from some account of monastic orders (perhaps from Abbas Wisbergensis in his chronicle of the year 1212, where the same error appears), adds "Waldensis' sect" to his list of "rabblement." See Guiliélm. de Podio Laur: c. 8, in Recueil des Historiens des Gaules et de la France, vol. xix. p. 200. And Vaissette His. gen. de Languedoc, vol. iii. p. 147: and compare with Chron. Abbat. Ursberg. in Bin. Concil. vol. x. col. 1533.—Ed.

(2) This prophecy has been collated with the Edition of 1563, p. 72. Some words are introduced from that edition, which is superior to any later ones, in fredom of style and force of language, —Ed.

Henry III. A.D. 1220.

ecclesiastical order did, every day, become worse and worse, and that priests did not teach, but destroy the law of God; and for these horrible crimes and impieties, she threateneth and prophesieth unto them God's most heavy wrath and displeasure, and doleful punishments." There is no cause why the spiritual papists should flatter themselves upon this, that she promised again to the ministers of the church those good things to follow, like as Johannes de Rupe scissa doth, and other such like prophets; for they say, it will come to pass, that they must repent before the times be amended. By which thing, undoubtedly, they mean the godly ministers in the reformed churches, who, for the most part, were of the spiritual number, and yet did forsake the dishonest life and those wicked idolatries. Now, whereas the priests and monks, that is, the whole rabble and spiritualty, do account Hildegard for a true prophetess, they ought to consider that by her they are more severely accused, not as by a woman, but as by God himself. And I pray you, what abomination, impiety, and idolatry have not been committed, since that time, by the spiritualty? I will note here a certain prophecy of hers, taken out of the common places of Henry Token, because we see it manifestly fulfilled in our time. She prophesieth of the reformation of religion, and saith that it shall be most godly.

A prophecy of the decay of the Romish church.

"Then shall the crown of apostolical honour be divided, because there shall be found no religion among the apostolical order, and for that cause shall they despise the dignity of that name, and shall set over them other men and other archbishops; insomuch, that the apostolic see of that time (by the diminution of his honour) shall scarce have Rome, and a few other countries thereabout, under his crown. And these things shall partly come to pass by incursion of wars, and partly, also, by a common council and consent of the spiritual and secular persons. Then shall justice flourish, so that, in those days, men shall honestly apply themselves to the ancient customs and discipline of ancient men, and shall observe them as the ancient men did." The gloss agreeth therewith.

These things thus premised, now will we come to the prophecy of the aforesaid Hildegard, concerning the begging friars above mentioned, reciting her words, not only as they are in a book printed lately in Germany, but also, as myself have seen and read, and still have the same to show written in old parchment leaves, agreeing to the same book word for word, in such sort, as the thing itself most evidently declareth a great iniquity of time. The words of her prophecy be these:—

Hildegard prophesying of friars and monks.

In those days shall arise a senseless people, proud, greedy, without faith, and subtle, that shall eat the sins of the people; holding a certain order of foolish devotion under the dissimulated cloak of beggary, preferring themselves above all others by their feigned devotion; arrogant in understanding, and pretending holiness, walking without blushing or the fear of God, in inventing many new mischiefs strong and sturdy. But this order shall be accursed of all wise men, and Christ's faithful. They shall cease from all labour, and give themselves over unto idleness, choosing rather to live through flattery and begging. Moreover they shall altogether study how they may perversely resist the teachers of the truth, and, with the mighty, kill them; how to seduce and deceive the nobility, for the necessity of their living, and pleasures of this world: for the devil will graft in them four principal vices; that is to say, flattery envy, hypocrisy, and backbiting. Flattery, that they may have large gifts given them. Envy, when they see gifts given to others, and not to them. Hypocrisy, that by false dissimulation they may please men. Backbiting, that they may extol and commend themselves, and dispraise others, for the praise of men, and seducing of the simple. Also they shall instantly preach, but without devotion or example of the martyrs; and shall report evil of secular princes, taking away the sacraments of the church from the true pastors, receiving alms of the poor, diseased, and miserable; and also associating themselves with the common people, having familiarity with women, instructing them how they may deceive their husbands and friends by their flattery and deceitful words, and rob their husbands to give it unto them, for they will take all these stolen and evil-gotten goods, and say, "Give it unto us, and we will pray for you;" so that they, being curious to hide other men's faults, do utterly forget their own. And alas, they will receive all things of rovers, pickers, spoilers, thieves, and robbers; sacrilegious persons, usurers, and adulterers; heretics, schismatics, apostates,[1] noblemen, perjurers, merchants, false judges, soldiers, tyrants, princes living contrary to the law, and of many perverse and wicked men, following the persuasion of the devil, the sweetness of sin, a delicate and transitory life, and satiety even unto eternal damnation.

All these things shall manifestly appear in them unto all people, and they, day by day, shall wax more wicked and hard-hearted: and when their wickedness and deceits shall be found out, then shall their gifts cease, and they shall go about their houses hungry, and as mad dogs looking down upon the earth, and drawing in their necks as doves,[2] that they might be satisfied with bread. Then shall the people cry out upon them: "Woe be unto you, ye miserable children of sorrow! the world hath seduced you, and the devil hath snaffled your mouths; your flesh is frail, and your hearts without savour; your minds have been unstedfast, and your eyes delighted in much vanity and folly; your dainty bellies desire delicate meats; your feet are swift to run unto mischief. Remember when you were apparently blessed, yet envious; poor in sight, but rich; simple to see to, but mighty flatterers, unfaithful betrayers, perverse detractors, holy hypocrites, subverters of the truth, overmuch upright, proud, shameless, unstedfast teachers, delicate martyrs, confessors for gain; meek, but slanderers; religious, but covetous; humble, but proud; pitiful, but hard-hearted liars; pleasant flatterers, peacemakers, persecutors, oppressors of the poor, bringing in new sects newly invented of yourselves; merciful thought, but found wicked; lovers of the world, sellers of pardons, spoilers of benefices, unprofitable orators,[3] seditious conspirators, drunkards, desirers of honours, maintainers of mischief,[4] robbers of the world, unsatiable preachers, men-pleasers, seducers of women, and sowers of discord; of whom Moses, the glorious prophet, spake very well in his song, "A people without counsel or understanding: would to God they did know and understand, and foresee the latter end to come." You have builded up on high; and when you could ascend no higher, then did you fall, even as Simon Magus, whom God overthrew, and did strike with a cruel plague; so you, likewise, through your false doctrine, naughtiness, lies, detractions and wickedness, are come to ruin. And the people shall say unto them, "Go, ye teachers of wickedness, subverters of the truth, brethren of the Shunamite, fathers of heretical pravity,[5] false apostles, which have feigned yourselves to follow the life of the apostles, and yet ye have not followed their steps, not in the least: ye sons of iniquity, we will not follow the knowledge of your ways; for pride and presumption hath deceived you, and insatiable concupiscence hath subverted your erroneous hearts." And when you would ascend higher than was meet or comely for you, by the just judgment of God, you are fallen back into perpetual opprobrium and shame

This Hildegard, whose prophecy we have mentioned, lived about A.D. 1146, as we read in Chronico Martini.

(1) A coarse epithet is here omitted; in Latin, "scorta et lenæ."—Ed.
(2) "Doves"—"Turtles," Edition 1563.—Ed. (3) "Orators," "makers of prayer," Idem.
(4) "Maintainers," &c. "curious in men's faults," Idem.
(5) "Heretical pravity," "Heresies," Idem.

Henry III.

A.D. 1220.

Cross-bearing friars.

About the time that these Franciscans and Dominic Friars, above mentioned, began, sprang up also the Cross-bearers,[1] or Crutched Friars, taking their original and occasion from Innocent III.; which Innocent raised up an army (signed with a cross on their breast) to fight against the Albigenses, whom the pope and his sect accounted for heretics, about the parts of Toulouse. What these Albigenses were, it cannot be well gathered by the old popish histories: for if there were any who did hold, teach, or maintain against the pope, or his papal pride, or withstand and gainsay his beggarly traditions, rites, and religions, &c. the historians of that time, in writing of them, do, for the most part, so deprave and misreport them (suppressing the truth of their articles), that they make them and paint them forth to be worse than Turks and infidels. This, as I suppose, caused Matthew Paris, and others of that sort, to write so of them as they did: otherwise it is to be thought (and so I find in some records) that the opinions of the said Albigenses were sound enough, holding and professing nothing else, but against the wanton wealth, pride, and tyranny of the prelates, denying the pope's authority to have ground of the Scriptures: neither could they away with their ceremonies and traditions, as images, pardons, purgatory of the Romish church, calling them, as some say, blasphemous occupyings, &c. Of these Albigenses were slain, at times, and burned, a great multitude, by means of the pope, and Simon Ecclesiasticus, with others more. It seemeth that these Albigenses were chiefly abhorred of the pope because they set up a contrary pope against him about the coasts of Burgarorum: for the which cause the bishop called Portinensis, being the pope's legate in those quarters, writeth to the archbishop of Rouen, and other bishops, as hereunder written.[2]

(1) The Albigenses have been represented by some authors under the most revolting colours, and have been accused of every crime against religion, morality, and social order. But it is a singular testimony in their favour, that after the people, designated by this name, had continued to attract public notice by their opposition to the church of Rome, for many years, and when Pope Innocent III. first resolved to put them down by fire and sword, by stirring up a crusade against them, he denounced them as enemies to the orthodox faith, and inveterate heretics, but made no allusion whatever to their moral turpitude; on the contrary, he spoke of their professed rectitude and virtue. Innocent was elected pope in the beginning of the year 1198. In the April of that year he addressed a letter to the archbishop of Auch, inviting him to pursue the heretics of Gascony and the neighbouring regions with the temporal sword—"et etiam si necesse fuerit per principes et populum eosdem facias virtute malerialis gladii coerceri,"—but not a word against their moral conduct. In the same month and year Innocent sent another letter to the archbishop of Aix, and letters also to all the bishops and archbishops of the south of France, to awaken their zeal against the innumerable adversaries of the Romish church ("innumeros populos") who peopled their dioceses. In these we have the following description of the objects of his displeasure: "Qui, iniquitatem suam justitiæ specie palliantes, ut salutentur in foro, et vocentur ab hominibus Rabbi, et soli recta sapere ac justè vivere videantur, magisterium ecclesiæ Romanæ refugiunt," &c. See Recueil des Hist. des Gaules, vol. xix. p. 350; and Epist. Innocentii. III. lib. i. Ep. 81, 94.—Ed.

(2) *A Letter of the Bishop Portinensis concerning the Albigenses.*—"Venerabilibus patribus, Dei gratia Rothomagensi archiepiscopo et ejus suffraganeis episcopis; salutem in Domino Jesu Christo. Dum pro sponsa veri crucifixi vestrum cogimur auxilium implorare, potius compellimur lacerari singultibus et plorare. Ecce quod vidimus loquimur, et quod scimus testificamur. Ille homo perditus, qui extollitur super omne quod colitur, aut dicitur Deus, jam habet perfidiæ suæ preambulum hæresiarcham, quem hæretici Albigenses papam suum nominant, habitantem finibus Burgarorum et Croaticæ, et Dalmatiæ, juxta Hungariorum nationem. Ad eum confluunt hæretici Albigenses, ut ad eorum consulta respondeat. Et enim de Carcasona oriundus vices illius antipapæ gerens Bartholomæus, hæreticorum episcopus, funestam ei exhibendo reverentiam, sedem et locum concessit in villa quæ Porlos appellatur, et seipsum transtulit in partes Tholosanas. Iste Bartholomæus, in literarum suarum undique discurrentium tenore, se in primo salutationis alloquio intitulat in hunc modum: Bartholomæus servus servorum, M. sanctæ fidei salutem. Ipse etiam inter alias enormitates creat episcopos, et ecclesias perfide ordinare contendit. Rogamus igitur attentius, et per aspersionem sanguinis Jesu Christi, et propensius obsecramus, authoritate domini papæ qua fungimur, in hac parte districte præcipientes, quatenus veniatis Senonas in oct. apostolorum Petri et Pauli proxime futuris, ubi et alii prælati Franciæ, favente Domino congregabuntur, parati consilium dare in negotio prædicto, et cum aliis qui ibidem aderunt providere super negotio Albigensi. Alioqui inobedientiam vestram domino papæ curabimus significari. Datum apud Plauvium, 6, nonas Julii."

Forasmuch as mention is here made of these superstitious sects of friars, and such other beggarly religions, it might seem not altogether impertinent, being moved by the occasion hereof, as I have done in Hildegard before, so now to annex also to the same, a certain other ancient treatise compiled by Geoffery Chaucer, by the way of a dialogue or questions, moved in the person of a certain uplandish and simple ploughman of the country. That treatise, for the same, the author entitled Jack Upland, wherein is to be seen and noted, to all the world, the blind ignorance and variable discord of these irreligious religions, how rude and unskilful they are in matters and principles of our christian institution, as by the contents of this present dialogue appeareth; the words whereof in the same old English wherein first it was set forth, in this wise do proceed. Wherein also thou mayest see, that it is no new thing, that their blasphemous doings have by divers good men, in old time been detected, as there are many and divers other old books to show.

Henry III

A.D. 1220

The blind ignorance of friars described

A Treatise of Geoffery Chawcer, intituled, Jacke Upland.

I, Jacke Upland, make my mone to very God and to all true in Christ, that antichrist and his disciples (by colour of holines) walking and deceauing Christes church by many false figures, were through (by antechrist and hys) many vertues bene transposed to vices.

The fruits of antichrist

But the fellest folke that euer antechrist found, bene last brought into the church and in a wonder wise, for they bene of diuers sectes of antechrist, sowne of diuers countreys and kindreds. And all men knowne well, that they be not obedient to byshops, ne liege men to kinges. neyther they tyllen, ne sowne, weden, ne repen, woode, corne, ne grasse, neither nothing that man should helpe · but onely themselues their lyues to sustayne. And these men han all maner power of God as they seyn in heuyn and in yerth, to sell heuyn and hell to whom that them liketh, and these wretches wete neuer where to bene themselfes.

Antichrist's brood

And therefore (frere) if thine order and rules bene grounded on Goddys law, tell thou me, Jacke Upland, that I aske of thee, and if thou be, or thinkest to be, on Christes side, keepe thy paciens.

Patience proveth master trier

Saint Paule teacheth, that all our deedes should be do in charite, and els it is nought worth, but displeasing to God and harme to our owne soules And for that freres challenge to be greatest clerkes of the churche, and next following Christ in liuing: men should for charite axe them some questions, and praye them to grounde theyr aunsweres in reason and in holy write, for els their aunswere woulde nought bee worth, be it florished neuer so fayre. and as methinke men might skilfully axe thus of a frere.—

The friar must answer according to God's word

1. Frere, how many orders be in erth, and which is the perfitest order? Of what order art thou? who made thyne order? What is thy rule? Is there any perfecter rule then Christ himselfe made? If Christes rule be most perfite, why rulest thou thee not therafter? Without more why, shall a frere be more punished if he breke the rule that hys patron made, then if he breke the heestes that God hymselfe made?

Friars may better break God's law than man's law

2. Approueth Christ any more religions then one, that S. James speaketh of? If he approueth no more, why hast thou left his rule and takest an other? Why is a frere apostata that leuyth his order and taketh an other sect, sith there is but one religion of Christ?

There is but one religion

3. Why be ye wedded faster to your habites then a man is to hys wife? For a man may leaue his wife for a yeare or two as many men done: and if you leue your abite a quarter of a yeare, ye should beholden apostatase.

The friar more bound to his habit than the man to his wife

4. Makith your habite you men of religion or no? If it do, then euer as it wereth, your religion wereth, and after that your habite is better, your religion is better, and when ye haue liggin it beside, then lig ye your religion beside

If the habit make

Henry III. A.D. 1220.

you, and byn ye apostatase: why bye ye you so precious clothes? sith no man seekith such but for vayne glory, as S. Gregory sayth.

What betokeneth your great hood, your scaplery, your knotted girdle, and your wide cope?

5. Why use ye all one colour, more then other christen men do? What betokeneth that ye bene clothed all in one maner of clothing?

the friar religious, as his habit weareth, so doth his religion. Holiness of all hypocrites consisteth in clothing, and outward appearance.

If ye say, it betokenith loue and charite, certes then ye be oft hipocrites, when any of you hateth other, and in that ye woole be sayd holy by your clothing.

Why may not a frere weare cloathing of an other sect of freres, sith holiness stondeth not in the clothes?

6. Why hold ye silence in one house more then an other, sith men ought ouer all to speke the good and leaue the euil?

Why eate you flesh in one house more then in an other? if your rule and your order be perfite, and the patron that made it?

7. Why gete ye your dispensations to haue it more esy? Certes, other it seemeth that ye be unperfite, or he that made it so hard, that ye may not hold it; And seker, if ye holde not the rule of your patrons, ye be not then her freres, and so ye lye upon your selues.

All friars found liars.

8. Why make ye you as dede men when ye be professed, and yet ye be not dede, but more quicke beggers then ye were before? And it seemeth euil a dede man to goe about and begge.

Friars be dead men and quick beggars.

9. Why will ye not suffer your nouices heare your councels in your chapter house ere that they haue bene professed, if your counsels byn true and after Gods law?

10. Why make ye you so costly houses to dwell in? sith Christ did not so, and dede men should haue but graues, as falleth it to dead men, and yet ye haue more courtes then many lordes of England: for ye mowe wenden through the realme, and each night well nigh lyg in your owne courts, and so mow but right few lordes do.

Graves become dead men, and not courtly houses.

11. Why hyre ye to ferme your limitors, geuing therefore ech yeare a certayne rent, and will not suffer one in an others limitation, right as ye were your selfes lordes of countreys?

Why be ye not under your bishops visitations, and liege men to our king?

Friars not the king's liegemen.

Why axe ye no letters of brether heds of other mens prayers, as ye desire that other men shoulde aske letters of you?

Friars need on men's prayers.

If your letters be good, why graunt ye them not generally to all maner of men for the more charitie?

12. Mow ye make any man more perfite brother for your prayers then God hath by our beleeue? By our baptisme and his own graunt? If ye mow, certes then ye be aboue God.

Friars greater and better than God.

Why make ye men beleue that your golden trentall song of you, to take therefore ten shillings, or at the least five shillings, wole bring soules out of hel, or out of purgatory? If this be soth, certes ye might bring al soules out of payne, and that wull ye nought, and then ye be out of charitie.

O uncharitable friars!

13. Why make ye men beleue that he that is buryed in your habite shall neuer come in hell, and ye wyte not of your selfe whether ye shall to hell or no? and if this were sothe, ye shuld sell your hye houses to make many habites for to saue many mens soules.

14. Why steale ye mens children for to make hem of your sect, sith that theft is against Gods hestes, and sith your sect is not perfite? ye know not whether the rule that ye bynde hym to, be best for him or worst.

Friars steal men's children.

15. Why underneme ye not your brethren for their trespas after the law of the gospell, sith that underneming is the best that may be? But ye put them in prison oft when they do after God's law, and by Saint Augustines rule, if anye did amisse and would not amend him, ye should put hym from you.

16. Why couete ye shrifte and burying of other mens parishens, and none other sacrament that falleth to christen folke?

Shrift and burials were more gainful than the ministering of the sacraments.

Why bussy yee not to here to shrift of pore folk as wel as of rich lords and ladyes? sith they mowe haue more plenty of shrift fathers then poore folke mow.

Why say ye not the gospell in howses of bededred men, as ye do in riche mens that mow go to churche and heare the gospell?

Why couete you not to bury poore folke among you? sith that they bene most holy (as ye fayne that yee beene for your pouerty.)

17. Why will ye not be at her diriges as ye have bene at rich mens? sithe God prayseth him more then he doth other men.

What is thy prayer worth? sithe thou wilt take therefore, for of all chapmen ye nede to be most wise for dread of simonie.

What cause hast thou that thou wilt not preach the gospell, as God sayth that thou shouldst? sith it is the best lore and also our beleue.

Why be ye evil apayd that secular priests shuld preach the gospell? sith God himselfe hath bodden hem.

18. Why hate ye the gospell to be preached, sithe ye be so much hold therto? For ye wyn more by yere with 'In Principio,' then with all the rules that euer your patrons made, and in this minstrels bene better then ye, for they contrarien not to the mirthis that they maken, but ye contrarien the gospell both in word and deede.

19. Frere, when thou receuest a peny for to say a Masse, whether sellest thou Gods body for that peny, or thy prayer, or else thy trauell? If thou sayest thou wolt not trauell for to say the mass, but for the peny, that certes if this be soth, then thou louest to little mede for thy soule, and if thou sellest Gods body, other thy prayer, then it is very simonie, and art become a chapman worse then Judas that solde it for thirty pence.

20. Why writest thou her names in thy tables that yeueth the mony? sith God knoweth all thing: for it seemeth by thy writing, that God would not reward him, but thou write in thy tables; God wold els forgetten it.

Why bearist thou God in honde and sclaundrest hym that he begged for hys meet? sithe he was Lorde ouer all, for then had he bene unwyse to haue begged, and haue no neede thereto?

Frere, after what law rulest thou thee? Where findest thou in Gods law that thou shouldest thus beg?

21. What maner men needeth for to beg?

For whom oweth such men to beg?

Why beggest thou so for thy brethren?

If thou sayest, for they haue neede, then thou doest it for the more perfection, or els for the lest, or els for the meane. If it be the most perfection of all, then should al thy brethren do so, and then no man needed to beg but for himselfe, for so should no man beg but him neded. And if it be the lest perfection, why louest thou then other men more then thy self? For so thou art not wel in charitie, sith thou shouldst seeke the more perfection after thy power, liuing thy selfe most after God. And thus leauing that imperfection thou shouldest not so beg for them. And if it is a good meane thus to beg as thou doest, then should no man do so, but they bene in this good meane, and yet suche a meane graunted to you may neuer be grounded on Gods law; for then both lerid and lewd that bene in meane degre of this world, shoulde goe about and beg as ye do. And if all shoulde doe so, certes well nigh all the world should goe about and beg as ye done, and so should there be ten beggers against one yeuer.

Why procurest thou men to yeue thee their almes, and sayest it is so needefull, and thou wilt not thyselfe wynne thee that mede?

22. Why wilt not thou beg for poore bedred men that bene poorer then any of youe sect? That liggen and mow not goe about to helpe himselfes, sith we be all brethren in God, and that bretherhed passeth any other that ye or any man coulde make, and where most neede were, there were most perfection, either els ye hold them not your pure brethren, but worse, but then ye be unperfit in your begging.

Why make ye so many maysters among you? sithe it is agaynst the teaching of Christ and his apostle?

23. Whose bene all your rich courtes that ye han, and all your rich juells? sithe ye seyne that ye han nought ne in proper ne in common. If ye sayne they bene the popes? why gether ye then of poore men and lords so much out of the kinges hand to make your pope riche? And sithe ye sayne that it is great perfection to have nought in proper ne in commen? why be ye so fast about to make the pope that is your father rich, and put on him imperfection? sithen ye sayne that your goodes bene all hys, and he should by reason be the most perfite man, it seemeth openlich that ye ben cursed children so to

Poor men have no souls saith my fellow friar.

These be they that will not enter themselves, nor suffer other men that would.

The friar getteth by 'In Principio,' and yet hateth the gospel.

Judas, for thirty pence, but the priest and friar for fourpence, selleth Christ.

The friar writeth because God forgetteth.

Better to labour and give, than to loiter and beg, Master Friar.

Friars beg from all men to make the pope rich.

sclaunder your father and make hym imperfect And if ye sayne that the goodes be yours, then do ye ayenst your rule, and if it be not ayenst your rule, then might ye haue both plough and cart, and labour as other good men done, and not so to beg by losengery, and idle as ye done. If ye say that it is more perfection to beg, then to trauell or to worch with your hand, why preach ye not openly and teach all men to doe so? sithe it is the best and most perfite life to the helpe of their soules, as ye make children to beg that might haue bene riche heyres.

If it be imperfection to be rich, why do the friars desire to make the pope perfect?

Why make ye not your festes to poore men and yeueth hem yeftes, as ye done to the rich? sith poore men han more nede then the rich.

What betokeneth that ye go tweyne and tweyne together? If ye be out of charitie, ye accord not in soule.

Why beg ye and take salaries thereto more then other priestes? sith he that most taketh, most charge hath

If Francis' order be contrary to Christ's testament, then is Francis accursed

24. Why hold ye not S. Fraunces rule and his testament? sith Fraunces sayth, that God shewed him this liuing and this rule and certes if it were Gods will, the pope might not fordoe it, or els Fraunces was a lyer that sayd on this wise. And but this testament that he made accorde with Gods will, or else erred he is a lyer that were out of charitie and as the law saith, he is cursed that letteth the rightfull last will of a dead man. And this testament is the last will of Fraunces that is a dead man, it seemeth therefore that all his freres bene cursed

He that is more holy in hand than in heart, is false to God

25 Why will you not touch no coyned mony with the crosse, ne with the kings hed, as ye done other juels both of gold and siluer? Certes if ye despise the crosse or the kinges hed, then ye be worthy to be despised of God and the king, and sith ye will receiue mony in your harts, and not with your handes, it seemeth that ye holde more holines in your hands then in your hartes, and then be false to God

A subject to exempt himself from the laws of his prince smelleth of treason

26 Why haue ye exempt you from our kinges lawes and visiting of our byshops more then other christen men that liuen in this realm, if ye be not gilty of traitory to our realme, or trespassors to our byshops? But ye will haue the kinges lawes for the trespasse do to you, and ye wyll haue power of other byshops more then other priestes, and also haue leaue to prison your brethren, as lordes in your courtes, more then other folkes han, that bene the kinges liege men.

Friars are forced to be thieves

27. Why shall some sect of your freres pay eche a yeare a certayne to her generall prouinciall or minister, or els to her soueraignes? but if he steale a certayne number of children (as some men sayne) and certes if this be sothe, then ye be constreined upon a certayne payne to do theft agaynst Gods commandment, "Non furtum facies"

Works of supererogation.

28 Why be ye so hardy to graunt by letters of fraternitie to men and women, that they shall haue part and merite of all your good dedes, and ye witten neuer whether God be apayd with your dedes because of your sinne? Also ye witten neuer whether that man or woman be in state to be saued or damned, then shall he haue no merite in heuyn for hys owne dedes ne for none other mans And all were it so, that he should haue part of your good dedes: yet shuld he haue no more then God woulde geue him after that he were worthy, and so mich shall ech man haue of Gods yeft without your limitation. But if ye will say that ye bene Gods fellowes, and that he may not doe without your assent, then be ye blasphemers to God.

God is the limiter of meed and reward, and not the friar

Friars will not pray, but for them that be of their fraternity

29. What betokeneth that ye haue ordeyned, that when such one as ye haue made your brother or sister, and hath a letter of your seale, that letter mought be brought in your holy chapter and there be rad, or els ye will not praye for him And but ye willen praye especially for all other that were not made your brethren or sistren, then were ye not in right charitie, for that ought to be commen, and namely in ghostly thinges.

30. Frere, what charitie is this, to ouercharge the people by mighty begging under color of preaching or praying, or masses singing? sith holy write biddeth not thus, but euen the contrary. for all such ghostly dedes shuld be done freely, as God yeueth them freely?

31 Frere, what charitie is this to beguile children or they commen to discretion, and bynde hym to your orders that byn not grounded in Gods law against her frendes will? sithen by this folly bene many apostataes, both in wil and dede,

and many bene apostataes in her will during al her lyfe, that would gladly be discharged if they wist how, and so many bene apostataes that shoulden in other states haue byn true men.

32. Frere, what charitie is this, to make so many freres in euery country to the charge of the people, sith persons and vicares alone, ye secular priests alone, ye monks and chanons alone, with bishops aboue them, were inough to the church to doe priestes office. And to adde moe then inough is a foule error, and great charge to the people, and this openly agaynst Gods will that ordayned all thinges to be done in weight, number, and measure. And Christ himselfe was apayd with twelve apostles and a few disciples, to preach and to doe priestes office to all the whole worlde, then was it better do then is now at this tyme by a thousand dele. And right so as foure fingers with a thumbe in a mans hand helpeth a man to worch, and double number of fingers in one hand should let hym more, and so the more number that there were passing the measure of Gods ordinaunce, the more were a man letted to worke: Right so (as it seemeth) it is of these new orders that ben added to the church without grounde of holy write and Gods ordinaunce.

Friars do make apostates. The number of friars superfluous, and as necessary as ten fingers on one hand.

33. Frere, what charitie is this to the people, to lye and say that ye follow Christ in pouerty more then other men done, and yet in curious and costly howsing, and fine and precious clothing, and delicious and liking feeding, and in treasure and iewels, and rich ornamentes, freres passen lordes and other rich worldly men, and soonest they should bryng her cause about (be it neuer so costly) though Gods la w be put abacke.

See how fast the friar followeth Christ in his poverty.

34. Frere, what charitie is this, to gather up the books of holy write, and put hem in treasory, and so emprison them from secular priestes and curates, and by this cautel let hem to preach the gospell freely to the people without worldly mede, and also to defame good priestes of heresie, and lyen on hem openly for to let hem to shew Gods law by the holy gospell to the christen people?

Friars are the hinderers of preaching the gospel.

35. Frere, what charitie is thys, to fayne so much holines in your bodely clothing (that ye clepe your habite) that many blynd fooles desiren to die therein more than in another: and also that a frere, that leuith his habite late founden of men, may not be assoyled till he take it agayne, but is apostata as ye seyn, and cursed of God and man both: The frere beleueth truth, and patience, chastitie, meeknes and sobriety, yet for the more part of his life he may soone be assoyled of his prior, and if he bring home to his house mich goad by the yeare (be it neuer so falsly begged and pilled of the poore and nedy people in countries about) he shal be hold a noble frere. O Lord whether this be charitie?

What holiness is in a friar's coat.

36. Frere, what charitie is this, to prease upon a riche man, and to entice him to be buryed among you from hys parish church, and to such riche men geue letters of fraternitie confirmed by your generale seale, and thereby to beare him in hand that he shall haue part of all your masses, mattens, preachinges, fastinges, wakinges, and all other good dedes done by your brethren of your order (both whiles he liueth, and after that he is dead) and yet ye wytten neuer whether your dedes be acceptable to God, ne whether that man that hath that letter be able by good liuing to receiue any parte of your deedes, and yet a poore man (that ye wyte well or supposen in certaine to haue no good of) ye ne geuen to such letters, though he be a better man to God than such a rich man: neuerthelesse, this poore man doth not retche thereof. For as men supposen suche letters and many other that freres behotten to men, be full false deceites of fryers, out of all reason, and Gods law and christen mens fayth.

Why friars so much desire to have rich men buried in their friaries.

Friars' behests are false deceits.

37. Frere, what charitie is this, to be confessours of lordes and ladies, and to other mighty men, and not amend hem in her liuing, but rather as it seemeth, to be the bolder to pill her poore tenauntes, and to liue in lechery, and there to dwell in your office of confessour for wynning of worldly goodes, and to be holde great by colour of suche ghostly offices; this seemith rather pride of freres, than charitie of God.

Friars desire to be lords and ladies' confessors.

38. Frere, what charity is this to sayne, that who so liueth after your order, liueth most perfitely, and next followeth the state of apostles in pouertie and penaunce, and yet the wisest and greatest clerkes of you wend or sed, or procure to the court of Rome to be made cardinals or bishops of the popes chaplaines, and to be assoyled of the vowe of pouertie and obedience to your ministers, in the which (as ye sayne) standeth most perfection and merites of

Friars and Pharisees say one thing and do another.

Henry III. your orders, and thus ye faren as Phariseis that sayen one and do an other to the contrary.

A.D. 1220. Why name ye more the patrone of your order in your Confiteor when ye beginne masse, then other sayntes, apostles, or martyrs, that holy churche hold more glorious then hem, and clepe hem your patrons and your auowries.

Dilemma. Frere, whether was S. Frauncis in making of hys rule that hee set thine order in, a foole and a lyer, or else wyse and true? If ye sayne that he was not a foole, but wise; ne a lyer but true: why shewe ye contrary by your doyng? whan by your suggestion to the pope ye sayde that your rule that Fraunces made was so harde that ye might not liue to hold it without declaration and dispensation of the pope. And so, by your deede ne lete your patrone a foole that made a rule so harde that no man may well keepe, and eke your dede proueth him a lyer, where he saith in his rule, That he tooke and learned it of the Holy Ghost. For how might ye for shame pray the pope undoe that the Holy Ghost bit, as when ye prayed him to dispense with the hardnes of your order?

Which is the best order of friars? Frere, whiche of the foure orders of freres is best to a man that knoweth not which is the best, but would fayne enter into the best, and none other? If thou sayst that thine is the best, then sayst thou that none of the other is as good as thine; and in this ech frere in the three other orders wolle say that thou lyest, for in the selfe maner eche other freere wolle say that hys order is best. And thus to eche of the four orders bene the other three contrary in this poynt: in the which if anye sayth sooth, that is one alone, for there may but one be the best of foure. So followeth it that if each of these orders aunswered to this question as thou doest, three were false, and but one true, and yet no man should wyte who that were. And thus it seemeth, that the most part of freeres byn or should be lyers in this poynt, and they should aunswere thereto. If you say that an other order of the freres is better than thine, or as good; why tooke ye nat rather therto as to the better, when thou mightst haue chose at the beginning. And eke why shouldest thou be an apostata to leaue thine order and take thee to that is better, and so why goest thou not from thine order into that?

Friars never agree one with another.

The friar thinketh his rule perfecter than Christ's, because he leaveth the one and followeth the other. Frere, is there any perficter rule of religion than Christ Gods sonne gaue in his gospell to his brethren? Or then that religion that Sainct James in his epistle maketh mention of? If you say yes, then puttest thou on Christ (that is the wisdome of God, the Father) unkunning, unpower, or euil will: for than he could not make his rule so good as an other did his. And so he had unkunning, that he might not so make his rule so good as an other man might, and so were he unmighty, and not God, as he would not make his rule so perfite as an other did his, and so he had bene euil willed, namely to himselfe.

For if he might, and could, and would, haue made a rule perfite without default, and did not, he was not Gods Sonne Almighty. For if any other rule be perfiter then Christes, then must Christes rule lack of that perfection by as much as the other weren more perfiter, and so were default, and Christ had fayled in making of his rule: but to put any default or failing in God is blasphemie. If thou say that Christs rule, and that religion of that S. James maketh mention of, is the perfitest; why holdest thou not thilke rule without more. And why clepest thou the rather of S. Francis or S. Dominickes rule or religion or order, then of Christes rule or Christes order?

Frere, canst thou any default assigne in Christs rule of the gospell (with the which he taught al men sekerly to be saued) if they kept it to her ending? Dilemma. If thou say it was to hard, then sayest thou Christ lyed; for he sayd of his rule: "My yoke is soft, and my burthen light." If thou say Christes rule was to light, that may be assigned for no default, for the better it may be kept. If thou sayest that there is no default in Christes rule of the gospell, sith Christ himselfe saith it is light and easy: what neede was it to patrons of freres to adde more thereto? and so to make an hardar religion to saue fryers, then was the religion of Christes apostles and his disciples helden and were saued by. But if they wolden that her freres saten aboue the apostles in heauen for the harder religion that the kepen here, so wold they sitten in heauen aboue Christ himselfe, for they mo and straight observaunces, then so should they bee better then Christ himselfe with mischaunce.

Friars would sit in heaven, above the apostles.

Go now forth and frayne your clerkes, and ground ye you in God's law, and gyf Jack an aunswere, and when ye han assoiled me that I haue sayd sadly in truth, I shall soile thee of thine orders, and saue thee to heauen.

If freres kun not or mow not excuse hem of these questions asked of hem, it seemeth that they be horrible gilty against God, and her euen chrisen. For which giltes and defaultes it were worthy that the order that they call theyr order were fordone. And it is wonder that men sustayne hem or suffer hem lyue in such maner. For holy writ biddeth, that "Thou doe well to the meke, and geue not to the wicked, but forbed to giue hem bread, least they be made thereby mightier through you."

After these digressions, now to return to the course of our story again. As this King Henry succeeded King John, his father, so after Innocent, the pope, came Honorius III, A.D. 1216, then Gregory IX., A.D. 1227. After Otho, the emperor (whom the pope had once set up, and after deprived again,) succeeded Frederic II., A.D. 1197, as it is partly before touched. In the days of these kings, popes, and emperors, it were too long to recite all that happened in England, but especially in Germany, betwixt Pope Honorius, Gregory, and Frederic, the emperor; the horrible tragedy whereof were enough to fill a whole book by itself. But still we mean (God willing) somewhat to touch concerning these ecclesiastical matters, first beginning with this realm of England.

Otho, the emperor, set up and deposed again by the pope.

After the kingdom of England had been subjected by King John, as hath been said, and made tributary to the pope and the Romish church, it is incredible how the insatiable avarice and greediness of the Romans did oppress and wring the commons and all estates and degrees of the realm, especially beneficed men, and such as had any thing of the church; who, what for their domestical charges within the realm, what for the pope, what for the legates, what for contributing to the Holy Land, what for relaxations, and other subtle sleights to get away their money, were brought into such slavery, captivity, and penury; that whereas the king neither durst, nor might remedy their exclamations by himself: yet, notwithstanding, by his advice, Simon Montfort and the earl of Leicester, with other noblemen, not forgetting what great grievances and distresses the realm was brought into by the Romans, thought to work some way how to bridle and restrain the insatiable ravening of these greedy wolves. Wherefore they devised their letter, giving strait commandment to the religious men, and to such as had their churches to farm, that henceforth they should not answer the Romans on account of such farms and rents any more, but should pay the said farms or rents unto their own proctors appointed for the same purpose; as by their writings sent abroad to bishops or chapters, and other ecclesiastical houses, may appear, in this form and effect as followeth.

A Complaint of the Nobles of England against the intolerable Covetousness of the Pope and Prelates of Rome.[1]

A.D. 1229.

To such and such a bishop, and such a chapter. "All the university and company of them, that had rather die than be confounded of the Romans, wisheth health. How the Romans and their legates have hitherto behaved themselves toward you and other ecclesiastical persons of this realm of England, it is not unknown to your discretions, in disposing and giving away the

(1) The Latin copy of this complaint of the nobles of England is at p. 72, in the Edition of 1563. —ED.

Henry III.

A.D. 1220.

benefices of the realm after their own lust, to the intolerable prejudice and grievance both of you and all other Englishmen. For whereas, the collation of benefices should and doth properly belong to you and other your fellow-bishops (ecclesiastical persons), they, thundering against you the sentence of excommunication, ordain that you should not bestow them upon any person of this realm, until in every diocese and cathedral-church within the realm, five Romans (such as the pope shall name) be provided for, to the value of, every man, an hundred pounds a year. Besides these, many other grievances the said Romanists do inflict and infer, both to the laity and nobles of the realm, for the patronages and alms bestowed by them and their ancestors, for the sustentation of the poor of the realm, and also to the clergy and ecclesiastical persons of the realm, touching their livings and benefices. And yet the said Romanists, not contented with the premises, do also take from the clergy of this realm the benefices which they have, to bestow them on men of their own country, &c.

Wherefore, we, considering the rigorous austerity of these aforesaid Romanists, who, once coming in but as strangers hither, now take upon them not only to judge, but also to condemn us, laying upon us unportable burdens, whereunto they will not put one of their own fingers to move; and laying our heads together upon a general and full advice had among ourselves concerning the same; have thought good (although very late) to resist or withstand them, rather than to be subject to their intolerable oppressions, and to the still greater slavery hereafter to be looked for. For which cause we straitly charge and command you, as your friends going about to deliver you, the church, the king, and the kingdom, from that miserable yoke of servitude, that you do not intermeddle or take any part concerning such exactions or rents to be required or given to the said Romans. Letting you to understand for truth, that in case you shall (which God forbid) be found culpable herein, not only your goods and possessions shall be in danger of burning, but you, also, in your persons shall incur the same peril and punishment as shall the said Romish oppressors themselves. Thus fare ye well.

Example never to take part against the king with foreign power.

Thus much I thought here to insert and notify concerning this matter, not only that the foul and avaricious greediness of the Romish church might the more evidently unto all Englishmen appear; but that they may learn by this example how worthy they be so to be served and plagued with their own rod, who, before, would take no part with their natural king against foreign power, by which now they are scourged.

Cardinal Otho legate.

To make the story more plain; in the reign of this Henry III. (who succeeding, as is said, King John, his father, reigned fifty-six years), came divers legates from Rome to England. First, Cardinal Otho, sent from the pope with letters to the king, like as other letters also were sent to other places for exactions of money.

The pope requireth two prebendships in every cathedral church.

The king opening the letters, and perceiving the contents, answered, that he alone could say nothing in the matter, which concerned all the clergy and commons of the whole realm. Not long after a council was called at Westminster, where the letters being opened, the form was this:[1] "We require to be given unto us, first, of all cathedral churches two prebends, one for the bishops' part, the other for the chapter: and likewise of monasteries, where be divers portions, one for the abbot, another for the covent: of the covent, so much as appertaineth to one monk, the portion of the goods being proportionally divided; of the abbot likewise as much." The cause why he required these prebends was this: "It hath been," saith he, "an old

(1) "Petimus imprimis ab omnibus ecclesiis cathedralibus duas nobis præbendas exhiberi, unam de portione episcopi, et alteram de capitulo: et similiter de cœnobiis ubi diversæ sunt portiones abbatis et conventus; a conventibus quantum pertinet ad unum monachum, æquali facta distributione bonorum suorum, et ab abbate tantundem."

Henry III

A.D. 1220

slander, and a great complaint against the church of Rome, that it hath been charged with insatiable covetousness, which, as ye know, is the root of all mischief, and all by reason that causes be wont commonly not to be handled, nor to proceed in the church of Rome, without great gifts and expense of money. Whereof seeing the poverty of the church is the cause, and the only reason why it is so slandered and evil spoken of, it is therefore convenient that you, as natural children, should succour your mother. For unless we should receive of you and of other good men as you are, we should then lack necessaries for our life, which were a great dishonour to our dignity," &c.

Note the cause why the pope is compelled to crave money of other countries.

When those petitions and causes of the legate were propounded, in the aforesaid assembly, at Westminster on the pope's behalf (the bishops and prelates of the realm being present), answer was made by the mouth of Master John Bedford on this wise: 'that the matter there proponed by the lord legate especially concerned the king of England, but in general it touched all the archbishops, with their suffragans, the bishops, and all the prelates of the realm. Wherefore, seeing that both the king, by reason of his sickness, was absent, and, also, that the archbishop of Canterbury with divers other bishops were not there, therefore, in the absence of them, they had nothing to say in the matter, neither could they so do without prejudice of them who were lacking.'—And so the assembly for that time brake up.

A council at London called.

Not long after, the said Otho, Cardinal De carcere Tulliano, coming again from Rome, with full authority and power, indicted another council at London, and caused all prelates, archbishops, bishops, abbots, priors, and other of the clergy to be warned unto the same council, to be held in the church of St. Paul's at London about the feast of St. Martin. The pretence of this council was for redress of matters concerning benefices and religion; but the chief and principal intent was to hunt for money: for, putting them in fear and in hope, some to lose, some to obtain spiritual promotions at his hand, he thought gain would rise thereby, and so it did, for in the mean time (as Matthew Paris, in his life of Henry III., writeth) divers precious rewards were offered him in palfreys, in rich plate and jewels, in costly and sumptuous garments richly furred, in coin, in victuals, *[1]and such like things of value well worthy of acceptation; wherein one endeavoured to go beyond another in munificence, not considering, by means of the servility wherewith they were oppressed of those popish shavelings and shameless shifters, that all was mere pillage and extortion.* Insomuch that the bishop of Winchester, (as the story reporteth), on only hearing that he would winter in London, sent him fifty fat oxen, a hundred coombs of pure wheat, and eight tun of chosen wine, toward his housekeeping. Likewise other bishops also, for their part offered unto the cardinal's box after their ability.

Great rewards given to the cardinal.

The time of the council drawing nigh, the cardinal commanded, at the west end of Paul's church, an high and solemn throne to be prepared, rising up with a glorious scaffold upon mighty and substantial stages strongly builded, and of great height. Thus, against

(1) These words are not in the editions of Foxe previous to 1596.—Ed.

Henry III.

A.D. 1220.

the day assigned, came the said archbishops, bishops, abbots, and other of the prelacy, both far and near throughout all England, wearied and vexed with the winter's journey, bringing their letters procuratory; who being together assembled, the cardinal beginneth his sermon. But before we come to the sermon, there happened a great discord between the two archbishops of Canterbury and York, about sitting at the right hand and the left hand of the glorious cardinal, for the which the one appealed against the other. The cardinal, to pacify the strife between them both, so that he would not derogate from either of them, brought forth a certain bull of the pope: in the midst of which bull was pictured the figure of the cross. On the right side of the cross stood the image of St. Paul, and on the left side that of St. Peter: "Lo," saith the cardinal (holding open the bull with the cross), "here you see St. Peter on the left hand of the cross, and St. Paul on the right side, and yet is there between these two no contention, for both are of equal glory. And yet St. Peter, for the prerogative of his keys, and for the pre-eminence of his apostleship and cathedral dignity, seemeth most worthy to be placed on the right side. But yet because St. Paul believed on Christ when he saw him not, therefore hath he the right hand of the cross: for blessed be they (saith Christ) who believe and see not," &c. From that time forth the archbishop of Canterbury enjoyed the right hand, and the archbishop of York the left; wherein, however, this cardinal is more to be commended than the other Cardinal Hugo mentioned a little before, who, in a like contention between these archbishops, ran away.

Contention about sitting on the right hand of the cardinal.

Why St. Paul standeth on the right hand of the pope's cross. Why the archbishop of Canterbury hath the right hand, and the archbishop of York the left.

Thus, the controversy having ceased and been composed between these two, Otho the cardinal, sitting aloft between these two archbishops, beginneth his sermon, taking this theme of the prophet; "In the midst of the seat, and in the circuit about the seat, were four beasts full of eyes before and behind," &c. Upon this theme the cardinal proceeded in his sermon, sitting like a god in the midst. He compared those about him to the four beasts about the seat, declaring how they ought to have eyes both before and behind; that is, that they must be provident in disposing of secular things, and circumspect in spiritual matters, continuing and joining wisely things past with things to come; and this was the greatest effect of this clerkly sermon. That done, he giveth forth certain statutes for ordering of churches, as for the dedication of temples, for the seven sacraments, for the giving of orders, for the farming of benefices, for collations and resignations of benefices and vicarages, priests' apparel, and single life, for eating of flesh in religious houses, and for archdeacons, bishops, proctors, and other like matters. But the chief intent of all his proceeding was this, that they should be vigilant, provident, and circumspect, with all their eyes (both before and behind), to fill the pope's pouch, as appeared not only by this, but all their other travails besides; insomuch that the king, dreading the displeasure of his commons for the doings of the legate, willed him to repair home to Rome again, but yet could not so be rid of him, for he, receiving new commandments from the pope, applied his harvest, still gleaning and raking whatsoever he might scrape; writing and

Note the theme of the prophet applying to God, how the cardinal applieth it to himself.

Scripture clerkly applied.

sending to bishops and archdeacons in the form and tenor as hereunder followeth.[1]

And moreover, note again the wicked and cursed trains of these Romish rakehells, who, to pick simple men's purses, first send out their friars and preachers to stir up, in all places and countries, men to go fight against the Turks: whom, when they have once bound with a vow, and signed them with the cross, then send they their bulls, to release them, for money, both from their labour and from their vow, as by their own style of writing is hereunder to be seen.[2]

Note the crafty practice of Romish prelates to prowl for money.

The cause why the pope was so greedy and needy of money, was this; because he had mortal hatred, and waged continual battle at the same time against the good emperor, Frederic II., who had to wife King John's daughter, sister to King Henry III., whose name was Isabella. Therefore, because the pope's war could not be sustained without charges, the pope was the more importunate to take money in all places, but especially in England; insomuch that he shamed not to require the fifth part of every ecclesiastical man's living, as Matthew Paris writeth. And not only that, but also the said Pope Gregory, conventing with the citizens of Rome, so agreed with them, that, if they would join with him in vanquishing the aforesaid Frederic, he would (and so did) grant unto them, that all the benefices in England which were or should be vacant (namely, pertaining to religious houses), should be bestowed at their own will and commandment on their children and kinsfolks. Whereupon it followeth in the aforenamed history,[3] that "the pope sent in commandment to the archbishop of Canterbury and four other bishops, that provision should be made for three hundred Romans in the chief and best benefices in all England at the next voidance, so that the aforesaid archbishop and bishops should be suspended in the mean time from all collation or gift of benefices, until the aforesaid three hundred were provided for;" whereupon, the archbishop at that time, seeing the unreasonable oppression of the church of England, left the realm and went into France.

Fifth part of every spiritual man's living given to the pope.

Three hundred Romans placed in the best benefices of England

Again, mark another similar or more easy sleight of the pope in procuring money. He sent one Petrus Rubeus, at the same time, with a new device, which was this: not to work any thing openly,

A Romish sleight of the pope to get English money

(1) *A Letter of the Cardinal to Bishops and Archdeacons, in which the censure of the Church is well applied.*—"Otto miseratione divina, &c Discreto viro *N* episcopo vel *N* archidiacono salutem Cum necesse habeamus de mandato summi pontificis moram trahere in Anglia longiorem, nec possimus propriis stipendiis militare, discretionem vestram qua fungimur autoritate rogamus, ut procurationes vobis debitas in episcopatu, vel archidiaconatu vestro colligi faciatis nostro nomine diligenter, eas quam citius poteritis, nobis transmissuri, contradictores per censuram ecclesiasticam compescendo Proviso, quod quælibet procuratio summam 4 marcarum aliquatenus non excedat, et ubi una ecclesia non sufficiet ad procurationem hujusmodi habendam, duæ pariter unam solvant.—Datum Lond 15 Kal Mar Pont D Gregor Papæ 9."

(2) "*N* episcopus dilectis in Christo filiis omnibus archidiaconis per diocesim suam constitutis, salutem Literas domini legati suscepimus in hæc verba, Otto miseratione divina, &c Cum sicut intelleximus nonnulli cruce signati regni Angliæ, qui sunt inhabiles ad pugnandum, ad sedem apostolicam accedant, ut ibidem a voto crucis absolvi valeant, et nos nuper recepimus a summo pontifice in mandatis, ut tales non solum absolvere, verum et ad redimenda vota sua [note the style of Rome], compellere debeamus, volentes eorum parcere laboribus et expensis, fraternitatem vestram qua fungimur, monemus, quatenus, partem prædictam a summo pontifice nobis concessam faciatis in nostris diocesibus sine mora qualibet publicari, ut prefati cruce signati ad nos accedere valeant, [immo maleficium et naufragium, pecuniæ,] beneficium super his juxta formam nobis traditam accepturi.—Datum Londini 15. Kal Mart. Pont D N Papæ Gregor 9."

(3) "Unde infra paucos dies misit Dom Papa sacra præcepta sua domino Cant Archiep Eliensi et Lincol et Salisb episcopis, ut trecentis Romanis, in primis beneficiis vacantibus, providerent, scientes se suspensos a beneficiorum collatione donec tot competenter provideretur."

Henry III — A.D. 1220

but privily to go betwixt bishop and bishop, abbot and abbot, &c., telling in their ears, such a bishop, such an abbot, hath given so much and so much unto the pope's holiness, "trusting that you also will not be behind on your part," &c By means of this it is incredible to think what a mass of money was made out of the realm unto the pope.

At length the aforesaid bishops, abbots, and archdeacons, feeling their own smart, came to the king, whose father before they did resist, with their humble suit, lamentably complaining of the immeasurable exactions of the pope, and especially against Petrus Rubeus and his fellow, Otto the legate; desiring the king, that, seeing the matter touched not themselves alone, but the whole church, and seeing the valuation of churches was known better to their archdeacons than to themselves, therefore they desired a general calling and talk to be had in the matter. In the octaves of St. John the Baptist, the day and place were assigned when and where they should talk; at which day and place the prelates of England, conventing together, durst not give any direct denial of that contribution, but after a modest sort did insinuate certain exceptions against the same.

Exceptions alleged for not contributing to the pope

I. They say, that forasmuch as the contribution is demanded to war against him who was joined by matrimony with their prince, they were not bound so to do.

II. That the said contribution tended to the shedding of christian blood, as the form of the bill implied an intention to fight against the emperor.

III They refuse because it was against the liberty of the church, for so it is in the bill, that they who would not contribute, should be excommunicated.

IV. Because that when of late they gave the tenth part of their goods, it was with this protestation, that they should contribute to the pope no more hereafter

V. Because they had contributed before; and if they should now contribute again, it were to be feared lest an action twice done should grow into a custom, as is in the law, "Lege nemo," &c.

VI For so much as they shall have causes continually to seek to Rome through the emperor's land; it were to be feared lest the said emperor by the way would work their annoyance

VII. Because the king hath many enemies abroad, and for his wars hath need of much money at home, it is not convenient that the goods of the realm should be alienated out of the realm.

VIII. Because that could not be done without prejudice to the patrons of their churches, not knowing whether their patrons did or would agree unto the same.

IX. Lastly, because they hear say, that the general state of the church is in danger, for which they understand there shall be shortly a general council, wherein such matters shall be determined. and. therefore, if they should contribute now, it should be to the hinderance and damage of the church

The legate and his fellow hearing these allegations, seeing their own confusion, were the less importunate.

Not long after this followed a general council at Lyons, called by Pope Innocent IV., in which council the English nation did exhibit certain articles of their grievances not unworthy to be known.[1]

Articles exhibited in the Council of Lyons: the grievances sustained from the Pope.

I. The kingdom of England is grieved that the pope, being not contented with his Peter-pence, requireth and extorteth from the clergy great exactions

(1) "Gravatur regnum Angliæ, eo quod Dom Papa non est contentus subsidio illo, quod vocatur denarius beati Petri," &c.

(and more is likely), both without the consent of the king, and against the customs of the realm.

II. The church and kingdom of England is grieved, that the patrons of the same cannot present, as they were wont, unto their churches, on account of the pope's letters: but the churches are given to Romans, who know neither the realm nor the tongue thereof, both to the great peril of souls, and robbing away the money out of the realm.

III. It is grieved, for that the pope, promising by the tenor of his letters, that in requiring of pensions and provisions in the realm of England, he would require only twelve benefices, now, contrary to the tenor thereof, many more benefices and provisions are bestowed away by him.

IV. The realm is grieved and complaineth, that in the benefices in England, one Italian succeedeth another, the Englishmen being not only excluded, but also compelled, for the determining of their matters, to seek to Rome, contrary both to the customs of the realm, and also to the privileges granted by the pope's predecessors to the king and kingdom of England.

V. The fifth grievance is, for the oft recourse of that infamous legate, by whom both faith and fidelity, the ancient customs of the realm, and the authority of old grants, statutes, laws, and privileges, are embezzled and abrogated, whereby an infinite number in England be grievously afflicted and oppressed.

He meaneth percase, Otho, or Master Martinus.

VI. The said realm is also grieved by general tallages, collections, and assessments, made without the king's consent; the appellation and contradiction of the king's proctors, to the contrary notwithstanding.

VII. The aforesaid realm complaineth and is grieved, that in the benefices given to Italians, neither the old ordinances, nor relief of the poor, nor hospitality, nor any preaching of God's word, nor care of men's souls, nor service in the church, nor yet the walls of the churches be kept up and maintained, as the manner and custom of the same realm requireth. Over and above these aforesaid grievances, there came, moreover, from the pope, other fresh letters, charging and commanding the prelates of England to find, of their proper costs and charges for one whole year, some, ten armed soldiers, some five, some fifteen, to be ready at the pope's commandment where he should appoint.

The Babylonish captivity and slavery of England under the pope.

After these and other grievances and enormities of Rome, the states of England, consulting together, direct their letters to the pope, for reformation thereof. First, the abbots and priors; then, the bishops and suffragans; afterwards, the nobles and barons; last of all, the king himself. But as the proverb is, "Venter non habet aures,"[1] so the pope's purse had no ears to hear. And, as our common saying goeth, "As good never a whit, as never the better," so went it with the pope, who, not long after the same, sent for new tallages and exactions to be collected; which thing when it came to the king's ear, he, being moved and disturbed vehemently withal, writeth in this wise to the bishops severally, to every one in his diocese.[2]

The Letter of King Henry III. to the Bishops.

Henry III., by the grace of God, to the reverend in Christ, the bishop of N—. Whereas we have heretofore written unto you, once, twice, thrice, as well by our privy seals, as by our letters patent, that you should not exact or collect for the pope's behalf, any tallage or other help of our subjects, either of the clergy, or of the laity, for that no such tallage or help either can or is used to be exacted in our realm without the great prejudice of our princely dignity, which we neither will nor can suffer or sustain: yet you contemning and vilipending our commandment, and contrary to the provision made in our last council at London, granted and agreed upon by our prelates, earls, and barons, have, that notwithstanding, proceeded in collecting the said your taxes and tallages. Whereupon, we do greatly marvel and are moved, especially seeing you are not ashamed to do contrary unto your own decrees; whereas you, and

King Henry III. commandeth that no tax nor tallage be sent to the pope.

(1) The French say, "Ventre affamé n'a point d'oreilles."—Ed.

(2) "Henricus tertius Dei gratia, &c., venerabili in Christo, N. episcopo salutem. Licet alias vobis," &c.

Henry III.

A.D. 1220.

other prelates in the said council, in this did all agree and grant, that no such exactions should be hereafter, until the return of our and your ambassadors from the court of Rome, sent thither purposely of us, and in the name of the whole realm for the same, to provide redress against those oppressions. Wherefore, we straitly will and command you, that from henceforth you do not proceed any more in collecting and exacting such tallages or helps, as you will enjoy our favour, and such possessions of yours as, within this our kingdom, you have and hold. And if you have already procured or gathered any such thing, yet that you suffer not the same to be transported out of our realm, but cause it to be kept in safe custody, till the return of the said ambassadors, under pain of our displeasure in doing the contrary, and also of provoking us to extend our hand upon your possessions, further than you will think or believe. Moreover, willing and charging you that you participate and make common this our inhibition, with your archdeacons and officials, which we here have set forth for the liberties of the clergy and of the people, as knoweth God, &c.

At length, the ambassadors who were at Rome came home about the latter end of December, bringing word that the pope, hearing what was done in the council of Winchester and by the king, was greatly displeased with him and the realm, saying, "Rex Anglorum, qui jam recalcitrat et frederisat, suum habet consilium; ego vero et meum habeo, quod et sequar," &c. Whereupon, when the ambassadors began to speak in the king's behalf, from that time they were half counted for schismatics, and could no more be heard in the court of Rome. The king, hearing this, was marvellously incensed therewith, commanding, by general proclamation throughout all his realm, that no man should hereafter consent to any tax or subsidy of money for the court of Rome. When this came to the pope's ear, upon a cruel rage he directed his letters to the prelates of England, charging that under pain of suspense or interdiction, they should provide the same sum of money to be collected against the feast of Assumption, the charge being given to the bishop of Worcester, to be executor of the said curse. The king, who lately intended to stand to the liberties of the church, now, for fear of the pope, and partly for the persuasions of the said bishop of Worcester and other prelates, durst not stand to them, but gave over. Moreover the greedy gulf of the Romish avarice waxed so immeasurable, that at length the pope shamed not, upon the censure of his curse, to ask the third part of the church goods, and the yearly fruit of all vacant benefices. The chief doers and legates in England, were Otho, Stephanus Capellanus, Petrus Rubeus, the nuncio, Mag. Martin, and Mag. Marinus, Johannes Anglicus Episcopus Sabinensis; of whom, to speak further (for that I have much more to write), I think best for the present to defer, lest in opening all the detestable doings and pestilent workings of those men, I might, perhaps, not only molest good ears, but also infect the air. Yet one thing concerning the said Otho I cannot well overpass.

The pope's saying against King Henry.

Henry again restraineth the pope's taxes.

The pope taketh on, against the king.

The king compelled to give over to the pope.

The pope asketh the third part of the church goods.

A story of Cardinal Otho at Oxford.

This Otho, as he left no place unsought, where any vantage might be got: so, amongst all others, he came to Oxford, where lying in the house of Osney, he was received with great honour; the scholars presenting him honourably with such dishes and rewards as they had, thinking to gratify the cardinal after the best manner. This being done before dinner, and the dinner ended, they came reverently to see and welcome him, supposing that they also should again, of him, with like courtesy be entertained. As they came to the gate, the

Henry III. A.D. 1220.

porter, being an Italian, with a loud voice, asketh what they would have? They said, they came to see the lord legate. But Cerberus, the porter, holding the door half open, with proud and contumelious language thrust them out, and would not suffer them to enter. The scholars, seeing that, by force thrust open the gate and came in; whom when the Romans, who were within, would have repelled with their fists, and such staves as they had in their hands, they fell to alarum and by the ears together, with much heaving and shoving, and many blows on both sides. In the mean time, while some of the scholars ran home for their weapons, there chanced a poor scholar, an Irishman, to stand at the gate waiting for his alms, whom when the master-cook saw at the gate, he, taking hot scalding water out of the pan where the meat was sodden, did cast it in his face. One of the scholars, a Welshman, who came with his bow and shafts, seeing that, letteth drive an arrow, and shooteth this Nabuzardan (that master of cooks) clean through the body, and slayeth him out of hand. The cook falling dead, there was a mighty broil and a great clamour throughout all the house. The cardinal, hearing the tumult and great noise about him, like a valiant Roman, runneth as fast as he could into the steeple, and there locketh the doors fast unto him, where he remained till midnight. The scholars, in the mean while, not yet at all pacified, sought all corners about for the legate, exclaiming and crying out, "Where is that usurer, that simoniac, that piller and poller of our livings, that prowler and extortioner of our money, who perverteth our king, and subverteth his kingdom, enriching himself with our spoils?" All this heard the cardinal, and held his peace. When the night approaching had broken up the field, the cardinal coming out of his fort, and taking his horse, in the silence of the night, was privily conveyed over the river towards the king, conveying himself away as fast as he could. After the king heard this, he sendeth to Oxford a garrison of armed men, to deliver the Romans who were there hidden for fear of the scholars. Then was Master Otho, a lawyer, with thirty other scholars, apprehended, and carried to Wallingford castle, and from thence had in carts to London, where, at length, through much entreaty of the bishops, they, being brought barefoot to the legate's door, had their pardon, and the university was released from interdiction. Thus much concerning the pope's legate in England.

Skirmish between the scholars of Oxford and the cardinal's men.

The cardinal runneth away.

Thirty scholars taken and had to prison.

Thus partly you have heard, and do understand the miserable thraldom and captivity of this realm of England, and the clergy of the same, who before refused to take part with King John their natural prince, against the foreign power of the pope, and now how miserably they are oppressed and scourged of the same pope, whose insatiable extortion and rapacity did so exceed in pilling and polling of this realm long after this, that neither the king now could help them, nor could the pope with any reasonable measure be content; insomuch that writers record, that in the days of Sudbury, archbishop of Canterbury, A.D. 1360, the pope by his proctors gat from the clergy, in less than one year, more than sixty thousand florins, of mere contribution; besides his other avails and common revenues out of benefices, prebendaries, first-fruits, tributes, Peter-pence, collations, reservations, relaxations, and such merchandize, &c.

Threescore thousand florins contributed to the pope, in one year, by the clergy.

Henry III. A.D. 1220.

And yet the state of this realm of England, although most miserable, was not so lamentable, but that the case of Germany and of the Emperor Frederic II. was then as much or more pitiful, who in the same time of King Henry III. was so persecuted and disturbed by Pope Innocent, Honorius, Gregory, Celestine, and Innocent IV., that not only with their curses and excommunications most wretchedly they did infame, impugn, and assault him, but also in open field continually did they war against him, and all with Englishmen's money. Albeit, concerning the troubles of this emperor, being a foreign story and pertaining to other countries, I have not much to do nor to write therein, having enough already to story at home. Yet I cannot but lament and marvel to see the ambitious presumption and tragical fury of those popes against the emperor.[1]

Mention was made a little before of the Albigenses keeping about the city of Toulouse. These Albigenses, because they began to smell the pope, and to control the inordinate proceedings and discipline of the see of Rome, the pope therefore recounting them as a people heretical, excited and stirred up about this present time and year, A.D. 1220, Louis, the young French king, through the instance of Philip II., his father, to lay siege against the said city of Toulouse to expunge and extinguish these Albigenses, his enemies; whereupon Louis, according to his father's commandment, reared a puissant and mighty army to compass about and beset that city, and so did. Here were the men of Toulouse in great danger; but see how the mighty protection of God fighteth for his people against the might of man: for after that Louis, as Matthew Paris testifieth,[2] had long wearied himself and his men in waste, and could do no good with all their engines and artillery against the city, there fell, moreover, upon the French host, by the hand of God, such famine and pestilence both of men and horses, besides the other daily slaughter of the soldiers, that Louis was forced to retire, and, with such as were left, to return again home to France, from whence he came. In the slaughter of his soldiers, besides many others, was earl Simon Montfort, general of the army, to whom the lands of the earl of Toulouse were given by the pope; he was slain before the gate of the city with a stone; and so was also the brother of the said Simon, at the same time, while besieging a castle near Toulouse, slain with a stone in like manner. And thus was the siege of the Frenchmen against Toulouse broken up.[3]

Louis, the French king, fighteth against the Albigenses.

Besiegeth Toulouse. The hand of God fighteth for his people.

The siege against the Albigenses broken up.

While the siege of these Frenchmen could do no good against the city of Toulouse, it happened at that time that the Christians, marching towards the Holy Land, had better success in laying their siege to a certain tower or castle in Egypt, near to the city Damietta, that seemed by nature, for the situation and difficulty of the place, inexpugnable: which, being situate in the midst of the great flood Nilus, hard by the city called Damietta, could neither be come to by land, nor be undermined for the water, nor by famine subdued, for the nearness of the city; yet, notwithstanding, through the help of God and the policy of man, erecting scaffolds and castles upon tops of

(1) This paragraph in single asterisks is from the Edition of 1563, p. 73, and is followed by a short abstract of the ecclesiastical and civil history of this country to the time of Wickliff, given more fully in later Editions.—Ed.

(2) Ex Matth. Paris. in Vita Hen. III.

(3) Ex Matth. Paris.

masts, the Christians at last conquered it, and after that also the city Damietta, albeit not without great loss of christian people. (A.D. 1219.) In the expugnation of this city or fort, among others that there died was the landgrave of Thuring, named Louis, the husband of Elizabeth, whom we use to call St. Elizabeth. This Elizabeth, as my story recordeth, was the daughter of the king of Hungary, and married in Almain, where she lived with the aforenamed Louis, landgrave of Thuring, whom she, through her persuasions, provoked and incensed to take that voyage to fight for the Holy Land, where he in the same voyage was slain. After his death, Elizabeth, remaining a widow, entered the profession of cloisterly religion, and made herself a nun; so growing and increasing from virtue to virtue, that after her death all Almain did sound with the fame of her worthy doings. Matthew Paris addeth this also, that she was the daughter of that queen, who, being accused to be naughty with a certain archbishop, was therefore condemned with this sentence pronounced against her;[1] although it be hard in English to be translated as it standeth in Latin,—"To kill the queen will ye not to fear, that is good; and if all men consent thereunto, not I myself do stand against it." Which sentence being brought to Pope Innocent, thus in pointing the sentence, which otherwise seemeth to have a double understanding, he saved the queen; thus interpreting and pointing the same, "Reginam interficere nolite, timere bonum est, et si omnes consenserint, non ego, contradico." That is, "To kill the queen will ye not, to fear, that is good: and if all do consent thereto, yet not I, I myself do stand against it," and so escaped she the danger. This queen was the mother, as is said, of Elizabeth the nun, who, for her holy nunnishness, was canonized of the pope's church for a saint in Almain, about A.D. 1220.[2]

Damietta taken by the Christians. The story of St. Elizabeth.

The mother of St. Elizabeth accused of adultery.

The queen saved by favourable interpretation of a double sentence. Elizabeth canonized a saint in Almain.

And this by the way. Now to proceed further in the years and life of this King Henry. The next year following, which was A.D. 1221, the king went to Oxford, where he had something to do with William, earl of Albemarle, who had taken the castle of Biham: but at last, for his good service he had done in the realm before, he was released by the king, with all his men, at the intercession of Walter, archbishop of York, and of Pandulph, the legate.[3] About that year entered first the Friar Minorites, or Grey friars, into England, and had their first house at Canterbury, whose first patron was Francis, who died A.D. 1127. His order was confirmed by Pope Honorius III., A.D. 1224.

A.D. 1221.

The Grey friars first enter England. The order confirmed.

About the first coming of these Dominic and Grey friars Franciscan into the realm (as is in Nicolas Trivet testified), many Englishmen at that time entered into their orders, among whom was Johannes de Sancto Egidio, a man famously expert in the science of physic and astronomy, and Alexander de Hales, both Englishmen and great divines. This Johannes making his "sermon ad clerum," in the house of the Dominic friars, exhorted his auditory with great persuasions unto wilful poverty, and to confirm his words the more by his own example, in the midst of his sermon he came down from the pulpit and put on his friar's habit; and so, returning into the pulpit again,

(1) "Reginam interficere nolite timere bonum est, et si omnes consenserint non ego contradico."
(2) Ex Matth. Paris. (3) Ex tabula pensili in æde divi Pauli.

Henry III.

A.D. 1221.

made an end of his sermon. Likewise Alexander Hales entered the order of the Franciscans, of whom remaineth yet the book entitled "De Summa Theologiæ," in old libraries.

Charter-house monks founded.

Moreover, not long after, by William Longspey, who was the bastard son of King Henry II., and earl of Salisbury, was first founded the house of the Carthusian monks, at Heitrope, A.D. 1222. After his death, his wife Ela was translated to the house of Henton, in Berkshire, A.D. 1227; which Ela also founded the house of nuns at Lacocks, and there continued herself abbess of the place. The bishop of London, named William, at the same time gave over his bishopric, after whom succeeded Eustace in that see.[1]

Two condemned at a council in Oxford.

In the town of Oxford, where the king then kept his court, Simon Langton, archbishop of Canterbury, held a council, where was condemned and burned a certain deacon, as Nicholas Trivet saith, for apostasy; also another rude countryman, who had crucified himself, and superstitiously bare about the wounds in his feet and hands, was condemned to be closed up perpetually within walls.[2] About the same year also, Alexander, king of Scots, married Joan, sister to King Henry.

Not long after began the new building of the minster of Salisbury, whereof Pandulph, the pope's legate, laid the first five stones; one for the pope (such was the fortune of that church to have the pope's stone in its foundation); the second, for the young King Henry; the third, for the good earl of Salisbury; the fourth, for the countess; the fifth, for the bishop of Salisbury; which was about the same year above mentioned, A.D. 1221.[3]

Dissension between the citizens of London and Westminster.

In the same year, about St. James's tide, arose a dissension between the citizens of London and the men of Westminster, the occasion whereof was this:—A certain match between these two parties was appointed, to try which party, in wrestling, could overcome the other. Thus, in striving for mastery, each party contending against the other, as the manner is in such pastime, it happened that the Londoners got the victory, and the other side was put to foil, but especially the steward of the abbot of Westminster; who, being not a little confounded therewith, began to forethink in his mind how to be revenged again of the Londoners. Whereupon, another day was set, which was at Lammas, that the Londoners should come again to wrestle; and whoso had the victory should have the bell-wether,[4] which was the price of the game appointed. As the parties were thus occupied in their play, the steward suddenly bringeth upon the Londoners, unawares, a company of harnessed men prepared for the same beforehand, and letteth drive at the Londoners; who, at length, being wounded and grievously hurt, after much bloodshed were driven back again into the city. This contumely thus being received, the citizens, eagerly struck with ire and impatience, ran to the common bell, and by ringing thereof assembled their commons together, to consult with themselves what was to be done in that case so contumelious; wherein, when divers sentences were given diversely, Serle, at that time mayor of London (a wise and discreet man), gave this counsel, that the abbot of Westminster should be talked withal, who if he would rectify

Wholesome counsel of the mayor of London.

(1) Flor. Historiæ. (2) Nicholas Trivet. (3) Ex Chron. de Sal.
(4) Usually, the best sheep in the flock.—Ed.

Henry III. A.D. 1222.

the injury done, and satisfy for the harm received, it should be to them sufficient. But contrary, one Constantine, a great man then in the city of London, in much heat exciting the people, gave this sentence, that all the houses of the abbot of Westminster, but especially the house of the steward, should be cast down to the ground. In fine, that which he so unadvisedly counselled, was as madly performed, for the furious people, according to his counsel, did. This tumultuous outrage, as it could not be privy, coming to the knowledge of Hubert de Burgh, lord chief justice of England, above mentioned, he coming with a sufficient strength of armed soldiers to the city of London, sent to the mayor and aldermen of the city to will them to come unto him; who so obeying his commandment, he required of them the principal beginners of the riot. To whom Constantine, there being present, answered, that he would warrant that which was done; sorrowing, moreover, that they had not done more than they did in the matter. The justice, upon this his confession, commanded him, with two others, without any further tumult, to be taken; and so, along with the same two, he was hanged, he offering for his life fifteen hundred marks.

refused by wild heads.

Constantine executed at London for riot.

The said Hubert, earl of Kent, and lord chief justice, although he was a faithful and trusty officer to his prince, and had the whole guiding of the realm in his own hands, the king, as yet, being in his minority, yet afterwards, what indignation he sustained for this his severity and other things, both of the nobles and of the commons, and how sharply he was tossed and trounced of his prince, it is a wonder to see, as in its due place and time (by the Lord's leave) hereafter shall appear.[1]

Discord and contention among churchmen.

As mention hath been made of the wrangling between the commoners of London and Westminster, both time and occasion bring me in remembrance something to speak likewise of the ecclesiastical conflicts among churchmen; nothing inferior in my mind, nor less worthy to be noted than the other. For so I read in Matthew Paris, and in the Flowers of History, that at what time this wrestling was among the citizens for the sheep, the like contention kindled and inflamed between Eustace, bishop of London, and the chapter of Paul's, on the one side, and the abbot of Westminster, with his covent, on the other, about spiritual jurisdiction and subjection; to wit, whether the monastery of Westminster were exempted from the subjection and jurisdiction of the bishop of London or not. This controversy at last coming to a compromise, was committed to the arbitrement of Stephen, archbishop of Canterbury, Philip, bishop of Winchester, Thomas of Merton, and Richard, prior of Dunstable; and at length it was thus agreed: that the monastery of Westminster should be utterly exempted from the jurisdiction of the bishop of London, and that Staines, with the appurtenances thereto belonging, should appertain to the monastery of Westminster. Also, that the manor of Sunbury should be due and proper to the church of St. Paul, and also that the church of St. Margaret, with all the lands belonging to the same, should be exempted from all other jurisdiction, but of the bishop of Rome only: and so was this matter decided. A.D. 1222.[2]

(1) Ex Matth. Paris. (2) Ibid.; ex Flor. Historiarum.

Henry III. A.D. 1223. The same year, as writeth Matthew Paris, horrible tempests, with thundering and lightning and whirlwinds, went throughout all the land, so that much harm was done; churches, steeples, towers, houses, and divers trees, with the violence of the winds, were blown up by the roots. In Warwickshire, a certain wife, and eight others in her house, were slain. In Grantham, the church was set on fire by lightning most terrible, with such a stink left behind, that no man could, for a long time after, abide it. The author addeth, that manifest marks of the tempest did remain long after in that monastery to be seen. Some also write that fiery dragons and spirits were seen then flying in the air.

Horrible tempest in England.

A.D. 1223. Louis, king of France, false to his promise.

A.D. 1223, Philip, the French king, died, after whom his son Louis succeeded to the crown; to whom King Henry, sending his message, and desiring him to remember his promise and covenant made of rendering again the lands lost in Normandy, could obtain nothing at his hands. Whereupon Richard, earl of Cornwall, also William, the king's uncle, earl of Salisbury, with divers other nobles, made over into France, where they recovered Poictiers, and kept Gascony under the king's obedience.[1]

A.D. 1224. Wardship first granted to the king.

In the same year, or as Fabian giveth it, the next year following, which was A.D. 1224, by virtue of a certain parliament, it was granted of the lords and barony of the land, that the king and his heirs should have the ward and marriage of their heirs, which then was called, and afterwards proved to be, 'initium malorum,' the beginning of harms.

In the same year, according to Gisburn and other writers, the said king, holding another parliament at Oxford, by the advice of his council and his clergy, did grant and confirm, under his great seal, two charts of the old liberties and customs of this realm, for ever to be kept and observed, the one called 'Magna Charta,' the other 'Charta de Foresta;' the contents whereof fully in the beforenamed author be expressed. For this cause was granted again by the whole parliament, a fifteenth of all his subjects, as well of laymen as also of the clergy.

Here is to be noted, that these liberties were afterwards broken, and confirmed again by the said king, A.D. 1236.

A.D. 1226 died Pope Honorius III., a great adversary of Frederic the emperor, after whom succeeded Gregory IX., more grievous than his predecessor. In this year also died Louis VIII., the perjured French king, at the siege of Avignon; whom the pope now, for the second or third time, had set up to fight against Reimund, the good earl of Toulouse, and the heretic Albigenses of that country; for so the pope calleth all those who hold not in all points with his glorious pride, usurped power, and ungodly proceedings. The origin of it was this, as in Matthew Paris appeareth. In the days of Philip, the French king, this Reimund, earl of Toulouse, was disdained by the pope for holding with the Albigenses; and therefore, by the instigation of the pope, the lands of the earl were taken from him, and given to Simon Montfort, and instruments were made upon the same; but when the said earl Reimund would not be removed from the right of his possessions by unrighteous dealing, the pope setteth Philip II., the French king, to make open war against him. Where-

(1) Ex Matth. Paris.; Nich. Trivet; Flor. Hist.

upon Louis, the French king's son,[1] was sent with a great power, as is above declared, to besiege the city of Toulouse; but being repulsed from thence by the marvellous hand of God fighting for his people, he could not prevail, and so returned home, after he had lost the most part of his army by pestilence and other calamity, as hath been before described. Thus continued the good earl still in quiet possession till this present time, A.D. 1226; in the which year the pope, not forgetting his old malice against the earl, and no less inflamed with insatiable avarice, directeth down his legate, Master Romanus, to the parts of France, for two several purposes; one to extirpate the earl, the other to enlarge his own revenues. Thus the legate, being entered into France, beginneth to summon a council, willing the French king, with the archbishops, bishops, and clergy of France, to appear before him at Bitures; to whom eftsoons repaired six archbishops, with the bishops and suffragans of nine provinces, to the number of a hundred, besides the abbots, priors, and proctors of all the covents of France, to hear the pope's will and commandment. But because there was a discord feared to rise, saith Matthew Paris, about pre-eminence of sitting, for that the archbishop of Lyons challenged the superior place above the archbishop of Sens, also the archbishop of Rouen above the archbishop of Bitures, and above the archbishop of Narbonne; therefore the session was holden there not in manner and form of a council, but of a certain parley or consultation. Thus the meek and holy council being set, and the pope's majesty's letters read and declared, appeareth before them Reimund, earl of Toulouse, of the one part, and Simon Montfort, on the other part. This Simon required to be restored unto him the lands and possessions of the said Reimund, which the pope and Philip, the French king, had given to him and to his father before, having good evidences to show for the same, confirmed by the donation of the pope and of the king; adding moreover, that the earl Reimund was deprived and disinherited in the general council at Rome for heresy, which is called the heresy of the Albigenses. At least, if he might not have the whole yielded unto him, yet the most part of his lordships he required to be granted him.

The pope raiseth war, A.D. 1226. The pope's wicked malice against the christian earl of Toulouse.

Mark, reader, the right nature of Pharisees striving for the chief place.

The pope giveth the right possession away from the owners.

To this the earl Reimund answered again, offering himself ready to all duty and office both toward the French king and to the church of Rome, whatsoever to him did duly appertain. And moreover, touching the heresy wherewith he was there charged; he did not only there offer himself, in that council, before the legate, but most humbly did crave of him, that he would take the pains to come into every city within his precinct, to inquire of every person there the articles of his belief; and if he found any person or persons holding that which was not catholic, he would see the same to be corrected and amended, according to the censure of holy church, to the uttermost. Or if he should find any city rebelling against him, he, to the uttermost of his might with the inhabitants thereof, would compel them to do satisfaction there for. And as touching himself, if he had committed or erred in any thing (which he remembereth not

Reimund the good earl of Toulouse answereth for himself.

Albigenses falsely suspected of heresy.

(1) This Louis (afterwards Louis VIII. of France) was the eldest son of Philip II. To him the barons of England offered the crown, in the miserable days of King John. John died A.D. 1216, and Louis was defeated on the 19th of May in the following year, by the Lord Protector Pembroke, and compelled to evacuate the kingdom.—ED.

Henry III — A.D. 1226

that he had done), he offered there full satisfaction to God and the church, as became any faithful christian man to do; requiring, moreover, there, before the legate, to be examined of his faith. But all this, saith Matthew Paris, the legate despised; neither could the catholic earl, saith he, there find any grace, unless he would depart from his heritage, both for himself, and for his heirs for ever. In fine, when it was required, on the contrary part, that he should stand to the arbitrement of twelve peers of France, Reimund answered, that if the French king would receive his homage, which he was ready at all times to exhibit, he was contented therewith. For, otherwise, they would not, said he, take him as one of their society and fellow-subjects.

After much altercation on both sides about the matter, the legate willeth every archbishop to call aside his suffragans to deliberate with them upon the cause, and to give up in writing what was concluded. This being done accordingly, the legate denounceth excommunication on all such as did reveal any piece of that which was there concluded, before the pope and the king had intelligence thereof.

These things, thus in hudder mutter among themselves, concluded, the legate gave leave to all proctors of covents and chapters to return home, only retaining with him the archbishops, bishops, and abbots, and certain simple prelates, such as he might be more bold withal, to open, and of them to obtain, the other part of his commission; which was, indeed, to obtain of every cathedral church two prebendships,—one for the bishop, the other for the chapter. In monasteries also, after the like sort, where the abbot and covent had divers and several portions, to require two churches; one for the abbot, the other for the covent; keeping this proportion, that how much should suffice for the living of one monk, so much the whole covent should find for their part, and as much the abbot likewise for his. And, forasmuch as he would not seem to demand this without some colour of cause, his reason was this: that because the court of Rome had long been blotted with the note of avarice, who is mother of all evil, for that no man could come to Rome for any business, but he must pay for the expedition of the same; therefore, for the removing away of the occasion of that slander, the public help of the church must necessarily be required.

Mark, reader, the practice of prelates, for thy learning

The proctors and parties thus sent home by the legates, marvelling with themselves why the bishops and abbots should be staid, and they sent home, and suspecting no less than as the matter was indeed, conferred their counsels together, and devised with themselves to send certain unto him in the behalf of all the cathedral and conventual churches in France; and sent to the said legate this message, to signify to him, that they were credibly informed he came with special letters from the court of Rome for the obtaining of certain prebendaries in every cathedral and conventual church; which being so, they much marvelled that he would not in the public council make manifest to them those letters which specially concerned them, as much as the others. Wherefore, their request was to him in the Lord, that no such offensive matter might arise by him in the French church; knowing this, that the thing he enterprised could not be brought to effect without great offence

The clergy of France answering to the legate

taken, and inestimable damage to the church of France. "For grant," said they, "that certain will assent unto you, yet their assent standeth in no effect concerning such matters as touch the whole; especially seeing both the states of the realm, with all the inferior subjects, yea, and the king himself, they are sure, will withstand the same, to the venture, not only of their honour, but of their life also; considering the case to be such, as upon the offence whereof standeth the subversion both of the realm public, and of the whole church in general." Declaring, moreover, the cause of this fear to arise hereof, for that in other realms such communication hath been with bishops and prelates for the procuring of such prebendships, whereas neither the prince nor the subjects were made any thing privy thereto.

In conclusion, when the matter came to debating with the legate, the objections of the inferior parties against the cruel exaction were these in brief effect, as in Matthew Paris are noted.

Inferiors evermore bold to speak than the rich.

First, They alleged their great damages and expenses which they were like to sustain thereby, by reason of the continual procurators of the pope, who, in every diocese, must not live of their own, but be sustained by the charges of the cathedral churches, and other churches also; and many times they, being but procurators, will be found as legates.

Objections of the clergy of France against the pope's exaction.

Item, By that means, they said, great perturbations might ensue to the covents and chapters of cathedral churches in their elections; forasmuch as the pope's agents and factors being in every cathedral church and chapter-house, perhaps the pope would command the agent or factor in person to be present at their elections, and so might trouble the same in delaying, and deferring, till it might fall to the court of Rome to give; and so there should be placed more of the pope's clientels in the churches of France, than of the proper inhabitants of the land.

Item, By this means they affirmed, that all they in the court of Rome should be richer, and should receive more for their proportion than the king of the realm: by reason of which abundance of riches, it was like to come to pass, that as the worm of rich men is pride, so, by the means of this their riches, the court of Rome would delay and drive off great suits, and would scarcely take any pains with small causes; the experiment whereof is evident, for that now also they use to delay their matters, when they come with their gifts, and being in assurance to receive. And thus should justice stand aside, and poor suitors die at the gates of the court of Rome, thus flowing and triumphing in full abundance of all treasure and riches.

Item, Forasmuch as it is meet and convenient to have friends in the court of Rome, for the better speeding of their causes; therefore they thought to keep them needy, whereby their gifts may be the sweeter, and their causes sooner despatched.

Item, As it is impossible to stop the fountain of greedy desire, it was to be feared, either that they would do that by others, which they were wont to do by themselves, or else, that they should be forced to give greater rewards than before; for small gifts, in the sight of great rich men, are not looked upon.

Item, Where he alleged the removing away of the slander which

Henry III.

A.D. 1226.

goeth on the court of Rome: by this means rather the contrary were to be feared, wherein they alleged the sentence of the verse, that great riches stop not the taking of much, but a mind contented with a little:

"Quod virtus reddit, non copia sufficientem,
Et non paupertas sed mentis hiatus egentem."

Further, they alleged that great riches would make the Romans mad, and so might kindle among them sides and parts-taking; so that, by great possessions, sedition might follow to the ruin and destruction of the city, whereof some experiment they had already.

Item, They added, that although they would condescend and oblige themselves to that contribution, yet their successors would not be so bound, nor yet ratify that bond of theirs.

Lastly, They conclude the matter by desiring that the zeal of the universal church, and of the church of Rome, would move him: for, if this oppression of the church should be universal, it were to be doubted lest an universal departing might follow from the church of Rome, which God forbid, say they, should happen.

God grant, say we.

The legate hearing these words, being therewith something moved, as seemed, excused himself, that he, being in the court, never agreed to this exaction; and that the letters, hereof, came not to him before he was in France, whereat he said he was greatly sorry: adding this withal, that the words of his precept included this secret meaning in them, thus to be understood and taken, "so far forth as the empire and other realms would agree unto the same;' and as for him, he would stir no more in the matter, before it were proved what other countries would say and do therein.

The cardinal repulsed and defeated in France.

And thus much concerning the second part of the blind commission of this legate, touching his exaction of prebendships in every cathedral and conventual church; wherein, as ye hear, he was repulsed.[1]

The pope raiseth war against the earl and people of Toulouse.

Now to return to the first part of his commission again, which was concerning Reimund, the godly earl of Toulouse,—thus the story proceedeth: that while the legate was in hand with this matter of the pope's money, in the mean season, certain preaching friars were directed by the said Romanus, the pope's legate, into all France, to incite and stir up the Frenchmen to take the cross upon them, and to war against the earl of Toulouse, and the people thereof, whom they accounted for heretics. At their preaching, a great number of prelates and laymen signed themselves with the cross, to fight against the people of Toulouse, being thereto induced, as the story saith, more for fear of the French king, Louis VIII., or favour of the legate, than for any true zeal of justice. For so it followeth in the words of Matthew Paris:[2] "For to many," saith he, "it seemed an abuse to move war against a faithful christian man, especially, seeing in the council of Bitures, before all men, he entreated the legate, with great instance, that he would come into

Testimony of the author for the clearing of Reimund and of the Albigenses.

(1) Ex Matth. Paris. p. 62.

(2) "Videbatur enim multis abusio, ut hominem fidelem Christianum infestarent, præcipue cum constaret cunctis, eum, in concilio nuper Bituriensi, multis precibus persuasisse legato, ut veniret ad singulas terræ suæ civitates, inquirens a singulis articulos fidei: et si quempiam contra fidem inveniret," &c.

every city within his dominions, and there inquire of every person the articles of his faith; where, if he found any man to hold any thing contrary to the catholic faith, he promised a full satisfaction to be had thereof, according to the censure of the church, to the uttermost."

The unreasonable tyranny of the pope against the people of Toulouse.

Yet all this notwithstanding, the proud legate, contemning this so honest and reasonable purgation of the earl Reimund, ceased not by all manner of means to prosecute the pope's fury against him and his subjects, stirring up the king and the Frenchmen, under pain of excommunication, to war against them. Louis, the French king, thus being enforced by the legate, answered again, that he, for his own safety, would not achieve that expedition, or adventure against the earl, unless it were first obtained of the pope to write to the king of England; commanding him, that, during the time of that expedition, he should invade and molest no part of his lands and possessions which he at that time did hold, whether by right or by wrong, or howsoever they were holden, while the time of the said war against the heretics (as they were then termed) did endure, but rather should aid and assist him with counsel and money in that enterprise. All this being done and accomplished, the French king and the legate (crossing themselves to the field) appointed a day peremptory for the French army to meet together at Lyons, under pain of the pope's excommunication, and, with horse and harness, to set upon the people of Toulouse, against the Ascension day next ensuing.

Excommunication abused.

Louis, the French king, and Romanus, the pope's legate, march against the Albigenses. Earl of Toulouse excommunicated.

When the Ascension day was come, which was the day peremptorily appointed, the French king, having prepared at Lyons all things necessary for his army, marcheth forward with a great and mighty host; after whom also cometh the legate, with his bishops and prelates. The number of fighting men in his army, besides the victuallers and waggoners, was fifty thousand men. The legate, by the way, openly excommunicated the earl of Toulouse, and all that took his part; and, furthermore, interdicted his whole land. Thus the king marched forward till he came into the province of Toulouse; and the first city which he came unto there of the earl's was Avignon, which city they thought first to besiege, and so in order afterwards, as they went to destroy and waste all the whole province belonging to the earl. And first the king demanded of them to have his passage through their city; feigning himself in peaceable wise, but for the expedition of his journey, to pass through the same. The citizens, consulting with themselves what was to be done, at length gave answer, that they mistrusted their coming, and supposed that, in deceit, they required the entrance of their city, and for no necessity of their journey.

City of Avignon besieged.

The king, hereat being much offended, swore an oath, that he would not depart thence till he had taken the city; and immediately, in those places where he thought most meet, he began to make sharp attacks, with all manner of saultable engines; the citizens again within manfully defended themselves, and casting stone for stone, and shooting shot for shot, slew and wounded many of the Frenchmen. Thus, when they had long besieged the city, and could not win the same, at length victuals in the French camp began to fail,

Henry III.
A.D. 1226.

and many of them died for hunger; for the earl of Toulouse, as a wise man of war, hearing before of their coming, took into the town all the provision that was abroad, and left nothing, without, to serve for their defence and succour; he ploughed up the fields, that there should no stover[1] be found to serve their horses; he put out of the town all the old people and young children, lest they should want victuals that kept the town, and before their coming sent them far away, so that within the town they had plenty, and without, they died for famine. And, besides, in seeking far for their forage, many fell into the hands of them that kept the city, who secretly lay in wait for them abroad, and slew many of them; besides that, a great number of cattle and horses died for want of forage; and also poor soldiers, who had no great store of money, died for want of victuals. By the mortality and the stench, both of men and cattle, grew great infection and pestilence among them; insomuch that the king himself, and also the legate, were greatly dismayed, thinking it to be no little shame, as well to the realm of France, as also to Rome, that they should so depart and break up their siege. Thus again thought the soldiers, that much better it were for them to end their lives by battle, than thus to starve and die like dogs; wherefore, with one consent, they purposed to give a new assault at the bridge that goeth over the Rhone into the town, to which place they came in such numbers, that either by the debility of the bridge, or by the subtlety of the soldiers that kept the town, three thousand of them, with bridge and all, fell armed into the violent stream, and were drowned. What was there, then, but joy and gladness on the citizen's part, and much lamentation and heaviness on the other part? Shortly after this, the citizens of Avignon (when they saw a convenient time, whilst their enemies were eating meat) came suddenly upon them out of the town, and slew of them two thousand, and took to the town again with safety. But the legate, with his company of prelates, like good men of war, practised no other martial feats, but all to be cursed,—the earl of Toulouse, his cities, and his people. Louis VIII. the king, to avoid the pestilence that was in the camp, went into an abbey not far off; where, shortly after, he died. Of his death there are sundry opinions; some saying, that he was poisoned; some, that he died of a bloody-flux, A.D. 1226; whose death, notwithstanding, the legate thought to keep secret and conceal, till the town might be surrendered and given up: for he thought himself shamed for ever if he should depart before the town were won. Wherefore, after he had encouraged the soldiers afresh, and yet after many sharp assaults could not prevail, he bethought him how by falsehood he might betray them, and sent unto them certain heralds, to will them that they should among themselves consult upon articles of peace, and bring the same to their camp, whose safe conduct they faithfully promised and warranted, both of coming, and going. When they had given their pledges for the same, the messengers from the citizens talked with the legate, who promised them, if they would deliver up their city, they should have their lives, goods, and possessions in as ample manner as now they enjoyed the

Famine and pestilence in the French camp.

The French soldiers destroyed at the siege of Avignon.

Louis, the French king, dieth at the siege of Avignon.

The false dealing of the pope's legate in betraying the city of Avignon.

(1) "Stover," fodder.—ED.

same. But the citizens and soldiers refused to be under the servitude of the French king, neither would so deliver up their city to those of whose insolent pride they had so good experiment. After much talk on both sides, and none likely to take effect, the legate requested them, and friendly desired, that he and his prelates who were about him, might come into their city to examine what faith and belief they were of, and that he neither sought nor meant any other thing thereby, but their own safeties, as well of body as soul, which thing he faithfully swore unto: "For," saith he, "the rumour of your great infidelity hath come to the lord pope's ear, and therefore desired he to make true certificate thereof." Hereupon the citizens, not mistrusting his faithful oath and promise made unto them, granted entrance to him and the residue of the clergy, bringing with them no weapon into the town. The soldiers of the camp, as it was agreed before, made themselves ready, so that at the entrance of the prelates in at the gate, nothing regarding their oath and fidelity, the others suddenly were ready, and with violence rushed in, slew the porter and warders, and, at length, won the city and destroyed the same, and slew many of them that were within. When by falsehood and policy they had thus gotten this noble city, they carried the king's corpse to Paris, where they buried the same. Of the whole number of the French soldiers who in this siege were destroyed by famine, pestilence, and drowning, be recounted more than two and twenty thousand: "Whereby," saith Matthew Paris, "it may evidently appear that the war was unjustly taken in hand."

Perjury of the papists. The city of Avignon taken.

After these things finished, and after the funeral of the king celebrated at Paris, it followeth in the History of Matthew Paris, that the said legate, Romanus, was vehemently suspected and grievously defamed as having abused himself with Blanca, the king's mother:[1]—"But it is ungodly," saith he, "to suspect any such thing of him, because his enemies so rumoured the same abroad; but a gentle mind expoundeth things doubtful in the better part."

To pass on to the year following, which was A.D. 1227, first it is to be noted, that in this year King Henry, beginning to shoot up unto the twentieth year of his age, came from Reading to London, where he began to charge the citizens of London for old reckonings; namely, for giving or lending one thousand marks to Louis, the French king, at his departing out of the realm, to the great prejudice of him and of his kingdom; for the recompense whereof they were constrained to yield to the king the full sum of the like money. That done, he removed to Oxford, where he assembled a great council, there denouncing and protesting before them all, that he was come to sufficient age no more to be under tutors and governors, but to be his own man, requiring to be freed from the custody of others. This being protested against and resisted, forthwith he, by the counsel of Hubert the chief justice, whom he then made earl of Kent, removed from his company the bishop of Winchester, and others, under whom he was moderated; and immediately, in the same council, by the sinister persuasion of some, he doth annihilate and make void the charters and liberties, before, by him granted;

The king claimeth to be freed from governors, and to be his own man.

(1) "Sed impium est, hoc credere, quia æmuli ejus hoc disseminaverunt; benignus autem animus dubia in melius interpretatur."

Henry III.

A.D. 1228.

pretending this colour, for that they had been granted and sealed in the time of his minority, at a time when he had the rule neither of himself, nor of his seal; whereupon much muttering and murmuring was among the multitude, who did all impute the cause to Hubert, the justice. Moreover, it was at the same time proclaimed, that whosoever had any charter or gift sealed in the time of the king's minority, should come and renew the same again under the new seal of the king, knowing otherwise, that the thing should stand in no effect. And finally, for renewing of their seals, they were taxed not according to their ability, but according to as it pleased the justice and others to levy upon them.

Revoketh the liberties which he had granted.

Moreover, besides this general subsidy of the fifteenth, granted to the king through the whole realm, and besides all the contribution of the Londoners, divers other parcels and payments he gathered through several places; as of the burgesses of Northampton he required a thousand and two hundred marks, for his helping of them, and so of others likewise. All this preparation of money was made toward the furnishing of his voyage to recover Normandy: and yet, because he would gratify the city of London again with some pleasure, he granted that the citizens thereof should pass toll-free, saith Fabian, throughout all England; and if, of any city, borough, or town, they were constrained at any time to pay their toll, then the sheriffs of London were to attach every man coming to London of the said city, borough, or town, and him with his goods to withhold, till the Londoners were again restored of all such money paid for the said toll, with all costs and damages sustained for the same.[1]

Citizens of London freed from toll. A.D. 1228.

I declared before, how after the death of Honorius succeeded Pope Gregory IX., between whom and the people of Rome this year arose a great sedition, insomuch that about the feast of Easter they thrust the pope out of the city, pursuing him unto his castle at Viterbium, where also they invaded him so valiantly, that they chased him to Perugia. Then having no other remedy wherewith to revenge his persecutors, fiercely he did excommunicate them.[2]

The pope's church may be judged by their dissensions and schisms. No peace in the pope's church.

Here, by the way, is to be observed and considered, christian reader, not only by this sedition, but by so many other schisms, divisions, tumults, fightings, brawls, and contentions in the church of Rome from the first beginning of the pope's usurped power, and that not only within the city of Rome, but universally almost in all popish monasteries, colleges, churches, and covents under the pope subjected, continually reigning amongst them, what is to be thought of their religion and holiness, having so little peace, so great disquietness, dissensions, and wrangling amongst them, as in stories manifest it is both to behold, and wondrous to consider.

Dissension between the prior and covent of Durham and the king.

Forasmuch as I have here entered into the mention of this schismatical commotion between the pope and his citizens, it followeth moreover, in the History of Matthew Paris, who maketh relation of a like brawling matter, which befell the same year and time, A.D. 1228, between the prior and covent of Durham, and this King Henry III., upon this occasion. After the death of Richard, bishop of Durham, the prior and chapter of the said church came to the king, to obtain

(1) Ex Fabiano, par. 7. (2) Ex Matth. Paris. p. 69.

license for the electing of their bishop. The king offered them one Lucas, a chaplain of his, requiring them instantly to elect him for their bishop. To this the monks answered, that they would receive no man, but by their order of canonical election; meaning, belike, by their canonical election, when they either elect some monk out of their own company, or else some monkish priest after their own liking. Contrary, the king again sendeth word unto them, and bound it with an oath, that they should tarry seven years without a bishop, unless they would admit the aforesaid Lucas to that place of dignity. All which notwithstanding, the monks, proceeding in their election, refused the said Lucas; and preferred another clerk of theirs, named William, archdeacon of Worcester, and him they presented to the king: but the king, bringing in exceptions and causes against that party, would not admit him. Then the monks, in all hasty speed, sent up to Rome certain of their covent, to have their election ratified by the authority apostolical. On the other side, the king, likewise hearing, sendeth also to Rome against the monks, the bishop of Chester and the prior of Lentony on his behalf, to withstand the purpose of the monks. And so the matter, being traversed with great altercation on both sides, did hang in suspense, saith mine author; till at length thus it was concluded between both, that neither Master William nor yet Lucas should be taken, but that Richard, bishop of Sarum, should be translated to Durham, and be bishop there. A.D. 1228.[1]

The monks of Durham send to Rome against their king.

The like stir also happened, both the same year, and for a like matter, between the monks of Coventry and the canons of Lichfield, about choosing their bishop, which of them should have the superior voice in the election of their prelate. After much ado, the cause, at length being hoisted up to Rome, had this determination; that the monks of Coventry, and the church of Lichfield, should choose their bishop by course, each party taking turn, the one after the other: provided, notwithstanding, that the prior of Coventry should always have the first voice in every election; whereas the old custom was, saith mine author, that the covent with the prior of Coventry was wont to have the whole election of the bishop without the canons. This was A.D. 1228.[2]

In that year died Stephen Langton, archbishop of Canterbury, by whom, as is recorded by Nicholas Trivet, the chapters of the Bible, in that order and number as we now use them, were first distinguished. The said Langton also made postils[3] upon the whole Bible. The same prelate, moreover, builded the new hall, in the palace of Canterbury.

The chapters of the Bible first distinguished by Stephen Langton.

After the death of this Langton ensued another variance about the election of the archbishop of Canterbury, between the monks of Canterbury and the king; the perturbation whereof as it was no less seditious, so the determination of the same was much more costly. After the death of Langton, the monks of Canterbury, obtaining license of the king to proceed in the election of a new archbishop, did choose one of their own society, named Master Walter Hemesham; whom, when the monks had presented unto the king, he, after long deliberation, began to object against that election, saying, first,

Dissension between the monks of Canterbury and the king.

(1) Ex Matth Paris (2) Ibid fol 68 (3) "Postils," Marginal notes —Ed

Henry III. A.D. 1228.

that the monks had elected such a one as was neither profitable to him, nor his kingdom. Secondly, he objected against the party elect, that his father was convicted of felony, and hanged for the same. Thirdly, that he stood in causes against his father, King John, in the time of the interdict. Moreover, the bishops, his suffragans, charged the party elect, that by a certain nun, he had had children; adding further, that the election of the archbishop was without their presence, which ought not to be. But the archbishop, stoutly standing to the election, appealed up to Rome, and eftsoons taking with him certain monks, presented himself to the pope's own proper person, there to sue his appeal, instantly entreating that his election might stand confirmed by his authority pontifical; but the pope, understanding that the said election was resisted by the king and the bishops, deferred the matter until he did hear further of the certainty thereof. The king and the bishops, having intelligence that the archbishop with his monks were gone to Rome, thought good to articulate the aforesaid objections above alleged, in writing; and, sealing the same with the seals both of the king and of the bishops, to exhibit them to the bishop of Rome. The messengers of these letters were the bishops of Rochester, of Chester, and the archdeacon of Bedford, Master John, &c., who, coming to Rome, and exhibiting their message with their letters unto the pope (consideration being had upon the same), were commanded to wait attendance against the next day after Ash Wednesday: then to have a resolute answer concerning the cause, which was the second day of March the year following; that is, A.D. 1229. In the mean season, the king's proctors ceased not with all instance to labour the pope and his cardinals to be favourable to the king's side; but finding them somewhat hard and strict in the matter, as is the guise of that court, they began to misdoubt their speeding. Wherefore, consulting together with themselves upon the premises, they came to the pope, promising in the king's behalf, to be given and granted to him out of the realms both of England and Ireland, the tithe or tenth part of all the goods within the said realms moveable, to sustain his wars against the emperor, so that he would incline favourably to the king's suit and petition herein. "But the pope," saith Matthew Paris, "who boiled with desire above all measure, to have the emperor, his enemy, cast down, being cheered with such great promises," (O auri sacra fames!) "granted his consent to them;"[1] who, sitting then in his consistory, had these words which here follow.

King Henry sendeth to the pope.

Tithe of all moveable goods in England and Ireland promised to the pope.

It is pity the pope will take no bribes.

The Pope's Answer to the Election of Walter, Archbishop of Canterbury.

There hath come, of late, to our intelligence, the election of a certain monk named Walter, to be archbishop of Canterbury; whereupon, after that we heard and advised, as well those things which the said monk hath said for himself and for his election; as also, on the contrary side, the objections and exceptions of the bishops of England, alleging against him and against his election; namely, of the bishop of Chester, the bishop of Rochester, and John, archdeacon of Bedford: we, upon the same, committed the examination, touching the person of the man, unto our reverend brethren Lord Cardinal

No, but when your darling Thos. Becket

(1) "At dominus papa, qui rebellem imperatorem super omnia æstuabat dejicere, tantis promissionibus exhilaratus, trahitur ad consensum."

Albany, Lord Cardinal Thomas de Sabina, and Master Peter. And when the aforesaid elect, coming before them, was asked of them, first concerning the Lord's descending into hell, whether he descended in flesh, or without his flesh, he answered not well. Item, being asked touching the making of the body of Christ on the altar, he answered, likewise, not soundly. Being asked, moreover, how Rachel wept for her children, she being dead before, he answered not well. Item, being asked concerning the sentence of excommunication denounced against the order of law, he answered not well. Again, being required of matrimony, if one of the married parties be an infidel, and do depart, he answered, thereto, not well. Upon these articles, he was (as is said), diligently examined of the cardinals; to the which we say he answered not only not well, but also very ill. Forasmuch, therefore, as the church of Canterbury is a noble church, and requireth a noble prelate, a man discreet and modest, and such as ought to be taken out of the bosom of the church of Rome; and forasmuch as this new elect (whom not only here we pronounce to be unworthy, but also should say more of him, if we would proceed with him by the rigour of the law) is so insufficient, that he ought not to be admitted to such a room: we do utterly infringe, annihilate, and evacuate his election, always reserving to ourselves the provision of the said church.[1]

Henry III. A.D. 1229.

Came, he was heard without such communication.

The election of Walter, archbishop of Canterbury, dissolved by the pope, for the king's money.

Thus, the election of Walter being frustrated and dissolved, the king's procurators, bringing forth the letters of the king and of the suffragans of the church of Canterbury, presented the same unto the pope for the ratification of Richard, chancellor of Lincoln, to be appointed archbishop of Canterbury; whom they, with great commendation of words, did set forth to be a man of profound learning and knowledge, of an honest conversation, and, which was greatest of all, that he was a man much for the profit of the church of Rome, as also for the realm of England. The said Richard being thus commended to the pope by the letters procuratory of the king and of the bishops, had the consent of the pope and of the cardinals, and so was made bishop of Canterbury before he was elected. Whereupon the said Pope Gregory, in his behalf, directeth down his letters to all and singular the suffragans of the church of Canterbury, declaring thus, and beginning first with a lie, that 'forasmuch as, by the fulness of ecclesiastical power, the charge of pastoral office is committed to him in general upon all churches, he, therefore, for the solicitude he beareth, as well to all other churches in general, as in an especial manner to the metropolitan church of Canterbury, repudiating and disannulling the former election of Walter, the monk, upon just causes, hath provided for that see a man, as, in all other good gifts, perfect and excellent, by the report of them that know him, so, for that function, very fit and commodious; and willeth and commandeth them, and all others, by his authority apostolical, with all devout reverence to receive him, and humbly to obey him. A.D. 1229.'[2]

The effect of the pope's letters to the suffragans of Canterbury.

The pope beginneth with a lie.

These things thus finished at Rome, the pope, not forgetting the sweet promises made of the English silver which he so greedily gaped for, omitting neither time nor diligence, in all speedywise sendeth, unto the king of England, Master Stephen, his own chaplain and trusty legate, to require and collect the aforesaid tithes of all the moveable goods both of England, Ireland, and Wales, which were promised to him before; therewith to maintain his war against Frederic, the emperor. And, to the intent he might inflame all christian realms with the like hatred which he bare against Frederic,

This was a *dear* archbishop of Canterbury, bought with the tithes of all England.

(1) Hæc ex Matth. Parisiensi ad verbum. (2) Ex Matth. Paris.

Henry III

A.D. 1229

the emperor, he sendeth also with the said Stephen special letters, full of manifold complaints and grievous accusations against the said emperor, whereof more (Christ granting) shall be showed hereafter. Upon the coming of this Stephen, the legate, the king assembled all his earls and barons, with the archbishops, bishops, abbots, priors, templars, hospitallers, parsons, vicars, and others, such as held of him *in capite*, to appear before him at Westminster, to hear and to commune of the matter; in the assembly of whom the pope's patent letters were brought forth and read; wherein he required the tenths of all the moveables in England, Wales, and Ireland, as well of the clergy as of the laity, to maintain his expedition against the aforesaid Frederic, the emperor. As he pretended to achieve and to take in hand this expedition for the cause of the universal church, and happily had begun the matter already; and forasmuch as the riches of the apostolic see did not suffice for the accomplishing of so great an enterprise, he therefore, enforced by mere necessity, did implore the aid and help of all the true obedient and natural chickens of the church of Rome, lest the members thereof, together with the head, should be subverted. These letters of the pope, to this effect, being openly recited and explained by the pope's chaplain, which he, with much more allegation and persuasion of words, did amplify to his uttermost, the king, saith mine author, in whom all men did hope for help to their defence, became then as a staff of reed; for, much as he had obliged himself to the same before for the election of his archbishop, now could he say nothing against it, but held his peace. The earls, barons, and all the laity utterly refused so to bind their baronies to the church of Rome: but the bishops, abbots, priors, with other prelates of the church, first, requiring space and respite to deliberate for three or four days, at length, for fear of the pope's curse (although they durst not utterly withstand) had brought to pass to have concluded for a sum of money much less, had not Stephen Segrave, one of the king's counsellors, craftily convented with the legate, and by subtle means brought it so to pass, that the whole tenths were gathered and paid, to the inestimable damage, saith Matthew Paris, both of the ecclesiastical and temporal state; the means whereof, saith the author, were these: the legate showing to the prelates his procuratory letters, to collect and gather up all the aforesaid tenths in the name and authority of the pope, declared, moreover, the full authority to him granted by the virtue of his commission, to excommunicate all such, and to interdict their churches, whosoever did gainstand or go contrary to the said collection. Whereupon, by the said virtue legantine, he sendeth to every shire his proctors, to gather the pope's money, or else to excommunicate them who refused to pay. And, forasmuch as the present need of the pope required present help without delay, he sendeth moreover to the bishops and prelates of the realm, on pain of interdiction, forthwith to procure and send to him either of their own, or by loan or usance, or by what means soever, so much money, in all post speed, for the present use of the pope; and after, to take up again the said money of the tenths of every single person, by the right taxing of their goods. Upon this, the prelates, to avoid the danger, having no other remedy, were driven to sell their chalices, cruets,

The pope requireth the tenths of all the moveables in England, Wales, and Ireland

False pretence of the pope, under the name of the church, wreaking his own cankered malice

The king's mouth stopped

Excommunication abused

The pope's extortion.

copes, jewels, and other church plate, and some to lay to mortgage such things as they had, some also to borrow upon usance, to make the money which was required. Moreover the said Stephen, the pope's chaplain, as reporteth Matthew Paris, brought with him into England, for the same purpose, such bankers and usurers; who, lending out their money upon great usury, did unreasonably pinch the English people, which merchant usurers were then called Caursini. Briefly, such strait exaction was then upon the poor Englishmen, that not only their present goods were valued and taxed, but also the corn yet growing in the field against the next harvest was tithed. Only the earl of Chester, named Ranulph, stood stoutly against the pope, suffering none within his dominion, either layman or clerk, to yield any tenths to the pope's proctors.[1] And this was the end of the strife between the monks of Canterbury and the king for the election of their archbishop, which was about A. D. 1229; in which year was finished the new church of Coventry, by Alexander, bishop of the said city, and partly by the help of the king, which church Richard, his predecessor, a bishop of Coventry, had begun.

Usurers brought into England by the pope.

Corn upon the ground tithed to the pope A.D. 1229.

The Frenchmen about this time again prepared themselves towards Provence, to war against the aforesaid Reimund, earl of Toulouse, and to drive him out of his possessions; and, hearing that he was in his castle of Saracene, they marched thither all their power, thinking there to enclose and compass him about; but the earl, being privy to their conspired purpose, set for them by the way, appointing certain ambushments in woods, not so secretly as strongly, there to wait and receive the coming of the Frenchmen, and to give them their welcome. Thus when the French were entered the wood, the earl, with his train of well armed and able warriors, suddenly did fly upon them unawares, and gave them a bitter meeting, so that, in that conflict, five hundred of the French soldiers were taken and many slain. Of their servitors, to the number of two thousand men with their armour were taken, of whom some lost their eyes, some their noses, some their ears, some their legs, and so were sent home; the rest were carried away prisoners into the castle. "And to be brief," saith the history, "thrice in the same summer were the Frenchmen discomfited, put to flight, and taken and imprisoned by the aforesaid Reimund the godly earl.[2] Wherein is to be seen and to be praised the gracious protection of the Lord our God against the furious papists, who is glorious always in his saints.[3]

The pope's French army, thinking to destroy Reimund, is destroyed by the way.

(1) Ex Matth Paris, fol 74 (2) Ibid p 69

(3) We must conclude that our author extols rather the goodness of God in giving the victory, than the cruel manner in which earl Reimund improved it But while we shrink with disgust at these excesses inflicted upon the French soldiery, it must be remembered that Reimund, the seventh earl, was influenced more by political motives, than by the force of that love, which is taught in the pure doctrines of the gospel of Christ Without this holy principle, we cannot be surprised that the atrocious severities which his predecessor suffered, and which he saw inflicted upon his own people by the papal power, fostered within him a spirit of unrelenting rigour, which might in time become the dominant principle of his nature Let us for a moment glance at some of the hideous scenes to which a most bitter persecution had familiarised his mind, and then let any candid reader judge whether the papists have not more cause to blush at the name of pope Innocent III, the founder of the Inquisition, than the Albigenses have at the name of the earls Reimund "The subjects of Raymund (VIth) earl of Toulouse, and of some other great personages in his neighbourhood, so generally professed the Waldensian doctrines, that they became the peculiar objects of papal vengeance The inhabitants of Toulouse, Carcassone, Beziers, Narbonne, Avignon, and many other cities, who were commonly called the Albigenses, were exposed to a persecution more cruel and atrocious than any recorded in history"—(Milner, Ch Hist vol iii p 484) The first victims of the destructive and insidious machinations of the Inquisition, instituted about this period (A D 1206), were the people of the earl Reimund "The beginning of the thirteenth century" (continues the above author), "saw thousands of persons hanged or

Henry III

A.D. 1229.

The same year, the king, being at Portsmouth, had assembled together all his nobility, earls, barons, and knights of England, with such an army of horsemen and footmen, as hath not been lightly seen, thinking to recover again the countries of Normandy and Gaunt, and other possessions which King John, his father, before, had lost; but, when the captains and marshals of the field would take shipping, there were not half ships enough to receive the host. Hereupon the king was vehemently inflamed with anger, laying all the fault on Hubert, the lord chief justice, who, under the king, had all the government of the realm, calling him 'old traitor,' charging him that he would be the let of his voyage, as he was before, when he took of the French queen five thousand marks to stay the king's journey into Normandy. In so much was the rage of the king kindled against him, that, drawing his sword, he made at him to run him through, had not Ranulph, the earl of Chester, stopped the king. Hubert withdrew himself away till the king's rage was past. This was about Michaelmas, at which time arrived Henry, earl of Normandy, in the haven of Portsmouth, in the month of October; who should have conducted

Inconstancy of princes towards those that be chief about them

burned by these diabolical devices, whose sole crime was, that they trusted only to Jesus Christ for salvation, and renounced all the vain hopes of self-righteous idolatry and superstition." We will not relate details too terrible and disgusting to peruse, they may be found elsewhere but a brief extract from Stockdale's History of the Inquisition (p. 191) will give the reader some idea of the horrors of this ordeal. "When the accused was condemned to the torture, they conducted him to the place destined for its application, which was called The Place of Torment. It was a subterraneous vault, the descent to which was by an infinite number of winding passages, in order that the shrieks of the unhappy sufferers should not be heard. In this place there were no seats but such as were destined for the inquisitors, who were always present at the infliction of the torture. It was lighted only by two gloomy lamps, whose dim and mournful light served but to show to the criminal, the instruments of his torment. one or more executioners attended, as the case required. These executioners were clothed nearly in the same manner in which penitents are dressed,—in a large robe of black buckram, their heads and faces concealed under a cowl of the same colour, with holes for the eyes, the nose, and the mouth. This spectre-like figure seized the criminal, and stripped him of his clothes," &c. The same author (p. 47) observes, in reference to the persecutions of the Albigenses, "The siege of Beziers commenced. it was urged by all the fury of persecution, and sustained with all the energy of despair. The contest was too unequal. upon the 22d of July, 1209, a day ever memorable in the annals of Europe, the ramparts were forced, and the crusaders entered the city. Bleeding humanity attempts in vain to discredit the sad story of the scene which followed. Men, women, children, old and young, were murdered without mercy and without distinction. Not even the temples of the Almighty were respected, the unhappy victims were slaughtered upon the very altars to which they had fled for refuge, and when the troops were wearied with massacre, they fastened the doors of the churches, wherein thousands were immured, and setting fire to the buildings, the conflagration completed the destruction of those whom the sword had spared."—"After this, we need not be astonished to hear, that upwards of sixty thousand victims perished on that day." Nor are these cruelties to be attributed to the spirit of an uncultivated age, for the reader may now be referred to one of the enemies of the Albigenses, who defends the enormities here described. we mean the Right Rev. John Milner, D.D. In the Seventh Edition of his "Letters to a Prebendary," p. 72, this Romish writer, in speaking of the Albigenses, observes,—"It was against these pests of society and human nature, that fires were first lighted in the West, &c., and it was to repress and rout out these, &c. that the crusade of *our* Simon de Montfort and the Inquisition were set on foot, and that the canons, &c. were passed." And in the next page, this writer (who assures us that persecution is no tenet of the Romish church,) speaks of the "much lamented persecution of the Albigenses, to which, however, we are indebted for the continuance of society and the human race," &c.—"Three hundred thousand pilgrims, induced by the united motives of avarice and superstition, filled the country of the Albigenses with carnage and confusion for a number of years." "The castle of Menerbe, on the frontiers of Spain, for want of water, was reduced to the necessity of surrendering to the pope's legate. A certain abbot undertook to preach to those who were found in the castle, and to exhort them to acknowledge the pope: but they interrupted his discourse, declaring that his labour was to no purpose. Earl Simon (Montfort) and the legate then caused a great fire to be kindled. and they burned a hundred and forty persons of both sexes. These martyrs died in triumph, praising God that he had counted them worthy to suffer for the sake of Christ."—(Milner's Church History, vol. iii. p. 492.) The sixth earl Reimund, after a life of suffering and persecution, died in peace, A.D. 1222. His successor, the subject of the present history, pressed on all sides by the enemies of the truth and "the sinful seat of Rome," was constrained, A.D. 1229, to purchase an ignominious peace, by sacrificing a portion of his possessions to Louis IX., the French king, and making the accustomed *peace offering* to Pope Gregory IX. We come then to this conclusion. Our author, who, only on a foreign shore could escape the sanguinary rage of the papists in Queen Mary's reign, praises God for their defeat, and attaches to them the epithet "furious," in his recollections of wrongs and injuries suffered by his fellow-protestants. Reimund, the victim of papal cruelty, insult, and rage, in the flush of victory, surrounded by an infuriated soldiery, permitted the barbarities here related, against his prisoners. The church of Rome, in the written decrees of her councils—in the calm deliberations of her primates—in the mournful dungeons of the Inquisition—in cold blood—in premeditated crime, has made herself "drunk with the blood" of innocent millions whose "witness is in heaven, and whose record is on high."—Ed.

the king, upon his allegiance and oath, into Normandy, but he, with others of the king's army, counselled the king not to take that voyage towards winter, but rather to defer it to the Easter following; wherewith the king was stayed and well contented, and pacified again with Hubert, the justice, &c.[1]

Henry III

A. D. 1230

Fabian recordeth this year the liberties and franchises of the city of London to be confirmed by the king; and to each of the sheriffs to be granted two clerks, and two officers, without any more.[2]

Then followed A. D. 1230, in which, upon the day of the conversion of St. Paul, as saith Matthew Paris, as a great multitude of people for the solemnity of the day were congregate in the temple of St. Paul, the bishop then being at his mass, a sudden darkness with such thickness of clouds fell in the air, that scarcely one man might see another in the church. After that followed cracks of thunder and lightning so terrible, leaving such a scent in the church, that the people, looking for doomsday, thought no less but that the steeple and whole church would have fallen upon their heads; insomuch that running out of the church, the people fell down together by thousands, as men amazed, not knowing for the time where they were; only the bishop and his deacon stood still at their mass, holding fast by the altar.[3]

A sudden terror among the people in Paul's church by thunder and lightning.

Of the death of Stephen Langton, and of the troublesome election of the next archbishop, also of the costly and chargeable bringing in of Richard to succeed in his room, which did cost the whole realm of England the tenths of all their moveables, sufficient hath been declared before. This Richard, being now confirmed in his seat, came to the king, complaining of Hubert, the lord chief justice, oft mentioned before, for withholding from him the castle and town of Tunbridge, with the appurtenances to the same belonging, and other lands of the earl of Clare, late deceased, which lands appertain to the right of his see, and to the church of Canterbury; for which the said earl with his ancestors were bound to do homage to him and to his predecessors: and, therefore, he required the keeping of the aforesaid castle, with the domains thereof, to be restored to him. To this the king answered, that the said earl did hold of him *in capite*, and that the castles being vacant of earls and barons, with their heirs, did belong to his crown, till the lawful age of the said heirs. The archbishop, when he could get no other answer of the king, did excommunicate all such as invaded the aforesaid possessions, with all others that took their part, the king only excepted. This done, eftsoons he speedeth himself to Rome, there to prosecute his suit before the pope. The king hearing thereof, not long after sendeth up master Roger Cantelu, with certain other messengers, unto Rome against the archbishop.

A D 1231.

Complaint of Richard, archbishop of Canterbury, against Hubert lord chief justice

Excommunication abused.

Thus Richard the archbishop, coming before the pope's presence, beginneth first to complain of his king, for that he committed all the affairs of his realm to the disposition and government of Hubert, his justice, using only his counsel, all his other nobles despised.

Against the said justice, moreover, he complained, laying to his charge: first, that he had married a wife, being the kinswoman of her whom he had married before; also that the said Hubert, the

(1) Ex Matth Paris (2) Ex Fabiano (3) Ex Matth Paris fol 75

Henry III. justice, did invade, hold, and wrongfully detain such possessions as belonged to the see and church of Canterbury.

A.D. 1231. As touching the wife of this Hubert, here is to be noted, that he married the elder sister of the king of Scots: which, as it seemeth, could be of no great kin to her whom he married before.

Further, he complained of certain bishops, his suffragans, who, neglecting their pastoral function, did sit on exchequer matters belonging to the king, and exercised sessions and judgments of blood.

Over and besides, he complaineth of beneficed persons, and clerks in orders, for having many benefices joined with cure of soul: and that they also, taking example of the bishops, did intermeddle in secular matters, and in judgments of laymen.

Of these and such other defaults he required redress to be had. The pope, weighing the cause of the archbishop, and considering it to stand upon right and reason, at leastwise seeming so to his purpose, commanded incontinent his petitions and requests to be despatched according to justice.

Against these complaints of the archbishop, the king's attorneys alleged and defended as much in favour of the king as they might, but could do no good: such favour found the archbishop in the pope's sight, being, as the story reporteth, of a comely personage, and of an eloquent tongue, that he obtained whatsoever he asked. Thus the archbishop, with all favourable speed being despatched from Rome after his own will and desire, returned homeward; who, in his journey, within three days of his setting forth, departed in the house of Grey friars at St. Gemmes, and so his cause departed with him: who, winning his suit, lost his life; for whom it had been better, I suppose, to have tarried at home. And here of him an end, with all his complaints also.[1]

Respect of persons doth much with the pope.

After the death of this Richard, the monks of Canterbury, according to the manner, address themselves to a new election, at which was chosen Radulph Nevil, bishop of Chichester, who was the king's chancellor, much commended in stories as a man faithful, upright, and constant, who from the way of justice declined neither to the right hand nor to the left, but was upright and sincere both in word and deed.[2] This Radulph, thus chosen of the monks, was presented unto the king to be their archbishop, wherewith the king was right well contented, and glad also of this election, and forthwith invested him for archbishop of the church of Canterbury. But this investing of the king was not enough, unless he should also be confirmed by the pope. Wherefore the monks, ready to take their journey unto Rome, came to the new archbishop, requiring his help for their expenses by the way, and to know what service he would command them to the court of Rome. But he, fearing in his mind the same not to be without some scruple of simony and ambition, said, he would not give a halfpenny, and, holding up his hands to heaven, thus prayed, saying, "O Lord God, if I shall be thought worthy to be called, although indeed unworthy, to the seat and office of this church, so be it as thou shalt dispose it. But if, otherwise, in this troublesome office of chancery, and this my inferior ministery, whereunto I have been assigned, I shall seem more necessary for this

A rare example of a good archbishop.

(1) Ex Matth. Paris. (2) Ibid.

thy kingdom and people, I refuse not my labour; thy will be done!"

A.D. 1231.

The monks, beholding the constancy of the man, notwithstanding they had of him no money, yet refused not their travail and journey to Rome, to have their election confirmed by the pope's authority. The pope inquiring of Simon Langton (brother of Stephen Langton, archbishop of Canterbury, before mentioned) respecting the person of this man, it was reported to him by the said Simon (maliciously depraving the good man behind his back), declaring to the pope, that he was a courtier, unlearned, hasty and fervent in his doings, and one who, if he should be promoted to that dignity, would go about, with the help of the king and of the whole realm, to remove and bring the realm of England from under the yoke of the pope and the church of Rome, and so to bereave the see of Rome of the tribute, to which King John had once subjected himself and his realm, at the time he yielded his crown to the hands of Pandulph, the legate. With these and such other words Simon Langton falsely and maliciously depraved the godly bishop. The pope hearing with one ear, and crediting what he heard, without further inquisition made of the other party accused, sendeth immediately to the monks of Canterbury to proceed in a new election, and to choose them another archbishop, such as was an wholesome pastor of souls, profitable unto the church of England, and devoted to the church of Rome: and thus was the lawful election of this good archbishop made frustrate; too good, peradventure, to serve in that place whereunto he was elected.

Simon Langton, archbishop of York, a malicious backbiter of Ralph, archbishop elect.

Rash judgment of the pope.

After the repulse of this Radulph, the Canterbury monks, entering on a new election, agreed for John, their prior, to be their metropolitan, who, going up to Rome to have his election confirmed by the pope, was for three days together examined of the cardinals; and when they could find no insufficiency in him, touching those things wherein they tried him, yet, notwithstanding, the pope, finding fault with his age (he peradventure being more aged himself), repealed him, for that he said he was too old and simple to sustain that dignity.[1] What was the age of this person, I find not in the author expressed; yet it is to be supposed, that he, who was able to take that journey to Rome and home again, was not so greatly to be complained of for his age, but that he was able sufficiently to take pains in keeping the chair of Canterbury.

Two elections refused by the pope.

In the former parts of the preceding story partly, before, hath been declared, partly, hereafter, shall further appear (Christ willing) how the church of England and the commons of the same were grieved and miserably afflicted by the intolerable oppressions of the pope, who, through his violent extortion, had procured the best benefices to be given to his Romans, and the chief fruits of them to be reserved to his own coffers. What complaints thereof have been made, ye have heard before; but yet no redress could be had. Such was the insatiable avarice of these Roman rake-hells, prolling, and polling, wheresoever they came, with their provisions and exactions out of measure, and never satisfied; insomuch that here in England, whosoever lacked, their barns were always full of corn; and what penury soever pinched the people, they were sure to have enough. And these importunate

The pope's intolerable exactions in England.

(1) Ex Matth. Paris.

Henry III — A.D. 1231 — exactions and contributions of these Italian harpies, besides the Peter-pence, besides the common tribute, daily more and more increased, to the great grievance of the realm, insomuch that the wealth of this land was almost clean sucked up, and translated to the court of Rome, Neither was the king ignorant hereof, but could not help the matter. Wherefore it was devised by some of the nobles, as appeareth in the story of Matthew Paris,[1] this aforesaid year, A.D. 1231, that certain letters, under the pretensed colour of the king's authority, should be sent abroad, willing and commanding, that such corn and grain, with other revenues, as were taken up for the pope, should be staid and forthcoming by a certain day in the said letters appointed; which letters are thought to proceed chiefly by the means of Hubert, lord chief justice of England, who then, next under the king, ruled most of the affairs of the realm. The words and contents of the letters be these:—

Hubert, lord chief justice, a worker against the pope.

Copy of a Letter, written under the King's authority, to restrain the Benefices of the Romans within the Realm.

After divers and sundry griefs and oppressions which this realm, as you know, hath sustained by the Romanists, and yet doth, as well to the prejudice of the king himself, as also of the nobility of the same, concerning the advowsons of their churches, and about their tithes who also go about to take from the clerks and spiritual men their benefices, and to bestow them upon their own nation and countrymen, to the spoil and confusion both of us and our realm: we, therefore, by our common consents, have thought good (although very late) now, rather than any longer to suffer their intolerable oppressions and extortions, to resist and withstand the same, and, by the taking from them their benefices through all England, in like manner to cut short and bridle them, as they had thought to have kept under and bridled others · whereby they may desist any longer to molest the realm. Wherefore, we straitly charge and command you, as touching the farming of their churches, or else the rents belonging to them, which either you have presently in your hands, or else do owe unto the said Romanists, that, from henceforth, you be no more accountable to them, or pay to them from henceforth the same; but that you have the said your rents and revenues ready by such a day, to pay and deliver unto our procurators thereunto by our letters assigned, and that all abbots and priors have the same in readiness at the time appointed, in their own monasteries and that all other priests, clerks, and laymen, at the churches of the Romanists, be there ready to pay. And further, know ye for certainty, that if ye refuse thus to do, all that you have besides shall be by us burned and spoiled And besides, look, what danger we purpose shall fall upon them, the same shall light upon your necks, if you refuse thus to do Farewell.

When this was done, they sent their letters abroad by certain soldiers thereunto appointed, to the which letters they had devised a new seal with two swords engraved, and between the swords was written in Latin, "Behold these two swords, ready to take vengeance of all those that shall withstand the form and order in these letters contained."

A.D. 1232. At that time, the sixteenth day before the kalends of January, about the beginning of the year A.D. 1232, there was held at St. Alban's a great consistory of abbots, priors, and archdeacons, with divers both of the nobility and clergy, by the pope's commandment, for the celebration of a divorce between the countess of Essex and her husband. At the breaking up of which consistory, when every man

A Roman priest, canon of Paul's, taken and robbed by soldiers.

(1) Ex Matth Paris. fol 79

was about to depart thence, there was a certain clerk, whose name was Cincius, a Roman, and also a canon of Paul's in London, taken by some of the said university not far off from St. Alban's, and was carried away from his company by the soldiers. But Master John, archdeacon of Norwich, a Florentine, hardly escaping from that company, got to London, where he hid himself, and durst not be seen. Cincius, after five weeks, when they had well emptied his bags, was safely sent again without any more hurt to London.

Barns of a Roman parson broken up, and the corn distributed to the poor.

Not long after this, about the beginning of January, the barns of a certain beneficed man, a Roman, and parson of Wingham, being full of corn, were broken up by a like company of armed soldiers, and the corn brought out to be sold, and given away to the poor people. The farmer, seeing this, and not able to resist, complaineth to the sheriff of the shire of this injury done to his master, and of the breaking of the king's peace: whereupon the sheriff sent certain of his men to see what was done. Who, coming to the empty barns, and there finding the aforesaid soldiers, to them unknown, who had sold away the most part of the corn at an easy price, and some for charity had given to the poverty of the country about, required of them what they were, who so durst presume to break the king's peace. Whom the others then called secretly apart, and showed them the king's letters patent (pretending at least the king's name and seal), wherein was forbidden that any man should presume to stop or hinder them in that purpose. Of this the sheriff's servants being certified, quietly returned from whence they came.

This coming to the knowledge of Roger, bishop of London, he, with the assistance of other bishops, proceedeth in solemn excommunication, first against them that robbed Cincius, the Roman; then of them who spoiled the barns of the parson of Wingham, another Roman; thirdly, he excommunicated them that forged the letters and seal of the king above specified.

General spoil of the Roman parsons in England.

Neither yet, for all this, did that cease, but the same year, about the Easter following, all the barns in England which were in the hands of any Roman or Italian, were likewise wasted, and the corn sold to the best commodity of the poor commons; of the which, great alms were distributed, and many times money also, together with corn, was dispersed for the needy people to gather up; neither was there any that would or durst stand against them. As for the Romans and Italians themselves, they were stricken in such fear, that they hid themselves in monasteries and cells, not daring to complain of their injuries received; but held it better rather to lose their goods, than to lose their lives. The authors and workers of this feat were, to the number of fourscore, armed soldiers, of whom the principal captain was one naming himself William Withers, surnamed Twing.

The pope's choler. A furnish vicar of mild Christ.

This coming to the pope's knowledge, he was not a little stirred therewith, and sendeth his letters immediately to the king upon the same, with sharp threatenings, and imperious commandments, charging him for suffering such villany within his realm, straitly enjoining him, under pain of excommunication, to search out the doers hereof with all diligence, and so to punish them that all others by them may take example. Likewise he sendeth the same charge to Peter, bishop of

Henry III. A.D. 1232.

Winchester, and to the abbot of St. Edmund, to inquire in the south parts. Also to the archbishop of York, and to the bishop of Durham, and to Master John, canon of York, a Roman, to inquire in the north parts for the said malefactors, and, after diligent inquisition made, to send them up to Rome, there to appear before him.

Inquisition made for the spoiling of the pope's corn.

Thus, after earnest inquisition made of all parties, and witnesses sworn and examined, many were found culpable in the matter, of whom some were factors, some consenters, some bishops and chaplains to the king, some archdeacons and deans, with others who were soldiers and laymen. Among them were certain sheriffs and undersheriffs, who, with their servitors under them, were apprehended and cast into prison by the king. Many for fear fled and escaped away, who, being sought for, could not be found; but the principal of this number aforesaid, was supposed to be Hubert, the lord chief justice; who, both with the king's letters and his own, fortified the doers thereof, that no man durst interrupt them. Moreover, in the society of those who were noted in these doings, was the same Robert Twing above mentioned, a comely young man and a tall soldier; who, of his own voluntary accord, with five other servitors whom he took with him abroad to work that feat, came unto the king, openly protesting himself to be the author of that deed-doing; and said he did it for hatred of the pope and the Romans, because that by the sentence of the bishop of Rome, and fraudulent circumvention of the Italians, he was bereaved of the patronage of his benefice, having no more to give up than one; wherefore, to be revenged of that injury, he enterprised that which was done; preferring rather justly to be excommunicated for a season, than to be spoiled of his benefice for ever. Then the king, and other executors of the pope's commandment, gave him counsel, that seeing he had so incurred the danger of the pope's sentence, he should offer himself to the pope to be absolved of him again, and there to make his declaration unto him, that he, justly and canonically, was possessed of that church. The king, moreover, with him sent his letters testimonial unto the pope, witnessing with the said soldier, and instantly desiring the pope in his behalf, that he might with favour be heard; at the request whereof, Pope Gregory afterwards both released him from the sentence, and restored unto him his patronage, writing unto the archbishop of York, that he might again enjoy the right of his benefice, in as ample a manner as he did, before it was taken from him.

Robert Twing spoiled of his benefice by the Romans.

The bishops go about to get Hubert out of the king's favour.

Hubert de Burgh, lord chief justice, being one of those who held against the Romish priests, as is before signified, was there-for not a little noted of the bishops; who, to requite him with the like despite again, after their accustomed manner of practice, went about by subtle working to shake him out of the king's favour. And first cometh Peter, bishop of Winchester, to the king, grievously complaining of certain about the king; but especially of the aforesaid Hubert, the king's justice: insomuch that he caused him to be removed from his office, notwithstanding he had the king's seal and writing for the perpetuity of the same, and procured Stephen Segrave to be placed in his function. And after a few days, the king, more and more incensed against him, called him to give account of all the treasure for which he was accountable by his exchequer office: also,

Objections laid against Hubert by the king.

of all such debts, by him due, from the time of his father, till his time: also, of all the lordships which were in the possession of William, earl of Pembroke, chief justice before him. Item, of the liberties which he did hold at that time in forests, warrens, shires, and other places, how they were kept, or how they were made away with. Of prices likewise, also of losses committed through his negligence, and of wastes made contrary to the king's profit; of his liberties, how he did use them. Item, of injuries and damages wrought against the clerks of Rome and other Italians, and the pope's legates; for the redress whereof he would never adjoin his counsel, according as pertained to his office, being then chief justice of England. Also of scutages, gifts, presents, scapes of prisoners. Item, of maritages which King John committed to his keeping at the day of his death, and which were also in his time committed unto him. To these demands Hubert answered, that he had King John's own hand to show for his discharge, who so approved his fidelity, that he never called him to any, but clearly discharged him from all such counts. Whereunto answered the bishop of Winchester, saying, "the charter of King John hath no force after his death, but that ye may now be called to a reckoning by this king for the same."

Henry III. — A.D. 1232.

Note, that in Winchester the king's charter is no longer in force than whilst he liveth.

Over and besides these, other greater objections were laid to his charge by the king; as for sending and writing unto the duke of Austria, that he might marry his daughter, to the prejudice of the king, and of the realm, who dissuaded that she might not be given him. Item, for counselling the king not to enter into Normandy with his army, which he had prepared for the recovery of lands there belonging to his right, whereby great treasure was there consumed in vain. Item, for corrupting the daughter of the king of Scots, whom King John, his father, committed unto his custody for him to marry. Item, for stealing from him a precious stone, which had a virtue to make him victorious in war, and for sending the same unto Leoline, prince of Wales: and that by his letters sent to the said Leoline, William Brewer, a nobleman, was caused there traitorously to be hanged. These, with other crimes, whether true or false, were suggested to the king against the said Hubert by his adversaries; whereunto he was required to answer by order of law. Hubert then, seeing himself in such a strait, refused to answer presently, but required respite thereunto, for that the matters were weighty which the king objected to him: which was granted to him till the fourteenth day of September; but, in the mean time, Hubert, being in fear of the king, fled from London to the priory of Merton. "And thus Hubert, who before, for the love of the king, and the defence of the realm," saith mine author, "had got the hatred of all the nobles of England, now being out of the king's favour, was destitute of comfort on every side; save only that Lucas, archbishop of Dublin, with instant prayers and tears, laboured to the king for him." By this example, and many like, is to be seen, how unstable and variable a thing the favour of mortal and mutable princes is: to teach all such as have to do about princes, how to repose and plant their trust, not in man, but in their Lord God, by him to find help in Christ, the true prince of all princes, who never faileth. A like example was Clito, servant of King Alexander; also Joab, of King David;

Other crimes objected to Hubert.

Princes' favour not to be trusted to.

Henry III — A.D. 1232.

Belisarius, of Justinian; Harpagus, of Astiages; Cromwell, of King Henry, with innumerable more, who in histories are to be found.

The king's displeasure against Hubert.

When the day was come that this Hubert should answer, keeping among the monks of Merton, he durst not appear. Then was it signified unto him from the king, that he should come up and appear in the court, there to answer to his charge. Whereunto he answered again, that he misdoubted the king's anger, and therefore he did fly to the church, as the uttermost refuge for all such as suffer wrong; from whence he would not stir, till he heard the king's wrath to be mitigated towards him. With this the king, moved and sorely displeased, directed his letters, in all haste, to the mayor of London, commanding him, at the sight thereof, to muster and take up all the citizens that could bear harness in the city, and to bring to him by force of arms the aforesaid Hubert, either quick or dead, out of Merton. Whereupon, the mayor immediately causing the great bell to be rung, assembled together the people of London, and opening before them the king's letters, commanded them to prepare and arm themselves in all readiness for the executing of the king's will and message.

Message to the mayor of London.

Old grudge borne in mind.

The citizens, hearing this, were therewith right glad and ready, for they all had great hatred to Hubert, because of the execution of Constantine, their citizen, before mentioned. Notwithstanding, certain of the citizens, namely, Andrew Buckerell, John Travers, and others, men of more grave and sage discretion, wisely pondering with themselves, what inconvenience might rise hereof, went in haste to the bishop of Winchester, lying then in Southwark, and, waking him out of his sleep, desired his counsel in that so sudden and dangerous distress; declaring unto him what peril might thereby ensue, as well to the church of Merton, as also to the city, by the fury of the inordinate and fierce multitude, which would hardly be bridled from robbing and spoiling, neither would spare shedding of blood. Unto whom again, the bloody bishop gave this bloody counsel, saith Matthew Paris: "Dangerous it is," quoth he, "both here and there; but yet see that you obey and execute the precept of the king; I counsel you plainly." At this counsel of the bishop, they, being amazed, went with an evil will about the business enjoined; but the people, inflamed with hatred, gladly coveted to be revenged, and to shed the blood of Hubert.

Good advice of discreet citizens.

Cruel counsel of Peter, bishop of Winchester.

Causes of displeasure between Hubert and the bishop of Winchester.

The cause why Peter, bishop of Winchester, was so cruelly set against the justice, was partly for the damages he had done to the Roman priests, as before is touched; partly, also, for the old grudge, because the king coming to his lawful age before (through the counsel of this Hubert) loosed himself from the government of the said bishop, who had him then in custody. And thus rose up the grudge and displeasure of this bishop towards him.

On the morrow, the Londoners, issuing out of the city, to the number of twenty thousand, set forth toward the abbey of Merton, where Hubert was lying prostrate before the altar, commending himself to God.

In the mean season, while the citizens were on their journey, raging against the poor earl of Kent, it was suggested to the king by

Radulph, bishop of Chichester, and lord chancellor, that it was dangerous to excite the vulgar and unruly multitude, for fear of sedition; lest, peradventure, the rude and heady people, being stirred up, will not so soon be brought down again, when the king would have them. Moreover, what shall be said, quoth he, among the Frenchmen and other nations, which of great things love to make greater, and of evil things to make them worse than they are? but thus jestingly and mockingly: "See what a kind bird is the young king of England, who seeketh to devour his old nurse, under whose wings he had been brought up and nourished in his youth." And thus the king, by this persuasion, changing his counsel, sent in all hasty wise after the army again, willing them to retract their journey, and to retire. And thus the Londoners, although much against their wills, returned home, missing their purpose.[1] Herein is to be observed another notable example of God's working providence; for when the king, saith the history, had sent by two messengers or pursuivants to revoke and call back again the army of the Londoners, going with greedy minds to shed the blood of the innocent justice: one of the messengers, posting with all speed possible with the king's letters, overtook the army; and coming to the fore-ward where the captains were, by virtue of the king's letters stayed their course and bloody purpose, whereby they could proceed no further. But the other messenger, crafty and malicious, bearing hatred to the said Hubert, and rather wishing him to be slain than to be delivered, lingered by the way on purpose, although commanded to make haste; and when he came, went only to the middle sort, more like a messenger meet to serve a dead man's errand, than to serve the turn of those who be alive. And so in like manner, by the just hand of God it fell upon him; for this messenger stumbling with his horse, riding but at a soft or foot pace, and rather walking than riding, fell down backwards from his horse's back, and there brake his neck and died. This merciful message of the king was (as is said) sent by the instigation of Radulph, bishop of Chichester, lord chancellor, a virtuous and a faithful man, and one that could skill to have compassion on the miseries of men; of whom it was declared before, that he, being elected archbishop of Canterbury, would not give one halfpenny to their expenses by the way, to get his election confirmed by the pope; and who afterwards by the said pope was defeated and frustrated of his election, as relation was made before. Thus, through God's providence, by the means of the king's letters, the army returned, and Hubert's life (contrary to this expectation) was preserved.

Sage counsel of an earl to the king. Juxta versum, saith the story, Alis ales, alis alium ne longius ales.

The marvellous working of the Lord's help in time of need

A notable example of God's just punishment

After this, the archbishop of Dublin, with much labour and great suit, entreated and obtained of the king to grant, unto the said Hubert, respite, till the twelfth day of January, to provide himself with his answer to such things as were commenced against him. Then Hubert, trusting to enjoy some safety, by the king's permission to him granted, to breathe himself a little, and to walk abroad, took his journey towards St. Edmundsbury, where his wife was; and, passing through the county of Essex, was inned there in a certain town belonging to the bishop of Norwich. Of this, when the king was certified, fearing lest he would raise up some commotion

The archbishop of Dublin again maketh intercession for Hubert

(1) Ex additament.s Matth. Paris fol 81.

Henry III.

A.D. 1232.

in the realm, he sendeth in hasty anger after him Sir Godfred Crancombe, knight, with three hundred men; commanding, under pain of hanging, that they should apprehend him, and bring him to the tower of London: which commandment to accomplish, there lacked no haste. Hubert, having intelligence of their coming (rising out of his bed, naked as he was) ran unto the chapel standing near unto the inn, where he holdeth with the one hand the cross, with the other hand the sacrament of the Lord's body. Then Godfred, with his aforesaid armed soldiers, entering into the chapel, willed him to come out. When he would not do this, with violent hands he drew him out of the chapel, and taking the cross and the sacrament out of his hands, fast bound him with fetters and gives under a horse's belly, and brought him, as they were commanded, to the tower. And so, certifying the king what they had done (who then tarried up waking for them), he rejoiced not a little thereat, and went merrily to his bed.

Hubert flieth to the church for refuge.

Violently drawn out of the church, and cast into the tower of London.

On the morrow, Roger, bishop of London, having knowledge how, and in what order, he was taken violently out of the chapel, cometh unto the king, blaming him boldly, for violating the peace of holy church, and protesting, that, unless the party were loosed again, and sent to the chapel from whence he was drawn, he would enter sentence of excommunication against all the deed doers.

The king compelled to send Hubert again to his sanctuary.

The king, as he did not deny his transgression herein, so he sendeth him, albeit against his will, out of the tower, unto the said chapel again, and by the same soldiers who brought him out before. This done, he giveth straight charge and commandment, under pain of hanging, to the sheriffs of Hertford and Essex, that they, in their own persons, with the strength of both shires, should watch and compass about the chapel, and see that the said Hubert might no ways escape; which commandment of the king was accomplished with all diligence. But Hubert took all this patiently, and continued in the chapel praying both night and day, and commending his cause unto the Lord; whom he desired so to deliver him from that instant danger, as he always sought the king's honour by his faithful and trusty service. And, as he continued in his prayer, so the king, continuing in his rage, commanded that no man should entreat for him, or make any mention of him in his presence. Notwithstanding this, Lucas, archbishop of Dublin, his true, and almost only friend, ceased not to pray and weep to the king for him, desiring the king at least to intimate to him, what he purposed should be done with Hubert. Whereunto the king answering, said, That of these three things, one he should choose: Whether he would abjure the realm of England for ever, or be condemned unto perpetual prison, or else, confess himself openly to be a traitor? But Hubert hereunto said, That he would choose none of these articles, as one who knew himself neither guilty nor worthy of any such confusion: but, to satisfy somewhat the mind of the king, he would be contented to depart the realm for a season; but to abjure the realm, he would not so do.

Example of a constant friend in time of need.

Three things put to Hubert.

In this mean time it befel that Ranulph, earl of Chester and Lincoln, one of his sorest enemies, died. Hubert all this while remained in the chapel, enclosed and guarded about with the power, as is said, of two shires, and so continued, till at length, by the commandment of the king, his two servitors, who ministered unto him within the chapel, were taken from him. Then Hubert, seeing no other remedy but there to starve for famine, offered himself of his own accord to the sheriffs, saying, that he would rather put himself in the king's mercy, than there desperately perish for hunger. And so was he taken, and being fast bound in fetters, was brought again, and clapped, by the king's commandment, in the tower of London.

Hubert reduced again to the tower.

Not long after this, word was brought unto the king by certain, that the said Hubert had much treasure lying in the house of the new Templars in London. Whereupon, the king, to try out the truth thereof, sendeth for the prior or master of the house; who, not daring to deny, confessed that there was indeed treasure brought into the house, but the quantity and number thereof he could not tell. The king, desirous to seize upon the treasure, required and charged the master with his brethren, with threatening words, to bring forth the treasure to him, saying, that it was taken and stolen out of his treasury. But they answered again, that the treasure was committed with trust and faith unto their hands, and therefore they neither would, nor ought, to let it go out of their hands, being trusted withal, without the assent of him who committed the same unto them. When the king could get no other answer at their hands, neither durst show any further violence against them, he sendeth unto Hubert in the tower, requiring of him the aforesaid treasures. To whom he, answering again mildly, yielded both himself, his treasures, and all that ever he had, unto the king's will and pleasure; and so, sending word unto the master and brethren of the temple, willeth them to take all the keys, and deliver the goods, with all that there was, unto the king, who, receiving the same, and taking an inventory of that which was received, caused it to be brought to his treasury, whereof the number both of the plate, of the coin, and of the jewels, was of price unknown. The enemies of Hubert, supposing thereby to take advantage against him to bring him to his end, came with open complaint unto the king, crying out against Hubert, that he was a thief, a traitor, and a robber of the king's treasure, and, therefore, by right was worthy to be hanged: and thus cried his accusers daily in the king's ear. "But the hearts of kings," saith the wise man, "are in the hands of the Lord," to be ruled, not after man's will, but as it pleaseth God to direct them. And so this king, having now his will and fill upon poor Hubert, and somewhat coming more unto himself, answered again in this wise: "That there was no such need to deal so straitly with him, who from the time of his youth first served mine uncle, King Richard, then my father, King John, in whose service (as I heard say) beyond the seas, he was driven to eat his horse;[1] and who, in my time, hath stood so constantly in defence of the realm against foreign nations; who kept the castle of Dover against King Louis, and vanquished the Frenchmen upon the seas; also at Bedford and at Lincoln he hath done such service. And if against me he hath dealt any thing untruly, which yet is not evidently proved, yet he shall never be put by me to so villanous a death. I had rather be counted a king foolish and

Bereft of all his treasures.

God ruleth the hearts of kings.

The king's answer in defence of Hubert.

A worthy word of a king.

(1) Matth. Paris. fol. 61.

Henry III. — A.D. 1232. simple, than be judged a tyrant or a seeker of blood, especially of such as have served me and mine ancestors, in many perils so dangerously, weighing more the few evils which yet be not proved, than so many good deserts of his evident and manifest service, done both to me and to the whole realm." Thus the king, somewhat relenting to poor Hubert, his old servant, granted unto him all such lands as he had had given him by King John, his father, and whatsoever else he had by his own purchase.

The king's mind relenteth toward Hubert. Thus Hubert, after long trouble, a little cheered with some piece of comfort, set Lawrence, his trusty friend that never left him, one that belonged to St. Alban's, to be his steward and overseer of those possessions granted to him by the king. Shortly upon the same, after the king's mind was seen thus something to relent, the envy also of the nobles, being now partly satisfied, began to turn to mercy; insomuch that four earls, to wit, Earl Richard, the king's brother; William, earl of Warreine; Richard, earl Marshal; and William, earl of Ferrers, became sureties to the king for him; upon whose Hubert put in the castle of Devizes. surety he was transferred to the castle of Devizes, where he was under the keeping of four soldiers by them appointed, having the liberty of the castle. But the bishop of Winchester, who always hunted after the life of Hubert, craftily cometh to the king, and desireth the custody of that castle, making no mention of Hubert, to the intent, that by the keeping thereof he might the sooner despatch A.D. 1233. him. Hubert having thereof some inkling, breaketh the matter to two of his servants; who, with compassion tendering his misery, watched their time, the keepers being asleep, and conveyed him by night upon their backs, fettered as he was, into the parish church Conveyed into the parish church. of the town, and there remained with him. The keepers, when they missed their prisoner, were in great perplexity, and, after diligent search, finding him at length where he was in the church, Brought back to the castle. with violent force drew him from thence to the castle again; for which injury to the church, the bishop of Sarum, understanding the order of the matter, cometh to the castle where the keepers were, and required that Hubert should be brought again into the church from whence he was taken. Which when the keepers refused to do, saying, they would rather he should hang than they, the bishop gave sentence of excommunication against them. This done, he, with the bishop of London, and other bishops, goeth immediately to the king, complaining of the injury done to Hubert, and especially of the contumely against holy church; neither would they leave the king before they had obtained that he should be brought back again into the church, and so he was. Not long after, the king, in great displeasure, sendeth to the sheriff of the shire to keep him well watched in the church, till he either came forth, or there perished with famine.

Delivered out of prison, and carried into Wales. It befel, in the mean season, that great dissension arose between the king and the nobles of the realm, by reason whereof Hubert was taken and carried away by Richard, earl Marshal, into Wales, and there remained until the king at length was reconciled with his nobles, and so received, along with the rest, the said Hubert again into his favour.[1] Of this dissension more shall be showed (Christ willing) hereafter.

(1) Ex Matth. Paris, et ex Floribus Historiarum.

As the beginning of this trouble of Hubert's first sprang out of 'exing the pope's barns, so likewise Roger, bishop of London, uspected for the same cause, was forced to travel up to Rome, here to purge himself before the pope; where, after much money onsumed, and being robbed also by the way, he got nothing else, ut lost his labour, and so came home again. There, doing the part of good bishop, after his return from Rome, he attempted to expel and xclude out of his diocese all those Italian usurers, called, as is before aid, Caursini. These Caursinites coming with the pope's legates nto England, and lending their money to religious houses, colleges, nd churches, had their debtors bound unto them in such sort as was f much advantage to them, and much injury to the others, as in the orm of their obligations in the story of Matthew Paris is largely xpressed.[1] Against these Caursinites the bishop of London being orthily inflamed with zeal of justice, first, with loving admonition, vent about to reclaim them for the wealth of their souls, and afterwards with sharp words he began to charge them. But they, lisregarding christian counsel, and despising the bishop's threatenings, vould not leave the sweetness of their occupation; wherefore the ishop, proceeding to the sentence of excommunication, precisely nd strictly charged them to depart his diocese. But they, again, eing confident and emboldened upon the pope's defence, not only et at light his excommunication, but also wrought such ways with he pope that they caused the said bishop of London, being both ged and sickly, to be cited peremptorily to appear beyond the seas, here to answer to such objections as they should infer against him. And thus, the bishop, minding rather to cover than to open the faults of the church, and partly being let with infirmity and age, was compelled to let the cause fall.

Henry III. A.D. 1233.

Roger, bishop of London, goeth to Rome to purge himself before the pope.

Usurers excommunicated and expelled by the bishop of London.

And thus much of the pope's merchants here in England, who were not so busy here for their part, but the pope, the great master of these merchant usurers, was as busy for his. And although his barns here in England were destroyed, and his bank something decayed, yet he thought to win it up in another way, for he proclaimed, the same year, a general visitation through all the religious houses, exempt or not exempt, universally pertaining to his jurisdiction; where, by the cruel dealing of the visitors, many were compelled to appeal and to travel up to Rome, to the great expenditure of their money, and the filling of the pope's coffers. But as touching this visitation, to make short, saith the story, it tended not to any reformation so much as to the deformation of the universal order:[2] "While all those who before, through all parts of the world, followed only the rule of Benedict, now, through new devised constitutions, are found in all places so divided and divers, that of all monasteries, and other churches of religion, scarce may two be found which do agree in one rule and institution of life."

General visitation of the pope through all religious houses.

Great diversity among religious orders.

All the while that Hubert, above mentioned, was secluded from the king, Peter, bishop of Winchester, bare all the rule, and above all other alone was accepted. This bishop being in such principal

(1) Matth. Paris. fol. 65.

(2) "Dum omnes, qui in diversis orbis partibus unicam Benedicti secuti fuerant regulam, per novas constitutiones ita inveniantur ubique discordes, quod ex omnibus cœnobiis, vel aliis religiosorum ecclesiis vix duo habeantur in norma vivendi concordes."—Ex Parisiensi.

Henry III.

A.D. 1233.

favour with the king, as by whose counsel all things were administered, removed the natural servitors who were Englishmen, out of their offices, and placed other strangers, namely, of Pictavia, and of other countries, in their room. Among those who were thrust out, was William, under-marshal, who supplied the room of Richard, lord great Marshal of England; for which cause the said Lord Richard was mightily offended. Also Walter, treasurer of the king's house, was not only expelled, but also amerced in a hundred pounds, and put from all his holds and munitions, which he had by the king's patent granted to him.

Old servitors of the king put out and discharged.

Moreover, by the counsel of the said bishop of Winchester, all the old counsellors, as well bishops, as other earls and barons, and all the nobles, were rejected from the king in such sort, that he would hear and follow no man's counsel, but only the said Peter, bishop of Winchester, and his cousin, Peter de Rivallis; whereby it came to pass, that all the greatest holds and munitions in the realm were taken from the old keepers, and committed to the custody of the said Peter. Then the bishop of Winchester, to plant and pitch himself more strongly in the king's favour, adjoined to his fellowship Stephen Segrave, succeeding in the place of Hubert, the justice: also Robert Passelew, who had the keeping of the treasure under the aforesaid Peter Rival. So, by these three, all the affairs of the realm were ordered. Moreover, to make their party more sure, by them it was provided, that soldiers and servitors from beyond the sea, as Pictavians and Britons, were sent for, to the number of two thousand, who were placed partly about the king, partly were set in castles and holds within the realm, and had the oversight and government of shires and baronies, who then oppressed the nobles of the land, accusing them to the king for traitors; whom the simple king did easily believe, committing to them the custody of his treasures, the sitting in judgments, and the doing in all things. When the nobles, thus oppressed, came to complain of their injuries to the king, by the means of the bishop of Winchester, their cause was nothing regarded; insomuch that the said Winchester, moreover, accused certain bishops also to the king, so that he did flee and shun them as open traitors and rebels.

The king forsaketh his nobles and sticketh to strangers.

These things standing thus out of order, Richard, the noble Marshal of England, with others of the nobles joining with him, seeing these oppressions and injuries daily growing, contrary to the laws and wealth of the realm, came to the king, and blamed him for retaining such perverse council about him of the Pictavians and other foreigners, to the great prejudice of his natural subjects, and of the liberties of the realm; humbly desiring and beseeching him, that he, with as much speed as might be, would reform and redress such excesses, whereby the whole realm seemed to lie in danger of subversion. Otherwise, if he refused to see correction thereof, he, with other peers and nobles, would withdraw themselves from his council, so long as he maintained the society of those foreigners and strangers about him.

Richard, earl marshal, admonisheth the king.

To this Peter Winchester, answering again, said, that the king right well might call unto him what foreigners and strangers him listed, for the defence both of his kingdom, and of his crown; and

Disdainful answer of the bishop.

what number of them he would, as by whom he might be able to bridle his proud and rebellious subjects, and so to keep them in awe and good order.—When the earl and the nobles could get no other answer of him, in great perturbation they departed, promising among themselves, that in this cause, which so touched the state of the whole realm, they would with constancy join together, to the parting with their lives.

Henry II

A.D. 1233

of Winchester

After this, the aforesaid Peter, bishop of Winchester, with his accomplices, ceased not by all means to inflame the king's heart to hatred and contempt of his natural people, whom they so vehemently perverted, that he, accounting them no other than his enemies, sought, by all diligence, the utter destruction of them, sending daily for more garrisons of the Pictavians, till in short space they replenished well near the whole land, whose defence the king only trusted unto: neither was any thing disposed in the realm, but through the guiding of this Peter, and of the Pictavians.

Petrus de Rupibus, bishop of Winchester, perverter of the king, by picked counsel

The king, thus guarded and strengthened with these foreign aliens and strangers, proclaimed a parliament to be holden at Oxford, where the nobles were warned to be present. They, considering the indignation of the king conceived, would not appear. Again, they were required the first, second, and third time to present themselves. The assembly proceeded, but they came not for whom the king looked. In this assembly or parliament, it was plainly told the king, by a Dominic friar preaching before him, that unless he removed from him the bishop of Winchester, and Peter Rival, his kinsman, he should not, neither could, long enjoy peace in his kingdom. This, although it was bluntly spoken by the friar against the bishop, yet his remedy he had; the friar had nothing to lose. Yet was there another chaplain of the court, who perceiving the king somewhat mitigated by the former preaching, and after a courtlike dexterity handling his matter, being a pleasant conceited man, thus merrily came to the king, asking a question, "What is the thing most pernicious and dangerous of all other things to them that travel by the seas?" "That," said the king, "is best known to such as travel in that kind of traffic." "Nay," saith he, "this is easy to be told." The king demanding what it was, "Forsooth," quoth he, "stones and rocks," alluding merrily, but yet truly, to the bishop of Winchester, whose name and surname was Petrus de Rupibus, for 'Petræ' in Latin signifieth stones, and 'Rupes,' rocks. Notwithstanding, the king, either not perceiving the meaning, or not amending the fault, again sendeth to his nobles, to have them come and speak with him at Westminster. But they, fearing some train to be laid for them, refused to appear, sending plain words to the king by solemn message, that his grace, without all delay, should seclude from him Peter, bishop of Winchester, and other aliens of Pictavia, or, if he would not, they, with the common assent of the realm, would displace him with his wicked counsellors from his kingdom, and have, within themselves, tractation for choosing a new king.

Merry apothegm of the king's chaplain

Message of the nobles to the king

The king, at the hearing of this message, being mightily moved, partly to fear, partly to indignation, especially having the late example of King John, his father, before his eyes, was cast into great perplexity, doubting what was best to be done. But Winchester,

War raised by him against his nobles

Henry III. A.D. 1233.

with his wicked counsel, so wrought with the king, that he proceeded with all severity against them; insomuch that, in a short time, the sparkles of poisoned counsel kindling more and more, grew to a sharp battle between the king and Richard, earl Marshal, with other nobles, to the great disquietness of the whole realm. This war was presignified by terrible thundering and lightning, heard all England over in the month of March, with such abundance of rain and floods accompanying the same, as cast down mills, overcovered the fields, threw down houses, and did much harm through the whole realm.

Great thunders and floods in England.

To prosecute here, at large, the whole discourse of this war between the king and the earl marshal, which continued near the space of two years; to declare all the parts and circumstances thereof; what troubles it brought, what damages it wrought unto the whole realm, what trains were laid, what slaughter of men, what waste of whole countries ensued from Wales unto Shrewsbury, how the marshal joined himself with Llewellyn, or Leoline, prince of Wales, how the Pictavians were almost all slain and destroyed, how the king was distressed, what forgery wily Winchester wrought by the king's letters to entrap the Marshal, and to betray him to the Irishmen, amongst whom he was at length slain: for all this I refer to other authors, who at large do treat of the same, as Matthew Paris, Florilegus, and others.[1] This is to be noted and observed (which rather pertaineth to our ecclesiastical history), to see what sedition and continual disquietness there was in those days among almost all christian people, being under the pope's catholic obedience; but especially, to mark the corrupt doctrine then reigning, it is to be marvelled, or rather lamented, to see the king and the people then so blinded in the principal point and article of their salvation, as we find in stories, which, making mention of a house or monastery of converts builded the same year by the king at London, do express in plain words, that he then did it "for the redemption of his soul, of the soul of King John, his father, and for the souls of all his ancestors:"[2] whereby may be understood in what palpable darkness of blind ignorance the silly souls redeemed by Christ were then enwrapped, who did not know, nor yet were taught, the right doctrine and first principles of their redemption.

Why monasteries were builded.

Mention was made a little before of dissolving the election of John, prior of Canterbury, who was chosen by the monks to be archbishop of the said church of Canterbury, but by the pope was defeated. After him one John Blund was elected, who, travelling up to Rome this year, A.D. 1233, to be confirmed of the pope, was also repealed and unelected again, for that it was thought in England,

Archbishop of Canterbury elected by the chapter, unelected by the pope.

(1) A brief abstract of fifty years of these melancholy times will serve to recal, to the recollection of the reader, the events to which our author here alludes. The king, at an early age, came to the throne, A.D. 1216. Excess and extravagance pervaded the court. The people were oppressed—the clergy suffered the most disgraceful extortion from Pope Gregory IX.—violence and rapine troubled the realm—the baronial aristocracy seconded the ambitious designs of the earl of Leicester, A.D. 1258—they usurped the power of the throne—a civil war, accompanied with its usual horrors, succeeded—the king and his brother Richard were defeated and taken prisoners, at Lewes, on the 14th May, A.D. 1264—in the following year the earl of Leicester called a parliament, distinguished as the one to which deputies from the boroughs were first summoned—and on the 4th of August that nobleman fell in the battle of Eversham, fighting against Prince Edward (afterwards Edward I.), upon which King Henry was restored to the throne.—Ed.

(2) "Pro redemptione animæ suæ et Regis Johannis patris sui, et omnium antecessorum suorum.'—Ex Matth. Paris. fol. 86.

and so complained of to the pope, that he had received of Peter, bishop of Winchester, a thousand marks, and had another thousand promised him of the said Winchester, who by his money thought to make him on his side, and also wrote to the emperor to help forward his promotion in the court of Rome. Notwithstanding, both he, with his giving, and the other, with his taking of bribes, were both detected and disappointed of their purpose. For the pope, hating then the emperor, for the same cause, admitted not the election; pretending as the cause, that he was proved to hold two benefices without his dispensation. After him, by the commandment of the pope, one Edmund, canon of Salisbury, was ordained archbishop, and had his pall sent to him from the pope. This Edmund, for his virtues, was afterwards canonized by the popish monks there for a saint, and called St. Edmund. About this time, also, Robert Grosthead was made bishop of Lincoln.

Henry III — A. D. 1233. — Corruption of bribes.

This Edmund, accompanied with other bishops, during this trouble between the king and his nobles, being in council at Westminster, in the year next ensuing (A.D. 1234), came, uttering their minds boldly, in the name of the lords, and declaring unto the king, as became his faithful servants, that the counsel, which he then followed, was not sound or safe, but cruel and dangerous, both to him, and to the state of the realm, meaning the counsel of Peter Winchester and Peter Rival, with other adherents. A D 1234.

Faithful Counsel of the Bishops given to the King.

1. For that they hate and contemn the English nation, calling them traitors and rebels, and turning the king's heart from the love of his natural subjects, and the hearts of them from him, as appeareth by the earl marshal and others, sowing discord among them

2 Item, By the said counsel, to wit, by the aforesaid bishop and his fellows, King John, the king's father, lost first the hearts of his barons, after that lost Normandy, and afterwards, other lands also, and in the end wasted all his treasure, so that since that time the regiment of England had never any quiet after

3. Item, By the said counsel also, in their time and memory, the kingdom of England had been troubled and suspended, and in conclusion, she that was before the prince of provinces, became tributary, and so, war ensuing upon the same, the said King John, his father, incurred great danger of death, and at last was extinguished, after lacking both peace of his kingdom and of his own heart.

4. Item, By the said counsel the castle of Bedford was kept a long time against the king, to the great loss both of men and treasure, beside the loss of Rupella, to the shame of the realm of England.

5. Item, Through their wicked counsel, at this present, great perturbation seemed to hang over the whole realm, for else, if it had not been for their counsel, and if true justice and judgment might have been ministered unto the king's subjects, these tumults had never been stirred, and the king might have had his land unwasted, and his treasure unconsumed.

6. Item, In that faith and allegiance, wherewith they were obliged unto him, they protested unto him, that his said council was not a council of peace, but of division and disquietness, to the end that they who otherwise, by peace, could not aspire, by disturbing and disheriting others, might be exalted.

7. Item, For that all the castles, forts, munitions, also all the officers of the exchequer, with all other the greatest escheats of the realm, were in their hands, of the which if the king would demand account, he should prove how true they were.

8. Item, For that neither by the king's seal nor commandment, except it

Henry III.

A.D. 1234.

bore withal the seal of Peter Rival, almost any business of any weight could be despatched in the realm, as though they counted their king for no king.

9. Furthermore, by the aforesaid counsel, the natural subjects and nobles of the realm were banished the court, which it was to be feared would grow to some inconvenience both to the king and to the realm; forasmuch as the king seemed to be more on their side, than they on his, as by many evident conjectures may appear.

10. Item, It was not well to be taken and liked, the said council standing of strangers and aliens, that they should have in their power both the king's sister, and many other noblemen's daughters, and other women marriageable, with the king's wards and marriages, which they bestowed and divided among themselves and men of their affinity.

11. Item, The said council, regarding neither the laws nor the liberties of the realm, confirmed and corroborated by excommunication, did confound and pervert all justice: wherefore it was to be feared, that they would run under excommunication, and the king also, in communicating with them.

12. Item, Because they kept neither promise, nor faith, nor oath with any person, neither did observe any instrument made, never so formal, by law, nor yet did fear any excommunication; wherefore they were to be left for people desperate, as who were departed from all truth and honesty.

"These things," said the bishops, "we, as your faithful subjects before God and men, do tell and advertise your grace, desiring and beseeching you, that you will remove and seclude from you such counsel: and as the custom is of all other kingdoms to do, that you will so govern in like manner your kingdom by your own natural liege people, and such as be sworn unto you of your own realm. For thus," said they, "in verity we denounce unto you, that unless in short time you will see these things reformed, we, according to our duty, will proceed by the censure of the church against you and all others that gainstand the same, tarrying no other thing, but only the consecration of this our reverend archbishop."

Excommunication denounced by the bishops against the king.

These words of the bishops thus said and finished, the king required a little time of respite, wherein to advise with himself about the matter, saying, that he could not, on such a sudden, remove from him his council, before he had entered with them account of his treasure committed to them; and so that assembly brake up.

His answer.

It followed then, after this communication so broken up, that the king resorted to the parts of Norfolk, where, coming by St. Edmundsbury, where the wife of Hubert, the justice, was, he being moved with zeal of pity toward the woman, who very humbly behaved herself to the king, did grant her eight manors,[1] which her husband before with his money had purchased, being then in the custody and possession of Robert Passelew, one of the king's new counsellors above specified. It was not long after this, that Edmund, the archbishop, was invested and consecrated in the church of Canterbury; who, shortly after his consecration, about the month of April, coming with his suffragans to the place of council, where the king with his earls and barons were assembled, opened to him the cause and purpose of his coming, and of the other prelates, which was, to put him in remembrance of their former talk had with him at Westminster; denouncing, moreover, to him expressly, that unless with speed he would take a better way, and fall to a peaceable and godly agreement with the true and faithful nobles of his realm, he immediately, with the other prelates there present, would pass the sentence of excommunication against him, and against all them that would be enemies to the same peace, and maintainers of discord.

The pity of the king toward the wife of Hubert.

Edmund consecrated archbishop of Canterbury, afterwards canonized by Pope Innocent IV.

Excommunication rightly practised.

The king, after he heard the meaning of the bishops, with humble

(1) "Manor places."—Old editions.—Ed.

and gentle language answered them, promising to condescend to them in all things. Whereupon within few days after, the king, coming to some better remembrance of himself, commanded the aforenamed bishop of Winchester to leave the court, and to return home to his bishopric, there to attend unto the spiritual charge and care of his flock committed to him. Moreover, he commanded Peter Rival, the bishop's cousin, some stories say his son, who had then the disposing of all the affairs of the realm, to render unto him his castles, and to give account of all his treasures whereof he had the keeping, and so to void the realm; swearing, moreover, unto him, that if he had not been beneficed, and within orders of the church, he would have caused both his eyes to be plucked out of his head.

Peter Rival called to account of the king's treasures.

Henry likewise expelled the Pictavians out of the court, and from the custody of his munitions, sending them home into their country, and bidding them no more see his face. Thus the king, wisely despatching his wicked counsellors, first did send Edmund, the archbishop, with the bishops of Chester and of Rochester, into Wales to Llewellyn, and to Richard, earl Marshal, and others, to treat with them of peace. Also he received back to his service men of his natural country, to attend about him, offering himself willing to be ruled by the counsel of the archbishop and the bishops, by whose prudence he trusted his realm should be reduced again to a better quietness.

Pictavians and strangers sent home by the king.

But in the mean time, while these things were doing in England, the aforesaid Richard, earl Marshal, by the falsehood of the bishop of Winchester, and Peter Rival, forging the king's letters to the Irishmen against him, and partly by the conspiracy of Gilbert de Marisco, being circumvented by the Irishmen in war, and there taken and wounded, was by them, through the means of his surgeon, slain.

Richard, earl Marshal, fraudulently slain in Ireland.

Great slaughter at the same time there was of them who were called Catini, about the parts of Almain. These Catini were esteemed of Pope Gregory and the papists to be heretics, but what their opinions were, I find it not expressed in Matthew Paris.

Catini, slain about Almain, judged of the papists for heretics.

In like sort the Albigenses before mentioned, accounted also by the pope's flock to be heretics, with their bishops, and a great number and company of them, were slain by commandment of Pope Gregory IX., at the same time, in a certain plain in Spain.[1]

Albigenses slain in Spain.

How the archbishop of Canterbury, with two other bishops, was sent into Wales, for entreaty of peace, ye heard before; at whose return, after the time of Easter, the king going toward Gloucester to meet them by the way, as he was in his journey at Woodstock, there came messengers from Ireland, declaring to the king the death of Richard, earl Marshal, and the order thereof, through the forged letters of Winchester, and others; whereat the king made great lamentation and mourning, to the great admiration of all them that were by, saying and complaining, that he left not his like in all the realm again.

After this, the king proceeding in his journey, came to Gloucester, where the archbishop, with the other bishops, coming to the king, declared to him the form and condition of peace, which they had concluded with Llewellyn, which was this:—If the king would be

The saying of Llewellyn king of Wales

(1) Ex Matth Paris. fol. 87.

Henry III. A. D. 1234.

reconciled before with the other nobles with whom he was confederate, such as the king had banished out of his realm, to the end that the concord might be the more firm between them: thus, said they, was Llewellyn contented, although with much ado and great difficulty, to receive the league of peace, saying and protesting this unto them, that he feared more the king's alms than all the puissance both of him and of all his clergy in England.

Peace concluded between the king and his nobles.

This done, the king, there remaining with the bishops, directed his letters to all the exiles and banished lords, and to all his nobles, that they should repair to him about the beginning of June, at Gloucester, promising to them his full favour, and reconcilement to them and to their heirs; and, that they might suspect no fraud therein, they should have their safe conduct by the archbishop and bishops. Whereupon, through the mediation of the said archbishop and the bishops, first cometh to the king Hubert, earl of Kent, offering himself to the king's good will and favour, whom the king, with cheerful countenance, received and embraced, restoring him not only to his favour, but also to his household and counsel, with his livings and possessions, from which he had been disseized before. Then Hubert, lifting up his eyes to heaven, gave praise and glory to God, by whose gracious providence he, being so marvellously preserved through so great distresses and tribulations, was again so happily reconciled to the king and to his faithful friends. After him, in like sort, came in Gilbert Basset, a nobleman; Richard Suard; also Gilbert, the brother of Richard Marshal, who was slain; which Gilbert recovered again his whole inheritance, as well in England as in Ireland, doing his homage to the king, and his service due for the same; to whom also was granted the office of the high marshal court, belonging before to his brother Richard.

Hubert, earl of Kent, restored to the king's favour.

Giveth thanks to God.

Falshood and murder cometh out. Kings many times abused by wicked counsel.

In the same council or communication, continuing then at Gloucester, the said Edmund, archbishop of Canterbury, bringing the forged letters, wherein was betrayed the life of Richard, earl Marshal, sealed with the king's seal, and sent to the great men of Ireland, read the same openly, in the presence of the king and all the nobles. At the hearing whereof, the king, greatly sorrowing and weeping, confessed there in truth, that being forced by the bishop of Winchester and Peter Rival, he commanded his seal to be set to certain letters presented unto him, but the tenor thereof, he said and swore, he never heard; whereunto the archbishop answering, desired the king to search well his conscience, and said, that all they who were procurers, or had knowledge of those letters, were guilty of the death of the earl Marshal, no less than if they had murdered him with their own hands.

Bishop of Winchester and others called to answer.

Then the king, calling a council, sent his letters for the bishop of Winchester, Peter Rival, Stephen Segrave, and Robert Passelew, to appear and yield account for his treasures unto them committed, and for his seal by them abused. But the bishop and Rival, keeping themselves in the sanctuary of the minster church of Winchester, neither durst nor would appear. Stephen Segrave, who succeeded after Hubert, the justice, and was of the clergy before, after became a layman, and now, hiding himself in St. Mary's church, in the abbey of Leicester, was turned to a clerk again. Robert Passelew covertly hid himself in a certain cellar of the New Temple, so secretly, that none could tell where he was, but thought he was gone to Rome. At length, through the aforesaid Edmund, archbishop of Canterbury, measures were taken that a remote day was granted, by the king, for them to answer. On that day, first appeared Peter Rival, then Stephen Segrave, after him Robert Passelew, each of whom severally, one after another, showed themselves; but not able to answer for themselves, like traitors they were reproved, and, like villains, were sent away.[1]

Henry III. A.D. 1234.

VARIANCE BETWEEN POPE GREGORY IX. AND THE CITIZENS OF ROME.

While peace between the king and the nobles was thus reconciled in England, dissension and variance the same time and year began in Rome, between the pope and the citizens of Rome. The cause was, that the citizens claimed, by old custom and law, that the bishop of Rome might not excommunicate any citizen of the city, nor suspend the said city, with any interdiction, for any manner of excess.

To this the pope answered again, "Quod minor Deo est, sed quolibet homine major;" to use the very words of mine author, "Ergo, major quolibet sive, ne etiam rege, vel imperatore." That is, "That he is less than God, but greater than any man: ergo, greater than any citizen, yea also, greater than king or emperor." And forasmuch as he is their spiritual father, he both ought, and lawfully may, chastise his children when they offend, as being subjected to him in the faith of Christ, and reduce them into the way again, when they have strayed out of course.

Moreover, the citizens allege again for themselves, that the potestates of the city, and the senators, do receive of the church of Rome, a yearly tribute, which the bishops of Rome were bound to pay to them, both by new, and also ancient laws. Of this yearly tribute they have been ever in possession, before the time of this Pope Gregory IX.

The pope bound to pay to Rome yearly tribute.

Hereunto the pope answered, and said, that although the church of Rome, in time of persecution, for their defence and the cause of peace, was wont to respect the head rulers of the city with gentle rewards, yet ought not that now to be taken for a custom; for that custom only ought to stand, which consisteth not in examples, but in right and reason.

Further and besides, the citizens said that they, at the commandment of the senators, would appropriate their country with new and larger limits, and enfranchise the same, being enlarged with fines and borders.

To this the pope again made answer, that certain lordships, and cities, and castles, be contained within the compass of the said limits, as the city Viterbium and Montcaster, which they presume to appropriate within their precinct; but, to ascribe to them, and usurp that which pertaineth to others, is against right and justice.

For these and such other controversies rising between the pope and the Romans, such dissension was kindled, that the pope, with his cardinals, leaving the city of Rome, removed to Perusium, as partly before is recited, thinking there to remain and to plant themselves;

Flieth the city of Rome.

(1) Ex Matth. Paris. fol. 91.

Henry III.

A. D. 1234.

Warreth against the Romans

but the Romans, prevailing against him, overthrew divers of his houses in the city, for which he did excommunicate them. The Romans, then flying to the emperor, desired his aid and succour; but he, belike to pleasure the pope, gathering an army, went rather against the Romans. Then the pope's army, whose captains were the earl of Toulouse (to purchase the pope's favour), and Peter the aforesaid bishop of Winchester (whom the pope, for the same end, had sent for from England, partly for his treasure, partly for his practice and skill in feats of war), and the emperor's host joined together, and bordering about the city of Rome, cast down the castles or mansions belonging to the citizens round about the suburbs, to the number of eighteen, and destroyed all their vines and vineyards about the city. At this the Romans, being not a little offended, brast out of the city, with more heat than order, to the number of one hundred thousand (as the story reporteth), to destroy Viterbium, the pope's city, with sword and fire. But the multitude, being unordered, and out of battle-array, and unprovided for jeopardies which by the way might happen, fell into the hands of their enemies, who were in wait for them, and of them destroyed a great number; so that on both parts were slain to the number of thirty thousand; but the most part was of the citizens. This dissension thus begun, was not soon ended, but continued long after.[1]

Church of Rome degenerated from the image of the true church

By these, and such other stories, who seeth not how far the church of Rome hath degenerated from the true image of the right church of Christ, which, by the rule and example of the gospel, ought to be a daughter of peace, not a mother of debate; not a revenger of herself, nor a seeker of wars, but a forgiver of injuries, humbly and patiently referring all revenge to the Lord; not a raker for riches, but a winner of souls; not contending for worldly mastership, but humbling themselves as servants; not vicars of the Lord, but jointly, like brethren, serving together, bishops with bishops, ministers with ministers, deacons with deacons, and not as masters, separating themselves by superiority one from another, but briefly communicating together in doctrine and counsel, one particular church with another; not as a mother, one over another, but rather as a sister church one with another, seeking together the glory of Christ, and not their own. Such was the church of Rome at first, in the old ancient beginning of her primitive state, especially while the cross of persecution yet kept the bishops and ministers under, in humility of heart, and fervent calling upon the Lord for help; so happy was that Christian then, who with liberty of conscience only might hold his life, how barely soever he lived. As for the pride and pomp of the world, as striving for patrimonies, buying of bishoprics, gaping for benefices, so far was this off from them, that then they had little leisure, and less list, so much as once to think upon them. Neither did the bishops, then, of Rome, fight to be consuls of the city, but sought how to bring the consuls unto Christ, being glad if the consuls would permit them to dwell by them in the city. Nor did they then presume so high as to bring the emperors' necks under their girdles, but were glad to save their necks, in any corner, from the sword of the emperors. Then lacked they outward peace, but abounded in inward consolation,

Difference between the church of Rome that was, and the church of Rome that is

(1) Ex Matth Paris fol 92.

God's Holy Spirit mightily working in their hearts. Then was one catholic unity of truth and doctrine amongst all churches, against errors and sects; neither did the east and west, nor distance of place, divide the church, but both the east church and the west church, the Greeks and the Latins, made all one church. And, albeit there were then five patriarchal sees appointed for order sake, differing in regions, and peradventure also in some rites one from another; yet all these consenting together in one unity of catholic doctrine, having one God, one Christ, one faith, one baptism, one spirit, one head, and linked together in one bond of charity, and in one equality of honour; they made altogether one body, one church, one communion, called one catholic, universal, and apostolic church. And so long as this knot of charity and equality did join them in unity together, so long the church of Christ flourished and increased, one being ready to help and harbour another, in time of distress, as Agapetus and Vigilius, flying to Constantinople, were there aided by the patriarch; so that, all this while, neither foreign enemy, neither Saracen, nor soldan, nor sultan, nor caliph, nor corasmine, nor Turk, had any power greatly to harm it.

East church West church

Catholic church

But through the malice of the enemy, this catholic unity did not long continue, and all by reason of the bishop of Rome, who, not contented to be like his brethren, began to extend himself, and to claim superiority above the other four patriarchal sees, and all other churches in the world. And thus, as equality amongst christian bishops was by pride and singularity oppressed, so unity began, by little and little, to be dissolved, and the Lord's coat, which the soldiers left whole, to be divided. Which coat of christian unity, albeit of long time it hath been now seam-ript before, by the occasion aforesaid, yet notwithstanding, in some sort it held together in some mean agreement, in subjection to the see of Rome, till the time of this Pope Gregory IX., A.D. 1230, at which time this rupture and schism of the church brake out into a plain division, utterly dissevering the east church from the west church, upon this occasion.

Schism between the Greek church and the church of Rome

Equality, mother of concord

There was a certain archbishop elected to an archbishopric among the Greeks, who, coming to Rome to be confirmed, could not be admitted unless he promised a very great sum of money. Which when he refused to do, and detested the execrable simony of the court of Rome, he made his repair home again to his own country, unconfirmed, declaring there to the whole nobility of that land, the case how it stood. For the further confirmation of this, there were also others, who, coming lately from Rome, where they had proved the same, or worse, came in and gave testimony to his saying. Whereupon all the churches of the Greeks, at the same time hearing this, departed utterly away from the church of Rome, which was in the days of this Pope Gregory IX., insomuch that the archbishop of Constantinople, coming afterwards to the general council at Lyons, there openly declared, that whereas before time he had under him above thirty bishoprics and suffragans, now he had not three; adding, moreover, that all the Greeks, and certain others, with Antioch, and the whole empire of Romania, even to the gates, almost, of Constantinople, were gone from the obedience of the church of Rome, &c.[1]

The cause and occasion why the Greek church utterly brake from the Romans

All Greece gone from the obedience of the church of Rome.

(1) Ex Matth Paris fol 112, &c fol. 186

Henry III.

A.D. 1234.

Germanus, patriarch of Constantinople, writeth to Pope Gregory IX.

By the occasion of the aforesaid separation of the Greeks from Pope Gregory, it happened shortly after (A.D. 1237), that Germanus, archbishop and patriarch of Constantinople, wrote to the said Pope Gregory IX., humbly desiring him to study and seek some means of unity, how the seamless coat of the Lord Jesus thus lamentably rent, not with hands of soldiers, but by discord of prelates, may be healed again; offering this, moreover, that if he will take the pains to stir out, he, for his part, notwithstanding his old age and feeble body, would not refuse to meet him in the mid way, to the intent that the truth on both sides being debated by the Scriptures, the wrong part may be reduced, the slander stopped, and unity re-formed between them.

The pope setteth the west church to fight against the east church.

This request of the patriarch, as it was both godly and reasonable, so it had been the bishop's part again, with like humility, to have condescended to the same, and to have been glad with all his might to help forward the reformation of christian unity in the church of Christ, and so to have showed himself the son of peace: but the proud bishop of Rome, more like the son of discord and dissension, standing still upon his majesty, refused thus to do; but wrote again in answer to his letters, with great disdain, seeking nothing else but how to advance his see above all other churches; and not only that, but, also, shortly after, he sent forth his preaching friars, to move all Christians to take the sign of the cross, and to fight against the Greeks, no otherwise than against the Turks and Saracens; insomuch that, in the Isle of Cyprus, many good men and martyrs were slain for the same, as by the letters of the said Germanus, patriarch of Constantinople, is to be seen.[1]

The patriarch's letter to the pope, and the pope's answer thereto, being long and tedious to read, are omitted here, but are extant in the history of Matthew Paris;[2] the summary effect whereof, notwithstanding, I thought here briefly to notify, for the simple and unlearned multitude, who, not understanding the Latin, may hereby perceive the fault of this schism not so much to rest in the Greek church, as in the church of Rome, as by the contents of this letter may appear.

SUBSTANCE OF A LETTER OF GERMANUS, THE PATRIARCH OF CONSTANTINOPLE, TO POPE GREGORY IX., A.D. 1237.

In this letter the said Germanus, patriarch of Constantinople, writing to Pope Gregory, first after his reverend salutation and preamble following upon the same, entering then upon the matter, showeth the occasion of his writing, which was by five observant friars repairing thither, whom he, gently receiving into his house, had conference with them touching this discord between the two churches, how it might be reduced again to unity; and afterwards, perceiving the said friars to make their journey towards Rome, he thought, therefore, by them to write his letters, wherein first lamenting this division in the house of God, and reciting the inconveniences which come thereof, by the example of Judah and Israel, Jerusalem and Samaria, Cain and Abel, Esau and Jacob, also of other such like, both private and public societies, where brother fighteth against brother, like as among

The inconvenience of discord.

(1) Ex Matth. Paris. fol. 112. (2) Ibid. fol. 3, et 111.

fishes the greater devoureth the lesser; he proceedeth then further gently to exhort Pope Gregory to the study of unity. *Henry III.*

And forasmuch as the pope had accursed, belike, those churches of the Greeks before, he therefore, taking his ground upon the words of St. Paul, [Gal. i.] where he accurseth every such person and persons, whatsoever they be, either man or angel of heaven, that shall preach any other gospel than hath been preached, willeth the pope to stand with him upon the same ground of the apostle's curse; so that if the stroke of that curse have lighted upon him or his churches, he desireth him to show the wound, and to help to wipe away the blood, to minister some spiritual plaster, to bind up the sore, and to save his brethren from perishing who lay in danger, according to the saying of the wise man, "A brotherly friend is tried in adversity." A.D. 1237.

"But if we (saith he), of the Greek church be free from the stripe of this curse of the apostle, and you Italians, and of the Latin church, be stricken therewith and lie thereby in danger of destruction, I trust that you, through ignorance and wilful obstinacy, will not so suffer yourselves to be separated from the Lord, but rather will suffer a thousand deaths before, if it were possible for a man so often to die."

Whether the church of the Greeks or the pope's church lieth more under the danger of God's curse.

And as touching this great discord between us, if either contrariety of doctrine, or swerving from the ancient canons, or diversity of rites received of our forefathers, be any cause thereof, we here take heaven and earth to witness, that we for our parts are ready, and desire also, upon due trial of profound truth of God's word, and invocation of the Holy Ghost, to join hands with you, or you to join with us. But, to say the very truth, and to tell you plainly, this we suppose, that many mighty and noble potentates would sooner incline to your obedience, were it not that they feared your unjust oppressions, your insatiable exactions, and inordinate provisions wherewith you wring your subjects, by reason whereof have risen amongst us cruel wars, one fighting against another, desolation of cities, bulls and interdictions set upon church-doors, division of brethren, and churches of the Grecians left without service, where God should be praised. So that now only one thing lacketh, which I believe to be predefined and appointed from above long before to us Grecians, the time I mean of martyrdom, which also now hasteneth fast upon us, that the tribunal of tyrants should be opened, and the seats of torments be set, that the blood of martyrs should be spilled, and we brought to the stage of martyrdom, to fight for the crown of glory."

The Greeks afraid of the pope's oppressions.

The patriarch of Constantinople prophesieth of the martyrdom of the Grecians.

"This that I do speak, and wherefore I speak it, the noble island of Cyprus doth already know and feel, which hath made many new martyrs, and hath seen valiant soldiers of Christ, who of long time before, passing through water and tears of sorrow, now at last have also passed through fire, and so entered into the heavenly rest. How say you, be these good and seemly, O holy pope! the successor of St. Peter, the apostle? Is this the bidding of that good Peter, the meek and humble disciple of Christ? Doth he thus instruct the seniors and elders in his epistle, where he writeth in this wise? "The elders which are among you, I beseech, which am also a fellow-elder with them, and witness of the sufferings of Christ, and also a partaker of the glory that shall be opened: feed the flock of God which is amongst you, having care and sight over it, not of coaction, as compelled against your wills, but willingly, of your own accord; not for filthy lucre' sake, but freely and heartily; neither as bearing dominion and lordship over the church, but showing yourselves as an example to the flock; and when the chief Pastor shall appear, you shall receive an incorruptible crown of eternal glory." [1 Pet. v. 1, 4.] And this is the doctrine of Peter, as they shall see who do not obey it. As for us, the other part of the said epistle is sufficient: wherein he willeth them to rejoice which are in heaviness through manifold temptations, that the trial of their faith being much more precious than gold that perisheth, and is tried in fire, may be their laud, honour, and glory, at the appearing of the Lord Jesus. [1 Pet. i. 7.] But bear with me,

The pope's persecution in the isle of Cyprus.

The tyranny and avarice of the pope chastened by the words of St. Peter.

Henry III

A.D. 1237

I pray you, O holy father, and of all your predecessors most meek, and suffer my words though they be something sharp, for they be sighings of a sorrowful heart."

"Wherefore, gird about your loins with fortitude, and light up the candle of your discretion, and seek the groat that is lost, of the unity, I mean, of faith. And we will also with like compassion join with your holiness, and I will not spare this weak body of mine, in pretending any excuse either of age or the length of the way: for the more laborious the travail is, the more crowns it bringeth. And St. Paul saith, 'Every man shall receive reward according to his travail.'"

He exhorteth the pope to come and meet with him, that they might confer together about the unity of faith.

"Neither are we ignorant, if it please your holiness, that like as we Grecians, for our parts, do labour in all respects to keep and observe the sincerity of true faith and doctrine, not to err, nor swerve in any part or point from the statutes of the blessed apostles and ancient fathers, so the church, likewise, of old Rome doth, for her part, labour also, we know well, to follow the sincere verity of christian doctrine, and thinketh herself to err in nothing, nor to need any remedy or reformation. And this we know is the judgment and sayings of both the churches, as well of the Greeks as of the Latins. For no man can see any spot in his own face, without he stoop down to the glass, or else be admonished by some other, whether his face be blotted or no. Even so have we many great and fair glasses set before us: first, the clear gospel of Christ, the epistles of the apostles, and divinity books of ancient writers. Let us therefore look into them well, they will show every man's mind and judgment, whether he go right or wrong. The God of peace tread down Satan speedily under our feet. The Author of peace confound the sower of discord. He that is the cause of all goodness destroy the hater of all that which is good, and which giveth cause of offence and slander. And he who is God of all joy and peace, send us, who are shepherds of his sheep reasonable, the angel of peace, and the messenger of great glad tidings, as he did in the Nativity of Christ to the shepherds of brute sheep and unreasonable; and make us worthy to sing that joyful song of God's praise, "Glory to God in the highest; on earth peace; good-will to men," and to receive one another with an holy kiss. The grace of our Lord Jesus Christ, and the peace of God the Father, and the communion of the Holy Spirit, be with you always. Amen."[1]

The Greek church sound and sincere in doctrine.

He exhorteth the church of Rome to look her face in God's glass, that is, to try their doctrine by God's word.

SUBSTANCE OF ANOTHER EPISTLE OF GERMANUS, PATRIARCH OF CONSTANTINOPLE, AND PRIMATE OF THE GREEK CHURCH, TO THE CARDINALS OF ROME.

Another letter, the said Germanus, patriarch of Constantinople, written also, at the same time, to the pope's cardinals, wherein he first commendeth them for their wisdom and counsel, and then showeth what utility cometh by giving good counsel, he saith:

"Forasmuch as God, many times, that which he hideth from one, inspireth to another, so that that good thing which by the Almighty God is sparingly dispensed to divers, through common counsel and conference spreadeth to the public utility of many," &c.

After this, eftsoons, he beginneth to exhort them, that they, like charitable ministers, and discreet counsellors, will take in hand the spiritual armour of God, to cast down the stop and partition wall of the old discord between the Greek and Latin church, and that they will be a mean to the bishop of Rome, that they who have been so long dissevered by dissension, may now be conjoined in unity of peace, in brotherly charity, and in communion of faith.

"Concerning this matter, I have (saith he) already written to his holiness. And now, I beseech the King of heaven, who took the shape of a servant to help his miserable servants, and was exalted upon the cross to raise them up

(1) Ex libro Matth. Paris manuscripto, ff. 3 et 111.

who were fallen into the profundity of desolation, that he will vouchsafe to put from your hearts all elation of mind, extolling itself over and above the unity of your brethren and fellow-servants, and to enlighten your consciences with the true light of understanding, that we may altogether agree in one, and that there be no schism amongst us. Let us, therefore, as we are instructed, so abide in one mind, that it be not said of us, as it was of the Corinthians before us, 'I hold of Paul, I of Apollos, I of Cephas, and I of Christ;' [1 Cor. i. 12;] but that all we, as we hold the name of Christ, and are called Christians, so may also abide in that wherein we are instructed, in one mind; that is, to follow love and charity in Christ Jesus, having always in our hearts the words of the apostle, saying, 'One Lord, one faith, one baptism.'"

"And now to be plain with you in that I have to say, I shall desire you not to be offended with me in uttering the truth as a friend unto you. 'The words,' saith Solomon, 'of a wise man telling truth, be like to nails which be driven in deep:' and truth for the most part breedeth enemies; and, therefore, though I am partly afraid, yet will I simply confess the truth unto you. Certes, this division of christian unity amongst us, proceedeth of no other cause but only of the tyranny, oppression, and exactions of the church of Rome, who of a mother is become a stepdame, and hath put her children from her whom long time she nourished (after the manner of a ravening bird, which driveth her young from her); which children, how much the more humble and obedient they are to her, the less she esteemeth them, and treadeth them underfoot, not regarding the saying of the gospel, 'Whoso humbleth himself shall be exalted.'" [Luke xviii. 14.]

The tyranny and oppression of the church of Rome is the only cause of breaking unity between the Greek church and the Latin.

"Let modesty, therefore, something temper you, and let the avarice of the court of Rome, although that cannot well out of the flesh which is bred in the bone, yet surcease a while, and let us together condescend to the trial of the truth; which truth being found out on both sides, let us constantly embrace the same."

"For why? we have been altogether sometimes, both Italians and Grecians, in one faith, and under the same canons, having peace with each other, and defending one another, and confounding the enemies of the church. At what time, many flying out of the west parts (while the tyranny of the heretics endured) made their concourse to us, and were received; and part fled unto you, that is, old Rome, as to a strong tower of refuge, and so received they comfort in both places, and one brother was thus received into the bosom of another, by mutual love for their defence."

The old amity and concord between the east church and the west.

"Then, afterwards, when Rome had been often distressed by the barbarous and heathen nations, the Grecians were ever ready to rescue and deliver them. Did not Agapetus and Vigilius flee unto Constantinople by reason of the dissensions then at Rome, and being honourably received, were here defended under our protection? although the like kindness was never yet showed on your part to us again in our like necessities. Notwithstanding, we ought to do good to them also that be ungrateful; for so doth the sea participate her smooth and calm tides even unto the pirates, and so 'God causeth the sun to shine upon the just and unjust.' But, alas for sorrow, what bitter division is this, that hath thus sequestered us asunder? One of us detracteth another, shunning the company one of another, as the damnation of his soul. What a mortal hatred is this that is come among us? If you think we are fallen, then do you help to lift us up, and be not to us a stumbling-block to our bodily ruin, but helpers unto the spiritual resurrection of our souls; so shall we acknowledge ourselves bound unto you to give you condign thanks accordingly."

Agapetus and Vigilius fled to Constantinople for succour.

"But if the blame and first origin of all this offence proceedeth from Rome, and the successors of Peter, the apostle; then read ye the words of St. Paul to the Galatians, saying, 'When Peter came to Antioch I withstood him to the face, because he was to be rebuked.' [Gal. ii. 11.] Howbeit this resistance was no cause of any discord, or breach between them, but the cause rather of further search and profounder disputations, provoking temporal agreement; for they were fast joined together in the bond of charity in Christ, agreeing in faith and conformity of doctrine, separated by no ambition or avarice, in which points, would God we also were like unto them! This to us, in our minds, gendereth a great offence, that you gaping so greedily after terrene possessions, scrape together all that you can scratch and rake. You heap up gold and

Paul rebuketh Peter.

Henry III.

A.D 1237.

silver, and yet pretend that you be the disciples of Him who said, 'Gold and silver I have none,' &c. [Acts iii. 6.] You make whole kingdoms tributary to you, and kings and princes your vassals. You augment your money by usury, and by feats of merchandise. You unteach by your deeds that which you teach in words."

He meaneth of the kingdom of England, and others which were made tributary to the see of Rome. The immoderate avarice of the court of Rome. Peter's faith shaken.

"Moderate yourselves, therefore, with more temperance, that you may be an example to us and to all the world. You see how good a thing it is for one brother to help another. Only God alone needeth no help or counsel, but men need to be holpen one of another. And were it not that I do reverence the blessed apostle Peter, the chief of Christ's apostles, the rock of our faith; I would here put you in remembrance how greatly this rock was shaken and removed from the foundation at the sight of a silly woman; and Christ of his secret purpose permitted the same, who, by the crowing of the cock, brought him again to remembrance of that which was foretold him, and raised him from the slumber of desperation. Then he, being thus waked, washed his face with tears, confessing himself, before God and all the world, to be a true pattern of repentance, who before bare the keys of the kingdom, saying thus unto us, 'May not he which falleth, rise again? Oh you which are fallen, rise up and behold me, and hearken unto me, travelling towards Paradise; the gates whereof to open I have received power.'"

Peter an ensample of repentance.

"And thus do I write unto you, not for any instruction, but only to put you in remembrance: for I know how God hath endued you with all wisdom and knowledge; as Solomon saith, 'Give only occasion to the wise, and he will learn wisdom: teach the just man, and he will be glad to take instruction.'"

Christian countries and nations in the east which are not under the bishop of Rome.

"This one thing more I will say, and so make an end: There be great and mighty nations that are of like mind and opinion with us. First, the Ethiopians, who inhabit the chief part of the east. After that the Syrians, and others besides, of greater number than they, and more disposed to virtue, as the Hiberi, Alani, Gothi, Charari, with innumerable people of Russia, and the kingdom of great victory, that of the Volgarians. All these are obedient unto us as their mother church, persisting hitherto constantly in the ancient and true orthodox faith immoveable."

Christ the only head of the church.

"The God of all holiness, who for our sakes became man, and who only is the head of his church and congregation, vouchsafe to gather us again together in unity, and grant that the Grecian church, together with her sister church of old Rome, may glorify the same Christ, the Prince of Peace, by the unity of faith, to the restitution of sound and wholesome doctrine, wherein many years agone they have agreed and were united. God grant unto you brotherly charity, and the hand of the most mighty God govern you all, holy cardinals, till that ye joyfully arrive in the haven of everlasting tranquillity. The grace of God be with you all. Amen."[1]

The pope proclaimeth war against the Greek church. The archbishops of Antioch and Constantinople excommunicate the pope. Five things to be considered.

Shortly after the sending of these letters, pope Gregory prepared to send men of war, signed with the cross, to fight against the Grecians; whereupon the archbishop of Antioch, with the said Germanus, solemnly excommunicated the pope, after he first had excommunicated them.[2] In the mean time, by the tenor of these letters of the patriarch sent to the pope and to the cardinals, it is evident to all men who have eyes in their heads to see: First, how the whole universal church of Christ, from the east parts to the west, in ancient times, were altogether united in one consent of doctrine, and linked together in brotherly charity, one church brotherly to help another, both with temporal aid and spiritual counsel, as the case required. Neither was then any one mother-church above other churches, but the whole universal church was the mother-church, and spouse of the Lord, to every faithful believer; under which universal church, in general, were comprehended all other particular churches in special, as sister churches together; not one greater than another, but all in like equality, as

(1) Ex Matth. Paris. fol. 111. (2) Ibid. fol. 118.

God gave his gifts, so serving one another, ever holding together the unity of faith and sisterly love. And so long was it, and rightly might so be called, the catholic church, having in it true unity, universality, and free consent. Unity in doctrine, universality in communicating and joining together of voices, consent in spirit and judgment. For whatsoever was taught at Rome, touching faith and salvation, it was no other than was taught at Antioch, Syria, &c.

The true catholic church, where it was, and what. Unity, universality, and consent. The church hath her name of catholic, whereby, and when

Secondly, how in process of time, through occasion of the tyranny and violent oppression of the bishops of Rome, this ring of equality, being broken, all flew in pieces, the east church from the west, the Greek from the Latin; and that which was one before, now was made two; unity turned to division, universality to singularity, and free consent to dissension.

Thirdly, here is also to be noted, after this pitiful breach of equality, how many and what great nations departed from the communion of the church of Rome, and especially about this time above specified of pope Gregory IX., A.D. 1230; so that both before and after that time, many councils were holden, and many things concluded in the west church, whereunto the one half of Christendom, lying in the east parts, did never agree; and contrary, many councils holden by them, which in the Latin church were not received; so that the church now, as she lost the benefit of universal consent, so also she lost the name of 'Catholic.' Whereupon this question is to be asked, namely, whether, when the council of Lateran, under pope Innocent III., ordained the doctrine of transubstantiation and auricular confession, here, in the west church, without the free consent of the east church, the same doctrine is to be counted catholic or not? &c.

Whether the doctrine of transubstantiation, made without the free consent of the east churches, be catholic or no?

Fourthly, in the departing of these churches from the bishop of Rome, here also is to be noted, that the same churches of the Greeks, notwithstanding they sequestered themselves, and fell out with the church of Rome, and that justly, yet they kept their unity still with their God, and retained still the true 'ὀρθοδοξίαν,' that is, the true and sincere doctrine of faith; ready to debate and try the truth of their religion by the Scriptures, as they here, in their own writings, desire to have the truth examined, according as ye have heard. Wherefore the church of Rome hath done them open wrong, which being offered so gently to try, and to be tried, by the truth of God's word, not only would stand to no trial, nor abide conference, but also hath excommunicated those as heretics, who appear here to be more orthodox Christians than themselves.

Fifthly, these things thus standing, then have we to conclude that the church of Rome falsely pretendeth itself to be catholic: for if the name of catholic must needs import an universal consent of the whole, how can that be catholic where the consent of so many famous and true christian churches hath been lacking; and, furthermore, where the consent that hath been amongst themselves, hath rather been coacted than any true or free consent? Which is easy to be proved; for let these fires and faggots cease, let kings and princes leave to press their subjects with the pope's obedience, let the Scripture and the bishops alone, every one in his own diocese, govern their flock after the rule of God's word, and how few be there in this west end of the world, trow you, that would not do the same that these Grecians,

The church of Rome proved not to be catholic.

The proceedings of Rome stand upon no free consent, but are coacted.

Henry III. A.D. 1237.

Ethiopians, and Syrians, have done before us ?—And thus much of this patriarch's letters, sent to pope Gregory, concerning the Greek church.

The miserable state of the west parts of Christendom under the pope.

When I consider the doings of these Grecians, as I cannot but commend their wisdom, and judge their state happy and blessed, in shaking off from their necks the miserable yoke of the pope's tyranny; so, on the other hand, considering with myself the wretched thraldom of these our churches here in the west part of the world, under the bishop of Rome; I cannot tell whether more to marvel at, or to lament, their pitiful state, who were brought into such oppression and slavery under him, that neither could they abide him, nor yet durst cast him off. So intolerable were his exactions, so terrible was his tyranny, his suspensions and excommunications so much like a madman's dagger, drawn at every trifle, that no christian patience could suffer it, nor nation abide it. Again, so deeply did he sit in their consciences, they falsely believing him to have the authority of St. Peter, that for conscience' sake neither king nor Cæsar durst withstand him, much less poor subjects once mute against him. And although his takings and spoilings, namely, in this realm of England, were such, that neither the laity nor spiritualty could bear them, yet was there no remedy; but bear them they must, or else the pope's sentence was upon them, to curse them as black as pitch.

Excommunications like a fool's dagger.

The false persuasion of the pope's supremacy, cause of much wretchedness.

In reading the histories of these times, any good heart would lament and rue to see the miserable captivity of the people; what they suffered under this thraldom of the bishop of Rome, whereof part hath been showed before; more, God willing, shall follow hereafter, and some part here presently I express.

A BRIEF TABLE OR DECLARATION OF THE POPE'S UNREASONABLE GATHERINGS, EXACTIONS, AND OPPRESSIONS, IN THE REALM OF ENGLAND, IN THE DAYS OF KING HENRY III.[1]

And first, to begin with the elections of the bishops, abbots, deans, and priors within this realm: it cannot be told what mass of money grew to the pope's coffers thereby, especially in this king's days; forasmuch as in his time scarcely any election happened, either of archbishop, bishop, abbot, or any room of dignity, but, when the covent or chapter had chosen one to their mind, the king, who had married a stranger, and sought therefore to prefer strangers, would set up another. By reason of this, when the other part was fain to appeal to Rome, and there to plead the case, no small rivers of English money, besides expenses and travel by the way, went flowing to the pope's see. And though the election went never so clear, yet the newly elect must needs respect the holy father with some gentle reward, and further, by his oath was bound every three years, either in his own person, or by another, to visit 'limina apostolorum.'

So in the house of St. Alban's, when John Herford was elected abbot, their public election was not enough, but for the confirmation of the same, the monks were fain to send Reinold, the physician,

(1) The substance of the facts here recorded appear to be contained in the Harl. MSS. Brit. Mus. No. 419, Art. 9: "Concerning the wicked and unreasonable demeanour of divers popes, against christian princes, the foundation of divers orders, beginning of new ceremonies, and some other historical observations," with a note: "Written probably by Matthew Paris."—Ed.

and Nicholas, a monk, to Rome, with a sufficient bag of money, through the mediation whereof the election might stand, and the new abbot was sworn every third year, by himself or another, to visit the dorsels[1] of the apostles.

Another such contention happened between the king and the monks of Winchester, about the election of William Rale, whom the monks had chosen, but the king refused, willing to place a stranger, and therefore sent to Rome his messengers, namely, Theobald, a monk of Westminster, and Master Alexander, a lawyer, with no small sum of money, to evacuate the election of the aforesaid William Rale; commanding, moreover, that the gates of Winchester should be shut against him, and that no man should be so hardy, there, as to receive him into his house. Whereupon the said William, being excluded, after he had laid his curse upon the whole city of Winchester, made his repair to Rome, where, for eight thousand marks promised to the pope, his bishopric (spite of the king's heart) was confirmed, and he received.[2] A.D. 1243.

Eight thousand marks given out of the bishopric of Winchester to the pope.

After the death of Stephen Langton, archbishop of Canterbury, ye heard before how the monks had elected Walter, a monk of Canterbury. But the king, to stop that election, sent up his proctors, Mr. Alexander Stanes, and Mr. Henry Sandford, bishop of Rochester, to the pope, to evacuate that election, and to appoint Richard, chancellor of Lincoln. Which proctors perceiving at first how hard and unwilling the pope and cardinals were thereunto, and considering how all things might be bought for money, rather than the king should fail of his purpose, they promised on the king's behalf to the pope, for maintaining his wars against Frederic, the emperor, a disme, or tenth part of all the moveables in the realm of England and Ireland. At the contemplation of this money, the pope, eftsoons, thinking to pass with the king, began to pick quarrels with the aforesaid Walter, for not answering rightly to his questions about Christ's descending to hell, the making of Christ's body on the altar, the weeping of Rachel for her children, she being dead before; also about the sentence of excommunication, and certain causes of matrimony; his answers whereunto, when they were not to the pope's mind, he was put back, and the king's man preferred, which cost the whole realm of England and Ireland the tenth part of their moveable goods, by reason whereof, what money was raised to the pope's Gazophylacium,[3] I leave to the estimation of the reader.[4] A.D. 1229. And yet, for all this, the said Richard, the costly archbishop of Canterbury, within less than two years after, falling out with the king about the castle and lordship of Tunbridge, went and complained of him to the pope; in the traverse whereof it cost the king a great piece of money, and yet missed he his purpose. In that journey the said archbishop, returning homeward, by the way, departed. A.D. 1231.

Tenth part of all movables in England and Ireland given to the pope.

Money spent at Rome between the king and the archbishop of Canterbury.

Of the like dissension ye heard before, between the king and the covent of Durham, for not choosing Master Lucas, the king's chaplain, whom the king offered to be their bishop; about the suit whereof,

The costly elections of bishops.

(1) "The dorsels of the apostles." "Limina apostolorum." The arrival of the abbot, every third year, to visit, with a full purse, the seats of the apostles, was both agreeable and advantageous to the pope.—Ed.

(2) Ex Matth. Paris. fols. 164, 240.

(3) The ecclesiastical treasury.—Ed.

(4) Ex Matth. Paris. fol. 71.

Henry III. A.D. 1237.

when much money was bestowed on both sides well-favouredly, the pope, defeating them both, admitted neither Master William nor Master Lucas, but ordained the bishop of Sarum to be their bishop. A.D. 1228.[1]

Money coming to the pope for the election of the bishop of Coventry and Lichfield.

Between the monks of Coventry and the canons of Lichfield, arose another like quarrel, which of them should have the superior voice in choosing their bishop; in which suit, after much money bestowed in the court of Rome, the pope, to requalify each party with some retribution for their money received, took this order indifferently between them, that each party by course should have the choosing of their bishop. A.D. 1228.[2]

Edmund, archbishop of Canterbury, condemned at Rome in a thousand marks.

What business arose likewise between Edmund, archbishop of Canterbury, and the monks of Rochester, about the election of Richard Wendour, to be their bishop; and what was the end thereof? First, the archbishop was fain to travel himself to the pope, and so did the covent also send their proctors, who, probably being better moved, weighed down the cause, so that the good archbishop in that affair against the monks, and partly in another cause against the earl of Arundel, was condemned of the pope in a thousand marks, whereof the greatest part, no doubt, redounded to the pope's coffers. A.D. 1238.[3]

The fifth part of the goods of the clergy granted to the pope.

After the return of the said Edmund, archbishop of Canterbury, from Rome, it chanced that the monks of Canterbury had elected their prior without his assent; for which he did excommunicate the monks, and evacuate their election. Not long after this, the pope's exactors went about to extort from the churchmen the fifth part of their goods to the pope's use, fighting then against the emperor. This cruel exaction being for a great while resisted by the prelates and clergy, at length the aforesaid archbishop, thinking thereby to get the victory against the monks, was contented to yield to the said exaction; adding, moreover, of his own, for an overplus, eight hundred marks, whereupon the rest of the clergy were fain to follow after, and contribute to the pope's exactors. A.D. 1240.[4]

Great expense of money in the court of Rome, between the bishop of Lincoln and the cathedral church.

In the church of Lincoln (which see, before the Conquest, was at Dorchester, and afterwards by William Rufus translated from thence to Lincoln) rose a grievous contention between Robert Grosthead, then bishop, and the canons of the cathedral church, about their visitation, whether the bishop should visit them, or the dean; which matter being put to arbitrators, could not be composed before the bishop and the chapter, after their appeal made unto the pope, had both gone to Rome, where, after they had well wasted their purses, they received at length their answer, but paid full sweetly for it. A.D. 1239.[5]

At what time the canons of Chichester had elected Robert Passelew to be their bishop, at the king's request, the archbishop with certain other bishops, taking part against the king's chaplain, repelled him, and set up Richard Witch. Upon this, what sending and going there was unto Rome, and what money bestowed about the matter, as well on the king's part as on the bishop's, read the story thereof in Matthew Paris.[6]

(1) Ex Matth. Paris. (2) Ibid. fol. 68. (3) Ibid. fol. 114.
(4) Ibid. fol. 132. b. (5) Ibid. fol. 119. (6) Ibid. fols. 182, 184, 186.

Henry III. A.D 1237

Robert Grosthead, bishop of Lincoln (of whom relation was made before), having a great care how to bring the privileged orders of religious houses within his precinct under his subjection and discipline, went unto Rome, and there, with great labour and much effusion of money, as the story saith, procured of the pope a mandate, whereby all such religious orders were commanded to be under his power and obedience. Not long after, the monks, who could soon weigh down the bishop with money, not abiding that, sent their factors to the pope, who, with their golden eloquence so persuaded him, and stirred his affections in such sort, that soon they purchased to themselves freedom from their ordinary bishop. Robert Grosthead having intelligence of this, made up to Rome, and there complaining to the pope, declared how he was disappointed and confounded in his purpose, contrary to promises and assurance made to him before; to whom Pope Innocent, looking with a stern countenance, made this answer: "Brother," said he, "what is that to thee? Thou hast delivered and discharged thine own soul. It hath pleased us to show favour unto them. Is thine eye evil, for that I am good?" And thus was the bishop sent away with a flea in his ear, murmuring with himself, yet not so softly, but that the pope heard him say these words: "O money! money! what canst not thou do in the court of Rome?" Wherewith the pope being somewhat pinched, gave this answer again: "O ye Englishmen! Englishmen! of all men most wretched; for all your seeking is how ye may consume and devour one another."[1] A.D. 1250.

How prettily the pope can take with both hands.

Money may do much at Rome. The pope's answer to Robert Grosthead.

It happened moreover the same year that the said Robert Grosthead excommunicated and deprived one Ranulph, a beneficed person in his diocese, being accused of incontinency; who, after the term of forty days, refusing to submit himself, the bishop wrote to the sheriff of Rutland to apprehend him as one contumacious. The sheriff, because he deferred or refused so to do (bearing favour to the party), and being therefore solemnly excommunicated by the bishop, uttered his complaint to the king. Whereat the king taking great displeasure with the bishop for excommunicating his sheriff, and not first making his complaint to him, sendeth forth a substantial messenger, Master Moneta, such as he was sure would speed, unto Pope Innocent; by virtue of whose words, the pope, easy to be entreated, sendeth down a proviso to the abbot of Westminster, charging that no prelate or bishop in the realm of England should molest or enter action against any of the king's bailiffs or officers, in such matters as to the king's jurisdiction appertained. And thus was the strife ended, not without some help and heap of English money; so that no wind of any controversy here stirred in England, were it never so small, but it blew some profit for the pope's advantage.[2] A.D. 1250.

Justice perverted by the pope's authority for money.

In like manner no little treasure grew to the pope's coffers by the election of Boniface, the queen's uncle, a Frenchman, to be archbishop of Canterbury, A.D. 1243, and of Ethelmare, the queen's brother, to be bishop of Winchester, against the wills of the prior and covent there, A.D. 1250, besides many such other escheats, which made England poor, and the pope rich.

Money coming to the pope, by the election of two prelates, both strangers.

(1) Ex Matth. Paris. fol. 230. (2) Ibid. fol. 231.

Henry III.

A.D. 1237.

I come now something likewise to touch briefly of the pope's dispensations, provisions, exactions, contributions, and extortions in England in this king's days, for to discourse all, it is not one book will hold it.

Marriage with Elenor the king's sister, a nun, made good by the pope for money.

Simon Montfort, earl of Leicester, had married Elenor, the king's sister, and daughter of King John, who by report of stories had taken the mantle and ring; wherefore the king, and his brother Richard, earl of Exeter, were greatly offended with the marriage. The earl Simon seeing this, made a hand of money, and posting over to Rome, after he had talked a few words in Pope Innocent's ear, the marriage was good enough; and letters were sent to Otho, the pope's legate here, to give sentence solemnly with the earl. Notwithstanding, the Dominic friars, and others of the like religious fraternity, withstood that sentence of the pope stoutly, saying, that the pope's holiness was therein deceived, and souls were in danger; that Christ was jealous over his wife; and that it could not be in anywise possible that a woman who had vowed marriage with Christ, could afterwards marry with another, &c. A.D. 1238.[1]

What inconvenience cometh by the pope's dispensations.

As there was nothing so hard in the wide world, wherewith the pope would not dispense for money, so, by the said dispensations, much mischief was wrought abroad; for, by reason thereof, the people relying upon the pope's dispensation, little regarded what they did, what they promised, or what they swore. This well appeared in the case of this King Henry III.; who, being as great an exactor of the poor commons as ever was any king before him or since, and thinking thereby to win the people sooner to his devotion, most faithfully promised them once or twice, and thereto bound himself with a solemn oath, both before the clergy and laity, to grant unto them the old liberties and customs as well of Magna Charta, as of Charta de Foresta, perpetually to be observed; whereupon, a fifteenth was granted to the king. But, after the payment was sure, the king trusting, by the pope's dispensation, for a little money, to be discharged of his oath and covenant, went from what he had before promised and sworn.

In like manner, the said king, another time, being in need of money, signed himself with the cross, pretending and swearing deeply in the face of the whole parliament, that he would himself personally fight in the Holy Land against the Saracens. But, as soon as the money was taken, small care was had for performance of his oath, it being put into his head by certain about him, that he needed not to regard that perjury, forasmuch as the pope, for one or two hundred pounds, would quickly discharge him thereof.[2]

Wilful perjury maintained by the pope's dispensations.

Enormities which spring from them.

Out of the same corrupt spring of these popish dispensations, have proceeded also many other foul absurdities, for there were many young men in those days who enjoyed benefices, and yet were not priests; and when, by the procurement of Robert Grosthead, bishop of Lincoln, the said young men should be forced, whether they would or not, to enter orders, they, laying their purses together, sent to Rome, and obtained of the pope a dispensation to remain still as they were; that is, to have the fruits of benefices to find them at school or university, and yet being themselves neither ministers to take charge,

(1) Ex Matth. Paris. fol. 114. (2) Ibid. fol. 273.

nor yielding any service for their profits taken.[1] Besides innumerable heaps of enormities more, proceeding from the pope's dispensations, as dispensing one man to have sundry bishoprics, encroach on pluralities of benefices, making children parsons, legitimatizing bastards, with other such things, the particulars whereof, for brevity' sake, I do omit till further opportunity.

THE INTOLERABLE OPPRESSION OF THE REALM OF ENGLAND BY THE POPE'S EXACTIONS AND CONTRIBUTIONS, AND OTHER SLEIGHTS, USED IN THE TIME OF KING HENRY III.

Although these emoluments, thus rising daily to the pope's purse by simony and bribery, by elections and dispensations, might seem sufficient to satisfy his greedy appetite; yet so insatiable was the avarice of that see, that he, not yet contented herewith, over and besides all this, sent almost every year some legate or other into this realm to take for his advantage. Insomuch, that during all this king's time, the realm was never long without some of the pope's leaguers, with all violence exacting and extorting continual provisions, contributions, and sums of money to be levied out of cells, abbeys, priories, fruits of benefices, and bishoprics, and also laymen's purses, to the miserable impoverishing both of the clergy and temporalty, as hereunder followeth.

First, after Pandulph, was sent into this realm Cardinal Otho, procured by the king, without the assent of his nobles, to assist him in certain affairs he had to do. At receiving of this legate, great preparation was made; many rich and precious gifts in scarlet, in plate, in jewels, in money, and in palfreys, were given him; whom the king also himself went as far as the sea-side to receive, bowing down his head in low courtesy to the cardinal's knees; to whom also the bishop of Winchester for his part gave, towards keeping his house, fifty fat oxen, an hundred semes of wheat, and eight great vessels of pure wine. This legate, at his first coming, beginneth first to bestow such benefices as he found vacant upon those whom he brought with him, without respect to whether they were meet or unmeet.[2] A.D. 1237.

The receiving of Otho the pope's legate into the realm.

After this, the pope, hearing how the nobles and commons of the realm began to stomach the cardinal for his excessive procurations and exactions, sent for him home; but the king, because he stood in fear of his nobles, and thought to have a stay by the cardinal against all occurrents, entreated him to stay while he wrote to the pope to obtain further license for him to tarry; and so he did, not without some English money, ye may be sure.

In this mean time of vacation, Otho, thinking to lose no time, but to gather also some crumbs in Scotland, made as though he would set things there in order, which were in the church of Scotland, to be reformed; and so cometh to the king of Scots,[3] being then in York with King Henry, to have leave to enter. Unto him the king thus made answer, that he never saw to his remembrance, any pope's legate in his land, neither was there any such need (God be praised) for such to be sent for. Matters there were well enough, and needed no help of his. And as he could never learn either in the days of his

Otho seeketh to come into Scotland.

The king of Scots' answer to him.

Scotland hitherto never

(1) Ex Matth. Paris. fol. 256. (2) Ibid. fol. 103. (3) Alexander II.—Ed.

Henry III.

A.D. 1238.

father, or any his predecessors, that any such entrance to any legate was granted; so he, for his part, would not now begin. "But yet, notwithstanding, forasmuch as I hear," said he, "that you are a good man, this I tell you before, that if you will needs adventure in, do it warily, and take heed to yourself, lest it happen to you otherwise than I would wish; for they be a savage and unruly people, given much to murder, and shedding blood, whom I myself am scarcely able to bridle; so that if they fall upon you, I shall not be able to help you; for how they also invaded me, and sought to expel me from my kingdom, ye heard of late. And therefore I warn you before, take heed betime what you think best to do." After the cardinal heard the king speak these words, he plucked in his horns, and durst proceed no further, but kept him still by the side of King Henry. Notwithstanding, shortly after, the same legate coming to the borders of Scotland, there called the bishops to him, and so, when he had well filled his bags, came back again.[1]

troubled with any pope's legate.

Otho stopped from going into Scotland.

It was not long before license came from Pope Gregory to his legate Otho, for his longer abode here in the realm (as welcome as water in the ship), with new authority also to proceed in the pope's affairs; who, first showing the bishops and the clergy his letters of longer tarrying, required of them, forasmuch as no man, said he, warreth of his own charges, to be supported with new procurations; which was, to have, of every able church, four marks; and where one church was not able to reach thereto, that other churches should join withal to make up the said money. Notwithstanding, the bishops a great while stood in the denial thereof.[2]

Oppressions of the cardinal.

A.D. 1238.

Besides he assembled together all the black monks of St. Benedict's order, giving to them strict orders, which shortly after, for money, he released to them again.[3]

Moreover, by the said Otho, and the pope's other exactors, with special bulls directed down for the same, the collation of benefices being taken out of the hands of the patrons, they were given to light and vile runagates, coming from Italy and other places, such as it pleased the pope and his legate to bestow them upon; to the great prejudice of the ancient liberty and right of the true patrons thereof. Whereupon the earls, and barons, and nobles of the realm, addressed letters unto Pope Gregory IX. by Sir Robert Twing, knight, for redress of such wrongs and injuries; who otherwise should be forced, they said, to invocate the succour of their king, who both was able, and was no less willing, according to his duty, they trusted, to reform such enormities, and to defend the liberties of his realm. The tenor of the letters is to be read in Matthew Paris.[4]

Nobles of England write to the pope for collation of benefices wrested out of their hands.

Not long after, A. D. 1240, came a new precept from Pope Gregory, by Peter Rubeus, the pope's nuncio, to the aforesaid Otho, that all the beneficed clergy, as well in England as in France, should pay to the pope the fifth part of their revenues. Whereupon when the clergy made their complaint to the king, seeking to be relieved by him, the king answered them, that he neither would, nor durst stand against the pope in any case; and so without all hope of succour he sent them away.[5] Then were the archbishops, bishops,

Peter Rubeus, the pope's carrier. All beneficed men in England compelled to give the fifth part of their

(1) Ex Matth. Paris. fols. 106, 123. b. (2) Ibid. fols. 123, 128, 132. (3) Ibid. fols. 116, 119. (4) Ibid. fol. 128. a. (5) Ibid. fol. 132.

Henry III. A.D. 1240.

abbots, and prelates of the church commanded to assemble together at Reading, there to hear the pope's pleasure and commandment concerning the payment of this fifth part, where, in the end, the matter concluded thus: the prelates desired a further time to be given them to advise upon the matter, and for that season the assembly brake up.[1] Many excuses and exceptions were alleged by the clergy; first, that whereas the money was gathered to fight against the emperor, they ought not to contribute their money contrary to the liberties of the church. Item, that forasmuch as they had paid a tenth not long before unto the pope, upon condition that no more such payments should be required of them, much less now the fifth part should be exacted of them, because an action twice done, maketh a custom. Item, that seeing they had oftentimes to repair unto the court of Rome, if they should give this money against the emperor, it would turn to their danger when going through his land. Item, that seeing their king had many enemies, against whom they must needs relieve the king with their money, they could not so do if the realm were thus impoverished. All these excuses, with divers others, notwithstanding, they were compelled at length to conform themselves to the pope's good pleasure, through the example given by Edmund, archbishop of Canterbury, who, to obtain his purpose against the monks of Canterbury, with whom he was then at strife, began first to yield to the legates eight hundred marks for his part, whereby the rest also were fain to follow after.[2]

revenues to the pope. A.D. 1240. Excuses of the clergy, why they would not contribute to the pope.

Furthermore, the same year, the pope agreed with the people of Rome, that if they would aid him against Frederic the emperor, whatever benefices were to be given in England, the same should be at their arbitrement to be bestowed upon their children. Whereupon commandment was sent to the aforesaid Edmund, archbishop, and to the bishops of Lincoln and Sarum, that all the collations of benefices within the realm should be suspended, till provision were made for three hundred children of the citizens of Rome to be first served. Upon this so miserable request, the said Edmund, archbishop of Canterbury, for sorrow to see the church so oppressed, departed the realm, and so continuing in France, died at Pontigny.[3] This Edmund was afterwards made a saint, and canonized by pope Innocent IV.

Three hundred children of Rome, placed in benefices in England.

Edmund, archbishop of Canterbury, dieth in exile, afterwards canonized.

This done, Peter Rubeus, the pope's nuncio, and Ruffinus, went into Scotland, from whence they brought with them three thousand pounds for the pope's use about All-hallow-tide the same year. At that time, moreover, cometh another harpy from the pope to England, named Mumelius, bringing with him three and twenty Romans here into the realm to be beneficed. Thus, what by the king on the one side, and what by the Cardinal Otho, Peter Rubeus, Ruffinus, and Mumelius, on the other side, poor England was in a wretched case.[4]

Twenty three Romans brought to England to be beneficed.

Another pretty practice of the pope to prowl for money, was this: the aforesaid Peter Rubeus, coming into religious houses and into their chapters, caused them to contribute to the pope's holiness, by the example of this bishop and that abbot, pretending that he and he, of their own voluntary devotion, had given so much and so much,

(1) Matth. Paris. fol. 122. (2) Ibid. fols. 132, 136. (3) Ibid. fol. 134. b. (4) Ibid. fol. 137.

Henry III. A.D. 1240.

and so seduced them.[1] Also the pope craftily suborned certain friars, authorized with full indulgence, that whosoever had vowed to fight in the Holy Land, and was disposed to be released of his vow, needed not to repair to Rome for absolution, but paying so much money as his charges would come to in going thither, he, resorting to the said friars, might be assoiled at home. A.D. 1240.

The pope for money releaseth Christians of their vows.

Now all these troubles laid together, were enough to vex the meekest prince in the world, besides which, by way of access to the king's molestation, he had much ado with the prelates and clergy of his realm, who were always tampering with his title, especially in their assemblies and councils; to whom the king, to restrain them from that presumption, did both send and write, as appeareth by the evidence of record, commencing, "Rex misit Galfridum de Langley,"[2] &c. That is, the king sent Geoffry Langley to the archbishop of York and to other bishops purposed to meet at Oxford, to appeal for him, lest, in the said council there called, they should presume to ordain something against his crown and dignity. This was done A.D. 1241.[3] In the same year came a commandment apostolical to the house of Peterborough, that they, at the pope's contemplation, must needs grant him some benefice lying in their donation, the fruits whereof were worth at least an hundred pounds, and if it were more it should be the better welcome; so that they should be as the farmers, and he to receive the profits. In fine, the covent excused themselves by the abbot, being then not at home. The abbot, when he came home, excused himself by the king being the patron and founder of the house. The king being grieved with the unreasonable ravening of these Romanists, utterly forbade any such example to be given.[4] But what happened? The abbot, being for this accused to the pope by one of the legates, and coming up about four years after, in the time of Pope Innocent, to the council of Lyons, was so rated and reviled, and so shamefully thrust out of the pope's court, that for sorrow he fell sick upon the same, and there died.[5]

Abbot of Peterborough thrust out of the pope's court.

In the time of this council of Lyons, pope Innocent IV., forasmuch as the instrument or obligation, whereby the realm of England stood tributary to the pope, was thought to be burned in the pope's chamber a little before, brought forth either the same, or another chart like unto it; whereunto he straitly charged and commanded every English bishop there present at the council, severally to set his hand and seal. This unreasonable petition of the pope, albeit it went sore against the hearts of the bishops, yet (see in what miserable subjection the pope had all the bishops under him) none of them durst otherwise do, but accomplish the pope's request therein, both to their own shame, and with prejudice to the public freedom of the realm. Amongst which bishops, the longest that held out, and last that put to his seal, was the bishop of London. This act, when the king and the nobility understood, they were mightily and worthily therewithal offended.[6] A.D. 1245.

The obligation of king John's tribute to the pope burned.

The bishops of England put their hands and seals to the pope's bill.

After that time Cardinal Otho was sent for by pope Gregory in all haste to come to the general council; two others in his room

(1) Matth. Paris. p. 134. (2) Turris Lond.
(3) The passage in asterisks is not found in the Editions previous to 1596.
(4) Ex Matth. Paris. fol. 143. (5) Ibid. fol. 184. (6) Ibid. fol. 192.

remained here, whose names were Peter Rubeus, and Petrus de Supino, of whom the one, bearing himself for the pope's kinsman, brought out his bills and bulls under the pope's authority, to such an abbot, or to such a prior, or to such and such a bishop, and so extorted from them a great quantity of gold and silver. The other, to wit, Petrus de Supino, sailed to Ireland, from whence he brought with him a thousand and five hundred marks for the pope's use, A.D. 1241.[1] All which money notwithstanding, gotten by both the collectors, in the carriage of it up to Rome, about the death of pope Gregory, fell into the hands of Frederic, the emperor; who caused it to be restored, as nearly as he could, to those from whom it was taken.[2]

Henry III. A.D. 1241.

A thousand five hundred marks brought out of Ireland for the pope.

After these came in Master Martin, a new merchant from the new pope Innocent IV. (A.D. 1244) armed with full power to suspend all prelates in England from giving benefices, till the pope's kinsmen were first preferred; neither would he take the fruits of any benefice, unless it were above the value of thirty marks. At his first coming, he required prelates, and especially religious houses, to furnish him with horses and palfreys, such as were convenient for the pope's especial chaplain and legate to sit upon; also with plate, raiment, provision for his kitchen and cellar, &c.; and such as refused, or made excuses, he suspended, as the abbot of Malmesbury, and the prior of Merton. All prebends that were void he sought out and reserved for the pope's behoof; among which was the golden prebend of Sarum, belonging to the chancellor of the choir, whom he preferred to the bishopric of Bath, and so seized upon the prebend, being void, against the wills both of the bishop and the chapter.[3] Moreover, he brought with him blanks in paper and parchment, signed in the pope's chamber with his stamp and seal; wherein he might afterward write to whom, and what he would,[4] requiring, furthermore, of the king, in the pope's behalf, to help his holiness with a contribution to be taxed amongst his clergy, of at least ten thousand marks;[5] and, to the end that the pope might win the king sooner to his devotion, he writeth in the king's behalf to the nobles and commons of the realm, that they should not fail, upon pain of his great curse, to confer such subsidy of money to the assistance of the king, as he then had demanded of them; but they stood stiff in not granting it him.

Another messenger for the pope's money. A.D. 1244.

His extortion upon the clergy of England.

Contribution of ten thousand marks for the pope.

The pope craftily holdeth with the king, that the king might hold with him.

While the insatiable avarice of the pope thus made no end in gathering riches and goods together in England; the nobles and barons, with the community as well of the clergy as the laity, weighing the miserable state of the realm, and particularly of the church, the clergy of which now neither had liberty left them to choose their own ministers, nor yet could enjoy their own livings, laid their heads together, and so exhibited an earnest intimation to the king; beseeching him to consider the pitiful affliction and oppression of his subjects under the pope's extortion, living in more thraldom than ever did the people of Israel under Pharaoh. Whereupon, the king beginning at last to look up, and to consider the injuries and wrongs received in his realm, through the avarice of the court of Rome, directeth to pope Innocent IV. the following letter.

Intimation given to the king touching the insupportable oppression of the realm by the pope.

(1) Ex Matth. Paris. fol. 247. b. (2) Ibid. fol. 151. (3) Ibid. fols. 167, 180.
(4) Ibid. fol. 178. b. (5) Ibid.

Henry III.

A.D. 1244.

King Henry's Letter to Pope Innocent IV.[1]

To the most holy father in Christ, and lord Innocent, by the grace of God, chief bishop: Henry, by the same grace, king of England, &c., greeting and kissings of his blessed feet. The more devout and obsequious the son showeth himself in obeying the father's will, the more favour and supportation doth he deserve to find again at his father's hands. This therefore I write, for that whereas both we and our realm have ever and in all things been, hitherto, at the devotion and commandment of your fatherhood; and that, although in some certain affairs of ours and of our kingdom, we have found your fatherly favour and grace sometimes propitious unto us, yet in some things again, as in provisions given and granted to your clerks of foreign nations, both we and our kingdom have felt no small detriment; by reason of which provisions, the church of England is so sore charged and burdened, that not only the patrons of churches, to whom the donations thereof do appertain, are defrauded of their right, but also many other good works of charity thereby do decay, for that such benefices as have been mercifully bestowed upon religious houses to their sustentation, are now wasted and consumed, by your provisions.

The king offereth to kiss the pope's feet.

Damage caused by the pope in the realm of England.

Wherefore, forasmuch as your see apostolic ought to be favourable to all that be petitioners to the same, so that no person be wronged in that which is his right, we thought therefore to be suitors to your fatherhood, most humbly beseeching your holiness, that you will desist and surcease for a time from such provisions to be exacted. In the mean season, may it please your fatherhood, we beseech you, that our laws and liberties (which you may rightly repute none other but your own) you will receive to your tuition, to be preserved whole and sound, nor to suffer the same, by any sinister suggestion in your court, to be violated and infringed. Neither let your holiness be any whit moved there-for with us, if, in some such cases as these be, we do or shall hereafter resist the tenor of your commandments; forasmuch as the complaints of those who daily call upon us, do necessarily enforce us thereunto; who ought, by the charge of this our office and kingly dignity committed to us of Almighty God, to foresee that no man, in that which is his right, be injured, but truly to minister justice to every one, in that which duly to him appertaineth.—This letter was sent the eight and twentieth year of the king's reign.[2]

A man would think that this so gentle and obedient letter of the king to the pope, would have wrought some good effect in his apostolical breast, to withdraw his provisions, and to have tendered the king's so reasonable and honest request: but, how little all this prevailed to stop his insatiable greediness and intolerable extortions and oppressions, the sequel well declareth. For, besides that, shortly after, the pope sent Master Martin with blanks, being bulled for contribution of ten thousand marks, in all haste to be paid also, even immediately upon the receiving of this letter.[3] It followeth in mine author, that the said pope Innocent IV., after all this great submission of the king, and such manifold benefits and payments yearly out of this realm received, was not ashamed to take of David, prince of North Wales, five hundred marks a year, to set him against the king of England, exempting him from his fealty and obedience due to his own liege lord and king, to whom both he and all other Welshmen had sworn subjection before, as by the seals and obligations as well of that David himself, as of other Welsh lords, in this behalf doth appear.[4]

The pope setteth Welshmen against the king of England.

In the mean while Master Martin did not let sleep his business, in making up his market for the pope's money of ten thousand marks, but was still calling upon the prelates and clergy, who, first excusing

(1) "Sanctissimo in Christo patri, ac Domino Innocentio, Dei gratia summo pontifici: Henricus eadem gratia rex Angliæ, &c., salutem et pedum oscula beatorum," &c.
(2) Ex Matth. Paris. fol. 172. (3) Ibid. (4) Ibid.

themselves by the absence of the king and the archbishop of Canterbury, afterwards being called again by new letters, made their answer by the dean of Paul's, their prolocutor:— *Henry III.* A.D. 1244.

First, That the poverty of the realm would not suffer them to consent thereto.

Item, Whereas they had given before a contribution to cardinal Otho, for paying the pope's debts, and knew the said money to be employed to no such end as it was demanded for, more cause they had now to misdoubt, lest this contribution in his hands, who was a much inferior messenger than the cardinal, would come to the same or a worse effect. Excuses and reasons against contributions

Item, If they should now agree to a new contribution, they feared lest it would grow to a custom, seeing that one action twice done maketh a custom.

Item, Forasmuch as a general council is shortly looked for, where every prelate of the realm must needs bestow both his travel and expenses, and also his presence, to the pope, if the prelates now should be bound to this tax, they would not be able to abide this burden.

Item, Seeing it is alleged, that the mother church of Rome is so far in debt, reason and right it were, that the mother so oppressed should be sustained by all her devout children meeting together in the general council; as by help of many, more relief might come than by one nation alone.

Lastly, They alleged, that for fear of the emperor and his threatenings, they durst not consent to the said contribution.

While these things were thus in talk between the pope's priests and the clergy of England, cometh in John Mariscal and other messengers from the king, commanding, in the king's name, that no bishop, that held his baronage of the king, should infiefed his lay fee to the court of Rome, which they owed only to him.[1]

Not long after this (A.D. 1245), the whole nobility of the realm, by general consent, and not without the king's knowledge also, caused an injunction to be laid on all the ports by the sea-side, that no messenger with the pope's letters and bulls from Rome, should be permitted to enter the realm; whereupon, some were taken at Dover, and there stayed. Notwithstanding, when complaint thereof was brought to the king by Master Martin, the pope's legate, there was no remedy but the king must needs cause these letters to be restored again, and executed to the full effect.[2] An injunction laid on the ports of England, to stop the pope's letters, yet all would not serve

Then the king, upon advice, caused a view to be taken through every shire in England, to what sum the whole revenues of the Romans and Italians amounted, which, by the pope's authority, went out of England: the whole sum whereof was found yearly to be threescore thousand marks, to the which sum the revenues of the whole crown of England did not extend.[3] Sixty thousand marks yearly going out of England to the pope and his Italian clerks

The nobles, then, understanding the miserable oppression of the realm, and being assembled together at Dunstable for certain causes, sent one Fulco, in the name of the whole nobility, unto Master Martin, the pope's merchant, with this message: That he, without delay, upon the same warning, should prepare himself to be

(1) Matth Paris fol 139 (2) Ibid fol. 183 (3) Ibid fol 185 a

Henry III. A.D. 1245.

gone out of the realm, under pain of being cut all to pieces. At which message the legate being sore aghast, went straight to the king, to know whether his consent was to the same or not. Of whom when he found little better comfort, he took his leave of the king, who bade him adieu in the devil's name, saith Matthew Paris, and thus was the realm rid of Master Martin.[1] A.D. 1245.

The proud words of the pope against the French king and the king of England.

As soon as pope Innocent IV. had hereof intelligence by the complaint of his legate, he was in a mighty rage; and furthermore, remembering how the French king and the king of Arragon, not long before, had denied him entrance into their land, and being, therefore, in displeasure with them likewise, he began in great anger to knit his brows, and said, "It is best that we fall in agreement with our prince, whereby we may the sooner bring under these little petty kings (istos regulos), and so the great dragon being pacified, these little serpents we shall handle at our own pleasure as we list."

Immediately after this followed the general council of Lyons, to which the lords and states of the realm, with the consent of the commonalty, sent two bills; one containing a general supplication to the pope and the council; the other, with the articles of such grievances as they desired to be redressed, whereof relation is made sufficiently before. The other bill of the supplication, because it is not before expressed, I thought here to exhibit for two causes: First, that men, now in these days, may see the pitiful blindness of those ignorant days, wherein our English nation here did so blindly humble themselves and stand on courtesy to the pope, whom rather they should have shaken off, as the Grecians did. Secondly, that the pride of the pope might the better appear in its true colours, who so disdainfully rejected the humble suit of our lords and nobles, when they had much more cause rather to disdain and stamp him under their feet. The tenor of the supplication was this.

The Copy of the Supplication written in the names of all the Nobles and Commons of England, to Pope Innocent IV. in the General Council at Lyons, A.D. 1245.

To the reverend father in Christ, Pope Innocent, chief bishop; the nobles, with the whole commonalty of the realm of England, send commendation, with kissing of his blessed feet.

Our mother, the church of Rome, we love with all our hearts, as our duty is, and covet the increase of her honour with as much affection as we may, as to whom we ought always to fly for refuge, whereby the grief lying upon the child, may find comfort at the mother's hand; which succour the mother is bound so much the rather to impart to her child, how much more kind and beneficial she findeth him in relieving her necessity. Neither is it to the said our mother unknown, how beneficial and bountiful a giver the realm of England hath been now of long time for the more amplifying of her exaltation, as appeared by our yearly subsidy, which we term by the name of Peter-pence. Now the said church, not contented with this yearly subsidy, hath sent divers legates for other contributions, at divers and sundry times, to be taxed and levied out of the same realm: all which contributions and taxes, notwithstanding, have been lovingly and liberally granted.

Superstitious founding of monasteries in England.

Furthermore, neither is it unknown to your fatherhood, how our forefathers, like good catholics, both loving and fearing their Maker, for the soul's health as well of themselves, as of their progenitors and successors also, have founded

(1) Ex Matth. Paris. fol. 185, b.

monasteries, and largely have endowed the same, both with their own proper lands, and also with patronages of benefices, whereby such religious persons, professing the first and chiefest perfection of holy religion in their monasteries, might with more peace and tranquillity occupy themselves devoutly in God's service, as to the order appertained: and also the clerks, presented by them to their benefices, might sustain the other exterior labours for them in that second order of religion, and so discharge and defend them from all hazards: so that the said religious monasteries cannot be defrauded of those their patronages and collations of benefices, but the same must touch us also very near, and work intolerable grief unto our hearts.

Injuries received by the pope.

And now see, we beseech you, which is lamentable to behold, what injuries we sustain by you and your predecessors, who, not considering those our subsidies and contributions above remembered, do suffer also your Italians and foreigners, who be out of number, to be possessed of our churches and benefices in England, pertaining to the right and patronage of those monasteries aforesaid: which foreigners, neither defending the said religious persons whom they ought to see to, nor yet having the language, whereby they may instruct the flock, take no regard of their souls, but utterly leave them of wild wolves to be devoured. Wherefore, it may truly be said of them, that they are not good shepherds, whereas they neither know their sheep, nor do the sheep know the voice of their shepherds; neither do they keep any hospitality, but only take up the rents of those benefices, carrying them out of the realm, wherewith our brethren, our nephews, and our kinsfolks, might be sustained, who could and would dwell upon them, and employ such exercises of mercy and hospitality as their duty required, of whom a great number now for mere necessity are laymen, and fain to fly out of the realm.

Benefices wickedly given away to Italians.

Threescore thousand marks yearly given to Italians out of the church of England.

And now, to the intent more fully to certify you of the truth, ye shall understand that the said Italians and strangers, receiving of yearly rents out of England not so little as threescore thousand marks a year, besides other avails and excises deducted, do reap in the said our kingdom of England more emoluments of mere rents than doth the king himself, being both tutor of the church, and governor of the land.

Italians received more in this land of mere rents, than did the king's crown.

Furthermore, whereas at the first creation of your papacy we were in good hope, and yet are, that by means of your fatherly goodness we should enjoy our franchises and free collation of our benefices and donatives, to be reduced again to the former state; now cometh another grievance which we cannot but signify unto you, pressing us above measure, which we receive by Master Martin, who, entering late into our land without leave of our king, with greater power than ever was seen before in any legate, although he beareth not the state and show of a legate, yet he hath doubled the doings of a legate, charging us every day with new mandates, and so most extremely hath oppressed us: First, in bestowing and giving away our benefices, if any were above thirty marks, as soon as they were vacant, to Italian persons. Secondly, after the decease of the said Italians, unknown to the patrons, he hath intruded other Italians therein, whereby the true patrons have been spoiled and defrauded of their right. Thirdly, the said Master Martinus yet also ceaseth not to assign and confer such benefices still to the like persons; and some he reserveth to the donation of the apostolic see; and extorteth, moreover, from religious houses, immoderate pensions, excommunicating and interdicting whosoever dare gain-stand him.

Detestable dealings of the pope's legate in England.

Complaint of the pope's legate.

Wherefore, forasmuch as the said Master Martin hath so far extended his jurisdiction, to the great perturbation of the whole realm, and no less derogation to our king's privilege, to whom it hath been fully granted, by the see apostolic, that no legate should have to do in his land, but such as he by special letters did send for: with most humble devotion we beseech you, that as a good father will always be ready to support his child, so your fatherhood will reach forth your hand of compassion to relieve us, your humble children, from these grievous oppressions.

And, although our lord and king, being a catholic prince, and wholly given to his devotions, and to the service of Christ Jesus our Lord, so that he respecteth not the health of his own body, will fear and reverence the see apostolic; and, as a devout son of the church of Rome, desireth nothing more than to advance the estate and honour of the same: yet, we who travail in his affairs, bearing the heat and burden of the day, and whose duty, together with him, is

Henry III. A.D. 1245.

to tender the preservation of the public wealth, neither can patiently suffer such oppressions, so detestable to God and man, and grievances intolerable, neither by God's grace will suffer them, through the means of your godly remedy, which we well hope and trust of you speedily to obtain. And thus may it please your fatherhood, we beseech you to accept this our supplication, who in so doing shall worthily deserve of all the lords and nobles, with the whole commonalty of the realm of England, condign and special thanks accordingly. A.D. 1245.[1]

Stout words of the lords to the pope.

This supplication being sent by the hands of Sir R. Bygot, Knight, and W. de Powick, Esquire, Henry de la Mare, with other knights and gentlemen, after it was there opened and read, pope Innocent, first keeping silence, deferred to make answer thereunto, making haste to proceed in his detestable excommunication and curse against the good emperor Frederic. Which curse being done, and the English ambassadors waiting still for their answer, the pope told them flatly they should not have their request fulfilled. At this the Englishmen, departing in great anger, swore, with terrible oaths, that they would never more suffer any tribute, or fruits of any benefices (speaking of those whereof the noblemen were patrons) to be paid to that insatiable and greedy court of Rome, worthy to be detested in all worlds.[2]

The pope in anger with England. The bishops of England set their seals to the pope's tribute.

The pope, hearing these words, albeit making them no answer, thought to watch his time, and did. First, incontinently upon the same, during the said council, he caused every bishop of England to put his hand and seal to the obligation made by king John for the pope's tribute, as is above specified; threatening, moreover, and saying, that if he had once brought down the emperor Frederic, he would bridle the insolent pride of England well enough.

*[3]But here, on occasion of this council at Lyons, that the reader may see upon what slippery uncertainty and variableness the state of the king did depend; it is material to interlace the form of a letter, sent by Henry III. to the prelates of his land, before they were transported over sea to Lyons; wherein may be gathered, that the king doubted they would be shoving and heaving at his royalty, and, therefore, directed these letters unto them, otherwise to prepare their affections,—the tenor whereof followeth.

Charge to the Prelates of England about to assemble in the Council at Lyons, that they should ordain nothing to their King's prejudice.

The king to the archbishops, bishops, and to all other prelates of his land of England, appointed to meet at a council at Lyons, greeting: you are, as you know, bound unto us by oath, whereby you ought to keep all the fealty that you can unto us, in all things concerning our royal dignity and crown. Wherefore we command you, upon the fealty and allegiance wherein you are firmly bound unto us, enjoining that you do your uttermost endeavour, as well to get as to keep, and also to defend the right of us and our kingdom; and that neither to the prejudice of us, nor of the same kingdom, nor yet against us or our rights, which our predecessors and we, by ancient and approved custom, have used, you presume to procure or attempt any thing in your council at Lyons: nor

(1) Ex Matth. Paris. fol. 188. (2) Ibid. fol. 193.
(3) This passage in single asterisks is not found in the editions which were published previous to A.D. 1596.
(4) "Rex archiepiscopis, episcopis, et omnibus aliis prælatis terræ suæ Angliæ, conventuris ad concilium Lugdunense, salutem. Vinculo juramenti nobis (ut nostis) adstricti," &c.

Henry III. A.D. 1246.

that you give assent to any that shall procure or ordain ought in this case, upon your oath aforesaid, and the loss of your temporalities, which you hold of us. Wherefore, in this behalf, so behave yourselves, that for your good dealing and virtue of thankfulness, we may rather specially commend you, than for the contrary by you attempted, which God forbid, reprove your unthankfulness, and reserve vengeance for you in due time. Witness ourself, &c. the nine and twentieth year of our reign."

In like sort wrote he to the archbishops and bishops, &c. of Ireland and Gascony.*

After this council, in the beginning of the next year (A. D. 1246), pope Innocent came to Cluniack, where was then appointed a secret meeting or colloquy between the pope and Louis, the French king (who was then preparing his voyage to Jerusalem), in which colloquy the pope sought all means to persuade the French king, in revengement of his injury, to war 'contra regulum,' as he termed it; that is, against the weak and feeble king of England; either to drive him utterly from his kingdom, or else so damnify him, that he should be constrained, whether he would or no, to stoop to the pope's will and obedience; wherein he also would assist him with all the authority he was able. Nevertheless, the French king to this would not agree; first for the consanguinity that was between them, for their two queens were sisters; secondly, for the truce that they had taken; thirdly, for fear of the emperor, lest he should take his part; fourthly, for that it could not be without the spilling of much christian blood; and, lastly, because he was preparing his voyage to the Holy Land, where his coming was already looked for. And thus the French king, denying the pope's bloody request, refused not only to enter upon a war with the king and the realm of England, but also, shortly after, concluded with him longer truce. A. D. 1246.[1]

The pope stirreth up Louis the French king against the king of England.

Straight upon the neck of this followed the exaction of Boniface, archbishop of Canterbury, that he had bought of the pope; which was, to have the first year's fruits of all benefices and spiritual livings in England for the space of seven years together, until the sum should come to ten thousand marks; whereat the king at first was greatly grieved, but in conclusion, he was fain at last to agree with the archbishop, and so the money was gathered.[2]

First fruits for seven years gathered for the archbishop of Canterbury.

Over and besides all other exactions, wherewith the pope miserably oppressed the church of England, this also is not to be silenced; how the pope, sending down his letters from the see apostolic, charged and commanded the prelates to find him, some five, some ten, and some fifteen, able men, well furnished with horse and harness, for one whole year, to fight in the pope's wars. And, lest the king should have knowledge thereof, it was enjoined them, under pain of excommunication, that they should reveal it to none, but to keep it secret to themselves.[3]

Prelates of England charged to find horse and harness for the pope's war.

The pope still, notwithstanding, partly being belaboured by suitors, partly of his own mind thinking it good to give somewhat to the king and people of England, as fathers are wont to give something to their babes to play withal to keep them still, sent down this releasement to the king, that hereafter, whensoever any of the pope's nephews or cardinals were to be beneficed in any church of

The pope's bait laid for more money.

(1) Ex Matth. Paris. fol. 196 (2) Ibid. fol. 197. (3) Ibid. fol 206.

Henry III. A.D. 1246.

England, either he or the cardinals should first make the king privy thereto, and instantly crave his good will in obtaining the procuration, or else the same to stand as of no effect.[1] Howbeit, all this seemed to be done but of policy, to get the king's favour, whereby he might be suffered more freely to pass with greater exactions, as afterwards appeared. For when the aforesaid pope, Innocent IV., had knowledge, about that time, of certain rich clerks leaving great substance of money, who died intestate, as of one Robert Hailes, archdeacon of Lincoln, who died, leaving thousands of marks, and much plate behind him, all which, because no will was made, came to temporal men's hands; also of Master Almarike, archdeacon of Bedford, who was found worth a great substance when he died; and likewise of another, one John Hotosp, archdeacon of Northampton, who died suddenly intestate, leaving behind him five thousand marks, and thirty standing pieces of plate, with other infinite jewels besides: he sent forth upon the same a statute to be proclaimed in England, that whatsoever ecclesiastical person henceforth should decease in England intestate, that is, without making his will, all his goods should redound to the pope's use.[2]

A new law of the pope to seize upon all the goods of clergy who die intestate.

Furthermore, the pope, not yet satisfied with all this, addresseth new letters to the bishop of Winchester, and to William, bishop of Norwich, for gathering up, amongst the clergy and religious houses in England, six thousand marks to the behoof of the holy mother church, without any excuse or delay, by virtue of obedience. This tallage being greatly grudged by the clergy, when it came to the king's ear, he eftsoons directeth contrary letters to all the prelates, commanding them, on pain of forfeiting their temporalities to the king, that no such subsidy-money should be gathered or transported out of the realm. But the pope again, hearing hereof, in great anger writeth to the prelates of England, that this collection of money, upon pain of excommunication and suspension, should be provided, and brought to the new Temple, in London, by the feast of the Assumption next ensuing.

Six thousand marks to be gathered of the clergy of England for the pope.

The pope in a chafe.

And furthermore, forasmuch as he perceived the king to go about to withstand his proceedings, taking thereat great disdain, he was, at the same time, about to interdict the whole land; to whom then one of his cardinals, called Johannes Anglicus, an Englishman born, speaking for the realm of England, desired his fatherhood for God's sake to mitigate his moody ire, and with the bridle of temperance to assuage the passion of his mind: "which," said he, "to tell you plain, is here stirred up too much without cause. Your fatherhood," quoth he, "may consider that these days be evil. First, the Holy Land lieth in great perils to be lost. All the Greek church is departed from us. Frederic, the emperor, is against us, the mightiest prince this day in all Christendom. Both you and we who are the peers of the church, are banished from the papal see, thrust out of Rome, yea, excluded out of all Italy. Hungary, with all coasts bordering about it, looketh for nothing but utter subversion by the Tartarians. Germany is wasted and afflicted with inward wars and tumults. Spain is fierce and cruel against us, even to the

The miserable troubles of Christendom.

(1) Matth. Paris. fol. 202. (2) Ibid. fol. 203.

cutting out of the bishops' tongues.[1] France by us is so impoverished, that it is brought to beggary; which also conspireth against us. Miserable England, being so often plagued by our manifold injuries, even much like to Balaam's ass, beaten and bounced with spurs and staves, beginneth at length to speak and complain of her intolerable griefs and burdens, being so wearied and damnified, that she may seem past all recovery; and we, after the manner of Ishmael, hating all men, provoke all men to hate us."[2]

Notwithstanding all these words of Johannes Anglicus, his cardinal, the pope's choleric passion could not yet be appeased, but forthwith he sendeth commandment, with full authority, to the bishop of Worcester, that in case the king would not speedily surcease his rebellion against his apostolical proceedings, he would interdict his land; so that in conclusion, the king, for all his stout enterprise, was fain to relent at last, and the pope had his money.[3]

Power given to the bishop of Worcester to interdict the land. The king fain to relent to the pope.

A.D. 1246.

Ye heard before of the Greek churches, under the empire of Constantinople, how they sequestered themselves from the company of the Romish church, insomuch that Germanus, the patriarch of Constantinople, and the archbishop of Antioch, did excommunicate the bishop of Rome: and after the said Germanus, another bishop of Constantinople, at the council of Lyons, protested, that whereas before there were thirty suffragans belonging to that province, now there were not three that held with the church of Rome. This breach, albeit it chiefly burst out in the time of pope Gregory IX. (A.D. 1230) to open war and bloodshed, yet the same had begun, and so continued, long before, in such sort that in the time of pope Innocent III., if any priest had said mass in their churches, they would wash the altar afterwards; as appeareth by the acts of the Lateran Council. Wherefore pope Innocent, now, (as his other predecessors had done before) bearing an old grudge against those churches of the Greeks, and neither willing by conference to try with them, nor able by learning to match with them, thought by force of arms to subdue them, and sent the provincial of the Grey Friars, with other associates of the same order, into England, with his precept authentical, containing in it these articles.[4]

The Grecians used to wash their altars, if any Latin mass had been said upon them.

I. That the said provincial, or his friars, should inquire about all usurers being alive; and of all such evil-gotten goods gained "per usuriam pravitatem," should make attachment, for the use and preparation, for this war against the Greeks; excommunicating all them by district censures[5] of the church who repugned against it.

II. That all they who took the badge of the cross, for the recovery of the said empire of the Greeks, or who, with goods and cattle, would help sufficiently unto the same, should be absolved of all their sins.

III. That all the goods left in the testaments of them that were departed, being gotten by usury, should be taken up to the subsidy of the empire aforesaid; and whosoever repugned against the same, should be excommunicated.

IV. That such goods as in the testaments of the dead were left, or which should be left the three next years to come, for restitution of such goods as the dead had evil gotten, they should take up for the subsidy of the empire aforesaid, excommunicating, &c.

V. That such goods as were left to be distributed in godly uses, after the

(1) Of Spain, he meaneth, because the king of Arragon a little before had cut off the tongue of a certain bishop that did reprehend him. (2) Ex Matth. Paris. fol. 207. (3) Ibid. fol. 204.
(4) Ex actis concilii Lateranensis, cap. 4. (5) Confined to certain districts.—Ed.

Henry III. A.D. 1246.

arbitrement of executors, by the wills of the dead, or were not in their wills deputed to any certain places or persons named, nor yet were bestowed by the said executors to the aforesaid uses, they should collect to the use and subsidy aforesaid, and give certificate to the see apostolic of the quantity thereof; excommunicating all repugners and rebellers against the same.

VI. That they should diligently inquire of such men's goods evil gotten or evil come by, as were alive, and them they should attach for the subsidy aforesaid, in case the party, who ought to be satisfied for those goods evil gotten, could not be found, giving certificate thereof, and excommunicating, &c.

VII. That the said provincial, or his friars, should have full power to absolve those that were excommunicated, who wittingly had done any fraud touching the collection aforesaid, so that the said persons did make due satisfaction to the deputies aforesaid.[1]

What man, having eyes, is so blind, that he seeth not these execrable dealings of the pope to be such as would cause any nation in the world to do as the wise Grecians did, and perpetually to renounce the pope, and well to consider the usurped authority of that see not to be of God? But such was the rude dulness then of miserable England, for lack of learning and godly knowledge, that they, feeling what burdens were laid upon them, yet would play still the ass of Balaam, or else the horse of Æsop, which, receiving the bridle once in its mouth, could afterward neither abide its own misery, nor yet recover liberty. And so it fared with England, under the pope's thraldom: as partly by these stories above hath been declared, partly by other in the like case following is to be seen.

An unreasonable exaction of the pope.

For so it followeth in the history of Matthew Paris, how the pope taking more courage by his former abused boldness, and perceiving what a tame ass he had to ride upon, ceased not thus, but directed a new precept the same year (A.D. 1246) to the prelates of England, commanding by the authority apostolic, that all beneficed men in the realm of England, who were resident upon their benefices, should yield to the pope the third part of their goods, and that they who were not resident should give the one half of their goods, and that for the space of three years together; with terrible comminations against all them that did resist; and ever with this clause withal, "non obstante," which was like a key that opened all locks. The sum cast together was found to amount to sixty thousand pounds; which sum of money could scarcely be found in all England to pay for king Richard's ransom.[2] The execution of this precept was committed to the bishop of London, who, conferring about the matter with his brethren in the church of Paul, as they were busily consulting together and bewailing the importable burden of this contribution, which it was impossible for them to sustain, suddenly come in certain messengers from the king,—Sir John Lexinton, Knt., and Lawrence Martin, the king's chaplain,—straitly, in the king's name, forbidding them, in any case, to consent to this contribution, which should be greatly to the prejudice and desolation of the whole realm.[3]

Threescore thousand pounds exacted of the clergy for the pope.

This was done, about the first day of December. In the beginning of the next year, (A.D. 1247,) about February, the king called a parliament, where by common advice it was agreed, that certain ambassadors should be sent to Rome, to make manifest to the court of Rome the exceeding grievances of the realm, delivering, moreover, this letter to

A parliament.

(1) Ex Matth Paris fol 205 (2) Ibid fol 207 (3) Ibid

the pope in the name both of the temporalty and also of the clergy, as here followeth.

Another Letter sent to Pope Innocent IV., in the names of the whole Clergy and Commonalty of England, A.D. 1247.[1]

To the most holy father in Christ, and lord Innocent, by God's providence chief bishop; the whole commonalty, both of the clergy and laity within the province of Canterbury, send devout kissings of his blessed feet. Like as the church of England, since she hath first received the catholic faith, hath always showed herself faithful and devout in adhering to God, and to our holy mother the church of Rome, studying with all kind of service to please and to serve the same, and thinking never otherwise to do, but rather to continue and increase as she hath begun: even so now, the same church, most humbly prostrate before the feet of your holiness, entirely beseecheth your clemency to accept her petition, in sparing this imposition of money, which so manifold ways for the subversion of other nations, by the commandment of your holiness, is laid upon us; considering that not only it is importable, but also impossible which is enjoined us. For although our country sometimes yieldeth forth fruit for the necessary sustentation of the inhabitants, yet it bringeth forth neither gold nor silver, neither were able to bring forth, of long time, so much as now-a-days is required; which also being burdened and overcharged of late days, with another such like imposition, but not so great as this, is not able any whit to answer unto that which is exacted. More fools you, in giving to the church so much.

Furthermore, besides this commandment of your holiness, there is required of the clergy a subsidy for our temporal king, whose necessities neither possibly we can, nor honestly we ought, to forsake; whereby he may both withstand the invasion of the enemy, and maintain the right of his patrimony, and also recover again that which hath been lost; in consideration whereof, we have directed the bearers hereof to the presence of your holiness with our humble supplication, to explain to you the dangers and inconveniences which are like to ensue upon the premises, which by no means we are able to sustain, although notwithstanding we know ourselves by all bonds of charity to be obliged to your devotion and obedience. And, because our general community hath no seal proper, we have signed therefore these presents with the public seal of the city of London.[2]

The like letters were sent also unto the cardinals to the same effect. The pope understanding these things, and perceiving that there was no striving against such a general consent, and yet loth to forego his sweet harvest, which he was wont to reap in England, craftily devised to send this answer again unto the king, much like to the same which he sent before, which was, that although the pope in time past, upon his own will and pleasure, to the importable grievance of the realm of England, hath every where, and without respect, through the whole land, made his provisions in giving their benefices unto his Italians, yet now, the Lord be praised, that tempest, said he, is overblown: so that hereafter, if the pope shall grant his provision for any of his nephews or cardinals, they shall come first and make their instant suit unto the king, without all enforcement, so that it shall stand wholly in the king's free arbitrement to do herein what he thinketh good, &c.[3] The pope's answer to the king of England.

This answer of the pope, albeit it was but a subtle shift for the time, yet neither did he long stand to what he had thus promised to the king; for shortly after, and within few days of the same, and The pope false to his promise.

(1) "Sanctissimo patri in Christo, ac domino Innocentio, Dei providentia summo pontifici; universitas cleri et populi per provintiam Cant. constituti devota pedum oscula beatorum Cum Anglicana ecclesia," &c.

(2) Ex Matth. Paris. fol. 209.

(3) Ibid. b.

Henry III.

A.D. 1247.

in the time also of the said parliament holden at Winchester, the pope sent two English friars into the realm, whose names were John and Alexander, with full authority, after the largest sort, for new contributions; who, first pretending lowly submission to the king, while they had leave granted to range about the realm, but afterwards coming to the bishops and rich abbots, showed themselves forth in their full authority, in such sort as they became rather tyrants than extortioners.

Subtle practices of the pope to get money.

Among others, coming to Robert, bishop of Lincoln, who of all others bare a special mind to the order of observants, these two friars, as proud as Lucifer, bringing forth the terrible mandate with the pope's bulls, required and eke commanded, under the pope's mighty curse, to have the gathering in his diocese of six thousand marks. Likewise of the abbot of St. Alban's they required four hundred marks, under great penalty, and that in short time to be paid.

The bishop of Lincoln's answer to the friars.

The bishop, although well liking, before, that order of friars, yet seeing the impudent behaviour, and more impudent request of those merchants, thus answered to them again, 'that this exaction, saving,' saith he, 'the pope's authority, was never heard of before, and neither was honest, nor yet possible to be performed; and, moreover, was such as did not only concern him, but the whole public state of the clergy, and of the whole realm in general; and therefore it should be absurdly and rashly done of him to give them answer herein, before the king and the rest of the council, with others to whom the matter generally did appertain, were made privy thereunto,' &c., and so for that time he shook them off.[1]

The abbot of St. Alban's maketh great suit to the pope for the four hundred marks that he should pay.

Furthermore, as touching the abbot of St. Alban's, when he also alleged the same causes, he pretended, moreover, that he would appeal, and so did, to the pope and his cardinals. Whereupon immediately was sent down, from pope Innocent, another legate, called Johannes Anglicus, an English friar and cardinal; who, bringing down a new special precept to the aforesaid abbot, cited him either to appear at London the morrow after St. Giles's day, or to disburse to the use of the pope the aforesaid four hundred marks. By reason whereof the abbot was driven to send his proctors again, with a new supplication, to the pope at Lyons; who in the end, through great instance of monied friends, agreed with the abbot for two hundred marks, besides his other charges borne; and so was that matter compounded, little to the abbot's profit.[2]

To recite all damages and grievances received from the bishop of Rome in this realm of England, neither is any history sufficiently able to comprehend, nor if it were, scarcely is there any that would believe it. Notwithstanding, to those above declared, this one I thought to commit likewise to memory, to the intent that they who now live in this age may behold and wonder, in themselves, to see into what miserable slavery, passing all measure, not only the subjects, but kings also of this realm were brought, under the intolerable yoke of the pope's tyranny, which in those days neither durst any man cast off, nor yet was able to abide, as by this example ensuing, with infinite others like to the same, may appear.

After pope Innocent IV. had taken such order in the realm, that

(1) Ex Matth. Paris. fol. 210. (2) Ibid. fol. 213.

Henry III.

A.D. 1247.

all prelates of the church were suspended from collation of any benefice, before the pope's kinsfolks and clerks of Italy had been provided for; it happened A. D. 1248, that the abbot of Abingdon had a commandment from the pope, to bestow some benefice of his church in all haste on a certain priest of Rome, which the abbot, as an obedient child unto his father, the pope, was pressed and ready to accomplish accordingly. But the Roman priest, not contented with such as fell next to hand, would tarry his time, to have such as were the principal and for his own appetite, having a special eye to the benefice of the church of St. Helen in Abingdon, which was then esteemed worth a hundred marks a year, besides other vails[1] and commodities belonging to the same, the collation whereof the priest required by the authority apostolical to be granted unto him.

How this realm of England was oppressed by the pope.

As this passed on, the incumbent chanced at last to die and the benefice to be empty; which eftsoons being known, the same day cometh a commandment, with great charge from the king to the abbot, to give the benefice to one Ethelmare, the king's brother by the mother's side, who at the same time was possessed of so many benefices, that the number and value thereof was unknown. The abbot, here, being in great perplexity, and not knowing what to do, whether to gratify his king or to obey the pope, took counsel with his friends; who, well advising of the matter, gave him counsel to prefer the brother of his prince and patron, so that the king would undertake to stand in his defence against the pope, rather than the Romish priest, whom always he should have lying there as a spy and watcher of him, and like a thorn ever in his eye; and so the king assuring the abbot of his undoubted protection and indemnity against all harms, the benefice was conferred forthwith on the king's brother.

The Roman priest, not a little aggrieved thereat, speedeth himself in all haste to the bishop of Rome, certifying him what was done, and partly also (as the manner is of men), making it worse than it was; upon whose complaint the pope, directly, in great anger, cited up the abbot personally to appear before him, to answer to the crime of disobedience. The abbot trusting to the king's promise and protection (who neither could help him in that case, neither durst oppose himself against the pope), being both aged and sickly, was driven to travel up to the court of Rome, in great heaviness and bitterness of mind. Where, in conclusion, after much vexation and bitter rebukes, besides great expenses, he was fain to satisfy the pope after his own will, compounding to give him yearly fifty marks in part of making amends for his trespass of disobedience.[2]

The abbot of Abingdon condemned in fifty marks for denying an English benefice to the pope's nephew.

To this also may be added another like fact of the pope, as outrageous as this, against the house of Binham. For when the benefice of Westle, in the diocese of Ely, was void by the death of the incumbent, who was an Italian, and one of the pope's chamber, the donation of which benefice belonged to the priory of Binham; another Italian, who was a bastard and unlearned, born in the city of Genoa, called Heriggetto de Malachano de Volta, brought down the pope's letters to Berardo de Nympha, the pope's agent here in England, with strict charge and full authority, commanding him to see the said benefice conferred in any case on Heriggetto. Yea,

A detestable extortion of the pope used against the priory of Binham, in Norfolk.

(1) "Vails," additional profits.—ED.

(2) Ex Matth. Paris. fol. 222.

Henry III.

A.D. 1247.

and though the benefice had been given already, yet, notwithstanding, the possessor thereof should be displaced, and the said Heriggetto preferred: yea, also, "non obstante," that the said pope himself had before given his grant to the king and realm of England, that one Italian should not succeed another in any benefice there, yet, for all that, the said Heriggetto, upon pain of excommunication, was to be placed therein.[1]

The Grecians excused and purged in parting from the church of Rome.

And thus much hitherto of these matters, through the occasion of the east churches and the Grecians, to the intent all men that read these stories, and see the doings of this western bishop, may consider what just cause these Grecians had to seclude themselves from his subjection and communion; for what christian communion is to be joined with him who, so contrary to Christ and his gospel, seeketh for worldly dominion, so cruelly persecuteth his brethren, is so given to avarice, so greedy in getting, so injurious in oppressing, so insatiable in his exactions, so malicious in revenging; stirring up wars, depriving kings, deposing emperors, playing 'rex' in the church of Christ, so erroneous in doctrine, so abominably abusing excommunication, so false of promise, so corrupt in life, so void of God's fear; and, briefly, so far from all the parts of a true evangelical bishop? For what seemeth he to care for the souls of men, who setteth in benefices boys and outlandish Italians; and further, one Italian to succeed another, who neither did know the language of the flock, nor would once abide to see their faces? And who can blame the Grecians then for dissevering themselves from such an oppressor and giant against Christ?

The miseries of England through subjection to the church of Rome.

England plagued by the pope when it needed not.

Whose wise example if this realm had then followed, as they might, certes our predecessors had been rid of an infinite number of troubles, injuries, oppressions, wars, commotions, great travails and charges, besides the saving of innumerable thousands of pounds, which the said bishop full falsely had raked and transported out of this realm of ours. But, not to exceed the bounds of my history, because my purpose is not to stand upon declamations, nor to dilate common places, I will pass this over, leaving the judgment thereof to the further examination of the reader. For else, if I listed to prosecute this argument so far as matter would lead me, and truth peradventure would require me to say, I durst not only say, but could well prove the pope and court of Rome to be the only fountain and principal cause, I say, not only of much misery here in England, but of all the public calamities and notorious mischiefs which have happened these many years throughout all these west parts of Christendom, and especially of all the lamentable ruin of the church, which not only we, but the Grecians also, this day do suffer by the Turks and Saracens. Whosoever well considereth by reading of histories the course of times, and vieweth withal the doings and acts passed by the said bishop of Rome, together with the blind leading of his doctrine, shall see good cause not only to think, but also to witness the same. Only one narration touching this argument, and yet not transgressing the office of my history, I mind (the Lord willing) to set before the reader's eyes, which happened even about A. D. 1244, in the time of this king Henry's reign.

The pope and court of Rome the principal cause of all the public calamities throughout Christendom.

(1) Ex Matth. Paris. fol. 240.

In that year it chanced, that Louis, the French king, son to queen Blanch, fell very sorely sick, lying in a swoon or trance for certain days, in such sort that few thought he would have lived, and some said he was gone already. Among others, there was with him his mother, who, sorrowing bitterly for her son, and given somewhat, as commonly the manner of women is, to superstition, went and brought forth a piece of the holy cross, with the crown and the spear; which piece of the holy cross Baldwin, emperor of Constantinople, whom the Grecians had deposed a little before for holding with the bishop of Rome, had sold to the French king for a great sum of money, and blessing him with the same, also laid the crown and the spear on his body, making a vow withal in the person of her son, that if the Lord would visit him with health, and release him of that infirmity, he should be croised or marked with the cross, to visit his sepulchre, and there solemnly to render thanks in the land which Christ had sanctified with his blood. Thus as she, with the bishop of Paris, and others there present, was praying, behold the king, who was supposed by some to be dead, began with a sigh to pluck to his arms and legs, and so stretching himself began to speak, giving thanks to God who, from on high, had visited him, and called him from the danger of death. As the king's mother with others there took this to be a great miracle wrought by the virtue of the holy cross; so the king amending more and more, as soon as he was well recovered, received solemnly the badge of the cross, vowing for a freewill sacrifice unto God, that he, if the council of his realm would suffer him, would, in his own person, visit the Holy Land: forgetting belike the rule of true Christianity, where Christ teacheth us otherwise in the gospel, saying, that "neither in this mount, nor in Samaria, nor at Jerusalem, the Lord will be worshipped, but seeketh true worshippers, who shall worship him in truth and verity." A. D. 1244.[1]

The sickness of Louis the French king.

The superstition of the king's mother.

The king recovereth.

The people of France blinded with a false miracle.

The vain vow of Louis, the French king.

After this was great preparation and much ado in France toward the setting forth to the Holy Land. For after the king first began to be croised, the most part of the nobles of France, with divers archbishops and bishops, with earls, and barons, and gentlemen, to a mighty number, received also the cross upon their sleeves. Amongst them was the earl Atrebacensis, the king's brother, the duke of Burgundy, the duke of Brabant, the countess of Flanders, with her two sons, the earl of Brittany, with his son, the earl of Barensis, the earl of Soissons, the earl of St. Paul, the earl of Druis, the earl of Retel, with many noble persons besides. Neither lacked here whatsoever the pope could do, to set forward this holy business, in sending his legates and friars into France, to stir the people to follow the king, and to contribute to his journey. Whereupon it was granted to the king to gather of the universal church of France, by the pope's authority, the tenth part of all their goods for three years' space together, upon this condition, that the king likewise would grant to the pope the twentieth part for so many years after, to be gathered of the said church of France. This was agreed to A.D. 1246.[2]

Great preparation in France toward a voyage to the Holy Land.

Shortly after this, A.D. 1247, followed a parliament in France, where the king with his nobles being present, there was declared how the king of Tartarians, or Turks, hearing of the voyage of the French

(1) Matth. Paris. fol. 182. (2) Ibid. fol. 204, b.

king, writeth a letter to him, requiring that he will become his subject. In that parliament the time was prefixed for taking their journey, which should be after the feast of St. John Baptist, the very next year ensuing. Also they that were croised were sworn to persist in their purpose, and the sentence of the pope's great curse was denounced on all them that went from the same.[1] Furthermore, for better speed in his journey, the king through all his realm caused it to be proclaimed, that if any merchant or other person had been injured at any time by the king's exactors, either by oppression, or borrowing of money, let him bring forth his bill, showing how or wherein, and he should be recompensed. At this time William Longspath, a worthy warrior, with the bishop of Worcester and certain other great men in the realm of England, moved by the example of the Frenchmen, prepared themselves likewise to the same journey.

Time of the king's voyage appointed.

The next year after, A.D. 1248, the French king yet still remaining in his purposed journey, lady Blanch, his mother, also the bishop of Paris, his brother, with the lords of his council, and other nobles, and his special friends, advertised him with great persuasions to alter his mind touching that so adventurous and dangerous a journey, for that his vow, said they, was unadvisedly made, and in time of his sickness, when his mind was not perfectly established: and what jeopardies might happen at home it was uncertain; the king of England being on the one side, the emperor on the other side, and the Pictavians in the midst, so fugitive and unstable: and as concerning his vow, the pope should friendly dispense with him, considering the necessity of his realm, and the weakness of his body. Besides all this, his mother, upon her blessing required him, and his brethren, of all love, desired him to stay at home, and not in his person to adventure; others might be sent in his room, with no less furniture to achieve that enterprise, and to discharge him of his vow, especially seeing at the making thereof that his senses were feeble, his body weak, and reason, through sickness and very death, almost decayed.

Persuasions given to the French king to turn his voyage.

To whom the king again said, "forasmuch as you say, that for feebleness of my senses I took this vow upon me: lo, therefore, as you here will me, I lay down the cross that I took." And putting his hand to his shoulder, he tore off the badge of the cross, saying to the bishop, "Here, Sir, I resign to you the cross wherewith I was signed;" at the sight whereof there was no small rejoicing of all that were there present. To whom the king then, both altering his countenance and his speech, thus spake: "My friends," said he, "whatsoever I was then in my sickness, now I thank God I am of perfect sense, and reason sound, and now I require my cross again to be restored unto me:" saying, moreover, that no bread should come into his head before he were recognised again with the same cross, as he was before. At the hearing of this, all there present were astonied, supposing that God had some great matter to work, and so moved no more questions unto him.

The king's answer to his lords, laying down and taking up his cross again A.D. 1248.

Upon this drew nigh the feast of John Baptist, which was the time fixed for the setting forth. And now being in readiness, the king, in a few days after, was entering his journey; but yet one thing lacked,

Setteth forth on his journey.

(1) Matth Paris fol. 211.

for the king, perceiving the mortal variance between the pope and good Frederic, the emperor, thought best first, before his going, to have that matter appeased, whereby his way both might be safer through the emperor's countries, and also less jeopardy at home after his departure; and therefore, upon the same, he took first his way to Lyons, where the pope was, partly to take his leave, but most especially to make reconcilement between the emperor and the pope.

Here is to be noted by the way, that as touching the good emperor there was no let nor stay; who rather sought all means how to compass the pope's favour, and never could obtain it; insomuch that before he should be excommunicated in the council of Lyons, he not only answered sufficiently by Thadeus, his attorney, discharging himself against whatsoever crimes or objections could be brought against him, but so far humbled himself to the pope and the council, that for all detriments, damages, losses, or wrongs done on his part, what amends soever the pope could or would require, he would recompense it to the uttermost. This would not be taken.

Furthermore, if the pope, he said, could not abide his tarrying in his own dominions and empire, he would go fight against the Saracens and Turks, never to return into Europe again; offering there to recover whatsoever lands and kingdoms did, at any time, belong to Christendom, so that the pope only would be contented that Henry, his son, who was nephew to Henry, then king here in England, should be emperor after him. Neither could this be admitted.

The emperor offereth the French king and king of England to be his sureties.

Then he offered, for truth of his promise, to put in the French king and the king of England to be his sureties, or else for trial of his cause, to stand to their award and arbitrement. Neither would that be granted. At least he desired, that he might come himself and answer before the council; but the proud pope in no case would abide that, saying, that he did not yet find himself so ready and meet for martyrdom to have him to come thither to the council; for if he did, he would depart himself.[1]

This obstinate rancour and devilish malice of pope Innocent and his predecessor against that valiant emperor and against the Grecians, what disturbance and mischief it wrought to the whole church, what strength it gave to the Saracens and Tartarians, how it impaired christian concord, and weakened all christian lands, not only the host of the French king did find shortly after, but Christendom, even to this day, may and doth feel and rue. Neither can in stories be found any greater cause, which first made the Turks so strong, to get so much ground over Christendom as they have, than the pestilent working of this pope, in deposing and excommunicating this worthy emperor. For, as there was never emperor for a long time, who more victoriously prevailed in bridling, and keeping under, these enemies of Christ, or would have done more against them than the said Frederic, if he might have been suffered: so, after the deposing and excommunicating of him, when the French king neither would abide at home, as he was counselled, neither was yet able, without the help of others, to withstand the force and multitude of the said Saracens and Tartarians being now joined together, neither yet could the emperor be suffered by the pope to rescue the king: it followed thereof, that the

Beginning of the Turks' victories over Christendom.

(1) Ex Matth. Paris. fol. 787.

Henry III. A.D. 1249.

good king being taken prisoner, and all his army destroyed, the Turks thereupon got such a hand, and such a courage against the Christians, that ever since they have burst in further upon us, and now have prevailed so far, as neither the power of the pope, nor of all Christendom, is able to drive them out; as hereafter, by the sequel of my story, is further to be declared.

Pope Innocent IV. would not be reconciled with the emperor.

In the mean time, to return to where before we left off, when the French king, coming thus unto the pope at Lyons to entreat for the emperor, could find no favour, he took his leave, and with great heaviness departed, setting forward on his journey to Marseilles, and so sailed to the isle of Cyprus, where he remained all that winter, and there falling into penury and lack of victuals, he was fain to send to Venice, and other islands by, for provisions. The Venetians gently sent unto him six great ships laden with corn, wine, and other victuals requisite, besides the relief of other islands more. But especially Frederic, the emperor, understanding their want, so furnished the French camp with all plenty of necessaries, that it had abundance. Whereupon, the French king, moved with the kindness of the emperor, wrote special letters to the pope in the emperor's behalf; but the hard heart of the pope would not relent. Blanch, the king's mother, hearing in France what the emperor had done to her son, sent him most hearty thanks, with presents and rewards manifold.[1]

The French army relieved by the emperor Frederic. The French king again entreateth the pope for the emperor.

Damietta gotten again by Frenchmen.

In the mean time, about the beginning of October, A.D. 1249, the Frenchmen took Damietta, being the principal fort or hold of the Saracens in all Egypt. After the winning of Damietta, the prince and people of the Saracens, being astonished at the loss thereof, offered to the Christians great ground and possessions more than ever belonged to Christendom before, so that they might have Damietta restored to them again. But the pride of the earl of Artois, the king's brother, would in no case accept the offer of the Saracens, but required both Damietta, and Alexandria, the chief metropolitan city of all Egypt, to be delivered unto them. The Saracens, seeing the pride and greediness of the Frenchmen, in no case would abide it: which turned afterwards to the great detriment of our Christians, as in the end it proved.[2]

Death of certain of the French captains.

First, in the isle of Cyprus, and in the journey before, died the earl of Palatine, and one of the twelve peers of France, also the earl of St. Paul and Blesse, who had under him fifty ensigns, who were all after his death scattered abroad and dispersed; also died Johannes de Denis, a valiant captain, with many other noble personages, both men and women, who, by altering the air and diet, there deceased.[3]

A.D. 1250. Victory of the French over the Saracens.

The next year ensuing, A.D. 1250, about Ash Wednesday, the Frenchmen, issuing out of their tents by the city of Damietta, flew upon the Saracens, who besieged them, and after a great number of the enemy had been slain, with victory and great spoils returned to their tents again. Now, within the city of Damietta was the queen with her ladies, and the pope's legate and the bishops, with a garrison of horsemen and footmen, for the defence of the city strongly appointed. The next day, the Frenchmen supposing to have the like hand of the Saracens, as they had the day before, gave a fresh assault upon them, but in that conflict the Saracens had so strongly

French discomfited by the Saracens.

(1) Matth. Paris. p. 226. (2) Ibid. fol. 229. (3) Ibid.

appointed themselves, that the Frenchmen lost ten times more than they got the day before, and so, after a great slaughter of their men, retired unto their tents again. Whereupon, the Saracens began to take great heart and courage against our men, stopping also the passages round about the city of Damietta, that no victuals could pass unto them. In like manner the Soldan also, gathering the galleys about Alexandria and all the land of Egypt, so enclosed the seas, that no intercourse should be to them by water.

At length, after long talk and consultation between them on both sides, the Soldan advised them betimes to resign unto him the city of Damietta, with the furniture which they found therein, and they should have all the country about Jerusalem, with all the captives of the Christians, in a friendly manner restored unto them: wherewith the Christians, said he, ought to be contented, and to seek no further, but only to have the land of Jerusalem; which being granted to them, they should not encroach into other lands and kingdoms, to which they had no right. This form of peace, as it liked well the meaner sort of the poor soldiers, and divers others of the said council and nobility; so the proud earl of Artois, the king's brother, in no case would assent thereto, but still required the city of Alexandria to be yielded to them; to which the Egyptians would by no means agree.

The Frenchmen again well offered by the Soldan.

The earl of Artois and the pope's legate again refuse the form of peace offered.

From that time the French army, being compassed about by sea and land, began every day more and more to be distressed for lack of victuals and with famine, being driven to such misery that they were fain to eat their own horses in Lent-time, which should have served them for other uses; neither could any Christian, nor Frederic, being deposed by the pope, send them any succour. Furthermore, the more misery the Christians were in, the more fiercely did the Saracens press upon them on every side, detesting their forward wilfulness, insomuch that divers of the christian soldiers, not able to abide the affliction, privily conveyed themselves, as they could, out of the camp to the Saracens, who were gladly received and relieved; some were suffered still to keep their faith, and some married wives amongst them, and for hope of honour did apostate to their law, and so wrought no little harm to the Christians. The Soldan, being perfectly instructed by these fugitives of all things belonging to the king's army, sent him word in derision, asking where were all his mattocks, forks, and rakes, his scythes, ploughs, and harrows, which he brought over with him, or why he did not use them, but let them lie by him to rust and canker? All this, and much more, the king with his Frenchmen were fain to take well in worth. It happened, shortly after, that this Soldan died, being poisoned by his own servants, which was to the Christians an aggravation of their miseries; for, albeit the said Soldan had been a cruel tyrant to the Christians, yet was he hated of his own people, whereby his strength was the less. After him succeeded another much more cruel; who, as he was better loved, so he became much stronger, by a general confederacy of all the Saracens who were in the east parts, joining now together, so that when the Christians desired now to have the form of peace before proffered, he flatly denied them. And so the French host, which at first began to be feared,

The Frenchmen eat their own horses in Lent-time

The Soldan's message deriding the Frenchmen

The Soldan dieth, a worse followeth

The French desire again the

Henry III.

A.D. 1250.

by their pride and over-greediness growing more and more into contempt amongst their enemies, now were utterly despised.

Peace offered before, and could not have it.

The Christians, thus seeing all things to go backward with them, and how the infidel Saracens daily did prevail, began to murmur against God, and some also, who were well settled before, to stagger in their religion, casting out these words of infidelity: "How is this," said they, "that the Lord hath left us in whose cause we fight? How often within the time of remembrance have we been confounded by these Saracens and infidels, who, with shedding of our blood, have enjoyed great spoils and victories? First, this city of Damietta, which we Christians had gotten dearly, with effusion of so much christian blood, afterwards we were constrained for nought to resign again. After that, the army of the Templars, fighting for the holy temple against the Saracens, near to Antioch, was vanquished, and the standard-bearer slain in the fields. Again, within these few years, our Frenchmen, fighting in like manner against the Saracens at the city of Gaza, were put to the worst, and many afterwards out of captivity ransomed by Richard, duke of Exeter, brother to Henry III., king of England. Then came in the Chosmorins, sent by the Soldan of Babylon, who, by a wile, invaded the Christians in the city of Jerusalem, where almost all the christian army in the Holy Land were destroyed And now here, our most christian king, together with the whole nobility, is like to be in danger utterly to be overthrown. And how is it that the Lord thus standeth against us, and fighteth with them? Hath he more regard of them than of us?"[1] Such murmuring words of an unstable faith many there began to cast out, as taking displeasure on account of their sufferings: but not considering, on the other side, what idolaters they were, what pride and discord was amongst them, what cruelty and murder they had showed at home in persecuting the poor Albigenses, what superstition they first brought out with them, with what idolatry they proceeded, putting their trust in masses, in the pope's indulgences, in worshipping of images, and in praying to saints. And what helps then could they look for at God's hand, who had images in their temples, to fight against them who had none? or what marvel if the Lord of hosts went not with their army, committing such idolatry every day in their pavilions to their sacramental bread and wine as they did, and fighting with the strength of their own merits, and not by the power of their faith in Christ alone, which is the only victory that overcometh the world? [1 John v. 4.] Finally, having in their camp the legate of him whom the Lord taketh to be his enemy: as by example of Frederic, the emperor, may be well perceived; who, after he was accursed by pope Gregory a little before, coming the same time to war against the Saracens in Palestine, God's blessing wrought so mightily with him, that without any bloodshed he recovered Jerusalem, and set all the country about it in great quietness, till at last the popish Templars, who at the pope's setting on, went about to betray him to the Soldan of Babylon, lost all again by their own malicious mischief, which the emperor before had gotten.[2]

Victories over the Templars and keepers of Jerusalem.

Why the Lord did not prosper the Christians fighting against the Saracens.

(1) Ex Matth. Paris. fol. 231. (2) Ex Matth. Paris.

Henry III — A.D. 1250.

But let us proceed further in this holy progress. The French king with his army seeing himself distressed, and no good there to be done against the Soldan of Egypt, after he had sufficiently fortified the city of Damietta with an able garrison left with the duke of Burgundy, he removed his tents from thence to go eastward. In his army also followed William Longspath (of whom mention was made before), accompanied with a picked number of English warriors, retained unto him: but such was the disdain of the Frenchmen against this William Longspath and the Englishmen, that they could not abide them, but flouted them in opprobrious manner, with "English tails," insomuch that the good king himself had much ado to keep peace between them.

Grudge between the French and the English soldiers.

The original cause of this grudge between them began thus: there was, not far from Alexandria in Egypt, a strong fort or castle, replenished with great ladies, and rich treasure of the Saracens; this hold it chanced the said William Longspath, with his company of English soldiers, to get, more by good luck and politic dexterity, than by open force of arms; whereby he and his retinue were greatly enriched. When the Frenchmen had knowledge hereof, they, being not made privy thereto, began to conceive a heart-burning against the English soldiers, and could not speak well of them after that. It happened, not long after, that the said William had intelligence of a company of rich merchants among the Saracens, going to a certain fair about the parts of Alexandria; having their camels, asses, and mules, richly laden with silks, precious jewels, spices, gold and silver, with cart-loads of other wares, besides victuals and furniture, whereof the soldiers then stood in great need. He, having secret knowledge hereof, gathered all the power of Englishmen unto him that he could, and so, by night, falling upon the merchants, some he slew with their guides and conductors, some he took, some he put to flight. The carts with the drivers and the oxen, and the camels, asses, and mules, with the whole carriage and victuals, he took, and brought with him, losing in all the skirmish but one soldier, and eight of his servitors; some of whom, notwithstanding, he brought home wounded to be cured.

Booty gotten by the English soldiers about Alexandria.

Venturous act of William Longspath.

Enriched by Saracens' goods.

This being known in the camp, forth came the Frenchmen, who all this while loitered in their pavilions, and meeting their carriage by the way, took all the aforesaid prey wholly unto themselves, rating the said William and the Englishmen, for so adventuring and issuing out of the camp without leave or knowledge of their general, contrary to the discipline of war. William said again, he had done nothing but what he would answer to, whose purpose was to have the spoil divided to the behoof of the whole army. When this would not serve, he being sore grieved in his mind, so cowardly to be spoiled of that for which he had so adventurously travailed, went to the king to complain. But when no reason or complaint would serve, by reason of the proud earl of Artois, the king's brother, who, upon despite and disdain, stood against him, he, bidding the king farewell, said he would serve him no longer. And so William de Longspath with the rest of his company, breaking from the French host, went to Acre. Upon whose departure, the earl of Artois said, "Now is the army of Frenchmen well rid of these tailed people." Which words,

Wronged by the French.

Departeth to Acre.

Despiteful word of the king's brother against the English.

Henry III — spoken in great despite, were evil taken of many good men that heard him.[1]

A.D. 1250. — Before the arrival of the French army in the land of Egypt, the Soldan of Babylon, having beforehand intelligence of their coming, committed the custody of Damietta to a certain prince of his whom he specially trusted, committing also to his brother the keeping of Cairo and Babylon. It followed now after the taking of Damietta, that the Soldan of Babylon accused the prince who had the custody thereof, before his nobles, of treason, as giving the city unto the Christians; who, notwithstanding, in judgment did sufficiently clear himself, declaring how he was certified that the king would land at Alexandria, and therefore bent all his power to prevent the king's arrival there; but, by stress of weather, he missing his purpose, and the king landing about Damietta, by reason thereof the city was taken unprovided, he, notwithstanding, with his company resisting as well as they might, till they could no longer, and so departed, cursing (said he) Mahomet and his law. At these words, the Soldan, being offended, commanded him to be had away as a traitor and blasphemer, and to be hanged, albeit he had sufficiently purged himself by the judgment of the court. His brother, who was the keeper of Cairo and Babylon, being therewith not a little grieved, and bearing a good mind to the christian religion, devised, in himself, how to give the said city of Cairo with Babylon to the French king; and so, in most secret wise, he sent to the king, showing his full purpose and what had happened: and, furthermore, instructing the king in all things how and what he should do; and, moreover, requiring the sacrament of baptism, meaning indeed good faith, and sending also away all the christian captives which he had with him in prison. The king, being glad hereof, sent in all haste for William Longspath, promising a full redress of all injuries past, who upon hope of some good luck, came at the king's request, and so joined again with the French power.

Damietta taken by the Christians.

The keeper or tribune wrongfully put to death.

The tribune of Cairo desireth to be christened.

William Longspath sent for, and cometh.

THE LAMENTABLE OVERTHROW AND SLAUGHTER OF THE FRENCH ARMY FIGHTING AGAINST THE INFIDELS, THROUGH THE SINISTER COUNSEL OF THE POPE'S LEGATE.

To make the story short, the king, setting forward from Damietta, directed his journey towards Cairo, slaying by the way such Saracens as were set there to stop the victuals from Damietta. The Soldan, in the mean time, hearing of the courageous coming of the French host, as being in great hope to conquer all, sent unto the king by certain that were next about him, offering to the Christians the quiet and full possession of the Holy Land, with all the kingdom of Jerusalem, and more; besides other infinite treasure of gold and silver, or what else might pleasure them, only upon this condition, that they would restore again Damietta, with the captives there, and so would join together in mutual peace and amity. Also they should have all their christian captives delivered up, and so both countries should freely pass one to another with their wares and traffic, such as they chose to adventure. Furthermore, it was firmly affirmed and spoken,

Fair offers of the Soldan to the French.

(1) Ex Matth Paris. fol 233, 234.

that the Soldan, with most of his nobles, was minded no less than to leave the filthy law of Mahomet, and receive the faith of Christ, so that they might quietly enjoy their lands and possessions. The same day great quietness would have entered, no doubt, into all Christendom, with the end of much bloodshed and misery, had it not been for the pope's legate, who (having commandment from the pope, that if any such offers should come, he should not take them) stoutly "*et frontose contradicens*," (as the words be of the story) in nowise would receive the conditions offered.[1]

Henry III.

A.D. 1250.

The pope's legate causes all this mischief.

Thus, while the Christians unprofitably lingered the time in debating this matter, the Soldan, mean while, got intelligence of the compact between the tribune of Cairo and the French king; whereupon he sent in all haste to their city to apprehend the tribune till the truth were fully tried, which seemed to him more apparent, for that the christian prisoners were already delivered. Hereupon the Soldan being in some better hope and less fear, refused that which before he had offered to the Christians; albeit, they with great instance afterward sued to the Soldan, and could not obtain it. Then the Soldan, being wholly bent to try the matter by the sword, sent to the east parts for an infinite multitude of soldiers, giving out by proclamation, that whosoever could bring in any christian man's head, should have ten talents, besides his standing wages. And whosoever brought his right hand should have five. He that brought his foot should have two talents, for his reward.

The Christians refusing good offers, could not have them when they would.

Cruel proclamation of the Saracens against the Christians.

After these things thus prepared on both sides to the necessity of war, the king cometh to the great river Nile, having gotten together many boats, thinking by them to pass over, as upon a sure bridge. On the other side the Soldan pitched himself to withstand his coming over. In the mean time happened a certain feast amongst the Saracens, in which the Soldan was absent, leaving his tents by the water-side. This being foreseen by a certain Saracen, lately converted to Christ, serving with earl Robert, the king's brother, and showing them withal a certain shallow ford in the river Nile, where they might more easily pass over; the said earl Robert, and the master of the Temple, with a great power, amounting to the third part of the army, passed over the river, after whom also followed William Longspath, with his band of English soldiers. These, being together joined on the other side the water, encountered the same day with the Saracens remaining in the tents, and put them to the worse. After this victory, the French earl, surprised with pride and triumph, as though he had conquered the whole earth, would needs advance, dividing himself from the main host, thinking to win the spurs alone; to whom certain sage men of the Temple giving contrary counsel, advised him not so to do, but rather to return and take their whole company with them, and so should they be more sure against all deceits and dangers, which there might be laid privily for them. The manner of that people (they said) they better knew, and had more experience thereof than he; alleging, moreover, their wearied bodies, their tired horses, their famished soldiers, and the insufficiency also of their number, which was not able to withstand the multitude of the enemies, especially at this present brunt; in

The earl of Artois, with the third part of the christian army, passeth over the Nile.

Victory of the Christians against the Saracens.

Good counsel given, but not followed.

(1) Ex Matth. Paris. fol. 233.

Henry III. A.D. 1250.

which the adversaries did well see the whole state of their dominion now to consist either in winning all, or losing all; with other such like words of persuasion. When the proud earl did hear this, being inflamed, with no less arrogancy than ignorance, with opprobrious taunts he reviled them, called them cowardly dastards, and betrayers of the whole country; objecting unto them the common report of many, who said, that the land of the holy cross might be won to Christendom, were it not for the rebellious Templars, with the Hospitallers and their fellows.

Rebukes of earl Robert, to them that gave him good counsel.

To these contumelious rebukes the master of the Temple answered again for himself and his fellows, bidding him display his ensign when he would, and where he durst, for they were as ready to follow him, as he to go before them. Then began William de Longspath, the worthy knight, to speak: desiring the earl to give ear to those men of experience, who had better knowledge of those countries and people than he had, commending also their counsel to be discreet and wholesome, and so turning to the master of the Temple began with gentle words to mitigate him likewise. The knight had not half ended his talk, when the earl, taking the words out of his mouth, began to fume and swear, crying out on these cowardly Englishmen with tails. "What a pure army," said he, "should we have here, if these tails, and tailed people were purged from it?" With other like words of great villany and much disdain. Whereunto the English knight answering again, "Well, earl Robert," said he, "wheresoever you dare set your foot, my step shall go as far as yours; and, as I believe, we go this day where you shall not dare to come near the tail of my horse:" as in the event proved true.[1]

Worthy answer of the English knight to him.

A number of French soldiers sent to Damietta, drowned or slain by the way.

In the mean time the French king, intending to set forward his army, thought best to send away such as were feeble and lacked armour, unto Damietta, by boats. The Soldan, hearing thereof, prepared a great number of boats to be carried, by wain and cart, to the water-side; who, meeting them by the way, drowned and destroyed by wildfire every one, so that of all that company of our Christians, of whom some were burned, some slain, some drowned, not one escaped alive, save only one Englishman, named Alexander Giffard; who, although he was sore wounded in the chace in five places in his body, yet escaped to the French camp, bringing word unto the king what was done. And this was upon the water.

Mansor assaulted by the French.

Now upon the land: seeing earl Robert would needs set forward, weening to get all the glory unto himself before the coming of the host, they invaded first a little village or castle which was not far off, called Mansor. The country boors and pagans in the villages by, seeing the Christians come, ran out with such a main cry and shout, that it came to the Soldan's hearing, who was nearer than our men did think. In the mean while the Christians, invading and entering into the munition uncircumspectly, were pelted and pashed[2] with stones by them that stood above; whereby a great number of our men were lost, and the army sore maimed, and almost in despair. Then, immediately upon the same, cometh the Soldan with all his main power; who, seeing the Christians' army to be divided, and the

(1) Ex Matth. Paris. fol. 236. (2) "Pashed," struck.—Ed.

Henry III

A.D. 1250.

one brother separated from the other, had that which he long wished for, and thus enclosing them round about so that none should escape, had with them a cruel fight. Then the earl began to repent him of his heady rashness, but it was too late; who, then seeing William the English knight, doughtily fighting in the chief brunt of the enemies, cried unto him most cowardly to fly, "seeing God," said he, "doth fight against us." To whom the knight, answering again, "God forbid," saith he, "that my father's son should run away from the face of a Saracen." The earl then, turning his horse, fled away, thinking to escape by its swiftness, and so taking the river of Thafnis, oppressed with harness, there sunk and was drowned. Thus the earl being gone, the Frenchmen began to despair and scatter. Then William de Longspath, bearing all the force of the enemies, stood against them as long as he could, wounding and slaying many a Saracen, until at length his horse being killed, and his legs maimed, he could no longer stand; who yet notwithstanding, as he was down, mangled their feet and legs, and did the Saracens much sorrow, till at the last after many blows and wounds, being stoned of the Saracens, he yielded his life. After the death of him, the Saracens setting upon the residue of the army, whom they had compassed on every side, devoured and destroyed them all, insomuch, that scarcely one man escaped alive, saving two templars, one hospitaller, and one poor rascal soldier, who brought tidings hereof to the king.

Earl Robert's army enclosed by the Soldan of Babylon

Earl Robert cowardly flying away, is drowned

The manly courage and death of William Longspath

These things being known, in the French camp, to the king and his soldiers; first of their drowning who were sent to Damietta, then of the ruin and slaughter of the army, with the king's brother, near the town of Mansor, there was no little sorrow and heaviness on every side, with great fear and doubt in themselves what it was best to do. At last, when they saw no remedy, but they must stand manfully to revenge the blood of their brethren, the king, with his host, passed over the flood of the Nile, and coming to the place where the battle had been, there they beheld their fellows and brethren, pitifully lying with their heads and hands cut off. For the Saracens, for the reward before promised by the Soldan or Sultan, unto them that could bring the head or hand of any Christian, had so mangled the Christians, leaving their bodies to the wild beasts. Thus, as they were sorrowing and lamenting the rueful case of their christian fellows, suddenly appeareth the coming of the Soldan, with a multitude of innumerable thousands, against whom the Frenchmen eftsoons prepare themselves to encounter, and so the battle being struck up, the armies began to join. But, alack for pity! what could the Frenchmen here do, their number at first so maimed, their hearts wounded already with fear and sorrow, their bodies consumed with penury and famine, their horses for feebleness not able to serve them? In conclusion, the Frenchmen were overthrown, slain, and despatched; and, seeing there was no flying, happy was he that first could yield himself. In this miserable conflict, the king, with his two brethren, and a few that clave unto him, were taken captives, to the confusion of all christian realms, and presented to the Soldan. All the residue were put to the sword, or else stood at the mercy of the Saracens, whether to be slain or to remain in woeful captivity. And this was the end of that sorrowful battle, wherein almost all the nobility of France were slain,

Sorrows in the French camp for loss of their brethren

Heads and hands of the Christians cut off

Pitiful slaughter of the French

The king with his two brethren taken by the Soldan

Henry III A.D. 1250.

and in which there was hardly one man of all that multitude who escaped free, they being either slain or taken prisoners. Furthermore, they that were slain or left half alive, had every one his head and hand cut off upon the Soldan's proclamation above mentioned.

The Soldan or Sultan, after the taking of the French king, fraudulently suborning an army of Saracens to the number of the French army, with the arms and ensigns of them that were slain, made towards Damietta, where the duke of Burgundy, with the French queen, and Otho, the pope's legate, and other bishops and their garrisons were remaining; supposing, under the show of Frenchmen, to be let in: but the captains, mistrusting their hasty coming, and misdoubting their visages, not like those of the Frenchmen, shut the gates against them, and so returned they, frustrated in their intent.

The purpose of the Soldan was, if he might have gotten Damietta, to send the French king up higher into the east countries to the Caliph,[1] the chief pope of Damascus, to increase the titles of Mahomet, and to be a spectacle or gazing-stock to all those quarters of the world. The manner of Caliph was, never to let any christian prisoner come out, whosoever came once in his hand. But forasmuch as the Soldan missed his purpose, he thought, by advice of council, to use the king's life for his own advantage in recovering the city of Damietta, as in the end it came to pass. For although the king at first was greatly unwilling, and had rather die than surrender Damietta again to the Saracens, yet the conclusion fell out, that the king was put to his ransom, and the city of Damietta was also resigned; which city, being twice won and twice lost by the Christians, the Soldan or Saladin afterwards caused it to be utterly razed to the ground. The ransom of the king, upon condition that the Soldan should see him safely conducted to Acre (which I take to be Cesarea), came to sixty thousand marks. The number of Frenchmen and others who miscarried in that war, by water and by land, came to eighty thousand persons.[2]

Damietta resigned to the Saracens. Sum of the king's ransom. Number of the French slain.

And thus have ye the brief narration of this lamentable peregrination of Louis, the French king, in which, when the Frenchmen were once or twice well offered by the Soldan, to have all the kingdom of Jerusalem, and much more, in free possession; they, not contented with that which was reasonable and sufficient, for greediness to have all, lost all; having at length no more than their naked bodies could cover, lying dead upon the ground, and all through the original cause of the pope, and Otho, his legate. By their sinister means and pestilent pride, not only the lives of so many Christians were then lost, but also to the said pope is to be imputed all the loss of other cities and christian regions bordering in the same quarters: forasmuch as, by the occasion hereof, the hearts of the Saracens, on the one side, were so encouraged, and the courage of the Christians, on the other, so much discomfited, that in a short space after, both the dominion of Antioch and that of Acre, with all other possessions belonging to the Christians, were lost, to the great diminishing of Christ's church.

The two Soldans' variance about the French king.

During the time of this good king lying at Acre, or Cesarea, Almighty God sent such discord betwixt the Soldan of Halaphia and the Soldan of Babylon, for letting the king so escape, that the said Soldan or Saladin of Babylon, to win the king unto his side, entered

(1) See Note 1, p 29[illegible]—ED

(2) Hæc Matth. Paris fol 237, 238.

Henry III. A.D. 1250.

into a league with him (whom both his brethren, and almost all his nobles at home had forsaken), and remitted his ransom, and also restored unto him such prisoners as were in the said battle found to be alive.[1] Thus the Lord worketh, where man commonly forsaketh.[2]

Another cause, moreover, why the ruin of this French army may worthily be imputed to the pope, is this: when Louis, the French king (perceiving what a necessary friend and helper Frederic, the emperor, might be to him in these his affairs against the Saracens), was an earnest suitor for him to the pope to have him released, neither he, nor the king of England, by any means could obtain it. And, although the emperor himself offered to pope Innocent, with all humble submission, to make satisfaction in the council of Lyons, promising, also, to conquer all the dominions of the Saracens, and never to return into Europe again, and there to recover whatsoever the Christians had lost, so that the pope would only grant his son Henry to be emperor after him: yet the proud pope would not be mollified; but would needs proceed against him with both swords; that is, first, with the spiritual sword, to accurse him, and then with the temporal sword, to depose him from his imperial throne. Through the occasion whereof, not only the French king's power went to wreck, but also such a fire of mischief was kindled against Christendom, as yet to this day cannot be quenched; for, after this overthrow of the French king and his army, the Christians of Antioch, and of other christian regions thereabouts, being utterly discouraged, gave up their holds and cities; whereupon the Saracens, and after them the Turks, got such a hand over Christendom, as, to this day, we all have good cause to rue and lament. Besides this, where divers Christians were croised to go over and help the French king, the pope, for money, dispensed with them to tarry still at home.

How Frederic the emperor might have served in good stead against the Saracens, but the pope would not suffer him.

Tyranny and devilish mischief of the pope against the emperor.

But as I said, the greatest cause was, that the emperor, who could have done most, was deposed by the pope's tyranny; whereby all those churches in Asia were left desolate, as touching the which emperor Frederic, because we have divers and sundry times made mention of him before, and for that his story is strange, his acts wondrous, and his conflicts tragical, which he sustained against four or five popes, one after another, I thought (not out of story) in a whole narration to set forth the same, for the reader to consider what is to be judged of this cathedral see of Rome, which had wrought such abominable mischief in the world, as in the sequel of the story following, faithfully translated out of Latin into English, is to be seen.

THE WHOLE TRAGICAL HISTORY OF FREDERIC II., THE EMPEROR OF GERMANY, TRANSLATED OUT OF THE LATIN BOOK OF NICHOLES CISNERUS.

A.D. 1193 to 1250.

Frederic II. came out of the ancient house of the Beblins or Ghibellines; which Ghibellines came out of the most famous stock of the French kings and emperors. He had Frederic Barbarossa to his grandfather, whose son, Henry VI., was emperor after him; who of Constantia, the daughter (or as some write, the niece) of Roger I., king of Sicily, begat this Frederic II.

(1) This was the seventh and last principal crusade.—ED. (2) Matth. Paris. fol. 261.

This Constantia was fifty years of age before she conceived him; whom the emperor Henry VI., to avoid all doubt and surmise that of her conception and childing might be entertained, and to the peril of the empire ensue, caused his regal tent to be pitched abroad in a place where every man might resort; and, when the time of his queen's travail approached, Constantia, in presence of divers ladies and matrons, and other gentlewomen of the empire, a great number, was brought to bed and delivered of this Frederic, the seventh day before the kalends of January, A.D. 1193, who, by inheritance, was king of Naples, Apulia, Calabria, and Sicily.

Henry's father, shortly after he was born, obtained of the princes, electors, that by their oath unto him given, they would choose his son Frederic for their emperor after his decease; and so they did, and immediately called him Cæsar, being yet but in his cradle.

This Henry when he died, which was shortly after the birth of Frederic, committed the protection of him to Constantia, his wife, to Philip, his brother, chief governor of Etruria, and to the bishop of Rome, then Innocent III. A.D. 1197.

Constantia, not long after the death of Henry, her husband, being sickly, and growing into age, and thereby not so well able to govern the troubled and unquiet state of the empire, resigned; and willed by her testament the safety both of her son Frederic, and also of his dominions, to the protection and government of Innocent III., thinking thereby safely to have provided.

Conspiracies of pope Innocent against Frederic during his minority.

This pope Innocent, as soon as he had the protection of the young emperor and his seigniories, became, instead of a patron and protector to him and his dominions, both an enemy and a conspirator. The examples are many: one is, he persuaded Sibylla, the late wife of Tancred (whom Henry put out from the kingdom of Sicily,) to recover the same again, and that she should thereunto require Philip, the French king's aid; whereupon one Walter, being of the noble house of the earls of Brenno, who, in the province of Barrencecis, had great living, and marrying with Ateria, the eldest daughter of Tancred, once king of Sicily (as is said), now, by the instigation, counsel, and aid of the French king, with the pope (well hoping to recover the kingdom) entered and invaded with great power Campania and Apulia. At this time, also, the same worthy protector, Innocent III., sent his legates with letters of excommunication against all those that would not admit and take the said Walter for their king.

Another instance is, that where the princes, electors, and other nobles, as before is said, had promised by their oath to Henry, that they would make Frederic, his son, emperor after his decease, the pope seeing they were endeavouring to bring this to pass, absolved them all from the oath which they had taken and given for the election of Frederic, the emperor, as one not content he should obtain the same. And further, he raised slanders and defamations against Philip, whom the electors had chosen to govern the empire during the minority of Frederic his nephew. He wrote his epistle, which is yet extant, to the duke Barthold of Zaringia, to be emperor, who, because the latter gave place to Philip, he went about to procure that Otho, the son of Henry Leo, should be made emperor, and that the princes and lords, electors of Germany, would crown him forthwith, after the manner of Aquitaine. He deprived all such bishops as he knew to favour Philip as emperor, in the defence of his nephew's right; but Philip, whose cause was better, his skill in martial affairs greater, and who in power and strength was mightier, after divers and great conflicts, occasioning the marvellous disturbance and vastation of the whole empire, by God's help, put the other to the worse. All these calamities and mischiefs Conrade de Lichtenau, at that time living, in his annals, most pitifully complaineth of, and accuseth the bishop of Rome and his adherents of being the chief authors and devisers of this great and lamentable mischief; who, to make themselves rich by the spoil thereof, sought by all means, and desired the same.

Not long after, a peace was concluded between Philip and Otho, and Philip was again reconciled to the pope; which Philip, within a while after, between Otho and him, was murdered in his chamber and slain. After this event Otho was again brought to the imperial seat, and newly elected for emperor, with the counsel and consent of this Innocent III., and so continued till a great variance and discord chanced to arise between the said Otho and the pope, whereupon Innocent sought, by all means, how against Otho, likewise, he might work mischief, and bring him to his end. The occasion of this sudden change and alteration my author maketh no mention of, but that Otho (now being of great power) invaded and destroyed the dominions of Frederic, as Flaminia, Picenum, Umbria, Etruria, but chiefly Campania and Apulia, because those properly appertained to the inheritance of Frederic. A.D. 1214.

Philip slain

A.D. 1208

Variance between Otho and the pope

Thus you see how, first, by the counsel and consent of pope Innocent, and by his instigation, besides his secret conspiracies, this good Frederic and his dominions were hurt and damaged. Then, again, through his default what damage he sustained by Otho, who, by him and his means, was made so strong as he was: notwithstanding the great trust he was put in, for the protection both of Frederic and his dominions.

At this time Frederic was come unto the age of twenty years; who in his youth, by the provision of Constantia, his mother, was so well instructed in letters, and with other arts and virtues so endued, that, at these years, there appeared and did shine in him excellent gifts both of wisdom and knowledge. He was excellently well versed in the Latin and Greek tongues, although at that time learning began to decay, and barbarousness to increase. He had also the German tongue, the Italian tongue, and the Saracen tongue. He daily exercised and put in practice those virtues which nature had planted in him, as piety, wisdom, justice, and fortitude: insomuch that he might well be compared and accounted among the worthiest and most renowned emperors, his predecessors.

Frederic's learning and knowledge

Fazellus, the historian of Sicily in this time,[1] writeth, that Frederic was again, after this, had in great honour and estimation with Innocent; but yet, notwithstanding, he had no sure confidence in him, for that he had the suspected name of Frederic, his grandfather, often in remembrance, and for that reason was very desirous to have him far from Italy.

Suspected for his grandfather's sake

(1) Fazellus flourished in the sixteenth century.—Ed

Henry III.

A.D. 1220 to 1250.

When Frederic had gathered his power, he purposed to set upon Otho, his enemy. Otho hearing of this, came out of Italy, with his army into Germany, thinking to meet Frederic as he was weary of travelling, at the river Rhine, and to stop his passage; but he was deceived in his expectation, and Frederic was crowned, as the manner of Aquitaine is, before he came. After that, Frederic, in the winter time, took his journey to Frankfort; and after many meetings held in Nuremburg, and after Otho was dead, he settled the empire; and the whole country of Germany he in a manner appeased. And then, with all his nobles and princes, he returned to Rome, and by Honorius III. was with great solemnity consecrated and called Augustus. A.D. 1220. This Honorius succeeded Innocent III. in the papal see, and was a great help to Frederic, although he loved him not, in order to revenge himself upon Otho.

Death of Otho, and consecration of Frederic the emperor.

After his consecration Frederic II. gave many great and liberal gifts, as well to the bishop of Rome himself, as also to the court of Rome. He likewise gave and confirmed by his charter to the church of Rome, the dukedom of Fundanum; for, by the insatiable covetousness of the Romish bishops, this wicked use and custom grew up, that unless the emperors, elect and crowned, would give them such like great and large gifts, they could not obtain of them their consecration or confirmation, which for that intent they devised.

Furthermore, Frederic, the emperor, willing to show himself more bountiful and liberal to the church, and not wishing to restrain any privilege that might benefit the same, gave and admitted those constitutions which the pope himself would desire, and are yet extant in their civil law, by which doings he delivered, to their hands, a sword (as it were) to cut his own throat: for the bishops of Rome, now, having even what they listed, and all in their own hands, might, by the pain of proscription, bring what emperor or king they listed under "coram nobis," and keep them by their own laws, as if they were bound in certain bands, out of which they might not start. For whatsoever he were who, for the diminution of the liberties of the church was excommunicated, and so continued a year's space, he should be within the danger of this proscript, and should not be released before he had made satisfaction, and were admitted by the pope to the church and congregation of good men again. Whereby it came to pass, that whatever emperor, in the government of his dominions, should in any point displease, or do contrary to the will of the bishop of Rome, he then, as enemy to the church was excommunicated; and, unless within a year he were reconciled to them again, by this their principal law, he was in the proscript; and often it chanced that princes, to avoid the pain of this proscript, were ready to do whatsoever the pope would have them, and commanded them to do.

Frederic gave, through his liberality, a sword to cut his own throat.

Canon of proscription granted and confirmed by Frederic.

After the consecration of Frederic was with great solemnity finished, and that the pope and church of Rome, in all ample manner, as is partly described, were gratified, and yet larger constitutions to them confirmed, he departed from Rome, and went into Italy, there to set in order and settle the cities and great towns, for the better tranquillity of himself, and safety of his subjects; and from thence, into his own provinces and dominions, where he heard of certain, who began to raise and make new factions against him; amongst whom were found Thomas and Richard, the brethren of Innocent III., the earl of Anaquinos, who held back certain castles in the kingdom of the Neapolitans from him by force; which castles he besieged and beat down, and took from them all that he found in them. Richard he took, and sent as prisoner into Sicily; but Thomas escaped, and came speedily to Rome; whither also repaired certain bishops and others who were conspirators against Frederic; as also such others as the fear of the emperor's laws and their own guilty consciences caused to fly, and who were (that notwithstanding) by this bishop of Rome, Honorius III., to recompense the liberality of the emperor bestowed upon him, under his nose succoured, maintained, and defended. This when Frederic understood, he began to expostulate with the bishop, considering the unseemliness of that deed of his; against whom the pope, on the other side, was so chafed and vexed, that immediately, without further delay, he thundereth out against him, like a tyrant, his curses and excommunications.

The liberality of Frederic well recompensed of Honorius III Frederic expostulateth, the pope curseth

Fazellus declareth the detestation or defiance to happen between them, somewhat otherwise. There were (saith he) amongst those who were found traitors to the emperor, certain bishops, who, flying to the pope, requested his aid: whereupon the pope sent his legates to the emperor, and requested him, that he would admit and receive to favour those bishops whom he had banished and put out of their offices; and that he would not intermeddle with any ecclesiastical charge wherewith he had not to do: and said further, that the correction and punishment of such matters appertained to the bishop of Rome, and not to him; and, moreover, that the oversight of those churches in that kingdom, from which he had expelled the bishops, pertained and belonged unto him.

To this Frederic replieth, "that forasmuch as now, for four hundred years and more, from the time of Charlemagne, all emperors and kings in their dominions might lawfully commit to apt and fit men, for the same, such ecclesiastical functions and charges as within their territories and kingdoms fell vacant, he looked to have the like privilege and authority also, that others his predecessors had before him." And, he further said, "that he had the same and like authority in the empire that his father Henry, and Frederic his grandfather, and others his predecessors before them had; neither had he so deserved at the hands of the church of Rome, nor at those of Honorius himself, as to be deprived of those privileges which his ancestors before him had, and kept." And further, Frederic being chafed and moved with these demands of the pope, breaketh forth and saith, "How long will the bishop of Rome abuse my patience? When will his covetous heart be satisfied? Whereunto will his ambitious desire grow?" with other like words besides, repeating certain injuries and conspiracies, both against him and his dominions, as well by Honorius as by Innocent III. his predecessor; as also other like injuries of popes practised towards his ancestors. "What man," saith he, "is able to suffer and bear this so incredible boldness, and intolerable insolency of so proud a bishop?" "Go," saith he, to the

The emperor replieth to the pope's demand

Strife between the pope and the emperor for the election and deprivation of bishops.

Henry III. A.D. 1221 to 1250.

legates, "and tell Honorius, that I will hazard both the seigniory of my empire, and crown of my kingdom, rather than I will suffer him thus to diminish the authority of our majesty."[1]

Now, because much disquietness and controversy hath arisen, for the most part, throughout all Christendom, in every kingdom and realm severally, for and about the authority of choosing and depriving of bishops (as may be seen by the example of this Frederic), which the pope only and arrogantly challengeth to himself, and saith, it doth not appertain to another, I thought good, not with silence to overpass, but somewhat to say, and to prove the authority of christian kings and princes, in this behalf, to be both sufficient and good; which thing, not only by the holy Scriptures, is right easy to be done, but also, that it is by synodal decrees and councils, divers and sundry, established and confirmed, may easily be proved; as, by the ancient custom and manner of the primitive church, may also be further corroborated and made good.

Election of bishops to be in princes and their subjects.

Hereunto appertain certain places collected and gathered out of the decrees of Gratian, and especially in these canons, the twelfth, thirteenth, fourteenth, twenty-sixth, twenty-seventh, thirty-second, and sixty-third distinctions. Furthermore, when christian kings and princes began to embrace Christ's religion, both for honour and order's sake it was granted, that when the people desired such ministers as were convenient, and by them thought meet, that they who were then in the ecclesiastical function, and chiefest in authority, should either confirm such as were presented, or else themselves should place fit men in their churches as need required. Thus did the emperors of Constantinople (receiving the order and manner from Constantine the Great), use and give the right of ecclesiastical function with the consent both of the people and of ecclesiastical persons; and long they so retained the same, as in the case of Honorius, the emperor, to Boniface;[2] also, in the examples of Pelagius and Gregory the Great, of whom one was appointed bishop of the church of Rome, in the reign of Justinian, the emperor,[3] when Totila was governing Italy; and the other, in the time of Maurice, the emperor, when the Lombards possessed it.[4]

And whereas Gratian, in the beginning of the ninety-sixth and ninety-seventh distinctions, doth declare, that the rescript of Honorius the emperor, is void and of none effect, for that he determined the election of the bishop of Rome, contrary to the authority of the holy canons, when as yet neither to the civil magistrate, nor to any of the ecclesiastical order, can there be read of any license given them to dispense it withal; each man may plainly see and discern his great folly and want of understanding. As if, at that time, any decrees were made which should debar emperors from the constituting of the ecclesiastical ministers, or that it were doubtful whether the emperors, at that time, had past any constitutions touching the causes of ecclesiastical discipline, and the same laws then put in use; when the contrary most manifestly (both by the laws and histories of that age and time, as well of the church as of the empire,) may appear. And, that we need not

(1) Thomas Fazellus lib. 8. (2) Can. 8. dist. 79. et can. 2. dist. 97.
(3) Justinian flourished from A.D. 527 to 565; Mauritius, from A.D. 582 to 602.—ED.
(4) Chap. 15, 21, 24.

seek far for the matter, this thing is sufficiently proved by these titles; 'De sacro sanctis Ecclesiis,' 'Episcopis,' 'Clericis,' besides other ecclesiastical chapters and matters touching religion, all which are to be seen in the books of the principal and chiefest constitutions, collected and set forth by Justinian. Amongst which, many of the chapters are said to be accepted and allowed by Honorius and Theodosius: so, in like case, the twenty-first canon in the sixty-third distinction doth declare, that the Grecian emperors, who next ensued after Justinian, did observe that manner of ordaining and electing the bishop of Rome, although at that time "Interpellatum erat," it was somewhat spurned at.

The election decreed by one hundred and fifty-three bishops in the council of Lateran to be in the emperor.

Among the emperors, mention is made of Constantine, surnamed Pogonatus.[1] Charlemagne, in like manner, followed their steps in the same; as in the twenty-second canon, and the same distinction is declared. And further, at a synodal council in Lateran (Adrian being high bishop, where were convented and assembled one hundred and fifty-three other bishops), it was decreed, "that the power and authority of creating the bishop of Rome, and ordaining of all other prelates and ecclesiastical orders, should be in the power and will of Charlemagne as well in Italy, as in his other dominions and provinces; and that whosoever was not promoted and allowed by him, should not be consecrated by any; and that those who repugned and disobeyed this decree, should incur the most sharp pain of proscription and publication of law." The worthy example of this is extant in the eighteenth canon and eighteenth title. Yet, notwithstanding, Stephen IV., author of this rescript against the said decree, without the emperor's consent, was made bishop of Rome; who, to the intent he might elude the decreed and solemnized penalty, thereby to excuse himself, went into France to Louis the Pious, son of Charlemagne, and at Rheims crowned he him with the imperial diadem. (A. D. 814.) Neither could this bishop here stay himself, but spying the great lenity of the emperor, essayed to make frustrate the aforesaid constitution. For his purpose was, and so he brought to pass, as in the twenty-seventh canon and the same distinction appeareth, that it "might be lawful for the ecclesiastical order, with the people and senate of Rome, without the authority of the emperor, to choose the bishop of Rome; reserving, that he should not be consecrated without the will and consent of the emperor." Thus it is manifest, that the bishops of Rome themselves, not regarding, but despising the strict penalty and sanction of the aforesaid decree of the Lateran council, were not only the first that brake the same, but also, by contrary rescripts and constitutions, laboured and endeavoured to extol and set up themselves above all others.

Bishop of Rome the breaker of the decrees of the council.

Lothaire reneweth the Lateran decree for election of bishops.

Hereupon Lothaire, afterwards being emperor and nephew to Charlemagne, coming into Italy, there to dissolve the conspiracy and confederacy of Leo IV., about the translation of the empire, renewed, and established again, the synodal decree of Lateran, touching the jurisdiction of the emperor for the election of the bishop of Rome and other ecclesiastical persons; and hereof it came, that those epistles were written by Leo, in the sixteenth and seventeenth canons,

(1) Constantine Pogonatus, A. D. 668 to 685, Charlemagne, A. D. 786 to 814 — ED.

Henry III. A.D. 1221 to 1250.

and the same distinction, who also, as in the ninth canon and tenth distinction, made a profession, that the same imperial precepts should be kept in all ages. This Leo, when he was reproved of treason and other evils, pleaded his cause before Louis, emperor of Rome, and son of Lothaire above recited.[1]

But after this, as time grew on, the bishops of Rome nothing relinquishing their ambitious desires; Otho, the first emperor of that name, deprived and put from the see of Rome that most filthy and wicked bishop, John XIII., both for divers and sundry wicked and heinous acts by him committed, as also for his great treasons and conspiracies against his royal person, and did substitute in his place Leo V.; who, calling a synod at Lateran, in the same temple and place where the other before was kept, did promulgate a new constitution with consent of the senate and people of Rome, concerning the emperor's jurisdiction in the aforesaid election, which is contained in the twenty-third canon, and sixty-third distinction. By this the old right and power of the emperor in the election of the bishop of Rome, and other ecclesiastical prelates, was again, with sharper and stricter sanction, confirmed and ratified. Again, John XVIII., whom Crescentius the Roman, usurping the imperial crown, had made bishop by the consent of the people of Rome and the ecclesiastical order, having his nose cut off, and his eyes put out, and being so thrust out of the capitol, was again, of Otho III., established and made bishop. But when, notwithstanding, the bishops of Rome would not alter their old accustomed disposition, but with all their industry endeavoured to abrogate that jurisdiction of the emperor over the bishop of Rome (as people loath to be under subjection), Henry III. (Leo IX. being then constituted bishop, A.D. 1049), did once again ratify the same, and caused the bishop, who extolled himself before all his fellow bishops, to stoop and give place to Moguntius.

The election once again ratified to be in the emperor's jurisdiction.

So after the death of Henry III. emperor of Germany, Nicholas II., although in his decree (which in the first canon and twenty-third distinction is recited) he gave the primacy for the election of the bishop of Rome, by the means of the priests and people of Rome, unto the cardinals; yet he would, after that, that the prerogative therein should be reserved to Henry IV., the young emperor, from whom the empire afterwards was for a time wrested and taken.

The election hitherto in the emperors, beginneth to fall by Hildebrand.

But now, after this, when Hildebrand, who was called Gregory VII. was pope (A.D. 1073), this prerogative of the emperors in their election, which, before, in the creation of Alexander the bishop, was neglected and broken, the bishop of Rome not only did seek to diminish the authority thereof, but also to evacuate and quite undo the same; for he not only aspired to that dignity without the consent and appointment of the emperor, but also made restraint that no emperor, king, duke, marquis, earl, or any civil magistrate, should assign and appoint any one, to any ecclesiastical function and charge; and that none of his prelates should be so hardy, as to take them at any of their hands; as in question sixteen, canons seven, nine, and ten may be seen.

Henry IV. again challengeth the election.

Yet, notwithstanding, after this horrible monster Hildebrand was proscribed and thrust out of the papal seat, and Clement III. put in

(1) 2 Quest. 7. can. 40.

his stead, Henry again challenged his imperial prerogative of election. But when the bishops who succeeded this Hildebrand, led on by his example, began to derogate from the imperial prerogative of election, and when Henry, on the other side, by all the means possible, sought to defend and maintain the same, by the subtle fraud and mischievous policy of the bishops, who set the son against the father, and found means to steal from him the hearts of his nobles and subjects, and to set them all against him, and especially the princes of Germany, he was deposed and disappointed of his purpose.

And although Henry V., coming to Rome, brought Paschal II. (A.D. 1099) to that point, that he both in public council, and in writing sealed, and by oath confirmed, restored again to the emperors of Rome the prerogative of election, and giving of ecclesiastical dignities: yet, notwithstanding, after that Henry, the emperor, was gone from Rome, Paschal, the pope, greatly repenting and sorrowing for that he had done (in allowing and confirming the privileges of emperors through fear), touching the giving and disposing of ecclesiastical functions, excommunicated the emperor, and, in a synodal council at Lateran, ordained and decreed, that he should be had and accounted a wicked enemy, who would take any ecclesiastical function or preferment at the hands of a civil magistrate; whereupon were made these decrees, question sixteen, chapters seven, thirteen, fourteen, fifteen and sixteen.

Priests accursed that take any benefice at the hands of a layman

Therefore, when these decrees touching the designation of bishops in spite and contempt of the emperor, were practised and put in use, and when now (especially by the means and procurement of the bishops) intestine and civil wars began to rise in the empire, the imperial jurisdiction in this matter was not only weakened and much debilitated, but also, in a manner, utterly broken and lost. For when Henry V., the emperor, was sharply of Lothaire, and his vassals, the bishops, beset, and laid unto by the provocation of the pope, and was mightily, by the bishops that took his part on the other side, requested and entreated (in hope of public peace and tranquillity), that he would condescend and somewhat yield to the pope's demands: he, at length (the more was the pity), that he might be reconciled and have peace with pope Calixtus II. (A.D. 1119), in the city of Worms, parted from and with that his prerogative or jurisdiction of giving ecclesiastical preferments to the pope and his prelates, now more than three hundred years (from the time of Charlemagne) in the hands of the emperors of Rome; and until this time, with great fortitude and princely courage conserved and kept; which resignation turned to no small detriment both of the church of Christ and the christian commonwealth.

Henry V resigneth his prerogative of election.

Then first, and never before, the bishop of Rome obtained and quietly enjoyed that prerogative of election and bestowing of benefices, which he so long before, with such great policies, now secretly, now openly, and now with force, had sought for. And Gratian showeth, in the twenty-ninth and thirtieth canons, with what sufficient and good authority he will prove, that before this time the same authority was given to the city of Rome for the election of the pope without the consent of the emperor; and what good stuff he putteth in the latter, and how subtilly that papistical flatterer, or pontifical parasite,

The election gotten to the bishops of Rome.

Henry III.

A.D. 1221 to 1250.

hath forged the same, both Carolus Molineus sufficiently in divers places hath noted, and by the observation of times may, by an ordinary historiographer, who hath read the French and German histories, soon be espied and discerned. For first, five bishops, one after another, succeeded this Gregory IV., upon whom the twenty-ninth canon is entitled or fathered; that is, Sergius II., John VIII., Adrian II., John IX., and Adrian III.; which Adrian, by force wresting the authority of the election from the people, was made pope; whereas Gregory (specially to be noted) would not take on him the papacy before the emperor had consented to his election. After this, Molineus compareth Raphael Volateran with the thirtieth canon, which again is suspected. For why? When Eugenius was bishop, who was the successor of this Paschal, with whom Louis the Pious is said to have made a league or paction, the same Louis, with his son Lothaire, together with the help of the king of the Romans at Rome, made laws, both for all his subjects in the empire, as also for the Romans themselves; speaking nothing of the renewing of the decree made by Lothaire. Then again, how could Leo IV. write to Lothaire and Louis, the emperors, that counterfeit or forged decree beginning with 'Constitutio,' &c., when in the same, mention is made of Henry the Fowler, and of Otho I., who reigned more than fourscore years after them; and of Leo IV.,[1] bishop of Rome.

Gratian a forger of canons.

How shameless and impudent Gratian is, in forging the decrees.

Now with what face dare this fond fellow Gratian make Otho I. to be the author of the thirty-first canon, when Otho deprived John XII. of the papacy; and not only took nothing from the imperial jurisdiction concerning the election, nor from the city of Rome, nor any other bishops subject to the Roman empire, but added somewhat more thereunto, as was said before. And yet, so shameless and senseless was this Gratian, that he durst obtrude and lay before the reader such manifest fraud and evident legerdemain (feigned and made of his own brains in the compiling of this decree), being so necessary, as he thought, for the dominion and primacy of the Roman bishops, in the stead of good and true laws; neither fearing that the same might be after his days reprehended, neither, to his great shame and discredit, to him attributed. Where also by the way is to be noted, that as this graceless Gratian, to please these holy fathers, and to erect their kingdom, would give such an impudent attempt to the blinding and deceiving of all posterities, inserting for grounded truths and holy decrees such loud lies and detestable doctrine, what may be thought of the rabble of the rest of writers in those days? what attempts might hope of gain cause them to work, by whom, and such like, is to be feared the falsifying of divers other good works now extant, in those perilous times written?

The election wrested from the emperor.

Thus, when the bishops had once wrested this authority out of the emperor's hands, they then so fortified and armed themselves and their dominion, that although afterwards Frederic I., grandfather to this good emperor Frederic II. as also Louis the Pious, and Henry of Luxemburg (as men most studious and careful for the dignities of the empire, unfeigned lovers and maintainers of the utility of the commonweal, and most desirous of the preservation and prosperity of

(1) Leo IV. A. D. 847 to 851.—Ed.

the church) did all their endeavours, with singular wisdom and strength, as much as in them lay, to recover again from the bishop of Rome this authority of the imperial jurisdiction lost, most cruelly and wickedly abusing the same, to the destruction of the empire, the undoing of the commonwealth, and the utter subversion of the church of God; yet could they not be able to bring the same to pass in those dark and shadowed times of perverse doctrine and errors of the people, and most miserable servitude of civil magistrates.

Henry III.

A.D. 1221 to 1250.

What Rome catcheth, that she keepeth

The same and like privilege also in the election of their bishops and prelates, and in the disposing of ecclesiastical offices, as the emperor of Rome, had every prince and king in their several dominions possessed. For, by the decree of the council of Toledo, which in the twenty-fifth canon and sixty-third distinction is mentioned, the authority of creating and choosing bishops and prelates in Spain, was in the power of the king of Spain. The like also by the histories of Clovis, Charlemagne, Louis IX., Philip Augustus, Philip the Fair, Charles V., Charles VI., and Charles VII., kings of France, is apparent and well known; for all these kings had the chief charge and government of the French church, and not the bishops of Rome.

Not without good cause desired they to muzzle the people in ignorance

Every king and prince in their several kingdoms, had also till that time the prerogative of election

And by our English histories also, as you heard, it is manifest, that the authority of choosing ecclesiastical ministers and bishops was always in the kings of England, till the reign of king Henry I., who, by the labour and procurement of Anselm, archbishop of Canterbury, was deprived and put from the same.

Also the princes of Germany and electors of the emperor, till the time of Henry V., had all (every prince severally in his own empire and province) the same jurisdiction and prerogative, to give and dispose ecclesiastical functions to their prelates at their pleasure; and after that, it appertained to the people and prelates together. And how in the reign of Frederic the prelates got unto themselves alone this immunity, John of Aventine, in his Seventh Book of the Annals of the Boiores, doth describe.

Also it is probable, that the kings of Sicily had the same faculty in giving and disposing of their ecclesiastical promotions and charge of churches;[1] and that because Frederic defended himself against the tyranny of the bishop of Rome, therefore (as Fazellus saith) he was excommunicated by Honorius; but that Platina and Blondus allege other causes, wherefore he was excommunicated by Honorius, I am not ignorant: howbeit he who will compare their writings with those of others, who write more indifferently between Honorius and him, shall easily find, that they more sought the favour of the Roman bishops, than to write a verity. But now again to the history of Frederic.

Nicolaus Cisnerus affirmeth, that whilst Frederic the emperor was in Sicily, his wife Constantia died at Catiana or Catana. In the mean time the Christians, who with a great navy sailed into Egypt, and took the city Heliopolis, commonly called Damatia, and long ago named Pelusinum, being in good hope to have driven the Sultan, or Soldan, out of Egypt, had a great and marvellous overthrow by the conveying of the water of the river Nile (which then overflowed into their camp), and were fain to accord an unprofitable truce with

Death of Constantia, wife of Frederic

Great overthrow of the Christians in Egypt.

(1) Andreas de Isthmia ad prim. constit. Neap. nu. 12.

Henry III.

A.D. 1227 to 1250.

the Soldan for certain years, and to deliver the city again; and so departing out of Egypt, they were fain to come to Acre and Tyre, to the no small detriment and loss of the christian army. Hereupon John, surnamed Brennus, king of Jerusalem, arrived in Italy, and prayed aid of the emperor against his enemies, in whom he had great hope to find a remedy for the evils and calamities before declared; and from thence he went to Rome to the pope, declaring unto him the great discomfiture and overthrow past, as also the present peril and calamity that they were in, desiring also his aid therein. By means of this king John (as Cisnerus saith), the emperor was reconciled again to the pope, and made friends together; to whom also that king gave Joel, his daughter, in marriage, who came of the daughter of Conrad, king of Jerusalem, and marquis of Montserrat, with whom he had for dowry the inheritance of the kingdom of Jerusalem, as right heir thereunto by her mother; by whom also he afterwards obtained the kingdom of Naples and Sicily, and promised that, with as much expedient speed as he might, he would prepare a power for the recovery of Jerusalem, and be there himself in person; which thing to do, for that upon divers occasions he deferred (whereof some think one thing, some another), pope Honorius, unto whom he was lately reconciled, purposed to have made against him some great and secret attempt, had he not been by death prevented; upon whom were made these verses:—

Frederic and the pope made friends.

> "O pater Honori, multorum nate dolori,
> Est tibi decori vivere, vade mori."

Gregory IX. as great an enemy to Frederic as Honorius.

After Honorius III. succeeded Gregory IX., A.D. 1227, as great an enemy to Frederic as was Honorius; this Gregory came of the race whom the emperor, as before ye heard, condemned of treason which they wrought against him. This pope was scarcely settled in his papacy, when he threatened Frederic greatly with excommunication, unless he would prepare himself to go into Asia according to his promise, as ye heard before, to king John of Jerusalem; and what the cause was why the pope so hastened the journey of Frederic into Asia, you shall hear hereafter. In effect, he could not well bring that to pass, which in his mischievous mind he had devised, unless the emperor were further from him. Notwithstanding, Frederic, it should seem, smelling a rat, or mistrusting somewhat (as well he might), alleged divers causes and hindrances, as lately and truly he did to Honorius.

Frederic refuseth to go into Asia at the pope's bidding. The pope is angry.

Fazellus, a Sicilian writer, saith, that the special cause of the emperor's stay was, for the oath of truce and peace during certain years, which was made between the Saracens and Christians, as you heard, which time was not yet expired.

The cause of the stay of the emperor's journey into Asia.

The same Fazellus also writeth thus of king John of Jerusalem, that when his daughter was brought to Rome, the emperor and the pope were reconciled together. And being called up to Rome to celebrate the marriage, pope Gregory, as the manner of those proud prelates is, offered his right foot unto the emperor to kiss. But the emperor, not stooping so low, scarcely with his lip touched the upper part of his knee, and would not kiss his foot; which thing the pope took in very evil part, and was therewith marvellously offended. But as no opportunity at that time served to revenge his conceived grudge and old malice, he dissembled the same, as he might for that time, thinking to recompence it fully, as time would serve and fall out for that purpose.

After this, it happened that the emperor, hearing how the Christians were oppressed by the Soldan in Syria, and that from Arsacida there came a great power against the christian princes, made the more haste, and was with more desire encouraged to set forward his journey into Asia. Wherefore, assembling the nobility of the empire at Ravenna and Cremona, he gave in commandment to Henry, his son, whom not long before he caused to be created Cæsar, that he should persuade the nobles and princes of the empire, that they all would be ready to put to their helping hands, in furthering this his journey and enterprise. This writeth Fazellus; howbeit, some others affirm that these things were done in the time of Honorius. But, howsoever the matter is, this thing is manifest; that Frederic, to satisfy the pope's desire, who never would give over, but by all means sought to provoke him forward, gave him at length his promise, that by a certain time he would prepare an army, and fight himself against those who kept from him the city of Jerusalem (which thing he also confesseth himself in his epistles, and also how he desired and obtained, of the peers and nobility of the empire, their aid thereunto), and he also appointed a convenient time when they should be at Brundusium.

Preparation of the voyage of Frederic, and stay thereof.

In the mean season, he with all his power and endeavour made speedy and hasty preparation for the wars. He rigged and manned a puissant navy; he had the most picked men and best soldiers that were in every country, and made warlike provision and furniture for every thing that to such a voyage and expedition appertained. Neither was the matter slacked, but, at the time appointed, great bands assembled and mustered, both of German soldiers and others, who, under their captains appointed, set forth and marched to Brundusium (their generals were Thuringus, and Sigibert, and Augustine the bishop); where they for a long time lying, and attending the emperor's coming, being let by infirmity and sickness, great pestilence and sundry diseases molested them, by reason of the great heat and intemperance of that country, and many a soldier there lost his life, among whom also died Thuringus, one of their generals. The emperor, when he had somewhat recovered his health, with all his navy launched out, and set forward to Brundusium. And when he came to the straits of Peloponesus and Crete, being islands lying in the sea, and there for lack of convenient wind was staid, suddenly the emperor (his diseases growing upon him again) fell sick; and sending before, all or the most part of his bands and ships into Palestine, promising them most assuredly to come after and follow them as soon as he might recover and get never so little health, he himself with a few ships returned and came to Brundusium, and from thence, for want of health, went into Apulia.

Great sickness in the emperor's army.

When tidings hereof came to the pope's ear, he sent out his thundering curses and new excommunications against the emperor. The causes whereof I find noted and mentioned in his own letters; that is, how that when he had robbed and taken from Brundusium the prince of Thuringia, his horses, his money, and other rich furniture of

The pope excommunicateth the emperor for staying his voyage.

Henry III.

A.D. 1227 to 1250.

his house at the time of his death, he sailed into Italy; not for the intent to make war against the Turk, but to convey his prey that he had stolen and taken away from Brundusium; and so, neglecting his oath and promise which he had made, and feigning himself to be sick, he came home again: and that by his default also, Damietta was lost, and the host of the Christians sore afflicted. Fazellus, besides these causes spoken of before, doth write that the pope alleged these also; that he seduced a certain damsel who was in the queen's nursery, and that he slew his wife Joel when he had whipped her in the prison, for declaring the mischievous act to her father king John. But all the writers, and also Blondus himself doth declare, that this Joel died after the publication of the proscript and excommunication; wherefore the pope could not without great shame allege as the cause the death of Joel, for undoubtedly the truth is, that she, of her son Conrad, died in childbed. Then Frederic, to repel and avoid the aforesaid slanders, sendeth the bishop of Brundusium and other legates to Rome, whom the pope would not suffer to come to his presence, neither yet to the councils of the cardinals to make his purgation. Wherefore the emperor, to purge himself of the crimes which the pope did so falsely accuse him of, both to all christian kings, and especially to the princes of Germany, and all the nobles of the empire, writeth his letters (which are to be seen), that those things are both false and also feigned, and of the pope's own head invented; and showeth, how that his ambassadors with his purgation could not be suffered to come to the pope's presence; also doth largely describe, how unthankful and ungrateful the bishops of Rome were towards him for the great benefits, which both he and also his predecessors had bestowed upon them and the Roman church; which letter, for that it is over tedious here to place, considering the discourse of the history is somewhat long, the sum of the purgation is this:—

The emperor purgeth himself of crimes which the pope laid against him, by his letters dedicated to all christian princes.

He protesteth and declareth universally, that he had always great care for the christian commonwealth, and that he had determined even from his youth to fight against the Turks and Saracens; and for that occasion he made a promise to the princes electors of Aquitaine, how that he would take the war upon him. Afterwards he renewed his promise at Rome, when he was consecrated by Honorius, then when he married the daughter of the king of Jerusalem, who was an heir of the same. And because that kingdom might be defended and kept from the injuries of the enemies, and because he favoured it even as he did his own, he prepared a huge navy, and gathered together a strong army of men, neither did he neglect any thing that belonged to the furniture of the war. But when the time was come, and his band was gathered together, his sickness would not suffer him to be there; and afterwards, when he had recovered the same, and came to Brundusium, and from thence without any disturbance went forthwith to sea, he fell into the same sickness again, by which he was hindered of his purpose, which thing (saith he) he is able to prove by sufficient testimony. How the pope also doth lay the losing of Damietta, and other things which prospered not well with him, unjustly to his charge; whereas he had made great provision for that journey, both of soldiers and of other necessary things. But he that will understand these things more plainly, among other epistles of Petrus de Vineis, written in the name of Frederic, let him read these especially which begin thus: "In admirationem, et justitiam, et innocentiam, et levate oculos." And truly, even as Frederic the emperor declareth in his letters concerning this matter, all the old writers of Germany do accord and agree in the same.

Matthew Paris also briefly collecteth the effect of another letter which he wrote to the king of England, complaining unto him of the excommunication of the pope against him, whose words are these:—

And amongst other catholic princes (saith he) he also wrote his letters unto the king of England, embulled with gold; declaring in the same, that the bishop of Rome was so inflamed with the fire of avarice and manifest concupiscence, that he was not contented with the goods of the church, which were innumerable; but also that he shamed not to bring princes, kings, and emperors, to be subjects and contributors to him, and so to disherit them, and put them from their kingly dignities: and that the king of England himself had good experiment thereof, whose father (that is to say, king John) they so long held excommunicate, till they had brought both him and his dominions under servitude, and to pay unto him tribute. Also that many have experience of the same by the earl of Toulouse and divers other princes, who so long held their persons and lands in interdict, till they might bring them into like servitude. I pass by (saith he) the simonies and sundry sorts of exactions (the like whereof was never yet heard) which daily are used amongst the ecclesiastical persons, besides their manifest usury, yet so cloaked and coloured to the simple sort, that therewithal they infect the whole world. They be sugared and embalmed simonists, the insatiable horse-leeches or blood-suckers, saying, that the church of Rome is our mother and nurse, whereas it is indeed the most polling court in the universal world, the root and right mother of all mischief; using and exercising no motherly doings or deeds, but bringing forth the right exercises of a wicked step-dame, making sufficient proof thereof by her manifest fruits to all the world apparent. Let the barons of England consider whether this be true or not, whom pope Innocent by his bulls, encouraged to rise and rebel, with one consent, against their sovereign lord and prince king John, your father, as an obstinate enemy to the church of Rome. But, after that the king (far out of square), remembering himself, had crouched unto him, and obliged both himself and kingdom to the church of Rome, more like a woman than a man; and that the wise barons whom the pope had first maintained and stirred up, without all shame, either of the world, or fear of God, had done the same, he sought how he might with gaping mouth devour and consume the sweet fat from them, whom he had miserably to death betrayed and disherited, as the manner of the Roman bishops is; by whose greedy avarice it came to pass, that England, the prince of provinces, was brought under miserable subjection and tribute. Behold the manners and conditions of our Roman bishops; behold the snares wherewith these prelates do seek to entangle men withal, to wipe their noses of their money, to make their children bondmen, to disquiet such as seek to live in peace, being clothed with sheep's clothing, when indeed they be but ravening wolves, sending their legates hither and thither to excommunicate and suspend; as having power to punish whom they list, not sowing the seed, that is the word of God, to fructify, but that they may bribe and poll men's persons, and reap that which they never did sow. Thus cometh it to pass, that they spoil the holy churches and houses of God, which should be a refuge for the poor, and the mansion-houses of saints, which our devout and simple parents to that purpose builded and ordained to the refection of poor men and pilgrims, and to the sustentation of such as were well disposed and religious. But these degenerate varlets, whom only letters have made both mad and malapert, do strive and gape to be both kings and emperors.

A letter of the emperor to the king of England.

Many kingdoms have experience of the pope's practices.

The church of Rome the mother of mischief.

King John's submission to the pope blamed by the emperor.

Who be the ravening wolves in sheep's clothing.

Doubtless the primitive church was builded and laid in poverty and simplicity of life, and then as a fruitful mother begat she those her holy children, whom the catalogue of saints now maketh mention of; and verily no other

Christ's church builded in humility.

Henry III.

A.D. 1227 to 1250.

foundation can be laid of any other church, than that which is laid by Jesus Christ. But this church, as it swimmeth and walloweth in all superfluity of riches, and doth build and raise the frame in all superfluous wealth and glory, so is it to be feared lest the walls thereof in time fall to decay, and when the walls be down, utter ruin and subversion follow after. Against us, He knoweth, who is the searcher of all hearts, how furiously these Catholics rage and go to work, saying, and therefore excommunicating me, that I will not take upon me the journey I have promised beyond the seas; whereas inevitable and most urgent causes and perils, as well to the church of God, as also to the empire, besides the annoyance of mine infirmity and sickness, do detain me at home, and stay the same, but especially the insolency of the rebellious Sicilians. For why? neither do we think it safety to our empire, nor expedient to the christian state, that we should now take our journey into Asia, leaving behind us at home such intestine and civil wars; no more for a good surgeon to lay a healing plaister to a grievous wound new made and stricken with the sword. In conclusion, also, this he addeth, admonishing all the princes of the world, that they would beware and take heed (by their avaricious iniquity) of like peril and danger to themselves, because that, as the proverb is, "It behoveth him to look about, that seeth his neighbour's house on fire."[1]

The pope's church is all superfluity: ergo, the pope's church is not Christ's church.

But now, that Frederic the emperor might in very deed stop the mouth of the cruel pope, who did persist and go forward still in his excommunication against him; and that he might declare to the whole world, how that the last year he delayed not his journey by his own voluntary will, but by necessity; when he had devised and prepared all things meet for the war, and that he had gathered together, and levied a great army of men, he departed from thence to Brundusium, committing the government of his kingdom to Reinald, the son of duke Spoletus, and to Anselm, a baron of Instigensis, and came by sea to Cyprus, with his host.

Another journey of the emperor to Jerusalem.

From Cyprus, the emperor with his whole navy sailed to Joppa, which city he fortified, because the passages by land were stopped and kept by the enemies, and by sea he might not pass nor travel, by means of the extreme weather and tempest; whereby it came to pass, that within short space they lacked victuals, and were sorely afflicted with famine. Then fell they to prayer, and made their humble supplication to God; with whose tears his wrath being appeased, the great tempest, and long continued foul weather ceased, whereby (the seas being now calm) they had both victuals in great plenty, and all other necessary things for their need brought unto them; whereby immediately it came to pass, that both the emperor and his army, as also the inhabitants of Joppa were greatly refreshed and animated, and, on the other side, their enemies being disappointed of their purpose, were greatly discouraged; insomuch that the king of Egypt, who with great power, accompanied by Scarapho, his brother, prince of Gaza, and the prince of Damascus, their nephew, with many other dukes and nobles, had encamped themselves within one day's journey of Joppa, thinking to besiege the same, were contented upon the coming of the emperor's heralds to them, to treat of a peace; whereupon ambassadors were sent unto them with the emperor's demands right profitable to the christian commonweal. The Saracens, immediately consulting upon the same, yielded thereto; so that a peace for ten years was concluded, and confirmed by solemn oath on the behalf of both princes, according to their several usages and manner: the

The emperor oppressed by famine, and by prayer miraculously relieved.

Peace during ten years, between

(1) Matth. Paris, p. 69.

form and condition of which articles of peace, briefly collected, are these:—

The Turks and Christians.

I. That Frederic the emperor should be crowned and anointed king of Jerusalem, according to the manner of the kings of Jerusalem before him.

II. That all the lands and possessions which were situate betwixt Jerusalem and Ptolomaida, and the greatest part of Palestine, and the cities of Tyre and Sidon, which were in Syria, and all other territories which Baldwin IV. at any time had occupied there, should be delivered unto him, only certain castles reserved.

III. That he might fortify and build what fortresses and castles, cities and towns, he thought good in all Syria and Palestine.

IV. That all the prisoners who were in the Saracens' hands, should be ransomed freely, and sent home. And again, that the Saracens might have leave, without armour, to come into the temple where the Lord's sepulchre is, to pray; and that they should still hold and keep Chratum, and the King's Mount.

Letters of Frederic to the princes and pope of his success.

Frederic now, because he thought the conclusion of this peace to be both necessary and also profitable for all Christians, and had also gotten as much thereby as if the wars had continued, sent his legates with letters into the west, to all christian kings, princes, and potentates, as also to the bishop of Rome, declaring unto them the circumstance and success of his journey and wars, as partly ye have heard; requiring them that they also would praise and give God thanks for his good success and profitable peace concluded: and he desireth the pope, that forasmuch as he had now accomplished his promise, neither was there now any cause wherefore he should be with him displeased, that he might be reconciled and obtain his favour.

The emperor crowned king of Jerusalem.

In the mean season the emperor, with all his army, marcheth to Jerusalem, where, upon Easter-day, A.D. 1229, he was, with great triumph and comfort of all his nobles, and also of the magistrates of that kingdom (only the patriarch of Cyprus, the king's legate, and Oliver, the master or captain of the Temple, with his company excepted), solemnly and with great applause crowned king.

After this, the emperor re-edifieth the city and walls thereof, which by the Saracens were beaten down and battered. He also furnisheth it with munition, buildeth up the churches and temples that were ruinous, and fortifieth Nazareth and Joppa with strong garrisons, victuals, and all other things necessary.

The first secret practice of pope Gregory IX.

Now see and behold, I pray you, whilst Frederic was thus occupied in the kingdom of Jerusalem, what practices the pope had in Italy; not, I warrant you, any whit at all careful in the affairs of the christian commonwealth, but studying and labouring what mischief and spite he might work against the emperor, whom of set purpose he had so occupied (partly for hate, and partly to enrich himself) in Asia and Jerusalem, so far out of Italy, ye may be sure. First, he caused the soldiers which the emperor sent for out of Germany to the maintenance of the holy wars, to be stayed as they passed through Italy, hindering them of their journey, and taking from them, and spoiling them of all such provision as they had. And not only this, but he sent secretly also his letters into Asia to those that were of his own faction; that is, to the patriarch of Jerusalem, and to the soldiers that kept the temple and the hospital, enticing and inciting them to rebel against the emperor; which thing Blondus himself, that popish parasite or historiographer, dissembleth not nor hideth. But furthermore, he

Henry III. A.D. 1229 to 1250.

persuaded the princes of the Saracens that they should make no league nor accept any truce with Frederic, neither deliver up to him the crown and kingdom of Jerusalem, which letters, as they were manifest testimonies of his treachery and treason towards him whom God had instituted and made his liege lord and sovereign, and mightiest potentate upon earth; so was it his will that he should come to the knowledge thereof, and that those letters should fall into his hands. And that he kept the same letters for the more credible testimony thereof, in the same his last epistle to the christian princes, he protesteth. The copy of which letters, amongst his other epistles, you shall have expressed.

The emperor withstandeth the secret treason which the pope had wrought against him at Jerusalem.

Neither were the pope's letters written to that leavened and factious sect in vain; for the patriarch and his collegioners, who took their name from the Temple, did mightily contend against Frederic. They raised a tumult in Ptolomaida against him; they accused him and his legates openly of treason; and did malapertly and boldly withstand the right worthy and good order he made amongst them. But as God would, by the help of the inhabitants of Pisa and the Genoese, and the Dutch soldiers, both their false accusations were refuted, and also their seditious purpose and tumult repressed. And this was the cause that when all other men rejoiced and were glad of the emperor's coronation, they, as wicked confederators, were heavy thereat, and were obtrectors of his worthy laud and fame.

The second treason of the pope against Frederic.

The pope, when he had thus conspired against Frederic, and had betrayed him to the public enemy of all christian men,—the Turk, could not dissemble this his mischievous act, nor content himself therewith, but would devise and practice yet another. For, by reason of those slanders (which a little before I mentioned) of the death and slaughter of his wife Joel, he incited John Brennus, his father-in-law, to make war against him, who caused the subjects of his empire to withdraw from him their allegiance, as also the inhabitants of Picenum, and those of Lombardy. And thus, joining themselves together, they craved further aid of the French king, whereby they made a great power. That done, they divided their host into two armies, invading with the one the empire, and with the other the proper territories and ditions belonging to the inheritance of Frederic; John Brennus and Pandulph Savellanus leading the one, as generals, into Campania and the kingdom of Naples; and the other, with John Columma, cardinal, his legate, and that Thomas, before convicted of treason, being his lieutenant, he sendeth into Picenum.

The pope's generals and leaders of his host.

Of this treason of the pope against Frederic doth also Matthew Paris make mention, during his wars in Asia, who, saith he, purposed to have deposed him, and to have placed "any other, he cared not whom (so that he were the child of peace and obedience), in his stead."[1] And for the more certainty thereof, the said Matthew Paris[2] repeateth the letter which a certain earl of Styria wrote unto him concerning the same, which letter hereunder ensueth word for word.

To the high and mighty prince, Frederic, by the grace of God, emperor of Rome, and ever Augustus, and most puissant king of Sicily, Thomas, earl of Actran, his faithful and trusty subject in all things, humble salutation. After

(1) "Alium quemlibet filium pacis et obedientiæ loco ejus subrogare." Matth. Paris
(2) Ibid. fol. 71.

your departure, most excellent prince, Gregory, the bishop of Rome, and public enemy to your magnificence, gathering together a great power and host of men by Johannes Brennus, late king of Jerusalem, and other stout captains, whom he hath made generals of the same his host, as a foreign enemy invading your dominions and the possessions of your highness' subjects, against the law of christianity, hath purposed and determined to vanquish and subdue you with the material or temporal sword, whom he cannot master and overcome with the spiritual sword, he saith. For the aforesaid John Brennus, gathering out of France and other provinces near adjoining a great army, giveth unto them of the treasure he hath gotten together (by what means I cannot tell) great wages, in hope to recover and get from you the empire. And furthermore, the same John and others, the captains of the see apostolical, invading your land, burn and destroy all as they go, driving away, and taking for their booties, all that they can come by, as well cattle as other things; and such as they take prisoners, they constrain, by afflicting them with grievous punishments, to ransom themselves for great sums of money; neither spare they man, woman, nor child, but take and keep your towns and castles, having no regard that you be in the service of Jesus Christ. And further, if any make mention of your majesty unto him, he saith, there is none other emperor but himself. Your friends and subjects, most excellent prince, much marvel hereupon; yea, and also the clergy themselves of the empire, do marvel with what conscience or upon what consideration the bishop of Rome can do the same, making such bloody wars and slaughter upon christian men; especially seeing that Christ commanded Peter, when he struck with the material sword, to put up the same into the scabbard, saying, "All that strike with the sword, shall perish with the sword;" or else, by what law he daily can excommunicate such as are pirates, burners of men's houses, and robbers, when he is the patron and maintainer of such himself: hereat they greatly muse and marvel. Wherefore, most mighty and renowned emperor, I beseech your highness to consider your own safety, for that the said John Brennus hath laid and fortified all the ports and havens with no small company of men and soldiers; that if (not knowing thereof) your grace should arrive in any of them, the same garrisons of his may apprehend and take you as a prisoner, which thing to chance, God forefend.

What meaning the pope had to send Frederic to fight against the Turk.

Thus, whilst the host of this hostile enemy the pope was encamped in the dominions of Frederic, he received the letters which Frederic by his legates sent into Europe, as you heard, whereby he understood the good success he had in Asia; who not only took no delectation at all therein, but was also in a vehement perturbation therewith. Whereby manifestly it may appear, what was the cause and meaning of the pope, that he was so solicitous and urgent to have Frederic the emperor, make a voyage into Asia. Doubtless even the same that Pelias had, when by his instigation he procured Jason, with all the chosen youth and flower of Greece, to sail into Colchis to fetch away the golden fleece; and that by the opportunity of his absence he might use, or rather abuse, his power and tyranny, and that Frederic might either be long afflicted and molested in the Asiatic war, or that he might perish and lose his life therein, was what he sought, and all that he desired.

The pope chafeth and fretteth at the prosperous success of the emperor.

And when he saw that fortune neither favoured his fetches, nor served his longing lust, he was as a man bereft of his wits, specially at these tidings of the prosperous success of the emperor. He tore and threw all his letters on the ground, and with all opprobrious words rebuked and reviled the legates for the emperor their master's sake; which thing also Blondus himself denieth not, though he writeth altogether in favour of the pope. And to the intent that he might cover this his rage and unbridled fury with some cloak and colour of justly deserved dolour, he feigned himself to be much

Henry III. A.D. 1229 to 1250.

displeased therewith, as though the emperor therein had only respected his own private commodity, not regarding the utility of the Christians; because the Saracens had license, although without armour and weapon, to repair unto the sepulchre of Christ, and had left for them somewhat near the same a hostelry or lodging place; "for which occasion," saith Blondus, "his lord pope rebuked the emperor's legates by the name of traitors and other like opprobrious words." Now go to, friend Blondus; by what strong arguments prove you and your lord pope, either that the peace which the emperor hath concluded was against the christian commonwealth, or that the emperor was a traitor? But who is it that seeth not these things, either by reading of old and ancient writers, or else partly by me who have gathered and collected the same out of divers monuments and histories, and plainly perceiveth not the conspiracies and treasons of your good lord the pope, so notable and filthy, as also his manifest shame and infamy? What? there be divers that write how the pope commanded these legates of Frederic to be put secretly out of the way, and also how he commanded divers soldiers, returning out of Asia, to be slain, to the intent that none should hear the report of that good news which was in Asia, nor any go thither to tell the fetches he had in hand at home. But I will make report of no more than of those things which all the writers, with most consent, agree upon. This is most certain, that the pope caused this rumour to be spread of the death and taking of the emperor upon this consideration, that he might allure unto him the fidelity of those cities in the kingdom of Naples, which yet kept their allegiance unto Frederic, of whom they should now hope for no longer refuge. And of that doth the emperor, in his epistle entitled 'Levate oculos,' greatly against him complain.

Blondus reproved, who wrote so greatly in the pope's favour.

The third practice of pope Gregory.

Great are these injuries of the pope against Frederic, and most wicked treasons. But herewith could not his cruel and tyrannical mind be contented, nor his lust satisfied, but it so far exceeded, as scarcely is it credible that it could: for he presumed not only to set variance between Henry (whom Frederic his father had caused to be made king of Germany) and him, but also by his allurements, he caused him to become an enemy to him. To whom when his father had assigned the duke of Boioria, named Louis, to be his overseer and counsellor, neither knew he amongst all the princes of Germany a man more faithful to him in his office and duty, or more virtuous, or more grave and apt to be in authority: Henry, fearing lest he should understand and know of these secret counsels, which he with his conspirators had in hand against his father, or that he should utter the same to him, or that he should go about to dissuade him from what he was purposed to do by authority of the court and senate of Rome, he put him out of office. And this was the fetch of all their policy, that together and at one instant, but in divers and sundry places far one from another, sharp and cruel war might be made against the emperor, so that his power being distract to the appeasing of variable contention, he might himself be the easier oppressed of a few.

Setteth the son against the father, as a good father of peace.

Henry Cæsar at the pope's enticement putteth from him his trusty counsellor.

When the emperor now understood what stir the pope kept in all his dominions in his absence, and that he had somewhat reformed and appeased the troubles which he secretly had wrought him in the kingdom of Jerusalem, thinking to prevent the pope's purpose in that he went about, and also to confirm the friendship towards him of them whom in his absence he found his trusty subjects; he left in Asia, Renaldus with his garrisons, commanding all the other bands to be under his appointment; and with all speed he came forth in certain gallies to Calabria. During the time of his being there, who unlooked for came thither, he assembled his power, and made with his friends all the speedy preparation that he might. From thence he went to Berletta, where he tarried twenty days, to whom came the duke of Spolitanum with all his garrisons; and so from thence with all his power he came into Apulia, and removed John Brennus, his father-in-law, from the siege of Calatia, and within a short time, by God's help, recovered again all his holds and dominions there. And from thence going into Campania, he winneth Beneventum, and as many other towns and holds as the pope had there, even almost to Rome, and so, after that, Umbria and Picena. And now, although the emperor, being moved thereunto upon good occasion and upon the pope's worthy desert, had gotten and recovered this so likely an entrance upon the pope's dominions, whereby he might have revenged him of all the injuries done to him; yet, notwithstanding, because he preferred nothing before the christian and public tranquillity, for the love of which he restrained his wrath, so vehemently urged and kindled, he sendeth unto him his legates to entreat a peace, declaring unto him, that if there were no other conceived grudge towards him than what he dissembled and pretended, he promiseth that he would make him a voluntary account of all things that ever he had done in his life, and that he would and was contented to submit himself unto the church; and also that for this cause he willingly offered unto him both duty and observance. Furthermore, to the entreating of this peace, and deciding of all controversies, he sent to the pope eight or ten of the noblest and chiefest about him who were princes and dukes of the empire; as Barthold, the patriarch of Aquileia, and his brother Otho, prince of Dalmatia and Istria, Eberhardus Juvanensis, Sigifridus, Reginoburgensis, Sibbotus Augustanus, a worthy prelate, Leopold of Austria and Styria, and Bernhardus, being all dukes; besides others of the nobility to accompany them.

The emperor returneth secretly out of Asia.

God prospereth Frederic in all his affairs.

But yet so great was the insolence and pride of the stubborn pope, that by no gentleness or beneficence he could of those princes be brought that year to the profitable concord of the church and Christian commonweal. O worthy head! that challengeth all authority to himself in the church of Christ, and in respect of his own wilful revenge, setteth nothing by the health and utility of all Christendom! Then, therefore, when nothing could be done in the matter, and the most part of these noblemen departed from Rome, the next year after, with much ado, a peace was made and concluded between them, by the help and industry of Leopold of Austria, Herman, captain of the Dutch soldiers, and the president of Messania. The pope then absolving the emperor Frederic of his excommunication, took therefore of him one hundred and twenty thousand ounces of gold, restoring to him again the titles both of his empire, and also of his kingdoms. Now, considering the uncourteous dealing of the

The pope refuseth peace with the emperor.

The price of the emperor's absolution.

Henry III. A.D. 1229 to 1250.

pope with Frederic the emperor herein, who can sufficiently muse and marvel at the shamelessness of Blondus, who hath the face to write, that the pope, notwithstanding, had dealt more gently and courteously with Frederic than was meet, or beseemed him to do? Who is it that doth not see his manifest flattery, coloured neither with reason, nor secret dissimulation? But much more truly and better writeth Cuspinian concerning this matter, who saith, that the pope doth occupy very profitable merchandize, who for so much money selleth what he received freely, paying nothing therefor, if he had received it of Christ indeed, as he saith he had.

And yet although the emperor Frederic concluded with the pope this unprofitable peace for himself, yet he performed those things that were agreed upon faithfully and diligently. But the pope, who thought it but a trifle to break his promise, would not stand to the conditions of that peace he made. For by the way, to pass over other things, neither had he restored, as he promised, the customs of the land of Sicily, neither yet the city Castellana, which he, before the peace concluded between them, did occupy and enjoy. And this Frederic in his epistles testifies, and also Fazellus in his eighth book, writing of the affairs of Sicily. Still, notwithstanding, Frederic, for the quietness and utility of the commonwealth, purposed with himself to bear and suffer these small injuries, and further studied all he could, as well by liberal gifts as otherwise, to have the pope to be to him a trusty friend. As when the Romans and others of the ecclesiastical number made war against the pope for certain possessions which he kept of theirs, he coming to him at Reate, and as one that tendered the unity of the church, and thinking to help the pope at his earnest request in these matters, sent his legates unto them, willing them to lay down their armour which against the pope they bare. And when that would not serve, at the pope's further request and desire, he levied an army against them at his own charge, and drave them from the siege of Viterbium; with other such like assured tokens of amity and friendship which he showed him; who, notwithstanding, as soon as the emperor was departed with a small company which he took with him into Sicily, leaving with him the greater part of his army for the maintenance of his wars, concluded a peace with the Romans unknown to the emperor, whom he had procured to travail and labour therein with great expenses; affirming, that without his will and commandment, the emperor had expelled them, and driven them out of the territories of Viterbium. And hereof doth Frederic also himself make mention in his second and third epistles, where he complaineth of the injuries of the pope towards him. Therefore greater commendation had Blondus deserved, if he had written of these treacheries of the pope, than (forgetting himself, as unto liars it often chanceth) in that he writeth both contrary to himself in the effect of this matter, and contrary to the verity of Frederic's story, which saith, that the Romans were incited to these tumults by his enticing and setting on. As though simple men of understanding could not, both by the offering of his son as a hostage, by the great preparation of the wars, and by the event especially of the thing itself, gather the contrary. But too, too impudent, will Blondus needs show himself.

What beneficence the emperor useth to have the pope's friendship, which he shall never get.

A well recompensed good turn of the pope to the emperor.

Whilst these things were done in Italy and Sicily, great rebellions were moved in Germany against the emperor by Henry Cæsar and Frederic of Austria, his sons being the chief authors thereof. For Henry, being disappointed and shaken off by his lord pope and other conspirators, by reason of the peace between his father and him, as ye heard, began now to make open challenge for the empire. And for that cause, as before is said, he put from him Louis, whom he knew to be unto the emperor, his father, so loving and assured a friend, who as willingly (perceiving and smelling what mischief he went about) forsook his court, and came to Boioria; who had not there remained a year, but was, as he walked abroad at a certain time, stabbed with a dagger by one Kelhemius, and presently died, his servants not being far from him, of whose death divers diversely write. Notwithstanding, the sequel doth show them to write most truly, who affirm the said striker to be suborned by Henry Cæsar, who coming unto him in the habit of a messenger, delivered unto him certain letters, which he feigned to be sent from the emperor; and whilst Louis was reading the same, he struck him with a dagger, and gave him his mortal wound, and with speed fled upon the same. After the death of Louis succeeded in that dukedom his son Otho, who, when solemnly, according to the manner of the Boiores, he should have been created, was also hindered by the same Henry Cæsar, who forbade the assembly of the magistrates and citizens the same. They, notwithstanding, neglecting his unjust restraint, created him; wherefore he first besieged Reginoburg, and, with another company, sacked, burnt, and wasted Boioria; with many more such great outrages and rebellions.

The emperor's sons rebel against their father.

Wicked murder by Henry Cæsar, for true and faithful service.

Outrage against the emperor his father.

When intelligence was brought of these things to the emperor, he sent his legates, and commanded that both the Cæsar, his son, and other princes of Germany who had assembled their armies, should break up and disperse the same; and because he saw and perceived now manifestly his son made so apparent rebellion against him, and fearing greater insurrections to ensue in Germany, he thought good to prevent the same with all expedition; wherefore he determined to go in all haste to Germany with his army, from whence he had now been absent fourteen years, and hereunto he maketh the pope privy. The pope promised the emperor hereupon, that he would write letters in his behalf to all the princes of Germany; but persuaded him to the uttermost of his power, that he should in no case go into Germany himself. For why? his conscience accused him that he had written to the nobles of Germany, even from the beginning of his papacy (for the hate and grudge he had against the emperor), that they should not suffer him, nor any of his heirs to enjoy the empire; and further, he had stirred them all up to rebel against him, and had moved Henry, the emperor's son, by his bribes and fair promises, to conspire against his father. And to conclude, he was the author and procurer of the conspiracy which the Lombards made then against him; and fearing lest these things should come now to the emperor's ear, he was greatly troubled and careful. But the emperor not thinking it good at so needful a time to be absent, he (all doubt set apart) with his second son Conrad, went speedily into Germany. Assembling there a council in the city of Nuremburg, Henry Cæsar, his son, after his conspiracy was manifestly detected, which he had in

The emperor fourteen years out of Germany.

The pope feareth that his treason should be spied by the emperor.

Henry Cæsar condemned of treason, and dieth in prison.

Henry III

A.D. 1229 to 1250.

practice with the Longobards (whereof the pope was chief author), was by judgment and sentence of seventy princes condemned of high treason, and being commanded by his father to be bound, was as prisoner brought to Apulia, where not long after (A.D. 1242) he died in prison; in whose stead the emperor ordained Conrad, his second son, Cæsar, by consent of all the peers and princes. Furthermore, by public commandment he renounced Frederic of Austria for his son, and caused him to be proclaimed an enemy to the public weal. And further, when he saw that punishment would neither cause him to remember himself, nor to acknowledge his abuse, the emperor, with a great army, accompanied by divers of the noblemen of Germany, took from him all Austria and Styria, and brought them again under his own obedience and fidelity.

Frederic of Austria proclaimed an open enemy to his father, and disherited.

The same year the emperor married his third wife, named Isabel, the daughter of king John of England. Then, when he had set Germany in a stay and quietness, he left there Conrad Cæsar, his son; and with his host returneth again into Italy, there to punish such as with Henry, his eldest son, had conspired against him; whose treasons were all detected at the condemnation of Henry Cæsar, his son, chiefly set on by the pope. When the pope had understanding that the emperor with warlike furniture marched toward Italy, although he feigned himself reconciled, and to be a friend to Frederic, yet was he, notwithstanding, to him a most secret and infestive enemy; and, understanding that he brought with him such a power both of horsemen and footmen to do execution on such as he understood had been conspirators against him in the late tumult and rebellion, those who were faulty herein and guilty, and all others who took their parts, he admonished to join themselves together, and that they should furnish strongly their cities with garrisons, that they should send for aid to their friends, and that, with all the force they were able, they should prepare them for the war. The rest of the cities also in Italy, whether they were the emperor's or his own, he endeavoureth to make them all his, and proper to himself.

The emperor marrieth king John's daughter of England.

The pope again beginneth to play his part.

Furthermore, unto the emperor the pope sendeth his ambassadors; to whom, under the pretence of nourishing a peace, he had given secret commandment that they should interdict him and his host, as soon as he came within the borders of Italy; to the preservation of which peace, saith he, he had but lately promulgated a subsidy to be gathered among the Christians, when he began the holy war. And also to say, not by way of entreaty, but commandingly, that what cause of controversy he had with the Longobards, the same he should commit to him, and stand to his arbitrement. Whereunto the emperor replying maketh the legate this answer:—

"Shortly after," saith he, "the peace was made between the pope and me, he called me for a chief defence both of the church and himself, against the Romans who made war with him; and at his request, with mine own proper charge I maintained that war, and gave his enemies the overthrow." And further he said, that he should not do well, through the pretence of peace, to be a hindrance to him from that which both by law and right he might and ought to do; but rather he ought to dispose himself, with force to restrain and expel those who gathered them together as rebels, thinking to exclude themselves from the subjection both of him and the empire; and that such rebels, as both had restrained the soldiers whom the emperor sent for when he was in Asia, and divers others also whom for necessary causes he had called to him, whom they had so wickedly dealt with and abused, he (as they had deserved) should rather desire to see punished and reformed, than to maintain them (under colour of peace), being such wicked and manifest evil doers. And touching that he demandeth of him, that he should commit and defer so great a cause, wherein the wealth and safety of the empire consisteth, to his arbitrement, by him to be determined, without either assignment of any time when, or adding thereunto any condition or exception for not doing the same, neither the diminishing and impairing the dignity and regality of his empire considered, he could not but marvel; seeing that neither it appertained to his calling and faculty, nor to the benefit or commodity of the empire. To this effect also writeth Frederic in his last epistle to the pope; the effect whereof amongst other epistles you may read.

Secret conspiracy of the pope against the emperor. And in the same letters of his he showeth, that when the emperor at a certain time had been with the pope, at his going away he requested, that when he came again, he would come into Italy only with his household-band and family; for that if he should come as before he did accustom with his army, he should terrify them overmuch; "amongst whom," saith he, "you may assure yourself to be in great safety, and find all things in rest and quiet;" when quite contrary, as the emperor for a certainty had tried, he had there all things ready and prepared for his destruction; so that when he pretended unto him the greatest friendship, he was busiest in conspiring his death. The certain time when the pope had this exercise in hand against the emperor, I cannot search out, neither may it be in his epistles undated easily found out; but that no man need to doubt of the certainty thereof, I have referred you to the emperor's epistle, where he maketh mention of the same.

The emperor marcheth into Italy, notwithstanding the pope's forbidding. The emperor then, as he had determined, prosecuted his purpose and marched into Italy, where he brought under his subjection those cities that against him rebelled, as Mantua, Verona, Ternisium, Patavium, and others. And then he afterwards set upon the great host of the Mediolanenses, the Brixians, the Placentines, and other confederators, unto whom the pope's legate, Georgius Longomontanus, had joined himself, from whom he took one thousand prisoners, and also, their general, being the chief magistrate in the city of Mediolanum, and Petrus Tenopolus, the duke's son of Venice; and slew divers captains more, and took all their ensigns. And in this battle, especially at the recovering of Marchia and Ternissana, he used the friendly aid of Actiolinus. A.D. 1239.

The emperor loth to break the peace. The pope, now somewhat dismayed at this overthrow of his confederates and mates, though not much, yet somewhat began to fear the emperor; and whereas before, that which he did he wrought secretly and by others, now he goeth to work with might and main to subdue and deprive the emperor. And although the emperor saw and perceived what inward hate and mortal malice he bare towards him, not only in that he so apertly stood with his conspirators against him, but also that on every side he heard, and from all parts was

Henry III. A. D. 1239 to 1250. brought him certain word how greatly he laboured against him, as with opprobrious words, naughty reports and slanders, to the intent to pull from him the hearts and fidelity of his subjects, and make those that were his friends his enemies; neither that he meant at any time to take up and cease from such evil and wicked practices: yet, notwithstanding, that there should be no default in him found for the breach of the league and peace between them a little before concluded, he sendeth four legates to the bishop of Rome, who should answer unto and refute those iniquitous objections which he laid unto him, as also make him privy unto his purpose, and what he meant to do, thereby to declare his innocency towards him, in such causes, and his simplicity.

The pope refuseth to speak with the emperor's legate. The bishop, when he understood these ambassadors to be not far off from Rome, and knew the cause of their coming, thinking with himself, that in hearing the excuse and reasonable answer of the emperor, perhaps he might be provoked to desist from his purpose, and so degenerate from others of his predecessors, he refuseth to speak with them; and at the day appointed pronounceth the sentence of proscription against him, depriving him of all his dignities, honours, titles, prerogatives, kingdoms, and whole empire. And, that the pope had no occasion hereunto, as well Pandulph and Colonucius, as the letters of the emperor himself, do both right well declare; for it may appear he dedicated as it were himself to his utter ruin and destruction, when he did solicit against Frederic, Jacobus Tenopolus, the Venetian duke, whom, for the displeasure he took with the emperor in the imprisoning of his son, he was in good hope he should allure unto him, he being in that so troublous time such a comforter and aider unto him, that, as Blondus writeth in a certain epistle gratulatory, he calleth him lord of the fourth part of Croatia and Dalmatia, and lord of half the Roman empire; and calling unto him the Venetian and Genoese legates, he made a peace betwixt them, Hireth galleys to spoil the coasts of the emperor. who for certain causes about their sea-coasts were at variance, and covenanted with them upon this condition, that at their public charges they should rig and man five and thirty galleys, which should spoil and burn all along the sea-coasts of the kingdoms and dominions of Frederic.

Edict against the emperor. But the pope, when he saw the good will and fidelity which the duke of Venice bare unto the emperor, and saw also what aid the emperor had of him, neither that he was like to win him to his purpose, then had he recourse again to his old crafty practices and subtleties. And further, he devised to put forth an edict at Rome to the universal church and people, the beginning whereof is, "Ascendit de mari bellica bestia;" wherein he declareth the causes wherefore he curseth and giveth the emperor to the devil of hell, and hath dejected him from all his princely dignity. He in the same accuseth him of so many and so huge a heap of mischiefs, as to nominate them my heart detesteth. And, besides that, he restraineth his sovereign lord and emperor of the appellation which every private man by law may have. He slandereth him with charges of treason, perjury, cruelty, sacrilege, killing of his kindred, and all impiety; he accuseth him as a heretic, a schismatic, and a miscreant; and, to be brief, what mischief soever the pope can devise, with that doth he

Henry III.

A.D. 1239 to 1250.

charge him and burden him. "All this doth he," saith the pope, "that when he hath brought our holiness and all the ecclesiastical estate to beggary, he might scoff at, and deride the religion of Christ, which as a miscreant he detesteth." And now, because the pope had a great and special trust in Albertus Behavus, of the noble house called Equestri (as crafty an apostle as the best), as one whom he saw ready to lean to his lust, to him the pope delivered two other mandates in several letters sealed, in which he commanded all bishops, prelates, and others of the clergy, that they should solemnly recite the same in their churches instead of their sermon, that by his decree he had excommunicated Frederic out of the fellowship of christian men, put him from the procuration or government of the empire, and that he had released all his subjects from their allegiance and fidelity towards him. And furthermore he chargeth them and all other christian men, under pain of cursing and damnation, that they neither succour the emperor, nor yet so much as wish him well. Thus he, being the pope's special and trusty servitor, and made to his hand, caused a most horrible confusion and chaos of public unquietness, as shall hereafter appear.

Threateneth to curse those that wish well to the emperor.

Amongst all the noblemen of Germany at that time, was Otho, the governor of the Rhine and duke of Boiora, towards the emperor both most serviceable, and also a prince of great honour, riches, and estimation. This prince both with fair promises and also rewards, he enticed from him; for that he was made by him to believe, that Louis, his father, of whom we spake before, was by the emperor murdered and slain. And the same Otho again caused three other princes and dukes to revolt from the emperor to the pope, who were neighbours, and nearly adjoining unto him: Uvenceslaus and Belus, princes of the Hungarians, and Henry, duke of Polonia. To whom came also Frederic, of Austria, his son, who, because he was proscribed or outlawed by the emperor his father, and had his dukedom wasted and burned, as you heard, was easily won to the pope. These, gathering a council (when they had thought to have translated the empire unto the king's son of Denmark), desired to have the pope's legates sent from him, to the effect of that election.

Divers princes of Germany, by the pope's means, forsake the emperor.

The emperor was at Patavium when news was brought to him of what the pope had done at Rome. He therefore commanded Peter of Venice, his secretary (on Easter-day), to make a narration to the people of his great and liberal munificence to the bishops and church of Rome, and again, of the injuries done by them towards him, in recompense thereof; of his innocency also in that whereof he had accused him, and of the unseemliness of such an act or deed, of the right use of the ecclesiastical censure, and of the errors and abuses of the church of Rome. By which oration of his, he so removed the cloud from many men's hearts of blind superstition, and the conceived opinion of holiness of the church of Rome, and bishops of the same, and also of their usurped power and subtle persuasion, that they both plainly saw and perceived the vices and filthiness of the church of Rome, and of the bishops of that see, as also their fraudulent deceits, and flagitious doings, most vehemently lamenting and complaining of the same. Albert maketh mention of certain verses which were sent and written between the bishop of Rome and

What good the oration of Peter of Venice did for the emperor.

Henry III.

A.D. 1239 to 1250.

the emperor, which verses in the latter end of this present history of Frederic you shall find.

The emperor, moreover, both by his letters and legates, giveth intelligence unto all christian kings, to the princes of his own empire, to the college of cardinals, and to the people of Rome; as well of the feigned crimes wherewith he was charged, as also of the cruelty of the bishop of Rome against him. The copy of which letter or epistle here follows.

The Emperor to the Prelates of the World, to bridle the Pope, and restrain him of his will.

In the beginning and creation of the world, the inestimable foreknowledge and providence of God (who asketh counsel of none) created in the firmament of heaven two lights, a greater and a less; the greater he created to govern the day, and the less to govern the night: which two do their proper offices and duties in the zodiac, so that although oftentimes the one be in an oblique aspect unto the other, yet the one is not an enemy to the other; but rather doth the superior communicate his light with the inferior. Even so the same eternal foreknowledge hath appointed upon the earth two regiments, that is to say, priesthood and kingly power; the one for knowledge and wisdom, the other for defence; that man, who is made of two parts (over-wanton and dissolute), might have two reins to govern and bridle him withal, that peace, thereby, and love might dwell upon the face of the earth. But, alas! the bishop of Rome, sitting in the chair of perverse doctrine or pestilence, that pharisee anointed with the oil of iniquity above the rest of his consorts in this our time, who for his abominable pride is fallen from heaven, endeavoureth with his power to destroy and undo all, and thinketh, I believe, to stellify again himself there, from whence he fell. His purpose is to darken and to shadow the light of our unspotted life, whilst that (altering the verity into lies) his papal letters, stuffed with all untruths, are sent into sundry parts of the world; by his own corrupt humour, and upon no reasonable cause, blemishing the sincerity of our religion. The lord pope hath compared us unto the beast rising out of the sea, full of names of blasphemy, and spotted like a leopard. But we say, that he is that monstrous beast of whom it is said, and of whom we thus read: "And there shall come another red horse out of the sea, and he that shall sit on him shall take peace away out of the earth: let them therefore that dwell upon the earth destroy him." For, since the time of his promotion, he hath not been the father of mercy, but of discord; a diligent steward of desolation, instead of consolation, and hath enticed all the world to commit offence. And, to take the words in right sense and interpretation, he is that great dragon that hath deceived the whole world; he is that Antichrist, of whom he hath called us the forerunner; he is that other Balaam hired for money to curse us; the prince of darkness, who hath abused the prophets. This is the angel leaping out of the sea, having his vials filled with bitterness, that he may both hurt the sea and the land; the counterfeit vicar of Christ, that setteth forth his own imaginations. He saith, that we do not rightly believe in the Christian faith, and that the world is deceived with three manners of deceivers, whom to name, God forbid we should open our mouth; seeing that openly we confess only Jesus Christ, our Lord and Saviour, to be the everlasting Son of God, coequal with his Father and the Holy Ghost, begotten before all worlds, and in process of time sent down upon the earth for the salvation of mankind; conceived, not by the seed of man, but by the Holy Ghost; who was born of the glorious Virgin Mary, and after that suffered and died, as touching the flesh; and by his godhead, the third day, he raised from death that other nature which he assumed in the womb of his mother. But we have learned that the body of Mahomet hangeth in the air, and his soul is buried in hell: whose works are damnable and contrary to the law of the Most High. We affirm also, that Moses was the faithful servant of God, and a true teacher of the law; and that he talked with God in Mount Sinai, unto whom the Lord said at the bush; [Exod. iii. 4.] "I am the God of thy father, the God of Abraham," &c.; by whom also God wrought miracles in Egypt, and delivered the law written to the Israelites; and that, afterwards,

Man being made of two parts hath two several regiments; God's word, and the material sword.

Apology of the emperor to the pope's edict, beginning "Ascendit de mari," &c.

Antichrist long ago descried to the world by the emperor.

Confession of the emperor's faith, whereof he was accused by the pope.

with the elect, he was called to glory. In these and other things our enemy and envier of our state, causing our mother, the church, to accuse her son, hath written against us venomous and lying slander, and sent the same to the whole world.' If he had rightly understood the apostle's meaning, he would not have preferred his violent will, which beareth such sway with him, before reason; neither would he have sent out his mandates at the suggestion of those who call light darkness, and evil good; who suspect honey to be gall, for the great good opinion they had conceived of that holy place, which indeed is both weak and infirm, and converteth all truth into falsehood, and affirmeth that to be, which is not.

The pope, under pretence of his holiness, deceiveth simple souls and ignorant men.

Truly my opinion, so indifferent on every side, ought not in any case to be infringed and averted from the faith, to such enemies of so corrupt a conscience. Wherefore we greatly are enforced not a little to marvel, which thing also doth much disquiet us to see; that you, who are the pillars and assistants in office of righteous dealing, the senators of Peter's city, and the principal beams in God's building, have not qualified the perturbation of so fierce a judge; as do the planets of heaven in their kind, which, to mitigate the passing swift course of the great orb or sphere of heaven, draw a contrary way by their opposite movings. In very deed, our imperial felicity hath been, almost even from the beginning, spurned against, and envied at by the papal see and dignity: as Simonides, being demanded why he had no more enemies and enviers of his state, answered and said, "Quia nihil feliciter gessi:" "because," saith he, "I have had no good success in any thing, that ever I took in hand." And so, for that we have had prosperous success in all our enterprises, for which the Lord's name be blessed (especially in the overthrow, of late, of our rebellious enemies, the Lombards, to whom, in their good quarrel, he promised life and absolution, with remission of their sins), is the cause wherefore this apostolical bishop mourneth and lamenteth. And now not by your counsels, I suppose, he laboureth to impugn this our felicity, but out of his own power of binding and loosing, whereof he glorieth so much, he impugneth it. But, presently, where power and ability are wanting to redress, there doth abuse take place. We see him, who was so mighty a king, and the worthiest prince amongst all the prophets, desire and crave the restitution of God's holy spirit, when he had polluted the dignity of his office. But the proverb is, "Uti indissolubilia non solvuntur, ita inligabilia non ligantur:" "As things indissoluble are not to be loosed, so things that cannot be bound, are not to be bound;" which thing is manifestly proved in him. For why? the Scriptures of God do instruct men how to live, they mortify our souls which are immortal, and quicken the same which are dead for want of life. And, doubtless, he is able to humble and bring down those that are unworthy of dignity, as much as him pleaseth, and when him pleaseth. Doubtless if the bishop of Rome were a true bishop indeed, innocent, unpolluted, and not associated with wicked livers and evil men, his life should declare him so to be. He would not then be an offerer of dissentious sacrifice, but a peaceable offerer of love and charity, and would cense, not with the incense of grief and hatred, but with the sweet smelling incense of concord and unity, neither yet would alter "Suum pontificium in maleficium:" that is, "make of a sanctified office an execrable abuse." If he were such a bishop as he ought to be, he would not wrest or abuse the preaching of the word to the fruit and gain of his own dissension, neither should we be accused for being such an enemy of our mother, the true church, as is laid unto her son's charge by such a bishop. Which true and mother church, with all reverence, we honour, and benignity embrace, so beautified and adorned with God's holy sacraments. Some singular persons, notwithstanding, feigning themselves to be our brethren by that mother, and who yet are not, but are unlawfully begotten; such, I say, as are subjects and slaves to corruptible things (putting them from amongst us) we utterly reject: especially for that injuries by them done are not only transitory and mundane, wherewith our majesty is so molested, vexed and grieved. Wherefore we cannot so easily mitigate our mood, neither ought we, in very deed, so to do, and therefore are we enforced the more to take the greater revenge of them. You, therefore, that are men of grave and deliberate counsel, having the excellent gift (as from God) of wisdom and understanding; refuse you that roaring enemy of ours in these his proceedings, whose beginnings are so wicked and detestable, wisely comparing things past

The answer of Simonides applied.

The emperor prophesieth of the pope's fall.

Utterly rejecteth the pope and church of Rome.

Henry III.

A.D. 1239 to 1250.

with those to come. Otherwise, you that are under our subjection, as well of our empire, as our other dominions, shall feel and perceive (both of my chief enemy and persecutor, as also of the princes that are his fautors and adherents) what revenge by sword Frederic Augustus shall take upon them, God so permitting.

Calleth a parliament or council to express the pope's malice.

This done, he commands, by proclamation, a solemn parliament or council of all the princes, and other nobility of the empire, at Ægra; whither came Conrad Cæsar, Moguntine the Presul, the Saxon dukes, the lords of Brandenburgh, Misna, Thuringia, and the legates of all the nobles of Brabant, to aid the emperor. But the princes Boiemus and Palatinus, being dissuaded by the legates, unto whom the Austrians had joined themselves, refused to come to the council holden at Ægra; and being at their wits' end, not knowing well what they might do, they at last forsook the emperor, and took part with the pope and the other conspirators. Then Frederic of Austria, the emperor's second son (whom he disinherited as ye heard), by the aid of the Boiors, and Bohemians, recovered again the dukedoms of Austria and Styaia, putting to flight and discomfiting the emperor's bands and garrisons which he had there. And although the cardinals (especially that honest man, Albertus Boiemus,) had allured to the pope, Otho the duke of Boiora, as ye heard, and divers other noblemen of Germany; yet, notwithstanding, certain bishops in Boiora, as Eberhardus Juvanensis, and Sigrefridus Reginoburgensis, being at that time the emperor's chancellor, Rudicenus Ratheviensis, Conradus Frisingensis, and others, left not, nor yet forsook the emperor. All these the aforesaid Albert not only did excommunicate, but also, by process, sought to bring them up to Rome before the pope, giving commandment to their collegioners and cloisterers, that they should deprive them of their offices, and choose such others in their stead as would obey the pope. All which things the pope, understanding by Albert, and of this their fidelity to the emperor, corroborated and confirmed the same, commanding them to choose other bishops in their stead.

Bishops of Germany are obedient to their prince.

But the bishops and prelates, with one consent contemning the pope's mandates and writs, and also the curses and threatenings of Albert, accused, reproved, and greatly blamed his temerity, and also tyranny which he usurped against the churches of Germany, and especially against the good emperor; that, without his consent, he durst be so bold as to meddle in churches committed to the emperor's government against the old and ancient customs; and that he had excommunicated the emperor without just cause; that he had condemned the emperor's faithful subjects as enemies to the church, for standing with their liege and sovereign prince (which allegiance they might not violate without horrible iniquity), and so had sought to disquiet them likewise in their charges and administrations; and had also in that quarrel given such defiance to the emperor. They accused and condemned the same Albert also, for a most impudent impostor and wicked varlet, and for a most pestiferous botch and sore of the christian commonweal; and they do give him to the devil as a ruinous enemy, as well of the church, as of his own natural country; and further, think him worthy to have his reward with the rest of the pope's pursuivants, being the most wicked inventors and devisers of

Bishops of Germany excommunicate the pope's legate and cardinal.

mischief that were in all Germany. This done, they make relation hereof to the emperor by their letters; and further, they advertise all the princes of Germany (especially those who were of the pope's faction or rebellion, and were the favourers of Albert), that they should take heed, and beware in any case of his subtle deceits, and pernicious deceivable allurements, and that they should not assist the pope, for all his words, against the emperor. And doubtless, by the counsel of the high prelate or archbishop of Boiora, whose name was Juvanensis, and by his industry and persuasion, Frederic of Austria was again reconciled to the emperor, his father; from whose aid and obedience after that, by no promises, threatenings, bribes, nor pains, no, nor for the execrable curses of the pope's own holy mouth, he would be induced or removed. But Albert prosecuteth still his purposed mischief, alluring and inciting by all means possible (and that not amongst the worst but the best), friends to the pope, and enemies to the emperor. Unto some he gave their tithes to fight against the emperor, to others he gave the glebe-lands of benefices, and to others he gave the spoil of such colleges and monasteries as took not part with the pope; and to some others also he gave the colleges and monasteries themselves. And assuredly I find by Johannes Aventinus,[1] that there were certain of the pope's own birds, who had their ecclesiastical tithes taken from them; and others who had the rents and revenues of their colleges plucked away by force, to the maintenance of the pope's quarrel against the emperor. Hereby was there a window opened to do what they listed, every man according to his ravening and detestable lust, and all things lay open unto their greedy and insatiable desires. Who listeth to hear more hereof, let him read Aventinus, in his book before noted, and there shall he see what vastation grew thereby to the whole state of Germany, who largely treateth of the same.

Juvanensis, the bishop, a true subject to his prince.

The pope's means used to maintain the war against his lord and master.

While these things were thus working in Germany, Frederic, leaving in Lombardy Actiolinus, with a great part of his host, he (passing, with the rest, by the Apennines) came to Etruria, and settled the same, after that he had allayed certain insurrections there; and from thence he came to Pisa, where he was with great amity and honour received and welcomed. This city was always assured and faithful to the emperors of Germany. The pope, hearing of the emperor's coming into Etruria, and knowing what power the emperor had also left in Lombardy, with a great army besieged the city Ferraria, that always loved the emperor full well; which city, when the pope's legate had assaulted sharply for the space of five months, and could not win the same, he devised with himself to send for Salingwerra out of the town by way of a parley, promising his faith and truth to him for his safe return; who, by the persuasion of Hugo Rambartus, that said without peril he might do the same (being but by way of parley), was coming to the legate; but he, preventing him in his journey, took him prisoner, contrary to his truth and fidelity. And thus gat he Ferraria, and delivered the keeping thereof to Azones Astensis. And that the pope's legate thus falsified his truth, and circumvented the captain and old man

Besiegeth Ferraria.

Fidelity of papists learned by this base example.

(1) Lib. 7. Annalium Boiorum.

Henry III.

A.D. 1239 to 1250.

Salingwerra, the same is confessed of the pope's friendly historiographers, to be but a stratagem or warlike policy. But to return again. About the same time also the Venetian navy, at the Mount Garganum, chased twelve gallies of the emperor's, which were appointed to the keeping of that coast, and spoiled, burned, and wasted all the region; and, further, took one of the emperor's great ships, being driven by tempest and weather into the haven Sipontinum, fraught with men and munition.

The emperor's galley taken by the pope.

Frederic again getting on his side the Lucenses, the Volaterans, the Genenses, the Aretines, and divers cities besides in Etruria, to help that country, came to Pisa and Viterbium, which took part with him. Some say, that the names and factions of Ghibellines and Guelphs sprang from Frederic, that, by them, he might spy and know, having recourse to all the towns and cities in Italy, which took part with and favoured the pope, and which, the emperor; and he called the one by the name of Ghibellines, and the other by the name of Guelphs. But because both Blondus and Platina, and some others, bring no sufficient proof thereof, but only slender conjecture, I rather cleave to the opinion of Nauclerus, Hermanus, Antoninus, Florentinus, and such other writers, who say, that these Guelphs and Ghibellines, in Italy, took their beginning of Conrad III., Frederic, his great uncle, being emperor; and that these Guelphs were dedicated to the pope by Guelph, the younger brother of Henry the Proud; and that those who were called the Ghibellines were appointed, either by Conrad himself, or else by his son, being brought up in the lordship of Vaiblingen. But to our purpose.

The Ghibellines and Guelphs.

The pope, when he understood that Frederic was come to Viterbium, was very heavy; for he feared he would come to Rome, the good will of which city the pope much mistrusted. He therefore caused a supplication to be drawn, portraying, about the same, the heads of Peter and Paul; and with a sharp and contumelious oration he much defaced the emperor; promising them everlasting life, and giving the badge of the cross to as many as would arm themselves, and fight against the emperor, as against the most wicked enemy of God and the church. Now when the emperor, marching somewhat near to Rome's gates, beheld those whom the pope had, with his goodly spectacle of St. Peter and St. Paul, and with his alluring oration, stirred up and marked with the badge of the cross to come forth in battle against him; disdaining to be accounted as the enemy of the church, who had been thereunto so beneficial, giving a fierce charge upon them, he put them soon to flight; and as many as the emperor took (cutting off that badge from them), he caused to be hanged. From thence marching into Campania, and his own kingdoms, he levied a great mass of money, and mustered new bands, and augmented his army; and in these bands he retained the Saracens also. And to the intent he might find the Saracens the more trusty to him, he appointed them to inhabit in a city named Luceria. For which thing, although the papistical writers do greatly blame and opprobriously write of Frederic, yet, notwithstanding, Nicholaus Machiavellus doth write, that for this cause he retained them,—lest, through the pope's execrable curses,

The pope afraid of the emperor's coming into Italy

The emperor hangeth all the crossed soldiers.

Retaineth the Saracens in his wars against the pope.

he should be quite destitute of soldiers, as was Frederic Barbarossa, his grandfather, a little before, when he was excommunicated by Alexander, the pope, as ye have heard.

After this, when the emperor had greatly afflicted by battle the pope's ecclesiastical consorts, such as conspired with the pope against him, and had wasted and destroyed Beneventum, the Mount Cascenum and Sora, because they took part with the pope against him; Frederic, when he had manned the city of Aquila, marched forth with a great host both of horsemen and footmen to Picenum, that he might vanquish his enemies in Italy; and, by the way, he besieged the strong town of war, named Asculnum, which was also converted to the pope's faction and rebellion. He there, having understanding of what the pope's assistants had done with the princes electors, and other princes of Germany, especially with Wenceslaus, king of Bohemia, and Otho Palatine, writeth his letters unto them. In these he first showed, how those contumelies and spiteful words, which the pope blustered out against him, are lighted upon himself, and how the bishops of Rome have taken to them of late such heart of grace, and are become so lofty, that not only they seek to bring emperors, kings, and princes, under their obedience, but also seek how to be honoured as gods; and say that they cannot err, neither yet be subject or bound to any religion; and that it is lawful for them to do all things they list; neither that any account is to be sought or demanded of their doings, or else to be made of them to any; so impudent are they in these their affirmations. And further, as princes, they command (and that under pain of cursing), that men believe every thing they say, how great a lie soever it be; insomuch that, by this covetousness of his, all things go backward, and the whole state of the commonweal is subverted, neither can there any enemy be found more hurtful or perilous to the church of God than he. He wrote unto them, furthermore, that he (to whom the greatest charge and dignity was in the whole commonweal appointed and committed), seeing and perceiving to his great peril, their good hearts, wills, and practices towards him, would, with all the power and ability that God had given him, do his endeavour, that he who, in the likeness of the shepherd of the flock, and the servant of Christ, and chief prelate in the church, showeth himself so very a wolf, persecutor, and tyrant, may be removed from that place, and that a true and careful shepherd of God's flock may be appointed in the church. Wherefore he exhorteth them, that if they desire the safety and preservation of the whole state of the commonweal and empire, they be unto him no hinderers, but furtherers of his purpose and proceedings; lest, otherwise, they also should happen to fall into the same snare of servitude with the bishop of Rome. And further, he gave them to know, that if the pope should aspire to that he sought for (that is, to be an emperor and king over kings), yet should that be no stay of his insatiable desire, but he would be as greedy and ravenous as now he is; therefore, if they be wise, they should withstand him betimes, lest hereafter, when they would, it should be too late, neither should they be able to withstand his tyranny.—The effect of this epistle I took out of Aventinus, who more largely dilateth it,

The effect of a letter sent by the emperor to the princes of Germany.

No enemy more hurtful to the church of God than the pope.

The emperor voweth to remove the pope, and put in another more careful shepherd.

Henry III.

A.D. 1239 to 1250.

and also writeth that the emperor (by his legates) sent the same to Wenceslaus.

Boiemus relenteth at the emperor's letter. Otho and the pope against the emperor.

Boiemus, somewhat relenting at this letter, promiseth to accomplish the emperor's biddings and precepts, and forthwith gathereth the assembly of princes and nobles at Ægra; where, by common consent, they think to renovate with the emperor a new league and covenant. And furthermore, they find Otho Boius (who was absent, and would not be at this their assembly) to be the author of this defection, and an enemy to the commonweal. Otho then, seeing himself not able to stand against Cæsar and the other princes with whom he was associated, desiring aid of the pope by his letters, came with all speed to Boiemus, his kinsman; whom, when he could not persuade unto him again, neither would he to their parts also be won, he obtaineth, notwithstanding, thus much at their hands: that the league and covenant which they were in hand to make with the emperor, might for a time be deferred, and that another assembly might be made, whereat he also would be, and join himself with them. Thus had they, who killed, as you heard, his father, bewitched also his son, and brought him to be both a rebel and a traitor. In the mean season, the pope sent his rescript unto the king of Bohemia and to Otho, tending to this effect; that in no case they should either forsake him or the church, to take the emperor's part. And so much prevailed he by the means of Bohuslaus and Budislaus, who were the chief of the senate regal, and by his fair promises and bribes to such as he before had made towards him, that again at Libussa, by Boiemus and Boius, new assemblies were gathered for the creation of a new emperor, in spite of Augustus the emperor, and Cæsar, his son. And while this was thus in hand, Conrad Cæsar casteth Landshuta, the wife of Otho, then absent, in the teeth, for great benefits and possessions which her husband had, and possessed by his ancestors; and that unless her husband took a better way with himself, and showed his obedience to the emperor, his father, he should not enjoy one foot of that land which now he had by his predecessors. The promotion and dignities which Otho had by the ancestors of Conrad Cæsar came thus: Frederic Barbarossa, A.D. 1180, at a parliament holden at Reginoburg, condemned Henry Leo of high treason, and deprived him of his dominions of Boiora and Saxony, and gave Boiora to Otho Wiltaspachius, because he had done him such faithful service in his Italian wars. After that, Louis, the son of this Otho, obtained of this emperor Frederic II., in recompense of his assured and trusty fidelity, the dition of 'Palatinatum Rheni,' so called; who gave also Agnes, the daughter of Henry, earl of Palatine, to Otho, his son, in marriage. This Henry was the son of Henry Leo, the traitor, unto whom Henry VI., the father of Frederic, gave in marriage Clementia, the daughter of his brother Conrad, Palatine of the Rhine, and gave him the keeping of the palace of the same. And as touching the inheritance of Boiora, he had also now long possessed that, by the heirs of Otho Wiltespachius. But to our purpose again.

By what means Otho attained so great possession by the emperor and his ancestors.

The governor of Agrippina revolteth to the pope.

At the same time, also, the governor of Colonia Agrippina revolted to the pope; who, not long after, in a skirmish between Brabantinus and him, was vanquished and taken prisoner. And doubtless, Frederic of Austria, after he was received into favour again with the emperor (keeping most constantly his promise and fidelity renewed), during this time made sharp war upon the Hungarians, who took part with the pope, and greatly annoyed them. As these things thus passed in Germany, the emperor, when he had gotten Ascalum, and led his host into Flaminia, having Ravenna at his command, from thence came to Faventia, which city never loved the emperor (the circuit of whose walls is five miles in compass), and pitched his camp round about it. Although the siege was much hindered by austerity of the time and weather (it being in the very dead of winter) still, notwithstanding, through his great fortitude and courage, so animating his soldiers in the painfulness of the laborious siege, he endured out the same, who thought it no little shame, having once made that enterprise, to come from thence without any assault given. And therefore, when now the winter (so extremely cold and hard) was nearly ended, and the spring-time hard at hand, and when, by long battery, he had made the same in divers places assaultable, the citizens (being greatly discouraged, and in no hope of the defence thereof) sent their legates to the emperor, craving pardon for their offence, and that he would grant them their lives, and so yielded themselves to his mercy.

The emperor's great lenity and clemency.

The emperor, having against them good and sufficient cause of revenge, yet because his noble heart thought it to be the best revenge that might be, to pardon the offence of vanquished men, considered it better to grant them their requests, and to save the city and citizens, with innumerable people, than by arms to make the same his soldiers' prey, to the destruction both of the city and great number of people therein. So doth this good emperor in one of his epistles, "Adacta nobis," confess himself. Which epistle, to declare the lenity and merciful heart of so worthy a prince, if with great and marvellous provocations and wrongs he had not been incited, I thought good, in the midst of the history, here to have placed. But thus I have kept you long herein, and yet not finished the same.

The emperor forced to make money of leather

In this siege the emperor, having spent and consumed almost all his treasure, both gold and silver, caused other money to be made of leather, which on the one side had his image, and on the other side the spread eagle (the arms of the empire), and made a proclamation, that the same should pass from man to man for all necessaries instead of other money; and therewithal promised, that whosoever brought the same money unto his exchequer, when the wars were ended, he would give them gold for the same, according to the value of every coin limited; which thing afterwards truly and faithfully he performed, as all the historiographers do agree.

The pope sendeth for foreign aid, and is prevented.

Thus when the pope, as before is said, had stopped his ears and would not hear the emperor's legates who came to entreat for peace, but rejected and despised his most courteous and equal demands; neither yet had he left any wily policy unattempted or force unpractised, by means of which, with his confederates, he thought himself either able to revenge or resist: he, by his legates, calleth to a council at Rome, all such prelates out of Italy, France, and England, as he thought to favour him and his proceedings; that hereby, as his last shift and only refuge, he by their helps might deprive Frederic of his empire, as an utter enemy to God and to the church. All which

Henry III.

A.D. 1239 to 1250.

things Frederic having understanding of, and knowing that these assemblies would be put to the destruction and supplanting of him, he determined to stop and hinder their passage to Rome, as well by sea as by land, all that ever he might; so that all the passages by land being now stopped and prevented, he commanded his son Henry, with certain galleys, to go and keep the coasts of Sardinia, which kingdom the Italians call Entimum: and from thence to go to Pisa, and with the Pisans to rig out a navy to meet (if it were possible) with such as should come to aid the pope at Rome. The pope's champions, understanding that by land they could not safely repair to Rome, procured of galleys and ships out of Genoa (having Gulielmus Braccius for their chief captain or admiral) forty sail for their defence; thinking hereby, that if they should happen to meet with any of the emperor's ships or galleys, which should lie for them in wait, they should be able to make their part good, and give them also the repulse. Encius, in like manner, and Huglinus, being captain and admiral of the Pisan navy for the emperor, launched forth to sea with forty ships and galleys: and, betwixt the isles of Lilium and Mons Christi, which lie between Liburnium and Corsica, they met with the Genoese ships; and straightways fiercely began to grapple with and board them, in which fight, at length, were three of the Genoese ships both bilged and sunk, and twenty-two taken and brought away, with all the riches and treasure in them. In these were taken three of the pope's legates, whereof two were cardinals; the legates were Jacobus Columna, Otho Marchio, and Gregory of Romania, all cruel enemies against the emperor, and many more prelates were taken with them; besides a great number of legates and procurators of cities, with an infinite number of monks and priests, besides of Genoese soldiers six thousand, with divers others.

The emperor riggeth forth a navy.

A great victory at sea against the pope's confederates.

Pandolphus Colonutius, in describing the circumstances of the great loss and misfortune of these champions of the pope by sea, amongst the rest declareth; that besides the great prey and booty which the takers had from them, they also found many writings and letters against Frederic, which much helped them in the defence of those causes, wherein they had laboured against him. The like mischance also, almost about that time, happened on the pope's side, by the emperor's soldiers who lay in the garrison at Ticinum, thus: There went forth upon a time out of Ticinum into the borders of the Genoese, certain bands to give them alarms in the country; which bands the scurriers of Mediolanum (where lay a great garrison of the pope's) descrying, told the captain of the town, that now there was a very opportune and fit time to give an assault to Ticinum; "since," say they, "the greatest part are now gone foraging." Whereupon they immediately calling together the captains and such as had charge, set their soldiers in array, and marched forward to Ticinum. And now, when they were come almost thither, the Ticinian bands (whom they thought to have been far off foraging) returned and met with them, and fiercely gave a full charge upon them: who, being dismayed at the suddenness of the matter, fought not long, but gave over and fled. In which skirmish were taken, besides those that were slain, three hundred and fifty captains, who were brought prisoners into Ticinum with all their ensigns.

Another victory by land at Ticinum.

News hereof was brought to the emperor not long after, who then was removing from the siege of Faventia (as ye heard) to the city of Benonium, thinking to destroy the same. But upon the hearing this good news, he altereth his purpose, and thinking to have hereafter a more convenient time, leadeth his army towards Rome; and in the way he reconcileth to him the city of Pisarum. But Fanum, because the townsmen shut their gates and would not suffer the emperor to come in, he took by force and destroyed. For the emperor, seeing that neither by petition made to the pope, nor yet by his lawful excusation, he could do any good with him, thought that by his sudden coming thither, and with fear of the peril imminent, he might be brought to some uniformity, and caused to leave off his accustomed pertinacity. And although the emperor was too strong for him, yet, because he regarded nothing more than the public tranquillity of the empire, and that he might then take the Tartarian wars in hand, if he could by any means conclude, he refused not so to entreat a peace with him, as though he had been both in force and fortune much the pope's inferior.

The emperor thinketh to make the pope afraid.

While this ruffle was betwixt the emperor and the pope, Ochodarius, the son of the emperor of the Tartars, with a great power and provision made, invaded the borders next adjoining to him, and there won Roxolanum, Bodolium, Mudanum, with divers other cities, towns, and villages, destroying, wasting, and burning the countries all about; killing and slaying man, woman, and child, and sparing none of any sex or age. (A.D. 1241.) At this sudden invasion, the people being in great fear and perplexity, having no city, no refuge, nor aid to stand in defence for them, were fain to leave all they had, and disperse themselves into woods, and fly to marshes and mountains, or wherever any succour else did offer itself to them. And by this time the Tartarian host was come as far as Uratislavia, where Henry of Polonia and the duke of Silesia, with their armies, met with them; who, for the inequality of the number and small strength they were of, had soon an overthrow, and, almost all their soldiers being slain, they themselves were taken and put to the sword. From thence they came to Moravia, and from thence to the kingdom of Bohemia, which country, while the king kept himself in strong defenced forts, and durst not come abroad, they invaded, and destroyed all Hungary; putting to flight and vanquishing Colmannus, the brother of Belus IV. the king of Hungary, by whom also was great spoil made in both the Pannonias, Misiarum, Bulgaria, and Servia. When Belus, the king of Hungary, had gotten to Pola (which is a city of Istria), unto Otho, the duke of Dalmatia, he sent his legates to Frederic, the emperor; promising that if he would send him aid, so that the Tartarians might be expelled, Hungary should ever after be under the jurisdiction of the emperor: which thing if he refused to do, that then Hungary would be in great danger of being subjected to the Tartarians, to the no little peril of the whole empire. And he said further, that the cause wherefore he with more instance required the same, was, that so many christian men and countries made such pitiful lamentation in this their great calamity and misery, and that there was none able to help them; "which," saith he, "is as great shame as may be to the whole christian state and empire." And also he

The Turk invadeth Christendom with a great and mighty power.

Unmerciful slaughter of the Christians.

The king of Hungary craveth aid of the emperor.

said, that if the malice of this barbarous people were not suppressed, then he thought they would make invasion upon the empire and the provinces of the same.

The emperor, although he thought it very requisite, that with all convenient speed this mischief should be remedied and prevented; yet, notwithstanding, his great enemy the pope, with his confederates, was the only let and hinderance thereof. For when he saw and perceived that he himself could do no good, and only laboured in vain in seeking peace with the pope, he gave commandment to Boiemus and Boius, to entreat and persuade him, that considering the imminent peril like to ensue, by reason of such civil dissension, to the whole state of Christendom, he would take up and conclude a peace, and mitigate somewhat his fierce and wrathful mood. Wherefore, when he saw further, that neither by entreaty, nor by any other means, the pope would desist from his stubborn and malicious froward purpose, he writeth again to the king of Hungary, that he was right sorry, and greatly lamented their miserable state, and that he much desired to relieve the need and necessity that he and all the rest stood in. But, as the cause why he could not redress the same, nor stand him then in any stead, he blamed greatly the bishop of Rome; who refusing all entreaty of peace, he (the emperor) could not, without great peril to himself, depart out of Italy, lest that when he should come to the aid of him (by the pope's mischievous imaginations), he should be in peril of losing all at home.' Notwithstanding, he sent Conrad Cæsar, king of Bohemia, and other princes of Germany, to resist and withstand the enemy, as much as in them lay. The great army and number of such soldiers, as wore the cross by the pope's assignment, deferred their journey against the Tartarians, and had commandment given unto them by one Albert, the pope's procurator, to tarry and abide at home, until they should be called for in battle to fight against the emperor. To conclude, this was the loving zeal and affection of the pope and his adherents, in this time of calamity, towards the christian state and commonwealth; that he had rather bend his force, and revenge his malice upon the christian and good emperor, than he himself either withstand, or suffer and permit by conclusion of any profitable peace, that this most bloody and cruel Tartarian should be let and restrained from such great havoc, spoil, and slaughter of the christian men: and yet, forsooth, these men will seem to have the greatest regard of all others to the christian preservation, and think to have the supremacy given therein! What thing else is this, but manifest mockery and deceiving of the people? But, notwithstanding, even in the midst of this spoil and havoc of Polonia, Bohemia, and Hungaria, was it determined, that at Libussa, the princes confederate should be assembled, about the deposing of the emperor, and the creation of another.

The pope's fault that the Turk is not resisted.

Had rather fight against the emperor than against the Turk.

But now, notwithstanding the provident foresight and wise policy of the emperor (as you heard before) in restraining the passages both by sea and land, who had special regard thereunto, and gave most strict charge that none should pass without privy search and examination, as one having sufficient trial, as well in his own person, as by the example of his predecessors, what great mischief and dissension, by their legates every way sent out, they had procured, both to the

The emperor and his predecessors have trial of the pope's subtle practices.

imperial state and dignity, and to the whole country of Germany; yet found they such means, and wrought such policies, that they had not only secret passage and repassage with their letters and spies into all Christendom where they listed, but they also so laboured the matter and handled the same, that the long continued league of amity between the French king and the emperor, whose predecessors, as also they themselves, had many years reverently observed it in christian concord and unity, was, by this seditious prelate and arrogant vicar of Satan, now either utterly infringed, or else in variable suspense; as by their letters to each other, and here ensuing, is to be read and seen; which, for the more probability of this history of Frederic (not being long or greatly tedious), I thought meet here to insert.

Henry III.

A.D. 1241 to 1250.

The Epistle of the French King to Frederic the Emperor, touching the Imprisonment of certain Cardinals of France.

Hitherto, noble emperor, hath the good opinion and great confidence (many years in mutual love established betwixt us) lasted and continued well, hoping that no such cause should rise betwixt us to hatch either hatred or other occasion offensive between your highness's empire, and our kingdom. Especially, seeing that all our predecessors, kings of France, late of most worthy memory, till these our days, have been so zealously affected to the most high and regal state of your empire; and also that we, after whom God hath placed successively to reign as king, have been no otherwise minded nor affected towards the same. None otherwise also on their behalf have the ancient and renowned emperors of Rome, our neighbours and your predecessors, showed themselves towards us (each other esteeming the empire and kingdom of France as one), and faithfully conserving together the unity of peace and concord; insomuch that there hath not chanced between them, these many years, so much as one spark of discord and dissension. But this notwithstanding, we, for our part, cannot but greatly marvel, and not without good cause are troubled and vexed, that, without desert or any offence, you have taken the prelates of our realm upon the sea, making their repair to the see apostolical, to the which, as well by their faith as their obedience they stand bound and are obedient, neither could they withstand the pope's commandment; these have you imprisoned, and so still detain the same: whereat (we do your majesty to wit) we are not well pleased, neither yet take it in so good part, as you peradventure think we do. For by their own letters we understand, they had contemplated nothing prejudicial to your imperial estate and celsitude, although the pope had prosecuted therein more than became him to do. Wherefore, seeing that there is no cause why you should detain them; it is meet, and becometh no less your magnificence, that you restore unto us and set at liberty the said prelates of our realm; wherein also you shall appease our grudge, and keep us your friend, who account the displeasure you do to them as our own and proper injury. For why? It were a great dishonour to our realm and kingly estate, if we would wink hereat and overpass the same with silence. Wherefore, if you will consider and respect the thing that we have said, we doubt not but that you will release the bishop of Penestrum, with the other legates and prelates of the church, whom you, to our prejudice, do detain. In desiring our aid, doubtless we gave unto them a manifest nay; neither could they obtain in our kingdom any thing at all which seemed to be against or prejudicial to your majesty. Let therefore your imperial providence ponder in the balance of justice those things which we write unto you, neither let our lawful request unto you be frustrated or made in vain. For our realm and kingdom of France is not so debilitated or impoverished that it will be spurned at, or trodden under your feet. Fare ye well.

Long continued league between the empire and kingdom of France.

The king, without great allurement of the pope, would not so have written to the emperor.

The Rescript of the Emperor to the same Letter of the King of France.

Our imperial magnificence hath perused your kingly letters; wherein if we had not found manifest contradiction, they might peradventure have obtained

French king's letters con-

Henry III. A.D. 1241 to 1250.

at our hands all that they required. But even as with a little leaven a whole lump of dough is soured; so a manifest untruth alleged hath made the whole argument of your letter both faulty and unsavoury. It is apparent that you wanted the virtue of mediocrity in the conclusion of the same your grace's letters; for that they themselves bewray no less than we give you manifestly to understand, and many more besides do know. It is notorious also, and to all the world revealed, in what sort that apostolical father hath impugned our innocency, as well with the one sword as with the other; and that how, whilst we at his commandment took our journey beyond the seas, the same our great enemy and hostile adversary invaded our kingdom of Sicily; and the same, not in one place or two, but in divers and sundry parts thereof hath wasted, spoiled, and destroyed. After this, when with great entreaty at our return from Asia, we had concluded a peace with him, which with us at his own pleasure he made, and had taken and received our devotion for the same, which in serviceable manner we granted him; the said apostolical father, that notwithstanding, hath since that time rather aggravated his displeasure toward us, than any thing at all qualified the same; and further hath, to our deprivation and subversion, excogitated and devised against us all the mischief he might or hath been able, no cause in all the world given of us to provoke the same; and further hath he promulgated, to our great defamation and shame, as well by his letters as legates, the sentence of excommunication against us unto all nations. Lastly, he, aspiring to our imperial state, and conspiring our supplantation, hath made war against us, as against king David, God's anointed; and hath, unto a private council, for that purpose, called all the prelates he can get, as one that meaneth to set all the whole world together by the ears. But such is the marvellous wisdom of God, by whom we live and reign, who beholding the wicked purpose he went about (confounding the crafty in their craftiness), hath given into our hands as well your prelates of the realm of France, as also of other regions and provinces; all whom we imprison and detain, as enemies and adversaries to our imperial crown and person. For where there desisted not to be a persecutor, there hath not wanted also a sufficient withstander and defender. Let not, therefore, your kingly highness marvel, although Augustus detaineth in prison your French prelates, who have endeavoured themselves to conspire, and so to disturb our imperial estate and regiment. Fare ye well.

[Margin: trary to themselves. A good apostolical father with a two-handed sword. One hundred and twenty ounces of gold, as before you heard. The crafty compassed in their craftiness.]

When Frederic now saw there was no other remedy, and that in vain he laboured to have peace with the pope, he prosecuteth this war to the uttermost; and when he had gotten Tudertum, and reconciled the same, he destroyed the towns of Geminum and Narvia, and giveth the spoil of them to his soldiers, he gently received the yielding up of Siburnum, and wasteth all the country round about Rome. The pope herewith dismayed, and troubled with such as otherwise dissuaded and counselled him, and seeing that things prospered not so well with him and against the emperor as he wished and desired, being in despair of obtaining his purpose, died for very anger and thought. A.D. 1241.

[Margin: Death of Gregory IX. A.D. 1241.]

What opinion the prelates of Germany at that time had of this Gregory is extant and to be seen, in the oration of Eberhard, bishop of Juvavence, which he made to the nobility of Bojoria, in the parliament at Reginoburgh, written by Johannes Aventinus in his seventh book. Doubtless he not only brought great and ruinous calamities on the whole christian commonwealth and also the empire, whilst he sought thus to depress and bridle the emperor and advance his papal see and dignity, but he also brought into the church of God much horrible impiety, blasphemy, and wickedness, whereof both Blondus, Platina, Balæus, and others make mention; and, amongst others, that most the detestable canticle, 'Salve Regina!' in which he attributeth the honour and worship proper only to Christ, unto the Virgin, his mother.

This is he in whose name the book of the decretals was set out, which (to omit the opinion of divers other learned men) Johannes Balæus calleth 'the sink or puddle of foolishness and impiety!' Doubtless Carolus Molinæus (a man of singular judgment both in that law which in tribunal courts and judgments is used, as also in this), painted forth the decree of this Gregory in his book of 'Annotations unto Platina,' whose words thereof are these:—"Doubtless divers chapters in the same book of decretals be mangled and imperfect, that many contentious arguments therein might lurk."[1] For when the ambitious desire of reigning like kings took them, they studied nothing else but how to enlarge and advance their see and dominion (oft shaken and weakened through contention with the empire itself and other kingdoms), and this purpose and end had they, and none other, in all their constitutions; the proof whereof Molinæus declareth in his book 'De Regibus Galliæ et Angliæ.' But many more examples by the emperors, princes, and lords electors of the empire may be gathered, whereof to speak, more convenient place shall serve hereafter.

Carolus Molineus upon the decretals of pope Gregory IX.

In the stead of this Gregory was placed Celestine IV., born in Mediolanum, amongst the Castellians; who, as Blondus declareth, with feigned promises, offered a league with Frederic, and, on the eighteenth day after he was created pope, died.

Thus when the author of all this conspiracy was gone, Frederic now thinking himself free and void of that fear which before he had, and not daring to be absent out of Italy, with all his endeavour levieth an army, and prepareth his furniture and other necessaries for the delivery of the Christians, so mightily oppressed, as ye heard, by the Turks or Tartarians. The latter, hearing of the coming of the emperor, left the straight way through Hungary, by which they came, and returned by the river Danube to Taurica, and so through the fens of Meotida, and by the river Tanaum, into Sarmatia Asiatica. When the cardinals had now for a long time protracted the creation of the pope, and would not agree upon the same, the emperor put them in remembrance of their duty, and blameth them for their disagreeing, and exhorteth them to be more careful for the christian commonwealth. His two epistles touching this matter are extant; whereby appeareth, that only for the care and desire he had for peace and the christian unity and state, he did the same; and for that, peradventure, the cardinals refused to make peace with him before they had created a new pope. The one letter, for more brevity, I have omitted, and have here inserted the other.

The emperor prepareth an army to fight with the Tartars

An Epistle invective of the Emperor unto the Cardinals, because they could not agree upon the creation of the Pope.

Unto you I write, O you children of Ephraim! who evil have bent your bows, and worse have shot your arrows, filthily turning your backs in the day of battle: unto you I speak, O you children of Belial, and dispurpled flock! you insensible people, and assistants of the great judge! unto you I write, O you dissentious cardinals! whom the world for your deserts doth hate; for whose cause the whole world being at variance is evil spoken of. Doubtless, I cannot speak unto you, but to your detraction, because I am worldly, and you spiritual. I am unperfect, wherefore I must do as the unperfect world doth: neither can

(1) "Certum est, multa capita in iis mutila et decurtata esse, ut invidiosum argumentum lateret," &c. Carolus Molineus upon the Decretals of Gregory IX.

Henry III.

A.D. 1241 to 1250.

the part be dissonant to the whole, nor I contrary to myself that write. Attend ye, therefore, to my rude epistle, wanting the dignity of rhetorical style. My provoked tongue brasteth forth into words, before my conceiving spirit hath delivered the same; and so, not attending to the higher regiment, hath hastened to express my words not fully conceived or premeditate. Thus, I say, a troubled mind oftentimes doth beget unordered talk, and untimely uttereth the same. This, therefore, it is that our heart hath conceived, that we believe, and all men confess, that Jesus Christ, the Mediator between God and man, who came from heaven to make peace upon the earth, is not divided and at variance, being also the Master and Lord of the apostles. But Satan, being divided in himself, that blustering prince is amongst you, as those to whom he ministereth; he, even he, the persuader of discord and dissension, that man-killer, father of lies, and spirit of darkness, that hath divided your tongues, and set dissension amongst yourselves; neither do ye good one to another, nor yet to the world, being by you into so perilous a state brought; and the little ship of Peter, which is tossed upon the sea by the vehement winds, you nothing regard; which ship, though it need not indeed utterly to fear drowning, yet suffereth it by your negligence many great storms and perilous tempests. Doubtless, if ye would diligently consider how the nations and people whom ye were wont to judge, in scorn shake their heads at you; every one of you would be ashamed of another. And to say the truth, they cannot do too much to detect your so detestable opprobry: for whilst every one of you aspireth to the chair, every one is at variance with his fellow; and whilst one of you cannot agree with another, none is promoted; and whilst none is promoted, the cathedral dignity vanisheth. And thus by your discord, the peaceable state and concord of the church is confounded, and the perfection of the faith and religion, whereby ye should live, perisheth. And surely, through your default it perisheth, so that where nature hath placed the sense and understanding to be, that part, like a monster, remaineth with you both senseless and headless. And no marvel, for why your hearing is impaired, and that sound of the mouth which shrilly was heard throughout the whole earth, is utterly dumb, and become a scoffing echo. For why, the thunderings of Peter and Paul are now no more heard, the preachers are become dumb dogs, and are commanded to silence. Perhaps you have hands ready to receive, but there be no bribes; for why, those that were wont to come from Saba, and bring gold with them, now come no more, seeing the Lord is not in the manger, and the celestial shining star refusing to be their guide. Moreover, ye want feet to walk withal, for seeing there is no man to give you ought, you will not remove one foot for any man's pleasure. Fie, shameless people! the least and simplest beast may learn you obedience, for the birds have their captain, and the silly bees their king; but you will come under no government, &c.

Peter's ship, by the dissension of the cardinals, greatly afflicted.

Peter's shrill voice turned into a scoffing echo.

The emperor releaseth the cardinals from prison.

The emperor, after this, at the request of Baldwin, the emperor of Constantinople, who came to Frederic to Parma, released the cardinals out of prison, thinking not only to gratify the emperor Baldwin, but also that thereby things would the better grow to public tranquillity on every side. When the cardinals were all assembled at Avignia, they made Sinibald, a Genoese, pope, whom, by a contrary name (for that he had determined, as I suppose, to be hurtful to the common-
A.D.1243. wealth), they called Innocent IV. Of this election, when Frederic understood, he was well pleased therewith; and for that he had, in all this troublous time, been his friend, the emperor well-hoped that the christian commonwealth should by him have been brought to much peace and concord. Wherefore he sent both his legates and letters gratulatory unto him, giving him to understand how well it contented and pleased him that he was made pope; and what peace and quietness thereby he promiseth (as it were to himself) he maketh full relation thereof; offering again unto him observance, help and aid in all things, commending his dignity to the public state and quietness of the christian commonwealth and empire.

Rejoiceth at the pope's election.

He also wrote his letters to Otho, duke of Boioria, who a little before was reconciled to the emperor, that he who was elected pope was a good man, a lover of peace, and studious as well for the tranquillity of the christian commonwealth, as of the empire.

Henry III.

A.D. 1243 to 1250.

The legates of Frederic, also, with the furtherance of Baldwin, the emperor of Constantinople, laboured very diligently for the conclusion of the promised peace; and, to be brief, every man was in good hope and looked for no less. But far otherwise fell the matter out, and contrary to all their expectations, for the pope, set on and encouraged by the cardinals and others against Frederic, secretly, and amongst themselves, wrought contrary to what they openly pretended, and not a little disappointed both Frederic and others of their expectation, and of the good opinion they had of the pope's holiness. For, while the emperor's legates attended the answer of their peace before promised, Rainerus, the cardinal, went secretly to Viterbium with a certain number of soldiers, and took the town, which before was on the emperor's part.

The pope taketh Viterbium while the emperor hoped for peace.

The emperor having understanding hereof, mustereth his bands, and with a sufficient power entereth the pope's dominion, again to recover Viterbium: but yet, taking this war so in hand (not thinking thereby to expel all conditions of peace), at the request of certain of the cardinals he was contented to leave Viterbium, it being furnished by the emperor with warlike provision before his departure, and came to Aqua. From thence he sent again other ambassadors to Rome, and with them also the emperor of Constantinople, with the earl of Toulouse, who he thought were able to do much with the pope in the prosecuting of this peace. But although at the time of Easter the matter seemed to have been got through, and peace concluded, for that his legates had sworn in the behalf of the emperor (and as he willed them), that he would submit himself to the pope; and again, although the cardinals and others commonly called and named him Frederic, the christian Prince, yet all this was no more but for a further fetch and purpose, not that they meant indeed to conclude any peace with him, or to go through therewithal, but that through this dissimulation and likelihood of peace, which they understood the emperor much desired, he should set free and open the passages which he straitly kept, so that no man could pass and come to Rome, whither a great multitude daily resorted and flocked for religion's sake. But when all came to all, and the legates perceived that no conclusion of peace was simply purposed on their behalf, they began to despair of the matter; letting the emperor so to understand. The emperor, notwithstanding, doubted not, but if he might himself speak with the pope, he upon reasonable conditions should well enough accord with him; wherefore he by his legates and letters desired him to appoint a place where the emperor might resort to him. The pope seemed to be contented herewithal, and appointed a day at Fescennia, where they would talk together; and the pope promised that he would be there before him, and expect the emperor's coming. But the pope (a bitter enemy to the said Frederic), in the mean while, had made a confederacy with the French king against him; who when he knew those three galleys to be ready and brought unto Centincellas, which he before had spoken for unto the Genoese, secretly in the night, with his company, hastening thither in post speed, he took ship, and first came to Genoa,

Dissimulation of the subtle pope Innocent IV.

The pope mocketh the emperor, and goeth to Lyons, where he proscribeth him.

Henry III.

A.D. 1245 to 1250.

and from thence to Lyons in France; where he (to answer the steps of his predecessors), calling a council, with a loud voice summoneth Frederic, and, appointing him a day, commanded him there personally to plead his cause.

And yet although he understood that the sudden departing of the pope out of Italy made plain demonstration of no conclusion or meaning of a peace; and although he also knew the council which the pope had called, wherein he was himself both plaintiff and judge, and at the same council, those whom the pope had by bribes allured foreshowed the destruction of the emperor; with many other such evident demonstrations, of the pope's both envious and hateful heart towards him: yet the most modest emperor, using the innocency and uprightness of his cause, and as one most desirous of peace and christian concord, sent the patriarch of Antioch, who lately was come out of Syria, the bishop of Panormia, and Thadeus Suessanus, the president of his court, a most skilful and prudent civilian, to the council at Lyons; who signified unto them that the emperor would be there for the defence of his own cause: but as the day was very short, he required a time more convenient for him thither to repair. The emperor, also, being onward on his way, and come as far as Taurinum, sent before him other messengers, as the master of the Flemish order, and Peter de Vineis, to give them understanding of the emperor's coming, and to entreat that he would prorogue the day of hearing, till he might conveniently travel thither. But for any thing that could be either said or done, or upon how just cause soever required, the pope would not give so much as three days' space, in the which time the ambassadors assured them of the emperor's presence; as though there had been no common proviso for every man in that case by the law to have used upon any reasonable hindrance. For what should I longer protract the time? When the day by them appointed was come, the pope with his confederates (whom for money and bribes he had gotten to that council)—against God's law, against christian doctrine, against the prescript of the law both of nature and of reason, against the rule of equity, against the order of law appointed, against the constitutions of emperors and also the decrees of the empire, without any observation of the law, or granting dilatory days, without probation of any crime, or his cause being suffered to be pleaded unto, or hearing what might be answered therein—the pope taking upon him to be both adversary and judge, condemned the emperor being absent, and, *in his full heat of fury and malice, denounced him accursed; and moreover deprived him of his imperial dignity, charging him with heinous crimes of perjury and sacrilege, writing also letters and libels of defamations to all kings, princes, and potentates.*[1] What more wicked sentence was ever pronounced? What more cruel act, considering the person, might be committed? What thing more brutish and vile could have been imagined or devised? And yet hereat were those bishops nothing ashamed; but, meaning to leave their doings in writing, as an impudent testimony to their posterity, established the same for a law to continue.

The emperor cometh to make his appearance before the pope.

But mark what vengeance God took upon this wicked judge. The writers of the Annals record, that when Frederic, the emperor,

Vengeance falleth on the pope.

(1) For this, with the two last parentheses in the paragraph next above, see Edition 1563, p. 73.—Ed.

and Conrad, his son, being Cæsar, were both dead, the pope gaping for the inheritance of Naples and Sicily, and thinking by force to have subdued the same, came to Naples with a great host of men; where was heard in the pope's court manifestly pronounced this voice, "Veni miser ad judicium Dei." "Thou wretch, come to receive thy judgment." And the next day after, the pope was found dead in his bed, all black and blue, as though he had been beaten with bats; as before, in the history of king John, is declared.

When the emperor had understanding of this cruel and tyrannical sentence of the pope passed and pronounced against him, considering his furious purpose and mind therein, he thought good, by his letters, to let all christian princes and potentates understand, as well what injurious and manifold displeasure he had sustained by the four popes in all their times, as also the cruelty and tyranny of this pope, in pronouncing the sentence of judgment and condemnation against him (passing the bounds both of justice, equity, and reason); which letter, as he wrote the same, hereunder followeth.

The Letter of the Emperor to the French King and other Princes, in consequence of the Sentence given against him in the Council of Lyons by the Pope and Cardinals.

Although we suppose not the contrary, but that both by true certificate and common rumour you have heard of the indifferency of our cause and good handling thereof: yet for that more credit is commonly given to what the eye seeth, than to what the ear receiveth, we thought good to present unto you the naked truth of such things as the popes successively have put forth, and forged against us. For the perusing and consideration of which my case and letter, I beseech your gentleness amongst other times of leisure, that you will spy out some fit and convenient time. And all others whatsoever who shall have desire to hear princes' counsels and affairs, let them in like sort attentively consider. First, whether our predecessors have been destitute or not, of godly zeal, just dealing, and righteousness: and whether we may not lawfully revenge ourselves, being so much provoked, of such evils and injuries as have been wrought against us. Secondly, let them consider whether Christ's vicar doth follow Christ's steps or not; and whether Peter's successors do follow his example or not; and also by what law, equity and right, that sentence which they have pronounced against us, may be maintained and allowed: as also what name they may justly give it, and whether that may be said to be a sentence, which is given by an insufficient judge or not. For, although we acknowledge that the Lord hath given full power in spiritual things unto his church, that whatsoever the same bindeth in earth, is bound in heaven, and whatsover the same looseth, is also loosed; yet we read neither by God's law, nor by any law of man, that we ought of duty to be subject unto him, or that an empire ought at his pleasure to be transformed and transposed, or that he may give any such sentence or judgment to punish princes temporally, and deprive them of their kingdoms. For why? Although our consecration belongeth unto him by right and custom (as he challengeth), yet our deposing and depriving doth no more belong to him, than doth that presumption belong to any other prelate of other realms, which do consecrate and anoint their kings, as the custom and manner is. Or in case it were so (we nothing hindered hereby) that he had such power: hath he that power to the intent to revenge himself upon whomsoever his malicious mind consenteth, and without all equity and law, to bring them under his jurisdiction? He hath proceeded of late against us, as is said, but not by the order of accusation, forasmuch as neither was there any sufficient accuser, neither went there out any inscription or process before; neither yet by denunciation, forasmuch as there lacked a lawful denouncer; neither yet by the way of inquisition, for that there went before it no manifest accusation. But he, peradventure, will say, that all

Henry III

A.D. 1245 to 1250.

things that he layeth against us were manifest and notorious. But that we deny, and nothing to be notorious, but that which may, by a sufficient number of witnesses, be approved and tried. For so may every judge himself (contemning the order of law) affirm what he lists to be notorious, and thus condemn whom he lists There were against us (as well it may be said in council) certain false witnesses, although not many, of whom the bishop of Calin was one, whose near kinsman or nephew (by our laws condemned for treason to be hanged) maketh also to us an infestive enemy.

With such like effect prosecuting the rest of his epistle, which for brevity's sake I omit. This policy the pope used, to vex and disturb both the country of Germany, and the whole empire; and not only so, but also utterly to destroy and subvert the same, by the ruinous decay whereof, the pope and his prelates thought to make up their mouths. And thus, while Germany was now newly again divided, some taking part with Frederic, the emperor, and Conrad Cæsar, his son, and other nobles and princes of the empire, some, with those who by the pope's procurement should be the electors of the new emperor; others with neither, as men not minding nor tending to the public utility, but to serve their own purposes, armed themselves; and thus was the public peace and quiet broken and disturbed, and altogether in tumult and hurly-burly. For whilst the one part laboured by all force to retain the dominion by public and common consent first to him committed, the other part in like sort endeavoured themselves, with all their force and power, to use and occupy the same, according to the decree of the bishop of Rome, and to take it from Frederic. Thus great conflicts grew on all sides.

Germany altogether in hurly-burly through the pope's malicious mind

By these civil wars, Germany suffered no little calamity; in every place was manslaughter and murder, the country spoiled, the towns and villages set on fire and burnt, the churches and temples wherein the husbandmen had put their goods and substance, violated and robbed: houses were pulled down, the goods divided, and every man's cattle driven away. To conclude, in this turmoil and contention of deposing and choosing another emperor, in this faction of princes, and this liberty of wearing armour, in this licence of hurting and sinning, the impudent boldness of divers private soldiers, and especially of such as were the horsemen, then counted the better sort of soldiers, was so great, and their unbridled and unsatiable desire in robbing, spoiling, and taking of booties, catching and snatching all that came to hand, so much, that nothing could be sure and in safety that any good man enjoyed. Wherefore, a little before the death of William, the king (A.D 1256), threescore cities and towns belonging to Louis Palatine, duke of Boiora and the Rhine, and Otho, his son, and other princes, of whose names Aventinus, in his seventh book of the Annals of the Boiores, maketh mention, joined themselves in a league for the expelling of these rebels, and repressing of their so great injurious rapines and slaughter of men; of which army the said Louis being captain, he chased and drave the whole rout of them to the uttermost parts of Germany, and pulled down and overthrew their castles and fortresses, and every other place where they had intrenched themselves.

Spoiled by civil dissension through the pope's practices against the emperor.

William, earl of Holland, made king of the Romans, by the pope.

Robbers and rebels chased out of Germany.

Otho Boius, yet notwithstanding, keepeth his promise and faith, most constantly, made before to the emperor Frederic and Conrad,

Fidelity of Otho to the emperor

his son; whereupon Philip Javavensis, Albert, and others, calling a council at Mildorsus, by the pope's commandment, sent for Otho unto them, unto whom they opened the pope's pleasure and commandment. To all which, when he had heard, Otho answered: "I cannot marvel at some of you enough, that when, as heretofore, you persuaded me to leave and forsake the part I took with the bishop of Rome, whom you yourselves affirmed to be Antichrist, and that I should take part with the emperor, why you yourselves will not keep your fidelity and promise made unto those good princes:" and he said, that he perceived in them a great inconstancy and levity, both in their words and deeds, who now call that thing wicked, unjust, and violently wrong, that but lately they thought equal, just, and right. He said further, that they were overcome with pleasures, corrupted with superfluity, won with bribes, gaping for honour and estimation; and that they neither regarded honesty, godliness, nor their duty and office, but studied how to make dissension and commotions, and longed after war and bloody battle.

His answer to the legates.

He said further, that for his part he would obey God and his prince, to whom he had sworn fidelity; and that he nought esteemed the feigned holiness and detestable practices of such prelates. He said he believed in Christ, and would trust to his mercy; and that he believed how those whom they cursed and gave to the devil, were in greatest favour with God. Howbeit, and notwithstanding those prelates took in good part this expostulation of his, and seemed to bear Otho no malice or grudge for what he had said, but to be desirous of peace and unity, yet, not long after, Otho was cursed as black as all the rest, and counted as bad as the worst.

Excommunicated for turning from the pope to take the emperor's part.

Albert, the pope's champion, now in Germany, playeth not only *rex* amongst the citizens, but also bethought him of a mischievous device against Conrad Cæsar, the emperor's son. When by fraud and subtilty he had gotten and taken many of the rich burgesses and citizens of Reginoburgh, who bare the emperor good will, and had sent them prisoners to Staffum, Conrad, joining with other noblemen of the empire (after he had spoiled and wasted much of his lands and others his companions), drave him so near, that upon certain other conditions he delivered again the citizens. And, shortly after, coming again to Reginoburgh, and being received and welcomed into the college of Doctor Hamaranus, Albert, with certain of his confederates, by the means of Ulric, a chief officer of the monks, came in the dead of the night into the chamber, where the Cæsar with a few others about him did lie, and falling upon them, some they took, and others they slew; and finding no other body in the chamber or lodging, they thought that Cæsar had been slain among the rest. But he hearing the noise, forsook his bed, and hid himself under a bench, and so escaped their hands. The next day he outlawed or proscribed the bishop and his mates, and also the monks' bailiff for treason, and seized upon all the goods of the house. But, at the suit of the guiltless monks, he released all to them again, taking by way of fine one hundred pounds. Ulric lost his office, and Albert, to escape danger of punishment, took upon him the habit of a monk. Conrad Hochenfolseus, who was the murderer of these men, though he escaped the punishment of man's hand, yet the

Cæsar in danger of Albert.

Albert, to escape punishment, taketh the order of monkery.

Henry III. A.D. 1246 to 1250.

vengeance of God for the fact he escaped not. For as he rode in the day time abroad, he was suddenly stricken with a thunderbolt and died.

The emperor suppresseth these tumults.

During all this busy and contentious time, it may well be gathered, that Frederic, the emperor, lay not still, but had his hands full: who, notwithstanding, by God's help, overcoming and suppressing these or the greater part of these rebellious popish tumults, and having done strait execution on those especially who had conspired against his person, called a council, and setting in some stay the troublesome affairs of his kingdom, came to Cremona with Frederic, prince of Antioch, Richard, earl of Umbria, the governor of Flamminia, and Encius, king of Sardinia, with a great number of soldiers and men of war besides. And besides, he took with him (whom he sent for out of every part) the wisest, most virtuous, and best learned men that there were, thinking with them to have gone himself to Lyons to the pope, and there to have with him communication, as well concerning the sentence definitive, as also about the conclusion of any peace, if by any means he might. And when all things were prepared and ready, he took the journey in hand, and came to Taurinum, having with him both a great army of soldiers, and also a great company of legates and ambassadors. From thence sending his carriages before, within three days' journey of Lyons, he was certified that Parma was taken and kept by the outlaws of divers and sundry factions of the pope, his near neighbours and friends; as by the pope's legate, and other citizens, as of Brixia, Placentia, and such like. Which when he understood, and that the pope herein was the only and chief doer, he saw manifestly it should little prevail to attempt any further the thing he went about, and then, at length, when he saw no other remedy, putting from him all hope of peace, he determined himself to the wars with all his force and might. Thus altering his purpose and journey, he took the straightest way into Lombardy, and, with an army of sixty thousand men, besieged Parma. And to the intent he might more aptly and near the town plant his siege and battery without disturbance, first he intrenched his camp, and fortified the same about with bulwarks and other defensible munition. After that, he caused divers victualling-houses and taverns in his camp to be slightly builded of timber; and without the camp he appointed the place where the market should be kept, and all victuallers resort that would. He appointed places for their churches and temples, and in seemly manner adorned the same: and for the most part their tents were builded with wood, so that it was like another Parma. All which things when he had finished, which was not long in doing, for this happy and prosperous success he called and named it Victoria, and had thought to have made the same to be in the stead of the city of Parma, which he purposed to have made level with the ground. And in the beginning, both there and elsewhere, all things prospered well with Frederic, and had good success; for he sharply laid to their charges who defended and kept the city of Parma. And further, Robert Castilion, who was the emperor's lieutenant in Picenum, near unto Auximum, discomfited the pope's army, and slew of them more than four thousand, and took many such as were of the confederate cities prisoners. And when the

Parma taken and kept by the pope's legate and other friends of his.

The emperor altereth his journey from Lyons to Parma.

The pope's army discomfited by the emperor's lieutenant.

factions or companies of the Ghibellines and Guelphs in Florence were at controversy, when Frederic of Etruria came to the Ghibellines, to whom they had sent for aid, the Guelphs therewith dismayed, fled from thence to Bononia, whose goods and substance came all to the emperor's coffers, and Florence also itself to the emperor's obedience. But this good success and prosperous fortune lasted not long, for as at a time when Frederic, to recreate himself (who seldom had his health), rode about the fields with certain of his horsemen to hawk and hunt, many of the emperor's soldiers, thinking nothing less than of such a matter to be attempted of a many starvelings within the town of Parma, wandered and ranged unarmed out of their city Victoria about the fields. The soldiers in Parma, having this occasion offered, with all force and speed possible entered the emperor's camp or town Victoria; which being not very strongly fenced, nor having gates to shut against them, was a thing easy enough to do. The sudden strangeness of the matter much abashed the soldiers, and they rang out their larum-bell. The first assault was given upon Marcus Malaspina's charge, whom, when the emperor, returning in all haste, found to be hard beset, he had thought to have rescued; but when that was perceived of the enemy, they bent all their force together on that side, insomuch that the emperor was forced to take to the trench, lest he should have been of the enemy environed. From thence he retired into the city or camp, where he had thought to have gathered further aid; but the enemy giving not so much time thereunto, with all force entered the city Victoria. The emperor now, when the enemies were entered, left the camp, and came to Dominum, who, when they had killed and slain a great number of the emperor's soldiers, and had burnt and destroyed the same camp Victoria, came again to Parma. The emperor then suspecting this thing to be wrought by treason, whereby the enemy had understanding as well of the emperor's absence, as also of the negligence of his soldiers, imprisoned certain of the chiefest about him, amongst whom also was Petrus de Vineis. Yet, whilst he was at Dominum, gathering together his soldiers, and the residue of his bands, Encius getteth a great victory over the Mansuanos, who coming to the rescue of Parma, lost fifty of their ships, and all that they had in them.

Negligence of the soldiers offereth an occasion to the enemy.

Discomfiture of the emperor at Victoria.

Imprisoneth divers of his captains.

After this also, Richard, in another conflict in Picenum, discomfited the pope's soldiers, and slew their captain, Hugolinus, besides two thousand others slain and taken prisoners. When now Frederic had gathered again, and new mustered his bands at Dominum, he marched forth to Cremona; and, notwithstanding that there he understood of the good success and victory that Encius had at Rhegium, yet for that he perceived the defection and backsliding of all or most part of Lombardy from him, he determined to take his journey into Apulia; and when he had there levied a strong and sufficient power, he purposed to make his speedy return again into Lombardy. Therefore, in his journey through Etruria into Apulia, he joined with his son Frederic, who besieged Capras, and took the same, and led with him divers of the chiefest captains prisoners; and after that, subduing Miniatum unto the obedience of the empire, he came into Apulia.

Capras taken by the emperor.

Henry III.

A.D. 1250.

When news was brought him thither, that Encius his son (coming to aid the Mutinenses against the Bononians) was taken prisoner two miles off from Mutina, and that in his absence, the pope's captains, with their bands and garrisons, went throughout all Lombardy, Emilia, Flamminia, and Etruria, to stir and procure the cities to revolt from the obedience of the emperor, and working the same, partly by subtle policies, and partly by force and sinister means, to bring them to his purpose: he determined with himself, with all the force and power he might by any means procure and make, to begin afresh, and prosecute this war to the uttermost. Neither was it to be doubted (as Pandolphus Colonucius writeth) but that he would have wrought some marvellous exploit and great attempt, but that he was of this his purpose (whereunto he was both willing and bent) prevented by unlooked-for death. For when he fell into this ague, being at a certain castle of his in Apulia, called Florentinum, and seeing by the extremity thereof his days to be short, *[1] being poisoned, as some think, by means of the pope,* he remembered that which was once showed him, how he should die at Florence; whereupon he made and ordained his testament. And when unto Conrad and other his children he had given and appointed the great and innumerable mass of money which he had collected and levied for the maintenance of his wars, and godly purpose, as it is called, and unto them also had given all other his kingdoms and dominions (to every one according to his age), the emperor, Frederic II., departed this wretched and miserable world, A.D. 1250.[2]

The emperor purposeth to make some great attempt.

Prevented by death. A.D. 1250.

Pandolph writeth, that Frederic was very willing to die, and, as they made certain report to him who were present at his death, that his mind was altogether set and bent on the heavenly joy and felicity. The same thing also Gulielmus Putranus, Andreas Pandalus, and Manardus the bishop, being Italian writers, do all affirm; of whom this last writeth, that he assuredly believeth Frederic to be one of the number of God's elect.

Frederic said to be one of God's elect.

The writers, notwithstanding, are of sundry judgments and opinions touching this good emperor's death. Some write, that he was traitorously poisoned by his cup-bearer, being hired thereunto. Others, that he was strangled with a pillow by Manfred, the son of Pherus. But Pandulph, as good a writer as the best, maketh no mention of any poison that was given him, but only that he died of an ague. The last opinion of Manfred he manifestly refuteth, and showeth that there is no manner of likelihood of the same; and further, that the contrary is affirmed by divers other writers who were of that time. He died A.D. 1250, the thirteenth day of December, in the seven and fiftieth year of his age, and seven and thirtieth year of his reign, whose corpse was brought to Panormum, and there entombed.

Sundry opinions of the death of Frederic the emperor.

Frederic had three wives, the first was Constantia, the daughter of the king of Arragon, of whom he begat Henry, the duke of Suevia, and king of the Romans: the other Jole, the daughter of Johannes Brennus, king of Jerusalem, by whom he had the inheritance of Jerusalem, Naples, and Sicily; of whom he begat Conrad, duke of Suevia, king of Jerusalem and Naples, being Cæsar: the third Isabella,

The issue of Frederic the emperor.

(1) Edition 1563, p. 74.—Ed. (2) Foxe erroneously gives 1268 in some Editions.—Ed.

Henry III

A.D. 1250.

the daughter of king John of England, by whom he had a son named Henry, who is said to have died in his childhood. This Frederic had not his peer in martial affairs and warlike policies to be compared unto him, amongst all the princes of that age: a wise and skilful soldier he was, a greater endurer of painful labours and travails, most bold in greatest perils, prudent in foresight, industrious in all his doings, prompt and nimble about that he took in hand, and in adversity most stout and courageous. But as in this corruption of nature few there be that attain perfection, neither yet is there any prince almost of such government and godly institution both in life and doctrine as is required of them: so neither was this Frederic without his fault and human fragility, for the writers impute to him some fault of concupiscence, wherewith he was stained and spotted.[1] And it appeareth that he was not clear thereof, forasmuch as by sundry concubines, he had sundry children; as Encius, the king of Sardinia, Manfred, the prince of Sarentinum, and Frederic, king of Antioch. And this is all that I find of the description of Frederic by Colonucius, which he affirmeth that he gathered out of good and probable authors. But as touching the heinous acts and flagitious deeds which the pope burdeneth him withal, and in his sentence against him maketh mention of, Frederic not only purgeth himself thereof, but also divers historicians (as well German writers as Italian) affirm the same to be false, and of the pope's own brains invented, to do him skath and teen withal.[2] Of this matter those things which Pandulph, touching the commendation or dispraise of Frederic, writeth, I thought good out of Italian to translate, whose words be these:

Frederic a most puissant prince.

Not without his faults

"Albeit the emperor Frederic was endued with many goodly gifts and virtues, yet notwithstanding was he accounted an enemy of the church, and a persecutor of the same: of which Innocent IV., in his sentence, hath pronounced him guilty, and the same sentence have other popes registered in their six books of Decretals, and established the same for a law, how that he ought to be taken for no less. Therefore, peradventure, it should not become me to falsify or call in question that which others have confirmed, or else to dispute and argue much of that matter. Yet, notwithstanding, as much as his acts and deeds in writing declare, and the books of the chiefest authors affirm, as also his own epistles do testify, I cannot precisely say, whether the bishops of Rome so call him and judge him there-for; or else for that he was somewhat too bold in speaking and telling them but the truth, and reproving the ecclesiastical order of their great abuses; or else, whether for that he would have had them go somewhat more near the conditions and lives of the ancient fathers of the primitive church and disciples of Christ; or whether because he defended and stood with them for the prerogative and dignities belonging to the empire or not, or else whether they stood in fear and awe of the great power he was of in Italy, which thing indeed Gregory IX., in a certain epistle of his, confesseth: but of these things let them judge and discern, who shall read the monuments and histories of Frederic. Truly," saith he, "when I consider

Pandolph touching his praise and dispraise.

(1) Our author adverts to the vices of Frederic with unjustifiable partiality.—ED.
(2) "Do him skath, or skare," &c.—Bring upon him injury and sorrow.—ED.

Henry III. A.D. 1250.

The pope's church, compared with Christ's church, are like black and white.

with myself that Christ (whose vicars the Roman bishops boast themselves to be) said unto his disciples, that they should follow him, and also imitate his example, as of their master and teacher; and commanded them, furthermore, how they should not draw the sword, but put up the same into the scabbard; and further gave them in precept, that they should not only forgive injuries seven times, but seventy times seven, to those that offended them; and when I now compare the lives of the bishops of Rome, how near they follow him whose vicar they say they be; and consider so many and great conspiracies, treasons, rebellions, disloyalties, lyings-in-wait, and treacherous devices, so many legates of the popes (being ecclesiastical persons) who will needs be called the shepherds of Christ's flock, to be such warriors and captains of soldiers in all parts of Italy, Campania, Apulia, Calabria (being the emperor's dominions), in Picenum, Æmilia, Flamminia, and Lombardy, to be sent out against him, and also when with myself I meditate the destruction of so many great and famous cities, the subversion of such commonweals, the slaughter of so many men, and the effusion of so much christian blood; and lastly, when I behold such victorious, prosperous, and fortunate emperors to stand, and so many miserable, unfortunate, and vanquished popes put to flight, I am persuaded with myself to think and believe, that the judgments of God are secret and marvellous, and that to be true, which Æneas Sylvius, in his history of Austria writeth, that there is no great and marvellous slaughter, no notorious and special calamity, that hath happened either to the public weal, or to the church of God, of the which the bishops of Rome have not been the authors. Nicholas Machiavel also saith, 'That all the ruinous calamities and miserable chances, that the whole christian commonweal, and also Italy hath suffered, have been brought in by the popes and bishops of Rome.'"

* [1] Divers of the said emperor's letters are dispersed in sundry places in the story of Matthew Paris, yet to be seen; whereof I thought to insert these few words, written to the French king concerning antichrist. Wherein, in process of his letter, these words follow—

"We marvel much at the prudence and wisdom of the Frenchmen, that you do not consider more quick than others, the pope's subtle deceits; or that you do not attend to, and mark his greedy covetousness. For his insatiable ambition purposeth no less than to subdue all realms christened under his jurisdiction, as consequently well may be gathered by the crown of England, brought under his girdle; yea, and furthermore presumptuously and shamelessly doth he achieve, to bring and subdue the majesty of the imperial crown, under his authority and dominion," &c.

Besides this, divers other letters he writeth, not so much charging the pope, as *proving* him to be, the beast and the adversary prefiguring Antichrist.* The aforesaid Pandolph continues:—"Many epistles of Frederic there be, which he wrote unto the bishops of Rome, to the cardinals, and to divers other christian princes, all which I have read; and in them is to be seen nothing contrary unto christian doctrine, nothing wicked and ungodly, nothing injurious to the church of God, nothing contumelious or arrogantly written. But indeed I deny not that his letters are fraught and full

(1) For this passage, and the extract from the emperor's letter, see Edition 1563, p. 74.

Henry III — A.D. 1250.

of pitiful complaints and lamentations, touching the avaricious ambition of the ecclesiastical persons, and pertinacity of the bishops of Rome; and that he would receive and take no satisfaction nor yet excuse, in the defence of the right and privilege of the empire, which he maintained: also of their manifold and infinite conspiracies which they practised both secretly and openly against him, and of the often admonitions which he gave to the whole multitude and order ecclesiastical, to attend upon and discharge their functions and charges. And those who are still further desirous to know and understand the truth, and who covet to search out the renowned virtues of magnificent princes, let them read the epistle of Frederic, dated to all christian princes, which thus beginneth, 'Collegerunt principes, pontifices et Pharisæi concilium:' and another, wherein he persuadeth the college of cardinals to take up the dissension between the emperor and the pope, which beginneth, 'In exordio nascentis mundi;' and also another which thus beginneth, 'Infallibilis veritatis testem;' besides yet another, 'Ad Reges et principes orbis Christiani;' with divers others, wherein may well be seen the princely virtues of this so worthy a peer; all which epistles collected together in the Latin tongue, I wish the learned sort to read, whereout they may pick no little benefit and commodity to themselves. In his epistle last recited, these are his words:[1]—'Think ye not that we so earnestly desire or crave this peace at your hands, as though our majesty were terrified with the pope's sentence of deprivation; when God, upon whom we trust and invocate, is our witness, and judge of our conscience, that when we went about to reform the ecclesiastical state, but especially the ringleaders of the same, and should restrain their power, and extirpate their great tyranny, and reduce the same to the state and condition of primitive church, we look for no less at their hands.'—For these causes peradventure, those who had the government of the ecclesiastical dignity, decreed and pronounced Frederic to be an enemy to the church: of which (as I have said) I leave to others to judge." Hitherto Pandolphus Colonucius.

Deserved commendation upon the epistles of Frederic.

Frederic purposed with the hazard of the state to reform the church of Rome

And doubtless examples to the contrary do appear, namely, that Frederic was no enemy to the church of Rome, for that he both gave large and great gifts thereunto, and also franchised the same with great privileges and immunities, which things, by his own constitutions, statutes, and customs, may be perceived and understood. But rather, contrariwise, that the bishops of Rome most filthily recompensed again the same his great liberality and princely benevolence, which he gave and bestowed upon the same, as partly in the discourse of this history you have heard; who, notwithstanding they so molested and tired him with such and so many injuries as you have seen, he nevertheless, forgiving and pardoning all the same, for the great zeal he had to the common christian wealth, whereat he more laboured than at any other thing, sought by all means he might to have peace, although it were to his own great hinderance. Therefore, seeing he was of necessity by the bishops of Rome provoked to that war, if he did them any skath in revenge of his imperial dignity, let them thank

Sheweth himself no enemy but a friend to the church of Rome

Self do, self have, the proverb is

(1) "Non existimetis id me a vobis ideo contendere, ac si ex sententia pontificia privationis majestas nostra sit perculsa. Cum enim nobis sit rectæ voluntatis conscientia cumque Deum nobiscum habeamus, eundem testem invocamus id nos spectasse, cum totum ordinem ecclesiasticum, tum presertim primores, nervis potentiæ dominationisque eorum succisis extirpatisque tyrannidis radicibus, ad primitivæ ecclesiæ conditionem et statum revocaremus."

their own selves, who might otherwise have remedied the same. Notwithstanding upon this occasion divers writers (both Italian and German, who at that time sought for fat benefices, and ever since, even unto these our days, have done the like, by flattery rather to obtain that which they hunted for, than to bear true and faithful testimony of things as they were indeed) took great occasion to write and slander this good emperor. But let us pass over these parasites, and return to those, who, although they themselves were of that calling, I mean of the ecclesiastical order, yet notwithstanding (for that they rather preferred the study of verity, and to reverence the truth before popish authority and flattering servitude), greatly extolled and commended this good emperor Frederic. So did Nicolaus Cusanus, a cardinal, in his writing, affirm this emperor to be another Charlemagne, both for his wisdom and also diligent regard to the commonweal. So also writeth Ægidius Biturigum, the bishop, in his books of the institution and bringing up of a prince, which he wrote to the French king, exhorting him and all others to take pattern of this most worthy and excellent prince · in commendation of whose worthy praise and virtue these verses are written on his tomb.

Hope of gain allureth many to flatter and write untruths.

Si probitas, sensus, virtutum gratia, census,
Nobilitas, orti possent resistere morti,
Non foret extinctus Fredericus, qui jacet intus.

Wherefore, inasmuch as it appeareth by the approved writers of whom I have made mention, who and what manner of prince this emperor Frederic was, and that because he diligently laboured, as well in the preservation of the christian commonweal, as in the conservation of the imperial dignity, he procured to himself the great hatred and displeasure of the Roman bishops (who have been to all the good emperors for the most part utter foes and enemies), and with what wicked slanders and other injuries both by them, and by their ministers they continually molested him—this lesson ought to be ours, that having the same in our memory, we imitate and follow his virtues, hating and detesting the wicked and flagitious doings of those holy fathers that will so be called, and bishops of Rome; desiring God that he will so guide the hearts of all kings and princes, that they may, by his grace, advance and set forth his glory, and reform the corrupt and vicious manner and order of the church to all sincerity and purity both of life and doctrine.

These verses which here ensue were sent and written between the emperor and pope Innocent IV., which, because to the learned they are both commodious and profitable, at the end of this history I thought good to place.

Fredericus Imper. Innocent IV. Papæ.

Fata monent, stellæque docent, aviumque volatus,
  Totius subito malleus orbis ero:
Roma diu titubans longis erroribus acta
  Corruet, et mundi desinet esse caput.

Innocent. Papa Frederico Imper.

Fata silent, stellæque tacent, nil prædicat ales,
  Solius est proprium nosse futura Dei:
Niteris incassum navem submergere Petri:
  Fluctuat, at nunquam mergitur illa ratis.

Fama refert, scriptura docet, peccata loquuntur,
Quod tibi vita brevis, pœna perennis erit.
Quod divina manus potuit, sensit Julianus,
Tu succedis ei, te tenet ira Dei.
FRE. fremit in mundo, DE. deprimit alta profundo,
RI. mala rimatur, CUS. cuspide cuncta minatur.

Fredericus Innocentio.

Fata monent, stellæque docent, aviumque volatus,
Lapsurum te mox ad stygis antra nigræ:
Cymba Petri non est, sed Christi, quæ natat undis
Fluctuat, at nusquam mergitur illa ratis.
Fama refert, tua scripta docent, peccata nefanda
Interitum ostendunt, exitiumque tuum
Strangulat Adrianum musca; annon ira tonantis
Cogitat, et de te sumere supplicium?
Carcere suspendit sese Benedictus, et alter
In stupro captus, saucius ense perit.
Sylvestrum extinguit Satan sceleratior ipse.
Ergo tuis factis præmia digna feres.
Innocuum te voce notas, cum sis nociturus
Orbi terrarum christianoque gregi.

Fredericus Innocentio de integro.

Esses si membrum, non te caput orbis et urbis
Jactares, cum sis orbis et urbis onus.
Nunc membrum non es, sed putre cadaver et ulcus,
Ense recidendum, ridiculumque caput.
A Daniele βδέλυγμα, nefasque caputque malorum
Diceris, a Paulo filius exitii.
Nos solum christum nostrum caput esse malorum
Totius orbis te caput esse facis.
Et caput est unum, quod Paulus dicit ubique;
Tu vecors balatro, dic mihi quale caput?
Corporis ergo caput monstrosi, monstra parisque,
Monstra paris monachos, scorta nefanda foves.
Est tua religio stuprum, ira, superbia, cædes,
Error, deliciæ, fulmina, turpe lucrum.
Ex his ergo liquet Christum te spernere: Christo
Hostem esse invisum, dedecorique Deo.
Rex tandem veniet cœlo delapsus ab alto,
Tunc non defendent te, sacra, missa, cruces;
Non in sublimi surgentes vertice cristæ,
Non diploma potens, non tua sacra cohors
Nec diadema triplex, nec sedes sanguine parta,
Nullus honos solii, purpura nulla tui
Triginta argenteis Christum vendebat Iudas,
Tu Christi vendis corpora pluratui
Corpora tu vendis Christi parvo ære, polumque,
Cœlestes genios, sidera, jura, Deos.

Certain preachers in Suevia.

As ye have heard of the iniquity and raging pride of the popish church against this lawful emperor; so now shall ye hear (Christ willing) how God beginneth to resist and withstand the corruption of that whorish church, by stirring up certain faithful teachers in sundry countries; as in the country of Suevia about the time of this emperor (A. D. 1240), or near upon the same, where were many preachers, mentioned in the chronicle of Urspergensis, and also in Crantzius,[1] who preached freely against the pope. These preachers (as Crantzius saith) ringing the bells, and calling the barons together in Hallis of Suevia, there preached that the pope was a heretic, and

(1) Lib. VIII. cap. 16 et 18.

Henry III. A.D. 1250. that his bishops and prelates were Simoniacs and heretics; and that the inferior priests and prelates had no authority to bind and loose, but were all seducers. Item, that no pope, bishop, or priest, could restrain men from their duty of serving and worshipping God, and therefore, such cities or countries as were then under the pope's curse, might, notwithstanding, lawfully resort to the receiving of sacraments as well as before. Item, that friars, Dominic and Franciscan, did subvert the church with their preaching; and, as the indulgence of the pope and his popelings was of no regard, so, that remission which they did preach unto them, they preached it not from the pope, but as from the Lord. And thus much I thought here to recite, whereby it may appear how the resisting of the pope's usurped power and corrupt doctrine is no new thing in these days in the church of Christ.

Resistance against the pope no new thing in Christ's church.

Arnoldus de nova villa condemned of heresy.

And not long after these rose up Arnoldus de Nova Villa, a Spaniard, and a man famously learned and a great writer (A. D. 1250), whom the pope with his spiritualty condemned among heretics for holding and writing against the corrupt errors of the popish church. His teaching was, that Satan had seduced all the world from the truth of Christ Jesus. Item, that the faith which then christian men were commonly taught, was such a faith as the devils had; meaning perhaps (as we now affirm) that the papists do teach only the historical faith, which is the faith 'Historiæ, non fiduciæ.' Item, that christian people (meaning belike, for the most part) are led by the pope into hell. Item, that all cloisterers are void of charity and damned; and that they all do falsify the doctrine of Christ. Item, that the divines do evil in mixing philosophy with divinity. Item, that masses are not to be celebrated; and that they ought not to sacrifice for the dead. Certain other opinions there are, which the slanderous sects of monks and friars do attribute unto him; but (as they are wont in all others to do) rather upon envious taking, than of any just cause given.[1]

Johannes Semeca, the gloss-writer of the pope's decrees, excommunicated.

And as this Arnold was condemned, so also at the same time, Johannes Semeca, the gloss-writer of the pope's decrees, and provost of Halberstat, was excommunicated and deprived of his provostship, for resisting pope Clement IV. in gathering certain exactions in Germany; and therefore he appealed from the pope to a general council, and had many great favourers on his side, till at last both the pope and he died.

Gulielmus de S. Amore.

Consequently, in this order and number followeth the worthy and valiant champion of Christ, and adversary of Antichrist, Gulielmus de Sancto Amore, a master of Paris, and chief ruler then of that university. This Gulielmus in his time had no small ado in writing against the friars and their hypocrisy, but especially against the begging friars, both condemning their whole order, and also accusing them, as those that did disturb and trouble all the churches of Christ by their preaching in churches against the will of the ordinaries and pastors, by their hearing of confessions, and executing the charges of curates and pastors in their churches. All the testimonies of Scripture that make against Antichrist, he applieth against the clergy of prelates, and the pope's spiritualty. The same Gulielmus is thought to be the author of the book, which is attributed to the school of

(1) Vide librum de testibus veritatis.

Paris, and entitled, 'De periculis Ecclesiæ;' where he proveth by nine and thirty arguments, that friars be false apostles.

Henry III.

A.D. 1250.

Moreover, he doth well expound this saying of Christ, "If thou wilt be perfect, go and sell away all thou hast, and come follow me," declaring there, poverty to be enjoined us of Christ; 'non actualem, sed habitualem;' not in such sort as standeth in outward action, when no need requireth, but in inward affection of heart when need shall require. As though the meaning and precept of our Lord were not, that we should cast away actually all that we have; but that, when the confession of the name of God and the glory of Christ shall so require, then we be ready to leave and relinquish what things soever for the sake of him, &c. As when he requireth in us, after the like phrase, the hatred of father and mother, and of our own lives, he biddeth us not to dishonour father or mother, much less to hate them; but that then, when case shall require, we set all things behind the love of Christ. Many other worthy works he compiled, wherein albeit he uttered nothing but what was truth, yet, notwithstanding, he was by Antichrist and his rabble condemned for a heretic, exiled, and his books burnt; whose heretical arguments, as they called them, that thou mayest better judge thereof, hereunder I thought good to place. Against false prophets, with signs to know them by, these his words do follow:—

The place of the gospel expounded, 'Go and sell all and come follow me.'

For because these seducers (saith he) name themselves to be apostles, and say that they are sent of God to preach, to absolve and dispense with the souls of men, by means of their ministry, read the saying of the apostle: [2 Cor. xi. 11.] "For such apostles are subtle and crafty workmen, disguising themselves to be like the apostles of Christ." Therefore, we mean to show some certain infallible and probable tokens, by the which false apostles may be discerned from the true preachers and apostles of Christ.

The first sign or mark is, that such as be true preachers do not enter into simple women's houses laden with sin, and take them as it were captive, as many of the false preachers do; as in the second epistle of St. Paul to Timothy, the third chapter, is manifest, saying, "Of those sorts are they, which enter into women's houses," &c. Therefore those preachers who come into women's houses, to the intent they may take them captive, be not true preachers, but false apostles.

First sign and token to know a false prophet by.

The second sign and token is, that those that be true preachers do not deceive simple men with painted and flattering words, whereby they prefer their own trash and tradition, as all false prophets do, as in the last chapter to the Romans appeareth, saying, "By their pleasant and sugared talk, and by their blessing and crossing, they deceive and beguile the hearts of innocent men and women."[1] Glossary: "With gay glorious words they extol and set forth their traditions, whereby they deceive simple men." Very greatly do they deceive the souls of simple men, who cause them to enter into their sect, which they term religion. And they who before led a naughty life, by reason of their ignorance or simplicity, after their entrance, become subtle and false deceiving hypocrites, entering together with the rest into poor men's houses; yea, and oftentimes they become worse than the others. Whereupon, [St. Matthew xxii. 15,] "Woe be unto you Scribes and Pharisees, hypocrites, which go about," &c. Therefore they who do this, are no true messengers, but false apostles.

Second sign. True preachers do not deceive simple men with painted and flattering words.

The third sign is, that the true apostles, if they be reproved, suffer the same patiently, saying, "The tokens of my apostleship are accomplished among you, in all patience and sufferance;" [2 Cor. xii. 12,] meaning that patience which pertaineth to the manners of the preachers. Therefore they, who suffer not correction or punishment, be no true apostles, but rather show themselves to be no Christians at all; "No man can say that Jesus is the Lord, but by the Holy

The third sign is, that they take in good part when they be reproved.

(1) "By good words and fair speeches deceive the hearts of the simple." Rom. xvi. 18.—Ed.

Henry III. A.D. 1250.

Ghost." [1 Cor. xii. 3.] Glossary: "It is meet that Christians should be humbled, to the intent that they may suffer themselves to be reproved, and not to be holden up with yea and nay." And also such men do show themselves to be carnal, and not spiritual at all, although they feign themselves to be spiritual. "Therefore am I become an enemy unto you." [Gal. iv. 16.] Notwithstanding the Glossary saith, "No carnal man will be reproved, although he err." Wherefore, those preachers who suffer not correction, seem not to be true apostles, but false prophets.

The fourth, that they commend not themselves.

The fourth sign is, that true apostles commend not themselves [2 Cor. x. 12]. "For we dare not join ourselves, nor yet compare ourselves unto others which commend and boast of many of their acts, when God alloweth none of them at all." Also true preachers, although they be indeed praiseworthy for their good deserts, in the consciences of men are they praiseworthy, and not to the outward show alone; "We commend ourselves," saith the apostle, "to the consciences of all men." [2 Cor. iv. 2.] Then they do not commend themselves in comparison of others. Wherefore the Glossary saith, upon the same place, "Those that deserve no commendation, but in comparison of others, do challenge to themselves other men's deserts and praise." Wherefore it is said, "Even as our well-beloved brother Paul, according to the wisdom that God hath given unto him, hath written unto you." [2 Peter iii. 15.] Glossary: "The chiefest of the apostles hath here forgotten his papal authority, and also his keys that were delivered unto him; for he is astonied as it were at the great wisdom given unto his brother Paul." For indeed it is the manner of the elect children of God, to be more in love with the virtues of other men, than with their own. Wherefore it is written, "Let those that are superiors esteem of themselves in all humility." [Phil. ii. 2.] They therefore that do the contrary, saying, 'That their state or doings be better than other men's,' although they be preachers, yet are they no true apostles indeed, but false prophets.

The fifth, they need no letters commendatory.

The fifth sign is, that true apostles need no letters of commendation; nor yet desire to have themselves praised by men, as saith the apostle, "We need not the letters of commendation of any man," [2 Cor. iii. 1,] that is to say, of false prophets.

The sixth, they preach not except they be sent.

The sixth sign is, that true apostles do not preach unless they be sent, as "How shall they preach, unless they be sent?" [Rom. x. 15.] Glossary: "There be no true apostles, but those that be sent: for they have no need of signs who are true witness-bearers, but those that be not sent and do preach are false prophets."

The seventh, when those false prophets preach, that were never sent.

The seventh sign is, forasmuch as false prophets have their authority in their own names; wherefore it is written, "For we dare not boast of ourselves, or make comparison." [2 Cor. x. 12.] Glossary: "That is to say, with those that be false prophets, not taking their authority from God, but usurping the same, desirous to bear rule, claiming in their own name their authority." And, therefore, although peradventure by presumption, they say that they are sent of God, as all heretics will say; yet, notwithstanding, unless they shall prove their sending either by spiritual prophecy, as John the Baptist did, saying, "I am the voice of a crier in the desert;" as out of the prophet Isaiah, in John's gospel is alleged [chap. i. 23], or else by miracles, as Moses did, who turned his rod into a serpent, and again, from a serpent to a rod [Exod. vii. 10, 12], they ought to be excommunicated, till such time as they cease from preaching. Yet notwithstanding, a miracle ought not to be a sufficient testimony of their sending, forasmuch as they be done oftentimes, and that of evil and wicked men, (1 Quæst. 1.) we may perceive towards the end. But miracles ought to be suspected, forasmuch as our Saviour saith, "Then shall false prophets arise," &c. [Matth. xxiv. 11.] Therefore they who do challenge authority in their own name, forasmuch as they have not their authority from God, are not true apostles, but false preachers.

The eighth, that they pretend great holiness in superstition.

The eighth sign is, that false prophets, pretending great wisdom and holiness to be in superstition, have named their own traditions to be religion, which are rather to be counted sacrilege or church robbery, and do usurp unto themselves, for due deserts of other men, by boasting and bragging among strange and unknown people. Wherefore the apostle speaking of false prophets [Col. ii. 8], saith, "According to the precepts of men, which having a face of wisdom consist in superstition, interlaced with humility." Glossary: "That is to say, mingled with feigned religion, that it might be called religion, when in very deed it is nothing else but sacrilege, because it is contrary to all authority;" that is, contrary to God himself, that any man should desire to have government of a multitude without public commandment, as [Deut. xxiii. 24], "Thou hast entered into thy neighbour's vineyard." Glossary: "That is to say, into the church of another bishop." May a man warn and admonish others, or else correct that congregation which is not lawful for him to govern, nor yet to take so great a charge upon him? No. And that it is not lawful to enter into another bishop's diocese, it is apparent, because it is not lawful for the archbishop so to do. To this effect appertaineth that which is read [6 Quæst. 3.] And also it is written [9 Quæst. 2] throughout. Therefore those preachers, who, against God and his divine Scriptures, do call their own traditions religion, are not apostles, but false prophets.

The ninth sign is, by the authority which they have: for although they be no preachers of the gospel or ministers of the sacraments, yet they will live by the gospel, and not by the labour of their own hands, contrary to the text, [2 Thess. iii. 8.] "Neither have we eaten any man's bread for nought, or of free cost." Glossary: "Then those false prophets ought much more to live by their labour, who have not that authority which we ought to have; that is to say, to live by the gospel." And St. Augustine speaketh of this more expressly, in his book *De opere Monachorum*, in these words: "Those our brethren do claim to themselves (very rashly as me thinketh) that they have any such authority, to live by the gospel. If they be preachers of the gospel, I grant that indeed they have such authority; if they be ministers of the altar, if they be disposers of the sacraments, they cannot well but take to themselves this authority, as also manifestly to challenge the same; if, at least, they have not wherewithal to sustain this present life, without labour of their hands." As though he would have said, if they be not such manner of men, then have they no authority to live by the gospel. Therefore those preachers who have not authority to live by the gospel, or minister the sacraments, because they have no congregation whereby to take charge of souls, and yet, for all that, will needs live upon the gospel; they be no true apostles, but false prophets.

That when they neither preach nor minister, yet they live upon other men's labour.

The tenth sign is, that false teachers rejoice more to be commended themselves, than that the word of God should have the commendation and praise. But they that are true preachers and apostles are far otherwise minded, "Not seeking the praise of men," &c. [1 Thess. ii. 4.] And herein he toucheth those false prophets, who desire rather to be commended themselves, than that the word of God which they preach should have the commendation: but he is an apostle, who not seeking the glory of this present world, but for the glory to come, doth abase himself, to the intent that the preaching and word of God might be commended and exalted. They, therefore, who desire to have praise and to be commended of others, rather than that the word of God should have the praise, be not true apostles, but false prophets.

That they take that to themselves, which pertaineth to the word of God.

The eleventh sign is, that true apostles preach only for God's cause, and for the health of souls, and for no temporal gain, as St. Paul saith, [2 Cor. ii. 5,] "We preach not ourselves," &c. Glossary: "Our preaching tendeth not to our glory and gain, but only to the glory of Christ." But the preaching of Christ, by those that are false prophets, tendeth to the contrary. Whereupon it is said, [Phil. i. 18,] "Whether it be upon occasion given, or else for the Verity's sake, let Christ be preached," &c. Glossary: "False prophets do preach the gospel upon some occasion, as either by seeking some commodity at the hands of men, or else because of getting goods, honour, or praise among men." Notwithstanding, however, that they be ready and willing, as it should seem, to bear and sustain injuries, yet they seek not so much the health of him to whom they preach, as in very deed they do their own commodity and gain. Whereupon St. Paul saith, [2 Cor. xii. 14,] "Because I seek not the things that be yours." Glossary: "That is to say, not your treasure, as gold and silver, but only you yourselves." For, otherwise, it could by no means be gathered that they should understand him to speak or mean of their substance, because he more esteemeth them than their money, to the intent that they might understand his great good will towards them. Therefore these evil and naughty preachers who preach for worldly gain or honour, or else for the praise and commendation of men, be no true apostles, but false prophets. But it may be asked, how shall men understand when these good fellows preach for their

They preach for gain, and not for God's cause.

Henry III. A.D. 1250.

own vain-glory's sake? It may be answered thus, when they preach before they be called [2 Cor. x. 17], "Whosoever boasteth, let him boast and rejoice in the Lord." Glossary: "Which thing he cannot by any means do that hath not his authority from God." For if any such prophet preach, he seeketh his own glory, and that may easily be perceived. Because he is not called of God, he hath no such authority of him; that is to say, of his church or congregation, as [Heb. v. 4], "No man taketh to himself any dignity, but he that is called of God, as Aaron was." Glossary: "He is called of God, that is, lawfully chosen of the congregation."

They counterfeit to love, where they hate.

The twelfth sign or token of a false prophet is, because such prophets do counterfeit themselves to have greater care and love to men's souls, than they have that be their very governors and pastors, although they have no charge at all of them; against whom the apostle speaketh [1 Thess. ii. 7], "We are become meek and loving towards you, even as the nurse which giveth her child suck." Glossary: "A woman nurseth other men's children for wages, and not for love alone; but she giveth her own suck of very love without respect of money." Therefore those preachers who feign themselves to have a greater love and affection to the souls of men, than they that have the charge over them, seem not to be true apostles. The apostles study neither for eloquence, nor for the curious placing of their words, but false prophets do both, as [1 Cor. xiv. 23], "If the simple and ineloquent man," &c. Glossary: "The apostles were not eloquent, but false prophets are full of curious eloquence." Also upon the same subject another gloss: "The Corinthians were led away from the gospel by over nice eloquence." [2 Cor. vi. 4.] "Let us show ourselves before all men as the ministers of God." Glossary: "The ministers of God do not flatter as false prophets do." And for this occasion those that be true apostles have not their abiding in princes' courts and noblemen's houses, knowing this saying of Christ [Matt. xi. 8], "Behold, those that are clothed with silks dwell in kings' courts." Glossary: "And therefore true apostles are not conversant in princes' courts, and noblemen's houses." Hard and strait life with the preaching of the gospel loveth not to come near princes' palaces, and noblemen's houses. Oftentimes it cometh to pass that courtiers are found great flatterers; therefore those preachers that have their abode in princes' courts, or that in any other place are used to flatter, are not true apostles, but false prophets.

They circumvent men, to have their goods, and care for nothing else.

The thirteenth sign is, that true apostles or messengers do not circumvent or subtlely go about to deceive men, that they should give unto them their goods, either in their lifetime, or else at the time of their death, as [2 Cor. vii. 2], "We have falsely deceived no man." Glossary: "By the subtle and deceitful getting away of your substance, as false prophets do, who get away from you those things that be yours under pretence of great friendship." Also [Matt. xxiii. 14], "Woe be unto you, Scribes and Pharisees, you hypocrites, which spoil widows' houses by your long prayers;" who mean nothing else by your superstition, but that you may spoil and rob the people. [Luke xx. 47], "Which devour widows' houses by dissembling of your long prayer." Glossary: "Who make over-long prayers, to the intent they may seem more devout, and that they may get both money and great commendation of all such as be sick and troubled with the burden of their sins; whose prayers be turned into sin, which neither are profitable for themselves nor any other, but rather shall have for making those prayers greater damnation, forasmuch as by the same they deceive others." For by this, that they receive and take both gold and silver, it appeareth that they preach not for souls' health sake, but only for filthy lucre and gain sake. [Matt. x. 9], "Be ye possessors neither of gold nor silver." Glossary: "If they then have these things, they cannot seem or be thought to preach for the health of the soul, but for lucre's sake." And so saith Jerome upon the prophet Malachi, "Because some prophets took money, their prophecy became divination;" that is to say, their prophecy appeared not to be prophecy, but divination, or enchantment: that is, that such prophecy proceedeth not from God, but from the devil. And this appeareth in [1 Quæst. 1.] having this beginning, "Nunquam Divinatio," &c. Therefore those preachers who circumvent and beguile men, to the intent that they should give them their goods, either in their lifetime, or after their death, are not true apostles, but false prophets.

The fourteenth sign is, that false prophets, when any verity is preached, with which for the most part they are not acquainted, or that toucheth them, then begin they to chase and bark against the same. Whereupon the apostle [Phil. iii. 2], saith, "Behold the dogs," &c. Glossary: "Understand you that they are not dogs by nature, but by their usage and conditions, barking against the truth, which they were never acquainted with." And so he compareth them right well to dogs, because dogs follow rather custom than reason; so false apostles do keep the custom of the law, and do bite and bark against the truth, as though they were without the gift of reason. Also [2 Tim. iv. 3], "They get them instructors according to their own desires." Glossary: "Which may teach them what things they themselves are willing to hear, because the truth seemeth nothing pleasant unto them." Therefore those preachers who bark against the late revealed truth, which toucheth them very near, and therefore cause the same to be hidden and kept under, are not true apostles, but false prophets.

They cannot abide to have the truth preached.

The fifteenth sign is, that the true apostles do not force any to receive or hear them who be unwilling, but send them away rather, lest they should seem to seek after some earthly and transitory thing. [Matt. x. 14], "Whosoever will not receive you, get you out of that city, and shake the dust from off your feet," &c. Glossary: "That you may thereby show that the desire of earthly things hath no power in you." Therefore those preachers who strive and wrestle, as it were, to the intent they would be received and heard, are not true apostles, forasmuch as the apostle saith [1 Cor. xi. 16], "If any man appear among you to be over-contentious or full of strife, such custom have we none, nor yet the congregation of Christ."

False prophets enforce those to hear who are not willing.

The sixteenth sign is, that the apostles did not procure the indignation of those princes, by whom they were esteemed and regarded, against such persons as would not receive them and hear them; as we read in the lives of Simon and Jude, the apostles. The chief ruler, being very angry, commanded a very great fire to be made, that the bishops might be cast into the same, and all others who went about to defame the doctrine of the apostles of Christ. But the apostles fell down before the emperor, saying, "We beseech you, sir, let not us be the authors or causers of this destruction or calamity; nor let us who are sent to be the preservation of men, and to revive those that are dead through sin, be killers of those that be alive." Therefore those preachers who seek to stir up the displeasure of princes, against those whose favours now they enjoy, who will not receive and hear them, or rather, whom they themselves hate, are not true apostles, but false prophets.

They cause princes to hate and punish them that will not hear them.

The seventeenth sign is, that the apostles of Christ have not only the knowledge of those things which God hath already done, but also of those things which he will hereafter do, as in the Apocalypse [chap. iv. 6.], "The beasts were full of eyes both behind and before." Glossary: "Obtaining the knowledge of those things which God had done, as also what he would do, hereafter, in the end of the world." Therefore those that say they know not the perils of the church in the latter time which are prophesied before, or that they care not for them, or else, if they know them, have not eyes behind and before, are no true apostles; therefore when they call themselves apostles, they are false prophets.

False prophets do not know either what God hath done, or yet will do, as true prophets do.

The eighteenth sign is, that true apostles do not desire the riches and goods of them to whom they preach, whereby they are discerned from wolves, that is to say, from false prophets. [Acts xx. 8.] "I have desired no man's gold nor silver." Glossary: "By this are wolves discerned, for they desire such things." And again in the same place; "For those things which I have need of, and those which were with me, these hands have ministered." Glossary: "This example also of labouring is a spectacle for bishops whereby they are discerned from wolves." For such as ask or beg of those to whom they preach, or set any other to ask or beg in their names, do seem to commit simony, like Gehazi, of whom it is read [2 Kings v. 20], that he craved certain apparel of Naaman, the Syrian, to whom his master Elisha had restored the benefit of health, notwithstanding he had gotten those garments unwitting to his master. Whereupon Gregory Nazianzen saith, [1 Quæst. 1] "Qui isti debetur." But some man perhaps will say, cannot the preacher ask money, or money's worth, of those to whom he preacheth? Or at the least, may not he beg? To this may be

That they preach for money, and are not to be discerned from wolves.

Henry III.

A.D. 1250.

answered; if the preacher by authority preach and feed his flock as a true pastor with the food of God's word, he may take money or money's worth; but then it is not begging or craving, but it is by authority, as [2 Tim. ii. 6], "It is meet that the husbandman that tilleth the ground, should first and after others, receive the commodity of his increase." Glossary: "He putteth the virtuous preacher out of doubt, not preaching for the intent to make merchandise of the gospel, and giveth him to understand, that it is lawful for him to take of them whom he feedeth as his flock what things soever he hath need of, and doth it not in begging or craving, but by good authority." It is manifest that it cannot in any place of the holy Scripture be found, that the preacher ought to beg. But begging is forbidden of all the apostles of Christ, and is abhorred by Solomon and by St. Augustine, and reproved by divers other holy men. Therefore it is manifest that the true apostles do not desire the temporal goods of them to whom they preach, neither do they beg nor crave the same. They, therefore, that require any thing of them to whom they preach, or else set any other man to ask for them, or in their names, do not seem to be true apostles, but false preachers.

If the preacher do his duty in preaching, he may take lawfully for his necessary things.

The nineteenth sign is, that true apostles are patient in tribulation, neither do they render evil for good. [Matt. x. 16.] "Behold, I send you as sheep among wolves." Glossary: "They, that occupy the place of preaching, ought not to procure any evil toward their brethren, as the example of Christ teacheth" [1 Pet. ii. 23], "Who, when he was reviled, reviled not again, but did submit himself to him that judgeth justly." They therefore that suffer not injury, but rather do wrong themselves, are not true apostles, but false apostles.

True apostles do not render evil for good, as false do.

The twentieth sign is, that true apostles at their first coming are evil entertained, as the Lord saith [Matt. xxiv. 9], "Ye shall be hated of all men for my name's sake." But at length such get the victory, according to that saying, [1 John v. 4,] "Every thing that is of God overcometh the world." They, therefore, that in the beginning rejoice and are well entertained, but in the end are rejected, seem not to be true apostles, but false.

True apostles are not so well entertained as false prophets be.

The twenty-first sign is, that true preachers go not to preach unto those who have preachers appointed unto them, because they have not to rejoice of a company belonging to another man's charge; as [Rom. xv. 20], "I have preached the gospel where Christ was not before preached, lest I should build upon another man's foundation." And again St. Paul saith [2 Cor. x. 15], "We are not boasters, nor busy in other men's matters." Glossary: "Where another man had laid the foundation." Likewise in the same chapter [16], "Not having pleasure to boast of other men's labours," that is to say, of those which he committed to the government of another man. Likewise Augustine saith; "Honour ought to seek thee, and not thou honour." Also Chrysostom; "Authority is in love with such a man as refuseth her, and yet abhorreth her not." They therefore that procure and have a desire to preach unto the people committed to another man's charge, which is an office of honour, especially in councils, synods, and great assemblies, also in kings' and princes' courts, and prelates' palaces, are not true apostles, but false teachers.

True preachers build not upon any other man's foundation.

Authority loveth them that refuse her, and yet abhor her not.

The twenty-second sign is, that true apostles, when they know themselves to do much good in the church and congregation of God, yet, notwithstanding, are not puffed up with pride [Ezek. iii. 9]; "O son of man, I have made thy face as an adamant stone." The adamant stone, when it draweth iron unto it, is not thereby either lifted up or altered. Likewise a true preacher, when he draweth unto him, by his preaching, sinners whose hearts are as hard as iron, is never the more lifted up or higher minded therefore. But as in Luke [chap. xvii. 10], "When ye have done all that ye can, and as well as ye can, yet say that you are unprofitable servants;" and in Psalm xcv. "Not unto us, Lord, not unto us, but to thy name be given the glory." They therefore that do arrogantly boast themselves of their fruit, and of the benefit they have done in the church of God, saying, "We have given light to the universal church, which was blind before our time, and we have put out the flame of sin in the church of God" (when perhaps they have more furthered hypocrisy than either truth or verity), they are not true prophets, but false, of whom it is spoken in the Psalms, "The mouth of them that speak proud things," &c.

True prophets are not proud and vain-glorious, as false prophets be.

The twenty-third sign is, that true apostles do not seek the favour of the world, nor yet how to please men, as [Gal. i. 10], "If I should please men,"

False prophets always are men-pleasers.

that is to say, "if I had a desire to please men, I should not be the servant of God." Whereupon the apostle says to the Colossians [chap. iii. 22], "Not as men-pleasers." Glossary: "Seeking to please, because we have not the pleasing Spirit." Therefore those preachers that seek the favour of the world, and do labour to this intent that they might please men, are not true apostles, but false.

Henry III.

A.D. 1250.

The twenty-fourth sign is, that true apostles, when they have meat and drink, they are contented, neither do they desire over-dainty fare, according to the saying in Luke [chap. x. 8], "Eating and drinking those things that are set before you." Glossary: "The gospel condemneth not altogether costly and delicate fare, yet it so alloweth the same, that if we have meat and drink, we ought not to grudge, but to be therewith content." Therefore those preachers, who, although they neither be sent, nor have authority to preach, are yet offended when they have not fine and delicate fare, are not true apostles, but false preachers.

True prophets eat what is set before them, and give God thanks, unlike false prophets.

The twenty-fifth sign is, that true apostles do love more the law of God than their own estimation amongst their neighbours; according to that in the Proverbs [chap. vii. 2, 3], "Keep my law as the apple of thine eye, and bind the same upon thy fingers, and write the same in the table of thy heart." Whereupon also the Psalmist [Psalm cxix. 72], "The law of thy mouth is dearer unto me than thousands of gold and silver." Glossary: "Charity doth more love the law of God, than the desire of gold and silver a thousand fold." He, therefore, that seeth the gospel of Christ trodden under foot, which is the eternal glad tidings, to be taken away by that cursed one, and doth neglect and contemn the same, or else, peradventure, consenteth unto the same to the outward appearance of the world; and yet, because he will keep his temporal dignity and estimation, refuseth not to stir up strife and contention about the same, and so to be evil spoken of, seemeth not to be an apostle of Christ, but rather a false prophet, if he be a preacher.

False prophets love more their own estimation, than that the word of God should be truly taught.

The twenty-sixth sign is, that true apostles seek not after such fine lodgings and wealthy habitations, where they may have all things at their commandments; but rather such honest resting places where they may have necessary things for themselves, with their good wills of whom they have them. And they take nothing of such whom they see to be so ready and liberal in giving, nor think that they do him more pleasure in receiving the gift, than the others do in giving them the same; according to that in Matthew [chap. x. 11], where it is said, "Into what city or town soever ye shall enter, inquire out those that be of good report in the same, and abide you with them so long as you tarry in the same city or town." Glossary: "Your host, with whom ye lodge, ought to be chosen by the good report of neighbours, lest your preaching be evil spoken of, by reason of his infamy; neither ought such men to run from house to house." But whom shall we call "worthy of good report?" Glossary: "Him who knoweth better to do other men good, than to receive a good turn of another;" and this is he which giveth willingly, for Christ's cause, and not in respect of any commodity. Also true apostles receive nothing of such men as lie weltering in their sins, but rather of those that are washed and cleansed from their sins; whereupon that saying [2 Cor. viii. 5], "They have given themselves first to the Lord." Glossary: "Because they now, amending their old errors and vicious manners, have vowed themselves unto the Lord, and afterwards gave of that which they had to their brethren; for otherwise they ought not to have taken any thing of them, because gifts do blind the eyes; but those that give, where there is no cause of reproof in their doings, have no just cause to give." Therefore those preachers that seek how to come by dainty fare, and do receive bribes and rewards of naughty men that have this world at will, to the intent that those preachers may cover and hide their faults, and who get of others what they can by subtlety, or who give indeed to remove the shameless importunity of the craver, or else for avoiding of present shame, rather than for any love they have to God, are not true apostles, but false prophets; according to that in the Corinthians [2 Cor. ix. 7], "The Lord doth love a willing giver." Glossary: "He that giveth for present shame, or else that he may be free from the importunacy of him that asketh, doth lose his substance and merit: wherefore he that hath respect to these things, doth not seek the fruit and profit of the giver, but the gift itself, as saith the apostle [Phil. iv. 17], "Seek not the gift, but the fruit or benefit of the giver."

They are not contented with necessary things, but look after superfluous.

Henry III.

A.D. 1250.

The twenty-seventh sign is, that true apostles do not endeavour themselves to seek and enjoy the fruit of other men's labours that they may be fed thereby, because that the belly is such men's god, according to those words [2 Thess. iii. 2], "We have heard of some amongst you which walk inordinately, not labouring at all, but living delicately, or idly." Glossary: "On other men's labours;" and deserve they to be fed? The discipline of the Lord cannot away with that doing; for the belly is their god, which provide to have more than necessary dishes of meat. Therefore those preachers who so do, are not true apostles, but false.

Those be false prophets, whose belly is their god.

The twenty-eighth sign is, that true apostles do not rejoice only on account of the miracles or other excellent works which the Lord doth by them, but they rather rejoice for the salvation which they look for from the Lord, than that by doing those miracles they desire any honour; according to that which is written in Luke [chap. x. 20], saying, "Rejoice ye not for that the spirits be subject unto you, but because your names are registered in heaven." They therefore that boast of their own miracles, or of any that belong unto them, for this cause, that they are saved by the doing of them, as many do say, seem not to be true apostles, but false.

True prophets rejoice not in miracles, as false prophets do.

The twenty-ninth sign is, that the true apostles do never seek their own glory in this life, but the glory of Christ. "He that speaketh of himself doth seek his own glory; but he that seeketh the glory of him which sent him," that is, of whom he is sent, "is a true apostle." [John vii. 18.] Therefore those who seek the things that pertain to the glory of this world, of the which one is to be assistant to those that bear rule and authority, or according to the saying of Boetius, 'De consolatione;' "Those that do desire to be extolled," either they reign and bear rule themselves, or else do desire to be near about them that have such dominion. Another is, they desire to have the fame and victory of that for which they have nothing at all deserved before God; whereupon is written that saying of the apostle [Gal. v. 26], "Let not us become desirous of vain-glory." Glossary: "To be desirous of vain-glory, is to have victory without any merit or desert;" and those, I say, that do such things, seem not to be true apostles, but false.

True prophets seek not their own glory.

The thirtieth sign is, that true apostles care not for the solemnities of men, neither for their salutations, nor feastings, nor any other benefit of theirs. They therefore who love and seek the company and fellowship of men, their feastings, and other their commodities, do not seem to be true apostles, but false.

True prophets seek the solemn salutations of men.

The one and thirtieth sign is, that true apostles do not commonly resort to other men's tables, lest they should, for a meal's meat, become flatterers [2 Thess. iii. 9], "That we should give an example to follow us." Glossary: "He that cometh oftentimes to another man's table, being given to idleness, cannot choose but flatter him that feedeth him." But Christ's religion calleth men to liberty and to no such bondage; they therefore that resort oftentimes, and that of their own minds, to other men's tables, living idly, are not true apostles, but false.

False prophets resort to other men's boards and flatter for a meal's meat.

The two and thirtieth sign is, that true apostles do not hate their enemies, and such as hate them; which doctrine the Lord taught [Matt. v. 44], saying, "Love your enemies, do well to them which hate you;" but false prophets do hurt and defame their neighbours, as saith Jeremiah [chap. xii. 10, 11], "The prophets of Jerusalem have defiled the whole earth." Glossary: "They are not contented to hurt their neighbours only, but also whom they before this time have hated, they defame and speak evil of in every place they come to." Therefore those preachers who hate them whom they think are their enemies, and that defame them, are not true apostles, but false preachers.

True prophets do not hate their enemies.

The thirty-third sign is, that false prophets, when they are examined and proved whether they be true apostles or liars, take that very grievously, and persecute all those that can prove them to be so, and also do stir up and provoke others to persecute the same men; who also join themselves together by secular power, even as certain false prophets did in the primitive church against the bishop of Ephesus, to whom the Lord said [Rev. ii. 2, 3], "I know," that is to say, I do allow, "thy works and thy labour;" that is, thy tribulation, "because thou canst not away with those that be evil men." Glossary: "But that thou hast a desire to amend them, or else to expel them—"and hast examined those which say that they are apostles, and are but liars, and also hast suf-

True prophets do not persecute men.

fered this patiently." Glossary: "The evils which these false prophets, joined together by secular power, do bring in, are not the doings of true apostles, but false prophets."

The thirty-fourth sign is, that true apostles go not to preach to those who are converted already by other men, but rather do convert those who are not yet converted, lest that they should build upon another man's foundation; as St. Paul [Rom. xv. 20] saith; "I have laboured so, that from Jerusalem to Illyricus, I have replenished the gospel in every place." Glossary: "That is, I have preached the same abundantly, in whom the great virtue of the Holy Ghost appeareth, because so many nations (that is, the Gentiles), have received the gospel by my preaching." "But I have preached the gospel there where Christ was not preached before, lest I should build upon another man's foundation." Glossary: "I should not preach to those that were converted by another man." Also [2 Cor. x. 15], "We are not such as boast and glory in other men's labours." Glossary: "Where another man laid the foundation, for that should be to boast inordinately." Also in the same place, "not thinking to boast where another man hath government, but in those things which are put in experience." Glossary: "Of other preachers;" because the apostle did preach to those to whom the gospel was never preached, that he might get praise by his own proper labour. Therefore, those preachers who go not to that people who have need to be converted, but to those who are converted already, who have apostles of their own, that is to say, bishops and priests, and yet do boast over another man's flock, are not true apostles, but false prophets.

True prophets preach to those who be not yet converted.

The thirty-fifth sign is, because true apostles, when they are sent, go to their own diocese, and not to another man's diocese, even as Paul being sent, went to the Gentiles when he purposed to preach [Acts xiii. 2], "Separate Paul and Barnabas for the business which I have chosen them unto." Glossary: "According to the appointment and decree of James, Cephas, and John, went he forth to be a teacher unto the Gentiles." But those preachers that stand upon their feet, that is to say, those preachers which have but small worldly substance, for which cause they are more ready to go which way soever it shall please the Lord to send them, I say the Lord hath sent them to preach, not to those that be sufficiently learned, but to those that are infidels; as we read in Ezekiel [chap. ii. 2, 3], "After that, the Spirit of the Lord set Ezekiel upon his feet," In quam spem situs unus tangitur, "and he said unto him, O son of man, behold I sent thee to the nations which have start back from their profession, which have gone from me;" that is, to the Jewish heretics, and to those nations that sometimes have been Christians, as the Egyptians, the Babylonians, and all those that observe the law of Mahomet. Therefore, if such go to those that are already instructed, having both apostles, bishops, and priests of their own; they go not into their own diocese, but into another man's diocese, and are not true apostles, but false preachers. And it is greatly to be feared, lest the church be in hazard and danger by such, unless they be thrust out of the same betimes; even as Jonas, when he was sent to Nineveh, by the Lord, which is interpreted, large or wide, and leadeth to the hill, that is, to the infidels we spake of before. They go not to those infidels according to the commandment of the Lord, but they turn another way, and take their journey into Tarshish, which is interpreted, seeking after joy and pleasure; that is, they go unto those who receive them with joy and gladness, and do well provide for them, that is to say, to godly and devout Christians; and, therefore, it is to be feared lest the ship in which they be (that is, the church) be in great peril, unless they be thrown forth. And therefore the apostle spake of such false prophets not without good cause [2 Tim. ii. 16], "And shun thou those." Glossary: "That is, such men as those be."

True prophets chiefly preach in their own diocese, and not in other men's.

The thirty-sixth sign is, because true apostles do not boast, neither do they attribute unto themselves any thing, but that God hath wrought the same by them. Paul [Rom. xv. 18], saith, "I dare not say any thing but that which Christ hath wrought and accomplished by me." Glossary: "That is, I speak only those things which by me (that is, by my ministry) Christ hath wrought." They therefore that boast of many things, and do attribute much unto themselves which they never did, are not true apostles, but false prophets.

False prophets attribute to themselves that which they never did.

The thirty-seventh sign is, that true apostles do not apply themselves, or lean to logical or philosophical reasons. Therefore those preachers who do

They cleave to

Henry III. A.D. 1250.

endeavour themselves to such kind of reasons, are not true apostles, but false prophets.

logical reasons. They love carnally, not spiritually.

The thirty-eighth sign is, that true apostles do not love carnally, or after the flesh, but hate what thing soever doth resist them in the service of God. "He that doth not hate his father and mother, his son and sister, and also himself, he cannot be my disciple." Luke xiv. 26. Glossary: "That is, he that doth not hate whatsoever doth resist or let him in the service of God, is not worthy to be a disciple, neither can he abide in that office." Therefore forasmuch as true preachers are the true disciples of the Lord, it must needs follow that the preachers who do promote their nephews and kinsfolk (how unworthy soever they be) to ecclesiastical promotions and livings, contrary to the will of God, or do any other thing that letteth or hindereth them in the service of God, are not true apostles, but false prophets.

They hunt after the friendship of this world.

The thirty-ninth sign is, that true apostles do not hunt for the friendship of this world, for he that is the friend of this world is the enemy of God; therefore those preachers, who purchase the friendship of this world, are not true apostles, but false prophets; and forasmuch as the Scripture is infallible, saying [Matt. xxiv. 35], "Heaven and earth shall perish, but my words shall endure for ever;" and the Holy Ghost, which spake by the apostles, cannot lie; (for prophecy, for the most part, is not spoken by the will of man, but holy men of God spake by the inspiration of the Holy Ghost, as it is read in Peter) [2 Pet. i. 21], it remaineth, that all men who are bound to defend the church, may rise up in the defence of the same, according to that in the Proverbs [chap. xxiv. 11], "Deliver those that are led to death, and cease thou not to rescue those who are drawn to destruction." Neither may he allege vain accusations, because it is said in the same place, "If he say he is not able or strong enough, he that beholdeth the thoughts of men's hearts, shall know it," &c. Whatsoever perisheth in the church of God for want of preachers, all that shall be demanded of them at the day of judgment; as Jacob confesseth to Laban, whose sheep he fed [Gen. xxxi. 39], "I did restore all thy loss, and that which was stolen I made answer for." "I will demand his blood at thy hands." Ezek. iii. 24. This is said to the pastor or prelate. But if the other things, which we have spoken of before, could not move the prelates and cardinals, this at least should move them; because that then the spiritual power which doth consist, for the most part, in the exercise of preaching, in hearing confessions, and in enjoining of penance, shall be taken away from them by little and little (for by piecemeal doth the wolf devour the poor and needy man) [3 Quæst. 1], when the authority ecclesiastical, therefore, shall be quite taken from them and disposed to others, such as either by their order, or apostolical grant do challenge to have the same; then doubtless shall neither the jurisdiction of civil causes and pleadings, nor any authority that such prelates have yet remaining, neither yet the possessions of the temporal goods of the church any longer remain amongst them. Shall such have the temporal goods of the church who minister not the spiritual treasure thereof? [1 Cor. ix. 13], "Know ye not that they which kill the sacrifice ought to eat of the sacrifice? and they that serve at the altar are partakers of the altar?" For as the body without the soul cannot stand; so corporal things without spiritual things cannot continue [1 Quæst. 1] if any shall take away the same.

Whatsoever doth perish in the church of God for want of preachers shall be required.

A detestable book of the friars called 'Evangelium æternum.'

Thus have you had the thirty-nine arguments, for which the said Gulielmus was condemned, and his books burned. In his days there was a most detestable and blasphemous book set forth by the friars (mentioned also in Matthew Paris), which they called 'Evangelium æternum,' or 'Evangelium Spiritus Sancti;' that is, 'The everlasting gospel,' or 'The gospel of the Holy Ghost.' In which book many abominable errors of the friars were contained, so that the gospel of Jesus Christ was utterly defaced, which, this book said, was not to be compared with this everlasting gospel, no more than the shell is to be compared with the kernel, or than darkness to light. Moreover, that the gospel of Christ shall be preached no longer than fifty years, and that then this 'everlasting gospel' should rule the church. Item, that whatsoever was in the whole Bible, was in the said gospel contained. At length this friar's gospel was accused to the pope, and so six persons chosen out of the whole university to peruse and judge of the book, as Christianus Canonicus, Baluacensis, Odo de Doaco, Nicolaus de Baro, Johannes de Sicca Villa, a Briton, Johannes Belim, a Gaul; among whom this Gulielmus was one, who mightily impugned this pestiferous and devilish book. These six, after the perusing of the book, were sent up to Rome. The friars also sent their messengers thither, where they were refuted, and the errors of the book condemned; but so that the pope, with the cardinals, commanded the said book to be abolished and condemned, not publicly (tendering the estimation of the religious orders, as of his own most chief champions), but that they should be burned in secret wise, and that the books of the aforesaid Gulielmus should be burnt also.

The eternal and spiritual gospel of the friars condemned, with much ado by the pope

Besides his other books, we have two sermons of his yet remaining, one upon the gospel of St. Luke, of the Pharisee and the Publican, the other upon the epistle read in the church on May-day; where, in the first, he resembleth the Pharisees to our monks, and that he proveth by all the properties of the Pharisees described in the gospel. The Publican he resembleth to the laity, such as, because they are sooner reduced to acknowledge their sins, the more hope they have of mercy. The other, because they stand confident in their own righteousness, are therefore further from their justification. In the latter sermon he setteth forth and declareth what perils and dangers be likely to fall upon the church by these religious orders of monks and friars.

Among others of that age who withstood the bishop of Rome and his antichristian errors, was one Lawrence, an Englishman, and a master of Paris; another was Petrus Johannes, a minorite. Lawrence lived about A.D. 1260, who in his teaching, preaching, and writing, did stoutly defend the part of the aforesaid Gulielmus, and the rest of his side, against the friars. For this purpose he wrote two books, one in the defence of Gulielmus, the other upon this argument and title, 'To beware of false prophets,' &c. Certain other things also he wrote, wherein, by divers proofs and testimonies, he argued and proved, that the coming of Antichrist was not far off. Petrus Johannes lived about A.D. 1290, who taught and maintained many things against the pope, proving, that he was Antichrist, and that the synagogue of Rome was great Babylon. He wrote on Matthew, on the Epistles, and on the Apocalypse. Mention of this Petrus Johannes is made in Nicolaus Emericus, in his book of the Inquisitions. And he saith, moreover, that Michael Cesenas (of whom, Christ willing, shall follow hereafter) took of him a great part of his opinions; and because the pope could not burn him alive, after his death he caused his bones to be taken up and burned.

Lawrence, an Englishman, condemned by the pope.

The pope, Antichrist

The synagogue of Rome, great Babylon

Petrus Johannes burned after his death.

To these is to be added Robertus Gallus, who being born of a right noble parentage, for devotion's sake was made a Dominic friar, about the same year (A.D. 1290). This man, as appeareth by his writing, had divers and sundry visions, whereof part is annexed with the visions and prophecy of Hildegard. His visions all tend against

Robertus Gallus prophesieth

The pope described.

Henry III

A. D. 1250

the spiritualty of Rome; where, in the first chapter, he plainly calleth the pope an idol, who having eyes seeth not, neither lusteth to see the abominations of his people, nor the excessive enormity of their voluptuousness, but only to see to the heaping up of his own treasure, and having a mouth, speaketh not; but saith, I have set good men over them (which is sufficient for me), to do them good either by myself, or by some other. And it followeth in the same chapter, "Woe to that idol! woe to the mighty and proud! who shall be equal in all the earth to that idol? He that exalteth his name in earth, saying, Who shall bring me under? Is not my house compared with the mighty potentates of the land? I am higher than dukes; knights on horseback do service unto me; that which my fathers had not before me, that I have done to me. My house is strewed with silver; gold and pearl are the pavement of my palace."

Again, in the twelfth chapter, and also in the first, under the name of a serpent, he painteth out the pope, whom he declareth to extol himself above measure, and to oppress the few that be godly, and to have many false prophets about him; who, neglecting the word and name of Christ, do preach and extol him only, obscuring the name of Christ. The church of Rome and the pope he describeth in these words: "I was praying," saith he, "on my knees, looking upward to heaven, near to the altar of St. James in Paris, on the right side of the altar, and saw in the air before me, the body of a certain high bishop, all clothed in white silk; who, turning his back on the east, lifted up his hand towards the west, as the priests are wont in their mass, turning to the people, but his head was not seen. And as I was considering advisedly, whether he had any head or no, I perceived a certain head in him all dry, lean and withered, as though it had been a head of wood. And the Spirit of the Lord said to me, 'This signifieth the state of the church of Rome.'"

The visions of Robertus Gallus

State of the church of Rome described

Moreover, the same author in his visions, well describing the manner of the school sophisters and sobornists, addeth in this wise: "Another day, as I was in like contemplation as before, I beheld in spirit; and behold, I saw a man apparelled like to the other before, who went about having fine bread and excellent wine that hanged about him on both sides; and the same, having in his hand a long and hard flint stone, was gnawing hungerly upon the same, as one being hungry is wont to bite upon a loaf of bread; out of which stone came two heads of two serpents, the Spirit of the Lord instructing me and saying, 'This stone purporteth the frivolous, intricate, and curious questions, wherein the hungry do travail and labour, leaving the substantial food of their souls.' And I asked what these two heads did mean? And he said, 'The name of the one is Vainglory, the name of the other is, The Marring and Dissipating of Religion.'"

School-men and frivolous questions described

Also, concerning the reformation of the church, this vision he declareth. "It happened, as I was in the same city in the house of a certain nobleman, a Briton, and was there speaking with certain, I saw a cross of silver very bright, much like to the cross of the earl of Toulouse. But the twelve apples, which did hang beside the arm of the cross, were very vile, like the apples which the sea is wont

Reformation of the church presignified.

to cast up. And I said, 'What is this, Lord Jesus?' And the Spirit answered me, 'This cross which thou seest is the church, which shall be clear and bright in pureness of life, and shall be heard and known all over through the shrill voice of the preaching of sincere verity.' Then, being troubled with the apples, I asked what these apples so vile did signify? And he said, 'It is the humiliation of the church.'"

This godly man did forewarn (as in a certain chronicle is declared) how God would punish the simony and avarice of the clergy, with such a plague, that rivers should run with blood. It is said, that there is remaining a great volume of his visions which are not yet abroad; for these that be abroad, are but a brief extract out of his visions and revelations. *Simony and avarice of the clergy to be punished.*

After that we have thus long strayed in these foreign stories of Frederic, and in the tractation of other matters pertaining to other countries, it is time that we return to our own country again.

THE STORY OF ROBERT GROSTHEAD, BISHOP OF LINCOLN.

Following the continuation of time and course of the church, we will now join to these good fathers and writers, the history of the learned bishop of Lincoln, named Robert Grosthead,[1] a man famously learned, as that time served, in the three tongues, both Latin, Greek, and Hebrew, also in all liberal sciences; whose works and sermons even to this day are extant, which I have seen in the library of the queen's majesty at Westminster, wherein is one special sermon written and exhibited in four sundry scrolls addressed to the pope, and to other four cardinals, beginning "Dominus noster Jesus Christus." Nicholas Trivet, in his Chronicle, writing of this bishop, affirmed that he was born in Suffolk, in the diocese of Norfolk: who giving him the praise of being a man of excellent wisdom, of profound doctrine, and an example of all virtue, witnesseth that he being master of arts, wrote first a commentary on the latter books of Aristotle; also that he wrote tractations concerning the spheres, and the art of computations, and that he set forth divers books concerning philosophy. Afterwards, being doctor in divinity, and expertly seen in all the three tongues, he drew sundry treatises out of the Hebrew glosses, also translated divers works out of the Greek, as the testament of the twelve patriarchs, and the books of Dionysius, commenting upon the new translation with his own gloss.[2] *Robert Grosthead, a Suffolk man.* *His books and works.*

This godly and learned bishop, after divers conflicts and agonies sustained against the bishop of Rome, after the example of Frederic, of Gulielmus de Sancto amore, of Nicholaus Gallus, and others after named, at length, after great labours and travails of life, finished his course, and departed at Bugden in the month of October, A.D. 1253. Of his decease thus writeth Matthew Paris,[3] "Out of *Death of Grosthead*

(1) Robert Grosthead or Grossteste was born about A.D. 1175, was made bishop in 1235, and died 1253.—ED.

(2) Many other works and volumes were written by the said Grosthead, as "De oculo Morali," "De dotibus," "De cessatione legalium," "Parvus Cato," "Annotationes in Suidam," "In Boetium," "De potestate Pastorali," "Expositiones in Gen. et in Lucam," with a number more, besides divers epistles, sermons, and invections sent to the pope for his immeasurable exactions, wherewith he overcharged and oppressed the church of England.

(3) Matth. Paris. fol. 278.

Henry III — A.D. 1253

the prison and banishment of this world (which he never loved) was taken the holy bishop of Lincoln, Robert, at his manor of Bugden, in the even of St. Dionisius; who was an open reprover of the pope and of the king, a rebuker of the prelates, a corrector of the monks, a director of the priests, an instructor of the clerks, a favourer of scholars, a preacher to the people, a persecutor of the incontinent, a diligent searcher of the Scripture, a mall to the Romans, and a contemner of their doings." What a mall he was to the Romans, in the sequel hereof (Christ willing) shall appear. The story is this:—It so befel, that among other daily and intolerable exactions, wherein pope Innocent IV. was grievous and injurious in manifold ways to the realm of England, he had a certain cousin or nephew (so popes were wont to call their sons) named Frederic, being yet young and under years, whom the said Innocent the pope would needs prefer to be a canon or prebendary in the church of Lincoln, in this time of Robert, bishop of the said church; and that, upon the same, the pope directed letters to certain of his factors here in England, for the execution thereof; a copy of which letters by chance, yet not by chance, but by the opportune sending of God, came to my hands as I was penning this present story, written in the end of an old parchment book, and otherwise rarely I suppose to be found;[1] it is thus in English.

Six years' troubles of Grosthead with the pope A D 1253

The Pope's unreasonable Letter to his Factors in England.

Unto our well-beloved sons, the archdeacon of Canterbury, and to Master Innocent, our scribe, abiding in England, greeting and apostolical benediction. Forasmuch as our well-beloved son G of S Eustace, deacon cardinal, upon our

(1) "Dilectis filiis archdiacono Cant et Magistro Innocent scriptori nostro in Anglia commoranti salutem et apostolicam benedict Cum dilectus filius noster G Sanct Eustachii diaconus cardinalis dilecto [recte dictum fortassis filio!] filio Frederico de Lavania, clerico, nepoti nostro, de speciali mandato nostro canonicatum Lincolniens cum plenitudine juris canonici duxerit conferendum, ipsum per suum annulum corporaliter et præsentialiter investiens de eodem, ut ex tunc canonicus Lincolniensis existat, et plenum nomen et jus canonici consequatur ibidem, ac præbendam, si qua vacaverit in ecclesia Lincol a tempore quo dudum literæ nostræ super receptione, ac provisione facienda sibi in eccles eadem de præmissis venerab fratri nostro episcopo Lincoln præsentatæ fuerunt, alioqui post vacaturam conferendam sibi donationi apostolicæ reservarit. decernendo irritum et inane, si quid de præbenda hujusmodi a quoquam fuerit attentatum, nec non et in contradictores et rebelles excommunicationis sententiam ubique promulgando, prout in literis ejusdem exinde de constitutis [confectis] plenius continetur

"Nos ipsius Frederici devotis supplicationibus inclinati, quod ab eodem cardinale factum est super hoc et ratum et gratum habentes, idem authoritate apostolica duximus confirmandum Quocirca discretioni vestræ per apostolica scripta mandamus, quatenus eundem Fredericum, vel procuratorem suum ejus nomine in corporalem possessionem prædictorum canonicatus et præbendæ authoritate nostra inducatis, et defendatis inductum, contradictores per censuram ecclesiasticam appellatione post posita compescendo Non obstantibus aliquibus consuetudinibus vel statutis, juramentis, vel confirmationibus sedis apostolicæ, seu quacunque alia infirmitate roboratis, vel quod dictus Fredericus præsens non fuerit ad præstandum juramentum de observandis consuetudinibus ejusdem eccles consuetis, sive si prædicto episcopo vel capitulo ipsius ecclesiæ communiter vel singulatim, seu aliis quibuscunque personis a dicta sede indultum existat, quod ad receptionem vel provisionem alicujus compelli nequeant, sive quod nullus alius in eorum ecclesia nemini providere valeat vel quod interdici, suspendi, aut excommunicari non possint, per literas apostol sub quacunque forma verborum obtentas, vel obtinendas, etiamsi totus tenor indulgentiarum hujusmodi de verbo in verbum in iisdem literis sit insertus, sive quibus aliis indulgentiis quibuscunque personis, dignitati, vel loco, sub quacunque forma verborum concessis a sede apost vel etiam concedendis, per quas effectus hujusmodi provisionis posset impediri aliquatenus vel differri Tamen volumus, ea de certa scientia, quantum ad provisionem factam et faciendam Frederico prædicto in ecclesia Lincoln viribus omnino carere Cæterum, si aliqui prædicto Frederico vel procuratori super præmissis, vel aliquo præmissorum, aliquatenus duxerint apponendum illos ex parte nostra citari curetis, ut peremptorie infra duorum mensium spacium post citationem vestram personaliter compareant coram nobis, eidem Frederico super præmissis legitime responsuri Non obstantibus privilegiis, sive quibuslibet indulgentiis personis regni Angliæ generaliter vel cujus alii personæ, vel dignitati, vel loco specialiter a prædicta sede sub quacunque forma verborum concessis Quod non possunt ultra mare, seu extra civitatem vel diocesin suam in judicium evocari per literas apost sub quacunque forma verborum obtentas, quod privilegium et indulgentias eisdem personis de certa scientia nullatenus volumus suffragari, et constitutione edita de duabus dictis in concilio generali non obstante Diem autem citationis et formam nobis, vestris literis tenorem præsentium continentibus fideliter intimetis Quod si non ambo his exequendis interesse poteritis, alter vestrum nihilominus exequatur"—Datum Perus 7 Cal Febr pontificat. nostro anno decimo.

special commandment hath given and granted to our well-beloved son Frederic de Lavania, a clerk and our nephew, a canonship in the church of Lincoln, with full power and grant of the same, investing him also corporally and presently with his own ring in the said canonship, to be from henceforth canon of Lincoln, and to have full power over the said canonship in the church, and a prebend when any shall fall in the church of Lincoln, from that time since which our letters of late concerning this receiving and provision to be given to him in the said church, were lately presented and exhibited to our reverend brother, the bishop of Lincoln, or else after the next avoiding, the said prebendship to be reserved to the apostolical donation; and to be given to him, making it void and frustrate if the said prebendship shall be given to any other man beside, and also denouncing the sentence of excommunication against all them that shall rebel and gainsay the same, as in the letters of the said cardinal is more fully contained

Henry III

A D 1253

Well said peradventure to a son

We, therefore, graciously inclined by the devout supplication of the said Frederic, ratifying and gratefully approving that which hath been done by the said cardinal in the premises, we thought good by the authority apostolical to confirm the same. Wherefore we give all commandment by our letters apostolical to your wisdoms, that you will see the said Frederic (or his proctor in his behalf) to be really and corporally possessed in the said canonship or prebend by our authority, and also defend the said party being therein possessed, denouncing the sentence of excommunication against all such as shall withstand the same, all manner of customs or statutes to the contrary notwithstanding, corroborated either with oath, or confirmations of the see apostolic, or by what stay or let soever; or whether that the said Frederic be not present to take the oath accustomed to be given for observing the customs of the said church, or whether it be given and granted by the said see to the aforesaid bishop, or to the chapter of the said church jointly and severally, or to what person or persons else; that no man, by compulsion, should have admission or provision for any person in their church whereby they cannot be interdicted, suspended, or excommunicated by the letters apostolical obtained, or to be obtained hereafter, under what form or words soever, yea, although the whole tenor of the said indulgence be inserted word for word in the said your letters, or by any other indulgences to what person or persons soever, of what estate, dignity, or place soever, under any manner or form of words, granted hereafter by the see apostolic, by the which indulgences the effect of the said provision may be by any manner of ways hindered or deferred · yet, of our certain knowledge, we will that they shall want their strength in the provision made or to be made for the said Frederic, in the church of Lincoln. And if any, upon the premises or any of them, shall allege against the foresaid Frederic, or his procurator, that you will cause them to be cited on our behalf, so that they, being cited peremptorily, shall within the space of two months from your citation, personally appear before us according to law, to make answer to the said Frederic upon the premises any privileges or indulgences whatsoever given and granted, either generally to the kingdom of England, or peculiarly to any other person of what state, degree, and place soever, granted by the aforesaid see, under whatsoever manner and form of words for them not to be called up beyond the sea, or out of their own city or diocese by letters apostolical, under whatsoever form of words obtained, to the contrary in any wise notwithstanding. All which privileges and indulgences, we will, in no case, shall stand in any force or effect to the said parties. Moreover, the day and form of the citation we will that ye do faithfully intimate unto us by your letters containing the tenor thereof, and if both of you cannot be present at the execution hereof, yet we will, notwithstanding, that one of you do execute the same without fail.—Dated the seventh Kal., February, the tenth year of our popedom.

Excommunication abused

As there is no man who hath any eyes to see, but may easily understand in reading this letter of the pope, how unreasonable his request is, how impudently he commandeth, how proudly he threateneth, how wickedly he oppresseth and racketh the church of God, in placing boys and strangers in the ministry and cure of souls, and also in making them his provisors, to raven up the church goods; so is it

Henry III. A.D. 1253.

no great marvel, if this godly bishop, Robert Grosthead, was offended therewith; who, in my mind deserveth herein a double commendation, not only that he so wisely did discern error from sincerity and truth; but also that he was so hardy and constant to stand to the defence thereof against the pope, according as in this his answer to the pope again may appear, as followeth.

Commendation of Grosthead.

The Answer of Bishop Grosthead to the Pope.

Salutem. May it please your wisdom to understand, that I am not disobedient to any of the apostolic precepts, but both devoutly and reverently, with the natural affection of a son, obey the same, and also am an utter enemy to all those that resist such apostolic precepts, as a child zealous of his father's honour. And truly, I am no less than bound thereunto by the precept and commandment of God. For the apostolic precepts are none other, nor can be, than consonant and uniform to the doctrine of the apostles, and of our Saviour Christ, who is the master and lord of all the apostles; whose type and person, especially in the consonant and uniform hierarchy of the church, the lord pope seemeth to bear; our Lord and Saviour Jesus Christ, saying the same, 'whosoever is not with me, the same is against me.' Therefore, against him neither is nor can be the most divine sanctity of the see apostolical. The tenor, then, of your aforesaid apostolical letter is not consonant to true sanctity, but utterly dissonant and disagreeing with the same. First, for that the clause of this your letter, and many such other letters (which clause always ye so much do urge) '*non obstante*' induced and brought in upon no necessity of any natural law to be observed, doth swarm and flow with all inconstancy, boldness, pertinacity, impudency, lying, and deceiving, and is also a sea of mistrust as giving credit to no man. And as it swarmeth with these, so doth it in like manner with innumerable other vices which hang and depend upon the same; moving and disturbing the purity of the christian religion and of the life agreeable to the same, as also the public tranquillity of men. Moreover, next after the sin of Lucifer (who shall be in the latter time, to wit, of Antichrist, the child of perdition, whom the Lord shall destroy with the breath of his mouth) there is not, nor can be, any kind of sin so repugnant and contrary to the doctrine of the apostles and holy Scripture, and to our Saviour Christ himself more hateful, detestable, and abominable, than to destroy and kill men's souls, by defrauding them of the mystery of the pastoral office, which, by the ministry of the pastoral cure, ought to save and quicken the same. Which sin, by most evident places of the Scripture, such men are discerned and known to commit, who, being in the authority of the pastoral dignity, do serve their own carnal desires and necessaries with the benefit of the milk and wool of the sheep and flock of Christ, and do not minister the same pastoral office and charge to the benefit and salvation of those their sheep. The same, therefore, by the testimony of the Scripture is not the administration of the pastoral ministry, but the killing and destruction of the sheep. And that these two kind of vices be most vile and wicked (although after a differing sort), and far exceeding all other kind of wickedness, hereby it is manifest, for that the same are directly contrary to two virtues most chiefly good, although differing in themselves, and unlike each other; for that is called most wicked, which is contrary to a thing most good. As much then as lieth in the offenders, the one of their offences is directly against the Deity, who of himself is always essentially and supernaturally good; the other is against the deification and the image of God in man, who is not always, but by the participation of God's lightsome grace, essentially and naturally good. And forasmuch as in things being good, the cause of good is better than the effect, and as again in evil things, the cause of evil is worse than the effect of evil, proceeding thereof, hereby it is manifest: that the inducers of such wicked destroyers of God's image and deification in the sheep of Christ (that is, the church of God) are worse than those chief destroyers, to wit, Lucifer and Antichrist.

And as in these degrees of wickedness how much more excellent such be, who, having a great charge committed to them of God (to edification, and not to destruction) are more bound to keep away and exclude such wicked

Henry III.

A.D. 1253.

destroyers from the church of God: so much is it also of that, that this holy seat apostolic, to whom the Lord Jesus Christ hath given all manner of power (to edification, as the apostle saith, and not to destruction) can command, or will to go about any such thing, urging unto so great wickedness, so odious, detestable, and abominable to our Lord Jesus Christ, and also so pernicious to mankind. For this should be a great defection, corruption and abuse of the said seat and fulness of power, and an utter separation from the glorious throne of our Lord Jesus Christ, and a near neighbourhood unto the two most principal princes of darkness, sitting in the chair of pestilence, prepared for the pains of hell. Neither can any man who is subject and faithful to the said see, and not cut away from the body of Christ, and from the said holy see, with sincere and unspotted conscience obey such manner of precepts and commandments, or whatsoever other attempts proceeding, yea, though from the high order of angels themselves, but rather ought of necessity with all their strength to withstand and rebel against the same. Wherefore, my reverend lord, I, like an obedient child, upon my bound duty of obedience and fidelity which I owe to both the parents[1] of this holy apostolic see, and partly for love of unity in the body of Christ joined with the said see, do not obey, but withstand, and utterly rebel against these things in the said letter contained; and especially which urge and tend to the aforesaid wickedness, so abominable to the Lord Jesus Christ, so repugnant to the holiness of the holy apostolic see, and so contrary to the unity of the catholic faith. Neither for this cause can your discretion determine any extremity to me, because all my doing and gainsaying in this matter is no resistance nor rebellion, but a childly obedience to the divine precept, and honour due both to father and mother.[2] Briefly therefore repeating my words, I say, that this holy apostolic see cannot do any thing but to edification, and nothing at all to destruction: for this is the fulness of power, to be able to do all things to edification. But these which you call provisions be not to edification, but to manifest destruction. The holy apostolic see, therefore, neither can nor ought to attempt any such thing, because flesh and blood, which cannot enter into the kingdom of God, hath revealed the same, and not the Father of our Lord Jesus Christ which is in heaven.

Power given to ministers to edification only, not to destruction.

Two principal princes of darkness, Lucifer and Antichrist.

Then followeth it in the story both of Matthew Paris, and of Florilegus, that when this epistle came to the knowledge of the pope, he, fuming and fretting with anger and indignation, answered with a fierce look and proud mind, saying, "What old doating frantic wretch is this, so boldly and rashly to judge of my doings? By sweet St. Peter and St. Paul, were it not that upon our own clemency and good nature we are restrained, we should hurl him down to such confusion, that we would make him a fable, a gazing stock, an example and wonderment to all the world. For is not the king of England our vassal? and to say more, our mancipal or page" (to use the very words of mine author) "who may at our pleasure and beck both hamper him, imprison him, and put him to utter shame?" When the pope, in his great fury and rage, had uttered this amongst his brethren, the cardinals, who were scarcely able to appease the furious violence of the pope, with mild moderation of words said unto him: that it was not expedient for them to proceed against that bishop in such rigorous manner. "For," said they, "to confess the truth to your holiness, it is but very truth that he affirmeth, neither can we condemn him for it. He is a catholic man, yea, also a holy man: more holy and also religious than we ourselves; a man of excellent wit and excellent life; so that it is thought, among all the prelates he hath not his better, nor yet his like. This is not unknown both to the French and English clergy universally, neither can our

Well sworn, master pope!

Giles, a cardinal, defendeth Grosthead to the pope.

(1) He meaneth either Christ and the church, or Peter and Paul.
(2) That is, both to Christ and his church.

Henry III. A.D. 1253.

contradiction prevail against him. The truth of this his epistle perhaps is known now to many, and shall stir up many against us: for he hath the name of being a great philosopher, and singularly seen in all the tongues, both Greek, Latin, and Hebrew; zealous in justice, a reader of divinity in the schools, a preacher amongst the people, a lover of chastity, and a persecutor of simony." These words spake L. Giles, a Spanish cardinal, to the pope, and others besides, moved by their conscience to speak. And this counsel they gave to the pope, that he should dissemble and wink at these things, as one not seeing or regarding them, lest otherwise perhaps some tumult might rise and spring therefrom; especially seeing this is manifest and known to all men, that at last there must needs come a defection and parting from the church of Rome.

The godly talk of Grost-head in his sickness.

Not long after this, about the canicular days,[1] this reverend and godly Robert, bishop of Lincoln, lying at his manor place in Bugden, fell grievously sick; and thereupon within few days departed. In the time of his sickness he called to him a certain friar of the preaching order, named Master John Giles, a man expert and cunning both in physic and divinity; partly to receive of him some comfort of his body, and partly to confer with him in spiritual matters. Thus, upon a certain day, the bishop conferring with the foresaid Master John, and reciting to him the doings and proceedings of the pope, did grievously rebuke and reprehend his fellow brethren, the preaching friars, and the other order also of the minorites; that, forasmuch as their order, being planted in wilful poverty of the spirit, to the intent that they should more freely carp at and reprove the vices of the mighty, and not flatter or spare them, but sharply rebuke and reprehend the same; the said friars, contrary to their profession, did not boldly enough cry out and inveigh against the abuses of their superiors and men of power, nor did uncover or detect their faults and wickedness; and therefore, said the bishop, I judge them to be no better than manifest heretics. And he addeth moreover, demanding of Master John, "What is heresy?" and that he should give him the true definition thereof. Whereat when the friar did stay and pause, not remembering the solemn definition of that matter, the bishop thereupon inferreth, giving the definition in Latin by the true interpretation of the Greek word:[2] "Heresy is a sentence taken and chosen of man's own brain, contrary to holy Scripture, openly maintained, and stiffly defended." And this definition given, consequently he inferred, sharply reprehending the prelates of the church, but especially the Romans, who commit the charge of souls unto their kinsfolks, being both in age unworthy, and in learning insufficient. "To give," saith he, "the charge of souls unto a boy, is a sentence of a prelate chosen and taken of man's own head, only for carnal and earthly respect, and also is contrary to holy Scripture, which forbiddeth any such to be made ministers or pastors, who are not sufficient to drive away the wolves. And, moreover, it is also openly maintained, because it is manifestly borne abroad and commanded, with charts imbulled both with wax and lead; and finally, it is stiffly defended. For if any man shall dare to presume to withstand the same, he is suspended

Definition of heresy.

(1) "Canicular days," the dog-days.—Ed.

(2) "Heresis Græce, electio, Latine, est sententia humano sensu electa, scripturæ sacræ contraria, palma docta, pertinaciter defensa."

and excommunicated, and open war cried out against him: therefore to whom the whole definition of a heretic doth agree, he is a very heretic. But every faithful christian man ought to set himself against a heretic as much as he may. Wherefore, he that can resist him and doth not, he sinneth, and seemeth to be a favourer thereof, according to the saying of Gregory; 'He lacketh not conscience of secret society, who ceaseth to resist open impiety.' But the friars, both Franciscans and Dominics, are most chiefly bound to withstand such, seeing both of them have the gift of preaching committed to them by their office, and be more apt to the said office, by reason of their poverty; and, therefore, they do not only offend in not resisting such, but also are to be counted maintainers of the same, according to the sentence of the apostle to the Romans, saying, 'Not only they which commit such things, but also they that consent, are worthy of death.' Wherefore it may be concluded, that as well the pope, unless he cease from that vice, as also the same friars, unless they show themselves more earnest and studious in repelling the same, are alike worthy of death; that is, perpetual damnation. 'Item,' saith the canon decretal, 'That upon this vice of heresy the pope both may and ought to be accused.'"

Saying of Gregory.

The pope accused of heresy.

After this the vehemency of his disease more and more increasing, and because the nights were something longer, the third night before his departure, the bishop feeling his infirmity to grow upon him, willed certain of his clergy to be called to him, thereby to be refreshed with some conference or communication. Unto whom the bishop, mourning and lamenting in his mind for the loss of souls through the avarice of the pope's court, said on this wise, as by certain aphorisms.

Certain Aphorisms or Articles of Robert Grosthead against the Bishop of Rome.

1. Christ came into the world to save and win souls: ergo, he that feareth not to destroy souls, may he not worthily be counted Antichrist?

2. The Lord created the whole world in six days, but in restoring of man he laboured more than thirty years. Wherefore he that is a destroyer of that, about which the Lord so long laboured, is not he worthy to be counted the enemy of God, and Antichrist?

3. The pope shameth not impudently to annihilate and disannul the privileges of his holy predecessors, of Roman bishops, by this obstacle, 'Non obstante,' which is not done without the prejudice and manifest injury of them. For in so doing he doth reprove and destroy that which so many and such holy men have builded up before, and thus seemeth he to be a contemner of the saints. Worthily therefore he that contemneth shall be contemned, according to the saying of Isaiah, "Woe to thee that dost despise, for shalt not thou thyself be despised?" And who shall keep his privileges, who so breaketh the privileges of others?

The pope accused of his wicked clause, "Non obstante."

4. The pope answering thereunto, thus defendeth perhaps his error: "He that is equal, hath no superiority over his equal; therefore no pope hath power to bind me, being pope as well as he." To this I answer again (quoth the bishop), it seemeth to me, that he that now presently is sailing in the dangerous seas of this world, and he that is safely arrived in the haven, having past all jeopardies, are not both like and equal. Grant that some popes be saved (God forbid any should say to the contrary), then saith our Saviour: "He that is least in the kingdom of heaven is greater than John the Baptist, a greater than whom did never rise amongst the children of men." Is not therefore some pope greater, being a giver and confirmer of privileges, than this that is

And for arrogating more than his due; and proved not to be equal, but inferior to his predecessors.

Henry III. A.D. 1253.

alive? Truly, methinks, he is greater; therefore he hath dominion over his inferior.

5. Doth not the pope thus say, speaking of all his predecessors for the most part; "This our predecessor, and this our predecessor of most worthy memory," &c. And again, "We," saith he, "cleaving to, or following the steps of our predecessors," &c. And why then do such popes as come after, destroy these foundations which their predecessors have laid?

Accused of undoing the acts of his predecessors. The pope alive, is inferior to his predecessors, therefore has no authority to infringe their privileges. Men more ancient in time, ought to be had in higher reverence.

6. Many apostolic men coming after, have confirmed some privilege granted by others; and be not many bishops, being already saved by the grace of God, to be counted greater and better than one bishop who hath not yet attained, but standeth in danger to obtain, that which the others have got already?

7. Also our forefathers, the bishops of the apostolical see, in preferment of time, go before the others who in time come after; and those whom the estimation of ancient time doth advance, such are we bound to esteem and to have in more reverence. This did the holy man Benedict well consider; who in his rule preferreth such as came first in time, whatsoever men they were, before them who, albeit more ancient in years, came after them into the order, and commandeth them to be their superiors, and to have the pre-eminence. Which being so, as it is true and certain, how cometh then this injurious and rash presumption, which dare repeal and disannul the old privileges of many ancient holy bishops, in time and in reverence going before them?

The pope accused of maintaining usury.

8. Moreover, and though many popes have been grievous to the church, yet this pope, more especially, hath brought it most into servitude, and, in manifold ways, hath damnified the same. For these Caursini, these open usurers, whom our holy forefathers and doctors have seen, and whom we have seen, and namely our learned master in France, preacher; also the abbot of Flay, a Cistercian, Master Jacobus de veteri, and Master Stephen, archbishop of Canterbury, in the time of his banishment, and also Master Robert Curcun, with his preaching banished out of France (for before that time these kind of usurers were never known in England), the same Caursini, these wicked usurers, I say, were by this pope induced, supported and maintained; so that if any do speak against them, he is miserably tossed and trounced for his labour, whereof partly Roger, bishop of London, hath some experience.

Again usury.

9. The world doth know, that usury is counted a detestable thing in both the Testaments, and is forbidden of God. But now the pope's usurers or exchangers, the very Jews crying out against them, being openly suffered in London to exercise their usury, to the great damage and detriment of all ecclesiastical persons, but especially of houses of religion, compelling such as be in poverty to counterfeit and to put their seals to forged writings, which is no less than to commit idolatry and to renounce the Verity, which is God himself. As for example: I borrow an hundred marks[1] for a year, instead of a hundred pounds; I am compelled to make my writing and to seal the same, confessing that I have received and borrowed one hundred pounds, to be repaid again at the year's end to such a man, &c. And if it shall chance that your occupying be such that within a month you bring again the principal to the pope's usurer, he will receive no less, notwithstanding, than his full hundred pounds; which condition of usury is much worse than that of the Jews, for to the Jew what principal you bring, he will require no more than proportionably for the commensuration of so much time wherein his money hath been out of his hands.

Crafty practice of usurers. Pope's usurers worse than the Jews.

Crafty subtlety of the pope to get money.

10. Moreover, we have seen and known the pope to have given in charge and commandment to the friars, preachers, and Minorites, to inquire diligently for such as lie sick and are likely to die; and so coming to them diligently to persuade them to make their wills and testaments favourably to the profit and subsidy of the Holy Land, and to take the cross upon them; that if they do amend, they may wring them in the law, and if they die, they may wrest the money from their executors.

Men signed to the Holy Land, sold for money like sheep by the pope.

11. We have known likewise and seen men, that have taken the vow and sign of the cross upon them, to be sold to laymen, as sheep and oxen were wont in time past to be sold in the temple. We have also seen with our eyes the pope's letter, in which we have found this to be written: that they, who

(1) A mark was thirteen shillings and fourpence.—ED.

bequeath any thing to the behoof or subsidy of the Holy Land, shall receive so much indulgence as they have disbursed money.

12. Over and besides all this, the pope, in divers and sundry his letters, hath willed and commanded prelates to receive into ecclesiastical benefices, and to provide some such living in their churches, as shall be sufficient to such and such strangers (being both absent and also unworthy), who have neither learning, nor yet the language of the country: whereby they are neither able to preach, nor to hear confessions, nor to keep residence to refresh the poor and the wayfarers.

Remission of sins sold for money.

The pope injurious to churches in his provisions and reservations.

13. We know and have seen ourselves, that the pope hath written to the abbot of St. Alban's to provide for one called John de Camezana, whom we never saw, some competent benefice. Whereupon, in few days after, when provision was made for him in a certain church, worth forty marks by the year and more, the party being not therewith contented, complained to the pope; who then writing to the aforesaid abbot, commanded him to provide for the aforesaid Master John some better thing, reserving, notwithstanding, the gift of the former benefice to himself.

Also to the abbot of St. Alban's.

The pope accused of violent extortion.

14. Again, not long after came also to the house of the aforesaid abbot, two other persons like begging vagabonds, bringing with them the pope's letters; in the tenor whereof the abbot was commanded, that, incontinently upon the sight thereof, he should give and disburse to the said persons for the expedition and dispatch of his affairs ten marks in hand, without any delay or sticking: which persons uttering unto the abbot proud and threatening words, he was fain to agree with them and send them away.

Of troubling and corrupting learned men of the spirituality, with his temporal affairs

15. Also, of men who are both holy and well learned, who have left the world for the following of God in such order as they ought not to turn back again, the pope maketh his collectors[1] and bankers to get in his money, which charge they are compelled against their wills to take upon them, lest they should seem to be disobedient; and so of spiritual men they are made more secular than the most secular. And so the baseness of their chimmers and scapillers,[2] which they wear, doth prove them to be liars; whilst, under the habit of poverty and humiliation, there lurketh the spirit of pride and elation. And because no legate may be sent into England, but being first required of the king, the pope sendeth sophistical legates, and such as be disguised and counterfeit in apparel, and are guarded with great might and power: neither is it hard to bring forth examples thereof; for so many such daily do come into the realm, that to hear the names of them recited, it would be tedious for any man to hear.

The pope accused for unlawful dispensations.

16. Furthermore (as we have seen ourselves) the pope granteth for secular favour, that a man may have a bishopric, and yet be no bishop consecrated, "Sed electus sempiturnus," that is, "Elect for ever:" which is as much to signify, to have the milk and the wool of the sheep and not to keep the wolves away from the sheep; to retain the rents of a bishop, and not discharge the function of a bishop.

And when this godly bishop had thus reproved these and such other detestable enormities of the court of Rome; as all kinds of avarice, their usury, their simony, their extortion, all kinds of filthiness, fleshly lust, gluttony, and their sumptuous apparel reigning in that court; "then," saith he, "this old verse may be truly verified upon it:

> 'Ejus avaritiæ totus non sufficit orbis,
> Ejus luxuriæ meretrix non sufficit omnis.'

> 'All the world cannot suffice, their greedy covetous mind,
> Nor all the drabs and naughty packs, their filthy lusting kind.'"

Afterwards he went about further to prosecute, how the aforesaid court, like a gulf never satisfied (ever gaping so wide, that the flood of Jordan might run into his mouth), aspired how to usurp the goods

(1) Tolners.—Old Edition.
(2) "Chimmers and Scapillers." "Simarre" in French is a long gown or robe A "scapulary" is that part of the dress which covers the shoulders.—Ed.

Henry III — A.D. 1253.

of them that die untested, and of legacies bequeathed without form of law; and whereby more licentiously to bring this to pass they used to join the king to be fellow and partaker with them in their spoils, extortions, and robbings "Neither," saith he, "shall the church be delivered from the servitude of Egypt but by violence and force, and with the bloody sword. And albeit," saith he, "these be yet but light matters, yet, shortly, more great and grievous things than these shall be seen."

Death of Robert Grosthead, bishop of Lincoln

And in the end of this his prophesying, which he scarcely could utter without sighing, sobbing, and weeping, his tongue and breath began to fail, and so, the organ of his voice being stopped, he made an end both of his speech and life.[1]

And, forasmuch as mention hath been made before of the insatiable avarice of the pope's court by his inordinate provisions and reservations, it is testified by Matthew Paris, that the aforesaid Robert Grosthead, being bishop of Lincoln, caused to be viewed and considered diligently by his clerks, what the revenues of foreigners and strangers within England, set in by the pope, came to by the year; and it was found and evidently tried, that this pope now present, Innocent IV., did impoverish the universal church throughout Christendom, more than all his predecessors from the time the pope first began, so that the revenues of foreigners and clerks, placed by him here in England, mounted unto the sum of threescore and ten thousand marks and above, whereas the mere revenues of the crown came not to thirty thousand.

What the yearly revenues the pope's clerks here in England came to

Of this Robert Grosthead writeth Cestrensis (lib. vii.), that partly for that it grieved him to see the intolerable exactions of the pope in this realm; and, partly, because he refused to admit a certain young nephew of the pope to be canon of his church (as hath been before recited), he, therefore, writing unto the pope, and signifying that he could not admit any such persons into his church, who neither knew themselves nor the tongue of the people, nor the charges committed unto them, was called up to Rome, and there excommunicated; who, then appealing from the pope, shortly after departed, A.D. 1253. It chanced, within two years after his decease, that the said pope Innocent being asleep, a certain bishop, apparelled bishop-like, appeared unto him, and striking him with his staff on the left side, said, "Surge miser, veni in judicium:" that is, "Rise, wretch! and come to thy judgment." The next day, the pope was found amazed, as a man stricken on the side with the stroke of a staff. This Robert, though he was greatly commended for his sanctity, and, as Cestrensis saith, for his miracles, yet was he not permitted in the court of Rome to be inscribed in the catalogue of saints. And thus much out of Cestrensis concerning this matter.

The pope stricken with the staff of Grosthead, bishop of Lincoln

Matthew Paris, and the author of Flores Historiarum, prosecuting this story more at large, add this unto it, and say, that pope Innocent, the year following (which was A.D. 1254), being passing angry, contrary to the mind of his brethren the cardinals, would have the bones of this bishop of Lincoln cast out of the church, and purposed to bring him into such spite and hatred of the people, that he should be counted an ethnic, a rebel, and a disobedient person throughout

A.D. 1254

(1) Ex Matth Paris

the whole world; and thereupon caused he his letters to be written and sent down to the king of England, knowing that the king would gladly serve him therein, to have the spoil of the bishop and of his church. But, in the night following, the said bishop of Lincoln appeared unto him as coming in his pontificalibus,[1] and with a severe countenance, stern look, and terrible voice, speaking unto him being in his rest, and smiting him on the side with a vehement stroke with the end of his cross staff, thus said, "O thou lazy, bald, wretched, doting old pope![2] hast thou purposed to cast my bones out of the church to the shame and slander of me? How cometh this rash wilfulness into thy head? It were more meet for thee, being thus advanced by God, and honoured, to make much of the zealous servants of God, although departed. The Lord will not suffer thee henceforth to have any more power over me. I have written unto thee in the spirit of humility and love, that thou shouldst correct thy manifold errors; but thou, with a proud eye and disdainful heart, hast despised my wholesome admonitions. Woe to thee that despisest, shalt not thou also be despised?" And so the bishop departing from the pope, stricken, as is said, on the side, left him for half dead, and so lying in sorrow and lamentation. Whereupon his chamberlains being amazed, hearing these things, came running to the pope to know what ailed him. To whom the pope, much troubled and vexed in his spirit, said, that great terrors in his sleep vehemently disturbed and molested him, in such sort that he thought he should never recover it, nor be restored to himself again. "Oh," said he, "how sore is my side, and how eagerly it vexeth me, as being run through with a spear!" Neither did the pope eat or drink all that day, but feigning himself to be sick of a burning ague, kept in. And yet the indignation of the ireful hand of God, saith the story, so left him not. For after these wholesome admonitions given to him by the servant of God, the pope, not regarding them, but all set upon war, the suppression of his enemies, and on secular affairs, gave his mind wholly unto them; and yet all his labours, counsels, and expenses bestowed upon them, could never prosper after that day, in what he went about; for the pope, at that time, having war with the Apulians, all his army, fighting under the pope's nephew as their captain, were slain and confounded to the number of many thousands; whose lamentable slaughter all the country of the Romans did much bewail. The pope, not yet quiet in his mind, directeth his journey towards Naples, although sorely vexed in his side, like a man sick of a pleurisy, or smitten rather with a spear, neither could any physic of his cardinals help him. For Robert of Lincoln, saith the story, did not spare him; and he who would not hear him gently correcting him being alive, did feel his stripes when he was dead; so that he never after that enjoyed any lucky or prosperous day, till the time of his death, nor yet any prosperous or quiet night until the morning. And so continued he until his death, which shortly after ensued, he being at Naples, A.D. 1255, or as Nicholas Trivet recordeth, 1254. And thus have ye the whole discourse between Robert Grosthead and pope Innocent.

The pope's new and true style given by Grosthead, bishop of Lincoln

The pope disquieted in his mind.

God's revenge on pope Innocent.

The pope's army vanquished and confounded.

Death of pope Innocent IV.

(1) Ex Matth Paris Ex Flor Hist.
(2) As our author gives "Senibalde papa miserrime" for the substance of this speech, a less free and harsh translation than appears in the original, is here retained.—Ed

Henry III.

A.D. 1255.

A note concerning the appearing of dead men.

In this story is to be noted, gentle reader, that although in Cestrensis, Matthew Paris, and Flores Historiarum, it is expressly testified and reported, that the pope was smitten with the staff of Robert, the aforesaid bishop of Lincoln, yet thou must wisely understand; that, howsoever God's hand dealeth here in this world in punishing his enemies, or howsoever the images of things not seen but fantasied, offer themselves to the secret cogitation of man, his senses being asleep (by the operation or permission of God working after some spiritual influence in our imaginations), certain it is, that no dead man materially can ever arise again or appear before the judgment-day, to any man, with his staff or without his staff, to work any feat, after he have once departed this life.

Dissension between the archbishop of Canterbury and the church of Lincoln.

Excommunication abused.

After the death of this Robert Grosthead, bishop of Lincoln, there was great dissension between Boniface, the archbishop of Canterbury, and the canons of the said church of Lincoln, about the right of giving prebendships, and about the revenues of the said church, the bishop's see being then vacant; which right and power the archbishop claimed to himself, but the canons of that church, maintaining the contrary side, stood against him; and, for the same, were excommunicated of the archbishop. Among whom, one Master Wolf, resisting the archbishop to the face, in the name of all the other canons, made up his appeal to Rome, where much money on both sides was spent. At length, after this Grosthead, Henry Lexinton was elected to the see of Lincoln.

A child crucified by the Jews at Lincoln.

A child circumcised by the Jews, and kept a whole year to be crucified.

The Jews expelled out of France.

About this time the wicked Jews at Lincoln had cruelly crucified, whipped, and tormented a certain child, named Hugo, of nine years of age, A.D. 1255, in the month of August.[1] At length the child being sought and found by the mother, being cast into a pit, two and thirty of those abominable Jews were put to execution. Of this Matthew Paris reciteth a long story. The same or like fact was also intended by the Jews at Norwich, twenty years before, upon a certain child, whom they had first circumcised, and detained a whole year in custody, intending to crucify him; for which the Jews were sent up to the tower of London, of whom eighteen were hanged, and the rest remained long in prison.[2] Of this wicked Jewish people I find also, in the book Flores Historiarum, that about this year they began first to be expelled out of France, by the commandment of the French king, he being then in Palestine, warring against the Turks; on the occasion of its being objected by the Turk, against him and other christian princes, that they retained the Jews among them, who *did* crucify our Saviour, and warred against those who did *not* crucify him.[3] Of the Jews here, moreover, king Henry the same year exacted to be given unto him eight thousand marks, on pain of hanging; who, being much grieved therewith, and complaining that the king went about their destruction, desired leave to be given them by the king, that they might depart the realm, never again to return.

The Jews ask leave to depart the realm of England.

But the king committed the doing of that matter unto earl Richard, his brother, to enforce them to pay the money whether they would or not. Moreover mention is made, in the story entitled 'Eulogium,' of the Jews at Northampton, who had among themselves

(1) Ex Gualt. Gisburn. (2) Ex Nich. Trivet.
(3) Ex Flor. Histor. Ex Cestrensi, lib. vii. cap. 34.

Henry III. A.D. 1255.

prepared wildfire, to burn the city of London; for which divers of them were taken, and burned in the time of Lent, in the said town of Northampton. This was two years before, or about A.D. 1253. And forasmuch as mention here is made of the Jews, I cannot omit what some English stories write of a certain Jew, who not long after this time (about A.D. 1257), fell into a privy at Tewkesbury upon a sabbath day; who, for the great reverence he had to his holy sabbath, would not suffer himself to be plucked out. And so lord Richard, earl of Gloucester, hearing thereof, would not suffer him to be drawn out on Sunday for reverence of the holy day. And thus the wretched superstitious Jew, remaining there till Monday, was found dead.

Jews burned at Northampton.

Further, to note the blind superstition of that time, not only among the Jews, but also among the Christians; to omit divers other stories, as of Walter Gray, archbishop of York, who coming up to the parliament at London, A.D. 1255, with inordinate fasting did so overcharge nature, and pined himself, and (as the story mentioneth) did so dry up his brain, that he, losing thereby all appetite of stomach, going to Fulham, there, within three days, died, as by the compiler of Flores Historiarum is both storied and reprehended; let this only be added, which, by the aforenamed author, and in the same year, is recorded of one named Peter Chaceporce, who, dying in France, A.D. 1255, left by bequest in his testament six hundred marks for lands to be purchased to the house of Merton, for God to be served there perpetually, "Pro anima ejus et omnium fidelium;" that is, "For his soul's health, and all faithful souls." As one who would say, christian faith were not the ordinary means sufficient to salvation of faithful souls, without the choir service of the monks of Merton.

Superstitious fasting noted in Walter, archbishop of York.

Superstition in seeking salvation by wrong means.

Ye have heard it often complained of before, how the usurped power of the pope hath violently and presumptuously encroached upon the church of England, in giving and conferring benefices and prebends to his Italians and strangers, to the great damage and ruin of Christ's flock in manifold ways. This violent injury and oppression of the pope, as by no lawful and gentle means it could be reformed, so, by occasion and means inordinate, about this time it began somewhat to be bridled. The matter whereof was this, as it is by the collector of Flores Historiarum recited. In the forty-fourth year of the reign of this king Henry III., the bishop of London, named Fulco, had given a certain prebend in the church of St. Paul to one Master Rustand, the pope's messenger here in England; who entering into the profession of the grey friars, and shortly after dying on the other side of the sea, the pope immediately conferred the said prebend on one of his specials, a stranger, as was the other before. About the same instant it befel, that the bishop of London deceased, whereby the bishopric, now vacant, fell into the king's hands, who, hearing of the death of the aforenamed Rustand, gave the said prebendship, given of the pope before, to one John Crakehale, his under-treasurer; who, with all solemnity, took his installation, not knowing as yet that it was bestowed by the pope before. Not long after, as time grew, this being noised at Rome, forthwith cometh down a certain proctor, named John Gras, with the pope's embulled letters, to receive the collation of the benefice, by his commission

The pope injurious to the church of England.

The same prebendship of St. Paul's given by the pope and the king at one time to two different persons.

Henry III

A.D. 1255.

The pope's donation preferred before the king's

procuratory given by the pope, wherein John Crakehale had been already installed, as is aforesaid, by the king's donation. This matter coming in traverse before Boniface, archbishop of Canterbury, he, after inquiring and searching which donation was the first, and finding the pope's grant to be the former, gave sentence with him against the king; so that, in conclusion, the Roman clerk had the advantage of the benefice, although the other had long enjoyed the possession thereof before. Thus the pope's man being preferred, and the Englishman excluded, after the party had been invested and stalled after the use and manner, he, thinking himself to be in sure possession of his place, attempted with the rest to enter the chapter-house, but was not permitted so to do; whereupon the pope's clerk, giving place to force and number, went to the archbishop to complain. This being known, certain recluses pursued him; and he being so compassed about, one in the thickness of the throng, being never after known, suddenly rushing upon him, so pareth off his head, a little above his eyes, that he fell down dead; the same also was done to another of his fellows in flying away. This heinous murder being famed abroad, strait inquiry thereof was made, but the deed-doer could not be known; and although great suspicion was laid upon Crakehale, the king's chaplain, yet no proof could be brought. But most men thought that bloody fact to be done by certain ruffians or other light persons about the city or the court; disdaining perhaps that the Romans were so enriched with Englishmen's livings, by whom neither came relief to any Englishman, nor any godly instruction to the flock of Christ. And, therefore, because they saw the church and realm of England in such subjection, and so much to be trodden down by the Romans and the pope's messengers, they thought thereby something to bridle, as with a snaffle, the pope's messengers from their intemperate ranging into this land.[1]

Two Roman clerks going to complain, are slain by the way

The story of Matth Paris here ceaseth

Here, by the way, is to be noted, that until the death of this aforesaid Fulco, bishop of London, continueth the history of Matthew Paris, monk of St. Alban's, which was to the year of grace 1260. The residue was continued by another monk of the same house, but not with such like commendation, worthy to make any authentic story; as I have seen it noted in a written book.

It were too curious and tedious to prosecute in order what happened in every year, through this king's reign; as how it was provided by the king, that whosoever could expend fifteen pounds from land by the year, should be bound to find the king a soldier; that watch should be kept every night in cities; that whosoever was robbed, or otherwise damnified in any part of the country, he that had the custody thereof should be compelled to make up the loss again, or else to pursue the malefactor.[2] (A.D. 1253). Item, how the king making his voyage into Gascony, his expenses were reckoned to amount to two hundred and seventy thousand marks, beside thirty thousand marks bestowed upon his brethren by the mother's side, and besides other great gifts given abroad. By reason of this, great taxes, and tolonies, and tenths were required of his subjects; especially of the churchmen, who, being wont to receive tithes of others, now were constrained to give tithes to the laity.[3] (A.D. 1254.)

(1) Ex Flor. Hist (2) Ibid. (3) Ibid

Item, how in the year following, the Londoners, offering one hundred pounds for a gift to the king, with a precious cup of gold, at his return out of France, were shortly after compelled by the king to pay three thousand marks for the escape of a certain prisoner, being a clerk condemned; which clerk being granted by the king to the bishop, and he having no prison sufficient for him, borrowed of the Londoners the prison of Newgate, to have him kept therein; who escaping, there was demanded of them, as it is said, this recompense. (A.D. 1255.) Item, how the king, greatly complaining of his debts the same year, required the whole tenths which should be gathered in three years, to be taken up all at once; at whose request the nobles and commons agreed to strain themselves, so that the charter of their liberties and customs might be ratified, and fully by him confirmed; and so for that year they were.[1] Item, how pope Alexander III., to destroy the city Michera, with king Manfred, the son of Frederic the emperor, sent forth the same year Octavian, his cardinal, with a puissant army; who, coming to the city with his siege, through the counsel of Marchisius, one of the chief captains, discharged a great part of his host, whereby the most of the pope's army was slain and destroyed; almost all, save only the family of Marchisius.[2] A.D. 1255.

Pope Alexander III. maketh war.

The pope's army slain.

Many other things during the time of this king might be heaped together, as the rising of Llewellyn, king of Wales, and of the Welshmen against Henry III., and wasting the land unto the town of Chester, who destroyed divers of the English horsemen taken in the marsh; with whom at length they came to agreement by means of Octobonus, that his successors should only be called princes of Wales, and should do the king homage, and that Henry should receive of him three thousand marks. And this being established in writing, was confirmed by the pope's seal, A.D. 1257.[3]

The king of Wales warreth against the king of England.

A.D. 1257

About the same time such famine and lack of victuals oppressed the land, that a somme[4] of corn was then sold for six and twenty shillings; insomuch that the poorer sort were forced to eat nettle-roots, thistle-roots, and whatsoever they could get.[5] Some authors, however, refer this to A.D. 1262.

Hereunto, moreover, might be added, how pope Alexander, abusing and mocking the king's simplicity, made him believe that he would make his son Edmund, king of Apulia, so that he would sustain the charges and cost thereof, to maintain the war which thereto should appertain; whereby the king, cast in a sudden hope, caused his son incontinently to be proclaimed king of Apulia; and upon the same sent up to the pope all the riches he could well procure in his realm. And thus was the realm, in manifold ways, miserably impoverished to enrich the pope.[6] About this season, Richard, earl of Exeter, the king's brother, was made king of Almain by the electors.

Pope Alexander, to get money, maketh the king believe his son should be king of Apulia.

The king's brother made king of Almain

Here might be showed, moreover, and added to the stories above, how the next year (A.D. 1259), as Nicholas Trivet writeth, the king entering into France, required the restitution of such lands in Normandy and Anjou as of old right were due to him, and wrongfully

(1) Ex Flor. Hist. (2) Ex Flor Hist., et Matth. Paris. (3) Ex Polychron. 17.
(4) A beast's load.—ED. (5) Ex Authore Eulogii. (6) Ex Flor. Hist.

Henry III. A.D. 1257.

withholden from him. But the French king again alleged, saying, that the country of Normandy, in old time, was not given away from the crown of France, but was usurped, and by force extorted, by Rollo, &c. In conclusion, the king, fearing and suspecting the hearts of his nobles, and looking for nothing but rebellion at home, durst not try with them, but was compelled to agree with them upon such conditions of peace as he could get; which were these: that he should have of the French king thirteen hundred thousand of Turin pounds, with so much lands besides, as came to the value of twenty thousand pounds in yearly rent; so should he resign fully and purely, into the hands of the French king, all such lands and possessions as he had in France. Whereby the king, giving over the style and titles which he had in those parts, ceased then to be called duke of Normandy, or earl of Anjou.

What civil discord worketh. Resignation of the earldom of Normandy and Anjou.

Albeit that be true which Gisburn writeth, that the king afterward repenting of his deed, did never receive the money all his life, neither did he cease during his life to entitle himself duke of Normandy; but after him, his son Edward and his successors, in their style, left out the title to be called duke of Normandy.[1]

Conflict and skirmish between the Northern Welshmen and the Southern men, at Oxford.

Besides many other matters omitted, here I overpass also the sore and vehement conflict, not between the frogs and the mice of which Homer writeth, but the mighty pitched field, fought A.D. 1259, between the young students and scholars of the university of Oxford, having no other occasion, as I read in Matthew Paris, but only the diversity of the country where they were born; for the Northern men joining with the Welshmen, to try their manhood against the Southern, fell together in such a broil, with their ensigns and warlike array, that in conclusion divers on both sides were slain. This heavy and bloody conflict during and increasing among them, the end was this: that the Northern lads with the Welsh had the victory. After that fury and fiery fierceness had done what it could, the victors bethinking at length with themselves, partly what they had done, partly how it would be taken of the higher powers, and fearing due punishment would fall upon them, especially seeing the brother of Llewellyn, prince of Wales, and son of Griffin, was newly dead in prison; drawing their counsel and helps together, they offered to king Henry four thousand marks, to Edward, his son, three hundred, and to the queen two hundred, to be released of their trespass. But the king answered them again, that he, setting more price on the life of one true subject, than on all which by them was offered, would in no wise receive their money. And so the students without hope of peace went home with small triumph, learning what the common proverb meaneth, "Dulce bellum inexpertis." Notwithstanding, the king being then occupied in great affairs and wars, partly with Llewellyn and the Welshmen, partly inwrapped with discord at home with his nobles, had no leisure to attend to the correction of these university men.[2] Likewise, concerning the dissension following in the next year (A.D. 1260) in the university of Paris, between the students there and the friars, the number of whom then did so much increase, that the commons were scarcely able to sustain them with their alms. Also, between the universities both of Oxford and

Variance between the students and the friars in Paris. Between the Uni-

(1) Ex Gisburnensi. (2) Ex Matth. Paris.

Cambridge, for a certain prisoner taken out of prison by strength, and brought into sanctuary the same year, as is testified in Matthew Paris. (A.D. 1259.) In like manner touching the variance between the archbishop of Canterbury, and the chapter of Lincoln. Again, between the said archbishop of Canterbury, and the chapter and bishop of London; and how the said bishop at his consecration would not make his profession to the archbishop but with this exception, "Salvis jure et libertate ecclesiæ Londinensis, quæ pro posse meo defendam in omnibus," &c.[1] All which wranglings and dissensions, with innumerable others reigning daily in the church in those days, if I had leisure enough to prosecute them as I find them in stories remaining, might sufficiently induce us to understand what small peace and agreement were then joined with the doctrine and religion of those days, during the state and reign of Antichrist.

Henry III. — A.D. 1257.

versities of Oxford and Cambridge. Between the archbishop of Canterbury and the chapter of Lincoln. Between the archbishop of Canterbury and the chapter of London. Little peace in the pope's church.

These, with many such other matters, which here might be discoursed and storied at large, being more foreign than ecclesiastical, for brevity I do purposely contract and omit, cutting off all such superfluities as may seem more curious to write upon, than necessary to be known.

Histories profitable for example

This that followeth, concerning the pitiful and turbulent commotion between the king and the nobles, which lasted a long season; because it is lamentable and containeth much fruitful example both for princes and subjects to behold and look upon, to see what mischief and inconvenience groweth in commonweals, where study of mutual concord lacketh, that is, where the prince regardeth not the offending of his subjects, and where the subjects forget the office of christian patience in suffering their prince's injuries by God's wrath inflicted for their sins: therefore, in explaining the order and story thereof, I thought it not unprofitable to occupy the reader with a little more tarriance in perusing the full discourse of this so lamentable a matter, and so pernicious to the public weal.

Occasion of commotion between the king and his nobles.

And first, to declare the occasions and first beginning of this tumult, here is to be understood, that which before was signified, how king Henry married with Elenor, daughter of the earl of Provence, a stranger, which was about A.D. 1234; whereupon a great door was opened for strangers, not only to enter the land, but also to replenish the court, to whom the king seemed more to incline his favour, advancing them to more preferment than his own natural English lords; which thing to them was no little grievance. Moreover, before was declared how the king, by Isabel, his mother, who was a stranger, had divers brethren, whom he nourished up with great livings and possessions, and large pensions of money; which was another heart-sore to divers, and also an hindrance. Over and besides hath also been declared, what unreasonable collections of money from time to time, as quindecims, subsidies, tenths, amercements, fines, payments, loans, and taxes, have been levied by the king, as well on the spirituality, as on the lay sort, partly for maintaining the king's wars against Wales, Scotland, and France, and to recover Normandy; partly for helping the king's debts, voyages, and other expenses; partly for the kingdom of Apulia, which was promised the king's son by the pope; partly for moneying and supporting the

(1) Flor. Hist.

Henry III. A.D. 1257

pope in his wars against the emperor: by reason of all which sundry and importable collections, the commonwealth of the realm was utterly excoriated, to the great impoverishment of poor Englishmen; neither did it a little vex the people, to see the king call in so many legates from Rome every year, who did nothing else but transport the English money unto the pope's coffers. Besides all this, what variance and altercation have been between the king and his subjects about the liberties of Magna Charta and De Foresta, granted by king John, and after confirmed by this king, in the former council holden at Oxford, hath been before declared.

Perhaps this also might be some cause, namely, that the king, considering and bearing in mind the old injuries done by the lords and barons to his father king John before him, did bear some grudge on that account, or some privy hatred to the nobility, to revenge his father's quarrel; but of things uncertain I have nothing certainly to affirm. This is certain by truth of history, that the year next ensuing (A.D.
A.D. 1260. 1260), thus writeth Nicholas Trivet: That the king's justices, called Itinerarii, being sent thither to execute their office, were from thence repelled: the cause being alleged, that they were against the king in proceeding and enterprising against the form of the provisions enacted and established a little before at Oxford.

*[1] In this year it pleased the king, after suit to him made, to license a university or academical school to be planted in the town of Northampton; and of a special favour which he pretended to bear (and like enough did indeed) unto the scholars that went there to seat themselves, and to prosecute the exercises of studies, he wrote his letters mandatory unto the chief officers and others of the said borough in the said students' behalf; the tenor whereof followeth agreeing with the record:

The King's Letter to the Mayor, Bailiffs, and others the Inhabitants of Northampton, in the behalf of certain Scholars minded to plant themselves there, as in a University.[2]

The king to his beloved and trusty the mayor, bailiffs, and other honest men, his subjects of Northampton, greeting: Whereas certain masters and other scholars do purpose to tarry in your town corporate, there to exercise scholarly discipline, as we hear: we, hereupon, regarding the service of God, and the great profit of our kingdom, taking in good part the coming thither of the said scholars, and liking well their abode there, do will and grant that the said scholars, in the said town corporate, under our protection and defence, do safely and securely abide, and there exercise and do such things, as to such scholars shall belong. And therefore we command you and straitly charge you, that when the said scholars shall come unto you, to tarry in your said corporate town, you receive them courteously, and as becometh the state of scholars use them, not doing or suffering to be done unto them any impediment, molestation, or grievance. In witness whereof we have caused these our letters patent to be made. Witness the king, at Windsor, the first day of February, in the five and fortieth year of his reign.*

Strangers have all the

It befel, moreover, in the same year, above other times, as Walter Hemingford writeth, that a great number of aliens coming out of

(1) This passage in asterisks is not in the Editions published previous to the year 1596.
(2) "Rex dilectis et fidelibus suis majori, ballivis, et cæteris probis hominibus suis de Northampton, salutem. Cum quidam magistri et alii scholares proponant," &c.—Turris Lond.

France and other provinces, resorted to England, and had here the doing of all the principal matters of the realm under the king.[1] Unto them the rewards and reliefs, and other emoluments of the land, did most chiefly redound; which thing to see, did not a little trouble and vex the nobility and baronage of England, insomuch that Simon Mountfort, earl of Leicester, offering to stand to death for the liberties and wealth of the realm, conferred together with other lords and barons upon the matter; who, then coming to the king after an humble sort of petition, declared to him how all the doings of his realm, and his own affairs, were altogether disposed by the hands, and after the wills of strangers, neither profitable unto him, nor to the weal-public, forasmuch as his treasures being wasted and consumed, he was in great debt, neither was able to satisfy the provision of his own house, but was driven to tally for his own cates, to the no small dishonour of his own state. "And now, therefore," said they, "please your highness to be informed by our advice, and to commit your house to the guiding and government of your own faithful and natural subjects, and we will take upon us to discharge your whole debt within one year, of our own proper goods and revenues, so that we, within five years, may clear ourselves again. Neither will we diminish your family, but rather increase it with a much greater retinue; providing so for the safety, and seeing to the custody, of your royal person, as your highness shall find and understand our diligence most trusty and faithful unto you in the end."

Henry III.

A. D. 1260.

Wealth of the realm under the king.

The appeal of the nobles to the king.

To these words, so lovingly declared, so humbly pretended, so heartily and freely offered, the king as willingly condescended, assinging to them both day and place where to confer and to deliberate further upon the matter, which should be at Oxford, the fifteenth day after Easter. On that day, and at that place, all the states and lords, with the bishops of the realm, were summoned to appear in the said town of Oxford, on behalf of the king and the realm convented together; where, first of the king himself, then of the lords, an oath was taken, that what decrees or laws in the said assembly should be provided to his profit of the king and of the realm, the same universally should be kept and observed to the honour of God, the utility of his church, and the wealth of the realm. Besides these lords and the king, were also nine bishops, who swearing to the same, did excommunicate all such as should gainstand the said provisions there made; the king, holding a burning taper in his hand, and the lords openly protesting to rise with all their force against all them that should stand against the same.

The king yieldeth to his lords.

A parliament at Oxford.

Provisions or laws made there.

The king sweareth unto them.

There were at that time in the realm four brethren of the king's (the most of them by the mother's side) who would in no case agree hereunto, but in anger departed privily unto Winchester. The nobles hearing thereof, in all speedy wise pursued them, fearing lest they should take the city of Winchester, and forcibly keep the same. Wherefore the lords preventing their purpose, and seeing them stiffly to persist in their stubborn sentence, wrought no other violence against them, but, returning to Oxford, prescribed to them these conditions: That they, departing the realm, should repair to their

The king's brethren against the said provisions.

(1) Ex Gualt. et Gisburn.

Henry III. A.D. 1260. own lands and possessions, which they had beyond the sea; and that forthwith they should put this injunction in execution. Notwithstanding that the king made for them great intercession, yet it took no place. And because this should seem to proceed of no special displeasure against them, they enacted, moreover, that all strangers and aliens, of what state or condition soever, should forthwith void the realm on pain of death. Divers other provisions at the same time were ordained and established; that if any did hold of the king in whole or in part, and should chance to depart, his heir being under age, the wardship of him should belong to the king, as hath partly before been specified.

God grant this law may take place again. Moreover, it was there decreed, that the wool of England should be wrought only within the realm, neither should it be transported out to strangers.[1]

Item, That no man should wear any cloth, but which was wrought and made within the realm.

And this, for the wealth of the realm. *Item*, That garments too sumptuous should not be brought in or worn.

Item, That all excessive and prodigal expenses, wasted upon pleasure and superfluity, should be eschewed by all persons.

Divers in this council poisoned. Many other laws and decrees, saith the author, in this assembly were ordained, wherein they continued the space of fifteen days; and many of them were poisoned, of whom was the abbot of Westminster, a man in that order much commended. Also William, brother to the earl of Gloucester: also the earl himself, being poisoned, hardly escaped with his life, his hair and nails falling off his body; whereof the author not long after was taken, and duly executed at Winchester. In the mean time, the nobles considering those dangers and jeopardies, were constrained to break off for that time, appointing the fourteenth day of October next following to convent together at London with weapon and harness, to prosecute and finish the residue that was in the said council to be concluded. All which, at the time and place appointed, was fully accomplished, and the acts thereof in order of writing promulgated, and so committed to execution.

The king repenteth of his oath. After the promulgation whereof, many things therein displeased the king, and it began to repent him of his oath. But because he could not at that present otherwise choose, he dissembled for a season. A.D. 1261. Thus, time passing on, within a year following (A.D. 1261), the king seeing himself more and more to grow in debt, and not to be relieved according to promise made, but especially being edged, as may be thought by his brethren, taking it to stomach, sent up to the pope, both for him and his son Edward to be released of their oath made before at Oxford. Sueth to the pope to release him from his oath. Absolution abused. The benefit of which absolution being easily obtained, or rather bought at the pope's hand, the king, stepping back from all that was before concluded, calleth another parliament at Oxford, where he, before the lords and nobles, declared how in the late council of Oxford they had agreed among themselves for the common utility of the realm and of the king, as they pretended, for the increasing of his treasure, and his debt to be diminished; and thereupon bound themselves with an oath, causing also himself and his son Edward to be bound unto the same. But now,

(1) Ex Hist. Gualt. Gisburnensis.

Henry III. A.D. 1261.

by experience proving and trying the matter to be otherwise than their promise was, and that they, contrary to their covenant made, sought not so much the profit of him and of the realm, as their own, taking him not as their lord, but going about to bring him under their subjection as an underling; and for that, moreover, his treasure greatly decreasing, his debts increased, and his princely liberality was cut short and trodden under foot: they should not marvel therefore, if he henceforth would be no more ruled by their counsel, but would provide himself with some other remedy, such as he might. And moreover, as touching the oath wherewith he and his son stood bound unto them, he had sent already to Rome, and had obtained absolution and dispensation of the same, both for him and his son Edward, and for all others that would take his part. And therefore he required of them to be restored again to that state and condition he had enjoyed in times past.

Further answer of the nobles to the king.

To this again gave answer the state of nobility on the other side, being in the same place present; in the number of whom was Simon Montfort, earl of Leicester, Richard Clare, earl of Gloucester, Humphrey Ronne, earl Ferrence, with a great number of barons, as lord John Fitz-John, lord Hastings, lord Geffery Lucy, lord John Vescy, lord William Segrave, Hugh Spencer, lord Robert Vespoint, with divers and many more; whose answer to the king again was this: That the provisions made at the council of Oxford, whereunto they were sworn, they would hold, defend, and maintain to their lives' end; forasmuch as they did sound, and also were agreed upon, both to the honour of God, to the profit of the prince, and the stable wealth of the realm. And thus on both sides discording amongst themselves, they would so have departed, had not certain of the bishops, coming between both, laboured to make up the matter. By whose means (saith Gisburn), and procurement, the determination of the cause was brought in compromise, and referred to Louis, the French king, to judge betwixt them, who, hearing both the allegations (saith he), like no equal judge but a partial friend, inclined wholly and fully to the king's sentence, and condemned the nobles. But the author of Flores Historiarum saith, that by the mediation of certain discreet men, two were chosen, one for one side, the other for the other, to whom a third also was annexed, who hearing, as well what was brought of the king's part, as also what was answered of the other, should define between them both; and so peace was between them concluded till the coming of Edward. All this while the pope's absolution for the king, although it was granted and obtained at Rome, yet was it not brought down in solemn writing, neither was prince Edward as yet returned out of France into England.

Controversy between the king and the nobles compromised.

At length, the writing of the king's absolution being brought from Rome, the king soon commanded the same to be published throughout the realm, and sendeth to the French king and other strangers for help; moreover, he seizeth all his castles into his own hand, rejecting the counsel of the lords, to whose custody they were before committed; also removing the former officers, as the justices and the chancellor, with others placed before by the lords, he appointed new in their stead.

The pope releaseth the king from his oath.

To this aforesaid absolution procured from Rome for the king and

Henry III. A.D. 1261.

his son, Edward, returning out of France at that time, did not give his consent, but held with the lords; who then putting themselves in arms, with a great power repaired to London, keeping there in the suburbs and places about, while the king kept within the tower, causing the city gates to be watched and locked, and all within the said city, being above the age of twelve years, to be sworn unto him. But, at length, through the means of certain coming between, this tumultuous perturbation being somewhat appeased, at least some hope of peace appeared; so that the matter was taken up for that time without war or bloodshed. Notwithstanding, some false pretensed dissemblers there were, who secretly disclosing all the counsels and doings of the lords unto the king, did all they could to hinder concord, and to kindle debate; by the means of whom the purpose of the lords came not to so good effect, as otherwise it might.[1]

Wicked make-baits.

*[2]In this year the archbishop of Canterbury, with his suffragans (after their wonted manner), standing against the king, had made their appeal to Rome: whereupon the king was fain to answer by proxy, as appeareth by this brief note, drawn out of record:—"Rex constituit Johannem Hemingford procuratorem suum in causa appellationis," &c. "The king hath appointed and made John Hemingford his proctor in a cause of appeal which is moved in the court of Rome, between the king on the one part, and the archbishop of Canterbury with his suffragans on the other, about certain ordinances, constitutions, and decrees lately in a council provincial at London by them published, to the prejudice of the king's right, his dignity royal, the liberties, laws, and customs of his kingdom."[3]

Ordinances in a provincial council at London against the king's right.

This matter no doubt was laboured very diligently by the said John Hemingford, who was to that end authorized by the king to make his abode at Rome, during the time that any manner of process was held and maintained against him to the impeaching of his royalty; whereof the king had a special regard, perceiving the waywardness of his own clergy, or rather rebelliousness in daring to decree and ordain laws against him, and therefore he was the more careful to have all matters depending in the court of Rome concerning him and his to be earnestly followed, insomuch that he joined to the aforesaid Hemingford, in the charge of procuration, one Roger Lovel: unto which two, residing at Rome, the king sent his letters, charging them so to manage his affairs, as that nothing might pass to the derogation of his royal title. The copy of the said letter followeth, agreeing with the prototype or original.

A Letter of the King sent to his Proctors at Rome, concerning a Case of his in the said Court depending.[4]

Against the proceedings in the court of Rome tending to the hurt and prejudice of the king.

The king to Master John of Hemingford, and Roger Lovel, his proctors, pleading in the court of Rome, greeting: Forasmuch as upon you, our trusty and vowed servants, the defence of our right and honour doth lie; and, as we hear, certain of our realm, pleading in the court of Rome, do move divers matters to the prejudice of our right and honour, presuming and intending to prevail against us, we command you, and straitly charge you, that on our behalf you straitly forbid all and every of them, that they presume not any further to undertake such things as tend to the hurt of our majesty, and the

(1) Ex Flor. Hist. (2) In no Edition before that of 1596.—Ed. (3) Ex Flor. Hist.

(4) "Rex magistris Johanni de Hemingford, et Rogero Lovel procuratoribus suis, in curia Romana agentibus, salutem, etc. Cum vobis tanquam fidelibus nostris," etc.—Turris Lond.

derogation of our honour, but wholly forbear so to do, as they will avoid our indignation, and the peril of them and theirs. This inhibition also we will (by you all and every of you, as often as you shall see needful), to be made known, and, thereupon, by you or some of you to be certified of the contemners of the same. Witness the king at Westminster, the six-and-twentieth of March, in the six-and-fortieth year of his reign."* *Henry III.* A. D. 1262.

In this present year also (as affirmeth the forenamed author) it was rumoured abroad that all the bishops of England went about to recover, out of the hands of religious men, all such churches and benefices, as were to them impropriated or appropriated;[1] and that they, for the expedition of the same, had sent up to Rome both messengers and money, nothing misdoubting to obtain their purpose. But, as little good fruit in those days used to spring out of that see, so I do not find that godly suit and labour of the bishops to take any fruitful effect. Bishops going about to recover benefices appropriated by religious houses.

The same year died pope Alexander, after whom succeeded pope Urban IV. Of this Urban the king also obtained (or rather revived) a new releasement from his oath made to the provisions and statutes of Oxford; which being granted, he commandeth incontinently all the aforesaid laws and provisions throughout England to be dissolved and broken.[2] This done, the king, with the queen, taketh his voyage into France, where he fell into great infirmity of sickness, and the most part of his family were taken with the quartan fever, of which many died; in the number of whom, was Richard, the worthy earl of Gloucester and Hereford, after whom succeeded Gilbert Clare, his son. A.D.1262.

The Welshmen this year (A. D. 1262), breaking into the borders of England, did much annoyance in the lands of Roger lord Mortimer, but mightily again by him were expelled, not without great slaughter of the invaders. About which time, the king, through some discreet counsel about him, inclined to peace and concord with his nobles, granting, of his mere voluntary will, the constitutions and provisions of Oxford to take place in the realm, directing his commandment to every shire. Albeit the realm yet was not altogether pacified for all that. The Welsh rebel. The provisions of Oxford again granted by the king.

In the latter end of this year, the king's palace at Westminster was burnt, and for the most part was all consumed with fire, which seemed to many an evil prognostication against the king.[3] Palace at Westminster burnt with fire.

In some English chronicles it is also recorded, that the same year five hundred Jews at London were slain for taking usury more than two pence a week for twenty shillings, being before forbidden by the king to take above that rate by the week. Usury punished.

After this (A. D. 1263) the barons of England, confederating themselves together for maintaining the statutes and laws of Oxford, and partly moved with old grudge conceived against the strangers (maintained by the king and the queen, and Edward their son, in the realm of England), joined powers in all forcible wise, and first invaded the said strangers, namely, those who were about the king. Their goods and manors they wasted and spoiled, whether they were persons ecclesiastical or temporal; among whom, besides others, was A.D.1263. The nobles rise up against the strangers, having the commodity of the realm.

(1) Ex Flor. Historiarum.
(2) A new release of the king's oath from Rome, with this epitaph: "Hic pudor Hypoliti, Paridis gena, sensus Ulyssis; Æneæ pietas, Hectoris ira jacet."
(3) Ex Flor. Hist.

Henry III.

A.D. 1263.

Peter, a Burgundian (bishop of Hereford, a rich prelate), with all his treasure apprehended and spoiled: also his countrymen, whom he had placed to be canons of the same church. With like order of handling, other aliens also, to whom had been committed the custody of divers castles, as Gloucester, Worcester, and Bridgenorth, were spoiled, imprisoned, and sent away. Briefly, whosoever he was in all the land that could not utter the English tongue, was of every rascal disdained, and happy if he might so escape; by reason whereof it so came to pass, that a great number as well of other foreigners, as especially religious men, and rich priests (who here had gathered much substance) were urged to that extremity, that they were glad to flee the land; in the catalogue of whom was one most principal, named John Maunsel, a priest notoriously grown in riches and treasures not to be told, having in his hand so many and rich benefices, that hardly any bishop of this realm might compare with him in riches. This priest, notwithstanding he kept with the king at London, yet was compelled privily to avoid the realm, and was pursued by Henry, the son of Richard, king of Almain. Certain other strangers there were, to the number of two hundred and more, who, having the castle at Windsor, there immured and entrenched themselves, to whom at length, prince Edward also joined himself.

Peter, a Burgundian, a rich English bishop.

John Maunsel a rich priest.

In the mean time while this stir was abroad, the king keeping then in the Tower, and seeing the greatest part of his nobles and commons with the Londoners to be set against him, agreed to the peace of the barons, and was contented to assent again to the ordinances and provisions of Oxford; albeit the queen, by all means possible, went about to persuade the king not to assent thereto; who, as it seemed, was a great worker in kindling this fire of discord between the king and the barons: insomuch, that when the said queen Elenor should pass by barge from the Tower to Windsor, the Londoners standing upon the bridge, with their exclamations, cursing and throwing of stones and dirt at her, interrupted her course, causing her to return to the Tower again. Notwithstanding, the peace yet continued with the nobles and the king, the form whereof was this: First, that Henry, the son of Richard, king of the Romans, should be delivered up by the king and queen. Secondly, that the castles again should be committed to the custody of Englishmen, not of strangers. Thirdly, that the provisions and statutes decreed at Oxford, should as well by the king, as by all others, inviolably be observed. Fourthly, that the realm henceforth should be ruled and governed not by foreigners, but by personages born within the land. Fifthly, that all aliens and strangers should void the land, not to return again; except only those, whose abode should by the common assent of the king's trusty subjects be admitted and allowed.

The king again agreeth with the nobles.

The queen a great cause of this debate.

Form of the peace concluded between the king and the nobles.

Thus the king and the nobles, joining together after this form of peace above prefixed, although not fully with heart, as after appeared, put themselves in arms, with all their power to recover the castle of Windsor out of the strangers' hands. But Edward, mid-way between London and the castle, meeting with his father and the barons, entered into communication upon the matter; which being finished and he thinking to return into the castle again, by the policy of the earl of Leicester, and William, bishop of Worcester, was not permitted to re-enter: whereupon the strangers within the hold (destitute of all hope to withstand the great force approaching) rendered the castle unto the king and the barons, upon this convention: that with horse and harness they might be suffered safely to depart the land, not to return any more. This being granted, certain of the barons conducted them in their journey towards the sea side, and there they left them.

Henry III.

A. D. 1263.

Windsor Castle recovered out of the hands of strangers.

In the same year, about the beginning of October, the king and queen made over to France, with Simon Mountfort and other nobles, to hear and stand to the arbitrement of Louis, the French king, concerning the controversy between the states of England; and all through the procurement of Elenor, the queen. For she, not forgetting the old contumely of the Londoners, exclaiming against her upon the bridge, wrought always what revenge she could against them.

"Manet alta mente repostum
Judicium Paridis."[1]

Concerning the arbitrement of this matter referred to the French king, part hath been said before, and more shall be said (Christ willing) hereafter. Some stories do add, moreover, that the king continuing long in France, word was sent to him out of England, that unless he returned again to the realm, they would elect a new king; whereupon the king, returning out of France to Dover, would have entered the castle, but was stopped. Wherefore the king, in fierce anger and great indignation, prepared his power towards London, where Simon Mountfort, the worthy earl of Leicester, through a subtle train, was almost betrayed and circumvented in Southwark, by the sudden pursuing of the king's army, had not the Londoners, with more speed, breaking bars and chains, made way to rescue him; by the means of whom the earl at that time escaped the danger.

Now to come to the sentence of the French king: Forasmuch as the arbitrement of this matter was committed to him, as hath before been specified, he, with a great assemblage both of French and English persons about him, considering and poising the cause on both sides, between the king and the nobles, clearly and solemnly pronounced on the king's side against the barons; ordaining that the king of England all this while had suffered wrong, and that he should be restored again to his pristine state, notwithstanding the provisions made at Oxford, which he ordained to be repealed and abrogated.[2]

Sentence of the French king with the king of England, against the barons.

The sentence of the French king thus awarded, as it gave to the king of England with his retinue no little encouragement, so it wrought in the nobles' hearts great indignation; who, notwithstanding that partial decreement of the French king, sped themselves home out of France to defend themselves with all their strength and power. And not long after followeth also the king, by whose train Simon Mountfort, earl of Leicester, as is above recited, was well nigh circumvented in Southwark. Then the king calling his council together at Oxford (from whence he excluded the university of students for a season, who were then at Northampton, as you heard before) there consulted, conferring with his friends and counsellors, what way was best to be taken. And hearing that the barons were assembled in

War betwixt the king and the barons beginneth.

The university of students removed for a time from Oxford to Northampton.

(1) Virg. Æneid. i. 26. (2) Ex Flor. Historiarum, Gisburn. et aliis.

Henry III. A.D. 1264. great numbers in the town of Northampton, he went thither with his host and his banners displayed, accompanied by Richard, his brother, king of Almain, also by Edward, his son, John Comyn of Scotland, with many other Scots—John of Dalliolo, Lord of Galoway, Robert of Bruce, Lord Walter of Anand, Roger of Clifford, Philip of Marmion, John of Waus, Roger of Laiburne, Henry Percy, Philip Basset, Roger of Mortimer, and William of Wallace, and many others. Therefore the king commanded the barons that were within, to yield unto him presently the city and the pledges, or else he would immediately destroy them. But they, counselling with the younger Simon de Mountfort, who, by his father's commandment, had got the residue thither to take counsel together (for his father and the earl of Gloucester were not yet come), boldly and with one mind answered, that they would not obey the king's will, but would rather defend themselves and the city, if need were, even to the death. The noblemen of the king's part hearing this, sent word again, that at least they should come to the wall of the city to speak to the king, if, by any means, peace might be made. They, suspecting no deceit, followed their counsel, and leaving their holds, came to the wall towards the meadow, for there lay the king and his strong host hard by. But, in the mean space, whilst divers matters were reasoned and treated of between the king and the lords, the lord Philip Basset, who before was appointed to work that feat, with mattocks and other instruments of iron, and with men prepared for the onset, near to the monastery of St. Andrew, did undermine the wall of the city; and by this means the wall soon fell down, and there was made a great plain, so that in one forefront there might have gone together on a row forty horsemen. Of this subtlety the alien monks that were there, were thought to be the workers, because they made way and entrance for them that came in; but when they that passed by saw this, and that the king's banners were erected ready to enter in, there was a great howling made, and the noise of the people came to the ears of the barons, and they made speed to resist them; but it was all in vain, because they were already prevented by a great company of their enemies. But Simon Mountfort the younger, after he had valiantly fought a while in the midst of his enemies, with Peter Mountfort, and a few that were with him, when Edward the king's son came, was by his commandment taken and led away prisoner. But the clerks of the university of Oxford (which university by the barons' commandment was translated thither) did work against the king's men more hurt than the other barons, with their slings, long bows and cross bows; for they had a banner by themselves, and that was set up on high against the king. Wherewithal the king being greatly moved, sware at his entering in, that they should all be hanged; which when they heard, many of them shaved their crowns, and they that were able ran away as fast as they could, and when the king entered the city, many fled in their armour into the castle, others left their horse and harness, and ran into churches, and a few were slain, and those were of the common people; but there was not much bloodshed, because all things were done as upon the sudden. When the city was at length set in quiet, the king commanded his oath to be executed upon the clerks. But his counsellors said unto

Taking of Northampton by the king.

Simon Mountfort, the younger, taken prisoner.

The scholars of Oxford stout against the king.

him, "This be far from thee, O king! for the sons of thy nobles, and of other great men of thy kingdom were there gathered together into the university; whom if thou wouldst cause to be hanged or slain, even they that now take thy part would rise up against thee, not suffering, to the uttermost of their powers, the blood of their sons and kinsfolks to be shed." And so the king was pacified, and his wrath against the clerks was staid.

Henry III. A.D. 1264.

The students of Oxford spared.

In the same day, after little more than an hour, the king's host assaulted the castle, and the new hold-keepers were afraid, for that they had not victuals and other things necessary for their resistance; therefore they sent immediately messengers unto the king, and yielded themselves to the king's mercy. There were taken that day these knights and barons under written: lord William de Ferrers, lord Peter Mountfort, companion of the said Simon de Mountfort the younger, lord Baldwin de Wake, lord Adam de Newmarch, lord Roger Bertram; lord Simon, the son of Simon, a valiant warrior, who first erected his banner against the king; lord Berengarius de Watervile, lord Hugo Gubiam, lord Thomas Maunsel, lord Roger Botemlam, Nicholas Wake, lord Robert de Newton, lord Philip de Driby, and Grimbald de Pauncefoot. All these did the king take prisoners, and many more, of whom he committed some to the lord Nicholas of Haversham, to be kept in that castle well defended; some he led away with him; and some he sent to divers castles: Simon Mountfort he appointed to be cast into Windsor Castle. All these things, as touching the taking of Northampton, were done on the Sabbath day in Passion Week, being the third of April, A.D. 1264: and the king went forward even to Nottingham, burning and wasting the manors of the lords and others his enemies; and there he gathered together his nobles, and greatly increased his numbers.

The lords taken at Northampton.

When this ill luck was told, by them that from thence were run away to the earl Simon, who was coming towards Northampton with a great host, he was in a great rage, and yet was not discouraged; but immediately going to London, he caused a chariot to be made after the manner of litters or couches, wherein he might ride as though he were sick; for he feigned himself to be feeble and weak, whereas he was indeed a stout and valiant warrior; and there gathered to him other noblemen that were confederate with him, earls and barons, every one bringing with them their several arms, and preparing their engines of wood, they went to besiege Rochester; for the earl of Worcester, in the king's behalf, kept both the town and castle. When they had gotten the first gate and the bridge, they were partly wounded and compelled to retire; and there that valiant knight, Roger de la Bourn, was wounded, and very ill handled. Whilst they continued siege there awhile, it was told them that the king was coming towards London with a mighty host; and they said one to another, "If the king at his coming should take London, we shall be shut in as it were in a strait corner; let us, therefore, return unto London, that we may keep in safety both the place and the people." Therefore, appointing certain persons to keep the siege, they returned to London. At length when the king came, they went forth with the citizens to meet him, not with flowers and palms in their hands, but with swords and spears. The king shunned them, and after he had the castle of

Simon Mountfort feigneth himself sick.

Rochester besieged by the barons.

Henry III. A.D. 1264. The king shunneth London.

Kingston, which was the earl of Gloucester's, he went from thence to Rochester; where, after he had killed a few, he brake the siege, and from thence the king went to Tunbridge, and the town and castle now being given up to him, he took there the countess of Gloucester, and put her into an abbey, not to be kept in hold, but to go at liberty whither she would. He also left for the custody of the castle and city a great part of his host, to the number of above twenty picked ensigns, for that it was commonly said, that the earl of Gloucester would come out of hand to assault them. This being done, he continued on his journey to Winchester, where he received in peace the seamen of the haven towns. Three days after, upon the Sunday following, he came to the town of Lewes, and was received into the abbey, and his son Edward into the castle. Then the barons sent letters to the king the twelfth day of May, the tenor whereof followeth.

Letter of the Lords to the King.

To their most excellent Lord Henry, by the grace of God king of England, lord of Ireland, and duke of Aquitaine, his barons and others his faithful subjects, being willing to keep their oath and fidelity to God and him, send greeting and due obedience with honour and reverence. Whereas by many experiments it is manifest, that some of your grace's assistants have reported to your majesty many lies of us, working mischief, as much as in them lieth, not only against us, but against you also, and your whole realm: Be it known to your highness, that we have been always willing to defend the health and safeguard of your person, with all our power and fealty due to your grace, purposing to vex to the uttermost of our power and estate, not only our ill-willers, but also your enemies, and the enemies of your whole realm. If it be your good pleasure, give no credit to them; we shall be always found your faithful subjects. And we, the earl of Leicester, and Gilbert of Clare, at the request of others, for us and them have put to our seals.

These letters being read and heard, there was a council called, and the king wrote back to them, and especially to the two earls of Leicester and Gloucester, in manner and form following:—

The Answer of the King to the Lords.

Henry, by the grace of God king of England, lord of Ireland, duke of Aquitaine, &c., to Simon Mountfort, and Gilbert de Clare, and their confederates. Forasmuch as by the war, and general disquietness by your means raised up in our whole realm, and also the burnings and other hurtful enormities, it appeareth manifestly, that you keep not your fidelity to usward, nor care any thing for our health and safety; and for that ye have unorderly grieved our nobles, and others our faithful subjects sticking faithfully and constantly to us, as you have certified us; we, accounting their losses as our own, and their enemies as ours, and seeing these our aforesaid faithful subjects, for the keeping of their fidelity, do assist us manfully and faithfully against your unfaithfulness: we therefore care not for your fidelity or love, but defy you as our and their enemies. Witness myself, at Lewes, the day and year aforesaid.

Also Richard, king of Almain, and lord Edward, the son of king Henry, wrote to the barons in this wise:—

A Letter of Richard, King of Almain, and Prince Edward, to the Barons.

Richard, by the grace of God, king of the Romans, always Augustus, and Edward, eldest son of the king of England, and all the other barons and nobles constantly and faithfully in heart and deed cleaving to the aforesaid king of

England: to Simon Mountfort, and Gilbert de Clare, and to all and singular others their adherents in their conspiracy. By your letters which you sent to our lord, the noble king of England, we have understanding that you defy us; although before any such word, your defiance towards us was apparent enough by your cruel persecution, in burning our possessions and spoiling our goods. We therefore give you to wit, that we all and every one of us, do defy you all as our open enemies. And further, that we will not cease, wheresoever it shall lie in our power, to the uttermost of our force and might, to subvert your persons and all that you have. As touching what you lay to our charge, that we give neither faithful nor good counsel to our lord the king, you say not the truth. And if your lord Simon Mountfort or Gilbert de Clare, will affirm the same in our lord the king's court, we are ready to get safe conduct for you to come to the said court, to try and declare the truth of our innocency, and the falsehood of you both, as foresworn traitors, by some man equal with you in nobility and stock. All we are contained with the seals of the aforesaid lords, the lord Richard and the lord Edward. Dated the day aforesaid.

Battle of Lewes, betwixt the king and the barons.

Both which letters being read, they drew near to the king; for they were not far distant from Lewes. And because there was wanted to the king's store, provision for their horses, it was commanded them, on the Tuesday, to go forth to seek for hay and provender; who, when they were gone forth, were prevented by their enemies, and most of them killed; but the residue returning, saw their enemies coming, very early on the Wednesday morning, and making outcries, stirred up the king and his host to arm themselves. Then the barons, coming to the full plain, descended there, and girding and trimming their horses, made fit their harness to them. And there the earl Simon made the earl of Gloucester, and Robert de Vere, and many others new knights. This done, he divided and distinguished his host into four several battles, and he appointed noblemen to guide and govern each battle; and over the first battle were ordained captains, Henry Mountfort, the eldest son of the earl Simon, and Guido, his brother; lord John de Bruch the younger, and lord Humfrey de Bohun. Over the second battle, lord Gilbert Clare, earl of Gloucester, lord John the son of lord St. John, and lord William of Mountchersy. And over the third, in which the Londoners were, at their request the lord Nicholas Segrave was assigned; who required also very instantly, that they might have the first stroke in the battle, at the adventure, come what would. But over the fourth battle, the earl himself was captain, with the lord Thomas of Pilneston. In the mean season, came forth the king's host, preparing themselves, to the field, in three battles; of which Edward, the king's son, led the first, with the earl of Warwick, and Valence the king's brother; and the second the king of Almain guided, with his son Henry; but the king, with his nobles, guided the third; and the fourth legion the king appointed not, by reason he had left many of his chief soldiers behind him, to keep the castle and town of Tunbridge against the earl of Gloucester. The most part of the king's army were but young men, for the king thought not that his barons had been come so nigh to hand. Their armies being on both sides set in array and order, they exhorted one another on either part to fight valiantly; and after they had buckled together, the battle was great, and many horsemen were overthrown, even in a moment. But by and by Edward, the king's son, with his band, as a fierce young gentleman and valiant knight, fell upon his enemies with such force, that he compelled them to recoil

Henry III back a great way, so that the hindmost (thinking by reason of their giving back, that the foremost were slain), ran many of them away;

A.D. 1264. and taking water to pass over, almost threescore soldiers were drowned, and a few of them being slain, all the rest fled. Straightway the Londoners, who had asked the first fight, knowing not how the battle went, took to their heels, whom Edward pursued with his band, killing the hindmost of them, for the space of two or three miles; for he hated them because they had rebelled against his father, and disgraced his mother when she was carried by barge upon the Thames, from the Tower to Windsor, as is before recorded.

Whilst prince Edward was thus in chase of the Londoners, who had the vanguard of the barons' battle; in the mean time, the main battle of the barons set upon the king's main battle, of which the king of Almain, the brother of king Henry, had the leading; who being soon discomfited, and he with his son Henry, Robert de Bruce, and John Coven, with divers other captains taken prisoners, the rear-ward, wherein the king himself fought, being immediately so hardly beset, and he, seeing his knights and soldiers on every side about him beaten down and slain, and divers others of his soldiers to forsake the field and shift for themselves, thought good to take again to the town; and so retired into the abbey from whence he came, shutting and rampering up the gates, and caused the same to be strongly warded with soldiers. To be brief, the barons thus getting the field, after long fight, and many men on either side slain, entered also the town of Lewes, pursuing in chase such soldiers as thither fled for succour.

Richard, king of Almain, with his son, taken prisoners

The main battle discomfited, and the king fain to take to the abbey.

Prince Edward returning from the first chase, findeth all together lost

In the mean time, prince Edward returning from the chase of the Londoners, as ye heard, who desired to give the first onset, and espying the chariot of the earl Simon (which he caused purposely to be made for him), and the horses in the same, without either waggoner, or any other to govern the same, fell immediately upon the chariot, and brake it all in pieces, and slew two burgesses that were within the same. But when he came near to the place where the bloody battle had been fought, and saw the great discomfiture and overthrow, which, in his absence, with great mortality and slaughter, had happened, his heart was much dismayed, and his countenance altered. Yet notwithstanding, comforting and encouraging his knights and soldiers, of whom he had a valiant company, in battle array, he marched toward the town, against whom came the barons again with all their power; and thus was begun betwixt them a fresh field and a new battle, and many men were slain on either side. At length the earl de Warenna, with the king's two brothers, forsook the field and fled; after whom went more than seven hundred chosen soldiers, who were of their house and family, who the same day came to Pevensey, and there took shipping over the sea. Also Hugh Bigot, with divers others, fled, and left the valiant prince fighting in the field, which thing he also perceiving, took to the town; and when he found not the king his father, at the castle, he went from thence to the abbey where he was. In the mean season, the town was divided into parts, some fighting, some spoiling, some getting of booties, while scarcely one of them could know and discern another, whether he was friend or enemy. But when, within a while, the barons had assembled some

The prince fighteth a new battle.

He also is put to the worst, and fain to take to the town

company, they gave an assault upon the castle, thinking to have rescued John Gifford and others, whom the king's soldiers had taken prisoners, and put therein. But the soldiers within manfully defended the same, and in throwing out balls of wild-fire, which for the defence thereof they had, they also fired part of the town. Then the barons retired and left the castle, and purposed to have set upon the abbey, where the king and prince Edward, his son, were, which also was set on fire by the assault given to the castle; but yet it was shortly recovered and quenched. Then Edward, the king's son, perceiving the bold enterprise of the barons, prepared with the courageous knights and soldiers yet remaining and within the abbey, to issue out, and to give a new charge upon them. But the barons, perceiving that, sent unto the king messengers to entreat a truce for that day, and on the morrow to talk of and conclude a further peace between them. This battle was fought upon the nineteenth day of May.

The castle of Lewes besieged.

The next day, which was Thursday, there were sent on either side two preaching friars, between the king and the barons, with certain articles and demands of peace, so that with certain others, these conditions were agreed on: that on the morrow, being Friday, the prince should give himself as hostage for the king, his father, and others of his party, and that Henry, the king's son of Almain, should also give himself in like manner for his father; that those things which should be concluded upon for the benefit and commodity of the realm, and peaceable quietness thereof might be performed, and that all such prisoners as were taken on either side, should be freely ransomed and sent home.

Peace between the king and the barons.

The two princes given as hostages.

The next day, which was Saturday, the king discharged all his soldiers, and others that were with him in the abbey, licensing them to depart whither they listed. And furthermore, by the advice of his son and the barons, he gave commandment to those whom he had appointed to the keeping of Tunbridge, that they should make no attempt to the prejudice or hurt of the barons; but in hope of the peace which was now on the point of being concluded, they also should depart every man to his house and habitation. But they, giving no credit thereunto, went with their furniture to Bristol, where they kept themselves in garrison, until the escaping of Edward the king's son, out of prison. But first, before that, when they heard at Tunbridge, that the king was vanquished in battle, and that the Londoners in the fore-ward were put to flight by prince Edward (by a messenger that escaped from the same), and that also the same Londoners were at Croydon, they set upon them in the evening tide, and taking from them much spoil, slew also many of them.

The king's soldiers in Tunbridge, after spoiling the Londoners at Croydon, keep in garrison at Bristol.

But when Roger Mortimer's party began to decrease, and Simon the earl's party on the other side to increase, he bare himself more stoutly, for that both the king and all that was his, did depend upon the good will and favour of the earl, and led with him the king's son to such holds and castles, as he thought to be most strong, as though all were in his hands to do as he liked; and he kept the hostages more straitly than he was wont to do, insomuch that when it was blown abroad that the king's son was kept as prisoner, divers who were his friends, counselled him, that he should desire to disport himself at the barriers, that the people might have a sight of him. But he,

Earl Simon after this beareth himself so stout, that he imprisoneth the hostages of the king

Henry III. being narrowly guarded as he knew, and fearing some tumult to arise, thought good to refuse their counsel, and so did.

A.D. 1264. In this troublesome year, which was A.D. 1264, as the Londoners with the nobles were thus occupied in war and dissension, the malignant Jews, thinking to take advantage of that time, with privy treason conspired against the whole city and state of the nobles; and being taken so conspiring, were almost all slain that dwelt in the city of London. *[1] In this year also, Boniface, archbishop of Canterbury, the son of Peter, earl of Savoy, and a stranger, having been certain years beyond the seas in disgrace with the king of England, upon occasion of some misdemeanor belike, for he was, as Matthew Parker writeth of him, "Ut moribus gestisque peregrinus, sic nomine ipso et appellatione cæteris archiepiscopis dissimilis," the king being of a relenting nature, and bearing much with clergymen's insolencies, which, for a while, he might perhaps gainstand, but at last bear with them as supported by the court of Rome, did consult with his nobles about the return of the said Boniface into England conditionally, as followeth.

Acts passed in the King's Council, touching the Archbishop of Canterbury's return into England, under certain conditions.[2]

In the year of our Lord 1264, in the month of March, it was enacted in the presence of the renowned king of England, by the counsel of the peers, and states of the said realm, that the reverend father Boniface, by the grace of God archbishop of Canterbury, primate of all England, should return into England, and abide in the realm peaceably, upon the conditions under-written:—

First, therefore it is enacted, that the archbishop at his return, do without any difficulty release in form of law his sentences of excommunication, published against all persons whatsoever, occasioning much trouble in the realm of England; but yet so, that they who should be found excommunicated, be ready to make satisfaction for their excesses and defaults, and for the same receive, as they are bound by the canonical commandments of the archbishop, in form hereunder in the next article contained.

Secondly, it is enacted, that in making amends for defaults done to the churches and churchmen, within such places as are immediately subject unto his jurisdiction, the archbishop may arbitrate according to the counsel of all his suffragans, or the greater and sounder part; and of weighty affairs belonging to the church and realm of England, may in time to come after his return, order and dispose likewise by their counsel, and the counsel of other discreet men of the realm.

Thirdly, it is enacted, that he bring with him Master Henry Mortimer,[3] archdeacon of Canterbury, and Pont Sabler, his familiar clerks or household chaplains; and these clerks only, being strangers born, he keep and retain of his council and household.

Fourthly, it is enacted, that other clerks wheresoever, beneficed in the church of England, meaning and willing to return with the archbishop, may safely return and abide in their benefices, and expend the church goods within the realm as they are bound; carrying or sending nothing out of the realm, unless necessary occasion, allowed of the king's council, do so require.

Fifthly, it is enacted, that the archbishop or the clerks coming with him, shall bring nothing with them in letters, message or commandment, nor shall procure any thing else, during their abode in this realm, either by themselves, or by others, whereby any damage, danger, or prejudice, may redound to the king, or to any of his realm. And for memory of the premises, the seal of the said renowned king of England is hanged unto these presents.—By the whole council.

(1) This passage is not in the Editions previous to 1596.—Ed.
(2) "Anno Domini 1264, mense Martio, in præsentia illustris regis Angliæ, de concilio procerum et magnatum ejusdem regni actum est," &c.—Turris Lond.
(3) Henricus de mortuo mari.

Notwithstanding this conclusion, the archbishop did not presently return, but continued in Provence and elsewhere, behaving himself imperiously as a prelate of the right Romish stamp. In the mean time many matters incident to this place, were omitted and neglected, which personally by him should have been executed; but by reason of his absence the same were despatched by deputation, and the same ordered likewise according to his own fancy, which he preferred before the king's authority and commandment. The copy of a letter describing the contumacy of the said Boniface doth sufficiently testify this to be true, the same being set down agreeable to the prototype.

Henry III. A.D. 1264

A Letter of the King to Boniface, Archbishop of Canterbury, charging him to return into England, there personally to discharge his archiepiscopal function.[1]

The king to Boniface, archbishop of Canterbury, primate of all England, ;reeting. Although hitherto by patience we have suffered oftentimes bishops lect, abbots, and other prelates in our realm, for the benefit of their confirma-ion to be obtained, to pass over beyond sea unto you, we thought not to receive t your hands any such reward, as that against the right and custom of our ealm (to the which we mean not by this our patience, that prejudice shall any ray be procured or bred), you should attempt this to be followed. We do 1arvel therefore, and are moved that you, at the request of us, have refused to ommit the examination of the election of our well-beloved in Christ, Master Valter Gifford, late of Bath and Wells bishop elect, and the confirmation of ie same election, unto some discreet persons of our realm; we having detained, nd as yet detaining, the same Gifford against his will, that he might not repair ersonally unto you: whereunto common right and the very custom of the ealm ought to have led you unrequested, whilst you abide out of the realm. ,est, therefore, our too much patience might breed in you a contempt, we will ou to understand, that henceforward we mean to bear less with such dealing, specially in these days, wherein there is no safe passage for Englishmen unto ou through the parts of France, as it is reported. Wherefore we thought good) desire your fatherhood, and also to admonish you, giving you, moreover, in harge and commandment, and upon the fealty wherein you are bound unto us, rmly enjoining, that in respect of the aforesaid election and other ceremonies, ou come personally into England, to execute your office and charge, or send ome other in your room; or at least procure and cause some discreet persons f our realm, whom you shall repute more meet for this matter, to serve the irn for you in this behalf: lest, if with contumacy you refuse to hear our equests and commandments the second time, which you are by duty bound to bey, we be compelled to take indignation against you, as a contemner of the ghts, the liberties and the customs of our kingdom, and so to proceed against ou more sharply by way of revenge: neither will we suffer, if you should do therwise, that the revenues of your said archbishopric shall henceforth be onveyed unto you out of our realm, but as you refuse the burden, so will we 1 like sort do what we can to withdraw, hereafter, the profits and commodities 'om you during your abode out of our land. Finally, we, if need shall be, are eady to give you a sure and safe conduct. Witness the king at St. Paul's of ,ondon, the twenty-fifth of June, and the forty-eighth year of our reign.

Against the archbishop of Canterbury, abiding in a foreign country

Now after all this ado, we read that at last Boniface returned, and becoming more holy towards his end, he went with other bishops to he king, requesting him, that being mindful of the decay of his ingdom, by ecclesiastical livings bestowed upon strangers, he would ereafter prefer learned and godly men of his own nation. To whom he king answered that he would willingly do it. "Wherefore," said

The advice of Boniface disadvantageous to himself.

(1) "Rex Bonifacio Cantuariensi archiepiscopo, totius Angliæ," &c.—Turris Lond

Henry III. A.D. 1264.

he, "I think it meet that you, who are a stranger and unlearned, and also my brother Ethelmer, bishop of Winchester, whom I have preferred to such dignities only for kindred's sake, should first give examples to others, and forsake your churches, and I will provide other learned men to serve in them." This answer of the king so pierced this Boniface, that he always after lived a wearisome life in England; wherefore, perceiving himself to be misliked of the king and the people, he desired to return into his country, and thereupon, first felling and selling the woods, letting out the archbishopric, taking great fines of his tenants, and making a great mass of money of the clergy of his province, he went, with the curse of all men into Savoy; where, in the castle of St. Helen's, after he had misgoverned the see six and twenty years, six months, and sixteen days from his consecration, being nine and twenty years from his first election, he died the fifteenth of the kalends of August. And so ceased the troubles between the king and the said bishop, whose contumacy, with that of others of the like brood, doth largely appear in this book.

Boniface maketh spoil of the archbishopric, is hated, and dieth.

But to leave Boniface now dead, note ye this,* that in this year, after the death of pope Urban, succeeded (A.D. 1264) pope Clement IV.; who, as affirmeth Nicholas Trivet, was first a married man, and had a wife and children, and was the solicitor and counsellor to the French king; then, after the death of his wife, was bishop, entitled Podiensis; after that archbishop of Narbonne; and at last made cardinal; who being sent of pope Urban as a legate, for the reformation of peace, in his absence was elected pope by the cardinals. About this time flourished Thomas Aquinas, reader at Paris among the Dominic friars, and Bonaventure among the Franciscan friars.[1]

Death of pope Urban. Pope Clement IV. Pope Clement first a married man, with a wife and children. Aquinas and Bonaventure, readers at Paris.

*[2] Now, after all the aforesaid tumults and broils of the king and his barons, to the vexation of the whole land, it was thought meet and necessary that all parties at variance should be reconciled; whereupon, it was concluded amongst them as followeth.

A Form of Peace between the King and his Barons.[3]

This is the form of peace allowed by the king our lord, by the lord Edward his son, by all the prelates and peers, and by the whole commonalty of the realm of England, with common consent and agreement: To wit, that a certain ordinance or decree made in a parliament holden at London about the feast of the nativity of St. John Baptist last past, for the maintaining and keeping of the peace of the realm, shall continue all the days of the said king our sovereign lord, and the time of the lord Edward, after he shall be received as king, even till the end and term that shall be thought meet and convenient. The said ordinance or decree is this:

For the redressing of the state of the realm of England, let there be chosen or named three discreet and trusty persons of the realm, who may have authority and power from the lord the king to choose or name, in the king's behalf, nine counsellors; of which nine, three at least, by course or turns, may always be present in the court. And let the lord the king, by the counsel of the said nine, order and dispose of the keeping of castles, and the managing of all the affairs in his realm. Let the lord the king also, by the advice of the aforesaid nine, appoint justices, chancellors, treasurers, and other officers, greater and lesser in those matters that pertain to government of his court and realm.

(1) Ex Nich. Trivet.
(2) The next few pages, are not in the Editions previous to 1596.—Ed.
(3) "Hæc est forma pacis a domino rege, et domino Edwardo filio suo, prælatis et proceribus omnibus, et communitate tota regni Angliæ communiter et concorditer approbata," &c.—Turris Lond.

The choosers or namers shall swear first, that according to conscience they will choose or name such counsellors as they verily believe will be profitable and trusty in respect of God's honour, the church, the lord the king, and his realm. The counsellors likewise, and all the officers greater and lesser in their creation shall swear, that to the uttermost of their power they will faithfully execute their offices to the honour of God and of the church, and to the profit of the lord the king, and his realm, without bribe or gift; meat and drink, which are commonly wont to be set upon the table, excepted. And if so be that the aforesaid counsellors, or some or any of them, in the charge to them committed (whether they be he or she), have behaved themselves ill, or that upon some other occasion such officers are to be changed; the lord the king, by the counsel of the three former choosers or namers, may remove such as he shall see meet to be removed; and in their rooms by the same men's advice may appoint and place other persons trusty and serviceable.

And if so be that either the greater officers, or the lesser, do disorderly demean themselves in their offices, the lord the king, by the counsel of the aforesaid nine, may displace them, and without delay by the same advice set others in their room. And if so be that the three first or chief choosers or namers, in the choice or naming of counsellors, or perhaps the counsellors in the creating of officers, or in other affairs of the lord the king and the realm to be ordered or done, shall be at disagreement, then, whatsoever by consent of two parts shall be concluded or decreed, let the same be firmly kept and observed; so that of those two parts, one be a prelate of the church in the business belonging to the church: and if it so happen, that two parts of the said nine in some matter disagree, then shall they for their variance stand to the ordinance of the three first choosers or namers or the greater part of them. And if so be it seem expedient to all the prelates and barons, by consent, that some or one, in place of some or one of the three first namers be put and appointed, then let the lord the king, by the counsel of all the prelates and barons, ordain some others, or one other. And let the lord the king do all the premises by the advice of the said nine in manner above mentioned, or let them do it in the lord the king's behalf and by his authority, by this present ordinance to continue and hold out till such time as this agreement, made and afterwards sealed by the parties, be perfected by consent, or some other proviso be had, which the parties by consent shall judge allowable.

This ordinance was made at London, by the consent, will and commandment of the lord the king, and also of the prelates and barons, with the commonalty then and there present. In witness whereof R. Bishop of Lincoln, and H. Bishop of Ely, R. Earl of Norfolk and marshal of England, Robert de Vere, Earl of Oxford, Humphrey de Bohune, William de Monte Caniso, and the mayor of London, to this writing have set their seals. Acted in the parliament at London in the month of June A.D. 1264.

It is also ordained, that the state of the English church shall be reformed into a state meet and convenient. *Reformation of the church.*

It is also ordained, that the three choosers above named and counsellors, of whom mention is made in the said ordinance at London, and the keepers of castles and others the king's bailiffs be homebred. And as for strangers born, let them come, tarry, and depart peaceably, as well laymen willing to dwell upon their possessions, as clergymen residing upon their benefices. *No strangers to be keepers of the king's castles.*

Merchants also, and all others, to further and see to their affairs, shall come freely, and tarry peaceably; but yet conditionally, so they come without armour and a suspected multitude. And that none of them be received in any sort into any office or bailiwick in the realm, or otherwise in the king's house and service be entertained. As for the charters of general liberties and forests granted unto the homebred of late by the king, and the statutes made upon revoking of grievances, which the lord the king, the third year past, in every shire by his letters patent hath caused to be published, with the commendable customs of his realm, and a long time allowed, let them be for ever observed: and that it might be provided how they may be better and more soundly observed, it is also provided, that the lord the king, and the lord Edward, the barons and those that stand with them, let go all injury and rancour, so that they neither grieve, nor suffer to be grieved by any of theirs, any one of them by occasion of things done in the hurly-burly past, and also cause all their

Henry III.

A.D. 1264.

bailiffs at the undertaking of their bailiwicks, that they shall grieve none by the occasion aforesaid, but shall do justice and right to everybody with equality. And let there be good security provided how all these things may be firmly observed.

When this agreement was despatched, to set the realm in some quietness, a little leisure was allowed to look into the losses and damages of the church, whereupon it was provided as followeth.

Of the repairing of Trespasses committed against the Church.

It is provided by common assent of the king, of the prelates, earls, and barons of the land, that the trespasses which are committed against the church of England, by reason of the tumults and wars that have been in this realm of England, shall be reformed and amended in this manner.

There shall be chosen by the earls and great estates of the land, with the liking and assent of the prelates, three bishops authorized and having full power to establish and provide for such reasonable amends, as are to be made for the aforesaid trespass committed against holy church, so far forth as shall be fit and convenient.

Those that shall be found excommunicated, shall be absolved in form of right by such as have power and authority so to do.

The authority of the prelates shall be established in this manner: First, it shall be faithfully undertaken by the earls, justices, and the other laymen of the king's council, and other great barons of the realm, that all those things which the prelates that shall be chosen shall reasonably ordain and appoint by way of reformation, they themselves shall observe and fulfil, and shall do their endeavour faithfully to cause the same to be observed by others, and thereof they shall deliver their letters patent.

Moreover, unto the prelates, after they shall be chosen, full power shall be granted by the king, and the commonalty, the earls, barons, and great men of the land, to ordain those things which are needful and profitable to the full reformation of the estate of holy church, to the honour due to the fealty of our lord the king, and to the profit of the realm. And that the promise made by the king, and by the earls and barons aforesaid, and by the other great men of the land, may appear to be made in good faith, they shall thereof make their letters patent, to wit of things that have been done a year past before the last Easter.

If any be found that will not stand to the ordinance and appointment of the prelates in the causes, and according to the form aforesaid, he shall be compelled thereunto by doom of holy church; yea, if need be, he shall be thereunto forced by the secular power. And that it may the better be done, the justice shall have a hundred or more of choice men at arms, or serjeants, soldiers elect, to distrain the malefactors when by the said prelates he shall be required. Those soldiers to be sustained of the common goods of holy church, during the time they shall be employed in that business. And this ordinance shall continue for a year or two, till such time as matters be quieted, and that the provisions of the prelates, and the peace of the land be well observed.

Provided always, that the profits of benefices of holy church belonging to aliens, and others that have been enemies to the land, shall be collected and safely kept in the hands of the prelates, until such time as order be taken by common advice what is to be done therewithal. And for the more assurance and further testimony hereof, the king and the high estates of the land have unto this writing set their seals.

Besides all this it was considered, that non-residency being a default blameworthy, deserved reformation. To this the king having special regard, wrote his mind to the bishop of Hereford for the redress of the same; whose letter, because it is memorable, and convenient matter is therein contained for non-residents of our time, we have here introduced according to the record.

A Letter of King Henry III., directed to the Bishop of Hereford, concerning Non-residents.[1]

Henry III. A.D. 1264.

The king to the bishop of Hereford sendeth greeting. Pastors or shepherds are set over flocks, that by exercising themselves in watching over them day and night, they may know their own cattle by their look, bring the hunger-starved sheep into the meadows of fruitfulness, and the straying ones into one fold by the word of salvation, and the rod of correction; and to do their endeavour that unity indissolubly may be kept. But some there be who, damnably despising this doctrine, and not knowing to discern their own cattle from others, do take away the milk and the wool, not caring how the Lord's flock may be nourished; they catch up the temporal goods, and who perisheth in their parish with famishment, or miscarrieth in manners they regard not; which men deserve not to be called pastors, but rather hirelings. And that even we, in these days, removing ourselves into the borders of Wales to take order for the disposing of the garrisons of our realm, have found this default in your church of Hereford, we report it with grief; for that we have found there a church destitute of a pastor's comfort, as having neither bishop nor official, vicar nor dean, who may exercise any spiritual function and duty in the same. But the church itself (which in time past was wont to flow in delight, and had canons that tended upon days' and nights' service, and that ought to exercise the works of charity), at their forsaking the church, and leading their lives in countries far hence, has put off her stole or robe of pleasure, and fallen to the ground, bewailing the loss of her widowhood, and none among all her friends and lovers will comfort her. Verily while we beheld this, and considered it diligently, the prick of pity did move our bowels, and the sword of compassion did inwardly wound our heart very sorely, that we could no longer dissemble so great an injury done to our mother the church, nor pass the same over uncorrected.

Against non-residence of prelates.

Wherefore we command and straitly charge you, that all occasions set aside, you endeavour to remove yourselves with all possible speed unto your said church, and there personally to execute the pastoral charge committed unto you in the same. Otherwise we will you to know for certainty that if you have not a care to do this, we will wholly take into our own hands all the temporal goods, and whatsoever else doth belong unto the barony of the same church, which goods, for spiritual exercise' sake therein, it is certain our progenitors of a godly devotion have bestowed thereupon. And such goods and duties as we have commanded hitherto to be gathered and safely kept and turned to the profit and commodity of the same church, the cause now ceasing we will seize upon, and suffer no longer that he shall reap temporal things, who feareth not irreverently to withdraw and keep back spiritual things, whereunto by office and duty he is bound; or that he shall receive any profits who refuseth to undergo and bear the burdens of the same. Witness the king at Hereford, the first of June, in the forty-eighth year of our reign.

Non-residents strictly charged to be personally incumbent and abiding upon their cures note.

About this time (as appeareth by course of record, and thereby may well be gathered) a redress of certain sects was intended; among which one by name especially occurreth, and called the Assembly of Harlots; a kind of people of a lewd disposition and uncivil. Of their manners and life the king having been informed, addressed his letters to the sheriff of Oxfordshire, a place which they haunted, and wherein they practised their evil conversation; whose letter here followeth.

An assembly of ill-disposed people called Harlots, whereby may be gathered the ancientness of that name.

A Letter of King Henry III. to the Sheriff of Oxfordshire, concerning the Banishment of an unlawful assembly called Harlots, out of that Country.[2]

The king to the sheriff of Oxfordshire sendeth greeting. Because we understand that there be certain vagrant persons who call themselves Harlots, main-

(1) "Rex episcopo Hereford, salutem. Pastores gregibus præponuntur ut diei noctisque vigilas exercendo," &c.—Turris Lond.

(2) "Rex vic. Oxon. salutem. Quia intelleximus quod quidam, qui se harlotos appellant, vagi et otium foventes, in diversis partibus regni nostri, congregationes et conventicula, necnon contractus illicitos," &c.—Turris Lond.

Henry III A.D. 1264. taming idleness in divers parts of our realm, most shamelessly making their meetings, assemblies, and unlawful matches against the honesty of the church and good manners, which abuse we will not, neither ought we to suffer, we charge thee that on our behalf thou forbid the said Harlots henceforth in the said countries to make any more such meetings, conventicle, or contracts; or to presume according to their lewd manner and wonted fashion to rogue about our realm; and hereto thou shalt (if need be) bind them, as by law may be done. Wherein so behave thyself in this behalf, as we may commend thy diligence Witness the king at Reading the twenty-third of November, in the forty-eighth year of our reign.

What manner of persons these were, or what their conversation was, it doth not further appear; nevertheless by the premises it may seem to be some pretended order of religion. And it is most probable that the reproachful name of harlot had its beginning from hence.

To conclude with special matters of the church, wherein we have made somewhat the longer delay, by occasion of such necessary records as came to hand, and brought with them their necessary use, this one remembrance, notwithstanding, remaineth, no less worthy of note than the rest, and falling within the revolution of the forty-eighth year of this king's reign, a year of great trouble, as by the premises may be gathered.

You are therefore to note that at this time the prelates of England stood upon their pantofles, and jolly fellows (I tell you) they would be known to be. For in an inquisition made after the death of one Alfred of Lincoln, being, as is supposed, a baron of this realm, there is found, among other things, as followeth.[1] "The beforenamed Alfred held a certain piece of the park of Dunetish and Tilei of the abbot of Cerne, by service of holding his stirrup when the abbot should take horseback, and to give him place in the shire at such time as he should be present." The circumstances hereof being considered, together with the time when it was done, give probable cause to conjecture that the occasion of this matter came by this means: viz. That whereas the said abbot was desirous to enlarge his park, and could not so do but by purchasing part of some other ground next adjoining, whereof the said abbot was owner, he was therefore constrained either to lack that he liked, or to admit such conditions as pleased my lord abbot; who, like a lord, as you see, was content to let him have his land, reserving such service as is above said. Wherein should be noted the pomp of prelates in those days, and how near they drew in imitation to the pope, in whose footsteps they trod.

But leaving these affairs of the church and churchmen, into which we have gone somewhat largely, we will now enter into other troubles of the temporal state. You heard before of a pacification concluded between the king and his barons, A.D. 1264; the same having been admitted by mutual and common consent of the temporality and clergy. Nevertheless, as a sore not well searched and tented, but superficially and overly skinned, doth break out into a more dangerous botch, so it came to pass among the lords and barons; betwixt

(1) "Quod prædictus Alluredus tenuit quandam particulam parcæ de Dunetish et Tilei de abbate de Cerne, per servicium tenendi stropem suum, quando abbas debet ascendere equum suum, et dare ei locum in comitatu quando præsens fuerit"

whom no such firm reconciliation was made as was likely long to last; whereupon ensued, after secret grudge and privy hatred, open arms and conflicts.*

For in this year, the sons of Simon the earl, to wit, Henry, Simon, and Guido, being all puffed up, and with the pride of their success elevated, did that which not at all contented the earl of Gloucester; insomuch that he challenged Henry the eldest son of the earl Simon Mountfort at the barriers, to be tried at Northampton. But that challenge was taken up, lest some further inconvenience might have arisen thereof. But the earl of Gloucester, being moved therewith in his mind, sent unto his father the earl, that he should deliver him such prisoners, being noblemen, as he took at the battle of Lewes; among whom the king of Almain was named first. But he, by countermand, answered him, and said: that it might content and satisfy him, for that he had saved and preserved to him his lands, on the day the battle was fought at Lewes; and that furthermore he would not send him such prisoners as he demanded, and that he himself kept more noble than they in the castle of Dover. Among them was John Basset, who undermined and threw down the walls of Northampton, at that conflict, as is before specified.

Dissension between earl Simon and the earl of Gloucester.

The earl of Gloucester, being displeased, as soon as he heard this, sent incontinently to the lord Roger Mortimer, who always took the king's part, desiring that they two might talk together touching the benefit and commodity of the king. Roger, doubting some deceit, desired sureties and pledges for his safe return, if he would come to talk with him. When they met, and had a while talked familiarly, the earl of Gloucester showed him all that he was purposed to do, and that further, he lamented he had so much and so greatly offended the king; and that he would, with all his power and ability make amends for that offence, in the restitution of the king again to his kingly dignity, as much as he possibly might. Therefore they sent secretly to Robert, the brother of the earl of Gloucester, who was near about the earl Simon, and made him to consent with them therein. And, to work this thing more circumspectly, when opportunity might serve, Roger Mortimer sent to the king's son a horse excelling all others in footmanship, which he might be sure to trust, when he saw convenient time. Things being thus contrived, prince Edward desired leave of the earl to prove his courser against such time as he should ride at the tilt, as they might when they listed. As soon as he had got leave, and when with galloping and ranging the field, he had wearied divers of their horses, at last getting up upon the horse which for that purpose was sent, and spying a servant on horseback coming toward him with two swords, he turned about to his keeper, whose name was Robert de Rose, and to others his playfellows that were with him, saying, "My loving lords, thus long have I kept you company, and have been in your custodies; and now not purposing to use your companies any longer, I betake me to God." And quickly turning his horse about, put to the spurs, and away went he. The others pricked after apace, but yet came far enough behind, and overtake him they could not. At last, when they saw Roger Mortimer coming from his castle of Wigmore, accompanied with many armed men, to meet him, as before it was appointed, they

The earl of Gloucester and Roger Mortimer conspire against Simon.

Prince Edward escapeth out of the custody of earl Simon by a train.

Henry III. A.D. 1265.

returned home again as wise as when they came forth. And when this the prince's escape was divulged, much people came to him out of every quarter, with great joy thereof; amongst whom, the first was the earl of Gloucester, and the other soldiers of the king, who had now long lain at Bristol and thereabouts, and within a short space he had a great and a mighty host.

Earl Simon in all haste gathereth a power.

When the earl Simon understood this he much doubted and mistrusted himself; and sending into Wales, he got from thence a great many men, and augmented his power as strongly as he might, from every part of England. He sent also his son Simon, to the noblemen of the north parts, that with all possible speed he might bring them with him; who with a great company came to him, and at Kenilworth awhile they staid, and there pitched their tents. But leaving that town for a certain time, they went to Winchester, and spoiled the same, and then returned again to Kenilworth. And when this was declared to Edward the king's son, who was then at Worcester, by a certain spy, whom he had got after he came from Gloucester a little before; he prepared himself with his soldiers in the night season, to go to the place where the spy should bring him, which was into a deep valley, near unto the place where Simon and his company had pitched. And in the morning very early, when they were about to arm themselves, and prepare their horses, they heard a great noise of their enemies coming towards them. Then, thinking that the latter had prepared themselves against their coming, and so had been betrayed, they set forth in battle array, marching forwards, till they met certain of their enemies straggling in long wings, thinking to have gone a foraging, and to have sought for victuals; whom they took, and, with their fresh horses, new-mounted their soldiers who had had their horses tired with long travel, and so marching forward, came very early in the morning upon their enemies, whom for the most part they found sleeping; and laying lustily about them, they slew divers; some they took, the rest they put to flight, and fifteen of their chief ensigns they took, with many other rich spoils. But young Simon himself lodged in the castle, who, with a few, escaped and fled. And this was the fourth day before the nones of August, A. D. 1265.

The first enterprise of prince Edward after his escape.

The disposing of the prince's battle against earl Simon fought at Evesham.

But when Edward heard that earl Simon was coming toward Kenilworth, to join with his son's battle, he marched forward to meet him the third day after at Evesham, where he divided his host into three battles, he himself having the leading of one, the earl of Gloucester of the second, and Roger Mortimer of the third, who came upon their backs. The king's son Edward came northward, as though he came from Kenilworth to Evesham; and because he would not be descried, he caused his own standards and ensigns to be taken down, and young Simon's, which he had taken before, to be advanced. But the earl Simon's scurier, whose name was Nicholas, showed the earl that such bands and companies were marching towards him; who, thinking the same to have been his son Simon's power, not knowing of the overthrow which he had just had, gave small credit thereunto, till the said Nicholas, the better to descry them, went up to the abbey steeple of Evesham, where he might plainly discern them all and their standards. By this time they had mounted the hill which they had been labouring to attain, thinking to have that vantage when they should give their charge as they had purposed; Edward also had advanced again his own standards, and had pulled down Simon's, whereby they were the more easily descried and known. Then the aforesaid Nicholas cried aloud to the earl Simon, and said, "We are all but dead men; for it is not your son, as you suppose, that cometh, but it is Edward the king's son that cometh from one part, and the earl of Gloucester from another part, and Roger Mortimer from the third part." Then said the earl, "The Lord be merciful unto our souls, forasmuch as our bodies and lives are now in their hands;" and so saying, he commanded that every man should make himself ready to God, and to fight out the field, for that it was their wills to die for their laws, and in a just quarrel; and such as would depart, he gave leave to go their ways, that they should be no discomfiture to the rest.

Prince Edward's host descried, whereat the earl is much abashed.

Then came unto him his eldest son Henry, and comforted him; lesiring him to have no despair, nor yet mistrust in the good iuccess of this victory, with other such cheerful words. "No, my ;on," saith he, "I despair not; but yet, it is thy presumption, and .he pride of the rest of thy brethren that hath brought me to this :nd you see; notwithstanding, yet I trust I shall die to God, and n a righteous quarrel." After words of comfort given to all his host, ınd the oration made as is the manner, they all armed themselves. The king also, whom the earl always kept with him, he armed in an ırmour of his own; and then dividing their forces, they marched .owards their enemies. But before they joined, the Welshmen ran .heir ways, and thinking to escape over the river Dee, were there, ;ome drowned, and some slain. Then when the battle joined and :ame to handy strokes, within short space many of the earl's part 'ell and were slain; and the king himself being struck at, cried with ı loud voice to them, saying, "Kill me not, I am Henry your king." And with these the king's words, the lord Adam Monthaut knew him, ınd saved him. At his voice and cry came also prince Edward his on, and delivered him to the guard and custody of certain knights. In the mean season the earl Simon was hard bestead and beaten down, .nd also slain before Edward the prince came at him. Howbeit)efore he fell, when as he fought for life, and Henry his son, and ›ther noblemen on his part were about him, he brake out into these vords unto his enemies, saying, "What, is there no mercy and com›assion with you?" Who again answered, "What compassion should here be showed to traitors?" Then said he, "The Lord be nerciful unto our souls, our bodies are in your hands." And as soon s these words were spoken, they mangled his body, and divided his nembers, and cut off his head, which head Roger Mortimer sent unto is wife. And not far off from him also were slain Henry, his eldest son, he lord Hugh Spenser, the Lord Radulph Basset, the lord Thomas de Hestele, the lord William Mandeville, the lord John Beauchamp, the ›rd Guido Baillofer, the lord Roger Rowley, and many other noblenen besides, with a great multitude of people; the Lord knoweth ow many. This battle was fought in the month of August, and coninued from one o'clock till it was night; in the which was not so

The words of earl Simon to his son.

King Henry almost slain in the battle, at length known by his voice, and rescued by his son.

Earl Simon's son, and many more lords slain.

Henry III.

A.D. 1265.

much as one man on the earl's part, of any estimation, fortitude, and courage, but in that battle lost his life; except the lord John, who by the great grace of God escaped death. Neither is this to be forgotten, that the same day, being Tuesday, at that very hour, when the battle began, which was at one o'clock in the afternoon, there was such a darkness over all, such thunder and tempest, that the like before that time was never seen, being very calm and fair weather both immediately before and after; which seemed (saith mine author) to give plain demonstration of that which afterwards chanced and followed.

A.D. 1266.

A parliament summoned at Winchester, king Henry again restored to his regality.

After this great slaughter and overthrow there was a parliament summoned at Winchester by the earl of Gloucester, and others on his part. Here, by the way, is to be considered, that the king although he was in the camp of the earl of Leicester, being then in custody, and his son Edward with the earl of Gloucester, yet the king was on that side against his will, and therefore in the said parliament the king was restored to his kingly dignity, which was before that time under the custody of the barons. But after the battle was ended and done, certain of them that loved the earl, upon an old ladder gathered up such parts of his body as remained, and covering the same with an old gown, brought it to Evesham, where they, putting the same in a fair linen cloth, buried it in the church. But not long after, such as thought themselves not sufficiently revenged by his death, to wreak them of the dead corpse, took up the same and threw it into another place, saying, that he who was both accursed, and a traitor, was not worthy of christian burial.

The same year also died Walter Cantilupe, bishop of Winchester, after whom succeeded Nicholas of Ely, the king's chancellor.

The same year the king, perceiving that unless the castle of Kenilworth were recovered, and the boldness of them restrained who kept the same, many evils and inconveniences might ensue thereupon, to the prejudice of his kingdom, for that the number increased every day more and more, wasting and spoiling the country all about, gathered an army and came down to Warwick; where he tarried awhile expecting the meeting and assembling of his marquisses and lords, with ensigns and other saultable munition. When their bands were furnished and mustered, and all things ready, on the morrow after Midsummer-day he displayed his banner, and began his voyage, marching towards Kenilworth, and besieged the same. During the siege, by the advice and counsel of the king, the pope's legate, and other noblemen, twelve persons were chosen who should have the disposing of those things that pertained to the state of the realm, and to those that had lost their lands and inheritances; who amongst other things, made and established this one proviso, that was commonly called the Kenilworth decree: that all those who had lost their lands by attainder (although not yet attained) should fine there-for at the king's pleasure, and take their lands of him again; paying some two, some three, and some four years' revenues of the same, according to the quality of the crime and offence committed. All which provisions were established and confirmed as well by the corporal oath, as by signing of the same with the hands and seals of all the prelates and clergy of England, there assembled for that purpose by the pope's legate, upon the feast of All Saints. These

Kenilworth castle besieged by the king.

Kenilworth decree against the disinherited.

.ings finished, messengers were sent on the king's behalf, as well to ose that kept the castle of Kenilworth, as also to those that were sembled in the isle of Ely; willing them to come under the protection of the king's peace, and yield to the aforesaid provisos, tablished by the twelve commissioners; who altogether answered id said, that they would in nowise condescend thereunto, both as it is done without their consents, not being called unto it, and also as e said decree was over-strait and intolerable. Within a short space ter, great famine and pestilence chanced amongst those who kept ie castle, insomuch that they were without any hope of keeping the me; wherefore, soon after, the king sending again to them to yield ie castle and take their pardons, they, consulting together of their own tate, thus answered the king's messengers: "If it please the king id his council to permit us to send our messenger to the lord Simon Iountfort, who is beyond the sea, that he may come by a certain day ı the defence of this his garrison and fort, and that in the mean ace we be not disturbed by the king's army that hath environed us, ll the return of our messengers; if, by the day appointed, he come ot, we will yield up the same, so that we may be pardoned of life, mb, and moveables."

Gainsaid by divers

When the messengers were returned, and had declared to the king ıeir answer, he, consulting with his nobles about the matter, agreed nto their petitions, and caused the truce to be proclaimed throughıt all his camp, after sufficient hostages were on either side given ır the performance of the same; whereupon they set forward their ıessengers, as before was said they would. But after many of them ithin the castle had been very grievously vexed with the bloodyux, and other diseases, insomuch that the healthy men might not abide ıe corruption and annoyance of those that were diseased, they elivered up the castle before the return of the messengers, and were ermitted to go whither they would to refresh themselves, as men ıolested with great vexations and miseries. After the rendering up of ıe castle, the king committed the custody thereof to his son Edmund, nd so with his host departing from the siege, he came upon Christıas-even to Osney; where, with great solemnity and triumph he kept is Christmas during seven days, and from thence with his host came) Windsor, from whence after a few days he marched towards Ely; ı which island he besieged those who were disinherited, and sharply lso assaulted them.

Kenilworth yielded up to the king, before the return of the messengers out of France

The same year pope Clement IV. promoted Master Walter iifford, bishop of Bath, to be archbishop of York.

In this year also the church of England began to pay the tenths of ll her revenues, as well spiritual as temporal, to the king, to continue ır three years' space; and this was done by the authority apostolical.

The tenths granted to the king by authority apostolical

Within a while after, the barons who yet remained, gathered themelves together again; amongst whom John Daiwill (being a subtle nd stout man of war) began to have a name, and was well esteemed mongst them, who, altogether, did what mischief they might; and n the month of May they assembled at Chesterfield, under the said ohn Daiwill and the earl of Ferarence, upon whom the king's soldiers oming suddenly in the night, took them sleeping and slew many of hem. Then the said John Daiwill quickly arming himself came

New assembly of the barons at Chesterfield, where they had the overthrow.

Henry III. A.D. 1266.

forth, thinking with more defence both to save himself and to escape, who, in the way, struck the lord Gilbert Humsard such a blow with his demi-lance, that he felled both him and his horse to the ground, and so fled with a few more after him. Thus, while the poor soldiers fought and were slain, the barons fled away, and saved themselves. Also the earl Ferarence fled, and hid himself in a church; but being betrayed by a woman, he was taken forth, and led away prisoner. After this the king kept a parliament at Northampton, where he disinherited all those that took part with the earl Simon, and all their children. There also the pope's legate, Octobonus, held a convocation, and excommunicated all such bishops as had taken any part with Simon against the king; divers of whom he sent up to Rome, to be absolved of the pope; and further, the said legate caused to be proclaimed certain decrees which he himself had made, and also the new grant of pope Clement to the king and queen, of all the tenths for seven years to come. And shortly after, a tax also was fined upon the county of Norfolk; to the gathering whereof Walter, the bishop of Norwich, was appointed.[1]

The confederates of Simon Mountfort with their children disinherited by the king, and excommunicated by the pope's legate. Tenths granted by the pope to the king for seven years.

A.D.1267. Castle of Kenilworth again besieged.

A. D. 1267, king Henry again besieged the castle of Kenilworth, from the seventh day before the first day of July, until the beginning of December; whither came Octobonus, the pope's legate, by whose entreaty the same was delivered unto the king by Henry Hastings who stoutly had defended the same, and resisted the king, having pardon granted both for him and his, of his life, lands, goods and chattels. At this time also the barons again assembled with John Daiwill in the isle of Axioline, and proceeded till they came to Lincoln, which they also took, and spoiled the Jews, and slew many of them; and entering their synagogue, tare and rent the book of their law, and burnt the same, and all other writings and obligations which they could come by. Which thing when the king heard, he sent thither his son prince Edward; but as soon as they had heard that, they fled into the isle of Ely, and fortified the same with bulwarks as strongly as they might, at every entrance into the same. This was in the month of April, when Edward the king's son, came thither; who for the great abundance of waters in the same, could by no means enter the island, till at length, by the counsel of the inhabitants of that province, he caused with a number of workmen great trenches and ditches to be made, somewhat to convey away the water; and for a long time they used their counsel in making bridges with planks and hurdles, till at last they entered the island; upon which the barons fled to London, where of the Londoners they were well entertained. The rest who were in the island yielded themselves; amongst whom were Roger Wake, Simon the younger, and Peches, saving their lives and members. After this, both the king and Edward his son, came to London with a great power, but yet were kept out of the city by the barons and citizens for the space of forty days. And Octobonus, the legate (who for fear had fled into the Tower) they narrowly laid wait for, that he should not escape. At length, by the entreaty of the earl of Gloucester and other earls that were his friends, both the barons and citizens were pardoned, and admitted to the king's favour. Four bishops and eight other noblemen were also

Assembly of the barons at Axioline, and discomfiture of them. The Jews spoiled and slain at Lincoln. The barons fortify the island of Ely.

Assaulted and entered by prince Edward.

The king kept out of London forty days.

(1) Ex Scala Mundi.

chosen, such as were at Coventry first nominated, that they should order and dispose all matters betwixt the king and such as had lost their inheritance, as also the form of their peace and ransom; and proclamation was made, upon the feast of All Saints, of perfect peace and accord throughout all the realm.

Henry III

A.D. 1267.

Peace concluded between the barons and the king

In the fifty-second year of this king Henry's reign, eight days after the feast of St. Martin, he held a parliament at Marlborough, in the year above recited; where, by the advice of wise and discreet men, and with the consent of all the nobles, he ordained and enacted divers good and profitable statutes for the reformation and bettering of the state of the realm, and the execution of common justice, which are called 'the statutes of Marlborough.'

Statutes of Marlborough

The same year, upon St. Gregory's day, Octobonus, the legate, called a council at London, where were five archbishops, and a great number of bishops, abbots, and other prelates; which council also within three days brake up again.

Convocation holden at London by the legate

The same year, upon St. John the Baptist's day, Edward the king's son, and divers other noblemen of England, took upon them the cross by the legate's hands at Northampton, for the relief of the Holy Land, and the subversion of the enemies of the cross of Christ. This done, the legate that same year went out of England, not purposing after that to return again. This holy legate (saith mine author), who might well be resembled to a lynx, that monstrous beast whose quick sight penetrateth every thing, enrolled for perpetual memory the valuation of all the churches in the realm of England as narrowly as by any means possible he might inquire the certainty thereof. The same was he that made all the cathedral and conventual churches to pay pensions; so that those churches which gave not the vacancy of their benefices to their clerks and strangers, should pay unto them a certain yearly pension, during the vacancy of the benefices which they should have.

Valuation of all churches by Octobonus the legate

Pensions out of cathedral and conventual churches payed to the pope's clerks

The same year died pope Clement IV., after whose death the church of Rome was two years vacant; and then was chosen an archdeacon cardinal, whose name was Theaudus, as he was taking his journey into the Holy Land, and they called him Gregory X. A.D. 1271.

A.D. 1271

Then also did Edmund, earl of Lancaster and Leicester, and second son of king Henry, take to wife the earl of Albemarle's daughter, and the niece of the earl of Gloucester; at which marriage were the king and queen, with all the nobility of England.

Marriage of Edmund earl of Lancaster

The same year was the body of St. Edward, the king and confessor, by Walter Gifford, archbishop of York, and other bishops, entombed in a new and rich shrine of gold and silver, beset with precious stones, in the presence of Henry, the king of England. In the same year also fell a great rain and inundation of waters, such as hath not often been seen, which increased and continued the space of forty days, and more.

King Edmund the Confessor shrined

The same year died Walter de Laiwill, bishop of Sarum, the third day before the nones of January; after whom succeeded Robert of Northampton, the dean of the same church, and because the see of Canterbury was then vacant, he was confirmed by the chapter of Canterbury, which chapter had always the jurisdiction in

Bishop of Sarum consecrated

Henry III. A.D. 1271.

spiritual causes, during the vacancy of that see, in as ample manner as if the bishop himself had been alive. After this the bishop elect coming thither, thinking to have had his consecration, was, notwithstanding, put back for two causes; one was, because that there was present then no more than one bishop; the other was, that all the other bishops had appealed, that he might not be consecrated to their prejudice; that is, by the authority of the chapter of Canterbury, saying, that they would not be under the obedience of the monks.

After this, solemn messengers were for this cause sent to the cardinals of Rome, for that then the see of Rome was vacant; who received answer, that during the vacation of that see, the confirmation and consecration of the bishop elect pertained to the aforesaid chapter of Canterbury.

Death of lord Richard III., of Almain, the king's son, at Viterbium.

The same year also was the lord Henry, the son and heir of the lord Richard, king of Almain, and brother to king Henry III. slain at Viterbium, in a certain chapel hearing mass, by the lords Simon and Guido, sons of the lord Simon Mountfort, earl of Leicester.

During this king's reign, there was made a great and general expedition of divers and sundry christian princes to Jerusalem, taking upon them the Lord's character, that is, the cross; among whom was also Edward the king's son, for the which expedition was granted him a subsidy throughout all the realm; and the month of May, A.D. 1270, or as saith Florilegus, 1269, he set forward on his journey.[1]

Death of Boniface, archbishop of Canterbury.

Adam Chelindon elected in his stead.

About the time when prince Edward was preparing his journey toward Asia, Boniface, of whom ye heard before, the archbishop of Canterbury, ended his life in the country of Sabaudia, going probably to Rome, or coming thence. After his death, the monks of Canterbury, proceeding to a new election granted by the king, agreed upon the prior of their house, named Adam Chelindon. But the king and his son, prince Edward, consenting and speaking in the behalf of Robert Burnell, their chancellor, did solicit the matter with the monks, partly entreating, partly threatening them, to choose the said Robert to be archbishop. Notwithstanding, the monks being stout, would neither relent to their courteous request, nor yet bow to their boisterous threats, but constantly persisting in their former election, appealed from the king and prince to the pope. Prince Edward being now on his journey, and seeing himself thus frustrated by the monks, writeth back to the king, his father, devoutly praying and beseeching him in no wise to admit the election of the aforesaid monks. And so passing to Dover with Henry, the son of Richard, his uncle, king of the Romans, with their wives, they took their passage, in the month of August. After this the prior thus elected, but not admitted by the king, to be archbishop, went up to Rome.

Appellation from the king to the pope by the monks of Canterbury.

Chelindon goeth up to Rome.

In the mean time the monks, in the absence of their elect, ordained

(1) This was the last attempt at recovering the Holy Land. After an unsuccessful commencement this expedition was prosecuted with greater zeal by Louis IX., king of France, who died of the plague at Tunis, A.D. 1271; soon afterwards, his brother, Charles of Anjou, perished with his fleet at sea. Edward, afterwards Edward I., the son of Henry III., who had accompanied the French king, nothing daunted by these untoward events, proceeded to the Holy Land, and captured Acre; but being too enfeebled to follow up his victory with any prospect of success, he concluded a truce of ten years, with the Saracens. Edward returned to England, A.D. 1272, and found his father had just expired.—ED.

one Geffrey Pomenall to be their official; who, seeing himself advanced to that dignity, and bearing perhaps some old grudge against the prior of Dover, caused him to be cited up to appear in the chapter-house of Canterbury. The prior of Dover, seeing this citation to be prejudicial to him and to the church of Dover, and knowing that the monks of Canterbury have no such jurisdiction (the see of Canterbury being vacant), but that all things appertaining to that church ought to be reserved whole till the consecration of the new archbishop, therefore, for the state both of him and of his church, appealed up also unto Rome. But to return to the archbishop again.

Variance between the official of Canterbury, and the prior of Dover.

Appellation to Rome.

The second year after Chelindon, the aforesaid archbishop elect, remaining all this while at Rome, at last resigned up his election into the pope's hand (then Gregory X.), who gave the same to Robert Kilwardby. The latter coming to Dover, restored the prior of that house, who had been before excluded upon certain causes. By these contentions judge, good reader, of the religion of these men, and of these times. And now to return to our former story.

Chelindon resigneth to the pope. Robert Kilwardby, archbishop of Canterbury.

About this time came out the great Concordance, by an English friar, called John Dernington.[1]

The great Concordance.

It was above declared how a general voyage being proclaimed to war against the Turks, and a subsidy being collected in England on the occasion, prince Edward, with others, was appointed to take that voyage; and they were now on their way. At the Michaelmas following, Edward, with his company, came to Egermoth, which is from Marseilles eight leagues westward, and there taking ship again, having a merry wind and prosperous, within ten days arrived at Sunes at Tunis, where he was with great joy welcomed and entertained by the christian princes, who were for that purpose assembled, as also by Philip the French king, whose father Louis died a little before; by Charles, the king of Sicily, and by the two kings of Navarre and Arragon. And as the lord Edward came thither for his father the king of England, thither came also Henry, the son of the king of Almain, for his father; who, at his return from the voyage, was slain in a chapel at Viterbium, hearing mass, by the lords Simon and Guido, the sons of the lord Simon Mountfort, earl of Leicester.

When prince Edward demanded of these kings and princes what was to be done, they answered, "The prince of this city and of the province adjoining to the same, hath been accustomed to pay tribute unto the king of Sicily every year. And now as it hath been for the space of seven years unpaid and more, therefore we thought good to make invasion upon him. But the king, knowing the same tribute to be justly demanded, hath now, according to our own desires, satisfied for the time past, and also paid his tribute before-hand.

Then said he, "My lords! what is this to the purpose? Are we not here all assembled, and have taken upon us the Lord's character to fight against the infidels and the enemies of Christ? What mean you then to conclude a peace with them? God forbid we should do so, for now the land is plain and hard, so that we may approach the holy city Jerusalem." Then said they, "Now have we made a league with them; neither is it lawful for us to break the same; but

Expedition to invade the Turk, prevented by peace. Rage of the French king against

(1) Ex Eulogio.

Henry III. A.D. 1271.

let us return again to Sicily, that when the winter is past we may well take shipping to Acre." But this counsel nothing at all liked him, neither did he show himself well pleased therewith; but after he had made them a princely banquet, he went into his closet or privy chamber from amongst them, neither would be partaker of any of that wicked money which they had taken. They, notwithstanding, continuing their purpose, at the next merry wind took shipping, but for want of more ships, left two hundred of their men ashore, crying out and piteously lamenting for the peril and hazard of death they were in; wherewith prince Edward being somewhat moved to compassion, came back to the land, and received and stowed them in his own ships, being the last that went aboard. Within seven days after, they arrived in the kingdom of Sicily, over against the city Trapani, casting their anchors a league from thence in the sea, for that their ships were of great burthen, and thoroughly fraught; and from the haven of the city they sent out barges and boats to receive and bring such of the nobility to land as would; but their horses for the most part, and all their armour, they kept still on board. At length, towards evening, the sea began to be rough, and increased to a great tempest and a mighty, insomuch that their ships were beaten one against another's sides; and drowned there were of them, at that tempest, lying at anchor, more than a hundred and twenty, with all their armour and munition, with innumerable souls besides; and that wicked money also which they had taken before, likewise perished and was drowned. But the tempest hurt not so much as one ship of prince Edward's, who had in number thirteen, nor yet had one man lost thereby; for that as it may be presupposed, he consented not to the wicked counsel of the rest.[1] When in the morning the princes and kings came to the sea-side, and saw that all their ships were drowned, and their men and horses in great number cast dead upon the shore, they had full heavy hearts, as well they might. For of all their ships and mariners, who were in number fifteen hundred, besides the common soldiers, there were no more saved than the mariners of one only ship, and they in this wise: there was in that ship a good and wise matron (a countess or an earl's wife), who perceiving the tempest to grow, and fearing herself, called to her the master of the ship, and asked whether in attempting the shore, it were not possible to save themselves? Who answered, that to save the ship it was impossible, howbeit to save the men that were therein, by God's help, he doubted not. Then said the countess, "For the *ship* care no whit; save the *souls* therein, and have to thee double the value of thy ship." Immediately hoisting the sails, he with all force ran the ship aground, as near the shore as was possible. Thus, with the vehemency of the weather and the force he came withal, he brast the ship, and saved all that was within the same, as the master of the same ship had showed and said before.

Them turned into a money matter.

Clemency of prince Edward to the soldiers.

Great shipwreck of the Christians near Trapes.

Money evil got, as evil lost. "Non habet eventus sordida præda bonos."

Prince Edward preserved from tempest. His integrity rewarded of God.

Then the kings and princes (altering their purpose after this so great a shipwreck) returned home again every one unto their own lands; only Edward the king's son remained behind with his men and ships, which the Lord had saved and preserved. Then prince Edward (renovating his purpose) took shipping again, and within fifteen

(1) Ex Scala Mundi. Ex Gualto. Gisburn. Ex Flor. Hist.

Henry III. A.D. 1271.

days after Easter, arrived at Acre, and went on shore, taking with him a thousand of the best and most expert soldiers, and tarried there a month, refreshing both his men and horses, so that in this space he might learn and know the secrets of the land. After this he took with him six or seven thousand soldiers, and marched forward twenty miles from Acre, and took Nazareth; and those that he there found he slew, and afterwards returned again to Acre. But their enemies following after them, thinking to have set upon them at some strait or other advantage, they were by the prince premonished thereof, and returning again upon them, gave a charge, and slew many of them, and the rest they put to flight. After this, about Midsummer, when the prince had understanding that the Saracens began to gather at Cackhow, which was forty miles from Acre, he, marching thither, set upon them very early in the morning, and slew of them more than a thousand; the rest he put to flight, and took rich spoils, marching forward till they came to a castle named Castrum Peregrinorum, situated upon the sea-coast, and tarried there that night, and the next day they returned towards Acre. In the mean season the king of Jerusalem sent unto the noblemen of Cyprus, desiring them with speed that they would come and aid the Christians; but they would not come, saying, they would keep their own land, and go no further. Then prince Edward sent unto them, desiring that at his request they would come and join in aid with him, who immediately thereupon came unto him with great preparation and furniture for the war, saying, that at his command they were bound to do no less, for that his predecessors were sometime governors of their land, and that they ought always to show their fidelity to the kings of England. Then the Christians, being herewith animated, made a third 'viage', or 'rode,' and came as far as the fort called Vincula Petri, and to St. George's; and when they had slain certain there, not finding any to make resistance against them, they retired from whence they came.

Arriving at Acre, taketh Nazareth.

The nobles of Cyprus show their fidelity to the king of England.

When thus the fame of prince Edward grew amongst his enemies, and they began to stand in fear of him; they devised among themselves, how by some policy they might circumvent and betray him.[1] Hereupon the great prince and admiral of Joppa sent to him, feigning himself, under great deceit, to become a Christian, and that he would draw with him a great number besides, so that they might be honourably entertained and used of the Christians. This talk pleased the prince well, and persuaded him to finish the thing he had so well begun, by writing again; who also by the same messenger sent and wrote back unto him divers times about the same matter, whereby no mistrust should spring. This messenger, saith mine author, was one 'ex cote nutritus,' one of the stony-hearted, who neither feared God nor dreaded death. The fifth time when this messenger came, and was of the prince's servants searched, according to the manner and custom, to discover what weapon and armour he had about him, as also his purse, and when not so much as a knife could be found about him, he was had up into the prince's chamber, and after his reverence done, he pulled out certain letters, which he delivered to the prince from his lord, as he had done others before. This was about eight days after Whitsuntide, upon a Tuesday, somewhat before night; at

Guileful deceit of the Saracens practised against prince Edward.

(1) Ex Gisburn.; Scala Mundi.

Henry III. which time the prince was laid upon his bed, bare-headed, in his jerkin, for the great heat and intemperature of the weather.

A.D. 1271. When the prince had read the letters, it appeared by them, that upon the Saturday following, his lord would be there ready to accomplish all that he had written and promised. The report of this news, by the prince to the standers-by, liked them well, drawing somewhat back to consult thereof amongst themselves. In the mean time the messenger, kneeling and making his obeisance to the prince, who was questioning further with him, put his hand to the belt, as though he would have pulled out some secret letters, and suddenly he pulled out an envenomed knife, thinking to have stricken it into the prince's belly as he lay; but Edward, lifting up his hand to defend the blow, was stricken a great wound in the arm; and the messenger being about to fetch another stroke at him, the prince with his foot took him such a blow that he felled him to the ground. With that the prince gat him by the hand, and with such violence wrested the knife from him, that he hurt himself therewith in the forehead, and immediately thrust the same into the belly of the messenger and striker, and slew him. The prince's servants being in the next chamber not far off, hearing the bustling, came with great haste running in. And finding the messenger lying dead on the floor, one of them took up a stool and beat out his brains; whereat the prince was wroth, for that he struck a dead man, and one that was killed before. The rumour hereof, as it was strange, so it soon went throughout all the court, and from thence amongst the common people; wherefore they were very heavy and greatly discouraged. To him came also the captain of the temple, and brought him a costly and precious drink against poison, lest the venom of the knife should penetrate the lively blood, and in blamingwise said unto him, "Did I not show your grace before, of the deceit and subtlety of this people? Notwithstanding," saith he, "let your grace take a good heart; you shall not die of this wound, my life for yours." But straightway the surgeons and physicians were sent for, and the prince was dressed, and within a few days after the wound began to putrefy, and the flesh to look dead and black; whereupon those who were about the prince began to mutter amongst themselves, and were very sad and heavy. Which thing he himself perceiving, said unto them, "Why mutter you thus amongst yourselves? What see you in me, can I not be healed? Tell me the truth, be ye not afraid." Whereupon one said to him, "Your grace, you may be healed, we mistrust it not; but yet it will be very painful for you to suffer." "May suffering," said he again, "restore health?" "Yea," saith the other, "on pain of losing my head." "Then," said the prince, "I commit myself unto you, do with me what you think good." Then said one of his physicians, "Is there any of your nobles in whom your grace reposeth special trust?" To whom the prince answered "yea," naming certain of the noblemen that stood about him. Then said the physician unto the two whom the prince first named, the lord Edmund and the lord John Voisie: "And do you also faithfully love your lord and prince?" Who answered both, "Yea, undoubtedly." "Then," saith he, "take you away this gentlewoman and lady," meaning his wife, "and let her not see her lord and husband

Edward wounded with an envenomed knife by the Turks' messenger.

In peril of death by reason of his hurt, is comforted by the physicians.

until such time as I will you to let her;" whereupon they took her out of the prince's presence, crying out and wringing her hands. Then said they unto her, "Be ye contented, good lady and madam, it is better that one woman should weep a little while, than that all the realm of England should weep a great season." Then, on the morrow, they cut out all the dead envenomed flesh out of the prince's arm, and threw it from them, and said unto him, "How cheereth your grace? We promise you within these fifteen days you shall show yourself abroad (if God permit) on horseback, whole and well as ever you were." And according to the promise he made the prince, it came to pass, to the no little comfort and admiration of all his subjects. When the great Saladin heard of it, and that the prince was yet alive, he would scarcely believe the same; and sending unto him three of his nobles and princes, he excused himself by them, calling his gods to witness, that the same was done neither by him, nor his consent. The princes and messengers standing aloof off from the king's son, worshipping him fell flat upon the ground. "You," saith the prince, "do reverence me, but yet you love me not." But they understood him not, because he spake in English unto them, speaking by an interpreter. Nevertheless he treated them honourably, and sent them away in peace.

The prince restored to health, the Soldan forsweareth himself

Thus, when prince Edward had been eighteen months in Acre, he took shipping about the Assumption of Our Lady, as we call it, returning homeward; and, after seven weeks, he arrived in Sicily, at Trapani, and from thence travelling through Palistrina and Metines, and so through the midst of Apulia, till he came to Rome, where he was of the pope honourably entertained; from thence he came into France, whose fame and noble prowess was there much noised about among the common people, and envied of the nobility, especially of the earl of Chalons, who sent unto him, and required him that he might break a staff with him at the tilt in his country. This the prince, because he would not diminish his honour and fame, willingly consented to do, although he might have well alleged a sufficient excuse by means of his travail. It was therefore proclaimed, that prince Edward, by such a day, with those that were with him, had challenged all comers at the tilt and barriers. Hereupon great assemblies were made in the country all about; and divers, as well horsemen as footmen, had confederated among themselves, and conspired against the Englishmen, selling their horses and armour beforehand, and drinking one to another in 'boon viage,'[1] of the spoil of them whom they would take as their prisoners. Prince Edward, in the mean time, sent into England for divers earls and barons, who came unto him. When the day appointed was come, the prince had with him more than one thousand horsemen, who were knights, besides his footmen; but yet there were as many more, on the other side, both in horsemen and footmen. When the parties met, the French footmen, who had before conspired, began both to spoil, rifle, and kill. The Englishmen resisted and defended themselves, both with bows and slings; many of the Frenchmen they slew, and drove them to the gates of their city; the others they chased over a river, where many

The prince returneth to England.

A day of sport which turneth to good earnest.

Conspiracy of the Frenchmen against the Englishmen

(1) "Drinking one to another in boon viage," a common expression in old authors, in other words, "Drinking one another good success in the spoiling of those whom they had destined for their prisoners."—Ed

Henry III. — A.D. 1271.

of them were drowned. In the mean while the earl, with fifty of his knights who followed him, came forth and joined together, so many for so many, and a long time together they tried with it their swords, laying one on another. At last the earl, perceiving himself not able to match with the prince at arms' length, closed with him, and taking him about the neck, held him with his arms very straight. "What mean you, my lord," saith the prince, "think you to have my horse?" "Yea, marry," quoth the earl, "I mean to have both thee and thy horse." Hereat prince Edward, being indignant, lifted up himself, and gave him such a blow, that therewithal he, forsaking his horse, hung still about the prince's neck, till that he shook him off to the ground. Herewith the prince, being somewhat in a heat, left the press to take the air, thereby to refresh himself. But when he saw the injury of the Frenchmen towards his men, and how they had slain many of them, he then said unto them that they used rather the exercise of battle than of tourney. "Spare ye not, therefore," saith he, "from henceforth, any of them all, but give them again as good as they bring." Then they essayed to kill each other freely on either part, and let their swords walk. By this time the English footmen were again returned, and seeing the conflicts of horsemen, and many other Englishmen overthrown, they put themselves amidst the press; some paunching the horses, and some cutting asunder the girths of the Frenchmen's saddles, they overthrew the riders, and gave them holy bread. When the aforesaid earl had been horsed again by some of his men, and had got amongst the throng, prince Edward also rushed in amongst the thickest, and coped again with him, to whom he often spake and cried, that he should yield himself as vanquished; but that the earl would not do. Notwithstanding, when the earl's strength began to fail him, he was fain to yield himself unto a simple knight, according as prince Edward bade him, and all the rest of his horsemen and knights fled and saved themselves; howbeit, many of them in that place were slain; and so our men returned, having the victory. But when, after this, they thought to be quiet and at rest, they were killed by the citizens by twos and threes at once, as they walked in the streets. When the prince heard this, he sent for the mayor and burgesses, commanding them to see the same redressed, and that immediately; for otherwise, of his knighthood he assured them, that upon the morrow he would fire the city, and make it level with the ground. On this they went their ways, and set watchmen in divers places of the same to keep peace, by which means the prince and his men were in safety and quiet. Thus, in this pastime of tourneying and barriers, much blood was spilled, whereupon the name of the place was changed; so that it is not called 'Torniamentum de Chalons,' but 'Parvum Bellum de Chalons.'

Exercise of battle, instead of barriers and tourney.

Victory of the English against the earl de Chalons.

Prince Edward in Gascony at his father's death.

From thence the prince came to Paris, and was of the French king honourably entertained; and after certain days he went from thence into Gascony, where he tarried till he heard of the death of the king his father.

A.D.1272. Pope Clement IV. dies.

In the year of our Lord 1272, died pope Clement IV.: after whom succeeded pope Gregory X.; who, in the year following, called a general council at Lyons, about the controversy between the Greek church and the Latin church, and for the vacancy of the see apostolical. *Henry III*

A. D. 1216 to 1272.

CERTAIN NOTES OF OTHER OCCURRENCES CHANCED IN FOREIGN COUNTRIES ABROAD, WITHIN THE COMPASS OF THE YEARS AND REIGN OF THE AFORESAID KING HENRY III.

Having thus completed the life and history of king Henry III., with such accidents as happened within this realm, I thought good to adjoin unto the same, some other foreign matters not unworthy of note, incident in other countries during the time of the said king: namely, from A.D. 1216 unto this year, 1272. These I thought the rather not to be omitted, for that even from and about the beginning of this king's reign, sprang up the very well-springs of all mischief, the sects of monkish religions and other swarms of popish orders, which, with their gross and horrible superstitions, have encumbered the church of Christ ever since.

First, to omit the repetition of pope Innocent III., the great great grandsire of that foul monster transubstantiation and auricular confession, friars Dominic and Franciscan friars, Thomas Aquinas, Jacobus de Voragine, and Vincentius, with pope Honorius III. coiner of the canon law, and the cardinal Postiensis, as also Bonaventure, Albertus Magnus, with pope Urban IV., the first founder of the feast of Corpus Christi, and the procurer of the adoration of the body of Christ in the sacrament, besides Durandus and many more: it followeth further to be noted, that the Tartars, about A.D. 1240, issuing out of Muscovy into the parts of Poland, made great waste in Christendom, and this so much the rather, because the princes about Poland, being at variance amongst themselves, used no other remedy for their defence but heaps of masses, the invocation of the dead, and the worshipping of images, which indeed did not at all relieve them, but rather increase their trouble. *The Tartars make great spoil in Christendom*

In the year following, the whole nation of the Scythians, mustering like locusts, invaded the parts of Europe with two mighty armies, whereof the one, entering on Poland, made great havoc, and carried away many Christians from thence captives; the other overrunning Hungary, made no less spoil there. Add hereunto another fresh army of Tartarians, to the number of five millions,[1] who at the very same time joining themselves together, entered Muscovy and Cracow, and made most horrible slaughter, sparing neither sex nor age, neither noble nor ignoble within the land. From thence passing to Lower Sclavonia, they made great spoil there also, and thinking there to win the castle, were, by the miraculous working of the Lord, at the instance and prayers of good people, discomfited beyond all expectation of man, by thunder and lightning falling upon them from heaven in a most terrible manner. *The Scythians invade Europe like locusts*

The same year, immediately after Easter, another army of Tartars was gathered against Lignitz, drawing near to Germany; by the rumour whereof, the Germans, being put in great fears, were altogether dismayed, but yet not able to help themselves, because they lacked a good guide and governor amongst them. All this came

(1) Ex Annalibus Silesiæ

Henry III. A.D. 1216 to 1272.

to pass, especially by the mischievous practice of the Roman popes, raising variance and discord among them. Notwithstanding Henry, prince of Polonia and Silesia, gathering a power as well as he could, did encounter with him; but in the end his whole army was vanquished, and the king himself slain. Notwithstanding this overthrow of Christians, it pleased God to strike such a fear into the hearts of the Tartars, that they durst not approach any further or nearer into Germany, but retired for that time into their country again; who, recounting their victory by taking each man but one ear of every one of the Christians that were slain, found the slaughter so great, that they filled nine great sacks full of ears. Nevertheless, after this (A.D. 1260), the same Tartars, having the Muscovites for their guides, returned again into Polonia and Cracow; where, in the space of three months, they overran the land with fire and sword to the coasts of Silesia, and had not the princes of Germany put to their helping hand in this lamentable case, they had utterly wasted the whole land of Poland, and the coasts thereabout.

Henry of Polonia slain, and his army vanquished. Nine sacks full of the ears of Christians slain.

This year also, in the month of April, Richard, king of Almain, died at the castle of Berkhamstead, and was buried at the abbey of Hailes, which he built from the ground. The same year also, at Norwich, there arose a great controversy between the monks and the citizens, about certain tallages and liberties. At last, after much altercation and wrangling words, the furious rage of the citizens so much increased and prevailed, and so little was the fear of God before their eyes, that altogether they set upon the abbey and priory, and burned both the church and bishop's palace. When this thing was heard abroad, the people were very sorry to hear of so bold and naughty an enterprise, and much discommended the same. At last, king Henry, calling for certain of his lords and barons, sent them to the city of Norwich, that they might punish and see execution done on the chief malefactors; insomuch that some of them were condemned and burnt, some of them hanged, and some were drawn by the heels with horses throughout the streets of the city, and afterwards in much misery they ended their wretched lives. The same year Adam, the prior of Canterbury, and bishop elect, in the presence of Pope Gregory X. refused to be archbishop, although he was elected; wherefore the pope gave the archbishopric to friar Robert Kilwardby, the provost of the preaching friars, a man of good life and great learning. He was consecrated at Canterbury, on the fourth day of March, by six bishops of the same province. The same year also, at Michaelmas, the lord Edmund, the son of king Richard, of Almain, married the sister of Gilbert, earl of Gloucester. Also in this year, A.D. 1273, on the sixteenth day before the kalends of December, being the day of St. Edmund archbishop and confessor, died king Henry, in the fifty-sixth year of his reign, and was buried at Westminster, leaving behind him two sons and two daughters; to wit, Edward, the prince, and Edmund, earl of Lancaster and Leicester, Beatrice, and Margaret; which Margaret was married to the king of Scots. This king Henry, in his lifetime, began the building of the church and steeple of Westminster, but did not thoroughly finish the same before his death.

Richard king of Almain dies. Variance between the monks and the citizens of Norwich.

Execution at Norwich by the command of king Henry III.

Adam, prior of Canterbury refuseth to be archbishop of that see. Robert Kilwardby, archbishop of Canterbury.

Death of king Henry III.

EDWARD THE FIRST.[1]

Edward I. A.D. 1272.

In the time of the death of king Henry, Edward, his eldest son, was absent in Gascony, as a little before you heard; yet notwithstanding, by Robert Kilwarby, archbishop of Canterbury, and other bishops and nobles, he was ordained heir and successor to his father; on hearing of whose death, he returned home to his country, and was crowned A.D. 1274. On that occasion he laid down his crown, saying, he would no more put it on, before he had gathered together all the lands appertaining to the same. This Edward, who had always before been a loving and natural child to his father, whom he had delivered out of prison and captivity; hearing afterwards of the death of his son, and of that of his father, both together, wept and lamented much more for his father, than for his son, saying to the French king, who asked the cause thereof, that the loss of his child was but light; for children might afterwards increase and be multiplied, but the loss of his parent was greater, which could not be recovered.[2] So Almighty God, for his piety shown to his father, rewarded him again with great success, felicity, and long reign, insomuch that he being young, as he was playing at chess with a certain soldier of his, suddenly having occasion given, rose up and went his way; who had only just voided the place, when incontinent fell down a mighty stone from the vault above, directly upon the place where he had sat, able to have quashed him in pieces, if he had tarried ever so little more; in whose preservation, as I see present the hand and mighty providence of the living God, so, in the king's order again, I note a fault or error worthy of reprehension, in that he, after receiving such a lively benefit at the hand of the living Lord, and going therefore on pilgrimage to Walsingham, gave thanks not only to our Lord, but rather to a rotten block.[3]

Piety to parents rewarded of God.

A miracle of God in preserving king Edward.

False worship reprehended, God giveth the benefit, and a dumb stock hath the thanks.

Of the gentle nature of this courageous prince, sufficient proof is given by this one example. One day being in his disport of hawking, he chanced sharply to rebuke the negligence of one of his gentlemen, for what fault I cannot tell, about his hawk: the gentleman, being on the other side of the river, hearing his menacing words, was glad, as he said, that the river was between them. With this answer the courageous blood of this prince being moved, upon present heat he leaped straight into the flood, being both of a swift stream and of a dangerous deepness, and no less hard in getting out. Notwithstanding, either forgetting his own life, or neglecting the danger present, and having a good horse, he ventureth his own death, to have the death of his man. At length, with much difficulty recovering the bank, with his sword drawn he pursueth his provoker, who having not so good a horse, and seeing himself in danger of being taken, reineth up his horse, and returning back bareheaded unto the prince, submitteth his neck under his hand to strike. The prince, whose fervent

Example of princely clemency to be learned by kings and princes.

(1) Edition 1563, p. 74. Ed. 1583, p. 339. Ed. 1596, p. 310. Ed. 1684, vol. i. p. 386.
(2) Rob. Avesbury. Also from the Chronicles of Thomas Walsingham. p. 44. (3) Ibid.

Edward I. A.D. 1272. stomach the water of the whole river could not quench, a little submission of his man did so cool, that the quarrel dropped, his anger ceased, and his sword was put up without any stroke given. And so both returned to their game, good friends again.[1]

Wales subdued. The king's eldest son prince of Wales. In the beginning of his reign, the king had much ado in Wales, where he had divers conflicts with the Welshmen, whom he at last subdued, and cut down their woods, suppressed rebellions, and vanquishing their kings Llewelyn and his brother, ordained his eldest son Edward, born in the same country, to be prince of Wales. This Llewelyn, captain of the Welshmen here mentioned, rebelling against king Edward, asked counsel by way of conjuration, what event should come upon his attempt; to whom it was told, that he should go forward boldly, for doubtless he should ride through Cheapside in London, with a crown on his head. Which so came to pass; for, being slain, his head with a crown of silver was carried through Cheap to London Bridge. Vain prophecies not to be sought to. By this, men may learn not to seek or stick to these vain prophecies, which though they fall true, yet are they but the trains of the devil to deceive men.

About this time there was a great earthquake, and such a rot, that it consumed a great multitude of sheep in the land, through the occasion, as they say, of one scabbed sheep that came out of Spain. The king returning from Wales to England, ordered certain new laws for the wealth of the realm. Punishment for bakers and millers. Among many others, this was one: authority was given to all mayors, bailiffs, and other officers to see execution and punishment with the pillory on all bakers making bread under the assize; and with the tumbrel, on millers stealing corn, &c. The statute of mortmain first enacted. Within two years after this, the statute of mortmain was first enacted, which is as much as to say, that no man should give unto the church any lands or rents, without special license of the king.

A.D. 1279. Black-friars by Ludgate built. About this time, being the seventh year of king Edward's reign (A.D. 1279), Jews, for money-clipping, were brought to execution, and in the same year began the foundation of the Black-friars by Ludgate. Boston blemished with fire. The town of Boston was greatly wasted this year with fire. The halfpenny and farthing began first to be coined about the same time, which was the eighth year of this king's reign. The fourth year after this, the great conduit in Cheap began to be made. Westminster church finished. A.D. 1284. In the year following, the new work of the church of Westminster (begun as is before premised in the third year of Henry III.) was finished, which was sixty-six years in edifying. The Jews were utterly banished this realm of England at the same time, for which the commons gave to the king a fifteenth,[2] &c.

After that, the country of Wales was brought into full order and quiet, by the hewing down of the woods, and casting down the old holds, and building of new; which all was brought to a perfect end, about the twenty-fourth year of this king's reign. Then ensued another broil, as great or greater, with Scotland, to the great disquiet of the king and the realm of England for many years after. This trouble first began by the death of Alexander, king of Scots, who died without issue left alive. Although Fabian in the seventh

(1) Rob. Avesbury, Nich. Trivet, and Tho. Walsingham.
(2) Tho. Walsingham and Walter Gisburn.

book of his Chronicles affirmeth, that he left three daughters, the eldest married to Sir John Baliol, the second to Robert Bruce, the third to one Hastings. But this in Fabian is to be corrected, as which not only standeth not with itself, but is clearly convicted by the witness and history of Robert Avesbury and also by that of Gisburn.

Edward I. A.D. 1284.

For first, if king Alexander had left his eldest daughter married to Sir John Baliol, then what controversy might rise among the lords about succession, needing such diligent and anxious deciding by the king of England? Secondly, what claim or title could the king of Norway have to the crown of Scotland, who was one of the challengers, claiming the said crown in the behalf of Margaret, the niece of the aforesaid king Alexander, her grandfather, if the eldest daughter of the father had been left alive? Thirdly, what can be more plain, when by the affirmance of the aforesaid story it is testified, that king Alexander had two wives, of the second whereof he had no issue? Of the first, he had two children: Alexander, who died before his father; and Margaret married to the king of Norway, who died also before her father, of whom came Margaret, the niece of Alexander, and daughter to the king of Norway before mentioned; and she also died in the journey between Norway and Scotland, the fourth year after the decease of her grandfather. Wherefore, as this matter standeth most clear, so let us now, returning from whence we digressed, prosecute the rest that followeth. After that, Alexander thus, as is said, departing without issue, and also Margaret his niece in Norway being deceased, the matter came into great doubt among the nobles of Scotland (especially twelve by name), to whom the right of the crown should next pertain. After much variance among parties, at length the election and determination of the matter was committed to the judgment of king Edward of England; who, after sufficient proof made to the Scots, and firm evidence brought out of all the ancient histories both of England and Scotland, testifying from time to time that he was chief head and sovereign of the realm of Scotland; first, by necessity of the law, and by all their consents, took full possession of the same. And that done, he adjudged the right of the crown to John Baliol, who descended from the daughter of David, earl of Huntingdon, brother to David, king of Scots, in the days of king Henry II. This earl David had three daughters, Isabel, married to Robert Bruce; Margaret, to Allen earl of Galloway; and Ellen, to Henry lord Hastings. Allen earl of Galloway had Ellen, married to Roger Quincy, earl of Winchester, constable of Scotland; and Dorvagile, married to John Baliol, father to Edward, king of Scots.

Lack of succession, what disturbance it worketh in a realm.

The king of England proved by old records chief head of Scotland. A.D. 1291.

When these things were thus finished in Scotland, and Sir John Baliol, as most rightful inheritor, had received the crown of Scotland at the hands of king Edward thankfully, and for the same, in the presence of the barony of England and of Scotland, doing unto the said king Edward his homage, and swearing to him fealty: the Scots, with their new king, returned into Scotland, and king Edward removed again to England. A.D. 1292.

Sir John Baliol made king of Scotland by king Edward. King of Scots doth homage to the king of England.

But not long after, the falseness of this Scottish king soon appeared, who, repenting him of his homage done, untruly forsook his former

Edward I. A.D. 1295. oath and promise, and made war against king Edward, through the counsel of the abbot of Melros. Wherefore the king, with a great host, sped him into Scotland, and in process laid siege to the town of Berwick, which the Scots did eagerly defend, not only to the discomfiture, but also to the derision of the king and his English host. But in conclusion, the Englishmen prevailed and won the town, where were slain of the Scots the number of five and twenty thousand. While the king was there busied in winning other holds about the same, he sent part of his host to Dunbar, where the Englishmen again had the victory, and slew of the Scots twenty thousand: Gisburn saith but ten thousand; so that very few were lost of the English company. The king, with a great number of prisoners returning into his realm, shortly after sped him over unto Flanders, where he sustained great trouble through the French king, till truce for a certain space was between them concluded. But, while king Edward was thus occupied beyond the seas, the French king, resorting to his practised manner, set the Scots secretly against the Englishmen to keep the king at home; which Scots, making themselves a captain named William Wallace, warred upon the borders of Northumberland, where they did much hurt. At length the king, returning from Bourdeaux into England, shortly after took his journey into Scotland, where meeting at York with his host, he marched into the realm of Scotland, winning, as he went, towns and castles, till at length coming to the town of Falkirk on Mary Magdalen's day, he met with the power of Scotland, and had with them a sore fight, but, through God's providence, the victory fell to the right cause of Englishmen: so that of the Scots were slain in the field, as it is of divers writers affirmed, above the number of thirty and two thousand; and of Englishmen, but barely twenty-eight persons.[1] Whereupon the king, again taking possession and fealty of the whole land, returned home.

Falseness of the Scottish king.

Town and castle of Berwick won by Englishmen.

Falseness justly punished.

The Scots rebel again.

Second voyage of king Edward into Scotland. A.D. 1298.

And yet the false untruth of the Scots would not thus be ruled, but rose up in a new broil; the king, therefore, was forced to march his power again, the year following, into Scotland, where he so suppressed the rebellion of the lords and of the commons, that they, swearing to the king's allegiance, presented themselves in great companies, and put themselves wholly at the king's grace and mercy: so that the king, thinking himself to be in peaceable possession, and in a great surety of the land, caused to be sworn unto him the rulers of the boroughs, cities, and towns, with other officers of the land, and so returned unto Berwick, and from thence into England, and lastly to Westminster.

Notable victory against the Scots. A.D. 1299. The Scots sworn to the king's allegiance.

These martial affairs between England and Scotland, although they appertain not greatly to the purpose of our story ecclesiastical, yet thus much, by the way, I thought briefly to notice, that what followeth in the sequel hereof, might the better be understood by these premises.[2] As the Scots were thus warring and raging against the king, and saw they could not make their party good, they sent privily to pope Boniface for his aid and counsel: who immediately sendeth down his precept to the king, to this effect, that he should hereafter cease to disquiet or molest the Scots, for that they were a people exempt, and

The pope's message to the king.

(1) Ex Fabiano. (2) Ex Chron. Tho. Walsingham et Avesbury.

roperly pertaining to his chapel; and therefore it could not other- ise be, but that the city of Jerusalem must needs defend its own itizens; and, as the Mount Sion maintains such as trust in the Lord, :c. Whereunto the king briefly maketh answer again, swearing ith an oath, that he would to his uttermost keep and defend that hich was his right, evidently known to all the world, &c. Thus he Scots, bearing themselves bold upon the pope's message, and also onfederating themselves with the Frenchmen, passed over that year.

Edward I.

A.D. 1299.

The king's answer.

n the following year (which was the twenty-ninth year of the king's eign), the said pope Boniface directeth his letters again to the king, herein he doth vindicate the kingdom of Scotland, to be proper to he church of Rome, and not subject to the king of England; howing, therefore, that it was against God, against justice, and also rejudicial to the church of Rome, for him to have or hold dominion ver the same; which he proved by these reasons:

The pope challengeth Scotland to be free from the dominion of England.

"First, that when king Henry, the father of this king, received id of Alexander, king of Scots, in his wars against Simon Mountfort, e recognised and acknowledged in his letters patent, that he received he same of king Alexander, not of any duty, but of special favour.

"Item, when the said king Alexander, coming to England, did omage to the said king Henry; he did it not as king of Scotland, ut only for certain lands of Tindal and Penrith, lying in England.

"Item, whereas the said king Alexander left behind him Margaret is heir; being niece to the king of England, and yet under age; yet he tuition of the said Margaret was committed not to the king of England, but to certain lords of Scotland, deputed to the same.

"Moreover, when any legacy was directed down from Rome to he realm of England, for collecting of tenths or other causes, the said egacy took no place in the realm of Scotland, and might well be esisted (as it was in king Alexander's days), except another special commission touching the realm of Scotland, were joined withal. Whereby it appeareth, that these be two several dominions, and not subject under one.

"Adding, furthermore, that the kingdom of Scotland, at the first, was converted by the relics of the blessed apostle St. Peter, through he divine operation of God, to the unity of the catholic faith.

"Wherefore, upon these causes and reasons, pope Boniface, in his etters to the king, required him to give over his claim, and cease his wars against the Scottish nation, and release all such, both of the spiritualty and the laity, as he had of them prisoners. Also, to call home again his officers and deputies, which he had there placed and ordained to the grievance of that nation, to the slander of all faithful people, and no less prejudice to the church of Rome. And if he would claim any right or title to the said realm, or any part thereof, he should send up his procurators specially to the same appointed, with all that he could for himself allege, unto the see apostolic, there to receive what reason and right would require."

The king, after he had received these letters of the pope, assembled a council or parliament at Lincoln, by the advice of which council and parliament, he addressed other letters responsal to the pope again; wherein first, in all reverend manner, he desireth him not to give light ear to the sinister suggestions of false reports, and imaginers of

A.D. 1301. The king replieth to the pope.

Edward I. A.D. 1301.

Scotland all one with England.

mischief. Then he declareth, out of old records and histories from the first time of the Britons, that the realm of Scotland hath always, from time to time, been all one with England, beginning first with Brutus in the time of Eli, and Samuel, the prophet: which Brutus, coming from Troy to this isle, called then Albion, afterwards called by him Britannia, had three sons; Locrinus, to whom he gave that part of the land, called then of him Lœgria, now Anglia; Albanactus, his second son, to whom he gave Albania, now called Scotia; and his third son, Camber, to whom he gave Cambria, now called Wales.

"And thus much concerning the first division of this isle, as in ancient histories is found recorded. In which matter, passing over the death of king Humber, the acts of Dunwald, king of this realm, the division of Belyn and Brenne, the victories of king Arthur, we will resort," saith the king, "to more near times, testified and witnessed by sufficient authors, as Marianus Scotus, William Malmesbury, Roger Abyndon, Henry Huntingdon, Radulph de Bizoto and others, all of whom make special declaration, and give manifest evidence of the execution of this our right," saith he, "and title of superiority ever continued and preserved hitherto.

"And first to begin with Edward the Elder, before the conquest, son to Alured (or Alfred), king of England, about A.D. 907, it is plain and manifest, that he had under his dominion and obedience the king of Scots: and here is to be noted, that this matter was so notorious and manifest, that Marian the Scot, writing that story in those days, granteth, confesseth, and testifieth the same: and this dominion continued in that state twenty-three years. At that time, Athelstan succeeded to the crown of England, and having by battle conquered Scotland, he made one Constantine, king of that party, to rule and govern the country of Scotland under him; adding this princely word, that it was more honour to him to make a king, than to be a king.

"Twenty-four years after that, which was A.D. 947, Eldred, the king our progenitor, Athelstan's brother, took homage of Irise, then king of Scots.

"Thirty years after that, which was A.D. 977, king Edgar, our predecessor, took homage of Kynald, king of Scots. Here was a little trouble in England by the death of St. Edward, king and martyr, destroyed by the deceit of his mother-in-law, but yet within memory.

"Forty years after the homage done by Kynald to king Edgar, that is to say, A.D. 1017, Malcoline, the king of Scots, did homage to Canute our predecessor. After this homage done, the Scots uttered some piece of their natural disposition, whereupon (by war made by our progenitor St. Edward the Confessor, thirty and nine years after that homage done, that is to say, A.D. 1056), Malcoline, king of Scots, was vanquished, and the realm of Scotland given to Malcoline his son, by our said progenitor St. Edward, unto whom the said Malcoline made homage and fealty

"Within forty years after that, William the Conqueror entered this realm, whereof he accounted no perfect conquest until he had likewise subdued the Scots; and, therefore, in the said year (which was A.D. 1068), the said Malcoline, king of Scots, did homage to the said William the Conqueror as to his superior, by conquest king of England.

"Twenty and five years after that, which was A.D. 1093, the said Malcoline did homage and fealty to William Rufus, son to the said William the Conqueror; and yet after that, he was for his offences and demerits deposed, and his son substituted in his place, who likewise failed in his duty; and, therefore, was ordained in that estate, by the said William Rufus, Edgar, brother to the last Malcoline, and son to the first, who did his homage and fealty accordingly.

"Seven years after that, which was A.D. 1100, the said Edgar, king of the Scots, did homage to Henry I., our progenitor.

"Thirty-seven years after that, David, king of Scots, did homage to Matilda, the emperatrice, as daughter and heir to Henry I. Wherefore being afterwards required by Stephen, then obtaining possession of the realm, to make his homage, he refused so to do, because he had before made it to the said Matilda, and thereupon forbore. After David's death, which ensued shortly after, the son of the said David made homage to the said king Stephen.

"Fourteen years after that, which was A.D. 1150, William, king of Scots, and David his brother, with all the nobles of Scotland, made homage to the son of Henry II., with a reservation of their duty to Henry II., his father. *Edward I.* A.D. 1301.

"Twenty-five years after that, which was A.D. 1175, William, king of Scotland, after much rebellion and resistance according to their natural inclination (king Henry II. then being in Normandy), acknowledged finally his error, and made his peace and composition, confirmed with his great seal, and the seals of the nobility of Scotland, making therewith his homage and fealty.

"Within fifteen years after that, which was A.D. 1190, the said William, king of Scots, came to our city of Canterbury, and there did homage to our noble progenitor king Richard I.

"Fourteen years after that, the said William did homage to our progenitor king John, upon a hill beside Lincoln, making his oath upon the cross of Hubert, then archbishop of Canterbury, being there present, and a marvellous multitude assembled for that purpose.

"Twenty-six years after that, which was A.D. 1230, Alexander, king of Scots, married Margaret, the daughter of our progenitor Henry III., at our city of York, at the feast of Christmas: at which time the said Alexander did his homage to our said progenitor, who reigned in this realm fifty-six years. And, therefore, between the homage made by the said Alexander, king of Scotland, and the homage done by Alexander, son to the said king of Scots, to us at our coronation at Westminster, there was about fifty years. At that time, the said Alexander, king of Scots, repaired to the said feast of our coronation, and there did he his duty as is aforesaid."

Besides these letters of the king, the lords temporal also, in the name of the whole commonalty and parliament, wrote another letter to the pope answering to that in which the pope arrogated to him to be judge respecting the title to the realm of Scotland, which the king of England claimed unto himself; which letter also I thought good to annex in the words here following.

The Lords Temporal, and the whole Barony of England to the Pope.

The holy mother church, by whose ministry the catholic see is governed, in her deeds, as we throughly believe and hold, proceedeth with that ripeness in judgment, that she will be hurtful to none, but, like a mother, would every man's right to be kept unbroken as well in others as in herself. Whereas, therefore, in a general parliament called at Lincoln of late by our most dread lord Edward, by the grace of God the noble king of England, the same our lord caused certain letters received from you to be read openly, and to be declared seriously before us, about certain businesses touching the condition and state of the realm of Scotland: we did not a little muse and marvel with ourselves, hearing the meanings concerning the same, so wondrous and strange, as the like we have not heard at any time before. For we know, most holy father, and it is well known as well in this realm of England, as also it is not unknown to other persons besides, that from the first beginning of the realm of England, the certain and direct government of the realm of Scotland in all temporal causes, from time to time, belonged to the kings of the same realm of England, and realm of Scotland; as well in the times of the Britons, as also of Englishmen. Yea rather, the same realm of Scotland of old time was in fee to the ancestors of our aforesaid lords, kings of England, now to [the lord Edward] himself. Furthermore, the kings of the Scots, and the realm, have not been under any other than the kings of England; and the kings of England have not answered, nor ought to answer for their rights in the aforesaid realm, or for any their temporalities before any judge ecclesiastical or secular, by reason of free pre-eminence of the state of their royal dignity, and custom kept without breach at all times. Wherefore, after treaty had, and diligent deliberation of the contents in your aforesaid letters, this was the common agreeing and consent with one mind, and shall be without fail in time to come, by God's grace: that our aforesaid lord the king ought by no means to answer in judgment in any

A letter of the lords temporal to the pope.

Edward I. A.D. 1301.

case, nor should bring his aforesaid right into doubt, nor ought to send any proctors or messengers to your presence: especially seeing that the premises tend manifestly to the disinheriting of the right of the crown of England, and the plain overthrow of the state of the said realm, and also hurt of the liberties, customs, and laws of our fathers; for the keeping and defence of which we are bound by the duty of our oath made, and we will maintain them with all power, and will defend them, by God's help, with all strength. And further, we will not suffer our aforesaid lord the king to do, or by any means to attempt the premises, being so unaccustomed, unwont, and not heard of before. Wherefore, we reverently and humbly beseech your holiness that ye would suffer the same our lord, king of England, who among other princes of the world, showeth himself catholic and devout to the Romish church, quietly to enjoy his rights, liberties, customs, and laws aforesaid; without all impairing and trouble, and let them continue untouched. In witness whereof we have set our seals to these presents, as well for us, as for the whole commonalty of the aforesaid realm of England. Dated at Lincoln, in the year of our Saviour 1301, and in the twenty-eighth of Edward I.

A.D. 1302. The pope setteth king against king.

The year following (A.D. 1302), the said pope Boniface, the eighth of that name, taking displeasure with Philip the French king, excited king Edward of England to war against him, promising him great aid thereunto. But he (as mine author saith) little trusting the pope's false unstable affection toward him well proved before, put him off with delays.[1] Whereupon, the French king fearing the power of king Edward, whom the pope had set against his friendship, restored unto him again Gascony, which he wrongfully had in his hands detained. Concerning this variance here mentioned between the pope and the French king, how it began first, and to what end it fell out, the sequel hereof (Christ willing) shall declare, after I have finished the discourse begun between England and Scotland.

Another Scottish rebellion suppressed.

In this year the aforesaid William Wallace, who had done so many displeasures to the king before, continuing still in his rebellion, gathered great multitudes of the Scots to withstand the king, till at length in the year following he was taken, and sent up to London, and there executed for the same. After this, the king held his parliament at Westminster, whither came out of Scotland the bishop of St. Andrews, Robert Bruce above mentioned, the earl of Dunbar, the earl of Arles, and sir John Comming,[2] with divers others, who voluntarily were sworn to be true to the king of England, and to keep the land of Scotland to his use against all persons. But shortly after the said Robert Bruce, who, as is said, married the second daughter of earl David, forgetting his oath before made unto the king, within a year or two after this, by the counsel of the abbot of Stone and the bishop of St. Andrews, sent up unto pope Clement V., for a dispensation of his oath made; insinuating to him, that king Edward vexed and grieved the realm of Scotland wrongfully; whereupon the pope wrote unto the king to leave off such doings. Notwithstanding this inhibition to the pope, the king, prosecuting his own right, after he had understanding of the doings of the Scots and of the mischief of Robert Bruce who had slain with his own hands sir John Comming, for not consenting with him and other lords at his parliament, arrayed his power and strength of men, preparing himself toward Scotland; where, joining with the said sir Robert and all his power of Scotland in a plain, near unto St. John's Town, he put him to flight, and so chased the Scots, that of them were slain to the

The pope dispenseth with due and true obedience of subjects towards their prince.

The pope's inhibition neglected in England.

Another rebellion of the Scots.

(1) Ex Rob. Avesbury. (2) "Comming," or Comyn.—Ed.

number of seven thousand. In that victory, such bishops and abbots as were taken he sent to the pope; the temporal lords and other Scots he sent to London, &c. Sir Robert Bruce, after this discomfiture, when he had thus lost both the field and his chief friends, seeing himself not able to make his party good, fled into Norway, where he abode during the time that king Edward lived. When this noble Edward had thus subdued the Scots, he yielded thanks to God for his victory, and so setting the land at rest and in order, he returned unto London; which was in the thirty-fifth and last year of his reign. A.D. 1307.

Edward I. A.D. 1307.

Again subdued

Now to return to that which I promised before touching the variance and grievous dissension between Philip the French king and pope Boniface VIII. After the bishopric of Rome had been long void through the dissension of the cardinals, for the space of two years and three months; at length pope Celestine was chosen successor to pope Nicholas IV. This Celestine, in his first consistory, began to reform the clergy of Rome, thinking to make it an example to all other churches; wherefore, he procured to himself such hatred among his clergy, that this Boniface, then called Benedict, speaking though a reed in his chamber wall, nightly admonished him, as it had been a voice from heaven, that he should give over his papacy, as being a burden bigger than he could wield.

A.D. 1292 to 1307.

A grievous variance between Philip and Boniface

This pope Celestine after he had sat six months, by the treachery and falsehood of this Boniface was induced to give up and resign his bishopric, partly for the voice spoken of before, partly for fear; being told by certain craftily suborned in his chamber, that, if he did not resign, he would lose his life; who, then, after his resignation, going to live in some solitary desert, being a simple man, was vilely taken and thrust into perpetual prison by pope Boniface, craftily pretending that he did it not for any hatred to Celestine, but that seditious persons might not have him as their head to raise up some stir in the church; and so he was brought to his death.[1] Wherefore, this Boniface was worthily called the eighth Nero; of whom it was rightly said, he came in like a fox, reigned like a lion, and died like a dog.

Pope Celestinus V

Crafty juggling among popes and cardinals.

The eighth Nero

This pope Boniface succeeding (A.D. 1294), or rather invading after Celestine, behaved himself so imperiously, that he put down princes, and excommunicated kings, who did not take their confirmation at his hand. Divers of his cardinals he drove away for fear; some of them as schismatics he deposed and spoiled of all their substance. Philip, the French king, he excommunicated, for not suffering his money to go out of the realm; and therefore cursed both him and his to the fourth generation. Albert, the emperor, not once or twice, but thrice sought at his hands to be confirmed, and yet was rejected, neither could succeed, unless he would promise to drive the French king out of his realm. In the factious discord in Italy between the Guelphs and Ghibellines, which the part of a good bishop had been to extinguish, so little he helped to quench the smoke, that he of all others was the chiefest firebrand to increase the flame; insomuch that upon Ash Wednesday, when Porchetus, an

Mischief done by pope Boniface

Guelphs and Ghibellines, two factions in Rome

(1) Ex Massæo

Edward I. A.D. 1303 to 1307.

archbishop, came and kneeled down before him to receive his ashes, pope Boniface looking upon him, and perceiving that he was one of the Ghibellines' party, cast a handful of ashes in his eyes, saying, "Memento, homo, quod Gibellinus es," &c. That is, "Remember, man, that a Ghibelline thou art, and to ashes thou shalt go." This pope, moreover, first ordained the jubilee at Rome, in the solemnizing whereof on the first day he showed himself in his Pontificalibus, and gave free remission of sins to as many as came to Rome out of all parts of the world. The second day (being arrayed with imperial ensigns) he commanded a naked sword to be carried before him, and said with a loud voice; "Ecce potestatem utriusque gladii," that is, "Lo! here the power and authority of both the swords."

Jubilee first begun in Rome.

The pope claimeth and practiseth the power of both swords.

From that very year, as most stories do record, the Turks do begin the first count of their Turkish emperors, whereof the first was Ottoman, as you shall hear discoursed hereafter by God's grace in the history of the Turks.

Pope Boniface VIII. author of the book of decretals.

By this said pope Boniface, divers constitutions and extravagancies of his predecessors were collected together, with many of his own newly added thereto, and so made the book called "Sextus decretalium," &c. By him also first sprang up pardons and indulgences from Rome.

These things premised of Boniface the pope, now will I come to the occasion of the strife between him and the French king. Concerning which, first I find in the history of Nicholas Trivet, that, A.D. 1301, the bishop of Oppanuham, being accused of a conspiracy against Philip the French king, was brought up to his court, and committed to prison. The pope, hearing this, sendeth word to the king by his legate to set him at liberty. The French king, not daring to the contrary, looseth the bishop; but when he had done that, he dischargeth both the bishop and the legate, commanding them to leave his realm, whereupon pope Boniface revoketh all the graces and privileges granted either by him or his predecessors before to the kingdom of France; also, not long after he thundered out the sentence of his curse against him; and, moreover, cited all the prelates, all divines, and lawyers both civil and canon, to appear personally before him at Rome, at a certain day, which was the first of November. Against this citation the king again provided, and commanded by strait proclamation, that no manner of person should export out of the realm of France either gold, or silver, or any other manner of ware or merchandise, upon pain of forfeiting all their goods, and their bodies at the king's pleasure; providing withal, that the ways and passages should be diligently kept, that none might pass unsearched. Over and besides, Philip defeated the pope by giving and bestowing prebends, and benefices, and other ecclesiastical livings, contrary to the pope's profit; for which cause, the pope writeth to the aforesaid king in form and effect as followeth:—

Philip, the French king, excommunicated.

Letter of Pope Boniface to Philip, King of France.

Boniface, bishop, and servant to God's servants, to his beloved son Philip, by the grace of God, king of France, greeting and apostolical blessing. Fear God, and observe his commandments. We will thee to understand, that thou art subject to us both in spiritual things and temporal, and that no gift of benefices or prebends belongeth to thee; and if thou have the keeping of any being vacant, that thou reserve the profits of them for the successors; but if thou have given away any, we judge the gift to be void, and call back, how far soever thou hast gone forward. And whosoever believeth otherwise, we judge them heretics.[1] Edward I. A.D. 1303 to 1307.

Unto this letter of the pope, king Philip IV. maketh answer again in manner and order as followeth:—

King Philip's Reply to Pope Boniface.

"Philip, by the grace of God, king of France, to Boniface, not in deeds behaving himself as pope, little friendship or none:—To Boniface, bearing himself for chief bishop, little health or none. Let thy foolishness know, that in temporal things we are subject to no man, and that the gifts of prebends and benefices, made and to be made by us, were and shall be good, both in time past and to come. And that we will defend manfully the possessor of the said benefices, and we think them that believe or think otherwise, fools and mad men.—Given at Paris, the Wednesday after Candlemas, A. D. 1301.

After these and other writings passing to and fro between the French king and the pope, within a year and a half after, the king summoneth a parliament, sending down his letters to his sheriffs and other officers, to summon the prelates and barons of the realm unto the said court of parliament, according to the tenor of the king's letters here following:—

The Summons of a Parliament by Philip the French King.

A.D. 1303. A parliament summoned by king Philip at Paris.

Philip, by the grace of God, king of France, &c. Whereas we would take counsel with the prelates, barons, and other our faithful subjects, about weighty matters and hard, and such as belong greatly to our right, and touching our honour and state, and the liberties and laws of this our realm, churches, and ecclesiastical persons, and would also go forward and proceed in the aforesaid matters according to their counsel: we command you, that ye diligently in our behalf require and straitly charge all the prelates in your bailiwick, and also all and singular abbots and priors of the same your aforesaid bailiwick (to certain of whom we have directed down our special letters for the same cause), that as they favour our honour, the good estate both of the realm, of themselves and of the church, they repair to us in their own persons, all lets and delays set aside, and all other business left off: showing to them, moreover, that we can judge none of them to be either to us faithful subjects, or friends to the realm, who shall fail herein, or withdraw themselves in the aforesaid business, counsels, and helps in time. Wherein, if peradventure any shall slack or refuse to resort and come toward us within eight days from the time of this charge given by you, or your commandment; then we require you to seize all his temporal goods in our hand, and so seized to hold them until you receive other commandment from us.—Given at Paris, the Monday before the Nativity of St. John Baptist, A. D. 1303.

A Declaration of Master William Nagareta, made against Pope Boniface VIII., with his Appellation also made at Paris, before the King and his Council in the Church of Paris.

The appeal of Nagareta made against pope Boniface VIII.

In the name of God, Amen. In the year of our Lord, 1303, indictione secunda, the 12th day of March, and the ninth year of the popedom of the most holy father the lord Boniface VIII., by God's providence pope, and in the presence of us common notaries and witnesses under written, the nobleman, Master William Nagareta knight, a worshipful professor of the laws, standing before the most excellent prince, the lord Philip, by the grace of God most noble king of France, spake with lively words, and gave in writing these things that follow:[2]—

(1) Ex lib. Stephan. Aufrefreril.

(2) Ex registro.

Edward I. A.D. 1303 to 1307.

There have been false prophets among the people, as there have been also among you false teachers, &c. St. Peter, the glorious prince of the apostles, speaking to us by the Spirit, told us things to come; that like as there were false prophets in former times, so there should come among you false teachers, bringing in sects of destruction, by which the way of truth shall be defaced, and covetously they shall make merchandise of you with feigned words; and further added, that such masters did follow the way of Balaam of Bosor, who loved the reward of wickedness, and had his bridled ass to correct his madness, which, speaking in a man's voice, did stop the foolishness of the prophet. All which things as they be showed to us by the greatest patriarch himself, your eyes see them fulfilled this day according to the letter. For there sitteth in St. Peter's chair the master of lies, causing himself to be called Boniface, that is, a well-doer, whereas he is notable in all kinds of evil doing, and so he hath taken to himself a false name; and where he is not a true ruler and master, he calleth himself the lord, judge, and master of all men. And coming in contrary to the common order appointed by the holy fathers, and also contrary to the rules of reason, and so not entering in at the door into the Lord's sheepfold, he is not a shepherd or hireling, but rather a thief and robber. For he (the true husband of the Romish church yet living) deceived him that was delighted in simplicity, and enticed him with feigned flatterings and gifts to let him have his spouse to be his wife, against the Truth, who crieth, "Those whom God hath coupled, let no man separate:" and at length, laying violent hands upon him, persuading him falsely that that thing which the deceiver said, came from the Holy Spirit, was not ashamed to join to himself with wicked practice that holy church, which is mistress of all churches, calling himself her husband, whereas he cannot be; for Celestine, the true Romish bishop, agreed not to the said divorce, being deceived by such great subtlety; nothing is so contrary to agreement as error and deceit, and as the man's laws bear witness of it, I need not to speak of his violence. But because the Spirit inspireth where he will, and he that is led by the Spirit, is not under the law; the holy universal church of God, not knowing the crafts of that deceiver, stumbling and doubting whether it came from the Holy Ghost that Celestine should leave off his government, and the sins of the people deserving it, for fear of a schism, suffered the aforesaid deceiver; although, according to the doctrine of our Lord, by his fruits he might be known, whether he came to the said authority by the Holy Ghost or otherwise: his fruits, as it is plainly here written beneath, are now manifest to all men, by which it is apparent to the world that he came not in by God, but otherwise; and so came not in by the sheepfold. His fruits are most wicked, and his end is death; and therefore it is necessary that so evil a tree, according to the Lord's saying, should be cut down and cast into the fire. This cannot avail as his excuse, which is said by some men, that the cardinals did agree upon him again, after the death of the said Celestine the pope, seeing that he could not be her husband, whom it is manifest he had defiled by adultery, her first husband yet living, and she being worthy to have the promise of marriage kept unto her. Therefore, because that which is done against the Lord turneth to the wrong of all men, and especially to so great a mischief, by reason of the consequence, in that she is judged by the people both a woman adulterous or defamed, I, like a bridled ass, by the power of the Lord, and not by the voice of a mere man, being not able to bear so great a burden, take in hand to rebuke the madness of the said false prophet Balaam, who, at the instance of king Balak, that is, of the prince of devils, whom he serveth, is ready to curse the people blessed of the Lord. I beseech you, most excellent prince, and lord Philip, by the grace of God king of France, that like as the angel of God in time past met in the way, with a sword drawn, the prophet Balaam going to curse God's people; so you, who are unwilling to execute justice, and therefore are like the angel of the Lord, and the minister of power and office, would meet with a naked sword this said wicked man, who is far worse than Balaam, that he perform not that evil which he intendeth to the people.

An invective against placing Boniface VIII. in the papal see.

The pope well compared to Balaam who was wont to curse God's people for reward of money.

Articles propounded against pope Boniface.

1. I propound that the aforesaid man, who nameth himself Boniface, is no pope, but wrongfully keepeth the seat which he indeed hath, to the great damage of all the souls of God's holy church. I say also, that this entering was in many ways faulty, and that he entered not in at the door, but otherwise; and, therefore, is to be judged a thief and a robber.

2. I propound also, that the said Boniface is a manifest heretic, and utterly cut off from the body of the holy church, because of many kinds of heresies, which are to be declared in convenient time and place.

3. I propound also, that the said Boniface is a horrible simoniac; and such a one as hath not been since the beginning of the world: and the mischief of this sin in him is notorious to all the world (which thing is manifest to all that will plainly understand), insomuch that he, being openly slandered, said openly, "that he could not commit simony."

4. I propound also, that the said Boniface, being wrapt in infinite, manifest, and heinous sins, is so hardened in them, that he is utterly incapable of being corrected; and that he lieth in dungeon of mischief so deep, that he may not be suffered any longer without the overthrow of the state of the church. His mouth is full of cursing, his feet and steps are swift to shed blood. He utterly teareth in pieces the churches, which he ought to cherish; wasting wickedly the goods of the poor, and making much of wicked men that give him rewards; persecuting the righteous, and among the people not gathering but scattering, bringing in new sects of destruction that have not been heard of; blaspheming the way of truth, and, by robbery, thinking himself equal to the Lord Jesus Christ, who is blessed for ever. And he, being most covetous, thirsteth for gold, coveteth gold, and by some device getteth gold of every people, and utterly disregarding the worshipping of God, with feigned words, sometimes by flattering, sometimes by threatening, sometimes by false teaching; and only to get money withal, he maketh merchandise of us all, envying all things but his own; loving no man, nourishing war, persecuting and hating the peace of his subjects. He is rooted in all unspeakable sins, contending and striving against all the ways and doctrines of the Lord: he is truly that abomination of the people, which Daniel, the Lord's prophet, described.

The nature of this pope, and all popes by his lineage painted out.

The pope thinketh himself equal with Christ.

Therefore I answer, that laws, weapons, and all the elements, ought to rise against him, who thus overthroweth the state of the church; for whose sins God plagueth the whole world. And, finally, nothing remaineth to him, being so unsatiable, to satisfy him withal; but only the insatiable mouth of hell, and the fire that cannot be quenched, continuing for ever. Therefore, seeing that in a general council it so becometh, and I see this wicked man to be damned, who offendeth both God and all men, I ask and require as instantly as I can, and beseech you, my lord and king, that ye would declare these things to the prelates, doctors, people, and princes, your brethren in Christ, and chiefly to the cardinals and all prelates, and call a council; in which (when the aforesaid wicked man is condemned), by the worshipful cardinals, the church may be provided with a shepherd, and for that council I offer myself ready lawfully to pursue the aforesaid things. And whereas the said man, being in the highest dignity, in the mean time cannot be suspended by his superior; therefore, by the means aforesaid, he certainly ought to be taken and suspended for those things, seeing his state is called into judgment.

The pope the abomination of desolation.

I beseech and require the said cardinals by you, and I presently require them and the church of God, that this wicked man being put in prison, the church of Rome may be provided with a vicar, who may minister those things that shall appertain, until the church of God be provided with a bishop, utterly to take away all occasion of a schism. And, lest the said wicked man should let and hinder the prosecuting thereof, I require these things of you, my lord king, affirming you to be bound to do this, for many causes: first, for the faith's sake; secondly, for your kingly dignity, to whose office it belongeth to root out such wicked men; thirdly, for your oath's sake, which ye made for the defence of the churches of your realm, which the aforesaid raviner utterly teareth in pieces; fourthly, because ye be the patron of the churches, and, therefore, ye are not only bound to the defence of them, but to the calling for again of their goods, which this man hath wasted; fifthly, ye, following the footsteps of your ancestors, ought to deliver your mother, the Romish church, from so wicked a band wherein by oppression she is tied and bound. I require that a public instrument may be made of these requests by the notaries, under the witness of the worshipful men that be here present.

These things were done and spoken, as is aforesaid, at Paris, in the king's house of Lupara. After this protestation of Master Nagareta,

Edward I. A.D. 1303 to 1307.

immediately ensued the appeal of the king, pronounced and published against the said Boniface, in form as followeth:—

The Appeal made by the French King and certain Nobles, Lovers of the Realm, against Pope Boniface VIII.

The appellation of the French king and nobles against pope Boniface VIII

In the name of God, Amen. In the year of our Lord 1303, indictione prima, the 13th day of June, and the ninth year of the popedom of Boniface VIII. By the tenor of this public instrument, be it unto all men known, that the most noble prince and lord, Philip, by the grace of God, king of France, the famous and reverend fathers in Christ, archbishops and bishops, religious men, abbots and priors here undernamed, in the presence of us common notaries hereunder written, especially called and required for this purpose, as it is contained in the subscriptions here under, the famous and noblemen, the lord Louis, son of the French king, Guido of St. Paul and John Drocem, earls, and William of Plesiano, lord of Vitenob., knight: moved, as they said, with a fervent faith, with affection of sincere love and zeal of charity to be showed to the holy Romish church, and having pity from their heart on their mother, the universal church, which, as they say, is oppressed dangerously under the rule of the said lord Boniface, and suffereth outrageous defacing and loss; and pitying the right faith, in which stands the salvation of souls, and which, alas! for pity, in their times miserably pineth away and perisheth for the lack of wholesome government of the church through all Christendom; and earnestly taking pains, as they say, for the repairing and enhancing of the catholic faith: especially, seeing it was necessary for the same church, for the foundation of the faith, and the health of the souls, that none should rule the fold of the Lord's flock, but the true and lawful shepherd; and, also, because the same church was the spouse of Christ that hath no spot or wrinkle, all error, offence, wickedness, and wrong, should be put away; and their salvation, peace, and quietness, through God's mercy, might be procured to the whole world, which they say, lieth in wars and darkness by the wicked deeds, cursed works, and hurtful examples of the said Boniface: they say and lay against the said Boniface heresy, and other divers horrible and accursed faults, wherein they affirm him to be entangled and commonly and notoriously reported; the king himself being present with archbishops, bishops, and other dignitaries and churchmen, assembled to treat of their own matters, and matters of their churches, besides barons, earls, and other noblemen, whose names are under written.

The said William propounded and objected against Boniface, swearing by the holy gospel of God, which he corporally touched, that he could prove all and every the premises to be true. And the said William of Plesiano swore further this oath, that he believed he could prove the premises, and that he would pursue to the full end against the said Boniface in the general council, where, when, and before whomsoever of right it ought to be done: requiring earnestly the said king, as a champion of the faith, and defender of the church; that for declaring of this truth to the praise of God's name, to the increase and promoting of the catholic faith, to the honour and wealth of the universal church, and of all christian people, and the congregation of the said general council, he would help and bestow his profitable labour, with soldiers and such like, for the love of men, and zeal to justice, because his kingly house was ever a ruler of the truth, and that he would earnestly require the archbishops, bishops, and other prelates, and that he would be effectually instant with them.

The earls and knights themselves besought earnestly many of the same prelates (as they were pillars of the church and the faith) that they would help and effectually bestow their labour to the calling and assembling of the said council by all ways and means lawful, according to the ordinances of the holy fathers, and decrees of the canons. But when the prelates heard and fully understood such objections, oppositions, and requests, as aforesaid; and considered that such a matter was not only most hard, but needed wise counsel, they departed out of the same place. But on the Friday following, the fourteenth day of the same month of June, the aforesaid lord king being present, and also the lords, archbishops, bishops, abbots, priors, and many witnesses hereunder written at the same time being present, and in the presence of us, common notaries here subscribed, and being especially called and required for this purpose: the aforesaid William of Plesiano, knight, said, propounded, affirmed, objected, and read; as was contained more fully in a certain paper which he held in his hand, whose tenor was after this sort:— *Edward I.* A.D. 1303 to 1307

The Protest of William of Plesiano, knight, against Pope Boniface VIII.

I, William of Plesiano, knight, say, propound, and affirm, that Boniface who now ruleth the apostolic see is a rank heretic in heresies, and by heresies: outrageous deeds, and wicked doctrines hereafter to be declared, which thing to be true, I believe I am able to prove; or else, such things as these shall sufficiently prove him a full heretic in a convenient place and time, and before whom of right this can or ought to be done. This thing I swear on the holy gospel of God presently touched by me.

1. That he believeth not the immortality of men, and of Christian souls, but thinking much like as the Sadducees did believe, that there is no everlasting life, and that men cannot get at length joy, but that all the lot and part of comfort and gladness is in this world: and by this means he affirmeth, that it is no sin for the body to live daintily in all dainties. And out of the abundance of this leaven, he was not ashamed to say and openly to confess, that he had rather be an ass, or a dog, or any other brute beast, than a Frenchman; which thing he would not have said, if he believed a Frenchman had a soul that could enjoy everlasting life. This thing he taught many men who acknowleged this at the point of death, and the common report goeth of him thus in these things.

Pope Boniface had rather be a dog than a Frenchman.

2. Also, he believeth not faithfully, that by the words ordained of Christ, and spoken over the host, after the fashion of the church by a faithful priest lawfully ordered, the body of Christ is there; and therefore it cometh to pass, that he giveth no reverence to it, no not a little, when it is lifted up by the priest; yea, he riseth not to it, but turneth his back to it, and makes himself and his seat to be honoured where he sitteth, rather than the altar where the host is consecrated; and he is commonly reported to do this.

3. Also, he is reported to say, that whoredom is no sin, no more than rubbing of the hands together, and thus commonly runs the voice and rumour.

4. Also, he said often, that to thrust down the king and Frenchmen, it it could not be otherwise done, he would overthrow himself, the whole world, and the whole church. And when he had said so, some that stood by said, "God forbid;" he answered, "God grant." And when good men that heard the words replied against him, that he should not say so, because the church of God and all Christian men should suffer great slander thereby, he answered, "I care not what slanders soever come, so that the Frenchmen and their pride be destroyed; for it is necessary that slanders and offences come."

5. Item, he re-called and allowed a book made by Master Arnold of Newton, containing and smelling of heresy, condemned by the bishop of Paris, and reproved by the masters of divinity, and burned openly by Boniface himself: and in the full consistory of cardinals being likewise reproved, condemned, and burned, yet he allowed it, being written again, and containing the same fault.

6. Item, that he might make the most damnable remembrance of him perpetual, he caused his images of silver to be set up in the church, by this means bringing men to idolatry.

7. Item, he hath a private devil, whose counsel he useth in all things, and through all things.

8. Item, he said once, that if all men were on one side, and he on another, they could not deceive him neither in law nor in deed: which thing could not be done except he used a devilish art; and of this he is openly reported.

9. Item, he is a witch, asking counsel of soothsayers both men and women; and thus he is commonly judged

10. Item, he said openly, that the Romish pope could not commit simony, which it is heretical to say: this is a sin reproved as well in the Old

Edward I. A.D. 1303 to 1307.

Testament as in the New, and generally in the holy councils. Also he is wont to make merchandise of prelates' livings, dignities, superiorities, and benefices (to the which holy orders be necessarily joined), and of absolutions and dispensations, like as usurers and merchants use to buy and sell common things in the market; and of this common rumour reports him.

11. Item, he hindereth with all his might among Christian men the special embassage of Christ, made to his own sons, saying, "Peace I leave to you," and soweth discord and wars; wherefore it was once said before him, that certain parties would friendly agree after a good sort, but he prevented the peace: and when the other party did humbly beseech him, that he would give license to agree, he said, he would not: yea, if the Son of God or Peter the apostle would come down to the earth and command him, he would say, "I will not believe thee."

12. Item, because the French nation (being manifestly a most Christian nation) followeth not his errors in the faith, he reckoneth and openly calleth all and every of them Paterniani.

13. Item, he is infected with a most horrible sin, and of this fault he is † most commonly and openly reported.

14. Item, he hath caused many murders of clerks to be done in his presence, commending them and rejoicing at their death: and if they were not deadly wounded at the first by his servants, as oft as he saw them smiting he said, "Smite!" "smite!" by which example many were slain.

15. Item, when he had condemned a certain nobleman, he forbad the sacrament to be given him at the point of death, he desiring it and being penitent, saying, "that the sacrament of penance was not necessary to salvation."

16. Item, he compelled certain priests to show unto him the confessions of men, and he afterwards published them openly, contrary to the will of them that were confessed, to their shame and confusion, and compelled them to redeem their sins; insomuch that once he deposed a certain bishop of Spain, for the faults that he confessed to a certain cardinal, confessing unto him a certain privy horrible fault under 'Benedicite,' and compelled the cardinal, against his will, to declare his confession; and yet afterwards he restored the same bishop again to his place for a little money. Wherefore he is thought to play the heretic in the sacrament of penance.

17. Item, he fasteth not on the fasting-days, nor Lent, but eateth flesh indifferently, and without cause suffereth his household and friends to eat, saying, "It is no sin:" doing in this thing against the general state of the holy church.

18. Item, he oppressed the order of the cardinals, and hath oppressed the order of black and white monks, of grey friars and preachers, and said oft, "that the world was destroyed by them, and that they were false hypocrites, and that good could never chance unto any that would be confessed to them, or who would be familiar with them, or would keep them in their house:" and he never said good word of any prelate, religious man, or clerk, but ever rebuketh and slandereth them, taking away their good name; and, to compel them to redeem their faults, he is glad of their accusations: and this is the common voice and report of him.

19. Item, of old time, he going about to destroy the faith, conceived a hate against the French king, even to the abhorring of the faith; because of the light of faith which is there, and because of the great witness and example of Christianity, which is and hath been there. And before he had this seat he is proved to have said, that if he were pope, he would overthrow all Christendom, rather than not overthrow and destroy the nation, which he calleth the pride of the French.

20. Also, it is reported that when the ambassadors of the king of England, in the name of the said king, did require and entreat for the tenth of the realm of England to be given him; he answered, "That he would not give them the tenth, but on this condition, that he would make war with them against the French king." And besides this, he is reported to have given great sums of money to certain persons, to cause that peace should not be betwixt the said kings. He himself also, with all his might, hath letted it, by messengers, letters, and other ways that he could, yea by giving bribes.

21. Item, he is reported also to have commanded Frederic who keepeth the isle of Sicily, that if he would betray Charles the king, and break the peace which he made and swore that he would keep with him, and would stir against the king, and kill the Frenchmen, that then he would give him aid, help, and counsel; and for so doing he would give and grant him the said kingdoms.

22. He confirmed also the king of Almain to be emperor, and said openly, that he did it to destroy the nation, which he calleth the pride of the Frenchmen, who say, that they are subject to none in temporal things; wherein, saith he, they lied on their own heads: declaring, moreover, that whosoever (yea if it were an angel from heaven) would say, that all kings of the world were not subject to the same king of Almain, he were accursed.

Pope Boniface an enemy to the Frenchmen,

23. Further, he brake the agreements of peace betwixt the king of Almain and the French king, in which either of them should have their own saved, and what encroachings soever had been on either side should be brought to a due state, and under an oath orderly given and taken: he is reported to have commanded the same king of Almain, that he should not keep these conditions of peace, but be an enemy, and go about to sow debate among christian men.

and to peace.

24. Item, it is openly reported, that the Holy Land was betrayed through his fault, and came to the enemies of God and of the faith; and that he suffered this for the nonst[1] and denied to give aid to the Christians who defended it; spending the treasures and money of the church, which should have been bestowed for that use as the patrimony of Christ, in persecuting faithful Christians and friends of the church; and, therewith, would enrich his friends.

25. Item, he is openly reported to use simony, not only in bestowing of benefices, but in giving of orders, and making dispensations. He hath set to sale all benefices of the church, and would bestow the church commonly on him that would offer most: and he made his servants prelates of the church, not for wealth of the faith, nor to thrust down infidels, but to oppress the faithful, and to enrich his kindred by the church goods, and with the patrimony of him that was crucified; and presumed to make them marquises, earls, and barons, and was not afraid to build them strong holds, rooting out and oppressing many noblemen and others.

26. Item, it is commonly reported, that he hath divorced many marriages lawfully made, to the contempt, hurt, and slander of many; and he did promote his nephew to a cardinalship, being married, unlearned, and altogether unworthy to live; and openly married one that was divorced, and compelled him to make a vow of chastity, and after that he is reported to have had two bastards by her, and so goeth the common rumour of him.

27. Item, it is commonly reported, that he handled ungently his predecessor Celestine of holy memory, leading an holy life (peradventure knowing in conscience that he could not forsake his popedom, and therefore Boniface himself had no lawful entrance to the see), and imprisoned him, and there quickly and privily caused him to die. And of this the common rumour and report is through all the world, that he caused many and great men living a regular life (who disputed of this, whether he might renounce the popedom or not) to be set in prison, and there to die.

Boniface a murderer of his predecessor.

28. Item, he is reported to have railed at religious persons leading a regular life without a reasonable cause to the world, to the slander of many.

29. Item, he is reported to have said, that he would within short time make all the Frenchmen either martyrs, or forsakers of their faith.

30. Item, it is commonly reported, that he seeketh not the health of the souls, but the destruction of them.

These things being propounded and read, the same William protested, said, declared, appealed, and added these words, reading them in writing.

I, William of Plesiano, knight, protest that I do not propound nor speak

The protestation.

(1) "For the nonst," for the purpose; designedly.—Ed.

Edward I. A.D. 1303.

the aforesaid things for any special hate of Boniface himself, for I hate not him, but his aforesaid evil deeds, nor do I seek his injury or slander, or any man's else: but I speak it of zeal for the faith, and for the devotion that I have to the holy church of God, and the holy Romish see; as well for those things that I have seen and heard of credible men of his doings, and by likely presumptions gathered of the aforesaid things, and many and divers other things to be declared in their due place and time. And I sware by the holy gospel of God (which I touch with my hand), that I believe him to be a rank heretic; and that I also believe that the aforesaid things, and such others, may prove against him such things as shall be sufficient to prove him a heretic, according to the state of the holy fathers. I swear also that I will pursue against him, by the laws, the aforesaid things in the general council that shall be assembled, in a place that shall be safe and sure for me, to the honour of God and increase of the christian faith, saving the right, honour, and state of the holy apostolical see, in all things. Wherefore, earnestly and with reverence I require you, my lord the king (to whom belongeth the defence of the holy mother the church, and the catholic faith, for of that ye shall make account in the last judgment), and you, my lords the prelates, who be the pillars of the faith, and who ought to be judges of the aforesaid things, together with other reverend fathers, the catholic prelates of the holy church, in the general council to be assembled; that ye would procure and take diligent pains that a general council may be gathered in a fit and safe place and convenient time, before which the aforesaid things may be propounded, brought forth, and proved, against the said Boniface, as is premised. And I earnestly also require you, my lord king, that ye would require the same prelates present and absent, in what country soever they be, or to whom it belongeth, and that ye would effectually induce them manfully to labour, and to require others faithfully, that the aforesaid council for the aforesaid matters might be gathered in such sort as is aforesaid. And because, so long as this is deferred to be proved, I suspect Boniface himself, lest he being angry and moved for the aforesaid things against me and my partakers, procurers, and helpers, my friends and familiars, should go about by some means to stay and stop my good purpose and theirs from going forward; therefore, by these writings before you my lord the king and divers prelates, and before your common notaries here present, I provoke and appeal to the said holy general council apostolic and catholic that shall be, and to the holy apostolic see, and to him and them to whom of right I may or ought; and I earnestly require, once, twice, and thrice, that testimonial letters may be given me from you; supposing myself, my followers, favourers, familiars, friends, procurators, and all them that will hereafter follow me, my goods and theirs, to be under the protection and keeping of St. Peter and St. Paul, and the said holy council to be assembled by the holy Romish see, and the catholic apostolic pope that shall be: sticking, nevertheless, and willing to stick, to the appellation and appellations, process and processes made hereupon by the nobleman, Master William of Nagareta, knight, inasmuch as they shall be found and made lawful, and yet not forsaking this present appellation.

Pope Boniface proved a heretic.

When these things were thus read and done, the king answered and required the prelates, provoking and appealing, and making request, provocation, and appellation, as is contained in the paper underwritten, both there and then with other prelates: all which things are more fully contained in these writings following, and were read to them that heard it, whose tenor is such:

The King's Answer, or the Appeal of Philip, the French King, from the Pope.

We, Philip, by the grace of God, hearing and understanding the objections propounded by our beloved faithful knight William of Nagareta, against Boniface, now having the regiment of the Romish church: although we would gladly cover with our own cloak the filthy parts of such a father; yet, for the love of the catholic faith, and great devotion that we bear to the holy Romish and universal church, our mother, and spouse of Christ, and to all faithful men, following the steps of our ancestors, who doubted not to shed their own blood for the increase and defence of the church's liberty and the faith; and coveting to provide for the purity of the faith and state of the church; as also to avoid the hurt of the general slander, being not able to pass over any longer the premises with winking and dissembling, and my conscience driving to the same; seeing this estimate and opinion of him in these matters is not rashly of us conceived, but vehemently and plainly increased by many and continual cryings of credible men, and great authority oft and oftentimes beaten into us; fearing, moreover, the destruction of the faith, both of us and of all other subjects, and specially of the kings and princes of the world, who ought to reprove negligence, who acknowledge that we have received power given us from the Lord, to the promoting and increasement of it; we agree to your requests in his behalf, and to the calling and assembling a council for the glory of God (saving the honour and reverence that is due to the holy Romish church in all things), whereby the truth may appear in the premises, and all error avoided; that the state of the universal church, and all Christianity, and matters of faith, and the Holy Land, may be provided for, and the slanders and jeopardies hanging over us may be withstood; we be ready, and offer ourselves gladly, as much as in us is, to bestow our labour and diligent pains thereabout; earnestly requiring and beseeching, in the merciful bowels of Jesus Christ, you archbishops and other prelates here present, as children of the church and pillars of faith, called of the Lord to the promoting, increase, and preserving thereof, to care for the same, that with all diligence ye would give heed, as becometh you, and effectually you would labour by all ways and fit means, to the calling and assembling of this council, at which we intend to be personally present. And lest the said Boniface, who hath boldly and wrongfully many times threatened to proceed against us, stopping and hindering our purposes and intent, lest any of his works of darkness, if there be any, should come to light, directly or indirectly hindering the calling and gathering of this council; or lest any state, being in the same realm, that will indeed proceed against us, or our state, churches, prelates, barons, and other faithful vassals, our subjects, our lands, or our realm, and the state of the realm, by abusing any spiritual sword, in excommunicating, suspending, or otherwise by any means for us and our well-willers, and them that will follow us, we provoke and appeal in writing to the aforesaid general council, which we instantly desire to be called, and to one lawful chief bishop that shall be, or to any other to whom we should appeal; and yet not going from the appellation made by William of Nagareta, to whom we sticked then, and also yet stick; requiring earnestly a witness of our appellation of you prelates and notaries, expressly to renew such provocation and appellation when and before whom it shall be thought meet to you.

Then the archbishops within written, bishops, abbots, and priors, answered the premises (as it is found in the acts) provoked and appealed, agreed to, and protested; and made provocation and appellation, agreement and protestation, as is contained more fully in a certain paper there openly and plainly read, whose tenor followeth, with these words:—

The Protestation of the Prelates.

We, archbishops of Nicosen, Remen, Senorem, Narbonem, Turonem, and bishops of Landviren, Belnacen, Catolacen, Antisiodorem, Meldimen, Nurmen, Carnotem, Aurelianen, Ambiaven, Mornen, Silanen, Andeganen, Abricen, Constant, Ebroicen, Lexonicen, Sagien, Caloromont, Lemonicen, Avicen, Masticoren; and we, abbots of Cluniack, Premonstraten, of the greater monastery of the court of St. Dionese, in France, the Camped St. Victors, St. Genoveve, St. Marten, Landinoen, Figiacem, and Belliccm in Lemocinio, and friar Hugh, visitor of the houses of the order of Knights of St. John of Jerusalem, in France, and the father prior of St. Martin's in the Field, hearing these things which were said, propounded, and objected yesterday and to-day by you the lords, earls, and William aforesaid, against the lord Boniface VIII. and pope; being moved with such sayings, purposes, assertions, and your oaths, your request, and other lawful causes, and compelled by need, considering that the matter of our faith, which is Christ's, is handled in the premises: we that be called to part of this care, to the defence and maintenance of the faith of the souls of the realm, although unworthy, yet coveting to withstand the jeopardies that hang over us by reason of the premises and other causes, thinking the calling and gathering of the said council profitable and necessary, that the innocency of the lord Boniface himself may clearly be discussed, as we desire (our consciences bearing witness) that it may be determined of him by the council, touching such things as are laid against him, and that what they decree may be done according to the canons. We answer you, our lord king, and you our lords, earls, and William, that (the honour and reverence of the holy Romish church saved in all points) we agree to your due request in this behalf for the calling of the council, and are ready to give help and diligent labour to the calling and gathering of the said council, according to the decrees of the holy fathers, and to the lawful orders of the canons: not intending, by any means, to make parties of this matter, nor to stick to any that maketh parties.

Yet, lest the said Boniface being moved or provoked by these things, as we fear, by likely conjectures and threatenings made against us for the aforesaid things, that he will proceed against our parish churches and our subjects by some means, or cause to proceed against us by some authority of his own or others, by excommunication, suspension, interdicting, deposing, depriving, or by some other means and colour sought to some impeachment or trouble of the said council; and that we may sit in the said council to judge and do all other things that belong to the office of prelates; that our friends that stick to us, and would stick to us in all things, may remain safe for ourselves, our parish churches, our subjects, and those that stick to us, or would stick to us in this behalf, we provoke and appeal in writing to the aforesaid council that is to be gathered, and to him that shall be the true and lawful highest bishop, and to him or them to whom of right we should appeal, and earnestly require our appellations; committing us, our parish churches, our subjects, friends, and those that stick to us, our state and theirs, our right and goods, to the godly defence of the aforesaid council, and of him that shall be true and lawful highest bishop; and we protest to renew this appellation, where, when, and before whom, it shall be thought meet.

This was done at Paris, at Lupara, in the chamber of the said lord our king, indictione prima, the ninth year of this popedom, on the Thursday and Friday aforesaid, these noblemen being present; the lords of Avia and Bologne, the lords Martin and other earls named before, Matthew Dotera, Peter the lord chamberlain, Philip the lord of Wirtmos, and Henry of Bologne, knight, and also Master Philip, archdeacon of Bengem, Nicholas, archdeacon of Remein, William, treasurer of Anjou, Philip Beaspeare, Rainold of Bourbon, and John Montagre, and many more, both clerks and others, specially required and called to be witnesses to this.

After these things thus in parliament decreed and agreed, the prelates of the clergy consulting with themselves what was to be done in so doubtful a matter, and dreading the pope's displeasure for this which was done already, to clear themselves in the matter, contrived among themselves a letter to the pope, partly to certify him what there was done, and partly also to admonish him what he should do: the tenor of which letter contained these words following:—

The Form of a Letter which the Prelates of France, as well secular as religious, sent to Boniface, that he should cease his enterprise, wherein he was proceeding against the King.

To the most holy father and their dearest beloved lord, the lord Boniface, the chief bishop of the holy Romish church, and the universal church, his humble and devout archbishops, abbots, priors, conventuals, deans, provosts, chapters, covents and colleges of the cathedral and collegiate churches, regular and secular, of all the realm of France, being gathered together, do offer most devout kissings of your blessed feet. *Edward I.*

We are compelled, not without sorrow of heart and bitter tears, to signify unto your holiness that the most famous prince our dear lord Philip, by the grace of God, the noble king of France, when he heard and saw the apostolic letters sealed which were sent to him of late on your behalf by the worshipful man, the cardinal of Narbo, your notary and messenger, and were presented by the same cardinal to him, and certain other of his barons: upon the sight and perusing of those so bloody letters being read and declared to them sitting by him, both our lord the king and the barons themselves were highly moved with great marvelling and trouble. Insomuch that the said our lord the king, by the advice of his barons, commanded to be called before him the other barons then absent, and us also; that is to say, all archbishops, bishops, abbots, priors, conventuals, deans, provosts, chapters, covents, and colleges, as well of cathedral or collegiate churches, regular and secular, and also all the universities and commonalties of the towns of his realm; that we prelates, barons, deans, provosts, and two of the most learned of every collegiate and cathedral church, should appear personally, and should procure the rest likewise to appear, by their stewards, officers, and sufficient proctors, with full and sufficient commission at the appointed place and time. Further, when we and the other ecclesiastical persons aforesaid, and also the barons, stewards, officers, and proctors, and other of the commonalty of the towns were thus called, and when, according to the form of the aforesaid calling, by the king's commandment, we stood before the king this Wednesday, the tenth of this present April, in St. Mary's church in Paris: our lord the king caused to be propounded openly and plainly to all men, that it was signified to him from you among other things, by the aforesaid cardinal and by letters, that his kingdom, which he and his ancestors hitherto do acknowledge they hold of God only, now ought in temporalities to be subject to you, and held of you; and that ye were not content with these so marvellous and strange words, and not heard of from the beginning of the world by any dwellers within the same realm, but that ye went about to put them in practice; and that ye called to appear before you the prelates of the said realm, and doctors of divinity, and such professors of both laws, as were born within the said realm, for the correcting and amending of such excesses, faults, arrogancies, wrongs, and harms, as ye pretend to be done to the ecclesiastical prelates and persons ecclesiastical, both regular and secular, abiding within the realm and elsewhere, by our lord the king himself and his officers or bailiffs, and by his peers, earls, barons, and other nobles, with the commonalty and people of the said realm: to the intent that, by this means, the aforesaid realm might be made strong with precious jewels and durable treasures, which are to be preferred before the bucklers or any armour of strong men, that is to say, by the wisdom of prelates, and wise men and others; through whose ripe faithful counsel and circumspect foresight, the realm might be ruled and governed, the faith established, the ecclesiastical sacraments ministered, and justice executed, which by their being robbed of their goods and riches, and utterly spoiled, is in a doubtful case, and in jeopardy of miserable decay, and of being for ever destroyed.

A. D. 1303.

Among these and divers other griefs, which have been done by you and the Romish church, to him, to his realm, and the French church, both in reserving and wilful ordering of archbishoprics, bishoprics, and bestowing of great benefices of the realm upon strange and unknown persons, yea, and oft upon suspected persons, never being at the churches or benefices aforesaid, by reason whereof the decay of God's worship hath ensued, the godly wills of the founders and givers are defrauded of their godly purpose: the accustomed almsgiving is withdrawn from the poor of the said realm, the impoverishing of the realm followeth, and churches run in danger to be defaced, while they remain destitute of service; the prophets being taken away, and the fruits of them that serve them being appointed in the commodity of strangers: and, while prelates have not to give, and to reward men for their deserts, noblemen, whose ancestors founded the churches, and other learned men, cannot have servants: and that, for these causes, devotion began to be cold, and there was none in these days that would stretch out a liberal hand towards the churches; and,

Edward I. A.D. 1303.

furthermore, by the premises an evil example was given. Also he complained of new taxes, of pensions newly laid on the churches, of immeasurable bondages, exactions, and divers extortions, with other prejudical and hurtful novelties, by which the general state of the church is changed, in giving suffragans, as helpers to the higher prelates, whereby neither the bishops themselves nor the suffragans can do their duties, but for them they must run with gifts to the apostolical see. He complaineth also of divers causes and some articles long since, but true in the time that they were presented, that were done, and be done continually: and also not purposing to suffer so great a disinheriting of him and his successors from the realm, and so manifest a grief, they could not suffer any longer the evident loss of the honour of him and the realm, and said, that he was certain that it was known to the whole world, that he did maintain in this matter a just cause, as he had learned by the unanimous sentence of doctors in divinity, and masters of both laws, that were born within his realm, and others who among the doctors and cunning men of the world were accounted of the learned sort and more famous. Therefore he required us, all and every one, both prelates and barons, and others, earnestly as our lord; he prayed and gently begged as a friend, to consult and take diligent pains, that he might ordain wholesome things, both for the keeping of their old liberty, the honour and state of the realm and of the inhabitants thereof, for the easing of the griefs aforesaid, for redressing of the realm and the French church, by our counsel and his barons, to the praise of God's name, the increase of the catholic faith, the honour of the universal church, and promoting of God's religion: especially seeing such griefs were done by his officers and others of the realm, to the churches and churchmen, for the which he purposed a remedy of wholesome correction, before the coming of the aforesaid cardinal, and would now have put it in execution effectually, but that he might be thought to have done that for fear, or at your commandment, which thing ye cannot ascribe to yourself. Furthermore, he would spend not only his goods, but also his realm, yea his children if the case required; and therefore we should take heed to be ready with counsel and help in season, as we are bound by the duty of fidelity in these things, wherein it is manifest, that as all and every man's case is handled, generally and particularly their case is promoted, and every man's own interest is touched. And then he demanded by and by to be answered plainly and finally in these things, of all and every one.

Then the barons sitting aside with the officers and proctors aforesaid, at length, after they had taken counsel, coming to our aforesaid lord the king, and praising greatly and heartily thanking him for his laudable purpose and good will, answered with one voice: That for those things they were ready not only to spend their goods, but offered the same goods, riches, and also their persons to death, and not to flee any kind of torment. And said further, with one voice, that if our aforesaid lord the king would (as God forbid) suffer, or else willingly pass over those things, they themselves would in no case suffer it.

Then, when answer was asked of us afterwards, although we desired longer respite of deliberation of the king himself, our lord, and of the greatest of the aforesaid barons; and that for this intent, that in the mean while the pope's letters might have come to our lord the king; we answered, that we would not offend against the liberty of the realm, nor by any means innovate things contrary to the king's honour in this behalf.

We went about also to inform him with many godly words, and earnest persuasions, and with many kinds of help, and by sundry ways to bring him to keep the special bond of unity, which is known to have continued to these present days betwixt the holy Romish church, and his predecessors. But when we were denied any longer delay, and it was plainly and openly told to all men, that if any man were of a contrary mind, from thenceforth he should be manifestly counted for an enemy of the king and the realm: we, considering warily, and seeing plainly, that except our lord the king, and the barons aforesaid, were content with our answer, besides other dangers and great offences, whereof there could neither be number nor end, the devotion both of the Romish and French church, and also the whole obedience of the laity and all the people, from thenceforth should be taken away without recovery; not without great fear and doubt, we therefore thought good to answer thus:—

That we would help our lord the king with due counsel and convenient help for the preserving of his person, and of his earthly honour, and the liberty and laws of the said realm, like as we were (certain of us) by the duty of allegiance bound to him, who hold of him dukedoms, earldoms, baronies, fees, and other noble parts of the said realm, by the form of the oath, as all others do: yet we made humble suit to the same our lord the king, that seeing we were bound to obey the pope's holiness and your holy feet, he would suffer us to go, according to the tenor of your aforesaid calling."

Edward I. A.D. 1304.

Then on the king's and barons' behalf followeth answer, that in no case they would suffer us to go out of the realm, and that by no means they would bear to be handled so dangerously, yea rather to be altogether wasted.

Then we, considering so great an anger, and trouble so jeopardous and so great that none could be greater, both of the king, the barons, and other lay people of the realm; and now knowing plainly, that the old enemy of peace, who goeth about from the beginning of his fall sowing of darnel, to break the unity of the church, by troubling of peace, would break charity, and infect the sweetness of good works with the poison of bitter envy; and would overthrow mankind utterly, and would trouble with wickedness the band of lovely unity and singular friendship, which hitherto have had a happy increase betwixt the Romish church and our lord the king, and his predecessors, and the realm, to the praise of the highest God, the increase of christian faith, and the setting forth of the honour of the church, of the king, and of the realm; and that now, alas! a door was open, to the lamentable breaking and pitiful separating of great offences to rise on every side; that dangers are attempted against churches and churchmen, to spoil their goods and riches, with jeopardy of life; and seeing that the laity now do abhor and utterly flee the obedience of clerks, utterly banishing them from their counsels and doings, and have taken courage to condemn the ecclesiastical censure and process: all which jeopardies, with other sundry and divers dangers, which neither tongue is able to tell, nor writing can declare, we, seeing at hand, thought good in this point of greatest necessity, to run with weeping voice and lamentable sighs to the circumspect wisdom of your holiness: beseeching your fatherly mildness, and humbly praying you, that some wholesome remedy may be provided in the premises, by which the sound profitable agreement and mutual love, which hath continued so long betwixt the church, the king, and the realm, might be maintained in that old sweet concord; the state of the French church might continue in godly and quiet peace; and that he would vouchsafe to foresee how to withstand the dangers and offences aforesaid, that we and our states may be provided for, by the aforesaid commandment of your calling, by the study of your apostolic wisdom and fatherly love. The Almighty preserve your holiness to his holy church a long time.

These things thus discoursed and done, then followed the year of our Lord 1304. In that year, about the nativity of our Lady, came a garrison of harnessed soldiers well appointed, sent partly by the French king, partly by the cardinals of Columna, whom the pope before had deposed, unto the gates of Arvagium, where the pope did hide himself, because he was born in the town. The captains of this army were one Schaira, brother to the aforesaid cardinals, and William de Longareto, high steward to the French king, who invading the pope's town, and finding the gates open, gave assault to the pope's frontier, where the pope with his nephew, a marquis, and three other cardinals were immured. The townsmen, seeing all their intent and strength to be bent against the pope, caused the common bell to be rung, and so, assembling themselves in a common council, ordained Adolphus, one of the chiefest rulers of the town, for their captain, who, unknown to them, was a great adversary to the pope. This Adolphus bringing with him Reginald de Supine, a great lord in Campania, and the two sons of John Chitan, a nobleman, whose

A.D. 1304. Pope Boniface besieged.

Edward I. A.D. 1304.

father the pope had then in prison; at length joined he with the French company against the pope, and so beset his palace on every side. And first, setting upon the palaces of the three cardinals, who were then chief about the pope, they rifled and spoiled all their goods. The cardinals, by a back door, hardly avoided their hands: but the pope's palace, through munition and strength of the marquis, was somewhat better defended. At length the pope, perceiving himself not able to make his party good, desired truce with Schaira and his company, which was granted from one till nine. During this time of truce, the pope privily sendeth to the townsmen of Arvagium, desiring them to save his life; which if they would do, he promised so to enrich them, that they should all have cause never to forget or repent their benefit bestowed. To this they made answer, excusing themselves, that it lay not in their ability to do him any good, for that the whole power of the town was with the captain. Then the pope, all destitute and desolate, sendeth unto Schaira, beseeching him to draw out in articles, wherein he had wronged him, and he would make him amends to the uttermost. Schaira to this maketh a plain answer, signifying to him again, that he should in nowise escape with his life, except upon these three conditions. First, to restore again the two cardinals of Columna his brethren, whom he had before deprived, with all others of their stock and kindred. Secondly, that after their restitution, he should renounce his papacy. Thirdly, that his body should remain in his power and custody. These articles seemed to the pope so hard, that in no case he would agree to them; wherefore, the time of truce expired, the captains and soldiers, in all forcible means bending themselves against the bishop, first fired the gates of the palace, whereby the army, having a full entrance, fell to rifle and spoil the house. The marquis, in hope of saving his life, and the lives of his children, yieldeth him to the hands of Schaira and the other captain; which when the pope heard, he wept and made great lamentation. After this, through windows and doors, with much ado they brast in at length to the pope, whom they treated with words and threats accordingly. Upon this, he was put to his choice, whether he would presently surrender his life, or give over his papacy. But this he denied stiffly to do, choosing rather to die for it, saying to them in his vulgar tongue, "Eccle col, eccle cape;" that is, "Lo! here my neck, lo! here my head:" protesting, that he would never while he lived renounce his popedom. Then Schaira went about, and was ready to slay him, but, by certain that were about him, he was stayed; whereby it happened that the pope received no harm, although divers of his ministers and servants were slain. The soldiers, who ranged in the mean time through all corners of the pope's house, did lade themselves with such treasure of gold, silver, plate, and ornaments, that the words of my author (whom I follow) do thus express it;[1] "For all the kings of the earth together were not able to disburse so much out of their treasure in a whole year, as then was taken and carried out of the pope's palace, and out of the palace of the three cardinals, and the marquis." Thus Boniface, bereaved of all his goods, remained in their custody three days,

Brought to a strait.

Three conditions put to him.

Here may all kings, by the French king, learn how to handle the pope.

Boniface chooseth rather to die, than to give over his popedom.

The excessive treasures of the pope's house noted.

(1) "Quod omnes reges mundi non possent tantum de thesauro reddere infra unum annum, quantum fuit de papali palatio asportatum, et de palatiis trium cardinalium, et marchionis."—Ex Robert Avesb.

during which space, they had set him on a wild unbroken colt, his face turned to the horse's tail, causing the horse to run course, while the pope was almost breathless. Moreover, they kept him so without meat, that he was thereby nearly famished to death. After the third day, the Arvagians and people of the town mustering themselves together, to the number of ten thousand, secretly brast into the house where the pope was kept, and slaying the keepers, delivered the pope by strong hand, who then, being brought into the middle of the town, gave thanks with weeping tears to the people for his life saved; promising, moreover, that forasmuch as he was out of all his goods, having neither bread nor drink to put in his mouth, God's blessing and his, to all them that now would relieve him with any thing, either to eat or drink. And here now see what poverty and affliction can work in a man. The pope before, in all his pomp and most ruffling wealth, was never so proud, but now he was as humble and lowly, so that every poor simple man, as mine author testifieth, might have a bold and free access to his person. To make the story short, the pope, in that great distress of famine, was not so greedy of their victuals, as they were greedy of his blessing. Whereupon, the women and people of the town came so thick, some with bread, some with wine, some with water, some with meat, some with one thing, some with another, that the pope's chamber was too little to receive the offering; insomuch, that when there lacked cups to receive the wine, they poured it down on the chamber floor, not regarding the loss of wine, to win the pope's holy blessing. Thus pope Boniface, being refreshed by the town of Arvagium, took his journey from thence, accompanied with a great multitude of harnessed soldiers to Rome, where he shortly upon the same, partly for the fear he was in, partly for famine, partly for sorrow of so inestimable a treasure lost, died. After whom succeeded Benedict XI., of whom these verses are written: "A re nomen habe, benedic, benefac, benedicte. Aut rem perverte, maledic, malefac, maledicte," &c. And thus have ye the whole story of pope Boniface VIII., author of the Decretals, which story I thought the more diligently to set forth, that all the Latin church might see what an author he was, whose laws and decretals so devoutly they follow.

A pretty handling of the pope.

The pope delivered out of prison.

What poverty and affliction can do in plucking down the pride of man.

Pope Benedict XI.

Now, after the long debating of this matter between the French king and pope Boniface, let us proceed in our English story. About this time, in the days of king Edward, the church of Rome began daily more and more to rise up, and swell so high in pride and worldly dominion, that hardly any king in his own country could do any thing but as the pope pleased, who both had and ruled all, in all countries, but chiefly here in England; as partly by his intolerable tallage and pillage, before signified, may appear, partly by his injunctions and commandments sent down, also by his donations and reservations of benefices and church livings, also in deposing and disposing such as him listed, in place and office to bear rule: insomuch, that when the king and the church of Canterbury, in their election, had chosen one Robert Burnell, bishop of Bath, to be archbishop of Canterbury, pope Boniface, of his own singular presumptuous authority, ruling the matter after his pleasure, frustrated

The king's election in his own realm frustrate.

Edward I. A.D. 1304.

J. Peckham archbishop of Canterbury.

A point of practice in the court of Rome.

Ecclesiastical persons exempted by the pope, for not paying tribute to the king.

The pope proceedeth against the manifest word, in setting the clergy free from the king's tributes.

their election, and trusted in another, named John Peckham: for among all others, this had always been one practice of the court of Rome, ever to have the archbishop of their own setting, or such one as they might be sure of on their side, to weigh against the king and others, whatsoever need should happen. To this John Peckham, pope Boniface directed down a solemn bull from Rome, as also unto all other quarters of the universal church, in which bull was contained and decreed, directly against the rule of scripture and christian obedience, that no church or ecclesiastical person should henceforth yield to his king or temporal magistrate either any giving, or lending, or promising of tribute, or subsidy, or portion whatsoever, of the goods and possessions to him belonging; but should be clearly exempted and discharged from all such subjection of tallage or subvention to be exacted of them in the behoof of the prince and his affairs. This decree manifestly rebelled against the commanded ordinance of God, and the apostolic canon of St. Peter, and all other examples of holy Scripture. For as there is no word in the Scripture that excludeth spiritual men more than temporal from obedience and subjection to princes, so if it chance that the prince in his exacting be too rigorous or cruel in oppression, that is no cause for the clergy to be exempted, but to bear the common burden of obedience, and to pray to God to turn and move the prince's mind, and so, with prayer and patience, not with pride and disobedience, to help and amend that which is amiss. Concerning the bull of Boniface, if any there be who do not credit the same that contains what I allege, or would for his own mind see and read the same, the words thereof follow below.[1]

This bull being directed, as it is said, from Rome to the archbishop of Canterbury, and likewise through the whole universal church, under the pope's authority, it chanced, not long after, that the king held

(1) *The Copy of the Pope's Bull, wherein the Clergy are exempted from giving Tribute to Kings and Princes.*—"Bonifacius, &c. Ad sempiternam rei memoriam. Clericis, laicos infestos oppido tradidit antiquitas. Quod et præsentium experimenta temporum manifeste declarant, dum suis finibus non contenti nituntur in vetitum et ad illicita sua frena relaxant, nec prudenter attendunt quomodo sit eis in clericos ecclesiasticasve personas, et bona interdicta potestas. Quinimo ecclesiarum prælatis, ecclesiis, ecclesiasticisque personis regularibus et secularibus imponuntur onera gravia, ipsos talliant, et eis collectas imponunt, et ab ipsius suorumque proventuum, vel bonorum dimidiam, decimam, seu vicesimam, vel quamvis aliam portionem, quotam exigunt et extorquent, eosque moliuntur multifarie subjicere servituti, suæque subdedere ditioni. Et quod dolenter referimus, nonnulli ecclesiarum prælati, ecclesiasticæque personæ trepidantes, ubi trepidandum non est, transitoriam pacem quærentes; plus timentes majestatem temporalem offendere, quam æternam, talium abusibus non tam temerarie, quam improvide acquiescunt, sedis apostolicæ authoritate non obtenta. Nos igitur talibus actibus obviare volentes, de fratrum nostrorum consilio[1] apostolica authoritate statuimus; quod quicunque prælati, ecclesiasticæve personæ, vel seculares, quorumcunque ordinum, conditionis, seu status, collectas vel tallias, dimidiam, decimam, vicesimam, seu centesimam suorum et ecclesiarum suarum proventuum vel bonorum laicis solverint, vel promiserint, vel se soluturos excesserint, aut quamvis aliam quantitatem, portionem, aut quicquam ipsorum proventuum, vel bonorum æstimationem, vel valorem ipsorum, subventionis, subsidii, vel doni nomine, seu quovis alio timore, vel modo, vel quæsito colore absque autoritate sedis ejusdem: necnon imperatores, reges, seu principes, duces. seu comites, vel barones, potestates, capitaneas, officiales vel rectores quocunque nomine censeantur, civitatum castrorum, seu quorumque locorum constitutorum ubilibet et quis[2] alius cujuscunque præeminentiæ, conditionis et status, qui talia imposuerint et exegerint, vel receperint, aut apud ædes sacras deposita ecclesiarum vel ecclesiasticarum personarum ubilibet[2] arrestaverint, saysierint seu occupare præsumpserint, vel arestari, saysiri, aut occupari mandaverint, aut[3] occupata, saysita, seu arestata receperint: necnon omnes qui scienter in prædictis dederint consilium, auxilium, vel favorem, publice vel occulte, eo ipso sententiam excommunicationis[4] incurrunt. Universitates quoque quæ in his culpabiles fuerint ecclesiastico supponimus interdicto: prælatis, et personis ecclesiasticis supradictis, in virtute obedientiæ, et sub pœna depositionis districte mandantes, ut talibus absque licentia expressa dictæ sedis nullatenus acquiescant. A supradictis autem excommunicationis et interdicti sententiis nullis absolvi valeat, præterquam in mortis articulo absque sedis apostolicæ authoritate et licentia speciali," etc.—Ex Chron. Rob. Gisburnensis.

The Author's notes upon the same.

1. Apostolica authoritas frustra obtenditur, ubi apostolica scriptura contemnitur.
2. Quivis, pro quisquis, barbarismus apostolicus.
3. Flores Attici ex ipso Helicone desumpti, ἑτέρωσις Rhetorica.
4. Tauri cornu, wear the bull's horn.

his parliament at St. Edmundsbury, where was granted to him of all cities and boroughs an eighth, and of the commons a twelfth of their goods; only the clergy, by virtue of this bull, stood stout, denying to pay any thing to the king. This answer not well pleasing the king, he willeth them to deliberate better with themselves upon the matter, and, after long advisement, to give him an answer against the next parliament, which should be holden the next Hilary Term at London.

In conclusion, the parliament being assembled, the clergy persisted still in the denial of their subsidy, alleging the pope's bull for their warrant and discharge; whereupon the king likewise secludeth them from under his protection and the safeguard of his laws. And as concerning the archbishop of Canterbury, above mentioned, because he was found more stubborn than the rest, and was the inciter to the others, he seized upon all his goods, and caused an inventory of the same to be enrolled in the exchequer. Notwithstanding, divers of the other bishops relented soon after to the king, and contributed the fifth of their goods unto him, and were received again into favour.

Secluded from the king's protection.

The archbishop of Canterbury's goods confiscated.

In the life of this king's father, it was declared how the said king Henry III., after divers wars and commotions had with his barons, had granted certain liberties and freedoms written and contained in 'Magna Charta,' and in 'Charta de Foresta.' Concerning which matter, much business happened in this king's days also in the realm, between the king and his barons and commons. The occasion was this: A pack of wool which before paid but a mark to the king, was now by this king raised up to forty shillings. After this the king having to make a journey into Flanders, sent to his barons and divers others to give attendance, and service in the same, which they refused and denied to do. The king, notwithstanding, persisted in his purpose, and with such a power as he had, prepared toward his journey. On his way, at Winchelsea, the aforesaid earls, barons, and commons, sent him certain petitions contained in writing, under the names of the archbishops, bishops, abbots, and priors, and the earls and barons, with the commonalty of the realm. Therein, first, lamenting and complaining of their afflicted state and misery, after an humble manner they desired their lord the king to redress and amend certain grievances among them. And first, they declared in the name of the whole commons, that the premonitions or writs directed to them for their attendance upon his grace into Flanders, were not sufficient; for that there was no certain place in the said writs specified unto them, whither to come for making their provision, and preparing money and other things according to the same. And if the place had been to them signified, yet, because none of their ancestors ever served the king over into Flanders before, the commons therefore thought themselves not bound to any service in that country. And albeit they had been so bound thereunto, yet they were not able to do it, being so heavily oppressed with so many tallages, taxes, tolls, customs, and such prices of corn, oats, tin, wool, leather, oxen, kine, flesh, fish, &c.: and besides all this, having no penny of wages given them to relieve their charges. Over and besides the lack of the king's wages not paid them, their own poverty, like a heavy burden,

Variance between king Edward and his barons and commons.

Petitions of the barons and commons to the king.

Edward I. A. D. 1304.

did so miserably lie upon them, that some of them had no sustentation, some of them were not able to till their own ground. They alleged, moreover, that they were not now handled after the old laws and customs of the land, as their ancestors were wont to be. Many also found themselves grieved in that they were not used according to the articles contained in 'Magna Charta;' and again that the 'Charta de Foresta' was not observed nor kept, as it was wont to be. Wherefore most humbly they beseeched the king, both for his own honour and for the wealth of his people, that of these things they might find redress. For the custom, moreover, of wool, the whole commons bewailed to the king their grief, in that for every pack of wool there was fined to the king forty shillings, and for every sack of combed wool, seven marks; the which wool of England, as it doth rise up to the value of half the realm, so the toll of the same amounteth to the fifth part of the valuation of the whole land. And because, therefore, the commons wished the honour and preservation of their king (as they were bound to do), they thought it not good for his grace to sail over to Flanders, unless he had better assurance of their fidelity, especially at that time when the Scots were so busy; who, if they began to rebel, he being at home in his land, much more were they like to stir, he being abroad out of the land. And that, not on account of the Scots only, but also because the like peril was to be apprehended of other foreign nations and kingdoms, which as yet were in no firm peace with England.

Magna Charta. Charta de Foresta. Custom for wool.

To these petitions, the king said that he could as yet make no resolute answer, for that some of his council were gone over already to Flanders, some were in London. Notwithstanding, on his return from Flanders, which he trusted should be speedy, they should hear his answer, and know more of his mind concerning the same. In the mean time this he required of them, to keep good rule at home, while he was abroad. What answer the king had minded to make them at his return, it is uncertain, which peradventure had turned to a bloody answer, but occasion served otherwise, and turned all to agreement; for the Scots, with their captain, William Wallace, above specified, in the mean time, the king being absent, invaded the realm with such violence, that prince Edward, the king's son, who was left to rule in his father's stead, was forced to assemble a parliament, and to call for the earl of Hereford, the earl of Norfolk, high marshal of England; the earl of Essex, high constable; with other earls, barons, knights, and esquires, to entreat peace and concord between his father and them. On their coming up to London, with fifteen hundred well-armed soldiers, and obtaining the gates of the city with their own men, they fell at length to agreement with the prince, upon composition to have the articles of 'Magna Charta,' and of 'Charta de Foresta,' confirmed; and that, by his means and mediation, they might be assured of the king's displeasure to be removed from them. The aforesaid articles of 'Magna Charta,' with the other articles affixed, here follow.

The king's answer to the petitions of the barons and commons.

Articles contained in Magna Charta.

First, No tallage or subsidy by the king or his heirs to be imposed or levied hereafter within the realm of England, without the common assent of the archbishops, bishops, abbots, and other prelates, earls, barons, knights, burgesses, and commons of the realm.

Item, No taker or servitor of the king, or of his heirs, henceforth, within this realm, to take grain, wool, leather, or any goods of any man, without the will and consent of the owner. *Edward I. A.D. 1304.*

Item, No taking to be hereafter, under the name of tribute, for any pack of wool.

Item, To be granted by the king and his heirs after him, both to the clergy and laity of this realm, to have and to enjoy their laws, liberties, and customs, in as ample manner as they were wont at any time heretofore.

Item, If any decrees or statutes shall hereafter be made and set forth contrary to these aforesaid articles, the same to be void and of no effect for ever.

Besides these articles, in the same composition was also contained, that all grudge and displeasure between the king and barons for not going to Flanders ceasing, the earls and barons might be assured to be received again into the king's favour. *Agreement between the king and his barons.*

These things thus agreed upon, and also by mediation of the prince confirmed and sealed with the king his father's seal, all the variance was pacified, to the great comfort of the people, and no less strength of the realm against their enemies; and most chiefly to the commendation of the gentle and wise nature of the king, who, as he was gentle in promising his reconcilement with his subjects, so no less constant was he, in keeping that which he had promised. *Good nature of king Edward.*

After the death of John Peckham, archbishop of Canterbury, above mentioned, who in the parliament had resisted the king in the right of certain liberties pertaining to the crown, touching patronages and such church matters, succeeded Robert Winchelsey, with whom also the king had like variance, who accused him to the pope for breaking the peace, and taking part with them that rebelled against the king about usages and liberties of the realm. Wherefore the king being cited up to the court of Rome, and there suspended by means of the said archbishop, directed his letters again to the pope, taken out of the parliament rolls, where I find divers letters of the king to pope Clement, against the said Robert, archbishop of Canterbury, the contents whereof here follow in substance. And as this king was troubled in his time with both the archbishops, John Peckham, and also Robert Winchelsey; so it happened to all other kings for the most part, from the time of Lanfranc (that is, from pope Hildebrand), that every king in his time had some business or other with that see. As William Rufus and Henry I. were troubled with Anselm; Henry II. with Thomas Becket; king Richard and all England with William, bishop of Ely, the pope's legate; king John with Stephen Langton; king Henry III. with Edmund the archbishop, called St. Edmund;[1] likewise this king Edward I., with John Peckham and Robert Winchelsey aforesaid; and so other kings after him, with some prelate or other: whereby ye may understand, how and about what time the church of Rome, which formerly was subject to kings and princes, began first to take head above and against kings and rulers, and so hath kept it ever since. *Robert Winchelsey, archbishop of Canterbury. The king troubled with two archbishops of Canterbury. The church of Rome and Romish prelates set against kings and rulers. Kings of England commonly troubled with archbishops of Canterbury.*

By this John Peckham, above mentioned, it was ordained, that no spiritual minister should have any more benefices than one, which also was decreed by the constitutions of Octo and Octobonus, the pope's legates at that time in England. *Priests to have but one benefice.*

About the beginning of this king's reign, after the decease of

(1) Polychron, lib. vii.

Edward I. Walter, archbishop of York, William Wicewanger succeeding in that see, and minding to go on visitation, came to Durham, to visit the church and chapter there; but the clergy and the people of the city shut the gates against him, and kept him out, whereupon rose no small disturbance. The archbishop let fly his curse of excommunication and interdiction against them. The bishop of Durham again, with his clergy, despised all his cursings, grounding themselves upon the constitution of Innocent IV., 'De censibus et exactionibus:' and so they appealed to Rome, saying, That he ought not to be received there, before he had first begun to visit his own chapter and diocese, which he had not done; for the words of the constitution were—"We ordain and decree, that every archbishop that will visit his province, first must procure to visit his own church, city, and diocese."

A.D. 1304.

Variance between the archbishop of York and the clergy of Durham.

Inquisition made against ill rulers and false officers.

Among other things in this king that may be noted, this is not to be passed over; that where complaint was made to him of his officers, as justices, mayors, sheriffs, bailiffs, eschetors, and such other, who, abusing their offices, extortioned and oppressed the king's liege people otherwise than was according to right and conscience; the said king, not suffering such disorder to be unpunished, did appoint certain officers or inquisitors, to the number of twelve, which inquisition was called 'Traibaston,' or 'Trailbastoun;' by means of which inquisition divers false officers were accused, and such as were offenders were either removed from their place, or forced to buy again their office at the king's hand; to their no small loss, and great gain to the king, and much profit to the commonwealth.

Trailbastoun.

In the chronicle of Robert of Amesbury, it is recorded of the said king, that he being at Amesbury to see his mother, who was then in that monastery professed, there was a certain man who feigned himself blind a long time, brought to the presence of the said Elenor the king's mother, saying how that he had his sight restored at the tomb of king Henry, her late husband, insomuch that she was easily persuaded that the miracle was very true. But king Edward, her son, knowing the man a long time to be a vile dissembler, and a wicked person, used to lying and crafty deceiving, persuaded his mother not to give credit to the vile vagabond, declaring that he knew so well of the justice of his father, that, if he were alive, he would rather twice pluck out both his eyes, than once restore him one. Notwithstanding, the queen his mother, remaining still in the former fond persuasion, would hear or believe nothing to the contrary, but was so in anger with her son, that she bid him depart her chamber; and so he did. By the example whereof may easily be conceived, how and after what sort these blind miracles in those days, and since, have come up among the blind and superstitious people; for had not the king here been wiser than the mother, no doubt but this would have been extolled as a miracle, and perchance king Henry have been made a saint.

A false miracle well spied out by the king.

A true miracle.

But as this was a feigned miracle, and false no doubt, so, in the same author,[1] we read of another sort of miracle, sounding more near the truth, and so much the more likely, for that it served to the conversion unto christian faith, to which use all true miracles do

(1) Robert of Amesbury.

properly appertain. The miracle was this: In the last year of this king's reign, Cassanus, king of the Tartars (of whom come those whom we now call Turks) fighting against the Soldan, king of the Saracens, in the plain of Damascus, slew of them a hundred thousand; and again at Babylon, fighting with the said Soldan, he slew him in the field, and two hundred thousand of his Saracens, calling, himself, upon the help of Christ; and thereupon he became Christian. This Cassanus, I say, had a brother a pagan, who being in love with the daughter of the king of Armenia, a christian woman, desired of her father that he might marry with her. Whereunto the king her father would not agree, unless he promised to be a Christian. Notwithstanding, the other being stronger in power, and threatening to get her by war; the king at length was forced to agree. In conclusion, it happened that a child being born betwixt them, it was overgrown and all rough with hair, like the skin of a bear. The child being brought to the father, he commanded it to be thrown into the fire and burned, but the mother, desiring first to have it baptised, caused all things thereunto to be prepared. The infant being three times plunged in water, after receiving the sacrament of holy baptism, incontinently was altered and turned from all his hairy roughness, and appeared as fair and smooth-skinned as any other; the which, when the father had seen and beheld, he was christened himself, and all his house.

Victory against the Saracens.

In the reign of this king, Walter Merton, bishop of Rochester, built Merton College, Oxford. In the same reign also lived Henry of Gaudano, Arnold of Villa Nova, Dante, and others; also Scotus, called Duns, who, in his fourth book of Sentences, dist. 18, complaineth of the abuse of excommunication and of the pope's keys. "Whereas before, excommunication was not used but upon great and just causes, and therefore was feared; now," saith he, "it is brought forth for every trifling matter, as for not paying the priest's wages, &c. and therefore," saith he, "it groweth into contempt." Under the same king, about the beginning of his reign, the year was so hot and dry, that from the month of May till near the month of September, there fell no rain; insomuch that many died for heat, and the vulgar people, in their reckoning of years, did count the time from the said dry year long after.

Merton College built in Oxford.

After pope Benedict XI. above mentioned, succeeded pope Clement V., who, about A.D. 1310, translated the pope's court to Avignon in France, where it remained the term of seventy-four years. At the coronation of this Clement were present Philip king of France, Charles his son, and John duke of Britany, with a great number of other men of state and nobility; at which coronation, they being in the middle of the pomp or procession, a great wall broke down and fell upon them, by the fall whereof duke John and twelve others were slain, king Philip was hurt and wounded, and the pope being struck from his horse, lost out from the mitre upon his head a carbuncle, esteemed to the value of six thousand florins.[1] By this Clement it was ordained that the emperor, though he might be called king of the Romans, might not enjoy the title and right of the emperor, before he was by him confirmed; and that the emperor's

The pope's court translated to France.

Slaughter of nobles at the pope's coronation.

Emperor no emperor, unless confirmed by the pope.

(1) Platina. de Vit. Pont.

Edward I. A.D. 1306.

seat being vacant, the pope should reign as emperor, till a new emperor was chosen. By him the order of the Templars, who at that time were too abominable to be borne, was put down at the council of Vienna (A.D. 1312), as hereafter (Christ willing) shall be declared. He also ordained and confirmed the feast of Corpus Christi, assigning indulgences to such as heard the service thereof; and as pope Boniface before heaped up the book of decretals, called 'Sextus Decretalium,' so this Clement compiled the seventh book of the decretals, called by the same Clement, 'The Clementines.' In the time of this pope, the emperor Henry VI. was poisoned in receiving the sacrament, by a false dissembling monk called Bernard, that feigned himself to be his familiar friend; which was thought to be done not without the consent of the pope's legate. The emperor, perceiving himself poisoned, warned him to flee and escape, for else the Germans would certainly have slain him; who, although he escaped himself, yet divers of his order after that, with fire and sword, were slain.

The Templars put down. The feast of Corpus Christi. Septimus decretalium, called "The Clementines." Henry VI. emperor poisoned in the host.

As this pope Clement V. had now well provided, as ye have heard, against the empire of Rome to bring it under his girdle, insomuch that, without the pope's benediction no emperor might take the state upon him, he now proceeded further to intermeddle with the empire of Constantinople. He began by exercising his tyranny and power of excommunication against Andronicus Paleologus, emperor of Constantinople, A.D. 1306, declaring him to be a schismatic and heretic, because he neither would nor durst suffer the Grecians to make their appeal from the Greek church to the pope, neither would acknowledge him for his superior. By this it may appear, that the Greek church did not admit the pope's superiority as yet, nor at any time before; save only about the time of pope Innocent III., A.D. 1202, at which time the Frenchmen with their captain, Baldwin, earl of Flanders, joining together with the Venetians, were set against the Grecians, to place Alexius in the right of the empire of Constantinople, upon condition, as writeth Platina,[1] to subdue the Greek church under the church of Rome. This Alexius being restored, and shortly after slain, the empire came to the Frenchmen, with whom it remained the space of fifty-eight years, till the coming of Michael Paleologus in the days of pope Gregory IX., who restored the empire from the Frenchmen unto his pristine state again. During all this time of the French emperors, the Greek church was subject to Rome, as by the decretals of pope Gregory IX. may appear. Then followed after this, that the aforesaid Michael, emperor of Constantinople, being called up to a council at Lyons by pope Gregory X., about the controversy of the proceeding of the Holy Ghost (as is above specified) and obedience to the church of Rome; because the said Michael the emperor did there submit himself and the Grecians to the subjection of Rome, as testifieth Baptist Egnat, he thereby procured to himself such grudge and hatred among the Greek monks and priests, that after his death they denied him the due honour and place of burial.[2] The son of this Andronicus was Michael Paleologus above mentioned, who, as ye have heard before, because he was constrained by the Grecians not to admit any appellation to the bishop of Rome, was accursed by the pope's censures

Paleologus, emperor of Constantinople, excommunicated, with all his adherents, by pope Clement, for not suffering the Grecians to appeal to Rome. A.D. 1306.

Note the practice of the Romish prelates.

When and how long the Greek church was subject to Rome.

(1) Platina, in Vit. Innocentii. (2) Ex Baptist. Egnatio. Rom. Princ. l. 7.

as a heretic. Whereby it appeareth, that the Grecians, recovering their state again, refused all subjection at this time to the church of Rome, which was A.D. 1327. After this Clement V. followed pope John XXII., with whom Louis IV. the emperor had much trouble (A.D. 1328). After whom next in course succeeded pope Benedict XII., who on a time, being desired to make certain new cardinals, answered again; that he would gladly so do, if he also could make a new world. "For this world," said he, "is for these cardinals that be made already."[1] And thus much of the popes: now to return a little back to the king's story.

Edward I. A.D. 1307.

The Greek church denieth subjection to the church of Rome.

In the year of our Lord 1307,[2] which was the thirty-fourth of the reign of this king, in the beginning of Hilary term, the king kept a parliament at Carlisle, where great complaints were brought in by the nobles and ancients of the realm, concerning the manifold and intolerable oppressions of churches and monasteries, and exactions of money by the pope's legate, William Testa, otherwise termed 'Mala Testa,' lately brought into the realm of England. The coming of this William Testa was upon this occasion, as followeth: pope Clement, who, as ye heard before, had translated his court from Rome into France, where he had been archbishop before, because he contemned to come and remain at his own see, the princes of Rome thought him unworthy to enjoy Peter's patrimony; and so by that means falling into bareness and poverty, he lived only on the money of such bishops as came to him to be confirmed, and by such other shifts and gifts; so that partly by bishops and other religious persons, partly under the name of courtesy and benevolence, partly under the pretence of borrowing, he had within the first year nine thousand five hundred marks of silver; all his other charges and expenses, which he largely that year bestowed, being clearly borne.[3] Besides this, he sent the said legate, William Testa, into England with his bulls, in which he reserved the first fruits of the first year of all churches being vacant at any time, or by any man within the realms of England, Scotland, Wales, and Ireland, and also the fruits of abbeys and priories within the said realms, &c. Whereupon, the king with his nobles, seeing the inconvenience and harm therefrom ensuing to the whole realm: in the aforesaid parliament, holden at Carlisle, withstood the said legate, charging and commanding him by the assent of the earls and barons, that henceforth he should abstain from all such exactions; and that, as concerned his lord the pope, he would direct certain his messengers unto him purposely for the same matter appointed: by which ambassadors, the king wrote unto the aforesaid pope, declaring and admonishing him, as right and reason was, that he should not exact the first fruits of the churches and abbeys, by his predecessors and noblemen of the land founded for the honour and maintenance of God's service, for alms and hospitality: which otherwise, in so doing, should all be overthrown. And so by this means, the pope at that time changed his purpose concerning abbeys. The first fruits of English churches were, after that, granted to the king for two years, in which space he obtained them.

The pope's exactions complained of in parliament.

The pope's getting in one year.

The pope's legate sent into England.

First fruits first brought in by the pope.

King Edward withstandeth the pope and his legate.

First fruits of abbeys denied to the pope.

First fruits for two years granted to the king.

(1) Ex scripto Engethusensis. (2) Ex Nic. Trivet. (3) Ex Hist. quæ incipit ab Henrico Tertio.

Edward I. A.D. 1307.

During the parliament before specified, as men were talking many things of the pope's oppressions, which he had begun in the English church; in the full of the parliament, suddenly fell down among them, as sent from heaven, a certain paper, with this superscription.

An Epistle of Cassiodorus to the Church of England, concerning the Abuses of the Romish Church.

To the noble church of England, serving in clay and brick, as the Jews did in time past under the tyranny of the Egyptians; Peter, the son of Cassiodorus a catholic soldier, and devout champion of Christ, sendeth greeting, and wishing her to cast off the yoke of bondage, and to receive the reward of liberty.

To whom shall I compare thee, or to whom shall I liken thee, O daughter of Jerusalem? To whom shall I match thee, O daughter of Sion? Great is thy perturbation, like unto the sea. Thou sittest alone without comfort all the day long, thou art confounded and consumed with heaviness. Thou art given up into the hands of him from whence thou canst not rise, without help of one to lift thee up; for the Scribes and Pharisees sitting in the chair of Moses, the enemies of the Romans, are as thy heads and rulers, enlarging their guarded phylacteries, and seeking to be enriched with the marrow of thy bones, laying heavy burdens and not able to be borne, upon thy shoulders, and upon thy ministers, and they set thee under tribute, who of old time hast been free, beyond all honesty or measure. But marvel not thereat, for thy mother, who is the lady of people, like a widow having married and coupled herself to her subject, hath appointed him to be thy father: that is to say, the bishop of Rome, who showeth no point of any fatherly love towards thee. He magnifieth and extendeth, to the uttermost, his authority over thee, and by experience he declareth himself to be the husband of thy mother. He remembereth oft with himself the prophetical saying of the prophet, and hath well digested the same in the inward part of his breast: "Take to thee a great book, and write therein quickly with the pen of a man;" "Take the spoil, rob quickly." But is this it, which the apostle saith, that he was appointed for, where he writeth thus? "Every bishop, taken from among men, is appointed for men in those things that belong to the Lord:" not to spoil, nor to lay on them yearly taxes, nor to kill men; "but to offer gifts and sacrifices for sins," and to sorrow with them that be ignorant and do err. And so we read of Peter the fisher (whose successor he boasteth himself to be), that after the resurrection of Christ, he returned with other apostles, to the office of fishing; who, when he could take nothing on the left side of the ship, at the bidding of Christ, turned to the right side, and drew to land a net full of fishes. Wherefore the profitable ministry of the church is to be exercised on the right side, by the which the devil is overcome, and plenty of souls be lucrified and won to Christ. But certainly the labour on the left side of the ship is far otherwise; for in it the faith stumbleth, heaviness beareth rule, when that thing that is desired by seeking is not found. For who is so foolish as to think, that he can at one time serve both God and man, and that while, to satisfy his own will, he sticks to the revelations of flesh and blood, he can offer worthy gifts to Christ? And doubtless that shepherd who watcheth not for the edifying of the flock, prepareth another way to the roaring lion seeking whom he may devour. And now behold, I say, O daughter! the deeds of him that is called thy Father, such as have not been heard of before; he driveth away the good shepherd from the sheepfold, and placeth in their stead bishops, to rule, but not to profit, his nephews, cousins, and parents; some that know no letters, and others dumb and deaf, who understand not the plain voice of the sheep, not curing their wounds, that be hurt of the wolves: but like hirelings, plucking off the fleeces apace, and reaping that which other men have sown; whose hands, moreover, be always ready in their baskets and pouches, but their backs are turned from their burdens. By this it is manifest, that the priesthood is clean changed in these days, that the service of God is decayed, that alms are diminished and brought to nought, and the whole devotion of kings, princes, and Christians, is banished. May not this be thought wonderful in the eyes of all men; that whereas Christ commandeth tribute to be paid to kings for him and for Peter, the bishop of Rome now goeth about by dominion of his style, to subdue to him both realms and princes of realms, against His will, whose vicar he saith he is; and who refused the realms and judgments of the world, which this bishop, contrariwise, challengeth, claiming all that which he in his style writeth to be his? Alack, O daughter, what doth he yet more against thee? Mark, he draweth from thee whatsoever pleaseth him, and yet he thinketh not himself content, to have the tenth part only of thy goods from thee; except he have also the first fruits of the benefices of the ministers, whereby he may get a new patrimony, as well for himself as for his kindred, contrary to the godly wills of the first founders. Over and besides all this, he inferreth other execrable taxes and stipends for his legates and messengers, whom he sendeth into England; which not only take away the feeding and clothing of thee and thine, but also tear in pieces, like dogs, your flesh and skins. May not the prince be compared to king Nebuchadnezzar, who destroyed the temple of the Lord, and robbed away the silver and golden vessels thereof? The very same doth this man also; he robbed the ministers of God's house, and left them destitute of due help. In like manner doth he. Truly they be better who are killed with the sword, than they who be pined with hunger; for they are dead straight, but these are wasted with the barrenness of the earth. O daughter! all they that pass by the way, let them have pity and compassion on thee, for there is no sorrow like thy sorrow. For now thy face is blacker than coals, through much sorrow and weeping, and thou art no more known in the streets: thy aforesaid ruler hath placed thee in darkness, and hath given thee wormwood and gall to drink. O Lord! hear the sorrow and sighings of thy people, behold Lord, and descend, for the heart of this man is more obdurate than the heart of Pharaoh; for he will not suffer the people to depart, except in the fortitude only of thy hand, for he scourgeth them not only miserably upon the earth, but also, after their death, he intendeth to encroach upon the goods of all Christians, under the name and title of dying intestate, or making no will. Therefore, let the chivalry of England well remember how the Frenchmen in times past, directing their greedy eyes on the realm of England, laboured with all their power how to bring the same under their subjection. But it is to be feared, lest the new devices and practice of this new enemy supply that which hitherto hath been lacking in them; for by diminishing the treasure of the realm, and by spoiling of the church's goods, the realm shall be brought into such inability, that it shall not be able to help itself against the enemy. Therefore, O daughter! and you the ministers thereof, suffer not yourselves to be led any more into such miserable bondage. Better it is for the wealth of thee and thine, that the christian king and the powers of the realm, who have endued thee with great benefits, and you also, who are endued with their benefits, do labour, with all your power, how to resist the devices, conspiracies, arrogancy, presumption, and pride of the foresaid person; who, not for any zeal for God, but for the enriching of his parents and his own kindred (exalting himself like an eagle), by these and such other exactions goeth about, after another kind of extortion, to scrape up and devour all the money and treasure of England. Now, lest the dissembled simplicity of the realm in this behalf do bring utter subversion, and afterwards be compelled to seek remedy when it is too late, I beseech the Lord God of hosts to turn away the veil from the heart of that man, and to give him a contrite and an humble mind; in such sort, that he may acknowledge the ways of the true God, whereby he may be brought out of darkness, and be forced to relinquish his old sinister attempts; and that the vineyard, which the Lord's hand hath planted, may be replenished continually with the preachers of the word. Let the words of the Lord, prophesied by the mouth of Jeremy, stir up your minds to withstand and resist the subtle practices of this man, which words spoken by the Lord be these: "O thou pastor which hast scattered my people, and hast cast them out of their habitations, behold I will come and visit upon thee, and upon the malice of thy studies; neither shall there be any of thy seed which shall sit upon the seat of David, neither which shall have power any more in Judah. So that thy nest shall become barren, and utterly subverted, like Sodom and Gomorrah."

And if he, being terrified by these words, do not leave off from this which he beginneth, and doth not make restitution of those things which he hath received, then let all and singular persons sing for him being obdurate, to him that seeth all things, the hundred-and-eighth Psalm, "Deus laudem," &c. For truly as

Edward I. A.D. 1307

favour, grace, and benevolence, remitteth and neglecteth many things, so again the gentle benignity of man, being too much oppressed and grieved, seeking to be delivered and freed from the same, striveth and searcheth to have the truth known, and casteth off that yoke, by all means possible, that grieveth him, &c.[1]

What effect this letter wrought in them to whom it was directed, is not in story expressed. This, by the sequel, may be conjectured, that no reason or persuasion could prevail; but that the pope retained here still his exactions, whatever was said or written to the contrary.

And thus much being written hitherto of these acts and doings here in England, now to slip a little into matters happening at the same time in France, under the reign of the aforesaid king Philip above mentioned. Forasmuch as about this time (A. D. 1329)[2] was commenced a parliament by the said king of France against the pope, touching the jurisdiction, both temporal, pertaining to princes, and ecclesiastical, belonging to the church; I thought it not unprofitable for the reader to hear and learn the full discourse and tradition thereof, according as we have caused it to be extracted faithfully out of the true copy and records of Peter Bertrand, bishop of Edvenen, and chief doer and prolocutor in the said parliament upon the pope's side, against the king and state temporal.

A parliament in France, wherein is discussed, how far the jurisdiction ecclesiastical extendeth

Forasmuch as the high prelate of Rome, otherwise called antichrist, being then in his chief ruff, extolling himself above all princes and potentates of the world, as in other countries, so also in France, extended his usurped jurisdiction above the princely authority of the king, claiming to himself full government of both the states, as well secular as also ecclesiastical; the king, therefore, not suffering the excessive proceedings of pope Clement V. above specified, directeth his letters mandatory to the prelates and barons of the realm of France, to convene and assemble themselves together at Paris, about the beginning of December, the year above prefixed, the tenor of which letters of the king directed to the prelates, followeth in this form and manner.

The summons of Parliament by Philip, the French king.

Letter to the bishops and prelates

Philip, by the grace of God king of France, to our well-beloved bishop of Edvenen, greeting and salutation. Reverend father in God, right trusty and well-beloved, we greet you well. The more sight and knowledge you have in divinity and the holy Scriptures of God, with the practice and experience of other good qualities and virtues, you know the better a great deal, how that the clergy and laity of this our realm, as members of one body, ought to cleave and stick together, and how, by their helping hand, unity and peace should be maintained by all, and the contrary eschewed and avoided, every state contenting itself, and not encroaching one upon another. And because we are advertised, how that our barons and officers, as well in time past as of late, have diversely in divers points injured you, as in like manner, you and yours in many causes have wrongfully damaged them, by occasion whereof, the knot of unity and concord, which ought to have flourished among you, is quite loosed and undone; to the end therefore, that by God's grace, some good reformation and redress may be had herein, we, most studious of unity and concord, require you, and by these our letters command you, to appear personally before us at Paris, the fifteenth day of December next ensuing the date hereof, and

(1) Hæc Cassiodorus. Ex vetusto Chronico Albanensi.

(2) Our author here breaks into the chronological arrangement of his history, but reverts to A. D. 1307 at the close of this reign, at page 640.—ED.

there, before us, to make relation of such wrong as ye have received at the laity's hands. And we likewise straitly charge and command you, our barons, bailiffs, and officers, not to fail, but to make your personal appearances before us, on the day and at the place above written, and there to exhibit before us a bill of the complaints, wherewith you burden our prelates and clergy, with their officials; that we, with our council, consulting thereupon, with due regard may see redress therein; whereby perpetual love and charity may ever hereafter reign and remain among them for ever. Given at Paris the first day of September, A.D. 1329.

The parliament convened.

At the day in the letters above specified, the prelates and clergy assembled themselves before the king at his palace in Paris, that is to say, the lord Bituricen, the lord Auxitan, the lord Turonen, the lord Rothom, and the lord Senon, all archbishops: the lord Belvacen, the lord Cathalen, the lord Laudun, the lord of Paris, the lord Novionon, the lord Carnoten, the lord Constan, the lord Andegaven, the lord Pictaven, the lord Melden, the lord of Cameracen, the lord of St. Feri, the lord Brioce, the lord of Cabilion, and the lord of Edven, all bishops. After due reverence done unto the king's grace there sitting in his own person, with his barons and council about him, a certain noble and wise person, lord Peter de Cugneriis, being one of the king's council, rose up, and openly, in the parliament house, spake in the king's behalf on this wise, taking for his theme, "Render unto Cæsar, that which is Cæsar's, and unto God, that which is God's;" which he very skilfully prosecuted and applied, dividing it into two parts. First, that obedience and reverence is due unto the king; secondly, that there ought to be a difference between the jurisdiction of the clergy and laity, so that spiritual matters should be defined and ordered by the prelates and spiritual men, and temporal causes ruled and determined by the king, his barons, and temporal men. All this he proved by many reasons both of fact and law, as more fully appeareth beneath in the answer of the bishop of Edven. Finally, he concluded, that the clergy ought only to deal and have to do with spiritual matters; in defence whereof, the king's highness would stand their good lord and maintainer. His oration being ended, he repeated certain words in the French tongue, which imported that the king's will and pleasure was, in some points, to renew the temporal state and jurisdiction; and therewith he exhibited a certain bill in French, whereof also he gave a copy to the prelates, containing certain points and articles underwritten, the contents whereof he affirmed not to appertain to the order and jurisdiction of the spiritualty, but only to the temporalty, complaining that the clergy had wrongfully proceeded in the same. But notwithstanding the premises, and for all this his complaint, he said, that the prelates should have time to consult and deliberate thereupon with the king. The copy of the articles, with the answer ensuing upon the same, and the grievances of the kingdom of France, wrought by the clergy, and exhibited to the king, hereafter follow.

Lord Peter speaks in the parliament.

The oration divided into two parts: obedience to the king; difference between the jurisdiction of the states temporal and ecclesiastical.

Articles in the parliament propounded.

1. The cognition of causes real, whether they touch possession and their propriety, or not, by common law appertaineth to the jurisdiction temporal. But the prelates with their officials, infringe the temporal jurisdiction, by taking upon them the determination of such causes real; especially concerning possession and all other interdicts.

2. Item, When a temporal man is sued by any clerk or spiritual man for

Edward I. the possession of his land, obtaining an adjournment of the secular power, in the cause of novity or otherwise, the prelates' officials, stopping hereby

A.D. 1307. the temporal jurisdiction, at the instance of the clerk, call by process before them both the secular judge and the party; inhibiting them to proceed any further in the cause, under pain of excommunication and forfeiture of a certain sum.

Prelates intermeddle in temporal men's matters.

3. Item, Although the secular judge have the cognition of all laymen's matters, except in spiritual causes, yet will the bishops' officials, at the instance of any party, call such before them; and if the temporal men do except against their jurisdiction, alleging the incompetency of the judge, or if they require the cause to be remitted to those under whom they are, as the right judges, yet do the officials refuse to do this, and, even by excommunication, compel the parties to proceed before them.

4. Item, The bishops' officials at the instance of the clerks, alleging that they are injured in matters of inheritance by a layman, call by process the laity. And if it be alleged that those causes stand upon reality, being so indeed, and that for that consideration the cause ought to be remitted to the temporal law; this notwithstanding, the officials prohibit them, under pain of excommunication or some great forfeit, from proceeding, except before them.

5. Item, The bishops' officials take upon them to hear the plea of such contracts, as either be conceived in writings, or made by word of mouth in the temporal law; sending out their monition of excommunication against them that stand bound concerning the same contracts.

6. Item, The bishops and prelates decree provincial councils and synodal statutes, enacting and ordering therein many things to the high and great prejudice of the temporal jurisdiction, wherein they ought to have no cognition at all, neither to intermeddle themselves therewith.

7. Item, The aforesaid officials take upon them, before notaries, to swear persons for the performance of contracts and bargains made by them in places under the jurisdiction temporal, concerning the sale of inheritance or otherwise; encroaching thereby upon their jurisdiction, when verily they have nothing to do with any contracts and obligations, but with such as are made and agreed upon within the compass of their own seat and jurisdiction.

Ex officio.

8. Item, The said officials, by their mere office, call before them the laity, to answer to such matters of correction as shall be laid to their charge, the cognition whereof, as they say, doth appertain unto them; and when the said persons do appear before them, and deny the crime objected against them, the officials detain them and put them in prison; although in such cases they are to be released, and although imprisonment appertaineth only to the temporal power, and not to them.

Imprisonment pertaineth not to the clergy.

9. Item, In the cases aforesaid, although by making their purgations and other the process therein, they be found clear of that which is laid to their charge, and are acquitted; these said officials will in no wise discharge and dismiss them, before they have to the uttermost paid, for the writings and process in that behalf, a good piece of money; when by law it ought to be done gratis, and for nothing.

10. Item, It must not be forgotten to talk of the sentence of excommunication, which is decreed by virtue of one only citation, so often as a man faileth in his appearance.

11. Item, Mention is to be made of those kind of obligations 'De nisi; whereby a man is excommunicated by and by, if he make not payment at the day prefixed, although he be not able so to do.

12. Item, Whosoever by virtue of excommunication in the bishops' court is excommunicated, and who so excommunicated, do not satisfy the sum due about the excommunication, by and by the sum is doubled; and the secular power is charged by the bishops or their officials, that they, under pain of excommunication, compel the excommunicated, by attaching their goods, to pay the said sum, and not to miss a jot; which monition if the laity refuse to put in execution, they themselves are then excommunicated, and in no wise to be absolved, before they disburse that money which the principal excommunicated person should have paid.

13. Item, If the bailiffs, headboroughs, or other the king's officers and judges

of the temporalty, receiving the aforesaid monitions, do put the same in execution, and find those that be excommunicated to be beggarly and nothing worth; the said officers are bound, at their own proper costs and charges, to resort to the bishop's see or consistory, wheresoever it is, and there to take a corporal oath, that the parties excommunicated are nothing worth. This if they fail to do, those officers are sure to be excommunicated, and, thereby, forced to disburse the due of the first excommunicated persons.

14. Item, If two laymen be in suit together before a temporal judge, about an action either real or personal, and one of them after contestation of law, and great process therein, do appeal unto an ecclesiastical judge, he will presume then to detain before him the plea of such cases and actions, both real and personal, causing, by virtue of his monitions and authority, the temporal judge to cease and leave off from meddling therein; which, if the secular judge obeyeth not, he is pronounced excommunicate, and compelled to make satisfaction; by occasion whereof, the temporal jurisdiction is much annoyed and clean loseth the prerogative thereof; because, by law, no man may appeal from a spiritual judge to the temporal law.

Action real and personal.

No man may appeal from a spiritual judge to the temporal law by the pope's divinity.

15. Item, If a layman, inhabiter of any of the king's towns, procureth his debtor, being also a layman, to be arrested by virtue of secular justice in that place; and he who is so arrested appealeth, and causeth also his creditor to be arrested, the officials will take upon them to hear this matter; and if any thing be attempted concerning the appeal, they miss not to demand cost and satisfaction both of the justice, and also of him to whom the arrest was made. And if any of the prince's retinue compelleth them to resist this injury, they are straightways pronounced excommunicate.

16. Item, The said bishops have a number of officials under them, whom they term deans of the clergy, who usually cause all sorts of people throughout the king's dominions, only by word of mouth, to come before them, and that, sometimes, without commission; when in every diocese there ought to be but one seat or consistory, wherein matters should be heard and decided. And hereby it happeneth divers times, that many are wrongfully and without cause cited, to the end that they may pay money enough to rid themselves thereof; which is to the no small prejudice of the king's majesty's subjects, and of the temporal jurisdiction.

Deans of the clergy.

17. Item, The said rulers of the clerks seal up the houses of their clergy, which are situate in the king's towns, and other of his noblemen's villages, to the prejudice of the king's majesty's jurisdiction, and that of his nobility; for in such places the bishops have no such kind of jurisdiction.

18. Item, The said prelates, or their officials, do presume to seal up the moveable goods of married clerks, and of merchants; whereas, in such cases, the order thereof appertaineth to the temporal law.

Married clerks.

19. Item, They compel the laity to put in surety to answer before clerks in the spiritual court; yea, and chiefly the king's own servitors.

20. Item, They presume to hear and have the cognition of actions, which are real, or at least-wise mixed, that is, both real and personal.

21. Item, The said prelates go about to have cognition of such temporal men's matters as dwell in hospitals, almshouses, and the king's peculiars, and in villages of his subjects, although the plea thereof appertaineth to the king himself, and his subjects'; forbidding, under pain of excommunication and great forfeits, any man to be so hardy as to commence any suit against any of them, but before themselves, on pain of forfeiting a great sum of money.

22. Item, To the end the clergy and ecclesiastical rule should be multiplied, they confer a number of tonsures on children under age, some of them being sons of bondmen, others born bastards; yea, and to many more married folks, insufficient, unable, and unlearned.

23. Item, They do cause, by the governors of their clerks, widow-women to be inforced and defiled, and will have the discussing thereof: as in like manner, they will determine the matters of pupils applying their goods when they die, as they do the goods of those who die intestate, to their own use; the cognition whereof belongeth to the king himself, because those kinds of persons with their goods are in ward to the king, and under his tuition.

24. Item, They procure, through the said deans of the clergy, temporal men of the king's dominions, or elsewhere, without all order of law, to be maliciously,

Gins to get money.

Edward I. A.D. 1307.

apprehended; objecting against them that they have strayed from some article of christian faith, and forthwith shut them up: whereas their imprisonment appertaineth to the king till they be convicted thereof.

25. Item, They exercise their jurisdiction in all places, having no regard, either to the king's peculiar towns, or yet to his subjects; but run into every hole, when, by law, they ought to have no jurisdiction without their own limits and precinct.

26. Item, When these prelates or their officials, by virtue of their monitions, do charge the king's officers and his justices to execute any thing, if they do not perform that which is prescribed unto them, the forfeit which the monition containeth, is taken; yea, and excommunication denounced. And this is a new invention sprung up of late amongst them, much to the prejudice of the king and his subjects.

27. Item, When the bishops or their officials do prosecute a matter of office before themselves against any temporal man, and have no proof thereof, they compel many of the laity to depose what they know thereof, having no respect whether they be the king's burgesses, or not, or what they be; and yet will they not allow any charges and expenses for their pains taken in that behalf, but, if they appear not at their day, they are sure to be excommunicated.

28. Item, If malefactors be apprehended by any of the king's justices, and indicted of theft, and he, whose goods they were which were stolen, cometh before the king's sheriffs, and proveth them to be his, and that therefore the matter ought to be ordered by them: if, afterwards, the bishops, or their officials affirm the said felon or malefactor to be a clerk, they will, by virtue of their decrees or monitions, compel the king's sheriffs to restore and bring in the stolen goods; and if they do it not, they are pronounced excommunicate.

29. Item, If it happen that the king's sheriff or bailiff take an offender for his offence, and he affirmeth himself to be a clerk, although he never took any kind of tonsures or orders, wearing no habit appertaining thereunto; yet the bishops or their officials will cause the detainers of him, by their censures, to deliver unto them the said malefactor as their clerk.

30. Item, If it happen that the king's sheriff, or other his justice, take a thief or murderer, who beareth a clerk's mark and tonsure, and there-for delivereth him to the clergy to be ordered, it shall not be long before he be acquitted by them, although he afterwards recognise his deed; yea, and notwithstanding that his fellows and partners in that affair, being merely temporal persons, received justice for the same, and impeached him thereof; and so such malefactors are thereby encouraged to commit the like.

31. Item, If any complaineth and saith that he is spoiled, by and by the officials will decree a monition against the spoiler, by virtue whereof, some one of the deans of the clergy shall admonish him to restore the things comprised in the monition, and also minister to him an oath, whether he hath not spoiled the plaintiff of such things as, he saith, he was spoiled of. But if he refuse to take an oath before him, then the dean will straightways seal up the monition and excommunicate him; and by no means shall he be absolved before he restore, and satisfy the contents in the monition, whereof the plaintiff said first he was spoiled.

32. Item, If any for his offence be cast into prison by the secular power, although at the time of his taking he wore the temporal habit, and was in no orders, but all the days of his life had lived like a temporal man, yet, if he shall avouch and vow himself to be a clerk, to the intent to have more expedition at the clergy's hands, and to escape unpunished; the clergy will immediately give in command to the laity to restore unto them the malefactor, or else suspension shall be denounced throughout the whole township where the said malefactor shall be so imprisoned. And, for avoiding the jeopardy which might arise out of the said seizure, the secular judge is, of necessity, compelled to deliver up to them the offender, to the great prejudice of the king's temporal jurisdiction, to whom the cognition thereof might appertain, in case of resort and prerogative.

Resortum.

33. Item, When any offender is delivered by the temporal magistrates to the clergy, as, for instance, their clerk, his friends will make suit to the bishop's officials for him, and compound with them, by reason whereof they dismiss them unpunished, and so do worse and worse, although their fact was ever so notorious.

34. Item, As soon as any married clerk, being a merchant or of whatsoever other science he be, for any offence by him committed, is called before the secular judge, the said clerk obtaineth of the officials a monition, bringing with him some priest, who doth inhibit the secular judge under pain of one or two hundred marks, yea and of excommunication too, not to proceed further, nor to meddle in such causes, and not to molest such parties either in body or goods: and, if the judge obey not, he shall be suspended from hearing of mass in that place, although the matter concerneth the fact of merchandise.

35. Item, The said officials grant citations without number against the laity, in cases of warranties, personally to cite before them persons unknown; but, if the person be known, it is contained in the citation, that in no wise, and that under a great pain, they cause their adversary to be called before a secular judge, during the return of the citation.

36. Item, When one is excommunicated in any place, the officials grant out personal citations against those, who do participate, and are conversant with the excommunicated, causing a whole country for the space of eight miles round about to be cited together. And further, the friends and acquaintance of the party so excommunicated, sometimes forty, sometimes sixty, yea and sometimes a hundred at once, are compelled to make their purgation before them, that they do not participate or keep company with their friends the excommunicates. Whereby ensueth that many honest, old, and ancient men, for avoiding of troubles and expenses, do pay some twelve pence, some two shillings; by occasion whereof many vines are unlooked to, much ground is untilled, yea, and many good men are constrained to lay the key under the door, and run away.

37. Item, The said officials do burden many persons of good name and fame, with being usurers, whereby they are constrained to agree with them, to avoid the infamy that thereby might ensue.

38. Item, The aforesaid officials call by citation before them the honestly wedded, as well man as woman; charging them, that they have committed adultery to the perpetual infamy of their husbands and wives. And for nothing else but for extortion to wring money from them.

39. Item, Mention must be made of the multitude and number of proctors, who eat and devour up all the world with their citations, catching up clients, and keeping abroad in the countries, courts, and assizes; who, for money, return not the citations which by extortion they receive of them who are cited.

40. Item, There be many other griefs and enormities, which the chapters, abbots, priors, provosts, and other ecclesiastical persons in the realm of France, practise against the people; as, when they cause to be cited before them many of the king's burgesses, and others in divers places being privileged: that is to say, Baiocenses, Manmectans in Britain, Lugdons, Masticons, with other more. But especially the provosts of hospitals use this trick more commonly than any others do, whereby the people are much endamaged, and will be every day more and more, if remedy be not had therein.

41. Item, Ecclesiastical magistrates labour to have cognition of causes of injury, in whatsoever cause it be; whether the injury be committed by word or deed. Likewise they take upon them to hear the causes of married clerks, and of their wives, although they both use merchandise; and if at any time such couples be taken by the secular magistrates, the official causeth a suspension to be denounced in that parish, by force of the council Silvanecten.

42. Item, They challenge to have cognition concerning widows' goods, both moveable and unmoveable; and if it happeneth, at any time, that a merchant's widow, in any of the king's peculiars, by way of arrest, procureth any temporal man to be convented before the secular judge, and the matter be so far traversed, that he should have been condemned by the sentence of the secular judge, and then it come to the ear of the ecclesiastical magistrates, how and before whom the widow did summon him, the said temporal judge shall be constrained to withdraw the same, and by their monitions and censures, they will correct the same: and this oftentimes happeneth.

43. Item, Many of the tenants and inhabiters of the bishops' lands call one another to the court of the officials, by a kind of appellation, by virtue whereof the officials take upon them to proceed in the same, and to have cognition

Edward I. thereof, to the prejudice of the temporal jurisdiction of our sovereign lord the king.

A.D. 1307. 44. Item, If any man be apprehended by secular justice in shedding of blood; he is to be ordered by them, if he be lay; but if he be a clerk he is to be restored to the ecclesiastical judge. Whether he be a temporal man or a clerk, however, who is so taken, and appealeth to the officials' court, they will be so bold as to have cognition thereof, requiring herewith amends of the secular court, which undertook the aforesaid apprehension. If this be suffered, the malefactor shall never be punished, for, by and by, they will appeal, and, immediately after the appellation, fly and void away.

The clergy prejudicial to common justice.

Ex officio. 45. Item, When they cause many, by their office, to be cited before them, they will admit them to have no proctors; to whom, when they come at the day of appearance, they object the crime of usury; and except they answer as the promoters themselves will, they are trodden under foot (although they be mere laymen) and shall not be dismissed, before they fine even as the officials themselves list, although they be no usurers; but if any be usurers, they take of them satisfaction and bribes, and they be permitted to use their usury no less than before, so that they may have their old fees and bribes.

Usury craftily objected by the clergy against laymen.

46. Item, They procure their officers to apprehend clerks in whatsoever soil they be found, albeit by justice they may appeal therefrom: but if, by any, they be hindered of their will herein, they, by sentence of excommunication, do forthwith cause them to desist therefrom.

The prelates make the church a den of thieves.

47. Item, As often as any temporal magistrate doth apprehend any person, who afterwards, on being required by the clergy, is quietly delivered unto them, yet, for all that, the officials cause those magistrates to be denounced as excommunicate by law.

48. Item, The prelates give order for tonsures as well to men of thirty years as upward, as also to married men, when they come unto them, for fear of imprisonment and punishment due unto them for their criminal offences before committed; and this is oftentimes put in practice.

49. Item, If it happen that any of the king's servants or any others are excommunicate, who would fain be absolved, being glad to pay reasonably for the same, the clergy will not receive satisfaction but such as shall please them; whereby many of them remain still excommunicate.

50. Item, When two persons have been at strife and law together for the possession of land, and the matter contentious be put into the hands of the king, by some servant or officer of the king, for the taking up of the matter, then do the prelates admonish the one part not to trouble the other who is in possession. Otherwise, if he do, they do excommunicate him.

51. Item, The aforesaid prelates, deans, chaplains, and the rest of the clergy, put the king's officers to so much travail and expense in trying out the king's usurped jurisdiction, as they term it; that oftentimes many of them spend and consume, in the travail of the right and title thereof, all that they have, and more too.

52. Item, If any secular justicer in a true and just cause, at the request of the party, putteth in his helping hand, concerning the inheritance of clerks, the ecclesiastical judges and their ministers send out monitions in writing against the said justicer; yea, under pain of excommunication and forfeiture, to take away his hand and leave off; enjoining him further to suffer the other party quietly to enjoy the said things. Otherwise they denounce him excommunicate, and he shall not be absolved before he have well paid for it, even as pleaseth 'master official,' to the high prejudice of the authority of our sovereign lord the king.

Note the practice of officials to get money.

53. Item, The ecclesiastical magistrates, as soon as they hear that any rich or fat 'Cob' dies, or think that he will not live long, send out, forthwith, letters under seal to their chaplain, commanding him in no wise to presume to bury him, although he made his testament, and received the rites of the church. And when, afterwards, the friends and kinsfolks of the dead resort unto them to know the cause of their inhibition, they declare unto them that he was an usurer, and that he kept not the commandments of holy church: and so keep they the corpse of the dead long unburied, till his friends buy it out with good store of money, heaping and hoarding up by these means abundance of riches.

54. Item, If there be any violent shedding of blood in any church-yard,

whereby the interdict taketh place, the clergy cause a certain imposition to be levied on the parishioners there, for the salary towards the restoring thereof, although some of the parishioners be of an exempt jurisdiction; yea, and although he who shed blood be able to pay the whole tax which they levied, and more too.

55. Item, Certain chaplains affirm themselves to have certain apostolic privileges, by virtue whereof they may appoint what judges they will (yea, and oftentimes, of their own house), and so they be judges in their own cause; which is plainly against the law. By this oftentimes it happeneth, that after great process and expenses had and made in any great cause of inquest (more often about realty than otherwise), when they have notice by the proctors and advocates that they shall have the foil therein, they revoke forthwith those named judges, and so the king's subjects are damaged, and can have no justice or redress at their hands.

56. Item, If any temporal man call a clerk before a secular judge in case of inheritance, the ecclesiastical judge procureth a stop to be made therein, attributing to themselves the cognition thereof: and so by adjourning and removing, the layman is constrained to make satisfaction.

57. Item, The clergy challenge the cognition of such causes as married clerks, being merchants and artificers, do commence; when by law it doth appertain to the temporalty, especially about the trade of merchandise.

58. Item, They oftentimes make interdictions in many of the king's towns and holds, and cause the divine service to cease; contrary to the privileges granted by many of the high bishops of Rome to our sovereign lord and master, the king.

59. Item, To and for the maintainance and keeping of their temporalties, they appoint bailiffs and other officers, who, if they do offend, may not condignly be punished according to law and justice.

60. Item, The ecclesiastical judges have promoters belonging to them, who, when any man is excommunicated (be it right, or be it wrong) cause that no man shall work or do any thing for him that is excommunicated; whereby the lands and vines are oftentimes unlooked to and untilled, to the no small prejudice of the king and his common people.

61. Item, The aforesaid promoters cause citations to be made out, by virtue whereof they call, in one citation twenty, thirty, forty persons to appear, for participating with such interdicted persons; taking of some ten, of other some twenty shillings, as much as they be able to make: whereby the common people are much oppressed.

62. Item, The ecclesiastical judges cause all the advocates of their courts to be sworn, that none shall retain them of their counsel against any of them, without their license: whereby oftentimes, the poor man quite loseth his right, and the king's cause is delayed, because his solicitors cannot freely retain counsel, without special license.

63. Item, They will make inventories of their goods who die intestate, or without making of a will; and will have the possession of their goods, as well moveable as unmoveable, in their own hands, to distribute to the heirs, or to whom they list.

64. Item, The execution also of testaments they take into their own hands, taking inventories of dead men's goods, and keeping or disposing of them to the heirs after their pleasure. And they have officials properly deputed for the execution thereof.

65. Item, They sometimes will not give credit to testaments made before witnesses, unless they be first by their own officials approved.

After the Lord Peter had thus spoken, the prelates required to have time to answer thereunto: whereupon, the Friday next ensuing was appointed for the same. On that day the Bishop Edven (archbishop of Senon elect), in the name of the whole clergy, answered for them all before the king, holding his parliament that day at Vicenas; and thus he there propounded:—

Bishop Edven (archbishop of Senon elect) prolocutor for the prelates.

Edward I.

A.D. 1307.

Answer of the Prelates to the Lord Peter's Oration before Philip, the French King.

Repetition of the Lord Peter's oration above touched upon, p. 613.

Forasmuch as the Lord Peter de Cugneriis, of late propounding against the Church of France, took for his theme that which is written in the twenty-second chapter of Matthew, "Render unto Cæsar that which is Cæsar's, and unto God that which is God's;" by which words, he said, two points were to be noted: first, the reverence and subjection which the prelates ought to have to the king their sovereign; secondly, the division of the temporal jurisdiction from the spiritual, which first part he proved out of the second chapter of the first epistle of Peter, where it is written, "Submit yourselves unto every creature, for the Lord's sake, whether it be unto the king, as unto the superior, or unto governors, as unto them that are sent of him, for the punishment of evil doers, and for the praise of them that do well." The second point he proved by the words of our Saviour Christ in Luke (chap. xxii.), where the apostle saith, "Lord, behold, here are two swords. And he said unto them, It is enough;" signifying by the two swords the two jurisdictions; and likewise out of Matthew (chap. xvii.) where Christ would pay tribute for himself and Peter; giving hereby an example, how that ecclesiastical persons were bound to pay and yield to the temporal power the temporalties; which also is proved in the 11 Quæst. prim. cap. 'Si tributum' et cap. 'Magnum.'

Two gifts given, priesthood, empire.

And further, because this is proved by man's law, where it is said, two great gifts are bestowed, priesthood and empire; the priesthood to rule over matters divine, the empire to bear domination over human matters. Whereby he concluded, that seeing these jurisdictions are distinguished of God (the one being given and limited to the church, and the other to the temporalty), the church in no wise ought to intermeddle, or to have any thing to do with the temporal jurisdiction. For it is written in Proverbs (chap. xxii.), "You ought not to pass the old limits and bounds, which the forefathers have set." And well, by the way, he bringeth in this word, "old and ancient;" because customs brought in to the contrary, be of no force, but rather are counted abuses and corruptions. Neither can prescription take place, for that "jus fisci" is imprescriptible, neither can the king abrogate from himself such law, nor renounce his right; proving the same by many chapters contained in the 10. Dist. Wherefore seeing the king, at the time he was crowned, swore not only not to alienate or infringe the laws of his realm, but also to call in such laws as were alienated and usurped either by the church, or by any other; the king was bound by his oath to revoke the same abuses.

In particular he did exhibit many articles in writing, wherein, as he said, the church did usurp upon the jurisdiction temporal. To answer these premises with reconciling of the places whatsoever I say or shall say, under protestation, it is not to ground or make any final judgment or determination herein; but only to inform the conscience of our sovereign lord the king and his assistants here assembled, alleging what the apostle saith (1 Peter ii.), "Fear God and honour the king." By those words, the holy apostle St. Peter teacheth us two things: first, that love, fear, and obedience, are due unto God for the mightiness and puissance of his majesty, saying, "Fear God." Secondly, that special honour and reverence is due to the king, for the excellency of his dignity, saying, "Honour the king." But note you by the way, how the apostle placeth his words: first he saith, that fear is due unto God, because principally and in chief we ought to fear God. For if the king or any other should command things contrary to God, we ought to have no regard thereof, but to contemn the king, and fear God. For it is written, in the Acts of the Apostles (chap. v.), "We ought rather to obey God than men;" and also in the second book of Maccabees (chap. vii.) where it is said, "I will not obey the commandments of the king, but the law." The reason of this St. Augustine giveth, both in the gloss upon the Romans, and also in the 11. Quæst. 1. "He that resisteth the superior power, resisteth the will and ordinance of God." But put the case, thou art commanded to do that which thou mayest not do, or not to do that which thou oughtest to do: doubtless, thou must neglect the lesser power, and fear the higher, learning the degrees of worldly things. As for example, be it so that a proctor commandeth thee any thing, and the same be against the proconsul, thou oughtest not to follow it. Yea, and further, put the case that the proconsul commandeth one thing, the emperor another, and God willeth the third: thou must not care for them, but obey God, for God is the greater power. For they may threaten thee with prison, but God may threaten thee with hell fire: they may slay and kill thy body, but God may send thee, body and soul, to perpetual hell fire. And therefore worthily it is put first, "Fear God." And here the place in the last of Ecclesiastes is to be adjoined, where it is written, "Fear God and keep his commandments." And me thinketh that man is bound to fear God chiefly in three sorts: that is to say, first, in the bountiful bestowing of his gifts and benefits; secondly, in the evident promoting of his servants; and lastly, in the full rendering and restoring unto man what is his.

Fear of God standeth in three points.

First, I say, in the bountiful bestowing of his gifts and benefits. And for this cause the emperor Justinian writeth:[1] "Although there is nothing to be accounted good, which doth exceed and is too great, yet for a prince to bestow accordingly upon the church, it is very good." For why? the king and emperor is bound to bestow so much the more substance, how much the more God hath given to him, and to bestow the same both frankly, and especially to famous churches, wherein the best and greatest measure is of the Lord's gifts; that is, a great gift. And to this end Gregory enacteth a law [cap. 1. 'extra. de donationibus'], that nobility ought in a manner to prescribe this law to himself, to think himself bound, when he giveth, to give freely; and unless he still increase in giving, to think that he hath given nothing. [2]Wherefore Abel, as

(1) *A brief Recapitulation of Bishop Edven's Answer, with certain Notes in Reply to his Popish Reasons, addressed to the Reader.*

The answer of bishop Edven, in the name of the other prelates, to the oration and articles before objected by the lord Peter, consisteth of two parts. First, it declareth the fear due to God. Secondly, the honour due to the king. The first of these is, the fear of God, which, he saith, consisteth in three things. 1. In giving to God. 2. In honouring his ministers. 3. In restoring that which hath been taken away, &c. The second, which is the honouring of the king, he saith, consisteth in a double sort; that is, in words only, wherein is flattery. Also in deed; which again he divideth into four members. 1. When a man counselleth a king to that for which his dominion is loved. 2. When the king is counselled to that whereby his honour and excellency is not diminished. 3. When the king is counselled to that whereby his fame and renown is maintained. 4. When a king is counselled to that, whereby his conscience is not wounded, &c. And this is the order of his whole tractation. Now remaineth with like brevity, to recite the reasons and arguments in order, whereby he proveth the premises, with the subdivision of every member and part thereof. Wherein the studious reader may note both the subtle proceedings of these popish prelates, and also the feeble and impotent ground whereupon they build; whose building, as by this discourse and many others may appear, wholly and finally tendeth to this: To maintain their liberties, pomp, and estimation, above all other secular princes and persons.

First, as concerning fear to be given to God, which he divideth into three parts, in giving, in honouring, and restoring; for the first, he proveth that princes ought to give largely and without measure to the church, by these arguments.

By the testimony of Justinian: although nothing is good which is too much, yet, I answer, that in the time of Justinian, goods then given to the church, were the goods of the poor; wherein were used faithful distribution, voluntary giving, and necessary charity. But now, in our popish churches, revenues and lands given are not distributed to the poor; and yet are men compelled against their will to give still. And again, so little necessity is now to give to such, that almost all the wealth of realms is in their hands and houses; insomuch that they, flowing in such wealth, are now waxen so proud, that kings can scarcely bear any rule for them, as was proved before, that the pope's revenues here in England, amounted to more than three times double the stint of the king's crown. Wherefore by the counsel of Justinian, it was so then, and then might stand, "quod religio peperit divitias:" but now, as the time is altered, so that counsel holdeth not, "postquam nunc filia devoravit matrem;" that is, "after that the daughter hath devoured the mother." Finally, concerning men's giving to the church in these our popish days, four faults I note:

Four incommodities, in giving to the church.

First, that they give superfluously more than is sufficient to necessity of life.

Secondly, that they give to such as abuse it wickedly.

Thirdly, that in giving to them that need not, noblemen in mean time defraud their poor neighbours, who need indeed, and yet do not complain.

Fourthly, because of this title of giving, men have used, and yet do use, to put great hope of salvation therein, contrary to the testament of God in Christ's death, whereof examples are before.

(2) "Abel offered of the best to the Lord, and was blessed of God;" ergo, every great man that would be blessed of God, must offer of the best he hath unto the church. Answer: This argument, as it is far fetched, so it is soon answered, wherein three notes are to be observed.

Three things to be noted in offering to God and to the church.

First, that he who offereth unto the church of God, doth not therein offer unto God immediately as Abel did.

Secondly, neither is this to be granted, that he who offereth to all churchmen, offereth by and by to the church of God; for many times the churchmen are one, and the church of God is another. Lawrence, the martyr, showing forth the church of God, brought out the poor of the parish, and not the priests of the church.

The third note is; that if noble persons should offer unto God (by the example of Abel) that which is the best and fattest of the flock; then should they offer unto the Lord of their flocks only, and not of their lands. Yea, and to note the very truth, they are taught thereby to offer to God, neither cattle nor lands, but that which is the very best, that is, their own bodies for a lively sacrifice to God. He that offereth up to God a proud heart, and killeth it with the axe of humility, giveth unto him the best and fattest bullock he hath in all his flock. With like reason also I answer the place in Num. xviii. and of Chronicles [cap. ult.]

Edward I. A.D. 1307.

appeareth in Genesis iv., who offered of the best to the Lord, was blessed of God. And therefore other kings, the more they offered to God, the more they were both spiritually and temporally blessed of him: as we read of Joshua, David, Solomon, and others in the book of the Kings, and therefore it is so written in Numbers xviii.: "And ye shall separate unto the Lord's treasury, things that be chiefest and most principal." As likewise David saith in the first book of Paralipomenon,[3] the last chapter: "I have given all this with a glad heart, even with a good will, and now have I had joy to see thy people which here are present, offer with a free will unto thee." And no marvel, for David saith in that place: "For of thy hand we have received all, and to thee we give." And therefore it seemeth to me, because the kings of France, and the barons of the same, have given to God and his church more than any other; therefore they were happy and blessed above all other kings, and the more they did give to God, the more they received at his hands.

What benefit cometh by giving to the church.

Examples we have in Clovis, Charles, and St. Louis, how the more one giveth to God, the more one receiveth of him: For he, [Luke vi.] hath promised, "Give and it shall be given unto you:" Wherefore, a gift that a prince bestoweth upon the church is rendered again with triple increase, and that no less, in time of war, than in time of peace. I say in war time, because victory proceedeth of no other, but only of God; for it is written in the first book of Maccabees, (chap. iii.): "The victory of the battle standeth not in the multitude of the host, but the strength cometh from heaven." And likewise, in Exodus xvii., it is declared, "that when Moses held up his hands, Israel had the victory: but when he let down his hands, Amalek had the victory." To this end also serveth the last chapter of the second book of Maccabees, where Judas, being at the point to have the victory, thought he saw Onias and Jeremy, who had been high priests and very virtuous men, holding up their hands towards heaven, and praying for their people and all the whole city. Likewise, in peace time now, the long days of the king and of his sons, their peace, prosperity, and obedience, by the prayer of the church, is maintained and supported in the realm. For as long as Solomon was bent and given to building the house of God, so long he had peace; who thus in Proverbs xvi. teacheth us: "When a man's ways please the Lord, he maketh his very enemies to be his friends:" and also in 1 Esdras, chap. vi., where it is read, how the priests were commanded to offer sweet savours to the God of heaven, and pray for the king's life and his children. And well therefore may it be called a gift both favourable and irrevocable, whereby victory is given, life granted, and peace with security preserved. To serve God therefore, and liberally to give toward the worshipping of him, is the chiefest sign and token of Divine fear and love. "O ye that fear the Lord, believe him, and your reward shall not be empty." [Eccles. ii.]

In time of war.

In time of peace.

Secondly,[4] Concerning the fear of God, I would have you understand, that

that to offer up, or to separate unto the Lord's treasury, is not now to give to priests and chaplains of the church, who, peradventure, have more than they do well occupy; but to give liberally to the communion of saints who are needy, and are the true treasury of the church indeed, as Lawrence the true treasurer said.

(3) 1 Chronicles, xxxix. 17.—Ed.

(4) "By God's commandment we are bound in duty to honour our temporal fathers." *Ergo*, by the same duty we are bound much rather to honour our spiritual fathers, that is, priests and prelates. Answer: A father in common speech is diversely taken, as by age, by nature, by office. And to all these we of duty are bound to yield honour, reverence, obedience, submission; albeit not all after one sort, nor in like degree. For as we are bound to honour our fathers and mothers, so aged men and elders have also their honour and name of fathers; so magistrates and spiritual teachers, in their kind, have their honour and reverence. And St. Paul saith, [1 Tim. v.] "that such are worthy of double honour," "qui bene præsunt, et qui laborant in sermone." But, in this, two things are to be noted: Wherein this honour consisteth, and how far it extendeth. These spiritual fathers of the church think they be not honoured enough unless kings and emperors give and surrender unto them all the temporal rule and government, to do what they list, and none to control them: and unless noblemen and subjects endow them with temporal lands and possessions as much as they would have. And this they call honour, which they define only by giving temporally: where indeed it rather consisteth in giving spiritually, as to have a reverent opinion of their ministration, to yield a prompt obedience to their doctrine, to reverence them as the ministers of God, and not to despise, defame, or molest their persons; whereof St. Paul, also, about the same place speaketh, writing to Timothy, "Let no man despise thy youth," &c. And to Titus, "Let no man despise thee," &c. And this is to honour our spiritual fathers.

Two things to be noted in giving honour, wherein consisteth honour given to priests.

Secondly, To consider how far this honour extendeth: as no man doth deny, but that these pastors are worthy their double honour who rule well, so, if they administer not their office well, they are, under the oversight of the king bearing the temporal sword, worthy of double punishment. And yet to consider this double honour in them that rule well, how far it doth extend; if it be compared to the honour due to our parents, a case of necessity will soon decide it. For be it that our parents on the one side, and pastor on the other, stand in extreme need of the son's sup-

How far honour given to priests extendeth.

among the precepts of the Lord, the first and chiefest commandment of the second table is, to "honour thy father:" which precept is very well expounded in the Hebrews [chap. xii.], where it is not only meant of the fathers of our bodies, but also of the Father of Spirits. For as spiritual things do far exceed temporal matters; so much more a great deal the spiritual son is bound to reverence the spiritual father, and to be in subjection unto him, that he may live. And that the priests and prelates be the spiritual fathers, it is proved 2 Kings vi., where the king of Israel called Elizeus "father," saying: "My father, shall I smite them?" Unto this effect our Saviour [Luke x.] said to the apostles, whose successors the bishops are, "He that heareth you heareth me, and he that despiseth you, despiseth me;" also the apostle Paul [1 Thess. iv.], "He that despiseth you, despiseth not men, but God." Wherefore Justinian the emperor in another place saith, "We have great care to the church of God, that therein may be true doctrine and integrity of priest's life, which having, we trust that for our great gifts we shall receive such rewards at God's hands, as shall both be durable, and remain; yea and also what hitherto hath not happened." Blessed St. Jerome, in his register, writing to a certain emperor, which is also to be seen in the Decrees,[5] saith, "Let not the emperor disdain priests, but have special regard to them for His sake whose servants they be; and so let him rule over them, that due and condign reverence be given unto them. For they in the divine Scriptures are sometimes termed gods, sometimes named angels [Exod. xxii.], 'Then shall both their causes come before the gods.' Also Malachi ii., 'The priest's lips should be sure of knowledge, that men may seek the law at his mouth: for he is a messenger of the Lord of hosts.' And therefore it is no marvel, if we should vouchsafe to honour them, when God himself, in his speech attributing to them honour, termeth them gods and angels." And here is to be noted, how Constantine the emperor, when certain of his subjects presented unto him libels accusatory against the bishops, received them at their hands. But calling before him those bishops that were accused therein, in their sight he cast those libels into the fire, saying, "Depart you hence, and discuss these matters among yourselves; for it is not convenient and meet that we judge gods, because it is written, 'God stood in the synagogue of gods, and in the midst of them he did judge gods.'" In the same chapter it is declared, how that the Pagans, who worshipped golden and wooden gods, attributed great honour to the priests. What marvel is it then, if the godly and great and christian emperors do honour and reverence the priests of the true God? And, doubtless, it is their duty so to do. And it is reason, which the lord Peter, the last day, said in this point; that there are two powers, priesthood and dominion, the one spiritual, the other temporal, which no less differ one from the other, than the sun from the moon, the heaven from the earth, and gold from lead. And therefore if honour is due and to be given to the lesser power, by them that be underneath him: he that is chief of the higher power, of right good duty, is to be honoured and reverenced by all under him, as expressly is declared, cap.'Solit.' De mai. et obed. where answer is fully made to the allegation of the lord Peter, alleged by him to make for his own purpose, that is to say, "Be ye subject to all creatures for God's sake," &c. There he speaketh of the subjection which standeth upon the merit of virtue, and not upon the duty of necessity. For else, if he should speak of the subjection which is by duty of necessity; then must it needs follow, that every bishop ought to be subject to every beggarly rascal in the city of Paris. For the text is, "Be ye subject to all human creatures:" but a rascal is a human creature: ergo, bishops must be subject to a rascal. Of the dignity of a bishop, Ambrose talketh in his pastoral. "The honour," saith he, "and the majesty of a bishop is without all comparison. If you compare it to the royalty of a king, it is even as you would compare metal or lead to the beauty of gold; for that is to be seen, when kings and princes stooping under the knees of priests and kissing their right hand, think themselves to be defended by their prayer." And because the kings of France have, more than others, honoured and reverenced the prelates, they have, above all others, flourished

Second part of fearing God. Honouring spiritual fathers.

Honour to be given to priests.

Two powers, temporal and spiritual, and what difference between them both.

Double subjection upon merit of virtue, and upon duty of necessity.

Authority of a bishop and a king compared.

Pride of the prelacy.

portation, wherein he can help but the one: nature, I suppose, sooner will and ought to run, and the word of Christ will sooner drive us, to our father, than to the priest's corban [Mark vii.]: so that this distinction may have place here: That as the one standeth upon merit of virtue, so the other standeth upon mere duty of necessity.

(5) Decret. 11 Quest. cap. 1. "Sacerdotibus."

Edward I. A.D. 1307.

and prospered. It is said, Eccles. iv., "He that honoureth his father, shall rejoice in his sons." And it followeth there, "He that honoureth his father, shall live a long life." This is therefore the sign of the fear of God. And as it is written, Eccles. iv., "He that feareth God honoureth his parents."

Third part of fearing God.

Thirdly, I say, that a man ought to fear God, in the full reverencing and restoring unto man what is his; for he that doth not give to another what is his, but goeth about to usurp, doubtless he feareth not God. Contrary, he that restoreth all again, he is said to love and fear God. [Eccles. xviii.] "He that feareth God will do good things;" and in the Psalm, "I have been afraid of thy judgments, and have done judgment and justice." For as the lawyers say, which is true, "a thing may be made mine divers ways, as by succession, commutation, prescription, or any other acquisition, either by law or custom;" and so of the rest. And whereas the lord Peter, the last day, by distinction of jurisdiction, temporal and spiritual, endeavoured to prove that he who hath spiritual jurisdiction, ought not to have temporal; otherwise there were no distinction thereof, but rather a confusion of jurisdictions: I will therefore prove the contrary, that these jurisdictions are both compatible in one person, especially in an ecclesiastical man;[6] and this will I prove by the law of God, by the law of nature, canon law, civil law, custom and privilege. But first I allege, that in accidental forms, some of them are distinct, that they are not clean contrary, but unlike, as whiteness and sweetness. Other forms there be which are so distinct, that they are clean contrary one to the other, and are not compatible in one subject, for one contrary expels another, and importeth the negative of the other. Wherefore those things be contrary, which one from another are most of all distant and disagreeing, and which, in one susceptible, may come one after the other, but not together, as the philosopher teacheth in the Predicaments. But those forms which are so distinct that they be not contrary, but unlike, are compatible in one subject, as quantity and quality, which, being distinct in respect of their 'genus generalissimum,' yet may be in one person; and fortitude and temperance, being under one kind of moral virtue, are found to be in one man, as logic and grammar, which are also species and kinds in one genus, viz. of 'intellectus.' Therefore it is no good argument:[7] These forms be distinct, ergo, they be not compatible in one subject. And, therefore, that the jurisdictions temporal and spiritual are so distinct, that they are not contrary but compatible, it is evident hereby; because things contrary be so, that the one cannot be ordained to concur with the other, but rather the one confoundeth and destroyeth the other: but, in this case, jurisdiction temporal is ordained for the spiritual; and contrary, the spiritual for the temporal. Or rather, the one dependeth on the other, as the clearness of the moon doth on the brightness of the sun. Also the one jurisdiction so helpeth and comforteth the other, that there is no contrariety in them. And therefore it is no good consequence, because they are distinct, ergo, they are not compatible in one person. This also is to be proved *de facto*. "For the earth is the Lord's, and the plenty of the whole universal world, and all that dwell therein." It is proved likewise by this reason: for if the jurisdictions be not compatible, it should follow, that no ecclesiastical person should have any jot of temporal jurisdiction, neither land, tower, castle, lordship, nor any thing else; which is most absurd: and so by this means it should follow, that no ecclesiastical person should be in subjection unto the king, which were to the great derogation of the king's majesty's crown and dignity. It must needs be, therefore, that these jurisdictions be compatible, notwithstanding the distinction of them one from another. And thus much for answer to all these reasons, by the which lord Peter proved the distinction of these jurisdictions.

A thing made mine, divers ways.

Six proofs that the jurisdictions temporal and spiritual, are compatible in one person.

Forms being dislike and not contrary, may be compatible in one subject.

(6) "These jurisdictions temporal and spiritual, are compatible in one person." Answer: I grant "pro ratione subjecti:" that is, in the subject itself there is no cause to the contrary, but these vocations may both be exercised by one person, as they have been by the pope, one after the other, (and so may contrary forms also) and yet the pope's person hath been able to sustain them both. But now, here is to be considered, not, what the nature of the subject is able to bear by logic, but what order is taken herein by the will of God, whose order is this: that they, who with Peter are called to the feeding of the flock, should leave their fishing-nets, and fish for men; and that they who labour in the warfare of the Lord should not entangle themselves with the business of this life, whereby they may be more free to please him, whose soldiers they are. [Tit. ii.]

Two forms not contrary, may be compatible.

(7) "The jurisdictions temporal and spiritual, are so distinct that they are not contrary," &c. Answer: And what let is there then, but our queen now, and other kings hereafter, may have the government of both states, as well ecclesiastical as temporal? Seeing both the forms being compatible, may concur both in one subject; why not as well in the person of the king within the realm, as in the person of the pope without the realm?

These things premised, I proceed further to prove that a person ecclesiastical, who hath jurisdiction spiritual, may also have temporal jurisdiction; and that the jurisdiction temporal may be in an ecclesiastical person, I will prove by the Scriptures: and first out of the Old Testament, to the evident probation whereof, it is to be understood, that God, after the creation of the world and man, even unto Noah's time, would govern the world himself, as king, by the ministry of angels;[8] by reason whereof he gave and pronounced sentence himself against Cain. [Gen. iv.] Noah also, who offered burnt-offerings unto the Lord, and built an altar [Gen. viii.], which thing appertained only unto the priests, had the government and rule of all things, as well spiritual as temporal, which were in the ark.[9] Melchisedec likewise, who was the priest of the most high God, and also king of Salem [Gen. xiv.], had both the jurisdictions in his own hands.[10] For that master of history declareth: That all the first-begotten of Noah, even unto Aaron's time, were priests; who at meals and offerings blessed the people, and who only had the 'jus primogenituræ,' whereby the regiment of others was due unto them. Moses, in like manner, of whom it is said in the Psalm, "Moses and Aaron, among his priests," consecrated Aaron and his children to be priests; which Aaron did judge the whole people in temporal matters, yea, and that in causes of inheritance and real property, as appeareth in Numbers [chap. xxvii.], and many other places. To the same purpose serveth that passage [Deut. xvii.], where it is said, "If a matter be too hard for thee in judgment betwixt blood and blood, betwixt plea and plea, betwixt plague and plague, then shalt thou rise and go up to that place that the Lord thy God hath chosen, and shalt come to the priests, the Levites, and to the judge then being, and shalt ask, Who shall show unto us the truth of the judgment? and shalt follow their sentence. And if any man presumptuously shall refuse to obey the priest's commandments and the decree of the judge, the same shall die." Behold, how manifestly it doth appear, how not only the judgment appertaineth to a priest, between plague and plague, concerning the circumstances and irregularity of the law, but also betwixt blood and blood in matters criminal, yea, and betwixt plea and plea in civil matters; which thing doth appear to be in many judges out of the book of Judges. For Samuel, who was both a prophet and priest, was appointed judge for a long time over the people in matters temporal. And when the people desired a king, the Lord was highly offended with them, and said unto Samuel, "They have not refused thee but me, that I should not be king over them." Furthermore, as long as kings among the people of God used the advice and counsel of priests and bishops, it was well with them and their kingdom; but when they forsook and left the counsel of bishops and priests, then was their kingdom divided; and finally they were brought into captivity, in which captivity the people were altogether governed and ruled by the priests and prophets, as by Esdras and Nehemiah. And, last of all, by the means of the Maccabees, the kingdom and government were devolved and brought into the priests' hands, who were the kings and captains over the people, and had the government as well of spiritual matters as of temporal; as is read in Maccabees, of Mattathias and his sons, namely, of Judas, Machaby, Jonathan, Simon, and John the son of Simon, who, in all spiritual and temporal matters, were governors over the people of God. [1 Mac. ii.] Moreover, Jeremy, who was one of the priests, declareth after this manner [chap. i.]: "I have set thee over the people and kingdoms, that thou mayest root out, break, destroy, and make waste, and that thou mayest build up and plant." Besides this, in the time of judge Eliah, a priest in like manner had the judgment of temporal matters. And so much concerning the proof hereof, out of the Old Testament.

Proofs out of the Old Testament.

Melchisedec both king and priest, Ergo, the pope may have both jurisdictions.

Samuel a judge in temporal matters, Ergo, the pope may have both jurisdictions.

Secondly, I prove my former proposition by authorities taken out of the

(8) "God, after the creation of the world," &c., "even unto Noah's time," &c. Answer: If God unto Noah's time governing the world as king, gave sentence himself against Cain, as we say, how then did he that by the ministry of angels? If he did it by the angels his ministers, whether is more like then that it make for the pope, or rather for kings and princes, whom the Scripture thrice in one chapter calleth the ministers of God, to execute punishment on him that doth evil. [Rom. xiii.]

(9) "Noah also who offered," &c. Answer: If offering of burnt sacrifices to God do make a priest, then was Cain also, and Abel, Abraham, Isaac, and all the patriarchs, priests. If he had both temporal and spiritual jurisdiction over those that were in his ark, I marvel why he did not curse then the disobedient crow that returned not to him again.

Noah a priest, and had both jurisdictions in the ark.

(10) "Melchisedec likewise," &c. Answer: Melchisedec properly did bear a figure of Christ, both king and priest, and of none other.

Edward I. A.D. 1307.

New Testament. For Christ had not only both the powers, by divine nature, whereby he created all things out of nothing, and by consequence was God over all, but also by his humanity had both powers; for he was the priest after the order of Melchisedec, as it is said in the Psalms, and also is alleged to the Hebrews, who had both on his vesture and on thigh written, "King of kings, and Lord of lords." [Rev. xix.] By this vestment or thigh was meant his humanity, which was joined to his divinity, as the garment is to him that weareth it. He said of himself [Matt. xxviii.], "Unto me is given all power, both in heaven and in earth."[11] As also saith the apostle [Heb. i.], "Whom he made and constituted heir of all universal things." And again [Heb. ii.], "He hath made him not much inferior to the angels. He hath crowned him with glory and honour, and hath set him above the works of his hands: thou hast put all things in subjection under his feet, sheep and oxen, and all the whole cattle of the field." When therefore it is said, "He made all things subject unto him;" he excludeth nothing, as the apostle there saith. Whereby it is apparent, that as concerning his human nature, in the which he was made less than the angels, all things were subject to him. Also this appeareth in Philippians [chap. ii.]: "He humbled himself, wherefore God exalted him;" and it followeth, "That in the name of Jesus should every knee bow, both of things in heaven, and of things in earth, and of things under the earth." Behold here, that in that nature in which he did humble himself, he was exalted, "because every knee should bow down to him." This in like manner hath St. Peter, in Acts x., where he saith, "he was constituted of God, the judge of the quick and the dead." And he speaketh of the nature which God raised up the third day, as the whole Scripture proveth. And likewise St. Peter had this power given him, whom Christ constituted and made his vicar;[12] who also condemned by sentence judicially Ananias and Sapphira,[13] for lying and stealing. [Acts v.] Paul also condemned a fornicator convicted.[14] [1 Cor. v.] And that Christ would have the correction and judgment of such matters to appertain to his church, a text in Matthew xviii. expressly declareth, where it is said, "If thy brother trespass against thee, go and tell him his fault between him and thee: if he hear thee, thou hast won thy brother; but if he heareth not, then take with thee one or two, that in the mouth of two or three witnesses all things may be established: if he hear not then, tell it unto the congregation: if he hear not the congregation, take him as an heathen man and a publican. Verily I say unto you, whatsoever you bind on earth, the same shall be bound in heaven; and whatsoever you loose on earth, the same shall be loosed in heaven." Behold, how expressly it is commanded, that whensoever in any matter one offendeth the other, he being first charitably admonished, the matter must be published and referred to the order of the church and congregation.[15] But if the offender do not obey and hear the admonition, he is to be taken as a heathen and a publican: which is as much to say, like one that is excommunicated by the church and congregation, so that he may have no communion or participation with it. And that this was the intention of Christ, this seemeth much to prove, where, in giving the reason hereof, he immediately addeth, "Verily, I say unto you, whatsoever," &c. [omnia terminus distributivus], where note this term distributive, 'whatsoever;' so also the apostle argueth, in Hebrews ii., that if he ordained all things to be subject unto him, he excludeth nothing unsubjected.[16] Wherefore, thus I may argue: If all things that the church and congregation doth loose, be loosed, and every thing that the

Proofs out of the New Testament. Christ by his human nature had both powers.

(11) "Unto me is given," &c. Answer: That Christ hath all power given him, no man doubteth; but yet the same Christ saith, that his kingdom is not of this world; neither would he be made a king in this world, &c. "Non eripit mortalia, qui regno dat cælestia," &c.

(12) "Whom Christ, &c. made his vicar, &c." Answer: Here in one line be two lies. For Peter had not the very same power in heaven and earth as Christ had, neither was he the vicar of Christ.

(13) As the offence of Ananias and Sapphira was not temporal but spiritual; so did Peter kill them not judicially, that is, as a temporal judge; but spiritually, that is, by the power of the Spirit, which Spirit wrought by him, not as by a judge, but as a minister. And although this act of Peter was extraordinary for a singular example; yet, let any prelate with the like power of Spirit so do, and none will blame him.

(14) And so likewise the condemnation of Paul against the Corinthian, was only spiritual and not temporal.

(15) "Must be referred to the order," &c. Christ would have these causes to be referred to the hearing of the church, for spiritual admonition, but not for the temporal jurisdiction of the prelates.

(16) All things that the true church doth truly bind are bound, I grant: but first let the pope prove his church to be the true church, and himself to be the universal head thereof, and then let him claim the keys.

:hurch bindeth, is bound; there is nothing that the church may not loose and ›ind. Or by logic, thus I may reason: there is nothing bound by the church, hat is not bound in heaven; which argument is good by a certain rule of logic, vhich saith, that contraries, if the negation be put after, are equivalent; for very thing and nothing, whatsoever thing and no manner of thing, be conrary one to the other; and so nothing not, is as much as to say, all things. iecondly, I do prove it out of another text of Luke [chap. xxii.], which place ıe alleged to make for his purpose; but I will strike him with his own weapon; or where he said, That by the two swords the two powers, temporal and spiriual, were to be understood;[17] it was so indeed: but to whose hands would he, pray you, have these two swords committed? Truly to the hands of Peter nd the other apostles, &c. But the holy father the pope succeeded Peter and he other apostles, the bishops, disciples, curates, parsons, as in the Gloss appearth [Luke x.], whence I argue thus: that by the two swords, the two powers re meant; but Christ willed those two swords to be put into the church's ands: ergo, likewise the two powers. But you may reply and say, that Christ id reprehend Peter because he struck with a temporal sword and cut off an ar, saying unto him, "Put up thy sword," &c.[18] Which reason is of no force; or Christ did not will Peter to cast away the sword quite from him, but to put into the scabbard and to keep it, giving to understand thereby, that such ower, although it be in the church's hands, yet the execution thereof (as apertaineth to bloodshedding in the new law), he would have to appertain to the ecular judge: yet, perhaps, according to the discretion and will of the clergy.

Thirdly, I prove this by the intent of St. Paul [1 Cor. vi.], where he saith, ıat "they which have secular business, and contend one against another, ught to be judged by the saints." And that they should judge therein, he ıade this argument: "Know you not that the saints shall judge the world?"[19] ınd if the world be judged by you, are ye not good enough to judge small ifles? As though he would say, Do ye not know how that ye shall judge the ngels? How much more then may you judge things secular? And it followth; "If you have judgment of secular and worldly matters, take them who re despised in the church and congregations, and make them judges." Neither oth it make any thing against it, because the apostle in the same place infereth, "I say it to your shame;" for that is to be referred to those, where he iith, "Appoint those which are despised." Wherefore the apostle speaketh onically in this matter, as meaning thus: Sooner and the rather you ought to ın to the judgment of the despised who be in the church, than to the judgıent of those who be out of the church: ergo, the rather to resort to the ıdgment of the wise, who remain in the church and congregation. Wherefore ıe apostle by and by added, when he said, "I speak to your shame: what, ot one wise man amongst you that can judge between brother and brother?" leaning thereby, that there were some. By these, therefore, and many other ke reasons, which for brevity I omit, it appeareth that both the powers may e in an ecclesiastical man's hand: and that an ecclesiastical man is 'capax,' oth of the temporal and spiritual jurisdiction. Nor is it any matter if it be bjected, that Peter, and other apostles, and Christ himself, used little this temoral power: for in them there was not the like reason,[20] as now there is in us, ı is proved in the 22 Quæst. 1. cap., and in many other places of the law.[21] he apostles at first took no receipt of lands and possessions, but the price only ıereof;[22] which now the church, with very good reason, doth receive, and that the great merit both of the giver and offerer, as it appeareth in Constantine ıd others; in the which aforesaid chapter the reason of diversity is well proved, r that the apostles did foresee, that the church should be among Gentiles, and ot be only in Judea, &c. And further, at the beginning, Christ and his apostles

(17) The two swords do as much signify the two regiments, as do the two fishes wherewith Christ d feed four thousand persons.

(18) Christ bade Peter put up his sword, and not cast it away: *Ergo*, the church may have e temporal sword. Answer: God give you good morrow, I have brought you a capon.

(19) "Know ye not that the saints," &c. Answer: St. Paul here willing the Corinthians to plead eir matters, not before the heathen, but before the saints, meaneth the faithful of the congregaon, not only prelates.

(20) "In them there was not the like reason," &c. Answer: I grant that Christ and true ıristians is one thing; antichrist and his church is another thing.

(21) 22 Quæst. 1 cap. futuram.

(22) As ye say, the apostles had no leisure to take lands and possessions for preaching, but now r lordly loitering, you have leisure enough.

Edward I. A.D. 1307.

were wholly bent and given to our health, salvation, and erudition; little sticking or standing upon the exercise of every church's jurisdiction, having regard to that which is written in the Corinthians [chap. vi.], "All things are lawful unto men, but all things are not expedient." And likewise in Ecclesiastes [chap. viii.], we read, that "every thing hath his time." But now, through the grace of God, the whole people of the realm of France have submitted themselves to the christian faith; worthily therefore the church is occupied about administering justice, and punishing vice; for peace shall be the work of justice. [Isaiah xxxiii.] And in these judgments this only is to be considered, that the life of man be reformed. Thus you see how this our conclusion somewhat is confirmed by the Scriptures.

Probation by civil law and reason.

Now will I prove it by natural law and reason, and first after this manner: he seemeth most fit to play a good judge's part, who followeth nearest God;[23] for properly God is the ruler and director of all judgments, who saith [Prov. viii.] "By me the law-maker shall decree justice and just things:" but ecclesiastical persons follow next to God, and be nearest him; for that they be elected of God into a peculiar people, whereof it is said [1 Pet. ii.], "You are a chosen generation, a royal priesthood, a holy nation, and a peculiar people, that you should show the virtues of him that called you," &c. *Ergo*, It is most fit that persons ecclesiastical, and churchmen, should judge of such matters.

Moreover, secondly, none doubteth, but that the correction and punishment of sin belongeth to ecclesiastical persons; wherefore when such things be not committed without sin and offence of the one party, it is evident that the church may have cognition thereof. Also, whoso hath power to judge of the end, hath also power to judge of things ordained to the end; for the consideration of the things ordained to the end, riseth of the end. When therefore the body is ordained for the life and soul, and temporal things for spiritual, as for the end; the church which doth judge of spiritual things, may in like manner lawfully judge of temporal things. All which is sufficiently confirmed, in extra. cap. "Judiciis," where it is said, That the accessary followeth the nature of the principal; which appeareth sufficiently by example. Forasmuch, therefore, as these two jurisdictions be compared to two lights, that is to say, to the sun and moon, and all the whole clearness and brightness of the moon, both in form and virtue, dependeth of the sun, and in the sun, and that the brightness of the sun is not of the moon, or in the moon; it is plain that spiritual jurisdiction, which is compared to the sun, hath in it, both in form and virtue, the jurisdiction temporal, and not contrary. Many other like reasons might be brought in; but, since the time waxeth short, I will omit them.

Thirdly, I prove it by the civil law [Auth. Diffe. Jud. "Si tamen," ix. col.], where it is said, "If a secular judge be suspected, let the bishop of the city be joined unto him: but if he be negligent, then let the whole judgment be referred to the bishop." In like manner Theodosius the emperor enacted such a law, that whatsoever suitor being plaintiff in any kind of matter, whether at the beginning thereof, or after contestation of law, or when the matter came to confirmation or to sentence; if the plaintiff had once chosen the court and jurisdiction of the holy see, there without any doubt, though the defendant resisted and dissented, the matter before the bishops and other ecclesiastical judges should be determined and ended. Which law afterwards Charlemagne, who was king of France, confirmed in these words, "We will and command, that all our subjects, as well Romans and Frenchmen, as others under our dominion whatsoever, be by law and custom henceforth bound and charged to keep this for a perpetual and prescript law; 'That whosoever began, or commenced a suit,' &c. as is above mentioned," &c. [2 Quæst. 1. "Quicunque," &c. c. 2.] But you may object and say, that this law is abrogated, as the gloss seemeth there to imply. But all will not serve; for although this law is not introduced into the body of the law, yet for all that, it is not abrogated. But surely it is a privilege honourably granted to the whole universal church, which the emperor cannot take away, no more than any other liberty of the church.

23) "He seemeth most fit to play a good judge's part who followeth nearest God." 'Ecclesiastical persons follow next God. *Ergo*, Prelates of the clergy are most meet to bear temporal rule.—Answer: If God here be taken for that God, which is called the belly, I grant they seem to follow nearer. But if it be taken for the true God, not I, but their own fruits, life, and doctrine shall decide; and Isaiah also would deny their minor, and say, that this people draweth near to me with their lips, but their heart is far from me.

By the canon law also this privilege is confirmed [extra. de jud. c. "Timor. Novil."], and moreover, it seemeth to be confirmed by the civil law [c. de Sacros. "Si eccle. privilegium"); although it be not expressly, but generally named, and so it is clear by the civil law, that such jurisdiction doth pertain to ecclesiastical persons.[24] By canon law in like manner in places infinite [Distinct. 22. cap. "Omnes patriarchæ;" 2 Quæst. 5. ca. "Si quis Presbyte.;" 2 Quæst. 1. cap. "Relatum;" 25. Distinct. cap. "ecce." Extra de Judiciis. "Novit." De competenti foro. cap. "Licet;" et multis aliis]. Yea and further, the canon law so far proceedeth, that whosoever goeth about by custom to interrupt or hinder any, having such jurisdiction, incurreth sentence *ipso facto* of excommunication [ca. "Quoniam intelleximus de immunitate Eccle." lib. sext.]. Which is most plain by the notorious custom, time out of mind, in the days of the good and christian princes, where to violate such custom, it is plain sacrilege [2 Quæst. 1. Tit. i. &c. 2.] For by the law, custom winneth and gaineth jurisdiction, especially to him that is 'capax' thereof: yea and further, custom, time out of mind, is amongst all persons in place of written and confirmed law. Now, seeing the church of France hath in common been used, with the temporalty, to judge and decree both in actions personal and real touching the church, it is plain, that such custom winneth jurisdiction to it. *Ergo, &c.* But the Lord Peter avouched, that the custom could not prevail in this case, because here lacked true dealing. Besides, the said law is called imprescriptible, for that it is 'jus fisci.' But this maketh nothing against us; for the church of France rather challengeth this law by custom than by prescription; which custom seemeth rather to be brought in by the free will and election of the people, frequenting more the ecclesiastical consistories than the secular courts. Besides, this custom, in that it hath been oftentimes decided in judgment contradictory (judicium contradictorium), many of the barons dissenting and not consenting thereto, is much thereby confirmed. This custom, I say, of the church, hath been fast established by the consent and assent of the prelates, and then confirmed by the kings of France, your predecessors, and so peaceably observed of the church.

Probation by canon law. *Custom.*

And yet may the church challenge this by prescription, for that there are but three things which are required in prescription; that is to say, title, true dealing, and continuance of time. And it is without doubt, that the churches both purely have, and in times past had, a good title, as appeareth by the privilege granted by Theodosius the emperor, and confirmed by Charles, who gave in commandment, to keep the same inviolably, which title it hath both by divine, natural, and human law, as before is mentioned; wherefore it must needs have true dealing, when so many great and clear titles are known to condescend thereunto. Also there concurreth such continuance of time, that even against 'jus fisci,' it is prescriptible: for it hath not only continued for the space of a hundred years, but also more than six hundred years last past. Neither is this always true, this law is inprescriptible, especially of the church, which, inasmuch as it appertaineth to the spiritualty, is not subject to the king, but is much more noble, and far excelleth; even no less than the sun doth the moon, gold lead, and heaven the earth. And this is certain, and no less reason, that the higher and equal may duly prescribe law against him, that is either equal or lower in degree; as one king may do to another. Wherefore it appeareth, that the church may prescribe this, although it were 'jus fisci,' as indeed it is not.

Three things pertaining to prescription. 1. Titulus. 2. Bona fides. 3. Temporum continuatio. *The church not subject to the king.*

Finally, This is proved by privilege granted by Charlemagne, king of France, as before, and by Louis II., and by Philip your uncle, and by Louis and Philip your kinsmen, which privileges we have here ready to show. But perhaps you will say, that these things cannot agree: that the church hath this jurisdiction both by law, custom, and privilege, which all cannot well hang together; for if the church have it by one of these, it should follow, that the church lacketh it by another. But this may I answer two manner of ways; first, that the privilege may be double, one as a bringer in of a new law, and thus it cannot be reconciled; the other, as a confirmative and declarative of the old law; and this way it may well be agreed, which distinction may also take place in custom. Wherefore it may thus be answered, that although this jurisdiction is

Objection. *Answer.*

(24) "You are a chosen generation, a royal priesthood," &c.—Answer: This place of Peter was written not only to persons ecclesiastical, but to the whole congregation of the saints dispersed, as the words following may declare: "Qui eratis quondam non populus," &c.

Edward I. A.D. 1307.

due unto the church by law, it appertaineth also unto the same by privilege and custom, but yet not by such kind of custom and privilege which induceth a new law: but which declareth and confirmeth the old law. And if any will reply, demanding wherefore the church of France should more challenge this, than any other churches in other realms, which have no such prerogative; I can soon answer them. If the kings of France (whom God with singular grace, honour and privilege, far above all other princes, hath blessed and endued for three special causes, to wit, for their great faith and devotion unto God, for their honour and reverence to the church, and for their good justice showed unto the people) have granted to the church special liberties, or have permitted those which before were granted, peaceably to be kept and observed; why then they should have them, it is no marvel. Yea and further, their devotion unto the church hath been such, that the nearer the churches were unto them, the more liberties they enjoyed; and yet had these princes never the less on that account, but rather the more; which is evident, and redoundeth to the great honour and nobility both of the king and his realm.

French king more blessed than others in three things. 1. Faith to God. 2. Honour to the church. 3. Justice to the people.

I have oftentimes heard of others, how that four or five things do especially nobilitate and adorn this realm.

Five things ennoble the realm.

First, their sincere and inviolable faith; for it was at no time read, that the kings of France (since the receiving of the faith) did ever swerve from the same.

Secondly, the nobility of blood, which descended from Priam the king of the Trojans, and successively from Charlemagne and other royal kings.

Blood of France came out of Priam.

Thirdly, the unity and peace of concord, which especially, above all others, reigned and flourished in the realm of France.

Fourthly, the solemnity and pomp of the prelates and clergy.

Fifthly, the well-disposed readiness of the barons and subjects to obey.

If therefore the prelates of this realm should not have this law and privilege, but should be deprived thereof, then should the king and his realm lose one of his noble estates, whereby they are highly magnified, I mean the bravery, solemnity, and royalty of the prelates; for then, they should not only be neither pompous nor royal, but more beggarly and miserable than any others, the most part of their living consisting herein. I do conclude, therefore, that it is proved both by divine law, natural law, canon law, civil law, custom, and privilege, that the right of determining such temporal matters of the church may of right appertain to the church of France; and so I turn the lord Peter's theme against himself.

Besides this, I will propound that which is most plain and manifest; that whatsoever things be offered up to the church, and are converted to the dominion and property of the same, be God's, and appertain to him; forasmuch as they are said to be dedicated to and sanctified by him, as sufficiently throughout the Levites may appear, as declared [1 Sam. xxi.] concerning the bread offered to God, where it is said, "I have no common bread under my hands to eat, but holy bread." Wherefore it was not lawful for the laity to eat of the same bread, but in time of great necessity; which is also proved, where it is read, [Dan. v.] "Because king Belthazzar, and his lords, with his queen, drank in the golden and silver vessels, which his father Nebuchadnezzar had taken out of the temple of Jerusalem; in the same (very) hour there appeared fingers, as it had been of a man's hand, writing right over the candlestick upon the plain wall in the king's palace. And the king saw the palm of the hand that wrote; and that which was written was *Mene, Thekel, Phares*; the interpretation whereof is this, as there it appeareth: *Mene*, God hath numbered this kingdom and brought it to an end: *Thekel*, Thou art weighed in a balance, and art found too light: *Phares*, Thy kingdom is dealt in parts, and given to the Medes and Persians." The very selfsame night was Belthazzar, the king of the Chaldees, slain, and Darius succeeded in the kingdom of the Medes; the monarchy of the Assyrians being then translated unto the Medes. Whereby it appeareth, that those things which are offered up to the church, belong to God, and are so dedicated to him that no layman may use them; which if they do, they must look to receive vengeance at God's hand, as Belthazzar did.

These things now ended, I will argue out the lord Peter's theme, which was, "Give unto the emperor, that is the emperor's; and unto God, that is God's." But this jurisdiction, which, as I proved before, is diversely converted to the dominion and property of the French church, is now God's, and therefore to be reserved to and for him; wherefore, whensoever any goeth about to take away the same, the good and godly ought to answer, what Ambrose did to the Gothen soldiers, sent to him by the emperor, which was to this effect "If the emperor," quoth he, "had requested that which had been mine, I would not have denied him, albeit that whatsoever I have, all is the poor's; but because he demandeth those things which belong to God, wherein he hath no right or interest, I had rather he should imprison me, yea and cut off my head, than condescend to his request therein:" alluding to the history of Naboth [1 Kings xxi.], in which is to be seen how Naboth, the holy man, possessor of the vineyard, was requested by the king to give up his vineyard, who made answer, "I will not give unto thee the inheritance of my fathers," at which answer the king was marvellously offended. "Wherefore," quoth Ambrose, "if Naboth would not deliver his vineyard, shall we deliver to you the church of Christ? no, God forbid, that I should deliver you Christ's heritage. Naboth did not deliver the vineyard, nor surely will I deliver Christ's church." And further he addeth a good saying, "I can neither diminish nor add any thing to the church of God, for that I took not upon me the charge of keeping it besides this, it is my duty and office to consult with the high Emperor of Salvation in this matter what is to be done. and doubtless I may not deliver any thing to him, nor yet he receive any thing of me." [24 Quæst. ultimo capite "Convenior." et "Qui."] Wherefore, by these and the like reasons it appeareth, that not only jurisdiction spiritual, as the lord Peter falsely hath suggested, doth belong to God, but also, all other kind of jurisdiction whatsoever touching the church, whether it be by law, custom or privilege; insomuch that neither may we surrender the same to any, nor yet may the king at our hands take the same.

Ambrose in case denieth to obey the emperor.

Naboth denieth the king his vineyard

Further, the lord Peter affirmed, that Christ, for example sake, did pay tribute; which is untrue, as appeareth in Genesis xlvii., for the lands of priests were free from paying of all kind of toll and tribute And if the lord Peter well considered Matt. xvii., he should have found there, how that Christ did not only not pay tribute for example sake, but rather proved how he was not bound to pay any at all. To conclude, therefore, the children be free, but ye pay, to avoid slander and offence: wherefore the text saith. "Lest we should offend them, go to the sea," &c But peradventure it may be answered, that by the example of Christ, to avoid offence, ye ought to pay. But this is untrue, because there is a double offence of the weaklings and of the Pharisees for as concerning the offence of the weaklings, which cometh of ignorance and not of malice, some things are to be omitted for a time, till they be better instructed, as the apostle saith in Romans xiv But as concerning the offence of the Pharisees, who commit and offend of a pretenced malice, there is nothing to be omitted, as Christ saith in Matt. xvi., to whom his disciples saying, "Do you not know how that the Pharisees hearing this word are offended?" he answered them, "Behold, suffer them, they are blind, and leaders of the blind," for that in the time of Christ, the offence then was of little ones. but now is the offence of the Pharisees; wherefore, then it was to be suffered for avoiding of offence, but now not so. Now therefore it is apparent that the third token of the fear of God consisteth in the complete true restoring of goods. and of him who hath such fear whereby he restored to God his own, it is spoken in Eccles. xv. "The seed of the man that feareth God shall be brought to honour. but the seed which transgresseth the commandment of the Lord shall be shamed" And thus it fully appeareth, how loving fear and obedience is due unto God, for the excellency of his majesty, because the words be, "Fear God."

How offence ought to be avoided

Third note of the fear of God

Secondly, I do say, that especial honour and reverence are due unto the king, for his dignity's sake, which followeth in the theme. Now it is said, "Honour the king." I will allege Ecclesiastes x; where it is specified, "In the midst of the brethren the ruler is holden in honour among them;" wherefore it seemeth to me that there are two kinds of honours, one which proceedeth from the lips, and that is named flattery, wherefore it is spoken in Matt. xvii., "This people doth honour me with their lips, but their hearts are far from me." There is another kind of honour which is real, and cometh from the heart; and this is the very true honour indeed, wherewith the king ought to be honoured. But me thinketh, that he doth really, and *de facto* in very deed honour the king,

Honour of the king.

Two kinds of honours

Double honour, with lips and with heart

Edward I. A.D. 1307.

who wisheth and counselleth him to keep and do those things, whereby his dominion is beloved, his royalty not diminished, his honour and fame preserved, and his conscience not burdened; and he that persuadeth him contrary to these, I think doth not honour the king.

To proceed therefore further; I say first, that he doth *de facto* honour the king, who persuadeth him those things whereby he may be beloved of his subjects: for a prince ought to study rather to be beloved than feared. And what greater treasure can a prince wish, than to have the hearts of his subjects? according to the saying of Seneca,[1] "The love of the citizens is a fortress invincible, and a bulwark not saultable." What thing is more to be wished for, what is better than to live and reign, every man willing and rejoicing thereof? And in my opinion, there is nothing which causeth a prince more to be beloved, than if he keep and maintain his ancient liberties, and bring in no alteration; wherefore it is said [Prov. xxii.], "Thou shalt not remove the landmarks which thy fore-elders have set." This place the lord Peter alleged to make for himself, which I will prove to make against him, and that by this reason, ye ought not to transgress the old limits and bounds which the fathers have set, for novelty and alteration doth engender discord; and for this cause, in making of new alterations there ought to be both evident utility, and urgent necessity. If, therefore, the prince will abrogate and take away the liberties granted by his forefathers and predecessors, he shall not be of his realm beloved; as it appeareth by Rehoboam. [1 Kings xi.] All this, likewise, is to be seen in the Chronicles, how that by these means many kingdoms and dominions were translated from nation to nation, and from their own native regiment to the rule of strange people. And now for this time, certain it is, that your grand predecessors Charlemagne, St. Louis, Philip the Fair, Louis and Philip his sons, with many others, have sealed and confirmed this liberty of the church. Wherefore for a man to counsel and persuade your highness to spoil the church of any thing, it is even the next way to spoil and undo yourself, and bereave you of that by which your dominion is beloved; and for this cause I thought good to put your grace in remembrance of 1 Mac. ii. 51, where it is written, "Remember the works of your forefathers, which they have done in their generations, and you shall receive great glory and renown for ever." Note here, your highness, by the way, how king Philip, grandfather to St. Louis, fostered and kept in his realm St. Thomas, archbishop of Canterbury; who, because he stoutly defended the liberties of his church, was banished out of England; how much more, therefore, are you bound to defend and maintain your own prelates in their liberties ratified and confirmed by your grace's predecessors, according to the saying of Gregory [25 Quæst. cap. "Si."] "If I should destroy and pull down those things which my predecessors have built and ordained, I should not be called a builder and maker, but justly accounted a stroy-good and puller down, as the voice of the Lord saith, 'Every kingdom divided within itself shall be confounded.' All knowledge and learning divided one against the other, shall be destroyed." In another place he saith, "It is oversharp, and against all good manner and civility, upon what reason and excuse soever, to break and subvert those things which are well ordained; or, by his example, to teach others at their pleasures to dissolve old constitutions." Mark here a story about a castle which was given to St. Remige, for the church's use, by Clovis the king, which king Pepin afterwards desired to have by exchange and recovery; to whom the said St. Remige appeared in his dream, and highly blamed him for it, saying, "A better man than thou gave it me, and yet wilt thou take it away from me?" And with that he smote him, who the next day was found all black; since which time, no king of France durst even lie in that castle. Verily therefore, he doth not honour the king, who giveth him counsel to pass the old limits that his old fathers did set; yea, rather the king's majesty ought to say unto them, that which is written in John viii., "I do honour and glorify my father;" that is, in keeping the liberties of the church, as they did which granted them: "but you have dishonoured me," in counselling me that which seemeth best to please yourselves, as it is written in Ecclesiastes iv., "The worship of a man's father is his own worship, and where the father is without honour, it is the dishonour of the son."

A prince rather to be loved than feared

A sentence.

In alteration, what to be considered.

Mark here a fable.

(1) Seneca de Clementia ad Neronem.

Secondly, I say, that he truly doth honour the king, who counselleth him, whereby his power and dignity are not diminished; for as it is great honour to the king's highness to increase and augment his power, so is it as much dishonour for him to diminish any jot thereof; and therefore the emperors were wont to call themselves victorious, in augmenting and increasing their commonwealth. And to say that you and your predecessors could not grant these things to the church, it were too, too absurd, and to the too much derogation of your majesty's most honourable estate. And therefore for you, most sovereign lord, who hold and possess such ample right and title in the realm of France, both by election and inheritance, not to grant and leave this to your posterity, it were to the great debasing of your majesty's honour, crown, and dignity. Yea, if it were (as God forbid), it would follow, that your predecessors lived continually in sin; yea, and further, it were as much to say (which were too vile) that blessed St. Louis by whom all France is beautified, could not be justly canonized. For as the lord speaker declared, if he took his oath at his coronation both to alienate nothing, and also to call in that which was before alienated, which is inseparable from the crown, it should follow that he was foresworn, and consequently committed deadly sin, and so could never be canonized, which is too, too absurd to be talked of. And if reply be made, that he might have repented; it is soon to be answered, that his sin is read of, but of his repentance it is not found, as it is said of Solomon. But put the case that it be true what the lord Peter said, then it must needs follow, that your grace could bestow nothing, neither country, town, nor tower; and yet there be few who willingly would not receive them, notwithstanding their allegiance and homage, which they pretend to your highness. Keep, therefore, and confirm, most renowned prince! that which was granted by your noble progenitors, otherwise your royal honour shall decrease; that it may be verified in you which is read of in Romans xi., "I will honour my ministry."

Thirdly, I do affirm, that he rightly honoureth the king, who persuadeth him to that whereby his honour and renown is preserved. For, in matters of weight and of great importance, next after conscience we must have regard to name and fame, as it is written in Proverbs xxii., "It is better to have a good name than riches." A good name far surpasseth all things, and is above silver and gold; and St. Augustine saith, "Two things are necessary for thee, conscience and name; conscience for God, and name for thy neighbour; and therefore it is written in Ecclesiastes iv., "Labour to get a good name, for that will continue surer by thee than many great treasures of gold." A good life hath a number of days. That renown and name the Lord, who anointed your grace with the oil of gladness, hath in a very little time more abundantly blessed you with, than any other prince; wherefore you ought to be more vigilant and careful how still to keep and enjoy the same, for it is no less virtue to keep that which is gotten, than to seek and get; whereby not only while you live, but also when you are dead, your glorious renown may live for ever: yea and further, that by you nothing be done, whereby any blot or soil should creep into that your so great renown, applying that to your grace which is said in Proverbs x., "The memorial of the just shall have good report," &c. Beware therefore, most noble prince, and take heed that in your days and time, the liberties of the church be not taken away (which God forbid) or diminished in any jot; for if your glorious name should be blotted therewith, there be thousands who would chronicle the same to perpetual memory. Wherefore, most christian prince, if such as trusted after their death for no other life, but only for fame and renown, lived a life most godly and virtuous, how much more ought we Christians, who look after another life, by our well-doings here, to win us a perpetual name and memory after our death? And you besides, if you should dishonour your name and fame, what a matter were it, considering how the kings of France were ever counted the most christian princes, and most bountiful towards the church, giving examples to other princes how to enrich their churches and the liberties thereof. And now especially, if your grace, the church in some places being in great persecution, should (which God forbid), show light to others to pull and take away that which was given by your forefathers to the church, what might the world say? For then for the like reason might the emperor deprive the church of all which was given to it by Constantine the emperor. Also other kings would do the like in their realms.

Who honoureth the king.

Conscience and good name.

God forbid that your highness should give such example! And, for my part, I would rather wish myself to be dead, than give you such counsel, that in so pernicious and naughty a matter you should be example to others; especially, when the kings of France, your predecessors, were defenders always against such as went about to take away the liberties from the church, which is the office of a king. Hieronymus saith upon Jeremy [see also in the 24 Quæst. 5. cap. "Regnum" et cap. "Princeps"], after this manner: "Let the princes of the world know and understand, how they are bound to make an account to God for the church which they take upon them to keep." Note you also, and read some examples out of stories and commentaries, what regard the kings of France had in observing those things; and see you by their example, to follow and do the like; and then shall it be verified in your grace which is written in Ecclesiastes xxxvii., "A wise man shall obtain honour amongst his people:" as also in chap. iii.: "He that honoureth his mother, is like one that gathereth treasure together."

The fourth honouring the king.

Fourthly, I say, that he indeed doth honour the king, who persuadeth him to do that whereby his conscience is not hurt. For, above all things, a christian man ought to beware how he do that thing, which should be a grudge unto his conscience, because "the life is more than is meat." [Matt. vi.] And assuredly I believe, that your grace would not commit that thing willingly, wherewith your conscience should be burdened, for all the world's good, and that justly; for the more miraculously God hath called your highness to the state of a king, and hath endued you with his grace, so much the more care ought you to have, and take heed that you offend him not. Nor is it to be doubted, whether in doing the contrary, he will not be the more grievously displeased with you, as he was with Saul. [1 Sam. xv.] Consider, therefore, most sovereign lord, that at what time you were crowned, you sware only these things following, and no others.

Oath of the French kings.

First, that you would defend and maintain the canonical law, privilege, and justice, granted to the bishops and the church, and, as much as in you did lie, to enlarge and amplify the same: also, that by your arbitrement all christian people, at all times, should keep the true peace of God and his church: also, that you should forbid to all nations all kind of sacrilege, spoilings, and iniquities: also, that in all kind of judgments, you should will and command equity and mercy: also, that throughout your whole territory and jurisdiction, you should sincerely, with all your endeavour, study to exterminate, and cut off from the church the noted heretics: all which, and no other, your majesty swore to fulfil, at the time of your coronation, under the leave and correction of the lord Peter, who affirmed you were sworn to something else. Now therefore, seeing it is a canonical privilege of the church, and in the heart of the whole (Cano. 6. q. 1. "Quicunque litem habens") incorporate; when also, by custom which is canonical, it came in, that the church and spirituality, may have cognition in a number of cases, against which divers articles have been here laid in: if this amongst the laity should not be observed in the church, your grace's conscience thereby might be somewhat burdened. In like manner, if you be bound with all your whole might and power to procure, that the whole of Christendom should keep the true peace of God and his church, much more have you to procure the same amongst your own barons and people, who evermore were all one with the church. And as always, where any church was in honour and estimation, there were belonging to it twenty stout barons and knights, whose office, as it was to defend the church; so was it the part of the church to pray for them, and to offer sacrifice for them unto God. And to this end it was that blessed St. Louis so much laboured in his time; who, when the greatest barons of his realm had confederated to suppress these liberties of the church, and had consulted to give him, to that end, the hundredth part of their goods, would never condescend thereunto, but always dissuaded them therefrom; and, finally, by his authority sealed and confirmed these liberties of the church. Consider here, your majesty, how pope Innocent at that time proceeded against those barons. I dare be bold to say, that if there should be now dissension between the prelates and barons, it would not be long before the commonalty would usurp to rule and bear domination; as by experience it hath been seen in many places, and, likewise, by practice we of late time might have seen, at what time the people stomaching the spiritualty in the parts of Campania and Burgundy, at last rose, and made in every town a king; and therewithal caused the officers, who brought citations and absolutions from the pope and other, to be well banged; and not long after, made insurrection against the lord's temporal, and served them with the like sauce; until by the king's power they were suppressed, and many of them hanged. And this doubtless was in the days of Louis, the last king of that name. Truly the noblemen ought not to be grieved with that of which the church is possessed, for that there be few of them who have not their brothers and kinsfolks who live and are maintained by the goods and revenues of the church; amongst whom if they should divide their inheritance, perhaps they would bring little or nothing at all. Let the barons also consider, how there are but few who believe not in the church; for the church is one, as in Canticles vi., "My dove and darling is one." Wherefore without great peril of transgression can they not persuade and counsel such liberties of the church to be abrogated and taken away.

Edward I.

A.D. 1307

Arg. By the possessions of the church many brethren and kinsmen of the nobles be maintained. Ergo, Such possessions not to be grudged. Belief in the church not in our faith.

That therefore your majesty's conscience may remain pure and immaculate, may it please your highness, by your authority, to seal and confirm this good, ancient, and canonical privilege; and contrary attempts, if any be made by way of proclamation or otherwise, to revoke and call in; and further, to keep your mother, the church of France, in her ancient free choice, liberty and customs; and then by you, in all things, God shall be glorified and honoured; to whom be honour and glory for ever and ever: Amen. Who then will honour you, as is said, "Whosoever shall honour me, I will crown him with that glory, in which consisteth the true honour, and is granted to none unworthy;" whereunto, also, none is admitted but who is worthy, as blessed St. Austin saith; which honour grant he unto you and us, who is blessed world without end: Amen. And because a bill of many articles has been exhibited, whereof part doth infringe the whole ecclesiastical jurisdiction, to the defence thereof we will, according to Ecclesiasticus iv., stand even to the death, where it is said, "For the truth strive thou unto the death, and God shall fight for thee against thine enemies:" some other of them containing only alleged abuses (of which we believe none such to be), but if there be, we will see redress therein: therefore, for the honour of God, for the unburdening of our consciences, for the king's majesty's reverence, and for the people's profit and peace, all we here assembled have concluded to see remedy, that the aforesaid abuses, if any such be, shall be avoided, to the quietness of the people, and praise of Almighty God. To whom be honour and glory, world without end. Amen.

To the bill of articles exhibited.

Another Sitting of the Parliament.

On the Friday following, being December twenty-nine, the prelates assembled themselves again together at the king's palace in Paris, where the reverend father, the lord Peter Bertrand, by God's permission bishop of Edven, spake openly there before the king, sitting with his counsellors and barons about him; taking for his theme that which is written in Genesis xviii., "O Lord be not angry that I speak yet more," &c., which he applied to this end: That for the majesty of the king, the prudency of his council, and the insufficiency of himself (considering the weightiness of the cause) he trembled and was afraid to speak; yet nevertheless, trusting upon his accustomed clemency, he took to him boldness, and presumed to attempt that which was appointed for him by the prelates, beginning with the ninetieth Psalm: "Lord thou art our refuge," &c. This he prosecuted in extolling the king's person, and his miraculous attaining to the crown of France; preaching, further, how he ought to be the champion and defender of the faith: all which he proved in few words, by many reasons and authorities.

Bishop of Edven speaketh.

He afterwards touched upon those propositions which were propounded by the aforesaid lord Peter de Cugneriis, and for no other cause, as he protested, but only to inform the conscience of his sovereign lord and king, and to advise his grace concerning the same; not going about to make any final judgment, determination, or answer, whereby either sentence, order, statute, right to any man, or other process, might ensue or be grounded. And namely, the commencement of the theme of the lord Peter, where he affirmed that the words "Render unto the emperor what is the emperor's, and unto God what is his" [Mark xii.], signified the obedience and subjection to the king, with the difference of the spiritualty from the temporalty; whereof the first member was

Edward I. A. D. 1307. proved by a text in Peter [1 Pet ii.], where it is said, "Be ye subject to every human creature," &c, also by the cap. "Solite, extra de majo. et ob." and by the c. "Novit extra de judicus," cap "de sacerdotibus" 10. q 1, with the notes about the same. Moreover, he touched upon the distinction of both jurisdictions, whereof the lord Peter proved the temporal to pertain to secular men, the spiritual to the clergy, by the words of our Saviour Christ [Luke xxii.], where he said, "Behold two swords." Also for that Christ did pay tribute; teaching thereby, how that the temporalties were to be reserved to the temporal men [Matt. xvii 27], q. ca "Si tribut" ca. "Magnum" In like manner, he touched upon the law of Justinian, where it is written, that two great gifts were ordained and granted of God, a bishopric and a kingdom: the first to bear rule over God's matters, the other over worldly things, &c, and, moreover, that these two be the cases which in no wise could be altered or changed [Prov. xx.], de Tion mo. lib. 1. et ult · and where it is affirmed also, that of such princely right the king could not abrogate and deprive himself, for that it was imprescriptible, appertaining to the crown and his regal seat, considering how he took his oath at the time of his coronation, not only not to break or alienate the laws of his realm, but also to restore and revoke such as were broken and alienated.

To these reasons it was answered, that the jurisdiction and determination of civil causes (about which the controversy then was) belonged to the church, both by God's law and man's law. By God's law it was proved, even from Adam's time to Christ's coming, [per Innoc ca "licet extra de foro, compe;"] and from Christ's coming, to Peter's time and his successors, [22 di. c "omnes patriarchæ," Matthew xvi] But how the church, in the realms of catholic princes, attained unto the right and interest which at this present it doth enjoy, the law proveth, [2 q. ca. 5. "Si quis Presbyter." 11 q 1. "Relatum." 25 dist. "Ecce;"] which also is confirmed by the emperors in the body of the law [ff. 3. "Si causam." col 9. 23. q ult c. "his, et a quibus."]

The canon furthermore teacheth, how that St Peter commanded all the princes of the earth, and others, to obey and give place to the bishops: c. "omnes, extra de major. et ob" 16. dist. "duo sunt;" wherefore it was concluded, that in no wise this right is to be separated and taken away from the church. And albeit, in the realms of tyrannous princes, this state of the church is violated and not kept, yet in this blessed realm of France it hath been always, even to these days, duly observed · c. novit. extra. de "judicus." Thus jurisdiction the laws of Theodosius the emperor, and Charlemagne, have also confirmed. [extra de judicus c. "nonne. all." 11. q 1. "quæcunque," etc. fe. jurisdictio. c. "expresse,"] where it is mentioned, that the same Charlemagne, king of France and emperor, especially constituted the said law. And likewise to speak of customs, it hath been known from time out of mind, that the same hath belonged to the church of France; he, therefore, who shall go about to violate this law, committeth sacrilege [11. q. 1. ca. 1. et 2]. And let not the king's majesty marvel, if in this most noble realm of France this prerogative be due unto the church; as hereby his power and nobility is beautified. Anth. ut. ind sine quoquo suffia fi in principio, col. 2.

Besides this, our sovereign lord and king, at the time he was crowned, was sworn by the evangelists to keep and observe this canonical privilege of the church. Further, the barons, who in a manner are all sworn to the church, swore fidelity to the same · by which oath of fidelity they are bound to keep these liberties and rites of the church. When, therefore, every oath which tendeth not to the perdition of the soul, is to be kept, *a fortiori* that oath, which is taken in favour of the church, is much more to be observed c. "Si vero extra de jure jurando," 22. quæst. 4. c. ult. Besides this blessed Louis Philip of Arragon, Philip the Fair, Louis, Charlemagne, and Philip, confirmed these privileges, customs, and liberties of the church, who all were sworn at their coronations, as before, &c

These things considered, who can advise the king's majesty, without damning of his own soul, contrary to these liberties granted, and so confirmed to the church? To him belongeth great reward, whosoever bestoweth any thing upon the church [Antho. de non alie. ac permut re. ecce · ss "si munis," col. 3]: neither maketh it against us, where it is said, that there are two swords, &c.; neither yet doth the distinction between the bishopric and kingdom, because it is true that there are two swords, the power whereof is left to the church's hand, although the execution of the material sword is committed to the temporal and secular men [Matt. xxvi.], where Christ saith to Peter, "Convert and put up the sword into the place." But as touching the distinction betwixt the bishopric and kingdom, indeed it is true as much as appertaineth to the end, and to the execution of blood, but not concerning the beginning and subject: for that in one subject, both the powers are, may be, and ought to be; as is before proved.

Why Christ paid tribute.

To that point, where it is said, that Christ paid tribute, it is answered, that he paid it, not because he ought, or was bound thereunto, because it is certainly true, that the sons of the king (as he was) ought not to pay, but that he did this to avoid offence; yea also that the clergy are not bound hereunto [Esdræ 1. et ult.]; wherefore, such things do not infer a consequence. Neither yet maketh that against us, where it is said, that the king our sovereign lord and master cannot abdicate from himself this right, especially for that he was sworn thereunto at the time of his coronation, &c.; for it is answered, that he may well abdicate the same. And how doth he abdicate that from himself, which he giveth and bestoweth to God and the church? The land is the Lord's, and doubtless to give, is nothing else but to render to God and the church their own; for then, by that reason, the gift given to the church by Constantine is nought and nothing worth, which is false; and this is proved 16 dist. ca. Const., whereby it appeareth that an emperor and king may alienate things of the empire (ff. de legatis i. l. apud Julianum ss. ult.), and yet thereby the empire or kingdom not be damaged, for that the thing returneth to the pristinate state (ss. de pactis l. unus ss. pactus 35 dist. ab exordio): furthermore, by this reason propounded, all the kings of France who ever were, and especially blessed Louis, should be spotted; for, if that were true, (as God forbid,) then, all of them were perjured and died in mortal sin; which is too absurd.

Last of all, it hurteth not where it is said, that such things are imprescriptible. It is true, indeed, they cannot by subjects, or otherwise than by the church, be prescribed; but in this cause we talk not of subjects. Also seeing they may be alienated, they may be prescribed, especially the kings thus consenting, who have confirmed the same so long a time; which excludeth all right both fiscal and ecclesiastical. The prelates, therefore, all with one consent agree to and affirm the same as a verity to be maintained and defended, beseeching the king's majesty, their lord, both for his soul's health and the peace of the church, to maintain the same, and to keep the liberties of the church; desiring him to consider what commodity daily he receiveth by the church, and that his church never failed him yet, when he had needed help of the laity; showing the dangers and examples of those who did to the contrary. Furthermore, he beseecheth his highness to weigh how entirely his lord the pope loveth, and hath loved, his person and realm; affirming that never any one placed in the seat of Peter, loved better his realm, than he doth; alleging the text where it is said [Eccles. vi.], "Stand in the multitude of the priests, and believe them with thy heart."

Special answers to the articles premised by bishop Edven.

After this, in the said session, the aforesaid bishop of Edven, prolocutor, urged many things besides, and answered particularly to the articles above specified and exhibited by the lord Peter in writing to the king and parliament; which, because they touch more the subtilty of the law, and styles of the courts, than is necessary to this our history, and because we would not burden the volume with them, they containing no great profit in them, we have here, for the sake of brevity, omitted, passing to the next sitting, which was the following Friday, as ensueth. On that day the prelates assembled at Vicenas before the king, to hear the answer; where the aforesaid lord Peter de Cugneriis, being prolocutor for the king, spake on this wise, taking for his theme, "I am peace unto you, do not fear," &c.; which he prosecuted, admonishing that they should not be troubled by any thing that had been spoken, as the intent and mind of the sovereign lord their king was, to keep the rights of the church and prelates, which they had by law and by good and reasonable custom. Here,

Another day's sitting in the parliament.

Edward I. A.D. 1307. between the first and second conclusion, he went about to prove, that the cognition of civil causes ought not to appertain to the church; for that such things were temporal, and ought to pertain to the temporalty, as spiritual things to the spiritualty. And besides his other reasons, he alleged the 86 dist. cap. "Cum ad verum," declaring for a truth, that for this intent first the clerks' crowns were shaven, in sign that they should be free from all worldliness, and forsake all temporal things; alleging to that end, the 12, q. 2. Furthermore, he declared, that the bishops had cognition in certain cases expressed by law, wherefore, these said cases ministered a certain rule against him, alleging in proof thereof, De reg. juris. ff. de lega. 1. 1. "Ticie textoris." Also he affirmed, that by reason of sin, the decretal novit. could not make for them, for the same did speak of the king of France's state, which hath no superior, but in other persons it was, he said, otherwise. These things thus being proved, he concluded by saying, that, nevertheless, their lord and king was ready to hear the information of those, who would instruct him of any custom, and those customs which were good and reasonable he would observe.

Shaving of priests' crowns.

To this answer, because it did not seem to please and suffice the prelates, the bishop of Edven immediately replied for them all in manner following; First, commending the good and general answer, he spake in this wise: "The prince of the people shall be praised for the prudence of his talk," commending therewith, as touching the former good general answer of the king, his purpose and talk propounded. But as concerning the words of the lord Peter, which engendered and brought darkness and obscurity, and might give occasion to the temporal lords to break and infringe the rights and customs of the church, his answer seemed not full and plain to the prelates. Speaking, moreover, to the said Peter, he alluded to the words of the Virgin speaking in the Scripture thus to her son, "Why did you so to us?" And so he prosecuted the same, both marvelling with himself, and yet covertly complaining of his answer.

Afterwards, in reply to those things which the lord Peter affirmed, and first to the chapter, "Ad verum," he said, that it was before answered, touching the division of the two jurisdictions, that they may be in one subject, as before is proved. Neither doth that weigh which the lord Peter said, that these two jurisdictions could not be in one subject, because things that be in themselves diverse, and be under one genus, as a man and an ass, cannot be in one subject; but if they were under divers kinds, as whiteness and sweetness in milk, they might be well in one subject. It was answered, that this rule was not true, because justice and temperance are two divers virtues, and under one kind, and yet be in one subject. Besides these differing species, a man and an ass be not compatible in one subject. Also to that which was spoken concerning the shaving of the crown, it was answered, that the crown did betoken rule and excellency; and the shaving did signify, that they ought not to heap up store of temporal things, so as to apply their hearts thereunto; but that the temporal things ought to be subject to them, and not they to the temporalty, as is proved in the said chapter, "Duo sunt genera." Also as concerning the thing which was talked of "de regula," he answered, that this maketh for the church, as before was proved; yea, also, that the custom doth make the rule for the church; also that laws in all kind of sense do always except the custom, and, therefore, that his saying makes nothing against it.

And now as to that which the lord Peter spake about the decretal 'novit.,' that the case was only one of the king's person; yet, for all that, it is expressly said in the same text of every christian man: and although their law doth speak only of the pope, yet the same is applied to all bishops in their diocese. Wherefore the said bishop concluded and beseeched the king, that it would please his grace to give unto them a more plain and comfortable answer, and that they might not depart from his presence all pensive and sad, whereby occasion might be given to the laity to impugn the rites and liberties of the church, and that they doubted nothing hereof in the good nature and conscience of their sovereign lord and king. In the end, it was answered them, in the behalf of the king, that it was not his mind and intent to impugn the customs of the church.

The bishop finds fault with the king's answer.

On the Sunday following, the bishops assembled again before the king at Vicenas, where the lord bishop of Edven repeated their last supposition, with the last answer made them in behalf of the king, when the bishop of Byturien had given them to understand how the king willed them not to fear, as they should suffer no hinderance or damage in his time; yea, and how he would defend them in their rights and customs, because it should not be said, that he would give ensample to others, to impugn the church, assuring them, that even the king's grace willed him so to declare unto them. The said lord bishop of Sens, in the name of the whole prelates, gave humble thanks to the king for this, and the said bishop of Sens beseeched that such proclamations, which were made to the prejudice of the ecclesiastical jurisdiction, might be repealed and called in. Hereunto the king himself answereth with his own mouth, that they were not published at his commandment, neither did he know of them, nor ratify them. Thirdly, the bishop proposed, that those abuses which the temporalty complained of, should be so ordered and reformed, that every man should be well contented therewith. Last of all, he beseeched the king's highness, that he would of his gracious goodness give them a more comfortable and fuller answer. Then answered the lord Peter in the name of the king; that if the prelates and bishops would see reformation of those things which were to be amended (whereabouts he would take respite between then and the Christmas next following), his grace would innovate nothing in the mean season: and that if, in the aforesaid space, they would not correct and reform that which was amiss, his majesty would appoint such order and remedy, as should be acceptable both to God and his subjects. After this the prelates had leave of the king to depart, and went home.[1]

Gentle answer of the king to the bishop.

Final answer to the prelates.

And thus much concerning French matters, which because they be ecclesiastical, and bear with them some utility to the diligent reader (such as list to search, note and observe the acts of men, and the course of religion), I thought here to place and adjoin them next after the other contention between Philip the French king, and pope Boniface. Albeit as touching the perfect keeping of years and time,

(1) For the "Brief Recapitulation," &c., which, in some Editions, follows here, see the foot notes to pp. 621—629 of this volume.—Ed.

Edward I. A.D. 1307.

I am not ignorant that this aforesaid parliament, thus summoned and commenced against the French prelates, falling A.D. 1329, was to be referred rather to the reign of king Edward II., of whom now remaineth (by the grace of Christ) in order of history to prosecute, declaring first the instructions and informations of his father given to him at the time of his departing.

Death of king Edward A.D. 1307.

In the year of our Lord 1307, and the last year of the king, the aforesaid king Edward, in his journey marching towards Scotland, in the north fell sick of the flux, which increased so fervently upon him, that he despaired of life. Wherefore calling before him his earls and barons, he caused them to be sworn that they should crown his son Edward in such convenient time after his death as they might, and keep the land to his use, till he were crowned.

Godly lessons and precepts given to the young prince.

That done, he called before him his son Edward, informing and lessoning him with wholesome precepts, and he also charged him with divers points upon his blessing: first, that he should be courteous, gentle, upright in judgment, fair spoken to all men, constant in deed and word, familiar with the good, and especially to the miserable be merciful. After this, he gave him also charge not to be too hasty in taking his crown before he had revenged his father's injuries stoutly

The king ordereth his bones to be carried in the field against the Scots.

against the Scots; but that he should remain in those parts to take with him his father's bones, being well boiled from the flesh, and so being enclosed in some fit vessel, should carry them with him till he conquered all the Scots, saying, "that so long as he had his father's bones with him, none should overcome him." Moreover, he willed and required him to love his brothers, Thomas and Edmund; also to

Father's care in excluding wicked company from his son.

cherish and tender his mother Margaret, the queen. Over and besides, he straightly charged him upon his blessing (as he would avoid his curse) that he should in no case call to him again, or send for Peter Gaveston; which Peter Gaveston the king before had banished the realm, for his naughty and wicked familiarity with his son Edward, and for his seducing of him with sinister counsel; for which cause he had both banished Peter Gaveston utterly out of the realm, and also had put the said Edward his son in prison, and therefore so straightly he charged his son in nowise to send for this Gaveston, or to have him in any case about him. And finally,

Rash vow of king Edward his heart to be carried to the Holy Land.

because he had conceived in himself a vow to return in his own person to the Holy Land (which for his manifold wars with the Scots, he could not perform), therefore he had prepared thirty-two thousand pounds of silver, for the sending of certain soldiers with his heart unto the Holy Land. This thing he required of his son to see accomplished, so that the aforesaid money, under his curse and malediction, be not employed to other uses; but these injunctions and precepts the disobedient son did not at all observe or keep after the decease of his father. Forsaking and leaving off the war with the Scots, the son, with all speed, hasted him to his coronation. Also contrary to the mind of his nobles, and against the precept of his father, he sent for the aforesaid Peter Gaveston, and prodigally bestowed upon him all that treasure which his father had bequeathed to the Holy Land. He was, moreover, a proud despiser of his peers and nobles; and therefore reigned unfortunately, as by the sequel of the story here following, by the grace of Christ, shall be declared. Thus king Edward, the first of that name, leaving

Edward II — A.D. 1307.

›ehind him three sons, Thomas and Edmund by his third wife, and Edward by his first wife, whom he had sufficiently thus with precepts nstructed, departed this mortal life, A.D. 1307, after he had reigned ıearly thirty-five years; of whom this epitaph was written:

> "Dum viguit rex, et valuit tua magna potestas,
> Fraus latuit, pax magna fuit, regnavit honestas."

In the time and reign of this king many other things happened, which here I omit to speak of, as the long discord and strife between he prior of Canterbury, and the prior of Dover, which continued bove four years, together with much wrangling and unquietness etween them. Likewise another like contention growing up between ohn Romain, archbishop of York, and the archbishop of Canterbury: pon this occasion, that when John, archbishop of York, after his onsecration returned from the pope, coming to Dover, contrary to ıe inhibition of Canterbury, he passed through the middle of Kent, ith his cross borne up, although the story reporteth that he had the ing's consent thereunto, A.D. 1286.

Item, Between Thomas, bishop of Hereford, and John Pecham, archishop of Canterbury, arose another wrangling matter, in the time f this king; which bishop of Hereford, appealing from the archbishop) the pope, went up to Rome, and on his journey died. Who with ss cost might have tarried at home, A.D. 1282.

EDWARD THE SECOND.[1]

A.D. 1307.

Edward II., son of Edward I., who was born, as is aforesaid, at aernarvon, in Wales, after the departure of his father, entered upon ıe government of the land, A.D. 1307, but was not crowned before ıe following year, by reason of the absence of Robert Winchelsey, ho was banished by king Edward I.; whereupon the king, this prent year, writeth to the pope for the restitution of the said archshop, as, by an ancient law of the realm, the coronation of the king ›uld not proceed without the archbishop of Canterbury. Which dward, while he was personable in body and outward shape, so was he conditions and evil dispositions much deformed, as unsteadfast of his ord, and ready to disclose secrets of great counsel; also refusing the ›mpany of his lords and men of honour; much haunting among vilins and vile personages; and given, moreover, to overmuch drinking, ıd such vices as thereupon be wont to ensue. And as of his own ıture he was to the said vices disposed, so was he much worse by e counsel and familiarity of certain evil-disposed persons, as first of eter, or Pierce Gaveston beforementioned. Then, after him, of e two Spensers and others, whose wanton counsel he following, gave mself to the appetite and pleasure of his body, not ordering his mmonweal by gravity, discretion, and justice; which thing caused st great variance between him and his nobles, so that shortly : became to them odious, and, in the end, was deprived of his

Edward led by wicked counsel

(1) Edition 1563. p. 74. Ed 1583. p. 366. Ed. 1596. p. 336. Ed. 1684 vol. i. p. 416.—Ed.

Edward II A.D. 1307

kingdom. In the first year he took to wife Isabel, daughter of Philip, king of France; with whom, the year after, he was crowned at Westminster by the bishop of Winchester; as Robert Winchelsey, archbishop of Canterbury, had not returned home, being still in exile.

Peter Gaveston, a wicked doer about the king

The barons and lords, however, made first their request to the king to put Peter Gaveston from him, or else they would not consent to his coronation; whereupon he was forced to grant them at the next parliament to have their requests accomplished, and so he was crowned. In the mean season the aforesaid Peter or Pierce, bearing himself of the king's favour bold, continued triumphing and making light of all other states and nobles of the realm, so that he ruled both the king and the realm, and all things went as he would; neither had the king any delight nor did he keep company with any, but with him; with him only he opened all his mind, and conferred in all his counsels. This, as it seemed strange unto the lords and earls, so it inflamed their indignation so much against this Peter, that through the exciting of the nobles, the bishops of the land did proceed in excommunication against the said Gaveston, unless he departed the land. Upon this occasion the king, in that same first year of his reign, being grieved with the bishops, writeth to the pope, complaining that they had proceeded to excommunication of the said Peter unless he departed the realm within a certain time. What answer the king's letter had from the pope, I find not set down in story. Over and besides, it befel in the same year that the bishopric of York being vacant, the king gave the office of the treasure to one of his own clerks, whereof the pope, having intelligence, writeth to the king, commanding him to call back the same gift, and withal citeth up to Rome the said clerk, there to answer the matter to a nephew of one of his cardinals, upon whom he had bestowed the said dignity: whereunto the king maketh answer, "That if such citations, and the execution of the same, should proceed to the impeachment of our kingly jurisdiction, and to the prejudice of our lawful inheritance, and the honour of our crown (especially if the deciding of such matters which principally concern our estate, should be prosecuted in any other place than within this our realm by any manner of ways, &c.), certes, although we ourselves would wink thereat, or through sufferance permit matters so to pass our hands; yet the states and nobles of our kingdom, who, upon allegiance, are obliged and sworn to the protection and defence of the dignity of the crown of England, will in no wise suffer our right, and the laws of the land, so to be violated."

Besides this, the aforesaid pope wrote to the king, complaining that by certain counsellers of king Edward his father, when he was lying sick and utterly ignorant thereof, a certain restraint was given out, charging the nuncios and legates, whom the pope had sent for the gathering of the first-fruits of the benefices vacant within the realm, not hereafter to intermeddle therewith, &c. Whereunto the king maketh answer,—

Most holy father, it hath been given you to understand otherwise than the truth of the matter is For most true it is, indeed, that the aforesaid inhibition was ratified by good act of parliament holden at Karlin, upon certain causes concerning the execution of such collections, the said our father not only being not ignorant, but also witting, willing, and of his own mere knowledge ıgreeing to the same, in the presence not only of his own earls, barons and tates, and commons of the realm, but also your legates and liegers being alled thereunto.

Item, Upon other letters brought from the pope to the king, for he installing of one Peter de Subaudia, his kinsman, in the bishopic of Worcester, being then vacant; and withal requiring that if he said Peter would not accept thereof, the election should be eferred to the prior and convent of the same place.

The king therewith grieved, maketh answer by his letters to the ope, and sundry his cardinals: "That forasmuch as elections of relates to be placed in cathedral churches within his kingdom are ıot to be attempted without his license first had and obtained;" herefore he could not abide that any such strange and unaccustomed eservations should or could take place in his realm without manifest rejudice of his kingly estate; requiring further that he would not ause any such novelties to be brought into his kingdom, contrary o that which his ancestors before him have been accustomed to do.

Thus the time proceeded, and at length the parliament appointed ame, A.D. 1310, which was the fourth of this king's reign. The rticles were drawn by the nobles to be exhibited to the king, and vere the same as those contained in 'Magna Charta,' and in 'Charta le Foresta,' above specified, with such other articles as his father had harged him with before: to wit, that he should remove from him and is court all aliens and perverse counsellors, and that all the matters f the commonwealth should be debated by a common council of the ords both temporal and spiritual; and that he should stir no war out f England in any other foreign realm, without the common assent of he same, &c. The king perceiving their intent to be, as it was ndeed, to sever Peter Gaveston from his company; and seeing no ther remedy, but that he needs must yield and grant his consent, greed that the said Gaveston should be banished into Ireland. And o the parliament breaking up, the lords returned to their own ıomes, well appeased; because, though in the other articles they could ıot speed, yet, that they had driven Peter Gaveston out of the realm t this time, it did suffice them. A.D.1310.

This Peter Gaveston was a certain gentleman's son of Gascony; vhom, being young, king Edward I. (for the good service his father had lone him in his wars) received to his court, and placed with his son Edward now reigning. This Peter, in process of time growing up vith the prince, incensed and provoked him to much outrage and wantonness; by whose occasion first he began in his father's days to break he park of Walter, bishop of Chester, then chancellor of England, ınd afterwards executor to the king; for which deed the king (as is artly mentioned before) imprisoned his son, and condemned this Peter to perpetual banishment. Notwithstanding this, the young ing, after the death of his father, as ye have heard, sent for this Gaveston again; and withal he so persecuted this aforesaid bishop, that e clapped him in the tower, and seized upon all his goods. Moreover, he caused most strict inquisition to be made upon him for guiding his office, wherein, if the least crime might have been found, t would have cost him his life. And thus much of Peter Gaveston, ınd of his origin. Now to the matter.

Edward II. A.D. 1310.

The king thus separated from his old compeer, that is, from the company of Peter Gaveston now exiled into Ireland, continued in great mourning and pensiveness, seeking by all means possible how to call him home again, and conferring with such as were about him upon the same; who did insinuate to the king, that as the earl of Gloucester was a man well loved and favoured in all the realm, if a marriage might be wrought betwixt his sister and Peter Gaveston, it might be a mean both for him to obtain more friendship, and for the king to have his desire. To make short, Peter Gaveston in all haste was sent for, and the marriage, through the king's procuring, proceeded between the earl's sister, and the aforesaid Peter; albeit sorely against the earl's mind. Gaveston, thus restored and dignified, was so surprised in pride and exaltation more than ever before, that he disdained and derided all others, his rule and power more and more increasing; insomuch that he, having the guarding of all the king's jewels and treasure, conveyed out of the king's jewel-house at Westminster, a table and a pair of tressels of gold unto certain merchants beyond sea, with other jewels more to his behoof; to the great impoverishing both of the king and queen, and of the land. And above all that, he brought the king, by means of his wanton conditions, to manifold vices, as adultery, and the like. Wherefore the lords seeing the mischief that daily increased by occasion of this unhappy man, took counsel together at Lincoln, and there concluded to void him out of England, so that shortly after he was exiled again, and went into Flanders; for in France or his own country he durst not appear, for fear of Philip, the French king, to whom the queen of England, his daughter, had sent over great complaints of the said Gaveston, who had so impoverished her and the whole court, that she had not wherewith to maintain her estate. Upon this complaint, the French king, throughout all his dominions, laid strict watch to apprehend the said Gaveston; but he, not unwarned thereof, secretly coasted into Flanders, from whence it was not long before he was fetched again by the king, as in further process followeth; so much was the king's heart infatuated by this wicked person.

The pride of Gaveston. *He spoileth the king's treasure.* *Gaveston again banished the land.* *The queen complaineth to the French king of Gaveston.*

About this year, or the next before it, came in first the Crouched Friars; and also first began the knights of the order of St. John Baptist, otherwise called the knights of Rhodes, for that they, by manly knighthood, put out the Turks from the isle of Rhodes.

Crouched Friars. The knights of St. John, or, of Rhodes.

In the history of Edward I., this king's father, mention was made of pope Clement, who succeeded Benedict; also of the putting down of the Templars, which in this year happened by means of the French king; who, as he caused to be burned in the city of Paris this year fifty-four Templars, with the great master of the same order, so, by his procurement, the aforesaid pope Clement called a council at Vienna, where the whole order and sect of Templars being condemned, was shortly after, by the consent of all Christian kings, deposed all in one day. After that, the French king thought to make his son king of Jerusalem, and to convert to him all the lands of the said Templars. But Clement, the pope, would not thereto agree, transferring all their lands to the order of Hospitallers, for the great sum of money given for the same. The cause why these impious Templars were put down was so abominable

Templars burned at Paris; the horrible order put down.

Edward II. A.D. 1310.

nd filthy, that for reverence of chaste ears it were better not told, if t be true that some write. Another matter worthy to be noted of like bomination I thought here to insert, touching a certain nunnery in 'rance called Provines, within which, at the cleansing and casting of . fish-pond,[1] were found many bones of young children, and the bodies lso of some infants as yet wholly unconsumed; upon occasion vhereof divers of the nuns of the said nunnery, to the number of wenty-seven, were had to Paris, and there imprisoned: what became f them afterwards I find not in mine author, Arpontacus Burdegalensis.

Bones of children found in the fish-pond of a nunnery

In the same council also, it was decreed by the said Clement, that all eligious orders exempted should be subject to the common law as thers were; but the Cistercian monks, with money and great gifts, edeemed their privileges and exemptions of the pope, and so had them ranted.[2] These Cistercians sped better herein, than did the Mi-orites of the Franciscan order in their suit, of whom, when certain f them had offered unto the said pope Clement forty thousand florins f gold, besides other silver, that the pope would dispense with them o have lands and possessions against their rule, the pope asked hem, Where was that money?[3] They answered, In the merchant-ien's hands. So the space of three days being given them to bring orth these merchants; the pope absolved the merchants of their bond nade to the friars, and commanded that all that money should be mployed and should revert to his use; declaring to the friars that e would not infringe nor violate the rule of St. Francis lately canon-ed, neither ought to do it for any money. And thus the beggarly ch friars lost both their money and their indulgence.[4]

Cistercian monks redeem their exemptions

The Minorites deceived by pope Clement

One thief beguileth another.

Concerning this pope Clement V., Sabellicus writeth, that he xcommunicated the Venetians for aiding and preferring of Azoda nto the state of Ferraria; and wrote his letters throughout all urope, condemning them as enemies of the church, and giving their oods as a lawful prey unto all men, which caused them to sustain reat harm. But Francis Dandulus, a nobleman of Venice, being mbassador from the Venetians to the said Clement, for the obtain-ig of their absolution and the safeguard of their city and country, id for pacifying the pope's fury towards them, was fain so to humble imself before this proud tyrannical prelate, that he suffered a chain f iron to be tied about his neck, and to lie down flat before is table, and so to catch the bones and fragments that fell from his ible, as it had been a dog, till the pope's fury towards them was ssuaged; so that after that, in reproach, because he so humbled imself for the behalf and helping of his country, he was of some illed a dog. But the city of Venice showed themselves not unkind return to Dandulus for his gentle good-will declared to his ountry;[5] for, as he had abased himself before, in the vile and nominious condition of a dog, for his country's sake, so they extolled m with as much glory again when he returned home, decking and lorning him after the best array, with the chief princely ornaments the city, to make him amends for his former reproach received.[6]

Clement excommunicateth the Venetians for making a duke.

Pride and tyranny of Clement.

Francis Dandulus humbleth himself.

Piety of Dandulus to his country rewarded

Concerning the constitutions of this pope Clement, and his decretals

1) See also p 13 of this volume —Ed (2) Ex Chron Thomas Walsingham (3) Ibid
4) Ibid (5) Out of Sabellicus, and is alleged in the book named the "Image of Tyranny"
6) Sabel. Ennead. 9 lib 7.

Edward II

A.D 1311.

and Clementines, and how Henry the emperor, in his days, was poisoned in receiving the sacrament, ye have heard before. About this time Robert Winchelsey, archbishop of Canterbury, whom this king's father had banished before, was released, and returned home from Rome.

These things thus declared, let us proceed, by the Lord's grace, to the next year (A D 1311), and the fifth of this king's reign. In that year, counting the year from Michaelmas to the same feast again, as then the usage of the realm was, Peter Gaveston, who had wandered the countries about, and could find no safe resting-place (notwithstanding that, upon forfeiture of life and goods, he was utterly banished out of the realm, yet trusting to the king's favour, and the good will of the earl of Gloucester, whose sister he had married), secretly returning into England with a certain company of strangers, presented himself to the king's sight. On beholding him, the king for joy ran to him, and embracing him, did not only retain him, but also for his sake undid all such acts as had been, in the parliament before enacted.[1] The queen and the whole court seeing this doating of the king, made a heavy Christmas. After this return of Gaveston was noised among the commons, the peers and nobles of the realm were not a little stirred, casting with themselves what way it were best to take. If he were still suffered, they saw not only themselves rejected, but also that the queen could not enjoy the love of the king, neither could there be any quietness in the realm. Again, to stir up war in the land, it were not the best; to vex or disquiet the king also they were afraid But forasmuch as they could not abide that all the nobility should be so thrust out and vilipended for the love of one stranger, and also that the realm should be so spoiled and impoverished by the same, this way they took: namely, that Thomas, earl of Lancaster, should be elected among them as the chieftain, and chief doer in that business; to whom all other earls, and barons, and prelates also, did concordly condescend and consent, except only Walter, bishop of Coventry, whom Robert the archbishop, on that account, afterwards did excommunicate. This Thomas of Lancaster, by the public assent of the rest, sent to the king (then lying at York) humble petitions in the name, as well of the whole nobility as of the commons, desiring his grace to give the aforesaid Gaveston unto them; or else, according to the ordinance of the realm, that the land might be voided of him. But the tyrannous king, who set more by the love of one stranger than by his whole realm besides, neither would hearken to their counsel, nor give place to their supplications; but in all hasty fury removed from York to Newcastle, where he remained almost till Midsummer.

The counting of the year was, in old time, from Michaelmas

The archbishop of Canterbury excommunicateth the bishop of Coventry

In the meantime, the barons had gathered an host of sufficient and able soldiers, coming toward Newcastle; not intending any molestation against the king, but only the execution of the laws upon the wicked Gaveston The king, not having wherewith to resist their power, removeth in all speedy manner to Teignmouth, where the queen was; and, hearing there that Newcastle was taken, he taketh shipping, and saileth from thence, notwithstanding the queen there, being great with child, with weeping tears, and all instance, desireth

(1) Ex Chron Tho Walsingham

him to tarry with her, as safely as he might; but he, nothing relenting to her, took Peter, his compeer, with him, and coasted over to the castle of Scarborough; where, leaving Peter Gaveston to the safe keeping of his men, he himself journeyed toward the coast beside Warwick. The lords, hearing where Peter was, bend thither all their power; so that, at length, Gaveston seeing no remedy, but that he must needs come into their hands, yieldeth and submitteth himself; requiring only this one condition, that he might talk a few words with the king in his presence. Thus Gaveston being apprehended, the king hearing thereof, sent unto the lords, requiring his life to be spared; and that he might be brought to speak to him, and promised that on their so doing, he would satisfy their minds and requests in all things whatsoever. About this, advisement was taken: but the earl of Pembroke, hearing the king's promise, persuaded the barons to yield to his petition; promising himself, upon pain of losing all his lands, to take the charge upon him of bringing Gaveston to a conference with the king, and so to recommit him to them again: which when he had obtained, he taketh Peter Gaveston with him, to bring him where the king lay; and so coming to Dedington, not far from Warwick, he leaveth him in the keeping of his soldiers, while he that night went to his wife, being not far off from thence. The same night it chanced that Guy, earl of Warwick, came to the same place where Gaveston was left; who, taking him out of the hands of his keepers, carrieth him to the castle of Warwick, where incontinent they would have put him to death; but doubting and fearing the king's displeasure, they staid a little. At that time one of the company (a man of sage and wise counsel, as mine author writeth) standing up among them, with his grave oration declareth the nature of the man, the wickedness of his own condition, the realm by him so greatly endamaged, the nobles despised and rejected, the pride and ambition of the man intolerable, the ruin of things like to ensue by him, and the great charges and expenses they had been at, in so long pursuing and getting him; and now, being gotten and in their hands, he exhorteth them to use and take the occasion now present; as hereafter, being out of their hands, they might seek, and should not find it.

Peter Gaveston taken of the nobles.

The king entreateth for him.

Gaveston apprehended by Guy of Warwick.

Briefly, in such sort, he so persuaded the hearers, that forthwith he was brought out, and by common agreement beheaded in a place called Blakelow; which place in other stories I find to be called Gaveshead; but that name, as I think, was derived on this occasion afterwards. And thus he that before had called the earl of Warwick the black dog of Ardeine, was thus by the said dog worried, as ye have heard. His carcase the Dominic friars of Oxford had in their monastery interred for the space of two years; but, after that, the king caused the said carcase to be taken up and buried within his own manor of Langley. After this, great disturbance began to arise between the king and the lords; who having their power lying about Dunstable, sent stout message unto the king at London, to have their former acts confirmed. Gilbert, earl of Gloucester, the king's nephew (who neither did hold against the king, nor yet against the nobles), with the bishops and prelates of the realm, went between both parties with great diligence to make unity. At this time, also, came two cardinals

Gaveston beheaded.

His corpse buried in the king's manor of Langley.

Edward II

A.D. 1311.

from Rome, with letters sent unto them from the pope. The nobles answered to the message of the cardinals, lying then at St. Alban's; that, as touching themselves, they should be at all times welcome to them; but as touching their letters, forasmuch as they were men unlettered, and only brought up in war and feats of arms, therefore they cared not to see the same. Then message was sent again, that they would at least grant but to speak with the pope's legates, who purposely came for the intent to establish quiet and unity in the realm. They answered again, that they had bishops both godly and learned, by whose counsel only they would be led; and not by any strangers, who knew not the true cause of their commotion. And, therefore, they said precisely, that they would have no foreigners or aliens to be doers in their business and affairs pertaining to the realm. Yet, notwithstanding, through the mediation of the archbishop and of the earl of Gloucester, the matter at length was so taken up, that the barons should restore to the king, or to his attorney of St. Alban's, all the treasure, horses, and jewels of the aforesaid Gaveston taken at Newcastle; and so their requests should be granted. And so was the matter at that time composed.

The pope's letters and legates, not allowed by the nobles of England

Shortly after, Isabel the queen was delivered of a fair child at Windsor, whom Louis, the French king's son, (the queen's brother, with other Frenchmen there present) would have to be called by the name of the French king, but the English lords were contrary, willing him to be called by the name of Edward, his father. At the birth of this Edward there was great rejoicing throughout the land, and especially the king his father so much joyed thereat, that he began daily more and more to forget the sorrow and remembrance of Gaveston's death, and was, after that, more agreeable to the will of his nobles.

A.D. 1312

The king rules by foreign counsel.

Thus peace and concord between them began to be in a good towardness; which more and more might have been confirmed in process of time, had not Satan, the author and sower of discord, stirred up his instruments (certain Frenchmen, titivillers, and makebaits about the king), who ceased not, in carping and depraving the nobles, to inflame the king's hatred and grudge against them; by the exciting of whom the old quarrels being renewed afresh, the king, in his parliament called upon the same, began to charge the aforesaid barons and nobles with sedition and rebellion, and for slaying Peter Gaveston. Neither were the nobles less stout again in defending their cause, declaring that they in so doing had deserved rather thanks and favour with the king than any displeasure, in vanquishing such a public enemy of the realm; who not only had spoiled and wasted the king's substance, but also had raised much disturbance in the realm; and, forasmuch as they had begun with the matter to their so great labour and expense, they would proceed further, they said, not ceasing till they saw an end thereof. To be short: great threats there were on both parts, and a foul matter had like to have followed; but again, through the diligent mediation of the queen, the prelates, and the aforesaid earl of Gloucester, the matter was taken up and brought to reconcilement upon these conditions, that the lords and barons openly in Westminster Hall should humble themselves before the king, and ask pardon there of their doings, and that every man

Mediation for peace

The king reconciled with his nobles

here should receive a letter of the king's pardon, for their indemnity and assurance. And so passed over that year, within which died Robert Winchelsey, archbishop of Canterbury; in whose room Thomas Cobham was elected by the king and church of Canterbury to succeed; but the pope frustrating the election, placed Walter Reinold, bishop of Worcester.

A.D. 1313. In the mean time, the Scots hearing this civil discord in the realm, began to be busy, and to rebel anew through the means of Robert Bruce, who being chased out of Scotland by king Edward I., as is above premised, into Norway, was now returned again into Scotland, where he demeaned himself in such sort to the lords there, that in short process he was again made king of the realm, and warred so strongly upon those that took the king's part, that he won from them many castles and strong holds, and invaded the borders of England. The king, hearing this, assembleth a great power, and by water entereth the realm of Scotland; against whom encountered Robert Bruce with his Scots at Estrivelin, where was fought a strong battle, in the end whereof the Englishmen were discomfited, and so eagerly pursued by the Scots, that many of the noblemen were slain, as the earl of Gloucester, Sir Robert Clifford, Sir Edmund Maule, with other lords to the number of forty-two, and knights and barons two hundred and twenty-seven, besides men of name, who were taken prisoners; of common soldiers ten thousand, or, after the Scottish story, fifty thousand slain. After that, Sir Robert Bruce reigned as king of Scotland. About that time, and in that year, died pope Clement, who, keeping in the realm of France, never came to the see of Rome; after whose death the papacy stood void two years.

What discord doth in a common wealth.

The Scots rebel against England.

Englishmen overcome.

Pope Clement never sat in the see of Rome.

A.D. 1314. The Scots, after this, exalted with pride and fierceness, invaded the realm of England so sorely, killing and destroying man, woman, and child, that they came winning and wasting the north parts as far as to York. Besides this, such dearth of victuals and penury of all things oppressed the whole land, such murrain of sheep and oxen, that men were fain to eat horse-flesh, dogs, cats, mice, and what else they could get. Moreover, such a price of corn followed withal, that the king hardly had bread for the sustentation of his own household. Moreover, some there were that did steal children and eat them, and many, for lack of victual, died. And yet all this amended not the king of his evil living.

Miserable dearth and famine.

The cause and origin of this great dearth, was partly the wars and dissension between them and the Scots, whereby a great part of the land was wasted. But the chiefest cause was the intemperate season of the year, which, contrary to the common course, was so moist with abundance of rain, that the grain laid in the earth could have no ripening by heat of the sun, nor grow to any nourishment; so that they who had to eat, could not be satisfied with fulness, but eftsoons were as hungry again. They that had nothing were driven to steal and rob; the rich were constrained to avoid and diminish their households; the poor for famine died.[1] And not so much the want of victuals which could not be gotten, as the unwholesomeness of the same when it was taken, so consumed the people, that the quick were not sufficient to bury the dead; for the corruption of the meats,

Its origin.

(1) Ex Chron. Tho. Wals. in Vita Edwardi II.

Edward II — A.D. 1314

by reason of the unseasonableness of the ground, was so infectious that many died of the flux, many of hot fevers, divers of the pestilence. And not only the bodies of men thereby were infected, but also the beasts, by the putrefaction of the herbs and grass, fell into as great a murrain, so far forth as that the eating of flesh was suspected and thought contagious. A quarter of corn and salt, from the month of June to September, rose from thirty shillings to forty shillings. The flesh of horses was then precious to the poor. Many were driven to steal fat dogs, and to eat them. Some were said, in secret corners, to eat their own children. Some would steal other men's children to kill them and eat them privily. The prisoners and thieves that were in bonds, for hunger fell upon such as were newly brought in unto them, and, tearing them in pieces, did eat them half alive. Briefly, this extreme penury had extinguished and consumed (as it was thought) the greatest part of the people of the land, had not the king, by the statute of the Londoners, given forth commandment through all his land, that no corn should at that time be turned to the making of drink. Such a Lord is God, thus able to do, where he is disposed to strike. And yet we miserable creatures, in our wealth and abundance, will not cease daily to provoke his terrible Majesty.

But let us return again to the order of our story. After the Scots had thus plagued miserably, as ye have heard, the realm of England, they also invaded Ireland, where they kept up and continued war the space of four years. But in fine, the Irishmen (by aid sent to them from England) did quit themselves so well, that they vanquished the Scots, and slew Edward Bruce, and many of the nobles of Scotland, with many others, and drove the residue out of the country.

Scots driven out of Ireland

A.D. 1319 The king, about the twelfth year of his reign, assembled a new host, and went into Scotland, where he laid siege to Berwick. But in the mean time, the Scots, by another way, invaded the marshes of Yorkshire, robbing and harassing the country, and they slew much people. Wherefore the archbishop of York, and others, the abbots, priors, clerks, with husbandmen, assembled a great company, and gave them battle at a place called Mitton, where the Englishmen were discomfited, and many of them slain; but the archbishop and the abbot of Selby, and divers others there, escaped. So many spiritual men were slain there, that it was called the White Battle; for reason whereof, the king on hearing of it, and partly because winter did approach, was constrained to raise the siege; and so returned, not without great danger.

The White Battle of spiritual men in Yorkshire

At this time the two Spensers (sir Hugh Spenser the father, and Hugh Spenser the son) were of great power in England, and by the favour of the king practised such cruelty, and bore themselves so haughtily and proudly, that no lord of this land might gainsay them in any thing that they thought good; whereby they were in great hatred and indignation both with the nobles and the commons, no less than Peter Gaveston was before.

The two Spensers

Soon upon this came two legates from Rome, sent by pope John XXII., under pretence to settle an agreement between England and Scotland, who, for their charges and expenses, required of every spiritual person four-pence in every mark. But all their labour

The pope's legates spoiled of their ill-gotten treasure

nothing availed; for the legates, as they were in the north parts (about Darlington) with their whole family and train, were robbed and despoiled of their horses, treasure, apparel, and what else they had, and with an evil favoured handling, retired back again to Durham, where they staid awhile, waiting for an answer from the Scots. But when neither the pope's legacy, nor his curse, would take any place with the Scots, they returned again to London, where they first excommunicated and cursed as black as soot all those arrogant and presumptuous robbers of Northumberland. Secondly, for supplying of the losses received, they exacted of the clergy, to be given and paid unto them, eight-pence in every mark. But the clergy thereunto would not agree, seeing it was their own covetousness (as they said) that made them venture further than they needed. Still they were contented to relieve them as far as four-pence in a mark, as they promised before; further they would not grant: whereof the king being advertised, and taking part with his clergy, directed his letters to the said legates in form as followeth:[1]—

The pope's curse contemned by the Scots.

Clergy of England refuse to contribute to the pope's legates

Letter of the King to the Legates.

The king to Master Rigand of Asserio, canon of Aurelia, greeting We have taken notice of the clamours and lamentable petitions of the subjects of our realm, perceiving by the same that you practise many and sundry inconveniencies very strange, never heretofore accustomed, nor heard of in this our realm, as well against the clergy and ecclesiastical persons, as against the laity, even to the utter oppression and impoverishing of many of our liege people, which if it should be winked at, as God forbid, may, in process of time, be occasion of greater perils to ensue; whereat we are (not without cause) moved, and not a little grieved We forbid you, therefore, that from henceforth you practise not, nor presume in any case to attempt any thing within this our realm, either against our clergy or laity, that may in any manner of way tend to the prejudice of our royal person, or of our crown and dignity regal Witness the king at Windsor the sixth day of February, in the 11th year of his reign.

Per concilium.

A prohibition against strange taxes and impositions

Likewise in the same year the said king writeth to the same effect to the archbishop of Canterbury, as followeth:[2]—

Letter of the King to the Archbishop of Canterbury.

The king to the reverend father in God, W. by the same grace archbishop of Canterbury, primate of England, greeting We are credibly informed by many of our subjects, that certain strange impositions, never heard of before within any of our dominions, upon lands and tenements, goods and chattels, concerning the testaments and cases of matrimony, are brought into our realm to be executed upon our subjects by you or some others; which, if it should proceed to execution, would manifestly tend to the disherison and impeachment of our crown and dignity regal, and the intolerable damage of the subjects of our realm, to the due preservation of the which you are bound by solemn oath of allegiance. We therefore command and straitly charge you, that you proceed not in any case to the execution of any such letters, either in your own person, or by any other, nor yet presume, by colour of the same, to attempt any thing that may be prejudicial or hurtful to our crown or dignity regal And if you, or any other in your name, have done or attempted any thing by colour of the same, that ye call back and revoke the same forthwith without delay. Witness the king at Shene, the 17th of February, the eleventh year of his reign.

Per ipsum regem.

(1) Rex Magistro Rigando de Asserio, canonico Aurelian salutem, &c

(2) Rex venerabili in Christo patri, W eadem gra archiepiscopo Cant, &c

Edward II.

A.D. 1319.

The like letters in effect were directed to the archbishop of York, and to every other bishop throughout England; by force of which letters the greedy legates being restrained of their ravening purpose, taking what they could get, and settling a peace, such as it was, between the king and the earl of Lancaster, were fain to pack.

Besides the restraint above mentioned for strange impositions, there followed, moreover, the same year, the king's prohibition for the gathering of Peter-pence, directed to the aforesaid legate, the tenor whereof followeth.

A Prohibition for paying the Pope's Peter-pence.[1]

The king to Master Rigand of Asserio, canon of Aurelia, greeting: We are given to understand that you do demand and purpose to levy the Peter-penny within our realm, otherwise than the said Peter-penny hath been heretofore accustomed to be levied in the time of any our progenitors, exercising herein grievous censures ecclesiastical, to the great annoyance and damnifying of the subjects of our realm; for present remedy whereof our loving subjects have made their humble supplication unto us. And forasmuch as the said Peter-penny hath been hitherto accustomed to be gathered and levied upon lands and tenements within our realm after a due manner and form, we, not willing that any such unaccustomed impositions shall in any wise be made upon the lands and tenements of any of our subjects within our dominions, prohibit you, upon grievous pain, straitly charging that in no wise you presume to exact, gather, or levy the said Peter-penny in any other form or manner than hath been heretofore accustomed to be gathered and levied in the time of our progenitors, or since the beginning of our reign, until further order be taken in our high court of parliament by the advice of the nobles and peers of our realm, such as may well be taken without prejudice of our crown and damage of subjects. Witness the king at Westminster the first day of March.

Per ipsum regem et concilium.

Letters to the same effect were directed to the archbishops, deans, archdeacons, and the rest of the clergy.

Touching the first original of this Peter-pence, though mention be made before in the life of king Offa and others, yet to make a brief recapitulation of the same, according to the rolls as they come to our hands.[2] It is found recorded in ancient chronicles touching the Peter-pence of St. Peter (A.D. 793), that Offa, king of Mercia, travelled up to Rome in the time of pope Adrian I. to obtain the canonizing of St. Alban; and having performed his vow, visiting the college of English students which then flourished in Rome, he did give to the maintenance of the scholars of England, students in Rome, one penny out of every tenement within this realm, that had land belonging to it amounting to the yearly value of thirty pence. And for this his munificence he obtained of pope Adrian, that no person within his dominion public, repenting him for not performing enjoined penance, should therefore be banished.[3]

Read before in the lives of king Offa, and king Ethelwolf.

(1) "Rex Magistro Rigando." (2) De denariis beati Petri sic scriptum, &c.

(3) A.D. 857. "Adewulfus rex Westsaxonium. tempore Leonis papæ quarti Romæ singulis annis 300. Mancusas portari præcipit, taliter dividendas ibidem, viz. 100. Mancusas in honorem scilicet Petri specialiter ad emendum oleum, quo implerentur omnia luminaria ecclesiæ apostolicæ in vespera pasche et in galli cantu, et 100. Mancusas in honorem scilicet Pauli eisdem de causis, 100. Preterea mancusas præcipit exhiberi universali papæ ad suas eleemosynas ampliandas. Et sciendum, quod secundum antiquorum Anglorum interpretationem differunt mancusa, et manca, quia marcusa idem erat apud eos quod marca argentea: manca vero erat moneta aria, quadra, et valebat communiter 30. denarios argenteos."

Of this Peter-pence is found a transcript of the original rescript apostolical, the tenor whereof is this: "Gregorius episcopus servus servorum Dei, venerabilibus fratribus Cantuar. et Ebor. archiepiscopis et eorum suffraganeis et dilectis filiis abbatibus, prioribus, archidiaconis, eorumque officialibus per regnum Angliæ constitutis, ad quos literæ istæ pervenerint;

Concerning this Peter-pence, it is touched in the laws of king Edward the Martyr, chap. 10, when, where, of whom, and under what pain, this Peter-pence must be gathered; being but the king's mere alms, as is aforesaid. And thus much touching Peter-pence. Now for other letters written by the king to the pope, the same year, for other matters, as craving the pope's help in compounding the variance betwixt the two archbishops of Canterbury and York, for bearing the cross from the one province to the other, thus it followeth: that the king grievously complaineth, that such hurly-burly and uproar arose thereof, that they could not meet together in one place through the great multitude of armed men, assistants on both parts in the very bearing of the cross, to the great disturbance of the people.

Now after this long digression, to turn to our English matters again, mention was made before of the variance between the king and the carl of Lancaster, and of a peace concluded between them. But this peace did not long endure, which the king by his own default did break, sending to the Scots a privy messenger (who was taken in the way), to have the aforesaid earl of Lancaster, by their means made away with.

Pride of the Spensers.

In the mean time the lords and nobles of England, detesting the outrageous pride of the Spensers, whereby they wrought daily both great dishonour to the king, and hinderance to the commonweal, in such wise conspired against them, that gathering their power together, they made a request to the king, that he should remove the Spensers from his person. For this there was a parliament called at London, and the barons came together with a great company; at which parliament both the Spensers were banished the land for the term of their lives, and they took shipping at Dover, and so voided the land. But not long after, the king (contrary to the ordinance made in the parliament) sent for the Spensers again, and set them in high authority; and they ruled all things after their sensual appetites, nothing regarding justice or the commonwealth. The barons, therefore, intending again to reform this mischief, assembled their powers; but the king (making such hasty speed, and gathering his people so soon) was stronger than they, and pursued them so in divers places, that the barons, not fully joined together (some flying, and some departing to the king, some slain by the way), in the end were chased so eagerly, that in short space the aforesaid Thomas, earl of Lancaster, was taken, and put to death with the rest of the nobility, to the number of two and twenty of the greatest men, and chiefest captains of this realm; of whom only Thomas, earl of Lancaster,[1] for the nobility of his blood, was beheaded, all the other lords and barons being hanged, drawn, and quartered, &c. This bloody unmercifulness of the king toward his natural subjects, not only procured to him great dishonour

A.D. 1321. Twenty-two of the greatest nobility of the realm put to death by the king.

salutem et apostolicam benedictionem. Qualiter denarii beati Petri, qui debentur cameræ nostræ, colligantur in Anglia et in quibus episcopatibus et dioces. debeantur, ne super hoc dubitari contingat, et præsentibus fecimus annotari, sicut in registro sedis apostolicæ continetur. De Cantuar. dioces *7l.* 13*s.* sterlingorum. De London. dioces. 16*l.* 10*s.* De Roffens. dioces. 5*l.* 12*s.* De Norwicens. dioces. 21*l.* 10*s.* De Elienum. 5*l.* De Lincoln. 42*l.* De Cistrens. 8*l.* De Winton. 17*l.* 6*s.* 8*d.* De Exon. 9*l.* 5*s.* De Wigorne. 10*l.* 5*s.* De Hereford. 6*l.* De Bathon. dioces. 12*l.* 5*s.* De Sarisbur. 17*l.* De Coventre. 10*l.* 5*s.* De Eborac. 11*l.* 10*s.* Datum apud urbem veterem. 10 Kal. Maii Pontificatus nostri anno secundo. Summa, 30 marcæ et dimidi."

(1) Thomas, earl of Lancaster, came of Edmund, younger son of king Henry III.

Edward II. A.D. 1322. within the realm, but also turned afterwards to his much greater harm and hinderance, in his foreign wars against the Scots; and, finally, wrought his utter confusion, and the overthrow of his seat royal, as in the sequel of his end appeared, and worthily.

His cruel rejoicing. After the ruin of these noble personages, the king, as though he had gotten a great conquest (who then indeed began first to be overcome and conquered himself, when he so oppressed and cut off the strength and sinews of his chivalry), began to triumph not a little with the Spensers; and, to count himself sure as though he were in heaven, to exercise more sharp severity upon his subjects, trusting and committing all to the counsel only of the aforesaid Spensers, insomuch that both the queen and the residue of the nobles could little be regarded; who, as they grew ever in more contempt with the king, so they increased more in hatred against the Spensers; but strength and ability lacked to work their will.

A.D. 1323. The next year the king, being at York, after he had made Sir Hugh Spenser an earl, and Sir John Baldock (a man of evil fame) to be chancellor of England, raised a mighty host against the Scots; but for lack of skilful guiding, expert captains, and for want especially of due provision of victuals necessary for such an army, the great multitude, to the number reckoned of a hundred thousand (wandering through Scotland, from whence the Scots had conveyed all their goods and cattle into mountains and marshes), were so pinched and starved with famine, that a great part of the army, presently perished; and they that returned home, as soon as they tasted of meats, escaped not. The king not having resistance of his enemies, and seeing such a destruction of his subjects, was forced, without any act done, to retire. But in his retiring, Sir James Douglas and the Scots having knowledge thereof, pursued him in such wise, that they slew many Englishmen, and had well nigh taken the king himself. After this distress, the king, thus beaten and wearied with the Scots, would fain have joined in truce with the Scots; but because they stood excommunicated by the pope, he standing in fear thereof, desired license to treat with them of peace, notwithstanding the said excommunication: which license being obtained, a treaty was appointed by commissioners on both parts at Newcastle, at the feast of St. Nicholas next ensuing; and so truce was taken for twelve years. Whereupon this is to be noted by the way, gentle reader, not unworthy of observation, that whereas in former times, and especially in those of the late king Edward I., so long as the Scots were under the pope's blessing, and we in displeasure with his holiness for dealing with them, so long we prevailed mightily against them, even to the utter subversion in a manner of their whole estate. But now so soon as the pope took our part, and the Scots were under his curse and excommunication, then gat they greater victories against us than at any time either before or since; insomuch as that being before not able to defend themselves against us, they now pursued us into the bowels of our own country.

The king distressed again in Scotland.

The king purposing to erect a house of friars Augustine, within the town of Boston in Lincolnshire, first prayed the pope's license in that behalf.

Polydore Virgil, among other histories of our English nation hich he intermeddleth with, prosecuting also the acts and life of is present king, and coming to write of the queen's going over to France, inferreth much variety and diversity of authors and ory-writers concerning the cause thereof. Otherwise, he giveth mself no true certainty of that matter, neither yet toucheth he that hich was the real cause; by reason partly, that he being an Italian id a foreigner, could not understand our English tongue, and partly gain, being but one man, neither could he alone come to the sight all our Latin authors. One I am sure came not to his perusing, 1 old ancient Latin history fairly written in parchment, but without ame, belonging to the library of William Cary, citizen of London. n that story, the truth of this matter, without any ambiguity, is illy and with all circumstances expressed, as here briefly is inrted.

Polydore Virgil, an Italian, writeth out English stories.

The king of England had been divers and sundry times cited up the court of France, to do homage to the French king, for the ukedom of Aquitaine, and other lands which the king then held of 'rance; which homage because the king of England refused to ender, the French king began to enter all such possessions as the ing then did hold in France: whereupon great contention and onflicts there were, on both sides. At length, in this year now resent, a parliament was called at London, where, after much alteration, at last it was determined, that certain should be sent over, to it, the bishops of Winchester and Norwich, and the earl of Richmond, to make agreement betwixt the two kings; for the better help nd fortification of which agreement, it was thought good afterwards, at queen Isabel, sister to Charles, then the French king, should be ent over. Here is to be noted first, that the queen's lands and ossessions and castles a little before, upon the breach between the 'rench king and the king of England, were seized into the king's ands, and the queen put to her pension, &c. Thus the queen eing sent over with a few to attend upon her, only Sir John Cromwel, baron, and four knights, took their passage to France; by hose mediation it was there concluded, that the king of England, f he would not himself come to do his homage, should give to his on Edward the dukedom of Aquitaine and the earldom of Pontigny: nd so he to come to make his homage to the king, and to possess he same. This being in France concluded, was sent over by nessage to the king of England, with the king's letters patent djoined for the safe conduct of him or of his son. Upon this, leliberation was taken in the council of England; but the two Spensers fearing to take the seas with the king, or, without the king, o remain behind, for fear of the nobles, so appointed, that prince Edward, the king's son, was sent, which happened afterwards to their itter desolation, as it followed: for all things being quieted and ordered according to the agreement in France, king Edward of England, soon after Michaelmas, sendeth for his wife and his son igain out of France. But she, sending home most part of her family, efuseth herself to return; for what cause it is not fully certain, whether for indignation that her possessions and lands were seized to he king, as is before premised; or whether for fear and hatred of the Spensers, as is likely; or else for love and familiarity of Sir Roger

A.D. 1324.

The queen put to her pension. Sent to France.

Prince Edward made duke of Aquitaine and earl of Pontigny.

The queen and the prince refuse to return into England.

Edward II — A.D. 1324.

Mortimer. For here is to be noted, that the said Sir Roger Mortimer, with divers others of the barons' part, who had broken prison in England, were fled before into France, and now resorted unto the queen. The king seeing this, giveth forth in proclamation, and limiteth a certain day to the queen and his son to return; or else to be proclaimed traitors to the king and to the realm. Notwithstanding, the queen persisting in her purpose, denieth to return, unless the other nobles who were fled might be permitted safely also to return with her; whereupon the king immediately caused them both to be proclaimed traitors, and all them that took their parts.

Proclaimed traitors in England.

Here then began great hatred between king and king, between the king and the queen, much preparation of war, great spoiling on the sea, much sending between the pope and them; but that would not serve. Then the king, by the counsel of the Spensers, sendeth privily to procure the death of the queen and of his son, which should be wrought by the execution of the earl of Richmond, the queen's familiar; but as the Lord would, that imagination was prevented and utterly frustrated. Albeit, the queen, yet notwithstanding (whether misdoubting what corruption of money might do in the court of France; or whether the French king, being threatened by the king of England and by the pope, durst not detain her), removed from thence, and was received with Edward her son, joyously and honourably in the court or country of the earl of Heinault. There, by means of such as were about her, a marriage was concluded between the said Edward her son, being of the age of fourteen years, and Philip, the aforesaid earl's daughter. When this was noised in England, divers men of honour and name came over to the queen; and, soon after, the earl of Heinault prepared a crew of five hundred men at arms to escort over the young prince with his mother into England. Of this the fame sprang shortly through the realm; wherefore the king in all defensible ways made provision to have the havens and ports of his land surely kept, to resist the landing of his enemies. On the contrary side, the queen, with no less preparation, provideth all things to her expedition necessary; who, when she saw her time, speeding herself to the sea-coast with prince Edward her son, lord Edmund earl of Kent the king's brother, Sir Roger Mortimer, the lord Wygmore, and other exiles of England, accompanied also by the aforesaid Heinaulders, of whom Sir John of Heinault, the earl's brother, was captain, having with her of Englishmen and strangers the number of two thousand seven hundred and fifty-seven soldiers; she took shipping in those parts, and had the wind so favourable, that they landed in England at a port called Orwel, beside Harwich in Suffolk, in the dominion of the earl marshal, in the month of September; to whom, after her landing, resorted earl marshal the earl of Leicester, with other barons, knights, and bishops also; namely of Lincoln, Hereford, Durham, and Ely. The archbishop of Canterbury, though he came not himself, yet sent his aid and money. Thus the queen, well furnished with plenty both of men and victuals, setteth forward toward London; so that the further she came, the more her number daily increased, and the king's power contrarily decreased; insomuch that, as mine author affirmeth, not one almost in all the realm could be hired with any wages to fight on the king's behalf

The king conspires privily the death of the queen and of his son.

A.D. 1325. Prince Edward betrothed to the earl of Heinault's daughter.

The queen returning, landeth in England.

A.D. 1326. The king destitute of help and soldiers.

against the queen, neither did the queen's army hurt any man or child, either in goods or any other thing, by the way.

At the arriving of the queen, the king was in London, who first would not believe it to be true. Afterwards, seeing and perceiving how it was, he asketh help of the Londoners, who, after mature advisement, rendered this answer to the king again: that as touching the king, the queen, and their son, the lawful heir of the kingdom, they were ready, with all duty and service, to honour and obey. As for strangers and traitors to the realm, they would receive none such within their city gates. Furthermore, to go out of the city to fight, that, they said, they would not, unless it were so, that according to the liberties of their city, they might return home again before sunset. The king hearing this answer (which liked him not well), fortifieth the Tower of London with men and victuals, committing the custody thereof to John Ealtham, his younger son, and to the wife of Hugh Spenser, his niece; and leaving Walter Stapleton, bishop of Exeter, behind him, to have the rule of the city of London, he himself, hearing daily the great recourse of the people that drew to the queen, for more safeguard to himself, fled with a small company westward, towards Wales. But, before his departing from London, he caused a proclamation to be made, wherein all and singular persons were charged, upon forfeit of life and goods, every man with all his power to rise and invade the rebels and destroy them all, only the lives of the queen, his son, and his brother, reserved. Also that no man, upon pain pretaxate, should help, rescue, or relieve the said rebels, with goods, victuals, or otherwise. Item, it was also proclaimed, that whosoever would bring to the king the head and body of Sir Roger Mortimer, either dead or alive, should have out of the king's coffers a thousand pounds.

Answer of the Londoners to the king.

Liberties of the city of London in going to war.

The king's proclamation.

In contrariwise, the queen setteth forth another proclamation, wherein it was forbidden to take or spoil violently the value of any man's goods against the will of the owner, under pain of losing his finger, if it were three-pence; of his hand, if it were sixpence; of his head, if it were twelve-pence. Moreover, whosoever would bring to the queen the head of Hugh Spenser the younger, chopped off from his body, should receive of the queen for so doing, two thousand pounds. This done, the queen sendeth her letters to the city of London for aid and succour to subdue the oppressor of the realm, to which letters at first no answer was made. Again, she wrote the second letter, which was then tacked upon the cross in Cheap, which was then called the new cross; the copy and tenor of which letter was this:

The queen's proclamation.

Copy of a Letter that the Queen sent unto the Mayor and Citizens of London.

Isabel, by the grace of God, queen of England, lady of Ireland, and countess of Pountif. And we Edward, the first son of the king of England, duke of Guienne, earl of Chester, of Pountif, and of Mounstrell, to the mayor and all the commonalty of London, send greeting. Forasmuch as we have before this time sent to you by our letters, and how we come into this land in good array, and good manner, for the profit of holy church, and of our right dear lord and king, and all the realm, with all our might and strength to keep and maintain the realm, as all good people ought for to do; upon that, we pray you and desire you that ye would be helping to us for the health and profit of the realm; and

Edward II — A.D. 1326.

we have had none answer of you, nor know not your will in that part: wherefore we send to you again, and pray you, and charge you, that ye bear you so against us, that ye have no nor make cause us to grieve, but that ye be to us helping in all the ways that you may. And wete ye well in certain, that we, and also those that cometh with us into this realm, nothing for to done, but that shall be pleasing to God, and common profit to all the realm; not else, but for to destroy the Spensers, enemies to the realm, as ye well know. Wherefore we pray and charge you, in the faith that ye owe to our lord the king, to the crown, and to us, and upon all that ye may forfeit, that if Hugh Spenser, both the father and the son, our enemies, come within your power, that ye do them hastily to be taken, and safely kept, till we have ordained for them our will, as ye desire profit and honour of us, and of the realm. Understanding well, if it be so, that ye do our desire and prayer, we shall the more be beholden to you And also we shall do you profit and worship if that ye send us hastily word again of your will.

Given at Baldocke, the sixth day of October

Bishop of Exeter beheaded at the standard in Cheap

These aforesaid letters being published and perused, the bishop of Exeter,[1] to whom, as ye heard, was committed the rule of the city, sent to the mayor for the keys of the gates, using such sharp words in the king's name, that variance began to kindle between him and the citizens; so much so that the commons in their rage took the bishop and beheaded him and two of his household at the Standard in Cheap. Then the king went to Bristol, and ordained Sir Hugh Spenser the father, to keep the castle and town there; and the king, with Hugh Spenser the son, and Sir Robert Baldock, the chancellor, and the earl of Arundel, went into Wales. The queen's forces so pursued them, that they first took the town, yielded up to her; then they took Sir Hugh Spenser the father, whom, being drawn and torn, they at last hanged up at Bristol, in chains of iron. As the king was thus flying, the queen caused to be proclaimed throughout her army, that the king should come and appear, and so receive his kingdom again, if he would be comfortable to his liege subjects: who when he did not appear, prince Edward, his son, was proclaimed high keeper of the realm.

Hugh Spenser, the father, hanged in chains

The king taken in Wales

In the mean time Henry earl of Lancaster, and brother to the good earl Thomas, who before was beheaded, also lord William Souch, and Master Uphowel, were sent by the queen into Wales to pursue the king, and there they took him, and sent him to the castle of Kenilworth; and took Hugh Spenser the son, and Sir Robert Baldock the chancellor, and Sir John, earl of Arundel, and brought them all to the town of Hereford. Soon after, Hugh Spenser the son, was drawn, and hanged on a gallows fifty feet high, and afterwards beheaded and quartered, whose quarters were sent into the four quarters of the realm. Sir John of Arundel was beheaded, and Sir Robert Baldock was put in Newgate at London, where, shortly after, he pined away and died among the thieves. This done, a parliament was assembled at London, from whence message was sent to the king, that if he would resign up his crown, his son should have it after him; if not, another should take it, to whom the lot would give it: whereupon the king, being constrained to yield up his crown to his son, was kept in prison, and after had to Barkley; where he is said to have taken great repentance. After this message being sent, and the king half

Hugh Spenser, the son, executed

(1) This bishop of Exeter builded in Oxford two colleges, Exeter College, and Hart Hall, his name was Gualter Stapleton

condescending thereunto (the parliament notwithstanding prosecuting and going forward), there was a bill exhibited and put up, containing certain articles against the said king, then in prison in the castle of Barkley, touching his misbehaviour and imprudent governing of the realm; which bill openly before the lords and commons, by the speaker of the parliament house, was read. After long consultation thereupon amongst themselves touching those articles, and also for the better and more circumspect government of the realm from that time forth, it was consulted and agreed upon by the lords spiritual and temporal, and the commons there assembled, that the said Edward was a man not meet to be their king, nor from that time forth any more to bear the crown royal, or title of a king; but that Edward his eldest son, who there in the same court of high parliament was present, as he was rightful heir and inheritor thereunto, so should he be crowned king thereof in his father's stead, with these conditions thereunto annexed: that he should take wise, sage, and true counsellors unto him, that the realm might be better and more circumspectly governed, than before in the time of Edward his father it was; and that the old king, his father, should be honourably provided for and kept, so long as he lived, according as unto his estate it appertained, &c. These and other things thus finished and ended, the parliament breaketh up, and all things necessary, and to the coronation of a prince appertaining, were in speedy wise prepared, whereof more hereafter (Christ willing) shall be specified.

Edward II. A.D. 1326.

A bill exhibited in the parliament against the king.

The king deposed by the parliament, and his son Edward chosen king.

In the mean time as touching the king, who was yet in prison, it is thought by some writers, that the next year following, by the means of Sir Roger Mortimer, he was miserably slain, by a spit, as it is said, being thrust up into his body, and was buried at Gloucester, after he had reigned nineteen years.

In the time and reign of this king, the college of Cambridge, called Michael House, was founded and builded by Sir Henry Stanton, knight, to the use and increase of learning, a thing in a commonwealth very profitable and necessary to be had; the want and need whereof, many sundry times, is sooner felt in this realm of ours and other realms abroad, than is the discommodity thereof of most men commonly understood.

Michael House, in Cambridge, founded by Henry Stanton.

About the same time also was Nicolaus de Lyra, who wrote the ordinary Gloss of the Bible: also Gulielmus Ocham, a worthy divine, and of a right sincere judgment, as the times then would either give or suffer.

In the tractation of this king's history, it was declared before what grudge did kindle in the hearts of the barons against the king, for revoking such acts and customs as had been before in the parliament established, both for Peter Gaveston, and for the two Spensers. Also, what severe punishment the king did execute upon them for the same, in such cruel and rigorous sort, that as he spared none of those whom he could there find, so he never ceased all his life after to inquire out and to be revenged of all such as had been in any part or consenting to that matter. For this his extreme and implacable tyranny, he was in such hatred of all the people, that, as he said, he could not find one of all the commons to take his part, when need required. Among others who were for that matter troubled, was one Adam, bishop of

Tyranny odious to the people.

Edward II. A.D. 1326.

Hereford, who being impeached of treason with others besides, was at length arrested in the parliament to appear and answer to that which should be to him objected. Many things were there laid against him, for taking part with them that rose against the king, with more matters, and heinous rebukes, &c.; whereunto the bishop for a great while answered nothing.[1]

Form of words when a bishop challenges the privilege of the church against a secular judge.

At length the bishop, claiming the liberties and privileges of the church, answered the king in this form:[2]—"The due reverence of your princely majesty ever saved, I, an humble minister and member of the holy church of God, and a bishop consecrated (albeit unworthy), cannot, neither ought, to answer to these so high matters without authority of the archbishop of Canterbury, my direct judge next under the high bishop of Rome, whose suffragan also I am, and the consent likewise of the other my fellow-bishops." After these words by him pronounced, the archbishop and other bishops with him were ready to make humble intercession for him to the king, and did. But when the king would not be won nor turned with any supplication, the said bishop, together with the archbishop and the clergy, coming with their crosses, took him away, challenging him for the church, without any more answer-making; charging moreover, under the censures of the church and excommunication, none to presume to lay any further hands upon him. The king, moved with this boldness and stoutness of the clergy, commandeth, notwithstanding, to proceed in judgment, and the jury of twelve men to go upon the inquiry of his cause; who finding and pronouncing the bishop to be guilty, the king caused immediately all his goods and possessions to be confiscated unto himself: moreover, he made his plate and all his household provision to be thrown out of his house into the street; but yet he remained still under the protection and defence of the archbishop, &c.

The bishop rescued by the clergy.

The king proceedeth in judgment against the bishop.

This archbishop was Walter Winchelsey; after whom succeeded Simon Mepham, in the same see of Canterbury, A.D. 1327.[3]

After pope Clement V., by whose decease the Romish see stood vacant, as ye have heard, two years and three months, next was elected pope John XXII.,[4] a Cistercian monk, who sat in that papacy eighteen years. He was stout and inflexible, and given so much to the heaping up of riches, that he proclaimed them heretics who taught that Christ and his apostles had no possessions of their own in this world. At this time was emperor Louis of Bavaria, a worthy man, who, with this pope, and others that followed him, had no less contention than had Frederic before mentioned, in the time of king Henry III.; insomuch that this contention and variance continued the space of four and twenty years. The cause and first origin of this tragical conflict, arose upon the constitution of Clement V., the predecessor to this pope; by whom it was ordained, as is before mentioned, that emperors, by the German princes elected, might be called kings of the Romans, but might not enjoy the title or right of the empire to be nominated emperors, without their confirmation given by the pope. Wherefore, this emperor, because he used the imperial dignity in Italy, before he was

A new-found heresy, to say that Christ and the apostles had no proper possessions here.

(1) Ex Tho. Walsing.
(2) "Ego sanctæ ecclesiæ Dei minister humilis, membrum ejus, et episcopus consecratus, licet indignus, ad tam ardua nequeo respondere, nec debeo, absque D. Cant. archiepiscopi, post summum pontificem mei directi judicis, cujus etiam sum suffraganeus, autoritate, et aliorum parium meorum episcoporum consensu."

authorised by the pope, the said pope therefore excommunicated him. And notwithstanding the emperor oftentimes did proffer himself to make entreaty of peace and concord; yet the pope, inflexible, would not bend. The writings on both parts be yet extant, wherein the said bishop doth make his vaunt, that he had full power to create and depose kings and emperors at his pleasure. In the same time were divers learned men, who seeing the matter, did greatly disallow the doings of the bishops of Rome; among whom was William Ocham, whose tractations were afterwards condemned by the pope, for writing against the temporal jurisdiction of their see; as did another, named Marsilius Patavinus, who wrote the book entitled 'Defensor Pacis,' which was given into the hands of the said emperor; wherein the controversy of the pope's unlawful jurisdiction in things temporal is largely disputed, and the usurped authority of that see set forth to the uttermost. It is found in some writers, that a great cause of this variance first began, for that one of the emperor's secretaries, unknown to the emperor, in certain of his letters had likened the papal see to the beast rising out of the sea, in the Apocalypse. At length, when the emperor, after much suit made to the pope at Avignon, could not obtain his coronation, coming to Rome, he was there received with great honour; where he, with his wife, were both crowned, by the full consent of all the lords and cardinals present; and moreover, another pope was there set up, called Nicolas V. After these things done, the pope, not long after, departed at Avignon in France; after whom succeeded Benedict XII.,[1] a monk of the Benedict order, and reigned seven years; who, by the counsel of Philip, the French king, confirmed and prosecuted the censures and cursings that John, his predecessor, had published against Louis, the emperor: moreover, he deprived him of his imperial crown, and also of his dukedom of Bavaria. The emperor upon this cometh to Germany, and assembling the princes electors, dukes, bishops, nobles, and the learned, in a council at Frankfort, there declared before them, out of the ancient laws and customs of the empire, how it standeth only in the princes electors, and in no others to elect the kings or the emperors of the Romans (for in both these names there was no difference), so that the same electors, in choosing the king of the Romans, did also elect and choose the emperor; which emperor, so by them constituted, had lawful right, without any information of the apostolical see, to exercise the administration of the empire. And if he were lawfully elect, he ought to be anointed by the Roman bishop; which if he do refuse, then might he be anointed and declared emperor and Augustus by any other catholic bishop thereunto appointed, as by the old manner and custom hath been; especially seeing these injunctions are only certain solemnities added and invented by the bishops, for a token of unity between the church and empire, to govern and defend the faith together. Wherefore, in that the emperor sweareth to the bishop of Rome, in that is to be understood no homage or fealty made to the bishop, but only that it is a sacrament and a promise given to defend the faith;[2] which oath or sacrament so given, giveth no majority to the pope in any temporal rule, but only bindeth the emperor to be prompt and ready to defend

Strife between the pope and the emperor.

The emperor crowned against the will of the pope.

Is deprived and deposed.

A council at Frankfort.

The emperor's protestation.

(1) A.D. 1335.—ED. (2) Ex Hieron. Mario.; et ex Crantzio.

Edward II. A.D. 1326.

the faith and church of Christ, when need shall require obedience. Wherefore, whereas the pope leaneth only to the electors' authority to make the king of Romans, and taketh upon himself alone power to make the emperor; that, as it is newly brought in and devised of late by pope Clement V., so is it contrary both to all ancient order, and also derogatory to the liberty and majesty of the sacred empire. Again, neither is that also less absurd and contrary to all right and reason, that the pope, in time of the imperial seat being vacant, taketh upon him to have the whole and full doings of the empire, as lawful emperor for the time; which prerogative and function, by ancient orders of our ancestors, should properly and only appertain to the palatine of the Rhine: the constitution Clementine of the aforesaid pope Clement to the contrary notwithstanding. Then, in the end, for his own excuse, he, in the presence of them all, reciteth the public confession of his faith, to answer and purge himself of those objections laid to him by the pope. This did the meek emperor Louis in that council. Yet, all this notwithstanding, the said emperor remained still excommunicate, till the time that variance happened between this pope Benedict and Philip, the French king. Wherefore, to make his party good, at least to have some friends to flee to, he began to pretend favour and absolution, rather for necessity than for any good will to the emperor. But, not long after, this pope died; of whom this epitaph was made:—

"Hic situs est Nero, laicis mors, vipera clero,
Devius a vero, cupa repleta mero."

Trouble of Louis the emperor.

After Benedict followed pope Clement VI.,[1] a man most furious and cruel;[2] who renewing the excommunications of his predecessors, caused his letters to be set upon church-doors, wherein he threatened and denounced most terrible thunderbolts against the said Louis, the emperor, unless within three days he should satisfy to God and the church, and renounce the imperial possession of the crown. The emperor upon this cometh to Frankfort, and there, ready to stand in all things to the ordinance of the pope, sendeth his orators to the court of Rome, to entreat the pope's favour and good will towards him: to which messengers the pope answered again, that he would never pardon the emperor, before he gave over and confessed his errors and heresies, and, resigning up his empire to his hands, would submit himself, his children, and all his goods, to the will and pleasure of the bishop; promising that he should not receive again any part of the same, but upon his good grace, as his will should be to restore them.

Heresy of the pope's making, objected against the emperor.

The heresy here mentioned, which was to this emperor objected by the pope, was this; because (as is above touched upon) he used and executed the imperial dignity after his election, before he was by the pope confirmed. Over and besides, the pope sendeth to the emperor, by the said orators, a certain form of a bill contained in writing with certain conditions, which he commanded to be given into the hands of the emperor. Here, if the emperor Louis had had as much mind to set upon the pope with dint of sword, as he lacked

(1) A.D. 1342.—Ed. (2) Ex Chron. de sex. mundi ætatibus, cui tit. 'Rudimentum Novitiorum.'

neither occasion nor power so to do, what blood might have been spilt! But the good emperor, sparing the effusion of blood, receiveth gently the bill; and not only with his seal doth confirm it, but also sweareth to observe all the conditions thereof; which the pope hearing of, doth greatly marvel. But yet all this would nothing help to mollify the modest heart of this Pharaoh.

Edward II. A.D. 1326.

Proud heart of the pope.

The princes and electors, seeing the bill of the articles and conditions, whereof some sounded to the malicious defacing and destruction of the empire, and abhorring the wickedness thereof, desired the emperor to stand to the defence of the imperial dominion, as he had begun, promising that their assistance and aid to the uttermost thereunto should not lack. Upon that other orators were sent to pope Clement from the princes, desiring him to abstain from such manner of articles conceived against the state and majesty of the empire. The pope, surmising all this to spring from Louis the emperor, to the utter subversion of him and all his posterity, on Maundy-Thursday blustereth out most black curses against him; also he reneweth all the former processes of his predecessor against him, as against both a heretic and a schismatic: commanding, moreover, the princes electors to proceed in choosing a new emperor. The archbishop of Mentz, seeing the innocency of the emperor, would not consent to the violating of his majesty; wherefore he was deprived by the pope of all his dignities. The other bishops electors, as the archbishop of Cologne, who took eight thousand marks, with the duke of Saxony, who took two thousand marks, being corrupted with money by John, king of Bohemia, elected Charles, the son of the said John; whom pope Clement eftsoons in his consistory did approve. Who seeth not here what matter of war and bloodshed was ministered by the pope between these two emperors, if the patience of Louis had not been more prudent to quench the fire, than the pope was to kindle it? Charles, then the new emperor elect, sped him to Aquitaine, according to the custom, there to be crowned; but by the citizens there and the empress (the wife of Louis keeping thereabout) he was repelled. All this happened in the time and reign of Edward III., king of England; against whom the said Charles, with the French king, and the king of Bohemia, set on by the pope, encountered in war; where the king of England had against them a noble victory, and slew a great number of the Frenchmen and Almains, and put Charles, the new emperor, to flight. In the mean time, among the princes and citizens of Germany what sorrow and what complaints were against pope Clement and those electors, cannot be expressed; for as they were all together at Spires congregated in a general assembly, so there was none among them all, that allowed the election of Charles, or that cared for the pope's process; promising all to adhere and continue faithful subjects to Louis, their lawful emperor. But Louis, remembering his oath made before to the pope's bill, voluntarily and willingly gave over his imperial dignity, and went to Burgravia; where, shortly after, through the procured practice of pope Clement (as Hieronymus Marius doth write), poison was given him to drink; after which being drunk, when he would have vomited out and could not, he took his horse and went to hunt the boar, thereby, through the chasing and heat of his body, to expel the

The emperor accused by the pope for a heretic.

Faithful archbishop of Mentz.

Bribers corrupted with money.

The pope, a sower of discord and blood.

Again stirreth up wars.

Charles, the new emperor, put to flight by the Englishmen.

Louis, the right emperor, resigns his empire.

Is poisoned.

Edward II. A.D. 1326.

venom. And there the good and gentle emperor, wickedly persecuted and murdered of the pope, fell down dead,[1] whom I may well account among the innocent and blessed martyrs of Christ; for if the cause being righteous doth make a martyr, what papist can justly disprove his cause or faith? If persecution joined thereunto causeth martyrdom, what martyr could be more persecuted than he, who, having three popes like three ban-dogs upon him, at length was devoured by the same? The princes hearing of his death, assembled themselves to a new election, who, refusing Charles aforesaid, elected another for emperor, named Gunterus de Monte Nigro, who, shortly after falling sick at Frankfort, was likewise poisoned through his physician's servant, whom the aforesaid Charles had hired with money to work that feat. Gunterus tasting of the poison, although he did partly cast it up again, yet so much remained within him, as made him unable afterwards to serve that place; wherefore, for concord's sake, being counselled thereto by the Germans, he gave over his empire to Charles, for else, great bloodshed was likely to ensue. This Charles thus ambitiously aspiring to the imperial seat contrary to the minds of the states and peers of the empire, as he did wickedly and unlawfully come by it, so was he by his ambitious guiding, the first and principal mean of the utter ruin of that monarchy; for that he, to have his son set up emperor after him, convented and granted to the princes electors of Germany all the public taxes and tributes of the empire. This covenant, being once made between the emperor and them, they afterwards held so fast, that they caused the emperor to swear never to revoke or call back again the same: by reason whereof, the tribute of the countries of Germany, which then belonged only to the emperor for the sustentation of his wars, ever since to this day is dispersed diversely into the hands of the princes, and to the free cities within the said monarchy; so that both the empire being disfurnished and left desolate, and the emperors weakened thereby, they have neither been able sufficiently since to defend themselves, nor yet to resist the Turk, or other foreign enemies. Of this a great part, as ye have heard, may be imputed unto the popes, &c.[2]

Louis, emperor and martyr. *Gunterus de Monte Nigro, emperor.* *Is poisoned.* *Ruin of the German empire, and the first cause thereof.*

This pope Clement first reduced the year of jubilee to every fiftieth year, which before was kept but in the hundredth year; and so he being absent at Avignon (which he then purchased with his money to the see of Rome), caused it to be celebrated at Rome, A.D. 1350. In that year were numbered, of peregrines going in and coming out every day at Rome, to the estimation of five thousand. The bull of pope Clement, given out for this present year of jubilee, proceedeth in these words:—

The year of jubilee reduced to the fiftieth year. *Pilgrims in this year.*

What person or persons soever, for devotion sake, shall take their peregrination unto the holy city, the same day when he setteth forth out of his house, he may choose unto him what confessor or confessors either in the way or where else he listeth: unto the which confessors we grant, by our authority, plenary power to absolve all cases papal, as fully as if we were in our proper person there present. Item, we grant that whosoever being truly confessed shall chance by the way to die, he shall be quit and absolved of all his sins. Moreover, we command the angels of paradise to take his soul out of his body, being absolved, and to carry it into the glory of paradise, &c.

Abominable and blasphemous bull of pope Clement. *The pope commandeth the angels.*

(1) Louis of Bavaria died A.D. 1347.—ED.

(2) Hieronymus Marius.

And in another bull he saith,— *Edward II.*

We will, that no pain of hell shall touch him: granting, moreover, to all and singular person and persons signed with the holy cross, power and authority to deliver and release three or four souls, whom they list themselves, out of the pains of purgatory, &c. A.D. 1326.

O! blasphemy of the pope!

This Clement, as mine author affirmeth, took upon him so prodigally in his popedom, that he gave to his cardinals of Rome bishoprics and benefices which then were vacant in England, and began to give them new titles for the same livings he gave them in England; wherewith the king, as good cause he had, was offended, and undid all the provisions of the pope within his realm;[1] commanding, under pain of imprisonment and life, no man to be so hardy, as to induce and bring in any such provisions of the pope, any more within his land. And under the same punishment he charged the two cardinals to void the realm, (A.D. 1343). In the same year all the tenths, as well of the Templars as of other spiritual men, were given and paid to the king through the whole realm. And thus much concerning good Louis, emperor and martyr, and pope Clement VI., his enemy; wherein, because we have a little exceeded the course of years whereat we left off, let us return somewhat back again, and take such things in order as belong to the church of England and Scotland, setting forth the reign of king Edward III., and the doings of the church which in his time have happened, as the grace of Christ our Lord will assist and enable us thereto.

The king resisteth the pope.

Tenths of church goods given to the king.

This aforesaid king Edward II. in his time builded two houses in Oxford for good letters, to wit, Oriel-College, and St. Mary-Hall.

Oriel-College and St. Mary-Hall in Oxford builded by king Edw. II.

Here I omit also by the way the furious outrage and conflict which happened in the time of this king, a little before his death, A.D. 1326, between the townsmen and the abbey of Bury; wherein the townsmen gathering themselves together in a great multitude (for what cause or old grudge between them, the register doth not declare), invaded and sacked the monastery. And after they had imprisoned the monks, they rifled the goods and treasure of the whole house, spoiling and carrying away their plate, money, copes, vestments, censers, crosses, chalices, basons, jewels, cups, macers, books, with other ornaments and implements of the house, to a value unestimable:[2] in that conflict, certain also on both sides were slain. Such was the madness then of that people, that when they had gathered unto them a great concourse of servants and light persons of that country to the number of twenty thousand, to whom they promised liberty and freedom; by virtue of such writs as they had out of that house, first they got into their hands all their evidences, copies, and instruments, that they could find; then they took off the lead; that done, setting fire to the abbey-gates, they burned up nearly the whole house. After that they proceeded to the farms and granges belonging to the same abbey, whereof they wasted, spoiled, and burned to the number of two and twenty manor-places in one week; transporting away the corn, horses, cattle, and other moveables belonging to the same, the price whereof is registered to come to 922*l.* 4*s.* 11*d.*

Commotion between the town and abbey of Bury.

(1) Ex Chron. Wals. in Vit. Edw. III. (2) Ex Latino quodam registro.

Edward II. besides the valuation of other riches and treasures within the abbey, which cannot be estimated.

A. D. 1326. The abbot was all this space at London, in the parliament, by whose procurement at length such rescue was sent down, that twenty-four of the chief of the town (submitting themselves) were committed to ward; thirty carts-full of the townsmen were carried to Norwich, of whom nineteen were there hanged, and divers convicted were put to prison. The whole township was condemned in seven-score thousand pounds, to be paid for damages of the house. John Berton, alderman, and W. Herling, with thirty-two priests, thirteen women, and one hundred and thirty-eight others of the said town were outlawed; of whom divers, after grudging at the abbot for breaking promise with them at London, did confederate themselves together; and privily, in the night, coming to the manor of Chenington, where the abbot did lie, burst open the gates, and entering in, first bound all his family. After they had robbed him of all his plate, jewels and money, they took the abbot and shaved him, and secretly conveyed him away with them to London; where they, removing him from street to street unknown, from thence had him over the Thames into Kent: at length over the sea they ferried to Dist in Brabant, where they a sufficient time kept him in much penury, misery, and thraldom; till, at length, the matter being searched out, they were all excommunicated, first by the archbishop of Canterbury, then by the pope. At last it being known where he was, he was delivered and rescued by his friends out of the thieves' hands, and finally brought home with procession, and restored to his house again: and thus was that abbey with the abbot of the same, for what demerits I know not, vexed and afflicted about this time, as more largely I have seen in their Latin register. But thus much briefly; the rest I omit here,[1] passing over to the reign of the next king.

The abbot robbed, and stolen away to Brabant.

Restored again.

EDWARD THE THIRD.[2]

A. D. 1327. CONCERNING the acts and story of king Edward II., his deposition, and his cruel death, wrought by the false and counterfeit letter of Sir Roger Mortimer, sent in the king's name to the keepers, for the which he was afterwards charged, drawn, and quartered; I have written sufficiently before, and more, peradventure, than the profession of this ecclesiastical history will well admit. Notwithstanding, for certain respects and causes, I thought somewhat to extend my limits herein the more; whereby both kings, and such as climb to be about them, may take the better example by the same; the one to have the love of his subjects, the other to learn to flee ambition, and not bear themselves to brag of their fortune and state, how high soever it be: considering with themselves nothing to be in this world so firm and sure, that may promise itself any certain continuance, and that is not in perpetual danger of mutation, unless it be fastened by God's protection.

(1) About the latter end of this Edward II. ceaseth the history of Nic. Trivet, and of Flor. Hist.
(2) Edition 1563. p. 74. Ed. 1583. p. 374. Ed. 1596. p. 344. Ed. 1684. vol. i. p. 428.—ED.

After the suppression of this king, as is above expressed, Edward his son was crowned king of England, being about the age of fifteen, who reigned the space of fifty years, and was a prince of much and great temperance, in feats of arms very expert, and no less fortunate and lucky in all his ways, than his father was unfortunate before him. For liberality, also, and clemency, he was worthily commended; briefly, in all princely virtues, famous and excellent. Concerning the memorable acts of this prince, done both in war and peace, as how he subdued the Scots, had great victories by the sea, conquered France, A. D. 1332, won Calais, A. D. 1348, and translated the staple thither, took the French king prisoner, and how the French arms first by him were brought in, and conjoined with the English arms; also how the order of the garter first by the said king was invented and ordained, A. D 1356, also, A. D. 1357, how the king, in his parliament at Nottingham decreed, that all such, in Flanders or elsewhere, as had skill in making cloth, should peaceably inhabit the land, and be welcome (for three years before that, it was enacted, that no wool should be transported over the sea; which was, to bridle the pride of the Flemings, who then loved better the sacks of wool, than the nation of Englishmen): all these things, with other noble acts of this worthy prince, although in other chronicles they be fully treated of, yet, according to that order which I have begun (saying somewhat of each king's reign, although not pertinent to our ecclesiastical history), I have here inserted the same; making haste to other matters, shortly and compendiously abridging them out of divers and sundry authors together compacted, mentioned in this wise. *Edward III* A. D 1327.

The coronation and solemnity of king Edward III., and all the pomp thereof, was no sooner ended, but Robert Bruce, king of Scotland, understanding the state and government of the realm to be, as it was indeed, in the queen, the young king, the earl of Kent, and Sir Roger Mortimer; and that the lords and barons, as he was informed, did scarcely well agree amongst themselves, although he grew now in age, and was troubled with the falling disease, yet thought he this a meet time for his purpose, to make invasion: hoping for as good success and like victory now, as but lately before he had at the castle of Eustrivelin. Whereupon, about the feast of Easter, he sent his ambassadors with heralds and letters of defiance to the young king Edward III., the queen, and the council; declaring, that his purpose was, with fire and sword to enter and invade the realm of England, &c. The king, queen, and council, hearing this bold defiance, commanded in all speedy preparation musters to be made throughout all the realm; appointing to every band captains convenient, and at the city of York, by a day assigned them, commanding every man to be, with all their necessary furniture, ready and thoroughly provided. They directed their letters also with all speed to Sir John of Heinault, requiring him, with such soldiers and men-at-arms as he might conveniently provide in Flanders, Heinault, and Brabant, to meet the king and queen, upon the Ascension-day next ensuing, at their city of York. Defiance of the King of Scots

The king and queen made speedy preparation for this expedition; the noblemen provided themselves with all things necessary thereunto; the English captains and soldiers, their bands thoroughly

Edward III. A.D. 1327.

furnished, were ready at their appointed time and place. Sir John of Hemault lord Bedmount mustering his men as fast, was ready to take shipping, where, at Wysant, in English bottoms there lying for him ready, he went aboard, and with a merry wind landed at Dover, travelling from thence by small journeys daily, till he came, within three days after the feast of Pentecost, to the city of York, where the king and queen, with a great power of sixty thousand men, within and about the city of York, expected his coming; before whom, in courteous wise he presented himself, and mustered his troop, wherein he had to the number of five hundred good men-at-arms well appointed and mounted. His coming and furniture were well liked both by the king and queen; and he was, by the harbinger, appointed to be lodged, with his household retinue, in the abbey of white monks. To be brief, such grudge and variance arose between some of the king's soldiers and his, within the suburbs of the town being together lodged, that from the little to more, whilst the king and queen, with divers other of the nobles (strangers and others), were at dinner, the said fray so greatly increased, that the whole army, as many as were in the town then lodged, stood to their defence; so that there were slain of the English archers, in a short space, by the strangers, to the number of three hundred men. Whereupon, after the fray was, with much difficulty both of the king and queen, ended, such heart-burning grew between the parties, that the number of six thousand conspired together against them, thinking to have burned them in their lodgings, had they not been, by the great grace of God and discreet handling, otherwise prevented and let. Whereupon the Heinaulders were fain to take and keep the field, using as diligent watch and ward as though they had been among their hostile enemies. After this, the king set forward his army towards Durham, and encamped himself near about the same; who also sent the lord Vifford and the lord Mounbrey to Carlisle with a sufficient company to keep that entrance; and also the lord marshal of England to keep the town of Newcastle, with a sufficient company to defend the same, and the country adjoining. For well knew the king, that by one of these two entries the Scots must pass into England, standing both of them upon the river Tyne, twenty-four miles distant.

The king and queen at York, with an army of sixty thousand men, to meet the king of Scots

Great fray in York

Carlisle and Newcastle, then the keys of England, kept with garrisons

The Scots pass the Tyne, burning and spoiling the country

But the Scots privily with their army passed the river betwixt the two towns into England, few understanding thereof, till the great fires which the Scots had kindled and made in England, bewrayed them; who came burning and destroying the country all about as far as Stanhope park. This thing being declared to the king, he commandeth his host with all speed to march towards them; who so long travelled, that they came in sight each of other. The king also commanded the passages of the river to be so straitly and narrowly guarded, that by no means the Scots could retire and escape back again into Scotland, without battle given them of the king. But the Scots, understanding the great power of the king, kept always the advantage of the hills, retiring in the nights from one to another; so that, without great odds and advantage on the one side, and hazard to the other, the king could not set upon them.

The king's army and the Scots so near, that they see each other

Thus, in the day time, the Scots, keeping the advantage of the hills, and in the night time retiring to the advantage of other similar

Edward III. A.D. 1327.

ones, came near against that river where they first passed over, where they made a show to offer battle to the king upon the morrow. Hereupon the king being busied in putting his men and battles in readiness to fight the next morning, being almost wearied out in pursuing the Scots from place to place, the Scots, in the mean season, got over the river, and escaped the danger of the king. As this thing could not be done without great treason of some near about the king; so Sir Roger Mortimer was grievously suspected thereof, and, afterwards, it was laid to his charge. But to be short, by this means the Scots escaped the river; after whom it should have availed the king very little to have made pursuit, as the wily Scots knew full well. For joy thereof, the lord William Douglas, one of the Scottish generals, with two hundred horse, gave alarm in the king's camp; and came so near, that he cut certain of the lines of the king's tent in sunder with his sword, and retired to his company without great loss of any of his men. Then, on the morrow, the king, perceiving the Scots to be gone, came to the place where over-night they lodged, where were found five hundred great oxen and kine ready killed; five hundred cauldrons made of beasts' skins full of flesh, over the fire seething; a thousand spits full of flesh ready to be roasted; and more than ten thousand shoes of raw leather (the hair still upon the same), which the Scots had left behind; and five poor English prisoners tied to trees, and their legs broken. All which the king seeing, he left any further pursuing the Scots, and returned with his army to Durham, where he dismissed his army, and came again to London; sending with Sir John of Heinault two hundred men at arms for their better safeguard against the English archers (with whom at York, as you have heard, they frayed) till they had taken shipping; and so they returned home.

The Scots, through treason, escape out of England unfought.

Provision left in the Scottish camp.

The king returneth to London.

The king, then being at London, confirmed the liberties of the citizens, and ordained that the mayor should sit in all places as chief justice within the liberties of the same; and that what alderman soever had been mayor before, should be a justice of peace within his own ward.

Then the king, the queen, and the council, sent over to the earl of Heinault certain ambassadors, touching the solemnization of the marriage between the king and the lady Philippa, his daughter; who in such sort sped their message, that she was soon after conveyed over to England very honourably, and at Dover arrived. And from thence she came to London (some chronicles affirm to York), where, upon the day of the conversion of St. Paul, the year above specified, the marriage and coronation of the queen were with much triumph, during the space of three weeks, solemnized.

His marriage.

After this coronation and marriage, the king summoned his parliament to be kept at Northampton; whereat, by the means of Sir Roger Mortimer and the old queen, a peace was purchased for the Scots (who had for that purpose sent their ambassadors) to continue for four years. Also the king (then being within age) granted to release the Scots of all their homage and fealty unto the realm of England, which by their charter ensealed they were bound to; as also their indenture, which was called the Ragman Roll,[1] wherein were

Parliament at Northampton.

The Ragman Roll delivered to the Scots.

(1) "Ragman Roll," was a statute appointed by this king for hearing and determining all complaints of actions done five years before."—Ed.

Edward III

A.D. 1327.

specified the aforesaid homage and fealty to the king and crown of England, by the said king of Scots, nobles, and prelates, to be made; having all their seals annexed to the same. Also there was then delivered unto them the black cross of Scotland, which king Edward before, for a rich jewel and relic, had conquered and brought from Scone abbey; with all such rights and titles as any of the barons else had enjoyed in the said realm of Scotland, with many other things more, to the great prejudice both of the realm, and discontent of all the nobles and barons for the most part, more than the old queen, Sir Roger Mortimer and the bishop of Ely, who in such sort ruled the roast, that all the rest of the nobles and barons cast with themselves how best they might redress and remedy the great inconveniences, that unto the realm, by means of them, grew and happened.

The black cross of Scotland. The barons give up their titles in Scotland.

Hereupon the king and queen, and Sir Roger Mortimer, caused another parliament to be called at Salisbury, where the said Sir Roger Mortimer was made earl of March, against all the barons' wills, to prevent and disappoint the aforesaid purpose of them; but the earl Henry of Lancaster, with others, would not be at the same: wherefore it was laid unto their charges, that they went about to conspire the king's death.

Parliament at Salisbury. Earl Henry refuseth to come to it.

And further, because the king was under the government of the earl of Kent, his uncle, as well as under that of the queen his mother and the earl of March, and because they could not do in all things as they listed on account of the said earl the king's uncle, who loved the king and the realm, envy began to arise between the earl Mortimer and him; and, by Isabel the queen's practice, he found the means to persuade the king, that the earl of Kent (to enjoy the crown, as next heir unto the king) went about to poison him. To this the king giving easy credit, caused his said uncle to be apprehended; and, without making answer to his accusation and accusers, to be beheaded at Winchester, the third of October, in the third year of his reign. But the just judgment of God not permitting such odious crimes in him to be unpunished or undetected, so in fine it fell out, that Isabel the old queen, the king's mother, was found and understood to be with child by the said Mortimer. Complaint hereof was made to the king, as also of the killing of king Edward, his father, and of the conspiracy of Mortimer against the earl of Kent, the king's uncle, put to death before. Hereupon, divers other articles being laid against him, and manifestly read in the court, he was arraigned and indicted, and by verdict found guilty, having his judgment as in cases of high treason, and suffered death accordingly at London; where, upon London bridge, next unto Spenser's, his head obtained a place. The queen also, the king's mother, by good advice of the council, was restrained of her liberty, and within a certain castle not permitted once to come abroad: unto whom the king her son once or twice a year would resort, and visit her.

The earl of Kent put to death guiltless. Sir Roger Mortimer, earl of March, condemned, and put to death. The queen put in prison.

This year prince Edward was born at Woodstock; who in process of time and years grew to be a most valiant prince, and was, before he died, accounted throughout the world the flower of chivalry.

The birth of prince Edward.

After this the king prepared another army into Scotland in the year prefixed. But first he summoned king David of Scotland, who, in the last truce (four years to continue as you heard), his father then

Expedition of Edward into Scotland.

living, had married the lady Jane, sister to the king (termed Jane Makepeace), to do his homage to the king; but that he refused. Whereupon, not forgetting therewithal the scoffing rhymes, which daily from that time of truce the Scots had in their mouths, he did so much, that with an army well furnished he entered Scotland by the river Tweed; for the Scots had then the possession of the town of Berwick. The Scottish gigs and rhymes were these:—

> "Longbeards heartless, painted hoods witless;
> Gay coats graceless, make England thriftless."

To be short, the king wasted the land; burned, destroyed, and took towns and castles with small resistance or none; and, for the space of six months together, did in that land what he listed, without any battle offered to him: for the king of Scots was but a child, and not above the age of fifteen years, and wanted good captains that should have defended the realm; insomuch that they were all, saving those that kept in holds for their defence, fain to take the forest of Godworth; and there kept themselves as long as the king remained in Scotland. At length, when he had sufficiently wasted, and spoiled, and burned the same, he returned towards Berwick, about which he bent his siege, vowing not to discontinue the same, till he had gotten the town. *Wasteth and destroyeth the realm.*

The Scots who kept the same, after a certain time and many assaults made, were contented, upon certain conditions, to have delivered up the town; but that the king refused, unless, all conditions set apart, they would, with bag and baggage, depart. Hereupon they condescended to the king, that if by a certain time they were not by the king of Scots rescued, they would render up the town, and with bag and baggage depart; and so, the time having expired, frustrate of all hope and rescue, at the day appointed they did. The king then entered the town, and tarried there the space of twelve days; who, after he had appointed Sir Edward Baillew captain over the town, and leaving also behind him other knights, squires, and soldiers, as well to keep the same as other holds the king had conquered in Scotland and on the frontiers thereof, he returned with his people towards London, permitting every man to depart and go what way he liked. *Berwick besieged and yielded to the king.* *The king entereth the town.*

Then Sir Robert d'Artois, a nobleman of France, and descended of the blood royal, being in England with the king, ceased not oftentimes to advertise the king, and put him in memory of his good and right title to the inheritance of the crown of France. This Sir Robert, for a certain displeasure that Philip, the French king, took against him for a certain plea which by him was moved before the king, was fain, for the safeguard of his life, to flee the realm of France, and so come to the king's court. King Edward was not unwilling at all to hear thereof, but took delight oftentimes to reason and debate that matter with him concerning his right, title, and inheritance to the crown of France. But yet, notwithstanding, he thought it not good to make any attempt thereunto without advised and circumspect counsel; for that it contained matter of no small, but most difficult, importance: neither yet he took it to deserve the fame either of wisdom or prowess to let so good a title die, or so fit opportunity to *Sir Robert d'Artois, a nobleman of France, inciteth the king to prosecute his title in France.*

Edward III. A.D. 1327.

pass. Wherefore he, calling together certain of his council, used their deliberate advices touching the seriousness of this matter. In fine, it was by them thought good, that the king should send certain ambassadors over to the earl of Heinault, whose daughter he had married, as well to hear his advice and counsel herein; as also what friends and aid, by him and his means, in this so great an expedition to be begun in the empire, to him might be procured. The king hereunto condescended, and appointeth for this embassage the bishop of Lincoln with two other baronets, and two doctors; who in such speedy wise made their voyage, that in short space they returned again to the king with this answer, that not only the earl's counsel and advice should be herein pressed to the king of England their master, but also the whole country of Heinault. And further, for that to such an expedition as appertained, the province of Heinault was but a small matter to make account of—he said he would procure for the king greater aid and friendship in the empire; as the duke of Brabant his cousin-german and a puissant prince, the duke of Guerles, the archbishop of Cologne, the marquis of Juliers, &c., who are all good men of war, and able to make ten thousand fighting men, saith he. This answer well pleased the king, and made him joyous thereof; but this counsel of the king, as secret as it was, came to Philip the French king's ears; whereupon he stayed the voyage of the cross which he then had in hand, sending forth countermands to stay the same, till he knew further the purpose of the king of England.

The king deliberates with his council, concerning the title of France. Ambassadors sent to the earl of Heinault concerning it. They return an answer that pleaseth the king.

King Philip of France heareth of the king's purpose, and stayeth his voyage of the cross.

The king hereupon himself taketh shipping, accompanied as to a king appertained; and when he had consulted with all the aforesaid lords of the empire in this matter, and understood their fidelity, he made his repair to the emperor, at whose hands he was well entertained, and honourably received; whom the emperor appointed to be his lieutenant-general, having thereby more authority both to will and command such as for this his expedition he sted unto, and had made convention with. Philip, hearing this, prepared his army, and rigged his navy, that as soon as the king should enter into the dominion of France, they also might enter into England, requiting like for like.

King Edward assigned lieutenant-general of the empire.

The king of England, after the feast of St. John the Baptist, according to his purpose, prepared all things ready to such an expedition, conducting his army, and gathering a greater strength in the empire, as before to him was promised, using the emperor's authority therein, as his lieutenant-general; howbeit at the charge altogether of the king of England. The French king, as soon as king Edward had landed his army at Machelen in Flanders, hearing of the defiance which the king and other noblemen of the empire had sent unto him, sent certain ships lying ready thereunto, and waiting for such opportunity upon the coast of England; who, upon a Sunday, whilst the townsmen were at the church little looking for any such matter, entered the haven of Southampton, took the town and spoiled the same, committed most revolting excesses, burned, killed, took captives, and carried away rich spoils and great booties to their ships; and so again departed into France. Further, as the king of England had allied himself with the noblemen of the empire, and had the friendly favour of the emperor also thereunto, so the French

First voyage into France.

Southampton burned by the French. †

king made the like league and alliance with David, king of Scots (whom the king had so hardly dealt with in Scotland, as partly before you heard, keeping the most part of Scotland under his subjection), binding the said David, as well by writing as by oath and pledge, that without his consent he should make no peace, nor conclude any truce with the king of England. The French king again assured him of aid, and rescue, and help, and promised to recover his kingdom and dominion to his use; and forthwith sent certain garrisons and bands into Scotland to keep play with the Englishmen, and there to fortify divers places till further opportunity served. He also fortified with men, money, victuals, and munition, the town of Cambray, which he suspected would be besieged, lying so near upon the empire, as indeed it came to pass; for king Edward, departing from Machelen, set forward his host towards Heinault, and by the way assembled such power as in the empire he looked for, marching forward still till that they came to Cambray, and besieged it with forty thousand men, while another company, the Flemings, Brabanters, and Hollanders, went to St. Quintin. But in effect, neither there, nor at Cambray, nor elsewhere, any thing notorious was achieved, but the summer being well spent, and little prevailing in the siege of Cambray, being of situation strong and well defenced therewithal with men and munition, he broke up the siege, and marched further into the heart of France towards Mutterel. The French king having understanding of this, prepared himself to give battle to the king of England, who, with another great army, came to Vironfosse, where days were appointed to meet in battle; but in the end, nothing was done or attempted between the princes, and the king of England (without any battle either given or taken) returned with his army from thence to Ghent. Concerning the cause of the sudden removing of the king out of France, it seemeth most especially to arise from the pope; who at the same time sent down his legates, for the order of a peace to be made between the kings. At Ghent were gathered in council together, by the king's appointment, all the nobles as well of England, as of the empire, to consider what was best to be done; where this plain answer was made to the king of England: That unless he would take upon him the claim and title of France, as his lawful inheritance, and as king thereof prosecute his wars, it would not be lawful for them any further to aid the king of England, or to fight with him against the French king; for that the pope had bound them in two millions of florins of gold, and under pain of excommunication, that they should not fight against the lawful king of France. Whereupon, the king thought good, therefore, presently to make open challenge to the realm and crown of France; and further, to quarter and intermingle the arms of France with the arms of England in one escutcheon; whereupon king Edward immediately made answer to the pope again, directing unto him his letters, wherein he declareth at large his right and title to the crown of France, purging thereby himself and his cause unto the bishop. The copy and tenor of his letter is too long to express, but it is to be found in the story of Thomas Walsingham, remaining in the library of J. Stephenson, citizen of London, whoso hath list or leisure to peruse the same. Besides this letter to the pope, he, remaining

Edward III

A.D. 1327.

The Scots stirred against England by the French king

The pope, the cause of the king's removing out of France

A.D. 1340

The king of England taketh the title of France

Edward III. yet at Ghent, directed another to the peers and prelates of France in tenor as followeth.

A. D. 1340.

The Letter of King Edward to the Nobles and Commons of France.

Edward, by the grace of God, king of France and England, lord of Ireland: unto all prelates and ecclesiastical persons, to the peers, dukes, earls, barons, and to the commons of France, greeting. The high Lord and King above, to whom although his will be in his own power, yet would he that power should be subject unto law; commanding every thing to be given unto him which is his, declaring thereby that justice and judgment ought to be the preparation of the king's seat. Wherefore seeing the kingdom of France, through the providence of God, by the death of Charles, the last king of France of famous memory, brother-german to our lady mother, is fallen unto us by plain and manifest law; and forasmuch as lord Philip de Valois, being the son of the uncle of the aforesaid king, and so being far from the crown by a further degree of consanguinity, through force and usurpation hath intruded himself into the aforesaid kingdom, whilst we were yet in our minority, and so, contrary both to God and to justice, doth detain and occupy the same; and lest we should seem to neglect our own right and the gift given us of God, or not to submit our will to God's ordinance: we have thought good to acknowledge the title of France, and by supportation of the Almighty King have taken upon us the defence and regiment of the said kingdom; firmly purposing with ourselves, as every good man ought to do, graciously to minister justice to every one, according to the rites and laudable custom of the aforesaid kingdom. Also to renew the good laws and customs which have been in the time of Louis our progenitor; adding, moreover, that which shall seem expedient according to the condition and quality of the time. As to any change of coin, or any other inordinate exactions, we intend not to seek our profits by your detriments, when (the Almighty be praised for it) we abound and have enough. And as concerning the affairs of the realm, our purpose is not to proceed rashly, or by our own will, but by the discreet advice and counsel of the peers, prelates, nobles, and other our faithful subjects of the kingdom, so far forth as shall make for the honour of God, the defence and advancement of the church (which in all fulness of devotion we do reverence), and to the profit both public and private of all the subjects thereof, with full execution of justice by the grace of God to be executed upon all and singular persons, being earnestly careful for the honour, profit and tranquillity of you all. For, as the Lord knoweth nothing shall be more grateful to us, than that by our careful solicitude peace may be engendered, especially betwixt us, and universally among all christian men; so that by our concord the force and strength of all christian princes may be joined together for the recovery of the Holy Land, which our Saviour and Redeemer hath dedicated with his own proper blood, whereunto we will endeavour ourselves, through the grace of the Holy Ghost. And forasmuch as we have offered to the aforesaid lord Philip divers friendly and reasonable conditions of peace, whereunto he would neither condescend, nor agree to any conformation; yea, rather moveth against us unjust war, to the utter subversion of our state, we are forced of necessity, to the uttermost of our power, for the defence both of us, and recovery of our rights, to defend ourselves by force of battle; not seeking any slaughter of good and humble subjects, but desiring their safeguard and profit.

The title of France, how it came to king Edward.

Note the grossness of this time, when the blood of Christ was thought but only dedicated to the Holy Land.

For the which cause, all and singular such subjects of the kingdom of France, who shall submit themselves to us as the true king of France, within the feast of Easter next ensuing; professing unto us their fealty, and doing to us as to the king of France by duty appertaineth, so as our beloved subjects of Flanders have done already, or be ready to offer themselves so to do: all such we willingly admit and receive to our peace and grace, under our protection to be defended, them to maintain as is convenient from all molestation and unquietness whatsoever in person or goods, hereafter to be enforced either by us, or by our officers, upon whatsoever occasion of rebellion before passed. And, forasmuch as the premises cannot easily be intimated to all and singular persons, we have provided the same to be fixed upon church doors, and other public places, whereby the manifest notice thereof may come to all men, to the comfort of you that be to us devout, and to the true information of those who through sinister surmises of our enemies are otherwise informed of us.—Dated at Ghent the eighth day of February, in the year of our kingdom of France, the first; of England, the fourteenth.

This done, for that the winter then drew on, neither was there any hope, as the time served, of farther doing good, the king thought best for a season to return again to England with his company, giving over the wars until the next spring; and so he did, taking shipping, and arrived at Dover. When he came to London, it was declared unto him, of the great spoil the Frenchmen had made at Southampton; who answered again, "That within one year he doubted not but the same should be well paid for and recompensed." And according to the same purpose of his he lingered no time, but calling a parliament at Westminster, with much grudge and evil-will of his subjects there was for the maintenance of his wars granted to him a great subsidy, which was the fifth of every man's goods, and also the customs of his wools, two years beforehand, and the ninth sheaf of every man's corn. At the spring the king again prepared his army, and rigged his navy, purposing to land in Flanders. But the archbishop of Canterbury, then lord chancellor, having understanding of the French power upon the sea, lying for the king, gave him advertisement there, willing him to go more strongly, or else not to venture. But the king, not crediting the archbishop, and being angry with him therefore, said, "That he would go forward;" whereupon the bishop resigned the chancellorship, and removed himself from his council. Then the king, consulting thereupon further with the lord Morley his admiral, and others, hearing also the same of them, furnished himself with stronger power, and committed him to his ship, and did so much, that a few days before Midsummer, he was upon the sea with a great fleet. Before the town of Sluys, the French king, to stop his passage, had got ready a great navy, well nigh to the number of twenty score sail, and had made the Christopher of England, which before the Frenchmen took at Southampton, their admiral. Betwixt the two navies was a long and terrible fight, but, in the end, the victory, by God's grace, fell to the king of England, in which fight he himself was personally; so that of the number of thirty thousand Frenchmen, few or none were left and escaped alive, and two hundred sail of ships were taken, in one of which were found four hundred dead bodies.

Counsel of the archbishop to the king.

Battle upon the sea between king Edward and the French.

The French beaten.

After this great slaughter of the Frenchmen, of whom many for fear of the sword leaped into the sea, when no man durst bring tidings thereof to the French king, they who were next about the king did suborn his fool, to insinuate the understanding thereof by subtlety of covert words; which was thus. As the fool, being in the king's presence, was talking of many things, among other talk he suddenly burst out (being prompted by others) into a vehement railing against the Englishmen, calling them cowards and dastards, with many such opprobrious words tending to that effect. The king, not knowing whereunto the words of the fool did appertain, asked the fool, why he called the Englishmen such weaklings and cowards, &c. "Why," saith the fool, "because the fearful and cowardly

Edward III. A.D. 1340.

Englishmen had not the hearts to leap into the sea so lustily as our Normans and gentlemen of France had." By this the French king began to understand the victory on his part to be lost, and the Englishmen to be victors.

Words of the fool to the French king.

This victory achieved, the fame thereof spreading abroad in England, at first was not believed, till letters thereof came from the king, prince Edward his son being then at Waltham, directed to the bishops and prelates of the realm: the effect of which letters here followeth under written.

The Letter of King Edward to the Bishops of England.

The bountiful benignity of God's great clemency poured upon us of late, for your true certification and rejoicing, we thought good to intimate unto you. It is not unknown (we suppose) to you, and to others our faithful subjects, who also have been partakers with us of the same, with what storms of boisterous wars of late we have been tossed and shaken, as in the great ocean. But although the rising surges of the sea be marvellous, yet more marvellous is the Lord above, who, turning the tempest into calm, in so great dangers, so mercifully hath respected us. For whereas we of late did ordain our passage upon urgent causes into Flanders, the lord Philip de Valois our bitter enemy understanding thereof, laid against us a mighty navy of ships, intending thereby either to take us, or at least to stop our voyage; which voyage if it had been staid, it had been the cutting off of all the great enterprises by us intended and taken in hand, and, moreover, we ourselves had been brought to a great confusion. But the God of mercies, seeing us so distressed in such perils and dangers, hath graciously, and beyond man's expectation, sent to us great succour and strength of fighting soldiers, and a prosperous wind after our own desires, by the means and help whereof we set out of the haven into the seas, where we eftsoons perceived our enemies well appointed and prepared with a main multitude to set upon us, upon Midsummer day last past; against whom, notwithstanding, Christ our Lord and Saviour hath rendered to us the victory, through a strong and vehement conflict, in the which conflict, a mighty number of our enemies were destroyed, and well nigh all their whole navy was taken, with some loss also on our part, but nothing like in comparison to theirs; by reason whereof we doubt not but our passage by the seas hereafter shall be more quiet and safe for our subjects, and also many other commodities shall ensue thereof, as we have good cause to hope well of the same. For which cause we, devoutly considering the heavenly grace so mercifully wrought upon us, do render most humble thanks and praise to Christ our Lord and Saviour; beseeching him, that as he hath been, and always is, ready to prevent our necessities in time of opportunity, so he will continue his helping hand ever towards us, and so direct us here temporally, that we may reign and joy with him in heaven eternally. And, in like sort, we require your charity, that you also with us rising up to the praise of God alone, who hath begun so favourably to work with us to our goodness, in your prayers and divine service do instantly recommend us unto the Lord, travelling here in these foreign countries, and studying to recover not only our right here in France, but also to advance the whole catholic church of Christ, and to rule our people in justice; and that also ye call upon the clergy and people, every one through his diocese to do the same, invocating the name of our Saviour, that of his mercy he will give to us his humble servant a docible heart, so to judge and rule hereupon rightly, doing that which he hath commanded, that at length we may attain to that which he hath promised, &c.

This letter was written to the bishops A.D. 1340.

After this aforesaid victory on the sea, and that news thereof, with due thanks to our Saviour, had been sent into England: the king striking into Flanders, came to Ghent in Brabant, where he had left the queen, who joyfully received him, being a little before purified or churched, as we term it, of her fourth son, whose name was John, and commonly

Edward III

A.D. 1340.

Council at Villenorth

Flanders, Brabant, and Heinault, take part with king Edward

called John of Gaunt, and was earl of Richmond, and duke of Lancaster. At Villenorth the king assembled his council, whereat the noblemen of Flanders, Brabant, and Heinault conjoined together in most firm league, the one to help and defend the other with the king of England, against the French king, purposing and determining from thence to march toward Tournay, and it to besiege. But the French king, understanding their counsel, fortified and victualled the same before their coming thither. Furthermore the French king at the same time, to stop the siege of king Edward, sent with king David of Scotland a great power, to the intent to make invasion in England, thereby the sooner to cause the king to remove his siege. In the mean time king Edward wrote his letters to Philip de Valois, making unto him certain requests, as in the same his letters here following is to be seen; who, for that he wrote not unto him as king of France, but by the name of Philip de Valois, refused to answer him touching the same, as by their letters here placed may be seen.

The Letter of the King of England, to Philip de Valois, the French King, going to the Siege of Tournay.

Philip de Valois, of long time we have gently requested you by our ambassadors (by all the reasonable means we might), to the intent that you should have rendered unto us our lawful right and inheritance to the crown of France, which from us a long time you have by great wrong and force detained. And for that we well perceive you mean to persevere in the same your purpose and injurious detinue, without making any reasonable answer to our demand, we let you understand, that we are entered into the country of Flanders, as the sovereign lord of the same, and so pass through the country, and further signify unto you, how that by the help of our Saviour Jesus Christ and our righteous cause therein, and with the power of the said country, our people and allies, we purpose to recover the right which we have to that inheritance you detain from us by your injurious force, and therefore approach we towards you to make a short end of this our rightful challenge, if you also will do the like. And for that so great an host assembled as we bring with us on our part (supposing you also on the other part to do the like) cannot long remain together without great destruction both to our people and country, which thing every good Christian ought to eschew, especially princes and others who have the government of the same; avoiding by as short an end as may be, the mortality of Christian men, according as the quarrel is apparent between you and me; for the which causes here touched, let the challenge, if you think meet, between our own persons and bodies be discussed, that the great nobility and prowess of each other, may of every one be seen. And if you refuse this way, then let there, to finish this challenge, be a hundred of the best soldiers you can choose out of your part matched with so many of our liege subjects to try the same. And if of these two ways you refuse both the one and the other, then that you will assign unto us a certain day before the town of Tournay, to fight with us power against power, which may be within ten days next ensuing after the date of these our letters, offering the said conditions unto you above specified, as we would all the world to know and understand, not upon any orgoil, presumption, or pride we take therein, but for the causes before alleged, and to the end that (the will of our Saviour Jesus Christ betwixt us two herein declared and showed) rest and peace might grow amongst Christian men, the power and force of God's enemies may be abated, and in fine, the limits of Christianity enlarged and enfranchised. And therefore hereupon, consider with yourself, what way you will take concerning our aforesaid offers, and by the bearers of these our letters send unto us herein quick and speedy answer.—Given under our great seal at Chin in the plain of Leece, the twenty-seventh day of this present month of July.

Edward III.

The Answer of the Lord Philip de Valois, unto the Letter aforesaid.

A.D. 1340.

Philip, by the grace of God, king of France, to Edward king of England. We have seen the letters which you have sent unto our court to Philip de Valois, wherein are contained certain requests which you make to the said Philip de Valois. But for that the said letters come not as directed unto us, neither yet the said requests seem to be made unto us, which thing clearly by the tenor of the said letters appeareth, we therefore write unto you no answer touching the same. Notwithstanding this sufficeth, that we understand by the said letters of yours, as also other ways, that you are entered into our realm of France, to the great damage both unto us, our realm, and people (more proceeding of will than reason), and not regarding that which a liege-man ought to do unto his lord. For you are entered into our homage by you lieged unto us, acknowledging yourself, as reason is, a liege-man unto the king of France; and have promised unto us such obeisance as men are wont to do unto their liege lords, as more plainly by your letters patent appeareth, ensealed with your great seal, the which we have with us: for the which thing we will you to understand, that our purpose is, when it shall seem good unto us, to drive you out of our realm, to the honour both of us and our kingdom, and to the profit and commodity of our people. And this thing to do we have firm and assured hope in Jesus Christ, from whom we have all our power and strength. For by your unreasonable demand, more wilful than reasonable, hath been hindered and stayed the holy voyage to those parts beyond the seas, where a great number of christian men have been slain, the divine service diminished, and the service of the church less reverenced. And as touching that where you say, ye intend to have the obeisance of the Flemings, we think and believe that the good people and commons of that country will behave themselves in such sort towards our cousin the countess of Flanders, their lady, as it be not to their reproach; and to us their sovereign lord, they will respect their honour and loyalty. And that thing wherein they have done otherwise than well hitherto, hath been by the evil counsel of such people as neither regard the weal public nor honour of their country, but their own only gain and commodity.—Given in the field near adjoining to the priory of St. Andrew, under our privy-seal, in absence of our great seal, the thirtieth day of July, A. D. 1340.

The Scots invade England.

Mention was made a little before of David, king of Scots, whom the French king had supported and stirred up against the king and realm of England; which David, with the aid of the Scots and Frenchmen, did so much prevail, that they recovered again almost all Scotland, which before he had lost, when he was constrained to live in the forest of Gedworth many years before. Then invaded they England, and came with their army, wasting and burning the country before them, till they came as far as Durham; and then returned again into Scotland, where they recovered all their holds again, saving the town of Berwick. Edinburgh they took by a stratagem or subtle device practised by Douglas and certain others, who, apparelling themselves in poor men's habits, as victuallers with corn and provender and other things, demanded the porter early in the morning, what need they had thereof; who, nothing mistrusting, opened the outward gate, where they should tarry till the captain rose; and perceiving the porter to have the keys of the inward gate, they threw down their sacks in the outward gate, that it might not be shut again, and slew the porter, taking from him the keys of the town. Then they blew their horn as a warning to their bands, which privily they had laid not far off; who, in haste coming, and finding the gates ready opened, entered upon a sudden, and killed as many as resisted them, and so obtained again the city of Edinburgh.

And recover Edinburgh.

The Scots being thus busy in England, the French king, in the mean season, gathered together a puissant power, purposing to remove the siege from Tournay; and among others sent for the king of Scots, who came to him with great force, besides divers other noblemen of France; insomuch that the French king had a great army, and thought himself able enough to raise the siege, and thither bent his host. But the French king, for all this his aforesaid huge power and force, durst not yet approach the king so near, as either to give him battle, or remove his siege, but kept himself with his army aloof, in a sure place for his better defence. And notwithstanding the king of England wasted, burned, spoiled, and destroyed the country for twenty miles round about Tournay, and took divers and sundry strong towns and holds, as Ortois, Urses, Greney, Archies, Odint, St. Amand, and the town of Lille, where he slew above three hundred men at arms, and, about St. Omer, he slew and killed of noblemen, the lord of Duskune, of Maurisleou, of Rely, of Chastillion, of Melly, of Fenis, of Hamelar, Mountfaucon, and other barons, to the number of fourteen; and also slew and killed above one hundred and thirty knights, being all men of great possessions and prowess, and took other small cities and towns, to the number of three hundred: yet, for all this, Philip de Valois, the French king, durst neither rescue his towns, nor relieve his own men; but of his great army he lost (which is to be marvelled at, being in the midst of his own country), by famine and other inconveniences, and for want of water, more than twenty thousand men, without any battle by him given. Whereupon, at the entreaty of the said Philip, by his ambassadors sent to the king, and by the mediation of the lady Jane, sister to the said Philip, and mother to the earl of Heinault, whose daughter king Edward, as you heard, had married, a truce, containing the number of fourteen articles, for one year, was concluded, the king of England being very unwilling and loath thereunto. Yet, notwithstanding, partly by the instance of the aforesaid lady, but especially for that the king was greatly disappointed, through the negligence of his officers in England, who sent him not over such money as he needed for the continuance of his wars and payment of his soldiers' wages, the articles being somewhat reasonable, he agreeth to the truce; the conditions of which, as there concluded, here follow under-written.

Edward III.

A.D. 1340.

Tournay besieged.

Articles of Truce.

I. That during the said truce no tales or mistrust on either part shall be a detriment or cause of breach of the same.

II. Item, that during the said respite or truce either of the princes, their helpers, coadjutors, and allies whatsoever, shall remain and be in quiet possession of all such possessions, holds, territories, and lands, as at this present day they keep and enjoy within the realm and dominion of France, in what manner soever they have achieved the same, during the said truce.

III. Item, that the said princes, their aiders, coadjutors, and allies whatsoever, shall pass safely from one country to another, and all merchants with their merchandise, as well by sea as by land, as accustomably they have been wont; except such banished men as have been banished out of the said realms, or any of them for other causes than the wars between the said princes.

IV. Item, that the said two princes shall not procure, either by themselves or any other, any practice or other molestation to be made the one to the other, by the bishop of Rome, or any other belonging to the holy church whatsoever; either for the wars begun, or any other cause, nor for the service of any of their

Edward III. A.D. 1340.

allies, coadjutors, and aiders, or any of them. And that neither our holy father the pope, nor any other, shall disturb or molest either of the said two kings during the said time.

V. Item, that immediately after the truce be proclaimed in both the hosts, they may stand bound on either side, to keep and observe all and every such article as shall be therein contained.

VI. Item, that within twenty days next and immediately ensuing, each of the princes shall cause to be proclaimed in Gascony and Guienne, and other their lands, these articles of truce, to the intent they may be the better observed, kept, and known.

VII. Item, if by any the said princes, their allies, people, or coadjutors, any siege be laid in Gascony or the duchy of Guienne, or any other isles of the sea, Guernsey or Jersey, or any other, that the same sieges be raised as soon as they shall hear of this truce.

VIII. Item, that such as are thieves and fugitives out of the country of Flanders shall not return during the truce; and if they do, that then such as apprehended them shall see justice done upon them, and they shall forfeit all the goods they have in Flanders.

IX. Item, it is recorded that the debts due to Arras, Tresponois, or other titles of France, shall neither be demanded nor exacted during the said truce.

X. Item, that all such prisoners, as have been taken during these wars, shall be released out of prison, and sent home upon their faith and oath to return, if they be not ransomed during the said truce. And if any shall refuse so to do, that then the lord under whom he is, shall constrain him to return again to prison.

XI. Item, that all the bands, whatsoever they be, which be made before this said truce in the time of war, whether they be of goods spiritual or temporal, be released without restitution, during the said truce.

XII. Also, that these conditions of truce immediately may take effect between the English and Scots, their lords, aiders, and allies; and the same to endure until the nativity of St. John the Baptist; and that certain persons be appointed by a certain day to be at the marches of England and Scotland, to confirm the said truce, under such conditions as have been accustomed in those parts. And if the said Scots refuse so to do, that then they have no aid out of France during the said truce.

XIII. Item, that this said truce be proclaimed in England and in Scotland, within twenty-six days after the date hereof.

XIV. Item, it is accorded that within this truce be contained Espanels, Chatellon, Genovous, the bishop and the town of Cambray and castles of the same.

In witness whereof, we John, by the grace of God, king of Bohemia, and earl of Luxemburgh, Adulph, bishop of Liege, Radulph, duke of Loraine, Ayemes, earl of Savoy, and John, earl of Darminacke, on the one party; and B. duke of Brabant, C. duke of Gelre, D. marquis of Juliers, Sir John of Heinault, and Sir Beaumont, on the other party, betwixt the high and puissant princes of France and England, have sealed this instrument of truce and peace, and delivered the same accordingly in the church of Espleteline, on Monday the twenty-fifth day of September, in the year of grace 1340.

King Edward returneth from Tournay.

This truce thus finished, king Edward broke up his camp, removing his siege from Tournay, and came again to Ghent; from whence, very early in the morning, he, with a small company, took shipping, and by long seas came to the Tower of London, very few or none having understanding thereof. And being greatly displeased with divers of his council and high officers, as through their default he was constrained against his will, not having money to maintain his wars, to condescend unto the aforesaid truce, he commanded to be apprehended and brought unto him to the Tower, the lord John Stonehore, chief justice of England, and Sir John Poulteney, with divers others. The next morning he sent for L. R., bishop of Chichester, and the lord Wake, the lord treasurer, and divers other such that were in

Deceived by his officers.

authority and office, and commanded them all to be kept as prisoners in the said Tower, the said bishop only excepted; whom, for fear of the constitution of pope Clement, which commanded that no bishop should be by the king imprisoned, he set at liberty, and suffered him to go his way, and in his place substituted Sir Roger Boucher, knight, lord chancellor of England.

Edward III. A.D. 1340.

No bishop must be imprisoned by the pope's law.

The history treating of this matter reporteth thus: that the king had at this time under him evil substitutes, and covetous officers, who, attending more to their own gain than to the public honour and commodity of the realm, left the king destitute and naked of money. Of this crime also John Stratford, then archbishop of Canterbury, was vehemently noted and suspected; whether of his true deserving, or by the setting on of others, hereafter shall more appear; insomuch that the king, ardently incensed against him, charged him with great falsehood used against his person, as by these his letters written and directed to the dean and chapter of Paul's against the said archbishop, manifestly appeareth; the tenor of which letter here followeth underwritten.

Covetous officers.

John Stratford, archbishop of Canterbury.

The King's Letter to the Dean and Chapter of St. Paul's.

Edward, by the Grace of God, King of England and France, and Lord of Ireland, to his well-beloved in Christ, the Dean and Chapter of the Church of St. Paul in London, greeting in the Lord:

It is manifest by ancient histories, but more plainly it appeareth by those things which daily are practised amongst us, that many men abusing, through pride, the favour of princes, and honour bestowed upon them, have maliciously gone about to deprave the laudable endeavour of kings. And now, that the words which we speak may be more manifest unto our subjects, we suppose that neither you nor they have forgotten, that we, being established in our kingly throne in younger years, and coveting even then to guide this our regal charge taken upon us with wholesome counsels, have called unto us, John, bishop of Winchester, now archbishop of Canterbury, whom we supposed for his fidelity and discretion to exceed others; whose counsel in matters appertaining unto the health of our soul, as in matters also respecting the augmenting and conservation of our kingdom, both spiritually and temporally we used, and he was received of us into all familiarity. We found in him also such humanity, that he was saluted by the name of Father, and of all next unto the king had in honour. Now, afterwards, when by right of succession the kingdom of France should have descended unto us, and was by violent injury by the lord Philip of Valois holden from us; the said archbishop, by his importune instancy, persuaded us to enter into league of amity with the princes of Almain against the said Philip, and to commit ourself and ours unto the hazard of wars; promising and affirming that he would bring to pass, that the revenues of our lands, and other helps by him devised, should suffice abundantly for the maintenance of our said wars; adding moreover that our only care should be for the furniture of strong and able soldiers, such as were fit for the purpose, and expert in warfare: for the rest he himself would effectually procure money convenient to suffice our necessity, and the charges thereof. Whereupon, intending great exploits, we conveyed our army beyond the seas, and with marvellous great charges, as behoved, we set forward; we became also bound in great sums of money, making sure account of the aid aforesaid promised unto us. But, alas! unhappy is that man that reposeth confidence in man's deceitful staff of brittle reed; whereunto, as saith the prophet, if a man lean, it breaketh and pierceth the hand. Thus, being defrauded of our long looked-for subsidy, for very necessity's sake we were constrained to take upon us importable charges of debts by grievous usury. And so our expedition being staid, we were compelled to retire into England, desisting from our enterprises so valiantly begun.

Edward III.

A.D. 1340.

Now, when we were returned into England, we laid before our archbishop our manifold calamities and misfortunes before rehearsed, and thereupon called a parliament; wherein the prelates, noblemen, and others the faithful subjects of our dominions, granted unto us a new subsidy of corn, lamb, wool, &c., besides the tenth granted by the clergy; which subsidy, if it had been faithfully collected and obtained in due time, had greatly availed for the expedition of our said wars, the payment of our debts, and the confusion of our enemies. Our said archbishop promised diligently to do his endeavour, as well in collecting the same, as also in procuring other necessaries to serve to our purpose. Whereupon, trusting under these fair promises, having all things in a readiness, both men and furnished ships, we made sail towards Flanders; and, by the way, upon the dangerous seas, buckled with our enemies (sworn to the destruction of our English nation), over whom we triumphed and were victors, not by our merits, their multitude far exceeding ours, but by the merciful clemency of him that ruleth both wind and sea. Which being done, we passed from thence with a mighty power for the recovery of our right, and pitched our tents near unto the puissant city of Tournay; where, being detained for a time in the siege thereof, and wearied with continual toil, our charges still increasing, awaiting with silence our promised aid; day by day we hoped from our archbishop to receive succour in these our so great necessities. At length, being frustrate of all conceived hope, we signified unto our said archbishop, and others his adherents, by divers messengers and sundry letters, our great necessity and perils which we were in for lack of the said subsidy granted unto us. We added also the utility and honour which we saw might be achieved if we had received money in time. All this notwithstanding, we received from them no succour at all; for that preferring their private business and proper commodities, they cloaked their sloth, or rather, as I may call it, their fraud and malice, with vain excuses, and painted glozing words, like unto the deceitful, who, as saith Isaiah, use to deride with these words, 'Manda remanda,' &c.

By means whereof (alas for sorrow!) it came to pass, that while good hope of subduing our enemies graciously smiled upon us, we were constrained, penury prevailing against us, to take truce, to our shame, the hinderance of our expedition, and the no small rejoicing of our evil-willers; and so we returned into Flanders all void of money and oppressed with infinite debts, neither had we in our treasuries wherewith to discharge our necessities, nor yet to pay our soldiers' wages; insomuch that we were compelled to enter into the devouring gulf of usury, and to sustain on our shoulders great burdens of debts, heap upon heap. This being done, our faithful friends, companions in war, and partakers of our tribulations, came unto us, with whom we consulted diligently by what means we might best deliver ourselves from this dangerous storm of evil fortune. They all agreed, affirming certainly, that the protracting of our wars, and cause of our manifold necessity, happened unto us through the fault and negligence, or rather the malice, of the said archbishop (upon whose discretion the disposition of the whole kingdom seemed to depend) and other officers whom we had joined in counsel with him, touching the affairs of our kingdom; vehemently swearing and murmuring amongst themselves (for that we had left so long uncorrected the insolency of the bishops and other officers), that if remedy in these cases were not had with speed, they would withdraw themselves from our allegiance, and the covenant which they had sworn unto; to the utter subversion of our kingdom, our perpetual ignominy, and the everlasting shame of our English nation, which God, our most merciful Father, forbid should come to pass in our days, in whom is fixed immoveably the anchor of our hope.

Archbishop of Canterbury false to the king.

Whereupon, intending the due correction of our officers, we removed from offices, as seemed good to our wisdom, divers persons whom we suspected, in causes evident, of evil administration of justice, of subversion, and oppression of our subjects, of corruption, of bribes, and other heinous offences. Others, also, of inferior degree, offending in the premises, we caused to be detained in safe custody, lest by their liberty justice might be trodden under foot, and the inquisition of the truth concerning the premises not come to light. Forasmuch therefore as the knowledge of the truth in these cases might of none more certainly be known, than from the secret breast of our aforesaid archbishop, for that nothing pertaining to our information ought to lie hid from him, unto whom for so long a time had been committed the administration of our whole

Evil officers displaced by the king.

commonweal, and sum of our business, we sent unto him our faithful subject, Nicolas de Cantilupe, with special commandment from us, that, all delays set apart, he should forthwith make his personal appearance before us at our city of London. But he, as one always timorous, as well in prosperity as in adversity, and fearing where no fear was, untruly allegeth that some of our assistants had threatened him, and laid wait for his life, if at any time he departed from the church of Canterbury; which (God we take to witness, and a pure conscience) we never meant, nor any of our assistants.

Edward III.

A.D. 1340.

We suppose he touched thereby our cousin, although to all others, as well of the clergy as commonalty, through his malicious misdemeanours, he was become odious.

Archbishop of Canterbury odious to all the clergy.

Wherefore intending the safeguard of our subjects by letters, or otherwise, called before us, we appointed our trusty and well-beloved Ralfe Stafford, our harbinger, to offer unto him safe conduct, and, moreover, to present unto him our letters patent, under our seal; willing and commanding him thereby again personally to come before us, that we might be informed what of so long a time he had done touching the affairs of the kingdom. Whereunto, contemning our commandment and gentle request, he answereth, that neither he would in person appear, neither yet in any matter confer with us, except it were in a full parliament, which for divers reasonable causes could not then be called. Thus may you see this archbishop, whom our royal benignity had amplified with large honours, admitted into all familiarity, received into the bond of unanimity and friendship, upon whom, as on a father, our whole hope did consist (who, so long as we accomplished his will in all things, pretended towards us a face of counterfeit love, cloaked with dissembling benevolence, even as though he had been a loving father), how cruelly against reason he hath now forsaken us, requiting benefits with ingratitude, oppressing his benefactor with the arrogancy of fear; and, finally, according to the vulgar proverb, rewarded us as a horse in a satchell, as a snake in a man's bosom, and as fire cherished next the skin, reward their receivers. When we were first exalted unto the throne of our kingdom, descended unto us by right of inheritance (God's divine providence so working), we thought and always think it a detestable thing to abuse so high authority, but rather desire to govern with clemency, lenity, and moderation of justice, that peace, of all men desired, might firmly take place.

Denieth to come to the king.

Charged with dissembling and ingratitude.

Nevertheless, our said archbishop hath gone about to defame our innocency, and the fidelity and diligence of our faithful counsellors, prosecutors of true justice; openly declaring in his letters patent, and publishing abroad in divers places, that he was oppressed by the king's power contrary to justice, the clergy and commonalty confounded, and the church overcharged with divers grievous taxes and exactions. He subtilely usurped the name of a good pastor, when indeed he was nothing less, but rather, as it should seem, by his own confession, and the common opinion had of him, a very hireling. He cloaked his crafty subtleness with the zeal of defending the church, although he himself, in very deed, was the only cause, by his evil counsel and crafty devices, of the tribulation of the same. He also feigned that not long ago, certain writings were brought unto him to be sealed, containing in effect the defence and excusation of all such in general that were violators of the liberties of the church; hoping thereby to defame the opinion had of us and our faithful counsellors, to stir up sedition amongst the people, and finally to withdraw from us the hearts of our nobility. He gave commandment by his letters, that these things should be proclaimed in all places of great resort by divers special articles, contrary to his former order in his provincial council. Wherefore, respecting the integrity of our fame, intending to prevent the malice of the said archbishop, and also to decline from us the snares prepared for us and ours; we have thought good at this present (over and besides those which before are rehearsed) amongst so many which we omit, to declare unto you some of his perverse and wicked acts. When, in our minority, we were constituted over our dominions, he caused us through his unadvised counsel and rash persuasion (thereby to win excessive favour), to give away so many wasteful gifts, and so many unlawful alienations, that now, by means thereof, our treasury is clean consumed, the revenues of our exchequer without all order diminished, and he corrupted with bribes innumerable. Oftentimes also, without cause why, when neither necessity nor utility so required, only through his persuasion, we forgave divers men great

A defamer of the king.

Edward III. A.D. 1340.

sums of money due unto us; yea, and the rents and revenues which ought to have been conserved for our necessity and profit, we applied to the use of his friends, largely bestowing upon such as ill deserved it. Moreover, accepting as well persons as money, contrary to our mind and his oath of fidelity made unto us, he admitted unto public offices throughout our dominions persons unworthily, neglecting those that had well deserved. Many other things he rashly took in hand, to the detriment of our state, the hurt of our dignity royal, and no small damage of our subjects, by abusing his authority and office committed unto him. But if he persist in his proud obstinacy and stout rebellion, we shall hereafter, in convenient time and place, cause it to be more openly known; willing and commanding you to publish and cause to be published, all and singular the premises openly and distinctly in places where you shall think it expedient, and to set forth, as shall seem best to your godly wisdoms, our good intent for the suppressing of incommodities, and the furthering of the commodities of our subjects, that we may worthily commend your circumspect care herein.

The archbishop abuseth his office.

Teste me ipso apud Westm. 10, die Februar. Anno Regni nostri Angliæ 15, Regni vero Franciæ secundo.

By these aforesaid objections and accusations of the king, premised and laid against the archbishop of Canterbury, what is to be thought of the doings of the said archbishop, I leave it to thy judgment, gentle reader (as I said before), to be conjectured; forasmuch as our histories somewhat bearing with the said archbishop, seem either to be uncertain of the truth of the matter, or else covertly to dissemble some part of that they knew. And especially of Polydore Virgil I marvel, who, having so good occasion to touch the matter, doth so slightly pass it over without any word of mention. In which matter, if probable conjecture, besides history, might here be heard, it is not unlike but that some old practice of prelates hath herein been put in use, through some crafty conspiracy between the pope and the archbishop. And the rather it is to be gathered, for that as the pope was an enemy unto the king in this his challenge to the crown of France, so the archbishop against his prince (as for the most part always they have been) was a friend, as no man need to doubt thereof, unto the pope. Which thing also more probably may be supposed, because of the coming down of the two cardinals the same time, from the pope to the king of England, about the matter of further truce; whereof (Christ willing) more hereafter shall follow. Albeit the archbishop, this yet notwithstanding, subtilely and featly excuseth himself to the king of the aforesaid objections, and cunningly handleth the matter in words by his letter directed to the king as followeth.

Letter of the Archbishop of Canterbury to the King.

Redoubted sir, may it please your majesty to understand, that the most chiefest and special thing that keepeth kings and princes in the favour of God, and best preserveth them in their estate, is sage, wise, and deliberate counsel. And therefore saith the wise man concerning counsel in this wise, "Good men have thereby their safety." And it is written in the Book of Kings, how Solomon, who was the wisest prince that ever was, took unto him the most ancient and sage men of his realm to be his counsellors, by whose advisement and discretion he always kept the land of Israel in quiet, and in peace; and besides that, had all other kings and princes that bordered upon him, at his will and commandment. After whose death reigned Rehoboam his son, who neglecting the good counsel of his father, and the good advice of his sage and discreet counsellors, hearkened to such counsel as lighter and younger men persuaded him unto, who sought rather how to please and flatter him, than the quiet state of his realm; whereby he lost all the whole land of Israel, the twelfth part only excepted. In like manner have many kings of Israel, and other kingdoms beside, by rash and evil counsel come to great ruin and mischief. And sir, saving your princely patience, you may call to remembrance your own time; for by the wicked and sinister counsel to our late sovereign lord your father given (whom God forgive), which he took and followed, both against the law of his land, and the grand charter of the peers, and others his people of the land, some he put to shameful death, from others he took their goods, and such as fled he put unto their ransom; and what enemies he purchased thereby your grace well understandeth. And after this, sir, you know, even in your own time, how, by following and believing over-light counsel, you yourself lost the hearts of many of your subjects, from the which God deliver you, if it be his will. And after that time again until now, by the good advisement of your prelates, peers, and sage counsellors of your land, your grace's business and affairs have been so demeaned and ordered, that you have had the hearts again of all your subjects, as well spiritual as temporal, as much or rather more, than any of your grace's predecessors, kings of England, have had; so that, by means of the said good counsel, the good will and aid of your people, and the special grace of God, you have had the victory of all your enemies, as well in Scotland as in France, and all other places besides; so that unto this day (God's name be blessed for it) your grace hath been esteemed as one of the most noble princes in all Christendom. And now your grace, by the evil and perverse counsel of some such within the realm who are not so wise as they might be, and such also as consider and respect rather their own private commodity, than your grace's honour and safety of your realm, beginneth to apprehend divers clerks, peers, and other people of the land, and to direct process against them that is not beseeming, but contrary to the law of the land, which to keep and maintain you are bound by the oath you took at your coronation; and contrary to the grand charter, whereof all the realm are witnesses, and all the prelates of the same; and contrary to the sentence confirmed by the bull of our holy father the pope, which we have to show. All which things, as they are to the great peril and danger of your soul, so are they also to the utter debasing of your regal state and honour. And sir, although such as be your grace's governors and counsellors (being a calling above their degree) do give your grace to understand that their enterprises and yours do please and content your subjects and commons; yet your grace shall know for certain, and prove it your own self to be far otherwise than they bear you in hand. And that, unless God do remedy the same, if you prosecute your purpose begun in this order, you will lose the hearts of all your subjects, as also your good and rightful enterprise; and shall see such discord about the same, that you shall not be able to perform that you have begun, but rather force your enemies to seek your destruction, to lose your noble and renowned fame, and, in the end, your kingdom itself: which God forbid. Wherefore, sovereign lord and king, I beseech you that for the safeguard of your honour and realm, and enterprise begun, you will take unto you the most discreet and wisest men within your realm, and work by their advice and counsel, as before this time you have been accustomed; without the aid and counsel of whom you can neither maintain your enterprise, nor govern your realm. And because some such as are about your grace falsely devise against us treason and such like troubles (and therefore are of us excommunicate, and as persons excommunicate we do so esteem of them, as your spiritual pastor, we also desire you so to esteem and think of them); who also make like report of others that have been with your grace beyond the seas, that they have naughtily and falsely served you, whereby you have lost the town of Tournay, and much honour else, which you might have won and gotten there: may it please your grace to call before you the prelates and peers of your realm in some convenient place, where we and others may safely come and resort; and there also to make search and inquiry, in whose hands, after the beginning of your wars, the money, with what things else soever which was granted unto you in aid of the same your wars, until this present day, doth remain and is not laid out again; as also by whose default you were so forced to leave the said siege of Tournay, and that those who shall be found in any point faulty and guilty therein against you, as a good justicer, your grace will cause to be punished

Good counsellors necessary about a king.

Excommunication, in his own private cause, abused.

Edward III. A.D. 1340.

according to the law; and insomuch as appertaineth to us therein, we ask judgment of our peers (the state always of holy church, of us, and of our order reserved inviolate), according as we have written unto you herein. And for God's sake, sir, believe not either of us, or any other your true subjects else, more than that you shall understand the verity of; for if men should be punished without making answer to that which is objected against them, there should be then no difference in judgment betwixt the good doer and the bad.

And sir, may it please you well to consider of the great enterprise you have in hand, the great good will which you have need of for this cause, and of your great enemies the Scots, and the great jeopardy of your realm besides. For if your prelates, your nobles, and all the wise men of your realm were of one mind and will, without any discord or division amongst them, to dispose and set in order those things which are needful in so great affairs and business, they should have, all, enough to beat their heads about, for the maintenance of your great enterprise begun, the honour of you, and safeguard of your realm. And sir, may it please your grace not to be displeased that so rudely and grossly we declare unto you the verity; for why, the great love and affection which we bear unto you, and always have done the same, the preservation of your honour, and safeguard of your realm, as also for that we are, although unworthy, the primate of the whole realm of England, which thing appertaining unto us by our office (and we being your spiritual father), doth incite us the rather both to say and command that which may turn to the benefit of your soul, and profit of your realm and kingly estate. Thus the Holy Spirit save you, both body and soul, and give your grace both to hear and believe good counsel, and further, give you victory over all your enemies. Written at Cant., the first of January, by your grace's chaplain, the archbishop of the same.

Return of the king's army from Tournay.

And thus stood the case between the king and the archbishop of Canterbury, who coming thus, as is said, in secretwise into England from the siege of Tournay, his army in the mean while by ships was conveyed to Brittany. A great number of the troops, through unseasonable and inconvenient meats and drinks, were there consumed; to whom also no less danger happened on the seas in coming out of Brittany into England, by tempest, thunder, and lightning, stirred up, as is thought, by the necromancers of the French king.

A.D. 1341. Truce for three years between Edward and the French king.

About A.D. 1341, were sent from the pope two other cardinals to treat with king Edward for a truce of three years more to be concluded with the French king, besides the former truce taken before for one year; and all by the pope's means. For here is to be understood, that as it was not for the pope's purpose to have the king of England to reign over so many countries, so his privy support lacked not by all means possible, both by the archbishops and cardinals, and also by the emperor, to maintain the state of the French king, and to establish him in his possession.[1]

In the histories where these things be mentioned, it is also noted, that the same year there was here in the realm such plenty of victuals, that a quarter of wheat was sold for two shillings, a fat ox for a noble, and as some say, a sheep for four-pence. And thus far endureth the history of Ranulphus Cestrensis, called 'Polychronicon.'

A.D. 1342.

The year following, A.D. 1342, Louis of Bavaria, the emperor, who before had showed great courtesy to king Edward, in his first voyage over, insomuch that he made him his vicar or vicegerent general, and offered him also aid against the French king; now (either turned by inconstancy, or seduced by the pope) writeth to him contrary letters, wherein he revoketh the vicegerentship granted to him, and seeketh

(1) Ex Thom. Walsing. Ex Chron. Albanens.

all means in favour of the French king, and against king Edward; as by his letters here under written may better appear.

Letter of the Emperor to the King of England.

Louis, by the grace of God emperor of the Romans, always Augustus, &c. To Edward king of England, his beloved brother, greeting and unfeigned love. Although great and urgent business of our own do oppress us, and about the same our weighty affairs we are daily encumbered, yet with the discord and variance between your kingly dignity and the renowned Philip, the king of France our cousin, for your sake, we are not a little troubled. And the rather, the great charges which may hereafter grow both to you and to your kingdom thereby considered, both of men and money, unless the same be taken up, doth more easily provoke us to give ourself to the careful study of your affairs. Wherefore we give you to understand that the aforesaid Philip, at our request, hath given unto us, by his letters, authority and power to treat and conclude a peace between you, touching the variance begun: which peace (all the state diligently considered both of yourself, your kingdom, and subjects) we take and believe to be right expedient for you; moving therewithal your charity, and earnestly desiring you, that to this also you will give your consent, whereby we may bring you both to concord and unity, and establish between you a firm peace to endure; whereunto with willing mind we would apply ourself, and bestow our painful labour in prosecuting the same. And herein if you will condescend and agree unto our counsel, as we trust you will, it may please you by your letters to give unto us the like authority as is above said, to treat of peace or for the ordering of a truce for one year or two at least to continue. Neither let it move you, that between us and the said Philip of France a truce is taken; for, seeing that you without our consent took truce with him, we, by the advice of our princes who know the bonds, deeds, and covenants betwixt us, who also thought no less but that, saving your honour, we might do the same, have also made a league with the said Philip king of France; and for certain causes do revoke and call back the lieutenantship which we assigned unto you by our letters. Nevertheless, giving you for certain to understand that in our said treaties and peace concluded, we have so brotherly considered you, that, if you will agree and condescend unto our counsel, your cause, by our mean and help, shall be brought to good pass and effect; about which things further to confer with your brotherhood herein, we have sent a devout and religious man, Eliarhardus, reader and brother of the Heremites of St. Augustine, and chaplain of our court; whom, about the premises, we desire with speedy expedition to be sent unto us again.

Dated at Frankfort, the fourteenth day of June, in the twenty-fourth year of our reign, and the fourteenth of our empire.

Answer of the King of England to the Emperor.

To the high and mighty Prince Lord Louis, by the grace of God, Emperor of the Romans, always Augustus, Edward, by the same grace, King of France, and England, and Lord of Ireland, salutation and prosperous success.

We have reverently received your highness' letters, amongst other things containing, that the noble Philip de Valois, to the intent a peace and concord between us and him might be concluded, hath given unto you, by his letters, full power and authority thereunto at your highness' request; and that if the same might content us to do in like sort, your highness would travail to bring the concord to pass; and that it would not move us any whit at all, that your highness and the said Philip are in league together: forasmuch as we, without your assent and consent, you say, took truce with the said Philip, you have also done the like with him (which thing you might well do saving your honour, by the counsel of all your nobles and princes), and for certain causes you revoke again the lieutenantship which you committed unto us. Doubtless the zeal and good will you have to make this concord and agreement, we much commend; letting you to understand that we always have been desirous, and still are, to have a reasonable peace with the said Philip; which peace as much

Edward III

A.D. 1342.

as to us (our honour saved) appertained, we have in justice and by law prosecuted; and in very deed, it should be to us acceptable, and as we would wish, if by such a mediator as your celsitude is, it might be brought to pass. But, forasmuch as we understand the same our right and title to the kingdom of France to be manifest and clear enough, we purpose not to commit the same by any of our letters to doubtful arbitrement but while we well consider and revolve with ourselves, how, upon circumspect consideration (you manifestly beholding our just and rightful doing, and the strait dealing and obstinate purpose and injury of the said Philip), your gracious highness made a special league with us, and in our behalf, against the said Philip, adopting us of your great and bountiful love towards our person to be one of your sons, wherefore, that you should thus again alter and break the same, we cannot sufficiently marvel, seeing your invincible highness, being instituted of God to the laud and commendation of good men, and revenge of evil and wicked doers, hath made a league against us with the said Philip de Valois, our notorious and injurious enemy And as touching that which you say, that without your assignment and consent we took a truce, or days of respite, with the said Philip, which we ought not to have done, if your grace well consider the circumstance of the matter, we have done but as we might therein, for when we laid our siege to Tournay, it was requisite that we should follow their advice, whose aid and society therein we had Besides, the sudden and imminent necessity which we there stood in, and the distance of the place betwixt your highness and us furthermore was such, as that by no means we might attain the same, nor use your assent therein. Yea and further, if your grace well remember yourself, your grant unto us was such, that whensoever opportunity thereunto should serve, we migh treat of any peace, and grant what time we thought meet thereunto, without your consent therein; so that to conclude any final peace with the said Philip de Valois, without either your consent, or otherwise making your highness privy thereunto, it might not be lawful for us, which thing, without your said counsel, consent and advice, we never minded nor purposed to do, but have in all our doings done that which us beseemed, so far as by any means our power would stretch, hoping likewise that your brotherly benevolence for a time would have more lovingly supported us. It is thought also by some, that the revoking back again, or restraint of your aforesaid lieutenantship, was premature or done all out of time; when, according to your promise made to us herein by your letters imperial, you ought not so to have done, before the realm and kingdom of France, or at the least the greatest part thereof, were of us obtained and quietly in peaceable wise enjoyed These things premised, therefore, we desire you, according to your nobility, duly to consider, and hereafter to do, that which shall be thought both meet and convenient; because that (God willing) we mean to recompense and gratify both you and yours, according to the measure of your benevolence bestowed upon us. The Almighty grant unto your celsitude so much felicity as your heart desireth.

Dated at London the 18th day of July, in the second year of the reign of our kingdom of France, and of England the fifteenth.

In the mean time died pope Benedict XII., mentioned a little before; after whom succeeded in his room pope Clement VI. Of whom it is reported in stories, that he was very liberal and bountiful to his cardinals of Rome, enriching and heaping them with goods and possessions, not of his own, but with the ecclesiastical dignities and preferments of the churches of England;[1] for so recordeth the author, that he bestowed upon his cardinals the livings and promotions, such as were or should be vacant in the churches of England, and went about to set up new titles for his cardinals, here within this realm. But the king being offended therewith, made void and frustrate all those aforesaid provisions of the pope; charging moreover and commanding that no person whatsoever should busy himself with any such provisions, under pain of imprisonment and losing his life; which law was made the year following (A.D. 1344).

The king disannulleth the pope's provisions

(1) Ex Chron Albanens

It followeth then, that the said pope Clement again began to make new provisions for two of his cardinals of benefices and churches that should be next vacant, besides bishoprics and abbotships, to the extent of two thousand marks; whereupon the procurators of the said cardinals were sent down for the same. But the king and nobility of the realm, not suffering that, under pain of imprisonment caused the said procurators forthwith to depart the realm; whereupon the nobles and commons, shortly after, wrote a fruitful epistle to the pope, for the liberties and maintenance of the English church; whereunto, as saith the author, the pope and the cardinals were not able to answer. The argument and tenor of the letter, we have caused to be translated out of French into English, as ensueth.

Edward III. A.D. 1343.

The pope's procurators driven out of England.

Letter of the King of England, and of the Nobles and Commons of the same, to the Pope, against the Reservations and Provisions which he had in England.

To the most holy father in God, lord Clement, by the grace of God, of the holy church of Rome, and of the universal church, chief and high bishop: his humble and devout children, the princes, dukes, earls, barons, knights, citizens, burgesses, and all the commonalty of the realm of England, assembled at the parliament holden at Westminster, the fifteenth day of May last past; devout kissings of his holy feet, with all humble reverence and humility. Most holy father! the holy discretion, government, and equity, which appear to be in you, and ought of duty so to be (being so high and holy a prelate, and head of the holy church), by whom the holy universal church and people of God ought to be, as by the sunbeams, enlightened, give us good hope and likelihood, that the just petitions (to the honour of Jesus Christ and holy church, and your holiness also) by us declared, shall be of you graciously heard and considered, and that all errors and other iniquities should be quite taken away and removed; in stead whereof, fruitful exploits and necessary remedies (by the grace of the Holy Spirit which you in so high an estate have received) may be by you likewise graciously ordained and disposed. Wherefore, most holy father! all we (upon great deliberation and common assent) come unto your holiness, showing and declaring that the noble kings of England our progenitors, our ancestors, and we (according to the grace of the Holy Spirit to them and us given, every one according to his devotion) have established, founded, and endowed within the realm of England, churches, cathedrals, colleges, abbeys, priories, and divers other houses of religion in the same ordained; and to the prelates and governors of the same places, have given lands, possessions, patrimonies, franchises, advowsons, and patronages of dignities, revenues, offices, churches, with many and divers other benefices unto them given; whereby the service of God and the faith of Christ might have been honoured and had in reverence, that the hospitals and almshouses that are made, with all the churches and edifices, might be honestly kept and maintained, and that devout prayers might in those places be made for the founders, and the poor parishioners aided and comforted. And such only ought to have the cure thereof, as are able to hear confessions, and, in their own natural tongue, are otherwise meet to inform and teach their parishioners. And forasmuch as, most holy father! you cannot well come to the notice of divers such errors and defaults, neither yet understand the condition of the places, being so far off, unless your holiness be informed and advertised; we, having the perfect intelligence and understanding of the said errors and defaults of the places above mentioned, within the said realm, have thought meet to signify the same unto your holiness; that divers reservations, provisions and collations by your predecessors apostolic of Rome, and by you, most holy father! in your time have been granted (and that, more largely than they have been accustomed to be) unto divers persons, as well strangers, and of sundry nations, as unto some such as are our enemies, having no understanding at all of the tongue and conditions of them of whom they have the government and cure. By this a great number

Misappropriation of ecclesiastical property to foreigners.

Edward III

A.D. 1343

Decay of the church of England by the pope

of souls are in peril, a great many of their parishioners in danger, the service of God destroyed, the alms and devotion of all men diminished, the hospitals perished, the churches, with their appurtenances, decayed, charity withdrawn, the good and honest persons of our realm unadvanced, the charge and government of souls not regarded, the devotion of the people restrained, many poor scholars unpreferred, and the treasure of the realm carried out against the minds and intents of the founders All which errors, defaults, and slanders, most holy father! we neither can nor ought to suffer or endure. We, therefore, most humbly require your holiness, that the slanders, errors and defaults, which we have declared unto you, may be, through your great discretion, considered; and that it may please you, that such reservations, provisions, and collations may be utterly repelled, that from henceforth the same be no more amongst us used, and to take such order and remedy therein, that the said benefices, edifices, rights, with their appurtenants, may be to the honour of God by our own countrymen cured, defended, and governed And that it may further please your holiness by your letters to signify unto us, without delay and other protract of time, what your pleasure is touching this our lawful request and demand; that we may do our endeavour with diligence herein for the remedy, correction, and amendment of those enormities above specified. In witness whereof, unto these letters patent we have set our seals. Given in the full parliament at Westminster, the 18th day of May, A.D. 1343.

After these things thus passed over, the king shortly after sent over his procurators, the earl of Lancaster and Derby, Hugh Spenser, lord Ralph Stafford, with the bishop of Exeter, and divers others, to the pope's court, to discuss and plead about the right of his title before the pope, unto whom the said pope Clement VI, not long after, sent down this message: How that Louis, duke of Bavaria, the emperor, whom the pope had before deposed, had submitted himself to him in all things, and therefore deserved at his hands the benefit of absolution, and how the pope therefore had conferred and restored unto him, justly and graciously, the empire, which he before unjustly did hold, &c This message when the king did hear, being therewith moved to anger, he answered, saying, that if he also did agree and compound with the French king, he was ready to fight with them both, &c.[1]

The pope's message to the king

The king's answer

In the course of this year, pence, halfpence, and farthings began to be coined in the Tower; and in the year following, which was

A D 1344 A D 1344, the castle of Windsor, where the king was born, began to be repaired; and in the same house what was called the round-table was situated, the diameter whereof, from the one side to the other, contained two hundred feet; to the expenses of which house weekly was allowed a hundred pounds for the maintaining of the king's chivalry, till at length, by the occasion of the French wars, it came down to nine pounds a week. Provoked by the example of this, the French king began also the like round-table in France, for the maintaining of the knighthood. At the same time the said French king, moreover, gave free liberty throughout his realm to fell down trees for making ships and maintaining his navy, whereby the realm of England was not a little damnified.

The castle in Windsor enlarged, and the round-table builded

Tenths granted to the king by the clergy for three years

During the same year the clergy of England granted to the king tenths for three years; for which the king in recompense again granted to them his charter, containing these privileges: That no archbishop or bishop should be arraigned before his justices "sive ad sectam suam, sive partis," if the said clerk do submit and claim

(1) Ex Chron Albanen

his clergy, professing himself to be a member of holy church; who, so doing, shall not be bound to come to his answer before the justices. And if it shall be laid unto them to have married two wives, or to have married a widow, the justices shall have no power to proceed against them, to inquire into the matter; so that the cause shall be reserved to the spiritual court, &c.

Edward III. A.D. 1344.

By this, it is likely that priests had wives.

About this time, at the setting up of the round-table, the king made prince Edward, his eldest son, the first prince of Wales. All this while still continued the truce between the two kings, albeit it is likely to be thought that the French king made many attempts to infringe the same; whereupon Henry, earl of Lancaster, with six hundred men at arms, and as many archers, was sent over to Gascony, the year after (A.D. 1345), who there so valiantly is said to have behaved himself, that he subdued fifty-five townships unto the king; twenty-three noblemen he took prisoners, encountering with the Frenchmen at Allebroke. So courteously and liberally he dealt with the soldiers, that it was a joy to them, and a preferment to fight underneath him. His manner was, in winning any town, to reserve little or nothing to himself, but to disperse the whole spoil among his soldiers. One example in the author whom I follow is named; how the said earl at the winning of the town of Briers, where he had granted to every soldier, for his booty, the house with all the implements therein, which he by victory should obtain; among his other soldiers, to one named Reh, fell a certain house with the implements thereof, wherein were contained the mint and money coined for that country, to the value of a great substance; which when the soldier had found, in breaking up a house where first the gross metal was not yet perfectly wrought, he came to the earl declaring, to him the treasure, to know what was his pleasure therein. The earl answered, that the house was his, and whatsoever he found therein. Afterwards the soldier, finding a whole mint of pure silver ready coined, signified the same to the earl, forasmuch as he thought such treasure to be too great for his portion; to whom the said earl again answering, declared that he had once given him the whole house, and what he had once given, he would not call back again, as children use to play. And therefore bade him enjoy that which was granted to him; and if the money were thrice as much, it should be his own.[1] Which story, whether it were true or otherwise in those days, I have not to affirm. But certes, if in these our covetous and wretched days now present, any author should report the like act to be practised, I would hardly believe it to be true.

First prince of Wales.

A.D. 1345.

Henry, earl, after made duke of Lancaster, sent over to Gascony.

The liberal heart and constant voice of a worthy captain.

As the earl of Lancaster was thus occupied in Gascony, the Scots were as busy here in England, wasting and spoiling without mercy; who were thought, and not unlikely, to be set on by the French king; and therefore he was judged both by that, and by divers other ways, to have broken the covenants of truce between him and the king of England. Wherefore, the next year ensuing (A.D. 1346), king Edward, first sending his letters to the court of Rome, and therein complaining to the pope of Philip de Valois, how he transgressed and broke the truce between them made, which by evident probations he there made manifest, about the month of July made his

The Scots partly a mean of breaking truce.

A.D. 1346.

The second voyage of king Edward into France.

(1) Ex Chron. Albanen.

Edward III. A.D. 1346.

voyage into Normandy, in such a secret manner, that no man well knew whither he intended. There he first entered the town of Hogs, and from thence proceeded unto Cardoyne. About the twenty-seventh of July, by the river Cardoyne, he had a strong battle with the Normans and other Frenchmen, who, to stop his passage, defended the bridge; at which battle were taken of the lords of France, the earls of Ewe and Tankerville; and of knights with other men of arms, to the number of one hundred; of footmen six hundred; and the town and suburbs were beaten down to the hard walls, and all that could be borne away was transported to the ships.

The battle at Cardoyne.

A little before, mention was made how the French king began first to infringe the truce taken, and how the earl of Lancaster, upon the same, was sent into Gascony. Now, for the more evidence of the matter concerning the falling of the French king from the league, and other his wrongs and untrue dealing, it shall better, in the king's letter, appear; who, hearing word that the lord Philip de Valois, contrary to the form of truce taken at Vanes, had apprehended certain of his nobles of England, and had brought them to Paris to be imprisoned and put to death; besides other slaughters and spoilings made in Brittany, Gascony, and other places more: he, therefore, seeing the truce to be broken on the French king's part, and being thereto of necessity compelled, in the year above prefixed, the fourteenth of June, did publish and send abroad his letters of defiance, containing to this effect.

The King's Letters of Defiance against the French King.

To all and singular, to whom these presents shall come, public greeting. We think it is not unknown unto you all, that after the decease of Charles, late king of France, of famous memory, brother to our redoubted lady mother queen Isabel, queen of England; the crown of France, by just inheritance, hath fallen unto us, as to the next heir male now living after the said king. Now Philip de Valois, being but only son to the uncle of the aforesaid king Charles, and therefore, by degree of consanguinity, further off removed from the same (we being in the time of our minority), hath violently, by force and power, contrary to God and justice, usurped, occupied, and yet doth occupy the same; invading further, and spoiling our lands in the dukedom of Aquitaine, and joining himself with our rebellious enemies the Scots, seeking our subversion both by land and by sea, to the uttermost of his endeavour. And although we, to prevent the damages which might rise by war, have offered to the said Philip divers friendly ways of peace, to the intent we might better intend our purposed voyage against Christ's enemies the Turks; yet could we nothing prevail with him in obtaining any peaceable way of reformation, driving us off by crafty dissimulation, through false pretensed words, but performing nothing with heart and deed. Whereupon we, not neglecting the grace and gift of God, to defend the right of our inheritance, and to repulse the injuries of our enemy, have not refused by force of arms, coming down to Brittany, to encounter with him in open field. And so we being occupied in our wars, there repaired unto us the reverend father bishop of Prevest, and of Tusculane cardinals, and legates from pope Clement VI., to treat of some reformation of peace between us; at whose request we consented, agreeing to such forms and conditions of peace as then were taken between us, sending, moreover, our ambassadors to the court of Rome specially to treat of the same matter. And thus, while some hope of truce seemed between us to appear, news suddenly came unto us, which not a little astonished our mind, of the death of certain of our nobles and adherents, whom the said Philip unjustly and cruelly, at Paris, had commanded to be executed besides the wasting and spoiling our lands and subjects in Brittany, Gascony and other places; with innumerable wrongs and injuries, deceitfully intended gainst us, both by sea and land. By reason whereof, the truce on his part being otoriously broken, it is most manifest that it had been lawful for us, forthwith, o have set upon him with open war. Yet, notwithstanding, to avoid those ncommodities that come by war, we thought first to prove, if by any gentle neans some reformation might be had touching the premises. And therefore, undry times, we have sent ambassadors to the pope's presence for a treaty of eace and reformation to be had in those aforesaid excesses; requiring also, for he tractation thereof, certain terms of times to be appointed, always reserving o ourselves, notwithstanding, free liberty to resume war at our pleasure, ccording as the doings of the said Philip shall constrain us thereunto. And ow, forasmuch as the aforesaid terms be already expired, and yet no reasonble offer of peace appeareth, neither will the said Philip come to any conormity, being required and admonished, notwithstanding, by the pope's letter hereunto (as the pope by his letter hath written unto us), but always hath multiplied his conspiracy and obligations, using extremities against us; and, to mit here to speak of the excessive enormity of the pope's legate, who being ent by the bishop of Rome for the keeping of truce, and whose part had been ather to have quenched and stayed the discord, hath stirred up our enemy nore eagerly against us. In this, neither hath the bishop of Rome (saving his everence) as yet provided any remedy, albeit he hath been divers times equired of us so to do; which thing being so, we ought to be excused both efore God and man, if, for the defect of other remedy to be had, we shall be onstrained ourselves to find remedy against such wrongs and injuries, the ase of justice and necessity constraining us to give out these our letters of lefiance against the violator of the truce, and the unjust invader of our kingdom· protesting, that this we do, not upon any displeasure to the bishop of Rome, or o the apostolic see, but only for the moderation of equity, standing upon the lefence of our own right and lawful inheritance, intending always, rather to ave peace, if by any reasonable way it might be had. And thus much, for he stopping of slanderous fame and the mouths of backbiters, we thought good to signify, first to the high bishop of Rome, and the aforesaid cardinals, hat by them, as persons indifferent, and mediators, the same may be insinuated o the contrary part, and also unto your whole university in general, recomnending unto you all, the innocency of my cause, and the community of justice Dated at Westminster the fourteenth of June, the nineteenth year of our reign n England, and of France the sixth

The pope's legate stirreth up war

Like legate like pope.

And thus much for the king's letters. Now let us again return to his passage, from whence a little we have digressed. Concerning the which passage of the king, with the order of his acts achieved in the same, from the winning of Cadane or Cardoyne, unto the town of Poissy, it is sufficiently described by one of the king's chaplains and his confessor; who, being a Dominic friar, and accompanying the king through all his journey, writeth thereof as followeth.

A Letter of the King's Confessor touching his Acts-doing at Cardoyne.

Great cause we have to praise and laud the God of heaven, and most worthily to confess his holy name, who hath so wrought his mercy to us. For after the conflict had at Cadane, in the which many were slain, and the city taken and sacked, even to the bare walls, the city of Baia immediately yielded itself of its own accord, fearing lest their counsels had been bewrayed. After this the lord our king directed his progress toward Rouen; who being at the town of Lexon, there came certain cardinals to him, greatly exhorting him to peace; which cardinals being courteously entertained of the king for the reverence of the pope's see, it was thus answered to them again, that the king being very desirous of peace, had assayed by all ways and means reasonable how to maintain the same, and, therefore, hath offered conditions, and manifold ways of peace to be had, to the no small prejudice of his own cause; and yet is ready to admit any reasonable offer of peace, if by any means it may be sought, &c. With this answer the cardinals going to the French king, the king's adversary, to persuade with him in like manner, returned to King Edward, offering him in the French king's

The cardinals again entreat for peace

The king's answer to the cardinals

Edward III

A. D. 1346.

name, the dukedom of Aquitaine, in as full assurance as his father before him ever had it, besides further hope also of obtaining more, if treaty of peace might be obtained But forasmuch as that contented not enough the king's mind, neither did the cardinals find the French king so tractable and propense to the study of peace as they looked for, the cardinals returned, leaving the matter as they found it And so the king speeding forward in the way that his journey did lie, subdued the country and the great towns, without any resistance of the inhabitants, who did all flee and run away. Such fear God struck into them, that it seemed they had lost their hearts. In the same viage, as the king had gotten many towns and villages, so also he subdued castles and munitions very strong, and that with little stress. His enemy, being at the same time at Rouen, had reared a great army, who, notwithstanding being well manned, ever kept on the other side of the river Seine, breaking down all the bridges, that we should not come over to him. And although the country round about continually was spoiled, sacked, and with fire consumed by the circuit of twenty miles round about; yet the French king, being distant scarce the space of one mile from us, either would not, or else durst not (when he might easily have passed over the river), make any resistance for defence of his country and people. And so our king, journeying forward, came to Pusiake or Poissy, where the French king had likewise broken down the bridge, and keeping on the other side of the river would rest in no place

The French king showeth no careful study of peace

The king coming to Poissy

After the king's coming to Poissy, the aforesaid chaplain and confessor to the king, named Michael Northburgh (describing the king's voyage, and the acts of the Englishmen from the town of Poissy, to his coming to Calais), in his letters writeth in this wise.

A Letter of Michael Northburgh, the King's Confessor, describing the King's Voyage into France.

Salutations premised, we give you to understand, that our sovereign lord the king came to the town of Poissy, the day before the assumption of our Lady, where was a certain bridge over the water of Seine broken down by the enemy, but the king tarried there so long till that the bridge was made again, and while the bridge was in repairing, there came a great number of men at arms, and other soldiers armed, to hinder the same, but the earl of Northampton issued out against them and slew of them more than one thousand, the rest fled away, thanks be to God. At another time our men passed the water, although with much travail, and slew a great number of the common soldiers of France, about the city of Paris and country adjoining, being part of the French king's army, and thoroughly well appointed; so that our people have now made other good bridges upon our enemies, God be thanked, without any great loss and damage to us On the morrow after the assumption of our Lady, the king passed the water of Seine, and marched toward Poissy, which is a town of great defence, and strongly immured, and a marvellous strong castle within the same, which our enemies kept, and when our vanguard was passed the town, our rear-guard gave an assault thereunto, and took the same, where were slain more than three hundred men at arms on our enemies' part. The next day following, the earl of Suffolk and Sir Hugh Spenser marched forth upon the commons of the country assembled and well armed, and in fine discomfited them, and slew of them more than two hundred, and took sixty gentlemen prisoners, beside others After that, the king marched toward Grand Villers, and while he was there encamped, the king's vanguard was descried by the men of arms of the king of Bohemia, whereupon our men issued out in great haste, and joined battle with them, but were forced to retire. Notwithstanding, thanks be unto God! the earl of Northampton issued out, and rescued the horsemen with other soldiers, so that few or none of them were either taken or slain (saving only Thomas Talbot), but had again the enemy in chase within two leagues of Amiens, of whom we took eight, and slew twelve of their best men at arms the rest, being well horsed, took to the town of Amiens. After this, the king of England marched toward Pountife upon Bartholomew day, and came unto the water of Somme, where the French king ad laid five hundred men at arms, and three thousand footmen, purposing to ave kept and stopped our passage; but, thanks be to God! the king of England id his host entered the same water of Somme, where never man passed before, ithout the loss of any of our men, and, after that, encountered with the iemy, and slew of them more than two thousand; the rest fled to Abbeville, i which chase were taken many knights, squires, and men at arms. The same ay Sir Hugh Spenser took the town of Croylay, where he and his soldiers ew four hundred men at arms, and kept the town, where they found great ore of victuals. The same night encamped the king of England in the forest Cressy upon the same water, for that the French king's host came on the her side of the town near unto our passage; but he would not take the water us, and so marched toward Abbeville. Upon the Friday following, the king eing still encamped in the said forest, our scurriers descried the French king, ho marched toward us in four great battalions; and having then understanding our enemies (as God's will was) a little before the evening tide, we drew nto the plain field, and set our battles in array; and immediately the fight egan, which was sore and cruel, and endured long, for our enemies behaved iemselves right nobly. But, thanks be given to God! the victory fell on our de, and the king, our adversary, was discomfited with all his host, and put to ght; where also was slain the king of Bohemia, the duke of Loraine, the earl Dabeson, the earl of Flanders, the earl of Blois, the earl of Arcot with his vo sons; the earl of Damerler, the earl of Navers and his brother, the lord of ronard, the archbishop of Meymes, the archbishop of Saundes, the high prior France, the earl of Savoy, the lord of Morles, the lord de Guis, seignior de . Novant, seignior de Rosinburgh, with six earls of Almain, and divers other arls, barons, knights, and squires, whose names are unknown. Philip de alois himself, with another marquis, who was called lord elector among the omans, escaped from the battle. The number of the men at arms who were und dead in the field, besides the common soldiers and footmen, was one iousand five hundred and forty-two. All that night the king of England with is host, abode armed in the field where the battle was fought. On the morrow efore the sun rose, there marched toward us another great host, mighty and rong, of the Frenchmen; but the earl of Northampton and the earl of Norfolk sued out against them in three battles; and, after long and terrible fight, iem, in like wise, they discomfited by God's great help and grace (for otherise it could never have been); where they took of knights and squires a great umber, and slew above two thousand, pursuing the chase three leagues from ie place where the battle was fought. The same night also the king encamped imself again in the forest of Cressy, and on the morrow marched toward oulogne, and by the way he took the town of Staples; and from thence he iarched toward Calais, where he intendeth to plant his siege, and lay his attery to the same; and therefore our sovereign lord the king willeth and ommandeth you, in all that ever you may, to send to the said siege victuals onvenient, for, after the time of our departing from Chaam, we have travelled irough the country, with great peril, and danger of our people, but yet always ad of victuals plenty, thanks be to God there-for! But now, as the case standeth, 'e partly need your help to be refreshed with victuals. Thus fare you well.

Written at the siege before the town of Calais, the fourteenth day of September.

Siege of Calais.

After the siege and winning of Poissy, the third day of September, A.D. 1346, the king, through the midst of France, directed his assage unto Calais, as by the tenor of this letter you hear, and esieged the same; which siege he continued from the third of September aforesaid, till the third day of August next ensuing, upon he which day it was rendered up unto the said Edward III., and ubdued unto the crown of England; as after, the Lord willing, shall nore appear.

In the mean time, during the siege of Calais, David the Scottish ing, at the request of the French king, with a great army burst into he north parts of England; and first besieging the town of Liddell,

Edward III. A.D. 1346.

within six days obtained the greatest part of the town; and there taking all that he could find, with Sir Walter Salby, a valiant knight, who was the keeper of the hold, he caused him uncourteously to be put to the sword; and so from thence he proceeded further into England, till at length being met withal by William Surch, archbishop of York, and the lord Percy, and the lord Nevil, with other nobles of those parts (calling and gathering their men together) in the plain near to Durham, the seventeenth day of October in the year above mentioned, through the gracious hand of Christ, there they were subdued and conquered. In that conflict, the earls of Murray and Strathern, with the flower of all the chivalry, and the principal warriors of Scotland, were slain. Also the aforesaid king David, with the earls of Mentife and Fife, and other lords, and William Douglas Masklime a Fleming, and William Douglas, and many more men at arms were taken prisoners; and so the mischief which they intended to others, fell upon their own heads.

The Scots overthrown.

The Scottish king taken prisoner.

Moreover, during the said siege of Calais, the aforesaid pope Clement VI., writing to the king of England, went about under the pretence of peace to stop his proceedings; whose letters here follow.

Letter of the Pope to the King of England, in the behalf of the Frenchmen.

The pope recommends peace between England and France.

Clement the bishop, servant of God's servants, to his well-beloved son in Christ, Edward the puissant king of England, salutation and apostolical blessing. If you diligently consider, dear son! as ought a catholic prince to do, the slaughter of such an innumerable sort, bought with the precious blood of Christ our Redeemer; the loss of their substance and souls, and the lamentable perils which the dissensions and wars stirred up between you and our well-beloved son Philip, the noble king of France, have brought upon us, and yet daily do without intermission; and also the bewailing of so many poor people, crying out of orphans and pupils, lamentation of widows, and other miserable people who be robbed and spoiled, and almost famished; what exclamation they make with tears running down their cheeks, yelling and crying unto God for help; as also the destruction of churches, monasteries, and holy places, holy vessels, and other ornaments unto God's service dedicated; the sacrilegious robberies, sackings, and imprisonings, the spoiling of holy churches, and religious persons, with many other such innumerable, detestable, execrable mischiefs, offending the eyes of the Divine Majesty; all which, if your princely heart would consider and well remember, with this also, that catholic faith (especially in the east parts) and the Christians there abiding, by means of the same dissensions and wars, destitute of the helps of such catholic men as are in the west parts, are so afflicted of the infidels; seeing the other parts of Christendom so troubled with cruel persecutions, yea, and more cruel than ever it hath been (although in these times to amplify this our faith in the said east parts is cruel persecution showed, more than hath been of many years past), doubtless we believe it would pity your heart. And to the end that such and so great evils should no further proceed; nor yet that so great good as might be done by dilating of our aforesaid faith, in these times, should be let and hindered, we desire you that you would apply your mind to make some agreement and peace with the aforesaid king. For if, my well-beloved son! God hath given unto you prosperous success and fortune, ye ought rather to humble than to extol yourself; and be so much the more ready to incline to his peace, and to endeavour yourself to please God, who loveth peace, and delighteth in peaceable men; and to eschew the aforesaid evils, which without doubt do grievously offend him. Furthermore, we marvel greatly, that unto our reverend brother Anibaldus, bishop of Tusculane, and our beloved son Stephen, of the title of St. John and Paul, priest and cardinal of the apostolical see, being sent as legates by us and the same see apostolic, to entreat a peace, who diligently and faithfully labouring for the same, as lovers of verity, justice and equity, and therewithal regarders of your honour, could not be suffered, touching the entreaty of the same peace, to come unto your grace's presence.

Wherefore we desire your kingly highness more earnestly, and, for the mercy of God, with more vehemency we require the same, that you, taking up the aforesaid horrible evils, and preventing the sweetness of piety and compassion, may escape the vengeance of God's indignation, which were to be feared, if you should persevere in your former evils; as God forbid! And as touching the entreaty for peace, for which our aforesaid cardinals were sent unto you (howbeit secretly, lest it should be any derogation to your honour), we desire you to condescend thereunto, and that with all your affection you will incline your mind to the same, so pleasant unto God, so desired of the world; as also to you, the aforesaid king, and unto the catholic faith, profitable. And that the same peace by God's help and grace established and made perfect, you might essay your puissant strength about God's business in the aforesaid east parts (such good occasion serving, as before is said, in these our times), being such apt advancements of your honour, and happy increasing of your princely name; for we have heard it of you reported, that you behave yourself fervently in all your attempts. Thus we doubt not but that you will write unto us again touching the premises, and the purpose of your intention touching the same. Dated at Avignon, the eighteenth day of February, and the fifth year of our papacy.

Answer of the King of England, to the aforesaid Letter of the Pope.

Most holy father! we understand by the letters of the reverend fathers in God, the bishop of Tusculane, and Stephen of the title of St. John, priest, cardinals, and legates of the court of Rome, as also by the letters of your holiness sent unto us, that ye marvel greatly for that your said legates were of purpose sent unto us, and commanded to treat of a peace between our adversary of France and us, that we would not suffer them secretly to talk with us, for the safeguard of our honour, the intention of your heart being to make the aforesaid peace; complaining and bewailing therein the death of christian men, the loss of their goods, the peril of their souls, the lamentable wailings of the poor, of orphans, of widows, and the destruction of other pitiful persons, the pillage and robberies of churches, and other mischiefs innumerable; and especially, the diminishing of christian faith in the east parts, which, by the war between our adversary of France and us, is sore decayed, as the said letters plainly do import. And that forasmuch as God hath given us triumphant fortune, so much the more we ought to abase and humble our heart, and to be the readier to make and incline to a peace. As touching these things, holy father! we give your holiness to understand, that as well unto your aforesaid legates, as other messengers sent from you unto us, we have offered unto every one of them reasonable ways of peace, and every day declare the same, and that not secretly, but openly. For we doubt not to let our purpose be understood; for he that is the high Judge both of him and us, in whose disposition all things lie, hath given unto us the crown of France to our right and proper heritage; the which right our aforesaid adversary hath, by force, of long time detained from us, we seeking to obtain the same in peaceable wise; and yet do, if we might obtain the same in any good manner, rather for the benefit of christian men, and that the aforesaid evils might cease, which by his wrongful means only have increased and grown. Yet notwithstanding, as before this time you know, we assented to a truce, with certain articles contained in the same writing; all this he hath infringed; neither doth the wrong suffice him which he offereth us in our aforesaid heritage, but he endeavoureth himself, during the said truce, to invade our realm of England, and our other lands; and furthermore, maintaineth the Scots, and aideth them to the utter destruction of us, our people and lands aforesaid; wherein we were enforced, for the safeguard of our people and lands, by such lawful means as we may, to defend ourselves, and put him from his wicked purpose. And furthermore for the same, our quarrel being in the hands of God, have we come against him to conquer our inheritance of France; over whom God hath given us divers victories, as we have

King Edward exculpates himself.

Edward III. A. D. 1346.

trusted he would, by his right wise judgment and power. which thing he hath showed upon us (all chance of fortune set apart), in respect of our rightful title therein, and without our deserts; wherefore, with all humility of heart we give him thanks always therefore, most devoutly night and day praising his holy name, for we acknowledge the same cometh not by our strength and force. Wherefore, most holy father! we desire your holiness, and, so much as in us lieth, require the same, that you that supply the place of the Son of God on earth, and have the government of the souls of all christian men, and ought to be upright and equal towards all men, without exception of persons, that ye, I say, will receive good information and true, of the objections above said, and will put to your holy helping hand, as much as in you is, that our said adversary of France may acknowledge his wrong which he hath done to us herein, and that it may be by your aid redressed; and that he, in this his wrong, have no maintenance and aid at your hand. For if it be so, we then appeal unto the Judge of judges, who suffereth wrongs to be done for a time, for the sinful default of man, but in the end redresseth the same, leaving no good deed unrewarded, nor evil unpunished, most humbly requiring him to be to us a true and upright judge of all our controversies, for his mercies' sake, as in the mean time we repose our full trust and confidence in him. The Holy Spirit of God, &c.

The king appealeth from the pope to God

Moreover, during the siege of Calais, the French king had sent certain offers to the men of Flanders, that if they would relinquish the king of England, and adhere to him:

Offers made to the men of Flanders to forsake king Edward.

I He would remit all their former transgressions

II. He would unburden them of their interdict

III. He would send unto them such plenty of corn, that what was sold for twelve shillings with them, should be sold for four shillings, and that for six years.

IV. He would store them with plenty of French wool to make cloth for a small price, and that they might sell the said cloths, both in Flanders and in France, and that the Frenchmen should use the same cloth, forasmuch as all other manner of cloth should be forbidden in France, so long as any of that (made of French wool) might be found.

V. He would restore to them these three cities, Insulam, Rowocum, and Betony.

VI. He would defend them from all their adversaries; and in pledge of the same would send them money beforehand

VII Such as were able and forward men among them, he would retain and promote them, &c.

But these offers, seeming to proceed more of fair words to serve the present turn, than of any hearty truth, were not received. Then the lord John, prince and heir to the French king, during the aforesaid siege of Calais above mentioned, coming with a mighty army of Frenchmen, set upon the men of Flanders and Englishmen in the town of Cassel; in which conflict, enduring from morning to noon, the Frenchmen were vanquished, and the young dauphin driven back from whence he came. Of their number divers were slain and taken prisoners, whereas, on the other side, through the Lord's defence, not one is reported to have been grievously wounded.

The dauphin with the French discomfited at Cassel

A D 1347. As this passed on, not long after, about the seventh day of June, A.D. 1347, king Edward still continuing his siege against Calais, Philip the French king came down with a mighty army, purposing to raise the siege; where, not far off from the English host, he encamped himself. This done, two cardinals, Ambald and Stephan, procured for the very purpose, going between the two kings, gave to the king of England thus to understand: that if he would condescend to any reasonable way of peace, the French king was ready to offer such honest proffers unto him, as to reason and to his contentation should seem agreeable: but, in conclusion, when it came to talk, the nobles could not agree upon the conditions; wherefore the French king, seeing no other remedy, caused it to be signified to king Edward, that between that present Tuesday and the next Friday, if he would come forth into the field, he should have battle given him. Thus the place being viewed by four captains of either host for the battle to be fought; it so fell out, that the French king, on Wednesday at night, before the battle should join, secretly by night setting his pavilions on fire, returned back with his army out of the sight of the Englishmen.

The French king flieth before the battle

Upon the Friday following, those who were besieged in the town of Calais, seeing the king to be retired, upon whose help they trusted (being also in great penury and famine for lack of victuals, and otherwise, in much misery, vehemently distressed), surrendered the town to the king's hands; who, like a merciful prince, only detaining certain of the chief, the rest with the whole commons he let go with bag and baggage, diminishing no part of their goods, showing therein more princely favour to them, than they did of late in queen Mary's days unto our men, in recovering the said town of Calais again.

The town of Calais won.

After the winning thus of Calais, as hath been premised, king Edward, remaining in the said town a certain space, was in consultation concerning his voyage and proceeding further into France. But by means of the aforesaid cardinals, truce for a certain time was taken, and instruments made (so provided) that certain noblemen as well for the French king, as for the king of England, should come to the pope, there to debate upon the articles; unto which king Edward, for peace' sake, was not greatly disagreeing: which was A.D 1347.[1]

Truce between England and France

The year following, which was A.D. 1348, fell a sore plague, which they call the first general pestilence in the realm of England. This plague, as they say, first springing from the east, and so spreading westward, did so mightily prevail here in this land, beginning first at Dorchester, and the counties thereabout, that lightly, every day twenty, some days forty, some days sixty and more, dead corpses were brought and laid together in one pit. This beginning the first day of August, by the first of November it came to London; where the vehement rage thereof was so hot, and did increase so much, that from the first day of February, till about the beginning of May, in a churchyard then newly made by Smithfield, about two hundred dead corpses every day were buried, besides those which in other churchyards of the city were laid also. At length, by the grace of Christ, ceasing there, it proceeded from thence to the north parts; where also the next year after (A.D. 1349), it assuaged.

A.D 1348 Vehement pestilence in England

Burial-place, now called the Charterhouse churchyard.

After this, in the next year ensuing (A.D. 1350), the town of Calais was, by treason of the keeper of the castle, almost betrayed, and won from the Englishmen. Within the compass of that year died Philip the French king; after whom king John his son succeeded to the crown, who, the next year after, under false pretence of friendship, caused the constable of France, the earl of Ewe, to be beheaded; who, being taken prisoner before in war by Englishmen, and long

A.D 1350 Calais almost lost by treason

Death of the French king

A.D 1351

(1) Ex Thomas Walsingham

Edward III. A. D. 1351. detained in prison in England, was licensed by king Edward to visit his country of France. In the same year the town of Guines was taken by Englishmen, while the keepers of the hold were negligent and asleep.

A.D.1352. Victory of Sir Roger Bentele. The year following, the marshal of France with a great army was put to flight by Sir Roger Bentele, knight, and captain in Brittany, having only six hundred soldiers with him. In this battle were taken nine knights, and of esquires and gentlemen, one hundred and forty. The Frenchmen and men of Brittany by this victory were exceedingly discouraged and their pride cut down.

First duke of Lancaster. In the year after, Henry was made first duke of Lancaster, who before was earl of Derby and Lancaster; also divers good ordinances were appointed in the parliament at Westminster, which, afterwards, by avarice and partial favour of the head men, were again undone.

A.D.1354. Concord and agreement about A.D. 1354, began to come well forward, and instruments were drawn upon the same between the two kings; but the matter being brought up to pope Innocent VI., partly by the quarrelling of the Frenchmen, partly by the winking of the pope, who ever held with the French side, the conditions were repealed, which were these: That to the king of England, all the dukedom of Aquitaine, with other lands there, should be restored, without homage to the French king; and that king Edward again should surrender to him all his right and title, which he had in France. Upon this rose the occasion of the great war and tumult which followed after between the two realms.

A.D.1355. It followed after this (A.D. 1355),[1] that king Edward hearing of the death of Philip the French king, and that king John his son had granted the dukedom of Aquitaine to Charles his eldest son and dauphin of Vienna, sent over prince Edward with the earls of Warwick, Salisbury, and Oxford, and with them a sufficient number of able soldiers into Aquitaine, where he, being willingly received of divers, the rest partly by force of sword he subdued, partly received, submitting themselves to his protection.

Third voyage of king Edward into France. Not long after this, in the same year, word being brought to king Edward, that John the French king was ready to meet him at St. Omer, there to give him battle, he gathered his power, and set over to Calais with his two sons, Lionel earl of Wilton, and John of Gaunt earl of Richmond, and with Henry duke of Lancaster, &c., who being come to St. Omer, the French king, with a mighty army of his Francklings, hearing of his coming, the nearer he approached to them, the further they retired back; wasting and destroying behind them, to the intent that the English army in pursuing them, should find no victuals. By reason whereof, King Edward, following him by the space of nine or ten days unto Hadem, when neither he could find his enemy to fight, nor victuals nor forage for his army, returned to Calais; where war again being offered in the name of the king, upon unstable conditions, and yet the same not performed, king Edward seeing the shrinking of his enemy, from Calais crossed the seas into England, where he recovered again the town of Berwick, which the Scots before, by subtle train, had gotten. At that time

The French king refuseth to join in battle with king Edward.

(1) Chron. Adami Merimouth canonici D. Pauli de gestis Edw. 3.

was granted unto the king in parliament, fifty shillings for every sack or pack of wool that should be carried over, for the space of six years together; by the which grant, the king might dispend every day by estimation above one hundred marks sterling. And forasmuch as every year one hundred thousand sacks of wool were thought to be exported out of the realm, the sum thereof for six years' space was estimated to amount to £1,500,000 sterling.

Edward III. A.D. 1356

Fifty shillings for every sack of wool carried out of England

The same year, when king Edward had recovered Berwick and subdued Scotland, prince Edward being in Gascony, made towards the French king; who, notwithstanding all the bridges in the way were cast down, and great resistance made, yet the victorious prince making way with his sword, after much slaughter of the Frenchmen, and many prisoners taken, at length joining with the French king at Poictiers, with scarcely two thousand, gave the overthrow to the French king with seven thousand men at arms and more. In that conflict, the French king himself, and Philip his son, with Lord James of Bourbon, the archbishop of Sens, eleven earls, and twenty-two lords were taken; of other warriors and men at arms two thousand. Some affirm that in this conflict were slain two dukes; of lords and noblemen twenty-four; of men at arms two thousand and two; of other soldiers about eight thousand. The common report is, that more Frenchmen were there taken prisoners, than was the number of those who took them. This noble victory, gotten by the grace of God, brought no little admiration to all men.

The French king taken prisoner by prince Edward

It were too long, and little pertaining to the purpose of this history, to comprehend in order all the doings of this king, with the circumstances of his victories, of the bringing in of the French king into England, of his abode there, of the ransom levied on him, and on David the Scottish king; of whom, the one was rated at three millions of scutes, the other at a hundred thousand marks, to be paid in ten years: how the staple was after translated to Calais, with such like. I refer them that would see more, to the chronicles of Thomas Walsingham of St. Alban's, of John Froysard, and of Adam Merimouth, who discourse all this at large.

Every scute valuing six shillings and eight pence

Thus having discoursed at large all such martial affairs and warlike exploits, incident in the reign of this king betwixt him and the realms of France and Scotland; now, to return again to our matters ecclesiastical, it followeth, in order, to recapitulate and notify the troubles and contentions growing between the same king and the pope, and other ecclesiastical persons, in matters touching the church, taken out of the records remaining in the Tower, in order of years, as followeth. As where first, in the fourth year of his reign, the king wrote to the archbishop of Canterbury to this effect: that whereas king Edward I. his grandfather, did give to a clerk of his own, being his chaplain, the dignity of treasurer of York, the archbishopric of York being then vacant and in the king's hands, in the quiet possession whereof the said clerk continued, until the pope, displeased therewith, would have displaced him, and promoted to the same dignity a cardinal of Rome, to the manifest prejudice of the crown of England; the king therefore straitly chargeth the archbishop of York not to suffer any matter to pass, that may be prejudicial to the

Ecclesiastical affairs A.D. 1331 to 1360

Edward III. donation of his grandfather, but that his own clerk should enjoy the said dignity accordingly, upon pain of his highness' displeasure.

A.D. 1331 to 1360. The like precepts were also directed to these bishops following, namely, to the bishop of Lincoln, the bishop of Worcester, the bishop of Sarum, Monsieur Marmion, the archdeacon of Richmond, the archdeacon of Lincoln, the prior of Lewen, the prior of Lenton, to Master Rich of Bentworth, to Master Ihenco de Concoreto, to the pope's nuncio, to Master Guido of Calma. And withal, he wrote his letters unto the pope, as touching the same matter, consisting in three parts. first, in the declaration and defence of his right and title to the donation and gift of all manner of temporalties, of offices, prebends, benefices and dignities ecclesiastical, holden of him 'in capite,' as in the right of his crown of England: secondly, in expostulating with the pope for intruding himself into the ancient right of the crown of England, intermeddling with such collations, contrary to right and reason, and the example of all his predecessors who were popes before: thirdly, entreating him that he would henceforth abstain and desist from molesting the realm with such novelties and strange usurpations; and so much the more, for that, in the public parliament lately holden at Westminster, it was generally agreed upon, by the universal assent of all the estates of the realm, that the king should stand to the defence of all such rights and jurisdictions as to his regal dignity and crown any way appertained.

The pope's usurpations made the subject of frequent remonstrance

A.D. 1336. After this, in the ninth year of the reign of this king, pope Benedict XII. sendeth down letters touching his new creation, with certain other matters and requests to the king; whereunto the king answering again, declareth how glad he is of that his preferment; adding, moreover, that his purpose was to have sent unto him certain ambassadors for congratulation of the same; but that, being otherwise occupied by reason of wars, he could not attend his holiness' requests. notwithstanding, he minded to call a parliament about the feast of Ascension next, where, upon the assembly of his clergy and other estates, he would take order for the same, and so direct his ambassadors to his holiness accordingly.

A.D. 1337 The next year after, which was the tenth year of his reign, the king writeth another letter to the pope: that forasmuch as his clergy had granted him one year's tenth for the supportation of his wars, and for that the pope also had the same time to take up the payment of six years' tenths granted him by the clergy a little before, therefore the pope would vouchsafe, at his request, to forbear the exaction of that money for one year, till his tenth for the necessities of his wars were despatched

The same year he wrote also to the pope to this effect: that whereas the prior and chapter of Norwich did nominate a clerk to be bishop of Norwich, and sent him to Rome for his investiture, without the king's knowledge; therefore the pope would withdraw his consent, and not intermeddle in the matter appertaining to the king's peculiar jurisdiction and prerogative.

The pope sends legates to determine the patronage of benefices

After this, in the sixteenth year of this king, it happened that the pope sent over certain legates to hear and determine matters appertaining to the right of patronages of benefices; which the king perceiving to tend to the no small derogation of his right and of the liberties of his subjects, writeth unto the said legates, admonishing and requiring them not to proceed therein, nor attempt any thing unadvisedly, otherwise than might stand with the lawful ordinances and customs of the laws of his realm, and the freedom and liberties of his subjects.

Moreover he writeth the same year to other legates on their being sent over by the pope to treat of peace between the king and the French king, with request that they would first make their repair to the French king, who had so often broken with him, and prove what conformity the French king would offer, which, if he found reasonable, they should soon accord with him: otherwise he exhorted them not to enter into the land, nor to proceed any further in that behalf.

The year following, which was the seventeenth of his reign, ensueth another letter to the pope, against his provisions and reservations of benefices, worthy here to be placed and specified, but that the sum thereof is before set down, to be found in page 697. A.D. 1344

The year following, another letter likewise was sent by the king to the pope, upon occasion taken of the church of Norwich, requiring him to surcease his reservations and provisions of the bishoprics within the realm, and to leave the elections thereof free to the chapters of such cathedral churches, according to the ancient grants and ordinances of his noble progenitors.

Proceeding now to the nineteenth year of this king's reign, there came to the presence of the king certain legates from Rome, complaining of certain statues passed in his parliament, tending to the prejudice of the church of Rome, and the pope's primacy: viz. That if abbots, priors, or any other ecclesiastical patrons of benefices, should not present to the said benefices within a certain time, the lapse of the same should come to the ordinary or chapter thereof; or if they did not present, then to the archbishop; if the archbishop likewise did fail to present, then the gift to pertain not unto the lord pope, but unto the king and his heirs. Another complaint also was this: That if archbishops should be slack in giving such benefices as properly pertained to their own patronage in due time, then the collation thereof likewise should appertain to the aforesaid king and his heirs. Another complaint was. That if the pope should make void any elections in the church of England, for any defect found therein, and so had placed some honest and discreet persons in the same, that then the king and his heirs were not bound to render the temporalties unto the parties placed by the pope's provision. Whereupon the pope being not a little aggrieved, the king writeth unto him, certifying that he was misinformed, denying that there was any such statute made in that parliament. And further, as touching all other things, he would confer with his prelates and nobles, and thereof would return answer by his legates.

He complains of certain statutes passed in this reign

In the twentieth year of his reign, another letter was written to the pope by the king, the effect whereof, in few words to express it, was this: to certify him that, in respect of his great charges sustained in his wars, he hath by the counsel of his nobles, taken into his own hands the fruits and profits of all his benefices here in England. A.D. 1347

To proceed in the order of years: in the twenty-sixth year of this king, one Nicholas Heath, clerk, a busy-headed body, and a troubler A.D. 1353.

Edward III.

A.D. 1331 to 1360.

of the realm, had procured divers bishops, and others of the king's council, to be cited up to the court of Rome, there to answer such complaints as he had made against them. Whereupon commandment was given by the king to all the ports of the realm, for the restraint of all passengers out, and for searching and arresting all persons bringing in any bulls or other process from Rome, tending to the derogation of the dignity of the crown, or molestation of the subjects; concerning which Nicholas Heath, the king also writeth to the pope his letters, complaining of the said Heath, and desiring him to give no ear to his lewd complaints.

Nicholas Heath, a troubler of the realm.

The same year the king writeth also to the pope's legate resident in England, requiring him to surcease from exacting divers sums of money of the clergy, under the name of first fruits of benefices.

A.D.1358. Nicholas Stanway cites many honest men to Rome.

The thirty-first year of this king's reign, the king, by his letters, complaineth to the pope of a troublesome fellow named Nicholas Stanway, remaining in Rome, who, by his slanderous complaints, procured divers citations to be sent into the realm, to the great disturbance of many and sundry honest men; whereupon he prayeth and adviseth the pope to stay himself, and not to send over such hasty citations upon every light occasion.

To pass further, to the thirty-eighth year of the same king, thus we find in the rolls: that the king the same year took order by two of his clergy, to wit, John à Stock, and John of Norton, to take into their hands all the temporalities of all deaneries, prebends, dignities, and benefices, being then vacant in England, and to answer the profits of the same to the king's use.

The same year an ordinance was made by the king and his council, and the same was proclaimed in all port-towns within the realm, as follows:—

Order of council.

That good and diligent search should be made, that no person whatsoever, coming from the court of Rome, &c., do bring into the realm with him any bull, instrument, letters-patent, or other process, that may be prejudicial to the king, or any of his subjects; nor that any person, passing out of this realm towards the court of Rome, do carry with him any instrument or process that may redound to the prejudice of the king or his subjects; and that all persons passing to the said court of Rome, &c., with the king's special license, do notwithstanding promise and find surety to the lord chancellor, that they shall not in any wise attempt or pursue any matter to the prejudice of the king or his subjects, under pain to be put out of the king's protection, and to forfeit his body, goods, and chattels, according to the statute thereof made, in the twenty-seventh year, &c.

And thus much concerning the letters and writings of the king, with such other domestic matters, perturbations, and troubles, passing between him and the pope, taken out of the public records of the realm; whereby I thought to give the reader to understand the horrible abuses, the intolerable pride, and the insatiable avarice of that bishop, more like a proud Lucifer than a pastor of the church of Christ, in abusing the king, and oppressing his subjects with exactions unmeasurable; and not only exercising his tyranny, in this realm, but raging also against other princes, both far and near, amongst whom neither spared he the emperor himself. In the story and acts of that emperor Louis, mentioned a little before (p. 663), whom the pope did most arrogantly excommunicate upon Maundy-Thursday, and the

The pope characterised.

self-same day placed another emperor in his room; relation was made of certain learned men who took the emperor's part against the pope. In the number of them was Marsilius of Padua, William Ockam, John of Ganduno, Luitpoldus, Andreas Landensis, Ulricus Hangenor, treasurer of the emperor, Dante, Aligerius, &c.; of whom Marsilius of Padua compiled and exhibited unto the emperor Louis a worthy work, entitled 'Defensor pacis,' written in the emperor's behalf against the pope. In that book (both godly and learnedly disputing against the pope), he proveth all bishops and priests to be equal, and that the pope hath no superiority above other bishops, much less above the emperor; that the word of God only ought to be the chief judge in deciding and determining causes ecclesiastical; that not only spiritual persons, but laymen also, being godly and learned, ought to be admitted into general councils; that the clergy and the pope ought to be subject unto magistrates; that the church is the university of the faithful, and that the foundation and head of the church is Christ, and that he never appointed any vicar or pope over his universal church; that bishops ought to be chosen every one by their own church and clergy; that the marriage of priests may lawfully be permitted; that St. Peter was never at Rome; that the clergy and synagogue of the pope is a den of thieves; that the doctrine of the pope is not to be followed, because it leadeth to destruction; and that the corrupt manners of the Christians do spring and flow out of the wickedness of the spiritualty, &c. He disputeth, moreover, in another work, of free justification by grace; and extenuateth merits, saying, that they are no causes efficient of our salvation, but only a 'sine qua non,' that is to say, that works be no cause of our justification, but yet our justification goeth not without them. For the which his doctrine most sound and catholic, he was condemned (A.D. 1324), by the pope's decree 'Extravagant;'[1] concerning which man and his doctrine, I thought good thus much to commit to history, to the intent men may see that they who charge this doctrine now taught in the church with the note of novelty or newness, how ignorant and unskilful they be in the histories and order of times forepast.

Edward III. A.D. 1331 to 1360.

Articles of Marsilius against the pope.

Merits, not a cause of salvation, but only a 'sine qua non.' Marsilius condemned of the pope.

In the same part of condemnation, at the same time, was also John of Ganduno, A.D. 1330, and contained also in the aforesaid 'Extravagant' with Marsilius of Padua. This Johannes wrote much upon Aristotle and Averrois, and his books are yet remaining; and no doubt but he wrote also of divinity, but it is not unlikely that these works have been abolished.

In the same number and catalogue cometh also William Ockam, who flourished A.D. 1326, as is before mentioned, and who wrote likewise, in defence of Louis the emperor against the pope; and also in defence of Michael, general of the Grey-friars, whom the pope had excommunicated, and cursed for a heretic. Divers treatises were by the said Ockam set forth, whereof some are extant and in print, as his Questions and Distinctions; some are extinct and suppressed, as Ascentius reporteth,[2] "quod essent aliquando asperiora." Some again be published under no name of the author, being of his

Michael, general of the Grey-friars, excommunicated for a heretic.

(1) Cap. licet intra doctrinam.
(2) Ascentius in præfatione ejus autoris.

Dialogue between the soldier and the clerk, of Ockam's making. Eight questions disputed.

doing; as the dialogue between the soldier and the clerk; wherein it is to be conjectured, what books and works this Ockam had collected against the pope. Of this Ockam, John Sleidan in his history inferreth mention, to his great commendation, whose words be these: "William Ockam, in the time of Louis IV., the emperor, did flourish about A.D. 1326, who, among other things, wrote of the authority of the bishop of Rome; in which book he handleth these eight questions very copiously: First; whether both the administrations of the bishop's office, and of the emperor's, may be in one man? Secondly; whether the emperor taketh his power and authority only from God, or else of the pope? Thirdly; whether the pope and church of Rome have power by Christ to set up and place kings and emperors, and to commit to them their jurisdiction to be exercised? Fourthly; whether the emperor, being elected, hath full authority, upon the said his election, to administer his empire? Fifthly; whether other kings besides the emperor and king of Romans, in that they are consecrated of priests, receive of them any part of their power? Sixthly; whether the said kings in any case be subject to their consecrators? Seventhly; whether if the said kings should admit any new sacrifice, or should take to themselves the diadem without any further consecration, they should thereby lose their kingly right and title? Eighthly; whether the seven princes electors give as much to the election of the emperor, as succession rightfully giveth to other kings?—Upon these questions he disputeth and argueth with sundry arguments and reasons on both sides; at length he decideth the matter on the part of the civil magistrate, and by occasion thereof entereth into the mention of the pope's 'Decrees Extravagant;' declaring how little force or regard is to be given thereunto."

Gregorius Ariminensis.

Trithemius maketh mention of one Gregorius Ariminensis, a learned and a famous and right godly man; who not much differing from the age of this Ockam, about A.D. 1350, disputed on the same doctrine of grace and free-will as we do now, and dissented therein from the papists and sophisters, counting them worse than Pelagians.

Andreas de Castro and Burdianus.

Of the like judgment, and in the same time, was also Andreas de Castro,[1] and Burdianus upon the ethics of Aristotle; who both maintained the grace of the gospel, as it is now in the church received, above two hundred years since.

Eudo, duke of Burgundy.

And what should I speak of the duke of Burgundy, named Eudo, who, at the same time (A.D. 1350), persuaded the French king not to receive in his land the new found constitutions, 'Decretal' and 'Extravagant,' nor to suffer them within his realm; whose sage counsel then given, yet remaineth among the French king's records, as witnesseth Carolus Molineus.

Dante, an Italian.

Dante, an Italian writer, a Florentine, lived in the time of Louis, the emperor, about A.D. 1300, and took part with Marsilius of Padua against three sorts of men, who, he said, were enemies to the truth; that is, first, the pope: secondly, the order of religious men, who count themselves the children of the church, when they are the children of the devil their father: thirdly, the doctors of decrees and

(1) Super lit. i. Sent. dist. 45.

decretals.—Certain of his writings be extant abroad, wherein he proveth the pope not to be above the emperor, nor to have any right or jurisdiction in the empire. He confuteth the donation of Constantine to be a forged and a feigned thing, as what neither did stand with any law nor right; for which he was taken by many for a heretic. He complaineth, moreover, very much of the preaching of God's word being omitted; and that instead thereof, the vain fables of monks and friars are preached and believed by the people, and that so the flock of Christ is not fed with the food of the gospel, but with wind. "The pope," saith he, "of a pastor is made a wolf, to waste the church of Christ, and to procure, with his clergy, not the word of God to be preached, but his own decrees." In his canticle of purgatory, he declareth the pope to be the whore of Babylon; and as to her ministers, to some he applieth two horns, and to some four, as to the patriarchs, whom he noteth to be the tower of the said whore Babylonical.[1]

Donation of Constantine, a thing forged.

The pope the whore of Babylon.

Hereunto may be added the saying out of the book of Jornandus, imprinted with the aforesaid Dante; that forasmuch as Antichrist cometh not before the destruction of the empire, therefore such as go about to have the empire extinct, are in so doing forerunners and messengers of Antichrist. "Therefore let the Romans," saith he, "and their bishops beware, lest their sins and wickedness so deserving, by the just judgment of God, the priesthood be taken from them. Furthermore, let all the prelates and princes of Germany take heed," &c.

Also Antichrist.

An admonition to the Romans.

And because our adversaries, who object unto us the newness of our doctrine, shall see the course and form of this religion now received, not to have been either such a new thing now, or a thing so strange in times past, I will add to these above recited, Master Taulerus, a preacher of Argentine, in Germany, A.D. 1350; who, contrary to the pope's proceedings, taught openly against all men's merits, and against invocations of saints, and preached sincerely of our free justification by grace; referring all man's trust only to the mercy of God, and was an enemy to all superstition.

Taulerus of Germany.

With whom also may be joined Franciscus Petrarcha,[2] a writer of the same age, who, in his works and his Italian metre, speaking of Rome, calleth it the whore of Babylon, the school and mother of error, the temple of heresy, the nest of treachery, growing and increasing by the oppressing of others; and saith further, that she (meaning the pope's court) extolleth herself against her founders, that is, the emperors who first set her up, and did so enrich her; and seemeth plainly to affirm, that the pope was Antichrist, declaring that no greater evil could happen to any man, than to be made pope. This Petrarch was about A.D. 1350.

Franciscus Petrarcha.

Rome the mother and school of error.

And if time would serve us to seek out old histories, we should find plenty of faithful witnesses, of old and ancient time, to give witness with us against the pope, besides the others above rehearsed: as Johannes de Rupe Scissa, A.D. 1340; who, for rebuking the spiritualty for their great enormities, and for neglecting their office and duty, was cast into prison.

Johannes de Rupe Scissa cast into prison.

Illyricus, a writer in our days, testifieth that he found and read in

(1) Ex libris Dantis Italice. (2) Vide epistolam viginti Francisci Petrarchæ.

Edward III.

A.D. 1331 to 1360.

an old pamphlet, that the said Johannes should call the church of Rome the whore of Babylon, and the pope to be the minister of Antichrist, and the cardinals to be the false prophets. Being in prison, he wrote a book of prophecies, bearing the title, 'Vade mecum in tribulationem:' in which book (which also I have seen) he prophesied and admonished affliction and tribulation to hang over the spiritualty. And he pronounceth plainly, that God will purge his clergy, and will have priests that shall be poor and godly, and that shall faithfully feed the Lord's flock; moreover, that the goods of the church shall return again to the laymen. He prophesied also at the same time that the French king and his army should have an overthrow; which likewise came to pass during the time of his imprisonment. Of this Johannes de Rupe, writeth Froisart in his time, and also Wickliff; of whose prophecies much more may be said at more leisure, Christ willing, hereafter.

The church of Rome the whore of Babylon.

About the same year (A.D. 1340) in the city of Herbipoli, was one named Master Conrad Hager; who, as appeareth by the old bulls and registers of Otho, bishop of the said city, is there recorded to have maintained and taught, for the space of twenty-four years together, the mass to be no manner of sacrifice, neither that it profiteth any man either quick or dead; and that the money given by the dead for masses, be very robberies and sacrileges of priests, which they wickedly do intercept and take away from the poor; and he said, moreover, that if he had a stove full of gold and silver, he would not give one farthing for any mass. For the same his doctrine this good preacher was condemned and enclosed in prison; what afterwards became of him we do not find.[1]

The mass no sacrifice.

Conrad Hager cast into prison.

There is among other old and ancient records of antiquity belonging to this present time, a certain monument in verses poetically compiled, but not without a certain moral, entitled, 'Pœnitentiarius Asini,' 'The Ass's Confessor,' bearing the date and year of our Lord in this number, 'Completus, A.D. 1348.' In this treatise are brought forth the wolf, the fox, and the ass, coming to shrift and doing penance. First, the wolf confesseth him to the fox, who easily doth absolve him from all his faults, and also excuseth him in the same. In like manner the wolf, hearing the fox's shrift, showeth to him the like favour in return. After this cometh the ass to confession, whose fault was this; that he, being hungry, took a straw out from the sheaf of one that went in peregrination unto Rome. The ass, although repenting of this fact, yet, because he thought it not so heinous as the faults of the other, he hoped the more for his absolution. But what followed? After the silly ass had uttered his crime in auricular confession, immediately the discipline of the law was executed upon him with severity; neither was he judged worthy of any absolution, but was apprehended upon the same, slain, and devoured. Whosoever was the author of this fabulous tale, he had a mystical understanding of the same, for by the wolf no doubt was meant the pope; but the fox was resembled to the prelates, courtesans, priests, and the rest of the spiritualty. Of the spiritualty the lord pope is soon absolved; as, contrary, the pope doth soon absolve them in like manner. By the ass is meant the poor laity, upon whose back the

The pope and his spiritualty confederate against the laity.

The pope maketh the emperor and laymen asses.

(1) Ex bullis quibusdam Othonis Epis. Herbipoli.

strait censure of the law is sharply executed; especially when the German emperors come under the pope's inquisition, to be examined by his discipline, there is no absolution nor pardon to be found, but in all haste he must be deposed, as in these stories may partly appear before. And though the matter be not the weight of a straw, yet what saith the holy father, the wolf, if it please him to make any matter of it.

> "Immensum scelus est, injuria quam peregrino
> Fecisti, stramen subripiendo sibi.
> Non advertisti quod plura pericula passus,
> Plurima passurus, quod peregrinus erat.
> Non advertisti, quod ei per maxima terræ
> Et pelagi spacia, sit peragranda via.
> Non advertisti sanctos, nec limina sancta;
> Sanctorum sanctam sed nec Hierusalem.
> Ille retransivit eadem loca, tam violentum
> Ex inopinato sensit adesse malum.
> De papa taceo, cujus protectio talem
> Conduxit, cujus tu vilipendis opem.
> Totius ecclesiæ fuerit quam nuncius iste,
> Pertulit abstracto gramine damna viæ," &c.

And thus they, aggregating and exaggerating the fault to the uttermost, fly upon the poor ass and devour him. By this apology, the tyrannical and fraudulent practices of these spiritual Romanists are lively described.

Not long after these above rehearsed (about A.D. 1350) Gerhardus Ridder wrote also against the monks and friars a book entitled, 'Lacryma Ecclesiæ:' wherein he disputeth against the aforesaid religious orders, namely, against the begging friars; proving that kind of life to be far from christian perfection, for that it is against charity to live upon others, when a man may live by his own labours; and he affirmeth them to be hypocrites, filthy livers, and such as for man's favour, and for lucre' sake, do mix with true divinity, fables, apocryphas, and dreams of vanity. Also that they, under pretence of long prayer, devour widows' houses, and with their confessions, sermons, and burials, do trouble the church of Christ manifold ways. And therefore persuadeth he the prelates to bridle and keep short the inordinate license and abuses of these monastical persons, &c.

Michael Sesenas, and Petrus de Corbaria, condemned by the pope. Johannes de Poliaco.

I have, as yet, made no mention of Michael Sesenas, provincial of the Grey-friars, or of Petrus de Corbaria, of whom writeth Antoninus, 'in quarta parte summæ,' and saith they were condemned in the 'Extravagant' of pope John, with one Johannes de Poliaco. Their opinions, saith Antoninus, were these: that Peter the apostle was no more the head of the church, than the other apostles; that Christ left no vicar behind him or head in his church; and that the pope hath no such authority to correct and punish, to institute or depose the emperor. Item, That all priests, of what degree soever, are of equal authority, power, and jurisdiction, by the institution of Christ; but that by the institution of the emperor, the pope is superior, which supremacy by the same emperor also may be revoked again. Item, That neither the pope, nor yet the church, may punish any man, 'punitione coactiva:' that is, by extern coaction, unless they receive license of the emperor. This aforesaid Michael, general

Edward III. A.D. 1331 to 1360.

of the Grey-friars, wrote against the tyranny, pride, and primacy of the pope, accusing him to be Antichrist, and the church of Rome to be the whore of Babylon, drunk with the blood of saints. He said there were two churches; one of the wicked, flourishing, wherein reigned the pope; the other of the godly, afflicted. Item, that the verity was almost utterly extinct: and for this cause he was deprived of his dignity, and condemned of the pope. Notwithstanding, he stood constant in his assertions. This Michael was about A.D. 1322, and left behind him many favourers and followers of his doctrine, of whom a great part were slain by the pope; some were condemned, as William Ockam; some were burned, as Johannes de Castilione, and Franciscus de Arcatara.[1]

Opinion of Michael against the pope. Michael deprived and condemned. Martyrs Johannes de Castilione, Franciscus de Arcatara, burned.

With him also was condemned, in the said 'Extravagant,' Johannes de Poliaco above touched, whose assertions were these: That the pope could not give license to hear confessions to whom he would, but that every pastor in his own church ought to suffice. Item, that pastors and bishops had their authority immediately from Christ and his apostles, and not from the pope. Item, That the constitution of pope Benedict XI., wherein he granteth larger privileges to the friars above other pastors, was no declaration of the law, but a subversion; and for this he was by the said friars oppressed, about A.D. 1322.

After Simon Mepham, archbishop of Canterbury before mentioned, who lived not long, succeeded John Stratford. After him came John Offord, who lived but ten months; in whose room succeeded Thomas, and remained but one year, A.D. 1350; and after him Simon Islip was made archbishop of Canterbury by pope Clement VI., who sat seventeen years, and built Canterbury college in Oxford. This Simon Islip succeeded the bishop of Ely, named Simon Langham, who within two years was made cardinal. In his stead Pope Urban V. ordained William Wittlesey, bishop of Worcester, to be archbishop of Canterbury, A.D. 1366. In the same year, William, bishop of Winchester, elected and founded the new college in Oxford.

New College in Oxford founded.

Again, in the order of the popes, next unto pope Clement VI., before mentioned, about the same time (A.D. 1353), succeeded pope Innocent VI.; in the first year of which pope, two friars Minors or Franciscans were burned at Avignon, "Pro opinionibus," as mine author saith, "erroneis, prout D. Papæ et ejus cardinalibus videbatur," that is, "for certain opinions, as seemeth to the pope and his cardinals erroneous."[2] Of these two friars I find, in the Chronicles, "De actis Rom. pontificum," and in the History of Premonstratensis, that the one was Johannes Rochtayladus; or rather, as I find in 'Catalog. Testium,' cited out of the Chronicle of Henry of Hereford, his name to be Hayabalus;[3] who being (as that writer recordeth) a friar Minorite, began first in the time of pope Clement VI. (A.D. 1345) to preach and affirm openly, that he was, by God's revelation, charged and commanded to preach; that the church of Rome was the whore of Babylon, and that the pope, with his cardinals, was very Antichrist; and that pope Benedict, and the others before him his predecessors, were damned; with other such like words tending much against the pope's tyrannical majesty: and that the aforesaid Hayabalus being brought before the pope's face,

Two Franciscans burned at Avignon.

The church of Rome declared to be the whore of Babylon by God's revelation.

(1) In Extravag. Joan. 23. (2) Ex Chron. Wals. (3) Ex Chron. Henrici de Herfordia.

constantly did stand in the same, saying, that he was commanded by God's revelation so to say, and also that he would preach the same if he might. To whom it was then objected, that he had some heretical books, and so he was committed to prison in Avignon. In the time of his accusation it happened that a certain priest, coming before the pope, cast the pope's bull down before his feet, saying: "Lo here, take your bull unto you, for it doth me no good at all. I have laboured now these three years withal, and yet notwithstanding, for all this your bull, I cannot be restored to my right." The pope hearing this, commanded the poor priest to be scourged, and after to be laid in prison with the aforesaid friar. What became of them afterwards, the aforesaid writer, Henry of Hereford, maketh no mention; but I may probably conjecture that this priest and this friar, Rochtayladus, or rather Hayabalus, were the two, whom mine author, Thomas Walsingham, writeth to be burned at this time in Avignon, about the first beginning of this pope Innocent VI. Of this Rochtayladus I thought good here to infer the testimony and mention of John Froysard, written of him in his first volume, chap. 211, in these words:—

Rochtaylada, with another friar, martyrs

A priest, for casting the pope's bull before the pope's feet, scourged, cast into prison, and after, burned at Avignon A D 1354

There was, says Froysard, a friar minor, in the city of Avignon full of great clergy, called John of Rochtaylada,[1] the which friar pope Innocent VI. held in prison in the castle of Baignour, for showing of many marvels after to come; principally he showed many things to fall unto the prelates of the church, for the great superfluity and pride that was then used among them; and he also spake many things to fall of the realm of France, and of the great lords of Christendom, for the oppressions that they did to the poor common people. This friar, said he, would prove all his saying by the authority of the Apocalypse, and by other books of holy saints and prophets, which were opened to him by the grace of the Holy Ghost: he showed many things hard to believe, and many things afterwards befel as he said. He said them not as a prophet, but he showed them by authority of ancient Scriptures, and by the grace of the Holy Ghost, who gave him understanding to declare the ancient prophets, and to show to all christian people the years and times when such things should fall. He made divers books founded on great sciences and clergy, whereof one was made A.D. 1346, wherein were written such marvels, that it were hard to believe them; howbeit many things according thereto fell out after. And when he was demanded of the wars of France, he said that all that had been seen was not like that should be seen after; for, he said, that the wars in France should not be ended, till the realm were utterly wasted and spoiled in every part. The which saying was well seen after, for the noble realm of France was sore wasted and exiled, and specially in the term that the said friar had set; which was in 1356, and three years following. He said that in those years, the princes and gentlemen of the realm should not, for fear, show themselves against the people of low estate, assembled of all countries without head or captain; and they should do as they list in the realm of France: the which fell after, as ye have heard, how the companions assembled them together,

(1) Ex Johanne Froysardo, vol i cap ccxi

Edward III. and by reason of their robbery and pillage waxed rich, and became great captains.

A.D. 1331 to 1360.

Contention in France between the prelates and the friars.

About the same time happened in France a certain contention between the French prelates, and the friars of Paris, testified and recorded by Godfridus de Fontanis;[1] the brief effect of which story is this: the prelates of France conventing and assembling together in the city of Paris, after a long deliberation among themselves, caused, by the beadles, to be called together all the students, masters, and bachelors of every faculty, with the chief heads also of all the religious houses and friars in the university of Paris: who being all there congregated together in the house of the bishop of Paris, where there were present four archbishops, and twenty bishops, first stood up the bishop of Biturecense, who, there making his sermon, took for his theme the place of St. Paul to the Ephesians; "Fratres, ut sciatis quæ sit longitudo, latitudo, altitudo, et profunditas charitatis," &c. and concluded thereupon: first, that true charity would compel them to see and provide for their flocks: secondly, that the vigour of charity would arm them to withstand errors: thirdly, he concluded, that by duty of charity they were bound to give their lives for the souls of their flock committed to their charge: fourthly, that by the same charity every man ought to hold himself content with that which was his own, and not to intermeddle or busy himself further than to him appertained or belonged to his office. "For there," saith he, "all order ecclesiastical is dissolved; whereas men, not containing themselves in their own precincts, presume in other men's charges, where they have nothing to do." "But this charity," saith he, "now a-days waxeth cold, and all ecclesiastical order is confounded and utterly out of order. For many there be, who now a-days presume to thrust in themselves where they have nothing to do; so that now the church may seem a monster. For as in a natural body appeareth a monster, where one member doeth the office of another; so in the spiritual body, which is the church, it may be thought likewise; as when our learned and prudent brethren, to wit, the friars major and minor, do take upon them to usurp and occupy the office to us specially appertaining; namely, whereas the Scripture warneth us all, none to take upon him any office, except he be called thereunto of the Lord, as Aaron was. Wherefore we have heretofore oftentimes caused the said friars, both by the king himself in his own person, and also by other nobles, to be spoken to, and desired to surcease from doing and intermeddling in our office; and yet they would not, but have preached against our wills through all our diocese, and have heard confessions, saying, that they have the pope's privilege to bear them out therein. For the which cause we come to you, and not we here present only, but also we have the hand-writing, and the full consent of all our other fellow-bishops throughout the kingdom of France, to complain to you of this so great insolence and presumption of the friars: for that as we are, you shall be. Neither do I think that there be any of us prelates here now, who have not at sometime been taken out of this university of yours. We have desired, moreover, and caused to be desired of the aforesaid friars, that they would send their privileges

Sermon against the friars, Dominic and Franciscan.

(2) Ex scripto Godfri. de Fontanis.

to the see apostolic, to be interpreted and expounded more plainly by the lord pope: which they refused also to do. Wherefore to the intent you may the better understand and see what their privileges be, and how far they do extend, we have appointed the said privileges here openly to be read unto you."

Constitution of pope Innocent III.

Then stood up another in the public place, and there read the privileges of both the orders; and afterwards read also the constitution of pope Innocent III., written in the fifth of the decretals, and that beginneth, "Omnis utriusque sexus," &c.; which constitution was repugnant and contrary to the aforesaid privileges, as he there manifestly proved, declaring how both the said privileges were derogatory to that constitution.

Friars' privileges proved contrary to the pope's constitution.

This done, then rose up the bishop Ambianensis, a great lawyer, who discoursing from article to article, there proved by good law, that the said constitution stood in its full force and vigour, and ought not to be infringed by the friars' privileges in any part. And, therefore, by the virtue of that constitution, that the friars ought not so misorderly to intrude themselves in hearing confessions, in enjoining of penance, and in preaching in churches and dioceses, without special license of the bishop of the diocese, and curate of the parish: unto whose words never a friar at that time replied again. And so the bishop proceeding to his conclusion, desired the university to assist them in that case, wherein they were all determined (saith he) to stand firmly to the shedding of their blood, in resisting that misorder and injuries of the friars.—This happened the sixth day of December, which they dedicated to St. Nicholas.

Friars not to preach in churches without special license of them to whom the church belonged.

The next day being Sunday, one of the order of the Minorites, or Franciscans, went to the church of the Majorites or preaching friars (which was never seen before, the one order to come and resort to the other), where he made a sermon, beginning in the aforesaid matter to reply, and to expound in order through every article as well as he could; adding, moreover, and saying, that they went not so far in their privileges as they lawfully might. And he said moreover, that what time the said privileges were in obtaining at Rome, the bishop Ambianensis was there present himself, resisting the same with all his power; yea all the prelates also of France sent and wrote up to the court against the same, and yet did not prevail. For when the friars there presently declared and opened to the pope in what manner and how far they had used their privileges, the pope said, "Placet," that is, agreed unto the same. "And now," saith he, "the prelates require and demand of us to send up our privileges to the court; which were great folly in us. For in so doing, what should we else but give place and occasion to revoke again the authority which is given into our hands already? Furthermore, our warden and master is now lately dead, and the master here of the Dominic friars is not now present. Wherefore we dare not determine in such a weighty cause, touching the privileges of our order, without the presence of them. And therefore we desire you of the university to hold us therein excused, and not to be so lightly stirred against us, for we are not the worst and vilest part of the university," &c.

The friars' reply against the prelates.

The next day, being the eighth of the same month, which is also

Edward III.

A.D. 1331 to 1360.

dedicated to the conception of our Lady, it was determined likewise, that one of the Dominic friars should preach in the church of the Franciscan or Grey-friars: and so he did; tending to the same end, as the other friar in the other church had done before. Whereby it may seem that the proverb is well answered unto, whereof we read in the gospel: "Facti sunt amici Herodes et Pilatus in ipso die."

Herod and Pilate made friends in crucifying of Christ.

It was not long after, that the feast of St. Thomas the apostle followed, in whose vigil all the heads of the university again were warned the third day after to congregate together in the church of St. Bernard at the sermon time. Which being done, and the assembly meeting together, another sermon was made by a divine of the university, whose theme was, "Prope est dominus omnibus invocantibus eum in veritate," &c.; wherein, with many words and great authorities, he argued against those who would not be obedient unto their prelates, &c. The sermon being ended, then rose up again the bishop Ambianensis, who, prosecuting the rest of the theme, and coming to the word "in veritate," divided it into three parts, according to the common gloss of the decretals:—

Another sermon against the friars.

Bishop Ambianensis, in veritate, etc.

"Est verum vitæ, doctrinæ, justitiæque,
Primum semper habe; duo propter scandala linque:"

Showing and declaring by many authorities, both of canonical Scriptures and out of the law, and by evident demonstration of experience, that the friars first had no verity of life, because they were full of hypocrisy; neither had they verity of doctrine, because in their heart they bare gall, and in their tongue honey; neither verity of justice, because they usurped other men's offices. And thus concluding with the same, he caused again to be read the said privileges, with the constitution above specified. And so, expounding place by place, he did argue and prove that the said constitution in no part was made void or infringed by the privileges aforesaid. He added, moreover, that "whereas the friars say," saith he, "that I should be present in the obtaining of the privileges, I grant it to be true; and when word came to me thrice thereof, I went to the pope reclaiming and requiring the said privileges to be revoked; but the next day after, it pleased the pope to send me out abroad upon weighty affairs, so that then the matter had no end. After that, we sent also other messengers with our letters, for the same cause unto the court of Rome, whom the friars say not to have prevailed, but they lie therein; for the said messengers again brought us letters from the chief of the court of Rome, sealed with their seals; which letters we have divers times presented to our king, and will shortly show them unto you all, in which the lord pope hath promised the said privileges either to be utterly abrogated, or else to be mitigated with some more plain interpretation, of which we trust shortly to have the public bull or writ from the pope."

Verity consisteth in three parts.

The friars proved with a lie.

At last, the said bishop required and desired of all there, of what diocese or country soever they were, that they would copy out the aforesaid privileges, and send them abroad into their countries, that all men might see what they were, and how far they did extend. In fine, the matter coming into open disputation, it was concluded by Master Giles, one of the Augustine friars, who was thought to be

The friars' privileges confuted in disputation at Paris.

nost reasonable of all the other friars, in this wise: That after his ;entence, the prelates were in the truer part, &c.[1]

Concerning this wrangling contention between the university and 'riars of France here before mentioned, whereof partly the original :ause may be understood, by that which hath been said, to arise upon :ertain privileges granted by popes to the friars, to intermeddle in natters of parish churches; as to hear confessions, to preach and :each, with power thereunto annexed to gather for their labour, to ɔury within their houses, and to receive impropriations, &c., because t were too long here to describe the full circumstances thereof, also ɔecause the said contention did not only endure a long time in France, ɔut also came over into England; the whole discourse thereof more ımply (Christ willing) shall be declared in the beginning of the next ɔook, when we come to the story of Armachanus.

Seditious commotion between the townsmen and scholars of Oxford.

About the time and year that this brawl was in the university of Paris between the friars and prelates there, as hath been declared, the ike contention happened also in the university of Oxford in the year ıbove prefixed (A.D. 1354), save only that the strife among the nasters of Paris, as it rose upon friarly ceremonies, so it went no 'urther than brawling words and matter of excommunication; but this tumult, rising out of a drunken cause, proceeded further unto bloody stripes. The first origin of it began in a tavern, between a scholar and the good man of the house; who, falling together into altercation, grew to such height of words, that the student (contra jus hospitii) poured the wine upon the head of the host, and brake his head with the quart pot. Upon this occasion given, eftsoons parts began to be taken between the townsmen and the scholars, insomuch that a grievous sedition and conflict followed upon the same; wherein many of the townsmen were wounded, and to the number of twenty slain; and divers of the scholars also were grievously hurt. For the space of two days this hurly-burly continued. On the second day certain religious and devout persons ordained a solemn procession general, to pray for peace; yet, notwithstanding, all that procession, holy as it was, would not bring peace. In the which procession, the skirmish still waxing hot, one of the students, being hardly pursued by the townsmen, for succour in his flight came running to the priest or friar, who carried about, as the manner was, the pix; thinking to find refuge at the presence of the transubstantiated God of the altar there carried and imboxed. Notwithstanding, the god being not there present, or else not seeing him, or else peradventure being asleep,[2] the scholar found there small help; for the townsmen, in the heat of the chase, forgetting belike the virtue of the pope's transubstantiation, followed him so hard, that in the presence of the pix they brake his head, and wounded him grievously. This done, at length some peace or truce for that day was taken. On the morrow, other townsmen in the villages about, joining with the townsmen of Oxford, confederated together in great force and power to set upon the students there, and so did, having a black flag borne before them, and so invaded the university men; whereupon the scholars, being overmatched, and compelled to flee into their halls and hostels, were so pursued by their enemies, that twenty of the doors of their halls and chambers

Procession for peace, would bring no peace.

Transubstantiation will not help in time of need.

Conquest of the scholars of Oxford.

(1) Hæc ex Godfrido de Fontanis.

(2) "Asleep," as Baal was in days of old.—Ed.

Edward III. A.D. 1331 to 1360.

were broken open, and many of them wounded, and, as it is said, slain and thrown into the draughts; their books with knives and bills cut all in pieces, and much of their goods carried away. And thus the students of that university, being conquered by the townsmen of Oxford, and of the country about, departed and left the university, so that for a time the schools there, and all school acts, did utterly cease from all exercise of study, except only Merton college-hall, with a few others remaining behind.

The university of Oxford dissolved for a time.

This being done the twelfth day of February, the queen at the same time being at Woodstock was brought to bed, and purified on the first Sunday in Lent with great solemnity of justing.[1] About which time the bishop of Lincoln, their diocesan, hearing of this excessive outrage, sendeth his inhibition to all parsons and priests, forbidding them throughout all Oxford, to celebrate mass or any divine service in the presence of any lay person within the said town of Oxford, interdicting withal the whole town; which interdiction endured the space of a whole year and more.

The town of Oxford interdicted.

The king also sent thither his justices to examine and inquire into the matter, before whom divers of the laymen and clergy were indicted, and four of the chief burgesses of the said town were indicted, and by the king's commandment sent to the Tower of London, and were there imprisoned. At length, through much labour of the nobles, the king so took up the matter, that sending his writings unto all sheriffs in England, he offered pardon to all and singular the students of that university, wheresoever dispersed, for that transgression; whereby the university in a short time was replenished again as before. Moreover, it was granted to the vice-chancellor or commissary, as they term him, of the town and university of Oxford, to have the assize of bread, ale, wine, and all other victuals; the mayor of the said town being excluded. Also it was granted and decreed, that the commons of Oxford should give to the university of Oxford two hundred pounds sterling, in part of satisfaction for their excesses; there being reserved, notwithstanding, to every one of the students his several action against any several person of the townsmen, &c.

Assize of bread and ale granted to the commissary of Oxford.

About A.D. 1354, the king, with the consent of his council, called home again out of Flanders the staple of wool, with all things thereunto appertaining, and established the same in sundry places within the realm, namely, in Westminster, Canterbury, Chichester, Bristol, Lincoln, and Hull; which staple, after A.D. 1362, was translated over to Calais.

Of Simon Islip, archbishop of Canterbury, mentioned a little before, page 710, I read in the said author above specified, that he, by his letters patent, directed to all parsons and vicars within his province, straightly charged them and their parishioners, under pain of excommunication, not to abstain from bodily labour upon certain saints' days, which before were wont to be hallowed and consecrated to unthrifty idleness. Item, that to priests should be given no more for their yearly stipend, but three pounds, six shillings, and eight pence, which made divers of them to rob and steal, &c. A.D. 1362.

Not to abstain from bodily labour upon certain holy days.

A Parliament.

In the year following, king Edward kept his parliament at London

(1) "Great solemnity of justing," great show of piety.—ED.

in the month of October; wherein it was prohibited that either gold or silver should be worn in knives, girdles, brooches, rings, or in any other ornament belonging to the body, except the wearer might dispend ten pounds a year. Item, That none should wear either silks or costly furs, except such as might dispend one hundred pounds a year. Also that merchant adventurers should not export any merchandise out of the realm, or seek for wines in other countries; whereby other nations should be constrained rather to seek to us, &c. But none of this did take any great effect.

After this Simon Islip, as is above recorded, followed Simon Langham, then William Wittlesey; after whom next in place succeeded Simon Sudbury.

Nuns of St Bridget's order

Much about the same time the nuns of St. Bridget's order first began; about which time also was builded Queen's College in Oxford, by queen Philippa of England, wife to king Edward III., about A.D. 1360.

This lady Blanch was duchess of Lancaster.

Dead men excommunicated by the pope

Moreover, in the time of this pope Innocent, friar John Lyle, bishop of Ely, moved with certain injuries, as he thought, done to him by the lady Blanch, made his complaint to the pope; who, sending down his curse to the bishop of Lincoln and other prelates, to be executed upon the adversaries of the bishop of Ely, commanded them, that if they did know any of the said adversaries dead and buried, that notwithstanding, they should cause the same to be taken up: which also they performed accordingly, of whom some had been of the king's council; wherefore the king being displeased, and not unworthily, did again trouble and molest the said prelates. This coming to the pope's hearing, certain were directed down from the court of Rome, in behalf of the aforesaid bishop of Ely; who, meeting with the bishop of Rochester, the king's treasurer, delivered unto him, being armed, letters from the bishop of Rome, the tenor whereof was not known. This done, they incontinently voided away, but certain of the king's servants pursuing did overtake them; of whom some they imprisoned, some they brought to the justices, and so they were condemned to be hanged. Herein may appear what reverence the pope's letters in this king's days, had in this realm of England.[1] This pope Innocent ordained the feast of the Holy Spear, and of the Holy Nails.

The pope's messengers hanged

The feast of the Spear and of the Holy Nails

And here, to make an end of this Fourth Book, now remaineth, after our order and custom before begun, to prosecute the race of the archbishops of Canterbury, in this aforesaid Fourth Book contained; beginning where before we left off,[2] at Lanfranc.

A TABLE OF THE ARCHBISHOPS OF CANTERBURY IN THE FOURTH BOOK CONTAINED.

34. Lanfranc was archbishop of Canterbury for nineteen years. Polydore Virgil, lib. 9, numbereth this Lanfranc to be the thirty-third archbishop; but by the account of other authors, namely, by the chronicle of the monk of Dover, he seemeth to be deceived; as he was in the twenty-eight years of Dunstan, who indeed did sit but nineteen or twenty at the most. This error of Polydore seemeth to

(1) Ex Chro Walsing (2) Page 101

Edward III. A.D. 1360.

come by leaving out either Elsius, who was the twenty-third, or by leaving out Elfric, who was the twenty-sixth, as in some authors I find.

Moreover, here is to be noted, that although the said Elfric were left out, yet Lanfranc cannot be the thirty-third.

Note also, that in the previous table of the third book, after Siricius, you must put in St. Alured, whom, in the order of archbishops, I left out in the end of the third book, page 104.

This Lanfranc was an Italian, and a stout champion of the pope. After his stubborn dissension with Thomas, archbishop of York, he wrote against Berengarius, entitling his book 'Opus Scintillarum,' page 114.

Also the same Lanfranc builded the new church at Canterbury, and plucked down the old. By him was builded the church of St. Gregory. At length he was expelled by king William Rufus.

35. Anselm, for twenty years. Of this Anselm, and the strife between him and the king, look in page 144.

36. Radulph for eight years. Under Radulph the order of Cistercians began.

37. William Curboil, for thirteen years. By this William the new work of the church of St. Martin's, at Dover, was built.

38. Theobald, for twenty-four years. By this Theobald monks were first brought into the church of Dover. He was expelled by king Stephen. In his time the church of St. Gregory at Canterbury was burned.

39. Thomas Becket, for nine years. For the life and death of this Becket, see page 196.[1]

40. Richard, for ten years. This Richard was a monk. In his time Christ's Church, at Canterbury, was burned.

41. Baldwin, for seven years. Between this Baldwin and the monks was great discord. He suspended the prior from his priorship, and two and twenty monks from all service. He caused the sub-prior, with all his adherents, to be excommunicated through all Kent.

42. Hubert, for fourteen years. In the time of this Hubert the chapel of Lambeth was plucked down. Also the church of Dover was burned.

43. Stephen Langton, for twenty-two years. This Stephen, with the monks of Canterbury, was expelled by king John.

This Stephen, intending to give orders in the chapel of Lambeth, was stopped by the monks of Canterbury, through their appeal and prohibition. Wherefore he required Eustace, bishop of London, to minister the same orders in the church of St. Paul.

In his time fell great variance between the monks of Rochester and the monks of Canterbury, for the election of their bishop, which election the monks of Canterbury would not admit before the Rochester monks had presented the bishop's staff in the church of Canterbury; so that both the churches sent their messengers to the court of Rome.

44. Richardus Magnus, for four years. At the consecration of

(1) Ex Crickeladensi: Magnates in Anglia interdixerunt, ne quis Martyrem Thomam nominaret, ne quis ejus miracula prædicaret, interminantes minas mortis seu maximarum pœnarum omnibus confitentibus eum fuisse Martyrem, et miracula ejus prædicantibus, &c.

this Richard, contention arose between the bishop of Rochester and the bishop of Bath, who should consecrate him.

Item, between the said Richard and the monks of Canterbury fell a grievous discord, about certain liberties belonging to the archbishop.

The said archbishop, for certain quarrels against the king, went up to Rome, who died in Tuscia.

After this Richard, the election of three archbishops was disannulled at Rome; namely, of Radulphus de Nova Villa, of John, prior of Canterbury, and of John Blund.

45. Edmund of Abingdon for seven years. This Edmund was called St. Edmund, at whose election the prior of Dover, thinking to be present, as at the marriage of his mother, was not permitted by the monks of Canterbury. For that injury he appealed and went to Rome to complain, not against the elect, but against the election; where he obtained of the pope, for all the priors and successors of Dover, to have full interest in the election of the archbishops, besides other privileges which he obtained; percase not without some good store of money. Afterwards the monks of Canterbury accused him to the archbishop as though he stood against the person of the elect, and so obtained of the archbishop, being angry with him, to have brought him under the chapter of Canterbury, there to be punished. Whereupon the prior, seeing himself so destitute of all help of lawyers, was constrained in the aforesaid chapter to cry 'peccavi.' Then, being suspended from his priorship, he was at length sent home from Dover, being compelled first to set his hand to a certain composition between him and the aforesaid monks.

The said Edmund, archbishop, having also some quarrel against the king, went up to Rome, and died before his coming home.

46. Boniface, for twenty-five years. In the time of this Boniface, Pope Gregory wickedly granted to king Henry III. (for the getting of the kingdom of Sicily, which belonged not to him to give, nor to the other to take) tenths of goods, temporal and spiritual, for five years. Item, All the first year's fruits of churches that should be vacant for five years. Item, Half of all the goods of beneficed men, not resident on their benefices. Item, All legacies not distinctly given. And yet the kingdom of Sicily never came into his hands, which belonged to Manfred, son of Frederic the emperor. Strife there was between this Boniface and the prior of Canterbury, Item, Between him and the bishop of Roff. Item, Between him and the chapter of Lincoln: all which was afterwards agreed.[1]

Strife also in Winchester about choosing the bishop after the death of Avonarus, the king's brother.

Strife also in the convocation which Boniface did hold at Lambeth; in the which council were recited the statutes of Octobonus, and other new statutes made, against which John Hemelingford, the king's chaplain, with others besides, and Prince Edward on the king's behalf, did appeal.[2]

Under this Boniface, Tunbridge and Hadlow first came under the custody of the archbishop of Canterbury.

Master John of Exeter bought the bishopric of Winchester for

(1) Chron. Doverens. fol. 20, p. 2. (2) Ibid. fol. 21.

Edward III. A.D. 1360.

six thousand marks; which being known he was fain to pay the same sum again to the pope, and so was sent home.

Boniface the archbishop being in the parts of Sebaudia (A.D. 1262) there befell another altercation between the prior and chapter of Canterbury on the one part, and the prior and chapter of Dover on the other, which two houses were almost never in quiet, and all about certain liberties and privileges; as, for making the sub-prior, for receiving in of monks, and for visitations of the church of Dover.

A.D. 1268. Boniface, archbishop, interdicted the city of London, because in the same city the archbishop of York did hold up his cross, the archbishop of Canterbury being there present, the king holding then his parliament at Westminster.

This archbishop died in the parts of Sebaudia.

John, prior of Canterbury, was elected by the monks against the king's mind, but by the pope refused.

Adam Chilinden was elect, but he resigned his election to the pope.

47. Robert Kilwarby, friar, for six years. In the time of this Robert Kilwarby, appeal was taken against the chapter of Canterbury by the bishops of Winchester, Worcester, and Exeter; for which cause the said bishops went up to Rome to prosecute the appeal. The matter was, because they did not their obedience to the monks of Canterbury, the see being empty.

Walter Giffard, archbishop of York, going toward the general council, bore up his cross through the middle of Kent, in the time of this Robert, archbishop of Canterbury, A.D. 1272.

By pope Gregory X. in the general council at Lyons, all the orders of friars were put down, four orders only excepted, that is, Dominics, Franciscans, Carmelites, and Augustines.

This Robert Kilwarby, by the commandment of pope Nicholas, was made cardinal of Rome and bishop of Porvensis.

An untruth in Polydore Virgil. Here is to be noted an untruth in Polydore Virgil, who saith, that he was made cardinal by pope Gregory, which could not be.

Robert Burnel, bishop of Bath, was elected, but by the pope refused; for whom John Peckham, a Grey-friar, was placed in by pope Nicholas.

48 John Peckham, for thirteen years. In the first year of this friar Peckham, W. Wikewane, archbishop of York, coming from his consecration at Rome to Dover, bore up his cross through the midst of Kent, whereat was no little ado.

Robert Gernemine, archdeacon of Canterbury, went to law at Rome for the liberties and possessions of his archdeaconship two years, and there died.

In this time also another wrangling occurred between the monks of Canterbury and the monks of Dover, in the time of this John Peckham, for admitting certain novices of Dover into orders.[1]

This Peckham, holding a council at Lambeth, ordained divers statutes, and caused the ordinances of the council of Lyons, and of Boniface archbishop of Canterbury, and his predecessor, to be observed.

Great grief and hatred existed between this Peckham, and Thomas

(1) Ex Chr Monach Dover fol 42

bishop of Hereford, who, being excommunicated by Peckham, appealed to Rome, and went to the pope.

The prior and covent of Canterbury made their appeal against this archbishop Peckham, that he should not consecrate Walter le Schamele, the newly elect bishop of Salisbury, in any other place, except only in the church of Canterbury, but by their leave and license first obtained. Notwithstanding, the archbishop, nothing regarding their appeal, proceeded in the consecration of the said bishop near to the town of Reading, whereupon the prior and covent ceased not to prosecute their appeal against the archbishop.

Between Richard Ferrings, archdeacon of Canterbury, of the one part, and the barons of Dover of the other part, the same year fell out another like wrangling, for that the archdeacon claimed to visit the church of Dover: contrary the barons affirmed, that none had, nor should have, to do thereto, or order or dispose in spiritual matters, but only the archbishop, and the prior and covent of St. Martin.[1]

After the death of William Wicwane, archbishop of York, John de Roma succeeded; and coming from his consecration at Rome to Dover, bare his cross through the middle of Kent, contrary to the inhibition of John Peckham.

49. Robert Winchelsey was archbishop for nineteen years. This Robert, who was archbishop in the latter time of king Edward I., for certain displeasure the king had conceived against him, departed the realm, and in his banishment remained two or three years; and, about the beginning of the reign of king Edward II., he was restored again. (A.D. 1309.)[2] Thus few archbishops of Canterbury we find, with whom kings have not had some quarrel or other. "The cause between the king and him," saith mine author, "was this: That the king accused him to pope Clement of disturbing his realm, and of taking part with rebels," &c.[3]

This Robert also excommunicated Walter, bishop of Coventry, for holding with the king and Peter Gaveston against the ordinances of the barons; wherefore the said bishop appealed to the pope, against whom the archbishop sent Adam Mirimouth.

This Adam Mirimouth was compiler of the story of king Edward.

In the time of this Robert, archbishop, the order of Templars was abolished by pope Clement V. in the council of Vienna, with this sentence definitive: "Quanquam de jure non possumus, tamen ad plenitudinem potestatis dictum ordinem reprobamus."

50. Walter Reynald for fifteen years. After the decease of Robert Winchelsey, who departed A.D. 1312, Thomas Cobham, a learned man, was elected by full consent of the monks, who came to Avignon to have his election confirmed; but the pope reserving the vacant seat in his own hands, put in Walter Reynald, bishop of Worcester, chancellor of England, who governed the see fifteen years.

The chronicler of St. Alban's recordeth also, how in the days of this archbishop (A.D. 1319), certain lepers conspiring with the Turks and Jews went about to impotionate, and infect all Christendom, by envenoming their fountains, lakes, pits, barrels, and such other places; of the which crime divers of them being convicted, were worthily burned in France. About the same year, the said author maketh

(1) Ex cod. Chron. fol. 46. (2) Ex Chron. Rich. 2. (3) Ex Chron. St. Albani.

Edward III

A. D. 1360.

also relation, how, in the realm of England, much murrain prevailed among the beasts; insomuch that the dogs, feeding upon their flesh (infected belike by the waters and fountains), fell down dead incontinently; neither durst men, for that cause, almost taste of any beef. (A.D. 1318, 1319)[1]

This Walter, archbishop, taking part with the queen Isabel against king Edward her husband, died the same year in which he was deposed. (A.D. 1237.)[2]

After Walter the archbishop, as affirmeth the chronicle of St. Alban, succeeded Simon Mepham; of whom I marvel that Polydore maketh no word nor mention; belike he sat not long: after him followed,

51. John Stratford, for twenty-nine years. In the story of Adam Merimouth, it is recorded that this John Stratford, intending to visit the diocese of Norfolk, was not received by the bishop, the chapter and clergy there alleging that he observed not the ordinary canon therein. To whom the archbishop said again, he had the pope's letters, and showed the same. But the other answered, that those letters were falsely obtained, and tended to the suppression of the clergy, and therefore they would not obey: wherefore the archbishop excommunicated the bishop, suspended the prior, and interdicted the covent. (A.D. 1343.)

52. John Offord, ten months. Master John Offord, chancellor of England, was elected and confirmed archbishop of Canterbury, but not consecrated, and sat but ten months, about A.D. 1350, the time of the pestilence in England.

53. Thomas Braidwarden, archbishop for one year. This Thomas Braidwarden following after John Stratford, sat not long, but died within ten months, of the plague, as they say. This was called the first great plague in England, raging so sore in all quarters, that it was thought scarcely the tenth part of men to be left alive.

The first great plague in England

54. Simon Islip, for seventeen years. In the time of Simon Islip, who followed after Braidwarden, king Edward (A.D. 1362) is reported, after the blind superstition of those days, to offer in the church of Westminster the vestments wherein St Peter did celebrate mass; which belike were well kept from moths, to last so long.[3]

The vestments wherein St Peter said mass, or else the papists do lie

The same Simon Islip, among other constitutions, ordained through all churches and chapels, under pain of excommunication, that no man should abstain from bodily labours upon certain saints' days, as is before mentioned; which fact of his is not a little noted in our monkish histories.

This Simon built Canterbury College in Oxford.

THE CONCLUSION OF THIS FOURTH BOOK.

Antichrist in his pride. The loosing out of Satan

Forasmuch as Satan, being chained up all this while for the space of a thousand years, beginneth about this time to be loosed and to come abroad, according to the forewarning of St. John's Revelation: therefore, to conclude the Fourth Book, wherein sufficiently hath been described the excessive pride and pomp of Antichrist, flourishing in

(1) Ex Chro Alban (2) Ex Chro. Alban (3) Ex Chro Alban.

his ruff and security, from the time of William the Conqueror hitherto: now (Christ willing and assisting us thereunto) we mind in these latter books hereafter following, in order of history to express the latter persecutions and horrible troubles of the church, raised up by Satan in his minister Antichrist; with the resistance again of Christ's church against him. And so to prosecute, by the merciful grace of Christ, the proceeding and course of times, till we come at length to the fall and ruin of the said Antichrist; to the intent that if any be in such error as to think that Antichrist is yet to come, he may consider and ponder well the tragical rages, the miserable and most sorrowful persecutions, murders, and vexations, of these latter three hundred years now following; and then, I doubt not but he will be put out of all doubt, and know that not only Antichrist is already come, but also know where he sitteth, and how he is now falling apace (the Lord Christ be thanked for ever!) to his decay and confusion.

Edward III.

A.D. 1360.

END OF BOOK THE FOURTH.

ACTS AND MONUMENTS.

BOOK V.

CONTAINING

THE LAST THREE HUNDRED YEARS FROM THE LOOSING OUT OF SATAN.[1]

Edward III.

A. D. 1360.

Thus having discoursed in these former books of the order and course of years, from the first tying up of Satan unto the year of our Lord 1360, I have a little overpassed the stint of time in the Scripture appointed for the loosing out of him again. For so it is written by St. John [Apoc. xx.], that "after a thousand years, Satan, the old dragon, shall be let loose again for a season," &c.

The years and time of loosing out Satan examined.

For the better explanation of the which mystery, let us first consider the context of the Scripture; afterwards let us examine, by history and the course of times, the meaning of the same. And first, to recite the words of the Apocalypse; the text of the prophecy is

Apoc. xx.

this:—"And I saw an angel descending from heaven, having a key of the bottomless pit, and a great chain in his hand. And he took the dragon, the old serpent, which is the Devil and Satan, and bound him for a thousand years, and put him in the bottomless dungeon and shut him up, and signed him with his seal, that he should no more seduce the Gentiles, till a thousand years were expired. And after that he must be loosed again for a little space of time. And I saw seats, and they sat upon them, and judgment was given unto them; and the souls I saw of them which were beheaded for the testimony of Jesus." By these words of the Revelation, here recited, three special times are to be noted.

First, The being abroad of Satan to deceive the world.

Secondly, The binding up of him.

Thirdly, The loosing out of him again, after a thousand years consummate, for a time.

The place of the Apoc. xx. expounded, for the loosing out of Satan.

Concerning the interpretation of which times, I see the common opinion of many to be deceived by ignorance of histories, and the state of things done in the church; they supposing that the chaining up of Satan for a thousand years, spoken of in the Revelation, was meant from the birth of Christ our Lord. Wherein I grant that spiritually the strength and dominion of Satan, in accusing and condemning us for sin, was cast down at the passion and by the passion of Christ our Saviour, and locked up, not only for a thousand years,

(1) Edition 1563, p. 74 Ed. 1570, p. 493. Ed. 1576, p. 401. Ed. 1583, p. 397. Ed. 1596, p. 365. Ed. 1684, vol. i. p. 452.—Ed.

but for ever and ever. Albeit, as touching the malicious hatred and fury of that serpent against the outward bodies of Christ's poor saints (which is the heel of Christ), to afflict and torment the church outwardly; that I judge to be meant in the Revelation of St. John, not to be restrained till the ceasing of those terrible persecutions of the primitive church, at the time when it pleased God to pity the sorrowful affliction of his poor flock, being so long under persecution, the space of three hundred years, and so to assuage their griefs and torments; which is meant by the binding up of Satan, worker of all those mischiefs: understanding thereby, that forasmuch as the devil, the prince of this world, had now, by the death of Christ the Son of God, lost all his power and interest against the soul of man, he should turn his furious rage and malice, which he had to Christ, against the people of Christ, which is meant by the heel of the seed [Gen. iii.], in tormenting their outward bodies; which yet should not be for ever, but for a determinate time, when it should please the Lord to bridle the malice, and snaffle the power, of the old serpent, and give rest unto his church for the term of a thousand years; which time being expired, the said serpent should be suffered loose again for a certain or a small time. [Apoc. xx.]

What the loosing of Satan doth mean in Scripture.

And thus to expound this prophetical place of Scripture, I am led by three reasons:

Three reasons.

The first is, for that the binding up of Satan, and closing him in the bottomless pit by the angel, importeth as much as that he was at liberty, raging and doing mischief before. And, certes, those so terrible and so horrible persecutions of the primitive time universally through the whole world, during the space of three hundred years of the church, do declare no less. Wherein it is to be thought and supposed that Satan, all that time, was not fastened and closed up.

The first reason.

The second reason moving me to think that the closing up of Satan was after the ten persecutions of the primitive church, is taken out of the twelfth chapter of the Apocalypse; where we read, that after the woman, meaning the church, had travailed forth her man-child, the old dragon, the devil, the same time being cast down from heaven, drawing the third part of the stars with him, stood before the woman with great anger, and persecuted her (that is, the church of God) with a whole flood of water (that is, with abundance of all kinds of torments), and from thence went, moreover, to fight against the residue of her seed, and stood upon the sands of the sea; whereby it appeareth that he was not as yet locked up.

The second reason.

The third reason I collect out of the Apocalypse, chapter xiii., where it is written of the beast, signifying the imperial monarchy of Rome, that he had power to make war forty and two months; by which months is meant, no doubt, the time that the dragon and the persecuting emperors should have in afflicting the saints of the primitive church. The computation of which forty-two months (counting every month for a Sabbath of years; that is, for seven years, after the order of Scripture), riseth to the sum (counting from the passion of the Lord Christ) of three hundred years, lacking six; at which time Maxentius, the last persecutor in Rome, fighting against Constantine, was drowned with his soldiers, like as Pharaoh, persecuting the children of Israel, was drowned in the Red Sea. Unto the which forty-two

The third reason. Apoc. xiii.

Forty-two months in the Apoc. xiii. examined.

Edward III — A.D. 1360.

months, or Sabbaths of years, if ye add the other six years wherein Licinius persecuted in the East, ye shall find just three hundred years, as is specified before in the first book of this volume.

What time Satan was tied up

After the which forty and two months were expired, manifest it is that the fury of Satan, that is, his violent malice and power over the saints of Christ, was diminished and restrained universally throughout the whole world.

Thus then, the matter standing evident that Satan, after three hundred years, counting from the passion of Christ, began to be chained up, at which time the persecution of the primitive church began to cease, now let us see how long this binding up of Satan should continue, which was promised in the Book of the Revelation to be a thousand years, which thousand years, if ye add to the forty-two months of years, that is, to two hundred and ninety-four years, they make one thousand two hundred and ninety-four years after the passion of the Lord. To these, moreover, add the thirty years of the age of Christ, and it cometh to the year of our Lord 1324, which was the year of the letting out of Satan, according to the prophecy in the Apocalypse.

About what time and year Satan was let out, by the count of the Apocalypse

A TABLE CONTAINING THE TIME OF THE PERSECUTION BOTH OF THE PRIMITIVE, AND OF THE LATTER CHURCH, WITH THE COUNT OF YEARS FROM THE FIRST BINDING UP OF SATAN, TO HIS LOOSING AGAIN, AFTER THE MIND OF THE APOCALYPSE.

The first persecution of the primitive church, beginning at the thirtieth year of Christ, was prophesied to continue forty-two months; that is, till A.D. 294.

Ceasing of the last persecution

The ceasing of the last persecution of the primitive church by the death of Licinius, the last persecutor, began in the three hundred and twenty-fourth year from the nativity of Christ; which was from the thirtieth year of his age, two hundred and ninety-four years.

Binding up of Satan

The binding up of Satan after peace given to the church, counting from the thirty years of Christ, began A.D. 294, and lasted a thousand years, that is, counting from the thirtieth year of Christ, to the year 1294.

About which year, pope Boniface VIII. was pope, and made the sixth book of the Decretals, confirmed the orders of friars, and privileged them with great freedoms; as appeareth by his constitution, 'Super Cathedram.' A.D 1294.

Time of loosing him

Unto the which count of years doth not much disagree that which I found in a certain old chronicle prophesied and written in the latter end of a book; which book was written, as it seemeth, by a monk of Dover, and remaineth yet in the custody of William Cary, a citizen of London; alleging the prophecy of one Hayneard, a Grey-friar, grounded upon the authority of Joachim the abbot, prophesying that Antichrist should be born the year from the nativity of Christ 1260; which is, counting after the Lord's passion, the very same year and time when the orders of friars, both Dominics and Franciscans, began first to be set up by pope Honorius III. and by pope Gregorius IX., which was the year of our Lord, counting from his

The time of Antichrist examined

passion, A.D. 1226; and counting from the nativity of our Lord, was the year 1260. Whereof these verses, prophesying the coming of Antichrist, in the author were written:—

> "Cum fuerint anni completi mille ducenti,
> Et decies seni post partum virginis almæ.
> Tunc Antichristus nascetur dæmone plenus."

And these verses were written, as appeareth by the said author, A.D. 1285.

These things thus premised for the loosing out of Satan, according to the prophecy of the Apocalypse, now let us enter (Christ willing) upon the declaration of these latter times which followed after the letting out of Satan into the world; describing the wondrous perturbations and cruel tyranny stirred up by him against Christ's church, and also the valiant resistance of the church of Christ against him and Antichrist, as in these our books here under following may appear, the argument of which consisteth in two parts: first, to treat of the raging fury of Satan now loosed, and of Antichrist, against the saints of Christ fighting and travailing for the maintenance of truth, and the reformation of the church. Secondly, to declare the decay and ruin of the said Antichrist, through the power of the word of God; being at length, either in a great part of the world overthrown, or, at least, universally in the whole world detected.

Argument of the books after following

Thus then to begin with the year of our Lord 1360, wherein I have a little, as is aforesaid, transgressed the stint of the first loosing out of Satan: we are come now to the time wherein the Lord, after long darkness, beginneth some reformation of his church, by the diligent industry of sundry his faithful and learned servants, of whom divers already we have fore-touched in the former book; as Guliel. de Sancto Amore, Marsilius Patavinus, Ockam, Robertus Gallus, Robertus Grosthead, Petrus de Cugneriis, Johannes Rupescissanus, Conradus Hager, Johannes de Poliaco, Cesenas, with others, who withstood the corrupt errors and intolerable enormities of the bishop of Rome, besides those who about these times were put to death by the said bishop of Rome, as Castilio and Franciscus de Arcatara in the book before recorded; also the two Franciscans, martyrs, who were burned at Avignon, mentioned p. 710.

A.D. 1360

A brief rehearsal of faithful learned men, which withstood the proceedings of the pope

Now to these (the Lord willing) we will add such other holy martyrs and confessors, who following after in the course of years with like zeal and strength of God's word, and also with like danger of their lives, gave the like resistance against the enemy of Christ's religion, and suffered at his hands the like persecutions. First, beginning with that godly man, whosoever he was, the author of the book (his name I have not) entitled 'The Prayer and Complaint of the Ploughman;' written, as it appeareth, about this present time.

The author of the Ploughman's Prayer not known

This book, as it was faithfully set forth by William Tindal, so I have as truly distributed the same abroad to the reader's hands; neither changing any thing of the matter, nor altering many words of the phrase thereof. Although the oldness and age of his speech and terms be almost grown now out of use, yet I thought it best, both for the utility of the book to reserve it from oblivion, as also in his

Edward III

A.D. 1360

own language to let it go abroad, for the more credit and testimony of the true antiquity of the same; adding withal in the margin, for the better understanding of the reader, some interpretation of certain difficult terms and speeches, which otherwise might perhaps hinder or stay the reader. The matter of this complaining prayer of the ploughman thus proceedeth:—

An olde Booke intituled, the Ploughmans 'Prayer,'[1] written as it seemeth about Wickliffe's time.

The complaynt of Esai applied to these times

Iesu Christ that was ybore of the mayde Marye, haut on thy poore seruantes mercy and pitye, and helpe them in their great nede to fighte agaynst synne, and against the diuil that is autor of synne, and more nede nes ther neuer to cry to Christ for help, then it is right now. For it is fulfilled that God sayd by Isay the prophet: Ye ryseth vp erlich to folow dronkennes, and to drinke tyll it be euen, the harpe and other minstrelsyes beeth in your feastes and wyne. But the worke of God ye ne beholdeth not, ne taketh no kepe to the workes of hys hands. And therefore my people is take prisoner, for they ne had no cunnyng. And the noble men of my people deyeden for hunger, and the multitude of my people weren drye for thyrst, and therefore hell hath drawen abroade their soule, and hath yopened hys mouth withouten any ende. And eftsones sayth Isay the prophet: The word is floten away, and the hyghnes of the people is ymade sycke, and the earth is infect of his wonnyers, for they haue broken my lawes, and ychaunged my ryght, and han destroyed myne euerlastyng bonde and forward[2] betwene them and me. And therefore cursing shall deuoure the earth, and they that wonneth on the erthly shullen done synne. And therefore the earth tilyars shullen waxe woode, and fewe men shullen ben yleft vpon the earth. And yet sayth Isay the prophet, this sayth God, for as much as this peple nigheth me with their mouth, and glorifieth me with their lips, and their hart is farre from mee. And they han ydrad more mens commaundement, then myne, and more drawe to their doctrines, then myne. Therefore will I make a great wondring vnto this people, wisedome shall perish away from wise men, and vnderstanding of ready men shal bee yhid. And so it seemeth that an other saying of Isay is fulfilled, there as God bade him goe teach the people, and sayd goe forth and say to this people: Eares haue ye, and vnderstand ye not, and eyes yee haue sight ne know ye not. Make blynde the hart of this people, and make their eares heauy, and close their eyen, least he sea with his eyen, and yheare with his eares, and vnderstande with his hart, and by yturned, and ych heale hym of hys sicknesse. And Isay sayd to God: How long Lord shal this be? And God said: For to that the cities ben desolate withouten a wonnier, and an house wythouten a man.

Here is mychel nede for to make sorow, and to crye to our Lord Iesu Christ heitlich for helpe and for succour, that hee wole forgeue vs our sinnes, and geue vs grace and conning to seruen him better here after. And God of hys endles mercy geue vs grace and conning trulich to tellen which is Christes law in helping of mens soules, for we beth lewde men, and sinneful men, and vncunning, and if he woll be our helpe and our succor, we shullen wel perfaurme our purpose. And yblessed bee our Lorde God that hideth his wisedome from wise men, and fro ready men, and teacheth it to small children, as Christ teacheth in the gospel.

The law of Christ standeth on two parts

Christen men haue a law to keepe, the which law hath twe parties. Beleue in Christ that is God, and is the foundment of theyr law, and vpon this foundement, as he sayd to Peter, and the gospel beareth witnes, he woll byelden his church, and this is the first partie of Christes law. The second partie of this law beth Christes commaundmentes that beth written in the gospel, and more verilich in Christen mens hartes.

And as touching the beleue, we beleuen that Christ is God, and that there ne is no god but he. We beleuen neuerthelesse that in the Godhead there bene three persons, the Father, the Sonne, and the Holy Ghost, and al these three persons ben one God, and not many gods, and al they beth ylich mightie,

(1) This interesting document is given in every Edition but the First and the Third.—Ed.

(2) "Forward," that is, covenant.

ylich good, and ylich wise, and euer haue ben, and euer shullen ben. We beleuen this God made the world of nought, and man he made after hys owne likenesse in Paradise that was a lande of blisse, and gaue him that land for his heritage, and bad him that he shoulde not eate the tree of knowledge of good and euil, that was a midde Paradise.[1] Then the diuell that was fallen out of heauen for his pride, had enuie to man, and by a false suggestion he made man eate of this tree, and breake the commaundement of God, and tho was man ouercome of the deuil, and so he lost his heritage, and was put out thereof into the world that was a land of trauel, and of sorow vnder the feends thraldome, to be punished for his trespasse. There man followed wickednesse and sinne, and God for the sinne of man sent a floud into this world, and drownd al mankinde saue eight soules. And after this flud he let men multiply in the world, and so hee assayed whether man dread him or loued him, and among other he found a man that hight Abraham. this man he proued whether he loued him and drad him, and bad him that hee should offeren Isaac his son vppon an hil, and Abraham as a true seruant fulfilled the Lords commaundment: and for this buxumnesse and truth, God sware vnto Abraham that he would multiplie his seed as the grauel in the sea, and as the stars of heauen, and he behight to him and to his heires the land of behest for heritage for euer, gif they wolden ben his true seruauntes and keepe his hestes. And God helde him forward,[2] for Isaac Abrahams son begat Iacob and Esau: and of Iacob that is ycleped Israel, comen Gods people that he chose to be his seruants, and to whom he behight the land of behest. This people was in great thraldom in Egypt vnder Pharao that was king of Egypt and they crieden to God that hee shoulde deliueren them out of that thraldome, and so hee did: for he sent to Pharao, Moses and his brother Aaron, and bad him deliuer his people to done him sacrifices: and to fore Pharao he made Moses done manie wonders, or that Pharao would deliuer his people, and at the last by might hee deliuered his people out of thraldome, and led them through a desert towarde the land of behest, and there he gaue them a lawe that they shulden lyuen after, when they comen into their countrey, and in their way thither ward, the ten commaundementes God wrote himselfe in two tables of stone the remnant of the law he taught them by Moses his seruant how they shoulden doe euery chone to other, and gif they trespassed again the law, he ordeined how they shoulden be punished Also he taught them what maner sacrifices they should do to him, and he chose him a people to been his priests, that was Aaron and his children, to done sacrifices in the tabernacle, and afterward in the temple also. He chese him the remnant of the children of Leuy to ben seruaunts in the tabernacle to the priestes, and he said When ye come into the land of behest, the children of Leuy they shullen haue none heritage amongst their brethren, for I would be their part, and their heritage, and they shullen serue me in the tabernacle by dayes and by nightes, and he ordeined that priestes should haue a part of the sacrifices that wer offred in the tabernacle, and the first begotten beastes, both of men and beastes and other things as the lawe telleth. And the other children of Leuy that serued in the tabernacle, should haue tythings of the people to their lyuelode, of the which tythings they should geuen the priestes the tenth partie in forme of offeryng. The children of Leuy both priestes and other, should haue houses and crofts, and lesewes for their beastes in the land of behest, and none other heritage: and so God gaue them their land of behest, and bade them that they ne should worship no other God then him. Also he bade that they should kepe his commaundementes, and gife they did so, all their enemies about them shuld drede them and be their seruantes. And gife they worshipped false gods, and so forsaken his lawes, he behight them that he would bring them out of that land and make them serue their enemies, but yet hee said hee would not benemen his mercie away from them, if they would cry mercie and amend their defautes, and all this was done on Gods side.

Abraham

And here is much loue showed of God to man. And who so looketh the bible, hee shall finde that man showed him little loue againeward. for when they were come into their heritage, they forgetten their God, and worshipped false gods. And God sent to them the prophetes and his seruants feile times[3]

Gods loue to man

(1) "A midde Paradise," in the middest of Paradise (2) "Helde him forward," kept promise with him (3) "Feile times," oft times

to bid them withdrawen them from their sinnes, and other they haue slowen them, or they beaten them, or they led them in prison: and oft times God tooke vppon them great vengeance for their sinnes, and when they cried after helpen to God, he sent them helpe and succour. This is the generall processe of the Old Testament, that God gaue to his people by Moses his seruant. And all this testament and this doing ne was but a shadow and a figure of a new Testament that was giuen by Christ. And it was byhoten by Ieremie the prophet, as S. Paul beareth witnes in the epistle that he writeth to the Iewes. And Ieremie saith in this wise: Loe dayes shall come, God saith, and I will make a newe bande to the house of Israel, and to the house of Iuda, not like the forward that I made with their fathers in that day that I tooke their hande to led them out of the lande of Egypt, the which forward they maden vein, and I had lordship ouer them. But this shal be the forward that I wold make with them after those daies: I will giue my lawes with them in their inwardnesse, and I wil wryten them in their harts, and I wil be their God, and they should be my people, and after that a man shall not teach his neighbour ne his brother, for all (God saith) from the least to the most, should know me, for I will forgeuen them their sinnes, and will no more thinke on theyr sinnes.

This is the newe testament, that Christ, both God and man borne of the mayd Mary, he taught here in this world, to bring man out of sinne and out of the deuils thraldome and seruice, to heauen, that is, land of blisse and heritage to all tho that beleeuen on him and kepen his commaundementes, and for his teaching he was done to the death. But the third day arose againe from death to life, and sette Adam and Eue, and many other folke, out of hell, and afterward hee came to his disciples and comforted them. After he stied vp to heauen to his father, and tho he sent the Holy Ghost amonges his disciples: and in time comming he woll come and demen all mankinde after their workes, and after the word she spake vpon earth: some to blisse, within body and in soul euer withouten end, and some to paine withouten end, both in body and in soule.

This is our beleeue and all Christen mens, and this beleue is the first poynt of the newe Testament that ych christen man is holde stedfastly to beleue, and rather to suffer the death than forsaken this beleue, and so this beleue is the bread of spiritual life, in forsaking sinne, that Christ brought vs to life.

But for as much as mannes liuing ne stondeth not all onlych by bread, he hath y-giuen vs a draught of water of life to drinke. And who that drinketh of that water, he ne shall neuer afterward ben a thurst. For this water is the clere teaching of the gospel, that encloseth seuen commaundements.

Speciall precepts or lessons of the gospell.

The furst is this: Thou shalt loue thy God ouer all other things, and thy brother as thy selfe, both enemie and frend.

The second commaundement is of meekenesse, in the which Christ chargeth vs to forsake lordship vpon our brethren and other worldly worships, and so he did himselfe.

The third commaundement, is in stonding stedfastlich in truth and forsaking all falsenesse.

The fourth commaundement, is to suffer in this world diseases and wrongs withouten ageinstondinges.

The fifth commaundement is mercie, to forgeuen our brethren their trespasse, as often time as they gylteth, without asking of vengeance.

The sixth commandement is poorenes in spirite, but not to ben a begger.

The seuenth commaundement, is chastitie: that is a forsaking of fleshlych likinges displeasing to God. These commaundementes enclosen the ten commaundementes of the old law, and somewhat more.

Christes sheepe stopped from cleane water and compelled to drinke puddell.

This water is a blessed drinke for christen mens soule. But more harme is, much folke would drink of this water, but they mowe not come thereto: for God saith by Ezechiel the prophet: When iche geue to you the most cleane water to drinke, ye troubled that water with your feete, and that water is so defouled, ye geue my shepe to drinke. But the cleane water is yhid fro the shepe, and but gif God cleare this, it is dread least the shepe dyen for thurst. And Christ that is the wisedome of the father of heauen, and well of this wisdome that come from heauen to earth to teach man this wisedome, thorow the which man should ouercome the sleightes of the deuill that is principall enemy of mankind: haue mercy and pitye of his people, and shew if it be his wil how this water is troubled, and by whom: and sith[1] clere this water that his shepe mowne drinken herof, and kele the thurst of their soules. Blessed mote our Lord ben, for he hath itaught vs in the gospell, that ere than hee woulde come to the vniuersall dome, then should come manie in his name and sayen, that they weren Christ; and they shoulden done many wonders, and begilen manie men. And manie false prophets shoulden arisen and begylen much folke.

A Lord, yblessed mote thou ben of euerich creature: which ben they that haue ysaid that they weren Christ and haue begiled thus thy people? Trulich Lord I trow, thilke that sayen that they ben in thy steed, and binemen[2] thy worship, and maken thy people worshippen them as God, and haue hid thy lawes from the people. Lord, who durst syt in thy steede and benemen thee thy worship and thy sacrifice, and durst maken the people woorship them as gods? The Sauter telles, that God ne wole not in the day of dome demen men for bodilich sacrifices and holocaustes: But God saith, yeld to me sacrifice of herying, and yeld to God thine auowes, and clepe me in the day of tribulation, and ych wole defend thee, and shalt worship me.

The herying[3] of God standeth in three things. In louing God ouer all other things; in dreading God ouer all other thinges; in trusting in God ouer all other things.

These three points Christ teacheth in the gospel. But I trow men louen him but a little. For who so loueth Christ, he wole kepen his wordes. But men holden his wordes for heresie and follie, and kepeth mens wordes. Also men dreden more men and mens lawes and their cursings, then Christ and his lawes and his cursings. Also men hopen more in men and mens helpes, than they doe in Christ and in his helpe. And thus hath he that setteth in God's stede, bynomen God these three heryinges, and maketh men louen him and his lawes, more then Christ and Christes law, and dreden him also. And there as the people shulden yelde to God their vowes, he saith he hath power to assoylen them of their avowes, and so this sacrifice he nemeth[4] away from God. And there as the people should cry to God in the day of tribulation, he letteth them of their crying to God and bynemeth God that worship. This day of tribulation is whan man is fallen thorowe sinne into the deuils seruice, and than we shulden cry to God after help, and axen forgeuenes of our sinne, and make great sorrowe for our sinne, and ben in full will to doe so no more ne none other sin, and that our Lord God wole forgeuen vs our sinne, and maken our soule clene. For his mercie is endles.

The honouring of God standeth in three things.

But Lord, here men haue bynomen thee much worship: for men seyn that thou ne might not cleane assoylen vs of our sinne. But if we knowlegen our sinnes to priestes, and taken of them a penance for our sinne gif we mowen speake with them.

Against auricular confession.

A Lord! thou forgaue sometime Peter his sinnes and also Mary Magdaleine, and manie other sinfull men withouten shriuings to priestes, and taking penaunce of priests for their sinnes. And Lord thou art as mightie now as thou were that tyme, but gif any man haue bynomen thee thy might. And wee lewed men beleuen, that there nys no man of so great power, and gif any man maketh himselfe of so great power he heighteth[5] himselfe aboue God. And S. Paul speaketh of one that sitteth in the temple of God and highten him aboue God, and gif any such be, he is a false Christ.

Sinnes forgiue without shrift.

But hereto seyn priests, that when Christ made clean leprous men, he bade them go and shewe them to priestes. And therefore they seyn that it is a commaundement of Christ, that a man should shewen his sinne to priestes. For as they seyn, lepre in the old lawe betokeneth sinne in this new law. A Lord God! whether thine apostles knew not thy meaning as well as men done now? And gif they hadden yknow that thou haddest commanded menne to shriuen them to priests, and they ne taught not that commaundement to the people, me thinketh they hadden ben to blame: But I trow they knewen well that it was none of thy commandements, ne needfull to heale of mannes soule. And as me

Obiection of the priestes to maintain shrift. Answere to the obiection.

(1) "Sith," that is, afterwards. (2) "Binemen," that is, take away.
(3) "Herying," that is, worshipping. (4) "Nemeth," that is, taketh.
(5) "Heighteth," that is, exalteth.

Edward III

A.D 1360.

thinketh the law of lepre, is nothing to the purpose of shriuing: for priestes in the old lawe hadden certaine points and tokens to know whether a man were leprous or not: and gif they were leprous, they hadden power to putten them away from other cleane men, for to that they weren clene, and then they hadden power to receiuen him among his brethren, and offeren for him a sacrifice to God

This nys nothing to the purpose of shriuing. For there nis but one priest, that is Christ, that may knowe in certaine the lepre of the soule Ne no priest may make the soule cleane of her sinne, but Christ that is priest after Melchisedekes order ne no priest here beneath may ywit for certaine whether a man be cleane of his sinne or cleane assoyled, but gif God tell it him by reuelation. Ne God ordeined not that his priests shuld set men a penaunce for their sinne, after the quantitie of the sin, but this is mans ordinaunce, and it may well bee that there commeth good thereof. But I wote wel that God is much vnworshipped thereby. For men trust more in his absolutions, and in his years of grace, than in Christs absolutions, and therby is the people much apayred. For now, the sorrow a man should make for his sin, is put away by this shrift: and a man is more bold to doe sinne for trust of this shrift, and of this bodilich penance.

Penance for sin, is mans ordinance, not Gods.

An other mischiefe is, that the people is ybrought into this beleefe, that one priest hath a great power to assoylen a man of his sinne and clennere, then another priest hath

Mischiefes that come by auricular confession

An other mischiefe is this, that some priest may assoilen them both of sinne and paine, and in this they taken them a power that Christ graunted no man in earth, ne he ne vsed it nought on earth himselfe

An other mischiefe is, that these priests sellen forgeuenes of mens sinnes and absolutions for mony, and this is an heresie accursed that is ycleped simonie: and all thilke priests that axeth price for graunting of spirituall grace, beth[1] by holy lawes depriued of their priesthood, and thilke that assenteth to this heresye And be they ware, for Helyse the prophet toke no money of Naaman when he was made cleane of his lepre, but Giesi his seruaunt: and therefore the lepre of Naaman abode with him and with his heires euermore after.

Popish priestes charged with simony

Here is much matter of sorowe, to see the people thus far ylad away from God and worshupen a false god in earth, that by might and by strength hath ydone away the great sacrifice of God out of hys temple: of which mischiefe and discomfort, Daniel maketh mention, and Christ beareth thereof witnesse in the gospell Whoe that readeth it vnderstand it. Thus wee haue ytold apertlie, how he that saith he sitteth in Christes stede binemeth[2] Christ his worship and his sacrifice of his people and maketh the people worshepen hym as a God on earth.

Cry we to God, and knowledge we our sinnes euerichone to other as Seint Iames teacheth, and pray we hartilich to God euerichone for other, and then we shulen hopen forgeuenes of our sinnes. For God that is endlesse in mercy saith, that he ne will not a sinfull mans death, but that he be turned from his sin and liuen. And therefore, when he came downe to saue mankind, he gaue vs a law of loue and of mercie and bade, gif a man doe a trespasse, amend him priuilich, and gif he leue not his sinne, amend him before witnesse. and gif he ne amendeth not, men should tell to the church; and gif hee ne amendeth not than, men shuld shone his company as a publicane, or a man that is misbeleued, and this law was yfigured in the lawe of lepre, who that readeth it, he may see the sooth.

But Lord God, he that sitteth in thy stede, hath vndoe thy lawe of mercy and of loue, Lord, thou biddest louen enemyes as our self, and thou shewest in the gospell, there as the Samaritane had mercy on the Iewe. And thou biddest vs also prayen for them that cursen vs, and that defamen vs, and pursuen vs to death. And so Lorde thou didst, and thine apostles also. But he that clepeth himselfe thy vicar on earth, and head of thy church, he hath vndone thy lawe of loue and mercie. For gif we speaken of louing our ennemies, hee teacheth vs to fight with our enemies, that Christ hath forbodden Hee curseth and desireth uengeaunce to them that so dooth to him. Gif any man pursueth him, hee curseth him, that it is a sorowe a christen man to hearen the cursinges that

The pope breaketh the law of loue, and mercy

(1) "Beth," that is, be (2) "Binemeth," taketh away

they maken, and blasphemies in such cursing. Of what thing that I knowe, I may beare true witnesse.

But gif we speake of louing of our brethren, this is vndone by him that saith he is Gods vicar in earth. For Christ in the gospel biddeth vs, that we shoulden clepen vs no father vpon earth: but clepen God our father, to maken vs loue perfitlich together. And he clepeth himself father of fathers and maketh many religions, and to euerich a father. But whether is loue and charity encreased by these fathers and by their religions, or els ymade lesse? For a friar ne loueth not a monke, ne a secular man neither, nor yet one frier another that is not of the order, and it is agaynward.

The pope would be a father, but he beareth no loue.

A Lord! me thinketh that there is litle perfection in these religions. For Lord, what charitie hauen such men of religion, that knowen how they mowen against and sin, and fleen away fro their brethren that ben more vncunning then they ben, and suffren them to trauelen in the world withouten their councel as beastes? Trulich Lord, me thinketh that there is but little charitie, and then is there litle perfection. Lord God, when thou were on earth, thou were among sinfull men to drawen them from sin, and thy disciples also. And Lord, I trow thou ne grauntest not one man more cunning then another all for himselfe: and I wote well that lewd men that ben laborers, ne trauell not alonlich for him self. Lord our belief is, that thou ne were not of the world, ne thy teaching neither, ne thy seruants that lyueden after thy teaching. But all they forsaken the world, and so euerie christen man must. But Lord, whether thou taughtest men forsake their brethrens companie and trauell of the world, to lyuen in ease and in rest, and out of trouble and anger of the world, by their brethrens trauell and so forsaken the world?

To forsake the world is not to liue in ease from company.

A Lord! thou ne taughtest not a man to forsake a pore estate and trauel, to ben afterward a lord of his brethren, or ben a lords fellow and dwelling with lords, as doth men of these new religions. Lord thou ne taughtest not men of thy religion thus to forsake the world, to lyuen in perfection by them selfe in ease, and by other mens trauell. But Lord they sayen they ben ybound to thy seruise, and seruen thee both night and day in singing their praiers, both for them selfe and for other men, that done them good both quick and dead, and some of them gone about to teach thy people when they hauen leisure.

A Lord! gif they ben thy seruauntes: whose seruaunts ben we that cannot preyen as they done? And when thou were here on earth, for our neede thou taughtest thy seruants to preyen thy father priulich and shortlich: And gif there had been a better maner of praying, I trow thou wouldest haue taught it in help of thy people. And Lord thou reprouest hypocrits that preyen in long prayer and in open places, to ben yholden holy men. And thou seyst in the gospel, wo to you Pharises hypocrites. And Lord thou ne chargedest not thy seruaunts with such maner seruice: But thou seyst in the gospel, that the Pharises worshopen thee with their lippes, and their hart is farre from thee. For they chargen[1] more mens traditions than thy commaundementes.

And Lord, we lewed men han a beleefe, that thy goodnesse is endles: and gif we keepen thine hestes, than ben we thy true seruaunts. And though we preyen thee but a litle and shortlich, thou wilt thinke on vs, and granten vs that vs nedeth, for so thou behited[2] vs somtime: And Lord I trow, that pray a man neuer so many quaint praiers, gif he ne keep not thine hests he ne is not thy good seruaunt. But gif he kepe thine hestes, than he is thy good seruaunt, and so me thinketh. Lord that prayeng of long praiers ne is not the seruice that thou desirest, but keeping of thine hestes: and then a lewd man may serue God as well as a man of religion. *And so Lord our hope is that thou wilt assone heare a plowmans prayer and he keepe thyne hestes as thou wilt do a mans of religion,*[3] though that the plowman ne may not haue so much siluer for his prayer, as men of religion. For they kunnen[4] not so well preysen their prayers as these other chapmen: But Lord our hope is, that our praiers be neuer the worse though it be not so well sold as other mens praiers.

True seruice of God standeth not in long praiers, but in keeping Gods cōmandements.

Lord, Ezechiel the prophet saith that whan he spake to the people thy words, they turned thy wordes into songs and into tales: And so Lord men done now: they singin merilich thy words, and that singing they clepen thy service. But Lord I trow that the best singers ne herieth thee not most: But

Singing in churches falsly called Gods seruice.

(1) "Chargen," care for. (2) "Behited," promised.
(3) These words have been inadvertently omitted in every Edition since that of 1570, in which this document first appeared.—Ed. (4) "Kunnen," they can.

Edward III.

A.D. 1360.

he that fulfilleth thy words he heryeth[1] thee ful wel, though he wepe more then sing. And I trow that weeping for breaking of thy commaundements, be more pleasing seruice to thee, than the singing of thy words. And would God that men would serue him in sorrow for their sinnes, and that they shoulden afterward seruen thee in mirth. For Christ saith, yblessed ben they that maken sorrow, for they shoulden ben yconforted. And wo to them that ben merry and haue their comfort in this worlde. And Christ said that the world should ioyen, and his seruants shulden be sory, but their sorrow should be turned into joy.

Weeping for sins better seruice then singing in church.

A Lord! he that clepeth himselfe thy vicar vpon earth, hath yordained an order of priestes to doe thy seruice in church to fore thy lewd people in singing maten, euensong and masse. And therefore he chargeth lewd men in paine of cursing, to bring to his priests tythinges and offeringes to finden his priestes, and he clepeth that Gods part, and due to priestes that seruen him in church.

But Lord, in the old law, the tithings of the lewd people ne wer not due to priests, but to that other childer of Leuye that serueden thee in the temple, and the priest hadden their part of sacrifices, and the first bygetten beastes and other thinges as the lawe telleth. And Lord, S. Paul thy seruaunt saith, that the order of the priesthood of Aaron ceased in Christes comming and the lawe of that priesthood. For Christ was end of sacryfices yoffered vpon the crosse to the father of heauen, to bring man out of sinne and become himselfe a priest of Melchisedeckes order. For he was both king and priest without beginning and end, and both the priesthoode of Aaron, and also the law of that priesthood, ben ychaunged in the comming of Christ. And S. Paul seyth it is reproued, for it brought no man to perfection. For bloud of gotes ne of other beasts ne myght done away sinne, for to that Christ shadde his bloud.

The order of priestes, not made to offer Christs bodie.

A Lord Iesu, wether thou ordenest an order of priests to offren in the auter thy flesh and thy bloud to bringen men out of sinne, and also out of peine? And whether thou geue them alonelych a power to eate thy flesh and thy bloud, and wether none other man may eate thy flesh and thy bloud with outen leue of priestes? Lord, we beleuen, that thy flesh is very meate, and thy bloud very drinke, and who eteth thy flesh and drinketh thy bloud dwelleth in thee, and thou in him, and who that eateth this bread shall liue without end. But Lord thyne disciples seyde, this is an hard worde, but thou answerest them and seydest: when ye seeth mans soone stiuen vp there he was rather, the spirite is that maketh you liue, the words that ych haue spoken to you ben spirit and lyfe. Lord, yblessed mote thou be, for in this word thou teachest vs that he that kepeth thy wordes and doth after them, eateth thy fleshe and drynketh thy bloud, and hath an euerlasting life in thee. And for we shoulden haue minde of this liuing, thou gauest vs the sacrament of thy flesh and bloud, in forme of bread and wine at thy supper, before that thou shuldest suffer thy death, and took bread in thine hand, and saydest: take ye this, and eate it, for it is my body: and thou tookest wyne, and blessedst it, and saidest: this is the bloud of a newe and an euerlasting testament, that shall be shed for many men in forgiuenesse of sinnes: as oft as ye done this, doe ye this in mynde of me.

The sacrament of the bodie of the Lord abused.

A Lord! thou ne bede not thine disciples maken this a sacrifice, to bring men out of paynes, gif a priest offred thy bodie in the auter: but thou bede them goe and fullen[2] all the folke in the name of the father, and the sonne, and the holy ghost, in forgiueness of their sinnes: and teach ye them to keepe those thinges that ych haue commaunded you. And Lord, thine disciples ne ordained not priests principallich to make thy bodie in sacrament, but for to teach the people, and good husbandmen that wel gouern their housholdes, both wiues and children, and their meiny, they ordeind to be priests to teachen other men the law of Christ, both in word, in deede, and they liuedeyn as true christian men, euery day they eaten Christs body, and drinken his bloud, to the sustenaunce of liuing of their soules, and other whiles they tooken the sacrament of his bodie in forme of bread and wyne, in mind of our lord Iesu Christ.

Priests principally sent to preach, not to say maise, or to make the Lords bodie.

But all this is turned vpse downe: for now who so wil liuen as thou taughtest, he shal ben holden a foole. And gif he speake thy teaching, he shal ben holden an heretike, and accursed. Lord yhaue no lenger wonder hereof, for so they seiden to thee when thou were here some time. And therefore wee moten take in pacience their words of blasphemie as thou didest thy selfe, or else we

He that speaketh Gods teaching, is holden an heretike.

(1) "Heryeth," worshippeth. (2) "Fullen," baptise.

weren to blame. And truelich Lord I trowe, that if thou were nowe in the worlde, and taughtest as thou dyddest some time, thou shuldest ben done to death. For thy teaching is damned for heresie of wise men of the world, and then moten they nedes ben heretikes that teachen thy lore, and all they also that trauellen to liue thereafter.

And therefore Lord, gif it be thy will, help thine vnkunning and lewd seruaunts, that wolen by their power and their kunning, helpe to destroy sinne. Leue Lord, sith thou madest woman in helpe of man, and in a more frayle degree then man is, to be governed by mans reason: what perfection of charitie is in these priests and in men of religion, that haue forsaken spoushod that thou ordeynedst in Paradise betwixt man and woman, for perfection to forsaken traueile, and liuen in ease by other mens traueile? For they mow not doe bodilich workes for defouling of theyr handes, wyth whom they touchen thy precious bodye in the aulter.

What inconuenience by the vnmaried liues of priestes.

Leue Lord, gif good men forsaken the companye of woman, and needes they moten haue the gouernaile of man, then moten they ben ycoupled with shrewes, and therefore thy spoushode that thou madest in clennes from sinne, it is now ychaunged into liking of the flesh. And Lord, this is a great mischiefe vnto thy people. And yong priests and men of religion, for default of wiues maken many women horen, and drawn through their euel ensample many other men to sin, and the ease that they liuen in, and their welfare, is a great cause of this mischiefe. And Lord me thinketh, that these ben quaint orders of religion and none of thy sect, that wolen taken horen, whilke God forfends, and forsaken wiues that God ne forfendeth not. And forsaken trauail that God commands, and geuen their selfe to idlenes, that is the mother of all noughtines.

He complaineth of the idlenes of priestes.

And Lord, Mary thy blessed mother and Ioseph, touched oftentimes thy body, and wroughten with their hands, and liuedé in as much clennesse of soule, as our priests done now, and touched thy body, and thou touchedst them in their soules. And Lord our hope is, that thou goen not out of a poore mans soule that traueileth for his liuelode with his hands. For Lorde, our beliefe is, that thine house is mans soule, that thou madest after thine owne likenesse.

What is the true church of Christ.

But Lord God, men maketh now great stonen houses full of glasen windowes, and clepeth thilke thine houses and churches. And they setten in these houses mawmets of stocks and stones, to fore[1] them they knelen priuilich and apert, and maken their prayers, and all this they sayen is thy worship, and a great herying[2] to thee. A Lord! thou forbiddest sometime to make such mawmets, and who that had yworshipped such, had be worthy to be dead.

Lord in the gospel thou sayst, that true heriers[3] of God ne herieth him not in that hill beside Samaria, ne in Hierusalem neyther, but true heriers of God herieth him in spirite and in trueth. And Lord God what herying is it to bylden thee a church of deed stones, and robben thy quicke churches of their bodylich lyueloode? Lord God what herying is it, to cloth mawmettes of stocks and of stones in siluer and in gold, and in other good colours? And Lord I see thine image gone in colde and in hete in clothes all to broken, without shone and hosen, an hungred and a thrust. Lord what herying is it to teende tapers and torches before blinde mawmets that mowen not I seyen? And hide thee that art our light and our lanterne toward heauen, and put thee vnder a bushell that for darknesse we ne may not seene our way toward blisse? Lord what heryinge is it to kneele tofore mawmetes that mowe not yheren, and worshepen them with preyers, and maken thine quick images knele before them, and asken of them absolutions and blessings, and worshepen them as gods, and putten thy quicke images in thraldom and in traueil euermore as bestes, in cold and in heate, and in feeble fare to finden them in liken of the worlde? Lord what herieng is it to fetch deed mens bones out of the ground there as they shoulden kindelich rotten, and shrinen them in golde and in siluer: and suffren the quicke bones of thine images to rot in prison for default of clothings? And suffren also thy quicke images to perish for default of sustenance, and rooten in the hoorehouse in abhominable lecherie? Some become theeues and robbers, and manquellers that mighten ben yholpen with the gold and siluer that hongeth about deed mens bones and other blind mawmets of stocks and stones.

He complaineth of images in churches.

Lord here ben great abhominations that thou shewdist to Ezechiel thy

(1) To "fore," that is, before. (2) "Herying," worshipping.
(3) "Heriers," worshippers.

Edward III.

A.D. 1360.

prophet, that priests done in thy temple, and yet they clepen that thine heryeng. But leue Lord, me thinketh that they louen thee litle that thus defoulen thy quick images, and worshippen blinde mawmets.

He complayneth of false pastors that liue by their flocke, but feede not them.

And Lord another great mischief there is now in the world, an hunger that Amos thy prophet speaketh of, that there shall comen an hunger in the earth, not of bread ne thrust of drink, but of hearing of God's worde. And thy sheepe woulden be refreshed, but their shepheardes taken of thy shepe their liuelode, as tythings, &c. and liuen themselfe thereby where them liketh.

Of such shepheards thou speaketh by Ezechial thy prophet and seist: wo to the shepheards of Israel that feden themself, for the flocks of sheepe shoulden be yfed of their shepheards: but ye eaten the milke and clothen you with their wolle, and the fat sheep ye slow, and my flock ye ne fede not, the sicke sheep ye ne healed not, thilk that weren to broken ye ne knit not together, thilke that perished ye ne brought not againe: but ye ratled them with sternship and with power. And so the sheepe be sprad abroad in deuouring of all the beasts of the field. And Ieremie the prophet sayth: wo to the shepheards that dispearseth abroad and teareth the flocke of my lesew.[1]

A Lord, thou were a good shepheard, for thou puttest thy soule for thy sheep: but Lord thou teldest that thilk that come not in by the dore ben night theeues and day theeues, and a thefe as thou seest commeth not but for to steale, to slein, and to destroy. And Zacharie the prophet saith, that thou wouldest rerren vp a shepheard vnkunning, that ne wol not hele thy sheep that beth[2] sick, ne seeke thilke that beth lost. Vpon his arme is a swerd, and vpon his right eye: his arme shal waxe dry, and his right eye shal lese his light. O Lord, help, for thy shepe beth at great mischife in the shepheards defaute.

Against hirelings.

But Lord, there commeth hired men, and they ne feden not thy sheep in thy plenteous lesew, but feeden thy sheepe with sweuens[3] and false miracles and tales. But at thy trewth they ne comen not: For Lord, I trow thou sendest them neuer. For haue they hire of thy sheepe they ne careth but little of the feding and the keping of thy shepe. Lord of these hired men speaketh Ieremie the prophet, and thou seyst that worde by him. I ne send them not, and they ronne bliue:[4] I ne speake vnto them, and they propheciden. For if they hadden stonden in my counsell, and they had made my wordes knowen to the puple, ech would haue turned them away from their yuell way and from their wicked thoughts. For Lord, thou seyst that thy words ben as fire, and as an hammer breaking stones. And Lord, thou saist: Lo I to these prophets meeting sweuens of lesing, that haue ytold her sweuens, and haue begyled my puple in their lesing and in their false miracles, when I neither sent ne bede them. And these haue profitet nothing to my puple. And as Ieremie saith, from the lest to the mest[5] all they studien couetise, and from the prophet to the priest, all they done gyle.

Popish priestes neither teach themselues, nor will suffer others besides themselues to teach.

A Lord! here is much mischiefe and matere of sorow, and yet there is more. For gif a lewd ma wold teach thy people trewth of thy words as he is y hold by thy commandement of charity, he shal be forboden and put in prison gif he do it. And so Lord, thilke that haue the key of conning, haue y lockt the trewth of thy teaching vnder many wardes, and yhid it from thy children. But Lorde, sith thy teaching is ycome from heauen aboue, our hope is, that with thy grace it shall breaken these wardes, and show him to thy puple, to kele both the hunger and the thrust of the soule. And then shall no shepheard, ner no false hiridman begile thy puple no more. For by thy lawe I write, as thou ihightest[6] sometime, that fro the lest to the mest, all they shullen knowen thy will, and weten[7] how they shullen please thee euer more in certaine.

And leue Lord, gif it be thy will helpe at this nede, for there is none helpe but in thee. Thus Lord, by hym that maketh himselfe thy viker in earth, is thy commaundement of loue to thee and our brethren ybroken, both to him and to thy puple. But Lord God, mercy and patience that beth tweyne[8] of thy commaundements, beth destroyed, and thy puple hath forsake mercy. For Lord, Dauid in the Sauter saith: Blessed beth they that done dome and rightfulness in euerich tyme.

(1) "Lesew," that is, pasture. (2) "Beth," that is, bee. (3) "Sweuens," that is, dreames.
(4) "Bliue," quickly. (5) "Mest," most. (6) "Ihightest," promised.
(7) "Weten," know. (8) "Tweyne," that is, two.

Edward III

A D 1360

O Lord, thou hast ıtaught vs as rightfulnes of heauen, and hast ybeden vs forgeuen our brethren as oft as they trespassen against vs And Lord, thine olde law of iustice was, that such harme as a man did his brother, such he should suffer by the lawe, as eye for an eye, and tooth for a tooth. But Christ made an ende of this law, that one brother should not desire wracke of an other · but not that he would that sinne should ben vnpunished, for thereto hath he ordained kings and dukes and other lewd officers vnder them, whilke as Saint Paule saith, ne carien not the swerd in vaine, for they ben the ministers of God, and wrakers to wrath, to them that euil done And thus hath Christ ymade an ende of this olde law, that one brother may not suen another himselfe, for that[1] to wreken without sinne, for breaking of charitie. But this charitie Lord hath thy vicar ybroke, and says that we sinnen, but gif we suen for our right And we see I wot that thou taughtest vs some time to giue our mantell also, euer that we shoulden suen for our coate. And so Lord beleuen we, that we ben bounden to don by thy law, that is all charitie, and officers duty is to defenden vs from thilke theuery though we complainen not. But Lord, thy law is turned vpsedowne.

A Lord! what dome is it to slean a theefe that take a mans cattel away from him, and sufferen a spousebreaker to liue, and a lecheiour that killeth a womans soule? And yet thy law stoned the spousebreakers and leachours, and let the theeues liuen and haue other punishment.

He complaineth for punishing litle faults and to let great faultes escape

A Lord! what dome is it to slean a thefe for stealing of a horse and to let him liue vnpunished, and to maintaine him that robbeth thy poore people of their liuelod, and the soule of his food?

Lord, it was neuer thy dome to sayen, that a man is an heretike and cursed for breaking of mans law, and demen him for a good man for breaking thine hestes.

If he be an heritike that breaketh mans law, what is the Pope that breaketh Gods lawe?

Lord, what dome is it to curse a lewd man[2] if he smite a priest, and not curse a priest that smiteth a lewde man and leeseth his charitie

Lord, what dome is it to curse the lewd people for tythings, and not curse the parson that robbeth the people of tythings, and teacheth them not Gods law, but feedeth them with painting of stone walles, and songes of Latin that the people knowen not?

Lord, what dome is to punish the poore man for his trespasse, and suffer the rich to continue in his sinne for a quantitie of money?

Lord, what dome is it to slayn an vncunning lewed man for his sinne, and suffer a priest, other a clearke that doth the same sin, scape aliue? Lord the sinne of the priest or of the clearke is greater trespasse then it is of a lewd vncunning man, and greater ensample of wickednesse to the common people.

: Lord, what maner people be we, that neither keep thy domes and thy rightfulnes of the olde testament that was a lawe of drede, nor thy domes and thy rightfulnes of thy new testament that is a law of loue and of mercy but haue an other law, and taken out of both thy lawes that is liking to vs, and the remnant of heathen mens lawes, and Lord this is a great mischiefe

Against the canon law

O Lord thou sayest in thy lawe, deme ye not and ye should not be demed: for the same mesure that yee meten to other men, men shall meten to you againeward. And Lord thou sayst that by their worke we should know them. And by that we know that thou commaunded vs not to demen mens thoughts, nor their works, that were not against thy lawe expresly. And yet Lord he that sayth he is thy vicar, will demen our thoughts and aske vs what we thinke · not of the Lord, of thy hestes, for they caren little for them, but of him and of this whilke they set aboue thine, and maken vs accusen our selfe, or else they willen accursen vs, for our accusers mowen[3] we not knowne. And Lord thou saydest in thine old law, that vnder two witnes at the least or three, should stand euery matter. And that the witnes shoulden euer be the first that shoulden helpe to kil them

The popes lawe against Gods lawe, in causing men to accuse themselues

And when the Scribes and the Pharises some tyme brought before thee a woman that was ytake in spousebreaking, and axeden of the a dome, thou didst write on the earth, and then thou gaue this dome: He that is without sinne, throw first at her a stone, and Lord they went forth away from thee and the woman: and thou forgaue the woman her trespasse, and bad her goe forth and sinne no more.

(1) "For that," but (2) "A lewd man," a lay man (3) "Mowen," may

Edward III. A.D. 1360.

Sweet Lorde, if the priestes tooke keepe[1] to thy dome, they would be agast to demen men as they done. O Lord, if one of them breake a commaundement of thy law, he will aske mercy of thee, and not a peine that is due for the sinne, for peyne of death were too litle. O Lord, how daren they demen any man to the death for breaking of their lawes, other assent to such law? for breaking of thy law they will set men penaunce or pardon them, and mantaine them as often as they trespassen. But Lord, if a man once breake their lawes or speake against them, hee may done penaunce but once, and after be burnt. Trulych Lord thou sayst, but if euerie of vs forgeue not other his trespasse, thy father will not forgeuen vs our sins. And Lord when thou hong on the crosse, thou praiedst to thy father to haue mercie on thy enemyes.

The breaking of the popes lawe more punished, then the breaking of Gods lawe.

And yet they sain Lord, that they demen no man to the death; for they sain they ne mowen by their lawe demen any man to the death. A leeue Lord! euen so saden their forfathers the Pharises, that it ne was not lawfull for them to kill anie man. And yet they bidden Pilate to done thee to the death against his owne conscience, for hee would gladly haue iquitte thee, but for that they threatned him with the emperour and broughten against thee false witnes also. And he was an heathen man.

O Lord, how much truer dome was there in Pilate that was an heathen iustice, then in our kings and iustices that woulden demen to the death and berne in the fire him, that the priests delieuren vnto them withouten witnes or prefe? For Pilate ne would not demen thee: for that the Phariseis sayden that gif thou ne haddest not bene a misdoer we ne would not deliuer him vnto thee: for to,[2] they broughten in their false witnesses against thee. But Lord, as thou saidest sometime that it should ben lighter at domes day to Tyro and to Sydon and Gomorra, than to the cities where thou wrought wonders and myracles: so I dred, it shall be more light to Pilate in the dome, then to our kings and domes men that so demen without witnes and prefe. For Lord to demen thy folk for hereticks: is to holden thee an hereticke: and to brennen them, is to brennen thee, for thou saydest to Paul when he persecuted thy people: Saule, Saule, wherefore persecutest thou me, and in the dome thou shalt say, that ye haue done to the lest of mine, ye haue done to me.

Pilate more commended then the pope.

Thus Lord, is thy mercy and iustice foredone by him that sayth he is thy vicar in earth: for he neither keepeth it himself, nor nill not suffer other to doe it.

The third commaundement, that is patience and sufferance is also ibroken by this vicar. Lord thou biddest sufferen both wrongs and strokes withouten againstanding, and so thou diddest thy selfe to geuen vs ensample to sufferen of our brethren. For suffering nourisheth loue, and againstandeth debate. All thy lawe is loue, or els the thing that draweth to loue.

But Lord, men teachen, that men shoulden pleten for their right and fighten also therefore, and els they seyn, men ben in perill: and thou bid in the old law men fight for their countrey. And thy selfe haddest two swords in thy company when thou shouldest go to thy passion, that as these clerkes seyn, betokeneth a spirituall sword and a temporall sword, that thou gaue to thy vicar to rule with, thy church.

Lord this is a sleight speech, but Lord we beleuen that thou art king of blisse, and that is thine heritage and mankindes countrey, and in this world we ne bene but straungers and pilgrimes. For thou Lord ne art of this world, ne thy lawe neither, ne thy true seruants that kepen thy law. And Lord, thou were king of Iuda by inheritage if thou wouldest haue ihad it, but thou forsooke it and pletedest not therefore, ne fought not therefore.

But Lord, for thy kind heretage and mankindes countrey, that is a land of blisse, thou foughtest mightilich: In battaile thou ouercame thy enemie, and so thou wonne thine heretage. For thou that were a Lord mightiest in battail, and also Lord of vertues, are rightfullich king of blisse, as Dauid saieth in the Psalter. But Lord, thine enemie smote the despitefullich, and had power of thee and hang thee vpon the crosse as thou hadst ben a theefe, and benomyn thee all thy clothes, and sticked thee to the hart with a speare.

The pope breaketh patience.

O Lord, this was an hard assault of a battaile, and here thou ouercome by pacience mightilich thine enemies, for thou ne wouldest not done against the

(1) "Tooke keepe," that is, tooke heede. (2) "For to," that is, therefore.

ril of thy father. And thus Lord thou taughtest thy seruantes to fight for their ountry. And Lord this fighting was in figure itaught in the olde law. But ,ord men holden now the shadow of the old fighting and leuen the light of thy ghting, that thou taughtest openlich both in word and in deede.

Lord thou gave vs a sword to fighten against our enemis for our country, iat was thine holy teaching, and christen mens law. But Lord thy sword is ut in a shethe and in priestes ward, that haue forsake the fighting that thou aughtest. For as they seyn it is against their order to ben men of armes in hy battail, for it is vnsemelich, as they seyn, that thy vicar in earth, other his riests shulden suffer of other men. And therefore gif any man smyte him, ther any of his clerkes, he ne taketh it not in pacience, but anon he smiteth ith his sword of cursing, and afterward with his bodilich sword, he doth them death. O Lord me thinketh that this is a fighting against kinde, and much gainst thy teaching.

Christes vicar and his priestes will suffer nothing

O Lord whether axsedest thou after swerdes in time of thy passion to againe tond thine enemies? nay forsooth thou Lorde For Peter that smote for great oue of thee, had no great thanke of thee, for his smiting And Lorde thou ere mightie ynough to haue again stond thine enemies, for though thy ooking they fellen downe to the ground, Lord yblessed mote thou be Here iou teachest vs that we shoulden suffren: For thou were mightie ynow to haue gaynstande thine enemies, and thou haddest wepen, and thy men weren hartie haue smitten.

O sweet Lord, how may he for shame clepen him selfe thy vicar and head of e church, that may not for shame suffer? Sithe thou art a Lord, and suffer-dst of thy subjects, to giuen us ensample, and so did thy true seruantes.

O Lord, whether geue thou to Peter a spirituall swerd to cursse and a tem-oral swerd to sle mens bodies? Lord I trowe not, for then Peter that loued iee so much, wold haue smit with thy swerds but Lord, he taught vs to lessen them that cursen vs, and suffren, and not smiten. And Lord he fed thy eople as thou bed him, and therefore he suffred the death as thou didst.

No temporall sword geuen to Peter

O Lord, why clepeth any man him Peters successor that hath forsaken atience, and feedeth thy people with cursing and with smiting? Lord thou iydest in thy gospell, when thy disciples knewen well that thou were Christ, nd that thou mustest goe to Ierusalem, and sufferen of the Scribes and Phari-es, spittings, reprofes, and also the death. And Peter tooke thee aside, and aide, God forbidde that. And Lord thou saydest to Peter, goe behinde me athanas, thou sclaunderest me in Israel. For thou ne sauorest not thilke things[1] iat ben of God, but thilke that ben of men. Lord to mens wit it is vnrea-onable, that thou or thy vicar, gif thou madest any on earth, shoulden suffren f your suggetes.

A Lord! whether thou ordeynest an order of fighters to turn men to the eliefe? Other ordeinest that knightes shoulden sweare to fight for thy wordes? A Lord! whether bede thou, that gif a man turne to the faith that he should eue his goods and cattel to thy vicar that hath great lordships, and more then im needeth? Lord I wote well that in the beginning of the church men hat weren conuerted, threwen adown their goods afore the apostles feet, for al hey weren in charitie, and none of them said this is mine, ne Peter made imselfe no lord of these goods.

Faith commeth not by outward force

But Lord, now he that clepeth himselfe thy vicar vpon earth, and successor to 'eter, hath ybroke thy commaundment of charitie, for he is become a lorde. And hee hath also broken thy commaundement of mercy, and also of patience. 'hus Lord we be fallen into great mischiefe and thraldome, for our chief-ayne hath forsaken war and armes, and hath treated to haue peace with our nemies.

Pope breaketh the rule of charitie, of mercy, and of patience.

A Lord! gif it be thy wil, draw out thy swerd out of his shethe, that thy ser-iants may fight therewith against their enemies, and put cowardise out of our iarts: and comfort us in battail, or than[2] thou come with thy swerd in thy nouth, to take vengeance on thyne enemies. For gif we bene accorded with our nemies til that time come, it is dread least thou take vengeaunce both of them nd of vs together. A Lorde! there is no helpe now in this great mischiefe, ut onelych in thee

Lord, thou geuest vs a commandement of truth, in bidding vs say yea yea,

(1) "Thilk things," those thinges (2) "Or than," before that.

Edward III.

A.D. 1360.

nay nay, and sweare for nothing. Thou geue vs also a maundement of meekenes, and another of poorenes. But Lord he that clepeth himselfe thy vicar on earth, hath ybroken both these commandments, for he maketh a law to compel men to sweare, and by his lawes he teacheth that a man to saue his life, may forsweare and lye. And so Lord, through comfort of him and his lawes, the people ne dreadeth not to sweare and to lye, ne oft times to forswearen them. Lord here is lyttle truth.

The Pope breaketh the law of swearing.

O Lord, thou hast ybrought vs to a liuing of soules that standes in beleeuing in thee, and kepyng thy hestes, and when we breaken thyne hestes, then we slen our soule: and lesse harme it were to suffer bodilich death.

Lord, king Saule brake thine hestes, and thou took his kingdome from his heires euermore after him, and gaue it to Dauid thy seruaunt, that kept thine hestes. And thou saydst by Samuell thy prophet to Saule the king, that it is a maner of worshipping of false gods to breake thy hestes. For who that loueth thee ouer al things, and dreadeth thee also: hee nole[1] for nothing break thine hestes.

O Lord, gif breaking of thine hestes be herying of false gods, I trow that he that maketh the people breake thine hestes, and commaundeth that his hestes ben kept of the people, maketh himself a false god on earth: as Nabuchodonosor did sometime: that was king of Babilon.

But Lord, we forsaken such false gods, and beleuen that ther ne ben no mo gods then thou: and though thou suffer vs a while to bene in disease for knowledging of thee: we thanken thee with our hart, for it is a token that thou louest vs, to giuen vs in this world some penaunce for our trespas.

Lord, in the old law, thy true seruantes tooke the death, for they would not eaten swynes flesh that thou haddest forbidde them to eate. O Lord, what truth is in vs to eaten vncleen mete of the soul, that thou hast forbid? Lord thou sayst, he that doth sinne is seruant of sinne, and then he that lyeth in forswearing him selfe, is seruant of lesing: and then he is seruant to the deuil, that is a lyer and father of lesinges. And Lorde thou sayest, no man may serue two lords at ones. O Lord then euery lyer for the time that he lyeth, other forsweareth him selfe, and forsaketh thy seruice for drede of his bodily death, becommeth the deuils seruant.

Seruant of seruants, the popes stile abused.

O Lord, what trueth is in him that clepeth himselfe seruant of thy seruants, and in his doing, hee maketh him a lord of thy seruants: Lord, thou were both Lord and maister, and so thou said thy selfe, but yet in thy warkes thou were as a seruaunt. Lord this was a great trueth and a great meeknes: but Lord bid thou thy seruauntes that they shoulde not haue lordship ouer their brethren? Lord thou saidst kings of the heathen men han lordship ouer their subiects, and they that vse their power be cleped well doers.

But Lord, thou saidst it should not be so amongest thy seruaunts. But he that were most should be as a seruaunt. Thou Lord, thou taughtest thy disciples to be meeke. Lord in the old law thy seruaunts durst haue no lordship of theyr brethren, but if that thou bid them. And yet they shoulde not doe to their brethren as they did to thrailes[2] that serued them. But they should doe to their brethren that were their seruauntes as to their owne brethren. For all they were Abrahams children. And at a certaine time they shoulde let their brethren passe from them, in all freedom, but if they would wilfullich abiden still in seruice.

O Lord thou gaue vs in thy comming a law of perfect loue, and in token of loue thou clepedst thy selfe our brother. And to make vs perfect in loue, thou bid that we should clepe to vs no father vpon earth, but thy father of heauen wee should clepe our father. Alas Lord, how violently our brethren and thy children ben now put in bodily thraldom, and in despite as beasts euermore in greeuous trauell to find proud men in ease: But Lord, if we take this defoule and this disease in patience and in meekenes and kepe thine hests, we hope to be free. And Lord geue our brethren grace to come out of thraldom of sin, that they be fall in through the desiring and vsage of lordship vpon their brethren.

Pride of priests.

And Lord thy priests in the old law had no lordships among their brethren, but houses and pastures for their beasts: but Lord, our priests now haue great lordships, and put their brethren in greater thraldom then lewd men that be lords. Thus is meekenesse forsaken.

(1) "Nole," would not. (2) "Thrailes," that is to say, bondmen.

Lord thou biddest in the gospel that when a man is bid to the feast he should sit in the lowest place, and then he may be set hyer with worship when the lord of the feast beholdeth how his guests sitteth Lord it is drede that they that sit now in the highest place should be bidde, in time comming, sit beneath and that will be shame and vilenie for them. And it is thy saying, those that hyeth himselfe should be lowed, and those that loweth themselues should be an heyghed O Lord thou biddest in thy gospel to beware of the Pharisies, for it is a point of pride contrary to mekenes. And Lord thou sayst that they loue the first sittinges at supper, and also the principall chaires in churches, and greetings in cheping and to be cleped maisters of men. And Lord thou sayst be ye not cleped maisters, for one is your maister, and that is Christ, and all ye be brethren. And clepe ye to you no father vpon earth, for one is your father that is in heauen. O Lord this is a blessed lesson to teach men to be meke.

But Lord he that clepeth himselfe thy vikar on earth, he clepeth himselfe father of fathers against thy forbidding. And all those worships thou hast forbad. He approueth them, and maketh them maisters to many, that teach thy people their own teaching, and leaue thy teaching that is nedefull, and hiden it by quaint gloses from thy lewd people, and feede thy people with sweuens[1] that they mete, and tales that doth litle profite, but much harme to the people. But Lord, these glosers obiect that they desire not the state of mastry to be worshipped therby, but to profit the more to thy people when they preach thy word. For as they seggen the people will beleue more the preaching of a maister that hath taken a state of schole, then the preaching of another man that hath not taken the state of maistry.

Meeknes commended in ministers Vicar in earth not tollerable in the pope

Lord whether it be any nede that maisters beren witnesse to thy teaching that it is true and good? O Lord whether may any maister now by his estate of maisterie, that thou hast forboden, drawe any man from his sinne, rather than an other man that is not a maister, ne wole be none, for it is forbodden him in thy gospel? Lord thou sendest to maysters to preach thy people, and thou knowledgist in the gospel to thy father that he hath hid his wisedome from wise men and redy men, and shewed it to litle children. And Lord, maisters of the law hylden thy teaching folly, and saiden that thou wouldest destroy the people with thy teaching. Trulich Lord, so these maisters seggeth now for they haue written many books against thy teaching that is trueth, and so the prophecie of Hieremie is fulfilled, when he saith Truelich the false points of the maisters of the law hath wrought lesing. And now is the time come that S. Paul speaketh of, where hee saith. Time shall come when men shall not susteine wholesome teaching. But they shullen gather to hepe maisters with hutching eares, and from trueth they shullen turnen away their hearing, and turnen them to tales that maisters haue maked to showne their maistrye and their wisedome.

Mastership and lordship in preachers.

And Lord a man shall beleue more a mans workes then his words, and the dede sheweth well of these maisters that they desiren more maistrie for their owne worship than for profite of the people. For when they be maisters, they ne prechen not so oft as they did before. And gif they preachen, commonlich it is before rich men there as they mowen beare worship and also profit of their preaching. But before poore men they prechen but seldem, when they ben maisters: and so by their works we may seene that they ben false glosers.

And Lord, me thinketh that who so wole keepen thine hests him needeth no gloses: but thilke that clepen them selfe christen men, and lyuen against thy teaching and thine hestes needelich they mote glose thine hestes after their liuing, other else men shulden openlich yknow their hypocrisie and their falshod.

False glosers

But Lord, thou sayst that there is nothing yhid that shal not be shewed some time. And Lord yblessed mote thou be. For somewhat thou shewest vs now of our mischiefes that we ben fallen in through the wisedomes of maysters, that haue by sleightes ylad vs away from thee and thy teaching, that thou that were the maister of heauen taught vs for loue, when thou were here some time to heale of our soules, withouten error or heresie. But maisters of worldes wisedome and then founder, haue ydamned it for heresie and for errour.

O Lord, me thinketh it is a great pride thus to reproue thy wisedome and thy teaching. And Lord me thinketh that this Nabugodonosor king of Babilon that thus hath reproued thy teaching and thine hests, and commandeth on

(1) "Sweuens," that is, dreames

Edward III all wise to kepen his hests. maken thy people hearen him as a God on earth, and maketh them his thrales and his seruantes.

A.D 1360. But Lord, we lewd men knowen no God but thee, and we with thine helpe and thy grace forsaken Nabugodonosor and his lawes. For he in his proud estate wole haue al men vnder him, and he nele[1] be vnder no man He ondoth thy lawes that thou ordaynest to ben kept, and maketh his own lawes as him liketh and so he maketh him king aboue al other kings of the earth, and maketh men to worshippen him as a god, and thy great sacrifice he hath ydone away.

O Lord, here is thy commaundment of meekenes, mischiflich to broke: and thy blessed commaundement of poorenes is also to broken, and yhid from thy people Lord, Zacharie thy prophet saith, that thou that shouldest ben our king, shouldest bene a poore man, and so thou were. for thou saydest thy selfe, Foxes haue dens, and birdes of heauen nestes, and mans sonne hath not where to legge his head on. And thou saydest yblessed ben poore men in spirit, for thy kingdome of heauen is theiren. And woe to riche men, for they han their comfort in this world. And thou bade thy disciples to ben ware of all couetise, for thou saydest, in the abundance of a mans hauing, ne is not his lifelode. And so thou teachest that thilke that han more then them needeth to their liuing liuen in couetise. Also thou saiest, but gif a man forsake al thinges that he oweth, he ne may not ben thy disciple. Lord, thou sayest also that thy word that is sown in rich mens harts, bringeth forth no fruit. for riches and the businesse of this world maken it withouten fruit.

Pouertie of Christ not folowed

Couetise

O Lord, here bene many blessed teachinges to teach men to bene pore, and loue porenesse. But Lord harm is, poore men and poorenes ben yhated, and rich men ben yloved and honored. And gif a man be a poore man, men holden him a man without grace, and gif a man desireth poorenesse, men holden him but a foole. And if a man be a rich man, men clepen him a gratious man, and thilke that bene busy in getting of riches ben yhold wise men and ready: but Lord these rich men sayen that it is both leful and needful to them to gather richesse togither. For they ne gathereth it for themselfe, but for other men that ben needy, and Lord their workes shewen the truth For if a poore needy man would borowen of their riches, he nele[2] lean him none of his good, but gif he mow be seker to haue it again by a certeine day.

Pouertie counted folly

But Lord, thou bede that a man should lend, and not hoping yelding againe of him that hee lendeth to: and thy father of heauen wol quite him his mede. And gif a poore aske a rich man any good, the rich man will giue him but a litle, and yet it shall be little worth And Lord me thinketh that here is little loue and charitie, both to God and to our brethren.

For Lord, thou teachest in thy gospell, that what men doe to thy seruauntes, they done to thee. A Lord! gif a poore man axe good for thy loue, men geueth him a litle of the wurst For these rich men ordeinen both bread and ale for Gods men of the wurst that they haue. O Lord, syth al the good that men have commeth of thee how dare any man geue thee of the wurst, and kepe to himselfe the best? Howe may such men say that they gatheren riches for others need, as wel as himselfe, sith theyr works ben contrary to their words? And that is no great truth. And be ye seker these goods that rich men han, they ben Gods goods, ytake to your keeping, to loke how ye wolen be setten them to the worshipping of God. And Lord, thou sayest in the gospel, that who so is true in little, he is true in that thing that is more and who that is false in a little thing, who wole taken him toward things of a greater value? And therefore, be ye ware that han Gods goods to keepe. Spend yee thilke trulich to the worship of God, least ye leesen the blisse of heauen, for the vntrue dispending of Gods goods in this world

God is serued of the worst

A lesson for them that have goods well to spend them

O Lord, these rich men seggen[3] that they don much for thy loue. For many poore labourers ben yfound by them, that shoulden fare febelich, ne were not they and their readinesse forsooth me thinketh that poor labourers geueth to these rich men, more then they giuen them agaynward. For the poore men mote gone to his labour in cold and in heate, in wete and dry, and spend his flesh and his bloud in the rich mens works, vpon Gods ground, to find the rich man in ease, and in liking, and in good fare of meate, and of drink, and of clothing Heere is a great gift of the poore man, for he giueth his owne body. But what giueth the ryche man him agaynward? Certes feable meat, and feable drink,

(1) "Nele," that is, will not (2) Ibid (3) "Seggen," that is, do say.

and feable clothing. Whateuer they seggen, such be their werks, and here is litle loue. And whosoeuer looketh well about, all the worlde fareth thus as we seggen. And all men studieth on euery syde, how they may wex rich men. And euerich man almost is a shamed to ben holden a poore man.

And Lord, I trow for thou were a poore man, men token litle regarde to thee, and to thy teaching. But Lord thou came to geue vs a new testament of loue, and therefore it was semelich that thou came in poorenes, to proue who wold loue thee, and kepen thyne hests. For gif thou haddest ycome in forme of a rich man and of a lord, men wold rather for thy dread then for thy loue, haue ykept thine hests. And so Lord now thou might wel ysee which louen thee as they should in keeping thine hestes. For who that loueth thee in thy poorenes and in thy lownes, needes he mote loue thee in thy lordship and thy highnesse.

The pouerty of Christ rightly considered.

But Lord, the worlde is turned vpse downe, and men loue poore men but a litle ne poorenes neither. But men be ashamed of poorenes, and therefore Lord, I trow that thou art a poore kyng. And therefore I trow that he that clepeth himself thy vicare on earth, hath forsaken poorenes, as he hath do the remnaunt of thy law: and is become a rich man and a lord, and maketh his treasure vpon the earth that thou forbiddest in the gospel. And for his right and riches he will plete, and fight, and curse. And yet Lord, he will segge that hee forsaketh all thyngs that he oweth, as thy true disciple mete done after thy teaching in the gospel.

A poore king, and a proud uicar, how ioyne these two together?

But Lord thou ne taughtest not a man to forsaken his goods and plete for them, and fight, and curse. And Lord hee taketh on him power to assoyle a man of all maner things, but if it be of dette. Truely Lord, me thinketh he knoweth litle of charitie. For who that beth in charitie, possesseth thy goodes in common and not in proper at his neighbours nede. And then shall there none of them segge this is myne, but it is goods that God graunteth to vs to spenden it to his worship. And so if anie of them borroweth a porcion of those goods, and dispendeth them to Gods worship: God is apayed of this spending, and aloweth him for his true doing: And if God is a payed of that dispending that is the principal lord of those goods, how dare any of his seruants axen thereof accounts, other challenge it for dette? Serten, of one thing I am incerteine, that these that charge so much dette of worldly cattell, they know litle of Christes law of charitie. For if Ich am a bayly of Gods goodes in the world, if I see my brother in nede, I am hold by charity to part with him of these goodes to his nede: and if he spendeth them well to the worship of God, I mote be well apayd as though I my selfe had spended them to the worship of God. And if the principall Lord is well payed of my brothers doing, and the dispendyng of his goodes: how may I segge for shame that my brother is dettour to me, of the goodes that I tooke him to spende in Gods worship at his nede? And if my brother spendeth amisse the goodes that I take him, I am discharged of my deliuerance of the goodes, if I take him in charity thilk goodes at his nede. And I am hold to be sorie of his euill dispending, ne I may not axen the goodes, that I tooke him to his nede in forme of dette, for at his neede they were his as well as mine. And thus is my brother yholde to done to me gif he see me in nede, and gif we bene in charitie, litle should we chargen of dette. And ne we shold not axen so dettes, as men that knowen not God. And than we be poore in forsaking all thinges that we owen: for gif we ben in charitie, we wollen nother fight nor curse, ne plete for our goods with our brethren.

Christ a seruaunt vpon earth: the pope a lord.

The pope for his right and riches will plead, fight and c[urs]e.

Proprietie of goodes here, is not taken away, but charitie is required to help the neede of our neighbour.

O Lord thus thou taughtest thy seruauntes to lyuen. And so they lyueden while they hadden good shepheards, that fedden thy sheepe and robbed them not of their lifelode, as Peter thy good shepheard and thy other apostles. But Lord, he that clepeth himselfe thy vicar vpon earth and successour to Peter: he robbeth thy puple of their bodylich lyfelode, for he ordeneth proud shepherds to lyuen in ese by the tenth party of poore mens trauell. And he giueth them leue to lyuen where them lyketh. And gif men no wolen wilfullich geuen them the tithinges, they wolen han them against their will by maystery and by cursing, to maken them rich.

Lord, how may any man segge that such shepherdes that louen more the wolle then the sheepe, and feden not thy sheep in body ne in soul, ne ben such rauenours and theeues? And who may segge that the maintaynour of such shepheards, ne is not a maintenour of theeues and robbers? How wole hee

The pope a mainteyner of theeues and robbers.

Edward III. A.D. 1360.

assoile shepherds of their robbing without restitution of their goods, that they robben thy sheepe of against their will? Lord, of all shepherds, blessed mote thou be. For thou louedst more the sheepe then their wole. For thou feedest thy sheepe both in body and soule. And for loue of thy sheepe thou tooke thy death to bring thy sheepe out of wolues mouthes. And the most charge that thou goue to Peter was to feede thy sheepe. And so he did truelich, and tooke the deathe for thee and for thy sheepe. For he came into the fold of sheepe by thee that were the dore. And so I trow a few other did as he did, though they clepen themself successours to Peter, for their works showen what they ben. For they robben and sleen and destroyen: they robben thy sheepe of the tenth part of their trauell, and feden them self in ease. They sleen thy sheepe, for they pyenen them for hunger of their soul to the death. They destroyen the sheepe, for with might and with sternship they rulen thy sheepe: that for dred they ben dispearsed abrode in mountaines, and there the wilde beastes of the field destroieth them *and[1] devoureth them* for default of a good shepheard.

Christ a good shepeheard in deede.

Comparison between the popes sheepherds and Christ.

*O Lord, gif it be thy will deliuer thy sheepe out of such shepheardes ward that retcheth not of thy sheepe, they han their wolle to make themselfe riche. For thy sheepe ben in great mischiefe, and foule accombred with their shepheardes.

But for[2] thy shepheardes wolden ben excused, they haue ygetten them hyred men to feed thy people, and these comen in sheepes clothing. But dredles, their workes shewen that within forth[3] they ben but wolfes. For han they their hyre, they ne retcheth but a little howe sorilich thy sheepe ben kept. For as they seggen themselfe, they ben but hyred men that han no charge of thy sheepe. And when they shulden feden thy sheepe in the plenteous lesewe[4] of thy teaching, they stonden betweene them and their lesewe, so that thy sheepe ne han but a sight of thy lesewe, but eaten they shall not thereof. But they feden them in a sorry sowre lesewe of lesinges and of tales. And so thy sheepe fallen into greeuous sicknes through this euill lesewe. And gif any sheepe breake ouer into thy lesewe to tasten the sweetnesse thereof, anon these hyred men driue him out with houndes. And thus thy sheepe by these hyred men, ben ykept out of their kindlich lesewe, and ben yfed with soure grasse and sory baren lesewe. And yet they feden but seldome, and when they han sorilich fed them, they taken great hyre, and gone away from thy sheepe and letten them a worth.

And for dread least thy sheepe wolden in their absence go to thy sweet lesew, they han enclosed it all about so stronglich and so high, that there may no sheepe comen there within, but gif it be a Walisch leper[5] of the mountaines that may with his long legges lepen ouer the wallys. For the hyrid men ben full certain, that gif thy sheepe had ones ytasted the sweetnesse of thy lesewe: they ne woulde no more bene yfed of these hyred men in their sowre lesews, and therefore these hyred men keepen them out of that lesewe. For haden the sheepe ones ytasted well of that lesew, they woulden without a leder go thider to their mete, and then mote these hyred men sechen them another labour to liue by than keping of sheepe. And they ben fell and ware ynowe thereof, and therefore they feden thy sheepe with soure meate that naught is, and hiden from thy sheepe the sweetnesse of thy lesewe. And so though these hyred men gone in sheepes clothing, in their works they ben wolues, that much harme done to thy sheepe as wee haue ytold.

Wolues in lambeskins described.

O Lord, they comen as sheepe, for they seggen that they ben poore and haue forsaken the world to liuen parfetlich as thou taughtest in the gospel. Lord this is sheeps clothing. But Lord thou ne taughtest not a man to forsaken the trauelous liuing in poorenesse in the world, to liuen in ese with riches by other mens trauell, and haue lordship on their brethren. For Lord, this is more to forsaken thee and go to the world.

He complaineth against the valiant beggers the friers.

O Lord thou ne taughtest not a man to forsake the world to liuen in poorenesse of begging by other mens trauell that bene as feble as they ben. Ne Lord thou ne taughtest not a man to liuen in poorenesse of begging, that were strong inough to travayle for his lifelode. Ne Lord thou ne taughtest not a man to ben a begger to begge of men more then him needeth, to build great castles and make great feasts to thilke that han no need.

(1) From the second Edition of 1570, p. 500.—Ed. (2) "But for," but because. (3) "Within forth," inwardly. (4) "Lesewe," pasture. (5) "A Welch leaper."

O Lord thou ne taughtest not men this poorenesse, for it is out of charitie. But thy poorenesse that thou taughtest, norisheth charitie. Lord, sith Paul sayth, that hee that forsaketh the charge of thilke that ben homelich[1] with him, hath forsaken his faith, and is worse than a misbeleued manne: how then now these men seggen that they beleuen in Christ, that han forsake their poore feeble friends, and let them liue in trauell and in disese, that trauelled full sore for them, when they weren yong and vnmighty to helpen them self? And they wolen liue in ease by other mens traueil euermore begging withouten shame. Lord thou ne taughtest not this maner poorenes, for it is out of charitie. And all thy law is charitie and thing that nourisheth charitie: and these hyrdmen, these shepheards send about, to keep thy shepe and to feden them other whiles in sorryc bareyne lesewes. Lord thou ne madest none such shepheards, ne keepers of thy sheep that *weren[1] ireners about countries and wolden oder ones twyes a yere[2]* feed sorylich thy shepe, and for so litle trauel taken a great hire, and sithen all the yeare afterward, doe what them liketh, and let thy shepe perish for defaut of keping.

Wilfull pouertie abhorred.

But thy shepheards abiden still with their sheepe, and feeden them in thy plenteous lesewe of thy teaching, and gone byfore thy shepe, and teachen them the way into the plenteous and sweet lesewe, and keepen thy flocke from rauening of the wild beastes of the field.

O Lord deliuer thy sheepe out of the ward of these shepheards, and these hyred men, that stonden more to keepe their riches that they robben of thy sheep, than they stonden in keping of thy sheepe.

The propertie of good shepheards.

O Lorde when thou come to Ierusalem, sometime thou droue out of the temple, sellers of beastes and of other chaffre, and saydest: Mine house shoulden ben cleped an house of prayers, but they maden a den of theeues of it. O Lorde, thou art the temple in whom we shoulden prayen thy father of heauen. And Salomon's temple that was ybelded at Ierusalem, was figure of this temple. But Lord, he that clepeth himself thy vicar vppon earth, and sayth that he occupieth thy place here on earth, is become a chapman in thy temple, and hath his chapmen walking in diuers countreys to sellen his chaffare, and to maken him rich. And he saith, thou gaue him so great a power abouen all other men, that what euer he bindeth other vnbindeth in earth, thou bindest other vnbindest the same in heauen. And so of great power he selleth other men forgiuenesse of their sinne. And for much money hee will assoylen a man so cleane of his sinne, that he behoteth[3] men the blesse of heauen withouten any pain after that they be dead, that giuen him much money.

The pope is a chapman in Gods temple.

Bishoprickes and cherches, and such other chaffares he selleth also for mony, and maketh himselfe rich. And thus he beguiled the puple.

O Lord Iesu, here is much vntruth, and mischiefe, and matter of sorrow. Lord thou saidest sometime, that thou wouldest be with thy seruaunts vnto the end of the world. And thou saydest also, there as tweyne or three byn ygadred to gedder in thy name, that thou art in the midle of them. A Lord! then it was no need to thee to maken a liefetenant, sith thou wolte be euermore amongst thy seruaunts.

Note good reader if Christ be where 2 or 3 be gathered in his name, what neede is therof a lieuetenant.

Lorde, thou axedst of thy disciples, who they trowed that thou were. And Peter aunswered and saide, that thou art Christ God's sonne. And thou saydest to Peter, Thou art yblessed Symon Bariona, for fleshe and bloud ne showed not this to thee, but my father that is in heauen. And I say to thee that thou art Peter, and vppon this stone ych wolde bylde my churche, and the gates of hell ne shullen not auailen agens it.

The place of giuing to Peter ye keyes, expounded.

And to thee ych wole geue the keyes of heauen, and what euer thou bindest vpon earth shal be bound in heauen, and what euer thou vnbyndest on earth, shall be vnbounden in heauen. This power also was graunten vnto the other disciples as well as to Peter, as the gospell openlich telleth. In this place men seggen that thou graunted to Peters successors, the selue power that thou gaue to Peter. And therefore the bishop of Rome, that sayth he is Peters successour, taketh this power to him to bynden and vnbynden in earth what him liketh. But Lorde, ych haue much wonder how he may for shame clepen himself Peters successour. For Peter knowledged that thou were Christ and God, and kept the hestes of thy lawe: but these han forsaken the hestes of thy law, and hath ymaked a lawe contrary to thyne hestes of thy lawe. And so

(1) "Homelich," of his householde. (2) See Edition 1570.—Ed. (3) "Behoteth," promiseth.

Edward III. A.D. 1360.

hee maked himself a false Christ and a false God in earth. And I trowe thou gaue him no power to vndoe thy lawe. And so in taking this power vppon him, maketh him a false Christ and Antichrist.

For who may be more agens Christ, than he that in his words maketh himselfe Christes vicar in earth: and in his werkes vndoth the ordinaunce of Christ, and maketh men byleuen that it is needfull to the heale of mannes soules, to byleuen that he is Christes vicar in earth? And what euer he byndeth in earth is ybounden in heauen, and vnder this colour hee vndoth Christes lawe, and maketh men alwaies to kepen his law and hestes.

The pope proued a false Antichrist in earth.

And thus men may yseene that he is agenst Christ, and therfore he is Antechrist that maketh men worshupen him as a God on earth, as the proud king Nabugodonosor did sometime, that was king of Babylon. And therefore wee lewed menne that knowen no God but thee Iesu Christ, beleuen in thee that art our God, and our King, and our Christ, and thy lawes. And forsaken Antichrist and Nabugodonosor that is a false God and a false Christ, and his lawes that ben contrary to thy preaching.

The popes abbomination describ-ed.

And Lorde strength thou vs agenst our enemies. For they ben about to maken vs forsaken thee and thy law, other else to putten vs to death.

O Lorde, onelich in thee is our trust to helpe vs in this mischiefe, for thy great goodnesse that is withouten end.

Lord thou ne taughtest not thy disciples to assoylen men of their sinne, and setten them a penaunce for their sin, in fasting ne in praying, ne other almous dede: ne thy selfe, ne thy disciples, vseden no such power here on earth. For Lord, thou forgeue men their sinnes, and bede hem sin no more. And thy disciples fulleden[1] men in thy name, in forgiuenesse of her sins. Nor they took no such power vpon them as our priestes dare now. And Lord, thou ne assoyledest no man both of his sinne and of his peyne, that was due for his sinne, ne thou grauntedst no man such power here on earth.

Purgatorie.

And Lord me thinketh that gif there were a purgatorie, and any earthlich man had power to delieueren sinful men from the peynes of purgatory, he should and he were in charitie, sauen euerich man that were in way of salutation from thilke peynes, sith they make them greater then any bodilyche peynes of this world. Also gif the bishop of Rome had such a power, he himselfe should neuer comen in purgatory ne in hell. And sith we see well that he ne hath no power to keepen himselfe ne other men nother out of these bodilich peynes of the world, and he may goe to hell for his sinne as an other man may: I ne byleue not, that he hath so great a power to assoylen men of their sin as he taketh vpon him abouen all other men. And I trow that in this he hygheth him selfe aboue God.

Selling of bishopricks and benefices.

As touching the selling of bishopricks and personages, I trow it be a point of falsehed. For agenst Gods ordinance hee robbeth poore men of a porcion of their sustenance, and selleth it, other giueth it, to find proud men in idlenes that don the lewd puple little profite, but much harme as we told before. Thus ben thy commaundements of truth, of meekenesse, and of poornesse, vndone by him that clepeth himselfe thy vicar here vpon earth.

A Lord! thou gaue vs a commaundement of chastite, that is, a forsaking of fleschlich lustes. For thou broughtest vs to a liuing of soule that is ygouerned by the word. For Lord, thou ordeinedist women more frele than man to ben ygouerned by mans rule, and his helpe, to please thee and keep thine hestes. Ne thou ne ordainedist that a man should desire the company of a woman, and maken her his wife, to liuen with her in his lustis, as a swine doth or a horse. And his wife ne like him not to his lustes, Lorde thou ne gaue not a man leaue to departen him from his wife, and taken him another.

Mariage.

But Lord, thy mariage is a common accord betweene man and woman, to liuen togither to their liues end, and in thy seruice eyther the better for others helpe, and thilke that ben thus ycome together, bene ioyned by thee, and thilke that God ioineth, may no man depart. But Lord, thou sayst that gif a man see a woman to coueten her, than he doth with the woman lecherye in his hart. And so Lord, gif a man desire his wife in couetise of such lustes, and not to fly from whoredome, his weddins is lechery, ne thou ne ioynest them not together. Thus was Raguels daughter ywedded to seuen husbandes that the deuill instrangled. But Toby tooke her to liue with her in clennes, and bringing vp

A lesson how to marrye.

(1) "Fulleden," that is, baptised.

of her children in thy worship, and on him the deuill ne had no power. For the wedding was ymaked in God, for God, and through God. *Edward III.* A.D. 1360.

A Lord, the people is farre ygo from thys maner of wedding. For now men wedden their wiues for fairenes, other for riches, or some such other fleshlich lusts. And Lord, so it preueth by them for the most part. For a man shall not finde two wedded in a land, where the husband loues the wife, and the wife is buxum to the man, as they shoulden after thy law of marriage. But other the man loues not his wife, or the wife is not buxum to her man. And thus Lord is the rule of prefe, that neuer fayleth no preue whether it be done by thee or no. And Lord, all this mischiefe is common among thy people, for that they know not thy word, but their shepheards and hyred men fedden them with their sweuens[1] and leasings. And Lord, where they shoulden gon before vs in the field, they seggen their order is so holy for thy marriage. And Lord, he that calleth himself thy vicar vpon earth, will not suffren priests to taken them wyues, for that is against his law: but Lord, he will dispensen with them to kepen horen for a certaine somme of mony. And Lord, all horedome is forfended in thy lawe. And Lord, thou neuer forfendest priests their wiues, ner thy apostles neither. And well I wote in our land, priestes hadden wiues vntill Anselmus daies in the yeare of our Lord God, a leuen hundred and twentie and nine, as Huntingdon writes. And Lord, this makes people for the most part beleuen, that lecherie is no synne. Therefore wee lewd men prayen thee that thou wolt send vs shepheardes of thine owne that wolen feden thy flocke in thy lesewe, and gon before them selfe, and so written thy law in our harts, that from the least to the most all they mayen knowen thee. And Lord, geue our king and his lords, hart to defenden thy true shepheardes and thy sheepe from out of the wolues mouthes, and grace to know thee that art the true Christ, the sonne of thy heauenly father, from the Antichrist, that is the sonne of pride. And Lord, geue vs thy poore sheepe patience and strength to suffer for thy law, the cruelnes of the mischieuous wolues. And Lord, as thou hast promised, shorten these dayes. Lord we axen this now, for more need was there neuer.

Priests had wyues to the time of Anselmus.

I doubt not, gentle reader, but in reading this goodly treatise above prefixed, the matter is manifest and plain of itself without any further explication, what is to be thought and judged of this vicar of Christ, and successor of Peter, whom we call the bishop of Rome; whose life here thou seest not only to be disordered in all points, swerving from the steps and example of Christ the prince and bishop of our souls, but also whose laws and doctrines are so repugnant and contrary to the precepts and rule of the gospel, that almost there is no convenience between them; as in the perusing of this complaining prayer thou mayest notoriously understand. Wherefore, having no need to stand in any further expressing of this matter, but leaving it to thine own consideration and discretion, I will speed myself (Christ willing) to proceed toward the time of John Wickliff and his fellows, taking in the order of years as I go, such things by the way, as both happened before the said time of Wickliff, and also may the better prepare the mind of the reader to the entering of that story; where, first, I think it not inconvenient to infer a prophetical parable, written about this time, or not much before, which the author morally applieth unto the bishop of Rome. To what author this prophecy or moral is to be ascribed, I have not certainly to affirm: some say, that Rupescissanus (of whom mention is made before) was the author thereof, and allege it out of Froysard; but in Froysard, as yet, I have not found it. In the mean season, as I have found it in Latin expressed, because it painteth out the

(1) "Sweuens," that is, dreames.

Edward III. A.D. 1360.

pope so rightly in his feathers and colours; as I thought the thing was not to be omitted, so I took this present place, as most fit (although peradventure missing the order of years a little) to insert the same. The effect of the parable followeth here underwritten.

In the time of pope Innocent VI. above specified, this Johannes de Rupescissa, a friar, among his other prophecies marvellously forespake (as allegeth Froysard, who both heard and saw him) of the taking of John the French king, prisoner, and brought forth many other notable collections concerning the perils, mutations and changings in the church to come. At the time the pope kept him at Avignon in prison (where Froysard is said to have seen him, and to have spoken with him), the said Froysard heard in the pope's court this example and parable recited by the aforesaid friar Rupescissanus, to the two cardinals, to wit, cardinal Hostiensis, and cardinal Auxerrensis, which followeth in these words:

A Parable prophesying the Destruction of the Pope.

When, on a certain time, a bird was brought into the world all bare and without feathers, the other birds hearing thereof, came to visit her: and as they saw her to be a marvellously fair and beautiful bird, they counselled together how they might best do her good, since by no means without feathers she might either fly, or live commodiously. They all wished her to live for her excellent form and beauty's sake, insomuch that among them all there was not one that would not grant some part of her own feathers to deck this bird withal: yea, and the more trim they saw her to be, the more feathers still they gave unto her, so that by this means she was passing well penned and feathered, and began to fly. The other birds that thus had adorned her with goodly feathers, beholding her to fly abroad, were marvellously delighted therewith. In the end this bird seeing herself so gorgeously feathered, and of all the rest to be had in honour, began to wax proud and haughty; insomuch that she had no regard at all unto them, by whom she was advanced: yea, she punged them with her beak, plucked them by the skin and feathers, and in all places hurt them. Whereupon the birds sitting in council again, called the matter in question, demanding one of another what was best to be done touching this unkind bird, whom they lovingly with their own feathers had decked and adorned; affirming that they gave not their feathers, to the intent that she, thereby puffed up with pride, should contemptuously despise them all. The peacock therefore answereth first, "Truly," saith he, "for that she is bravely set forth with my painted feathers, I will again take them from her." Then saith the falcon, "And I also will have mine again." This sentence at length took place among them all, so that every one plucked from her those feathers which before they had given, challenging to them their own again. Now this proud bird, seeing herself thus to be dealt withal, began, forthwith, to abate her haughty stomach, and humbly to submit herself, openly confessing and acknowledging, that of herself she had nothing, but that her feathers, her honour, and other ornaments were their gift; she came into the world all naked and bare; they clad her with comely feathers, and, therefore, of right may they receive them again. Wherefore, in most humblewise, she desireth pardon, promising to amend all that was past, neither would she at any time hereafter commit that whereby, through pride, she might lose her feathers again. The gentle birds, that before had given their feathers, seeing her so humble and lowly, being moved with pity, restored again the feathers which lately they had taken away, adding withal this admonition, "We will gladly," say they, "behold thy flying among us, so long as thou wilt use thine office with humbleness of mind, which is the chiefest comeliness of all the rest: but this have thou for certainty, that if at any time hereafter thou extol thyself in pride, we will straightways deprive thee of thy feathers, and reduce thee to thy former state wherein we found thee." "Even so, O you cardinals!" saith

The pope compared to a bird feathered with other bird's feathers. The first rising and proud prosperity of the pope.

The decay of the pope described.

Johannes Rupescissanus, "shall it happen unto you: for the emperors of the Romans and Almains, and other christian kings, potentates, and princes of the earth, have bestowed upon you goods, lands and riches, that should serve God, but you have poured it out, and consumed it upon pride, and all kind of wickedness, riot and wantonness."

Edward III A.D. 1360.

The Life and Story of Armachanus, Archbishop and Primate of Ireland.

In the catalogue of these learned and zealous defenders of Christ against Antichrist above rehearsed, whom the Lord about this time began to raise up for the reformation of his church, being then far out of frame; I cannot forget or omit something to write of the reverend prelate, and famous clerk, Richard Armachanus, primate and archbishop of Ireland: a man for his life and learning so memorable, as the condition of those days then served, that the same days then, as they had but few as good, so had almost none his better. His name was Richard Fizraf, made primate and archbishop, as is said, of Ireland; first brought up in the university of Oxford in the study of all liberal knowledge, wherein he did exceedingly profit under John Bakenthorpe, his tutor and instructor. In this time the begging friars began greatly to multiply and spread, unto whom this Bakenthorpe was ever a great enemy; whose steps the scholar also following, began to do the like. Such was the capacity and dexterity of this Fizraf, that he, being commended to king Edward III., was promoted by him, first, to be archdeacon of Lichfield, then to be the commissary of the university of Oxford; at length, to be archbishop of Armagh in Ireland. He being archbishop upon a time, had cause to come up to London; at which time here, in the said city, was contention between the friars and the clergy about preaching and hearing confessions, &c. Whereupon, this Armachanus, being requested to preach, made seven or eight sermons; wherein he propounded nine conclusions against the friars, for which he was cited up by the friars before this pope Innocent VI., to appear; and so he did: who before the face of the pope valiantly defended, both in preaching and in writing,[1] the same conclusions, and therein stood constantly unto the death, as the words of John Wickliff, in his Trialogue, do well testify.[2] The like also Waldenus testifieth of him;[3] also Volateranus reporteth the same. Gulielmus Botonerus, testifying of him in like manner, saith, that Armachanus first reproved begging friars for hearing the confessions of professed nuns, without license of their superiors, and also of married women without knowledge of their husbands. What dangers and troubles he sustained by his persecutors, and how miraculously the Lord delivered him from their hands; insomuch, that they meeting him in the open streets, and in clear daylight, yet had no power to see him nor to apprehend him: in what peril of thieves and searchers he was, and yet the Lord delivered him; yea, and caused his money, being taken from him, to be restored again to him by portions

His commendation

Armachanus cited by the friars to appear before the pope

Troubles and persecutions of Armachanus.

Persecuted manifold ways, by the Lord

(1) For his numerous writings on this subject, see Catalogue of MSS. Angl et Hibern —Ed

(2) Ab Anglorum episcopis conductus Armachanus novem in Avinione conclusiones coram Innocentio VI. et suorum cardinalium cœtu, contra fratrum mendicitatum, audacter publicavit, verboque ac scriptis ad mortem usque defendit

(3) In fasciculo zizaniorum

in time of his necessity and famine: also in what dangers he was of the king's officers, who, coming with the king's letters, laid all the havens for him; yet how the Lord Jesus delivered him, showing him by what ways to escape them; moreover what appeals were laid against him, to the number of sixteen; and yet how the Lord gave him to triumph over all his enemies; how the Lord also taught him and brought him out of the profound vanities of Aristotle's subtlety, to the study of the Scriptures of God: all this, with much more, he himself expresseth in a certain prayer or confession made to Christ Jesus our Lord, in which he describeth almost the whole history of his own life; which prayer I have to show in old writing hand, and hereafter (Christ willing) intend, as time serveth, to publish the same.[1]

Thus what were the troubles of this good man, and how he was cited up by the friars to the pope, you have partly heard. Now, what were his reasons and arguments wherewith he defended his cause in the pope's presence, followeth to be declared; for the tractation whereof, first, I must put the reader in remembrance of the controversy mentioned before in the story of Gulielmus de Sancto Amore, p. 510; also in the story of the university of Paris contending against the friars, p. 712; for so long did this controversy continue in the church, from A. D. 1240, when the Oxford men began first to stand against the friars, to the time of this Armachanus, A. D. 1360; and after this time yet more did it increase. So it pleased the secret providence of God, for what cause he best knoweth, to suffer his church to be entangled and exercised sometimes with matters and controversies of no great importance; either to keep the vanity of men's wits thus occupied from idleness, or else to prepare their minds, by these smaller matters, to the consideration and searching out of other things more grave and weighty. Like as now in these our queen's days we see what tragedies be raised up in England about forms and fashions of ministers' wearings, what troubles grow, what placing and displacing there is about the same. Even so at this time happened the like stir about the liberties and privileges of the friars, which not a little troubled and occupied almost all the churches and divines throughout Christendom. This controversy, to the intent it may better be understood, all the circumstances thereof being explained, we will first begin, from the original and foundation of the matter, to declare by order and course of years, upon what occasion this variance first rising, in continuance of time increased and multiplied by gathering more matter, and burst out at length in this tumultuous contention among learned men.

Concerning therefore this present matter; first, it is to be understood, that (A. D. 1215), under pope Innocent III., was called a general council at Lateran, mentioned before (p. 334), in the days of king John. In that council, among many other things, was constituted a certain law or canon, beginning "Omnis utriusque sexus," &c. the tenor of which canon in English is thus:—

(1) *The beginning of the prayer in Latin is this* "Tibi laus, tibi gloria, tibi gratiarum actio, Jesu piissime, Jesu potentissime, Jesu dulcissime, qui dixisti, ego sum via, veritas et vita. Via sine devio, veritas sine nubilo, et vita sine termino. Quod tute viam mihi ostendisti, tute verum veritatem me docuisti, et tute vitam mihi promisisti. Via eras mihi in exilio; veritas eras in consilio, et vita eris mihi in præmio." [This beautiful prayer, which is in the MSS. of the Bodleian library, will be given in the Appendix.—ED.]

Be it decreed, that every faithful Christian, both man and woman, coming to the years of discretion, shall confess himself alone of all his sins to the priest of his own proper parish, once in the year at least, and that he shall endeavour, by his own self, to fulfil the penance, whensoever he receiveth the sacrament of the Eucharist, at least at the time of Easter, unless by the assent of his minister, upon some reasonable cause, he abstain for the time. Otherwise doing, let him both lack the communion of the church being alive, and christian burial when he is dead. Wherefore be it decreed, that this wholesome constitution shall be published accustomably in churches, to the end that no man, of ignorance or blindness, make to himself a cloak of excuse. And if any shall confess himself to any other priest than of his own parish upon any just cause, let him first ask and obtain license of his own priest. otherwise the priest shall have no power to bind him or to loose him, &c.

Note here, he calleth it not the sacrament of the altar.

In the time of this Innocent, and of this Lateran council, was Dominic, the first author and founder of the preaching friars; who laboured to the said pope Innocent for the confirmation of his order, but did not obtain it in his life time.

The next year after this Lateran council[1] died pope Innocent, A.D. 1216, after whom came Honorius III., who in the first year of his popedom confirmed the order of the friars Dominic, and gave to him and his friars authority to preach, and to hear confessions, with divers other privileges. And under this pope, who governed ten years, lived Dominic five years after the confirmation of his order, and died A.D. 1221. About that year the order of the Franciscan friars began also to breed, and to spread in the world, through preaching and hearing confessions.

After this Honorius, next followed Pope Gregory IX., about A.D. 1228, who, for the promoting of the aforesaid order of Dominics, gave out this bull, in tenor as followeth:—

The Bull of Pope Gregory in the behalf of the Dominic Friars.

Gregorius bishop, servant of God's servants, to his reverend brethren, archbishops, bishops, and to his well-beloved children, abbots, priors, and to all prelates of churches, to whomsoever these presents shall come, greeting, and apostolical blessing. Because iniquity[2] hath abounded, and the charity of many hath waxed cold, behold, the Lord hath raised up the order of our well-beloved children the preaching friars, who not seeing things of their own, but pertaining to Jesus Christ, for the extirpating of heresies, as well as for the rooting out also of other pernicious pestilences, have dedicated themselves to the preaching of the word[3] of God. We therefore, minding to advance their sacred purpose, &c., command you to see the said persons, gently to be received among you; and that your flocks committed to your charge do receive devoutly the seed of God's word out of their mouth, and do confess their sins unto them, all such as list, whom we have authorized to the same, to hear confessions, and to enjoin penance, &c. Dat. Perusii. An. Pont. nostri 8.

Friars to hear confessions, and enjoin penance

This pope Gregory died A.D. 1241, after whom came Celestine IV. and sat but eighteen days: then came Innocent IV., and sat eleven years and six months; who, although he began first to favour the friars, yet afterwards, being altered by certain divines of universities, prelates of churches, and curates, he debarred them of their liberties

Innocent IV against the friars.

(1) Friar Dominic, in the time of pope Innocent III., obtained not the confirmation of his order, but the order was first confirmed by pope Honorius III. The order of Franciscans was confirmed shortly after the Dominics.
(2) Iniquity hath abounded at Rome
(3) Nay, to the preaching rather of men's traditions against the word of God

Edward III — A.D. 1360.

and privileges, and gave out again precepts and excommunications, as well against the friars, as all other religious persons. And, not long after the same, he was despatched.

Alexander IV undoeth the acts of his predecessor

Innocent being thus removed out of the way, about A.D. 1254 succeeded pope Alexander IV., a great maintainer of the friars, and sat seven years. He revoked and repealed the acts and writings of pope Innocent his predecessor, given forth against the friars; wherewith the divines and students of Paris being not well contented, stirred up four principal doctors. the first and chief captain was Gulielmus de Sancto Amore, mentioned before (p. 510), against whom wrote Albertus Magnus, and Thomas Aquinas; and, at last, he was condemned by this aforesaid pope Alexander IV. in the Extravagant, "Non sine mulcta." The second was Simon Jornalensis; the third Godfridus de Fontibus; the fourth Henricus de Gandavo. These four, with other their accomplices, compiled a certain book against the begging order of friars, both Dominicans and Franciscans, entitled, 'De periculis Ecclesiæ,' containing fourteen chapters, whereof the fourteenth, which is the last, with thirty-nine articles against the friars, we have already translated and expressed, p. 511. Besides these thirty-nine articles, be other seven articles, moreover, to the said book annexed, under the name of the students of Paris against the friars, proving why the said friars ought not to be admitted into their society. These seven articles, because they are but short, I thought here better to place, than to omit them.

Four champions against the friars

Certain Articles given out by the Students of Paris, against the Friars, why they should not be admitted to their Society.

First, We say, they are not to be admitted to the society of our school, but upon our will and license, for our company or fellowship ought not to be coactive but voluntary and free.

Secondly, We say they are not to be admitted, forasmuch as we oft proved their community manifold ways to be hurtful and incommodious.

Thirdly, Seeing they be of a diverse profession from us, for they are called regular, and not scholastic, we, therefore, ought not to be joined and associated together in one scholastic office; forasmuch as the council of Spain doth say, "Thou shalt not plough with an ox and with an ass together," which is to say,—Men of divers professions ought not together to be matched in one kind of calling, or standing, for their studies and conditions be disagreeing and dissevered from ours, and cannot frame or couple together in one communion.

The friars make dissensions

Fourthly, We affirm by the apostle that they are not to be admitted, because they work dissensions and offences; for so saith the apostle [Rom. xvi.] "We desire you, brethren, that ye observe and take heed of such as make dissensions and offences about the doctrine which you have learned by the apostles, and avoid them; for such serve not the Lord, but their own belly." Gloss "Some they flatter, some they backbite, whereby they might feed their bellies." "That through their sweet and pleasant words, and by their benedictions, they may deceive the hearts of the simple." Gloss. "That is, with their fine sugared and trimly couched words they set forth their own traditions, wherewith they beguile the hearts of the simple innocents."

Devour men's houses, "Penetrantes domos"

Fifthly, We say they are not to be admitted, for that we fear lest they be in the number of them, who go about and devour men's houses: for they thrust in themselves into every man's house, searching and sacking the conscience and states of all persons · and whom they find easy to be seduced, as women, such they do circumvent, and lead them away from the counsels of their prelates, binding them either in act or oath: such we are warned by the apostle to avoid.

Sixthly, We say they are to be avoided, because we fear they are false prophets, who being neither bishops, nor parish priests, nor yet their vicars, nor sent by them, yet they preach (not sent) against the mind of the apostle [Rom. x.], saying, "How shall they preach except they be sent?" for else there appeareth in them no such great virtue, for the which they ought to be admitted to preach uncalled. Seeing therefore that such are so dangerous to the church, they ought to be avoided.

Edward III. A.D. 1360.

Preach uncalled.

Seventhly, We say they are not to be admitted, because they be a people so curious in searching and inquiring of other men's doings and spiritual demeanour. And yet be they neither apostles, nor yet successors of the apostles, as bishops; nor of the number of the seventy-two disciples of the Lord, nor their successors, that is, parish priests, nor their helpers, nor yet vicars. Wherefore, seeing they live thus in no order, by the sentence of the apostle we are commanded to avoid them [2 Thess. iii.], where he saith, "We admonish and denounce unto you, O brethren! in the name of our Lord Jesus Christ," (that is, as the gloss saith, "We command you by the authority of Christ,") "that you withdraw yourselves from every brother that walketh inordinately, and not after the tradition which you have received of us," &c. Look upon the common gloss of this place, and you shall find, that such are to be avoided till such time as they amend from so doing, &c.

Have no order of any calling in the church.

Besides these articles above rehearsed, certain propositions or conclusions were also propounded in the schools of Paris at the same time, solemnly to be disputed and defended against the friars; which, in a brief sum of words to collect them, were these:—

First, That the begging friars were not in the state of salvation.

Secondly, That they were bound to labour with their hands that could, and not to beg.

Thirdly, That they ought not to exercise the office of preaching, or to hear the confessions of them that will come unto them, although being licensed thereunto by the bishop of Rome, or by the diocesan; forasmuch as the same is prejudicial to the ministers and priests of the parishes.

Certain conclusions in the university of Paris to be disputed of against the friars.

All these aforesaid articles and conclusions, with the book set forth by these men of Paris, this pope Alexander IV. condemned to be abolished and burned, writing his precepts to the French king, and also to the university of Paris, in favour of the friars; willing and commanding the said friars to be restored to all their privileges and liberties in as ample manner, as before in pope Gregory's time.

Not long after pope Alexander IV., followed Clement IV., (A.D. 1263,) and sat three years: who also gave the privilege to the friars, beginning, "Quidam temere," &c.; in which privilege he condemneth those who say, that no man without license of his curate or minister ought to confess him to the friars, or that a subject ought to ask license of their ministers so to do, which was against the canon, "Omnis utriusque sexus," &c. made by pope Innocent III., before recited.

Another privilege given to the friars by pope Clement IV.

After this Clement, came pope Martin IV., (A. D. 1281,) who renewed again the canon, "Omnis utriusque sexus," in behalf of the curates against the friars.

Pope Martin IV. holdeth with curates against the friars.

This pope Boniface VIII. began to sit A.D. 1294, and sat eight years and nine months; who, taking side with the friars, gave them another privilege, beginning, "Supra cathedram," &c., in which he licensed the friars, that without license of vicars of churches they shall first present themselves to the prelates to be admitted; by whom, if they be refused the second time, then they, upon special

Pope Boniface holdeth with the friars again.

Edward III. A.D. 1360.

authority of this pope, shall be privileged, without either bishop or curate, to preach, to bury, and to hear confessions, whosoever will come to them; revoking all that was decreed by his predecessors before to the contrary notwithstanding.

By this pope Boniface, a certain Dominic friar was made cardinal, named Nicolaus de Tervisio, and, after the death of Boniface, he was also made pope, A.D. 1303, and surnamed pope Benedict XI.; who, seeing the constitution of Boniface, his predecessor, to gender dissension between the priests and friars, made another constitution, beginning "Inter cunctas," &c., revoking the constitution of Boniface, his predecessor. Upon this constitution of pope Benedict, Johannes Monachus, making a gloss, revoked also his other made before upon the constitution of pope Boniface.

Johannes Monachus revoketh his gloss.

Pope Clement V. holdeth with the friars, and repealeth the constitution of Benedict.

Again, after this Benedict XI. followed pope Clement V., (A. D. 1305,) and sat nine years; who, in his general council, holden at Vienna, revoked the constitution of Benedict, his predecessor, and renewed again the former decree of Boniface, by a new constitution of his, beginning "Dudum a Bonifacio VIII.,"[1] &c., which constitution, moreover, was confirmed afterwards by pope John XXII., A.D. 1316. This pope also caused Johannes de Poliaco to recant.

Upon this variable diversity of the popes (one dissenting and repugning from another) rose among the divines and schoolmen in universities great matter of contention, as well in the university of Paris, as the university of Oxford, about the begging friars, some holding one way, some another. But especially five principal opinions be noted of learned men, who, then disputing against the friars, were condemned for heretics, and their assertions reproved.

Diverse Opinions of Learned Men in this Age against Friars.

I. The first was the opinion of those who contended that the friars might not, by the license of the bishop of Rome and of the prelates, preach in parishes and hear confessions.

And of this opinion was Gulielmus de Sancto Amore, with his fellows, who, as it is said, were condemned.

The second opinion.

II. The second opinion was this, that friars, although not by their own authority, yet by the privilege of the pope and the bishop, might preach and hear confessions in parishes, but yet not without license of the parish priests.

Of this opinion was Bernard, glossing upon the canon, "Omnis utriusque sexus," before mentioned.

The third opinion.

III. The third opinion was, that friars might preach and hear confessions without license of the parish priests; but yet the said parishioners, notwithstanding, were bound by the canon, "Omnis utriusque sexus," to repeat the same sins again, if they had no other, to their own proper curate.

Of this opinion were many, as Godfridus de Fontibus, Henricus de Gandavo, Johannes Monachus Cardinalis, Johannes de Poliaco; which Johannes de Poliaco, pope John XXII. caused openly in Paris to recant and retract. This Johannes de Poliaco,[2] doctor of divinity in Paris, being complained of by the friars for certain articles or assertions, was sent for to the pope; where, time and place being to him assigned, he, in the audience of the pope and of friarly cardinals and other doctors, was strictly examined of his articles. To make

(1) Ex Clement cap. Dudum. (2) Ex libro fratris Engelberti.

the story short, he, at length submitting himself to the authority of the terrible see of Rome, was caused to recant his assertions openly at Paris: the assertions which he did hold were these. *Edward III.* — A.D. 1360.

First, that they who were confessed to friars, although having a general license to hear confessions, were bound to confess again their sins to their own parish priest, by the constitution "Omnis utriusque sexus," &c. His three assertions against the friars.

The second was, that the said constitution "Omnis utriusque sexus," standing in its force, the pope could not make away with, but parishioners were bound once a year to confess their sins to their priest. For the doing otherwise importeth a contradiction in itself.

The third was, that the pope could not give general license to hear confessions, but that the parishioner so confessed was bound to reiterate the same confession made, unto his own curate.

This he proved by these places of the canon law, 25 quest. i, "Quæ ad perpetuam."[1] Those things which be generally ordained for public utility, ought not to be altered by any change, &c. Item, the decrees of the sacred canons, none ought to keep more than the bishop apostolic, &c. Ibid. Item, to alter or to ordain any thing against the decrees of the fathers, is not in the authority or power, no, not of the apostolic see, Ibid.

IV. The fourth opinion was, that the friars, by the license of the pope and of the bishops, might lawfully hear confessions, and the people might be of them confessed and absolved. But yet notwithstanding, it was reasonable, convenient, honest, and profitable, that once in the year they should be confessed to their curates (although confessed before to the friars), because of the administration of the sacraments, especially at Easter. The fourth opinion.

Of which opinion was Gulielmus de monte Landuno. Henricus de Gaudavo also held it not only to be convenient, but also that they were bound so to do.

V. The fifth opinion was, that albeit the friars might at all times, and at Easter also, hear confessions as the curates did; yet it was better and more safe, at the time of Easter, to confess to the curates, than to the friars. The fifth opinion.

And of this opinion was this our Armachanus, of whom we presently now treat. And thus have ye, as in a brief sum, opened unto you, what was the matter of contention between the friars and the churchmen; what popes made for the friars, and what popes made against them; moreover, what learned men disputed against them in Paris, and other places; and what were their opinions.

The matter of contention about the friars stood in four points: first, preaching without license of curates; secondly, in hearing confession; thirdly, in burying; fourthly, in begging and taking of the people. The popes who maintained the friars were, Honorius III., Gregorius IX., Alexander IV., Clement IV., Boniface VIII., Clement V. The popes who maintained curates, were Innocentius III., Innocentius IV., Martinus IV., Benedictus XI.

The learned men who disputed against the friars were, Gulielmus de S. Amore; Bernardus super capitulum, "Omnis utriusque sexus;" Godfridus de Fontibus; Henricus de Gandavo; Gulielmus de Landuno; Johannes Monachus Cardinalis; Johannes de Poliaco and Armachanus. All these were condemned by the popes, or else caused to recant.

These considerations and circumstances hitherto premised, for the

(1) "Quæ ad perpetuam. Contra statuta patrum condedere vel mutare aliquid nec hujus quidem sedis potest autoritas."

Edward III. more opening of this present cause of Armachanus sustained against the idle beggarly sects of friars, in whom the reader may well perceive Anti-
A.D. 1360. christ plainly reigning and fighting against the church: it now remaineth, that as I have before declared the travails and troubles of divers godly learned men in the church striving against the said friars, continually, from the time of Gulielmus de Amore, hitherto; so now it remaineth, that forasmuch as this our Armachanus laboured, and in the same cause sustained the like conflict, with the same Antichrist, we likewise collect and open his reasons and arguments uttered in the consistory,[1] and in the audience of the pope himself, wherewith he maintaineth the true doctrine and cause of the church against the pestiferous canker creeping in by these friars after subtle ways of hypocrisy to corrupt the sincere simplicity of Christ's holy faith and perfect testament; which reasons and arguments, with the whole process of his doings, I thought good and expedient, for the utility of the church, more amply and largely to discourse and prosecute, for that I note in the sects, institutions, and doctrine of these friars, such subtle poison to lurk, more pernicious and hurtful to the religion of Christ and souls of Christians, than all men peradventure do consider.

Thus Armachanus, joining with the clergy of England, disputed and contended with the friars here of England (A.D. 1358) about a double matter; whereof the one was concerning confession and other excheats which the friars encroached in parish churches, against the curates and public pastors of churches. The other was concerning wilful beggary and poverty, which the friars then took upon them, not upon any necessity, being otherwise strong enough to work for their living, but only upon a wilful and affected profession, for which cause the friars appealed him up to the court of Rome. The occasion thereof did thus arise.

It befel that Armachanus, upon certain business coming up to London, found there certain doctors disputing and contending about the begging of Christ our Saviour. Whereupon he, being greatly urged and requested ofttimes thereunto, at request, made seven or eight sermons unto the people at London, wherein he uttered nine conclusions; whereof the first and principal conclusion was, touching the matter of the friars' privileges in hearing confessions. His conclusions were these:

Nine Conclusions of Armachanus against the Friars.

First, That if a doubt or question be moved for hearing confessions, which of two places is rather to be chosen; the parish church is to be preferred before the church of the friars.

Secondly, Being demanded, whether is to be taken, to hear the confession of the parishioners, the parson or curate, or the friar; it is to be said, rather the parson or the curate.

Thirdly, That our Lord Jesus Christ, in his human conversation was always poor, not that he loved poverty, or did covet to be poor.

Fourthly, That our Lord Jesus Christ did never beg, wilfully professing to be poor.

Fifthly, That our Lord Jesus Christ did never teach wilfully to beg, or to profess wilful beggary.

Sixthly, That Christ our Lord held the contrary, that men ought not wilfully or purposely, without mere necessity, to beg.

(1) Ex libro cui titulus, "Defensorium curatorum."

Seventhly, That it is neither wisdom nor holiness, for any man to take upon him wilful beggary, perpetually to be observed.

Eighthly, That it is not agreeing to the rule of the Observants, or Friars Minorite, to observe wilful poverty.

The last conclusion was touching the bull of pope Alexander IV., who condemned the libel of the masters of Paris: that the same bull touched none of these seven last conclusions.

Upon these nine conclusions premised, Armachanus being appealed, cited, and brought up to the presence of the pope, began to prove his aforesaid conclusions or assertions under protestation made.

I. That his intention was not to affirm any thing contrary to the christian faith or to the catholic doctrine, or that should be prejudicial or destructive to the orders of the begging friars, such as were approved by holy church, or confirmed by the high bishops; but only his intention was, to have the said orders reduced to the purity of their first institution. Concerning which matter, he desired his reasons to be heard; which, if they should be found weaker than the reasons of the friars, the punishment should be his. If otherwise, that then the friars might justly be rewarded for their slanderous obtrectation, and public contumelies, and injurious dealings, both privately and publicly, wrought and sought against him: and so taking for his theme, "Nolite judicare secundum faciem, sed justum judicium judicate," &c.; that is, "Judge not after the outward face, but judge true judgment," &c. (John vii.); he entereth on the probation of his conclusion: First, beginning with the former conclusion, "that the parish church was a place more fit and convenient for the confessions or burials of the parishioners to be used, than any other exempt church or place of the friars." This he proved by three causes: first, for the more sureness or certainty to the conscience of the parishioners confessed. Secondly, for the more utility and profit of the penitent. Thirdly, for the less incommodity ensuing, by confessions taken in parish churches, than in friars' churches.

The protestation of Armachanus. *His theme.* *The first conclusion proponed.* *Probation. Certainty. Utility. Commodity.*

I. As touching the first, for the more assuredness and certainty, thus he argued upon the place in Deuteronomy, "Unto that place which the Lord your God shall assign of all your tribes, to place his name and dwell therein; thither shall you resort, to offer up your oblations, tithes," &c. And in the same place God saith, "See thou offer not thy sacrifice in every place that liketh thee, but in that place alone which the Lord hath elected in one of the tribes; and thou shalt do in all things as I command thee." Also upon the words of Leviticus, [vi. 6,] which be these, "Whosoever sinneth of ignorance shall offer to the priest, and he shall pray for him, and he shall be forgiven," &c. Upon these places thus he argued: That forasmuch as the sacraments of the church are to be frequented and used in no other place, but only in that, which, by God himself peculiarly, is assigned and commanded for the same; and seeing that elect place in the law representeth the parish churches; neither can it be proved that the friars' church is the place prescribed of God, but only permitted by bishops of Rome; he concluded, therefore, that parish churches, for confessions and burials, were more sure and certain to the conscience of parishioners, than the exempt places of the friars.

First part of the first conclusion confirmed.

By another reason also he confirmed the same, for that while the parish church commonly standeth free from the pope's interdict, so do not the churches of the friars, which stand not so clear, but that they are under suspicion and doubt of the pope's interdict, by the Decretal, "De sepulturis," in sexto cap. "Animarum periculis." In that Decretal, all such conventual churches and church-yards of friars be interdicted, as do induce any person or persons, either by oath or promise made, to choose their burying places in their churches, as commonly the friars are reported to do; for else what parishioner would forsake his own church and parish where his ancestors do lie, to be buried among the friars, if the friars did not induce them so to do?

Confirmed by another reason.

Moreover, for the second part, concerning the utility of the place, that he confirmed in a double manner; first, for that confession, made within the parish church, hath a double merit of obedience, both for obeying the commandment of God in opening his confession (thus he speaketh according to the blindness of that time, for that auricular confession hath any commandment of God cannot

Second part of the first conclusion confirmed.

Edward III. A.D. 1360.

be proved), and also in obeying the commandment of God in observing the place by him appointed; which second merit of obedience lacketh on the friars' part.

Secondly, he proved it to be greater utility for a parishioner to confess him in his parish church, than with the friars; because, commonly, the number of christian people praying is ten times more in parish churches. Whereby it is to be thought, that each singular person may better be helped through more prayers, than in the oratories of the friars, &c.

Another confirmation of the second part of the first article.

Third part of the first conclusion proved.

Further, as touching the third part of the first conclusion or article he proved, that it had fewer incommodities for every man to resort to his parish church than to the friars; for that both great utility and more certainty (as hath been proved) did ensue thereof: which two being taken away (as must needs, in resorting to the friars' church), then two special commodities should be hindered, and so great incommodities thereof should follow. And thus much for the place of the friars.

Second conclusion or article. Three respects or causes to be proved.

II. Now to the second conclusion or article, touching the person of the friar, and of the ordinary curate. If the question be, which of these two is to be preferred in the office of ecclesiastical administration; the opinion of Armachanus was, that the ordinary curate was better than the extraordinary friar; and that for the three aforesaid respects, to wit, for certainty or assurance, for utility, and for incommodity, to be avoided.

First, that it is more safe and sure for the parishioners to resort to their ordinary or parish priest, he argued by three reasons; first, because the person of the lawful ordinary, or priest, is expressly of God commanded; whereas the person of the friar is not, and therefore is forbid.

Secondly, because the parishioner may more trust to his ordinary curate; as one who is more bound and obliged to provide, and to be careful for him, than any other extraordinary person.

Thirdly, because in the person of the ordinary curate, commonly there is no doubt of any interdict to bind him; whereas on the contrary, in the friar's behalf there is good matter to doubt, whether he stands bound under the pope's censure of excommunication or not, and that for divers causes, as by the chapter "Religiosi, in Clementino de decimis;" where it is decreed, that all such religious men who, having no benefices or cure of souls, presume to impropriate unto them (by any manner of colour or fraudulent circumvention), glebe-land, or other tithes due unto churches, and not appertaining to them, do incur the sentence of excommunication, *ipso facto*. Also by another chapter, "Religiosi, de privilegiis, in Clementino," where it is said, that all such religious men are excommunicated *de facto*, whosoever do absolve any against whom the sentence of excommunication hath been denounced by statute provincial, or synodal; as it is commonly said, that the friars, hearing men's confessions, are accustomed to do, in loosing them, whom the censures of prelates or their officials have bound. Whereof the said Armachanus bringeth forth an example in his own diocese: "For I," said he, "in mine own diocese of Armagh have as good as two thousand under me, who, by the censure of excommunication every year denounced against wilful murderers, common thieves, burners of men's houses, and such like malefactors, stand accursed; of all which number, notwithstanding, scarcely fourteen there be who come to me, or to any about me, for their absolution. And yet all they receive the sacraments as others do, and all because they be absolved, or because they feign themselves to be absolved, by none other than the friars; who, in so doing, are proved to be under the danger of excommunication, both the friars, and also the parishioners, if they, knowing thereof, do consent to their error."

Friars proved to be excommunicated by the pope's law.

Also out of the said Clementine, by three other places in one chapter, he proved the friars to be excommunicate, to wit, in the chapter "Cupientes, De pœnis, in Clementino." In which chapter, First, all such religious men are excommunicate, as, in their sermons, presume to withdraw their hearers from their tithes paying, due unto churches.

Secondly, in the said chapter all such friars are suspended from preaching, and so are excommunicate, who, within a certain time, did not make a concion to such as come to their confessions, in paying their tithes truly and duly to the church.

Thirdly, in the aforesaid chapter also, all such religious persons be bound in excommunication, who induce men by any manner of means, either by vow, oath, or promise, to choose their burials within their churches, or not to change the same, if they have made any such promise before. In all these three points he proved the friars to be culpable and excommunicate.

Moreover, that it is the more sure way for the parishioners to resort to their appointed curates, than to the friars, he argueth thus: for that the parish priest or curate, being better acquainted with his own parishioner than is a stranger, can better judge of the nature and disposition of his disease, and minister to him due physic of penance for the same, and also will be more careful in curing him.

Another proof that the parishioner may more safely go to his curate, than to the friars

Thus the first part of the second conclusion or article being proved and argued, Armachanus proceedeth further to prove the second part: "That it is better for the parishioners to leave the friars, and to resort to their own pastors. Which he proved by eight or nine reasons."

The second part of the second conclusion proved.

I. For that the ordinary pastor is properly appointed of God unto that ministry; whereas the friar is only permitted of man thereunto.

II. For that in resorting to the ordinary of the parish is a double reward of merit, whereas in coming to the friars there is but one.

III. Because the ordinary is more bound to his own flock, and is to be thought to be more tender and careful over them than a stranger.

IV. Because, in resorting to the person of his own ordinary, there is more assurance and certainty (as is above declared) than in resorting to another

V. Because, as Innocent (cap. "Si Animarum") saith, the coming to the curate or ordinary pastor is more easy and light, both in the night, and in necessity.

VI. Forasmuch as the parishioner must needs come to his curate at some time, and especially being in necessity, it is expedient and profitable that his former life before were known to him, rather than to the other.

VII. For that (as the said Innocent affirmeth) it striketh more shame of his sin, for the parishioner to be confessed to his curate whom he seeth every day, than to a friar unknown.

VIII Because it is more profitable, especially for them that live in matrimony, that he which heareth the confession of the one, should hear also the confession of the other; so that one hearing the confession of them both, as a spiritual physician taking two cures in one body, he may better know what spiritual counsel is to be administered to the one, after he had cured the other, &c.

These things thus proved, Armachanus then proceedeth to the third part; arguing how that greater detriments and inconveniences do ensue by confessions, burials, and other ecclesiastical functions exercised by the friars, than by those exercised by pastors and secular curates, serving in parishes; about which matter the said Armachanus learnedly and worthily inferreth a long discourse, proving and inferring how pernicious these orders of friars are to the whole state of the church, and what mischief cometh by the privileges of certain popes, who have privileged them to intermeddle in the office and function of ecclesiastical ministers, to preach, and to take alms and tithes of the people, and unpropriations from the church. All his reasons and arguments to prosecute in order as he hath left them in writing, would make a matter for a large book. Notwithstanding, because it shall not be unfruitful both for the time present, and for posterity, to know the manifold detriments and discommodities received from these friars, and to know what great benefit God hath done for us in unburdening the church of this monstrous generation, and especially because the book of Armachanus is rarely to be found, entitled, "Defensorium Curatorum," I have briefly therefore contracted out of the same certain of his reasons, such as seemed most pertinent and worthy of noting.

Third part of the second conclusion argued

And first, alleging the authority of Innocent IV., he importeth four inconveniences rising by the friars, which be these. contempt of the people against their ordinaries; decreasing of devotion; taking away of shame from the people by confessing to the friars; detaining of oblations, such as the people are wont to give at their confessions and burials, and which by right belong to the parish churches.

Item, By the said privileges of the popes, granted to the friars, many other great enormities do arise. As first, because thereby the true shepherds do not know the faces of their flock.

Edward III.

A.D. 1360.

Item, By the occasion of these privileges given to the friars, great contention, and sometimes blows arise between the friars and secular curates, about titles, impropriations, and other avails.

Harms that come to the world by the friars.

Item, By the occasion of the aforesaid privileges, divers young men, as well in universities as in their fathers' houses, are allured craftily by the friars their confessors, to enter their orders; from whence afterwards they cannot get out though they would, to the great grief of their parents, and no less repentance to the young men themselves. The example whereof Armachanus, in the said his treatise, inferreth of a certain substantial Englishman being with him at his inn in Rome; who, having a son at the university of Oxford, who was enticed by the friars to enter into their order, could by no means afterwards release him; but when his father and his mother would come unto him, they could not be suffered to speak with him, but under the friars' custody; whereas the Scripture commandeth plainly, that whoso stealeth any man and selleth him (being thereof convicted), shall be put to death [Exod. xxi.]; and, for the same cause, the father was compelled to come up to Rome to seek remedy for his son. And thus, saith Armachanus, it may appear what damage and detriments come by these friars unto the common people.

Example of the friars' theft in Oxford.

Friars hinderers of universities.

And no less inconvenience and danger, also, by the said friars ariseth to the clergy; forasmuch as laymen, seeing their children thus to be stolen from them in the universities by the friars, do refuse therefore to send them to their studies; rather willing to keep them at home to their occupation, or to follow the plough, than so to be circumvented and defeated of their sons at the university, "as by daily experience," saith he, "doth manifestly appear." "For whereas in my time," saith Armachanus, "there were in the university of Oxford thirty thousand students, now are there not to be found six thousand; the occasion of which so great decay is to be ascribed to no other cause but to this circumvention only of the friars above mentioned.

Thirty thousand students in Oxford, in the time of Armachanus.

Friars a great cause of decay of learning.

Over and besides this, another inconvenience as great or greater, the said Armachanus inferred to proceed by the friars, through the decay of doctrine and knowledge in all manner of faculties and liberal sciences, which thus he declared: for that these begging friars, through their privileges obtained of the popes to preach, to hear confessions, and to bury, and through their charters of impropriations, did grow, thereby, to such great riches and possessions, by their begging, craving, catching and intermeddling with church matters, that no book could stir of any science, either of divinity, law, or physic, but they were both able and ready to buy it up. So that every covent having a great library full stuffed and furnished with all sorts of books, and there being so many covents within the realm, and in every covent so many friars increasing daily more and more; by reason whereof it came to pass, that very few books, or none at all, remain for other students. This, by his own experience he thus testifieth, saying; that he himself sent forth to the university four of his own priests or chaplains, who, sending him word again, that they could neither find the Bible, nor any other good profitable book of divinity meet for their study, therefore were minded to return home to their country; and one of them, he was sure, was returned by this time.

Books not to be gotten for the friars.

Example what lack of books cometh by the friars.

Friars guilty in three faults: 1. Disobedience. 2. Avarice. 3. Pride.

Furthermore, as he hath proved hitherto the friars to be hurtful both to the laity, and to the clergy; so proceeding farther, he proveth them to be hurtful also to themselves: and that in three points, as incurring the vice of disobedience against God, and against their own rule; the vice of avarice, and the vice of pride. The probation of all which points he prosecuted in a long discourse.

Armachanus chargeth the friars with disobedience.

First, saith he, they are disobedient to the law of God, "Thou shalt not covet thy neighbour's house, ox, nor ass, nor any thing that is his;" in that they procure the pope's letters to preach in churches, and to take burials from churches, with license annexed withal to receive the avails which rise of the same, which properly belongeth to the right of parish priests.

Item, They are disobedient to this rule of the gospel: "So do to other, as thou wouldest have done to thee."

Disobedient to the rule of Scripture.

Item, They be disobedient against their own rule, which being founded upon strict poverty and beggary, this license obtained for them, to require necessaries of the people for their labours, is repugning against the same foundation.

Item, They be disobedient to the rule of the Scripture, which saith, "Let no man take honour unto him, except he be called, as Aaron." Also St. Paul saith, "How shall they preach, unless they be sent?" And how observe they this rule of obedience, who professing to keep the perfection of the gospel, yet contrary to the gospel procure to themselves privileges to run before they be sent?

Item, To their own rule they are disobedient; for where their chapter saith, that if any will take upon them this order, and will come to our brethren; let our brethren first send them to the provincials, to be examined of the catholic faith and sacraments of the church, &c.; contrary hereunto the friars have procured a privilege, that not only the provincials, but other inferiors, also, may take unto them indifferently whom they can catch; so far, without all examination, that almost at this day there is no notable house of friars, wherein is not either a whole, or half a covent of lads and boys under ten years old, being circumvented, who neither can skill of the creed nor sacraments.

Again, the rule of Francis saith, that his brethren Observants must observe not to preach in the diocese of any bishop, without the consent of the bishop; and, moreover, the said Francis, in his testament, saith, that if he had as much wisdom as Solomon, and found poor secular priests in the parishes where they dwell, yet he would not presume to preach without their will, and also would fear, love, and honour them, and all other as his masters, and so they be. Against which rule how the friars do disobey, how little they reverence bishops or secular priests, what privileges, exemptions, and immunities they procure against them, the world may see and judge.

Disobedient to their own profession.

Item, When none may be admitted to preach, or to hear confessions, unless they be entered into orders; and, seeing by the common law of the church, none must be admitted into holy orders, except he have sufficient title of living and clothing; the friars, therefore, having no such title, being wilful beggars, do disobey in both respects, that is, both in entering into such orders without convenient title, and in exercising the office of preaching without such lawful orders.

Moreover, the aforesaid Francis in his testament commandeth thus: "I command," saith he, "firmly by virtue of obedience, to all and singular my brethren wheresoever they be, that none of them presume to obtain in the court of Rome any letter or writing, either by himself, or by any other means, neither for the church, nor for any other place, nor under any colour of preaching, nor yet for the persecuting of their own bodies," &c. Against which testament of Francis, the Franciscans, in procuring their privileges from the bishop of Rome, have incurred manifest disobedience as all the world may see. Neither will this objection serve them, because the pope hath dispensed with Francis' rule. For if the testament of Francis, as he saith, came from God (and so should God have three testaments), how then can the pope repeal his precept, or dispense with his rule, when by the rule of the law, "Par in parem non habet imperium?"

Secondly, concerning the vice of avarice, manifestly it may be proved upon them, saith Armachanus; for else, seeing so many charges belong to the office of a secular parish priest, as to minister the sacrament at Easter, to visit the sick with extreme unction, to baptize children, to wed, with such others, wherein standeth as great devotion; how then happeneth it that these friars, making no labour for these, only procure to themselves privileges to preach in churches, to hear confessions, and to receive license to bury from parish churches, but because there is lucre and gain, in these, to be looked for, in the other is none?

Armachanus chargeth the friars with avarice.

Which also may appear by this, for, otherwise, if it were for mere devotion only that they procure license to bury from parish churches and to preach; why then have they procured withal, license to take offerings, oblations, and legacies for their funerals? And, for their preaching, why have they annexed also license to require and take, of the people, necessaries for their labour, but only that avarice is the cause thereof?

Another proof.

Likewise, for hearing of confessions, when all good men have enough to know their own faults, and nothing list to hear the faults of other; it is probably to be supposed, by this their privilege of hearing all men's confessions, that they would never have been so desirous of procuring that privilege, were it not that these friars did feel some sweetness and gain to hang upon the same.

Another proof.

Item, where the rule of friar Francis forbiddeth them to keep company with any woman, to enter into monasteries, to be godfathers and gossips to men and

Edward III. A.D. 1360.

women; how cometh it that they, contrary to their rule, enter into the secret chambers of queens and other women, and are made to know the most secret counsels of their doings, but that avarice and commodity have so blinded their eyes, and stirred their hearts?

Armachanus chargeth the friars with pride.

Thirdly, that the friars fall into the vice of pride and ambition, the said Armachanus proved thus:

To seek or to procure any high place in the church, is a point of pride and ambition.[1] "Nunquam sine ambitione desideratur primatus in ecclesia."

The friars seek and procure a high place in the church.

Ergo, the friars are proud and ambitious.

The minor he proveth, to have the state of preaching and hearing confessions is, in the church, a state of honour.

The friars seek, and have procured, the state of preaching and hearing confessions.

Ergo, the friars seek and procure a high place in the church, &c.

The third conclusion or article.

III. His third conclusion was, that "the Lord Christ in his human conversation was always poor, not for that he loved or desired poverty for itself," &c. Wherein this is to be noted; that Armachanus differed not from the friars in this, that Christ was poor, and that he loved poverty; but herein stood the difference, in manner of loving, that is, whether he loved poverty for itself, or not. Wherein the aforesaid Armachanus used four probations.

First, forasmuch as to be poor is nothing else but to be miserable, and seeing no man coveteth to be in misery for itself; therefore he concluded that Christ desired not poverty for itself.

His second reason was derived out of Aristotle:[2] Nothing, saith he, is to be loved for itself, but that which (all commodities being secluded which follow thereupon) is voluntarily sought and desired. But take from poverty all respect of commodities following the same, and it would be sought neither of God nor man. Ergo, he concluded, Christ loved not poverty for itself.

Thirdly again, no effect of sin, said he, is to be loved for itself. But poverty is the effect of sin. Ergo, poverty was not loved of Christ for itself.

Fourthly, no privation of the thing that is good, is to be loved for itself. Poverty is the privation of the thing that is good, that is, of riches, for God himself is principally rich. Ergo, poverty for itself was not loved of Christ.

His fourth conclusion against the friars.

IV. "The fourth conclusion was, that Christ our Lord and Saviour did never beg wilfully." Which he proveth by sundry reasons.

1. For that Christ in so doing should break the law, which saith, "Thou shalt not covet thy neighbour's house, his wife, his servant, his maid, his ox, his ass, or any thing that is his" [Exod. xx.]; the danger of which commandment he that beggeth voluntarily must needs incur.

2. Item, If Christ had begged voluntarily, he should have committed sin against another commandment, which saith, "There shall be no beggar, nor needy person among you," &c. [Deut. vi.]

3. Item, Christ in so doing should have transgressed the emperor's law, under which he would himself be subject (as appeareth by giving, and bidding tribute to be given, to Cæsar), forasmuch as the same emperor's law saith, "There shall no valiant beggar be suffered in the city."

4. Item, If Christ had been a wilful beggar, he had broke the law of loving his neighbour; whom he had vexed, having no need. For whoso, without need, asketh or craveth of his neighbour, doth but vex him, in such sort as he would not be vexed himself: which Christ would never do.

5. Item, If Christ had begged wilfully, he had moved slander, thereby, to his own gospel, which he with miracles did confirm; for then they that saw his miracle in feeding five thousand in the wilderness, would have thought much with themselves how that miracle had been wrought, if he who fed others, either could not, or would not feed himself.

6. Item, If Christ had begged wilfully, then he had done that which himself condemneth by Paul, for so we read, [1 Tim. vi.] that Paul condemneth them, who esteem piety to be gain and lucre; which all they do, who, under the colour of piety, hunt or seek for gain, when otherwise they need not.

7. Item, If Christ had begged wilfully, he had offended in declaring an

(1) Chrysost. in opere perfecto. (2) Arist. Ethic. lib. i.

untruth in so doing; for he that knoweth, in his mind, that he needeth not in deed, that thing which in word he asketh of another, declareth in himself an untruth, as who in word pretendeth to be otherwise than he is in very deed; which Christ without doubt never did, nor would ever do.

8. Item, If Christ had begged wilfully, that is, having no true need thereunto, then had he appeared either to be a hypocrite, seeming to be that he was not, and to lack, when he did not; or else to be a true beggar in very deed, not able to suffice his necessity. For he is a true beggar indeed, who, being constrained by mere necessity, is forced to ask of another that which he is not able to give to himself. But neither of these two agreeth to Christ.

9. Item, If Christ had begged wilfully, then why did Peter rebuke the mother of St. Clement, his disciple, finding her to stand among the beggars, whom he thought to be strong enough to labour with her hands for her living, if she, in so doing, had followed the example of Christ?[1]

10. Item, If Christ had begged wilfully, and if the friars do rightly define perfection of the gospel by wilful poverty, then was Clement, St. Peter's successor, to blame, who laboured so much to remove away beggary and poverty from among all them that were converted to the faith of Christ, and is specially, for the same, commended of the church.

Clement's example contrary to the friars.

11. Again, why did the said Clement, writing to James, bishop of Jerusalem,[2] command so much to obey the doctrine and examples of the apostles; who, as he showeth in that epistle, had no beggar or needy person amongst them, if christian perfection, by the friars' philosophy, standeth in wilful beggary?

12. Item, If Christ the high priest had begged wilfully, then did the holy church err wittingly, which ordained that none without sufficient title of living and clothing, should be admitted to holy orders. And moreover, when it is said, in the canonical decrees, that the bishop or clerk that beggeth, bringeth shame upon the whole order of the clergy.

13. Item, If Christ had wilfully begged, then the example of wilful poverty had pertained to the perfection of christian life, which is contrary to the old law, which commandeth the priests (who lived then after the perfection of the law) to have possessions and tithes to keep them from beggary.

14. Item, If Christ did wilfully beg, then beggary were a point of christian perfection: and so the church of God should err, in admitting such patrimonies and donations given to the church, and so in taking from the prelates their perfection.

15. Again, what will these friars, who put their perfection in begging, say to Melchisedec, who, without begging or wilful poverty, was the high priest of God, and king of Salem, and prefigured the order and priesthood of Christ?

16. And if beggary be such a perfection of the gospel, as the friars say, how cometh it, that the Holy Ghost given to the apostles, which should lead them into all truth, told them no word of this beggarly perfection, neither is there any word mentioned thereof throughout the whole Testament of God?

17. Moreover, where the prophet saith, "I never did see the just man forsaken, nor his seed go begging their bread:" how standeth this with the justice of Christ, which was most perfectly just, if he should be forsaken, or his seed go beg their bread? and then how agreeth this with the abominable doctrines of friars Franciscan, who put their perfection in wilful begging?

18. Finally, do we not read that Christ sent his disciples to preach without scrip or wallet, and bade them salute no man by the way; meaning that they should beg nothing of any man? Did not the same Christ also labour with his hands under Joseph? St. Paul, likewise, did he not labour with his hands, rather than he would burden the church of the Corinthians? And where now is the doctrine of the friars, which putteth the state of perfection in wilful begging?

V. The fifth conclusion of Armachanus against the friars, was this, "that Christ never taught any man wilfully to beg," which he proved thus: It is written, [Acts i.] "Christ began to do and to teach." If Christ, therefore, who did never wilfully beg himself, as hath been proved, had taught men otherwise to do; then his doing and teaching had not agreed together.

Fifth conclusion of Armachanus against the friars.

Item, If Christ, who never begged himself wilfully, had taught men this

(1) Ex vita S. Clementis. (2) Quæst. xiii. cap. 1.

doctrine of wilful begging, contrary to his own doing; he had given suspicion of his doctrine, and ministered slander of the same, as hath been proved before in the fourth conclusion.

Moreover, in so teaching, he had taught contrary to the emperor's just law, which expressly forbiddeth the same.

Sixth conclusion against the friars.

VI. The sixth conclusion of Armachanus against the friars was, "that our Lord Jesus Christ teacheth us, that we should not beg wilfully," which he proveth by seven or eight reasons.

1. Where it is written, [Luke xiv.] "When thou makest a feast, call the poor, weak, lame, and blind; and thou shalt be blessed: for they have not wherewith to reward thee again."

To this also pertaineth the decree of the apostle, [2 Thess. iii.] "He that will not work, let him not eat." Furthermore, the same apostle addeth in the same place: "For you have us for example, how we were burdensome to no man, neither did we eat our bread freely, but with labour and weariness, toiling both day and night, and all because we would not burden you," &c.

2. Item, Where we read in the Scripture the slothful man reprehended, [Prov. vi.] "Why sleepest thou, O sluggard? thy poverty and beggary are coming upon thee like an armed man," &c. And again, in the same book of Proverbs, "The slothful man," saith the Scripture, "for cold would not go to the plough, therefore he shall beg in summer, and no man shall give him," &c. Also in the said book of Proverbs, the last chapter, "The diligent labouring woman is commended, whose fingers are exercised about the rock and spindle." And all these places make against the wilful begging of sturdy friars.

The rule of friar Francis.

3. Item, Friar Francis, their own founder, in his own testament saith, "And I have laboured with mine own hands, and will labour, and will that all my friarlings shall labour and live by their labour, whereby they may support themselves in an honest way. And they that cannot work, let them learn to work, not for any covetousness to receive for their labour, but for example of good works, and to avoid idleness. And when the price of their labour is not given them, let them resort to the Lord's table, and ask their alms from door to door," &c. Thus much in his testament. And in his rule he saith, "Such brethren to whom the Lord hath given the gift to labour, let them labour faithfully and devoutly," &c. Wherefore it is to be marvelled how those friars with their wilful begging, dare transgress the rule and obedience of friar Francis, their great grandfather's testament.

4. Item, If Christ at any time did beg, or did lack, it was more because he would use a miracle in his own person, than because he would beg wilfully; as when he sent Peter to the sea to find a groat in the mouth of the fish; which thing yet he thought rather to do, than to beg the groat of the people, which he might soon have obtained.

5. Item, By divers other his examples he seemeth to teach the same, as where he saith, "The workman is worthy of his hire;" also, "The workman is worthy of his meat" [Matth. x. Luke x.]; and when he spake to Zaccheus that he would turn into his house. And so likewise in Bethany, and all other places, he ever used rather to burden his friends than to beg of others unacquainted.

6. Item, With plain precept, thus he sendeth forth his disciples, willing them not to go from house to house [Luke x.] as friars used now to, go. Many other Scriptures there be which reprove begging, as where it is said, "The foot of a fool is swift to the house of his neighbour". [Eccles. xxix.]; and in another place, "My child," saith he, "see thou want not in the time of thy life, for better it is to die, than to lack" [Eccles. xxi.]

7. Item, Where Christ, counselling the young man, bade him go and sell what he had, and give to the poor, and follow him if he would be perfect; he doth not there call him to wilful begging, but calleth him to follow him, who did not beg wilfully.

Seventh conclusion of Armachanus against the friars.

VII. The seventh conclusion of Armachanus is, "that no wise nor true holy man can take upon him wilful poverty to be observed always," which he proveth by four reasons.

1. That wilful beggary was reproved both by the doctrine of Christ and of the apostles, as in the conclusion before hath been declared.

2. Item, A man in taking upon him wilful beggary, in so doing should lead

himself into temptation, which were against the Lord's Prayer. Forasmuch also as Solomon [Prov. xxx.] saith, "O Lord, beggary and great riches give me not, but only sufficiency to live upon, lest if I have too much, I be driven to deny thee, and say, Who is the Lord? Again, if I have too little, I be forced thereby to steal, and perjure the name of my God." Wherefore saith Eccles. xxvii., "For need many have offended." And therefore they that choose wilful poverty, take to them great occasion of temptation.

Wilful beggary not to be permitted.

3. Item, They that take wilful poverty upon them, when they need not, induce themselves voluntarily to break the commandment of God, "Thou shalt not covet thy neighbour's house," &c. Again, where it is commanded, "There shall be no beggar among you," &c.

4. Item, He that taketh upon him needlessly and wilfully to beg, maketh himself unapt to receive holy orders, having, as it is said, no sufficient title thereunto, according to the laws of the church.

VIII. The eighth conclusion of this matter is, that it is not agreeing to the rule of the Friars Observant, to observe wilful beggary; which, saith he, may be proved, because friar Francis, both in his rule, and in his testament left to his Franciscans, doth plainly prefer labour before begging.

Eighth conclusion of Armachanus.

IX. The ninth and last conclusion of this matter is, that the bull of pope Alexander IV. which condemneth the book of the masters of Paris,[1] impugneth none of these conclusions premised. For the proof thereof he thus inferred:

Ninth conclusion.

1. That pope John XXIV., in his constitution, beginning thus, "Quia quorundam," affirmeth expressly, how pope Nicholas III. revoked and called back the said bull of pope Alexander IV., and all other writings of his, touching all such articles, which, in the same aforesaid constitution of this pope John, be contained and declared. Wherein also is declared how strait the poverty of the friars ought to be, which they call wilful poverty.

Pope Nicholas III. revoketh the bull of pope Alexander IV.

2. Item, It is manifest and notorious to all men, how the said pope Nicholas III., in his declaration showeth how the friars ought both to labour with their hands, and how, moreover, the said friars ought not to preach within the diocese of any bishop, wheresoever they be resisted: which being so, the conclusion appeareth that the bull of pope Alexander IV., as touching these articles, is void and of none effect. Besides these articles, there is nothing else in the said bull of Alexander, that I remember, which impugneth any of these conclusions premised.

"Many things more," said he, "I had besides these, both to object and to answer again to the same, and to confirm, more surely and firmly, these my reasons and assertions premised. But I have already too much wearied your holiness, and your reverend lordships here present; wherefore I conclude, and humbly and devoutly beseech you, according to my former petition premised in the beginning of this matter, that you judge not after the outward face, but judge ye true judgment.[2]

The end and conclusion of this oration of Armachanus before the pope.

NOTES TO BE OBSERVED IN THIS FORMER ORATION OF ARMACHANUS.

By this oration of Armachanus the learned prelate, thus made before pope Innocent and his cardinals, divers and sundry things there be, for the utility of the church, worthy to be observed. First, what troubles and vexations came to the church of Christ by these friars. Also what persecution followeth after, by means of them, against so many learned men and true servants of Christ. Furthermore, what repugnance and contrariety there was among the popes, and how they could not agree among themselves about the friars. Fourthly, what pestiferous doctrine, subverting well nigh the testament of Jesus Christ. Fifthly, what decay of ministers in Christ's church, as appeareth. Sixthly, what robbing and circumventing of men's

Notes to be observed.

Contrariety among the popes.

(1) Touching this book of the masters of Paris condemned, look p. 753.
(2) Ex libro Armachani, cui titulus, Defensorium Curatorum.

Edward III. A.D. 1360.

children, as appeareth. Seventhly, what decay of universities, as appeareth by Oxford (p. 760). Eighthly, that damage to learning, and lack of books to students, came by these friars, as appeareth. Ninthly, to what pride, under colour of feigned humility, to what riches, under dissembled poverty they grew, here is to be seen; insomuch that at length, through their subtle and most dangerous hypocrisy, they crept up to be lords, archbishops, cardinals, and at last also chancellors of realms, yea and of most secret counsel with kings and queens, as appeareth.

Whether the friars make up the body of Antichrist or no.

All these things well considered, now remaineth in the church to be marked; that forasmuch as these friars (with their new-found testament of friar Francis), not being contented with the testament of God in his Son Christ, began to spring up at the same time when Satan was prophesied to be let loose by order of the Scripture; whether, therefore, it is to be doubted that these friars make up the body of Antichrist, which is prophesied to come in the church, or not; which is much less to be doubted, because whoso list to try shall find, that of all other enemies of Christ, of whom some be manifest, some be privy, all be together cruel, yet is there no such sort of enemies that more sleightily deceiveth the simple Christian, or more deeply drowneth him in damnation, than doth this doctrine of the friars.

The death of godly Armachanus.

But of this oration of Armachanus enough. What success it had with the pope, by story it is not certain, but by his own life declared, it appeareth that the Lord so wrought that his enemies did not triumph over him. Notwithstanding, this by story appeareth, that he was seven or eight years in banishment for the same matter, and there died in the same at Avignon, of whom, a certain cardinal hearing of his death, openly protested that the same day a mighty pillar of Christ's church was fallen.

Testimony of a cardinal upon him.

After the death of Armachanus, the friars had contention likewise with the monks of Benedict's order[1] about the same year (A.D. 1360), and so removed their cause, both against the monks, and against the university of Oxford, unto the court of Rome; wherein, saith the author, they lacked another Richard.[2] By this that appeareth to be true, which is testified in the first volume of Waldenus, that long debate continued between the friars and the university of Oxford. Against the friars first stood up Robert Grosthead, bishop of Lincoln, above mentioned; then Sevallus of York; afterwards John of Baconthorpe, and now this Armachanus, of whom here presently we treat; and after him again John Wickliff, of whom (Christ willing) we will speak hereafter.[3] Against this aforesaid Armachanus wrote divers friars; Roger Conaway, a Franciscan, John Heyldesham, a Carmelite, Galfridus Hardby, a friar Augustine. Also friar Engelbert, a Dominican, in a book entitled 'Defensorium Privilegiorum,' and divers others. I credibly hear of certain old Irish Bibles translated long since into the Irish tongue,[4] which, if it be true, it is not likely to be the doing of any one but of this Armachanus. And thus much of this learned prelate and archbishop of Ireland, a man worthy, for his christian zeal, of immortal commendation.

Friars against the university of Oxford.

English writers against the friars.

Friars that write against Armachanus.

After the death of this Innocent, next was poped in the see of

(1) Ex Chron. Reg. Rich. II. (2) Ex Botonero. (3) Ex Waldeno.
(4) Testified by certain Englishmen, which are yet alive, and have seen it.

Rome pope Urban V., who, by the father's side, was an Englishman. This Urban had been a waiter a long time in the court of Rome; and when he saw no promotion would light upon him, complaining to a certain friend of his, he made to him his moan, saying, That he thought, verily, if all the churches of the world should fall, yet none would fall into his mouth. His friend afterwards seeing him to be pope, and enthronized in his threefold crown, cometh to him, and putting him in remembrance of his words to him before, saith, That whereas his holiness had moaned his fortune to him, that if all the churches in the world would fall, none would fall upon his head, "now," saith he, "God hath otherwise so disposed, that all the churches in the world are fallen upon your head."

Edward III. A.D. 1364.

Urban complaineth that no promotion would fall upon him. An answer to Urban, being made pope.

This pope maintained and kindled great wars in Italy, sending Egidius, his cardinal and legate, and after him Arduinus, a Burgundian, as his legate and abbot, with great puissance and much money, against sundry cities in Italy; by whose means the towns and cities which before had broken from the bishop of Rome were oppressed; also Barnabes and Galeaceus, princes of Milan, were vanquished.[1] By their examples, others being sorely afraid, submitted themselves to the church of Rome; and thus came up that wicked church to her great possessions, which her patrons would needs father upon Constantine, the godly emperor.

How the church of Rome came by their royal possessions.

In the time of this pope Urban V., and in the second year of his reign, about the beginning of the year of our Lord 1364, I find a certain sermon of one Nicholas Orem, made before the pope and his cardinals, on Christmas-even. In which sermon the learned man doth worthily rebuke the prelates and priests of his time, declaring their destruction not to be far off, by certain signs taken of their wicked and corrupt life. All the sayings of the prophets, spoken against the wicked priests of the Jews, he doth aptly apply against the clergy of his time, comparing the church then present to the spiritual strumpet spoken of in the prophet Ezekiel [chap. xvi.]; and he proveth, in conclusion, the clergy of the church then to be so much worse than the old synagogue of the Jews, by how much it is worse to sell the church and sacraments, than to suffer doves to be sold in the church. With no less judgment also, and learning, he answereth to the old and false objections of the papists, who, albeit they be never so wicked, yet think themselves to be the church which the Lord cannot forsake. All these things to the intent they may the better appear in his own words, I have thought good here to translate and exhibit the sermon as it was spoken before the pope.

A Copy of a Sermon made before Pope Urban V., the fourth Sunday in Advent, A.D. 1364, by Nicholas Orem.

"Juxta est salus mea, ut veniat, et justitia," &c. That is, "My saving health is near at hand to come, and my righteousness to be revealed," &c. [Isa. li.] After the sentence of St. Paul [Rom. ii.], and in divers other places, before the nativity of Christ, the whole world was divided into two sorts of men, the Jews and Gentiles. The Jews, who waited for the opening of the door of paradise by the blood of the Saviour to come: the Gentiles, who yet sitting in darkness were to be called to light, and to be justified by faith, as it is written in Romans, chap. v.

The world divided into two sorts of men before the incarnation of Christ.

(1) Ex Sabel. Ænead ix. lib. 8.

Edward III. A.D. 1364.

This salvation, pertaining both to the Jew and Gentile, God promised before time to the fathers by the prophets, to stir up the desire thereof in their hearts the more, and to increase their firm hope and faith in the same. As first, in Micah vi., the voice of the Lord crieth, "Health and salvation shall be to all men which fear my name." And Isaiah xlvi., "I will give in Sion salvation, and in Jerusalem my glory," &c., with divers other such places. And forasmuch as hope which is deferred many times, doth afflict the soul, and conceiveth weariness of long deferring; he, therefore, prophesying of the nearness of the coming thereof, saith moreover [Isa. xiv.], "His time is near at hand to come." Also [Hab. ii.], "He will come, and will not tarry." With many such other places more. So then the holy fathers being in Limbo, looked and hoped that he should bring out them that sat bound, and which in the house of prison sat in darkness, as we read in Isaiah xli. Then the time drew on, in which came the fulness of the Gentiles, and in which the Lord would declare the riches of this mystery hidden from the world, and from generations. [Col. i.] Wherefore the Lord, in this text, doth both certify our fathers of the coming of our Saviour, and doth comfort them touching the nearness thereof, and also teacheth the justification of the Gentiles by faith, approaching now near at hand, according to the words of my text, "my salvation is near." Which words were fulfilled then, what time the Lord did manifest his salvation, and did reveal his righteousness in the sight of all the Gentiles. And it is divided into three parts; of which the first speaketh of the nearness of his coming, where it is said, "my salvation is near." The second concerneth the mystery of the advent of Christ and his incarnation, where he saith, "ut veniat," &c. Thirdly, is considered the severity of God, his terrible revenging judgment to be revealed, where he saith, "ut reveletur," &c., which is to be expounded of his primitive justice, whereof speaketh Amos [chap. v.], saying, "And judgment shall be revealed like a flood, and righteousness like a strong stream." Wherefore, for our contemplation, let us receive, with joy the solemnity of his holy vigil, the word, I say, of God the Father, that is, Christ. To whom it is said [Isa. xlix.], "I have given thee to be a light to the Gentiles, and to be my salvation throughout the ends of the world:" and again [Isa. xlvi.], "My salvation shall not slack," &c.

Three heads.

The first part of his theme.

As touching the nearness thereof, it is in these days opened to us by the gospel, where we read in St. Matthew, When the virgin Mary was espoused unto Joseph, before they did come together, she was found with child by the Holy Ghost. By this it was evident to understand, that our Saviour ought shortly to proceed out of the chaste womb of the virgin, according as the prophet did foretel, saying, "Behold a virgin shall conceive and bring forth a son," &c. For as the grape, when it waxeth great and full, is near to the making of wine; and as the flower, when it shooteth abroad, hasteth to the fruit; so the salvation of the world, in the swelling and growing of the virgin's womb, began to draw nigh to mankind. For then appeared the grace and benignity of our Saviour, whom his mother was found to have in her womb by the Holy Ghost, as is declared in that which followeth by the angel, saying, "For that which is born of her is of the Holy Ghost."

The second part of his theme.

Touching the second part of that which is said, "ut veniat:" this may be applied to the contemplation of the mystery of Christ coming in the flesh; whereof speaketh Haggai the prophet [chap. ii.], "He shall come who is desired and looked for of all nations," &c. Albeit the same also may be applied to the second advent, spoken of in Isaiah [chap. iii.], "The Lord shall come to judgment," &c.; in memorial whereof the fourth Sunday was dedicated in the old time, of the fathers. And of this day of judgment it is written in the prophet Zeph. [chap. ii.], "The day of the Lord is near, great and mighty, it is approaching at hand, and wondrous short," &c. And albeit not in itself, yet it may be expounded in tribulations that go before, as preambles unto the same; as Gregory saith, "The last tribulation is prevented with many and sundry tribulations going before, although the end of all be not yet."

The third part of his theme.

Wherefore now coming to the third part of my sermon or theme, let us see, of those tribulations that go before the last coming of Christ, if there be any such tribulation approaching nigh at hand, whereof this last part of my theme may be verified, where he said, "Ut reveletur," that my righteousness shall be revealed; to wit, the righteousness primitive, that righteousness may be brought, and the prophecy of Daniel fulfilled [Dan. ix.], concerning which matter four things here come in order to be declared.

Four sub-divisions.

First, Concerning the revealing of tribulation, according to that part of my theme, "Ut reveletur," &c.

Secondly, Concerning the nearness of the tribulation coming, according to that part of my theme, "Quia juxta est," &c.

Thirdly, Of the false opinions of some upon this part of my theme, "Ut veniat," &c.

Fourthly, What means and consultation we ought to take, "Ut juxta est salus."

First sub-division.

As for the first, it is so notorious and so common in the Scriptures that the church should suffer and abide tribulation, that I need not here to stand in alleging any thing touching either the causes to be weighed, or the term to be conjectured thereof. As concerning which causes I will give two rules to be noted before, for the better opening of that which is to follow: The first rule is, that by the two kingdoms of the nation of the Hebrews which were in the old time, to wit, by the kingdom of Israel, whose head was Samaria, is signified in the prophets the erroneous synagogue; and by the second kingdom of Judah, of whose stock came Christ, whose head metropolitan was Jerusalem, is signified the true church. And this rule is not mine, but is an authentic gloss of St. Jerome, and also is the rule of Origen in the last homily upon the Old Testament, and is approved by the church.

The kingdom of Israel signifying the false church. The kingdom of Judah signifieth the right church.

The second rule is, that by the brothel-house and fornication mentioned in the prophets, are signified simony, and abused dispensations, and promotions of persons unworthy, for lucre's sake, or else for any other partial favour, who, by unlawful ways, by all laws of the world, come to office and honour. "Merx dicitur namque a merendo;" that is, because gain or price is derived of gaining; for the which gain or price, that is sold, which by nature ought not to be sold. Therefore, to give any thing for respect of gain or hire, which ought to be given freely for virtue's sake, is a kind of spiritual corruption, and as a man would say, a whorish thing; whereof the prophet [Isaiah, chap. i.] complaineth, speaking of Jerusalem, and saying, "The city which once was faithful and full of judgment, how is it now become a whorish city?" And in like manner Hosea also, the prophet [chap. ix.], "Jerusalem, thou hast fornicated and gone a whoring from thy God. Thou hast loved like a harlot to get gain in every barn of corn." And in many other places of Scripture, where fornication cannot be otherwise expounded.

These two rules thus premised, now let us mark the Scriptures, and, according to the same, judge of the whole state of the church, both what is past, and what is to come: First, treating of the causes of tribulation to come: Secondly, of the vicinity of time of the said tribulation to come.

Five states of the church described.

And first, concerning the state of the church, and of causes of tribulation, thus saith the Lord in the prophet Ezekiel [chap. xvi.], speaking to the church under the name of Jerusalem: "In the day of thy birth I came by thee, and saw thee trodden down in thine own blood," &c. Here he speaketh of the time of the martyrdom of the church. Then it followeth, "After this thou wast cleansed from thy blood, thou wast grown up, and waxen great; then washed I thee with water, I purged thy blood from thee" (speaking of ceasing of persecution), "I anointed thee with oil, I gave thee change of raiment, I girded thee with white silk, I decked thee with costly apparel, I put rings upon thy fingers, a chain about thy neck, spangles upon thy forehead, and ear-rings upon thine ears. Thus wast thou decked with silver and gold, and a beautiful crown set upon thine head. Marvellous goodly wast thou and beautiful, even a very queen wast thou: for thou wast excellent in my beauty, which I put upon thee, saith the Lord God," &c. This prophecy, or rather history, speaketh of, and declareth, the prosperity of the church.

1. The martyrdom of the church. 2. The prosperity of the church.

3. The corruption of the church.

And now hear the corruption and transgression of the church, for so it followeth: "But thou hast put confidence in thine own beauty, and played the harlot, when thou hadst gotten thee a name. Thou hast committed whoredom with all that went by thee, and hast fulfilled their desires; yea, thou hast taken thy garments of divers colours and decked thine altars therewith, whereupon thou mightest fulfil thy whoredom of such a fashion as never was done, nor shall be." Which whoredom can in no wise be expounded for carnal, but

Edward III.

A.D. 1364.

spiritual whoredom. And therefore, see how lively he hath painted out the corruption and falling of the church.

4. The correction of the church.

And therefore followeth now the correction and punishment of the church. It followeth, "Behold I stretch out my hand over thee, and will diminish thy store of food, and deliver thee over unto the wills of the Philistines, and of such as hate thee: and they shall break down thy stews, and destroy thy brothel-houses" (that is, the place wherein thou didst exercise this wickedness) "they shall strip thee out of thy clothes: all thy fair beautiful jewels shall they take from thee, and so let thee sit naked and bare," &c. [Ezek. xvi.] Here is plainly to be seen what shall happen to the church, and more followeth in the said chapter: "Thine elder sister is Samaria, she and her daughters upon thy left hand: but the youngest sister that dwelleth on thy right hand is Sodoma with her daughters, whose sins were these: pride, fulness of meat, abundance, and idleness, neither reached they their hand to the poor. And yet, neither Sodoma thy sister, with her daughters, hath done so evil as thou and thy daughters: neither hath Samaria" (that is, the synagogue) "done half of thy sins; yea, thou hast exceeded them in wickedness. Take therefore and bear thine own confusion," &c. Again in Ezek. [chap. xxiii.], after the prophet had described at large the wickedness, corruption, and punishment of the synagogue, turning to the church, he saith, "And when her sister saw this, she raged and was mad with lust * more than before; she was mad, that is, with fleshly lust,[1] * love of riches, and following voluptuousness. Her fornication and whoredom she committed with princes and great lords, clothed with all manner of gorgeous apparel; so that her paps were bruised, and her breasts were marred." And then speaking of her punishment, he saith, "Then my heart forsook her, like as my heart was gone from her sister also." And moreover, repeating again the cause thereof, he addeth, "Thy wickedness and thy fornication hath wrought thee all this," &c.

The like we find also in Isaiah, Jeremy, Ezekiel, and in all the other prophets, who, prophesying all together in one meaning, and almost in one manner of words, do conclude with a full agreement and prophecy to come, that the church shall fall, and then be punished for her great excesses, and be utterly spoiled, except she repent of all her abominations. Whereof speaketh Hosea [chap. ii.], "Let her put away her whoredom out of her sight, and her adultery from her breasts, lest I strip her naked, and set her even as she came naked into the world," (that is, in her primitive poverty). So if she do it not, it shall follow of her as in the prophet Nahum [chap. iii.], "For the multitude of the fornication of the fair and beautiful harlot, which is a master of witchcraft, yea and selleth the people through her whoredom, and the nations through her witchcraft." And it followeth upon the same, "Behold I come upon thee, saith the Lord of hosts, and will pull thy clothes over thy head, that they nakedness shall appear among the heathen, and thy shame amongst the kingdoms," &c. Wherefore by these it is to be understood that upon this church the primitive justice of God is to be revealed hereafter. And thus much of the first of the four members above touched.

The reformation of the church.

Second subdivision. Signs, that the tribulation of the church draweth near.

Now to the second member of my theme, "Juxta est;" concerning the nearness of time. Although it is not for us to know the moments and articles of time; yet, by certain notes and signs, peradventure, it may be collected and gathered, that which I have here to say. For the tractation whereof, first I ground myself upon the saying of the apostle Paul [2 Thes. ii.], where he writeth, "That unless there come a defection first," &c. By the which defection, Jerome[2] gathereth and expoundeth allegorically, the desolation of the monarchy of Rome: between which desolation, and the persecution of the church by Antichrist, he putteth no mean space. And now, what is the state of that commonwealth, if it be compared to the majesty of that it hath been, judge yourselves. Another gloss there is that saith, how by that defection is meant, that from the church of Rome shall come a departing of some other churches.

First sign. Except there come a defection first, how it is to be understood.

Second sign.

The second note and mark is this, when the church shall be worse in manners than was the synagogue; as appeareth by the ordinary gloss upon the third of Jeremiah, where it is written, "The backslider Israel may seem just and righteous in comparison of sinful Judah;" that is, the synagogue in comparison

(1) These words are inserted from the Second Edition.—Ed.
(2) Ultima quæst. ad inquisitiones Januarii.

of the church of God. Whereof writeth Origen saying, 'Think that to be spoken of us what the Lord saith in Ezekiel [chap. xvi.], "Thou hast exceeded thy sister in thine iniquities." Wherefore now, to compare the one with the other: First, ye know how Christ rebuked the Pharisees, who, as Jerome witnesseth, were then the clergy of the Jews, of covetousness, for that they suffered doves to be sold in the temple of God: Secondly, for that they did honour God with their lips, and not with their heart; and because they said, but did not: Thirdly, he rebuked them, for that they were hypocrites. To the first then, let us see whether it be worse to sell both church and sacraments than to suffer doves to be sold in the temple, or not. Secondly, whereas the Pharisees were rebuked for honouring God with their lips, and not with their heart, there be some who neither honour God with heart, nor yet with lips, and who neither do well, nor yet say well; neither do they preach any word at all, but be dumb dogs, not able to bark, impudent and shameless dogs, that never have enough; such pastors as have no understanding, declining and straying all in their own way, every one given to covetousness from the highest to the lowest. And thirdly, as for hypocrisy, there be also some whose intolerable pride and malice are so manifest and notorious, kindled up like a fire, that no cloak or shadow of hypocrisy can cover it, but they are so past all shame, that it may be well verified of them, which the prophet speaks, "Thou hast gotten thee the face of a harlot; thou wouldst not blush," &c.

The synagogue and church compared together in manners.

The third sign and token of tribulation approaching near to the church, may well be taken of the too much unequal proportion seen this day in the church; where one is hungry and starveth, another is drunk. By reason of which so great inequality, it cannot be that the state of the church, as it is now, can long endure; for, like as in good harmony, to make the music perfect, is required a moderate and proportionate inequality of voices, which if it do much exceed, it taketh away all the sweet melody; so, according to the sentence of the philosopher, by too much immoderate inequality or disparity of citizens, the commonwealth falleth to ruin. Contrary, where mediocrity, that is, where a mean inequality with some proportion is kept, that policy standeth firm and more sure to continue. Now, among all the politic regiments of the Gentiles, I think none more is to be found in histories, wherein is to be seen so great and exceeding odds, as in the policy of priests; of whom some be so high, that they exceed all princes of the earth; some again be so base, that they are under all rascals, so that such a policy or commonwealth may well be called Oligarchia.

Third sign.

Oligarchia, is where a few bear all the sway, and all the rest be nothing worth.

This may we plainly see and learn in the body of man, to the which Plutarch, writing to Thracinius, doth semblably compare the commonwealth. In the which body, if the sustenance received should all run to one member, so that that member should be too much exceedingly pampered, and all the other parts too much pined, that body could not long continue; so in the body of the wealth ecclesiastical, if some who be the heads be so enormously overgrown in riches and dignity, that the weaker members of the body be scantly able to bear them up, there is a great token of dissolution and ruin shortly. Whereupon cometh well in place the saying of the prophet Isaiah: "Every head is sick, every heart is full of sorrow;" of the which heads it is also spoken in the prophet Amos [chap. vi.], "Woe be to the secure, proud, and wealthy in Sion, and to such as think themselves so sure upon the mount of Samaria, taking themselves as heads and rulers over others," &c. And, moreover, in the said prophet Isaiah it followeth, "From the top of the head to the sole of the foot there is no whole part in all the body," to wit, in the inferiors, because they are not able to live for poverty; in the superiors, because for their excessive riches they are let from doing good. And it followeth in the same place, "But all are wounds, and botches, and stripes." Behold here the danger coming, the wounds of discord and division, the botch or sore of rancour and envy, the swelling stripe of rebellion and mischief.

The fourth sign is the pride of prelates. Some there have been who fondly have disputed of the poverty of Christ, and have inveighed against the prelates, because they live not in the poverty of the saints. But this fantasy cometh of the ignorance of moral philosophy and divinity, and of the defect of natural prudence; for that in all nations, and by common laws, priests have had, and ought to have, wherewith to sustain themselves more honestly than the vulgar sort, and prelates more honestly than the subjects. But yet hereby is not

Fourth sign.

Edward III. A.D. 1364.

permitted to them their great horses, their troops of horsemen, the superfluous pomp of their waiting-men and great families, which scarcely can be maintained without pride, neither can be sustained with safe justice, and, many, not without fighting and injuries inconvenient; not much unlike to that which Justin the historian writeth of the Carthaginians, "The family," saith he, "of so great emperors, was intolerable to such a free city." In semblable wise, this great pride in the church of God, especially in these days, doth move not so few to due reverence, as many to indignation; and yet more, to those things aforesaid: who think no less but to do sacrifice to God, if they may rob and spoil certain fat priests and persons, namely, such as neither have nobility of blood, and less learning to bear themselves upon, but are liars, servile and fraudulent, to whom the Lord speaketh by his prophet Amos [chap. iv.], "Hear you fat-fed kine of Samaria, ye that do poor men wrong, and oppress the needy, the day shall come upon you," &c.

Pride of prelates noted.

Fifth sign.

The fifth sign is, the tyranny of the prelates and presidents, which as it is a violent thing, so it cannot be long lasting. For as Solomon saith [chap. xvi.], "For it was requisite that, without any excuse, destruction should come upon those which exercised tyranny." The property of a tyrant is not to seek the commodity of his subjects, but only his will and profit. Such were the pastors that fed not the Lord's flock, but fed themselves; of whom and to whom speaketh the prophet Ezekiel [chap. xxxiv.], "Woe be unto those pastors of Israel that feed themselves. Should not the shepherds feed the flocks?" with many other threatenings against them in the same chapter. "Woe be unto them who rejoice at the transgressions of those whom it lieth in their power to condemn, neither do they seek what he is able to pay;" to whom crieth Micah the prophet [chap. iii.], "Ye hate the good and love the evil; ye pluck off men's skins, and the flesh from the bones; ye eat the flesh of my people, and flay off their skin; ye break their bones; ye chop them in pieces, as it were into a cauldron, and as flesh into the pot," &c. And, therefore, the aforesaid Ezekiel [chap. xxxiv.] pronounceth, "Behold, I will myself come upon the shepherds and require my sheep from their hands, and make them cease from feeding my sheep, yea the shepherds shall feed themselves no more; for I will deliver my sheep out of their mouths, so that they shall not devour them any more."

The tyranny of prelates noted.

Sixth sign. Promoting of unworthy ministers.

The sixth sign is the promoting of the unworthy, and neglecting them that be worthy. This, as Aristotle saith, is a great cause many times of the dissolution of commonweals. And oftentimes it so happeneth in the wars of princes, that the contempt and small regarding of the valiant, and the exalting of others that be less worthy, engender divers kinds and kindlings of sedition. For partly by reason of the same, partly of the other causes above recited, we have read not only in books, but have seen with our eyes, divers flourishing cities well nigh subverted; whereas good men be not made of, but are vexed with sorrow and grief by the evil: the contention at length bursteth out upon the prince, as Haymo reciteth out of Origen. This always hath been the perverse incredulity of man's hard heart, and that not only in hearing, but also in seeing: yet will they not believe that others have perished, unless they also perish themselves.

Seventh sign.

The seventh sign is, the tribulation of outward policy and commotions of the people, which in a great part has now happened already. And therefore, forasmuch as Seneca saith, "Men do complain commonly that evils only come so fast;" it is to be feared lest also the ecclesiastical policy be afflicted not only outwardly, but also in itself; and so that be fulfilled in us, which in Jeremy is prophesied [chap. iv.], "Murder is cried upon murder, and the whole land shall perish, and suddenly my tabernacles were destroyed, and my tents very quickly." And Ezekiel [chap. vii.], "Wherefore I will bring cruel tyrants from among the heathen, to take their houses in possession; I will make the pomp of the proud to cease, and their sanctuaries shall be taken. One mischief and sorrow shall follow another, and one rumour shall come after another: then shall they seek visions in vain at their prophets; the law shall be gone from their priests, and wisdom from their elders," &c.

Eighth sign. Refusing of correction in the clergy.

The eighth is, the refusing of correction, neither will they hear their faults told them, so that it happened to the princes and rulers of the church, as it is written in the prophet Zechariah, [chap. vii.] "They stopped their ears that they would not hear, yea they made their hearts as an adamant stone, lest they should hear the law and words which the Lord of hosts sent in his Holy Spirit by the prophets aforetime." Also Isaiah, witnessing after the same effect [chap. xxx.], saith, "For it is an obstinate people, lying children, and unfaithful children, that will not hear the law of the Lord, which say to the prophets, Meddle with nothing, and tell us nothing, that is true and right, but speak friendly words to us," &c. All this shall be verified when the prelates begin to hate them that tell them truth, and have knowledge; like unto such of whom Amos speaketh [chap. v.], "They bear him evil will, that reproveth them openly, and whoso telleth them the plain truth, they abhor him." And therefore saith the Lord, by Hosea, to the church of Jerusalem [chap. iv.], "Seeing thou hast refused understanding, I have refused thee also, that thou shalt no more be my priest. And forasmuch as thou hast forgotten the law of thy God, I will also forget thy children, and change their honour into shame. And so shall it be, like priest, like people," &c.; and many other sayings there be in the prophets, speaking of the dejecting and casting down of the priestly honour.

Truth shent.

Besides these aforesaid signs and tokens hitherto recited, there be also divers others; as the backsliding from righteousness, the lack of discreet and learned priests, promoting of children into the church, with others such. But these being already well noted and marked, you may easily judge and understand whether these times now present of ours be safe and clear from tribulation to be looked for, and whether the word of the Lord be true according to my theme, "My righteousness is near at hand to be revealed," &c. And thus much of the second part.

Lack of learned priests.

Now to the third part or member of my subdivision, which is concerning the false and perilous opinions of some, upon this word of my theme, "Ut veniat," &c.; which opinions principally be four, all repugning against the truth of the canonical scripture.

Third subdivision.

The first opinion is of such men, who, having too much confidence in themselves, do think and persuade with themselves, that the prelates be the church which the Lord will always keep and never forsake, as he hath promised in the persons of the apostles, saying, in Matthew [chap. xxviii.], "And I will be with you to the end of the world," &c. But this is to be understood of faith, whereof Christ speaketh in Luke [chap. xxi.], "I have prayed for thee, that thy faith shall not fail." Whereof we read in Ecclesiastes [chap. xl.], "Faith shall stand for ever," &c. And albeit charity wax never so cold, yet faith, notwithstanding, shall remain in a few, and in all distresses of the world; of the which distresses, our Saviour doth prophesy, in many places, to come. And lest, peradventure, some should think themselves to be safe from tribulation, because they be of the church; this opinion the Lord himself doth contradict in Jeremiah [chap. vii.], "Trust not," saith he, "in false lying words, saying, The Temple of the Lord, the Temple of the Lord." And a little after, "But you trust in words and lying counsels which deceive you, and do you no good."

The church, where it is, and in whom it consisteth.

The second opinion is of them who defer time; for this they will grant, that the church shall abide trouble, but not so shortly; thinking thus with themselves, that all these causes and tokens afore recited, have been before, at other times as well, in the church. For both by Gregory and Bernard, holy doctors, in time past, the prelates have been in like sort reprehended, both for their bribings, for their pomp and pride, for the promoting of children, and persons unfit unto ecclesiastical functions, and other vices more, which have reigned before this in the church of God more than now, and yet by God's grace the church hath prospered and stands. Do ye not see, that if a house have stood and continued ruinous a long season, it is never the more near the fall thereby, but rather to be trusted the better? Moreover, many times it cometh so to pass, in realms and kingdoms, that the posterity is punished for the sins of their predecessors. Whereof speaketh the book of Lamentations [chap. v.], "Our fathers have sinned and are now gone, and we must bear their wickedness," &c. Against this cogitation or opinion, well doth the Lord answer by the prophet Ezekiel [chap. xii.], saying, "Behold, thou Son of Man, the house of Israel saith in this manner, Tush, as for the vision that he hath seen, it will be many a day ere it come to pass; it is far off yet, the thing that he prophesieth. Therefore say unto them, thus saith the Lord God, The words that I have spoken shall be deferred no longer, look, what I have said shall come to pass, saith the Lord," &c. We have seen in our days things to happen, which seemed before incredible. And the like hath been seen in other times also,

Edward III. A.D. 1364.

as we read written in the book of Lamentations [chap. iv.], "The kings of the earth, nor all the inhabitants of the world would not have believed, that the enemy and adversary should have come in at the gates of the city, for the sins of her priests, and for the wickedness of her elders, that have shed innocent blood within her," &c. By Jerusalem, as is said, is meant the church.

The third opinion or error is very perilous and perverse, of all such as say "veniat," let come that will come; let us conform ourselves to this world, and take our time with those temporizers who say in the book of Wisdom [chap. ii.], "Come, let us enjoy our goods and pleasures that be present, and let us use the creature as in youth quickly," &c. Such as these be, are in a dangerous case, and be greatly prejudicial to good men in the church. And, if the heads and rulers of the church were so vile to have any such detestable cogitation in them, there were no place in hell too deep for them. This church, founded by the apostles in Christ, consecrated with the blood of so many martyrs, enlarged and increased with the virtues and merits of so many saints, and endued so richly with the devotion of so many secular princes, and so long prospered hitherto; if it now should come into the hands of such persons, it should fall in great danger of ruin, and they, for their negligence and wickedness, would well deserve of God to be cursed; yea here, also, in this present world, to incur temporal tribulation and destruction, which they fear more; by the sentence of the Lord, saying to them in the book of Proverbs [chap. i.], "All my counsels ye have despised, and set my correction at nought; therefore shall I also laugh in your destruction, when tribulation and anguish shall fall upon you."

Fourthly, another opinion or error is, of such as being unfaithful, believe not that any such thing will come. And this error seemeth to have no remedy, but that as other things and other kingdoms have their ends and limits set unto them, which they cannot overpass; so it must needs be, that such a domination and government of the church have an end, by reason of the demerits and obstinacies of the governors provoking and requiring the same; like as we read in the prophet Jeremy [chap. viii.], "There is no man that taketh repentance for his sin, that will so much as say, Wherefore have I done this? But every man runneth forth still like a wild horse in battle." And the same prophet, in chapter xiii. of his prophecy, "Like as the man of Inde may change his skin, and the cat-of-mountain her spots, so may ye, that be exercised in evil, do good." Whereunto also accordeth that which is written of the same prophet [chap. xvii.], speaking of Judah, signifying the church, "The sin of Judah," saith he, "is written in the table of your hearts, and graven so upon the edges of your altars with a pen of iron, and with an adamant claw;" which is as much to say, it is indelible, or which cannot be rased out; as also Ezekiel, speaking of the punishment [chap. xxi.], saith, "I the Lord have drawn my sword out of the sheath, and it cannot be revoked." Notwithstanding, all these signify no impossibility, but difficulty, because that wicked men are hardly converted; for, otherwise, the Scripture importeth no such inflexibility with God, but if conversion come, he will forgive. So we read in the prophet Jonas [chap. iii.], "Who can tell? God may turn and repent, and cease from his fierce wrath that we perish not." And to the like effect saith the same Lord in Jeremy [chap. xxvi.], "Look thou keep not one word back, if peradventure they will hearken and turn every man from his wicked way, that I also may repent of the plague which I have determined to bring upon them, because of their wicked inventions," &c. For the further proof whereof, Nineveh we see was converted, and remained undestroyed, &c. Likewise the Lord also had revealed destruction unto Constantinople by sundry signs and tokens, as Augustine in a certain sermon doth declare. And thus for the third part or member of my division.

Fourth subdivision.

Fourthly and lastly, remaineth to declare, some wholesome concluding, now upon the causes preceding: that is, if by these causes and signs, heretofore declared, tribulation be prepared to fall upon the church, then let us humble our minds mildly and wisely. And if we so return with heart and in deed unto God, verily he will rescue and help after an inestimable wise, and will surcease from scourging us, as he promiseth by his prophet Jeremiah [chap. xviii.], "If that people against whom I have thus devised, convert from their wickedness, immediately I will repent of the plague that I devised to bring upon them;" speaking here after the manner of men, &c. Now therefore, forasmuch as tribulation and affliction are so near coming toward us, yea lieth upon us already, let us be the more diligent to call upon God for mercy. For I think, verily, these many years, there have not been so many and so despiteful haters and evil willers, stout, and of such a rebellious heart against the church of God, as be now-a-days; neither be they lacking, that would work all that they can against it, and lovers of new-fangleness; whose hearts the Lord happily will turn, that they shall not hate his people, and work deceit against his servants; I mean against priests, whom they have now in little or no reputation at all, albeit many yet there be, through God's grace, good and godly; but yet the fury of the Lord is not turned away, but still his hand is stretched out. And unless ye be converted, he shaketh his sword; he hath bent his bow, and prepared it ready. Yet the Lord standeth waiting, that he may have mercy upon you [Isaiah xxx.] And, therefore, as the greatness of fear ought to incite us, so hope of salvation may allure us to pray and call upon the Lord, especially now, toward this holy and sacred time and solemnity of Christ's nativity: for that holy and continual prayer without intermission is profitable, and the instant devotion and vigilant deprecation of the just man is of great force. And if terrene kings, in the day of celebration of their nativity, be wont to show themselves more liberal and bounteous, how much more ought we to hope well, that the heavenly King, of nature most benign, now at his natal and birth-day, will not deny pardon and remission to such as rightly call unto him.

And now, therefore, as it is written in Joshua [chap. vii.], "Be ye sanctified against to-morrow," &c. And say unto him, as it is written in the first book of Samuel [chap. xxv.], "Now let thy servants I pray thee find favour in thy sight, for we come to thee in a good season." Moreover, ye may find what ye ask, if ye ask that which he brought, in the day of his nativity, that is, the peace of the church, not spiritual only, but also temporal; which the angelical noise did sound, and experience the same did prove, testified by Livy, Pliny, and other heathen story-writers, who all marvelled thereat, saying, that such an universal peace as that could not come on earth, but by the gift of God. For so God did forepromise in the prophet Isaiah [chap. lxvi.], "Behold, I will let peace into Jerusalem like a waterflood," &c. And in Psalm lxxi. "In his time righteousness shall flourish, yea and abundance of peace," &c.

Therefore now, O reverend fathers in the Lord! and you, here in this present assembly! behold, I say, the day of life and salvation; now is the opportune time to pray unto God, that the same thing, which he brought into the world at his birth, he will now grant in these days to his church, that is, his peace. And, like as Nineveh was subverted, and overturned, not in members but in manners, so the same words of my theme, "Juxta est justitia mea ut reveletur," may be verified in us, not of the primitive justice, but of our sanctification by grace; so that, as to-morrow is celebrated the nativity of our Saviour, our righteousness may rise together with him, and his blessing may be upon us, which God hath promised, saying, "My saving health is near at hand to come," &c.; whereof speaketh Isaiah the prophet [chap. li.], "My saving health shall endure for ever," &c. This health grant unto us, the Father, Son, and Holy Ghost! Amen.

This sermon was made by Master Nicholas Orem before pope Urban and his cardinals, upon the even of the nativity of the Lord, being the fourth Sunday of Advent, A.D. 1364, and the second of his popedom.

In the fifth year of this forenamed pope Urban, began first the order of the Jesuits. Unto this time, which was about A.D. 1367, the offices here in England, as that of the lord chancellor, the lord treasurer, and the privy seal, were wont to be in the hands of the clergy; but, about this year, through the motion of the lords in the parliament, and partly, as witnesseth mine author, for hatred of the clergy, all the said offices were removed from the clergy to the lords temporal.

The order of Jesuits. A.D. 1367.

The chief offices of the realm translated from the clergy to the lords temporal.

After the death of pope Urban, next succeeded pope Gregory XI., who, among his other acts, first brought back again the papacy out of

Pope Gregory XI.

Edward III. A.D. 1367.

France unto Rome, which had from thence been absent the space now of seventy years; being thereto moved, as Sabellicus recordeth, by the answer of a certain bishop, whom, as the pope saw standing by him, he asked, why he was so long from his charge and church at home, saying that, it was not the part of a good pastor, to keep him from his flock so long. Whereunto the bishop answering again, said, "And you yourself, being the chief bishop, who may and ought to be a spectacle to us all, why are you from the place so long where your church doth lie?" by the occasion whereof the pope sought all means after that to remove and to rid his court out of France again to Rome, and so he did.

The papacy reduced again from France to Rome.

Militzius a Bohemian, for the truth persecuted by the pope.

This Gregory XI., in a certain bull of his sent to the archbishop of Prague, maketh mention of one named Militzius, a Bohemian, and saith in the same bull, that this Militzius should hold opinion and teach (A.D. 1366), that Antichrist was already come. Also that the said Militzius had certain congregations following him; and that in the same congregations were certain harlots, who being converted from their wickedness, were brought to a godly life; which harlots being so converted, he used to say, were to be preferred before all the holy religious virgins.[1] And therefore he commanded the archbishop to excommunicate and persecute the said Militzius, who in foretime had been a religious man of Prague, and after forsook his order, and gave himself to preaching, and at length was by the aforesaid archbishop imprisoned.

Jacobus Misnensis, a learned man and a writer in the time of John Huss, maketh mention of this Militzius, and calleth him a worthy and a famous preacher. Also he citeth many things out of his writings, in which this good Militzius thus declareth of himself, how he was moved and urged by the Holy Ghost to search out by the sacred Scriptures, concerning the coming of Antichrist: and that he was compelled by the same Holy Spirit publicly to preach at Rome, and also before the inquisitor there to protest plainly, that the same great Antichrist, which is prophesied of in the Holy Scriptures, was already come. Moreover his saying was, "That the church through negligence of the pastors was desolate, did abound in temporal riches, but in spiritual riches was empty." Also, "That in the church of Christ were certain idols which destroyed Jerusalem, and defaced the temple, but hypocrisy caused that those idols could not be seen." Also, "That many there were who denied Christ, because that, knowing the truth, yet for fear of men, they durst not confess their conscience," &c. And thus much of good Militzius, living in the time of Gregory XI. and king Edward III., A.D. 1370.

The coming of Antichrist prophesied.

King Edward complaineth of the pope's reservation of benefices.

This king of England, holding a parliament in the third year of this pope, sent his ambassadors to him, desiring him, that he from henceforth would abstain from his reservations of benefices used in the court of England; and that spiritual men, within this realm promoted unto bishoprics, might freely enjoy their elections within the realm, and be confirmed by their metropolitans, according to the ancient custom of the realm. Wherefore, upon these, and such other matters, wherein the king and the realm thought themselves aggrieved, he desired of the pope some remedy to be provided, &c.

(1) Ex Bulla Gregorii XI.

Whereunto the pope returned a certain answer again unto the king, requiring by his messengers to be certified again of the king's mind concerning the same. But what answer it was, it is not in the story expressed, save that the year following, which was A.D. 1374, there was a tractation at Bruges upon certain of the said articles between the king and the pope, which did hang two years in suspense; and so at length it was thus agreed between them, that the pope should no more use his reservations of benefices in England, and likewise the king should no more confer and give benefices upon the writ, "Quare impedit," &c.; but, touching the freedom of elections to be confirmed by the metropolitan, mentioned in the year before, thereof was nothing done.

The pope put from his reserving of benefices in England. Quare impedit.

As touching these reservations, provisions and collations, with the elections of archbishops, bishops, beneficed men, and others, wherewith the pope vexed this realm of England, as before you have heard; the king, by the consent of the lords and commons, in the twenty-fifth year of his reign, enacted, that according to a statute made in the thirtieth year of his grandfather, Edward I., wherein was made an act against the ravenous pillage of the pope, through the same provisions, reservations and collations, &c. but not put in execution; by the which provisions, the state of the realm decreased more and more, the king's royalty and prerogative were greatly obscured and diminished, innumerable treasures of the realm transported, aliens and strangers placed in the best and fattest bishoprics, abbeys and benefices within the realm; and such, as either for their offices in Rome, as cardinalships, and such like, could not be here resident, or if resident, yet better away for causes infinite, as partly have been touched before; he not only revived the said statute made by Edward I. his grandfather, but also enlarged the same; adding thereunto very strait and sharp penalties against the offenders therein, or in any part thereof, as exemption out of the king's protection, loss of all their lands, goods, and other possessions, and their bodies to be imprisoned at the king's pleasure; and further, whosoever were lawfully convicted, or who, otherwise, for want of appearance by process directed forth, were within the lapse of this statute of 'Præmunire,' for so bore the name thereof, should suffer all and every such molestations and injuries, as men exempted from the protection of the king. Insomuch, that whosoever had killed such men, had been in no more danger of law for it, than for the killing of an outlaw, or one not worthy to live in a commonweal. Like unprofitable members were they then, yea, in that time of ignorance, esteemed in this commonweal of England, who would offer themselves to the wilful slavery and servile obedience of the pope; which thing in these days, yea, and that amongst no small fools, is counted more than evangelical holiness. He that listeth to peruse the statute, and would see every branch and article thereof at large discussed and handled, with the penalties due on account of it, let him read the statute of Provision and Præmunire made in the twenty-fifth year of this king's days. And let him read in the statutes made in the parliaments holden the twenty-seventh and thirty-eighth years of his reign; and under the same title of Provision and Præmunire he shall find the pope's primacy and jurisdiction within this realm more nearly touched, and

The law of præmunire, with the penalty thereof.

The pope's primacy here in England bridled.

Edward III. A.D. 1370.

much of his papal power restrained: insomuch that whosoever, for any cause or controversy in law, either spiritual or temporal, the same being determinable in any of the king's courts (as all matters were), whether they were personal or real citations, or otherwise, should either appeal or consent to any appellation to be made out of the realm to the pope or see of Rome, should incur the said penalty and danger of 'Præmunire.' Divers other matters wherein the pope is restrained of his usurped power, authority and jurisdiction within this realm of England, are in the said titles and statutes expressed, and at large set forth, whoever listeth to peruse the same, which for brevity's sake I omit, hasting to other matters.

St. Bridget.

About this time, being A.D. 1370, lived holy Bridget, whom the church of Rome hath canonized not only for a saint, but also for a prophetess; who, notwithstanding, in her book of Revelations,[1] which hath been oftentimes imprinted, was a great rebuker of the pope and of the filth of his clergy, calling him a murderer of souls, a spiller and a piller of the flock of Christ, more abominable than the Jews, more cruel than Judas, more unjust than Pilate, worse than Lucifer himself. The see of the pope, she prophesieth, shall be thrown down into the deep like a millstone, and that his assister shall burn with brimstone; affirming, that the prelates, bishops, and priests, are the cause why the doctrine of Christ is neglected, and almost extinguished; and that the clergy have turned the ten commandments of God into two words, to wit, "Da pecuniam," that is, "Give money." It were long and tedious to declare all that she against them writeth. Among the rest which I omit, let this suffice for all; where the said Bridget affirmeth in her revelations, that when the holy virgin should say to her Son, how Rome was a fruitful and fertile field; "Yea," said he, "but of weeds only and cockle," &c.

Da pecuniam.

Rome a fertile ground of weeds and cockle.

Catharina Senensis.

To this Bridget I will join also Catharina Senensis, a holy virgin, who lived much about the same time, (A.D 1379;) of whom writeth Antoninus.[2] This Catharine, having the spirit of prophecy, was wont much to complain of the corrupt state of the church, namely, of the prelates of the court of Rome, and of the pope; prophesying before of the great schism which then followed in the church of Rome, and endured to the council of Constance, the space of thirty-nine years; also of the great wars and tribulation, which ensued upon the same. And moreover, declared before, and foretold of this so excellent reformation of religion in the church now present. The words of Antoninus be these: "After this virgin, in her going to Rome, had told her brother of the wars and tumults that should arise in the countries about Rome, after the schism of the two popes; I, then, curious to know of things to come, and knowing that she understood by revelation what should happen, demanded of her, I pray you, good mother, said I, and what shall befall after these troubles in the church of God? And she said: 'By these tribulations and afflictions, after a secret manner unknown unto man, God shall purge his holy church, and stir up the spirit of his elect. And after these things, shall follow such a reformation of the holy church of God, and such a renovation of holy pastors, that only the cogitation and remembrance thereof,

The reformation of religion prophesied of before.

The prophecy of Catharine.

Note.

(1) Ex lib. revelationum Divæ Bridgitiæ. (2) Ex Anton. part. historiæ iii.

maketh my spirit to rejoice in the Lord. And, as I have oftentimes told you heretofore, the spouse, which now is all deformed and ragged, shall be adorned and decked with most rich and precious ouches and brooches. And all the faithful shall be glad and rejoice to see themselves so beautified with such holy shepherds. Yea, and also the infidels then, allured by the sweet savour of Christ, shall return to the catholic fold, and be converted to the true bishop and shepherd of their souls. Give thanks therefore to God; for after this storm he will give to his a great calm.' And after she had thus spoken, she staid, and said no more."

Edward III.

A.D. 1370.

Matthew Paris, a writer against the pope. Antichrist already come. The doctrine and protestation of Matthew.

Besides these aforenamed, the Lord, who never ceaseth to work in his church, stirred up against the malignant church of Rome, the spirits of divers other good and godly teachers, as Matthew Paris, a Bohemian born, who, about A.D. 1370, wrote a large book of Antichrist, and proveth him to be already come, and noteth the pope to be the same; which book one Illiricus, a writer in these our days, hath, and promiseth to put it in print. In this book he doth greatly inveigh against the wickedness and filthiness of the clergy, and against the neglecting of their duty in governing the church. The locusts mentioned in the Apocalypse, he saith, be the hypocrites reigning in the church. The works of Antichrist, he saith, be these, the fables and inventions of men reigning in the church, the images and feigned relics that are worshipped every where. Item, That men do worship, every one, his proper saint and saviour beside Christ, so that every man and city almost have their diverse and peculiar Christ. He taught and affirmed, moreover, that godliness and true worship of God are not bound to place, persons, or times, to be heard more in this place than in another, at this time more than at another, &c. He argueth also against the cloisterers, who leaving the only and true Saviour, set up to themselves their Franciscans, their Dominics, and such others, and have them for their saviours, glorying, and triumphing in them, and feigning many forged lies about them. He was greatly and much offended with monks and friars for neglecting or rather burying the word of Christ, and instead of him for celebrating and setting up their own rules and canons; affirming it to be very hurtful to true godliness, for that priests, monks and nuns do account themselves only spiritual, and all others to be lay and secular; attributing only to themselves the opinion of holiness, and contemning other men with all their politic administration, and the office as profane in comparison of their own. He further writeth that Antichrist hath seduced all universities and colleges of learned men, so that they teach no sincere doctrine, neither give any light to the Christians with their teaching. Finally, he forewarneth that it will come to pass, that God yet once again will raise up godly teachers, who, being fervent in the spirit and zeal of Elias, shall disclose and refute the errors of Antichrist, and Antichrist himself, openly to the whole world. This Matthew, in the said book of Antichrist, allegeth the sayings and writings of the university of Paris, also the writings of Gulielmus de Sancto Amore, and of Militzius before noted.

About the same time, or shortly after (A.D. 1384), we read also of Johannes of Mountziger, rector of the university of Ulm, who openly in the schools, in his oration, propounded that the body of

Edward III — A.D. 1370.

Johannes Mountziger protestant against the pope.

Christ was not God, and therefore not to be worshipped as God with that kind of worship called 'Latria,' as the sophister termeth it, meaning thereby the sacrament not to be adored, which afterwards he also defended by writing; affirming also, that Christ in his resurrection took to him again all his blood which in his passion he had shed. Meaning thereby to infer, that the blood of Christ, which in many places is worshipped, neither can be called the blood of Christ, neither ought to be worshipped. But by and by he was resisted and withstood by the monks and friars; who by this kind of idolatry were greatly enriched, till at length the senate and council of the city were fain to take up the matter between them.

Nilus, the archbishop of Thessalonica.

Nilus was archbishop of Thessalonica, and lived much about this time. He wrote a long work against the Latins; that is, against such as took part and held with the church of Rome. His first book being written in Greek, was afterward translated into Latin, and lately now into English, in this our time. In the first chapter of his book, he layeth all the blame and fault of the dissension and schism between the east and the west church, upon the pope. He affirmed that the pope would command only what him listed, were it never so contrary to all the old and ancient canons; that he would hear and follow no man's advice; that he would not permit any free councils to be assembled, &c. And that, therefore, it was not possible that the controversies between the Greek church and the Latin church should be decided and determined.

In the second chapter of his book, he purposely maketh a very learned disputation. For first, he declareth that he, no whit at all by God's commandment, but only by human law, hath any dignity, more than have other bishops; which dignity the councils, the fathers, the emperors, have granted unto him: neither did they grant the same for any other consideration, or greater ordinance, than because the same city then had the empery of all the whole world, and not at all for that Peter ever was there, or not there.

Secondarily he declareth, that the same primacy or prerogative is not such and so great, as he and his sycophants do usurp unto themselves. Also he refuteth the chief propositions of the papists, one after another. He declareth, that the pope hath no dominion more than other patriarchs have, and that he himself may err as well as other mortal men; and that he is subject both to laws and councils, as well as other bishops. That it belonged not to him, but to the emperor, to call general councils; and that in ecclesiastical causes he could establish and ordain no more than all other bishops might. And, lastly, that he getteth no more by Peter's succession, than that he is a bishop, as all other bishops after the apostles be, &c.

Jacobus Misuensis and Militzius.

I cannot, among other things, following here the occasion of this matter offered, leave out the memory of Jacobus Misuensis, who also wrote of the coming of Antichrist. In the same he maketh mention of a certain learned man, whose name was Militzius,[1] which Militzius, saith he, "was a famous and worthy preacher in Prague." He lived about A.D. 1366, long before Huss, and before Wickliff also. In his writings Jacobus declareth, how the same good man Militzius was, by the Holy Spirit of God incited, and vehemently moved to search out

(1) Ex Bulla Gregorii.

of the holy Scriptures the manner and coming of Antichrist; and found that now, in his time, he was already come. And the same Jacobus saith, that Militzius was constrained by the Spirit of God to go up to Rome, and there publicly to preach. And that afterwards, before the inquisitor, he affirmed the same; namely, that the same mighty and great Antichrist, which the Scriptures made mention of, was already come.

He affirmed also, that the church, by the negligence of the pastors, should become desolate; and that iniquity should abound, that is, by reason of Mammon, master of iniquity. Also, he said that there were in the church of Christ idols, which should destroy Jerusalem, and make the temple desolate, but were cloaked by hypocrisy. Further, that there be many who deny Christ, for that they keep silence; neither do they hear Christ, whom all the world should know, and confess his verity before men; who also knowingly do detain the verity and justice of God.

Militzius persecuted by the pope.

There is also a certain bull of pope Gregory XI. to the archbishop of Prague; wherein he is commanded to excommunicate and persecute Militzius and his auditors. The same bull declareth, that he was once a canon of Prague, but afterwards he renounced his canonship, and began to preach; who, also, for that he so manifestly preached of Antichrist to be already come, was of John, archbishop of Prague, put in prison, declaring what his error was; to wit, how he had his company or congregation to whom he preached, and that amongst the same were certain converted harlots, who had forsaken their evil life, and did live godly and well, which harlots he accustomed in his sermons to prefer before all the blessed virgins that never offended. He taught also openly, that in the pope, cardinals, bishops, prelates, priests, and other religious men was no truth, neither that they taught the way of truth, but that only he, and such as held with him, taught the true way of salvation. His postil[1] in some places is yet to be seen. They allege unto him certain other inconvenient articles, which notwithstanding I think the adversaries, to deprave him withal, have slanderously invented against him. He had, as appeared by the aforesaid bull, very many of every state and condition, as well rich as poor, that cleaved unto him.

About A.D. 1371, lived Henricus de Iota, whom Gerson doth much commend, and also his companion Henricus de Hassia, an excellent learned and famous man. An epistle of this Henricus de Hassia, which he wrote to the bishop of Normacia, Jacobus Cartsiensis inserted in his book 'De Erroribus Christianorum.' In the same epistle the author doth greatly accuse the spiritual men of every order, yea and the most holy of all others, the pope himself, of many and great vices. He said, that the ecclesiastical governors in the primitive church were to be compared to the sun shining in the day time; and the political governors, to the moon shining in the night. But the spiritual men, he said, that now are, do never shine in the day time, nor yet in the night time, but rather with their darkness do obscure both the day and the night; that is, with their filthy living, ignorance, and impiety. He citeth also out of the

(1) His glossary.—ED.

Edward III. A.D. 1370.

prophecy of Hildegard these words: "Therefore doth the devil in himself speak of you priests: Dainty banquets, and feasts wherein is all voluptuousness, do I find amongst these men; insomuch that mine eyes, mine ears, my belly, and my veins, be even filled with the froth of them, and my breasts stand astrut with the riches of them," &c. "Lastly," saith she, "they every day more and more, as Lucifer did, seek to climb higher and higher; till that every day with him, more and more, they fall deeper and deeper."

The citizens of Moguntina.

About A.D. 1390, there were burned at Bringa, thirty-six citizens of Moguntina, for the doctrine of Waldensis, as Brussius affirmeth; which opinion was nothing contrary to that they held before, wherein they affirmed the pope to be that great Antichrist, which should come; unless, peradventure, the pope seemed then to be more evidently convicted of Antichristianity, than at any other time before he was revealed to be.

A brief rehearsal of such as were put to death for holding against the bishop of Rome, before the time of Wickliff.

For the like cause, many other beside these are to be found in stories, who sustained the like persecutions by the pope, if leisure would serve to peruse all that might be searched. As where Masseus recordeth of divers, to the number of a hundred and forty, who in the province of Narbonne chose rather to suffer whatsoever grievous punishment by fire, than to receive the decretals of the Romish church, contrary to the upright truth of the Scripture.

What should I here speak of the twenty-four who suffered at Paris, A.D. 1210? Also in the same author is testified that in the following year there were four hundred under the name of heretics burned, eighty beheaded, prince Americus hanged, and the lady of the castle stoned to death.

Moreover, in the chronicles of Hoveden, and of other writers, be recited a marvellous number, who in the countries of France were burned for heretics; of whom, some were called Publicans, some Catharites, some Paterines, and others, by other names. What their assertions were, I find no certain report worthy of credit.

Eckhard, a friar, burned.

In Trithemius, it is signified of one Eckhard, a Dominican friar, who, not long before Wickliff's time, was condemned and suffered for heresy at Heidelburgh (A.D. 1330), who as he differeth not much in name, so may he be supposed to be the same, whom others do name Beghard, and is said to be burned at Erphord.

Of Albigenses, because sufficient mention is made before, of whom great number were burned about the time of king John, I pass them over.

A hermit disputing against the pope's sacraments. Ranulphus.

Likewise, I let pass the hermit, of whom John Bacon maketh relation,[1] who, disputing in Paul's Church, affirmeth "That those sacraments which were then used in the church, (A.D. 1360,) were not instituted by Christ." Peradventure, it was the same Ranulphus, mentioned in the Flower of Histories, and who is said to die in prison; for the time of them doth not much differ.

In Boetius, why the pope should so much commend a certain king, because for one man he had slain four hundred, shamefully mutilating the rest, I cannot judge, except the cause were that which the pope calleth heresy.

(1) 2 Dist. Quæst. 1.

But to let these things be passed over that be uncertain, because neither is it possible to comprehend all them who have withstood the corruption of the pope's see, neither have we any such firm testimony left of their doings, credibly to stay upon, we will now (Christ willing) convert our story to things more certain and undoubted; grounding upon no light reports of feeble credit, nor upon any fabulous legends without authority, but upon the true and substantial copies of the public records of the realm, remaining yet to be seen under the king's most sure and faithful custody: out of the which records[1] such matter appeareth against the popish church of Rome, and against its usurped authority, such open standing and crying out against the said see, and that not privily, but also in open parliament, in the days of this king Edward III.; that neither will the Romish people of this our age easily think it to be true when they see it, neither yet shall they be able to deny the same, so clear standeth the force of those records.

Partial dissimulation in our histories of the church of England.

Ye heard a little before (p. 683), how John Stratford, archbishop of Canterbury, being sent for, and required by the king to come unto him, refused to do so. What the cause was why he denied to come at the king's sending, is neither touched upon by Polydore Virgil, nor by any other monkish chronicler, writing of those acts and times; whose part had been, faithfully to have dispensed the simple truth of things done to their posterity. But that which they dissemblingly and colourably have concealed, contrary to the true law of story, the true cause thereof we have found out by the true parliament rolls declaring the story thus:

King Edward III., in the sixth year of his reign, hearing that Edward Baliol had proclaimed himself king of Scotland, required counsel of the whole state, to wit, whether it were better for him to assail Scotland, and to claim the demesing or demesnes of the same; or else by making him party to take his advantage, and thereby to enjoy the service, as other his ancestors before him had done. For this cause he summoned a parliament of all estates to meet at York, about the beginning of December. The king was already there, waiting for the coming of such as were warned thereunto; for the want of whose coming the parliament was adjourned till the Monday, and from thence to the Tuesday next ensuing. But forasmuch as most of the states were absent, the assembly required the continuance of the parliament, until the Utas of St. Hilary, then ensuing, at York, which was granted. And so a new summons was especially awarded to every person with special charge to attend, so that the affairs of the king and the realm might not be hindered because of the debate between the archbishop of Canterbury and the archbishop of York, for the superior bearing of their cross.[2]

The archbishop of Canterbury came not to the parliament at York, and all for bearing the cross.

In conclusion, for all the king's summoning, none other of all the clergy came, but only the archbishop of York, the bishops of Lincoln and Carlisle, and the abbots of York and Selby; so that hereunto came not the archbishop of Canterbury, nor any other of his province, and all for bearing the cross, whereby the same was not only a loss of the opportunity to Scotland, but also an importable charge to the whole estate by a new re-assembly. And thus much out of the records, whereby thou mayest easily judge (prudent reader) what is to be thought of these pope-holy catholic churchmen, being of the pope's brood and setting up; whom such frivolous causes of contention stir up both to such disquietness among themselves, and also to such disobedience against their prince: excuse them who can.[3]

The pope's provisions restrained.

It followeth, moreover, in the same records, concerning the abandoning of the pope's provisions,[4] how that the commons find great default at provisions

(1) Ex Archivis Regiæ Majestatis. (2) Ex an. 6. Regis Ed. III. tit. 1.
(3) Ex an. 6. Regis Ed. III. tit. 1. (4) Ex an. 17. Reg. Ed. III. tit. 39.

Edward III. A.D. 1370.

coming from Rome, whereby strangers were enabled within this realm to enjoy ecclesiastical dignities, and show divers inconveniencies ensuing thereby; namely, the decay of daily alms, the transporting of the treasure to nourish the king's enemies, the discovering of the secrets of the realm, and the disabling and impoverishing of the clerks within this realm.[1]

The church of England spoiled by the pope and his foreigners.

They also show how the pope had in most covertwise granted to two new cardinals within this realm (one named cardinal Peragotz), above ten thousand marks of yearly taxes. They therefore required the king and nobles to find some remedy, for that they never could nor would any longer bear those strange oppressions; or else to help them to expel out of this realm the pope's power by force.

The act of Edward I. revived for præmunire, tit. 60.

Hereupon the king, lords, and commons, sent for the act made at Carlisle, in the thirty-fifth year of king Edward I., upon the like complaint; thereby forbidding that any thing should be attempted or brought into the realm, which should tend to the blemishing of the king's prerogative, or to the prejudice of his lords or commons. And so at this time the statute called the Act of Provision, was made by common consent, which generally forbiddeth the bringing in of any bulls, or such trinkets from the court of Rome, or the using, enjoying, or allowing of any such bill, process, instrument, or such ware, as thereby at large doth appear; which sufficiently is touched before page 609.[2]

The penalty of the aforesaid statute[3] afterwards followed in the next parliament, which was this: the transgressors thereof were to lie in perpetual prison, or to be forejured the land; and that all justices of assize, gaol delivery, and oyer and determiner, may determine the same. Required withal, that the same act of provision should continue for ever.

Presentation within four months.

Item, In the said eighteenth year of the reign of king Edward, it was, moreover, propounded, that if any archbishop, or any person religious, or other, do not present within four months some able clerk to any dignity, where any person hath obtained from Rome any provision, bull, &c., but surcease the same, that then the king may present some able clerk.[4]

No election to be taken by the pope but only by the king.

Item, It was propounded in the said parliament, that if any bishop elect shall refuse to take any such bishoprics, otherwise than by such bull, that then such elect shall not enter or enjoy his temporalties without his special license.[5]

Dispositions of benefices only in the king's hand.

Also that the king shall dispose all such benefices and dignities of such aliens his enemies, as remain in the country of his enemies, and employ the profits thereof to the defence of the realm.[6]

Bulls from Rome forbidden.

Moreover, it was propounded, that commissioners be sent to all the king's ports, to apprehend all such persons as shall bring in any such instrument from Rome, and to bring them, forthwith, before the council to answer thereto.[7]

Deanery of York taken from the cardinal.

Propounded furthermore, that the deanery of York, which is to be recovered by judgment in the king's court, may be bestowed upon some able man within the realm, who will maintain the same against him (meaning the cardinal, who holdeth the same by provision from Rome, being the enemy to the king, and to the realm), and that the profits may be employed to the defence of the realm.[8]

The king's answer to the aforesaid petitions.

The king's answer. To all which petitions answer was made in form following: "It is agreed by the king, earls, barons, justices, and other wise men of the realm, that the petitions aforesaid be made in sufficient form of law, according to the petitions aforesaid."

Note in this answer of the king, good reader, that at the grant hereof the consent of the bishops is neither named, nor expressed, with the other lords of the parliament: and yet the parliament standeth in its full force, notwithstanding.

Notes of the Parliament holden in the Twentieth Year of King Edward III.

Alien monks to avoid.

To pass on further, in the twentieth year of the king's reign, in the parliament holden the same year, it was propounded; that all alien monks should

(1) 6 Edw. III. tit. 59. (2) Ibid. tit. 60. (3) An. Reg. Edw. 18, tit. 32. (4) Ibid. tit. 34. (5) Ibid. tit. 35. (6) Ibid. tit. 36. (7) Ibid. tit. 37. (8) Ibid. tit. 38.

avoid the realm by the day of St. Michael, and that their livings should be disposed of to young English scholars.[1] The livings of these, the king took to his hands.

Edward III. A.D. 1370.

Item, That the king may take the profits of all other strangers' livings, as cardinals and others, during their lives. The profits of whom were also in the king's hands.[2]

That such alien enemies, as be advanced to livings here in England (being in their own countries, shoemakers, tailors, or chamberlains to cardinals) should depart before Michaelmas, and their livings be disposed of to poor English scholars. The livings also of these remained in the king's hands.[3]

Livings of Romish strangers disposed to Englishmen.

The commons denied to make any payment to any cardinals, lying in France to treat of war or peace, which also was granted on the king's part as reasonable.

Item, It was propounded and fully agreed, that the yearly advancement of two thousand marks (granted by the pope to two cardinals, out of the provinces of Canterbury and York) should be restrained, and such as shall pursue for it to be out of the law.[4]

Cardinals deprived of their livings in England.

Likewise it was enacted and agreed, that no Englishman should take any thing in farm of any alien religious, or buy any of their goods, or be of their counsel, on pain of perpetual imprisonment.

Enacted further, That no person should bring into the realm, to any bishop or other, any bull, or any other letters from Rome, or from any alien, unless he show the same to the chancellor or warden of the Cinque Ports; upon loss of all he hath.

Finally, in the end of the said parliament the bishops were commanded, before the next convocation, to certify unto the chancery the names of such aliens and their benefices, and the values of the same.

Notes of the Five and Twentieth Year of King Edward III.[5]

The parliament of the twenty-fifth year of the reign of king Edward III., was begun on the sixth day of February, A.D. 1352. In that parliament, beside other matters, it was propounded, that remedy might be had against the pope's reservations, by which brokerage and means the pope received the first fruits of all ecclesiastical dignities: a greater consumption to the realm, than all the king's wars.[6]

The pope's first fruits and reservations more hurtful to the realm than all the king's wars.

Also that the like remedy might be had against such as in the court of Rome presume to undo any judgment given in the king's court, as if they laboured to undo the laws of the realm.[7]

Whereunto it was answered, that there was sufficient remedy provided by law.

Notes of the Eight and Thirtieth Year of King Edward III.

In the parliament holden at Westminster, the thirty-eighth year of Edward III., in the Utaves of Hilary, Simon, bishop of Ely, being lord chancellor, it was required by the king's own mouth, and declared to the whole estates, how daily citation and false suggestions were made to the pope, for matters determinable in his courts within the realm, and for procuring provisions to ecclesiastical dignities, to the great defacing of the ancient laws, to the spoiling of his crown, to the daily conveying away of the treasure, to the wasting of ecclesiastical livings, to the withdrawing of divine service, alms, hospitality, and other acceptable works, and to the daily increase of all mischiefs: wherefore, in person, and by his own mouth, the king required the whole estate to provide hereof due remedy.[8]

The request of the king for causes not to be determined at Rome. What mischiefs come by transporting causes to Rome.

It is to be noted finally in this parliament of the thirty-eighth year, that the act of provisors, brought in during this parliament, although in the printed copy [chapters 1, 2, 3, 4,] it doth agree with the record in manner, yet in the said records, unprinted, are more biting words against the pope: a mystery not to be known of all men.[9]

The printed statute of provision.

(1) An. 20. Edw. III. tit. 30. (2) Ibid. tit. 21. (3) Ibid. tit. 32, 33. (4) Ibid. tit. 31.
(5) Ex Arch. 25. an. Reg. Edw. III. (6) Ibid. tit. 14. (7) Ibid.
(8) Tit. 7. (9) Tit. 9.

Edward III.

Notes of the Fortieth Year of King Edward III.

A.D. 1370.

It followeth, moreover, in the said acts of king Edward III., and in the fortieth year of his reign, that another parliament was called at Westminster on the third of May, A.D. 1366,[1] the bishop of Ely being lord chancellor and speaker; who, on the second day of the said assembly, in the presence of the king, lords, and commons, declared how the day before generally they understood the cause of this their assembly, and now more particularly should understand the same; especially how that the king understood that the pope (for the homage which king John made to the see of Rome for the realms of England and Ireland, and for the tribute by him granted) meant, by process, to cite the king to Rome, to answer thereto; wherein the king required their advices, what were best for him to do, if any such thing were attempted. The bishops, by themselves, required a respite of answer, until the next day. So did the lords and commons every one of them by themselves.

The pope mindeth to send up for the king by process.

The next day the whole estates re-assembled together, and by common consent enacted in effect as follows, viz., That forasmuch as neither king John, nor any other king, could bring his realm and people into such thraldom and subjection, but by common assent of parliament, the which was not done,[2] and, therefore, because what he did was done against his oath at his coronation (beside many other causes); if, therefore, the pope should attempt any thing against the king, by process or indeed other matter, the king, with all his subjects, should, with all their force and power, resist the same.

King John could not, without consent of parliament, become tributary to the pope.

Here, moreover, is not to be omitted, how, in the said present parliament, the universities of Oxford and Cambridge on the one side, and the friars of the four orders mendicant in the said universities on the other side, made long complaints the one against the other to the king in parliament, and in the end submitted themselves to the king's order.[3]

Agreed that the king should resist the pope.

After this the king, upon full digesting of the whole matter, by assent of parliament, took order; that as well the chancellor and scholars, as the friars of those orders in the said universities, should, in all graces and other school exercises, use each other in friendly wise, without any rumour as before, and that none of those orders should receive any scholars into their said orders, being under the age of eighteen years.

Brawl between the four orders of friars and the two universities.

That the said friars shall take no advantage, nor procure bulls, or other process from Rome, against the said universities, or proceed therein; and that the king have power to redress all controversies between them from thenceforth; and the offenders to be punished at the pleasure of the king, and of the council.[4]

Friars subject to the king in all their controversies.

Notes of the Fiftieth Year of King Edward III.

In process of the aforesaid acts and rolls, it followeth more, that in the fiftieth year of the reign of king Edward III., A.D. 1376,[5] another great parliament was assembled at Westminster the twenty-fourth of April: where, Sir John Knyvet being lord chancellor of England, a certain long bill was put up against the usurpations of the pope, as being the cause of all the plagues, murrains, famine, and poverty of the realm, so that thereby was not left of persons, or other commodity within the realm, the third that lately was.

Against the usurpation of the pope. The cause of mischiefs in England.

II. That the taxes paid to the pope of Rome for ecclesiastical dignities, do amount to fivefold as much as the tax of all profits which appertain to the king, by the year, of his whole realm; and that for some one bishopric or other dignity, the pope, by way of translation and death, hath three, four, or five several taxes.[6]

Treasure of the realm conveyed away.

III. That the brokers of that sinful city for money promote many caitiffs, being altogether unlearned and unworthy, to a thousand marks living by year, where the learned and worthy can hardly obtain twenty marks, whereby learning decayeth.

IV. That aliens, enemies to this land, who never saw nor care to see their parishioners, have those livings, whereby they despise God's service, and convey away the treasure, and are worse than Jews or Saracens.

(1) Ex an. Reg. Ed. 40. tit. 7. videlicet. (2) Tit. 8. (3) Tit. 10. (4) Tit. 12.
(5) Ex Archivis Regiæ Majestatis, an. 50. Reg. Ed. tit. 94. (6) Tit. 97.

V. Also, it was put up in the said bill to be considered, that the laws of the church would have such livings to be bestowed for charity only, without praying or paying.

VI. That reason would that livings given of devotion should be bestowed in hospitality.

VII. That God had committed his sheep to the pope, to be pastured, and not shorn or shaven.

VIII. That lay patrons, perceiving the covetousness and simony of the pope, do thereby learn to sell their benefices unto beasts, none otherwise than Christ was sold to the Jews.[1]

The pope teacheth to sell benefices.

IX. That there is no prince in Christendom so rich, that hath the fourth part of so much treasure as the pope hath out of this realm for churches, most sinfully.[2]

Inestimable, what the pope hath here out of England.

X. Over and besides in the said bill, repeating again the tender zeal for the honour of the church, were declared and particularly named, all the plagues which have justly fallen upon this realm, for suffering the same church to be so defaced, with declaration that it will daily increase without redress.

XI. Whereupon with much persuasion this was desired, to help to re-edify the same; and the rather, for that this was the year of jubilee, the fiftieth year of the king's reign, the year of joy and gladness, than which there could be no greater.[3]

Reformation of the church of England desired in parliament.

XII. The means how to begin this was to write two letters to the pope: the one in Latin, under the king's seal, the other in French, under the seals of the nobles, importing their particularities, and requiring redress; of the which letter of the lords the effect may be seen in a like letter mentioned before, page 689.

XIII. And for a further accomplishment hereof, the means were, to enact that no money should be carried forth from the realm by letter of Lombardy or otherwise, on pain of forfeiture and imprisonment, and to enact the articles hereafter ensuing.[4]

Acts made for no money to be transported.

XIV. The king hath heretofore by statute provided sufficient remedy, and otherwise pursueth the same with the holy father the pope, and so mindeth to do from time to time, until he hath obtained, as well for the matters before, as for the articles ensuing, being in a manner all one.

XV. That the pope's collector and other strangers the king's enemies, and only leger spies for English dignities and disclosing of the secrets of the realm, may be touched.[5]

XVI. That the same collector, being also receiver of the pope's pence, keepeth a house in London, with clerks and officers thereto, as it were one of the king's solemn courts, transporting yearly to the pope twenty thousand marks, and most commonly more.[6]

The pope's collection, what it cometh to.

XVII. That cardinals, and other aliens remaining at Rome, whereof one cardinal is dean of York, another of Salisbury, another of Lincoln, another archdeacon of Canterbury, another archdeacon of Durham, another archdeacon of Suffolk, another archdeacon of York, another prebendary of Thame and Nassington, another prebendary of Bucks in the church of York, have divers of the best dignities of England, and have sent over to them yearly twenty thousand marks, over and above that which English brokers lying here have.[7]

The best dignities in England in the cardinals.

XVIII. That the pope (to ransom the Frenchmen, the king's enemies, who defend Lombardy from him) doth always at his pleasure levy a subsidy of the whole clergy of England.[8]

The pope maintaineth the king's enemies with the king's money.

XIX. That the pope, for more gain, maketh sundry translations of all the bishoprics, and other dignities within the realm.[9]

XX. That the pope's collector hath this year taken to his use the first fruits of all benefices, by collation or provision.

XXI. To renew all the statutes against provisors from Rome, since the pope reserveth all the benefices of the world for his own proper gift, and hath this year created twelve new cardinals, so that now there are thirty, where were wont to be but twelve; and all those cardinals, except two or three, are the king's enemies.

The law of præmunire renewed.

XXII. That the pope, in time, will give the temporal manors of those dignities

(1) Tit. 99. (2) Tit. 100. (3) Tit. 111. (4) Tit. 103. (5) Tit. 104.
(6) Tit. 105. (7) Tit. 106. (8) Tit. 107. (9) Tit. 108.

Edward III.

A.D. 1370.

to the king's enemies, since he so daily usurpeth upon the realm, and the king's regalities.[1]

XXIII. That all houses and corporations of religion, which, unto the king's reign now, had free election of heads, the pope hath encroached the same to himself.

English money payeth the pope's legacies.

XXIV. That in all legacies from the pope whatsoever, the English clergy bear the charge of the legates, and all for the goodness of our money.[2]

XXV. And so it appeareth, that if the money of the realm were as plentiful as ever it was, the collectors aforesaid, with the proctors of cardinals, would soon convey the same away.[3]

The pope's collector driven out of the realm.

XXVI. For remedy hereof it may be provided, That no such collector or proctor do remain in England, on pain of life and member; and that no Englishman, on the like pain, become any such collector or proctor, or remain at Rome.[4]

The pope's collector examined.

XXVII. For better information hereof, and namely touching the pope's collector, for that the whole clergy being obedient unto him, dare not displease him: it were good that Sir John Strensale, parson of St. Botolph's in Holborn, may be sent to come before the lords and commons of this parliament; who, being straitly charged, can declare much more, for that he served the same collector in his house five years.

Englishmen good asses.

And thus much of this bill, touching the pope's matters; whereby it may appear not to be for nought what hath been of us reported by the Italians and other strangers, who used to call Englishmen good asses: for they bear all burdens that be laid upon them.

Certain other Notes of Parliament.

Order against usury.

Item, In the said parliament it was provided also, that such order as is made in London against the horrible vice of usury, may be observed throughout the whole realm.[5]

Complaint against the bishop of York and his officers for their excessive taking for their admissions.

The commons of the diocese of York complain of the outrageous taking of the bishop and his clerks, for admission of priests to their benefices.

To these records of the parliament above prefixed, of the fiftieth year of this king Edward, we will adjoin also other notes collected out of the parliament in the year next following, which was the fifty-first year of this king's reign, and the last of his life, A.D. 1377,[6] the twenty-seventh day of January: although in the printed book these statutes are said to be made at the parliament holden, as above, in the fiftieth year: which is much mistaken, and ought to be referred to the one and fiftieth year, as by the records of the said year manifestly doth appear.[7]

The effect of the chancellor's oration.

In that parliament, the bishop of St. David's, being lord chancellor, made a long oration, taking his theme out of St. Paul, "Libenter suffertis incipientes," &c.: declaring in the said oration many things; as first, showing the joyful news of the old king's recovery; then, declaring the love of God toward the king and realm, in chastising him with sickness; afterwards showing the blessing of God upon the king in seeing his children's children; then, by a similitude of the head and members, exhorting the people, as the members of one body, to conform themselves unto the goodness of the head; lastly, he turned his matter to the lords and the rest, declaring the cause of that assembly: that forasmuch as the French king had allied himself with the Spaniards and Scots, the king's enemies, who had prepared great powers, conspiring to blot out the English tongue and name, the king, therefore, was willing to have therein their faithful counsel.

This parliament chiefly for the pope's usurpation against the king.

This being declared by the bishop, Sir Robert Ashton, the king's chamberlain, declaring that he was to move them on the part of the king, for the profit of the realm (the which words perchance lay not in the bishop's mouth, for that it touched the pope) viz., by protesting first, that the king was ready to do all that ought to be done for the pope; but, because divers usurpations were done by the pope to the king's crown and realm, as by particular bills in this parliament should be showed, he required of them to seek redress.

In this present parliament petition was made by the commons, that all

(1) Tit. 112. (2) Tit. 113. (3) Tit. 114. (4) Tit. 115. (5) Tit. 158. (6) Tit. 171. Ex Archivis Reg. Edw. III. reg. 5, tit. 36. (7) Anno reg. 51.

provisors of things from Rome, and from their ministers, should be out of the king's protection; whereunto the king answered, that the pope had promised redress, which if he did not give, the laws then should stand.[1]

It was also in that parliament required, that every person of what sex soever, being professed of any religion, continuing the habit for fifteen years, may, upon the trial of the same in any of the king's courts, be in law utterly forebarred of all inheritance, albeit he have dispensation from the pope; against which dispensation, is the chief grudge. Whereunto the king and the lords answered, saying, that they would provide.[2]

Against the pope's provisions from Rome.

Item, In the said parliament was propounded, that the statute of provisors made at any time may be executed, and that remedy may be had against such cardinals as, within the provinces of Canterbury and York, have purchased reservations, with the clause of 'Anteferri' to the value of twenty or thirty thousand scutes of gold against the pope's collector; who was wont to be an Englishman, and is now a mere Frenchman, residing at London, and who conveyeth yearly to the pope twenty thousand marks, or twenty thousand pounds; and who, this year, gathereth the first fruits whatsoever: alleging the means to meet these reservations and novelties, to be to command all strangers to depart the realm during the wars; and that no Englishman become their farmer, or send to them any money without a special license, on pain to be out of the king's protection. Whereunto was answered by the king, that the statutes and ordinances, for that purpose made, should be observed.[3]

Against the pope's dispensations.

By this 'Anteferri,' that is, 'præmunire,' is meant the pre-eminence above the king.

In these rolls and records of such parliament as were in this king's time continued, divers other things are to be noted very worthy to be marked, and not to be suppressed in silence; wherein the reader may learn and understand that the state of the king's jurisdiction here within this realm, was not straitened in those days (although the pope then seemed to be in his chief ruff) as afterwards, in other kings' days, was seen; as may appear in the parliament of the fifteenth year of this king Edward III., and in the twenty-fourth article of the said parliament: where it is to be read, that the king's officers and temporal justices did then both punish usurers, and impeach the officers of the church for bribery, and for taking money for temporal pain, probate of wills, solemnity of marriage, &c.; all the pretensed liberties of the popish church to the contrary notwithstanding.[4]

The pope's law of 'præeminire,' which now we corruptly call 'præmunire,' debarred by the king.

Punishment of the clergy in the temporal men's hands.

Furthermore, in the parliament of the twenty-fifth year it appeareth, that the liberties of the clergy, and their exemptions in claiming the deliverance of men by their book under the name of clerks, stood then in little force, as appeared by one Hawktine Honby, knight; who, for imprisoning one of the king's subjects till he made fine of twenty pounds, was on that account executed, notwithstanding the liberty of the clergy, which by his book would have saved him, but could not.

Clerks subject to temporal law.

The like also appeared by judgment given against a priest at Nottingham, for killing his master.

And likewise by hanging certain monks of Combe.[5]

Item, In the parliament of the fifteenth year, by the apprehending of John Stratford, archbishop of Canterbury, and his arraignment; concerning which his arraignment all things were committed to Sir William of Kildisby.[6]

The arraignment of the archbishop of Canterbury.

Besides these truths and notes of the king's parliaments, wherein may appear the toward proceedings of this king and all his commons against the pretended church of Rome; this is, moreover, to be added to the commendation of the king, how in the volumes of the Acts and Rolls of the king it appeareth, that the said king Edward III. sent also John Wickliff, reader then of divinity lectures in Oxford, with certain other lords and ambassadors, over into the parts of Italy, to treat with the pope's legates concerning affairs betwixt the king and the pope, with full commission: the tenor whereof here followeth expressed.[7]

John Wickliff sent with the king's ambassadors.

(1) An. reg. 51. tit. 35. (2) Tit. 62. (3) Tit. 78.
(4) Ex Actis Parliamenti in an. 15. Reg. Edw. III. tit. 24. (5) Ex Parliam. an. 23. Edw. III.
(6) Ibid. tit. 49. (7) "Rex universis, ad quorum notitiam præsentes literæ pervenerint," &c.

Edward III.

A.D. 1371.

The King's Letter authorizing John Wickliff and others to treat with the Pope's Legates.

The king, to all and singular to whom these presents shall come, greeting. Know ye, that we, reposing assured confidence in the fidelity and wisdom of the reverend father, John, bishop of Bangor, and other our loving and faithful subjects, Mr. John Wickliff, reader of the divinity lecture, Mr. John Guntur, dean of Segobyen, and Mr. Simon Moulton, doctor of law, Sir William Burton, knight, Mr. John Belknape, and Mr. John Honnington, have directed them as our ambassadors and special commissioners to the parts beyond the seas: giving to the said our ambassadors and commissioners, to five or six of them, of whom I will that the said bishop shall be one, full power and authority, with commandment special, to treat and consult mildly and charitably with the legates and ambassadors of the lord pope, touching certain affairs, whereupon, of late, we sent heretofore the said bishop, and William Ughtred, monk of Durham, and Master John Shepy, to the see apostolical: and hereof to make full relation of all things done and passed in the said assembly, that all such things which may tend to the honour of holy church and the advancement of our crown and this our realm, may, by the assistance of God and wisdom of the see apostolical, be brought to good effect, and accomplished accordingly. Witness ourselves, &c. at London, dated the twenty-sixth day of July, in the forty-eighth year of our reign.

By the which it is to be noted, what good will the king then bare to the said Wickliff, and what small regard he had to the sinful see of Rome.

Of which John Wickliff, because we are now approached to his time, it remaineth consequently for our story to treat, so as we have heretofore done of other like valiant soldiers of Christ's church before him.

The Story of John Wickliff.[1]

* Although[2] it is manifest and evident enough, that there were divers and sundry before Wickliff's[3] time, who have wrestled and laboured in the same cause and quarrel that our countryman Wickliff

(1) Latin Edition 1559, p. 1. Ed. 1563, p. 85. Ed. 1570, p. 523. Ed. 1576, p. 420. Ed. 1583, p. 424. Ed. 1596. p. 390. Ed. 1684, vol. i. p. 483.

(2) This passage, with the exception of a few words from later Editions, is the opening of the History of John Wickliff, in the edition of 1563, p. 85; and forms the commencement of the Latin edition of Foxe, entitled "Rerum in Ecclesia gestarum, quæ postremis et periculosis his temporibus evenerunt," &c.; published at Basle, in 1559. Perfect copies of the first English edition of Foxe are very scarce; it contains however many valuable and interesting details, suppressed or omitted in all succeeding editions; these are now carefully restored to their proper places, and materially enhance the value of the present work.—Ed.

(3) In the last six hundred years of which our author has treated, there is but little to cheer the mind in contemplating the progress of Christianity. The very name of religion must too often have been associated with the extortion of the legates of the Romish see; the worship of God, with the empty show of the popish service; and the ecclesiastical orders themselves, with impurity, hypocrisy, and deception. Nor is this a singular or prejudiced view of this interesting subject, but rather the result of the calm and deliberate inquiries of our most able historians. It pleased God, however, that upon this state of spiritual and moral darkness, the light of the Reformation should begin to dawn. Some bold and thinking men, amongst whom Wickliff stood so pre-eminent, began to grow weary of the yoke of the Romish church, and to discern the falsehoods of her creed, and the corruptions of her church government. This John Wickliff, to whose interesting times we are now introduced, was born about A.D. 1324, at a small village near Richmond, in Yorkshire, named Wyecliffe: his residence at Oxford commenced in 1340, and his theological lectures in 1372, in the reign of Edward III. In reference to the rise and spread of the doctrines of this Champion of the Truth, an extract from the learned Fuller is subjoined:—"The Romanists observe, that several advantages concurred to the speedy propagation of Wickliff's opinions; as, namely, the decrepid age of Edward the Third; the infancy of Richard, his successor, being but a child, as his grandfather was twice a child, so that the reins of authority were let loose. Secondly, the attractive nature of novelty drawing followers unto it. Thirdly, the enmity which John of Gaunt bore unto the clergy, which made him, out of opposition, to favour the doctrine and person of Wickliff. Lastly, the envy which the pope had contracted by his exactions and collections of ecclesiastical benefices. We deny not these helps were instrumentally active in their several degrees, but must attribute the main to divine providence blessing the gospel, and to the nature of truth itself, which, though for a time violently suppressed, will seasonably make its own free and clear passage into the world."—Fuller's Church History, Book IV.—Ed.

hath done, whom the Holy Ghost hath, from time to time, raised and stirred up in the church of God, to work against the bishop of Rome, to weaken the superstition of the friars, and to vanquish and overthrow the great errors which daily did grow and prevail in the world; amongst whom, in the monuments of histories, are remembered, Berengarius, in the time of the emperor Henry III., A.D. 1051; and John Scotus, who took away the verity of the body and blood from the sacrament; Bruno Audegavensis, Okleus II., Walden, Marsilius of Padua, John of Ganduno, Ocham, with divers others of that sect or school:[1] yet forasmuch as they are not many in number, neither yet very famous or notable, following the course of years, we will begin the narration of this our history with the story and tractation of John Wickliff; in whose time the furious fire of persecution seemed to take its first original and beginning. After all these then, heretofore rehearsed, through God's providence, stepped forth into the arena,[2] the valiant champion of the truth, John Wickliff;* whom the Lord, with the like zeal and power of spirit, raised up here in England, to detect more fully and amply the poison of the pope's doctrine, and the false religion set up by the friars. In whose opinions and assertions, albeit some blemishes perhaps may be noted; yet such blemishes they be, which rather declare him to be a man that might err, than who directly did fight against Christ our Saviour, as the pope's proceedings, and those of the friars, did. And what doctor or learned man hath been from the prime age of the church so perfect, so absolutely sure, in whom no opinion hath sometime swerved awry? and yet be the said articles of his neither in number so many, nor yet so gross in themselves and so cardinal, as those cardinal enemies of Christ, perchance, do give them out to be; if his books which they abolished, were remaining to be conferred with those blemishes which they have wrested to the worst, as evil will never said the best.

The blemishes of Wickliff made worse than they be.

This is certain and cannot be denied, but that he, being the public reader of divinity in the university of Oxford, was, for the rude time wherein he lived, famously reputed for a famous divine, a deep schoolman, and no less expert in all kinds of philosophy; the which doth not only appear by his own most famous and learned writings and monuments, but also by the confession of Walden, his most cruel and bitter enemy, who, in a certain epistle written unto pope Martin V., saith, "That he was wonderfully astonished at his most strong arguments, with the places of authority which he had gathered, with the vehemency and force of his reasons," &c. And thus much out of Walden. It appeareth by such as have observed the order and course of times, that this Wickliff flourished A.D. 1371, Edward III. reigning in England; for thus we do find in the Chronicles of Caxton: "In the year of our Lord 1371," saith he, "Edward III., king of England, in his parliament was against the pope's clergy: he willingly hearkened and gave ear to the voices and tales of heretics, with certain of his council, conceiving and following sinister opinions against the clergy; wherefore, afterwards, he tasted

The testimony of Walden, an enemy, in commendation of Wickliff.

The time Wickliff flourished. A.D. 1371.

(1) "Divers others:" Robert Grosthead, bishop of Lincoln; Armachanus, archbishop of Armagh; Nicholas Orem; the author of the Ploughman's Complaint, and others. See also p. 712; and the beginning of Book V. p. 727.—Ed.

(2) "In arenam prosiliit," in the Latin edition only, p. 1.—Ed.

Edward III

A.D. 1372.

and suffered much adversity and trouble. And not long after, in the year of our Lord," saith he, "1372, he wrote unto the bishop of Rome, that he should not by any means intermeddle any more within his kingdom, as touching the reservation or distribution of benefices; and that all such bishops as were under his dominion should enjoy their former and ancient liberty, and be confirmed of their metropolitans, as hath been accustomed in times past," &c. Thus much writeth Caxton. But, as touching the just number of the year and time, we will not be very curious or careful about it at present: this is out of all doubt, that at what time all the world was in most desperate and vile estate, and that the lamentable ignorance and darkness of God's truth had overshadowed the whole earth, this man stepped forth like a valiant champion, unto whom that may justly be applied which is spoken in the book called Ecclesiasticus, of one Simon, the son of Onias: "Even as the morning star being in the midst of a cloud, and as the moon being full in her course, and as the bright beams of the sun; so doth he shine and glister in the temple and church of God" [chap. l. v. 6.]

A description of Wickliff's time.

Thus doth Almighty God continually succour and help, when all things are in despair: being always, according to the prophecy of the Psalm [Ps. lx. v. 9.], "a helper in time of need;" which thing never more plainly appeared, than in these latter days and extreme age of the church, when the whole state and condition, not only of worldly things, but also of religion, was depraved and corrupted: that, like the disease named lethargy amongst the physicians, even so the state of religion amongst the divines, was past all man's help and remedy. The name only of Christ remained amongst Christians, but his true and lively doctrine was as far unknown to the most part, as his name was common to all men. As touching faith, consolation, the end and use of the law, the office of Christ, our impotency and weakness, the Holy Ghost, the greatness and strength of sin, true works, grace and free justification by faith, the liberty of a christian man, wherein consisteth and resteth the sum and matter of our profession, there was almost no mention, nor any word spoken. Scripture, learning, and divinity, were known but to a few, and that in the schools only; and there also they turned and converted almost all into sophistry. Instead of Peter and Paul, men occupied their time in studying Aquinas and Scotus, and the Master of Sentences. The world, leaving and forsaking the lively power of God's spiritual word and doctrine, was altogether led and blinded with outward ceremonies and human traditions, wherein the whole scope, in a manner, of all christian perfection, did consist and depend. In these was all the hope of obtaining salvation fully fixed; hereunto all things were attributed; insomuch that scarcely any other thing was seen in the temples or churches, taught or spoken of in sermons, or finally intended or gone about in their whole life, but only heaping up of certain shadowy ceremonies upon ceremonies; neither was there any end of their heaping.

The people were taught to worship no other thing but that which they did see; and did see almost nothing which they did not worship.

The church, being degenerated from the true apostolic institution above all measure, reserving only the name of the apostolic church, but far from the truth thereof in very deed, did fall into all kind of extreme tyranny; whereas the poverty and simplicity of Christ was changed into cruelty and abomination of life. Instead of the apostolic gifts and continual labours and travails, slothfulness and ambition had crept in amongst the priests. Beside all this, there arose and sprang up a thousand sorts and fashions of strange religions; being only the root and well-head of all superstition. How great abuses and depravations were crept into the sacraments, at the time they were compelled to worship similitudes and signs of things for the very things themselves; and to adore such things as were instituted and ordained only for memorials! Finally, what thing was there in the whole state of christian religion so sincere, so sound, and so pure, which was not defiled and spotted with some kind of superstition? Besides this, with how many bonds and snares of daily new-fangled ceremonies were the silly consciences of men, redeemed by Christ to liberty, ensnared and snarled; insomuch that there could be no great difference perceived between Christianity and Jewishness, save only the name of Christ: so that the state and condition of the Jews might seem somewhat more tolerable than ours! There was nothing sought for out of the true fountains, but out of the dirty puddles of the Philistines; the christian people were wholly carried away as it were by the nose, with mere decrees and constitutions of men, even whither it pleased the bishops to lead them, and not as Christ's will did direct them. All the whole world was filled and overwhelmed with error and darkness; and no great marvel: for why, the simple and unlearned people, being far from all knowledge of the holy Scripture, thought it quite enough for them to know only those things which were delivered them by their pastors and shepherds, and they, on the other part, taught in a manner nothing else but such things as came forth of the court of Rome; whereof the most part tended to the profit of their order, more than to the glory of Christ.

All good things defiled and spotted with superstition.

The christian faith was esteemed or accounted none other thing then, but that every man should know that Christ once suffered; that is to say, that all men should know and understand that thing which the devils themselves also knew. Hypocrisy was accounted for wonderful holiness. All men were so addicted unto outward shows, that even they themselves, who professed the most absolute and singular knowledge of the Scriptures, scarcely did understand or know any other thing. And this did evidently appear, not only in the common sort of doctors and teachers, but also in the very heads and captains of the church, whose whole religion and holiness consisted, in a manner, in the observing of days, meats, and garments, and such like rhetorical circumstances, as of place, time, person, &c. Hereof sprang so many sorts and fashions of vestures and garments; so many differences of colours and meats, with so many pilgrimages to several places, as though St. James at Compostella[1] could do that, which

The captains of the church seduced, as well as the inferior sort.

(1) "St. James at Compostella." This refers to a famous but most wearisome pilgrimage, much esteemed in former times, to the tomb of St. James at Compostella, in the province of Gallicia in Spain. The distance from Rome was about twelve hundred English miles, and yet from thence, as also from the most distant parts of Europe, have millions of Christians, to their own cost and misery, traversed rocks and mountains to visit that tomb.—See Dr. Michael Geddes' Miscellaneous Tracts, vol. ii.—Ed.

Edward III. A.D. 1372.

Christ could not do at Canterbury; or else that God were not of like power and strength in every place, or could not be found but by being sought for by running gadding hither and thither. Thus the holiness of the whole year was transported and put off unto the Lent season. No country or land was counted holy, but only Palestine, where Christ had walked himself with his corporal feet. Such was the blindness of that time, that men did strive and fight for the cross at Jerusalem, as it had been for the chief and only force and strength of our faith. It is a wonder to read the monuments of the former times, to see and understand what great troubles and calamities this cross hath caused almost in every christian commonwealth, for the Romish champions never ceased, by writing, admonishing, and counselling, yea, and by quarrelling, to move and stir up princes to mind war and battle, even as though the faith and belief of the gospel were of small force, or little effect without that wooden cross. This was the cause of the expedition of the most noble prince king Richard unto Jerusalem; who being taken in the same journey, and delivered unto the emperor, could scarcely be ransomed home again for thirty thousand marks. In the same enterprise or journey, Frederic, the emperor of Rome, a man of most excellent virtue, was much endamaged, A.D. 1179; and also Philip, the king of France, scarcely returned home again in safety, and not without great losses: so much did they esteem the recovery of the holy city and cross.

Palestine deemed holy for Christ's walking there.

Richard king of England.

Frederic, the emperor of Rome.

Philip, king of France.

Upon this alone all men's eyes, minds, and devotions were so set and bent, as though either there were no other cross but that, or that the cross of Christ were in no other place but only at Jerusalem. Such was the blindness and superstition of those days, which understood or knew nothing but such things as were outwardly seen; whereas the profession of our religion standeth in much other higher matters and greater mysteries What was the cause why Urban did so vex and torment himself? Because Antioch, with the holy cross, was lost out of the hands of the Christians; for so we do find it in the Chronicles, that at the time Jerusalem with king Guido and the cross of our Lord was taken, and under the power of the sultan, Urban took the matter so grievously, that for very sorrow he died. In his place succeeded Lambert, who was called Gregory VIII., by whose motion it was decreed by the cardinals, that (setting apart all riches and voluptuousness) "they should preach the cross of Christ, and by their poverty and humility first of all should take the cross upon them, and go before others into the land of Jerusalem." These are the words of the history; whereby it is evident unto the vigilant reader, unto what grossness the true knowledge of the spiritual doctrine of the gospel had degenerated and grown in those days; how great blindness and darkness were in those days, even in the first primacy and supremacy of the bishop of Rome: as though the outward succession of Peter and the apostles had been of greater force and effect to that matter. What doth it signify in what place Peter did rule or not rule? It is much more to be regarded that every man should labour and study with all his endeavour to follow the life and confession of Peter; and that man seemeth unto me to be the true successor of Peter against whom the gates of hell shall not prevail. For if Peter in the Gospel

The knowledge of the gospel grossly expounded by the Romanists.

do bear the type and figure of the christian church (as all men, in a manner, do affirm), what more foolish or vain thing can there be, than through private usurpation, to restrain and to bind that unto one man, which, by the appointment of the Lord, is of itself free and open to so many?

*But[1] let it be so that Peter did establish his chair and seat at Rome, and admit that he did the like at Antioch: what doth this place of Peter make, or help, to the remission of sins, to the interpretation of Scriptures, or to have the authority or keys of binding and loosing? The which things, if they be the works of the Holy Ghost and of christian faith, and not of the place, surely very foolishly do we then refer them unto the see of Rome; including, and hedging them in, as it were, within certain borders and limits, as though there was no faith, or that the Holy Ghost had no operation or power, in any other place but only at Rome. What doth it make matter, where Peter served the Lord? We ought rather to seek and know wherein Peter was acceptable unto his Lord, or wherefore? that we likewise, with all our whole power and endeavour, may go about by the same means and way, to do the like.

Wherefore if we do think or judge that Christ had given unto Peter any singular or particular privilege, which was not also granted unto the residue of the apostles, more for any private affection or love of the man (such as many times reigneth amongst us now-a-days), we are far deceived. But if that he, for the most high, divine, and ready confession, which not he alone, but for, and in the name of them all, did pronounce and express, obtained any singular privilege; then he who doth succeed in the place and chair of Peter, doth not, by and by, show forth Peter's faith; but whosoever doth nearest follow Peter in faith (in what chair or see soever he do sit), is worthily to be counted the successor of Peter, and is his successor indeed; in such sort and wise that he getteth thereby no kind of worldly honour. For the apostleship is an office, and no degree of honour; a ministry or service, and no mastership or rule; for as amongst the apostles themselves there was no pre-eminence of place or dignity, but that they altogether, with one mind, spirit, and accord, went about and did the work of their Master, and not their own business, so he who was the least amongst them was most set by, before Christ their witness.[2] Whereby their succession deserved praise before God, but neither dignity nor promotion in the world. For, as Polycarp answered very well in Eusebius, unto the under-consul, "How doth the profession of them (said he,) who have forsaken all things for Christ's sake, accord or agree with these worldly riches and earthly promotions?"

But the bishops in these days[3] (I know not by what means of ambition, or desire of promotion), have altered and changed the ecclesiastical ministration into a worldly policy, that even as prince succeedeth prince, so one bishop doth succeed another in the see, as by right and title of inheritance, flowing and abounding moreover in all

(1) These three paragraphs, with the few words at the close of the succeeding one, are reprinted, with the aid of the Latin, from the edition of 1563, p 87. See also the Latin edition of 1559, pp 33, 34 —Ed

(2) "Before Christ, witness to himself"—Edition 1563, p 87 "Sic ut qui minor inter ipsos foret, pluris haberetur apud Christum testem "—Lat Edition 1559, p 4 —Ed

(3) Edition 1563 —"Their days" Edition 1559.—"Illorum temporum."—Ed

Edward III. A.D. 1376.

kind of wealth and riches here in earth; being also guarded, after the fashion and manner of the world, with routs and bands of men, challenging unto himself rule and lordship, in such manner that the whole governance and rule of all things fully did rest and remain in his power and hands. All other pastors and shepherds of other churches had no power or authority, more than was permitted and granted unto them by him. He alone did not only rule and govern over all churches, but also reigned over all kingdoms; he alone was feared of all men; the other ministers of Christ were little or nothing regarded; all things were in his power, and at his hands only, all things were sought for. There was no power to excommunicate, no authority to release, neither any knowledge of understanding or interpreting the Scriptures, in any other place, but only in the cloister at Rome.*

The rising up of Wickliff in troublous times.

Thus, in these so great and troublous times and horrible darkness of ignorance, what time there seemed in a manner to be no one so little a spark of pure doctrine left or remaining, this aforesaid Wickliff, by God's providence, sprang and rose up, through whom the Lord would first waken and raise up again the world, which was overmuch drowned and whelmed in the deep streams of human traditions. Thus you have here the time of Wickcliff's origin: now we will also in few words show somewhat of his troubles and conflicts.

Wickliff, a divine of Oxford.

This Wickliff, after he had now a long time professed divinity in the university of Oxford, and perceiving the true doctrine of Christ's gospel to be adulterated and defiled with so many filthy inventions of bishops, sects of monks, and dark errors: and that he, after long debating and deliberating with himself (with many secret sighs, and bewailing in his mind the general ignorance of the whole world), could no longer suffer or abide the same, at the last determined with himself to help and to remedy such things as he saw to be wide, and out of the way. But, forasmuch as he saw that this dangerous meddling could not be attempted or stirred without great trouble, neither that these things, which had been so long time with use and custom rooted and grafted in men's minds, could be suddenly plucked up or taken away, he thought with himself that this matter should be done by little and little. Wherefore he, taking his original at small occasions, thereby opened himself a way or mean to greater matters. And first he assailed his adversaries in logical and metaphysical questions, disputing with them of the first form and fashion of things, of the increase of time, and of the intelligible substance of a creature, with other such like sophisms of no great effect; but yet, notwithstanding, it did not a little help and furnish him, who minded to dispute of greater matters. So in these matters first began Keningham, a Carmelite, to dispute and argue against John Wickliff.

By these originals, the way was made unto greater points, so that at length he came to touch the matters of the sacraments, and other abuses of the church; touching which things this holy man took great pains, protesting, as they said, openly in the schools, that it was his chief and principal purpose and intent, to revoke and call back the church from her idolatry, to some better amendment; especially in the matter of the sacrament of the body and blood of Christ. But this boil or sore could not be touched without the great grief and pain of the whole world: for, first of all, the whole glut of monks and begging friars was set in a rage and madness, who, even as hornets with their sharp stings, did assail this good man on every side; fighting, as is said, for their altars, paunches, and bellies. After them the priests and bishops, and then after them the archbishop, being then Simon Sudbury, took the matter in hand; who, for the same cause, deprived him of his benefice, which then he had in Oxford. *At[1] the last, when their power seemed also not sufficient to withstand the truth which was then breaking out, they ran wholly unto the lightnings and thunderings of the bishop of Rome, as it had been unto the last refuge of most force and strength. For this is their extreme succour and anchor-hold, in all such storms and troubles, when the outcries of monks and friars, and their pharisaical wickedness, cannot any more prevail.* Notwithstanding, he being somewhat befriended and supported by the king, as appeareth, continued and bore out the malice of the friars and of the archbishop all this while from his first beginning, till about A.D. 1377; after which time, now to prosecute likewise of his troubles and conflict, first I must fetch about a little compass, as is requisite, to introduce some mention of John of Gaunt, duke of Lancaster, the king's son, and lord Henry Percy, who were his special maintainers.

Edward III. — A.D. 1377.

Wickliff deprived of his benefice at Oxford.

Duke of Lancaster, and lord Henry Percy, great maintainers of Wickliff.

As years and time grew on, king Edward III., who had now reigned about fifty-one years, after the decease of prince Edward his son, who departed the year before, was stricken with great age, and with such feebleness withal, that he was unwieldly, through lack of strength, to govern the affairs of the realm. Wherefore, a parliament being called the year before his death, it was there put up, by the knights and other the burgesses of the parliament, because of the misgovernment of the realm (by certain greedy persons about the king, raking all to themselves, without seeing any justice done), that twelve sage and discreet lords and peers, such as were free from note of all avarice, should be placed as tutors about the king, to have the doing and disposing under him (six at one time, and in their absence, six at another) of matters pertaining to the public regiment. Here, by the way, I omit to speak of Alice Perris, the wicked harlot, who, as the story reporteth, had bewitched the king's heart, and governed all, and sat upon causes herself, through the devilish help of a friar Dominic; who, by the duke of Lancaster, was caused to be taken, and was convicted, and would have suffered for the same, had not the archbishop of Canterbury and the friars, more regarding the liberty of their church than the punishment of vice, reclaimed him for their own prisoner. This Alice Perris, notwithstanding she was banished by this parliament from the king, yet afterwards she came again, and left him not, till at his death she took all his rings upon his fingers and other jewels from him, and so fled away like a harlot. But this of her by the way.

Alice Perris, the king's concubine.

The king bewitched by a woman through the help of a friar.

These twelve governors, by parliament aforesaid being appointed to have the tuition of the king, and to attend the public affairs of the realm, remained for a certain space about him; till afterwards it so fell out, that they being again removed, all the regiment of the realm next under the king, was committed to the duke of Lancaster, the king's son; for as yet Richard, the son of prince Edward, lately departed, was very young and under age.

Twelve governors assigned about the king.

(1) See Edition 1563, p. 88. Lat. Ed. 1559, p. 5.—Ed.

Edward III

A.D. 1377.

This duke of Lancaster had in his heart of long time conceived a certain displeasure against the popish clergy; whether for corrupt and impure doctrine, joined with like abominable excess of life, or for what other cause, it is not precisely expressed; only by story the cause thereof may be guessed to arise by William Wickham, bishop of Winchester.[1] The matter is this:

A practice of the prelate against the duke of Lancaster

The bishop of Winchester, as the saying went then, was reported to affirm, that the aforesaid John of Gaunt, duke of Lancaster, was not the son of king Edward, nor of the queen; who, being in travail at Gaunt, had no son, as he said, but a daughter, which, the same time, by lying upon of the mother in the bed, was there smothered. Whereupon the queen, fearing the king's displeasure, caused a certain man-child of a woman of Flanders, born the very same time, to be conveyed, and brought unto her instead of her daughter aforesaid; and so she brought up the child whom she bare not, who now is called duke of Lancaster. And this, said the bishop, did the queen tell him, lying in extremity on her death-bed, under seal of confession; charging him if the said duke should ever aspire to get the crown, or if the kingdom by any means should fall unto him, he then should manifest the same, and declare it to the world, that the said duke of Lancaster was no part of the king's blood, but a false heir of the king. This slanderous report of the wicked bishop, as it savoureth of a contumelious lie, so seemeth it to proceed of a subtle zeal towards the pope's religion, meaning falsehood: for the aforesaid duke, by favouring of Wickliff, declared himself to be a professed enemy against the pope's profession; which thing was then not unknown, neither unmarked of the prelates and bishops then in England. But the sequel of the story thus followed:

William Wickham, bishop of Winchester deprived

"This slanderous villany of the bishop's report being blazed abroad, and coming to the duke's ear; he, therewith being not a little discontented, as no marvel was, sought again, by what means he could, to be revenged of the bishop. In conclusion the duke, having now all the government of the realm, under the king his father, in his own hands, so pursued the bishop of Winchester, that by act of parliament he was condemned and deprived of all his temporal goods; which goods were assigned to prince Richard, of Bourdeaux, the next in heritor of the crown after the king; and, furthermore, he inhibited the said bishop from approaching nearer to the court than twenty miles." Further as touching this bishop, the story thus proceedeth: "Not long after (A.D. 1377), a parliament was called by means of the duke of Lancaster, upon certain causes and respects; in which parliament great request and suit was made by the clergy, for the deliverance of the bishop of Winchester. At length, when a subsidy was asked in the king's name of the clergy, and request also made, in the king's behalf, for speedy expedition to be made for the dissolving of the parliament, the archbishop therefore accordingly convented the bishops for the tractation thereof. To whom the bishops with great lamentation complained for lack of their fellow and brother, the bishop of Winchester, whose injury, said they, did derogate from the liberties of the whole church; and therefore they refused to join themselves in

Liberties of the church a great matter.

(1) Ex Chron Monasterii Albani.

tractation of any such matters, before all the members together were united with the head; and, seeing the matter touched them altogether in common, as well him as them, they would not otherwise do. And they seemed, moreover, to be moved against the archbishop because he was not more stout in the cause, but suffered himself so to be cited of the duke." *Edward III.* A.D. 1377.

The archbishop, although he had sufficient cause to excuse himself, wherefore not to send for him, (as also he did,) because of the perils which might ensue thereof, yet being forced and persuaded thereto by the importunity of the bishops, directed down his letters to the aforesaid bishop of Winchester, willing him to resort unto the convocation of the clergy; who, being glad to obey the same, was received with great joy by the other bishops; and, at length, by means of Alice Perris, the king's paramour, above mentioned, having given her a good quantity of money, the said Winchester was restored to his temporalities again.

Bishop of Winchester sent for to the convocation.

As the bishops had thus sent for Winchester, the duke in the mean time had sent for John Wickliff, who, as is said, was then the divinity reader in Oxford, and had commenced, in sundry acts and disputations, contrary to the form and teaching of the pope's church in many things; who also, for the same had been deprived of his benefice, as hath been before noticed. The opinions which he began at Oxford, in his lectures and sermons, first to treat of, and for which he was deprived, were these: That the pope had no more power to excommunicate any man, than hath another. That if it be given by any person to the pope to excommunicate, yet to absolve the same is as much in the power of another priest, as in his. He affirmed, moreover, that neither the king, nor any temporal lord, could give any perpetuity to the church, or to any ecclesiastical person; for that when such ecclesiastical persons do sin, 'habitualiter,' continuing in the same still, the temporal powers ought and may meritoriously take away from them what before hath been bestowed upon them. And that he proved to have been practised before here in England by William Rufus; "which thing," said he, "if he did lawfully, why may not the same also be practised now?" "If he did it unlawfully, then doth the church err," saith he, "and doth unlawfully in praying for him." But of his assertions more shall follow, Christ willing, hereafter. The story which ascribed to him these assertions, being taken out, as I take it, of the monastery of St. Alban's, addeth withal: That in his teaching and preaching he was very eloquent, "but a dissembler," saith he, "and a hypocrite." The cause why he surmiseth him to be a hypocrite, was this:

John Wickliff sent for by the duke of Lancaster.

Example of William Rufus.

First, Because he resorted much to the orders of the begging friars, frequenting and extolling the perfection of their poverty.

Secondly, Because he and his fellows usually accustomed in their preaching to go barefoot, and in simple russet gowns.

By this, I suppose, may sufficiently appear to the indifferent, the nature and condition of Wickliff, how far it was from the ambition and pride, which the slanderous pen of Polydore Virgil reporteth in his nineteenth book of him, namely, that because he was not preferred to higher honours and dignities of the church, (conceiving therefore indignation against the clergy,) he became their mortal

The slanderous pen of Polydore.

Edward III. A.D. 1377.

enemy. How true was this, He only knoweth best, that rightly shall judge both the one and the other.

In the mean time, by other circumstances and parts of his life, we may also partly conjecture what is to be thought of the man. But however it was in him, whether true or false, yet it had been Polydore's part, either not so intemperately to have abused his pen, or at least, to have showed some greater authority and ground of that his report: for to follow nothing else but flying fame, so rashly to defame a man whose life he knoweth not, is not the part of a faithful story-writer.

Wickliff falsely charged with ambition by Polydore.

But to return from whence we digressed. Beside these his opinions and assertions above recited, with others which are hereafter to be brought forward in order, he began then something nearly to touch the matter of the sacrament, proving that in the said sacrament the accidents of bread remained not without the subject, or substance; and this, both by the holy Scriptures, and also by the authority of the doctors, but especially by such as were most ancient. As for the later writers, that is to say, such as have written upon that argument under the thousand years since Christ's time, he utterly refused them, saying, That after these years Satan was loosed and set at liberty; and that since that time the life of man hath been most subject to, and in danger of, errors; and that the simple and plain truth doth appear and consist in the Scriptures, whereunto all human traditions, whatsoever they be, must be referred, and especially such as are set forth and published now of late years. This was the cause why he refused the later writers of decretals, leaning only to the Scriptures and ancient doctors; most stoutly affirming out of them, that in the sacrament of the body, which is celebrated with bread, the accidents are not present without the substance; that is to say, that the body of Christ is not present without the bread, as the common sort of priests in those days did dream. As for his arguments, what they were, we will shortly, at more opportunity, by God's grace, declare them in another place, lest that with so long a digression we seem to defer and put off the reader. But herein the truth, as the poet speaketh very truly, had gotten John Wickliff great displeasure and hatred at many men's hands; and especially of the monks and richest sort of priests.

Wickliff beginneth to touch the matter of the sacrament.

The latter writers of the church to be misdoubted. The accidents not to be in the sacrament without the substance.

Albeit through the favour and supportation of the duke of Lancaster and lord Henry Percy, he persisted, hitherto, in some mean quiet against their wolfish violence and cruelty: till at last, (about A.D. 1377, the bishops, still urging and inciting their archbishop Simon Sudbury, who before had deprived him, and afterward prohibited him also not to stir any more in those sorts of matters, had obtained, by process and order of citation, to have him brought before them; whereunto both place and time for him to appear, after their usual form, was to him assigned.

The duke, having intelligence that Wickliff, his client, should come before the bishops, fearing that he being but one, was too weak against such a multitude, calleth to him, out of the orders of friars, four bachelors of divinity, out of every order one, to join them with Wickliff also, for more surety. When the day was come, assigned to the said Wickliff to appear, which day was Thursday, the nineteenth of February, John Wickliff went, accompanied with the four friars aforesaid, and with them also the duke of Lancaster, and lord Henry Percy, lord marshal of England; the said lord Percy also going before them to make room and way where Wickliff should come.

Thus Wickliff, through the providence of God, being sufficiently guarded, was coming to the place where the bishops sat; whom, by the way, they animated and exhorted not to fear or shrink a whit at the company of the bishops there present, who were all unlearned, said they, in respect of him (for so proceed the words of my aforesaid author, whom I follow in this narration), neither that he should dread the concourse of the people, whom they would themselves assist and defend, in such sort, as he should take no harm.[1] With these words, and with the assistance of the nobles, Wickliff, in heart encouraged, approached to the church of St. Paul in London, where a main press of people were gathered to hear what should be said and done. Such was there the frequency and throng of the multitude, that the lords, notwithstanding all the puissance of the high marshal, and only with great difficulty, got a way through; insomuch that the bishop of London, whose name was William Courtney, seeing the stir that the lord marshal kept up in the church among the people, speaking to the lord Percy, said, that if he had known before what masteries he would have kept in the church, he would have stopped him out from coming there; at which words of the bishop, the duke, disdaining not a little, answered the bishop, and said, that he would keep such mastery there, though he said 'nay.'

Striving of the lords to pass by the people.

The words of the bishop of London to the lord Percy.

At last, after much wrestling, they pierced through and came to Our Lady's Chapel, where the dukes and barons were sitting together with the archbishops and other bishops; before whom Wickliff, according to the manner, stood, to know what should be laid unto him. To whom first spake the lord Percy, bidding him to sit down, saying, that he had many things to answer to, and therefore had need of some softer seat. But the bishop of London, cast at once into a fumish chafe by those words, said, he should not sit there. Neither was it, said he, according to law or reason, that he, who was cited there to appear to answer before his ordinary, should sit down during the time of his answer, but that he should stand. Upon these words a fire began to heat and kindle between them; insomuch that they began so to rate and revile one the other, that the whole multitude, therewith disquieted, began to be set on a hurry.

Strife between the lord marshal and bishop of London.

Then the duke, taking the lord Percy's part, with hasty words began also to take up the bishop. To whom the bishop again, nothing inferior in reproachful checks and rebukes, did render and requite not only to him as good as he brought, but also did so far excel him in this railing art of scolding, that to use the words of mine author, "Erubuit dux, quod non potuit prævalere litigio;" that is, the duke blushed and was ashamed, because he could not overpass the bishop in brawling and railing, and, therefore, he fell to plain threatening; menacing the bishop, that he would bring down the pride, not only of him, but also of all the prelacy of England. And speaking, moreover, unto him: "Thou," said he, "bearest thyself so brag upon thy parents, who shall not be able to help thee; they shall

Strife between the duke of Lancaster and bishop of London, who overgoeth the duke in scolding.

(1) Ex Hist. Monachi D. Albani ex accommodato D. Matth. Archiepis. Cant.

Edward III.

A. D. 1377.

have enough to do to help themselves;" for his parents were the earl and countess of Devonshire.[1] To whom the bishop again answered, that to be bold to tell truth, his confidence was not in his parents, nor in any man else, but only in God in whom he trusted. Then the duke softly whispering in the ear of him next by him, said, That he would rather pluck the bishop by the hair of his head out of the church, than he would take this at his hand. This was not spoken so secretly, but that the Londoners overheard him. Whereupon, being set in a rage, they cried out, saying, that they would not suffer their bishop so contemptuously to be abused. But rather they would lose their lives, than that he should so be drawn out by the hair. Thus that council, being broken with scolding and brawling for that day, was dissolved before nine o'clock, and the duke, with the lord Percy, went to the parliament; where, the same day before dinner, a bill was put up in the name of the king by the lord Thomas Woodstock and lord Henry Percy, that the city of London should no more be governed by a mayor, but by a captain, as in times before; and that the marshal of England should have all the ado in taking the arrests within the said city, as in other cities besides, with other petitions more, tending to the like derogation of the liberties of London. This bill being read, John Philpot, then burgess for the city, standeth up, saying to those who read the bill, that that was never seen so before; and adding, moreover, that the mayor would never suffer any such things, or other arrest to be brought into the city; with more such words of like stoutness.

The duke threateneth to draw their bishop by the hair out of the church.

Petitions put up in parliament against the city of London.

Hasty counsel of the Londoners.

The next day following the Londoners assembled themselves in a council, to consider among them upon the bill for changing the mayor, and about the office of the marshal; also, concerning the injuries done the day before to their bishop.

In the mean time, they, being busy in long consultation of this matter, suddenly and unawares entered into the place two certain lords, whether come to spy, or for what other cause, the author leaveth it uncertain; the one called lord Fitz-Walter, the other lord Guy Bryan. At the first coming in of them the vulgar sort was ready forthwith to fly upon them as spies, had not they made their protestation with an oath, declaring that their coming in was for no harm toward them. And so they were compelled by the citizens to swear to the city their truth and fidelity: contrary to the which oath, if they should rebel, contented they would be to forfeit whatsoever goods and possessions they had within the city.

The oration of the lord Fitz-Walter to the Londoners.

This done, then began the Lord Fitz-Walter, in this wise, to persuade and exhort the citizens; first declaring how he was bound and obliged to them and to their city, not only on account of the oath now newly received, but of old and ancient good will from his great grandfather's time. Besides other divers duties, for the which he was chiefly bound to be one of their principal fautors; forasmuch as whatsoever tendeth to their damage and detriment redounded also no less unto his own: for which cause he could not otherwise choose, but that what he did understand to be attempted against the public profit and liberties of the city, he must needs communicate the same to them; who, unless they, with speedy circumspection, do occur, and

(1) This bishop of London was William Courtney, son to the earl of Devonshire.

prevent perils that may and are like to ensue, it would turn, in the end, to their no small incommodity. And as there were many other things which required their vigilant care and diligence, so one thing there was, which he could in no wise but admonish them of; which was this, necessary to be considered of them all: how the lord marshal Henry Percy, in his place within himself, had one in ward and custody, whether with the knowledge, or without the knowledge of them, he could not tell: this he could tell, that the said lord marshal was not allowed any such ward or prison in his house within the liberties of the city; which thing, if it be not seen to in time, the example thereof being suffered, would, in fine, breed to such a prejudice unto their customs and liberties, as that they should not, hereafter, when they would, reform the injury thereof.

These words of the lord Fitz-Walter were no sooner spoken, but they were as soon taken by the rash citizens; who, in all hasty fury, running to their armour and weapons, went immediately to the house of the lord Percy, where, breaking up the gates, by violence they took out the prisoner, and burned the stocks wherein he sat in the midst of London. Then was the lord Percy sought for, whom, saith the story, they would doubtless have slain if they might have found him. With their bills and javelins, all corners and privy chambers were searched, and beds and hangings torn asunder. But the lord Percy, as God would, was then with the duke, whom one John Yper, the same day, with great instance, had desired to dinner.

The citizens of London break up the lord Percy's house at Savoy

God's provision in saving his servants

The Londoners not finding him at home, and supposing that he was with the duke at the Savoy, in all hasty heat turned their power thither, running as fast as they could to the duke's house; where also, in like manner, they were disappointed of their cruel purpose. In the mean while, as this was doing, cometh one of the duke's men, running post haste to the duke and to the lord Percy, declaring what was done. The duke being then at his oysters, without any further tarrying, and also breaking both his shins at the form for haste, took boat with the lord Percy, and by water went to Kingston, where then the princess, with Richard the young prince did lie; and there declared unto the princess all the whole matter concerning the outrage of the Londoners, as it was. To whom she promised again, that such an order should be taken in the matter, as should be to his satisfaction. At the time the commons of London thus, as is said, were about the duke's house at Savoy, there meeteth with them a certain priest, who, marvelling at the sudden rage and concourse, asked what they sought. To whom answer was given again by some, that they sought for the duke and the lord marshal, to have of them the lord Peter de la Mare, whom they wrongfully had detained in prison. To this the priest answered again more boldly than opportunely: "That Peter," said he, "is a false traitor to the king, and worthy long since to be hanged." At the hearing of these words, the furious people, with a terrible shout, cried out upon him, that he was a traitor, and one that took the duke's part, and so falling upon him with their weapons, strove who might first strike him; and after they had wounded him very sore, they had him, so wounded, to prison; where, within few days, for the soreness of his wounds, he died.

The house of the duke of Lancaster searched by the Londoners

The duke and lord Percy fly to the prince

A priest in the duke of Lancaster's house cruelly killed

Edward III. A.D. 1377. Neither would the rage of the people thus have ceased; had not the bishop of London, leaving his dinner, come to them at Savoy, and putting them in remembrance of the blessed time, as they term it, of Lent, had persuaded them to cease and to be quiet.

The villany of the Londoners against the duke. The Londoners, seeing they could get no advantage against the duke, who was without their reach, to wreak their anger, took his arms, which in most despiteful ways they hanged up in the open places of the city, in sign of reproach, as for a traitor. Insomuch that when one of his gentlemen came through the city, with a plate containing the duke's arms, hanging by a lace about his neck, the citizens, not abiding the sight thereof, cast him from his horse, and plucked his escutcheon from him, and were about to work the extremity against him, had not the mayor rescued him out of their hands, and sent him home safe unto the duke his master. In such hatred then was the duke among the vulgar people of London.

The message of the princess to the Londoners. After this the princess, understanding the hearts and broil of the Londoners, set against the aforesaid duke, sent to London three knights, Sir Albred Lewer, Sir Simon Burley, and Sir Lewis Clifford, to entreat the citizens to be reconciled with the duke. The Londoners answered, that they, for the honour of the princess, would obey and do with all reverence, what she would require; but this they required and enjoined the messengers to say to the duke by word of mouth: that he should suffer the bishop of Winchester, before-mentioned, and also the lord Peter de la Mare, to come to their answer, and to be judged by their peers; whereby they might either be quit, if they were guiltless; or otherwise, if they be found culpable, they might receive, according to their deserts after the laws of the realm, what grief and displeasure the duke conceived and retained in his mind hereof. Again, what means and suit the Londoners on their part made to the old king for their liberties; what rhymes and songs in London were made against the duke; how the bishops, at the duke's request, were moved to excommunicate those malicious slanderers; and, moreover, how the duke at last was revenged of those contumelies and injuries; how he caused them to be brought before the king; how sharply they were rebuked for their misdemeanour by the worthy oration of the lord chamberlain, Robert Aston, in the presence of the king, archbishops, bishops, with divers other states, the king's children, and other nobilities of the realm; in conclusion, how the Londoners were compelled to this at length, by the common assent and public charges of the city, to make a great taper of wax, which, with the duke's arms set upon it, should be brought with solemn procession to the church of St. Paul, there to burn continually before the image of Our Lady; and, at last, how both the said duke and the Londoners were reconciled together, in the beginning of the reign of the new king, with the kiss of peace; and how the same reconcilement was publicly announced in the church of Westminster, and what joy was in the whole city thereof: these, because they are impertinent and make too long a digression from the matter of Wickliff, I cut off with brevity, referring the reader to other histories, such as that of St. Alban's, where they are to be found at large.

The duke revenged of the Londoners.

The Londoners caused to bear a taper of wax in procession, in honour of the duke.

As these aforesaid things, for brevity sake, I pass over, so I cannot

Edward III. A.D. 1377.

omit, though I will not be long, that which happened the same time and year to the bishop of Norwich, to the intent that this posterity now may see, to what pride the clergy of the pope's church had then grown. At the same time that this broil was in London, the bishop of Norwich, a little after Easter, coming to the town of Lennam, belonging to his lordship; being not contented with the old accustomed honour due unto him, and used of his predecessors before in the same town, required, moreover, with a new and unused kind of magnificence to be exalted: insomuch that when he saw the chief magistrate or mayor of that town to go in the streets with his officer going before him, holding a certain wand in his hand, tipped at both ends with black horn, as the manner was, he, reputing himself to be lord of that town, as he was, and thinking to be higher than the highest, commanded the honour of that staff due to the mayor, to be yielded and borne before his lordly personage. The mayor or bailiff, with other the townsmen, courteously answered him, that they were right willing and contented, with all their hearts, to exhibit that reverence unto him; and would so do, if he first of the king and council could obtain that custom, and if the same might be induced, after any peaceable way, with the good wills of the commons and body of the town: otherwise, said they, as the matter was dangerous, so they durst not take in hand any such new alteration of ancient customs and liberties, lest the people, who are always inclinable and prone to evil, do fall upon them with stones, and drive them out of the town. Wherefore, kneeling on their knees before him, there humbly they besought him that he would require no such thing of them; that he would save his own honour, and their lives, who, otherwise, if he intended that way, were in great danger. But the bishop, youthful and haughty, taking occasion, by their humbleness, to swell the more in himself, answered, that he would not be taught by their counsel, but that he would have it done, though all the commons (whom he named ribalds) said 'nay.' Also he rebuked the mayor and his brethren for mecocks and dastards, for so fearing the vulgar sort of people.

A story of the bishop of Norwich.

Example of pride in the pope's clergy.

The courtesy of the townsmen to the bishop.

The stout answer of the bishop to the township.

The citizens perceiving the wilful stoutness of the bishop, meekly answering again, said, they minded not to resist him, but to let him do therein what he thought good: only they desired him that he would license them to depart, and hold them excused for not waiting upon him, and conducting him out of the town with that reverence which he required, for if they should be seen in his company, all the suspicion thereof would be upon them, and so should they be all in danger, as much as their lives were worth. The bishop, not regarding their advice and counsel, commanded one of his men to take the rod borne before the mayor, and to carry the same before him: which being done, and perceived of the commons, the bishop after that manner went not far, but the rude people running to shut the gates, came out with their bows, some with clubs and staves, some with other instruments, some with stones, and let drive at the bishop and his men as fast as they might, in such sort, that both the bishop and his horse under him, with most part of his men, were hurt and wounded. And thus the glorious pride of this jolly prelate, ruffling in his new sceptre, was received and welcomed there: that is, he

The town of Lennam riseth against the bishop.

Edward III. — A.D. 1377.

was so pelted with bats and stones, so wounded with arrows and other instruments fit for such a skirmish, that the most part of his men, with his mace bearer, all running away from him, the poor wounded bishop was there left alone, not able to keep his old power, who went about to usurp a new power more than to him belonged. Thus, as is commonly true in all, so is it well exemplified here, that which is commonly said, and as it is commonly seen, that pride will have a fall, and power usurped will never stand. In like manner, if the citizens of Rome, following the example of these Lennam-men, as they have the like cause, and greater, to do by the usurped power of their bishop, would, after the same sauce, handle the pope, and unsceptre him of his mace and regality, which nothing pertain to him; they, in so doing, should both recover their own liberties, with more honour at home, and also win much more commendation abroad.[1]

Pride will have a fall. Power usurped will never stand. The usurped power of the pope would have a bridle.

This tragedy, with all the parts thereof, being thus ended at Lennam, a little after Easter (as is said), about the month of April, A. D. 1377, the same year, upon the 12th day of June, died the worthy and victorious prince, king Edward III., after he had reigned fifty-one years; a prince not more aged in years than renowned for many singular and heroical virtues, but principally noted and lauded for his singular meekness and clemency towards his subjects and inferiors, ruling them by gentleness and mercy without all rigour or austere severity. Among other noble and royal ornaments of his nature, worthily and copiously set forth of many, thus he is described by some, which may briefly suffice for the comprehension of all the rest:[1] "To the orphans he was as a father, compassionate to the afflicted, mourning with the miserable, relieving the oppressed, and to all them that wanted, an helper in time of need,"[2] &c. But, chiefly, above all other things in this prince, in my mind, to be commemorated is this, that he, above all other kings of this realm, unto the time of king Henry VIII., was the greatest bridler of the pope's usurped power, and outrageous oppression: during all the time of which king, not only the pope could not greatly prevail in this realm, but also John Wickliff was maintained with favour and aid sufficient.[3]

The death of king Edward. The commendation of king Edward.

But before we close up the story of this king, there cometh to hand that which I thought good not to omit, a noble purpose of the king in requiring a view to be taken in all his dominions of all benefices and dignities ecclesiastical remaining in the hands of Italians, and aliens, with the true valuation of the same, directed down by commission; whereof the like also is to be found in the time of king Richard II., the tenor of which commission of king Edward III., I thought here under to set down for worthy memory.

The king directed writs unto all the bishops of England in this form:

Edward, by the grace of God, king, &c. To the reverend father in Christ N., by the same grace bishop of L., greeting. Being willing upon certain causes to be certified what and how many benefices, as well archdeaconries and other dignities, as vicarages, parsonages, prebends and chapels, within your diocese, be at this present in the hands of Italians and other strangers, what they be, of what value, and how every of the said benefices be called by name; and

(1) Ex Chron. Monach. D. Albani.

(2) "Orphanis erat quasi pater, afflictis compatiens, miseris condolens, oppressos relevans, et cunctis indigentibus impendens auxilia opportuna."

(3) The reign of Edward III. closes here in the second and third editions.—Ed.

how much every of the same is worth by the year, not as by way of tax or extent, but according to the true value of the same; likewise of the names of all and singular such strangers being now incumbents or occupying the same and every of them; moreover, the names of all them, whether Englishmen or strangers, of what state or condition soever they be, who have the occupation or disposition of any such benefices with the fruits and profits of the same, in the behalf, or by the authority of any the aforesaid strangers, by way of farm, or title, or procuration, or by any other ways or means whatsoever, and how long they have occupied or disposed the same; and withal if any the said strangers be now residents upon any benefices: we command you, as we heretofore commanded you, that you send us a true certificate of all and singular the premises, into our high court of chancery under your seal distinctly and openly, on this side the feast of the Ascension of our Lord next coming, without further delay: returning unto us this our writ withal. Witness ourself at Westminster the sixteenth day of April in the forty-eighth year of our reign of England, and over France the thirty-fifth year. (A. D. 1375.)

Edward III.

A.D. 1377.

By virtue hereof, certificate was sent up to the king into his chancery, out of every diocese of England, of all such spiritual livings as were then in the occupation either of priors, aliens, or of other strangers; whereof the number was so great, as being all set down, it would fill almost half a quire of paper. Whereby may appear that it was high time for the king to seek remedy herein, either by treaty with the pope or otherwise; considering so great a portion of the revenues of his realm was, by this means, conveyed away and employed either for the relief of his enemies, or the maintenance of the foreigners; amongst which number the cardinals of the court of Rome lacked not their share, as may appear by this which followeth.

View of Ecclesiastical Benefices.

The lord Francis of the title of St. Sabine, priest and cardinal of the holy church of Rome, doth hold and enjoy the deanery of the cathedral church of Lichfield, in the jurisdiction of Lichfield, which is worth five hundred marks by the year; and the prebend of Brewood, and the parsonage of Adbaston to the same deanery annexed, which prebend is worth by the year fourscore marks, and the parsonage twenty pounds; which deanery with the prebends and parsonage aforesaid, he hath holden and occupied for the space of three years. And one Master de Ingrisa, a stranger, as proctor to the said cardinal, doth hold and occupy the same deanery with other the premises with the appurtenances, by name of proctor, during the years aforesaid, and hath taken up the fruits and profits, for the said cardinal, dwelling not in the realm. **Coventry and Lichfield.**

Lord William, cardinal of St. Angelo, a stranger, doth hold the archdeaconry of Suffolk, by virtue of provision apostolical, from the feast of St. Nicholas last past; he is not resident upon his said archdeaconry. And the said archdeaconry, together with the procurations due by reason of the visitation, is worth by year sixty-six pounds thirteen shillings and four pence. And Master John of Hellinington, &c., doth occupy the seal of the official of the said archdeaconry, &c. **Norwich.**

Lord Reginald of St. Adrian, deacon-cardinal, hath in the said county the parsonage of Godalming, worth by year forty pounds, and one Edward Teweste doth farm the said parsonage for nine years past. **Surren.**

The lord Anglicus of the holy church of Rome, priest and cardinal, a stranger, was incumbent, and did hold in possession the deanery of the cathedral church of York, from the eleventh day of November, A.D. 1366, and it is yearly worth, according to the true value thereof, four hundred pounds; and Master John of Stoke, canon of the said church, doth occupy the said deanery and the profits of the same, in the name or by the authority of the said lord dean, &c. But the said dean was never resident upon the said deanery since he was admitted thereunto. Item, lord Hugh of our lady in * * * deacon and cardinal, a stranger, doth possess the prebend of Driffield, in the said church of York, from **Ebor.**

Edward III. A.D. 1377. the seventh day of June, A. D. 1363: from which day, &c. John of Gisbourne, and George Coupemanthorp, &c., do occupy the said prebend, worth by year one hundred pounds; the said lord Hugh is not resident upon the said prebend.

Sarisbu. Item, Lord Simon of the title of St. Sixt, priest and cardinal, &c., doth possess the prebend of Wistow in the said church of York, worth by year one hundred pounds; and the aforesaid Master John of Stoke doth occupy the aforesaid prebend and the profits thereof, &c.; but the said lord Simon is not resident upon the said prebend.

Item, Lord Francis of the title of St. Sabine, priest and cardinal, a stranger, doth possess the prebend of Stransal, in the said church of York, worth by year one hundred marks. And Master William of Merfield, &c., doth occupy the said prebend, &c.; but the said lord Francis is not resident upon the said prebend.

Lord Peter of the title of St. Praxed, priest and cardinal, a stranger, doth hold the archdeaconry of York, worth by year one hundred pounds, and Master William of Mirfield, &c., for farmers.

The deanery of Salisbury. The deanery of the cathedral church of Sarum, with churches and chapels underwritten to the same deanery annexed, doth remain in the hands of lord Reginald of the title of St. Adrian, deacon and cardinal, and so hath remained these twenty-six years, who is never resident; his proctor is one Lawrence de Ingris, a stranger, and it is worth by year two hundred and fifty-four pounds, twelve shillings, and four pence.

Richard, bishop, doth hold the vicarage of Meere, to the deanery annexed, and hath holden the same for nineteen years; worth by year forty pounds.

Robert Codford, the farmer of the church of Heightredbury, to the same annexed, worth by year fifty pounds.

The church of Stoning and the chapel of Rescomp, to the same deanery annexed, worth by year seventy marks.

The chapel of Herst, to the same deanery annexed, worth by year forty pounds.

The chapel of Wokenbame, to the same deanery annexed, worth by year thirty-six pounds.

The chapel of Sandhurst, worth by year forty shillings.

The church of Godalming, to the same deanery annexed, in the diocese of Winchester, worth by year forty pounds.

Treasurer of the church of Sarum. The dignity of treasurer in the church of Sarum, with church and chapels underwritten to the same annexed, is in the hands of lord John of the title of St. Mark, priest and cardinal, and hath so continued twelve years, who was never resident in the same; worth by year one hundred and thirty-six pounds, thirteen shillings, and four-pence.

The church of Fighelden, to the same annexed, worth by year twenty-six pounds, thirteen shillings, and four-pence.

The church of Alwardbury with the chapel of Putton, worth by year ten pounds.

The prebend of Calve to the same treasurer annexed, worth by year one hundred pounds.

The archdeaconry of Berks, in the cathedral church of Salisbury, with the church of Mordon to the same annexed, is in the hands of lord William, of the title of St. Stephen, who was never resident in the same, worth by year eight score marks.

The archdeaconry of Dorset, in the church of Salisbury, with the church of Gissiche to the same annexed, in the hands of lord Robert, of the title of the Twelve Apostles, priest and cardinal, and is worth by year one hundred and three marks.

The prebend of Woodford and Willeleford, in the church of Salisbury, is in the hands of Robert, the cardinal aforesaid, and is worth forty marks.

The prebend of Heyworth, in the church of Salisbury, is in the hands of the lord cardinal of Agrifolio, who is never resident, worth by the year eighty pounds.

The prebend of Netherbarnby and Beminster, in the church of Salisbury, one Hugh Pelegrine a stranger, did hold twenty years and more, and was never resident in the same; worth by the year eight score marks.

The church prebendary of Gillingham, in the nunnery of Salisbury, lately holden of lord Richard, now bishop of Ely, is in the hands of the lord Peter of the title of St. Praxed, priest and cardinal, &c., worth by the year eighty pounds.

Lord William of the holy church of Rome, cardinal, a stranger, doth hold the archdeaconry of Canterbury, and is not resident; the true value of all the yearly fruits, rents and profits, is worth seven hundred florins. Canterbury.

The lord cardinal of Canterbury is archdeacon of Wells, and hath annexed to his archdeaconry the churches of Hewish, Berwes, and Southbrent, which are worth by year, with their procuration of visitations of the said archdeaconry, one hundred and sixty pounds. Bath and Wells.

Item, The lord cardinal is treasurer of the church of Wells, and hath the moiety of the church of Mertock annexed thereunto, worth by year sixty pounds.

Item, The lord cardinal of Agrifolio is archdeacon of Taunton, in the church of Wells, and is worth by year, with the procurations and the prebend of Mylmerton to the same annexed, eighty pounds.

Note. Like matter is also found in the time of king Richard II., upon what occasion it is uncertain; but, as it seemeth by record of that time, a new pope being come in place, he would take no knowledge of any matter done by his predecessors, that might any way abridge his commodity; and, therefore, this king was forced to begin anew, as may appear by this following.

Lord cardinal of Agrifolio is prebendary of the prebend of Soringham, together with a portion of St. Mary of Stow to the same annexed;[1] the fruits whereof, by common estimate, be worth by year one hundred and sixty-five pounds; Master John, vicar of Coringham, and Master Robert, parson of Ketelthorpe, and W. Thurly, be farmers. The archdeaconry of Stow.

Lord cardinal Albanum is prebendary of the prebend of Sutton, the fruits whereof be commonly esteemed worth by year four hundred marks. Roger Skyret of Buckingham, and William Bedeford of Sutton, do farm the same prebend. The lord cardinal Glandacen is prebendary of the prebend of Nassington, worth, by estimation, three hundred marks. Robert of Nassington, and John, son of Robert of Abethorpe, do occupy the same prebend. The archdeaconry of Northampton.

Lord cardinal Nonmacem is parson of Adderbury, worth, by estimation, one hundred pounds; Adam Robelyn, clerk, is his proctor, and occupation the same.

Lord cardinal of St. *** is prebendary of Thame, worth yearly, by common estimation, two hundred marks; John Heyward and Thomas *** a layman, do occupy the same prebend. The archdeaconry of Oxon.

Lord Peter de Yeverino, cardinal, is prebendary of Aylesbury, worth yearly, by common estimation, eighty marks. Holy Duse of Aylesbury doth occupy the same prebend. The archdeaconry of York.

The cardinal of St. Angelo hath the archdeaconry of Suffolk, and is worth by year, by common estimation, a hundred marks. The diocese of Norwich.

Lord cardinal Neminacem, treasurer of the church of Sarum, hath the archdeaconry of Sarum, with the church of Figheldon to his dignity annexed, which is let to farm to Grace, late wife of Edmund Swayne, deceased, paying yearly fifty marks. He hath also, in the same archdeaconry and county, the said church of Alwardbury, with the chapels of Putton and Farle to the same annexed, which is let to farm to the prior of the house of Ederose for the yearly rent of twenty-three pounds; he hath also the prebend of Calve in the said archdeaconry and county, worth by year one hundred pounds, and the farmer thereof is Raymund Peregrine. The diocese of Sarum.

Lord cardinal of Agrifolio hath the archdeaconry of Berks, worth by year one hundred and twenty marks, and it remaineth in his own hands. Item, He hath the prebend of Worth, worth by year a hundred pounds; Raymund Peregrine is farmer there.

Lord cardinal Gebanen hath the prebends of Woodford and Willeford in the county of Wiltshire, let to farm to John Bennet of Sarum, worth by year forty marks.

Lord Andomar de Rupy is archdeacon of Canterbury, to the which archdeacon belongs the church of Lymin within the same diocese, worth by year, after the taxation of the tenth, twenty pounds. The church of Tenham, worth by year, after the said taxation, one hundred and thirty pounds, six shillings, The diocese of Canterbury.

(1) An. 2. Rich. 2.

Edward III. A.D. 1375.

and eight-pence. The church of Hakington near Canterbury, worth by year twenty marks. The church of St. Clement in Sandwich, worth by year, after the taxations aforesaid, eight marks. The church of St. Mary in Sandwich, worth by year nine pounds, of the which the said archdeacon receiveth only six marks: the profits of all which premises Sir William Latimer, Knight, hath received, together with the profits arising out of the jurisdiction of the archdeaconry, worth by year twenty pounds.

The diocese of York.

Anglicus of the church of Rome, priest and cardinal, hath the deanery of the cathedral church of York, worth by year three hundred and seventy-three pounds, six shillings, and eight pence, and the prebend of Southcane, valued yearly at one hundred and sixty marks.

The diocese of Durham.

Lord cardinal Gebanen doth hold the church of Wearmouth, and the archdeaconry of Durham, worth by year two hundred marks. And John of Chambre, and Thomas of Harington, of Newcastle, be the farmers and proctors of the said cardinal.

(Ex Bundello Brevium Regis de an. 2. Rich. II. part i.)

END OF VOL. II.

LONDON:—R. CLAY, PRINTER, BREAD-STREET-HILL.

Lightning Source UK Ltd.
Milton Keynes UK
UKOW01f1938201017
311364UK00003B/59/P